MORAL REASONING

MORAL REASONING

A Text and Reader on Ethics and

Contemporary Moral Issues

David R. Morrow

Oxford   New York

OXFORD UNIVERSITY PRESS

Oxford University Press is a department of the University of Oxford.
It furthers the University's objective of excellence in research,
scholarship, and education by publishing worldwide.
Oxford is a registered trade mark of Oxford University Press
in the UK and certain other countries.

Published in the United States of America by Oxford University Press
198 Madison Avenue, New York, NY 10016, United States of America.

© 2018 by Oxford University Press

Library of Congress Cataloging-in-Publication Data

Names: Morrow, David R., author.
Title: Moral reasoning : a text and reader on ethics and contemporary moral
   issues / David Morrow.
Description: Oxford ; New York : Oxford University Press, [2017] | Includes
   bibliographical references.
Identifiers: LCCN 2016042676 (print) | LCCN 2017007212 (ebook) | ISBN
   9780190235857 (pbk.) | ISBN 9780190236120 (Ebook)
Subjects: LCSH: Ethics—Textbooks.
Classification: LCC BJ1012 .M639 2017 (print) | LCC BJ1012 (ebook) | DDC
   170—dc23
LC record available at https://lccn.loc.gov/2016042676

9 8 7 6 5 4 3 2 1

Printed by LSC Communications in the United States of America.

CONTENTS

Acknowledgments   ix
A Note to Instructors   xi
Preface   xiii

PART I: REASONING ABOUT MORAL AND NON-MORAL ISSUES   1

Chapter 1. An Introduction to Arguments   2

Chapter 2. Moral Arguments   14

PART II: WAYS OF REASONING ABOUT MORAL ISSUES   25

Chapter 3. Reasoning with Obligations   26

Chapter 4. Reasoning with Consequences   35

Chapter 5. Reasoning with Virtues and Vices   46

Chapter 6. Reasoning with Principles and Counterexamples   57

Chapter 7. Reasoning by Analogy   67

Chapter 8. Answering Moral Questions   76

PART III: MORAL THEORY AND MORAL REASONING   91

Chapter 9. Skepticism, Subjectivism, and Relativism   92

Chapter 10. Religion and Moral Reasoning   105

Chapter 11. Normative Theories, Part 1   114

Chapter 12. Normative Theories, Part 2   127

PART IV: APPENDICES   137

    Appendix 1. How to Write an Ethics Paper   138

    Appendix 2. Additional Case Studies   150

PART V: READINGS   161

    Tips on Reading Philosophy   162

    Moral Theory   164

        IMMANUEL KANT / *Grounding for the Metaphysics of Morals*   164

        JEREMY BENTHAM / *An Introduction to the Principles of Morals and Legislation*   171

        JOHN STUART MILL / *Utilitarianism*   175

        ARISTOTLE / *Nicomachean Ethics*   184

        STEPHANIE COLLINS / *Care Ethics: The Four Key Claims*   193

        MENCIUS / *Essential* Mengzi: *Selected Passages with Traditional Commentary*   205

        KWASI WIREDU / *The Moral Foundations of an African Culture*   216

    Moral Issues   226

      Sex   226

        YOLANDA ESTES / *Mutual Respect and Sexual Morality*   226

        TOM DOUGHERTY / *Sex, Lies, and Consent*   233

        ANNE W. EATON / *A Sensible Antiporn Feminism*   252

      Race   274

        J. L. A. GARCIA / *The Heart of Racism*   274

        LAURENCE THOMAS / *What Good Am I?*   294

        XIAOFEI LIU / *No Fats, Femmes, or Asians*   299

      Abortion   313

        MARY ANNE WARREN / *On the Moral and Legal Status of Abortion*   313

        DON MARQUIS / *Why Abortion Is Immoral*   320

        JUDITH JARVIS THOMSON / *A Defense of Abortion*   331

      Euthanasia   342

        SUSAN M. WOLF / *Physician-Assisted Suicide*   342

        JAMES RACHELS / *Active and Passive Euthanasia*   352

        J. GAY-WILLIAMS / *The Wrongfulness of Euthanasia*   357

Capital Punishment   360

    ERNEST VAN DEN HAAG / *The Ultimate Punishment: A Defense*   360

    STEPHEN NATHANSON / *An Eye for an Eye? The Morality of Punishing by Death*   366

    THADDEUS METZ / *African Values and Capital Punishment*   372

Torture   378

    HENRY SHUE / *Torture*   378

    ALAN M. DERSHOWITZ / *Should the Ticking Time Bomb Terrorist Be Tortured?*   389

    JEFF McMAHAN / *Torture in Principle and in Practice*   403

War   414

    JEFF McMAHAN / *The Ethics of Killing in War*   414

    CHERYL ABBATE / *Assuming Risk: A Critical Analysis of a Soldier's Duty to Prevent Collateral Casualties*   430

    BRADLEY JAY STRAWSER / *Moral Predators: The Duty to Employ Uninhabited Aerial Vehicles*   447

Animals   468

    PETER SINGER / *All Animals Are Equal*   468

    BONNIE STEINBOCK / *Speciesism and the Idea of Equality*   479

    ALASTAIR NORCROSS / *Puppies, Pigs, and People: Eating Meat and Marginal Cases*   486

Global Poverty   498

    ONORA NELL / *Lifeboat Earth*   498

    PETER SINGER / *Famine, Affluence, and Morality*   507

    FIONA WOOLLARD / *Saving Strangers: What Does Morality Demand?*   515

Climate Change   521

    WALTER SINNOTT-ARMSTRONG / *It's Not My Fault: Global Warming and Individual Moral Obligations*   521

    JOHN BROOME / *Private Morality and Climate Change*   535

    SARAH KRAKOFF / *Parenting the Planet*   546

Index   562

ACKNOWLEDGMENTS

Gratitude to one's benefactors, claimed W. D. Ross, is one of our basic moral obligations. Many people helped me write this book, and it is both an obligation and a pleasure for me to acknowledge their assistance.

This book would never have come into existence without the encouragement of my teacher, Steven Cahn, and my extremely patient editor, Robert Miller. I would not have been able to write it without the philosophical training I received from a great many teachers and colleagues and the pedagogical training I received from Steven Cahn, Alan Hausman, James Freeman, and hundreds of students at Hunter College and the University of Alabama at Birmingham. And none of that would have been possible without the support of my parents, Daniel and Felicia, and my wife, Melissa.

Many others have contributed in their own way, too. Thanks to Alyssa Palazzo at Oxford University Press for her deft handling of various editorial and logistical matters, Diane A. Lange for copyediting, and Holly Haydash, Elizabeth Kelly, and Kellylouise Delaney for the hard work of transforming a manuscript into a book. Thanks to Sol Herrera for the diagrams in Chapters 1 and 2, to Marshall Abrams for ideas about moral issues to include in the book, and to Thaddeus Metz for help learning about and explaining the ethics of *ubuntu*. Thanks to the many reviewers who helped shape and improve the book, including:

Tayo Basquiat, Bismarck State College
Michael Bradley, Georgia Perimeter College
Tom Buller, Illinois State University
Joni Doherty, Franklin Pierce University
Andrew Fenton, California State University, Fresno
Luisa Forrest, Richland College
Jeffrey Fry, Ball State University
Brett Fulkerson-Smith, Harper College
Dimitria Electra Gatzia, University of Akron
Clarence Johnson, Middle Tennessee State University
Keith Korcz, University of Louisiana, Lafayette
A.J. Kreider, Miami-Dade College
Sarah Mattice, University of North Florida
John Messerly, Shoreline Community College
Michael Barnes Norton, University of Arkansas, Little Rock
David O'Connor, Seton Hall University
Roger Paden, George Mason University

David Phillips, University of Houston
Michael Robinson, College of Western Idaho
Octavio Roca, Miami Dade College
Albert Spencer, Portland State University
Daniel Zelinski, Richard Bland College

Finally, thanks to whoever invented coffee.

A NOTE TO INSTRUCTORS

Students who slog through a typical applied ethics textbook will, with hard work, learn a lot about various moral theories, and they will read some very sophisticated arguments about pressing moral problems. Along the way, one hopes, they might also learn to think for themselves about difficult moral issues. There is something to be said for this standard approach, and instructors who prefer it have their pick of textbooks. But if your main goal as an instructor is to teach your students to reason about moral issues for themselves, the standard approach prioritizes the wrong things.

This book takes a different approach, focusing primarily and explicitly on training students to reason about moral issues. Some instructors who embrace this goal will want to retain a more traditional structure for their course: a quick introduction to argumentation in general, then metaethics and normative theory, followed by a discussion of moral reasoning, and finally a romp through some classic and contemporary papers from the applied ethics literature. If that's what you're looking for, it's easy to do by reading the chapters out of order. Or perhaps you want something a little less orthodox, which may or may not mean reading all of the chapters in order. Either way, the book is written so that you can read the chapters in any order, giving you the flexibility to structure your course as you see fit. The instructors' section of the book's companion web site provides a number of sample syllabuses to illustrate different ways of using the book.

As you think about how to use this book in your own teaching, please keep three things in mind:

1. **The chapters need not be read in the order in which they are printed.** The chapters and the readings had to be organized in one way or another, but there's no reason to feel bound by the order in which they're printed or to use everything in the book every time you teach your course. Most students will need to read Chapter 1 for a quick introduction to argumentation. Some instructors will want to follow that up with Chapter 9 on subjectivism and relativism and Chapter 10 on religion to help motivate the study of moral reasoning and dispel some common misconceptions. Some instructors prefer to discuss normative theory before turning to moral reasoning. I have found, however, that students don't fall into the subjectivist or relativist trap as often when they're simply presented with the tools of moral reasoning, rather than with normative theories that try to tell them what's right or wrong; that students are more receptive to critiques of subjectivism and relativism once they have some practice reasoning about moral issues; and that students find normative theory more interesting once they have some practice thinking philosophically about moral issues.

2. **The chapters on reasoning with obligation, consequences, and virtues are** *not* **chapters on deontology, consequentialism, and virtue ethics.** Professional philosophers are so used to thinking in terms of deontology, consequentialism, and virtue ethics that when we see a chapter entitled, say, "Reasoning with Obligations," it's almost impossible to avoid thinking, "Aha! Here's the chapter on deontology!" But if you read Chapter 3 thinking that it's going to explain deontology, you're going to come away disappointed; only Chapter 11 delves into detail on deontology. There are several reasons for presenting these techniques independently of the theories associated with them. First, none of these types of reasoning is actually restricted to adherents of the corresponding kinds of normative theory. Virtue ethicists and deontologists will often need to appeal to consequences (e.g., in discussing generosity or the obligation not to harm others), consequentialists may want to appeal to obligations (e.g., if they are two-level consequentialists or rule-utilitarians) or virtues (e.g., as Mill does in distinguishing the goodness of a person from the rightness of his or her actions), and so on. Second, presenting normative theories independently lets students focus on the techniques of moral reasoning without the significant cognitive burden of learning normative theories at the same time. Third, many students find abstract normative theories boring, difficult, or off-putting until they can see how the relevant concepts (about obligations, consequences, virtues, etc.) apply to their everyday lives. Fourth, while the limited overlap between the chapters on moral reasoning and the chapters on normative theory is redundant from an expert's perspective, it can help newcomers to moral philosophy reinforce and deepen their understanding of the central concepts of ethics.

3. **The applied ethics readings in Part V provide models of moral reasoning, not just substantive arguments about specific moral issues.** You might pick a few topics and work through the readings in detail, aiming to help your students form considered judgments about particular ethical issues. But you might instead pick readings from a range of different topics to illustrate the techniques of moral reasoning that your students will study throughout this text. (See the sample syllabuses on the textbook's companion web site for several different approaches to integrating the readings into the course.) Whatever you choose, connecting the *methods* of arguments from each reading back to the techniques developed in Part II will help develop your students' understanding of the reading and their capacity for moral reasoning.

In short, this book's structure works with many different ways of teaching your students to think through moral issues for themselves. Use your own pedagogical judgment to do what works best for you and your students.

PREFACE

I still remember the first thing my professor assigned us to read in my undergraduate Introduction to Moral Philosophy course. She asked us to read a famous essay by Peter Singer, a philosophy professor at Princeton University, in which he argues that morality requires even moderately well-off people to give a great deal of their income to organizations that fight global poverty.[1] (That same paper appears in Part V of this book.) After we'd read the paper, our professor asked for our reactions. One student raised her hand and said that she didn't like Singer's argument. "I don't like people telling me what to do," she said.

Our professor explained that moral philosophy isn't about telling anyone what to do. It's about giving *reasons* to try to convince people, including yourself, that they should (or should not) do something or value something. It's true that Singer was telling us what he thought we should do, but he wasn't saying that we should do it just because he said so. He was trying to give a rational argument. He was trying to convince us that some of the ideas we already accepted led logically to some surprising conclusions about what we ought to do. That, our professor explained, is what moral philosophy aims to do: show us, through rational argument, what we ought to do, what we ought to value, and how we ought to live.

This book aims to help you understand such arguments, tell which ones are good and which aren't, and come up with such arguments on your own. It aims to help you reason through moral issues for yourself, including both big, controversial topics like abortion and more day-to-day topics like whether you should volunteer some of your time at a local school or soup kitchen.

Thinking about moral issues can make people uncomfortable, especially when it involves confronting opposing views. When challenged to explain or defend their views, some people fall back on easy answers like, "That's just how I was raised," or "Well, those are *my* morals, and who are you to say what's right or wrong for me?" These conversation-killers suggest that there's nothing to discuss when it comes to morality—that morality is entirely subjective (or perhaps relative to one's culture) and, as a result, there's no point in trying to change anyone's mind about them. In fact, some people think it's *obvious* that morality is subjective. After all, people's moral beliefs differ widely and there's no decisive way to resolve disagreements about them. As we'll see in Chapter 9, however, these are actually highly controversial philosophical claims about the nature of morality.

Many moral philosophers—perhaps most of them—think that morality is not subjective. But even if it is, you can still use moral reasoning to see what your own values imply about particular cases, to discover whether your values conflict with one another, and to think hard about

---

[1] Peter Singer, "Famine, Affluence, and Morality," *Philosophy & Public Affairs* 1 (1972): 229–43.

why you value what you do. Even if this seems uncomfortable or unfamiliar at first, as you practice using the skills discussed in this book, you'll come to see that there is room for reasoning in morality, regardless of how you answer abstract philosophical questions about its objectivity.

To help you develop your moral reasoning skills, this book begins by introducing the basics of reasoning (Chapter 1) and extends those basic reasoning skills to apply to moral issues in particular (Chapter 2). Part II explores some more specific techniques for moral reasoning (Chapters 3–7), culminating in a general method for reaching well-reasoned judgments on moral issues (Chapter 8). Part III delves into deeper, more theoretical issues in moral philosophy, including questions of skepticism, subjectivism, and relativism (Chapter 9); the connections between religion and moral reasoning (Chapter 10); and some important philosophical theories about what makes actions right or wrong, people good or bad, and so on (Chapters 11 and 12). Two appendices will help you further develop your skills: Appendix 1 walks you through the process of writing a college-level paper on applied ethics, while Appendix 2 provides dozens of case studies for you to consider. Finally, Part V provides seven readings on moral theory and thirty more on specific moral issues, grouped thematically. Not only will these readings introduce you to some important arguments about morality and moral issues, but they will also serve as models of moral reasoning.

These materials provide both instruction in the skills of moral reasoning and ample opportunity to practice putting those skills into practice. Remember, though, that like reasoning in general, moral reasoning is a *skill*. You can always learn to do it better, and the way to do that is by practicing. The point of this book isn't to fill your head with facts or to tell what's right or wrong; it's to train you in a special and important skill—a skill that, I hope, you will use for the rest of your life, including in some of your most difficult moments.

DRM

PART I

Reasoning About Moral and
Non-Moral Issues

1 } An Introduction to Arguments

During the climactic courtroom scene in the film *Legally Blonde,* law student Elle Woods confronts the star witness in the trial of Brooke Taylor-Windham. The star witness is Brooke's stepdaughter, Chutney Windham, who has accused Brooke of murdering Chutney's father, Hayworth Windham. Chutney testifies that on the day of her father's murder, she returned home from her morning errands to an empty house. She got in the shower to wash her hair. When she got out of the shower, her stepmother was standing over her father's dead body, "drenched in his blood." She admits that she never heard a gunshot, which she says is because she was in the shower. Almost everyone in the courtroom seems to believe Chutney's story. That's bad news for Elle, who has pledged to defend Brooke's innocence.

Seemingly at a loss, Elle asks Chutney what else she had done on the day of the murder. Chutney reels off a list of errands—getting a latte, going to the gym, getting a perm. Elle's eyes light up; she sees her opportunity and she seizes it. Within two minutes, she forces Chutney into confessing that *she* had murdered her father in a botched attempt to kill her stepmother. How does she do it? In a series of rapid-fire questions, Elle establishes a set of facts that leads everyone in the courtroom to infer that Chutney is lying about being in the shower. These facts are:

1. Chutney had gotten a perm shortly before her father was murdered.
2. Chutney had been getting two perms a year every year for the past fifteen years.
3. Anyone who has had as many perms as Chutney would know that she should not wash her hair for twenty-four hours after getting a perm, because it would ruin her curls.

Once she gets Chutney to admit these facts, Elle says what everyone in the courtroom has come to recognize: Chutney was not in the shower at the time of the murder.[1]

What Elle does in that dramatic scene is to present the court with an excellent piece of **reasoning.** Reasoning is the art of showing that one claim is implied by some other claim(s). You can—and do—use this skill all the time, whether you're convincing other people to believe something (as Elle does), puzzling something out for yourself, or just thinking carefully about what is implied by some claim. Even though we all reason about all kinds of things all the time, each of us can always improve our reasoning skills through practice, training, and reflection. Most of this book is designed to help you reason more effectively about moral issues. This chapter, however, introduces some basic concepts and principles to help you improve your ability to reason about anything and everything.

---

[1]Robert Luketic, *Legally Blonde* (Beverly Hills, CA: MGM Studios), 2001.

ARGUMENTS

An individual piece of reasoning, such as Elle's reasoning in *Legally Blonde,* is called an **argument.** In everyday English, we use the word "argument" to refer to a disagreement or a verbal fight, as when we say that two roommates had an argument about whose turn it was to do the dishes. As it's used in academic discussions, however, the word "argument" means something very different. An argument is a set of **claims,** one of which is supposed to be implied by the others. A claim is just any statement that could be true or false, as opposed to something like a question or a command. To say that one claim implies another is to say that the first claim supports—that is, gives you a good reason to believe—the second. So, to give an argument is not simply to assert that something is true or to state that you believe something to be true; it is to offer *reasons* that (supposedly) show that something is true. To see how this works, take a closer look at Elle's argument in *Legally Blonde.* It consists of four claims: that Chutney got a perm on the day of the murder, that she'd had about thirty perms before, that anyone who'd had that many perms would know not to get her hair wet for twenty-four hours after getting a perm, and that Chutney did not take a shower when she got home after getting her perm. The first three claims are supposed to imply—that is, support or give a reason for—the fourth claim.

Every argument is made of up at least two claims, and each claim plays a distinct role in the argument. Exactly one of the claims is the **conclusion** of the argument. This is the claim that is supposed to be implied by the other claims. The other claims are called **premises.** (The word "premises" is pronounced PREM-ih-sees, and the singular form, "premise," is pronounced PREM-iss.) When giving or analyzing an argument, it's often helpful to present the premises and conclusion in a numbered list, with the conclusion at the end, like this:

ELLE'S ARGUMENT

1. Chutney had gotten a perm shortly before her father was murdered.
2. Chutney had been getting two perms a year every year for the past fifteen years.
3. Anyone who has had as many perms as Chutney would know that she should not wash her hair for twenty-four hours after getting a perm, because it would ruin her curls.
∴ 4. Chutney was not in the shower when her father was murdered.

Claims (1)–(3) are the premises of ELLE'S ARGUMENT. Claim (4) is the conclusion. We use the symbol ∴, which means "therefore," to show that (4) is implied by the previous claims. (You could also just write "Therefore.") The order in which you present the premises isn't terribly important—although sometimes ordering them one way rather than another will make it easier for readers to understand the argument. The point of providing a numbered list is simply that it makes it easier to talk about the argument. We can just say "claim (1)," rather than saying, "The claim that Chutney had gotten a perm on the day of her father's murder."

If this all seems very technical, here's a less technical but less precise way to think about arguments: an argument is a set of reasons given to convince someone that something is true. This is imprecise for two reasons: First, the conclusion is part of the argument, so technically speaking, the argument isn't *just* the sets of reasons given to convince someone of the conclusion. Second, someone could write out an argument without using it to try to convince anyone of anything. For instance, Elle might have considered various arguments that she *could* have used to defend her client without actually intending to use most of them to convince the jury of her client's innocence. She could also have thought about the arguments that the prosecution might have used against her client—but not because *she* was trying to convince anyone of the conclusion of those arguments. Still, in many cases, the goal is to convince someone that something is true.

ARGUMENTS vs. EXPLANATIONS

Thinking of arguments as sets of reasons given to convince someone of something is especially helpful when trying to distinguish arguments from **explanations.** While arguments help us see *that* something is true, explanations help us understand *why* something is true. Roughly, an explanation is a set of claims; some of which help us understand *why* one of the claims is true. In general, we ask for arguments to *support* claims about whose truth we are uncertain; we ask for explanations to help us *understand* claims that we already believe to be true.

To see this difference more clearly, imagine a chemistry teacher holding a ping-pong ball over an open flame. To many of her students' surprise, the ball catches fire and burns quickly. (Don't try this at home!) The students now know that ping-pong balls burn, but they don't know why. Some, perhaps, think that the plastic itself is flammable, while others suspect that the ball is coated with a flammable chemical. If the teacher tells the class that the ball is made of celluloid and that celluloid is an extremely flammable plastic, she will have *explained* the ball's flammability, enabling the students to *understand* something that they have already learned to be true—namely, that ping-pong balls are flammable. Later, one of the students goes home and tries to convince her little brother that ping-pong balls are flammable. When she says, "Our chemistry teacher held a ping-pong ball over a fire, and it burst into flame! She said that all ping-pong balls are flammable," she is giving an *argument* designed to *convince* her brother of something that he didn't yet believe. Note that the student can accomplish her goal of convincing her brother without getting her brother to understand *why* the balls are flammable. She only needs to get him to believe *that* they are flammable.

The point is that when you are trying to decide whether someone is offering an argument or giving an explanation, ask yourself about the goal of the person giving the argument or explanation. Is he or she trying to convince someone of something or get someone to understand why something is true?

Note, however, that it's possible for the same set of claims to be both an argument and an explanation. If the student had told her brother, "Ping-pong balls are flammable because they are made of celluloid, which is a highly flammable kind of plastic," she would be *both* trying to convince him that ping-pong balls are flammable *and* helping him understand why they're flammable.

UNDERSTANDING ARGUMENTS

Understanding an argument is more of an art than a science—but it's an art that anybody can learn with a bit of practice. The best way to get better at it is to practice finding arguments written in plain English and rewriting them as numbered lists of claims. This process is often called analyzing an argument, or **argument analysis.** The goal of analyzing an argument is *not* to determine how strong the argument is or whether you agree with its conclusion. The goal is simply to understand the argument—to take the argument apart into its different pieces and figure out how those pieces are supposed to fit together. This section offers some tips for doing that and gives some examples of the process.

The first thing to do when trying to analyze an argument is to identify the conclusion and the premise(s). Sometimes, people will use specific words that introduce the conclusion or premises of their arguments. Logicians (rather uncreatively) call these words or phrases **conclusion indicators** and **premise indicators,** respectively. Expressions like "so," "that's why," "this shows that," or (more formally) "therefore," "hence," and "thus" usually come before the conclusion of an argument. Consider, for instance, an argument that Obi Wan Kenobi makes in the Star Wars film *Return of the Jedi.* When Luke Skywalker complains that Obi Wan had lied to Luke about Darth Vader having murdered Luke's father, Obi Wan replies:

> Your father [Anakin Skywalker] was seduced by the dark side of the Force. He ceased to be Anakin Skywalker and became Darth Vader. When that happened, the good man who was your father was destroyed. So what I have told you [about Darth Vader murdering your father] was true.[2]

Here, the word "so" introduces the claim of which Obi Wan is trying to convince Luke—namely, that Obi Wan had told him the truth about his father. That's the conclusion of Obi Wan's argument.

Expressions like "because," "since," "for," or "given that" usually indicate a premise. Consider, for instance, the following argument from the novel *Candide.* The main character, Candide, offers this argument when he arrives in a strange land where gold and gems can be found everywhere, just lying on the ground:

> The king's children of this country must be well brought up, since they are taught to despise gold and precious stones.[3]

The conclusion of this argument is that the "king's children" in this strange country have been well brought up. The word "since" introduces the reason that Candide gives for this conclusion—namely, that the king's children have been taught to despise gold and precious stones. You don't need to agree that this is a *good* reason to think the king's children have been well brought up. Remember, analyzing an argument is different from deciding whether it's a good argument. The goal is just to understand what the person giving the argument is saying.

While conclusion indicators and premise indicators are often useful clues when analyzing an argument, you should always be careful when you find them. They don't *always* introduce conclusions or premises. Sometimes they introduce explanations ("The ping-pong ball caught fire because . . ."), relationships in time ("Since 1964 . . ."), and so on. Thus, even

---

[2]Richard Marquand, *Return of the Jedi* (Los Angeles: 20th Century Fox, 1980).
[3]Voltaire, *Candide.*

CONCLUSION INDICATORS AND PREMISE INDICATORS

Some Common Premise Indicators	Some Common Conclusion Indicators
because	therefore
since	hence
for	thus
given that	so
as implied by	that's why
for the reason that	consequently
entailed by the fact that	we may infer that
may be deduced from	implies that
on the assumption that	entails that
supposing that	it follows that

---

when you see a conclusion indicator or a premise indicator, you'll have to think carefully about whether it actually introduces a conclusion or a premise.

In many cases, you won't get conclusion indicators or premise indicators to guide you. Instead, you'll just need to read or listen carefully to discover the author's or speaker's main point; that's the conclusion of the argument. The premises are all of the reasons that the author or speaker gives to support his or her main point. Sometimes you'll need to try out different possibilities, asking yourself if it makes most sense to read a paragraph as an argument for one claim or another. It can take a while to get the hang of this, but even if you have trouble at first, you'll get better at it with practice.

Finally, note that an argument is sometimes presented along with a bunch of background claims, which are neither premises nor conclusions. They're just there to help you understand the meaning or importance of the argument. So, even if you know that a particular paragraph contains an argument, don't think that every single sentence needs to be either a premise in or the conclusion of that argument.

Argument Structures

Sometimes it's helpful, when analyzing an argument, to think about the structure of the argument—that is, about the way the premises fit together. Some arguments have two or more premises that provide independent reasons for the conclusion. Consider this bit of reasoning from the TV show *Pretty Little Liars:*

> Emily's friend Alison disappeared two years ago. But then she found a note in her locker that was signed "A." And the note contained information that only Alison could have known. Therefore, Alison must have written the note.[4]

The conclusion indicator *therefore* tells you that the last claim—that Alison must have left the note—is the argument's conclusion. To identify the argument's premises, consider which of the other claims could be considered reasons for thinking that Alison left the note. The fact

---

[4]"Pilot," *Pretty Little Liars*, ABC Family, June 8, 2010.

that the note contained information that only Alison could have known is a strong reason to think that Alison wrote it. So that's a premise. The fact that it was signed "A" might be considered a reason, too, even if it's not as strong a reason. (Again, our goal here is not to determine how good the argument is, but only to understand it.) The fact that Alison disappeared two years ago isn't a reason to think that Alison left the note; it's just background information. So if we wanted to write this argument out as a numbered list, it would look like this:

ALISON'S BACK

1. The note in Emily's locker was signed "A."
2. The note in Emily's locker contained information that only Alison could have known.
∴ 3. Alison wrote the note in Emily's locker.

Here, claim (1) and claim (2) are each providing reasons for claim (3).

In other cases, the reasons are chained together in a series, as in this half-joking argument from the commencement speech that J. K. Rowling delivered at Harvard in 2008:

> The famous British philosopher Baroness Mary Warnock delivered the commencement speech when I graduated from university twenty-one years ago. I don't remember a thing Warnock said. So, you probably won't remember a thing that I say today. So, it doesn't really matter what I say.[5]

Now, the main point of this argument is that it doesn't matter what Rowling says to the Harvard graduates. And since there's a conclusion indicator—*so*—in front of that claim, we can be confident that that's the conclusion. But notice that the word *so* also introduces the claim that the Harvard graduates probably won't remember what Rowling says. What's going on?

This argument proceeds in two steps: First, it moves from the claim that Rowling doesn't remember a thing that Warnock said to the claim that the Harvard graduates probably won't remember a thing that Rowling says. Second, it moves from the claim that the Harvard graduates probably won't remember a thing that Rowling says to the claim that it doesn't matter what Rowling says. The claim in the middle—that the Harvard graduates probably won't remember a thing that Rowling says—serves as both a conclusion and a premise. A claim that serves double duty like this is called a **subconclusion;** it is both implied by an earlier premise in the argument and serves as a premise for some further conclusion.

We could rewrite the argument this way:

ROWLING'S JOKE

1. Rowling doesn't remember a thing that Warnock said at her own graduation.
∴ 2. The Harvard graduates probably won't remember a thing that Rowling says at their graduation.
∴ 3. It doesn't really matter what Rowling says.

Finally, some arguments combine these approaches, as in this somewhat more complicated argument from the ancient Greek philosopher Aristotle:

> In lunar eclipses, the shadow on the moon is always curved. Since the eclipse is caused by the Earth's shadow, the shape of the shadow on the moon is determined by the shape of the Earth. Therefore, the Earth is spherical.[6]

---

[5]Paraphrased from J. K. Rowling, "The Fringe Benefits of Failure, and the Importance of Imagination," speech given at Harvard University, June 5, 2008, http://news.harvard.edu/gazette/story/2008/06/text-of-j-k-rowling-speech/.
[6]Paraphrased from Aristotle, *On the Heavens* II.14.

SOCRATES AND PLATO

Arguments are the tools of the trade in philosophy. Philosophers use them to try to discover the truth and to share it with others. The ancient Greek thinker Socrates (469–399 BCE), one of the founding figures in Western philosophy, used arguments to educate—and annoy—his fellow Athenians. He would strike up conversations with people in the street, asking them about things like courage, knowledge, or justice. Then he would give arguments to show that their ideas about those things were confused or incorrect. This habit probably contributed to the Athenians' decision to execute him in 399 BCE for corrupting the youth.

While Socrates did all his philosophizing by talking to people, his most famous student, Plato (ca. 429–347 BCE), wrote his ideas down in a series of dialogues, which are like short plays about people having philosophical discussions. Many of these dialogues feature Socrates as a main character. Through the arguments in these dialogues, Plato explored most of the central questions in philosophy, leading one famous philosopher to say that all of Western philosophy is just "a series of footnotes to Plato."

How should we analyze this argument? As usual, the first thing to ask is: What is the conclusion of this argument? The word *therefore* suggests that the conclusion is that the Earth is spherical. Before jumping to conclusions, though, let's make sure that it makes sense to read the paragraph that way. Is it reasonable to think that Aristotle's main point in this paragraph is that the Earth is spherical? How can we tell? One way is to ask whether the other claims in the argument could reasonably be understood as giving reasons for the claim that the Earth is spherical. The other claims are, first, that the shadow on the moon during a lunar eclipse is always curved; second, that the shadow is caused by the Earth; and third, that the shape of that shadow is determined by the shape of the Earth. It does make sense to see these as reasons for the claim that the Earth is spherical. So, we can analyze Aristotle's argument as follows:

ARISTOTLE'S ARGUMENT
1. In lunar eclipses, the shadow on the moon is caused by the Earth.
∴ 2. The shape of the shadow on the moon is determined by the shape of the Earth.
3. In lunar eclipses, the shadow on the moon is always curved.
∴ 4. The Earth is spherical.

You'll see that claim (2) is a subconclusion, implied by claim (1) and working together with claim (3) to imply the main conclusion, (4).

Just as you can't expect to shoot three-pointers with ease just because you've read a little bit about basketball, you shouldn't expect argument analysis to be easy just because you've read through a few examples. You'll need lots of practice. But this crash course on argument analysis should give you the tools to start thinking and talking about the structure of arguments.

EVALUATING ARGUMENTS

A good argument gives you good reason to accept its conclusion; a bad argument doesn't. How can you tell the difference? You need to **evaluate** the argument—that is, determine how good or bad the argument is. Beginners sometimes evaluate arguments based on whether they agree or disagree with the conclusion. But this gets things backwards: since an argument can give you reasons to accept a claim that you didn't already believe, evaluating an argument requires thinking about the premises and their connection to the conclusion.

In particular, evaluating an argument involves asking about the **acceptability,** the **relevance,** and the **sufficiency** of the premises. Very roughly, this means asking whether you have enough reason to believe that each premise is true; whether the premises, if they were true, would provide reasons to accept the conclusion; and if those reasons, taken together, would provide *enough* reason for you to accept the conclusion. There's a lot more to be said about each of these criteria, though, so it is worthwhile to think about them one at a time.

Premise Acceptability

Without getting too technical, to say that a premise is acceptable to a particular audience is to say that the audience already has a good enough reason to believe that premise. This means that premise acceptability is always relative to a particular audience. Many claims that are acceptable for a group of brain surgeons, for instance, won't be acceptable for a group of kindergarteners, since the kindergarteners don't know enough to realize that the claims are true.

We can identify six different ways that someone can have a good enough reason to believe a premise—that is, six different ways that a premise can be acceptable. First, a premise can be *known to be true by definition:* the claim that a triangle has three sides is true by definition. Second, a premise can be (easily) *knowable just by thinking about it:* the claim that 12 times 12 is 144 is knowable just by thinking about it, as is the claim that nothing can be completely red and completely green at the same time. Third, a premise can be acceptable *on the basis of one's own senses:* if you see that there is a monkey in the room, then the claim that there is a monkey in the room would be acceptable (for you) on the basis of your senses. Fourth, a premise can be acceptable *on the basis of reliable testimony:* if your (trustworthy) neighbors tell you that they just saw your dog walking down the street by itself, the claim that your dog is walking down the street by itself would be acceptable (for you) on the basis of their testimony. Reliable testimony could also include expert testimony: if a physics professor tells you that neutrinos are subatomic particles that have no electric charge, that gives you a good reason to believe that neutrinos have no electric charge. Fifth, a premise can be acceptable because it is *common knowledge,* meaning, roughly, that everyone in the audience can be expected to know it, even if they're not exactly sure how they first learned it. For instance, it's common knowledge—at least among Americans—that George Washington was the first president of the United States. (Be careful with this one, though! Not only will common knowledge vary from audience to audience, but common knowledge sometimes turns out to be wrong. It used to be "common knowledge" that the Sun went around the Earth!) Finally, a premise can be acceptable because it is *supported by a good argument.* After all, a good argument is one that gives you a good reason to believe something, so if you have a good argument for a premise, you have a good reason to believe it. If you're wondering whether a particular premise is acceptable for a particular audience, ask yourself whether the audience can be expected to believe the premise on the basis of any of these six ways. If so, the premise is acceptable for that audience; if not, not.

Finally, it's worth addressing two common confusions about premise acceptability. First, to say that a premise is acceptable is not quite the same as saying that it's true. On the one hand, a premise might be true even though the audience has no good reason to believe it. (Your average kindergartener, for instance, has no reason to believe that the first emperor of China's Qin dynasty died in 210 BCE.) On the other hand, a premise might be acceptable even if it turns out to be false, since we sometimes turn out to be wrong about things that we had very good reasons to believe. (If your friends are planning a surprise birthday party for you, they might initially give you good reason to think that they've forgotten your birthday altogether.) Second, to say that a premise is acceptable for a particular audience is not quite the same as saying that the audience actually accepts it. On the one hand, they might accept the premise even though it's not acceptable, since they might believe something that they don't have a good reason to believe. (Your paranoid neighbor might believe that you're trying to kill him, even though you presumably are not.) On the other hand, the audience might not believe something even though they have good reason to believe it. (Your stubborn friend might refuse to believe that narwhals are real even after seeing videos of them.) In short, to say that a premise is acceptable for a particular person is to say that, given the person's evidence, the person *ought* to believe that the premise is true.

Relevance

To say that a premise is (positively) relevant to the argument's conclusion is to say that the truth of the premise counts in favor of the truth of the conclusion.[7] Less formally, that means that *if* you believed the premise, you would have *some* reason to believe the conclusion—regardless of whether the premise is true or whether you actually believe it.

Relevance is most easily understood by contrasting it with obviously irrelevant claims—that is, claims whose truth has no bearing on the conclusion of an argument. Imagine that you are a detective investigating a kidnapping, and that you have identified a suspect. The claim that the missing child was last seen climbing into the suspect's van is relevant to the conclusion that the suspect really is the kidnapper. That is to say that if the claim is true, then that's a good reason to think that the suspect is the kidnapper. The claim that you're tired and would like to just arrest someone so you can go home is irrelevant; it does not count in favor of the truth of the claim that the suspect is the kidnapper.

There are two things to notice about relevance: First, you can say that a premise is relevant to the conclusion without saying that it's acceptable. Think about the kidnapping case again. If the claim about the child climbing into the suspect's van comes from an anonymous tip, you might not know whether to believe it. But you *do* know that it *would* count in favor of the claim that the suspect is the kidnapper *if* it were true. Second, you can say that premise is relevant to the conclusion without accepting the conclusion. After all, just because you have *some* reason to believe the conclusion doesn't mean that you have *enough* reason. There might be other possibilities that you can't yet rule out. That brings us to the final criterion in argument evaluation: sufficiency.

---

[7]One claim can be negatively relevant to another claim if the truth of the first claim counts against the truth of the second. That's not the kind of relevance you want in an argument, though.

Sufficiency

To say that an argument's premises are sufficient is to say that, taken together, they provide *enough* reason to believe the conclusion. This is to say more than that they provide some reason to believe it; it is to say that if you accept the argument's premises, then you rationally ought to accept the conclusion.

As with relevance, it can be easiest to understand sufficiency by thinking about arguments that fail on this criterion. Consider, for instance, the following argument:

MARTIAN MICROBES

 1. There used to be large amounts of liquid water on the surface of Mars.
 2. Liquid water is essential to life as we know it.
∴ 3. There used to be life on Mars.

The premises of this argument are both acceptable and relevant to the conclusion. But they are not sufficient. Just because Mars had one of the ingredients essential for life doesn't mean that it actually had life. Maybe it was missing other essential ingredients, or maybe life develops only very rarely in the universe. Given these other possibilities, the premises of martian microbes don't give us *enough* reason to accept its conclusion.

In general, if you think that an argument fails on the sufficiency criterion, you should be prepared to say what further premises would be needed in order to meet that criterion. For instance, you might think that MARTIAN MICROBES would meet the sufficiency criterion if it also stated that Mars still contains chemicals that were almost certainly created by living organisms. Since we don't (yet) have evidence of such chemicals, that claim would not be acceptable as a premise. But that's not the point here; the point is to figure out what sort of claims the argument would have to add to provide enough reason for us to accept its conclusion.

FALLACIES

An argument that violates one of the three criteria for a good argument might be a **fallacy.** A fallacy is, roughly, a deceptively bad argument. Many kinds of fallacies are so common that philosophers have given them special names. For instance, the fallacy of **wishful thinking** argues that a conclusion is true because it would be good if it were true; this violates the relevance criterion, since whether it would be good if something were true doesn't affect whether it *is* true. The fallacy of **appealing to ignorance** argues that a conclusion is true because it hasn't been proven false; this usually violates the sufficiency criterion, since something could be false even though it hasn't been *proven* false.

Throughout this book we'll discuss some fallacies that appear especially often in moral reasoning. To learn more about those fallacies or about other fallacies, see this book's companion web site for a link to online resources about fallacies.

When you encounter a fallacy, don't dismiss the argument right away. You can sometimes fix fallacious arguments by revising, deleting, or adding premises.

Cogency, Validity, and Soundness

An argument that meets all three of these criteria—premise acceptability, relevance, and sufficiency—is said to be **cogent.** That means, roughly, that someone who hears or reads the argument ought, rationally, to accept its conclusion; the argument's audience ought to think that its conclusion is true. Indeed, the conclusion of a cogent argument is very likely to be true. An argument that is cogent or nearly so is generally said to be a strong argument. An argument that is far from cogent is said to be a weak argument.

Some cogent arguments are special in that they are also **sound arguments.** Whereas all cogent arguments give us good reasons to think that their conclusions are true, a sound argument goes further by establishing its conclusion with certainty. If we know an argument is sound, we know *for sure* that its conclusion is true. To be sound, an argument must have true premises and be **valid.** Informally, people often say that an argument is "valid" when they really mean that it's cogent. Strictly speaking, to call an argument valid is to say something

---

THE RELATIONSHIPS BETWEEN COGENCY, VALIDITY, AND SOUNDNESS

The relationships between cogency, validity, and soundness can be visualized in a Venn diagram:

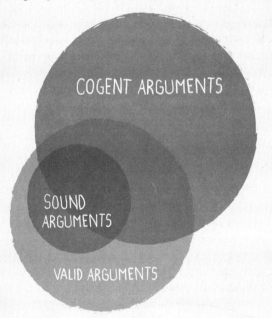

FIGURE 1.1   A visual representation of the relationships between cogency, validity, and soundness.

To test your understanding of the ideas of cogency, validity, and soundness, see if you can give examples of (kinds of) arguments that would fit into each of the five different areas of the Venn diagram.

much more specific: it is to say that its premises are connected to its conclusion so perfectly that it is *impossible* for the premises to be true while the conclusion is false. This doesn't mean that the premises *are* true—just that *if* they *were* true, then the conclusion *would have to be* true. To see the difference, suppose your friend told you about her new pet, Fluffy, and offered the following argument:

FLUFFY

1. Fluffy is a dolphin.
∴ 2. Fluffy is a mammal.

Since all dolphins are mammals, it's impossible for claim (1) to be true and claim (2) to be false. The truth of (1) would guarantee the truth of (2). Thus, your friend's argument is valid. Notice that we can know that the argument is valid without knowing whether Fluffy really is a dolphin—that is, without knowing whether the premise is actually true. If your friend were to introduce you to Fluffy and you confirmed that Fluffy really is a dolphin, then you would know that your friend's argument was not only valid, but also sound.

Remember, though, that not all cogent arguments are sound. Cogent arguments give you a good enough reason to believe their conclusions, but they do not necessarily establish their conclusions with certainty. And perhaps more surprisingly, not all sound arguments are cogent, since there are valid arguments whose premises are true but which no one has good reason to accept. (These would include, for instance, valid arguments about events in the distant past for which we have no evidence.)

The distinctions between cogency, soundness, and validity won't be crucial in most of this book, but it is worth understanding them for those cases when you do encounter a (supposedly) sound argument, since sound arguments are especially strong.

TERMINOLOGY TO KNOW

reasoning	conclusion indicator	fallacy
argument	premise indicator	wishful thinking
claim	subconclusion	appeal to ignorance
conclusion	argument evaluation	cogency
premise	premise acceptability	validity
explanation	relevance	soundness
argument analysis	sufficiency	

DISCUSSION QUESTIONS

1. Give an example of an argument that you've recently encountered in your classes or daily life. Write the argument as a list of numbered premises and a conclusion. Explain how you decided which claims were the premises and which was the conclusion.
2. Give an example of an explanation that you've recently encountered in your classes or daily life. Explain why you think it's an explanation rather than an argument.
3. Are all of the premises in ARISTOTLE'S ARGUMENT (p. 8) acceptable (to modern college students)? Are they all relevant? Are they sufficient? What about the premises in Elle Woods's argument from *Legally Blonde* (p. 3)? Are both arguments cogent? Explain your answers.
4. Why aren't all sound arguments cogent? Why aren't all cogent arguments sound?

2) Moral Arguments

"Dear Abby," the long-running advice column, printed the following letter in 1981:

> DEAR ABBY: I needed some Scotch tape, so I looked in my son's desk for some and noticed the beginning of a letter my son had written to his girlfriend. It read, "I am only interested in being stoned, spending money, and sex."
>
> I read no further.
>
> My first impulse was to confront him with this, but he would say I had no right to go snooping through his desk.
>
> I don't think I should go on ignoring this. I would appreciate some advice. He is eighteen-and-a-half.
>
> BEWILDERED FATHER[1]

People write to Abby when they aren't sure what to do about a problem they're facing. Some people might be looking for an easy answer. But others are looking for something more.

MORAL ARGUMENTS AND MORAL CLAIMS

Assuming that "Bewildered Father" wanted more than an easy answer, he might have wanted Abby to give him a **moral argument.** Recall from Chapter 1 that an "argument," in our sense of the word, is not a fight or even a disagreement. It's (roughly) a set of reasons given to convince someone that something is true. A *moral* argument, in particular, is any argument whose conclusion is a **moral claim.** Roughly, a moral claim is any claim about what is morally right, wrong, good, or bad. So, a moral argument gives reasons to think that a particular action (person, event, etc.) is morally right (or wrong or good or bad). That's just what Bewildered Father wanted from "Dear Abby."

. You encounter moral claims all the time: For instance, you might say that your friend made the right choice in a tough situation, meaning not just that it was the "smart" choice for your friend, but that your friend "did the right thing." You might get into a discussion with

---

[1] Abigail Van Buren, *The Best of Dear Abby* (New York: Phillips-Van Buren, 1981), 57.

a classmate about whether it's wrong to review copies of previous year's exams from your fraternity's files. You might decide, after getting to know someone, that he or she is a good person. You can surely think of a villain from a novel or a movie who is a bad person. All of these are moral claims.

The main goal of this book is to help you understand how to recognize and construct strong arguments for and against such claims—that is, how to reason well about moral issues. Talking about how to evaluate and construct moral arguments requires introducing a few concepts beyond those we introduced in Chapter 1 to discuss arguments in general. To begin with, we can get a bit more precise in our definition of "moral claim" by introducing more philosophical terminology.

Moral arguments can include two different kinds of moral claims: **deontic claims** and **axiological claims.** Roughly, deontic claims are about whether an action is morally right or wrong. Axiological claims (about morality) are about whether something is (morally) good or bad.[2]

Deontic claims can be divided into claims that an action is **morally wrong**, **morally obligatory,** or (merely) **morally permissible.** The first of these is straightforward: To say that an action is morally wrong is just to say that you ought not to do it. For example, murder is morally wrong. Philosophers often use the term "morally forbidden" as a synonym for "morally wrong," so they might say, "Murder is morally forbidden." We can understand the other two kinds of claims in terms of moral wrongness: An action is morally obligatory if it would be morally wrong *not* to do it. For example, imagine that you are standing on a busy street corner. You see that your best friend's 3-year-old nephew is about to run out into traffic, and you could easily stop your friend's nephew at no risk or cost to yourself. It would be wrong for you to let the boy run into the street, which entails that it is morally obligatory for you to stop him. If an action is merely morally permissible, then it is neither wrong nor obligatory. It wouldn't be wrong for you to do it, but it wouldn't be wrong for you *not* to do it, either. It's okay to do it and okay not to do it. For example, there would be nothing morally wrong with your becoming a doctor or a nurse, but it wouldn't be wrong for you to become something else instead; becoming a doctor or a nurse is merely morally permissible. (Sometimes when someone asks whether an action is morally permissible, they are just asking whether it's wrong or not; in that context, people would lump obligatory actions in with merely permissible actions. But as a technical term, "morally permissible" means the same as "neither wrong nor obligatory.")

Some moral theorists divide the category of morally permissible actions even further. They say that some permissible actions are **supererogatory,** while other permissible actions are **morally indifferent.** To say that an action is supererogatory is to say that it would be morally good or praiseworthy for you to do it, but it is not wrong for you not do it. For instance, it would be supererogatory for you to volunteer your time this weekend to help a struggling child learn to read. If you choose to spend your weekend doing other things, you won't have done anything *wrong*, but if you do spend it volunteering, you'll be doing something morally praiseworthy or admirable. To say that an action is morally indifferent is to say that it makes absolutely no difference, morally speaking, whether you do it or not. Neither

---

[2]In case you're interested in where these technical terms come from, the word "deontic" comes from the Greek word *deon*, which roughly translates to "duty" or "obligation." The word "axiological" comes from the Greek word *axia*, which translates to "value" or "worth."

BEING PERMISSIBLE vs. BEING PERMITTED

Many people confuse the idea of being morally permissible with the idea of something *actually* being permitted by society. That is, they interpret, "It is morally permissible to eat meat," as meaning, "Society permits people to eat meat." They interpret claims about an action's being morally wrong or morally obligatory along the same lines. While there are philosophical views according to which being permissible and being permitted amount to the same thing, those views are much more controversial and problematic than most people realize. To get a taste of why they're problematic, think about something that your society currently permits that you think is wrong or something that your society does not permit that you think is okay to do; if being permissible and being permitted were the same thing, it would be impossible to even think such thoughts, just as it's impossible to picture a four-sided triangle. For a more detailed discussion about the connection between morality and society's views about right and wrong, see Chapter 9. Also, see the boxed text about morality and the law later in this chapter.

doing an indifferent action nor omitting the action deserves praise or blame. Much of our moral reasoning does not require us to make such fine-grained distinctions. Often all that we need to know is whether an action is obligatory, forbidden, or neither.

It is worth your time to distinguish between these different kinds of claims because you will need to use slightly different strategies when arguing for different kinds of deontic claims. In Chapters 3–7 you will learn how to use various kinds of arguments to argue for moral claims. For instance, you will learn how to argue that an action is morally wrong by arguing that it violates the actor's obligations, that it exhibits especially bad character traits, or that it would bring about especially bad consequences (as compared to some alternative action).

Just as you use the idea of moral wrongness to understand claims about moral obligation and moral permissibility, you can think about arguing for those claims in terms of arguing for claims about moral wrongness. For instance, the way to argue that an action is morally obligatory is to argue that it would be wrong not to do it. The way to argue that an action is merely permissible is to argue *both* that it would not be wrong to do it *and* that it would not

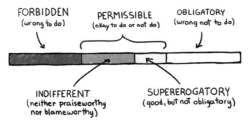

FIGURE 2.1   When you make a deontic claim, you are saying that an action falls into one of these categories.

be wrong to refrain from doing it. The way to argue that an action is supererogatory is to show *both* that it would be morally praiseworthy or admirable to do it *and* that it would not be wrong to refrain from doing it.

One thing that will sometimes help in constructing such arguments is to use *axiological* claims. Axiological claims are a second kind of moral claim, distinct from deontic claims.[3] Axiological claims include claims that something is morally good, morally bad, or morally neutral—that is, neither good nor bad—as well as claims that one thing is morally better than another. You can make axiological claims about all kinds of things, including people, character traits, events, and even states of affairs. For instance, you probably think that serial killer Jeffrey Dahmer was a bad person and that Adolf Hitler was even worse. You probably think that honesty and courage are morally good character traits, whereas cruelty is not. Slavery was a morally bad thing, whereas the abolition of slavery was a good thing. These are all examples of axiological claims.

In short, what makes an argument a moral argument is just that it has a moral claim—either a deontic or an axiological claim—as its conclusion. Learning to reason about morality is just learning to recognize and develop good arguments for and against different moral claims.

NORMATIVE AND DESCRIPTIVE CLAIMS

Moral claims are one type of **normative claim.** A normative claim is a claim about how the world *ought* to be or about what is *good* or *bad*. Any claim that says that the world ought or ought not to be a certain way, or that a person should or shouldn't do something, or that something is good or bad (in some way) is a normative claim. Normative claims are sometimes called "evaluative claims" because they *evaluate* some person, thing, or (possible) state of the world. Besides moral claims, other kinds of normative claims include aesthetic claims (which evaluate beauty and art), epistemological claims (which are evaluative claims related to knowledge and the justification of beliefs), and prudential claims (which evaluate actions in terms of their effect on the actor's own well-being). For example, "*Moonlight* is an excellent film" is an aesthetic claim but not a moral claim. "We ought not to believe things without good reason" is an epistemological claim; it tells you what you ought to do in order to have true beliefs. "You should always look both ways before crossing the street," "You ought to choose a career that makes you happy," and "You shouldn't bring a knife to a gunfight" are all prudential claims; they tell you what you should do if you want to ensure your own well-being. Finally, there are non-moral and non-aesthetic axiological claims, which say that something is good or bad, but not in a moral or aesthetic way. For instance, the overly enthusiastic narrators on infomercials are not trying to convince you that the latest

---

[3]Strictly speaking, not all axiological claims are moral claims. Some axiological claims, for instance, are about whether a particular piece of art is good art. See Figure 2.2. For simplicity, we'll ignore those kinds of axiological claims in this book, focusing only on claims about *moral* value.

kitchen gadgets are morally or aesthetically good, only that they are good tools to have in the kitchen.

Normative claims are usually contrasted with **descriptive claims.** A descriptive claim is a claim about how the world *is*, not how it ought to be. For instance, consider the claim that Stephenie Meyer, the author of the *Twilight* series, is extremely wealthy. This is a descriptive claim. It says something about the way the world is. By contrast, the claim that the *Twilight* series is the greatest work in all of Western literature is a normative claim. (Specifically, it's an aesthetic claim.) The claim that Meyer deserves her vast riches is also a normative claim. You don't have to agree with these claims to recognize that they are normative claims. All you have to notice is that they do more than just say how the world is; they *evaluate* the world. The first says that the *Twilight* series is a great work of literature—the greatest in Western history, no less. The second says that it is right or good for Meyer to have received so much money for writing the series.

The various kinds of claims we've discussed are shown in Figure 2.2.

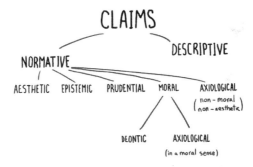

FIGURE 2.2   A visual representation of the relationships between different kinds of claims.

MORALITY AND THE LAW

Don't confuse claims about what's morally right or wrong with claims about what's legal or illegal. For one thing, claims about what's right or wrong are normative claims, whereas claims about what's legal or illegal are descriptive claims. They're making a statement what the law *is*, not what the law should be or whether we should obey any particular law. For another thing, something could be immoral without being illegal. For instance, many people would say that cheating on your spouse is generally immoral, but in many places it's not illegal. And while people generally have an obligation to obey the law, some actions are illegal without being immoral. Harriet Tubman's heroic work helping people escape slavery was illegal but not immoral.

MORAL PREMISES

Perhaps the most important thing to remember when analyzing and constructing moral arguments is that every moral argument needs to have at least one moral premise. (This is yet another reason why it's important to know what kinds of claims count as moral claims: you need to be able to tell whether any of the premises in an argument are moral premises.) People often leave the moral premise(s) unstated when they give a moral argument. This makes it all the more important to think carefully about what moral premises an argument includes or assumes.

The rule that every moral argument needs to have at least one moral premise is based on a principle called **Hume's Law**:

HUME'S LAW

You cannot derive an "ought" from an "is."

Hume's Law means that no argument for a normative conclusion—that is, for a conclusion about how things *ought* to be—can be a cogent argument unless it has at least one normative premise. For our purposes, that means that no moral argument is a cogent argument unless it has at least one moral premise. Of course, most moral arguments have some non-moral premises, too. Hume's Law allows this, as long as the argument also has at least one moral premise. The problem only arises when *all* of the premises are descriptive premises—that is, premises about the way the world *is* or *was* or *would be*, rather than how it ought to be.

When an argument violates Hume's Law—that is, when it has a normative conclusion but no normative premises—it is said to commit the **is/ought fallacy.**[4] The best way to respond to an argument that commits the is/ought fallacy is to ask what normative assumption(s) the argument is making—that is, what hidden normative premise(s) you need to add to the argument to get it to work.

Hume's Law strikes some people as obviously true, but it strikes others as obviously false. After all, the following strikes many people as a perfectly good moral argument:

PANDEMIC FLU

1. A pandemic flu would kill tens of millions of people.
2. Genetically engineering a pandemic flu virus would significantly increase the risk of a pandemic flu.
∴ 3. It is morally wrong to genetically engineer a pandemic flu virus.[5]

Notice, however, that neither of the premises is a moral premise. They are both about the way the world *is* or *would be*, not about how it *should* be. That is, neither says anything about

---

[4]People sometimes refer to the is/ought fallacy as the "naturalistic fallacy," but this can sometimes be confusing because people also use the term "naturalistic fallacy" to refer to other kinds of mistakes in reasoning.

[5]This argument is adapted from Martin Enserink, "Controversial Studies Give a Deadly Flu Virus Wings," *Science* 334 (2011): 1192–93.

DAVID HUME AND THE "IS/OUGHT PROBLEM"

Hume's Law is named for the Scottish philosopher David Hume (1711–1776), who was largely ignored in his lifetime but is now regarded as a major figure in the history of Western philosophy. In his most famous work, *A Treatise of Human Nature*, Hume develops provocative positions in the philosophical fields of metaphysics, epistemology, and ethics.

At the end of a section on ethics, Hume says that he can't resist adding "an observation, which may, perhaps, be found of some importance." Many authors, he notes, begin by talking about the way the world is and then shift to talking about the way the world ought to be, without explaining how their claims about how the world *is* lead to their claims about how the world *ought* to be. In technical terms, these authors move from descriptive premises to normative conclusions without explaining the connection between the two. Hume notes that such a move needs to be explained. That is why the principle that "you cannot derive an 'ought' from an 'is'" is called Hume's Law.

---

what is right or wrong, good or bad, etc. (You might think that (1) says something about what is good or bad. But just because a sentence is talking *about* something bad doesn't mean that the sentence *says* that the thing is bad. Premise (1) is simply predicting what *would* happen if there were a pandemic flu, not saying whether that would be good or bad. It would be logically possible for someone, such as a movie villain, to agree with premise (1) but think that the death of tens of millions of people would be just fine.)

What's really going on here is that the argument has a **hidden premise.** A hidden premise is a premise that is assumed but never explicitly stated in the argument. The hidden premise in this argument is a moral premise that connects the non-moral premises to the moral conclusion. It's important to determine, as best we can, exactly what the moral premise is. For instance, the hidden premise could be one of these two claims:

(H) It is always morally wrong to do anything that increases the risk that tens of millions of people will die.

(H*) It is morally wrong to significantly increase the risk that tens of millions of people will die unless there is a really good reason for doing so.

If we use (H) as the hidden premise of our argument, it will certainly connect (1) and (2) to the conclusion, (3). But there's reason to think that (H) might not be true. What if we could permanently end world poverty, cure cancer, and get mosquitos to stop biting people, but only at the cost of increasing the probability that 20 million people would die by a few billionths of 1 percent? It's not obvious that it would be wrong to do so. After all, poverty, cancer, and mosquito-borne illnesses kill millions of people every year. But if it would not be wrong to incur that risk to end poverty, cure cancer, and stop mosquitos from biting people, then (H) is, strictly speaking, false. Something closer to (H*) is more likely to be true. But if (H*) is true, then (1) and (2) might not be enough to support the conclusion, (3). We would need to know whether there is a really good reason to genetically engineer a pandemic flu virus. We would need to go look for more information before we could evaluate the argument.

CIRCULAR REASONING

An argument commits the fallacy of **circular reasoning** (also known as **begging the question**) when its premises include or assume the argument's conclusion. Circular reasoning often takes the form of smuggling the conclusion into the definition of a word in one of your premises. For instance, people sometimes argue that capital punishment is wrong because it is murder. But to call something murder is just to say that it is *unjustified* killing. Thus, the premise that capital punishment is murder is acceptable for you *only if* you already have good reason to believe that capital punishment is wrong. One helpful way to show that an argument commits this fallacy is to spell out the claim "Murder is unjustified killing" as a hidden premise in the argument, which makes it obvious that the argument's (explicit) premise assumes the truth of the conclusion.

As you can see, it makes a difference what claim you use, as a hidden premise. Some claims may "work" to connect the premises to the conclusion, but if they're unacceptable they won't make the argument cogent. Other claims might be acceptable but fail to connect the premises to the conclusion appropriately. Sometimes, you'll find a premise that is both acceptable *and* connects the premises to the conclusions. (That means you've found a strong argument!)

Identifying a particular claim as *the* hidden premise in an argument is tricky. The best way to do it depends in part on what you're trying to do. If you are trying to figure out exactly what someone else believes, you may need to ask them whether they accept (H), (H*), or some other alternative. If you're trying to figure out whether *you* should accept the conclusion of the argument, you should pick the hidden premise that makes the argument as strong as possible. That way, you'll be able to consider the best argument for the conclusion.

To see another example, consider this argument, which is commonly used in support of the death penalty:

DETERRENCE

   1. Executing convicted murderers deters some would-be murderers from killing people.
∴ 2. Executing convicted murderers is morally permissible.

The argument's only stated premise, (1), is a descriptive premise. It says that executing convicted murderers *causes* other people to decide not to commit murder. All causal claims—i.e., claims about what causes what—are descriptive claims. But the conclusion is a moral claim. So, we need to look for a hidden moral premise.

Here are several candidates:

(H_1) It is morally permissible to do whatever is necessary to prevent crime.

(H_2) It is morally permissible to do whatever is necessary to prevent murder.

(H_3) It is morally permissible to kill convicted murderers if doing so saves innocent lives.

Each of these would successfully connect (1) to (2). But (H$_1$) is surely false: Executing people on the spot for being suspected of shoplifting, graffiti, or jaywalking would probably deter all three of those activities to some extent. Yet it is clearly morally forbidden for a police officer to shoot someone on the spot just because he suspects the person has shoplifted a pack of gum.

Maybe (H$_2$) will fare better, since it focuses only on murder. It still has the problem that it endorses doing *whatever is necessary* to prevent murder. In ancient China, entire families could be executed for the crimes of a single family member. This would presumably be a more effective deterrent than just executing the criminal. But it would be morally wrong to do so, since it involves punishing people—quite severely!—for something that they didn't do.

What about (H$_3$)? This seems more promising. In fact, it's close to a premise suggested by the philosopher Ernest van den Haag, who argues that the death of an innocent murder victim is worse than the death of a convicted murderer.[6] Thus, if we can prevent the death of one or more innocent murder victims by executing a convicted murderer, it is morally permissible to do so.

Suppose, then, that we accept (H$_3$) as the hidden premise in DETERRENCE. We now have our work cut out for us in evaluating the argument. We will need to find out whether the death penalty does, in fact, deter would-be murderers. We will also need to think carefully about whether it is morally permissible to kill a convicted murderer in order to save innocent lives. Both of those are difficult tasks, but at least we now know where to start in evaluating DETERRENCE.

MAKING MORAL JUDGMENTS WITHOUT BEING JUDGMENTAL

The purpose of reasoning about moral issues is to form well-justified judgments about whether particular actions are right or wrong. Some people are uncomfortable making moral judgments. They worry that judging people's actions as right or wrong amounts to being judgmental. But you can make moral judgments about other people's actions without being judgmental.

Reaching the conclusion that someone else's action was morally wrong is not the same as judging that the person should be scolded or punished for doing it—much less that *you* should be the one to scold or punish the person. For instance, imagine that you see someone at a political protest carrying a sign with racist slogans on it. It would presumably be inappropriate for anyone (including you) to punish her for carrying the sign, since it's a form of protected free speech, but it would be appropriate for you to think that she's doing something wrong by carrying it. It might even be appropriate for you to tell her that you think it's wrong for her to carry that sign. Or imagine you overhear a stranger at a coffee shop admitting to a

---

[6]Ernest van den Haag, "On Deterrence and the Death Penalty," *The Journal of Criminal Law, Criminology and Political Science* 60 (1969): 141–47.

"THAT'S JUST, LIKE, YOUR OPINION, MAN"

Another reason that some people are uncomfortable making moral judgments is that they believe that all judgments about right or wrong are "just opinions." There are deep and important philosophical questions lurking here—questions about the distinction between "facts" and "opinions," for instance, and about whether moral claims can be true or justified. The idea that moral claims are "just opinions" is far more controversial, philosophically, than many people realize. We discuss these issues in Chapter 9. In the meantime, remember that just because something counts as "an opinion" doesn't mean that you can't give reasons for it. For instance, you might have views about whether one basketball player is better than another or which of two movies was funnier. Even if those are "just opinions," you can still give reasons for your views.

friend that he's been cheating on his wife. You might think that he's done something morally wrong, but you might also think that it is not your place to intervene. Similarly, determining that some action is morally obligatory is not the same as judging that someone should be forced to do it. For instance, you might agree with the philosopher Peter Singer that most Americans are morally obligated to donate a large share of their income to fight global poverty, but you could still think that it would be wrong for anyone to *force* people to do so. In general, you might form a moral judgment about someone else's action and yet do nothing to try to change that person's behavior.

In some cases, though, it might be appropriate—or even obligatory—to try to change someone else's behavior or to get someone else, like the police, to intervene. This only counts as "being judgmental" if you intervene in an overbearing or inappropriate way. For example, if you discover that a coworker has been stealing other people's lunches out of the office refrigerator, you might think it appropriate for you to tell him that he ought to stop. Whether you come across as judgmental depends on how to say it.

TERMINOLOGY TO KNOW

moral argument	morally permissible	is/ought fallacy
moral claim	supererogatory	hidden premise
deontic claim	morally indifferent	circular reasoning
axiological claim	normative claim	begging the question
morally wrong	descriptive claim	
morally obligatory	Hume's Law	

DISCUSSION QUESTIONS

1. Some people think that there are no supererogatory actions. Why might they think that? Are they right? Why or why not?
2. Is there a "bright line" between prudential claims and moral claims, so that we can always tell whether the claim is a prudential claim or a moral claim? Why or why not?

3. Why, exactly, can't a moral argument be cogent if it violates Hume's Law? That is, which of the criteria for cogency (pp. 8–12) would such an argument violate? Why?

4. Would "Murderers deserve to die" be a plausible hidden premise for DETERRENCE (p. 21)? Why or why not?

CASE STUDIES

See the Note About Case Studies on p. 150 for further instructions.

1. During a visit to a radio station in Manhattan in 2014, singer Ariana Grande signed autographs and posed for pictures, smiling and seemingly happy to be surrounded by adoring fans. According to the gossip column in the *New York Daily News*, however, Grande changed her tune once she stepped into the elevator. As soon as her fans were safely out of sight, she supposedly said, "I hope they all f—ing die." Evaluate Grande's action of pretending to be happy to see her fans when she actually couldn't stand to be around them. Give a moral argument to support your evaluation, being sure to use at least one normative premise.

2. Two parents in Silver Spring, Maryland, found themselves at the center of a national controversy when their 10-year-old son and 6-year-old daughter were found walking alone in their suburban neighborhood. The two kids were picked up by police while walking back from a park about a mile from their house. The parents, Danielle and Alexander Meitiv, endorse a style of parenting called "free-range parenting." They had previously allowed their children to walk together to other places in the neighborhood, such as the library and a 7-Eleven. They maintain that their children are mature enough to take such walks on their own and that the children face very little danger on the walks. Evaluate the parents' action of allowing their children to walk around their neighborhood without an adult. Give a moral argument to support your evaluation, being sure to use at least one normative premise.

3. Thomas More served as a close advisor to King Henry VIII of England in the decade before England split with the Catholic Church. As a devout Catholic, More disapproved of Henry's opposition to the Pope. Henry, in turn, disapproved of More's disapproval. In 1534, the Parliament of England passed a law that required More to take an oath that violated his Catholic faith in various ways. Refusal to take that oath amounted to treason. More refused to take the oath and was therefore executed. Moments before his execution, he described himself as "the king's good servant, but God's first." Evaluate More's action of refusing to take the oath demanded by Parliament. Give a moral argument to support your evaluation, being sure to use at least one normative premise.

4. The French film *Amélie* focuses on a young Parisian woman's attempts to make her friends and neighbors happy—usually without their realizing that she is involved. In one scene, Amélie listens to her elderly neighbor, Madeleine, tell the story of her late husband's adultery: in the 1970s, her husband ran off to the Bahamas with his secretary; he later died in an accident. Madeleine has lived alone, broken-hearted, ever since. When Amélie learns that the wreckage of a 1970s plane crash has recently been discovered and that mail from the crash was now being delivered to its intended recipients, she forges a love letter from Madeleine's husband. The letter apologizes for his (the husband's) infidelity, tells Madeleine that he has always loved her, and promises to return to her soon. Madeleine reads the forged letter and is delighted to learn that her husband still loved her after all; a great weight is lifted from her shoulders. Evaluate Amélie's act of forging a letter to mend Madeleine's broken heart. Give a moral argument to support your evaluation, being sure to use at least one normative premise.

PART II

Ways of Reasoning About Moral Issues

3) Reasoning with Obligations

When a corrupt Baltimore politician stands trial in the HBO series *The Wire*, he freely admits to stealing charitable donations. But, he explains, he didn't steal to enrich himself. He stole to help the struggling people of his run-down district in West Baltimore. The jury, despite having just heard the politician admit to the crime of which he was accused, found him not guilty of that crime.[1] This is an example, though a fictional one, of what lawyers call "jury nullification."

Jury nullification occurs when a jury declares a defendant not guilty, despite knowing that the court has clear evidence that the defendant is guilty. The jurors know that, according to the law, they should find the defendant guilty, but they decide to ignore the law and return a verdict of "not guilty." In the United States, at least, judges are not allowed to overrule a jury's acquittal, so there is nothing that the judge can do. The defendant simply gets away with breaking the law.

In the U.S. Supreme Court case *Sparf and Hansen* v. *U.S.* (1895), Justice John Marshall Harlan gave an argument much like this one:

JURY NULLIFICATION

    1. Jurors have both a legal and a moral obligation to apply the law to the facts of the case.
    2. Jury nullification occurs when a jury ignores the law.
∴ 3. It is morally wrong for a jury to engage in jury nullification.[2]

This argument relies on a special kind of moral premise: a moral premise that says that someone has a particular **moral obligation.** To say that someone has a moral obligation to do something is just to say that it is morally obligatory for *that person* to do *that thing*. For instance, premise (1) of JURY NULLIFICATION says that it is morally obligatory for *each juror to apply the law to the facts of the case*. As you'll recall from Chapter 2, to say that something is morally obligatory (for someone) is to say that it is would be morally wrong for that person *not* to do it. So premises (1) and (2) jointly entail that it would be morally wrong for a juror to fail to apply the law to the facts of the case.

---

[1] "Took," *The Wire*, HBO, February 17, 2008.

[2] It is unclear whether Justice Harlan meant to say that jurors have *both* a legal obligation and a moral obligation to apply the law or if he means that they have only a legal obligation. These are two different things. For the purposes of this argument, we will focus only on moral obligations. See *Sparf and Hansen* v. *U.S.,* 156 U.S. 51 (1895).

In general, reasoning with moral obligations makes it fairly easy to construct moral arguments. Most arguments that appeal to moral obligations use one of these two forms:

FORM 1

1. Person **P** has a moral obligation to do **X.**
2. The only way to do **X** is to do **Y.**
∴ 3. It is morally obligatory for person **P** to do **Y.**

FORM 2

1. Person *P* has a moral obligation to do **X.**
2. Doing action *Y* amounts to not doing **X.**
∴ 3. It is morally wrong for person *P* to do **Y.**

Filling in these forms involves identifying the relevant obligation and showing that doing **Y** is related to doing **X** in the relevant way. For instance, in JURY NULLIFICATION, the relevant obligation—what goes in the place of **X**—is the obligation to apply the law to the facts of the case. Action **Y** is jury nullification. By definition, jury nullification involves ignoring the law in deciding a case. So, it very clearly amounts to "not doing **X.**"

The philosophically difficult part of these arguments, of course, is establishing that someone has a particular moral obligation—that is, that "person **P** has a moral obligation to do **X.**" To help do that, we can divide moral obligations into two kinds: role-based obligations, which apply to people in virtue of their occupying certain roles, and general obligations, which apply to everybody.

MORAL THEORY: DEONTOLOGY

Some philosophers argue that morality should be understood primarily in terms of obligations. This philosophical view is known as **deontology,** which means "the study of duties," and people who hold this view are called deontologists. According to deontology, what matters most in morality is whether someone is or is not "following the moral rules." Therefore, deontologists claim, all arguments about what someone ought to do must ultimately depend on premises that appeal to obligations.

Deontologists disagree about exactly what "the moral rules" are, although this disagreement is often not as deep as it seems. That is, they disagree about exactly how to understand the obligations that people have, but in particular cases they frequently agree about which actions people are obligated to perform or not perform. Deontologists also disagree about how important it is that people follow the right rules for the right reason. For instance, some deontologists argue that a person who follows the rules only to avoid being punished is not really acting rightly. Other deontologists argue that such a person is acting rightly, even if his or her doing so does not necessarily make him or her a good person.

For more about deontology, see Chapter 11.

ROLE-BASED OBLIGATIONS

A moral obligation is a **role-based obligation** if all the people who occupy a particular role have that obligation and they have the obligation *because* they occupy that role. A role could include a job (e.g., a police officer), a civic role (e.g., a juror), a social role (e.g., a parent or friend), etc. Most people occupy many roles at once. For instance, a person could be a business executive, a daughter, a mother, a best friend, and a voter all at the same time.

Different roles come with different obligations. For instance, being a soldier carries the obligation of defending one's country, even if that means risking one's life. A parent has an obligation to ensure that his or her child is taken care of. And a juror, according to Justice Harlan, has an obligation to apply the law to the facts of the case before him or her. The jurors' obligation in JURY NULLIFICATION is a role-based obligation—one that they have *because* they are currently occupying the role of juror.

Appealing to social roles is often helpful in justifying premise (1) in an argument that follows FORM 1 or FORM 2 above. Recall that premise (1) had the form "Person *P* has a moral obligation to do *X*." If someone asked you why *P* has an obligation to do *X*, you might be able to identify a role that *P* occupies that carries an obligation to do *X*. For instance, suppose you said that the football player Tom Brady has an obligation to do his best (within the rules of the game) to help his team win. If someone asked you why Brady has this obligation, you could justify your claim by saying, "Professional athletes have an obligation to do their best (within the rules of the game) to help their teams win."

Many role-based obligations are straightforward and widely accepted. Few people would deny that politicians have an obligation to refuse bribes, that close friends have an obligation to help one another in times of need, or that elevator safety inspectors have an obligation to ensure that elevators are working properly. Other role-based obligations are more controversial. For instance, does a defense attorney have a moral obligation to defend her client to the best of her ability if she believes that her client is guilty of a serious crime? Parents have an obligation to protect their children, but if someone commits a crime, do his or her parents have a parental obligation to help their child conceal that crime from the police? There is no systematic way to answer these sorts of questions; they must be considered one at a time.

To see how this might work, consider another example—this one from bioethicist Daniel Callahan:

EUTHANASIA

1. Doctors have a special obligation never to use their medical knowledge to kill someone.
2. Physician-assisted suicide involves a doctor administering a lethal medication, at a patient's request, in order to kill the patient.
∴ 3. It is morally wrong for a doctor to participate in physician-assisted suicide.[3]

The normative premise in EUTHANASIA is that doctors have a special obligation—that is, a role-based obligation specific to the medical profession—never to use their medical knowledge to kill someone. But why should we accept that premise? Callahan argues that doctors' specialized medical knowledge gives them great power and that because society will not (or should not) grant them the privilege to use that power unless the power is limited, doctors

---

[3]Daniel Callahan, "Can We Return Death to Disease?" *Hastings Center Report* 19 (Jan.–Feb. 1989): 4–6.

have a special responsibility to use their medical knowledge only to "cure or comfort, never to kill."[4] In other words, Callahan appeals to a controversial role-based obligation in Euthanasia, and he backs that premise up with a further argument.

UNIVERSAL OBLIGATIONS

In contrast to role-based obligations, a **universal obligation** is a moral obligation that all persons have, regardless of the roles that they occupy.

Consider the following argument, which is adapted from an argument that philosopher Robert Arrington criticizes in his paper "Advertising and Behavior Control":

MANIPULATIVE ADVERTISING

1. Some kinds of advertising trick consumers into acting in ways that benefit the advertiser but don't necessarily benefit the consumer.
2. Tricking other people into acting in ways that benefit you but don't benefit them is manipulating them.
3. Everyone has a moral obligation not to manipulate others.
∴ 4. Some kinds of advertising are morally forbidden.[5]

Although MANIPULATIVE ADVERTISING is about the ethics of advertising, its main normative premise is not just about the obligations of advertisers; it's about an obligation that *everyone* has—namely, the obligation not to manipulate others. That is, the premise is about a universal obligation.

When using universal obligations in your moral reasoning, you can appeal to fairly specific ones, such as the obligation not to manipulate people, or you can appeal to more general ones. Various philosophers have tried to identify sets of general universal obligations that cover all of morality. While you may disagree with the exact lists that these philosophers have produced, they provide a helpful starting point for thinking about which obligations are genuinely universal. Each of these lists aims to provide a more or less complete list of the obligations that all people have, just in virtue of being people. You'll notice that the lists overlap quite a bit and that most of the obligations on each list are fairly uncontroversial. Appealing to one of these obligations in a moral argument is therefore a relatively safe move.

One major problem with these lists may have already occurred to you: it is possible for these obligations to conflict with one another—or with someone's role-based obligations. In fact, most of life's most difficult ethical problems involve conflicts among obligations. Consider MANIPULATIVE ADVERTISING again. Manipulating someone could be seen as a way of depriving others of freedom; it is a way of tricking them into doing something that they would not have done freely. That's why we all have an obligation not to manipulate others. But you might think that people who work at an advertising agency have a role-based obligation to produce advertisements that help their clients sell their products. They may even have promised the agency's clients that the agency would do everything it could to help sell the product. So it seems that the advertisers' obligation not to deprive others of freedom conflicts

[4] Callahan, "Can We Return Death to Disease?" 6.
[5] Robert L. Arrington, "Advertising and Behavior Control," *Journal of Business Ethics* 1 (1982): 3–12.

Table 3.1   Three Lists of Suggested Universal Obligations

W. D. Ross	Robert Audi	Bernard Gert
Fidelity (promise-keeping)	Prohibition of injury and harm	Do not kill
Reparation (making amends for wrongs done)	Veracity (not lying)	Do not cause pain
Gratitude (doing good or express-ing thanks to those who benefit us)	Fidelity (promise-keeping)	Do not disable others
Beneficence (promoting good outcomes)	Justice (not treating people unfairly)	Do not deprive others of freedom
Non-maleficence (not causing bad outcomes)	Reparation (making amends for wrongs done)	Do not deprive others of pleasure
	Beneficence (promoting other peo-ple's good)	Do not deceive others
	Gratitude (doing good or expressing thanks to those who benefit us)	Keep your promises
	Self-improvement (developing your talents and human capacities)	Do not cheat
	Enhancement of freedom (increasing freedom of persons)	Obey the law
	Respectfulness (treat others with respect)	Fulfill your role-based obligations

Sources: Adapted from W. D. Ross, *The Right and the Good*, ed. Philip Stratton-Lake (Oxford: Clarendon Press, 2002); Robert Audi, *The Good in the Right* (Princeton, NJ: Princeton University Press, 2004); and Bernard Gert, *Common Morality* (New York: Oxford University Press, 2004).

with their universal obligation to keep their promises and to fulfill their role-based obligation as employees of an advertising agency. What should they do?

One way out of this problem is to get clearer about the advertisers' obligations. What *exactly* is the relevant role-based obligation? Is it really to do "everything they could" to help their clients sell their products? Not quite: advertisers aren't obligated, for instance, to hold innocent people hostage until the hostages agree to buy their client's products. More generally, they aren't obligated to do anything illegal or immoral to help their clients sell products. We might say that their obligation is to do everything they can, short of breaking the law or behaving immorally, to help their clients sell their products. Since manipulating people is immoral, their role-based obligation doesn't require them to manipulate people. The apparent conflict between the advertisers' universal and role-based obligations was just an illusion.

This approach doesn't always work. Sometimes obligations really do conflict. For in-stance, sometimes the only way to avoid harming someone is to break a promise to someone else. Unfortunately, there is no general rule for deciding which obligation to satisfy when they conflict. It might be tempting to rank the obligations from most important to least im-portant, but some examples suggest that no such ranking is possible. For example, some-times it is more important to keep a promise than to benefit someone, especially when the promise is very important and the benefit is fairly small; at other times, it is more important to benefit someone than to keep a promise. Instead of relying on a general rule, the best we can do is puzzle through each situation on a case-by-case basis, trying to decide which obligation is most important in each case.

RESPECT FOR PERSONS

Some philosophers argue that our universal obligations all boil down to a single rule: always treat people with respect. That is, we should always treat each person with the kind of respect that it is owed to each person, just because they are persons. To see how this obligation gets used in a moral argument, consider the following argument, adapted from the philosopher Ann Garry:

PORNOGRAPHY

1. Pornography reduces women to mere sex objects.
2. Reducing a class of people to mere sex objects is degrading to the people of that class.
3. To degrade someone is to disrespect him or her.
4. Everyone is morally obligated to treat everyone else with respect.
∴ 5. Pornography is morally forbidden.[6]

There are various objections one might raise to this argument. For instance, one might deny that pornography in general "reduces women to mere sex objects" or that it "degrades" women. But the other two premises in the argument seem less controversial: to degrade someone is to disrespect him or her, and everyone is morally obligated to treat everyone else with respect. Some ways of treating others are obviously disrespectful, and it's hard to deny that we ought to treat others with respect.

Sometimes you can construct a powerful moral argument based on the universal obligation to respect other persons simply by pointing out that a behavior amounts to degrading, humiliating, insulting, coercing, or harming someone. All of these things are obviously ways of disrespecting someone. In other cases, however, a particular behavior may seem disrespectful even though it doesn't fit into any of those categories.

It turns out to be surprisingly hard to give a general account of what it is to show **respect for persons,** but several prominent philosophers have tried. Most famously, the great eighteenth-century German philosopher Immanuel Kant said that respecting persons requires treating them "always as ends in themselves, and never merely as means." Philosophers have offered various interpretations of this claim. At the very least, to say that persons are "ends in themselves" is to say that they are valuable for their own sakes, not just for what they can do for society (or for you or for anyone else). To treat someone "merely as a means" is to use or exploit that person, typically by treating them in ways that they do not, would not, or could not agree to be treated. Thus, one interpretation of Kant's rule is that we ought always to treat people as beings who have value in themselves, and so are not to be used or exploited

---

[6] Ann Garry, "Pornography and Respect for Women," *Social Theory and Practice* 4 (1978): 395–421.

IMMANUEL KANT

One of the giants of Western intellectual history, Immanuel Kant (1724–1804) taught philosophy in the city of Königsberg, which was a major city in the German kingdom of Prussia. Kant was famous in Königsberg for the regularity of his daily schedule. Supposedly people could set their clocks based on when Kant passed by their homes on his regular morning walk. Between 1781 and 1790, Kant published a series of books that revolutionized many areas of philosophy, including metaphysics, epistemology, and ethics. Kant's ideas continue to influence many philosophers today.

Kant's most famous idea in moral philosophy is the "categorical imperative," which is supposed to provide a single moral rule that applies to all rational beings regardless of their particular preferences. One way of understanding this rule is as requiring everyone to respect persons. For more on Kant's ethics and the categorical imperative, see Chapter 11.

---

exclusively for our own benefit—or even for someone else's benefit.[7] To reduce someone to a mere sex object, for example, reduces them to the state of a thing to be used for one's own gratification.

Although contemporary philosophers have developed very sophisticated interpretations of respect for persons, the basic idea is that respecting someone as a person requires that we take his or her goals and interests into account when deciding what to do. Some philosophers think that we have a general obligation to actively promote others' goals and interests. At the very least, respect for persons requires that we avoid interfering with or undermining others' goals and interests when we can. We may not simply use other people in any way we see fit, regardless of their goals and interests. This is what distinguishes treating someone as a person from treating him or her as a mere thing. In this way, other people's goals and interests create a kind of limit on what we are morally permitted to do.

This idea of respect for persons is, admittedly, a little vague. The idea behind saying that our only obligation is to treat persons with respect is not that this one obligation instantly clarifies what we ought to do. The idea is that the claim "You have an obligation to treat persons with respect" can serve as a basic premise in any moral argument. You can then develop an argument for or against particular actions (or institutions or whatever) by explaining how those actions (institutions, etc.) do or do not treat persons with respect. Thus, the idea that our most basic obligation is to treat persons with respect justifies one more form of obligation-based moral argument:

FORM 3

1. Everyone is obligated to treat persons with respect.
2. Doing X is not treating persons with respect because Y.
∴ 3. It is morally wrong for anyone to do X.

---

[7] To learn more about Kant's moral philosophy, see the discussion of Kantian deontology in Chapter 11 (pp. 119–22), as well as Kant's "Groundwork for the Metaphysics of Morals" in Part V of this book (pp. 164–170).

PERFECT vs. IMPERFECT OBLIGATIONS

Moral philosophers distinguish **perfect obligations** from **imperfect obligations.** A perfect obligation is one that you must fulfill in every case where it applies. An imperfect obligation is one that you must fulfill sometimes but not at every opportunity. For example, repaying your debts is a perfect obligation: whenever a debt comes due, you are obligated to repay it. Giving to charity, however, is (at most) an imperfect obligation: while you (arguably) act wrongly if you *never* give money to charity, you are not obligated to give to charity at every opportunity. To put this another way, you have some discretion over how and when to fulfill your imperfect obligations (like giving to charity) but not over how and when you fulfill your perfect obligations (like repaying your debts). When using normative premises about obligations, it will sometimes be important to consider whether the obligations you're discussing are perfect or imperfect obligations.

Think back to the earlier argument about pornography. If we replace X with "pornography" and Y with "it degrades women by reducing them to mere sex objects," PORNOGRAPHY fits FORM 3.

Thinking about such arguments in terms of FORM 3 is also helpful for evaluating those arguments. In any argument that fits FORM 3, the thing to focus on is the second premise. Do you really think that doing X is a way of failing to treat persons with respect? Does the argument offer a convincing explanation for thinking so? If not, can you come up with a convincing explanation? Or is the explanation obvious? Or do you think that doing X is actually consistent with treating persons with respect? For instance, is it possible to produce or view pornography without reducing women (or men) to the status of sex objects?

As this example illustrates, reducing all universal obligations to the obligation to treat persons with respect addresses the possibility of conflicting obligations, but it does not eliminate the need to think carefully about exactly what people ought to do (or not do).

TERMINOLOGY TO KNOW

moral obligation	universal obligation	perfect obligation
deontology	respect for persons	imperfect obligation
role-based obligation		

DISCUSSION QUESTIONS

1. What social roles do you occupy? What are some role-based obligations that you have because of those roles?
2. Review the three lists of universal obligations in Table 3.1. Are there any (supposed) obligations on any of the lists that you think are *not* universal obligations? Are there any obligations that you think *should* be on the lists but aren't?
3. Choose one of the lists of universal obligations in Table 3.1. Do you think there are any obligations on any of the lists that *always* take precedence over one of the others on that list? That is, can you

find two obligations on the list for which you think it is *always* more important to fulfill one rather than the other when they conflict?

4. What do you think it means to treat someone with respect? How do your ideas about respecting persons compare with Immanuel Kant's interpretation?

CASE STUDIES

See the Note About Case Studies on p. 150 for further instructions.

1. In July 2005, a helicopter carried a reconnaissance team of four U.S. Navy SEALs into hostile territory in Kunar Province, Afghanistan, as part of an anti-insurgent operation called Operation Red Wings. As the team moved into position, they encountered three unarmed Afghan goat herders. After determining that the goat herders were civilians, the team released them, as required by the U.S. military's rules of engagement. Knowing that the goat herders might report their position to hostile forces, the team retreated to a safer position. Shortly thereafter, hostile Afghan forces attacked the U.S. soldiers, quite possibly because the goat herders had alerted them to the soldiers' presence. Three of the four SEALs were killed. Another sixteen U.S. military personnel died trying to rescue them. Evaluate the SEALs' action of releasing the goat herders. Give a moral argument to support your evaluation, using at least one normative premise involving obligations.

2. Near the end of the novel *To Kill a Mockingbird*, the young narrator, Scout, and her brother, Jem, are walking home through the woods when they are attacked by a man named Bob Ewell. The kids' painfully shy neighbor, "Boo" Radley, rescues them. He wrestles Ewell's knife away from the attacker and kills him with it. When the kids' father discovers what's happened, he summons Sheriff Tate and explains the situation. Sheriff Tate believes the father's story. Legally, he ought to arrest Radley for killing Ewell, since the law requires that a jury decide whether Radley should be punished. But the sheriff knows what they will decide: they will acquit Radley, since he only killed to defend himself and the children. Furthermore, to put Radley on trial would cause the reclusive man great anguish, and it would stir up trouble in their little town. The sheriff can avoid all of that by writing in his official report that Ewell fell on his own knife after struggling with the kids; that's what he decides to do. Evaluate Sheriff Tate's decision to lie in his report in order to spare Radley and the town a trial. Give a moral argument to support your evaluation, using at least one normative premise involving obligations.

3. In the film *The Truman Show*, Jim Carrey plays Truman Burbank, whose entire life has been a wildly successful reality television show of sorts. What makes the show so unusual is that Truman doesn't realize he's on television. Unbeknownst to him, everyone in his life—even his own "friends" and "family"—are actors; the town in which he has lived his entire life is actually a giant television set. The show's creator, Christof, has engineered a nearly perfect life for Truman, carefully arranging every detail and then filming Truman with secret cameras. Evaluate Christof's action of creating a perfect life for Truman and then secretly filming it to make a television show. Give a moral argument to support your evaluation, using at least one normative premise involving obligations.

4. The 2013 Boston Marathon dissolved into chaos when two homemade bombs exploded near the finish line, killing three people and injuring almost three hundred more. The bombs had been built and placed by two brothers, Dzokhar and Tamerlan Tsarnaev. Tamerlan, the older of the two, later died in a shootout with police; Dzokhar was captured alive. Federal prosecutors charged Dzokhar with a long list of crimes and announced that they would seek the death penalty. Despite having no doubts about the younger Tsarnaev's guilt, lawyer Judy Clarke agreed to defend him in court. She wanted to do what she had done for a long list of America's most notorious criminals over the previous two decades—prevent the government from executing them. Clarke opposes the death penalty, and so she defends people, like Tsarnaev, who face execution, even when she believes that they are guilty and that she cannot prevent them from being convicted. Evaluate Clarke's action of choosing to defend Dzokhar Tsarnaev. Give a moral argument to support your evaluation, using at least one normative premise involving obligations.

4 ⟩ Reasoning with Consequences

Shocking pictures from the Abu Ghraib prison in Baghdad revealed that American military personnel were torturing prisoners during the early years of the Iraq War. Most people see torture as obviously wrong. Yet some people have defended torture in very special circumstances.

Imagine, for instance, that a fanatical, deranged criminal has planted a nuclear bomb under Paris. Unless it is quickly located and deactivated, the bomb will destroy the entire city. There is no way to evacuate the city's millions of inhabitants and priceless valuables, such as the art at the Louvre Museum. The only way to find the bomb in time would be to torture the criminal until he reveals its location. This is the imaginary scenario envisioned by contemporary philosopher Henry Shue in his paper on the immorality of torture.[1]

Shue implicitly invites us to consider an argument like the following:

TICKING TIME BOMB

1. Either the police torture the criminal or Paris is blown up.
2. If the police torture the criminal, then the criminal will suffer, but the police will save Paris.
3. If Paris is blown up, then millions of people will die; millions more will suffer deeply from the loss of friends and loved ones; and priceless buildings, artworks, etc. will be destroyed.
∴ 4. Either the criminal suffers but Paris is saved, or millions of innocent people die, millions more suffer, and countless priceless buildings, artworks, etc. will be destroyed.
5. It is much better for one criminal to suffer than for millions of innocent people to die, millions more to suffer, and all of those priceless things to be destroyed.
∴ 6. It is morally permissible for the police to torture the criminal.

Shue emphasizes that the circumstances in the "ticking time bomb" scenario are so unrealistic that we should never expect them to occur. In the scenario, the police *know* that the person they've arrested is the one who planted the bomb, they *know* that the bomb will detonate as planned and destroy Paris, they *know* that they can defuse it if they find it, and so on. Furthermore, ticking time bomb even assumes that torturing the criminal will work—that is, that he will honestly reveal the true location of the bomb in time for them to defuse it. Because these circumstances, taken together, are so unrealistic, Shue warns that we should not draw any general conclusions about torture from this argument. In particular, he insists that the

---

[1]Henry Shue, "Torture," *Philosophy & Public Affairs* 2 (1978): 141; reprinted in Part V of this book (pp. 378–88).

CONSEQUENTIALISM

While most philosophers agree that consequences matter morally, some philosophers believe that, ultimately, consequences are *all* that matter morally. Philosophers who believe this are called consequentialists, and the view they hold is called **consequentialism.** There are many different kinds of consequentialism. We discuss some of them in Chapter 11.

---

argument does *not* show that torture is permissible in more realistic circumstances. But he reluctantly admits that an argument like this one shows that in some very special cases torture would be morally permissible.

Let's look at the reasoning involved in TICKING TIME BOMB. It doesn't rely on premises about obligations. In fact, it might look like it doesn't have any normative premises at all. But that can't be right! If we look more closely, we'll see that premise (5) is a normative premise: it claims that one **state of affairs**—that is, one way that the world could be—is *better* than another state of affairs. This makes it a normative premise because it evaluates different ways that the world could be. (Using the terminology presented in Chapter 2, it is an *axiological* claim—that is, a claim about what is good or bad.) Premise (4) tells us that the police can achieve that better state of affairs by torturing the criminal. These two premises together are supposed to show that it is morally permissible for the police to torture the criminal.

This kind of moral reasoning relies on the *consequences* of an action to make a moral claim about that action. That is, it uses premises about what will happen as a result of performing some action to show that the action is morally forbidden, permissible, obligatory, or supererogatory. The key normative premises in this kind of argument claim that one state of affairs is better than another state of affairs. These premises matter because, other things being equal, if one action leads to a better state of affairs than another action, the first action is morally better.

The "**other things being equal**" clause—sometimes called a *ceteris paribus* clause—is crucial here. To say that "other things are equal" in two situations is to say that the two situations do not differ in any way that would matter for present purposes. The "other things being equal" clause entails that if the two actions differ in some other important way, then the one that has the better consequences might *not* be morally better.

The lesson here is that while it's important to take consequences into account in your moral reasoning, you need not rely *solely* on consequences in thinking about what to do. You can combine premises about consequences with the other methods of moral reasoning that we discuss in this book. In particular, you might use premises about obligations or other moral principles as **deontological constraints**—that is, as constraints or limits on what kinds of things you might do in order to bring about good consequences.

There are three major challenges involved in using consequences in your moral reasoning. The first challenge is that you need to *compare* the consequences of an action to the consequences of relevant alternatives. The second challenge is that it is sometimes hard to *measure* the goodness or badness of the consequences of an action. The third challenge is that many actions involve *uncertainty*. That is, it is sometimes hard to know exactly what will happen as a result of your action. We will address each of these challenges below.

FACING THE CONSEQUENCES OF YOUR ACTIONS

One common refrain in moral argument is that someone must "face the consequences" or "accept the consequences" of his or her action. In other words, they have to bear the burden of whatever happens as a result of their action. This is sometimes appropriate, but people often misuse it.

There are, arguably, two conditions under which it's appropriate to insist that someone must face the consequences of his or her action. The first is when the action itself is a morally bad action, such that someone who does it deserves to suffer as a result. The second is when someone tries to shift their burden unfairly onto someone else. For instance, suppose that a teenager makes a mess (literally or metaphorically). Because he doesn't want to have to clean up his mess, he tries to shift responsibility onto his sister. Since his sister didn't cause the mess, it would be unfair to make her clean it up. Instead, the boy ought to take responsibility for his actions and clean up his own mess.

Sometimes people abuse this idea by arguing as follows: "Action X has bad but preventable consequences. It would be wrong to prevent those consequences, however, because people who do X need to face the consequences of their actions." Arguments like this are often very weak: Imagine someone who breaks her ankle playing soccer and needs to get it treated to avoid a permanent injury. It would be ridiculous to say that it would be wrong for her to get her ankle treated because she needs to face the consequences of playing soccer.

In general, if you're going to argue that it would be wrong for someone to prevent some bad but avoidable consequences of his or her actions, you need to establish that the person really *deserves* to suffer those bad consequences or that avoiding the consequences amounts to shifting the burden *unfairly* onto someone else.

COMPARING CONSEQUENCES

Consider the following argument, adapted from the philosopher Bradley Strawser, who writes about military ethics.[2]

DRONE STRIKES

1. The use of uninhabited aerial vehicles (UAVs), or "drones," to wage war kills one civilian for every seventeen enemy combatants killed.
2. The use of special forces to wage war kills one civilian for every four enemy combatants killed.
3. The use of the regular army to wage war kills one civilian for every three enemy combatants killed.
4. If we are going to wage war, then other things being equal, it is better to kill fewer civilians than to kill more.
∴ 5. If we are going to wage war, it is better to use UAVs to do so rather than relying on the army or special forces.

---

[2]Bradley Jay Strawser, "Moral Predators: The Duty to Employ Uninhabited Aerial Vehicles," *Journal of Military Ethics* 9 (2010): 342–68; reprinted in Part V of this book (pp. 447–467).

SLIPPERY SLOPES

Stepping onto a steep, icy hillside isn't going to hurt you, but it might make it hard to get back up, leaving you no choice but to slide all the way to the bottom. So, if you don't want to end up at the bottom of the slope, you have a good reason not to take that first step. A **slippery slope argument** warns us not to take some apparently harmless step because it will lead to some undesirable outcome. A good slippery slope argument clearly identifies which seemingly harmless action we ought not to take; what bad outcome that action would lead to; and how taking that first step will lead to that bad outcome. A **slippery slope fallacy** is a slippery slope argument that lacks one of those three things. Most commonly, it relies on an implausible claim about how the first action will lead to the bad outcome. It is often unclear whether a slippery slope argument is fallacious or not. For instance, the argument that using marijuana is wrong because it will lead to using harder, more dangerous drugs is a slippery slope argument. Whether it commits the slippery slope fallacy depends on whether marijuana really is a "gateway drug" that leads to heavier drug use.

Notice that, just as TICKING TIME BOMB compared the consequences of torturing a criminal to the consequences of not torturing him, DRONE STRIKES compares the consequences of using drone strikes to the consequences of other ways of waging war. This is important because if you look *just* at the consequences of using drones to kill enemy combatants in war, you might quickly conclude that drone strikes are immoral. After all, they cause the deaths of innocent civilians, which is a very bad thing. When you compare it to the consequences of the alternative ways of waging war, however, the picture changes.

The relevant question here—as in any case where you are reasoning with consequences—is not just whether the consequences of an action are good or bad, but whether they are *better* or *worse* than the consequences of some other action. To figure that out, you need to think not just about the consequences of the particular action you're evaluating, but about what the alternatives are and what consequences each alternative would have.

To see how this kind of reasoning works, look at DRONE STRIKES again. Notice that if we are going to wage war, we have to choose between various ways of fighting enemy combatants. We can use drones; we can use special forces, like the Navy SEALS; or we can use "regular" soldiers. Those are our alternatives. The consequences of using special forces or "regular" soldiers are even worse than the consequences of using drones. Thus, *if* we are going to wage war, we ought to use drones to do so. When making this argument, Strawser admits that the really important question is often *whether* to wage war in the first place; drone strikes does not address that question.

MEASURING CONSEQUENCES

In DRONE STRIKES we are "comparing apples to apples." That is, the consequences that we are comparing come in easily measurable, comparable units—namely, civilian lives. Since killing civilians is a bad thing, it's easy to see it would be better if there were fewer civilian deaths rather than more. In other cases, you might find yourself having to "compare apples to oranges." This raises questions about how to measure the goodness or badness of the consequences of an action.

Consider the following argument about human cloning, adapted from the philosopher Dan Brock.[3] (Human cloning involves using one person's DNA to create a genetic "twin" of that person. Such twins would be similar to each other but not exactly alike, much as identical twins are not exactly alike even though they share the same DNA.)

HUMAN CLONING

1. Human cloning would cause psychological harms to the "later twin" (i.e., the person who is created via cloning).
2. Human cloning would expose the "later twin" to very serious medical risks.
3. Human cloning would lessen society's respect for human life.
4. Psychological harms and medical risks are bad for people.
5. Bad things would happen if society's respect for life were diminished.
∴ 6. Human cloning is morally forbidden.

In order to decide whether HUMAN CLONING succeeds in establishing its conclusion, we need to compare the harms that Brock identifies with the *benefits* of human cloning. Elsewhere in his paper, Brock lists several such benefits: Human cloning would provide another way for infertile couples to have children. It would enable couples in which one partner is a carrier for a serious genetic disorder to have children without risk of passing on that partner's disorder. Cloning could be used to make a "later twin" who would be a perfect donor for organs or tissues for transplantation. Cloning would enable people to clone children who died young.[4]

Do the bad consequences that Brock lists in HUMAN CLONING outweigh the good consequences listed above? You might find it hard to tell, since it's unclear exactly how much weight we should give to, e.g., alleviating infertility as opposed to avoiding psychological harms. The goodness and badness of these consequences is hard to measure and hard to compare.

Notice, however, that it is not always impossible to decide which of two unquantifiable consequences is better. For instance, pain and the destruction of beautiful wilderness are both bad, but neither is easy to quantify. Furthermore, it's hard to compare them. (Exactly how much pain is the destruction of one acre of beautiful forest worth?) But most people would probably agree that the state of affairs in which you have a mild headache for an hour is not as bad as the state of affairs in which 100,000 acres of old-growth forest is destroyed by slash-and-burn agriculture.

In cases like HUMAN CLONING, there is no simple, general procedure for determining which state of affairs is best. You might find, however, that after careful reflection on the various good and bad consequences of human cloning, you judge that the bad consequences outweigh the good or vice versa. If someone disagrees with you on this, there's usually not much you can do to convince them otherwise, except perhaps to get them to think more carefully about the various consequences or to imagine the consequences more vividly. Still,

---

[3]Dan Brock, "Cloning Human Beings: An Assessment of the Ethical Issues Pro and Con," in *Clones and Clones: Facts and Fantasies About Human Cloning*, eds. Martha C. Nussbaum and Cass R. Sunstein (New York: W. W. Norton & Co., 1998), 141–64.
[4]Brock, "Cloning Human Beings," 155–60.

JEREMY BENTHAM AND JOHN STUART MILL

The English philosopher Jeremy Bentham (1748–1832) is one of the founding fathers of a moral theory called **utilitarianism**, which he attempted to develop into a rigorous method for moral and political philosophy in his *Introduction to Principles of Morals and Legislation* (1789). The book offers an entirely "hedonistic" view of ethics: Bentham believed that pleasure and pain are the only kinds of consequences that matter in moral reasoning.

His most famous follower, John Stuart Mill (1806–1873), extended the theory of utilitarianism in various ways, such as by emphasizing the importance of rules and by arguing that while pleasure and pain are all that matter, some pleasures (e.g., poetry) are of higher *quality* than others (e.g., children's games). Besides writing on utilitarianism, Mill published well-known works in political philosophy, philosophy of science, philosophy of religion, and other fields.

Bentham and his friends and followers, including Mill, became known as the "philosophical radicals" for advocating such "radical" political reforms as abolishing slavery, extending the right to vote beyond wealthy men, and giving equal rights to women. Some of their desired reforms were accomplished through the Reform Act of 1832, which was passed into British law the day after Bentham died. Mill continued to fight for social reform for the rest of his life, even serving in the British parliament between 1865 and 1868.*

---

* For more on utilitarianism, see Chapter 11, as well as the excerpts from Bentham and Mill in Part V (pp. 171–83).

coming to your own judgment about the matter can still help you settle on your own view about whether human cloning is morally permissible.

Some philosophers have suggested rather complicated procedures for weighing the good and bad consequences of an action. To take one well-known example, the eighteenth-century British philosopher Jeremy Bentham devised what he called a "felicific calculus" (or "happiness calculus") for just this purpose. According to Bentham's procedure, you start by identifying everyone who is affected by action. Then you find out whether the action makes them more or less happy in the short term, how *much* happier or less happy it makes them in the short term, whether it leads to *future* happiness or unhappiness in the long term, how *much* future happiness, and so on. After you figure out the short- and long-term effects on each person's happiness, you add all those effects together to determine the action's "net effect" on the total amount of happiness in the world. That is, to determine which action has the best consequences, you need to convert all of the consequences into some common unit of measurement and then add all of those consequences together. This is obviously too difficult and time-consuming an activity to do before every decision you make, but many governments today use a procedure analogous to Bentham's, called "cost-benefit analysis," before implementing major new programs or policies.

Much of the time you won't need to use Bentham's felicific calculus, or any other complicated procedure, to determine which of several choices will have the best consequences. Sometimes giving the matter some careful thought, asking for advice from people with more experience, or doing just a bit of research will be enough.

DEALING WITH UNCERTAINTY

Most of the choices that we make in life involve another kind of challenge beyond the difficulty of comparing and adding up all of the consequences of a particular choice. The extra challenge is that we often don't know for sure what the consequences will be.

The key to thinking about actions with unknown consequences is a concept called **expected value.** When you have an action that could produce two or more different outcomes and you know (or can roughly estimate) the probability of each outcome occurring, you can calculate the expected value as the weighted average of the value of each outcome, with each value "weighted" by the probability of each outcome occurring. In plain English, that means that you need to figure out what the possible outcomes of the action could be (i.e., the "outcomes"); the value of each outcome (e.g., in dollars earned, lives saved, etc.); and the probability that each outcome will occur. Then you multiply each value by the probability that it will occur and add those numbers together.

It's easiest to grasp the idea of expected value by starting with a simple example involving money. We'll apply the idea to more morally important decisions later. Suppose that you have the chance to buy a raffle ticket for $5. Each ticket has a 1 in 100 (or 0.01) probability of winning a $50 gift certificate to your favorite restaurant. Applying the procedure outlined in the last paragraph, we see that the two possible outcomes are winning the raffle and losing. The value of your winning the gift certificate is $45. (That's $50 for the gift certificate minus the $5 you spent on the raffle ticket.) The value to you of "losing" the raffle is –$5. (That's the cost of buying the ticket.) The probability of your winning is 1 in 100, or 0.01; the probability that you'll lose is 99 in 100, or 0.99. To find the weighted average of the values, we multiply the value of each possible outcome by the probability of its occurring, and then we add those products together:

$$EV = \$45 * 0.01 + (-\$5)*0.99$$
$$EV = \$0.45 - \$4.95$$
$$EV = -\$4.50$$

Thus, the expected value of the raffle ticket is –$4.50. How do we interpret this number? Notice that it's not the amount of money you should expect to lose by buying the ticket. There is no situation in which you leave exactly $4.50 poorer than before the raffle began; either you leave $5 poorer or $45 richer. Rather, –$4.50 is the amount that you should expect to lose, *on average,* if you participated in this raffle many, many times.

Why is this number important? Given some plausible assumptions about how to compare two options and setting aside some complications, a choice that yields a higher expected value is better than a choice that yields a lower expected value. For instance, if buying a raffle ticket has an expected value of –$4.50, and you're only concerned about the money, then it's better for you to keep your $5.00 than to buy the ticket. If you keep your money, you'll have an expected net gain of $0, which is greater than the expected net loss of $4.50 that you'll suffer if you buy the ticket. (Again, "expected" is a technical term here. You shouldn't expect to lose exactly $4.50 in any single raffle. But the expected value of your net loss is $4.50.)

In many morally important cases, you'll want to think about expected value in something other than dollar terms. To see how this works, consider the following argument from the philosopher Shelly Kagan. Kagan is investigating the common idea that when it comes to big social issues, a single individual's actions don't matter, morally speaking, because one person "can't make a difference." In particular, Kagan is interested in the claim that even though animals raised on industrial farms suffer horribly, it's okay for people to eat them because no single individual can make a difference in the number of animals that are raised and slaughtered for food. Here is his argument:

EXPECTED CHICKENS

1. If I buy a (dead, prepackaged) chicken at the grocery store, there is a probability of 0.04 (or 1 in 25) that my purchase will prompt the store to order another case of 25 chickens from their supplier, who will raise and slaughter 25 more chickens as a result; and a probability of 0.96 (or 24 in 25) that my purchase will not prompt the store to order more chickens.[5]

∴ 2. The "expected number of chickens" to be raised and slaughtered because of my buying a chicken is 1.

3. The suffering that a single chicken endures in being raised on an industrial chicken farm and slaughtered in an industrial slaughterhouse outweighs the pleasure you get from eating that chicken.

∴ 4. The state of affairs in which you buy a chicken from the grocery store is worse than the state of affairs in which you buy a vegetarian alternative.

∴ 5. It is morally forbidden for you to buy a chicken from the grocery store.[6]

Kagan's point here is that the number of chickens produced by industrial chicken farmers depends on the number of chickens ordered by grocery stores, fast food restaurants, etc. The number of chickens ordered by grocery stores depends on the number of chickens purchased by customers. If, as Kagan suggests, your purchase of a chicken has a 1 in 25 chance of causing your grocery store to order another crate of 25 chickens, then the expected number of chickens killed as a result of your purchase is 1, since $25*(1/25) + 0*(24/25) = 1$. Since premise (4) asserts that the suffering of a single chicken outweighs the pleasure you would get from eating it, your buying the chicken makes the world a worse place. Therefore, Kagan concludes, you shouldn't buy the chicken.

As you can see, calculating and comparing the consequences of various actions is not an easy task. But since consequences matter in moral reasoning, it is important to do your best to take them into account. When it really is impossible for you to estimate the consequences of various actions well enough to know which has the best consequences, there's nothing wrong with withholding judgment. In fact, the world might be a much better place if people refrained from jumping to moral conclusions about cases in which the consequences of our actions are unclear.

One important role for expected value is in thinking about actions that carry a very small risk of a very bad outcome. Sometimes people cite such a risk to argue against an action. This is often not enough to show that the action is morally wrong. The probability of the bad consequence might be so small that the bad consequence is outweighed by the good

---

[5]Kagan picks 25 as a reasonable estimate of the number of chickens that come in a case. As a useful exercise in working with expected values, see whether his argument would still work if each case contained 100 chickens, so that your ordering a chicken had a 1 in 100 chance of prompting the store to order another case.

[6]Shelly Kagan, "Do I Make a Difference?" *Philosophy & Public Affairs* 39 (2011): 105–41.

consequences that are likely to occur. For instance, every time you get in your car, there is a small probability that you will be killed—a very bad consequence indeed! But the good consequences of your being able to drive places outweigh the small risk of death. This is why it's so important to think about probability and expected value when evaluating an action based on its possible consequences.

ACTS AND RULES

Sometimes it's important to think about the consequences of a society or institution having particular *rules*, rather than about the consequences of this or that person performing a particular action. Consider the following argument, adapted from David Hume.[7]

PROPERTY

1. If everyone felt free to take other people's possessions whenever they wanted or needed them, then we would lose many of the advantages of society.
2. It would be disastrous for everybody if we lost many of the advantages of society.
∴ 3. It is morally forbidden to take other people's possessions just because you want or need them—that is, it is wrong to steal.

It's easy to imagine cases, such as the case of a man who steals bread to feed his starving family, in which someone could do more good than harm by stealing. According to property, however, these cases are beside the point when we're thinking about the morality of stealing. What matters is that we all benefit tremendously from having a *rule* that prohibits people from stealing whenever they want or need to take someone else's possession. Because the consequences of having such a rule are better than the consequences of having a different rule, argues Hume, it is morally forbidden to break that rule.

Notice, however, that the relevant question is not always, "What would happen if everyone *actually* did that?" Often, you'll need to ask yourself, "What would happen if everyone *were allowed* to do that?" There are all kinds of actions such that if everyone did them the results would be disastrous, but merely allowing everyone to do them does not lead to disaster: if everyone chose not to have children, for example, it would literally mean the end of the human race, but merely *allowing* each person to remain childless does not lead to disaster. After all, many people will have children even if they are allowed to remain childless. On the other hand, if everyone were allowed to steal whenever they felt like it, many people *would* steal frequently, and the consequences would be disastrous. (Imagine a world in which everyone is constantly afraid that their things would be stolen and in which many people's things *are* stolen. What would such a world be like?) It's only when considering a rule that says that everyone *must* do something or must *not* do something that you should ask yourself about the consequences of everyone's actually doing (or not doing) that thing.

People are sometimes puzzled about how focusing on the morally best rules can lead to different conclusions than focusing on the morally best acts. Wouldn't the best rule, they ask, be the one that tells us to always act so as to bring about the best outcome? It turns out

---

[7]David Hume, *A Treatise of Human Nature*, III.ii.2.

the answer to that question is no. There are at least two reasons for this. The main reason, as spelled out by the economist and ethicist John Harsanyi, is that rules create expectations and incentives, which alter people's behavior, so that having certain rules in place changes which choices people confront.[8] For instance, if one professor allows students to rewrite plagiarized papers without penalty and another professor automatically fails any student who plagiarizes a paper, more students will submit plagiarized papers to the first professor than to the second. Thus, even though each professor would maximize overall happiness in any given instance of plagiarism by allowing the plagiarizing student to rewrite the paper without penalty, the second professor—the one who never allows this—will face this choice less often. The "price" of avoiding the additional plagiarism is that students who do plagiarize suffer a severe penalty. It is at least possible, though, that the overall happiness achieved by the second professor's policy is greater than that achieved by the first professor's policy, since fewer students will plagiarize their papers in the second professor's class. Property rights provide an even more important example, as Hume argues. The use of military drones provides yet another important example. One important objection to Strawser's DRONE STRIKES argument is that by lowering the chances that Americans would die during combat, rules allowing the use of drones incentivize the American military to attack more targets than they otherwise would, leading to more deaths overall than would result if there were a rule against using drones to kill people. The second reason that the best rule isn't the one that just tells you to bring about the best outcome is that people would have a very hard time putting such a rule into practice. They would spend a lot of time figuring out what to do and they would often get it wrong. Arguably, then, the best rules—those whose adoption would have the best consequences—include strict rules against theft, murder, and so on, even in cases where it might *seem* like such an action would bring about the best outcome.

TERMINOLOGY TO KNOW

consequentialism	deontological constraints	utilitarianism
state of affairs	slippery slope argument	expected value
other things being equal	slippery slope fallacy	

DISCUSSION QUESTIONS

1. Do you think the Parisian police should torture the suspect in the case from the beginning of the chapter? Why or why not? If the suspect refused to talk, even under torture, would it be permissible for the police to torture the suspect's child as a way to get the suspect to talk? Why or why not?

2. Do you think it is possible, at least in principle, to calculate the total costs and benefits of an action? Why or why not? If not, does that mean it's impossible to make decisions about what to do based on the consequences of your actions?

3. Some people object that making decisions based on expected value calculations can underestimate the importance of disasters with very low probabilities. (Do you see why?) To deal with this, some people suggest a different approach according to which you should look at the *worst* possible

---

[8]John C. Harsanyi, "Rule Utilitarianism and Decision Theory," *Erkenntnis* 11 (1977): 25–53.

outcome from each action and then choose the action whose worst outcome is the least bad. This is sometimes called a "maximin" approach. Is this better than using expected value? Why or why not?

4. Besides the examples discussed in this chapter, what are some other examples of rules that create important incentives or expectations? How do those incentives or expectations change people's behavior? Do those changes make the world better or worse overall, as compared to not having such a rule?

CASE STUDIES

See the Note About Case Studies on p. 150 for further instructions.

1. When Justin Combs turned 16, his father, Sean "Diddy" Combs, gave him a car worth $360,000 and a check for $10,000. Eleven days earlier, a massive earthquake had struck the Caribbean country of Haiti, killing over 200,000 people, harming millions more, and damaging hundreds of thousands of buildings. Justin quickly announced that he would donate the $10,000 he received to help relief efforts in Haiti. Evaluate Justin's act of donating the $10,000 to earthquake relief. Construct a moral argument to defend your evaluation, being sure to include at least one normative premise that appeals to the consequences of Justin's action.

2. The film *Inglorious Basterds* takes place during World War II. In one of the early scenes, a notorious Nazi, Colonel Hans Landa, arrives at a farmhouse in rural France. The farmer who lives there is hiding some Jewish neighbors, the Dreyfus family, under his floorboards. Colonel Landa makes clear that unless the farmer reveals the Dreyfus family's whereabouts, he will kill the farmer and his family and then find and kill the Dreyfus family. The farmer reluctantly shows Colonel Landa where the Dreyfus family is hiding. The Nazis kill them and let the farmer go. Evaluate the farmer's action of revealing the Dreyfus family's whereabouts. Give a moral argument to support your evaluation, using at least one normative premise involving consequences in your argument.

3. American teenager Abby Sunderland set out from Mexico in January 2010 to try to become the youngest person to sail around the world alone. Strong winds crippled her boat in the middle of the Indian Ocean, over 2,000 miles west of Australia. The Australian government and a French merchant ship coordinated a rescue effort; Abby was returned safely to the United States. The rescue effort cost somewhere between $200,000 and $300,000. Since international law requires that nearby ships must rescue sailors in distress at no cost to the distressed sailors, all of those costs will be borne by Australian and French taxpayers, not by Abby or her family. Evaluate the Australian government's action of rescuing her at great expense. Give moral arguments for each of your evaluations, using at least one normative premise involving consequences in each argument. (Hint: You might reach different conclusions if you evaluate the government's action on its own than if you evaluate the international law that required them to save Abby at the taxpayers' expense.)

4. The main character of the film *Slumdog Millionaire*, Jamal Malik, grew up very poor in the slums of Mumbai, India. When he was a boy, he traveled to Agra, India, where the Taj Mahal attracts millions of visitors every day. While Jamal was standing near a sign advertising tours of the Taj Mahal, a European couple mistook him for a tour guide and offered him cash to give them a private tour. Despite knowing almost nothing about the building, Jamal agreed. He showed them around, making up "facts" about the building and the grounds as he went. Realizing what a gold mine the tourists were, the boy started a fraudulent tour business, bilking unsuspecting tourists out of their money, which he shared with other poor children. Evaluate Jamal's act of giving fraudulent tours of the Taj Mahal. Give a moral argument to support your evaluation, using at least one normative premise involving consequences in each argument.

5 Reasoning with Virtues and Vices

Moments before winning a historic racing victory in the animated children's film *Cars*, Lightning McQueen comes to a screeching halt at the finish line. He has just realized that long-time champion Strip "The King" Weathers has suffered a terrible crash and is lying, battered, near the race track. As his rival Chick Hicks speeds past him to win the coveted Piston Cup, McQueen backs up to push The King across the finish line, explaining that "The King should finish his last race." The crowd goes wild, showering McQueen with attention and ignoring Hicks.[1]

What makes McQueen's actions so admirable? It's not that he had any obligation to help The King. It's not just that his actions have the good consequence of making everyone feel better about The King's last race. It's that McQueen's actions demonstrate an impressive degree of compassion. He gives up the Piston Cup, which he's dreamed about his entire life, in order to help someone else in a time of great need. His action also demonstrates significant wisdom, as he recognizes that in the grand scheme of things, the Piston Cup is not that important. In short, McQueen's actions demonstrate morally admirable character traits—the kind of character traits that make someone an excellent person. Philosophers call such traits **virtues.**

By contrast, McQueen's rival demonstrates morally deplorable character traits: He cruelly caused The King's crash to avoid finishing behind him yet again. He selfishly exploited McQueen's compassion to win the race himself. Afterward, he thoughtlessly demanded that everyone celebrate his victory rather than McQueen's sacrifice. These traits—cruelty, selfishness, thoughtlessness—are the kind of character traits that makes someone a bad person. Philosophers call such undesirable traits **vices.**

Virtues and vices provide yet another important way to reason about what to do. In their simplest forms, virtue- or vice-based arguments rely on normative premises like "You should act compassionately" or "You should not act cruelly." More generally, the fact that a particular action would demonstrate one or more virtues is a reason to do it, and the fact that an action would demonstrate one or more vices is a reason not to do it.

VIRTUES, DEONTOLOGY, AND AXIOLOGY

Since reasoning with virtues and vices is, in some ways, very different from reasoning in terms of obligations and consequences, it can sometimes be hard to square virtue- or vice-based reasoning with the conclusions of obligation- or consequence-based reasoning. Recall

---

[1] John Lasseter and Joe Ranft, *Cars* (Emeryville, CA: Pixar, 2006).

that in Chapter 2 we distinguished two kinds of moral claims: deontic claims are claims about whether an action is right or wrong—or, more specifically, whether it is morally obligatory, supererogatory, merely permissible, or morally forbidden; axiological claims are about whether something is good or bad. Many philosophers who think in terms of virtues and vices try to avoid deontic claims. They tend to more comfortable with claims about which actions or people are good or bad than with claims about what is morally obligatory or morally wrong. But sometimes, at least, it is possible to reach deontic conclusions from premises about virtues or vices. For the sake of understanding how reasoning in terms of virtues and vices relates to other kinds of moral reasoning, it's worth thinking about how to do this.

The most straightforward kind of reasoning here involves arguing that an action is morally wrong because it demonstrates a serious vice. Consider, for instance, the following argument, adapted from philosopher Rosalind Hursthouse's virtue-based analysis of the ethics of abortion.[2]

SHALLOW ABORTION

1. Aborting a pregnancy just so that one can carry on "having a good time" is shallow and immature.
2. One should not act shallowly, especially with respect to something as important as the creation of a human life.
3. One should not act immaturely, especially with respect to something as important as the creation of a human life.
∴ 4. It is morally wrong to abort a pregnancy just so that one can carry on "having a good time."

Notice that this argument focuses on a very specific type of action—namely, getting an abortion just for the sake of continuing "having a good time," rather than on abortions in general. The argument doesn't imply that it's *always* shallow or immature to get an abortion or that abortion is always wrong. Instead, the argument focuses on performing a particular action *for a particular reason*. This is very common in arguments about virtues or vices, since an action done for one reason can reflect a very different set of character traits than the same action done for a different reason. Nor does SHALLOW ABORTION say that it is *always* morally forbidden to act shallowly or immaturely. Instead, the second and third premise emphasize that being shallow and immature is especially bad in this context because it involves something very serious—namely, the creation of a human life.

If you want to use virtues or vices to show that an action is obligatory, the easiest thing to do is to show that *failing* to perform that action would demonstrate some serious vice. For example, in the film *Saving Private Ryan*, a heavily armed American soldier fails to intervene as an enemy soldier kills another American soldier with a knife. If you wanted to show that the heavily armed soldier was morally obligated to save his compatriot, you could argue that failing to do so in those circumstances was cowardly.

But in many cases, virtue-based arguments will not lead to conclusions about what is forbidden or obligatory. Consider, for instance, the case of the African American high school and college students who protested segregation by sitting at "whites-only" lunch counters

---

[2]Rosalind Hursthouse, "Virtue Ethics and Abortion," *Philosophy & Public Affairs* 20 (1991): 223–46.

THICK ETHICAL TERMS

Claims about virtues and vices blur the line between normative claims and descriptive claims. Recall from Chapter 2 that a normative claim is about how the world ought to be or about what is good or bad, whereas a descriptive claim is about how the world is, not how it ought to be or whether it is good or bad. Words like *brave* or *cruel*, however, both *describe* an action (or a person) *and* say something about whether the action (or person) is good or bad. To say that someone acted bravely, for instance, is to say that the person has faced danger, which is a non-normative, descriptive claim, and to praise the way they faced danger as good or right, which is a normative claim. Moral philosophers have a special name for words that are both descriptive and normative—they call them **thick ethical terms**. By contrast, **thin ethical terms** like *good* and *wrong* are purely normative. You can use them to make a normative claim about someone's action without saying anything non-normative about them.

Because virtue and vice terms are thick terms, premises that say that a particular action demonstrates some virtue or vice are normative claims. Therefore, you don't necessarily need an additional normative premise in arguments that use virtue- and vice-based reasoning.

throughout the South in 1960. These students faced intimidation and arrest. Writing about these students in his famous "Letter from a Birmingham Jail," Martin Luther King Jr. reasoned roughly as follows:

BRAVE DEMONSTRATORS

1. The students who voluntarily faced arrest and imprisonment for sitting at "whites only" lunch counters acted bravely.
2. One should act bravely.
∴ 3. The students' actions were morally good.[3]

VIRTUE ETHICS

Some philosophers think that we should understand morality primarily in terms of virtues and vices. The moral theory that focuses on virtues and vices is called **virtue ethics.** It is one of the three theories of ethics that receives the most attention in contemporary Western philosophy, along with deontology and consequentialism, and it also features prominently in Chinese philosophy. In contrast to the other main theories, virtue ethics places at least as much emphasis on being the right kind of person—that is, a virtuous person—as it does on doing the right thing. We explore virtue ethics in more detail in Chapter 11.

---

[3]Martin Luther King Jr., "Letter from a Birmingham Jail," April 16, 1963, https://kinginstitute.stanford.edu/king-papers/documents/letter-birmingham-jail

While King clearly admires and praises the students' protests, it is not clear that he wants to say that their actions were morally obligatory. That is, it's not clear that he thinks those who failed to protest segregation in this way were acting cowardly or doing something wrong. Perhaps if forced to express his ideas in terms of a deontic claim, he would have said that the students' actions were supererogatory—that is, admirable, but not obligatory.

IDENTIFYING VIRTUES AND VICES

Which character traits, exactly, are virtues? Which are vices? Different philosophers have offered different lists of virtues, but the lists tend to overlap significantly. Table 5.1 lists the virtues identified by three major historical philosophers—the ancient Greek philosopher Aristotle, the ancient Chinese philosopher Mencius, and the medieval Catholic philosopher Thomas Aquinas—as well as a list provided by contemporary philosopher Mark Alfano.[4] These lists are not necessarily complete or definitive, and you may disagree with some of the suggestions. Notice, however, that the lists overlap significantly, even though each of the four philosophers comes from a very different time and place.

You could easily come up with a list of vices by taking the lists of virtues in Table 5.1 and writing down the opposite of each trait. For instance, the opposite of courage is cowardice, the opposite of benevolence is malevolence (wishing others ill), the opposite of wisdom is foolishness, and the opposite of altruism is selfishness. But Aristotle argued that each virtue actually has *two* vices associated with it, one of which involves a deficiency or lack of the related virtue and the other of which involves an excess of the related virtue. Courage, for instance, is the virtue of facing danger in the right way, at the right time, and for the right reason. Cowardice is a lack of courage; it is an unwillingness to face danger when you should. But it is also possible to be *too* willing to face danger (e.g., by seeking it out unnecessarily or facing too much danger to protect things that are not worth the risk). That excessive willingness to face danger is called recklessness. Each virtue, then, is sometimes said to be a **golden mean** between two vices, striking just the right balance between a deficiency of some trait and an excess of it.

To better understand this idea, imagine that you and your roommate are throwing a party. One of your roommate's friends, whom you have never met, is the first to arrive. You welcome the friend into your home with a polite, "It's nice to meet you." The friend replies, "I wish I could say the same. Based on what I've heard, I think you're an awful person. And now I see that you're also ugly and have terrible taste in clothes. Really, I'm just here for the free food." Presumably, you wouldn't admire the friend for his honesty. In fact, you might think he's being a bit *too* forthcoming with the truth—that he should have kept some of that information to himself. And that is the key to the idea of the golden mean. Even virtues like

---

[4]These lists come from Martha C. Nussbaum, "Non-Relative Virtues: An Aristotelian Approach," *Midwest Studies in Philosophy* 13 (1988): 32–53; Mencius, *Mengzi: With Selections from Traditional Commentaries*, trans. Bryan van Norden (Indianapolis, IN: Hackett Publishing, 2008); Ralph McInerny & John O'Callaghan, "Saint Thomas Aquinas," in *Stanford Encyclopedia of Philosophy*, ed. Edward N. Zalta (Spring 2015 edition), http://plato.stanford.edu/archives/spr2015/entries/aquinas; and Mark Alfano, *Character as Moral Fiction* (New York: Cambridge University Press, 2013), 65.

Table 5.1. Lists of Virtues and Vices from Various Philosophers

Aristotle	Mencius	Aquinas	Alfano	
courage	benevolence	prudence	altruism	greatness of soul
moderation	righteousness	justice	beauty	honesty
justice	propriety	temperance	benevolence	hope
generosity	wisdom	courage	charity	humanity
hospitality		faith	chastity	humility
greatness of soul		hope	cleanliness	industry
mildness of temper		charity	compassion	justice
truthfulness			consideration	magnanimity
grace			contentment	mercy
friendliness			cooperativeness	modesty
good judgment			courage	obedience
intellectual virtue			courteousness	patience
practical wisdom			dignity	piety
			empathy	prudence
			endurance	reverence
			fairness	severity
			faith	sincerity
			fidelity	tact
			filial piety	temperance
			friendliness	tenacity
			frugalness	trustfulness
			generosity	trustworthiness
			gravitas	valor

ARISTOTLE

Another giant of Western intellectual history, the ancient Greek thinker Aristotle (384–322 BCE), wrote about philosophy, physics, biology, poetry, politics, and much more. He was a student of the great Athenian philosopher Plato, who was himself a student of the great philosopher Socrates. These three figures are often regarded as the most important philosophers of the ancient Western world. Like his teacher's, Aristotle's philosophical works continue to influence Western philosophy today. In addition, Aristotle's views on physical science played an important role in medieval Islamic and Catholic thought.

In moral philosophy, Aristotle is best known for his systematic account of virtue ethics.*

---

* For the details of Aristotle's ethical thought, see the excerpts from his *Nicomachean Ethics* in Part V of this book (pp. 184–93).

Table 5.2.   Vices Associated with Selected Virtues

Deficiency	Virtue	Excess
cowardice	courage	recklessness
meekness	mildness of temper	irascibility
impropriety	propriety	rigidity
gluttony	temperance	abstemiousness
miserliness	generosity	excessive liberality
suspiciousness	trustfulness	gullibility

honesty lie between two extremes. It is a middle way between dishonesty—the deficiency of not telling the truth enough—and what we might call bluntness or excessive truthfulness—the excess of telling the (whole) truth when doing so is cruel, dangerous, rude, or otherwise inappropriate. Honesty, by contrast, means knowing when to tell the (whole) truth and when to keep your thoughts to yourself.

With this in mind, we can do more than just identify the opposites of each virtue. Table 5.2 provides a list of vices corresponding to some of the virtues listed in Table 5.1.

The virtues and vices in these two lists provide a starting point for thinking about which character traits to use in your moral reasoning. If you think there are other character traits that count as virtues or vices, however, you should feel free to use those in your reasoning, too. In some cases—such as one of the examples in the next section—there might not be a ready-made name for a particular character trait. In those cases, you'll have to supply your own name for the trait.

USING VIRTUES AND VICES TO EVALUATE ACTIONS

Sometimes we use moral reasoning to evaluate what someone has already done. You can use virtue- or vice-based reasoning to evaluate someone's action by asking yourself which character trait(s) the person exhibited through his or her actions. Did she act bravely? Or recklessly? Was her action generous or selfish? And so on. When you think about these questions, however, it's important to remember that acting virtuously (or viciously) isn't just about doing what the virtuous (or vicious) person does. It's also about having the right (or wrong) motivations.

Consider, for example, the actions of Miracle Max in the film *The Princess Bride*. At one point in the film, the film's hero, Wesley, is on death's door. Two of his friends bring him to Miracle Max, hoping that the old man can revive him. They cannot afford to pay Max his usual fee, but they explain that Wesley needs to live in order to save his true love. Max is unmoved by this justification. But when he learns that reviving Wesley will cause great suffering and humiliation for a man that Max hates, Max gleefully agrees to help. By reviving Wesley, Max is doing the same thing that a generous and compassionate person would do, but he is not acting generously or compassionately. Acting generously or compassionately requires acting *for the sake of* helping someone; Max is acting for the sake of vengeance.[5]

---

[5]Rob Reiner, *The Princess Bride* (Burbank, CA: 20th Century Fox, 1987).

A more detailed example illustrates how to incorporate motivation into one's moral reasoning: Consider the act of running or working for a for-profit business. Although there are certainly many virtues involved in for-profit business, such as industriousness, conscientiousness, and honesty, many people don't think of working for a for-profit business as a virtuous thing in itself. Philosopher Jason Brennan, however, argues that for-profit work can be an important way of being virtuous, provided that it is done for the right reasons:

PROFIT FOR PROSPERITY

1. It is morally good to act out of civic virtue, which means acting in ways that promote the common good for the sake of promoting the common good.
2. Promoting conditions in which people are happier, live longer, and have more opportunity is a way of promoting the common good.
3. Running or working for a for-profit business can, in the right context, promote conditions in which people are happier, live longer, and have more opportunity.
∴ 4 Running or working for a for-profit business, in the right context and for the sake of promoting the common good, is morally good.[6]

The key normative premise in PROFIT FOR PROSPERITY is about a kind of virtue called civic virtue, which is usually understood, roughly, as a character trait that involves desiring to promote the common good. In PROFIT FOR PROSPERITY, Brennan takes "the common good" to include conditions in which people can satisfy more of their desires, live longer, and have the opportunity to do things like get an education, choose the kind of work they want to do, pursue their own goals, and so on. Premise (3) asserts that, given a properly structured and regulated market economy, working in a for-profit business can help achieve those things, both directly by providing things that satisfy people's desires, make them healthier, etc., and indirectly by contributing to long-run economic growth. So, Brennan concludes, running or working for a for-profit business is a way of exercising civic virtue, provided that it is done primarily for the sake of promoting the common good. (This isn't to say that people with civic virtue can't *also* have other motivations, such as a desire for money, just that those motivations cannot be the most important ones.) By contrast, someone who works for a for-profit business solely to make money, with little or no concern for the common good, is not exercising civic virtue by working for that business.

The general lesson to draw from Brennan's argument is that when we evaluate someone's action in terms of virtues and vices, we need to think not just about what they are doing but also about *why* they are doing it. The same action can count as virtuous when done from one motive but not when done from another.

On the other hand, it is possible to act from the right motivations but fail to act virtuously: acting virtuously requires not just acting for the right reason, but *doing the right thing* for the right reason. Take, for instance, the virtue of caring—that is, of being the kind of person who cares for other people, as a parent cares for a child or friends care for one another. Caring for others is not just a matter of feeling sympathy for them; it also requires listening to what they have to say, responding to their words and feelings appropriately, helping them fulfill their needs when appropriate, and so on.

Looking beyond the typical cases of care between family members or friends, consider the response by McDonald's executives to a mass shooting in a McDonald's in San Ysidro,

---

[6]Jason Brennan, "For-Profit Business as Civic Virtue," *Journal of Business Ethics* 106 (2012): 313–24.

CARING IN WESTERN, CHINESE, AND AFRICAN ETHICS

Some philosophers think that the best way to understand morality is to focus on caring and caring relationships. In contemporary Western philosophy, this view of morality is most commonly associated with feminist philosophy and is known as the ethics of care. Some care ethicists regard their view as a version of virtue ethics in which caring is the fundamental virtue. Others think of the ethics of care as an alternative theory of morality, distinct from the "big three" theories of consequentialism, deontology, and virtue ethics. We consider the ethics of care in more detail in Chapter 12, along with much older Chinese and African theories of morality that also give a prominent role to the virtue of caring and caring relationships.

California, in 1984. The shooting injured forty people, twenty-one of them fatally. When he learned of the massacre, McDonald's Executive Vice President Don Horwitz told his fellow executives that they should "do what's right for the survivors and families of the victims, and worry about lawsuits later." At great expense to the company, the executives suspended advertising across the country, paid the victims' hospital bills, helped families make funeral arrangements, paid to fly victims' relatives to be with their families, and even attended the funerals of eleven of the victims. They permanently closed the restaurant where the shooting occurred and solicited the local community's input about what to do with the building and the impromptu memorials that had been placed there. As business ethicist Sheldene Simola argues, the executives' actions successfully demonstrated the virtue of caring:

EXECUTIVE CARING

1. The McDonald's executives were motivated by a desire to attend to the needs of the victims and their families.
2. The executives listened to the victims and their families to identify their needs and wants.
3. The executives responded appropriately in fulfilling the victims' needs, often at great expense to their company.
∴ 4. The executives successfully demonstrated the virtue of caring in their response to the shooting in San Ysidro.[7]

There are many things that the executives *could* have done, even out of a sincere desire to help the victims, that would have failed to demonstrate the virtue of caring. Suppose, for instance, that the executives had offered to send all of the victims' families on an all-expenses paid trip to Disneyland in a sincere but inept attempt to cheer them up. The victims would likely have regarded this is an insensitive gesture that failed to recognize the depth of their grief and suffering. That way of responding to the victims' needs would therefore fail to demonstrate the virtue of caring.

The ability to recognize the appropriate way to act on a particular motivation is often called **practical wisdom.** It plays a central role in evaluating actions in terms of virtue and vice, as well as in using virtues and vices to think about what to do.

---

[7]Sheldene Simola, "Ethics and Justice and Ethics of Care in Crisis Management," *Journal of Business Ethics* 46 (2003): 351–61.

USING VIRTUES AND VICES TO DECIDE WHAT TO DO

In addition to using moral reasoning to evaluate something that someone has already done, we frequently use moral reasoning to decide what to do. You can use virtue- or vice-based reasoning to decide what you (or someone else) ought to do by reviewing the various options and asking yourself which of them would exhibit virtues and which would exhibit vices. Alternatively, you might start with a particular virtue, such as bravery or honesty, and ask yourself what would be the brave or honest thing to do in a particular situation.

When you do this, it's important to remember that having a particular virtue—say, bravery—involves more than just acting bravely. It even goes beyond having the right motivation, which we discussed in the last section. Not only does the brave person act bravely out of a desire to be brave, she values bravery and disapproves of both cowardice and recklessness. This affects her attitude toward people and actions that are cowardly or reckless. It leads her to feel pleased when people do brave things and even more pleased when they are rewarded for it. It leads her to want to promote bravery and discourage cowardice in other people, and so on. Because virtues require having many different kinds of attitudes and tendencies, moral philosophers say that virtues are **multi-track dispositions.**

To see how this complex set of attitudes plays a role in moral reasoning, consider the following argument from law professor R. Michael Cassidy. Cassidy is considering what prosecutors ought to do when trying to reach a plea bargain with someone accused of a crime. (A plea bargain involves a defendant agreeing to plead guilty to some crime in return for some benefit, such as a lighter sentence. As a condition of the plea bargain, prosecutors sometimes require the defendant to testify against other criminals, too.)

HONEST PROSECUTORS
1. It would be dishonest to let a defendant plead guilty to a crime that seriously misrepresents the defendant's actions (e.g., by making it seem like the defendant did something much less serious than he or she actually did).
2. It would be dishonest to try to intimidate or coerce the defendant into telling the court whatever the prosecutor wants the defendant to say (e.g., by pressuring the defendant to exaggerate the other defendants' crimes).
3. Since defendants who are testifying against others may have incentives to lie, the honest thing to do is to structure a plea bargain so as to reduce their incentives to lie (e.g., by explicitly stating that the plea bargain is null and void if the defendant lies on the witness stand).
4. One should act honestly.
∴ 5. Prosecutors should structure plea bargains so that (a) the defendant will not be charged with a crime that seriously misrepresents the actual offense; (b) the defendant is not compelled to offer a distorted version of events to the court; and (c) the defendant has incentives to be honest in his or her testimony.[8]

If you think of honesty simply as the tendency to tell the truth, you might have focused only on the first premise of HONEST PROSECUTORS. That is, you might have been concerned only

---

[8]R. Michael Cassidy, "Character and Context: What Virtue Theory Can Teach Us About a Prosecutor's Ethical Duty to 'Seek Justice'," *Notre Dame Law Review* 82 (2013): 635–98.

with what the prosecutors themselves are telling the court (and the public) about what the defendant did. But since being honest also means valuing honesty in other ways, being an honest prosecutor involves more than that. Premises (2) and (3) of HONEST PROSECUTORS reflects the fact that honest prosecutors would want the defendant to tell the truth on the stand, even if that makes it harder for the prosecutors to convict other criminals. Because they disapprove of dishonesty and of people who get what they want by being dishonest, truly honest prosecutors would not want to convict those other criminals by being dishonest or by getting someone else to be dishonest.

This illustrates the more general point that when you are thinking about what it is means to demonstrate a particular virtue, you should not focus exclusively on the most obvious ways of acting in accordance with that virtue. Truly exhibiting a particular virtue requires acting on a complex set of attitudes that affect a wide range of choices and actions.

TERMINOLOGY TO KNOW

virtue	thin ethical terms	practical wisdom
vice	virtue ethics	multi-track disposition
thick ethical terms	golden mean	

DISCUSSION QUESTIONS

1. Think of a person whom you really admire. Which of that person's character traits do you admire? Does the person have any character traits that you would count as vices?
2. Review the lists of virtues in Table 5.1. Are there any character traits on that list that you would not count as virtues? Are there any character traits that you would count as virtues but that don't appear on any of the lists?
3. Describe a time when you or someone you know acted out of a morally admirable motivation but ended up failing to achieve what you set out to do. Was your failure the result of bad luck, a failure of practical wisdom, or both?
4. Pick one of the virtues from Mark Alfano's list in Table 5.1. Describe a real or hypothetical situation in which that virtue would express itself as a multi-track disposition, as the virtue of honesty does in the example about plea bargains. What kinds of actions would someone who has the virtue perform (or refuse to perform) in that situation?

CASE STUDIES

See the Note About Case Studies on p. 150 for further instructions.

1. Wesley Autrey was standing on a New York subway platform when a stranger next to him had a seizure. Autrey and two other bystanders helped him through the seizure, but as the stranger stood up, he fell onto the tracks. Autrey leapt down onto the tracks, leaving his two young daughters with the two bystanders. He had intended to lift the stranger back onto the platform, but when he realized that a train was barreling into the station, Autrey pushed the stranger into the shallow drainage trench between the tracks and threw himself on top of him. Both men survived, though the train passed so closely over Autrey that it left grease on his hat. Afterward, Autrey explained that he had simply done what he thought was right when he saw someone who needed his help. Evaluate Autrey's act of saving the stranger by holding him down in the drainage trench. Construct a moral argument to support your evaluation, using at least one normative premise about virtues or vices.

2. Coyotes have recently become much more common in the suburbs of New York City. In the tiny town of Hawthorne, about an hour's drive north of Manhattan, a woman noticed a coyote hanging around her house. She felt sorry for the animal because it was all alone, so she started leaving food outside for it. This worried the other residents of Hawthorne, since the woman lived directly across from an elementary school. Although the animal never harmed anyone, the residents eventually had the animal trapped. News reports are unclear about whether the coyote was euthanized or merely relocated. Evaluate the woman's action of feeding the coyote that was hanging around her house. Construct a moral argument to support your evaluation, using at least one normative premise about virtues or vices.

3. During more than a decade as a member of the executive committee of FIFA, the governing body for international soccer, American Chuck Blazer raked in millions of dollars in bribes and other illegal income. When American law enforcement caught on and threatened to put him in jail for the rest of his life, Blazer struck a deal. Not only would he plead guilty to various offenses, he would go undercover at FIFA to secretly record meetings and collect information about other illegal activities, such as accepting bribes in connection with the selection of host countries for the World Cup. Blazer secretly funneled information about these criminal activities to the American authorities for nearly two years, eventually enabling them to charge over a dozen other FIFA officials with various crimes. Evaluate Blazer's action of secretly collecting information about his colleagues' crimes in order to reduce his own prison sentence. Construct a moral argument to support your evaluation, using at least one normative premise about virtues or vices.

4. World War II was still raging when 18-year-old Hiroo Onoda joined the Japanese army. The army sent Onoda to Lubang Island in the Philippines. A few months later, Japan's enemies captured the island. Only Onoda and three other Japanese soldiers escaped into the hills, where they decided to carry on the war effort using guerrilla tactics. A few months after that, the war ended. Onoda and his men, however, had no way of knowing this. When they found leaflets announcing the end of the war, the men thought they were fake. They continued their guerrilla war campaign, killing several people and destroying property over the years. Only in 1974, nearly three decades after the war ended, did Onoda leave his post—and then only when Japan sent his former commanding officer to order him to surrender. Evaluate Onoda's action of continuing to wage guerrilla war for nearly three decades after World War II ended. Construct a moral argument to support your evaluation, using at least one normative premise about virtues or vices.

6 } Reasoning with Principles and Counterexamples

When couples (or single women) undergo in vitro fertilization, doctors create multiple embryos, only some of which are implanted in the woman's womb. It is already possible to screen each embryo for some genetic diseases, such as cystic fibrosis and Tay-Sachs disease. If doctors identify such a disease in one of the embryos, they will implant one of the others. Suppose that it were also possible to screen the embryos for genes that affected traits like intelligence or attractiveness. Would it be morally permissible for would-be parents to select the embryo that has a greater genetic predisposition to be brilliant and beautiful?

The bioethicist Julian Savulescu argues that not only would it be permissible, it would actually be morally obligatory:

GENETIC SCREENING

1. Would-be parents are morally obligated to select the child, from among those children they could have, who is expected to have the best life, based on the information available to the parents at the time.
2. When undergoing in vitro fertilization, selecting the embryo that has the most favorable genes leads to having the child who is expected to have the best life, relative to other possible children the would-be parent(s) could have.
∴ 3. When undergoing in vitro fertilization, would-be parents are morally obligated to select the embryo that has the most favorable genes.[1]

The normative premise in GENETIC SCREENING says that would-be parents have a certain kind of obligation: to choose the "best" child from among the possible children they could have. Savulescu calls this premise the "principle of procreative beneficence." This principle is certainly not going to appear on any list of general obligations, such as those that we discussed in Chapter 4. Perhaps one could argue that it follows from the general obligation to promote good outcomes, or from a special parental obligation to do what it best for one's child, or even, perhaps, from the universal obligation to treat persons with respect. Different people can accept the principle of procreative beneficence without agreeing on exactly *why* would-be parents have an obligation to choose the "best" child.

---

[1] Julian Savulescu, "Procreative Beneficence: Why We Should Select the Best Children," *Bioethics* 15 (2001): 413–26. For the record, Savulescu thinks that even though parents morally ought to choose the "best" embryo, they should not be *legally* required or otherwise coerced into doing so.

A lot of moral reasoning, both in everyday life and in philosophical argument, involves moral principles of this kind—that is, principles that are more specific than the kinds we have considered in previous chapters but still broad enough to apply to a wide range of cases. In this chapter we will explore how to reason both with and about these sorts of principles—that is, how to use them in moral reasoning and how to reason about which principles to accept.

INTERMEDIATE MORAL PRINCIPLES

In previous chapters we explored moral arguments that rely on very general claims about obligations, appeals to the good or bad consequences of an action, or appeals to virtues or vices. These claims can be very vague, directing us to do things like "treat persons with respect" or "choose better consequences over worse consequences" or "act honestly." In many cases, we can apply those vague instructions directly to a particular action. In other cases, however, we need guidance from more specific moral principles. These **intermediate moral principles** are principles that help us apply more general moral principles to particular cases, especially when two or more general principles conflict; make claims about which kinds of actions are morally better than which other kinds of actions; specify which kinds of consequences matter, morally speaking; and so on. The idea of an intermediate moral principle is vague because it is something of a catch-all category: It can include any moral principle that doesn't fall into one of the more general categories of normative premises discussed in other chapters of this book.

Rather than try to offer a precise definition of "intermediate moral principles," it might be more helpful to give some examples. As a simple example, think of a situation where telling someone the truth would be unnecessarily harmful or hurtful. In that kind of case, we might wonder whether to tell an outright lie or simply to tell a misleading truth. Many people accept the intermediate moral principle that it is better to deliberately mislead someone (e.g., with a misleading truth) than to lie to them.[2]

When it comes to weightier cases involving, say, the obligation not to harm others, we sometimes need guidance in thinking about what kind of harms matter, morally speaking. Sometimes we even need guidance on seemingly straightforward issues, such as when killing someone counts as doing harm. For instance, when terminally ill patients are very close to death and are in great pain, doctors will sometimes ease their pain by administering large doses of powerful painkillers, even though they know that a large dose will hasten the patient's death. Does that count as killing the patient? If so, is it really harming the patient, since it reduces their suffering in their final hours?

To answer the second question, we might consider an intermediate moral principle suggested by philosopher Don Marquis. According to Marquis, someone's death harms that person when it deprives that person of a future of value; furthermore, this is one of the greatest harms that a person can suffer. So, given that it is generally wrong to harm others—and especially to inflict serious harm on them—killing someone is wrong when it deprives

---

[2]For a discussion of this principle, see Jennifer Saul, "Just Go Ahead and Lie," *Analysis* 72 (2012): 3–9.

that person of a future of value, except perhaps in extenuating circumstances (such as self-defense).[3] Using this principle, we get the "right answer" in a lot of important, uncontroversial cases: The principle implies that it is normally wrong to kill an adult human or a child or an infant. It implies that when someone is dying of cancer or some other disease, that is a bad thing for the person who is going to die, as opposed to just for their loved ones who will be left behind. It implies that it is probably wrong to kill certain kinds of animals, such as chimpanzees, but not others, such as fruit flies.

Marquis uses this intermediate principle in his own moral reasoning, as follows:

FUTURE OF VALUE

1. An abortion kills a fetus.
2. A fetus has a future of value.
3. It is usually morally forbidden to kill someone (or something) when he or she (or it) has a future of value.

∴ 4. It is usually morally forbidden to abort a pregnancy.

By using the intermediate moral principle in premise (3), rather than the more general moral principle that it is wrong to harm others, Marquis avoids many of the confusions that arise in trying to apply that more general principle.

To see another intermediate principle in action, let's return to the case of the doctors administering a large dose of painkillers to a terminally ill patient. To think about such cases, some ethicists turn to a famous principle known as the **doctrine of double effect.** The idea behind the doctrine of double effect is that most of our actions have two (or more) effects, only some of which we are specifically trying to bring about, and that when some of those effects are bad, it matters, morally, which of the effects we are trying to bring about. More specifically, the doctrine says that, under certain conditions, it is morally permissible to bring about a bad effect as a *side effect* of your action, even if it would be morally forbidden to bring about that bad effect as the intended consequence of your action (or as a direct means to that intended consequence). In the case of the doctors, for instance, some ethicists argue that even though it would be wrong to administer painkillers in order to bring about the patient's death, it is permissible to administer painkillers to ease the patient's pain, even when the doctors know that the side effect of the painkillers will be to hasten the patient's death.

Turning to a different example, intermediate moral principles are often helpful when more general obligations conflict. Consider, for instance, parents' obligation to promote their children's interests and everyone's obligation not to harm others or be unfair to others. These obligations conflict when parents can do things for their children that give them important advantages over other children, such as sending them to expensive college preparatory schools, hiring private tutors or coaches, and so on. On the one hand, these things benefit the child in question by, for example, increasing their chances of getting into a highly selective university or a highly competitive profession. On the other hand, they make it harder for other children to get into those universities and professions. This harms those other children, and, since it especially affects children whose parents cannot afford expensive schooling or tutors, it promotes unfairness.

---

[3]Don Marquis, "Why Abortion Is Immoral," *Journal of Philosophy* 86 (1989): 183–202; reprinted in Part V of this book (pp. 320–31).

To resolve this conflict, philosophers Harry Brighouse and Adam Swift suggest the following intermediate moral principle: parents are permitted to confer special advantages on their children only when those advantages result from activities that are important for developing healthy parent–child relationships. A simple example involves parents reading bedtime stories to their children. This gives a child various advantages over other children whose parents didn't read bedtime stories to them, but it is also just the kind of nurturing activity that helps develop a strong emotional bond between a parent and a child. Because reading bedtime stories promotes the parent–child bond, Brighouse and Swift's principle entails that parents are morally permitted to read bedtime stories to their children, even though doing so gives their children some competitive advantage over the children of parents who don't read them bedtime stories. By contrast, parents can develop a healthy relationship with their children without sending them to an elite preparatory school. Since sending children to such a school confers a significant advantage on the children, Brighouse and Swift's principle entails that it is wrong for parents to do so.[4]

This last example raises an important point about the evaluation of intermediate moral principles. There's something a little odd about saying that parents "are morally permitted to read bedtime stories to their children." *Of course* parents are morally permitted to read bedtime stories to their children! That seems so obvious as to be not worth pointing out, much less arguing for. Indeed, we would be very suspicious of any intermediate moral principle that implied that parents were forbidden from reading bedtime stories to their children. The existence of such clear-cut cases provides a method for testing intermediate moral principles, which we explore in the next section.

USING COUNTEREXAMPLES AND THOUGHT EXPERIMENTS

One common technique for evaluating an intermediate moral principle—or any principle, for that matter—is by looking for **counterexamples.** A counterexample is a real or imaginary case in which the principle seems to "get the wrong answer." If you can come up with a counterexample to an intermediate moral principle, you have provided a reason—maybe a decisive reason—to reject or modify the principle. (We'll look at ways to respond to counterexamples in the next section.)

To see how this works, consider the well-known principle **"an eye for an eye."** There are various ways of expressing this principle, but they generally amount to something like the following:

EYE FOR AN EYE

When one person wrongs another, the wrongdoer should suffer a punishment that is similar in degree and kind to the wrong he or she inflicted on the victim.

People often appeal to EYE FOR AN EYE to justify the death penalty. The thought is that when one person murders another, the only fitting punishment is for the murderer to die. The

---

[4]Harry Brighouse and Adam Swift, *Family Values: The Ethics of Parent-Child Relationships* (Princeton, NJ: Princeton University Press, 2014), 124*ff*.

philosopher Stephen Nathanson, however, points out that, based on EYE FOR AN EYE, we ought to "rape rapists, torture torturers, and burn arsonists whose acts have led to deaths."[5] But it is clearly morally forbidden, Nathanson suggests, for the government—or anyone else, for that matter—to do those things to anyone. So, those cases are counterexamples to EYE FOR AN EYE.

Sometimes you'll want to give a fairly detailed counterexample. One way to do this is to look for good examples in fiction, history, or scripture—especially examples with which your audience is already familiar. For instance, the ancient Chinese philosopher Mencius defends a principle of moderation in dealing with morally flawed people by citing two historical examples. The first, a man named Bo Yi, insisted so strongly on his own dignity that he would not even have a conversation with a bad person, much less work for one. The second, an otherwise virtuous man named Liuxia Hui, was so confident of his own incorruptibility that he would interact and even work for anyone, even a bad ruler. Mencius expects his audience to judge that both men made a mistake by being too extreme, and so he takes these two counterexamples to show that one should be willing to interact with bad people, but only up to a certain point.[6]

Alternatively, you can produce counterexamples by dreaming up an imaginary scenario—perhaps a very detailed scenario—and ask what the principle entails in that scenario. Philosophers call these imaginary scenarios **thought experiments** because they use the scenarios to "test" principles, much as scientists use experiments to test hypotheses. Consider, for instance, a famous thought experiment concocted by the philosopher James Rachels, who wants to argue against the following principle:

LETTING DIE

It is morally worse to kill someone than to let someone die.

To do this, Rachels asks us to imagine two scenarios. In the first scenario, Mr. Smith drowns his 6-year-old nephew in the bathtub in order to secure a large inheritance. This is an instance of killing (as opposed to letting die), and Smith's action is clearly wrong. In the second scenario, Jones sneaks into his 6-year-old nephew's bathroom, fully intending to drown the boy to secure his own large inheritance; but in this scenario the nephew slips in the tub, knocks himself unconscious, and drowns in the bath, without any intervention from Jones. This is an instance of letting the boy die (as opposed to killing him), but according to Rachels, Jones's action is just as wrong in the second scenario as Smith's is in the first. We seem to have a pair of cases in which killing and letting die are equally wrong. But according to LETTING DIE, this is impossible, since killing someone is worse than letting someone die. Thus, Rachels concludes, LETTING DIE must be incorrect.[7]

[5]Stephen Nathanson, *An Eye for an Eye?*, 2nd ed. (Lanham, MD: Roman and Littlefield, 2001); excerpts reprinted in Part V of this book (pp. 366–72).

[6]Mengzi, *Mengzi: With Selections from Traditional Commentaries*, translated by Bryan van Norden (Indianapolis: Hackett Publishing, 2008), 49.

[7]James Rachels, "Active and Passive Euthanasia," *New England Journal of Medicine* 292 (1975): 78–80; reprinted in Part V of this book (pp. 352–56).

MORAL INTUITIONS

Many of the arguments for and against intermediate principles rely on **moral intuitions** about particular cases, kinds of actions, or principles. Moral intuitions are, roughly, moral judgments that we make without going through any conscious process of reasoning. They contrast with conclusions that we reach only by explicit reasoning. Philosopher Gilbert Harman gives a famous example: If you saw some children set a cat on fire for fun, you would probably form an immediate judgment that the children were doing something morally wrong, without having to go through any conscious reasoning.*

Only some moral intuitions withstand scrutiny. You might change your mind about a judgment after you think about it for a while, learn more about the case, or just have a good meal and a nap. With other judgments, however, you will remain confident even after you've thought about it and eliminated distorting factors like bad moods. Some philosophers would say that only the judgments that withstand such scrutiny count as *real* moral intuitions. At any rate, those are the only ones worth using in moral reasoning.

People use moral intuitions not only to decide if some intermediate moral principle seems plausible or not but also to decide whether that principle gets the "right" or "wrong" answer in particular cases. We've seen several examples of this in this chapter. For instance, Marquis supports his moral principle about killing by showing that it agrees with our moral intuitions about various kinds of cases, and Nathanson argues against EYE FOR AN EYE by describing cases in which the principle conflicts with our moral intuitions—or, at least, with *his* intuitions. In such cases, the principles are said to have **counterintuitive** consequences—that is, logical consequences that run counter to (i.e., conflict with) our moral intuitions.

Moral philosophers disagree about exactly what role moral intuitions should play in justifying our moral beliefs. For discussion of one important suggestion, see the section on "reflective equilibrium" in Chapter 9 (pp. 96–98).

*Gilbert Harman, *The Nature of Morality* (New York: Oxford University Press, 1977), 4.

Some thought experiments get even more imaginative. The philosopher Robert Nozick was famous for his creative thought experiments. One well-known thought experiment was meant to provide a counterexample to the following principle:

NON-AGGRESSION

It is morally forbidden to use force against an innocent person.

Imagine, asks Nozick, that you are trapped at the bottom of a deep well. Someone picks up an innocent man and throws him down the well. If the man falls on you, he will survive but you will die. Fortunately for you, you happen to have a futuristic ray gun that can disintegrate the falling man instantly. Since the man is innocent, however, NON-AGGRESSION entails that it would be morally forbidden for you to use your ray gun to disintegrate him. This, Nozick suggests, is clearly a mistake, for you are permitted to disintegrate the falling man in self-defense.[8]

[8]Robert Nozick, *Anarchy, State and Utopia* (New York: Basic Books, 1974), 34–35.

Many people object to such fanciful thought experiments because they are too far removed from real life. The idea, however, is not that we might really encounter such a situation, but that the situation enables us to clarify the logical implications of a moral principle. These thought experiments abstract away from the messy details of real-life cases so that we can focus only on the things that are supposed to matter to a particular moral principle, as the difference between killing someone and allowing them to die matters in LETTING DIE.

When you are considering an intermediate principle, then, there are two kinds of potential counterexamples that you should consider. The first involve real-life cases, such as the historical figures that Mencius discusses. The second involve more imaginative and more detailed thought experiments, such as Rachels's paired cases of Mr. Smith and Mr. Jones or Nozick's case of the ray gun in the well.

RESPONDING TO COUNTEREXAMPLES

What do you do when you identify an apparent counterexample to a principle that you were using in your moral reasoning? One response, of course, is to abandon the principle—that is, to stop using it in your reasoning. But there are a number of other possible responses.

One option is to deny that the case or thought experiment really provides a counterexample at all. Sometimes this will be because the alleged counterexample rests on a misunderstanding of the principle. In that case, you'll need to explain why the principle does not get "the wrong answer" in the case described. More often, disputing the counterexample involves explaining why the case *seems* to disprove the principle in question but doesn't *really* do so. The philosopher Philippa Foot takes this approach in discussing James Rachels's thought experiment about Smith and Jones drowning their nephews. Recall that Rachels is trying to show that it is just as bad for Jones to allow his nephew to drown in the bathtub as it is for Smith to drown the boy himself. Foot admits that both men acted monstrously. That's why the case *seems* like a counterexample, because we recognize that Jones does something truly awful in allowing his nephew to drown. But, argues Foot, allowing the boy to drown is especially awful in this case because Jones has a role-based obligation to care for his nephew. And because he has this role-based obligation, his failure to save his nephew is just as bad as actively drowning the boy. Thus, the scenarios do not show that letting someone die is *generally* just as bad as killing someone. It shows only that there are special cases where it would be just as wrong for a particular person to let some other person die as it would be for the first person to kill the second.[9]

Along the same lines, you can deny that a counterexample is relevant by arguing that it simply involves a conflict between the principle in question and a more important principle. Mencius takes this approach when one of his disciples raises an apparent counterexample to a principle of ancient Chinese etiquette. (The distinction between etiquette and morality is blurry in ancient Chinese ethics.) The disciple asks whether it is forbidden for men and women's hands to touch each other (except, presumably, for men and women in special relationships with one another, such as husband and wife or mother and son). Mencius says

---

[9]Philippa Foot, "Killing and Letting Die," in *Abortion: Moral and Legal Perspectives*, ed. Joy L. Garfield and Patricia Hennessy (Amherst: University of Massachusetts Press, 1984), 177–85.

that it is. The disciple then asks what Mencius would do if his sister-in-law were drowning and Mencius could save her only by grasping her hand. The principle entails that Mencius should not save her, since that requires touching her hand with his. But surely, the disciple is suggesting, the right thing to do would be for Mencius to save his sister-in-law. Mencius agrees that "only a beast" would refuse to save his sister-in-law, but that this is a case where the need to save someone's life overrides the principle about people of different genders touching each other's hands.[10] Thus, the counterexample does not show that the principle is false. It only shows that the principle can sometimes be overridden by other principles.[11]

A different way to respond to an alleged counterexample is by "biting the bullet" and insisting that, even if they are counterintuitive, the principle's implications are correct. Recall that Don Marquis, whose views we discussed earlier in the chapter, says that it is wrong to kill something if and only if that thing has a future of value. A critic might object to this principle by giving an alleged counterexample involving a terminally ill person whose future involved nothing but intense pain. According to Marquis's principle, it would be permissible to kill such a pain. But, the critic would say, this is obviously incorrect, and so such a person is a counterexample to Marquis's principle. In response, someone who shared Marquis's view could simply insist that it *is* permissible to kill such a person. For if that were correct, then such a person would not be a counterexample to the principle, because the principle would not get the wrong answer in that person's case. This, of course, would not be the end of the argument. It would just shift the argument to whether it is, in fact, permissible to kill such a person.

A third way to respond to an alleged counterexample is to modify the principle in order to get the right answer in that case. Robert Nozick takes this approach after introducing his thought experiment about the ray gun and the well. Recall that he was initially considering a principle, which we called NON-AGGRESSION, according to which it is morally forbidden to use force against an innocent person. His thought experiment shows that there are cases in which NON-AGGRESSION gets the wrong answer. In response, he modifies NON-AGGRESSION to say that it is morally forbidden to use force against an innocent person *unless that person is an "innocent threat."* (An "innocent threat," says Nozick, is someone who, through no fault of their own, is going to cause you so much harm that you would be justified in using force against that person if he or she were doing it intentionally.)[12] This modified principle no longer gets the wrong answer in cases like the one that Nozick describes. That is, it is no longer open to that kind of counterexample.

These three ways of responding to counterexamples provide a method for testing and refining the intermediate moral principles that you use in your moral reasoning. By repeatedly testing a principle against possible counterexamples and modifying the principle when needed, you can often arrive at important, well-supported normative premises for moral arguments.

---

[10]Mencius, *Mengzi: With Selections from Traditional Commentaries*, trans. Bryan van Norden (Indianapolis: Hackett Publishing, 2008), 97.

[11]For further discussion of overriding obligations, see the section on Sir David Ross's theory of ethics in Chapter 11 (p. 118)

[12]Nozick, *Anarchy, State and Utopia*, 34–35.

TERMINOLOGY TO KNOW

intermediate moral principle
doctrine of double effect
counterexample

eye for an eye
thought experiment

moral intuition
counterintuitive

DISCUSSION QUESTIONS

1. Can you think of a popular saying or aphorism that expresses an intermediate moral principle (e.g., "Two wrongs don't make a right")? Can you come up with cases in which that principle "gets the right answer"? What about cases in which it "gets the wrong answer"? Can you come up with a modified version of the principle that avoids those "wrong answers"?

2. Do you think that Foot's reply to Rachels shows that his cases don't really provide a counterexample to LETTING DIE? If so, can you think of another pair of cases that *do* provide a counterexample? If not, explain why you think Foot's reply fails.

3. Can you think of an intermediate moral principle that has some counterintuitive consequence about which you are prepared to "bite the bullet"? That is, can you think of a case in which the principle seems to "get the wrong answer" but about which you're willing to accept that consequence of the principle anyway?

4. Some people argue that very unrealistic thought experiments, like Nozick's thought experiment about disintegrating someone with a ray gun, generate very useful moral intuitions because they eliminate other distracting elements that arise in more realistic scenarios. Other people argue that unrealistic scenarios generate unreliable moral intuitions because they're so divorced from real life. Who do you think is right about this? Why?

CASE STUDIES

See the Note About Case Studies on p. 150 for further instructions.

1. Before the government forced him to take them down, Cody Wilson had posted files on his organization's web that enabled anyone with a 3D printer to manufacture a working handgun. Wilson explains that he and his organization, Defense Distributed, were distributing the files in order to promote freedom by ensuring that people everywhere could access the weapons they needed to protect themselves, even against governments that wanted to ban firearms. He recognizes that somebody might one day use his weapons to kill someone, and he acknowledges that it would be very bad if that happened, but he insists that the need to protect civil liberties is important enough to justify that risk. Evaluate Wilson's action of enabling people to manufacture firearms with their 3D printers. Construct a moral argument to support your evaluation, using an intermediate moral principle (such as the doctrine of double effect) as a normative premise in your argument.

2. Each semester, about 500 students enrolled in sociology professor Patricia Adler's popular course on social deviance at the University of Colorado–Boulder. Like many courses on social deviance in sociology departments around the country, Adler's course included discussion of prostitution. For two decades, Adler's session on prostitution involved a skit designed to illustrate the wide range of experiences among sex workers. Adler solicited volunteers for the skit from among the undergraduate teaching assistants for the course. Each volunteer dressed up as a different kind of sex worker (e.g., a street-walking prostitute, a brothel worker, or an employee of an escort service) and worked with Adler to prepare a script for the skit. During the skit, which was performed in class, Adler interviewed each volunteer about his or her (fictional) experiences as a sex worker. The

university's administrators, claiming that a former teaching assistant had complained about the skit, expressed concerns that the skit was potentially offensive. Although accounts differ, Adler says that the university forced her to retire early. She is currently a professor emerita, meaning that she is retired from her official position but retains an affiliation with the university. Evaluate the university administrators' action of forcing Adler to retire early. Construct a moral argument to support your evaluation, using an intermediate moral principle as a normative premise in your argument. (Hint: If you can identify conflicting obligations or multiple virtues relevant to this case, consider developing an intermediate moral principle that specifies how to resolve those conflicts in cases like this one.)

3. The story of the Elgin Marbles is about 2,500 years long. Ancient Greek sculptors carved the statues out of marble during the construction of the Parthenon in Athens. The Parthenon was originally a temple to the ancient Greek goddess Athena. In 1800, the statues in the Parthenon came to the attention of Lord Elgin, the British ambassador to the Ottoman empire, which ruled Athens at the time. With the permission of the Ottoman government, Lord Elgin had the statues removed from the Parthenon and shipped to England. (Some people say that he secured that permission by bribing Ottoman officials.) In 1816, the British Parliament bought the marbles from Lord Elgin and deposited them in the British Museum in London, where they remain to this day. For decades now, Greece has demanded that the British Museum return the marbles to Athens. The museum has refused, insisting that Lord Elgin acquired the marbles from the legitimate government of the time and that the marbles provide the greatest public benefit by remaining in London. Evaluate the museum's action of refusing to return the Elgin marbles to Athens. Construct a moral argument to support your evaluation, using an intermediate moral principle as a normative premise in your argument.

4. The police responding to Bryant Heyward's 911 call had been told that armed men were trying to break into Heyward's mother's home. Someone had reported gunshots, and the officers observed a bullet hole in one of the windows. The officers were unsure, however, whether the intruders had entered the house and, if so, whether they were still there. As police circled around to the back of the house, 26-year-old Heyward, who is black, stepped out the back door holding the .40 caliber handgun that he'd picked up to defend himself and his mother from the intruders. One of the officers shouted, "Show me your hands!" But within a second or two, before Heyward could put down his gun, the officer fired two shots. One hit Heyward in the neck, partially paralyzing him. Evaluate the police officer's action of shooting Heyward so soon after encountering him. Construct a moral argument to support your evaluation, using an intermediate moral principle as a normative premise in your argument.

7 } Reasoning by Analogy

Each July from 1999 until 2005, Lance Armstrong climbed to the top of the podium in Paris to claim victory in cycling's biggest race, the Tour de France. But if you look at the record books today, you won't see Armstrong listed as the winner of those races. The international body in charge of cycling stripped Armstrong of all seven titles as punishment for doping—that is, for using banned substances to boost his athletic performance.

Most people disapprove of doping in professional sports. But some philosophers are not so sure that doping is unethical. One much-discussed argument in defense of doping goes like this:

DEFENSE OF DOPING

1. It is morally permissible for one athlete to hire better coaches than another.
2. Hiring better coaches is relevantly similar to doping in that both provide an advantage in athletic competitions.
∴ 3. Doping is morally permissible.

This argument defends doping by comparing doping with something that we already think is morally permissible—namely, hiring better coaches. Such an argument is called an **argument by analogy.**

In general, an argument by analogy compares two things in order to make a point about one of them. More specifically, an argument by analogy argues that because two things are similar in certain respects, they are also similar in some further respect. In ethics, people generally use arguments by analogy to show that some morally controversial action, such as doping, is right (or wrong) by comparing it to some other action that is uncontroversially right (or wrong). Less commonly, people use analogies to argue for other kinds of moral claims, such as the claim that something is good, that some person is brave, and so on.

Arguments by analogy have the following structure:

GENERIC ARGUMENT BY ANALOGY

1. **X** is **M.**
2. **X** is relevantly similar to **Y.**
∴ 3. **Y** is also **M.**

An argument by analogy will be a moral argument whenever **M** is some moral property, such as being morally permissible, being morally forbidden, being supererogatory, being morally

---

PRECEDENTS AND ANALOGIES IN LEGAL REASONING

In legal systems like those of the United States and the United Kingdom, which are known as "common law systems," the fact that a case is relevantly similar to a previous case has important legal implications. These implications depend on just *how* similar the two cases are.

When two cases are so similar as to be identical for legal purposes, the earlier case is said to provide a **precedent** for the later case. Very roughly, a precedent is a court ruling that constrains how courts should rule on legally identical cases in the future. Being identical *for legal purposes*, of course, does not require that the two cases are identical in every way. Roughly, it requires that the facts of the later case be the same as the facts in light of which the court made its decision about the earlier case.

When the facts of one case are not identical to the relevant facts of the earlier case, a court can still consider the earlier case as analogous to the later case. Whereas courts are more or less legally bound to respect earlier precedents, they are not bound by analogies. That is, when the facts are similar enough to make two cases analogous but different enough that the earlier case does not establish a precedent for the second, the court can issue a ruling in the second case that differs from the ruling in the first case.

The justification for requiring courts to respect precedents and consider analogies is, roughly, that the legal system should treat like cases alike. Exactly why it should do this, however, is a contested issue in the philosophy of law.

---

good, and so on (see Chapter 2). Sometimes the second premise of an argument will specify the way(s) in which **X** and **Y** are relevantly similar.

Consider how DEFENSE OF DOPING fits into the structure of GENERIC ARGUMENT BY ANALOGY. **X** in DEFENSE OF DOPING stands for "hiring better coaches." **M** stands for "being morally permissible." **Y** stands for "doping." And DEFENSE OF DOPING explains that **X** and **Y** are similar in that both provide an advantage in athletic competitions.

The idea behind arguments by analogy in ethics is that we should treat like cases alike. That is, if two cases are similar enough in relevant ways, we should make the same moral judgment about them. Or to put that the other way around, we shouldn't judge two cases differently unless we can identify morally relevant differences between them. In short, DEFENSE OF DOPING is accusing doping's critics of hypocrisy: there is no important difference, the argument suggests, between doping and hiring better coaches, so it is inconsistent to oppose one but not the other.

But how, exactly, do we determine whether two cases really are alike? More generally, how do we evaluate an argument by analogy?

EVALUATING ARGUMENTS BY ANALOGY

To understand how to evaluate arguments by analogy, let's take a look at another example. This one comes from an article published in the *Harvard Business Review* in 1968 by Albert Carr:

BLUFFING IN BUSINESS

1. When you are playing poker, it is morally permissible to deceive your competitors in certain ways (e.g., by bluffing about how good your cards are).
2. Business is relevantly similar to poker in that both involve strategic competition in which no one expects anyone else to be completely honest.
∴ 3. When you are engaged in business, it is morally permissible to deceive your competitors in certain ways (e.g., by withholding information in negotiations).[1]

How do we evaluate BLUFFING IN BUSINESS? That is, how do we determine whether the similarities between poker and business really do justify the conclusion that certain kinds of deception are morally permissible in business?

In keeping with the general rules for argument evaluation, which we discussed in Chapter 1, the first thing we need to do is determine whether the first premise is acceptable. In this case, it is clearly acceptable: it is permissible to bluff in poker. The strongest arguments by analogy start from such clearly acceptable premises. After all, you wouldn't get very far in arguing for deception in business if you compared it to another controversial practice, such as industrial espionage (i.e., spying on competing businesses). Don't just take the first premise for granted, though. Some allegedly uncontroversial cases turn out to be more controversial than they appear.

The more difficult part of evaluating an argument by analogy is determining whether the second premise is acceptable—that is, whether the two actions really are **relevantly similar.** Claiming that two actions are relevantly similar is not to say that they are exactly the same— all analogies are imperfect in one way or another. Rather, it is just to say that they are similar enough in the ways that are relevant to the moral property that is being claimed for both of them, such as being morally permissible, morally forbidden, or whatever.

Some arguments try to show relevant similarity by focusing on the features that make the first action morally permissible (or forbidden, or obligatory, or good, or whatever). After all, if you can explain what it is about an action that makes it permissible (or forbidden, etc.) and you can show that some other action resembles it in those ways, then you have at least some reason to think that the second action is also permissible (or forbidden, etc.). This is the approach that BLUFFING IN BUSINESS takes. It explains that bluffing is permitted in poker because none of the players expect any of the others to be completely honest; certain kinds of deception are simply part of the game. So, if business is similar to poker in that particular way—namely, in being the kind of activity where certain kinds of deception are "simply part of the game," which everyone expects from everyone else—then there's a strong case for thinking that poker and business are relevantly similar.

It remains, however, to think about whether there are important differences that outweigh the relevant similarities. There are, of course, many differences between poker and business. The question is whether those differences are relevant to the conclusion about bluffing. Here's one relevant difference between poker and business: arguably, society as a whole would be better off if business executives could be trusted to tell the truth all the time. But a similar level of trust among poker players wouldn't make society better off. In fact, by

---

[1] Adapted from Albert Z. Carr, "Is Business Bluffing Ethical?" *Harvard Business Review* 143 (1968): 155.

"YOU CAN'T COMPARE THIS TO THAT!"

Some people are too quick to dismiss analogies that strike them as far-fetched. People sometimes object that you "can't compare" the two things being compared in an analogy. This is especially true when they find the comparison offensive, as when someone compares something to slavery or Hitler.

Literally, of course, it isn't true that you *can't* compare the two things in the analogy. The point of saying that you "can't compare" two things is to say that the two things are so different that one cannot draw any conclusions about one from the other. But even if the two things are very different or if it really is offensive to compare them, that doesn't *by itself* show that the argument by analogy fails. And if the person does explain what relevant difference undermines the analogy, then the claim that you "can't compare" the two things adds nothing to the objection. So, in responding to outrageous analogies, the appropriate thing to do is focus on the important differences that undermine the analogy.

For instance, some people have compared the struggle for gay rights to the civil rights movement in order to argue for the importance of the gay rights movement. Others insist that "you can't compare" the two movements. It's true that there are important differences between the two movements, but in order to really dismiss the analogy, these critics would have to show *why* the differences between the two movements undermine whatever arguments people are trying to make with the comparison.

---

making poker less exciting, it might make society a little worse off. So although everyone expects certain kinds of deception in both poker and business, that expectation is beneficial to poker but detrimental to business. That's relevant to the conclusion because it suggests that deception in poker is better justified than is deception in business.

Reaching a final judgment about whether two things are relevantly similar requires making lists of all of the relevant similarities and differences you can think of. Then, for each similarity or difference, think about why it is relevant to the conclusion of the argument and about how important it is to the conclusion of the argument. Finally, you'll need to make an all-things-considered judgment about whether the similarities outweigh the differences. There is no mechanistic procedure for doing this, however, and so people will sometimes disagree about whether two things are relevantly similar—even if they have talked through all of the relevant similarities and differences. When that happens, there's not much you can do except look for other arguments.

EVOLVING ANALOGIES

Sometimes the best way to argue by analogy is to begin with a fairly simple analogy and develop it in response to objections. Developing the analogy involves making the comparison gradually more complicated so as to make the two actions (traits, etc.) being compared ever more similar. Consider, for instance, a famous analogy suggested by the work of the philosopher Peter Singer.[2] Imagine that you are walking alone in a remote area when you come upon a small child drowning in a shallow pond. You know that you can easily wade into the pond and rescue the child at no risk to yourself but that by doing so, you would suffer the minor inconvenience of getting your pants and shoes all muddy. It would be morally forbidden for you to leave the child to drown simply to avoid muddying your clothes. But, the argument goes, leaving the child to drown is relevantly similar to declining to donate money to global anti-poverty organizations, such as Oxfam. Those organizations save the lives of children who are dying of malnutrition and easily preventable diseases in very poor countries where such causes kill large numbers of people. Your donation, according to Singer, can save a life, and if you are even somewhat well-off, it comes at no great inconvenience to you.

DROWNING CHILD

1. If you were walking alone in a remote area and saw a small child drowning in a shallow pond, such that you could easily save the child's life at no risk to yourself, it would be morally forbidden for you to leave the child to drown.
2. Leaving the child to drown is like failing to donate to anti-poverty organizations, such as Oxfam, in that in both cases you are declining to do something that would save someone's life without your giving up anything important.
∴ 3. Failing to donate to anti-poverty organizations is morally forbidden.

Upon hearing this argument, many people hurry to point out differences between the case of the drowning child and the case of the starving child in some very poor country. Singer considers one such difference: in the case of the drowning child, you are the only one who can save the child, whereas in the case of the starving child, there are tens or hundreds of millions of other people who could save the child. In response, Singer tweaks the analogy a little bit. Imagine that the pond is surrounded by other adults, none of whom is doing anything to save the child, even though each could do so just as easily as you. This situation is a bit closer to the one in which we find ourselves with respect to the global poor. But even when other adults are standing around the pond, Singer contends, it would still be morally forbidden for you to refuse to save the drowning child. So it is still morally forbidden to fail to donate to anti-poverty organizations.

We can repeat this process for a number of other differences between the drowning child and the starving child. For instance, there is only one drowning child in the story; there are millions of starving children. Saving the drowning child solves the problem, but feeding one starving child does not. But suppose we change the analogy again. What if you came upon a pond filled with drowning children? Would you be justified in refusing to save even one just because there would still be many children left in the pond? Presumably not—and so it is wrong to fail to donate to anti-poverty organizations, even though doing so will not eliminate extreme poverty.

Working through this process not only helps you to develop and understand a more sophisticated argument by analogy, it also helps you separate the morally important aspects of the situation from the morally unimportant aspects.

---

[2]This analogy is based on: Peter Singer, "Famine, Affluence, and Morality," *Philosophy & Public Affairs* 1 (1972), 229–43; reprinted in Part V of this book (pp. 507–15). Strictly speaking, Singer's main argument does not depend primarily on this analogy. Instead, it is based on the principle that you should prevent very bad things from happening when you can do so without sacrificing anything of comparable moral significance.

GODWIN'S LAW AND EXAGGERATED ANALOGIES

You can only discuss something on the Internet for so long before somebody compares somebody to Hitler. (In fact, there's a popular name for this observation: Godwin's law of Nazi analogies, or "Godwin's law" for short.*) In almost every case, the comparison is supposed to be hyperbole—that is, an instance of exaggerating something to make a point. Some people might find some of these exaggerated analogies amusing, whether they refer to Hitler or something else outrageous. Such exaggerations might even be rhetorically effective in certain contexts because they can provoke strong emotions among people who agree with your conclusion.

Outrageous, exaggerated analogies are rarely cogent arguments, though. The relevant similarities between Hitler (or whatever) and the topic you're discussing are likely to be overwhelmed by the enormous differences between the two. Furthermore, outrageous analogies almost never succeed in changing anyone's mind for the same reason that they're so effective at galvanizing those who do agree with you: outrageous analogies provoke strong emotions, which can make it hard for people to take your argument seriously. So, when choosing comparisons, don't go for hyperbole or shock value; go for the closest, least offensive comparison that you can find to make your point.

*Mike Godwin, "Meme, Counter-Meme," *Wired*, July 1, 1994, http://www.wired.com/1994/10/godwin-if-2/.

USING ANALOGIES TO RESPOND TO MORAL ARGUMENTS

In addition to giving you a way to argue for or against specific moral claims, analogies provide a way to respond to others' moral arguments. The bioethicists J. Stewart Cameron and Raymond Hoffenberg provide a nice illustration of this technique in a paper on the ethics of buying and selling human kidneys.[3] Cameron and Hoffenberg observe that others have offered the following argument against allowing the buying and selling of kidneys:

DONOR RISK

    1. Donating a kidney involves a risk of death during or after donation.
    2. One should not undertake the risk of death for purely financial reasons.
∴ 3. It is morally forbidden to sell one's kidneys.

But, Cameron and Hoffenberg argue, DONOR RISK is relevantly similar to the following argument:

WORKER RISK

    1. Many jobs, such as construction work or mining, involve a risk of death.
    2. One should not undertake the risk of death for purely financial reasons.
∴ 3. It is morally forbidden to work as a construction worker or miner.

---

[3] J. Stewart Cameron and Raymond Hoffenberg, "The Ethics of Organ Transplantation Reconsidered: Paid Organ Donation and the Use of Executed Prisoners as Donors," *Kidney International* 55 (1999): 724–32.

Although they are about different actions, DONOR RISK and WORKER RISK are almost exactly the same. They even share the same normative premise. But, as Cameron and Hoffenberg point out, WORKER RISK does not seem like a very good argument. Most people would say that it is mistaken—that there is nothing wrong with working as a construction worker or miner. But if WORKER RISK is a bad argument, and it's relevantly similar to DONOR RISK, then DONOR RISK must also be a bad argument.

This kind of argument is called a **refutation by logical analogy,** and it's very useful in moral reasoning. Such an analogy aims to refute (that is, undermine) an argument by comparing it to another argument that is clearly a bad argument. In some cases, such as the analogy between DONOR RISK and WORKER RISK, one argument is so obviously mistaken and the two arguments are so similar that you won't need to explain exactly what's wrong with the mistaken argument. More complex cases, however, will require more thought.

The philosopher Judith Jarvis Thomson provides a more complex example of refutation by logical analogy.[4] Some people, Thomson notes, make the following sort of argument:

UNPROTECTED SEX

1. A woman who becomes pregnant as a result of consensual unprotected sex is partially responsible for the fetus's presence in her body.
2. If a woman is at least partially responsible for the fetus's presence in her body, then the fetus has the right to use her body.
∴ 3. It is morally forbidden for a woman who became pregnant as a result of consensual unprotected sex to get an abortion.

But, Thomson cautions, before we accept that argument, we should consider this argument:

OPEN WINDOW

1. If a homeowner opens a window in a stuffy room and a burglar climbs through the window, the homeowner is partially responsible for the burglar's presence in her home.
2. If a homeowner is at least partially responsible for the burglar's presence in her home, then the burglar has the right to use her home.
∴ 3. It is morally forbidden for the homeowner in this situation to force the burglar to leave her home.

As Thomson suggests, OPEN WINDOW is absurd. In particular, the second premise is clearly unacceptable: the mere fact that the homeowner is partially responsible, in the sense intended in premise (1), provides no reason to think that the burglar has any right to use her home.

But then Thomson offers the following argument by analogy:

REFUTATION

1. OPEN WINDOW is a bad argument.
2. UNPROTECTED SEX is relevantly similar to OPEN WINDOW.
∴ 3. UNPROTECTED SEX is a bad argument.

---

[4]The following arguments come from Judith Jarvis Thomson, "A Defense of Abortion," *Philosophy & Public Affairs* 1 (1971): 47–66; reprinted in Part V of this book (pp. 331–42)

The arguments here are sufficiently complex and the analogy sufficiently controversial that we need to think carefully about whether OPEN WINDOW and UNPROTECTED SEX really are relevantly similar.

Critics of REFUTATION might point out some important differences between OPEN WINDOW and UNPROTECTED SEX. One difference is that the burglar has entered the open window voluntarily, presumably knowing that it is wrong to do so. The fetus, on the other hand, had nothing to do with its presence in the woman's body, and unlike the burglar, it is innocent of any wrongdoing. Thomson recognizes this objection and tweaks the analogy a bit, much like Peter Singer tweaked his DROWNING CHILD analogy: Suppose that instead of a burglar, an innocent person accidentally stumbles through the open window. Even then, Thomson says, the homeowner is under no obligation to let the person stay.

There is another important difference between OPEN WINDOW and UNPROTECTED SEX, though. In the scenario described in OPEN WINDOW, forcing the burglar to leave the house will not lead to the burglar's death, whereas in the scenario described in UNPROTECTED SEX, forcing the fetus out of the womb will lead to the fetus's death. Some philosophers, at least, think this difference is important enough that REFUTATION fails. That is, they claim that REFUTATION does not show that UNPROTECTED SEX is a bad argument.

As with the evaluation of other kinds of argument by analogy, there is no checklist or automatic procedure for determining whether a refutation by logical analogy is successful. Sometimes, as in the case of Thomson's REFUTATION, it can be hard for different people to agree on whether the argument succeeds.

TERMINOLOGY TO KNOW

argument by analogy
precedent

relevantly similar

refutation by logical
analogy

DISCUSSION QUESTIONS

1. Why should courts abide by legal precedents? Are the reasons the same or different as the reasons for individuals to accept moral arguments by analogy?
2. Do all relevant differences between two actions weaken an argument from analogy that compares the two actions? Why or why not?
3. Do you think using an evolving analogy is a useful technique for developing your own arguments? Do you think it is an effective technique for convincing someone else of your conclusion? Why or why not?
4. Find a moral argument by analogy online (preferably one that does not involve Hitler). Construct an argument by logical refutation to undermine that argument.

CASE STUDIES

See the Note About Case Studies on p. 150 for further instructions.

1. In the film *Blue Jasmine*, Ginger goes to visit her sister, Jasmine, in New York City. The two have not seen each other in years. Having married a wealthy businessman, Jasmine now has little in common with her blue-collar sister and has even less interest in spending time with Ginger. During

her stay in New York, Ginger sees Jasmine's husband kissing another woman but decides not to tell Jasmine about it. Evaluate Ginger's act of deciding not to tell Jasmine that her husband is cheating on her.

2. After doctors put 13-year-old Daniel Hauser on chemotherapy to treat childhood Hodgkin's lymphoma, Daniel felt sick. With their son's agreement, Daniel's parents refused further chemotherapy, explaining that they would cure Daniel themselves using alternative, diet-based treatments. A Minnesota court ordered his parents to resume chemotherapy, arguing that chemotherapy was very effective in curing Daniel's kind of cancer. Daniel's mother, Colleen Hauser, took her son out of the state to evade the court order. Evaluate Colleen's action of taking her son out of the state to avoid court-ordered chemotherapy. Use an argument by analogy to support your conclusion.

3. The H5N1 flu virus—more commonly known as "avian flu" or "bird flu"—is one of the deadliest flu viruses known to humankind. About 60 percent of people who contract H5N1 die of the illness, compared to about 0.1 percent for a normal flu virus and about 2.5 percent for the "Spanish flu" that killed nearly 5 percent of the world's population in 1918. Fortunately, H5N1 is not easily transmitted between humans. Thus, it is much less contagious than most flu viruses. In 2011, how-ever, a team of researchers in the Netherlands intentionally developed a version of the virus that they believed would be highly contagious among humans. The researchers themselves describe it as "probably one of the most dangerous viruses you can make." They developed the highly contagious virus for two reasons, both related to protecting public health. First, they wanted to see how easy it was to mutate the virus in a way that makes it highly contagious; this would help public health experts estimate how likely it is that H5N1 will naturally start a pandemic. Second, the researchers wanted to know exactly what genetic mutations would make the virus highly contagious; this would help public health experts keep an eye out for strains of the virus that are close to becoming a major threat. Evaluate the researchers' act of developing a highly contagious version of the H5N1 virus. Construct an argument by analogy to defend your evaluation.

4. If you were using Facebook in January 2012, there's a chance that Facebook tried to manipulate your emotions. For one week that January, Facebook randomly selected almost 700,000 users, with-out their knowledge, to participate in an experiment. Facebook filtered the posts these users saw in their newsfeed. Some users saw more posts expressing positive emotions, such as happiness; others saw more posts expressing negative emotions, such as sadness or anger. Facebook's researchers then monitored these users to see what emotions they expressed in their own posts. In general, they found that users who saw more positive posts expressed more positive emotions themselves and those who saw more negative posts expressed more negative emotions. Technically, all Facebook users agree to let Facebook manipulate their newsfeed when they accept Facebook's terms and con-ditions upon signing up for an account. But none of the users involved in this study were specifically asked to participate or even informed that they were participating. Evaluate Facebook's action of secretly manipulating people's emotions for research purposes. Construct an argument by analogy to defend your evaluation.

8 } Answering Moral Questions

In the half-century since the first major survey about cheating in college, the share of college students who confess to having cheated at least once in college has stayed about the same: 75 percent.[1] That's three out of every four college students. Professors, of course, regard cheating as morally wrong. So do many students—presumably including some who cheat anyway. But some students think that cheating is morally permissible, at least under some circumstances. Who's right about the moral permissibility of cheating? How could you go about settling on a particular answer to this question? In the previous chapters we've considered different kinds of (short) moral arguments that you might give for one answer or another. In this chapter we'll consider a method for moral reasoning in which we bring many different arguments to bear on a single moral question in order to reach a well-reasoned final answer to that question.

The method involves six basic steps:

1. Gather **information** about your chosen issue.
2. Identify a specific moral **question** to answer.
3. Identify salient **answers** to your chosen question.
4. Identify important **arguments** for and against each answer.
5. Identify and evaluate important **objections** to each argument.
6. Draw a final **conclusion.**

Although this chapter presents these steps in order, the process of moral reasoning is usually less linear than that. You will often find yourself circling back to earlier steps as you work your way through the process.

This chapter explains each step in detail. The last part of the chapter applies the method to the topic of cheating in college to get a feel for how the method works in practice.

STEP 1. GATHER INFORMATION ABOUT YOUR CHOSEN ISSUE

Whether you start with a relatively narrow question (e.g., whether it's permissible for college students to cheat on exams) or a very general topic (e.g., cheating, global poverty, drugs, abortion, climate change, or prostitution), you'll need to begin by gathering information.

---

[1]James M. Lang, "How College Classes Encourage Cheating," *Boston Globe*, August 4, 2013, http://www.bostonglobe.com/ideas/2013/08/03/how-college-classes-encourage-cheating/3Q34x5ysYcplWNA3yO2eLK/story.html.

While you probably know a bit about your area of interest already, there is almost certainly a lot that you don't know. And especially with emotionally charged topics, there may be things that you *think* you know that turn out not to be true.

If you're starting with a broad topic, use this time to start focusing in on a particular issue within that topic. If you start off interested in the ethics of drugs, a bit of information-gathering will remind you that this is a *very* broad topic. Are you talking about illegal drugs, widely abused prescription drugs, or both? Are you talking about using drugs, abusing drugs, selling drugs, trafficking drugs, or something else? Narrowing your focus from a broad topic to a more specific issue will help you zero in on the particular information that you need to gather.

As you begin learning about your chosen issue, ask yourself what kinds of things you would need to know in order to make an informed moral judgment about the issue. You can use the classic questions of basic journalism—who? what? when? where? why? how?—to structure your search. For instance, when it comes to the issue of global poverty, you might need to know *who* is living in extreme poverty and *where* they live (i.e., how many people, in what countries, of what age, race, sex, etc.), exactly *what* living in extreme poverty is like, *why* so many people are so poor, and *how* various anti-poverty organizations are attempting to fight poverty. As you begin answering these basic questions, you're likely to come up with other questions—questions that you didn't think to ask initially. For instance, what caused the significant decline in global poverty over the last few decades? Which anti-poverty organizations can use your money most effectively? How would giving up small luxuries affect your life? Even if you think you've asked and answered all of the questions you can, you'll probably come up with more questions as you work through the process of moral reasoning. You can always go back to gather more information at that point.

A good way to start finding the information you want is to look for authoritative, non-partisan introductions to the issue, especially introductions from well-known and well-respected experts or organizations. (Partisan introductions from respected experts can also provide useful starting points, but be sure to check their sources and compare their claims to others'.) Relying on a casual web search isn't usually the best way to start, since many of the first sites to pop up will be biased in one way or another. A much better bet is to ask a librarian, since librarians are trained to be experts at finding reliable information. At the very least, start by looking for books, scholarly articles, and other sources available through your library. If you absolutely must rely on sources that you find through Google or another search engine, keep in mind that the information you're getting is likely to be incomplete and may well be biased; be sure to read widely, investigate the credentials of the web sites you visit, and actively seek out web sites on different sides of the issue. Don't rely on a single source for any crucial information.

In particular, beware of **confirmation bias** when collecting information. Confirmation bias is a universal psychological tendency to seek out or accept information that supports or confirms what we already believe (or want to believe) and to avoid or ignore information that conflicts with what we believe. Think about how false or misleading news stories spread on social media: people believe and share those news stories much more readily when the story supports their preconceived ideas about how the world works, and they're much more skeptical (and much more likely to investigate before sharing the stories) when the opposite is true. In light of this universal human tendency, gathering information about a moral issue requires actively resisting confirmation bias. That means seeking out information that conflicts with our preconceived views and, when it's supported by good evidence, taking that information seriously. It also means looking more skeptically at information that supports our preconceived views and refusing to accept important claims without evidence.

STEP 2. IDENTIFY A SPECIFIC MORAL QUESTION TO ANSWER

Once you've learned a bit about your chosen moral issue, you'll want to identify a specific moral question about that issue. The question could be as specific as asking about the morality of a particular person's action. For instance, if you are exploring the issue of police shootings, you might settle on the question, "Did police officer Timothy Loehmann act wrongly when he shot 12-year-old Tamir Rice in 2014?" Or it could be just a bit more general, asking about a specific kind of action: "Is it morally permissible for a woman to abort a pregnancy because the fetus has a serious genetic defect?" More general still, you could ask how or when a broader kind of action is permissible (or obligatory or forbidden): "Under what conditions is it permissible for a doctor to do something that will shorten a patient's life?" In some cases, you can even ask a very general question like: "Is it morally permissible to download movies, music, or video games illegally?" Be cautious about these very general questions, though. If you ask a question that is too big or too general, it will be too hard to reach a well-supported answer.

You can always revise your question later if it turns out to be too specific or too general or if you learn something new that brings up a more interesting question. In particular, if you start with a very general question, you'll probably find yourself making it more specific later on. For instance, you might refine the question about downloading media illegally as follows: "Is it morally permissible to download music illegally if you had previously purchased it but then lost it?" Similarly, if you start asking whether abortion is morally permissible, you may well end up refining the question to be about particular kinds of abortion or abortion under particular circumstances.

To see what a difference your question can make, compare Yolanda Estes's essay, "Mutual Respect and Sexual Ethics," with Tom Dougherty's, "Sex, Lies, and Consent," both reprinted in Part V of this book. In one sense, both philosophers are asking a question about sex and respect for persons. Estes asks a very broad question about what the obligation to respect persons entails for the ethics of sex. She ends up with a wide-ranging paper that covers many topics.[2] Dougherty asks a much narrower question about when it is wrong to deceive someone in order to get him or her to have sex with you.[3] He ends up with a paper that covers fewer topics, but it discusses them in much more detail.

---

[2] Yolanda Estes, "Mutual Respect and Sexual Ethics," in *College Sex and Philosophy: Philosophers with Benefits*, ed. Michael Bruce and Robert Michael Stewart (Oxford: Wiley-Blackwell, 2010), 209–19; reprinted in Part V of this book (pp. 226–33).

[3] Tom Dougherty, "Sex, Lies, and Consent," *Ethics* 123 (2013): 717–44; reprinted in Part V of this book (pp. 233–51).

It's worth waiting to choose your question until after you've gathered some information about your chosen issue. For instance, if you start out with the vague idea that you want to investigate the morality of eating meat, you might not initially realize the significant difference between animals raised on factory farms and those raised in less inhumane conditions. So until you've learned a bit about the issue, it might not occur to you to ask, "It is morally permissible to eat animals raised on factory farms?"

Also, be sure that your question is a normative one, rather than a descriptive one. That is, the question should be asking whether (or under what circumstances) something is good or bad, right or wrong, virtuous or vicious, and so on, as opposed to, for example, what causes people to behave in a certain way, whether attitudes toward that behavior differ between cultures, or other non-normative questions.

STEP 3. IDENTIFY SALIENT ANSWERS TO YOUR CHOSEN QUESTION

While you may think that you already know the answer to your chosen question, reasoning well about moral issues requires you to suspend judgment until you've considered the arguments for and against various answers. The idea, after all, is not to find arguments to support whatever you wanted to believe anyway. The idea is to follow the arguments where they lead, so that you end up with the best, most well-supported answer you can find. So the next step once you've identified a specific question is to identify salient answers to that question. A **salient answer** is a notable or important answer to the question—that is, one that merits your attention when you are thinking about the question.

A good way to start identifying salient answers is to make a list of commonly accepted answers to the question. You may find some of these answers implausible, but if the answer is commonly accepted, it is still worth including on your list. For instance, if you are asking about the conditions under which it is permissible for a woman to get an abortion, you might list the following answers: never; only when the pregnancy threatens the woman's life; in cases of rape or incest; when the fetus has a serious genetic defect; when the woman has a very serious reason for not being able to care for a child (e.g., because she cannot afford another child or because she is too young); or whenever the woman would rather not have a baby. You are unlikely to think that *all* of those answers are plausible, but each answer is accepted by quite a few people.

You can sometimes identify other salient answers by looking for smart people who have thought hard about the issue. They might have come up with answers that are not very commonly accepted. This is especially true when you are asking an open-ended question, such as, "What is the morally best way to deal with criminals?"

Finally, you can always come up with your own answers. If there's an answer that you think is plausible, despite not being widely accepted or endorsed by any expert that you've seen, add it to the list. As you do more research, maybe you'll discover that it's not as plausible as you thought. But you might also discover that it's a great idea that everyone else has overlooked.

There are several reasons to include answers that you don't think are plausible. First, as you do more research, you might discover that they're more plausible than you initially suspected. Second, investigating the arguments for those reasons can help you understand how smart people can accept them. (Remember, not everyone who disagrees with you is an uninformed idiot or moral degenerate! There are usually good arguments on different sides of an issue.) Third, if you're going to support a particular position, it's helpful to be able to explain what's wrong with the alternative positions. Doing that requires understanding the arguments for those positions and figuring out what's wrong with them.

THE IMPORTANCE OF DEFINING YOUR TERMS

As you focus in on a particular issue, you may need to define your terms carefully to zero in on exactly the right things. Dictionaries can help, but sometimes you'll need to get even more specific. Check how other people have defined the terms in the books and papers you've read during Step 1. If you need to stipulate a definition of your own, take care not to define your terms in a way that begs the question. (See p. 21.)

Defining your terms carefully can help you avoid the **fallacy of equivocation.** This fallacy occurs when an argument uses a single word or expression in two different ways but doesn't work when the two different meanings are made clear. As an illustration, consider the famous story in *The Odyssey* in which the one-eyed giant Polyphemus captures the hero Odysseus. Odysseus tells Polyphemus that his name is "Nobody." So when Odysseus attacks Polyphemus and other giants come running to help him, Polyphemus cries out that "nobody" is harming him. The other giants reason as follows:

1. Nobody is harming Polyphemus.
2. If nobody is harming Polyphemus, then Polyphemus doesn't need help.
3. If Polyphemus doesn't need help, then we should leave.
∴ 4. We should leave.

This seems like a cogent argument as long as you don't realize that the word *nobody* in premise (1) means something very different than it does in premise (2). If you replaced the word *nobody* in premise (1) with "a person who calls himself Nobody" but kept premise (2) as it is, the argument wouldn't work at all. Thus, the argument commits the fallacy of equivocation.

This example is a bit silly, but the equivocations that occur in more important moral arguments tend to be harder to see and take longer to explain. One well-known example occurs in arguments about abortion in which some people use the word *person* in importantly different ways in different premises.*

---

* For a discussion of this equivocation, see Mary Anne Warren, "On the Moral and Legal Status of Abortion," *The Monist* 57 (1973): 43–61; reprinted in Part V of this book (pp. 313–19).

STEP 4. IDENTIFY IMPORTANT ARGUMENTS FOR AND AGAINST EACH ANSWER

Here is where the real philosophical work begins. Now that you have a list of salient answers for your chosen question, you can begin to compile a list of arguments for and against each answer. One way to compile such a list is to create a new document in a word processor, create a section for each answer, and then start filling in arguments for and against each answer in the appropriate section. Or you might prefer to do things differently, such as with color-coded index cards or just a notebook.

There are three main ways to identify arguments related to each answer: brainstorming arguments by yourself; discussing the issue with other people; and reading others' arguments, especially in philosophical books and papers. We will consider each of these strategies below.

In coming up with your own arguments, consider the kinds of arguments discussed in Chapters 3–7. Does the action you're considering fulfill (or violate) any obligations? What are the consequences of performing (or not performing) the action? Would performing the action manifest (or fail to manifest) some virtues (or vices)? Are there any relevant intermediate moral principles, such as the principle that it is worse to cause harm than to allow it to happen? Can you think of relevant analogies that would support a particular answer to your question? Thinking about these sorts of questions can help you come up with a range of short arguments for and against each of the answers you identified in the previous step. Try to write the arguments out as a list of numbered premises, like the arguments in the earlier chapters. Notice that arguments for one answer will sometimes count as arguments against another answer, making your job a bit easier.

As discussed in Chapter 2, be sure that you clearly state the normative premise(s) of each argument.[4] One of the easiest ways to go wrong in moral reasoning is by leaving your normative premises unstated. At best, you're likely to miss the opportunity to develop your arguments as fully as possible. At worst, you might end up unintentionally relying on a normative premise that's indefensible.

Discussing your question with other people is another helpful way to identify relevant arguments. Your friends, family members, and classmates are likely to have ideas that didn't occur to you. Some of them may have had experiences or discussions that help them see aspects of the situation that hadn't occurred to you. Since these discussions can often arouse strong emotions—especially if you're talking to someone who disagrees with you—it's important to remind yourself (and others) that your goal here is not to prove the other person wrong but to better understand the reasons for and against different answers to your question. As you talk to other people, you might find it helpful to rephrase their arguments using the concepts introduced in Chapters 3–7. And, as with brainstorming your own arguments, be sure you've identified the normative premise(s) in other people's arguments.

---

[4] See especially pages 19–22.

In addition to brainstorming arguments on your own or with your friends and classmates, it's worth reading what other people have said after they have considered your issue for a while. After all, those people have already done much of the work of identifying important arguments. One obvious place to look for such arguments is in the philosophical literature—that is, at books and papers written by ethicists. Your professor and your librarians can point you to helpful web sites and databases that will enable you find books and papers that address the issue you're considering, if not the very question that you're trying to answer. Read these books and papers carefully looking for arguments for and against each of the answers you've considered. Once again, using the concepts from Chapters 3–7 can help you reconstruct the arguments you encounter.

In theory, there's no limit to how many arguments you can identify for each of the answers to your question. And there's no magic number about how many you *need* to identify for each one. But you should try to find at least a few arguments for each of the answers you've chosen, as well as a few arguments against each one. Confirmation bias applies here, too, so be sure to look especially carefully for arguments that support views you reject or undermine views you already suspect are correct.

You don't have to include every single argument that you can find. In some cases, an argument provides such a trivial reason that it's not worth mentioning. Focus on the arguments that seem most important. You might also have theoretical reasons for excluding certain arguments. Especially if you've already learned a bit about normative theories, you might think that certain kinds of ethical arguments are more important than others.[5] For instance, if you think that virtue ethics is the correct ethical theory, then you will see arguments about virtues and vices as most important; if you think that some other theory is correct, then virtues and vices will play a smaller role (or none at all) in your reasoning. But before you reject an argument on theoretical grounds, think for a moment about whether the argument can be rephrased in terms of your preferred theory. For instance, if you think that deontology is the correct normative theory, don't dismiss every argument that's presented in terms of virtues and vices. After all, an argument that a certain action is cruel could be easily translated into a deontological argument about the obligation not to harm others or the obligation to respect others.

STEP 5. IDENTIFY AND EVALUATE IMPORTANT OBJECTIONS TO EACH ARGUMENT

An **objection** to an argument is another argument that aims to undermine the first argument—that is, to show that the first argument doesn't work. To reach a truly well-supported answer to your chosen question, you'll need to consider not only the objections that might be raised to each argument, but the replies that might be made to each of those objections. As before, you can come up with these objections and replies on your own, in discussion with other people, or by reading books and papers about your chosen topic.

Objections come in two varieties. A **rebutting objection** tries to show that the conclusion of another argument is false. You've already compiled a list of these kinds of objections

---

[5] See Chapters 11 and 12 for discussions of normative theories.

KEEP YOUR EYE ON THE BALL

Objections sometimes commit one of two fallacies: the ***ad hominem* fallacy** or the **strawman fallacy.** Both kinds of fallacies involve criticizing something other than the argument you're actually trying to rebut or undermine. An objection commits an *ad hominem* fallacy when it criticizes the person who *gave* the argument, rather than the argument itself. (*Ad hominem* is Latin for "against the person.") Even bad people can give good arguments, so be sure your objection addresses the argument's flaws or failures, not the arguer's. An objection commits the strawman fallacy when it criticizes a misrepresentation of the argument rather than the real thing. The idea is to knock down an oversimplified or exaggerated version of the argument that is easier to rebut. But just as someone who knocks down a straw-filled scarecrow with a picture of boxing legend Manny Pacquaio's face on it hasn't actually beaten Pacquaio, someone who rebuts a distorted version of an argument hasn't rebutted the argument itself.

in the previous step when you identified arguments against each answer. An **undercutting objection** only tries to show that another argument is flawed in some way, without showing that the conclusion is false (e.g., by showing that its premises are unacceptable or irrelevant or that it commits some fallacy). Remember that an objection is an *argument*, with its own premises and conclusion. The way to tell rebutting objections and undercutting objections apart is by looking at their conclusions: the conclusion of a rebutting objection is that the conclusion of the original argument is false; the conclusion of an undercutting objection is merely that the original argument fails to adequately support its conclusion.[6]

It's easier to grasp all of this by looking at some examples. Consider the following, adapted from the philosopher Walter Sinnott-Armstrong:

NOT MY FAULT

1. Everyone's greenhouse gas emissions, taken together, will cause climate change that will do great harm to many people.
2. A single individual's greenhouse gas emissions will not make any difference in how much the climate changes.
∴ 3. Even though society has a collective obligation to reduce its greenhouse gas emissions, no individual person has a moral obligation to reduce his or her individual emissions.[7]

A rebutting objection to NOT MY FAULT would be an argument whose conclusion is that (at least some) individuals are morally obligated to reduce their individual greenhouse gas emissions. For instance, law professor Sarah Krakoff argues as follows:

---

[6]Technically, a rebutting objection also undercuts the argument it is trying to rebut, since it establishes that the premises fail to establish the conclusion. The difference, therefore, lies in whether the objection *also* aims to show that the conclusion is *false*.

[7]Walter Sinnott-Armstrong, "It's Not My Fault: Global Warming and Individual Moral Obligations," in *Perspectives on Climate Change*, ed. Walter Sinnott-Armstrong and Richard Howart (Amsterdam: Elsevier, 2005), 221–53; reprinted in Part V of this book (pp. 521–35).

LOVE THE PLANET

1. Reducing one's individual greenhouse gas emissions demonstrates the virtue of caring toward the planet and toward future generations; failing to reduce one's emissions demonstrates a lack of caring.

2. The planet and future generations are things toward which one ought to demonstrate the virtue of caring.

∴ 3. At least some people are morally obligated to reduce their individual greenhouse gas emissions.[8]

This argument doesn't attempt to show what, exactly, is wrong with NOT MY FAULT. Instead, it tries to show that NOT MY FAULT reaches the wrong conclusion by offering a different argument for a different and incompatible conclusion.

By contrast, philosopher Avram Hiller offers the following undercutting objection to NOT MY FAULT:

TINY CHANGES

1. The total amount of climate change is just the sum of the climate change caused by each individual's greenhouse gas emissions.

2. If each individual's greenhouse gas emissions made *no* difference to how much the climate changes, then all of our emissions, taken together, would not cause any climate change.

3. Our collective emissions, taken together, are causing climate change.

∴ 4. It is false that each individual's greenhouse gas emissions make *no* difference to how much the climate changes.[9]

Notice that TINY CHANGES doesn't even claim to show that individuals are morally obligated to reduce their greenhouse gas emissions. Instead, it only aims to show that premise (2) of NOT MY FAULT is false. (Notice also that because it's about a descriptive premise, TINY CHANGES doesn't need any normative premises.) This shows that NOT MY FAULT doesn't establish its conclusion, but it doesn't show that the conclusion is false. For all that TINY CHANGES has shown, there might well be other, better arguments for the claim that individuals are not obligated to reduce their emissions.

Once you identify some important objections to each of the arguments on your list, you'll need to evaluate them—that is, figure out how strong they are. The point of evaluating the objections is to see whether they succeed in defeating the original argument, either by rebutting it or by undermining it.

One way to evaluate objections is to think about how the author of the original argument might reply to each objection. There are various kinds of replies you might offer to an objection. First, you can simply admit that the objection defeats the argument, in which case you'll need to give up on the argument altogether. Second, you could acknowledge that the

---

[8]Sarah Krakoff, "Parenting the Planet," in *The Ethics of Global Climate Change*, ed. Denis G. Arnold (New York: Cambridge University Press, 2012), 145–69; reprinted in Part V of this book (pp. 546–61).
[9]Avram Hiller, "Climate Change and Individual Responsibility," *The Monist* 94 (2011): 349–68.

argument reveals an important flaw in the argument but revise the argument slightly to fix that flaw. This might mean tweaking the conclusion or some of the premises a little bit or adding some extra premises to provide some more support. (This is an especially important approach when the objection is that the argument commits some fallacy. It's often possible to "repair" a fallacious argument so that it avoids the fallacy. Try to reconstruct a non-fallacious version of the argument before you dismiss it altogether.) Third, you could argue that the objection is flawed. In that case, your reply will consist of an objection to the objection. Fourth, you can accept that the objection provides a good reason to think that the argument is weaker than it seems but insist that, overall, the argument still provides a good reason to accept its conclusion. Of course, you'll need to say something about *why* you think the original argument is stronger than the objection.

The process of thinking through objections often leads you to discover new answers to your question. In that case, add those answers to your list and then work through Steps 4 and 5 again for that answer.

STEP 6. DRAW A FINAL CONCLUSION

Once you've identified arguments for and against each answer and thought through the objections to each argument and the replies to each objection, you'll be in a position to decide which answer is best supported by the arguments. Unfortunately, there's no procedure or algorithm for doing this. Weighing all of the various arguments for and against the different answers is a matter of judgment. You'll need to ask yourself, "Given everything I've learned, which arguments do I honestly think are strongest?" Then, pick the answer that is supported by those arguments—whether or not it's the answer that you initially thought to be correct.

When people are considering a question for which they already accepted a particular answer, they are usually reluctant to give up that answer. This is a natural human response; it's hard to admit that you were wrong about something, especially if it's something you felt strongly about. But it's better to admit that you were wrong *and then change your view to the right one* than to go on believing something you now have good reason to believe is mistaken. Changing your mind in the face of good reasons isn't a sign of foolishness or weakness; it's a sign of intelligence and maturity.

AN EXAMPLE: IS IT WRONG TO CHEAT ON EXAMS IN COLLEGE?

Although we don't have space to work through this whole process here, we can at least walk through each of the steps to get a sense of what each one involves. To do that, let's return to the topic that opened the chapter: the ethics of cheating in college.

Step 1. Gather Information

There are lots of books and articles about cheating. One way to get started learning about cheating would be to search for a recent book, such as James Lang's *Cheating Lessons*.[10] As you read through Lang's book, you'll find references to studies of cheating and to other people who have written about the topic. Search your library databases or a search engine like Google Scholar to find books and articles by those people and for other books and articles that cite those people. Look for information about how common cheating is, whether it's becoming more common, how people cheat, why students cheat, how colleges are trying to deter cheating, and so on.

Step 2. Identify a Specific Moral Question to Answer

We'll want to focus our question specifically on cheating on assignments or exams for college courses. Since this is already a fairly narrow topic, we can start by asking, "Is it morally permissible to cheat on exams in college courses?" After further research, we might get even more specific (e.g., to ask about the circumstances under which it would be permissible to cheat), but for now, we'll start with this general question.

Step 3. Identify Salient Answers to Our Question

There are several obvious answers to our question. These include:

    a. Yes, it is always permissible to cheat on college exams.
    b. It is sometimes permissible to cheat on college exams.
    c. No, it is never permissible to cheat on college exams.

Answer (b) could be broken up into more specific answers, spelling out exactly when or under what circumstances it's permissible to cheat. You can probably come up with some of these by brainstorming or talking to your friends—for instance, when many other people in the class are cheating, when it's in a required course that's not part of your major, when you're in danger of failing the course if you don't cheat, when you had a good reason for being unable to study for an exam, and so on. (Remember, you don't have to think all of these answers are plausible. If you think that many people would accept the answer, you should put it on your list.) You'll discover other variations on answer (b) as you research arguments for and against the permissibility of cheating. For now, we'll treat answer (b) as a single answer, breaking it up later if necessary.

Step 4. Identifying Important Arguments for and Against Each Answer

We only have space here to explore a few arguments for and against the answers we've identified to our question about cheating. You'd want to find a lot more of them if you were really trying to figure out whether cheating is wrong.

---

[10] James M. Lang, *Cheating Lessons* (Cambridge, MA: Harvard University Press, 2013).

Here's an argument for the claim that cheating is always permissible, adapted from education writer and filmmaker Cevin Soling:

GRADES AS PUNISHMENT

1. If someone kidnapped you and asked you a series of questions while threatening to cut off a finger for each question you got wrong, it would be morally permissible for you to cheat on those questions.
2. College exams are like the kidnapper's quiz in that people are effectively forced to go to college now, where they're punished with bad grades if they don't give the right answers on their exams.

∴ 3. It is morally permissible for college student to cheat on their exams.[11]

Here's an argument for the claim that it's *sometimes* permissible to cheat, which was easy enough to come up with by brainstorming the reasons people might give for cheating.

UNFAIR DISADVANTAGE

1. College is a competitive situation in that people are competing to have the best grades in order to get scholarships, etc.
2. No one is ever morally obligated to put himself or herself at an unfair disadvantage in a competitive situation.
3. When other students are cheating on their exams, refraining from cheating puts a student at an unfair disadvantage.

∴ 4. It is morally permissible for college students to cheat on their exams when other students are also cheating.

Notice that both of these arguments double as arguments *against* the claim that it's never permissible to cheat.

Finally, here are two short arguments for the claim that it's never permissible to cheat, adapted from philosopher Brooke Sadler's paper, "The Wrongs of Plagiarism: Ten Quick Arguments."

CHEATING AS MANIPULATION

1. Cheating on exams deceives the instructor in order to manipulate him or her.
2. Deceiving someone in order to manipulate him or her is failing to treat that person with respect.
3. Everyone is morally obligated to treat other persons with respect.

∴ 4. It is morally forbidden for students to cheat on exams.[12]

VICIOUS CHEATERS

1. Cheating on exams demonstrates and/or encourages one or more vices, such as dishonesty, laziness, or cowardice; and it undermines virtues such as responsibility, diligence, perseverance, and self-respect.

---

[11] Cevin Soling, "Why I Think Students Should Cheat," *WIRED*, January 29, 2015, http://www.wired.com/2015/01/think-students-allowed-cheat/.

[12] Brooke Sadler, "The Wrongs of Plagiarism: Ten Quick Arguments," *Teaching Philosophy* 30 (2007): 285.

2. One should not act in ways that demonstrate or encourage vices and undermine virtues.

∴ 3. It is morally forbidden for students to cheat on their exams.[13]

These arguments double as arguments against the previous two answers.

All of these arguments need to be developed further. Some of the premises might need to be explained. (In what sense is cheating a form of manipulation?) Some of them need to be supported. (Is it true that no one is ever obligated to put themselves at an unfair disadvantage?) When you are first identifying arguments for and against different answers, though, you can start with fairly basic versions of each argument.

Step 5. Identify and Evaluate Objections to Each Argument

When we identified arguments for various answers to our question, we noted that each argument counts both as an argument *for* one answer and an argument *against* some other answer(s). Those answers count as rebutting objections. We should also look for undercutting objections to each argument.

As an example, here's an undercutting objection to UNFAIR DISADVANTAGE:

KEEPING UP WITH THE GAMBINOS

1. If a construction company is competing for a contract against a mafia-backed company that intimidates people into awarding them the contract, it would be wrong for the construction company to use similar threats of violence to get the contract.
2. When competing with the mafia, refusing to threaten people with violence puts a company at an unfair disadvantage.

∴ 3. It is false that people are never required to put themselves at an unfair disadvantage in a competitive situation.

This objection uses a counterexample to refute the intermediate moral principle that people are never required to put themselves at an unfair disadvantage in a competitive situation, which was the crucial normative premise in UNFAIR DISADVANTAGE. This is an undercutting objection because it doesn't show that the conclusion of UNFAIR DISADVANTAGE is false; it only shows that UNFAIR ADVANTAGE fails to establish that its conclusion is true.

How strong is this objection? The scenario presented in premise (1) does seem like a counterexample to the moral principle used in UNFAIR DISADVANTAGE, and so KEEPING UP WITH THE GAMBINOS does reveal a genuine problem with UNFAIR DISADVANTAGE. But the problem is fairly easy to work around: Someone could respond to this objection by revising UNFAIR DISADVANTAGE to argue that *except in special cases* (e.g., those involving physical violence), no one is required to put himself or herself at an unfair disadvantage.[14] The trick would be to spell out exactly *when* people are required to put themselves at an unfair disadvantage and show that cheating on exams is not such a situation. If you could do that, you would have a good reply to this objection; if not, the objection looks reasonably strong.

---

[13] Sadler, "The Wrongs of Plagiarism," 285.

[14] See the discussion about responding to counterexamples in Chapter 6 (pp. 63–64).

Step 6. Draw a Final Conclusion

Although we've looked at a number of arguments about the permissibility of cheating, we haven't done nearly enough work yet to reach a final conclusion. We would need to identify and evaluate more arguments on each side, consider whether we want to think about other possible answers to our questions (or slightly different questions!), look for objections, and so on. Once we'd done all that, we'd probably end up with a number of strong arguments on different sides of the question, and then we'd have to make an overall judgment about which arguments were strongest. Until then, it wouldn't be intellectually honest to draw a final conclusion.

TERMINOLOGY TO KNOW

confirmation bias	objection	*ad hominem* fallacy
salient answer	rebutting objection	strawman fallacy
fallacy of equivocation	undercutting objection	

DISCUSSION QUESTIONS

1. What are some concrete steps you can take to reduce confirmation bias while gathering information about a topic?
2. Why is it important to identify a specific question to answer before seeking out arguments on your chosen issue?
3. Do you think it's really worthwhile to include answers that you think are implausible when doing your research? Why or why not?
4. Since there is no algorithm to decide which answer is best supported by the arguments you've identified, it will sometimes be impossible for you to convince someone who disagrees with you about a moral issue. Does that mean that this entire book is just a waste of your time?

CASE STUDIES

The instructions for this chapter's case studies are slightly different than in the other chapters. Choose one of the following case studies, and then complete each of the following steps:

a. As usual, each case study asks you to evaluate a particular (kind of) action. For this chapter, identify *two different judgments* someone might make about that action (e.g., that it is obligatory *or* that it is supererogatory).
b. Identify at least one argument for *each* of the evaluations you identified in the previous step, as well as one argument against each evaluation.
c. Identify at least one undercutting objection to each of the arguments you identified in the previous step.

This process will not give you enough information to draw a final conclusion about the action in the case study, but it will give you practice with the method of moral reasoning presented in this chapter.

1. Julia Hill climbed a tree on December 10, 1997, and didn't come down for over two years. The 1,500-year-old giant redwood tree that she climbed lived in a section of pristine forest owned by the Pacific Lumber Company. To protest the company's plans to clear-cut the forest, Hill lived on a small platform in the tree for 738 days. Her supporters brought her food and other supplies, which she hauled up to her platform 180 feet above the ground. Hill eventually came down from the tree after striking an agreement with Pacific Lumber to preserve her tree and all of the others within a 250-foot radius. (Meanwhile, the company had also struck a deal with the government to set aside 10,000 acres nearby as a nature preserve.) Identify two possible evaluations of Hill's action of sitting in the tree to prevent Pacific Lumber from cutting it down. Then identify arguments for and against each evaluation, as well as objections to those arguments, as detailed in the instructions above.

2. Saying that the Yale School of Management changed his life by giving him a scholarship to earn his business degree, billionaire Chinese investor Zhang Lei donated $8,888,888 to the school in 2010—the largest alumni donation the school had ever received. Zhang's donation provoked cries of indignation in his native China, where he has been living and working since 2005. Chinese critics said that Zhang should have donated the money to Chinese schools that need it more than Yale does. Identify two possible evaluations of Zhang's action of donating money to Yale instead of to schools in China. Then identify arguments for and against each evaluation, as well as objections to those arguments, as detailed in the instructions above.

3. Florida man David Boyd ended up in the hospital after trying to break into someone's home. After a night of drinking, Boyd started shouting and banging on the door of a random house, apparently suffering from a delusion that the home's occupants had kidnapped Boyd's family. When no one answered the door, Boyd broke a window and began to climb in. One of the residents hit Boyd with a piece of wood, knocking him back out the window. In the process, Boyd suffered a large cut on his leg, which bled profusely. The homeowner saved Boyd's life by stemming the bleeding with a towel until the police arrived. Identify two possible evaluations of the homeowner's action of saving Boyd's life. Then identify arguments for and against each evaluation, as well as objections to those arguments, as detailed in the instructions above.

4. In the opening scene of the television series *House of Cards*, Congressman Frank Underwood discovers that his neighbors' dog has just been hit by a car. The dog is badly injured, and Underwood concludes that the dog is not going to survive. He sends his bodyguard to fetch the neighbors, but before they arrive he strangles the dog with his bare hands to spare it the "useless pain" of a long, drawn-out death. Identify two possible evaluations of Underwood's action of strangling the dog before the neighbors arrive. Then identify arguments for and against each evaluation, as well as objections to those arguments, as detailed in the instructions above.

PART III

Moral Theory and Moral Reasoning

9 \) Skepticism, Subjectivism, and Relativism

While interviewing a young job candidate in *The Devil Wears Prada*, fashion magazine editor Miranda Priestly (played by Meryl Streep) tells the job candidate, "You have no style or sense of fashion."

The job candidate starts to reply, "Well, um . . . I think that depends on what your . . ."

Priestly interrupts: "No, no. That wasn't a question."[1]

Many people would side with the job candidate on this issue: what kind of clothes look good, many people think, depends on your personal tastes, and there are no "right answers" when it comes to matters of personal taste. There may be "right answers" about what is *regarded* as fashionable in a particular place at a particular time, but those, it seems, are just truths about the personal tastes of the people who live there. It's not as if there are eternal truths about what kind of clothes look good, on par with truths of mathematics or physics; there are only truths about people's personal tastes—about what people think looks good.

Some people think that morality is like fashion in this sense—that in morality, as in fashion, there are no "right" or "wrong" answers. In this chapter, we will examine various kinds of **moral skepticism** that hold that there is no objective moral truth. We will pay particular attention to how moral skepticism relates to moral reasoning.

MORAL NIHILISM

The most extreme form of moral skepticism is **moral nihilism,** which is the view that there are no moral truths. This means that nothing is right or wrong, obligatory or forbidden, (morally) good or bad, and so on. This is not just to say that most people's moral beliefs are incorrect; it's to say that *all* moral beliefs are incorrect. In the nihilist's view, claims about which actions are right or wrong are like claims that someone is a witch. Whenever people say something like, "She's a witch!" they are saying something false, since there is no such thing as a witch. Likewise, according to the moral nihilist, whenever people say something like, "That action was morally wrong!" they are saying something false, since there is no such thing as morality, and so no such thing as a morally wrong action—or, for that matter, a morally right action.

---

[1]David Frankel, *The Devil Wears Prada* (Los Angeles, CA: 20th Century Fox, 2006)

A BAD ARGUMENT FOR MORAL SKEPTICISM

One common argument for moral skepticism starts from the frequency of irresolvable moral disagreements. For instance, two people might disagree about the permissibility of abortion, and there is nothing that either person can say to change the other one's mind. By contrast, people can resolve disagreements about, say, which of two race horses is faster: have the horses race each other—maybe several times. Whichever horse wins (or wins most often) is faster.

But moral disagreement—even irresolvable disagreement—is not enough to show that moral skepticism is true. To see why, notice that people disagree about all kinds of things about which we are not tempted to be skeptics. Even within our own society, people disagree about the age of the universe, whether humans evolved from earlier species, whether (or when) government spending helps the economy, and so on. In other times and places, people have disagreed about whether the Earth is flat; why some things are flammable; whether there are witches; and whether animals can be "spontaneously generated" from hay, rotten meat, or other substances. Many people are so deeply persuaded of their views on these matters that disagreements between them are no easier to resolve than are disagreements about morality. And yet, there is some fact of the matter about things like the age of the universe and the shape of the Earth.

With this in mind, compare these two arguments:

MORAL DISAGREEMENT

    1.   People disagree irresolvably about morality.
∴ 2.   There is no fact of the matter about morality—that is, moral skepticism is true.

PLANETARY DISAGREEMENT

    1.   People disagree irresolvably about the shape of the Earth—or they used to anyway.
    2.   There is no fact of the matter about the shape of the Earth—or at least, there used to be no fact of the matter.

These arguments share the same structure: each has a premise stating that people disagree irresolvably about some topic, and each concludes that there is no fact of the matter about that topic. But PLANETARY DISAGREEMENT is plainly a bad argument. The Earth has always been round, regardless of what anyone thought about it. The fact that people (used to) disagree about its shape is irrelevant to whether it has (or had) a definite shape. Since MORAL DISAGREEMENT shares the same structure as PLANETARY DISAGREEMENT, and PLANETARY DISAGREEMENT is clearly a bad argument, we should be very skeptical of MORAL DISAGREEMENT. In other words, we should not take persistent moral disagreement, all by itself, to show that moral skepticism is true.[*] If there are good reasons for moral skepticism, we will have to look elsewhere for them.

*This classic refutation by logical analogy is adapted from James Rachels and Stuart Rachels, *The Elements of Moral Philosophy,* 8th ed. (New York: McGraw-Hill, 2015).

The nihilist will happily admit that certain actions, such as theft, are *thought to be* wrong and certain others, like rescuing a drowning child, are *thought to be* morally right. According to the nihilist, however, all such beliefs are mistaken, just like beliefs that this or that person is a witch. People who hold such beliefs are making a mistake.

If moral nihilism is true, then there isn't much point to moral reasoning. It is like reasoning about which people are witches. While it might be useful when dealing with people who believe in morality, it won't help you discover the truth about what you morally ought to do, since there *isn't* anything that you morally ought to do.

But moral nihilism is a very hard position to accept. It entails that *anything* is permitted, that nothing anyone has ever done was morally wrong or morally praiseworthy, that nothing is morally better or worse than anything else, and so on. That probably conflicts with many of your deeply held commitments. For instance, no matter what you think about philosophical questions about the objectivity of morality, you probably live your life as if it were deeply wrong to kill people for fun, to steal from your close friends, and so forth. Philosophers have written a great deal about moral nihilism, but we don't have time to pursue the issue here. So for present purposes, we will simply follow the advice of the philosopher Charles Peirce that we "should not pretend to doubt in philosophy what we do not doubt in our hearts,"[2] and we will assume that moral nihilism is false.

MORAL SUBJECTIVISM

While few people actually accept moral nihilism, many people take themselves to accept **moral subjectivism.** Unlike the nihilist, the subjectivist accepts that there are moral truths but holds that these truths are determined by each person's beliefs or attitudes.[3] That is, to say "That action is wrong!" is to say something like "That action is wrong, according to me!" And as long as the speaker sincerely regards the action as wrong, that statement is correct, since the morality of the action is determined by the speaker's beliefs or attitudes. You could say that whereas the nihilist thinks that everyone's moral beliefs are equally wrong, the subjectivist thinks that everyone's moral beliefs are equally right.

Although some people regard it as common sense, moral subjectivism is actually a deeply problematic philosophical position. Some of its problems are technical problems in the philosophy of language, but some are more obvious. For instance, subjectivism implies that moral disagreement is impossible, since my moral claims are about what's right for me and yours are about what's right for you. (Indeed, many people think—mistakenly—that such disagreement is a *reason* for subjectivism; see the boxed text on page 93.) But it seems like

---

[2]Charles S. Peirce, "Some Consequences of Four Incapacities," *Journal of Speculative Philosophy* 2 (1868): 140–57.

[3]There are a lot of technical issues about moral subjectivism and its sophisticated cousins, such as expressivism, which we will gloss over in this section. For instance, some philosophers argue that if (certain kinds of) subjectivism are true, then moral "beliefs" aren't actually beliefs, and they can't really be true or false. Other philosophers argue that we can still use terms like *belief* and *true* to talk about morality, even if subjectivism is true. These debates belong to an area of moral philosophy known as metaethics. For simplicity's sake, we will help ourselves to the metaethical views that make it easiest to talk about moral reasoning, and we will use the term *subjectivism* loosely to cover a wide range of views.

ANOTHER BAD ARGUMENT FOR MORAL SKEPTICISM

Some people find moral subjectivism attractive because it seems to require tolerance. After all, if other people's moral beliefs are just as right as yours, they're not doing anything wrong by acting on them—even when their beliefs differ from yours—and so you ought to let them do as they wish.

This is a mistake. Moral subjectivism can't *require* tolerance because it denies the very existence of moral rules that apply to everyone, including rules like "You should tolerate people with different beliefs." In fact, if someone holds the view that they should *not* tolerate people with different beliefs, then according to moral subjectivism it would be *wrong* for that person to tolerate people with different beliefs. After all, their moral belief is that tolerance is wrong, and subjectivism says that their moral beliefs are correct (for them). So, far from requiring tolerance, moral subjectivism actually undermines arguments for tolerance. The thought that people ought to tolerate one another is therefore not a good reason to accept moral subjectivism. In fact, it's a reason to *deny* moral subjectivism.

we disagree with each other all the time, which suggests that subjectivism is false. Subjectivism also implies that someone who approves of recreational killing or even genocide is doing the right thing in killing people. Many people find these implications hard to accept.

Perhaps surprisingly, though, the truth of moral subjectivism would not make that much difference in our moral reasoning. Since a subjectivist holds that all of his or her moral beliefs are true, a subjectivist could still use moral arguments in many of the ways that non-skeptics do. Non-skeptics, for instance, might use moral arguments to figure out what to do in a particular situation, based on their moral beliefs. Subjectivists can do that, too. It's just that they disagree about when or how their reasoning would apply to other people. Non-skeptics might also use moral arguments to try to convince others that they should (or should not) do something. Since, as we saw in Chapter 1, the strongest arguments begin from premises that the argument's audience accepts or can be persuaded to accept, arguments aimed to convince someone *else* to do something should start from *that person's* beliefs, including their moral beliefs. Again, the skeptic and non-skeptic might disagree about whether that person's beliefs are correct (objectively or "for that person"), but they will use arguments in more or less the same way.

An example might clarify how this works. Imagine a person—call her Monique—who accepts that animal cruelty is wrong, and she defines animal cruelty as causing significant, unnecessary harm to sentient animals. (Sentient animals are those capable of feeling pain, including cats, dogs, pigs, cows, chickens, and many others.) Whether Monique is a subjectivist or not, she might wonder what this belief implies about eating meat from large, industrial "factory farms." And suppose she comes across the following argument, adapted from public health professor John Rossi and bioethicist Samual Garner.[4]

---

[4]John Rossi and Samual Garner, "Industrial Farm Animal Production: A Comprehensive Moral Critique," *Journal of Agricultural & Environmental Ethics* 27 (2014): 479–522.

FACTORY FARMING

1. Factory farms impose significant harms on billions of sentient animals every year, including: serious diseases and deformities, such as abcesses, lameness, broken bones, and so on; lives of great discomfort and frustration, caused by spaces so cramped and overcrowded that animals often end up fighting with each other; mutilations and surgeries, such as "debeaking," tail clipping, and castration, usually without anesthesia; and brutal deaths in slaughterhouses or, in the case of "unproductive" animals, shortly after birth.
2. The suffering endured by factory-farmed animals could be avoided by switching to different patterns of food consumption and production.
∴ 3. Factory farms cause significant, unnecessary harm to sentient animals.
4. It is wrong to cause significant, unnecessary harm to sentient animals.
∴ 5. Factory farming is wrong.

This argument shows that, given the brutality of factory farms, Monique's belief that animal cruelty is wrong commits *her* to thinking that factory farming is wrong. And this is true regardless of whether Monique is a subjectivist or not.

We can go one step further. Suppose that Monique wants to convince her friend Nina that factory farming is wrong, but Nina sees nothing wrong with being cruel to cows, pigs, chickens, or other farm animals. Nina does admit, though, that it is wrong to be cruel to dogs and cats. Even if Monique and Nina are both subjectivists, Monique might offer the following argument:

PIGS AND PUPPIES

1. It is wrong to cause significant, unnecessary suffering to dogs or cats.
2. Dogs and cats are relevantly similar to cows, pigs, and chickens in that both are capable of feeling pain.
∴ 3. It is wrong to cause significant, unnecessary suffering to cows, pigs, and chickens.[5]

This argument begins with a premise that Nina already accepts—namely, that is wrong to be cruel to dogs and cats. Thus, even if Monique and Nina were subjectivists, they could still regard PIGS AND PUPPIES as a reasonable way for Monique to try to convince Nina of the argument's conclusion.

In short, moral reasoning is still helpful when you want to figure out (or show someone) that a particular moral claim is or is not consistent with his or her existing moral beliefs—regardless of the answer to deep philosophical questions about the objectivity of those beliefs.

CONSISTENCY AND REFLECTIVE EQUILIBRIUM

The examples in the previous section highlight an important point about moral subjectivism: even if morality is subjective, moral reasoning can show you that some of your moral beliefs are **inconsistent**—that is, that some of your moral beliefs contradict some of your other

---

[5]This argument by analogy is a simplified version of the one found in Alastair Norcross, "Puppies, Pigs, and People: Eating Meat and Marginal Case," *Philosophical Perspectives* 18 (2004): 229–45; reprinted in Part V of this book (pp. 486–98). For more on arguments by analogy, see Chapter 7.

moral beliefs. If nothing else, such inconsistency can lead to practical problems, since inconsistent moral beliefs will sometimes lead to inconsistent conclusions about what you should do. To take a simple example, suppose that Stefan believes both that one should always tell the truth and should always be kind. It isn't hard to imagine cases in which being kind requires not telling the truth. What should Stefan do in such cases? It might seem that subjectivism requires him *both* to tell the truth *and* not to tell the truth. But that, of course, is impossible to do in these cases. So even a subjectivist has good reason to want to avoid such a situation.

One way to resolve this dilemma is to say that in order to figure out what he should do—that is, what would be right or wrong for him in this situation—Stefan needs to eliminate this inconsistency in his moral beliefs. For instance, he might give up the belief that he should *always* tell the truth in favor of the belief that he should tell the truth in every case except those in which a white lie is necessary to be kind. (This isn't the only way to resolve that inconsistency, of course. How else might Stefan reconcile his belief that he should be kind with the general idea that he should be truthful?) Figuring out which moral beliefs conflict with each other requires moral reasoning. So we can escape the problem of inconsistent moral beliefs by reasoning about what each of our moral beliefs requires of us.

Notice what this means for moral subjectivism. A crude form of moral subjectivism would say that *whatever* you think is right (or wrong) for you *really is* right (or wrong) for you. That is, you can't make a mistake about what's right or wrong for you. As we've just seen, this kind of crude subjectivism leads to serious problems. The more sophisticated moral subjectivist would say something like this: what is right (or wrong) for you depends not on what you *do* think is right (or wrong) but on what you *would* think is right (or wrong) for you after you went through the process of eliminating any relevant inconsistences in your moral beliefs. This means that you *can* make a mistake about what's right or wrong for you, even if (sophisticated) moral subjectivism is true.

The process of eliminating the inconsistencies in your moral beliefs is known in moral philosophy as the process of seeking **reflective equilibrium.** You are in reflective equilibrium when all of your moral beliefs "fit together" well, which means—at a minimum—that they do not conflict with one another. This includes both your beliefs about general moral principles (e.g., "You should always be kind") and the moral judgments you make about specific cases (e.g., "You shouldn't tell your sick grandmother that you wouldn't have come to visit her if your parents hadn't made you"). Going one step further, you are in "wide reflective equilibrium" when your moral beliefs fit together with one another *and* with all of your non-moral beliefs. Consider, for instance, the way that the non-moral premises in FACTORY FARMING (see p. 96) create an inconsistency between the belief that animal cruelty is wrong and the belief that factory farming is morally permissible.

Reflective equilibrium is very difficult to achieve. It may well be impossible to achieve *perfect* reflective equilibrium, in which *all* of your beliefs fit together well. But through moral reasoning we can always bring ourselves a little bit closer to reflective equilibrium.

Finally, notice that since reflective equilibrium is so hard to achieve, it's very hard for anyone to say exactly what moral beliefs they would hold in reflective equilibrium. It's quite possible that most people would end up with moral beliefs that are quite similar to everyone else's—or, at least, that there would be much less moral disagreement than there is now.

What does all of this mean for the moral subjectivist? It means that even if subjectivism is true, it won't make *that* much difference to our moral reasoning: You can still use moral reasoning to see what your moral beliefs tell you to do or think. You can't simply assume that something is right (or wrong) for you just because you believe it is right (or wrong). Rather, you need to see if that belief fits together well with your other moral beliefs, including both the moral principles that you accept and the particular moral judgments that you make. And you can't simply assume that moral disagreements are irresolvable, since the disagreements might disappear as both people move toward reflective equilibrium.

MORAL RELATIVISM

Some moral skeptics reject both nihilism and subjectivism, claiming that rather than being relative to each person's beliefs, morality is relative to culture. This view is known as **cultural relativism.** There are many different ways of formulating cultural relativism, but the basic idea is that a person's culture determines what is morally right or wrong for that person. To see what this means in practice, consider this famous story in which the Chinese philosopher Confucius discusses morality with a powerful nobleman in the ancient Kingdom of Chu:

> The Duke of She said to Confucius, "Among my people there is [a person] we call, 'Upright Gong.' When his father stole a sheep, he reported him to the authorities."
> Confucius replied, "Among my people, those who we consider 'upright' are different from this: fathers cover up for their sons, and sons cover up for their fathers. 'Uprightness' is to be found in this."[6]

Confucius was trying to tell the duke, in a polite way, that the people of Chu were mistaken about virtue; he was trying to say that virtue requires people to prioritize their family over the law. A cultural relativist, however, would say it was Confucius who was mistaken. Cultural relativism entails that it would be morally obligatory for someone from Chu to report a law-breaking relative to the authorities but that for someone from Confucius's native state of Lu it would be morally obligatory to help relatives cover up their crimes. And more importantly, cultural relativism says that these different people would have these different obligations *because* their respective cultures held different moral beliefs. Understanding this connection between moral beliefs and moral obligations is crucial to understanding cultural relativism.

One key to understanding this connection is to recognize that cultural relativism is not just the claim that different cultures have different moral beliefs. That much weaker claim is known as **descriptive cultural relativism,** since it is simply describing what moral beliefs people in a particular culture accept. Rather, cultural relativism is about *normative* claims. In particular, cultural relativism says that *not only* do different cultures have different moral beliefs, but these moral beliefs entail that corresponding normative claims *are true for the members of that culture.* (For this reason, what we will call "cultural relativism" in this chapter is sometimes explicitly labeled "**normative cultural relativism.**") Normative cultural relativism says that there *are* moral truths—and so moral nihilism is false—but that there are no *universal* moral truths that apply to all people at all times. Rather, there are only

---

[6]Confucius, *Analects: With Selections from Traditional Commentaries*, trans. Edward Slingerland (Indianapolis: Hackett Publishing, 2003), 147.

CONFUCIUS

Contemporary philosopher Bryan van Norden says that the ancient Chinese philosopher Confucius (ca. 551–ca. 479 BCE) had an influence on Chinese culture that is "comparable to the *combined* influence of Socrates and Jesus on the Western tradition."* Confucius (also known as Kongzi, which means "Master Kong") would probably be surprised to hear this. He spent his life trying to convince the rulers of China's many warring states to follow his political philosophy, which he regarded as little more than the collected wisdom of the ancients. He also taught many students, who compiled his sayings into a book of "collected sayings" called the *Analects*. Through these students Confucius inaugurated the Confucian tradition of philosophy, which would profoundly influence later Chinese thought and political practices.

Because Confucius emphasizes careful adherence to traditional forms of behavior, he is sometimes regarded as a cultural relativist. (This, too, would probably surprise him.) Some modern commentators argue, though, that Confucius focused on traditional behaviors not because cultural tradition makes those behaviors right in themselves, but because cultural tradition has established those behaviors as socially recognized ways of performing right actions, such as showing respect for other people.† This insight provides an interesting perspective on the connection between culture and morality, independently of the Confucian tradition.

We consider Confucian ethics, including the role of traditional behaviors, in more detail in Chapter 12.

---

* Bryan W. van Norden, ed., *Confucius and the Analects: New Essays* (New York: Oxford University Press, 2001), 3.
† Kwong-Loi Shun, "*Rén* and *Li* in the *Analects*," in *Confucius and the Analects: New Essays*, ed. Bryan W. van Norden (New York: Oxford University Press, 2001), 53–72.

the moral claims that are accepted by this or that culture, and each person ought to act (or judge) according to the rules of his or her own culture.

Nor is cultural relativism simply the view that people in different cultures have different moral obligations; it is the view that they have different moral obligations *because* their cultures have different moral beliefs. This connection between beliefs and obligations makes cultural relativism a far more radical and controversial view than most people initially realize. Think about your own reasons for accepting certain fundamental moral obligations. Why, for instance, do you think it is (usually) wrong to kill people? Most people would cite things like the harm that killing does to a person and his or her loved ones or the fundamental obligation to treat other people with respect. Some might say that it's just obvious that killing people is wrong, except perhaps in very special circumstances, such as self-defense. But according to cultural relativism, none of those things matter—at least, not in any fundamental way. What makes it wrong for you to kill someone, according to cultural relativism, is that your culture *believes* that it is wrong—or, at least, that it has some beliefs (e.g., about treating persons with respect) that entail that killing is wrong. If your culture did not have those beliefs, then according to cultural relativism it would not be wrong for you to kill people. Because of these implications, many people believe that cultural relativism is false.

BAD ARGUMENTS FOR CULTURAL RELATIVISM

Many of the most popular arguments for cultural relativism share the same structure—and the same flaws—as the arguments for moral subjectivism. For instance, people sometimes try to argue that (normative) cultural relativism is true *because* cultures disagree about morality. And some people try to argue that cultural relativism is true because it (allegedly) promotes tolerance, and we all have an obligation to tolerate other cultures. But those arguments for cultural relativism fail for the same reason that they fail as arguments for moral subjectivism—namely, that disagreement about some topic does not prove that there's no "fact of the matter" about the topic and that relativism undermines the very possibility of a universal obligation to tolerate others. See the boxed texts on p. 93 and p. 95 for a closer look at such arguments.

MORAL REASONING AND CULTURAL RELATIVISM

We can see further difficulties with cultural relativism when we consider what difference it would make to our moral reasoning if cultural relativism were true. The main difference is that it would allow arguments that follow patterns like this one:

RELATIVISTIC PATTERN

1. Culture **C** says that action **A** is morally permissible.
2. Person **P** is a member of culture **C.**
3. Doing **A** is morally permissible for person **P.**

You can easily come up with similar patterns for actions that culture **C** considers morally wrong, morally obligatory, courageous, cowardly, etc. One way to think of cultural relativism is as the view that arguments that resemble RELATIVISTIC PATTERN are generally—maybe even always—cogent. Is that kind of cultural relativism tenable?

One problem with RELATIVISTIC PATTERN is that it imposes no limits on what action **A** can be. If a culture approves of genocide, slavery, human sacrifice, forced religious conversion, honor killings of rape victims, "reeducation" of people with deviant moral beliefs, or literally anything else, then according to cultural relativism, those actions will be permissible—maybe even obligatory—for members of that culture. Consider, for instance, the Aztec practice of human sacrifice: The Aztecs, who once dominated what is now central Mexico, would kill people and remove their hearts as part of their religious rituals. Although it's hard to know for sure, scholars estimate that the Aztecs probably sacrificed tens of thousands of people each year. Cultural relativists would have to say that the Aztecs were morally permitted to perform those sacrifices because their culture approved of doing so. When the Spanish conquistador Hernán Cortés arrived at the edge of the Aztec empire in 1519, however, he and his fellow Spaniards did not approve of human sacrifice. So he resolved to conquer the Aztecs, force them to convert to Catholicism, and put an end to their practice of human sacrifice. The cultural relativist would *also* have to say that Cortés was right to conquer and convert the Aztecs, since *his* culture approved of doing so. In short, the cultural relativist must accept practices as shocking as human sacrifice *and* the violent suppression of such practices. Many people find that hard to accept, and so they reject cultural relativism.

Nor are cultural relativism's difficulties limited to cases of cross-cultural disagreement. Cultural relativism creates problems for thinking about disagreements or inconsistencies *within* a single culture's moral code. To see why, consider the following adaptation of an argument that the abolitionist Frederick Douglass gave in 1852 in his famous speech, "What to a Slave Is the Fourth of July?"

AGAINST SLAVERY

    1. American culture says that it is wrong for one person to oppress another.
    2. Holding someone as a slave is a form of oppressing that person.
∴ 3. It is morally forbidden for Americans to hold slaves.

Douglass's argument resembles RELATIVISTIC PATTERN, even if it doesn't follow it exactly: it draws a conclusion about the morality of some action (namely, slaveholding) from a premise about the moral beliefs of a culture (namely, mid-nineteenth-century American culture). Notice, though, that the conclusion is the exact *opposite* of what many Americans believed in 1852—and therefore the exact opposite of what cultural relativism might seem to entail about slaveholding in the United States in 1852! Thus, it might seem that cultural relativism entails that slaveholding both was and was not morally permissible for Americans in 1852.

WHICH CULTURE IS "YOUR CULTURE"? WHAT DOES IT BELIEVE?

Each of us belongs to many different cultures, many of which overlap. To which culture did Frederick Douglass belong, for instance? American culture generally? The culture of antebellum Maryland? African American culture? All of these? And would different answers to that question yield different conclusions about the morality of slavery for Douglass? For another example, think of the Italian American New York mobsters depicted in films like *The Godfather* or *Goodfellas*. Are their moral obligations determined by the moral beliefs of American culture at large? By the moral beliefs of New Yorkers? By the moral beliefs of Italian Americans in New York City? Or by the moral code of the mafia? What about pacifist Quakers in rural Pennsylvania? Is it morally forbidden for them to fight in wars, even though they are members of American society, and American culture as a whole regards fighting in wars as permissible—sometimes even praiseworthy? And how large a group does it take to count as "a culture" anyway? Does your clique of friends count as a culture? Do fraternities and sororities, individually or collectively, have their own culture? Do American college students constitute a distinct culture? Or American youth more generally?

Furthermore, even if you could figure out which culture is "your culture," you might still have questions about what your culture *as a whole* believes. If 51 percent of the people who share your culture believe that abortion is morally forbidden, does that mean that your culture believes it's forbidden? Or does it mean that your culture can't make up its mind? What if most people think it's forbidden but "cultural elites" think it's permissible?

Different cultural relativists will answer these questions differently, yielding slightly different versions of cultural relativism. In many cases, however, these questions have to be answered before you can apply cultural relativism to a particular moral issue.

To avoid such contradictions, cultural relativists would have to give some criteria for deciding which of a culture's moral beliefs apply to a particular action. One possibility is that more specific beliefs trump more general beliefs. For instance, the more specific belief that slaveholding is permissible might trump the more general belief that oppressing people is forbidden. This is not a terribly attractive position. For one thing, it contradicts the way we normally think about consistency in the case of individuals: if a slaveholder said that he personally agreed that oppressing people was wrong and admitted that slaveholding involved oppressing people, we wouldn't let him off the hook if he just shrugged his shoulders and said that he had a more specific belief that slaveholding was permissible. Logical consistency would require that he revise at least one of his beliefs. Furthermore, giving priority to the most specific belief would mean that, even if cultural relativism were true, no moral argument could be conclusive until we had done enough anthropological or sociological research to know that the relevant culture did not already have some belief about the argument's conclusion. For instance, even if you had an airtight argument showing that a culture's own moral code entailed that it was wrong to kill random people in the street, you would have to investigate the culture's *specific beliefs* about killing random people in the street to know whether it was really wrong for members of that culture to do so.

The alternative ways of avoiding contradiction involve allowing that, at least sometimes, more general beliefs trump more specific beliefs. And once we allow that, we must admit that arguments resembling RELATIVISTIC PATTERN are not generally cogent: from the mere fact that culture *C* approves of action *A*, we can no longer infer that action *A* is permissible for members of *C*. This is because culture *C* might have other, more general moral beliefs, that conflict with the belief that action *A* is permissible—which is precisely what Douglass showed in the case of antebellum American beliefs about slavery. Thus, on this approach, figuring out what is really right or wrong for members of some culture requires that we come up with an internally consistent set of moral beliefs based on the beliefs that the culture actually has. In short, we would need to figure out what the culture's beliefs would look like once they were brought into reflective equilibrium. It's very hard to know in advance what moral claims would be included in reflective equilibrium or how much different cultures' beliefs would differ after they were all made internally consistent. We can, however, be confident that they would not be exactly the same as they are now; and so, on philosophically sophisticated forms of cultural relativism, we cannot infer that an action is permissible for members of some culture simply from the fact that the culture *believes* it is permissible. Instead, even a cultural relativist will need to use moral reasoning, starting from moral beliefs that the relevant culture accepts, to try to figure out what is right or wrong for members of that culture.

MORAL REASONING AND MORAL OBJECTIVITY

So far, we have considered the connection between moral reasoning and various kinds of moral skepticism. We have seen that even if moral subjectivism or cultural relativism is true, it does not follow that every single one of a person's or a culture's moral beliefs is correct (for that person or for members of that culture). Thus, we would still need to use moral reasoning to try to bring our own or others' beliefs into reflective equilibrium.

This leaves open some deep and difficult philosophical questions about the objectivity of morality. Is there some objectively correct set of moral beliefs? If so, does pursuing reflective equilibrium bring us closer to those objectively correct beliefs? Those questions belong to the realm of **metaethics,** which tries to answer questions about the nature of morality and about moral language and thought. Fortunately, we don't need to resolve those questions to reason about particular moral issues. Different metaethical views will affect how we interpret what's going on when we make moral claims or reason about what to do, but, except for moral nihilism, they don't eliminate the need for moral reasoning.

TERMINOLOGY TO KNOW

moral skepticism	inconsistent	descriptive cultural relativism
moral nihilism	reflective equilibrium	normative cultural relativism
moral subjectivism	cultural relativism	metaethics

DISCUSSION QUESTIONS

1. Why might someone think that moral nihilism is true? Does moral nihilism have any logical consequences that you find hard to accept?

2. Moral subjectivism undermines the idea that everyone ought to tolerate everyone else. If morality is *objective*, does that also undermine the idea that everyone ought to tolerate everyone else? Why or why not?

3. If you could actually bring your moral beliefs into perfect reflective equilibrium, which of your current beliefs do you think you would be *most* likely to keep? Which are you least confident that you would keep?

4. The ancient Greek historian Herodotus famously tells the story of a meeting in which people from two different cultures, the Greeks and the Callatians, expressed outrage at the way members of the other culture disposed of their deceased parents' bodies. (The Greeks burned their dead, whereas the Callatians ate them.) Some people interpret the passage as evidence for cultural relativism, either of the descriptive or the normative kind. Is it good evidence for either kind (or both)? If so, which kind(s)? (Hint: Think about Confucius's reason for emphasizing traditional practices!)

CASE STUDIES

See the Note About Case Studies on p. 150 for further instructions.

1. The title character in the film *Vera Drake* works as a house cleaner for a wealthy family in England shortly after World War II. She frequently performs small acts of kindness for various people. On occasion, she also performs illegal abortions, free of charge, to young women whose pregnancies are a source of great personal difficulty for them (e.g., because they are very young or because the pregnancy resulted from an affair that they want to keep secret). Vera believes that she is providing an act of kindness for the women, but because she knows that her actions are illegal and that her family thinks abortion is morally wrong, she tells almost no one about what she does. Evaluate Vera Drake's action of providing secret, illegal abortions, free of charge. Give an argument to support your evaluation.

2. A 20-year-old woman drowned at a beach in Dubai in 1996 because her father forcibly restrained lifeguards from rescuing her. The father, who came from some other Asian country that police did not identify, explained his actions by saying that it would dishonor his daughter for a strange man

to touch her and that he preferred her to die rather than to lose her honor. Police arrested the man for preventing the rescue. Evaluate the father's action of restraining the lifeguards from saving his daughter's life. Give an argument to support your evaluation.

3. The Japanese town of Taiji has been a center for whaling since the 1600s. Today the town is best known for its annual dolphin hunting season. Each winter, fishing boats herd small groups of dolphins into a cove near Taiji and trap them there. The residents of Taiji then capture the dolphins one by one, killing most of them for food, using a technique that has been criticized as so cruel that it would be illegal to use on cattle in a Japanese slaughterhouse. All told, the residents of Taiji kill or capture about 2,000 dolphins this way each year. Animal rights activists regularly protest the dolphin hunt outside Japanese embassies and consulates around the world, including in the United States, calling for an end to the hunt. Evaluate the American protestors' action of trying to get the Japanese to end the dolphin hunt. Give an argument to support your evaluation.

4. In Mark Twain's *Adventures of Huckleberry Finn*, young Huck Finn promises to help an escaped slave, Jim, make it to Cairo, Illinois, where Jim would be free. As they near Cairo, Huck begins to feel guilty about committing what he and his culture believe to be the "sin" of helping Jim escape from his "rightful owner." Ultimately, Huck decides not to turn Jim in, despite having opportunities to do so. Evaluate Huck's action of helping Jim escape from slavery. Give an argument to support your evaluation.

10) Religion and Moral Reasoning

The hashtag #hajjselfie started trending on Twitter and Instagram in early October 2014. Young (and not-so-young) Muslim pilgrims used it to document one of the most important moments in many Muslims' lives: the pilgrimage to Mecca, known as the *hajj*, which all Muslims are required to undertake at least once in their lives, provided they are financially and physically able to do so. The *hajj* is so central to Islam that it is included as one of the so-called "five pillars" of the religion. (The other four are a declaration of faith, daily prayer, giving to the poor, and fasting during the Muslim holy month of Ramadan.) The Muslim obligation to perform the *hajj* exemplifies one of several ways in which religion matters to moral reasoning—namely, by providing new premises for moral reasoning. In this chapter we will consider this and other ways that religion relates to moral reasoning.

WHY RELIGION MATTERS TO MORAL REASONING

Religion affects moral reasoning in at least three ways: by providing new premises, by providing new or additional justification for premises that we (might) accept anyway, and by asserting non-moral claims (e.g., about the existence or nature of the soul) that have moral implications. This section will explore each of these topics.

Most religions, if not all, impose specific moral requirements on their followers or explicitly grant permission to do particular things. These requirements and permissions can serve as premises in moral reasoning. Some of these premises, such as the commandment to be honest or not to commit murder, are quite general and would probably be included in any list of moral obligations. Others are quite specific, such as the Jewish requirement to circumcise male infants or the Sikh prohibition against cutting your hair, and people would be unlikely to think of them as moral obligations if they had not been handed down in religious teachings. And some, such as the Christian commandment to "love the Lord thy God with all thy heart," certainly wouldn't count as moral obligations outside of a religious context. (Why would you be obligated to love God if God didn't exist?) For followers of a particular religion, these kinds of requirements and prohibitions provide important premises in reasoning about what they should do, even though people who follow other religions (or no religion) will reject many of the premises.

THE DIVERSITY OF RELIGIOUS TRADITIONS

While people often talk about "what Christians believe" or "what Islam requires," such claims usually hide a great deal of diversity within any particular religious tradition. Christianity, for instance, includes Catholics; Lutherans, Anglicans, Methodists, Baptists, and many other kinds of Protestants; Mormons; Eastern Orthodox Christians, Syriac Christians, and other Eastern Christians; and more. Islam includes Sunnis, Shiites, Sufis, and more, each of which encompasses a range of smaller denominations. Judaism has orthodox, conservative, and reform branches, among others; Buddhism includes both Mahayana and Theravada branches; and so on. Each of these denominations espouses subtly (or not so subtly) different versions of their respective religions. For instance, Catholics believe that the Pope is God's representative on Earth, whereas other Christians do not. And even when an organized religion takes an official stance on something, such as contraception or polygamy, some of its followers might believe differently. For instance, many Mormons disagree with some of the official teachings of the Mormon Church, many Catholics disagree with the Pope on certain issues, and so on. Finally, when religious scripture makes a claim, different followers of that religion might interpret that claim differently or give it more or less weight in their understanding of their religion.

With that in mind, claims about what some religion (or even a particular denomination) believes or what it requires of its followers should usually be taken as broad generalizations, which do not necessarily reflect the views of all denominations or all followers of that religion.

Religiously based normative premises can also supplement non-religious premises to help settle thorny moral questions that come up in non-religious contexts. For instance, questions about the morality of eating meat are not necessarily religious questions. There are many non-religious arguments for and against the moral permissibility of eating meat. Because thoughtful people disagree about which of those arguments are stronger, they disagree about the morality of eating meat. By taking a definite position on eating meat, a particular religious tradition can help settle the issue for its followers. Hinduism and Buddhism, for instance, generally prohibit eating meat; Judaism, Christianity, and Islam explicitly condone it, although with some limitations in the case of Judaism, Catholicism, and Islam.

What role should such religiously based normative premises play in your moral reasoning? Premises based on your own religious beliefs will be acceptable in your reasoning about what you yourself should do or in your reasoning with others who share your religious views. But, of course, such premises will carry no weight with those who do not share your religious views, and so you'll need to avoid them if you want to provide arguments that are rationally compelling to people who don't follow your religion.

In addition to providing new premises for our moral reasoning, religion offers one means of explaining or justifying normative premises that we would accept anyway, such as the claim that you ought to be kind to others or that it is wrong to commit adultery. Even if we accept such claims, we might be curious about exactly *why* adultery is wrong. Philosophers have developed various normative theories that bear on that question, but many religious traditions offer their own answers, too.[1] Consider, for instance, the following argument for the claim that it is wrong to commit adultery:

THOU SHALT NOT COMMIT ADULTERY

1. God commands us not to commit adultery.
2. You are obligated to obey God's commands.
∴ 3. You are obligated not to commit adultery.

Premise (1) in THOU SHALT NOT COMMIT ADULTERY is a common belief in many theistic religions. Premise (2), of course, might need some further justification, which different traditions provide in different ways. Within Christian traditions, for instance, people have argued that each of us is obligated to obey God out of a debt of gratitude or in deference to God's authority over us. Given arguments like these, Christianity and other theistic religions provide

---

OBJECTIVE OBLIGATION vs. SUBJECTIVE OBLIGATION

When you are evaluating the actions of people with very different religious beliefs, you may sometimes find it useful to distinguish between two senses of obligation, which moral philosophers call **objective obligation** and **subjective obligation**. Roughly, someone's objective obligation is simply what he or she is obligated to do, given the way things actually are, whereas someone's subjective obligation is what he or she *would* be obligated to do, *if* things were the way he or she believed them to be. When all of a person's (relevant) beliefs are correct, then his or her subjective obligation and objective obligation will be the same. But when a person holds false beliefs, his or her subjective obligation can sometimes differ from his or her objective obligation.

This distinction allows you to draw nuanced conclusions about people who act on sincere beliefs that you believe or know to be false. For instance, in the *Game of Thrones* series, Catelyn Stark is led to believe that Tyrion Lannister hired an assassin to murder her son. Therefore, she is (arguably) subjectively obligated to arrest Tyrion and bring him to justice. It turns out, however, that she has been misled and is acting on a false belief; Tyrion did not hire the assassin. So, given the way things *actually* are, Catelyn is not objectively obligated to arrest Tyrion.* (At the time, of course, Catelyn cannot possibly know that. That's why this distinction is only useful in evaluating other people's actions or your own past actions.)

In evaluating the actions of people with different religious beliefs, this distinction enables you to express the idea that, although *you* don't think they are obligated to do something (e.g., make a pilgrimage to Mecca or go door-to-door trying to convert others to their religion), you can understand why *they* believe themselves to be obligated to do so.

---

*George R. R. Martin, *A Game of Thrones* (New York: Bantam, 1996).

---

[1]To read more about philosophical theories that answer such questions, see Chapters 11 and 12.

reasons for accepting common normative premises, especially those about moral obligations. Nontheistic religions, such as most Buddhist traditions, can provide other kinds of arguments for common normative premises.

Religious teachings also affect moral reasoning in a less obvious way. Besides issuing moral commands, religions make non-moral claims that have important moral implications. For instance, many theistic religions claim that God created the universe and everything in it, including you. This is a non-normative claim about the origin of the world, but it has moral implications. Many religious believers argue that *because* God created you, you owe God gratitude or obedience. (This is one way that people argue for the second premise in THOU SHALT NOT COMMIT ADULTERY.) But other religions, such as Buddhism, do not include a creator God and so will need other reasons to think that you ought to obey those religions' moral requirements. Those reasons often rest on non-moral claims about the way the world is or the way it works.

To take another example, different religious teachings about the nature of the soul and the afterlife have profound moral implications. One particularly vivid way to see this difference is to consider a moral doctrine known as ethical egoism. Ethical egoism is the view that each person ought always to pursue his or her own self-interest. This isn't to say that you should *never* take others' interests into account. It's just to say that you should act for others' benefit only when doing so benefits yourself. Since it will generally be to your benefit to have other people like you and think well of you, it might seem that egoism requires you to be selfish, but in a manipulative and deceitful way that prevents others from realizing that you are only looking out for yourself. In particular, egoism seems to require that, when you can get away with it, you sometimes ought to do things, such as stealing, that are generally considered immoral. And if we ignore all religious claims about the way the world is, that might really be what egoism requires of us.

What would the egoist say, though, in light of the claims that each individual has a distinct, immortal soul that will enjoy (or endure) an eternal afterlife, and that the quality of that afterlife depends on the individual's actions in this life? (These claims, of course, are common in Christian and Islamic traditions.) If those claims are true, the greatest benefit you can get for yourself is a good afterlife, since that benefit will last forever. From an egoistic perspective, then, you ought to be willing to do *anything* to ensure a good afterlife—even if that means living a life of great sacrifice and suffering in this world. In fact, the most self-interested thing you can possibly do in these circumstances is to adhere to the moral requirements of your religion as closely as you can. (This is *not* to say that religious virtue is *selfish*. Religious virtue will require acting for the benefit of others. Nor is it to say that Western views of the soul entail ethical egoism. They don't. It's just to say that, given many Western views of the soul and the afterlife, it turns out to be in your own interest, narrowly construed, to be virtuous.) So, for the person who believes in an eternal afterlife whose quality depends on one's behavior in life, ethical egoism requires a life of religious virtue.

By contrast, consider how Buddhist teachings affect ethical egoism. One of the central teachings of Buddhism is the doctrine of *anātman*, which is usually translated as "no-self" or "non-self." Roughly, the idea is that what you think of as your "self" is really an illusion. To get a sense of what this means, think about a movie being projected onto a wall. For each frame, the projector projects a picture of a person onto the wall. In each frame, the person appears in a slightly different position, giving the illusion of movement. But there is no actual person that endures from one frame to the next; it's just a series of pictures that we *perceive* as forming a single, continuous whole. What you take to be your "self," in this view, is a bit like the person in a single frame of that movie: it disappears in an instant, to be replaced by another, very similar "self" an instant later. With this in mind, consider the following argument, sometimes attributed to the eighth-century Buddhist philosopher Shantideva:

NON-SELF

1. There is no self.
∴ 2. Suffering is not the suffering of anyone in particular.
∴ 3. "Your" suffering is no more or less important than any other suffering.
∴ 4. You ought to be just as concerned about eliminating suffering that is not "yours" as you are about eliminating "your own" suffering.[2]

The conclusion of NON-SELF entails that ethical egoism is false, since ethical egoism says that you should *only* be concerned about your *own* interests, whereas NON-SELF concludes that you should be equally concerned about everyone's interests (or, at least, their suffering). And this conclusion is supposed to follow from the non-moral Buddhist claim that there is no self.

This example illustrates the importance of non-moral religious claims in moral reasoning. Claims about the nature of the self are not moral claims. They're claims about the way the world really is. Given a non-religious Western perspective on the nature of the self, ethical egoism might seem to require deceit, manipulation, and perhaps the occasional act of theft (or worse). Given views of the soul and the afterlife common to many Western religions, however, ethical egoism seems to require a life of religious virtue. And given Buddhist views of the illusory nature of the self, ethical egoism is false—maybe even nonsensical.

In summary, religious thought provides several kinds of additional premises that are useful in moral reasoning: It provides additional normative premises that you would not or might not have accepted without religious support. It provides ways of justifying normative claims that you (or many others) would have accepted anyway. And it provides non-normative claims, such as claims about the nature of the self or the origin of the universe, that have important moral implications.

WHY MORAL REASONING MATTERS TO RELIGIOUS THOUGHT

Some people wonder why they need moral reasoning at all, since their religion already tells them how to live. There are at least three ways in which moral reasoning is still important, even for those whose religions give very explicit instructions about how to live.

The first and most obvious way that moral reasoning is important is in applying religious teachings to everyday life. Religious teachings tend to be fairly general, and people might disagree or be puzzled about exactly how to apply them in particular cases. For instance, what exactly does the Christian commandment to "love thy neighbor as thyself" require of a Christian who comes across a homeless man asking for help? Should she give the man

---

[2]For a presentation and discussion of this argument, see Stephen Harris, "Does *Anātman* Really Entail Altruism? On *Bodhivaryāvatāra* 8:101–103," *Journal of Buddhist Ethics* 18 (2011): n.p.

money? Should she provide him with food, clothing, or shelter? Should she donate her time or money to churches, non-profits, or other programs that provide those things? Or to programs that would help the man become able to care for himself? Answering these questions requires both interpretation of religious teachings and a bit of moral reasoning about what kinds of things are good, what counts as treating someone in a loving way, what other religious commandments might be relevant, and so on.

The second way in which moral reasoning matters to religious thought is more abstract. Moral reasoning can help religious people understand *why* their religion (or some other religion) requires or prohibits certain things. That is, it can help them understand their religion's moral teachings (or those of another religion) more deeply. Consider, for instance, the prohibition on suicide, which is found in nearly every major religion. Some religions, such as Islam, explicitly forbid suicide. In other religions, such as Christianity and Buddhism, suicide is taken to violate a more general rule against killing people. But because killing *yourself* seems importantly different from killing *someone else*, one might wonder *why* these religions condemn suicide. The twelfth-century philosopher Thomas Aquinas, one of the great theologians and philosophers of the Catholic tradition, offers the following reasoning:

AGAINST SUICIDE

1. Every organism naturally loves itself and seeks to keep itself intact.
∴ 2. Suicide is contrary to nature.
3. People should not act contrary to nature.
4. Every person is obligated to show charity (roughly, love and respect) for all persons, including himself.
5. Suicide manifests a lack of charity toward oneself.
∴ 6. It is morally forbidden to commit suicide.[3]

Premise (3) and, to a lesser extent, premise (4) are controversial, but both could be justified on either religious or non-religious grounds. Thus, AGAINST SUICIDE provides a way for everyone—Catholic or not—to understand the common religious prohibition on suicide. These sorts of arguments show that (at least many) religious commandments are not just arbitrary commands or requirements—there are good reasons for them.

This kind of argument also hints at the third way in which moral reasoning is important for religious people: it provides a way to find common ground with people of other faiths or of no faith. By reasoning from non-religious normative premises—or, at least, from normative premises that are accepted by many different faiths—people with different religious views can seek agreement about controversial moral issues. If you can provide a compelling argument for a moral claim, based entirely on normative premises that are independent of any particular religion, then you have a much better chance of convincing people who do not share your religious views. This is especially important in a pluralistic society that contains people from many different religions. In such a society, religiously based reasoning may be helpful in deciding *for yourself* what to believe about morality, but it is far less helpful in reaching an agreement with others about what is right or wrong. This is why it is important, especially in a pluralistic society, to learn to reason from non-religiously based normative premises, as we do in the rest of this book.

---

[3]Thomas Aquinas, *Summa Theologica* II.ii.64.5.

DIVINE COMMAND THEORY AND THE EUTHYPHRO DILEMMA

Does morality come from God? If there were no God, would "everything be permitted," as the Russian author Fyodor Dostoevsky says in *The Brothers Karamazov*? Some religious people think so. They hold a view known as **divine command theory.** This is the view that morality is *identical* with what God commands, much as the law is identical with what the government commands. Divine command theory entails that if there is no God, and so no divine commands, then there is no morality.

Many religious people reject divine command theory, as do most non-religious people. They believe that moral rules would apply with or without God's commands or even existence. One philosophical argument against divine command theory is known as the **Euthyphro dilemma,** because it is based on a similar argument that appears in the *Euthyphro*, a dialogue written by the ancient Greek philosopher Plato.

To understand the Euthyphro dilemma, it will help to start with a seemingly unrelated example. Think about the coach of the U.S. Olympic men's basketball team choosing players for the team. Let's agree, at least for the sake of argument, that he is going to pick the best male players possible. But are those players the best *because* the coach picked them? Or did he pick them *because* they're the best? Those might sound like two ways of saying the same thing, but they're not. The first option—that they're the best *because* the coach picked them—means that anybody the coach picked would have automatically been one of the best players; he could have picked Donald Trump, Elon Musk, and Justin Bieber, and those three would, *as a result of being chosen*, have been three of the best basketball players in the world. But that's obviously silly. A basketball player's ability is not determined by the coach's choosing him; rather, the coach chooses him because of his ability.

The Euthyphro dilemma, as applied to the connection between God and morality, starts from the assumption that God has commanded us to do what is right. The question is whether those things are right *because* God commands them or whether God commands them *because* they are right. Divine command theory says that they are right because God commands them. But many worry that this view makes God's commands arbitrary. It entails that if God had commanded us to rape, pillage, and murder, then those things would have been obligatory rather than forbidden. Furthermore, this view makes it hard to provide a non-circular reason to think that we are obligated to obey God's commands, since that would just amount to saying that God commands us to obey God's commands. Because of these two problems, many religious people conclude that God commanded the things he did because they are right, just as the Olympic coach picked his players because they were good. But if that's the case, then those actions are right *independently of God's commanding them*, just as the basketball players are good independently of the coach's choosing them. That is, they conclude that divine command theory is false; there is some deeper—or at least additional—reason that some actions are right and some are wrong.

None of this is to say that God is irrelevant to morality. Even if you accept that God commanded what he did because those actions were right independently of God's commands, you can still think that God plays an important role in providing moral knowledge and moral motivation. You can even believe that God provides additional commandments or generates further moral obligations that would not exist without God. The point of the Euthyphro dilemma is to show that morality exists independently of God and so can be (at least partly) understood and appreciated even by people who disagree about the nature or existence of God.

TERMINOLOGY TO KNOW

objective obligation   divine command theory   Euthyphro dilemma
subjective obligation

DISCUSSION QUESTIONS

1. Can you think of other ways in which religious claims matter to moral reasoning, besides those listed in this chapter? What about other ways in which moral reasoning can help religious people in contemporary society?
2. What is another example, besides the ones given in this chapter, of a non-moral religious claim that makes a difference in people's reasoning about a moral issue?
3. How might a defender of divine command theory respond to the Euthyphro dilemma? Do you find that response convincing? Why or why not?
4. Is the use of religious teachings in morality a form of cultural relativism? Why or why not?

CASE STUDIES

See the Note About Case Studies on p. 150 for further instructions. For these case studies in particular, you might find it helpful to distinguish between subjective and objective obligations.

1. Although songwriter Thao Nguyen's grandfather was cruel to his wife for years, their social circumstances made it impossible for her to divorce him. So for twenty years Nguyen's grandmother fought back the only way she could, by giving him the silent treatment. For two decades, though she cleaned and cooked and cared for him, she never said a word to him. Then Nguyen's grandfather fell sick and was admitted to the hospital. The doctors said that he didn't have long to live. Since Nguyen's grandparents were Catholic, her grandfather's family called a Catholic priest to the hospital to administer the last rites, which include a confession of sins. Since Nguyen's grandfather could no longer speak, the priest asked her grandmother to list her husband's sins so that the priest could absolve him of them. Nguyen's grandmother refused to tell him, even when the priest explained that unless he knew what her husband had done, he could not absolve his sins, and that if he did not absolve his sins, the man would go to hell. Evaluate Nguyen's grandmother's action of refusing to list her husband's sins, despite the priest's warning that her husband would go to hell if she refused. Construct an argument to support your evaluation.
2. The Shia branch of Islam allows people to enter into temporary marriage contracts, which last a fixed amount of time. (The other main denomination, Sunni Islam, prohibits such temporary marriages.) Because the contracts require that the husband give his bride a gift or dowry, some people regard such temporary marriages as a form of prostitution. Since Islam prohibits the kinds of romantic and sexual relationships that are common between young people in modern Britain, however, some young British Muslims are using temporary marriage contracts for a different purpose: when two young people want to date each other, they sign a temporary marriage contract, which allows them to get around the religious ban on dating in the modern British sense of the term. If the relationship works out, they can marry permanently. Evaluate the British Muslims' practice of using temporary marriage contracts as a way of dating. Construct an argument to support your evaluation.
3. The Aztecs dominated what is now central Mexico from the 1300s through the early 1500s. They believed that the gods required human sacrifices. More specifically, Aztec religion held that if the Aztecs did not provide human sacrifices, the gods would destroy the world and all of humanity.

(According to Aztec mythology, the gods had done this several times before, recreating the world each time.) To satisfy the gods' demands, the Aztecs are thought to have sacrificed thousands of people each year, including prisoners and slaves. Evaluate the Aztecs' practice of sacrificing people as part of their religious rituals. Construct an argument to defend your evaluation.

4. Philosopher Margaret Battin once answered her front door to find three college students outside. They were on a scavenger hunt. Happy to help, Battin supplied them with various odds and ends, such as a length of blue thread and a road map. Eventually, it came out that the students were from the Campus Crusade for Christ, and their real motivation for visiting Battin's house was to try to find people whom they could convert to Christianity. The scavenger hunt was just a ruse designed to make people more willing to have a conversation with the students. Evaluate the students' action of going door-to-door and using the scavenger hunt as a pretext for trying to convert people to Christianity. Construct an argument for support your evaluation.

11) Normative Theories, Part 1

In the film *Slumdog Millionaire*, two orphaned brothers, Jamal and Salim, band together with a girl named Latika to fend for themselves in the bustling streets of Mumbai, India. A man named Maman takes them in, but he turns out to be a gangster who forces the orphans to work for him as child beggars. When Salim learns that Maman plans to cut out Jamal's eyes because "blind [beggars] earn double," Salim helps Jamal to escape. Latika tries to flee with them, but Salim, who dislikes Latika, deliberately leaves her behind. Some years later, Jamal and Salim return to look for Latika in Mumbai, where they learn that Maman is preparing her for a life of prostitution. They confront Maman and rescue Latika.[1]

Salim and Jamal pretty clearly did the right thing in returning to rescue Latika, but even people who agree about that might disagree about *why* it was morally right.[2] Was it because their action had good consequences? Was it because they were making amends for leaving her behind? Was it because confronting Maman required great courage? Or was it for some other reason?

Answering these questions brings us to matters of **normative ethics,** which is the part of moral philosophy that aims to develop general theories about which actions or things are right or good. Normative ethics contrasts with **applied ethics** or practical ethics, which focuses on what (kinds of) actions one ought to do (or not do) in particular circumstances. Normative ethics not only provides you with a deeper understanding of ethics, it can sometimes help resolve particularly difficult moral problems.

This chapter examines the three normative theories that have received the most attention in recent Western philosophy: consequentialism, deontology, and virtue ethics. Note that when we focus on distinguishing the theories from one another, we will emphasize ways in which they disagree with one another, but that in many cases—perhaps most—all three theories would yield the same conclusion about *what* you ought to do, even if they disagree about *why* you ought to do it.

---

[1]Danny Boyle, *Slumdog Millionaire* (Burbank, CA: Warner Bros., 2009).
[2]If you've seen the movie, you may remember that after rescuing Latika, Salim kills Maman. That was, arguably, morally wrong. But since it wasn't a necessary part of rescuing Latika, we'll focus here just on the brothers' action of rescuing her.

CONSEQUENTIALISM

According to one kind of normative theory, morality is fundamentally about making the world a better place. This kind of theory, known as **consequentialism,** says that the rightness or wrongness of an action depends, ultimately, on the effects of that action or on the effects of something related to the action, such as a rule that permits the action. Consequentialism comes in so many varieties that it is best to think of it as a family of theories, tied together by a focus on the goodness or badness of consequences.

The most famous variety of consequentialism, known as **act utilitarianism,** provides a good introduction to this family of theories. Act utilitarianism is the view that an action is right if it maximizes the total amount of happiness in the world, counting everyone's happiness equally; otherwise, it is wrong. Traditionally, act utilitarians understand happiness as pleasure and the absence of pain. So, if you could perform several different actions right now, the morally right action would be the one that leads to the greatest overall balance of pleasure over pain, taking everyone's pleasure and pain into account; the other actions would be wrong.

To see how this works, consider Jamal and Salim's actions in *Slumdog Millionaire*. To simplify things, suppose that when they find out where Latika is, they have just two options: they can rescue Latika themselves or they can give up, leaving her as Maman's captive. Also for simplicity, let us assume that they are very confident that they *can* rescue Latika if they decide to do so.[3] To determine which of these options is the morally right one, act utilitarianism tells us to consider the effects of their possible actions on the happiness of everyone affected. The consequences of each option are summarized in Table 11.1, making some assumptions about what would happen in each case and how it would affect various people's happiness.

TABLE 11.1   Summary of Consequences from Each of the Brothers' Two Options

	Option 1: Rescue Latika	Option 2: Leave Latika with Maman
Jamal	Reunite with Latika, which would make Jamal very happy	Never see Latika again, and always feel bad that she got left behind
Salim, Jamal's brother	Rescue Latika, which would make Salim proud but not affect his happiness that much one way or the other	Never see Latika again, and perhaps feel a little bit of guilt about having left her behind
Latika, the brothers' childhood friend	Escape from her brutal captor and a life of forced prostitution, making her much happier for the rest of her life	Suffer greatly under Maman's control for many years, while being forced to work as a prostitute
Maman, the gangster	Lose Latika, leading to temporary anger and a minor loss of income	Earn some additional income from Latika's forced prostitution, making him slightly happier than he would otherwise be

---

[3]In many important decisions, uncertainty about the consequences of your action plays an important role. To learn more about handling uncertainty, see Chapter 4.

Rescuing Latika would make Latika and Jamal very happy, and it would make Salim somewhat happier, too. It would make Maman less happy, but not so much that it would out-weigh the gains to Latika and Jamal. (Notice that, because it requires us to count everyone's happiness equally, act utilitarianism requires us to take Maman's happiness into account, too, no matter how awful we think he is or how much we think he deserves to lose the income he would earn from Latika's prostitution.) Leaving Latika with Maman would make Maman slightly happier, but it would greatly reduce Latika's happiness for the rest of her life, and it would make both Jamal and Salim somewhat less happy. When we "add together" the gains and losses in everyone's happiness in each scenario, we see that rescuing Latika creates much more happiness than it destroys, whereas leaving her with Maman creates a great loss in happiness on balance. Thus, of the two options, rescuing Latika creates more happiness overall, taking into account both gains and losses. So, according to act utilitarianism, rescuing Latika is the right thing to do, and leaving her with Maman would be wrong.

In this particular case, act utilitarianism entails a fairly uncontroversial answer. In other cases, however, act utilitarianism has very surprising implications. In a famous example, you are asked to imagine that you have time to rescue exactly one of two people from a burning building. One person is someone who does a tremendous amount of good for society—say, a brilliant cancer researcher—and the other person is your mother (who, let's assume, is a per-fectly nice person but does only a normal amount of good for society).[4] Many people think it would be permissible, if not required, for you to save your mother rather than the cancer researcher, but because act utilitarianism requires you to count everyone's happiness equally, it entails that you are morally *required* to rescue the cancer researcher and leave your mother to burn. Act utilitarianism is therefore sometimes described as being "too demanding."

In other cases, act utilitarianism sometimes seems like it's not demanding enough. For in-stance, act utilitarianism implies that it is sometimes permissible to do things that strike most people as obviously wrong, such as framing innocent people for crimes, discreetly killing people to harvest their organs for needy transplant patients, and so on. Because many people think that a normative theory should respect our considered judgments about which things are right or wrong, these shocking conclusions lead many people to reject act utilitarianism.

One response to these worries is to adopt a different kind of consequentialism, known as **rule utilitarianism.** Rule utilitarianism is the view that, instead of focusing on particular actions, we should consider the consequences of having this or that set of rules for society. An action is right if and only if it is allowed (or required) by the rules whose adoption would create the most happiness overall, counting everyone's happiness equally.[5]

The story of Robin Hood illustrates the contrast between act utilitarianism and rule utili-tarianism. Assume that when Robin Hood stole from the rich to give to the poor, he increased his beneficiaries' happiness more than he decreased his victims' happiness. Act utilitarianism

---

[4]The inspiration for this example comes from William Godwin, *An Enquiry Concerning Political Justice, and Its Influence on General Virtue and Happiness*, Vol. 1 (London: G. G. & J Robinson, 1793), 126–28.

[5]Certain ways of spelling out rule utilitarianism turn out to "collapse" it into act utilitarianism. That is, on certain ways of specify-ing how rule utilitarianism works, it permits and requires exactly the same things that act utilitarianism does. See David Lyons, *Forms and Limits of Utilitarianism* (Oxford: Clarendon Press, 1965), 62–118. But this doesn't mean that *all* forms of rule utili-tarianism collapse into act utilitarianism, partly for the reasons explained at the end of Chapter 4. See Lyons, 136*ff.*; John C. Harsanyi, "Rule Utilitarianism and Decision Theory," *Erkenntnis* 11 (1977); and Brad Hooker, *Ideal Code, Real World: A Rule-Consequentialist Theory of Morality* (Oxford: Oxford University Press, 2000), 93–99.

would entail that Robin Hood acted rightly. A rule utilitarian, however, would consider the *rule* that allows people to steal from the rich to give to the poor. As the philosopher David Hume argues, rules that enforce strict property rights create enormous benefits for society: when society follows such rules, people feel less anxious about their belongings; they don't have to spend as much money on security; they invest their resources in productive ways, without worrying that the fruits of their investment would be taken from them; and so on. The result, Hume argues, is more overall happiness than would exist in a society whose rules allowed people to steal other people's possessions.[6]

There are other variations on consequentialism, too. For instance, some variations define the good differently (e.g., as preference-satisfaction rather than pleasure), while others consider something other than the sum total of happiness (e.g., such as the average level of happiness). Many of these variations are designed to help bring utilitarianism more in line with ordinary moral judgments.

There is one further distinction to keep in mind when thinking about consequentialism. All consequentialists are committed to the idea that what ultimately *makes* an action right or wrong is its connection to some kind of consequences (e.g., of the action itself, of the rules that allow it, etc.). Producing the best effects is therefore said to be the criterion of rightness for an action (or rule, etc.). Some consequentialists go further and say that when you are thinking about what to do, you should reason explicitly in terms of the effects of your actions (or of the effects of the adoption of a set of rules, etc.). Other consequentialists argue that you will bring about the best consequences if you usually reason in terms of obligations, virtues, relationships, or other values. The philosopher Peter Railton, for instance, argues that people will bring about the most happiness in the long run if they value their friends and family for their own sakes, rather than simply seeing relationships as a means to creating happiness.[7]

In short, consequentialism begins from the idea that morality is about making the world a better place. When it comes to put that idea into practice, however, there are many different consequentialist theories, each of which recommends a different way of figuring out what to do.

DEONTOLOGY

According to another kind of normative theory, morality is fundamentally about fulfilling your duties or obligations. This kind of theory, known as **deontology,** says that the rightness or wrongness of an action depends on its conformity with the moral rules—that is, on whether it violates the rules that specify the agent's moral obligations.

Contemporary deontology comes in two main varieties, which are sometimes called **Rossian deontology** and **Kantian deontology,** after the twentieth-century British philosopher W. D. Ross and the eighteenth-century German philosopher Immanuel Kant, respectively. We will explore each of these two types below.

[6]David Hume, *A Treatise of Human Nature* 3.2.2.
[7]Peter Railton, "Alienation, Consequentialism, and the Demands of Morality," *Philosophy & Public Affairs* 13 (1984): 134–71.

Rossian Deontology

Rossian deontology is the view that we have several basic ***prima facie* obligations** (e.g., to keep our promises, to avoid harming people), which are irreducible and unorderable. To unpack this definition, we need to understand what a *prima facie* obligation is and what it is for obligations to be irreducible and unorderable.

Let's start with the idea of a *prima facie* obligation. The Latin phrase *prima facie* (pronounced PREE-ma FAY-sha) literally means "on first appearance." The philosophical term *prima facie* obligation (or, equivalently, *prima facie* duty) doesn't quite follow the literal meaning, though. To say that you have a *prima facie* obligation to do something is, roughly, to say that you ought to do that thing unless some other, more important obligation requires you to do something else.[8] Ross himself articulated five kinds of *prima facie* obligations: fidelity (promise-keeping); reparation (making amends for harms we have done); gratitude (showing gratitude to our benefactors); beneficence (promoting good outcomes); and non-maleficence (not harming others).[9] The idea that these are *prima facie* obligations matters because in any given situation, you might have a number of *prima facie* obligations that conflict with one another. The most important obligation in some particular situation is said to be your "all-things-considered obligation" in that situation. That's the obligation that you ought, ultimately, to satisfy in that situation.

An example will help clarify the idea of a *prima facie* obligation. In Victor Hugo's novel *Les Misérables*, which was later turned into a musical and then a film, the poor peasant Jean Valjean steals a loaf of bread to feed his widowed sister and her seven starving children.[10] In doing so, he satisfies his *prima facie* obligation to promote good outcomes (by feeding his starving family), but he also violates his *prima facie* obligation not to harm others (by stealing from the baker who baked the bread). The idea of a *prima facie* obligation is that each of these obligations is a real obligation; the obligation not to harm others doesn't magically disappear just because Valjean has no other way to satisfy his obligation to promote good outcomes. Rather, both obligations are real, even if one is ultimately more important than the other.

Of course, in cases where you have only one *prima facie* obligation or where your *prima facie* obligations do not conflict, there's no puzzle about what you ought to do. Your *prima facie* obligation(s) just is (or are) your "all-things-considered" obligation(s).

The concepts of irreducible and unorderable obligations are easier to understand than that of *prima facie* obligation. Rossian basic obligations are irreducible in the sense that none of these basic duties can be reduced to or explained in terms of any simpler principle. We cannot explain our obligation to keep our promises, for instance, as a special case of our obligation to avoid harming people, since sometimes breaking a promise does not harm anyone. Rather, we ought to keep our promises *just because they are promises*. Rossian basic duties are unorderable in the sense that it is impossible to create an ordering or hierarchy of obligations that tells us when one kind of obligation takes priority over another. For instance, the obligation to avoid harming people usually takes priority over the obligation to help people, but as the example from *Les Misérables* suggests, this is not always the case.

---

[8]While Ross uses the expression "*prima facie*," some later philosophers use the expression "*pro tanto*" ("to that extent") instead. The expressions "*prima facie* obligation" and "*pro tanto* obligation" are now used interchangeably in moral philosophy.

[9]W. D. Ross, *The Right and the Good* (Oxford: Oxford University Press, 1930). Also see Chapter 3 of this book for Robert Audi's expanded list of Rossian obligations.

[10]Victor Hugo, *Les Misérables* (New York: Random House, 2000 [1862]), 73.

Kantian Deontology

The most famous deontological theory derives from Immanuel Kant. Like all deontologists, Kant is interested in finding rules that tell us how to live.

Some rules are what Kant calls **hypothetical imperatives.** You can think of an imperative, roughly, as a rule that tells you what to do. A hypothetical imperative is a rule that tells you what to do in the hypothetical situation where you want to accomplish some particular goal. (To say that a situation is hypothetical is to say that we are just *supposing* that it's true, without worrying about whether it really is true.) That is, it tells you what you should do *if* you want to achieve that goal. Here, for instance, is a hypothetical imperative: if you want to go to Antarctica, then you ought to take a boat or a plane. These imperatives don't assume that you *actually* want to go to Antarctica. They're just telling you what you should do *in the hypothetical situation* where you wanted to go there. We say that a particular hypothetical imperative "applies" to you—that is, it tells *you* what to do—if you happen to have the goal mentioned in the rule.

According to Kant, however, the rules of morality are not supposed to be hypothetical imperatives. The rules of morality are supposed to apply to everyone, independent of their particular goals, desires, preferences, and so on. A rule that applies to everyone independently of their goals is called a **categorical imperative.** (The term "categorical" here means "unconditional," "definite," or "conclusive," as opposed to hypothetical imperatives, which are conditional on your having some particular goal.) This raises an obvious question, though. *Are* there any such rules? What rule could possibly apply to everyone, all the time, regardless of what they want?

Kant reasons that any rule that applies to you independently of your goals and desires will automatically apply to everyone. After all, a hypothetical imperative applies to some people but not to others precisely *because* people's goals and desires differ. So, the key to finding a categorical imperative is finding a rule that applies independently of a person's particular goals and desires.

Kant says that there is exactly one such rule. The rule, which requires a bit of explanation, is that you should act only on a **maxim** that could be universalized without leading to a contradiction in your own will. Understanding this rule requires understanding three things: what Kant means by "maxim," what it means to universalize a maxim, and when universalizing a maxim leads to a contradiction in your own will. Unfortunately, it's not entirely clear what Kant means by any of these things, and so different philosophers offer different interpretations. The interpretation offered in this chapter is a standard one, but it is just one of several ways of interpreting Kant's ethics.

When you perform an action, the maxim of your action is, roughly, the principle that specifies your personal reason for performing that action. Some maxims are very general. For instance, you might act from "the maxim of self-love," which says that you will act in your own interest in order to promote your own happiness. Other maxims are fairly specific. For instance, a cashier might act from the maxim of giving correct change in order to avoid having customers complain to the store manager. Notice that each of these examples specifies both *what you are doing* and *why you are doing it*. That is, they describe both the action that you are doing and your *reason* for doing it. Thus, someone who does the same thing but for a different reason—such as someone who acts in his own interest in order to be better able to provide for his children or a cashier who gives correct change in order to treat her customers fairly—is acting on a different maxim.

In asking you to universalize the maxim of your action, Kant is simply asking you to imagine what would happen if everyone followed that maxim. In other words, he is asking you to imagine that when you choose to act on your maxim, you are also choosing for your maxim to become like a universal law of nature: everyone *must* obey it, much as everyone must obey the law of gravity.

It's harder to grasp the idea of being able to universalize your maxim without contradicting your own will. There are two ways that universalizing your maxim can lead to a contradiction: In some cases, universalizing the maxim undermines the maxim itself; it defeats the point of acting on the maxim in the first place. Kant's famous example here is the maxim, "I will falsely promise to pay someone back in order to get them to loan me money." To see how universalizing this maxim defeats the point of acting on it, imagine that Bart asks Lisa for a loan, promising to repay it within a year, even though he knows that he won't be able to do that. In the actual world, where promises are often sincere, Lisa might believe Bart's promise, and so his promise might get her to lend him the money. But if *everyone* acted on Bart's maxim, then a promise to repay a loan would be worthless. Lisa would know that the promise doesn't mean anything, because she knows that even someone who had no intention of repaying the loan would still promise to do so. And so, if the maxim were universalized, the action described in the maxim (namely, falsely promising to repay a loan) would not achieve the goal implied in the maxim (namely, getting someone to lend you money). Thus, if Bart willed for his maxim to be a universal law, he would be willing *both* that Lisa lends him the money *and* that Lisa would refuse to lend him the money. That would be a contradiction in Bart's will, and so it would violate the categorical imperative.

In other cases, universalizing your maxim might not undermine the maxim itself, but it might undermine your reason for adopting that maxim. Thinking back to the case from *Slumdog Millionaire*, suppose that Salim had adopted the maxim, "I will give up on rescuing Latika in order to avoid the difficulty and danger of rescuing her." What reasons might Salim have for adopting this maxim? One reason, suggested by Kant's discussion of a similar maxim,[11] is that Salim adopts his maxim out of self-interest, arriving at it via the following chain of reasoning:

1. I shall promote my self-interest.
2. Avoiding difficult or dangerous activities that only benefit others is in my self-interest.
∴ 3. I shall avoid difficult or dangerous activities that only benefit others.

1. I shall avoid difficult or dangerous activities that only benefit others.
2. Giving up on rescuing Latika will enable me to avoid a difficult, dangerous activity that will only benefit others.
∴ 3. I shall give up on rescuing Latika in order to avoid the difficulty and danger of rescuing her.

Since the first premise of the second argument comes from the first argument, the final conclusion (i.e., that Salim shall give up on rescuing Latika) is ultimately based on the first

---

[11]Kant's example is a maxim like, "Out of self-interest, I will not help others in need, even when I could easily do so." It is clear that Kant thinks this maxim cannot be universalized. Philosophers disagree about exactly how to interpret *why* Kant thinks this. Again, the interpretation offered here is just one among many.

premise of the first argument (i.e., that Salim shall promote his own interests). Since there is always a possibility that Salim will someday need someone's help—perhaps in a way that requires difficult or dangerous actions on that person's part—establishing a universal law that no one ever faces difficulty or danger to help someone else would undermine his *original* maxim of acting to promote his own interests. So Salim would be contradicting himself in a more subtle way if, in addition to willing that he act in his own interests, he also wills it to be a law of nature that no one ever faces difficulty or danger to help others: for the sake of promoting his self-interest, he would be willing that everyone acts in a way that would sometimes threaten his own self-interest.

Many people misunderstand Kant's point here. The question is *not* how you would *like* it if everyone acted the way you are acting. The question is whether you would end up *contradicting your own will* if you willed that everyone acted on your maxim. No (rational) person would want to contradict that person's own will, and so a rule against contradicting your own will applies to everyone, regardless of their interests. Thus, it is a categorical imperative. In fact, since Kant thinks that this is the *only* rule that applies to everyone, regardless of their interests, he calls it *the* categorical imperative.

Confusingly, however, Kant then offers several different versions of the categorical imperative, claiming that each is just a different "formulation" or way or expressing the same fundamental rule. The formulation that we've just seen—the one that expresses the categorical imperative in terms of acting only on maxims that you could universalize without contradiction—is called the **Formula of Universal Law.**

The most important statement of the categorical imperative, however, is called the **Formula of Humanity.** It says that you should always act so as to treat humanity, whether in your own person or someone else's, always as an **end-in-itself,** and never **merely as a means.** Like the Formula of Universal Law, this formulation needs some explanation, and as before, this explanation has several parts: what Kant means by "humanity . . . in your own person or someone else's," what it is for humanity to be an "end-in-itself," and what it is to treat someone "merely as a means."

While "treating humanity" with respect means treating individual persons with respect, you will more easily understand the Formula of Humanity if you keep in mind that, according to Kant, an individual's "humanity" comes from his or her capacity to make choices through rational reflection. So, when the Formula of Humanity tells us to treat humanity as an end-in-itself, it is saying that we should treat each person's *capacity for rational action* as an end-in-itself.

To say that something is an "end" is to say that it is a goal. If you adopt baking cupcakes as an end, for instance, your goal is to bake cupcakes. Your choosing that goal gives it value for you. To say that something is an end-in-itself is to say that it already exists and has value, independent of your goals. To treat something as an end-in-itself is to adopt a goal of protecting, promoting, and honoring that thing. Thus, to say that we should treat humanity as an end-in-itself is to say that we ought to protect, promote, and honor our own and others' capacity for rational action, regardless of whatever other goals we have. This means, at least, that we should never act in ways that undermine our own or others' capacity for rational action. We can further honor people's capacity for choosing their own goals by acting to promote that capacity and by helping them to achieve those goals.

To treat someone as a means is to use them to help you achieve your goals. We all do this all the time. For instance, when you buy food from someone else, you are using them as a means to your own ends. This is not a problem because the person who produced the food agreed to do so in exchange for money; they consented to participating in your plans. Kant objects, however, to treating someone *merely* as a means—that is, treating them as a mere thing, without any goals or interests of their own. This is usually interpreted as saying that we must not use people in a way to which they could not *possibly* give their free consent. In practice, this means that we may not deceive or coerce people. It is impossible for you to freely consent to do something if you have been deceived about what it is you're doing. For instance, in the final scene of *Hamlet*, Laertes tricks Hamlet into fighting a lethal duel; Hamlet does not know that Laertes's sword is tipped with poison.[12] And while Hamlet could, in principle, consent to fighting a lethal duel with poison-tipped swords, he could not consent to *unknowingly* fight such a duel, since doing so would require knowing that the duel involved poison-tipped swords. Similarly, if someone physically forces you to do something, you haven't consented, and if someone coerces you into doing something through threats of some kind, you do not give your *free* consent, if you have consented at all. It would be odd, for instance, to say that the victim of a robbery freely consents to the mugger's demand for cash.

These requirements are often summarized by saying that the Formula of Humanity requires us to "respect persons."[13] To respect persons, in this sense, is to refrain from deceiving or coercing them; to avoid acting in ways that undermine their ability to choose and pursue their own goals; and, at least sometimes and to some extent, to help promote their capacity for rational action and to help them achieve the goals they have chosen for themselves. And that, according to Kant, is the fundamental principle of morality.

VIRTUE ETHICS

The third major normative theory we'll discuss in this chapter is **virtue ethics.** It is often said that if deontology and consequentialism are about which acts you should do, virtue ethics is about what kind of person you should be. Virtue ethics also has a lot to say about which actions you should or shouldn't do, just as deontology and consequentialism do, but in virtue ethics, what you ought to do follows from the kind of person you ought to be, and the kind of person you ought to be is closely tied to the idea of living the best life possible for a human being.

The film *The Wolf of Wall Street* vividly illustrates some of the key ideas in virtue ethics. The film's main character, Jordan Belfort (played by Leonardo DiCaprio), rises from humble origins to build his own wildly successful company on Wall Street, making himself and his friends extremely wealthy. He marries the woman of his dreams, buys a mansion outside New York City, and starts a family, enjoying every luxury money can buy. From the outside, Belfort seems to be living the American dream; he seems to be living the kind of life that many parents would want for their children. In fact, however, Belfort is a terrible person

---

[12]*Hamlet*, V.2.
[13]See Chapter 3 for further discussion of putting the principle of respect for persons into practice.

whose success rests on dishonest and criminal behavior. He is a selfish, superficial, greedy, deceitful, arrogant, reckless, self-indulgent, drug-addicted criminal who mistreats his wife (who had initially been his mistress while he was married to someone else) and exploits his company's customers for personal gain.[14] He is not the kind of person many people would want to be or would want their children to be. And even before the law catches up with him, Belfort is not actually living the kind of life many people would want for their children—or, upon reflection, for themselves. Despite his superficial success, he is nowhere close to living the best life possible for a human being.

In ancient Greek philosophy, there was a word for living the best life possible for a human being: *eudaimonia* (pronounced you-die-MOH-nia or you-DIE-moh-nia). The word *eudaimonia* is very difficult to translate into English. It is sometimes translated as "happiness," but this is misleading, given the way contemporary English speakers use the word "happiness." After all, in one common way of talking about happiness, it would make sense to say that Belfort was happy, even though he wasn't living the best life possible for a human being. A better translation of *eudaimonia* is "flourishing," but it is perhaps best not to translate the word at all. Whatever we call it, *eudaimonia* plays an important role in many forms of virtue ethics, because it is, by definition, the best life possible and therefore the goal around which we ought to organize our lives. And so, for most Western traditions of virtue ethics, a central question of ethics is what *eudaimonia* is. That is, what *is* the best life possible for a human being?

As the example of Jordan Belfort suggests, one crucial ingredient in *eudaimonia* is being an excellent person, which virtue ethicists understand in terms of possessing some or all of the **virtues.** A virtue is, very roughly, a character trait that contributes to someone's being an excellent person, such as honesty, generosity, or courage, but this simplistic definition needs a lot of elaboration. To understand the nuances of the concept of a virtue, consider Abraham Lincoln's reputation as "Honest Abe." To know whether Lincoln actually had the virtue of honesty, we would need to know whether he consistently told the truth—but we would need to know a lot more, too. Most importantly, we would need to know *why* he told the truth; we would need to know what role honesty played in his deliberations about what to do. A lawyer and politician, such as Lincoln, might tell the truth all the time because he thinks a reputation for honesty will help him get business or get elected. While such a person performs honest actions, he does not count as an honest person, as far as virtue ethics is concerned, because a genuinely honest person values honesty for its own sake. If Lincoln had the virtue of honesty, he would be honest not merely as a way to get elected, but because he regarded the fact that something was "the honest thing to do" as a powerful reason for choosing to do it. Furthermore, a truly honest person would approve of others' acting honestly and would encourage them to do so. For instance, in his "Notes for a Law Lecture," Lincoln encourages aspiring lawyers to "resolve to be honest at all events; and if in your own judgment you cannot be an honest lawyer, resolve to be honest without being a lawyer."[15] This suggests that Lincoln really did possess the virtue of honesty: he had a stable disposition to act honestly, to weigh honesty heavily in his deliberations about what to do, and to value and encourage honesty

---

[14]Martin Scorsese, *The Wolf of Wall Street* (Hollywood: Paramount Pictures, 2013).

[15]Abraham Lincoln, "Fragment: Notes for a Law Lecture," in *Collected Works of Abraham Lincoln*, Vol. 2 (Ann Arbor: University of Michigan Digital Library Production Services, 2001), http://name.umdl.umich.edu/lincoln2.

in others. More generally, we can say that a virtue is a complex, stable disposition to act in a certain morally valuable way (e.g., honestly or generously), to treat some particular morally valuable feature of an action (e.g., its honesty or generosity) as a reason to choose that action, and to approve and encourage others to act in those ways and value those features of an action.

There is an additional requirement, as well, for the possession of a virtue. Truly virtuous people use good judgment in deciding how to exercise their virtues. The ability to use good judgment in this way is called **practical wisdom** (or, in Greek, *phronesis*). Honesty, for instance, is not just a matter of always saying exactly what is on one's mind; it is also a matter of knowing when to keep one's mouth shut and how to express certain truths in a way that won't hurt someone's feelings. Being genuinely honest, therefore, is a skill, and like any skill, being really good at it requires good judgment.

There are many ways someone can fail to have a particular virtue. Someone who chooses the right action but for the wrong reasons lacks the relevant virtue; Lincoln would not have been truly honest had he valued honesty only because it led to a good reputation. Someone who frequently chooses the wrong action, either because he does not place enough value on the relevant goal (e.g., truth telling) or because he is too often overcome by temptation, does not have the relevant virtue; Lincoln would not have been honest, obviously, if he had lied frequently. Someone who lacks practical wisdom might consistently try to choose the right action for the right reason but do so in inappropriate or clumsy ways that fail to exhibit the relevant virtue. And at the opposite extreme from virtue is someone who values something that is directly opposed to the virtue. For instance, someone who positively values misleading or manipulating others is dishonest. Such people not only lack the relevant virtue; they have a morally bad character trait, which is called a **vice**.

To return once more to the incident from *Slumdog Millionaire*, Jamal and Salim exhibited bravery, compassion, and loyalty in rescuing their old companion Latika. Doing so at least brought them closer to being genuinely brave, compassionate, and loyal—and so, closer to being excellent people. This, according to virtue ethics, is why rescuing Latika was the right thing to do. Had Jamal and Salim decided not to save Latika, whether out of fear, laziness, callousness, cruelty, or some other shortcoming, they would have acted wrongly.

TERMINOLOGY TO KNOW

normative ethics
applied ethics
consequentialism
act utilitarianism
rule utilitarianism
deontology
Rossian deontology

Kantian deontology
prima facie obligation
hypothetical imperative
categorical imperative
maxim
Formula of Universal Law
Formula of Humanity

end-in-itself
merely as a means
virtue ethics
eudaimonia
virtue
practical wisdom
vice

DISCUSSION QUESTIONS

1. Critics of utilitarianism—and especially of act utilitarianism—often say that the theory is too demanding in some ways and not demanding enough in others. Is this a good reason to reject act utilitarianism? Why or why not?
2. How is applying Kant's Formula of Universal Law different from asking how you would like it if everyone acted like you did? Why is that important to Kantian deontology?
3. Do you agree with virtue ethicists that being virtuous is essential to living the best life possible? Why or why not?
4. As noted at the beginning of this chapter, these three theories lead to the same conclusion in many cases. In what kinds of cases would consequentialism and deontology tend to yield different conclusions? What about consequentialism and virtue ethics? Deontology and virtue ethics?

CASE STUDIES

See the Note About Case Studies on p. 150 for further instructions, but note that the case studies in this chapter specifically ask you to base your argument on one of the normative theories discussed above.

1. The girl who saved young Jacques Hauser's life had to lie to do it. As Nazi soldiers approached their French village during World War II, the girl told Jacques that, if he was Jewish, he could hide in her family's house. He was Jewish, and so he did hide in her house. When the soldiers knocked on the girl's door and asked whether there were any Jews there, the family said there weren't. The soldiers left, and Jacques survived the war, eventually moving to the United States. Using one of the normative theories described in this chapter, evaluate the girl's action of hiding Jacques in her home and lying to the Nazi soldiers about it. Give an argument, based on the normative theory you've chosen, to support your evaluation.
2. Amy Strater's life fell apart after her teenage son, Blair, got into a petty online dispute with another computer hacker. The first sign of trouble came when pizzas started showing up at the Straters' suburban home in Illinois—pizzas that none of the Straters had ordered. The harassment escalated: Larger deliveries arrived, expecting payment. Someone called the police and the fire department to the Straters' home in the middle of the night. Someone hacked Tesla's Twitter account, instructing people to call the Straters' phones to receive a free Tesla. (The Straters received thousands of calls over a single weekend.) When someone posing as Blair emailed a bomb threat to his school, Blair spent three weeks in jail. When Amy warned her employer that the hackers might come after them, she lost her job. Her marriage fell apart from the stress of the months-long harassment. Blair blames the attacks on the notorious Finnish hacker Julius Kivimaki, but Kivimaki insists that he is only responsible for a few of the incidents, implying that other hackers have carried out the rest because they, too, dislike Blair. Using one of the normative theories described in this chapter, evaluate the hackers' actions of ruining Amy Strater's life because of their annoyance with her son. Give an argument, based on the normative theory you've chosen, to support your evaluation.
3. In the film *The Dark Knight*, the Joker quickly reveals himself to be an especially dangerous and devious criminal. In his first direct confrontation with the Joker, Batman has an opportunity to kill him, but he refuses to do so. Instead, he captures the Joker and turns him over to the police. The Joker escapes from police custody, kills many more people, turns Gotham City's heroic district attorney into a deranged villain, blows up a hospital, and creates all kinds of other mayhem before

Batman finally stops him. Using one of the normative theories described in this chapter, evaluate Batman's action of declining to kill the Joker when he had the chance. Give an argument, based on the normative theory you've chosen, to support your evaluation.

4. Fed up with phone scams and sales calls, Roger Anderson programmed his computer to talk to telemarketers. The computer tricks the telemarketers into thinking that a live human has answered the phone. It keeps the telemarketers talking by playing recordings of short statements like, "Right," "Yes," or "Uh huh." It can even tell when the telemarketer starts to get suspicious, at which point it throws in a longer recorded statement to try to convince the telemarketer that there's a real person on the line. Anderson initially developed the software as a fun prank. Eventually, he realized that it could be used to "fight back" against telemarketers and disrupt their annoying business model by keeping telemarketers tied up on useless calls. Now, he's set it up so that anyone can patch telemarketers through to his software, which he calls "Jolly Roger Telephone Co." Using one of the normative theories described in this chapter, evaluate Anderson's action of creating the Jolly Roger software "bot" and allowing anyone to connect telemarketers to it. Give an argument, based on the normative theory you've chosen, to support your evaluation.

12) Normative Theories, Part 2

The three theories discussed in the previous chapter—consequentialism, deontology, and virtue ethics—have received the most attention in recent philosophical discussion about normative ethics, but there are other important normative theories, too. This chapter explores five distinct normative theories: natural law theory, which has been particularly important in the Catholic tradition; contractarianism, along with its close relative, contractualism; the ethics of care, which emerged from feminist philosophy in the last few decades; Confucian ethics, one of the central moral traditions in Chinese philosophy; and the ethics of *ubuntu*, derived from an important tradition in African ethics. Each of these theories entails different views about what obligations we have, what kinds of consequences are good or bad, what counts as a virtue or vice, and what other moral principles should guide our thinking. Thus, each theory has slightly different logical consequences for the way we apply the kinds of moral reasoning discussed in Chapters 3–7.

NATURAL LAW THEORY

Some normative theories are not easily classified as consequentialist, deontological, or virtue-based because they combine elements of all of those theories. One such theory is **natural law theory.** While natural law theory is most commonly associated with the Catholic tradition, and especially with the medieval philosopher Thomas Aquinas, it is also found in ancient Greek and Roman sources and modern, non-Catholic sources.

SAINT THOMAS AQUINAS

The Catholic priest Thomas Aquinas (1225–1274) taught theology at the University of Paris during a critical period in the history of Western thought. By the Middle Ages, Catholic Europe had largely forgotten the works of the ancient Greeks, including the works of Aristotle. As those works were reintroduced from the Islamic world, where they had been preserved and studied for centuries, Catholic philosophers tried to reconcile these ancient Greek philosophies with their religious beliefs. Thomas Aquinas was central to synthesizing Aristotelian philosophy and Catholic theology, and his work influenced official Catholic doctrine for centuries.

Roughly, natural law theory says that some things are good for humans because of our human nature and that acting rightly consists in pursuing and promoting those good things in reasonable ways. The moral law comes, therefore, from our human nature. Furthermore, because all people are capable of reasoning and have at least some understanding of human nature, everyone is able to know, more or less, what is good and what is right. Different versions of natural law elaborate on that basic idea in different ways. In particular, they offer different lists of what things are good for human beings, and they offer different ways of understanding what it means to pursue those goods in reasonable ways.

Natural law theory resembles consequentialism because it emphasizes promoting the good. Most natural law theorists, however, think that there are a wide variety of goods, unlike many consequentialists, who tend to reduce all goods to some one fundamentally good thing, such as pleasure. Aquinas mentions life, procreation, knowledge, society, and reasonable action as goods.[1] More recent natural law theorists offer even longer lists, including such things as justice, friendship, health, appreciation of beauty, play, religion, the natural world, achievement, family, and so on. Natural law theorists argue that we can recognize these things as goods by reflecting on human nature. For instance, all humans—and indeed all living things—have a natural instinct to protect and preserve their lives, from which we can infer that life is good and worthy of protection.

Like consequentialism, natural law theory says that acting rightly is ultimately about pursuing or promoting good things, but like deontology, it also says that there are constraints on how we may pursue or promote those goods. Natural law theorists argue that we can identify these constraints through careful reflection on principles of **practical reasoning**—that is, principles for reasoning about what to do. That is, some ways of pursuing the good are intrinsically unreasonable, and so it would be wrong to pursue the good in those ways. For instance, the most basic principle of practical reasoning (according to natural law theory and common sense) is that you should pursue good things and avoid bad things. If you intentionally destroy something good, such as a life, then you have violated that basic principle of practical reasoning. It is therefore morally wrong, according to natural law theory, to intentionally kill a human being, whether through homicide, abortion, euthanasia, or suicide. Furthermore, killing is wrong even if you're doing so in an attempt to pursue or promote some other good.[2] Some natural law theorists argue that there are other general principles that can help us identify the constraints on pursuing goods. For instance, the contemporary natural law theorist John Finnis argues that there is one more basic principle of practical reasoning—namely, that one should love one's neighbor as oneself—and that we can figure out whether some way of pursuing a good is morally permissible by asking whether it is consistent with loving one's neighbor as oneself. Other natural law theorists think that recognizing the constraints on pursuing the good requires the kind of practical wisdom that virtue ethicists emphasize. There is no abstract argument that will prove that certain kinds of actions are unreasonable, but someone with practical wisdom will recognize them as such. Such a person could then frame general rules, such as rules against lying and murder. However they identify these constraints, natural law theorists agree that acting rightly requires responding to good things in reasonable ways.

---

[1]Thomas Aquinas, *Summa Theologica* IaIIae 94, 2.

[2]This idea leads to the famous Doctrine of Double Effect, which we discussed in Chapter 6 (see p. 59).

Most natural law theorists add one more important element to the theory: the natural law, they hold, was established by God or some other divine force. Although the details differ from one version to the next, the basic idea is that the moral law derives from our human nature, and human nature was designed by God. Thus, by acting in accordance with our human nature, we are following the plan that God laid out for us and for the universe. This means that morality comes from God but is at least partly knowable without knowing about God. In other words, someone who does not believe in God can come to know and understand the moral law, even though, according to natural law theory, the moral law is ultimately given by God.

CONTRACTARIANISM AND CONTRACTUALISM

There is another kind of normative theory according to which the rules of morality follow from facts about what is good for people. This kind of normative theory, known as **contractarianism** (pronounced con-track-TAIR-ian-ism), starts from the idea that it is good for everyone if we all agree to restrain our pursuit of our own self-interests. According to contractarianism, morality is created by a **social contract** that people accept (or would accept) because it enables everyone to avoid the undesirable situation in which everyone is simply looking out for his or her own interests. This social contract is usually understood as a hypothetical agreement—a sort of thought experiment that explains where morality comes from or why it is rational for each of us to abide by the moral rules.

Most versions of contractarianism start with three key assumptions about what people are like in a (hypothetical) world without a social contract. (Such a world is sometimes referred to as a **state of nature.**) Specifically, contractarianism usually assumes that, in a state of nature, individuals would be self-interested, rational, and able to benefit from cooperating with others. They are self-interested in the sense that, while they care about themselves and, perhaps, their own friends and family, they have no concern for others' well-being; whether others are doing well or badly is simply not of interest to them. They are rational in the weak

---

THOMAS HOBBES

The English philosopher Thomas Hobbes (1588–1679) is widely regarded as the founder of modern contractarianism. Having lived through the English Civil War of 1642–1651, Hobbes came to regard a stable society as essential to living a decent life. In his book *Leviathan*, Hobbes argued that unless we all agree to rules that constrain our pursuit of our own self-interest, everyone's life would be "nasty, brutish, and short." Notoriously, Hobbes argues that these rules should grant absolute authority to the government.* It is worth noting that Hobbes's ethical views could be regarded as a kind of natural law theory, since he argues for his ethical and political principles on the basis of some basic facts about human nature.

---

* Thomas Hobbes, *Leviathan* (Oxford: Oxford University Press, 2009 [1651]).

sense that they can reason well about how best to get what they want. This is important because of the third assumption—that individuals can benefit from cooperating with one another. If you and I can make ourselves better off by cooperating with each other, and we are both good at reasoning about how to get what we want, then it makes sense—even from an entirely self-interested perspective—for us to find a way to cooperate. Thus, the contractarian's three assumptions about human nature suggest that, if they were in a state of nature, people would find a way to cooperate with one another.

If you and I are purely self-interested, rational people trying to find a way to cooperate, a good place to start would be an agreement not to harm one another. We might agree to a set of rules that prohibit killing each other, injuring each other, taking each other's things without permission, cheating each other, and so on. This explains or justifies an important set of moral obligations, such as the obligation not to harm, deceive, or steal from others, that serve to protect people from one another. Furthermore, each of us might benefit even more if we agree to further rules stating that, at least sometimes, people ought to help one another. For instance, it might be wise for me—from a purely self-interested perspective—to agree to a rule that requires me to give you food if you're starving, provided you agree to give *me* food if *I'm* starving. The fact that rules like this would benefit each of us explains or justifies other kinds of moral obligations, such as the obligation of beneficence (i.e., doing good to others). Finally, if several people have agreed to these rules, it might benefit each of us if there is a rule that requires each person to make amends (or suffer some punishment) if he or she breaks the rules. A rule like that inspires confidence that everyone else will follow the rules, which makes the agreement more stable. This explains or justifies obligations to make amends for wrongdoing. Thus, according to contractarianism, most of the things that morality requires turn out to be things that each of us would agree to in a state of nature, even if we were entirely self-interested.

An important variation on contractarianism, known as **contractualism,** drops the assumption that people are purely self-interested. It retains the idea that morality is explained or justified by an agreement among independent persons. Instead of basing the agreement on self-interest, contractualism bases the agreement on the desire to treat one another as free and equal persons deserving of respect. To do that, according to the contractualist, we need an agreement whose rules no one could reasonably reject. For instance, women could reasonably reject a rule that says that they must be subservient to men. Thus, if some people wanted to include that rule in the social contract, they would not be treating women as free and equal persons deserving of respect. Therefore, contractualism entails that the social contract cannot include such a rule. By contrast, no one could reasonably reject rules prohibiting murder or theft. So, the social contract includes rules like those.

THE ETHICS OF CARE

In contrast to contractarianism, which famously treats people as if they were "mushrooms . . . sprung out of the earth without any obligation one to another,"[3] the **ethics of care** emphasizes the moral importance of good caring interpersonal relationships. Instead of taking

---

[3] Robert Filmer, *Observations Concerning the Original and Varied Forms of Government* (London: RRC, 1696), I.iii.

agreements between independent, self-interested parties as the model for morality, as contractarians do, care ethicists model morality on interpersonal relationships—especially caring relationships, such as the relationship between a mother and her child. And instead of focusing on abstract, impartial, rational rules that are supposed to apply in every case, as contractarians do, care ethicists emphasize the importance of emotion and judgment in responding to the particular needs of particular people in particular situations.

While care ethicists disagree among themselves about how best to understand the ethics of care, some common themes run through the different versions of the theory. The most important is that acting morally involves **caring** for others, where caring for someone is a complicated mix of feelings and actions. Part of caring for someone, in the relevant sense, involves *skillfully taking care of* him or her. That is, it involves acting to satisfy their needs and promote their interests, nurturing their development, etc., and involves doing so in a way that is responsive to the details of a situation, rather than through the mechanical application of abstract rules. Since recognizing and responding to someone's particular needs requires emotional intelligence, care ethicists insist that emotion is central to moral thought; if we don't listen to our emotions, we can't tell what the right thing to do is in a particular situation, because we can't tell how best to care for the particular person or people we're dealing with. Another part of caring for someone, in the relevant sense, involves *caring about* him or her. That is, it involves having certain kinds of feelings for a person and being disposed to feel happy when the person is doing well, anxious when the person faces risks or challenges, and so on. It is not enough, therefore, to simply take care of someone—even if you do it skillfully. Because the ethics of care requires both a disposition to perform certain kinds of actions skillfully and having the right motivations for performing those actions, some care ethicists think of it as a kind of virtue ethics.

Many care ethicists, however, stress the importance of looking beyond individual virtues to recognize the value of caring relationships themselves. Caring relationships come in many forms. In some cases, as between friends or lovers, these relationships might be mutually caring, with each person caring for the other in various ways. In other cases, as between parents and young children, one person in the relationship is caring for the other, in the relevant sense of caring, but even then, if the relationship is a genuinely caring relationship, the one being cared for will respond appropriately by recognizing, appreciating, and, if possible, acknowledging the care. In other words, genuinely caring relationships cannot be one-sided. A woman who skillfully and lovingly takes care of her husband is not in a caring relationship if the husband fails to properly respect, appreciate, and respond to the emotional and physical work she does on his behalf. Because the ethics of care values caring relationships, and not just acts of caring, it calls for us to encourage and sustain genuinely caring relationships, but it discourages people from sustaining a relationship that is exploitative, hostile, or destructive; doing so is a way of failing to care for oneself.

One major theoretical question in the ethics of care is about the uneasy relationship between care and justice. Care is primarily about interpersonal relationships with particular others, and it requires us to prioritize some people over others; justice is primarily about broader, social issues, and it requires us to treat everyone impartially. Different care ethicists explain the relationship differently, with some saying that care and justice are separate but equal values and others saying that respecting justice is part of extending care into broader social issues. Those who take the latter approach emphasize that when we care about several people—as, for instance, parents might care (equally) about each of their children—part of caring for them involves treating them fairly and equally. Thus, they argue, justice is simply one aspect of caring.

CONFUCIAN ETHICS

The ethics of care is only a few decades old, but in many ways it echoes one of the oldest traditions in moral philosophy: **Confucian ethics,** based on the teachings of the ancient Chinese philosopher Confucius (known in Chinese as Kongzi) and his followers, especially Mencius (known in Chinese as Mengzi).

The three central concepts in Confucian ethics are *rén,* which is often translated as good-ness, human-heartedness, or benevolence; *yì,* which is variously translated as righteousness, integrity, or justice; and *lǐ,* which is usually translated as ritual or ritual propriety. In the case of *rén* and *lǐ,* these translations can be a bit misleading, however, so it's often best to treat *rén* and *lǐ* as technical terms, rather than trying to translate them into English.

In Confucian ethics, *rén* is both a specific virtue related to benevolence toward others and the overarching virtue of the perfect person. The more specific virtue of *rén,* which is partly captured by the English word "benevolence," has two main aspects. First, it involves using an empathetic understanding of others' feelings to refrain from doing to them what you would not want done to yourself. Second, it involves conscientiously doing one's best to help others—especially in the sense of helping others to become more virtuous, just as you yourself (should) want to become more virtuous. More broadly, the person who has the virtue of *rén* in its overarching sense behaves correctly and virtuously in all of his or her interactions with other people; it is with this broader sense in mind that *rén* is sometimes translated as goodness.

If *rén* grows out of empathy for others, *yì* or integrity grows out of a sense of shame. Having the virtue of integrity requires doing what is right for its own sake, rather than for the sake of personal gain or some other ulterior motive. This complements *rén* in the following way: A benevolent person would treat others well out of a kind of love—that is, because they are motivated to promote the other person's well-being. A person of integrity would treat others well out of a sense of respect for others—that is, because they would be ashamed to fail to treat others appropriately. These two motivations can coexist, of course, so that someone can act out of both benevolence and integrity.

MENCIUS

For centuries, aspiring Chinese scholars had to study four ancient books in order to earn a position in the government bureaucracy. The *Analects* of Confucius was on the list; so were the collected sayings of Mencius (372–289 BCE), a student of Confucius's grandson. Mencius developed Confucian ethics in important ways, and, like Confucius, he spent his life trying to convince rulers to follow certain moral and political principles. He famously argued that human nature is good, meaning, roughly, that given the proper environment in which to grow, humans will naturally develop into virtuous people.*

---

* For details of Mencius's ethical thought, see the excerpts from *The Essential Mengzi,* reprinted in Part V of this book (pp. 205–16).

Perhaps the most distinctive element of Confucian ethics is its emphasis on *lǐ*. Originally, *lǐ* referred to formal ceremonies, such as government ceremonies or ceremonial sacrifices to the gods. In the Confucian tradition, it is important to perform such ceremonies according to tradition and with the right attitude; simply going through the motions doesn't count. For a modern equivalent, consider the traditions surrounding a ceremony like the singing of a national anthem: Tradition requires people to stand if they can, be silent and attentive, hold their hands over their hearts, and so on. But even someone who does all of these things can be "doing it wrong" if they roll their eyes, scowl, or feel annoyed at being interrupted by what they are doing; those things are thought to reveal an inappropriate lack of reverence for one's country. Over time, *lǐ* came to refer more generally to all conventions or traditions concerning interactions between people. For a modern example, consider how you greet someone. In Western societies, at least, traditional greetings involve handshakes or, for those you know well, a hug or a kiss. These traditional forms of interaction would count as *lǐ* in this broader sense. And as with the formal ceremonies, there are conventions about how and when you perform them, even if it is hard to put those conventions into words. A handshake can be firm and enthusiastic, limp and uninterested, or aggressively bone-crushing. Refusing to shake hands sometimes signals disrespect or contempt. A hug can be celebratory, macho, loving, or creepy. A kiss on the cheek can signal affection; a kiss withheld can signal anger or annoyance. Less intimately, consider conventions about how a server at a restaurant places food on the table. Placing a dish carefully in front of someone and saying, "I hope you enjoy it," signals respect and concern for the person's happiness; dropping it unceremoniously on the table and grunting, "Food's here," signals the opposite. In Confucian ethics, interacting with other people appropriately—that is, mastering *rén* in its broader sense—requires performing all of these interactions appropriately. That is, it requires a kind of easy but genuinely felt social grace. Someone who fails to perform *lǐ* correctly either doesn't recognize what the right thing to do is in a particular situation, doesn't have the proper feelings about it, or, at least, fails to communicate those feelings when it is important to do so.

Confucians understand all three of these concepts—*rén*, *yì*, and *lǐ*—through the lens of five kinds of relationships, which are taken as models for all relationships between people: ruler–subject, parent–child, elder sibling–younger sibling, husband–wife, and friend–friend. Except for the relationship between friends, each of these relationships is understood in the Confucian tradition to be asymmetrical. For instance, a parent's benevolence toward his or her child will take a very different form than the child's benevolence toward his or her parents. So, what you ought to do in any given situation depends on the specific relationship you have with people with whom you are interacting and on which role you play in that relationship. To return to the example of greetings, imagine that you've just met the president of the United States. Demonstrating a proper level of respect for the president would require offering a formal handshake and saying something like, "It's an honor to meet you." The president, by contrast, could demonstrate a different kind of respect for you with a less formal greeting that puts you at ease and makes you feel appreciated as an individual person, rather than just a face in the crowd. As this example illustrates, Confucian ethics calls for a careful, skillful responsiveness to the context of your actions and a deep concern for the specific people with whom you are interacting. Certain aspects of Confucian ethics can therefore be understood as requiring careful attention to various role-based obligations.

UBUNTU

Much as Confucian ethics presages the ethics of care in emphasizing appropriate concern for and interaction with particular people, many important traditions of African moral thought presage care ethicists' emphasis on the importance of good relationships. Some contemporary African philosophers have described the common thread in these traditions as the "ethics of **ubuntu**." In the Zulu and Xhosa languages of southern Africa, the word *ubuntu* means "human-ness." To have *ubuntu* is therefore to be human. But as with similar words in other languages—such as *mensch* in Yiddish or *onipa* and *eniyan* in the Akan and Yoruba languages of West Africa—the word *ubuntu* is not just about being biologically human. It has important normative connotations. To say that someone has *ubuntu* is to say that he or she has a morally good character—that he or she is a good person or exhibits human excellence. Thus, the morally best life is a life that best realizes *ubuntu*.

The contemporary ethics of *ubuntu* is a reconstruction of a very common theme in various cultures that are indigenous to sub-Saharan Africa. As with other normative theories, such as utilitarianism or deontology or Confucianism, it's best to think of the ethics of *ubuntu* as a family of theories, with many different African thinkers and different cultures embracing different versions of a recognizably common approach. Of course, even though the ethics of *ubuntu* captures a dominant theme in sub-Saharan thought, Africa is a vast and diverse place, and so some African thinkers and cultures hold views that are not recognizable as an ethics of *ubuntu*.

Many of the cultures that embrace an ethics of *ubuntu* have a saying along these lines: "A person is a person through other persons." This means that becoming a "real person" or living a genuinely human life requires acting so as to produce social harmony within your society. At a bare minimum, this entails many of the standard moral obligations implied by any other plausible normative theory—for example, that it is generally wrong to kill, to deceive, to steal, to break promises, and so on. As philosopher Thaddeus Metz explains it, however, promoting social harmony also involves two additional requirements that make the ethics of *ubuntu* distinctive: promoting social harmony involves promoting and honoring a sense of **shared identity** grounded in a particular kind of good will or **solidarity.**[4] Each of these two parts requires a bit of explanation.

A community has (or ideally should have) a sense of shared identity, in the relevant sense, to the extent that its members both regard themselves as members of a group that shares some important values, goals, and projects. To identify with such a group is to regard yourself has having various ethical obligations, responsibilities, rights, and privileges that arise from the collective aim of pursuing those goals and projects. Each individual is a member of many overlapping communities. You, for instance, are a member of a particular (extended) family; of a member of the larger set of relatives that include the extended families of your more distant family members, such as your grandmother's cousins; and so on, all the way out to the largest relevant group of which you are a member—namely, the human race. To reject the obligations and responsibilities associated with one of those communities is to reject your membership in that community, and vice versa. (Think, for instance, of Krusty the Clown's father in *The Simpsons*, who, outraged at his son's career choice, tells Bart, "I have no son!" Krusty's father doesn't mean this literally; rather, he means that he has rejected his identity as his son's father and, in doing so, rejected the obligations that come with being

---

[4] Thaddeus Metz, "Toward an African Moral Theory," *Journal of Political Philosophy* 15 (2007): 321–41.

someone's father.[5]) In general, promoting social harmony within your communities involves acting so as to enhance your own and others' sense that they belong to the group and share the obligations, responsibilities, rights, and privileges that arise from membership in that community; undermining that sense of belonging, either in yourself or another member of the community, undermines social harmony and demonstrates a failure to honor that social harmony as morally important. In addition to the commonplace moral obligations discussed above, this part of promoting and honoring social harmony also involves participating in and perpetuating the rituals, traditions, and cooperative social life of your community.

Acting out of good will, in the relevant sense, requires treating the fact that a fellow community member (or potential community member) needs help as a (very strong) reason for you to help that person. That is, you treat other people's problems as your problems, especially (but not only) when those other people are members of the groups with which you most strongly identify, such as your family. What makes such helpful behavior an act of good will, however, is the motivation for doing it. If the motivation is simply that you expect that helping others now will make them more likely to help you in the future, you are not acting out of good will. Instead, acting of good will requires helping others with their problems out of genuine concern for their well-being—helping them out of love, in a broad sense of the term.

Another important element of the ethics of *ubuntu* arises from the combination of valuing a shared identity and good will. The ethics of *ubuntu* places great value on harmonizing the interests of a society. A society, almost by definition, has some common interests. But even so, the interests of individual community members will sometimes come into conflict. If the community's members are to continue to identify with one another and share good will toward one another, it is important to find ways to resolve such conflicts in ways that satisfy everyone involved. This creates some distinctive contrasts with many Western views. For instance, whereas many Western normative theories entail that wrongdoers should be punished, either because they deserve it or because punishment will deter other would-be wrongdoers, the ethics of *ubuntu* sees that sort of punishment as divisive and destructive of social harmony. Thus, in the ethics of *ubuntu*, the preferred response to wrongdoing is reconciliation, with the goal of restoring harmony and especially good will between the wrongdoers and their victims.

In the ethics of *ubuntu*, a person who promotes and honors social harmony in these ways is said to be a "real person," much as a nineteenth-century Englishman might compliment another man for his outstanding moral character by calling him a "true gentleman." By contrast, someone who fails to do these things—someone who rejects his or her responsibilities to his or her society, acts selfishly or with inadequate regard for other's needs, or acts in ways that are destructive of his or her community—degrades himself or herself as a person, becoming "not a real person." And that, of course, is not a compliment.

TERMINOLOGY TO KNOW

natural law theory	ethics of care	*ubuntu*
practical reasoning	caring	shared identity
contractarianism	Confucian ethics	(in *ubuntu*)
social contract	*rén*	solidarity (in *ubuntu*)
state of nature	*yì* (righteousness)	
contractualism	*lǐ* (rites; ritual propriety)	

---

[5] "Like Father, Like Son," *The Simpsons*, FOX, October 24, 1991.

DISCUSSION QUESTIONS

1. Does natural law theory violate Hume's Law against deriving claims about what ought to be the case from claims about what is the case? Why or why not?

2. One central idea of contractarianism is that each person is better off if everyone follows some rules that constrain their pursuit of self-interest. Many philosophers have worried, however, about the person who thinks that as long as everyone else is obeying the rules, he or she would be better off by breaking the rules whenever he or she can get away with it. What, if anything, could the contractarian say to convince such a person that he or she should follow the moral rules?

3. Some critics of Confucian ethics worry that its emphasis on traditional rituals in social interaction makes it unduly conservative. Is this a valid criticism of Confucian ethics? Why or why not?

4. Whereas certain traditions in Western moral philosophy emphasize treating all persons equally and impartially, some of the theories discussed in this chapter encourage people to put the interests of their own social groups above those of others. Which theories do this? Is this a problem for those theories? Why or why not?

CASE STUDIES

See the Note About Case Studies on p. 150 for further instructions, but note that the case studies in this chapter specifically ask you to base your argument on one of the normative theories discussed above.

1. When doctors diagnosed 22-year-old single mother Christine Royles with an autoimmune disease, they added her to a list of people who needed a kidney transplant. Since that list had over 100,000 people on it, Royles decided to look for a donor herself. A complete stranger, Josh Dall-Leighton, saw Royles's advertisement on her car window and decided to donate his kidney to her. Doctors successfully performed the transplant later that year. Using one of the normative theories described in this chapter, evaluate Dall-Leighton's act of donating his kidney to a stranger. Give an argument, based on the normative theory you've chosen, to support your evaluation.

2. Christ Stoltzfoos ran a hardware store in Christiana, Pennsylvania. In keeping with the customs of his Amish community, Stoltzfoos avoided the trappings of modern life, refusing to use electric lights, cars, and so on. And like his fellow Amish, Stoltzfoos refused to interact with people whom the Amish community had officially decided to "shun" for violating those customs. For instance, Stoltzfoos would not permit people to shop in his store if they had been officially shunned. The Amish say that shunning is a way to pressure people to return to the community and accept the community's customs again. Using one of the normative theories described in this chapter, evaluate Stoltzfoos's practice of shunning those who have been officially declared to have violated Amish custom. Give an argument, based on the normative theory you've chosen, to support your evaluation.

3. According to prosecutors in Washington State, when State Trooper Daniel Tindall learned that his 18-year-old son, Wyatt, had repeatedly vandalized a classmate's family's car, he decided to help destroy evidence of his son's crime. Responding to a tip from the car's owner, police showed Tindall surveillance footage showing a masked teenager vandalizing the car. Tindall denied that the teenager was his son. Prosecutors claim that Tindall then found the clothing and ski mask that his son had worn in the video, hid the clothing, and burned the mask. Using one of the normative theories described in this chapter, evaluate Tindall's (alleged) action of covering up the evidence of his son's crime.

4. In Shakespeare's *Romeo and Juliet*, set in Italy in the 1500s, Romeo and Juliet fall in love despite their families' deep hatred for each other. Even though it will predictably lead to great tension between their families and probably even bloodshed, Romeo and Juliet decide to marry each other. Using one of the normative theories described in this chapter, evaluate Romeo and Juliet's action of getting married despite their families' mutual hatred. Give an argument, based on the normative theory you've chosen, to support your evaluation.

PART IV

Appendices

Appendix 1 } How to Write an Ethics Paper

On the Internet, controversy gets clicks. Perhaps that's why *Slate*'s education columnist Rebecca Schuman never shies away from controversy. Venting her frustrations in an angry, disdainful article in 2013, Schuman argued that professors should stop assigning papers in required courses. She claimed that students hate writing them, instructors hate grading them, and they don't help students learn anything anyway. So, she concluded, we should just replace them with exams.[1]

Schuman's essay touched a nerve in both students and instructors, eliciting hundreds of online responses. Many of the responses blasted Schuman's disrespect for her students. Some implied (or said) that Schuman's frustrations came from poorly designed writing assignments. Others suggested that the way to save the college essay is by being sure that students have the support they need to write good essays. In that spirit, this appendix aims to help you write a good argumentative essay about a moral issue.

THE GOALS OF AN ETHICS PAPER

Two years after Schuman published her end-of-semester rant against essays, writing professor John Warner published a blog post explaining why his first-year writing course didn't fully prepare students to write excellent papers in other courses. One issue, Warner suggests, is that each academic discipline (e.g., history, philosophy, sociology) requires something a little different from student papers. Without clear guidance about a discipline's goals and requirements, students often feel unsure about how to proceed.[2] That's why the first step in writing a good ethics paper is understanding the goal(s) of an argumentative essay in applied ethics.

For most essays in applied ethics, the main goal is to provide a strong, well-developed argument for a clear answer to a well-defined question about the morality of a particular (kind of) action.[3] If you browse through the essays in the back of this book, you'll notice that many

---

[1]Rebecca Schuman, "The End of the College Essay," *Slate*, December 13, 2013, http://www.slate.com/articles/life/education/2013/12/college_papers_students_hate_writing_them_professors_hate_grading_them_let.html.

[2]John Warner, "I Cannot Prepare Students to Write Their (History, Philosophy, Sociology, Poli Sci., etc. . . . .) Papers," *Inside Higher Ed*, December 15, 2015, https://www.insidehighered.com/blogs/just-visiting/i-cannot-prepare-students-write-their-history-philosophy-sociology-poly-sci-etc.

[3]Some essays will evaluate something other than an action—say, a person, policy, or institution. This appendix sticks to talking about "actions" for simplicity, but everything it says applies just as much to essays about the morality of other kinds of things.

of them share this goal. You should complete two parts of this three-part goal—namely, stating a "clear answer" to a "well-defined question"—in your introduction, which we'll discuss below. We'll examine the remaining part of the goal—namely, the "strong, well-developed argument"—in the sections on presenting your main argument and handling objections.

Essays in applied ethics sometimes have other goals. One common goal is to evaluate a particular argument for a specific conclusion. For instance, many philosophers have written papers about abortion whose main goal is not to say whether abortion is permissible or not but simply to criticize or defend the arguments presented in Judith Jarvis Thomson's "A Defense of Abortion." Other possible goals include: showing that taking a particular position on one topic, such as abortion, commits you to a particular position on some other topic, such as animal rights; showing that accepting a particular moral theory, such as those we explore in Chapters 11 and 12, would commit you to a particular answer to some moral question; or showing that certain moral principles, such as the principle that it is always better to mislead than to lie, are correct or incorrect. In every case, however, the key to writing a good ethics paper is to provide a strong, well-developed argument for a particular conclusion; the variations in this paragraph simply change what kind of conclusion you're arguing for.

Many of the papers you've written in high school or in other college courses have probably required something a little different. In high school, for instance, your teachers may have asked you to write papers that simply report all of the information you learned about a particular topic, such as the American Revolution or Martin Luther King Jr. Your English teachers may have required you to analyze a novel or poem, interpreting what the author was trying to say, explaining the symbolism in a poem, and so on. Your history teachers may have asked you to explain what caused some event, such as the fall of the Soviet Union. Some of these teachers may have asked you to argue for a particular claim, some may not; all of them probably asked you to do things that aren't necessary (or even helpful) in a philosophy paper. For instance, adhering too slavishly to the "five-paragraph essay" format commonly taught in high school is almost certainly unnecessary and quite likely unhelpful. Use as many paragraphs as you need to get the job done. If you're unsure about whether a rule you learned in a different class applies in your philosophy courses, ask your instructor. Your instructor will understand your concern best if you say something like, "My history professor asked us to do such-and-such in our papers. Is that important in a philosophy paper, too?"

Understanding what your essay is supposed to accomplish is a good start. Understanding some common parts of an ethics paper will help, too. The rest of this appendix walks through some of the key parts of a good ethics paper as well as a few comments about using quotations, citing sources, and academic writing style.

WRITING YOUR INTRODUCTION

Since the beginning of time, college students have been mystified about what to write in the introductions to their papers. As a result, they sometimes write sentences like the last one—clichéd opening lines that bore readers and make instructors cry. Fortunately, writing a good introduction isn't that hard if you have some guidance.

A good introduction should do two things: it should get your reader interested in what you're going to say, and then it should give them a clear idea of what you're going to say. Let's look at each of these requirements in order.

Getting your reader interested in what you have to say involves grabbing your reader's attention at the beginning and, if necessary, explaining why your topic is worth reading about. The kinds of clichés and broad generalizations that open many essays—such as claims about things that have happened "since the beginning of time" or platitudes about what things are like "in this day and age"—won't grab anybody's attention. There are many other approaches that do a better job. Here are three of them, with examples based on philosopher Tom Dougherty's essay, "Sex, Lies, and Consent," in which Dougherty argues that it is morally wrong to deceive someone in order to have sex with that person.[4] One approach is to start with a surprising or interesting fact. Dougherty, for instance, opens by noting that, on average, people on dating sites exaggerate their height by two inches and their income by $20,000.[5] (If you start with a surprising fact, be sure to cite your source, as Dougherty does!) Another approach is to give an example or tell a very short anecdote, based on real life or works of fiction, that illustrates an important aspect of your topic. Later in his paper, Dougherty cites an example from *The Three Musketeers* in which one of the characters, Milady de Winter, mistakes the main character, d'Artagnan, for her lover in a darkened room. D'Artagnan takes advantage of Milady's mistake to have sex with her.[6] Dougherty could easily have opened with this example, pointing out that in cases like that, deceiving someone in order to have sex is clearly wrong. If these options seem too gimmicky to you, you can always start your essay with a bold or pithy statement of your main conclusion. For instance, a few paragraphs into his paper, Dougherty writes, "Deceiving someone into sex is wrong."[7] He could have started with that sentence—or with the catchier phrase from a few lines earlier: "Lying to get laid is wrong." You can find other ways to start your introduction by paying attention to the opening lines of the essays in the back of this book.

Telling your reader what you're going to say in the essay means both stating your main conclusion and summarizing your argument for it. (Some instructors use the term **thesis statement** to mean "the statement of your main conclusion." Others use it to include *both* the statement of your main conclusion *and* the summary of your argument for that conclusion. On either meaning, you'll want to include a thesis statement in your introduction.) You don't need to go into a great amount of detail about your argument here, but after reading your introduction, your reader should be able to clearly state what question your essay is trying to answer, what answer you give to that question, and roughly what your reasons are for giving that answer. Even if you've done a lot of work beforehand to figure out what you want to say, your arguments might evolve as you write your essay. Therefore, you may want to write the introduction last—or at least come back and revise it after you've finished the essay, so that the introduction accurately reflects the rest of the paper.

---

[4]Tom Dougherty, "Sex, Lies, and Consent," *Ethics* 123 (2013): 717–44; reprinted in Part V of this volume (pp. 233–51).
[5]Dougherty, "Sex, Lies, and Consent," 717.
[6]Dougherty, "Sex, Lies, and Consent," 724.
[7]Dougherty, "Sex, Lies, and Consent," 718.

DEFINING KEY TERMS AND GIVING BACKGROUND INFORMATION

Depending on your topic, you might need to define some of the terms you'll use in your argument or provide background information about your topic. Sometimes you can do these things in the course of presenting your main argument. But when defining your terms requires a lot of careful distinctions or when you need to give a lot of background information, you might want to do it all at once, right after the introduction to your paper.

Defining the important terms in your argument ensures that your readers know what you're talking about. It also ensures that your readers know what you're *not* talking about. For instance, in arguing that the military sometimes has a moral obligation to use drones for military operations, philosopher Bradley Strawser specifies that, when talking about "drones," he means "uninhabited remote controlled weapons . . . which are under human control for, at the minimum, any particular lethal action the machine executes," and that he is "[p]rimarily . . . referencing those aircraft presently employed by the United States (and other) militaries."[8] Not only does this introduce the concept of a drone to readers who might not be familiar with it, it clearly excludes "fully autonomous" weapons that can "decide" for themselves when to kill someone. That's important because fully autonomous weapons raise more complicated moral issues; by defining his terms carefully, Strawser can avoid those issues.

Sometimes you'll need to spend even more time defining your terms in order to carefully distinguish your topic from closely related topics. In discussing physician-assisted suicide, for instance, Susan Wolf devotes several paragraphs to defining physician-assisted suicide and distinguishing it from similar concepts, such as euthanasia and terminal sedation.[9] This ensures that readers know exactly what Wolf is talking about in her arguments.

Just as the topic of your paper affects how much space you'll devote to defining key terms, it also affects how much background information you'll need to give. If your topic is especially technical (e.g., the ethics of genetic enhancement), your readers might need some background information just to understand your argument. If your topic is something that is changing rapidly (e.g., self-driving cars), you might need to bring your readers up to speed on the latest news. Third, if your topic is well known in some social circles but not well known in others (e.g., the ethics of "hook-up culture" on college campuses, about which older readers may know very little), you might need to provide a lot of background information. Finally, if your topic is one about which many people are misinformed or one where people disagree about the relevant descriptive facts (e.g., climate change), you'll want to explain the descriptive facts as you see them. That way, you can dispel misinformation—or at least help your readers understand where you're coming from.

---

[8]Bradley J. Strawser, "Moral Predators: The Duty to Employ Uninhabited Aerial Vehicles," *Journal of Military Ethics* 9 (2010): 342–68; reprinted in Part V of this book (pp. 447–67).

[9]Susan M. Wolf, "Physician-Assisted Suicide," *Clinics in Geriatric Medicine* 21 (2005): 179–92; reprinted in Part V of this book (pp. 342–52).

Don't go overboard in presenting background information. Remember, unlike many other papers that you may have written, the point of an ethics paper is not to tell your readers everything about your topic. The point is to present a well-developed argument for a particular conclusion. Therefore, you should only give as much background information as your readers need in order to understand your argument. A piece of information is necessary only if your readers need it to understand what a premise means, evaluate whether the premise is true, or see why the premise is relevant to the conclusion. Until you've written out your argument, you may not know exactly what information your readers will need. So, as with the introduction, you might want to write this section of the paper after you write the rest of the essay—or come back and revise the section after writing your main argument, adding any important information that's missing and deleting information that turns out to be unnecessary.

Since you'll only be presenting background information when your readers may not know—or may doubt—that information, it's essential that you back up each piece of information by citing reputable sources.

To find examples of effective presentations of background information, look for philosophical essays on very technical topics. For instance, in discussing the ethics of climate change, Sarah Krakoff spends several pages explaining the causes and effects of climate change. Presenting such thorough background information helps readers understand Krakoff's argument and helps dispel widely held misconceptions.[10] Look at her essay to see how she does it and how she cites her sources. By contrast, Walter Sinnott-Armstrong, also writing on climate change, introduces just the most essential background information for his topic.[11] (But notice how much more effectively Krakoff supports her claims by citing her sources!) While this won't achieve everything that Krakoff's more careful presentation does, it does give readers the information on which Sinnott-Armstrong bases his argument—and it leaves far more space for the arguments that are the real centerpiece of his essay.

PRESENT THE MAIN ARGUMENT(S) FOR YOUR CONCLUSION

The most important part of your essay presents the main argument(s) for your conclusion. The key to writing a really good ethics paper is to offer well-developed arguments. This requires putting a good deal of thought into your argument(s) *before* you write the first draft of your paper. If you've followed the method for moral reasoning described in Chapter 8, you've probably already done much of this work.

A **well-developed argument** is one in which each premise is clearly explained and well supported. "Developing" an argument means, first, explaining each premise clearly enough that your readers can understand exactly what you're claiming and, second, giving your readers good reasons to accept any premise that they might doubt. Sometimes you can support

---

[10]Sarah Krakoff, "Parenting the Planet," in *The Ethics of Global Climate Change*, ed. Denis G. Arnold (Cambridge, U.K.: Cambridge University Press, 2011), 145–69; reprinted in Part V of this book (pp. 546–61).
[11]Walter Sinnott-Armstrong, "It's Not My Fault! Global Warming and Individual Moral Obligations," in *Perspectives on Climate Change*, ed. Walter Sinnott-Armstrong and Richard Howards (Amsterdam: Elsevier, 2005), 221–53; reprinted in Part V of this book (pp. 521–35).

your premises by citing a reputable source. This works best for premises that make purely descriptive claims. For many normative premises, however, you will need to offer a moral argument.

Exactly how you present your main argument(s) is up to you. You might find it most effective to present the basic argument as a list of numbered premises, like many of the arguments discussed in this book. Then you can explain the various claims and present arguments for contentious premises afterward. Tom Dougherty takes that approach in "Sex, Lies, and Consent," introducing his main argument in the paper's first section and using the following sections to support each of its premises.[12] Skim that paper, in Part V of this book, to see how he does it. Alternatively, you might prefer to present the whole argument in paragraph form, clarifying and supporting each of the main premises as you go. Don Marquis takes this approach in "Why Abortion Is Immoral," explaining and arguing for each premise as he presents his main argument.[13] Skim Section II of that paper, in Part V of this book, to see how he does it.

EXPLAIN OBJECTIONS AND MEET THEM

No matter how strong your main arguments are, readers will undoubtedly have objections to them—that is, arguments *against* your arguments.[14] Developing your arguments also requires you to discuss and respond to these objections. If you've followed the method of moral reasoning presented in Chapter 8, you'll already have a long list of objections to your arguments. You don't need to present *all* of those in your paper. Instead, focus on objections that are either very common or particularly powerful—that is, objections that will or should cause many readers to question your arguments.

Some people discuss objections as they present their main arguments. For instance, in "Lifeboat Earth," Onora Nell draws an analogy between Earth and a well-stocked lifeboat to argue that people in wealthy countries have an obligation to donate money to fight global poverty. Immediately after presenting this analogy, she considers an objection about the differences between the Earth and a lifeboat. She explicitly introduces the objection by saying, "Some may object to the metaphor 'lifeboat Earth.' "[15] This ensures that the reader understands that she is merely expressing someone else's objection, rather than agreeing with it. Having introduced the objection, she then presents it as a complete argument: On a lifeboat, the objection goes, it is wrong for some people to hoard food and water because each person on the boat has an equal claim to the food and water on it. In the case of Earth as a whole, however, people do not have an equal claim on the world's resources, and so those who choose to keep their property rather than give it away are not acting wrongly.[16]

---

[12]Dougherty, "Sex, Lies, and Consent," 720*ff*.

[13]Don Marquis, "Why Abortion Is Immoral," *Journal of Philosophy* 86 (1989): 183–202; reprinted in Part V of this book (pp. 320–31).

[14]If you haven't read the section on "Objections" in Chapter 8, you should read it before continuing this section! (See pp. 82–85.)

[15]Onora Nell, "Lifeboat Earth," *Philosophy & Public Affairs* 4 (1975): 273–92; reprinted in Part V of this book (pp. 498–507).

[16]Nell, "Lifeboat Earth," 279.

Other authors wait to discuss objections until after they have presented their main argument. Sometimes they devote an entire section of the essay to discussing objections. For examples, take a quick look in Part V at Strawser's paper on drone warfare, Xiaofei Liu's paper on racial preferences on dating sites, or John Broome's chapter on ethics and climate change.[17] Because they wait to discuss objections until later in their essays, they can offer long, careful responses to each objection without interrupting the flow of their main argument.

Whichever way you choose to present your objections, remember that an objection is an *argument*, with its own premises and conclusion. It's often tempting to describe the objection in just a sentence or two so that you can move on to showing what's wrong with the objection. For instance, Nell might have just said, "Some may object to the metaphor 'lifeboat Earth' because it ignores the issue of property rights," and then jumped into her response. Doing so, however, would leave it up to the readers to figure out exactly how the objection works, which can leave them unsure about whether you've successfully responded to the objection. Even worse, failing to present the entire objection can leave *you* unsure about exactly how the objection works, in which case you might not give an adequate response. Again, take a look at the essays in Part V to see how they lay out objections as complete arguments.

Once you've presented an objection, you'll need to respond to it in some way. The most direct way to respond to an objection is to show what's wrong with it—that is, to point out some flaw in the argument. To see how this works, let's look at a detailed example from Strawser's essay on military drones. After arguing that militaries are morally obligated to use drones (rather than other methods) to carry out attacks, Strawser considers the following objection:

SLIPPERY SLOPE OBJECTION TO DRONES

1. It is morally forbidden to use fully autonomous weapons—that is, weapons (including drones) that can "decide" to use lethal force on their own.
2. Using drones to carry out attacks will eventually lead to the use of fully autonomous weapons.

∴ 3 It is morally forbidden to use drones to carry out attacks.[18]

If this objection is cogent, then Strawser's main conclusion is false, since militaries can't be obligated to use drones if they are forbidden from using them. Strawser replies to this objection by arguing that the second premise is unsupported and therefore unreliable.[19] Since the argument doesn't work without that premise, Strawser's reply successfully **rebuts** the objection—that is, it shows that the argument fails.

Occasionally, you'll find an objection to your argument that does not seem to have any flaws. In that case, you have three options, though each is problematic in its own way. The first is to admit that the objection provides a good reason to deny your conclusion but argue that your main argument provides an even stronger reason to accept your conclusion. But if you do this, be prepared to *argue* that your argument is stronger than the objection; simply saying so isn't enough. Another approach is to modify your conclusion slightly to

---

[17]See: Strawser, "Moral Predators" (pp. 447–67 in this volume); Xiaofei Liu, " 'No Fats, Femmes, or Asians'," *Moral Philosophy and Politics* 2 (2015): 255–76, reprinted in Part V of this book (pp. 299–313); John Broome, *Climate Matters: Ethics in a Warming World* (New York: W. W. Norton, 2012): 73–96, reprinted in Part V of this book (pp. 535–46).

[18]Strawser, "Moral Predators," 349.

[19]Strawser, "Moral Predators," 349–51.

accommodate the objection. This works only if the objection points out a rather minor prob-lem with your conclusion, so that you only need to introduce a little bit of nuance to avoid the objection. If you're going to take this approach, though, you should ask yourself whether you can't just go back and use the more nuanced conclusion from the beginning of the essay. (Sometimes you'll have a good reason; often you won't, in which case you can simply go back and revise your original conclusion.) The third approach is a bit more drastic. It only becomes necessary if none of the previous approaches works—that is, if the objection pro-vides a compelling reason to reject your conclusion and you cannot sidestep the objection by making minor changes to your conclusion. In that case, you'll need to rewrite your essay with a very different conclusion. If you've used the method of moral reasoning presented in Chapter 8, this usually won't be necessary, since you should have already picked the conclu-sion that was best supported by arguments, but sometimes you discover a new argument in the process of writing and realize that your conclusion was incorrect or unsupported. In that case, there's nothing to do but rewrite your essay.

WRITING A CONCLUDING SECTION

A concluding paragraph or section gives you a chance to drive home the main points that you want your readers to take away from your essay. In general, this isn't the place to introduce new ideas; it's certainly not the place to introduce new arguments. One simple approach to writing your concluding paragraph is to reiterate the main argument and restate the main conclusion. To see a nice example of this approach, skim Anne Eaton's "A Sensible Anti-porn Feminism" in Part V and then look at her last paragraph to see how it concisely restates her arguments and conclusion. A different approach is to comment on what your paper's argument means for how readers should live their lives. For an example of this approach, skim Peter Singer's "Famine, Affluence, and Morality" in Part V and then read his last two paragraphs.

QUOTING, PARAPHRASING, AND PLAGIARIZING

When writing an ethics paper, you will often use or engage with other people's ideas. Some-times you'll use an argument that someone else came up with. Sometimes you'll need to state someone else's view so that you can disagree with it or use their argument as an objec-tion to your own argument. When you use someone else's ideas in your essay, you can either quote that person or you can paraphrase or summarize that person's ideas. A **quotation** restates someone else's ideas in that person's own words, surrounded by quotation marks (if it's short) or set off as a block quote (if it's more than a few lines). **Paraphrasing** someone, by contrast, means restating their ideas in your own words.

Every time you use someone else's ideas, whether in a quotation or when paraphrasing, you *must* cite that person's work. If you do not cite that person's work, you are committing

plagiarism, which is passing off someone's else work or ideas as your own. Plagiarism is dishonest and deceptive; not only does it fail to give credit where credit is due, but it misleads your readers into thinking that you came up with something that you didn't and, sometimes, that you understand something that you don't. In an academic context, this is fraud. That said, a great deal of plagiarism is accidental; it occurs because some students aren't sure when or how to cite their sources. See the next section in this appendix for tips on citing other people's work.

Use quotations only when you have to. When writing an ethics paper, there are only a few cases when it is worth quoting another person's words directly. (You'll notice that the papers in the back of this book rarely quote other people, even when they're discussing their ideas.) The first case in which it's worth quoting someone is when you need to show that the other person *really said* what you're claiming they said. This is most important when you are criticizing that person's claims and you want to show that you're not misrepresenting what he or she said. The second is when the other person's words are unclear and you want to discuss various interpretations of what that person said. The third is when the other person has already expressed an idea so clearly and so concisely that attempting to paraphrase it only makes it longer. The fourth is when the other person has phrased an idea in an especially original or interesting way, which you think is worth sharing with your readers. In disciplines other than philosophy, you may have other reasons to use quotations (e.g., as evidence in a history paper or as an authoritative source on a technical matter), but if your quotations don't fall under one of the four cases above, think hard about whether there's a good reason to use the source's exact words.

When you do quote someone else, don't just switch from your own words to someone else's and then leave the quote to speak for itself. Instead, introduce the quotation using phrases like "Thomson writes . . ." or "Marquis argues. . . ." And once you've quoted someone, explain the quotation's meaning (if necessary) or its relevance to your argument, using your own words. And, of course, be sure to cite the source from which you're quoting.

If you want to use someone else's ideas but don't have a good reason to quote them, you should paraphrase their ideas instead. Doing this demonstrates, both to you and to your readers, that you really understand—or don't understand!—what the other person is saying. Paraphrasing is especially useful when the original source is hard to understand. Expressing someone else's ideas clearly and accurately can be difficult, but as with every other skill in writing, you can get better at it through practice. Sometimes you'll want to restate almost every sentence in your own words. (One word of caution: Don't start with a quotation and then change a word or two here and there. That will put you at the dangerous borderline between paraphrasing and plagiarizing. Instead, think carefully about what the author is saying and then start from scratch to express that same idea in your own words.) In other cases you can just briefly explain the main ideas, in your own words, rather than restating each point that the other person makes.[20] As with quotations, introduce your paraphrases by saying things like "Warren argues that . . ." or "Rachels claims that. . . ." And as with quotations, *be sure to cite your sources when paraphrasing or summarizing.* Even though you haven't used someone else's exact words, you have used someone else's ideas, and you need to acknowledge that person in a citation.

---

[20]Some people call this "summarizing" rather than "paraphrasing," but the distinction isn't that important.

CITING YOUR SOURCES

When you use an idea that isn't your own, whether by quoting or paraphrasing, you need to cite your source to acknowledge the person whose idea it is. You should add a citation after each quotation and after each paraphrase. Not only does this give credit where credit is due, it tells your readers where they can find the information or ideas that you've just presented. This is important in case your readers want to learn more about it, see the idea in context, or check that you've presented the idea accurately and fairly.

A good citation provides all of the information a reader would need to find the source from which you got the idea or information you've just presented. This usually means that the citation specifies the author(s) of the source, the title of the source, when the source was published, the book the source is in (if it's part of a book), the URL for the source (if it's online), or whatever else is needed to identify the source.

To make it easier to understand citations, different disciplines have adopted some common styles for formatting all of this information. In the humanities, including philosophy, the most common citation styles are "Chicago style," which comes from *The Chicago Manual of Style*, and "MLA style," which comes from the style guide of the Modern Language Association. You might also encounter "APA style," which comes from the style guide of the American Psychological Association, as well as others that are less common in the humanities. To learn how to cite sources in any of these styles, ask your instructor or librarian for help or search the web (e.g., by googling "help formatting citations in Chicago style" or even something more specific, like "citing Twitter in Chicago style").

In general, most citation styles require either that you add footnotes, endnotes, or use parenthetical citations. A footnote is a note at the bottom of a page, signaled by a little number like the one at the end of this sentence.[21] Endnotes are like footnotes except that they appear at the end of the paper instead of the bottom of the page. A parenthetical citation goes at the end of a sentence, wrapped in parentheses, and gives just enough information to know which source the idea or information came from—usually the author's last name, the year of publication, and a page number, if necessary. If you use parenthetical citations, you'll need to include a reference list (sometimes called a works cited list or, less commonly, a bibliography) at the end of the document.

One easy way to format citations is to use citation management software, which works together with your word processor (and sometimes your web browser) to collect and insert citations. Popular citation management tools include Zotero, EndNote, and Mendeley. Some of these are free, and others may be freely available through your library or university. It may take a little while to learn to use one of these software packages, but in the long run it can make things a lot easier for you.

If you are writing your essay for a class or for a particular publication, check with your instructor or the publication's editor to see if they prefer a particular citation style. If not, choose the style that you're most comfortable with. But whatever you do, pick a style and stick to it.

---

[21]It's best to insert footnotes using your word processor's footnote function, rather than trying to format them by hand! In Microsoft Word, for instance, look at the menu at the top of the window and choose Insert > Footnote.

STYLISH ACADEMIC WRITING

"Stylish academic writing" may seem like an oxymoron. A lot of academic writing is boring and difficult to read. It doesn't have to be that way, though. A few guidelines can help you write essays that are appropriately academic without being too dry or dense.

Avoid being too informal. Don't use slang or colloquial expressions. Use proper grammar. You probably shouldn't use the second person (i.e., the word *you*) or use contractions (e.g., *shouldn't* in place of *should not*).[22]

On the other hand, there are some "rules" of grammar and formal writing that are okay to break when writing an academic paper. Unless you're writing for an instructor who says otherwise, feel free to split infinitives and end sentences with prepositions, like *of*, *with*, or *to*, when doing so helps you express your ideas clearly. Go ahead and use the first person (i.e., the word *I*) when necessary, especially when you're explaining what you're doing or have done in a particular part of the essay (e.g., "I argued that . . ." or "I intend to show that . . ."). But don't use *I* unnecessarily. In particular, don't say things like, "In my opinion . . ." or, "I believe that Thomson's argument fails." Just say, "Thomson's argument fails."

Try to write sentences that use the **active voice.** A sentence in the active voice focuses on the person or thing doing the action; a sentence in the **passive voice** focuses on the person or thing to which the action is being done. (Compare "Beyoncé creates the best music videos," which is in active voice, to "The best music videos are created by Beyoncé," which is in passive voice.) A sentence is probably in the passive voice if it uses *to be* plus a verb that ends in *–ed*, as in *to be cited* or *to be quoted*, or a verb that ends in *–en*, as in *to be written* or *to be eaten.* If you're not sure if a sentence is in the passive voice, here's a test devised by ethics professor Rebecca Johnson: if you can make a grammatically correct sentence by adding "by zombies" to the end of the sentence, it's in the passive voice.[23] For instance, consider the sentence, "Descartes's theory of the mind was disproven," which uses the passive voice. (Notice how it focuses on what was done, rather than who did it. In fact, it doesn't even *tell* you who did it.) Adding "by zombies" gives us, "Descartes's theory of the mind was disproven by zombies," which is a grammatically correct sentence. To change it to active voice, we need to shift the emphasis to the person(s) or thing(s) that performed the main action of the sentence. For instance, "Zombies disproved Descartes's theory of the mind," while not historically accurate, is at least in the active voice.

Speaking of zombies, avoid what English professor Helen Sword calls "**zombie nouns.**"[24] Writers create zombie nouns when they take adjectives, like *formal*, or verbs, like *to argue*, and turn them into nouns, like *formality* or *argumentation*. Words ending in *–ity*, *–tion*, or *–ism* are often zombie nouns. Academic writers sometimes use zombie nouns because they help express complex, abstract ideas. But an essay that relies too heavily on zombie nouns shambles along slowly and clumsily, boring the reader to death. Zombie nouns also invite writers to indulge in *too* much abstraction, making their writing hard to understand. Think

---

[22]Wait! Aren't I being hypocritical here!? Not really. Different kinds of writing call for different levels of formality. This textbook is a little less formal than most academic writing. Notice, however, that the papers in Part V of the book are more formal, and they rarely use contractions or the word *you.*

[23]Rebecca Johnson, Twitter post, October 18, 2012, 2:26 pm, https://twitter.com/johnsonr/status/259012668298506240.

[24]Helen Sword, "Zombie Nouns," *New York Times*, July 23, 2012, http://nyti.ms/1cWsFsJ.

creatively about how you can use more concrete language (e.g., *critics* instead of *criticism* or even *arguments* instead of *argumentation*) and more exciting verbs. Sometimes you won't find a better way to express your idea, but often you'll come up with a more interesting way to say what you want to say.

Above all, don't try too hard to sound smart or stereotypically academic. Packing your prose with fancy words and complicated sentences usually just makes you look pretentious. Just try to express yourself as clearly as possible, and let your arguments show how smart you are.

TERMINOLOGY TO KNOW

thesis statement	quotation	active voice
well-developed argument	paraphrase	passive voice
rebut	plagiarism	zombie noun

Appendix 2 ⟩ Additional Case Studies

A NOTE ON CASE STUDIES

Many chapters in this book end with a set of "case studies." This appendix contains more case studies, grouped thematically. You'll find additional case studies on the textbook's companion web site. Each case study describes a real or fictional scenario and asks you to evaluate a particular action. Evaluating an action, in this context, means to form a judgment about how morally right or wrong (or good or bad) the action was. Each case study then asks you to support your evaluation with a moral argument, sometimes with specific instructions to use a particular kind of argument.

The simplest kind of evaluation would involve judging whether the act is morally obligatory, merely morally permissible, or morally wrong. You may find that you need a more nuanced conclusion—for instance, that the act was supererogatory or morally indifferent. (See pp. 14–17 for explanations of these terms.) In some cases you might find yourself making even more nuanced claims, such as, "Her action was morally wrong, but she did bring about a lot of good by doing it." Such an evaluation combines a judgment about whether the action was obligatory, wrong, or whatever with a judgment about how good or bad the action is, how praiseworthy or blameworthy the agent is, etc. Be sure, though, that you are focusing specifically on the action that you are asked to evaluate, rather than on some other aspect of the scenario (e.g., the actions of other people described in the scenario) and that you form a judgment about whether the act was right or wrong.

Note that you are not being asked to jot down the first judgment that comes to mind and then come up with some argument to support it. Instead, take some time to think carefully about the case. Use the tools you've learned from this book to figure out what arguments you could give for different judgments. Then decide what judgment is *best supported* by moral reasoning—that is, which judgment has the strongest arguments for it. In other words, you should use these case studies as an opportunity to practice key aspects of the "method for moral reasoning" presented in Chapter 8.

One final reminder: Some people don't like the idea of "judging" others' actions. But you can form judgments about others' actions without behaving in a judgmental way, as explained at the end of Chapter 2. You're not being asked to decide whether someone should be scolded, punished, stopped, or forced to do anything. In short, you're not being asked what exactly should be done in response to anyone's action; you're only being asked to determine whether an action is morally right or wrong.

BUSINESS AND MONEY

1. Ashley Madison is an online dating service for people who want to have extramarital affairs. At its peak, it boasted of almost 40 million users in over 50 different countries. But in July 2015, anonymous hackers announced they had stolen Ashley Madison's entire database, containing names, addresses, records of credit card transactions, and more—including information on people who had paid Ashley Madison a $19 fee to have all of their information deleted from the company's databases. Accusing the company of various fraudulent practices, the hackers demanded that the owners take down the web site permanently. They did not demand money or other compensation. The company acknowledged that it had been hacked but refused to take down the site. The hackers carried out their threat to release all of the information about the site's users. Marriages and careers were ruined. At least one person committed suicide after being exposed as a user of the site. Evaluate the company's decision to refuse the hackers' demands.

2. The infamous Triangle Shirtwaist Fire of 1911 killed 146 garment workers in New York City. The owners of the Triangle Shirtwaist Company, Max Blanck and Isaac Harris, had failed to maintain safe working conditions in their factory: There was no sprinkler system, some of the stairwells could not be opened from the inside, the fire escape was so rickety that it would collapse if there were too many people on it, and the fire hose inside the building was so old that it had rotted. When a fire broke out on one of the upper floors of the building, some twelve dozen women were burned alive or forced to jump to their deaths. Blanck and Harris worked on the top floor of the building, but they escaped by climbing onto the roof and jumping to an adjoining building. Evaluate Blanck and Harris's act of allowing working conditions in their factory to become so dangerous.

3. By the year 2000, Houston-based energy company Enron was one of the largest companies in the United States. What few people knew then, though, was that Enron's success rested in part on fraudulent and illegal accounting practices. In August 2001, one of the company's vice presidents, Sharon Watkins, emailed CEO Kenneth Lay to warn him that the company was about to collapse because of these practices, with disastrous financial consequences for many people. Lay met privately with Watkins and promised to have the company's lawyers investigate, and he secretly considered having Watkins fired for causing trouble. Watkins never took her concerns to law enforcement or the public, but she turned out to be right: in October 2001, a series of scandals rocked the company, ultimately leading Enron to file bankruptcy on December 2, 2001. Enron's shareholders lost tens of billions of dollars, and the company's 4,000 employees lost their jobs. Evaluate Watkins's action of warning Lay, but not anyone else, about the danger posed by Enron's fraudulent accounting practices.

4. Around the turn of the century, Indian pharmaceutical companies gave international efforts to fight HIV/AIDS a major boost. They began manufacturing generic versions of anti-retroviral drugs that had been developed by private companies in the United States and Europe. In 2000, before the Indian companies entered the market, those drugs cost about $10,000 per patient per year. Once Indian firms began to manufacture generic alternatives, the price plummeted to around $140 per patient per year, enabling organizations like Doctors Without Borders to provide life-saving medicines to many more people. Although these drugs were still patented in the United States and Europe, Indian law permitted Indian companies to manufacture them without paying royalties to the Western pharmaceutical companies that had developed the drugs. Those Western pharmaceutical companies therefore viewed the Indian firms' manufacturing as theft of intellectual property. Evaluate the Indian firms' (legally permissible) action of manufacturing generic versions of anti-retroviral drugs without paying royalties to the drugs' inventors.

5. Entrepreneur Kim Dotcom founded Megaupload in 2005 to allow people all over the world to upload, store, and share digital content. Eventually, the company's sites allegedly hosted some 12 billion files for over 100 million users and received about 50 million visits per day from around the world, raking in hundreds of millions of dollars. In January 2012, however, the U.S. government shut down the site, accusing it of facilitating digital piracy, and arrested Dotcom on various charges. According to the government, as well as an independent anti-piracy organization, the material shared through Megaupload's sites included a great deal of copyrighted media, such as music and movies. Google had cut off ad services to Megaupload's sites in 2007 due to the high levels of pirated materials on the site's servers. Assuming that Megaupload really did facilitate the illegal sharing of copyrighted materials, and that Kim Dotcom knew this, evaluate Dotcom's action of creating and maintaining the site.

WAR AND PEACE

6. As a soldier in the U.S. Army during the Iraq War, Private Bradley Manning had access to databases containing classified information. Manning came to believe that the public needed to see this information in order to understand the horrors of the wars in Iraq and Afghanistan. After contacting and being ignored by the *Washington Post* and the *New York Times*, Manning leaked over 250,000 classified U.S. diplomatic cables and various other files to Wikileaks, an anti-secrecy group, in 2009 and 2010. Wikileaks published the documents online for all to see, as Manning expected. Besides the diplomatic cables and other confidential messages, the files included videos of deadly U.S. airstrikes. One video, for instance, showed a U.S. attack helicopter mistakenly firing on journalists during a 2007 airstrike in Baghdad. The United States charged Manning with a range of crimes, from failure to follow Army regulations to "aiding the enemy." Manning pleaded guilty to some of these charges and entered no plea to the others, including the charge of aiding the enemy. He says that he only released documents that he thought would embarrass, but not harm, the United States. Evaluate Manning's act of leaking these classified documents to Wikileaks.

7. There was no time for Lt. Heather Penney and Col. Marc Sasseville to load their F-16 fighter jets with ammunition or missiles before they took off from Andrews Air Force Base on September 11, 2001. That left only one way for the fighter pilots to fulfill their mission of bringing down United Airlines flight 93: they were going to ram their jets directly into the hijacked plane. They considered ejecting before the planes collided. They rejected that plan, however, because it would mean that if the jets missed the airliner, there would be no way to stop it from reaching Washington, D.C. Fortunately for Penney and Sasseville, the passengers on flight 93 forced the hijackers to crash the plane themselves, so the fighter pilots didn't have to go through with their suicide mission. Evaluate Penney and Sasseville's action of taking off with the intent to ram flight 93, as ordered, to stop the airliner from reaching Washington, D.C.

8. Following the collapse of the Han dynasty toward the end of the second century, China fell into a prolonged and enormously destructive civil war. One of the major players in this war was a general named Guan Yu. Early in the war, Guan and two companions, Liu Bei and Zhang Fei, swore a solemn oath to regard one another as brothers and never to do anything to betray their friendship. Later in the war, Guan was captured by Liu Bei's powerful enemy, Cao Cao. Cao spared Guan's life and enticed him into serving in Cao's army by offering him generous gifts and titles. After serving Cao long enough to repay his mercy and generosity, however, Guan informed Cao that he was leaving his service and rejoining Liu Bei. By supporting Liu Bei against Cao Cao, Guan almost certainly prolonged the bloody civil war, leading to a great deal of additional death and suffering throughout China. Evaluate Guan's action of leaving Cao's service and rejoining Liu Bei.

9. During its invasion of the Palestinian-controlled Gaza Strip in 2014, the Israeli military sometimes targeted residential buildings that it believed had been used for military purposes. The military would issue warnings shortly before bombing the buildings, often by calling the people who lived in the building and telling them that they had five minutes to evacuate. (Sometimes people defied or ignored the warnings—even going onto the roof to act as human shields. In at least some cases, the Israeli military bombed the building anyway.) During the invasion, the military also scattered leaflets over areas of heavy fighting, explaining to residents that the military did not wish to harm them or their families and encouraging them to gather in specific areas of the city until the fighting was over. Evaluate the Israeli military's action of providing warnings to civilians to encourage them to evacuate bombing targets and areas of heavy fighting.

10. Taliban militants captured U.S. Army soldier Bowe Bergdahl on or around June 30, 2009. The exact details of his capture remain murky, but various sources indicate that Bergdahl walked off a small Army outpost in eastern Afghanistan and was captured soon thereafter. Although the U.S. military poured enormous resources into searching for Bergdahl, imposing serious hardships and grave risks on a great many American soldiers and Afghan civilians, the Taliban managed to evade the Americans and carry Bergdahl across the border into Pakistan. Nearly five years later, on May 31, 2014, the Taliban turned Bergdahl over to the U.S. government in return for the release of five prisoners from Guantanamo Bay. After his release, Bergdahl claimed that he had walked away from the outpost in an attempt to hike 20 miles to a larger base. He thought that his stunt would grab high-ranking officers' attention, which would enable him to explain that he thought his commanders had displayed reckless disregard for

his unit's safety. This, he thought, was the only way to protect his unit. Assuming that Bergdahl is telling the truth about why he disappeared, evaluate his action of trying to get his message across by walking away from his post into hostile territory.

CRIME AND PUNISHMENT

11. After stealing a stash of compact discs from a man's barn in 2011, two teenage thieves were shocked to find the discs contained large amounts of child pornography. The thieves took the discs to the police, confessing that they had stolen them. The police arrested the man from whom the discs were stolen and declined to press charges against the thieves. Evaluate the burglars' action of taking the discs to the police and confessing that they had stolen them.

12. A customer at a Home Deport in Auburn Hills, Michigan, watched as a security guard chased two men out of the store and into the parking lot. When the two men hopped into an SUV and tried to escape, the customer pulled out her handgun (for which she had a concealed carry permit) and starting shooting at the fleeing SUV. The two suspects escaped the scene unharmed, though one bullet did hit one of their tires. Prosecutors charged the customer, Tatiana Duva-Rodriguez, with reckless discharge of a firearm. At her trial, Duva-Rodriguez claimed that she had feared that she was witnessing something more serious than shoplifting and that she was "trying to help." Evaluate Duva-Rodriguez's action of shooting at the fleeing SUV.

13. As their subway train rumbled between stations on July 4, 2015, 18-year-old Jasper Spires tried to grab 24-year-old Kevin Sutherland's cell phone. Sutherland resisted and a fight broke out. Spires punched Sutherland until he fell to the floor, at which point Spires pulled out a knife and stabbed Sutherland thirty to forty times, killing him. The other passengers, terrified, huddled at either end of the car. No one tried to stop Spires, who then robbed other passengers and fled the scene at the next station. Evaluate the bystanders' failure to intervene in the stabbing.

14. When Noela Rukundo showed up at her own funeral, her husband was less thrilled than one might have expected. Just a few days earlier, the gangsters he'd hired to kill his wife had told him that she was dead. In truth, they'd never gone through with it. They kidnapped Rukundo in her native country of Burundi, held her hostage for two days, provided her with indisputable evidence that her husband had hired them to kill her, and then released her, saying that they refused to kill women. They kept the $7,000 that her husband had paid them. Evaluate the gangsters' action of taking Rukundo's husband's money, pretending to kill her, and then providing his wife with evidence of her husband's crimes.

FILM AND FICTION

15. In the novel *Make Your Home Among Strangers*, ambitious Lizet Ramirez kept her college applications secret from her Cuban-American parents. Upon receiving a full

scholarship to an elite liberal arts college in upstate New York, Lizet shocks and infuriates her family by announcing that she is leaving Miami to attend college, which they regard as a selfish betrayal. Evaluate Lizet's action of moving away from her family to attend an elite college on a full scholarship.

16. In the film *Reservoir Dogs*, Mr. Pink (played by Steve Buscemi) argues that he shouldn't have to tip servers in restaurants, as long as those servers make minimum wage. (Today, many servers in the United States officially make far less than minimum wage on the assumption that tips will make up the difference.) He says that they are simply doing their job, just like everybody else, and so there is no more reason to tip servers than to tip anybody else. Evaluate Mr. Pink's act of refusing to tip servers at restaurants.

17. In the film *Get Hard*, Darnell (played by Kevin Hart) runs a struggling car detailing business in a parking garage. With bad credit and no savings, Darnell is struggling to move his family out of a dangerous neighborhood. When one of his customers comes to him for help, Darnell sees an opportunity to make the money he needs to move to a better neighborhood. The customer, multimillionaire investment manager James King (played by Will Ferrell), has just been sentenced to ten years in a maximum security prison for securities fraud and embezzlement. King incorrectly assumes that Darnell has served time in prison because he is black. He begs Darnell to teach him what he needs to know to survive behind bars. Without correcting King's false assumption that he's been to prison, Darnell agrees to do so in return for $30,000. Evaluate Darnell's action of agreeing to teach King how to survive in prison despite lacking any special knowledge of how to do so.

18. In the novel *The Girl with the Dragon Tattoo*, which was adapted into films in both Sweden and the United States, teenage computer security expert Lisbeth Salander helps journalist Mikael Blomkvist uncover evidence linking billionaire industrialist and all-around terrible person Hans-Erik Wennerström to a range of international criminal activities. Blomkvist uses the evidence, which Lisbeth stole by hacking into Wennerström's computer, to write an exposé that ruins Wennerström. Lisbeth then hacks into Wennerström's secret bank accounts and steals hundreds of millions of dollars from him, which she keeps for herself. Evaluate Lisbeth's action of stealing Wennerström's (mostly ill-gotten) fortune.

TECHNOLOGY

19. Technology company FaceFirst won't tell you who its customers are. That's because many people find the company's technology creepy, and so FaceFirst's customers would rather that you not know what they're doing. FaceFirst's facial recognition software enables stores to identify shoppers using cameras set up at the front door or around the store. Some stores use the software to compare shoppers to a database of known shoplifters so that they can follow them around the store or even kick them out. In that case, the goal is to keep prices down by reducing theft. Other stores use it to identify loyal customers or big spenders so that they can offer them special service

or discounts. In that case, the goal is to provide a better experience to important customers. Evaluate the retail stores' action of using facial recognition technology to secretly identify customers and target some for (positive or negative) special treatment.

20. Anthony Elonis began writing violent lyrics and posting them to Facebook after his wife left him, taking their children with her. The lyrics included graphic, violent threats against his wife, his coworkers, local schoolchildren, and even an FBI agent who came to his home to investigate his behavior. But he also posted disclaimers that he was merely expressing his frustration and exercising his First Amendment right to free speech. Elonis continued his threatening lyrics even after his wife got a restraining order against him. Evaluate Elonis's action of posting threatening lyrics to Facebook. (Set aside the legal question of whether his posts were actually illegal. Focus instead on the *moral* evaluation of his actions.)

21. A pair of computer-security researchers publicly released a video and article through *WIRED* magazine, proving that (as of July 2015) they could hack into some Jeep Cherokees' control systems over the Internet, enabling them to track the vehicle, crank up the radio, control the windshield wipers, and even disable the brakes or the engine. The researchers explained that they released their video publicly to draw attention to the importance of cybersecurity in cars. They did not publicly release details about how to do any of these things. They had been in touch with Jeep about their work for months, and Jeep had already prepared a security update for the car's software, although drivers would need to contact Jeep or a Jeep dealer to install it. Evaluate the researchers' action of publicly releasing the video showing that Jeeps were vulnerable to hacking.

22. As a wildfire raged through British Columbia in the summer of 2015, a small, privately owned drone hovered near the fire for three hours. During that time, officials prohibited firefighting planes and helicopters from entering the area because of the risk of a crash. Similar incidents have hindered firefighting efforts throughout the American West. Not only do these drones hinder firefighting efforts, allowing the fires to grow larger and more destructive, they endanger firefighters' lives as they increase the risk of aircraft crashing directly into wildfires. Some of the drones presumably belong to curious and clueless hobbyists who just want a closer look, while others probably belong to people hoping to sell footage or pictures to local news outlets. Evaluate the drone operators' action of flying unauthorized, private drones over active wildfires.

23. American dentist Walter Palmer likes to hunt. In July 2015, he traveled to Zimbabwe, where, with the help of some local guides, he lured a lion out of a national park, shot it with a bow and arrow, and tracked the wounded animal for 40 hours before he finally killed it. The lion that Palmer killed turned out to be something of a celebrity: the 13-year-old male lion, named Cecil, was a well-known and beloved attraction at Zimbabwe's Hwange National Park. News of Cecil's death provoked international outrage. When journalists revealed Palmer's identity, some people found a way to strike back. Thousands of people posted negative reviews on the Yelp listing for Palmer's dental practice in Minnesota, leaving him with a one-star rating and a barrage of strongly worded comments. For instance, Yelp user "Joshua N." wrote, "Brought my lion here for dentistry and was horrified by the result. All kidding aside, I hope you die painfully." Evaluate the Yelp users' action of posting such reviews for Palmer's dental practice.

ANIMALS AND NATURE

24. New Yorkers used to know that the circus had come to town when the Ringling Bros. and Barnum & Bailey circus paraded its elephants through the Queens-Midtown Tunnel. As of 2016, however, circus-goers will no longer see elephants in Ringling Bros.' acts. The last performing elephants retired to the company's 200-acre Center for Elephant Conservation near Orlando, Florida, where they will live the rest of their lives amid friends and family. Although circuses have long faced criticism from animal rights groups about their treatment of the elephants, Ringling Bros. says that they retired the elephants only as a result of increasingly burdensome regulations about housing and transporting the elephants. Evaluate the company's action of retiring the elephants from the circus and moving them to their Center for Elephant Conservation.

25. When a 4-year-old boy slipped through the fence and jumped into the gorilla exhibit at the Cincinnati Zoo, a 450-pound silverback gorilla named Harambe ambled over and grabbed him. At one point Harambe dragged the boy across his enclosure, but at other times he stood over the boy in what some zoo visitors described as a protective manner. The zoo tried to coax the powerful gorilla out of his exhibit, but Harambe stayed put. They considered knocking Harambe out with a tranquilizer dart, but they feared that the gorilla might hurt or kill the boy in the ten minutes or so that it would take for the tranquilizer to take effect. So, in the end, the zoo's Dangerous Animal Response Team shot Harambe dead. Harambe had been one of about 175,000 Western lowland gorillas left in the world. The boy escaped with serious but non–life-threatening injuries. Evaluate the zoo's action of shooting and killing Harambe.

26. The Oregon National Primate Research Center houses thousands of monkeys that are used for biomedical research. The Center's Reproductive & Developmental Sciences division uses the monkeys to study serious problems that arise in human pregnancies, such as premature birth and stillbirth, with the goal of preventing and treating those problems. To do this, researchers often perform experiments that they expect will cause stillbirths, premature labor, and so on. In other cases, the researchers investigate the effects of potential treatments by performing cesarean sections ("C-sections") on pregnant monkeys and then killing the fetuses or baby monkeys to study their brains, lungs, and other tissues. All of these procedures are designed and performed in accordance with the Center's guidelines for the care and use of research animals. Evaluate the Center's action of disrupting monkey pregnancies and killing monkey fetuses or babies in order to study serious problems that arise in human pregnancies.

27. There are only about 5,000 black rhinos left in the world. On Monday, May 18, 2016, one of them died, shot by an American hunter named Corey Knowlton in the southern African country of Namibia. But even though the black rhino is critically endangered, Knowlton hadn't broken any laws. In fact, he had shot the rhino with the approval of Namibia's Ministry of Environment and Tourism. The Ministry had identified the specific rhino that Knowlton killed as eligible for hunting; the rhino was an older male who was no longer reproducing but posed a threat to younger males. The Ministry auctioned off a permit to hunt the rhino, which Knowlton bought for $350,000. That money will go toward anti-poaching and conservation efforts to

protect the black rhino species. Knowlton argues that by buying the permit and killing a dangerous, non-reproducing rhino, he was actually increasing the species' chance of survival. Evaluate Knowlton's action of buying the permit and hunting the rhino.

28. Some 5 billion passenger pigeons called North America home at the beginning of the nineteenth century, making it one of the most abundant birds on the planet. By 1914, however, hunting had driven the birds to extinction. That's when the last known passenger pigeon, known as Martha, died at the Cincinnati Zoo. She was preserved for future display, and now scientists are exploring ways to use DNA from her preserved remains to revive the species. Scientists believe they could create new passenger pigeons by cloning Martha's cells and using closely related species, such as rock pigeons, as surrogate parents. (Not all species are candidates for such "de-extinction." Passenger pigeons and woolly mammoths have been proposed as likely candidates; dinosaurs have not.) Evaluate the (proposed) action of using biomedical technology to revive species that humans drove to extinction.

MEDICINE AND BIOTECHNOLOGY

29. Citing philosophical reasons and sincere but misguided concerns about safety, some parents refuse to give their children the vaccines recommended by pediatricians and public health experts. Some of these parents base their refusal on misinformation that circulates widely online, such as a thoroughly discredited study published in 1999 that supposedly linked vaccines to autism. While refusing to vaccinate their children does protect their children from the very small risk of adverse side effects, it leaves their children vulnerable to childhood diseases that had been all but wiped out in the United States, including potentially fatal diseases such as pertussis (whooping cough) and measles. Furthermore, by making it possible for their children to pass the illnesses on to others—including babies who are too young to be vaccinated and people who can't be vaccinated because of other health issues—these parents are increasing others' risk of catching these diseases. Evaluate these parents' action of refusing to vaccinate their children. (Set aside people who refuse because of explicitly religious reasons.)

30. Rinat Dray went into labor with her third child in July 2011. Her first two children had been delivered by cesarean section, but Dray wanted to deliver the third naturally. Doctors, however, worried that her uterus would rupture during labor, endangering her baby. They tried to persuade her to have a C-section, but she refused. After a few hours of labor, the hospital's medical and legal staff overruled her refusal; the doctors wheeled her off to an operating room and delivered her baby boy by C-section. Evaluate the hospital's action of delivering Dray's baby by C-section against her wishes.

31. When they learned they were going blind, 45-year-old twins Marc and Eddy Verbessem were horrified. They were already deaf, and they communicated with each other using a special sign language that no one outside their immediate family could understand. Without their sight, they would lose their ability to communicate, and they would lose their independence. They would be confined to an institution for the severely disabled.

They decided that, given their special circumstances, going blind meant having nothing left to live for. Marc and Eddy lived in Belgium, where terminally ill patients can request euthanasia. Despite their aged parents' objections, Marc and Eddy eventually convinced several doctors to approve their request. The two died by lethal injection, with their parents and brother by their side, in December 2012. Evaluate Marc and Eddy's decision to carry out physician-assisted suicide to avoid becoming blind.

32. With a recently invented technique called CRISPR, scientists can now edit a cell's DNA with greater precision than ever before. Any changes made to a "germline" cell, such as an embryo or an egg cell, would not only affect any organism that develops from that cell, but could be passed on to that organism's descendants. In theory, therefore, it could be used to eliminate dangerous genetic diseases. But according to critics, it could also be used for more controversial purposes, such as creating genetically enhanced "designer babies." In 2015, Chinese scientists led by Huang Junjiu published the results of their attempt to use CRISPR to edit human embryos. All of the embryos, which Huang obtained from a local fertility clinic, were "non-viable," meaning that they could never have been used to produce a live birth. Huang's team attempted to edit the gene responsible for a fatal blood disease, and their research revealed serious difficulties in using CRISPR for medical purposes. Evaluate Huang's action of testing medical uses of CRISPR on non-viable human embryos.

PART V

Readings

Tips on Reading Philosophy

This section contains papers and excerpts from books written by historical and contemporary philosophers. Reading these papers and excerpts requires a somewhat different approach than reading most other things. For one thing, philosophers aren't usually telling a story, as novelists do, or providing you with a bunch of information to memorize, as many textbooks do. Instead, they are almost always giving *arguments*. Often these arguments aim to establish very controversial conclusions with careful and complex reasoning. With that in mind, here are six tips for reading philosophy well:

1. *Read slowly.* Reading philosophy takes a lot longer than reading most other things. It's often difficult to really understand a particular passage (or an entire paper) until you've read it several times. Don't be discouraged—it's like that for everyone.

2. *Don't multitask.* When you multitask while reading, your brain has to switch back and forth between what you're reading and whatever else you're doing. If you're just trying to absorb a bunch of information, that might not be so bad. But when you're trying to follow a long chain of reasoning, switching back and forth makes it *much* harder for your brain to keep track of the argument by connecting what you're reading now to what you read before. So, no matter how good you are at multitasking, reading philosophy will be much easier if you put everything else away for a while.

3. *Look for the main conclusion.* Most philosophical papers will tell you the author's main conclusion early on. (The excerpts from books are usually less clear about this, since the "main point" of an entire book is difficult to state succinctly.) When you figure out what the main conclusion is, make a note of it. You might even want to underline it or put a star in the margin. It will be much easier to follow the rest of the argument if you know what the conclusion is.

4. *Keep track of the arguments as you read them.* If you're reading a history textbook, you're probably learning information about what happened in the past, why those things happened, and so on. When you're reading philosophy, you're learning *arguments*. Those are the most important things that you should try to get out of each paper or excerpt. Use the tools introduced in Parts I and II of this book to reconstruct and keep track of those arguments.

5. *Be ready for the author to disagree with himself or herself.* Philosophers almost always raise objections to their own conclusions or arguments. Don't be surprised when a philosopher suddenly starts arguing *against* the position he or she was just arguing *for*. The author doesn't really think the objection works; he or she is usually just bringing it up in order to show why it fails or to introduce a slightly more nuanced version of the conclusion. (See pp. 82–85 for a discussion of objections and the various ways that philosophers typically respond to them.)

6. *Be prepared for authors to disagree with one another.* In many classes, your instructors assign readings mainly to convey information that they expect you to learn. That is, your instructors think that the claims in the

reading are true and they want you to believe those claims. That is not the case in a philosophy class. Your instructors assign readings because they want you to understand and consider the *arguments* presented in the reading, not (necessarily) because they want you to accept the conclusions of those arguments. So don't be surprised if you read a paper one week that argues for the exact opposite conclusion from the one in the paper you read last week. The point is to study the arguments in both papers so that you can come to a well-reasoned judgment about which paper's conclusion is correct.

To help you with these tasks, Part V includes a short description and a few guiding questions before each reading as well as discussion questions after each reading. The description will give you a very brief idea about the main point of the reading. The guiding questions will direct your attention to key claims, arguments, and objections. Keeping these questions in mind as you read will help you navigate the reading. Thinking through the discussion questions afterward can help improve and deepen your understanding of the reading's arguments.

Moral Theory

Immanuel Kant (1724–1804)
Translated by James W. Ellington

Grounding for the Metaphysics of Morals

In these excerpts from the *Grounding for the Metaphysics of Morals*, philosophical giant Immanuel Kant searches for the fundamental rule of morality, which he calls the "categorical imperative." He argues that there is exactly one categorical imperative, which can be understood in three different ways.

GUIDING QUESTIONS

1. Kant begins by discussing the importance of a "good will" but spends the rest of the excerpt talking about "duty" (i.e., obligation). What is the connection, according to Kant, between the idea of a good will and the idea of duty?
2. What is the difference between a hypothetical imperative and a categorical imperative? What is the connection between a categorical imperative and a moral law?
3. What is the categorical imperative? That is, what does the categorical imperative tell you to do? (Kant gives more than one answer to this question. Look for at least three!)
4. Why does Kant discuss the examples of suicide, promise-keeping, developing one's talents, and helping others? That is, what purpose do those examples serve in the reading as a whole?
5. What does Kant mean when he says that something is "an end in itself" rather than a mere "thing"?
6. What is the "kingdom of ends" and what does it have to do with the categorical imperative?

FIRST SECTION

There is no possibility of thinking of anything at all in the world, or even out of it, which can be regarded as good without qualification, except a *good will*. Intelligence, wit, judgment, and whatever talents of the mind one might want to name are doubtless in many respects good and desirable, as are such qualities of temperament as courage, resolution, and perseverance. But they can also become extremely bad and harmful if the will, which is to make use of these gifts of nature and which in its special constitution is called character, is not good. The same holds with gifts of fortune; power, riches, honor, even health, and that complete well-being and contentment with one's condition which is called happiness make for pride and often hereby even arrogance, unless there is a good will to correct their influence on the mind and herewith also to rectify the whole principle of action and make it universally conformable to its end. The sight of a being who is not graced by any touch of a pure and good will but who yet enjoys an uninterrupted prosperity can never delight a rational and impartial spectator. Thus a good will seems to constitute the indispensable condition of being even worthy of happiness. . . .

A good will is good not because of what it effects or accomplishes, nor because of its fitness to attain some proposed end; it is good only through its willing, i.e., it is good in itself. When it is considered in itself, then it is to be esteemed very much higher than anything which it might ever bring about merely in order to favor some inclination, or even the sum total of all inclinations. Even if, by some especially unfortunate fate or by the niggardly provision of stepmotherly nature, this will should be wholly lacking in the power to accomplish its purpose; if with the greatest effort it should yet achieve nothing, and only the good will should remain (not, to be sure, as a mere wish but as the summoning of all the means in our power), yet would it, like a jewel, still shine by its own light as something which has its full value in itself. . . .

The concept of a will estimable in itself and good without regard to any further end must now be developed. . . .Therefore, we shall take up the concept of *duty*, which includes that of a good will. . . .

I here omit all actions already recognized as contrary to duty, even though they may be useful for this or that end; for in the case of these the question does not arise at all as to whether they might be done from duty, since they even conflict with duty. I also set aside those actions which are really in accordance with duty, yet to which men have no immediate inclination, but perform them because they are impelled thereto by some other inclination. For in this [second] case to decide whether the action which is in accord with duty has been done from duty or from some selfish purpose is easy. The difference is far more difficult to note in the [third] case where the action accords with duty and the subject has in addition an immediate inclination to do the action. For example, that a dealer should not overcharge an inexperienced purchaser certainly accords with duty; and where there is much commerce, the prudent merchant does not overcharge but keeps to a fixed price for everyone in general, so that a child may buy from him just as well as everyone else may. Thus customers

are honestly served, but this is not nearly enough for making us believe that the merchant has acted this way from duty and from principles of honesty; his own advantage required him to do it. He cannot, however, be assumed to have in addition [as in the third case] an immediate inclination toward his buyers, causing him, as it were, out of love to give no one as far as price is concerned any advantage other another. Hence the action was done neither from duty nor from immediate inclination, but merely for a selfish purpose.

On the other hand, to preserve one's life is a duty; and, furthermore, everyone has also an immediate inclination to do so. But on this account the often anxious care taken by most men for it has no intrinsic worth, and the maxim of their action has no moral content. They preserve their lives, to be sure, in accordance with duty, but not from duty. On the other hand, if adversity and hopeless sorrow have completely taken away the taste for life, if an unfortunate man, strong in soul and more indignant at his fate than despondent or dejected, wishes for death and yet preserves his life without loving it—not from inclination or fear, but from duty— then his maxim indeed has moral content. . . .

SECOND SECTION

Everything in nature works according to laws. Only a rational being has the power to act according to his conception of laws, i.e., according to principles, and thereby has he a will. Since the derivation of actions from laws requires reason, the will is nothing but practical reason. . . .

All imperatives are expressed by an *ought* and thereby indicate the relation of an objective law of reason to a will that is not necessarily determined by this law because of its subjective constitution (the relation of necessitation). Imperatives say that something would be good to do or to refrain from doing, but they say it to a will that does not always therefore do something simply because it has been represented to the will as something good to do. That is practically good which determines the will by means of representations of reason and hence not by subjective causes, but objectively, i.e., on grounds valid for every rational being as such. It is distinguished from the pleasant as that which influences the will only by means of sensation from merely subjective causes, which hold only for this or that person's senses but do not hold as a principle of reason valid for everyone. . . .

Now all imperatives command either hypothetically or categorically. The former represent the practical necessity of a possible action as a means for attaining something else that one wants (or may possibly want). The categorical imperative would be one which represented an action as objectively necessary in itself, without reference to another end.

Every practical law represents a possible action as good. . . . Now if the action would be good merely as a means to something else, so is the imperative hypothetical. But if the action is represented as good in itself, and hence as necessary in a will which of itself conforms to reason as the principle of the will, then the imperative is categorical. . . .

A hypothetical imperative thus says only that an action is good for some purpose, either possible or actual. . . . A categorical imperative, which declares an action to be of itself objectively necessary without reference to any purpose, i.e., without any other end, holds as an apodeictic practical principle. . . .

If I think of a hypothetical imperative in general, I do not know beforehand what it will contain until its condition is given. But if I think of a categorical imperative, I know immediately what it contains. For since, besides the law, the imperative contains only the necessity that the maxim[1] should accord with this law, while the law contains no conditions to restrict it, there remains nothing but the universality of a law as such with which the maxim of the action should conform. This conformity alone is properly what is represented as necessary by the imperative.

Hence there is only one categorical imperative and it is this: Act only according to that maxim whereby you can at the same time will that it should become a universal law.[2]

Now if all imperatives of duty can be derived from this one imperative as their principle, then there can at least be shown what is understood by the concept of duty and what it means, even though there is left undecided whether what is called duty may not be an empty concept.

The universality of law according to which effects are produced constitutes what is properly called nature in the most general sense (as to form), i.e., the existence of things as far as determined by universal laws.

Accordingly, the universal imperative of duty may be expressed thus: Act as if the maxim of your action were to become through your will a universal law of nature.[3]

We shall now enumerate some duties, following the usual division of these into duties to ourselves and to others and into perfect and imperfect duties.[4]

1. A man reduced to despair by a series of misfortunes feels sick of life but is still so far in possession of his reason that he can ask himself whether taking his own life would not be contrary to his duty to himself.[5] Now he asks whether the maxim of his action could become a universal law of nature. But his maxim is this: from self-love I make as my principle to shorten my life when its continued duration threatens more evil than it promises satisfaction. There only remains the question as to whether this principle of self-love can become a universal law of nature. One sees at once a contradiction in a system of nature whose law would destroy life by means of the very same feeling that acts so as to stimulate the furtherance of life, and hence there could be no existence as a system of nature. Therefore, such a maxim cannot possibly hold as a universal law of nature and is, consequently, wholly opposed to the supreme principle of all duty.

2. Another man in need finds himself forced to borrow money. He knows well that he won't be able to repay it, but he sees also that he will not get any loan unless he firmly promises to repay it within a fixed time. He wants to make such a promise, but he still has conscience enough to ask himself whether it is not permissible and is contrary to duty to get out of difficulty in this way. Suppose, however, that he decides to do so. The maxim of his action would then be expressed as follows: when I believe myself to be in need of money, I will borrow money and promise to pay it back, although I know that I can never do so. Now this principle of self-love or personal advantage may perhaps be quite compatible with one's entire future welfare, but the question is now whether it is right.[6] I then transform the requirement of self-love into a universal law and put the question thus: how would things stand if my maxim were to become a universal law? He then sees at once that such a maxim could never hold

as a universal law of nature and be consistent with itself, but must necessarily be self-contradictory. For the universality of a law which says that anyone believing himself to be in difficulty could promise whatever he pleases with the intention of not keeping it would make promising itself and the end to be attained thereby quite impossible, inasmuch as no one would believe what was promised him but would merely laugh at all such utterances as being vain pretenses.

3. A third finds in himself a talent whose cultivation could make him a man useful in many respects. But he finds himself in comfortable circumstances and prefers to indulge in pleasure rather than to bother himself about broadening and improving his fortunate natural aptitudes. But he asks himself further whether his maxim of neglecting his natural gifts, besides agreeing of itself with his propensity to indulgence, might agree also with what is called duty.[7] He then sees that a system of nature could indeed always subsist according to such a universal law, even though every man (like South Sea Islanders) should let his talents rust and resolve to devote his life entirely to idleness, indulgence, propagation, and, in a word, to enjoyment. But he cannot possibly will that this should become a universal law of nature or be implanted in us as such a law by a natural instinct. For as a rational being he necessarily wills that all his faculties should be developed, inasmuch as they are given him for all sorts of possible purposes.

4. A fourth man finds things going well for himself but sees others (whom he could help) struggling with great hardships; and he thinks: what does it matter to me? Let everybody be as happy as Heaven wills or as he can make himself; I shall take nothing from him nor even envy him; but I have no desire to contribute anything to his well-being or to his assistance when in need. If such a way of thinking were to become a universal law of nature, the human race admittedly could very well subsist and doubtless could subsist even better than when everyone prates about sympathy and benevolence and even on occasion exerts himself to practice them but, on the other hand, also cheats when he can, betrays the rights of man, or otherwise violates

them. But even though it is possible that a universal law of nature could subsist in accordance with that maxim, still it is impossible to will that such a principle should hold everywhere as a law of nature.[8] For a will which resolved in this way would contradict itself, inasmuch as cases might often arise in which one would have need of the love and sympathy of others and in which he would deprive himself, by such a law of nature springing from his own will, of all hope of the aid he wants for himself.

These are some of the many actual duties, or at least what are taken to be such, whose derivation from the single principle cited above is clear. We must be able to will that a maxim of our action become a universal law; this is the canon for morally estimating any of our actions. Some actions are so constituted that their maxims cannot without contradiction even be thought as a universal law of nature, much less be willed as what should become one. In the case of others this internal impossibility is indeed not found, but there is still no possibility of willing that their maxim should be raised to the universality of a law of nature, because such a will would contradict itself. . . .

[T]he proper and inestimable worth of an absolutely good will consists precisely in the fact that the principle of action is free of all influences from contingent grounds. . . .

Therefore, the question is this: is it a necessary law for all rational beings always to judge their actions according to such maxims as they can themselves will that such should serve as universal laws? If there is such a law, then it must already be connected (completely a priori) with the concept of the will of a rational being in general. . . .

The ends which a rational being arbitrarily proposes to himself as effects of this action (material ends) are all merely relative, for only their relation to a specially constituted faculty of desire in the subject gives them their worth. Consequently, such worth cannot provide any universal principles, which are valid and necessary for all rational beings and, furthermore, are valid for every volition, i.e., cannot provide any practical laws. Therefore, all such relative ends can be grounds only for hypothetical imperatives. . . .

Now I say that man, and in general every rational being, exists as an end in himself and not merely as a means to be arbitrarily used by this or that will. He must in all his actions, whether directed to himself or to other rational beings, always be regarded at the same time as an end. All the objects of inclination have only a conditioned value; for if there were not these inclinations and the needs founded on them, then their object would be without value. But the inclinations themselves, being sources of needs, are so far from having an absolute value such as to render them desirable for their own sake that the universal wish of every rational being must be, rather, to be wholly free from them. Accordingly, the value of any object obtainable by our action is always conditioned. Beings whose existence depends not on our will but on nature have, nevertheless, if they are not rational beings, only a relative value as means and are therefore called things. On the other hand, rational beings are called persons inasmuch as their nature already marks them out as ends in themselves, i.e., as something which is not to be used merely as means and hence there is imposed thereby a limit on all arbitrary use of such beings, which are thus objects of respect. Persons are, therefore, not merely subjective ends, whose existence as an effect of our actions has a value for us; but such beings for which there can be substituted no other end to which such beings should serve merely as means, for otherwise nothing at all of absolute value would be found anywhere. But if all value were conditioned and hence contingent, then no supreme practical principle could be found for reason at all.

If then there is to be a supreme practical principle and, as far as the human will is concerned, a categorical imperative, then it must be such that from the conception of what is necessarily an end for everyone because this end is an end in itself it constitutes an objective principle of the will and can hence serve as a practical law. The ground of such a principle is this: rational nature exists as an end in itself. In this way man necessarily thinks of his own existence; thus far is it a subjective principle of human actions. But in this way also does every other rational being think of his existence on the same rational ground that holds also for me; hence it is at the same time an objective principle, from which, as a supreme practical ground, all laws of the will must be able to be derived. The practical imperative will therefore be the following: Act in such a way that you treat humanity, whether in your own person or in the person of another, always at the same time as an

end and never simply as a means.[9] We now want to see whether this can be carried out in practice.

Let us keep to our previous examples.

First, as regards the concept of necessary duty to oneself, the man who contemplates suicide will ask himself whether his action can be consistent with the idea of humanity as an end in itself. If he destroys himself in order to escape from a difficult situation, then he is making use of his person merely as a means so as to maintain a tolerable condition till the end of this life. Man, however, is not a thing and hence is not something to be used merely as a means; he must in all his actions always be regarded as an end in himself. Therefore, I cannot dispose of man in my own person by mutilating, damaging, or killing him. . . .

Second, as concerns necessary or strict duty to others, the man who intends to make a false promise will immediately see that he intends to make use of another man merely as a means to an end which the latter does not likewise hold. For the man whom I want to use for my own purposes by such a promise cannot possibly concur with my way of acting toward him and hence cannot himself hold the end of this action. This conflict with the principle of duty to others becomes even clearer when instances of attacks on the freedom and property of others are considered. For then it becomes clear that a transgressor of the rights of men intends to make use of the persons of others merely as a means, without taking into consideration that, as rational beings, they should always be esteemed at the same time as ends, i.e., be esteemed only as beings who must themselves be able to hold the very same action as an end.[10]

Third, with regard to contingent (meritorious) duty to oneself, it is not enough that the action does not conflict with humanity in our own person as an end in itself; the action must also harmonize with this end. Now there are in humanity capacities for greater perfection which belong to the end that nature has in view as regards humanity in our own person. To neglect these capacities might perhaps be consistent with the maintenance of humanity as an end in itself, but would not be consistent with the advancement of this end.

Fourth, concerning meritorious duty to others, the natural end that all men have is their own happiness. Now humanity might indeed subsist if nobody contributed anything to the happiness of others, provided he did not intentionally impair their happiness. But this, after all, would harmonize only negatively and not positively with humanity as an end in itself, if everyone does not also strive, as much as he can, to further the ends of others. For the ends of any subject who is an end in himself must as far as possible be my ends also, if that conception of an end in itself is to have its full effect in me.

This principle of humanity and of every rational nature generally as an end in itself is the supreme limiting condition of every man's freedom of action. . . . [T]he ground of all practical legislation lies in the rule and in the form of universality, which (according to the first principle) makes the rule capable of being a law (say, for example, a law of nature). Subjectively, however, the ground of all practical legislation lies in the end; but (according to the second principle) the subject of all ends is every rational being as an end in himself. From this there now follows the third practical principle of the will as the supreme condition of the will's conformity with universal practical reason, viz., the idea of the will of every rational being as a will that legislates universal law. . . .

The concept of every rational being as one who must regard himself as legislating universal law by all his will's maxims, so that he may judge himself and his actions from this point of view, leads to another very fruitful concept, which depends on the aforementioned one, viz., that of a kingdom of ends.

By "kingdom" I understand a systematic union of different rational beings through common laws. Now laws determine ends as regards their universal validity; therefore, if one abstracts from the personal differences of rational beings and also from all content of their private ends, then it will be possible to think of a whole of all ends in systematic connection (a whole both of rational beings as ends in themselves and also of the particular ends which each may set for himself); that is, one can think of a kingdom of ends that is possible on the aforesaid principles.

For all rational beings stand under the law that each of them should treat himself and all others never merely as a means but always at the same time as an end in himself. Hereby arises a systematic union of rational beings through common objective laws, i.e., a kingdom that may be called a kingdom of ends (certainly only an ideal), inasmuch as these laws have in view the very relation of such beings to one another as ends and means.[11]

A rational being belongs to the kingdom of ends as a member when he legislates in it universal laws while also being himself subject to those laws. He belongs to it as sovereign, when as legislator he is himself subject to the will of no other.

A rational being must always regard himself as legislator in a kingdom of ends rendered possible by freedom of the will, whether as member or as sovereign. . . .

Hence morality consists in the relation of all action to that legislation whereby alone a kingdom of ends is possible. The legislation must be found in every rational being and must be able to arise from his will, whose principle then is never to act on any maxim except such as can also be a universal law and hence such as the will can thereby regard itself as at the same time the legislator of universal law. . . .

The practical necessity of acting according to this principle, i.e., duty, does not rest at all on feelings, impulses, and inclinations, but only on the relation of rational beings to one another, a relation in which the will of a rational being must always be regarded at the same time as legislative, because otherwise he could not be thought of as an end in himself. Reason, therefore, relates every maxim of the will as legislating universal laws to every other will and also to every action toward oneself; it does so not on account of any other practical motive or future advantage but rather from the idea of the dignity of a rational being who obeys no law except what he at the same time enacts himself.

In the kingdom of ends everything has either a price or a dignity. Whatever has a price can be replaced by something else as its equivalent; on the other hand, whatever is above all price, and therefore admits of no equivalent, has a dignity.

Whatever has reference to general human inclinations and needs has a market price; whatever, without presupposing any need, accords with a certain taste, i.e., a delight in the mere unpurposive play of our mental powers, has an affective price; but that which constitutes the condition under which alone something can be an end in itself has not merely a relative worth, i.e., a price, but has an intrinsic worth, i.e., dignity.

Now morality is the condition under which alone a rational being can be an end in himself, for only thereby can he be a legislating member in the kingdom of ends. Hence morality and humanity, insofar as it is capable of morality, alone have dignity. . . .

The aforementioned three ways of representing the principle of morality are at bottom only so many formulas of the very same law: one of them by itself contains a combination of the other two. . . . All maxims have, namely,

1. A form, which consists in universality; and in this respect the formula of the moral imperative is expressed thus: maxims must be so chosen as if they were to hold as universal laws of nature.

2. A matter, viz., an end; and here the formula says that a rational being, inasmuch as he is by his very nature an end and hence an end in himself, must serve in every maxim as a condition limiting all merely relative and arbitrary ends.

3. A complete determination of all maxims by the formula that all maxims proceeding from his own legislation ought to harmonize with a possible kingdom of ends as a kingdom of nature.

NOTES

1. A maxim is the subjective principle of acting and must be distinguished from the objective principle, viz., the practical law. A maxim contains the practical rule which reason determines in accordance with the conditions of the subject (often his ignorance or his inclinations) and is thus the principle according to which the subject does act. But the law is the objective principle valid for every rational being, and it is the principle according to which he ought to act, i.e., an imperative.

2. [This formulation of the categorical imperative is often referred to as the formula of universal law.]

3. [This is often called the formula of the law of nature.]

4. I understand here by a perfect duty one which permits no exception in the interest of inclination. Accordingly, I have perfect duties which are external [to others], while other ones are internal [to oneself]. [See the boxed text on p. 33 of this book for an explanation of perfect and imperfect duties. —DRM]

5. [Not committing suicide is an example of a perfect duty to oneself. . . .]

6. [Keeping promises is an example of a perfect duty to others. . . .]

7. [Cultivating one's talents is an example of an imperfect duty to oneself. . . .]

8. [Benefiting others is an example of an imperfect duty to others. . . .]

9. [This oft-quoted version of the categorical imperative is usually referred to as the formula of the end in itself.]

10. Let it not be thought that [do not do to others what you do not want done to yourself] can here serve as a standard or principle. For it is merely derived from our principle, although with several limitations. It cannot be a universal law, for it contains the ground neither of duties to oneself nor of duties of love toward others (for many a man would gladly consent that others should not benefit him, if only he might be excused from benefiting them). Nor, finally, does it contain the ground of strict duties toward others, for the criminal would on this ground be able to dispute with the judges who punish him; and so on.

11. [This is usually called the formula of the kingdom of ends.]

DISCUSSION QUESTIONS

1. What is Kant's initial argument that a good will is the only thing that is good in itself?

2. In illustrating the Formula of Universal Law, Kant discusses four different (alleged) moral duties: the duty not to commit suicide, the duty to keep your promises, the duty to develop your talents, and the duty to help others. Are you persuaded by his arguments that the Formula of Universal Law shows that each of those things is really a duty?

3. What is the connection, according to Kant, between the Formula of Universal Law and the Formula of the End in Itself?

4. In illustrating the Formula of the End in Itself, Kant revisits the four (alleged) duties that he used in explaining the Formula of the Universal Law. Are you persuaded by his arguments that the Formula of the End in Itself shows that each of those things is really a duty?

5. How is the Formula of the Kingdom of Ends related to the Formula of the Universal Law and the Formula of the End in Itself?

JEREMY BENTHAM (1748–1832)

An Introduction to the Principles of Morals and Legislation

Jeremy Bentham's *Introduction to the Principles of Morals and Legislation* is one of the earliest statements of the normative theory known as utilitarianism. In these short excerpts, Bentham explains the basic idea behind the theory and presents his "felicific calculus," which tells you how to calculate the amount of happiness or unhappiness that a particular action or law would bring about. Unlike most of the other readings in this section, this reading does not contain much of an argument; it is mostly just an explanation of Bentham's view.

GUIDING QUESTIONS

1. What is the "principle of utility," in your own words? What does Bentham mean by "utility"?
2. What is the purpose of the principle of utility, according to Bentham? Does Bentham want to apply it to individuals' actions, to laws, or to both?
3. In Chapter IV, Bentham explains the different factors that affect the overall goodness or badness of an action. He divides these into three groups, introduced in sections II, III, and IV, respectively. What is the difference between the factors introduced in section II and the factors introduced in section III? What is the difference between all of those factors and the one that's added in section IV?

CHAPTER I. OF THE PRINCIPLE OF UTILITY

I. Nature has placed mankind under the governance of two sovereign masters, pain and pleasure. It is for them alone to point out what we ought to do, as well as to determine what we shall do. On the one hand the standard of right and wrong, on the other the chain of causes and effects, are fastened to their throne. They govern us in all we do, in all we say, in all we think: every effort we can make to throw off our subjection, will serve but to demonstrate and confirm it. In

words a man may pretend to abjure their empire: but in reality he will remain subject to it all the while. The principle of utility[1] recognizes this subjection, and assumes it for the foundation of that system, the object of which is to rear the fabric of felicity by the hands of reason and of law. Systems which attempt to question it, deal in sounds instead of sense, in caprice instead of reason, in darkness instead of light.

But enough of metaphor and declamation: it is not by such means that moral science is to be improved.

II. The principle of utility is the foundation of the present work: it will be proper therefore at the outset to give an explicit and determinate account of what is meant by it. By the principle of utility is meant that principle which approves or disapproves of every action whatsoever, according to the tendency it appears to have to augment or diminish the happiness of the party whose interest is in question: or, what is the same thing in other words to promote or to oppose that happiness. I say of every action whatsoever, and therefore not only of every action of a private individual, but of every measure of government.

III. By utility is meant that property in any object, whereby it tends to produce benefit, advantage, pleasure, good, or happiness, (all this in the present case comes to the same thing) or (what comes again to the same thing) to prevent the happening of mischief, pain, evil, or unhappiness to the party whose interest is considered: if that party be the community in general, then the happiness of the community: if a particular individual, then the happiness of that individual.

IV. The interest of the community is one of the most general expressions that can occur in the phraseology of morals: no wonder that the meaning of it is often lost. When it has a meaning, it is this. The community is a fictitious body, composed of the individual persons who are considered as constituting as it were its members. The interest of the community then is, what is it?—the sum of the interests of the several members who compose it.

V. It is in vain to talk of the interest of the community, without understanding what is the interest of the individual. A thing is said to promote the interest, or to be for the interest, of an individual, when it tends to add to the sum total of his pleasures: or, what comes to the same thing, to diminish the sum total of his pains.

VI. An action then may be said to be conformable to the principle of utility, or, for shortness sake, to utility, (meaning with respect to the community at large) when the tendency it has to augment the happiness of the community is greater than any it has to diminish it.

VII. A measure of government (which is but a particular kind of action, performed by a particular person or persons) may be said to be conformable to or dictated by the principle of utility, when in like manner the tendency which it has to augment the happiness of the community is greater than any which it has to diminish it.

VIII. When an action, or in particular a measure of government, is supposed by a man to be conformable to the principle of utility, it may be convenient, for the purposes of discourse, to imagine a kind of law or dictate, called a law or dictate of utility: and to speak of the action in question, as being conformable to such law or dictate.

IX. A man may be said to be a partizan of the principle of utility, when the approbation or disapprobation he annexes to any action, or to any measure, is determined by and proportioned to the tendency which he conceives it to have to augment or to diminish the happiness of the community: or in other words, to its conformity or unconformity to the laws or dictates of utility.

X. Of an action that is conformable to the principle of utility one may always say either that it is one that ought to be done, or at least that it is not one that ought not to be done. One may say also, that it is right it should be done; at least that it is not wrong it should be done: that it is a right action; at least that it is not a wrong action. When thus interpreted, the words ought, and right and wrong and others of that stamp, have a meaning: when otherwise, they have none.

XI. Has the rectitude of this principle been ever formally contested? It should seem that it had, by those who have not known what they have been meaning. Is it susceptible of any direct proof? it should seem not: for that which is used to prove every thing else, cannot itself be proved: a chain of proofs must have their commencement somewhere. To give such proof is as impossible as it is needless. . . .

CHAPTER IV. VALUE OF A LOT OF PLEASURE OR PAIN, HOW MEASURED

I. Pleasures then, and the avoidance of pains, are the ends that the legislator has in view; it behoves him therefore to understand their value. Pleasures and pains are the instruments he has to work with: it behoves him therefore to understand their force, which is again, in other words, their value.

II. To a person considered by himself, the value of a pleasure or pain considered by itself, will be greater or less, according to the four following circumstances:

1. Its intensity.
2. Its duration.
3. Its certainty or uncertainty.
4. Its propinquity [i.e., closeness] or remoteness [in time].

III. These are the circumstances which are to be considered in estimating a pleasure or a pain considered each of them by itself. But when the value of any pleasure or pain is considered for the purpose of estimating the tendency of any act by which it is produced, there are two other circumstances to be taken into the account; these are,

1. Its fecundity, or the chance it has of being followed by sensations of the same kind: that is, pleasures, if it be a pleasure: pains, if it be a pain.
2. Its purity, or the chance it has of not being followed by sensations of the opposite kind: that is, pains, if it be a pleasure: pleasures, if it be a pain.

These two last, however, are in strictness scarcely to be deemed properties of the pleasure or the pain itself; they are not, therefore, in strictness to be taken into the account of the value of that pleasure or that pain. They are in strictness to be deemed properties only of the act, or other event, by which such pleasure or pain has been produced; and accordingly are only to be taken into the account of the tendency of such act or such event.

IV. To a number of persons, with reference to each of whom to the value of a pleasure or a pain is considered, it will be greater or less, according to seven circumstances: to wit, the six preceding ones; viz.,

1. Its intensity.
2. Its duration.
3. Its certainty or uncertainty.
4. Its propinquity [i.e., closeness] or remoteness [in time].
5. Its fecundity.
6. Its purity.

And one other; to wit:

7. Its extent; that is, the number of persons to whom it extends; or (in other words) who are affected by it.

V. To take an exact account then of the general tendency of any act, by which the interests of a community are affected, proceed as follows. Begin with any one person of those whose interests seem most immediately to be affected by it: and take an account,

1. Of the value of each distinguishable pleasure which appears to be produced by it in the first instance.
2. Of the value of each pain which appears to be produced by it in the first instance.
3. Of the value of each pleasure which appears to be produced by it after the first. This constitutes the fecundity of the first pleasure and the impurity of the first pain.
4. Of the value of each pain which appears to be produced by it after the first. This constitutes the fecundity of the first pain, and the impurity of the first pleasure.
5. Sum up all the values of all the pleasures on the one side, and those of all the pains on the other. The balance, if it be on the side of pleasure, will give the good tendency of the act upon the whole, with respect to the interests of that individual person; if on the side of pain, the bad tendency of it upon the whole.

6. Take an account of the number of persons whose interests appear to be concerned; and repeat the above process with respect to each. Sum up the numbers expressive of the degrees of good tendency, which the act has, with respect to each individual, in regard to whom the tendency of it is good upon the whole: do this again with respect to each individual, in regard to whom the tendency of it is good upon the whole: do this again with respect to each individual, in regard to whom the tendency of it is bad upon the whole. Take the balance which if on the side of pleasure, will give the general good tendency of the act, with respect to the total number or community of individuals concerned; if on the side of pain, the general evil tendency, with respect to the same community.

VI. It is not to be expected that this process should be strictly pursued previously to every moral judgment, or to every legislative or judicial operation. It may, however, be always kept in view: and as near as the process actually pursued on these occasions approaches to it, so near will such process approach to the character of an exact one.

VII. The same process is alike applicable to pleasure and pain, in whatever shape they appear: and by whatever denomination they are distinguished: to pleasure, whether it be called good (which is properly the cause or instrument of pleasure) or profit (which is distant pleasure, or the cause or instrument of, distant pleasure,) or convenience, or advantage, benefit, emolument, happiness, and so forth: to pain, whether it be called evil, (which corresponds to good) or mischief, or inconvenience or disadvantage, or loss, or unhappiness, and so forth.

VIII. Nor is this a novel and unwarranted, any more than it is a useless theory. In all this there is nothing but what the practice of mankind, wheresoever they have a clear view of their own interest, is perfectly conformable to. An article of property, an estate in land, for instance, is valuable, on what account? On account of the pleasures of all kinds which it enables a man to produce, and what comes to the same thing the pains of all kinds which it enables him to avert. But the value of such an article of property is universally understood to rise or fall according to the length or shortness of the time which a man has in it: the certainty or uncertainty of its coming into possession: and the nearness or remoteness of the time at which, if at all, it is to come into possession. As to the intensity of the pleasures which a man may derive from it, this is never thought of, because it depends upon the use which each particular person may come to make of it; which cannot be estimated till the particular pleasures he may come to derive from it, or the particular pains he may come to exclude by means of it, are brought to view. For the same reason, neither does he think of the fecundity or purity of those pleasures. Thus much for pleasure and pain, happiness and unhappiness, in general. We come now to consider the several particular kinds of pain and pleasure.

NOTE

1. [In a later edition, Bentham adds a footnote here explaining that it might have been better to call this the principle of "happiness" because it clarifies the principle's connection to pleasure and pain. —DRM]

DISCUSSION QUESTIONS

1. How do Bentham's views about human psychology, as explained in Chapter I, influence his moral philosophy?

2. In your own words, how does Bentham think we can compare the goodness or badness of different actions?

3. Bentham's principle of utility is sometimes paraphrased as saying that the right action is the one that produces "the greatest happiness for the greatest number." Is this an accurate way of explaining the principle of utility? Why or why not?

JOHN STUART MILL (1806–1873)

Utilitarianism

J. S. Mill originally published *Utilitarianism* in order to explain the theory of utilitarianism and defend it against its critics. These excerpts include parts of two different chapters. One chapter explains what utilitarianism is and defends it against various objections. It also introduces Mill's controversial idea that some pleasures are of higher quality than others. The other chapter discusses the relationship between utilitarianism and justice.

GUIDING QUESTIONS

1. What is the Greatest Happiness Principle, and what role does it play in Mill's moral philosophy?
2. How, according to Mill, does one determine which pleasures are of higher quality than others?
3. What are the major criticisms of utilitarianism to which Mill is replying in Chapter 2?
4. What is Mill's main point in Chapter 5? What is his argument for that main point?

CHAPTER 2. WHAT UTILITARIANISM IS

The creed which accepts as the foundation of morals, Utility, or the Greatest Happiness Principle, holds that actions are right in proportion as they tend to promote happiness, wrong as they tend to produce the reverse of happiness. By happiness is intended pleasure, and the absence of pain; by unhappiness, pain, and the privation of pleasure. To give a clear view of the moral standard set up by the theory, much more requires to be said; in particular, what things it includes in the ideas of pain and pleasure; and to what extent this is left an open question. But these supplementary explanations do not affect the theory of life on which this theory of morality is grounded—namely, that pleasure, and freedom from pain, are the only things desirable as ends; and that all desirable things (which are as numerous in the utilitarian as in any other scheme) are desirable either for the

pleasure inherent in themselves, or as means to the promotion of pleasure and the prevention of pain.

Now, such a theory of life excites in many minds, and among them in some of the most estimable in feeling and purpose, inveterate dislike. To suppose that life has (as they express it) no higher end than pleasure—no better and nobler object of desire and pursuit—they designate as utterly mean and grovelling; as a doctrine worthy only of swine, to whom the followers of Epicurus were, at a very early period, contemptuously likened; and modern holders of the doctrine are occasionally made the subject of equally polite comparisons by its German, French, and English assailants.

When thus attacked, the Epicureans have always answered, that it is not they, but their accusers, who represent human nature in a degrading light; since the accusation supposes human beings to be capable of no pleasures except those of which swine are capable. If this supposition were true, the charge could not be gainsaid, but would then be no longer an imputation; for if the sources of pleasure were precisely the same to human beings and to swine, the rule of life which is good enough for the one would be good enough for the other. The comparison of the Epicurean life to that of beasts is felt as degrading, precisely because a beast's pleasures do not satisfy a human being's conceptions of happiness. Human beings have faculties more elevated than the animal appetites, and when once made conscious of them, do not regard anything as happiness which does not include their gratification. I do not, indeed, consider the Epicureans to have been by any means faultless in drawing out their scheme of consequences from the utilitarian principle. To do this in any sufficient manner, many Stoic, as well as Christian elements require to be included. But there is no known Epicurean theory of life which does not assign to the pleasures of the intellect, of the feelings and imagination, and of the moral sentiments, a much higher value as pleasures than to those of mere sensation. It must be admitted, however, that utilitarian writers in general have placed the superiority of mental over bodily pleasures chiefly in the greater permanency, safety, uncostliness, etc., of the former—that is, in their circumstantial advantages rather than in their intrinsic nature. And on all these points utilitarians have fully proved their case; but they might have taken the other, and, as it may be called, higher ground, with entire consistency. It is quite compatible with the principle of utility to recognise the fact, that some kinds of pleasure are more desirable and more valuable than others. It would be absurd that while, in estimating all other things, quality is considered as well as quantity, the estimation of pleasures should be supposed to depend on quantity alone.

If I am asked, what I mean by difference of quality in pleasures, or what makes one pleasure more valuable than another, merely as a pleasure, except its being greater in amount, there is but one possible answer. Of two pleasures, if there be one to which all or almost all who have experience of both give a decided preference, irrespective of any feeling of moral obligation to prefer it, that is the more desirable pleasure. If one of the two is, by those who are competently acquainted with both, placed so far above the other that they prefer it, even though knowing it to

be attended with a greater amount of discontent, and would not resign it for any quantity of the other pleasure which their nature is capable of, we are justified in ascribing to the preferred enjoyment a superiority in quality, so far outweighing quantity as to render it, in comparison, of small account.

Now it is an unquestionable fact that those who are equally acquainted with, and equally capable of appreciating and enjoying, both, do give a most marked preference to the manner of existence which employs their higher faculties. Few human creatures would consent to be changed into any of the lower animals, for a promise of the fullest allowance of a beast's pleasures; no intelligent human being would consent to be a fool, no instructed person would be an ignoramus, no person of feeling and conscience would be selfish and base, even though they should be persuaded that the fool, the dunce, or the rascal is better satisfied with his lot than they are with theirs. They would not resign what they possess more than he for the most complete satisfaction of all the desires which they have in common with him. If they ever fancy they would, it is only in cases of unhappiness so extreme, that to escape from it they would exchange their lot for almost any other, however undesirable in their own eyes. A being of higher faculties requires more to make him happy, is capable probably of more acute suffering, and certainly accessible to it at more points, than one of an inferior type; but in spite of these liabilities, he can never really wish to sink into what he feels to be a lower grade of existence. We may give what explanation we please of this unwillingness; we may attribute it to pride, a name which is given indiscriminately to some of the most and to some of the least estimable feelings of which mankind are capable: we may refer it to the love of liberty and personal independence, an appeal to which was with the Stoics one of the most effective means for the inculcation of it; to the love of power, or to the love of excitement, both of which do really enter into and contribute to it: but its most appropriate appellation is a sense of dignity, which all human beings possess in one form or other, and in some, though by no means in exact, proportion to their higher faculties, and which is so essential a part of the happiness of those in whom it is strong, that nothing which conflicts with it could be, otherwise than momentarily, an object of desire to them.

Whoever supposes that this preference takes place at a sacrifice of happiness—that the superior being, in anything like equal circumstances, is not happier than the inferior—confounds the two very different ideas, of happiness, and content. It is indisputable that the being whose capacities of enjoyment are low, has the greatest chance of having them fully satisfied; and a highly endowed being will always feel that any happiness which he can look for, as the world is constituted, is imperfect. But he can learn to bear its imperfections, if they are at all bearable; and they will not make him envy the being who is indeed unconscious of the imperfections, but only because he feels not at all the good which those imperfections qualify. It is better to be a human being dissatisfied than a pig satisfied; better to be Socrates dissatisfied than a fool satisfied. And if the fool, or the pig, are of a different opinion, it is because they only know their own side of the question. The other party to the comparison knows both sides.

It may be objected, that many who are capable of the higher pleasures, occasionally, under the influence of temptation, postpone them to the lower. But this is quite compatible with a full appreciation of the intrinsic superiority of the higher. Men often, from infirmity of character, make their election for the nearer good, though they know it to be the less valuable; and this no less when the choice is between two bodily pleasures, than when it is between bodily and mental. They pursue sensual indulgences to the injury of health, though perfectly aware that health is the greater good.

It may be further objected, that many who begin with youthful enthusiasm for everything noble, as they advance in years sink into indolence and selfishness. But I do not believe that those who undergo this very common change, voluntarily choose the lower description of pleasures in preference to the higher. I believe that before they devote themselves exclusively to the one, they have already become incapable of the other. Capacity for the nobler feelings is in most natures a very tender plant, easily killed, not only by hostile influences, but by mere want of sustenance; and in the majority of young persons it speedily dies away if the occupations to which their position in life has devoted them, and the society into which it has thrown them, are not favourable to keeping that higher capacity in exercise. Men lose their high aspirations as they lose their intellectual tastes, because they have not time or opportunity for indulging them; and they addict themselves to inferior pleasures, not because they deliberately prefer them, but because they are either the only ones to which they have access, or the only ones which they are any longer capable of enjoying. It may be questioned whether any one who has remained equally susceptible to both classes of pleasures, ever knowingly and calmly preferred the lower; though many, in all ages, have broken down in an ineffectual attempt to combine both.

From this verdict of the only competent judges, I apprehend there can be no appeal. On a question which is the best worth having of two pleasures, or which of two modes of existence is the most grateful to the feelings, apart from its moral attributes and from its consequences, the judgment of those who are qualified by knowledge of both, or, if they differ, that of the majority among them, must be admitted as final. And there needs be the less hesitation to accept this judgment respecting the quality of pleasures, since there is no other tribunal to be referred to even on the question of quantity. What means are there of determining which is the acutest of two pains, or the intensest of two pleasurable sensations, except the general suffrage of those who are familiar with both? Neither pains nor pleasures are homogeneous, and pain is always heterogeneous with pleasure. What is there to decide whether a particular pleasure is worth purchasing at the cost of a particular pain, except the feelings and judgment of the experienced? When, therefore, those feelings and judgment declare the pleasures derived from the higher faculties to be preferable in kind, apart from the question of intensity, to those of which the animal nature, disjoined from the higher faculties, is susceptible, they are entitled on this subject to the same regard.

I have dwelt on this point, as being a necessary part of a perfectly just conception of Utility or Happiness, considered as the directive rule of human conduct. But it is by no means an indispensable condition to the acceptance of the utilitarian standard; for that standard is not the agent's own greatest happiness, but the greatest amount of happiness altogether; and if it may possibly be doubted whether a noble character is always the happier for its nobleness, there can be no doubt that it makes other people happier, and that the world in general is immensely a gainer by it. Utilitarianism, therefore, could only attain its end by the general cultivation of nobleness of character, even if each individual were only benefited by the nobleness of others, and his own, so far as happiness is concerned, were a sheer deduction from the benefit. But the bare enunciation of such an absurdity as this last, renders refutation superfluous.

According to the Greatest Happiness Principle, as above explained, the ultimate end, with reference to and for the sake of which all other things are desirable (whether we are considering our own good or that of other people), is an existence exempt as far as possible from pain, and as rich as possible in enjoyments, both in point of quantity and quality; the test of quality, and the rule for measuring it against quantity, being the preference felt by those who in their opportunities of experience, to which must be added their habits of self-consciousness and self-observation, are best furnished with the means of comparison. This, being, according to the utilitarian opinion, the end of human action, is necessarily also the standard of morality; which may accordingly be defined, the rules and precepts for human conduct, by the observance of which an existence such as has been described might be, to the greatest extent possible, secured to all mankind; and not to them only, but, so far as the nature of things admits, to the whole sentient creation. . . .

Unquestionably it is possible to do without happiness; it is done involuntarily by nineteen-twentieths of mankind, even in those parts of our present world which are least deep in barbarism; and it often has to be done voluntarily by the hero or the martyr, for the sake of something which he prizes more than his individual happiness. But this something, what is it, unless the happiness of others or some of the requisites of happiness? It is noble to be capable of resigning entirely one's own portion of happiness, or chances of it: but, after all, this self-sacrifice must be for some end; it is not its own end; and if we are told that its end is not happiness, but virtue, which is better than happiness, I ask, would the sacrifice be made if the hero or martyr did not believe that it would earn for others immunity from similar sacrifices? Would it be made if he thought that his renunciation of happiness for himself would produce no fruit for any of his fellow creatures, but to make their lot like his, and place them also in the condition of persons who have renounced happiness? All honour to those who can abnegate for themselves the personal enjoyment of life, when by such renunciation they contribute worthily to increase the amount of happiness in the world; but he who does it, or professes to do it, for any other purpose, is no more deserving of admiration than the ascetic mounted on his pillar. He may be an inspiriting proof of what men can do, but assuredly not an example of what they should.

Though it is only in a very imperfect state of the world's arrangements that any one can best serve the happiness of others by the absolute sacrifice of his own, yet so long as the world is in that imperfect state, I fully acknowledge that the readiness to make such a sacrifice is the highest virtue which can be found in man. . . .

The utilitarian morality does recognise in human beings the power of sacrificing their own greatest good for the good of others. It only refuses to admit that the sacrifice is itself a good. A sacrifice which does not increase, or tend to increase, the sum total of happiness, it considers as wasted. The only self-renunciation which it applauds, is devotion to the happiness, or to some of the means of happiness, of others; either of mankind collectively, or of individuals within the limits imposed by the collective interests of mankind.

I must again repeat, what the assailants of utilitarianism seldom have the justice to acknowledge, that the happiness which forms the utilitarian standard of what is right in conduct, is not the agent's own happiness, but that of all concerned. As between his own happiness and that of others, utilitarianism requires him to be as strictly impartial as a disinterested and benevolent spectator. In the golden rule of Jesus of Nazareth, we read the complete spirit of the ethics of utility. To do as you would be done by, and to love your neighbour as yourself, constitute the ideal perfection of utilitarian morality. . . .

The objectors to utilitarianism cannot always be charged with representing it in a discreditable light. On the contrary, those among them who entertain anything like a just idea of its disinterested character, sometimes find fault with its standard as being too high for humanity. They say it is exacting too much to require that people shall always act from the inducement of promoting the general interests of society. But this is to mistake the very meaning of a standard of morals, and confound the rule of action with the motive of it. It is the business of ethics to tell us what are our duties, or by what test we may know them; but no system of ethics requires that the sole motive of all we do shall be a feeling of duty; on the contrary, ninety-nine hundredths of all our actions are done from other motives, and rightly so done, if the rule of duty does not condemn them. It is the more unjust to utilitarianism that this particular misapprehension should be made a ground of objection to it, inasmuch as utilitarian moralists have gone beyond almost all others in affirming that the motive has nothing to do with the morality of the action, though much with the worth of the agent. He who saves a fellow creature from drowning does what is morally right, whether his motive be duty, or the hope of being paid for his trouble; he who betrays the friend that trusts him, is guilty of a crime, even if his object be to serve another friend to whom he is under greater obligations.

But to speak only of actions done from the motive of duty, and in direct obedience to principle: it is a misapprehension of the utilitarian mode of thought, to conceive it as implying that people should fix their minds upon so wide a generality as the world, or society at large. The great majority of good actions are intended not for the benefit of the world, but for that of individuals, of which the good of the world is made up; and the thoughts of the most virtuous man need not on these occasions travel beyond the particular persons concerned, except so far as is necessary to assure himself that in benefiting them he is not violating the rights, that is, the legitimate and authorised expectations, of any one else. The multiplication of happiness is, according to the utilitarian

ethics, the object of virtue: the occasions on which any person (except one in a thousand) has it in his power to do this on an extended scale, in other words to be a public benefactor, are but exceptional; and on these occasions alone is he called on to consider public utility; in every other case, private utility, the interest or happiness of some few persons, is all he has to attend to. Those alone the influence of whose actions extends to society in general, need concern themselves habitually about large an object. In the case of abstinences indeed—of things which people forbear to do from moral considerations, though the consequences in the particular case might be beneficial—it would be unworthy of an intelligent agent not to be consciously aware that the action is of a class which, if practised generally, would be generally injurious, and that this is the ground of the obligation to abstain from it. The amount of regard for the public interest implied in this recognition, is no greater than is demanded by every system of morals, for they all enjoin to abstain from whatever is manifestly pernicious to society. . . .

It may not be superfluous to notice a few more of the common misapprehensions of utilitarian ethics, even those which are so obvious and gross that it might appear impossible for any person of candour and intelligence to fall into them; since persons, even of considerable mental endowments, often give themselves so little trouble to understand the bearings of any opinion against which they entertain a prejudice, and men are in general so little conscious of this voluntary ignorance as a defect, that the vulgarest misunderstandings of ethical doctrines are continually met with in the deliberate writings of persons of the greatest pretensions both to high principle and to philosophy. We not uncommonly hear the doctrine of utility inveighed against as a godless doctrine. If it be necessary to say anything at all against so mere an assumption, we may say that the question depends upon what idea we have formed of the moral character of the Deity. If it be a true belief that God desires, above all things, the happiness of his creatures, and that this was his purpose in their creation, utility is not only not a godless doctrine, but more profoundly religious than any other. If it be meant that utilitarianism does not recognise the revealed will of God as the supreme law of morals, I answer, that a utilitarian who believes in the perfect goodness and wisdom of God, necessarily believes that whatever God has thought fit to reveal on the subject of morals, must fulfil the requirements of utility in a supreme degree. But others besides utilitarians have been of opinion that the Christian revelation was intended, and is fitted, to inform the hearts and minds of mankind with a spirit which should enable them to find for themselves what is right, and incline them to do it when found, rather than to tell them, except in a very general way, what it is; and that we need a doctrine of ethics, carefully followed out, to interpret to us the will of God. Whether this opinion is correct or not, it is superfluous here to discuss; since whatever aid religion, either natural or revealed, can afford to ethical investigation, is as open to the utilitarian moralist as to any other. He can use it as the testimony of God to the usefulness or hurtfulness of any given course of action, by as good a right as others can use it for the indication of a transcendental law, having no connection with usefulness or with happiness.

Again, Utility is often summarily stigmatised as an immoral doctrine by giving it the name of Expediency, and taking advantage of the popular use of that term to contrast it with Principle. But the Expedient, in the sense in which it is opposed to the Right, generally means that which is expedient for the particular interest of the agent himself; as when a minister sacrifices the interests of his country to keep himself in place. When it means anything better than this, it means that which is expedient for some immediate object, some temporary purpose, but which violates a rule whose observance is expedient in a much higher degree. The Expedient, in this sense, instead of being the same thing with the useful, is a branch of the hurtful. Thus, it would often be expedient, for the purpose of getting over some momentary embarrassment, or attaining some object immediately useful to ourselves or others, to tell a lie. But inasmuch as the cultivation in ourselves of a sensitive feeling on the subject of veracity, is one of the most useful, and the enfeeblement of that feeling one of the most hurtful, things to which our conduct can be instrumental; and inasmuch as any, even unintentional, deviation from truth, does that much towards weakening the trustworthiness of human assertion, which is not only the principal support of all present social well-being, but the insufficiency of which does more than any one thing that can be named to keep back civilisation, virtue, everything on which human happiness on the largest scale depends; we feel that the violation, for a present advantage, of a rule of such transcendant expediency, is not expedient, and that he who, for the sake of a convenience to himself or to some other individual, does what depends on him to deprive mankind of the good, and inflict upon them the evil, involved in the greater or less reliance which they can place in each other's word, acts the part of one of their worst enemies. Yet that even this rule, sacred as it is, admits of possible exceptions, is acknowledged by all moralists; the chief of which is when the withholding of some fact (as of information from a malefactor, or of bad news from a person dangerously ill) would save an individual (especially an individual other than oneself) from great and unmerited evil, and when the withholding can only be effected by denial. But in order that the exception may not extend itself beyond the need, and may have the least possible effect in weakening reliance on veracity, it ought to be recognised, and, if possible, its limits defined; and if the principle of utility is good for anything, it must be good for weighing these conflicting utilities against one another, and marking out the region within which one or the other preponderates.

Again, defenders of utility often find themselves called upon to reply to such objections as this—that there is not time, previous to action, for calculating and weighing the effects of any line of conduct on the general happiness. This is exactly as if any one were to say that it is impossible to guide our conduct by Christianity, because there is not time, on every occasion on which anything has to be done, to read through the Old and New Testaments. The answer to the objection is, that there has been ample time, namely, the whole past duration of the human species. During all that time, mankind have been learning by experience the tendencies of actions; on which experience all the prudence, as well as all the morality of life, are dependent. People talk as if the commencement of this course of experience had hitherto been put off, and as if, at the moment when some man feels tempted to meddle with the property or life of another, he had to begin considering for the first time whether murder and theft are injurious to human happiness. Even then I do not think that he would find the question very puzzling; but, at all events, the matter is now done to his hand.

It is truly a whimsical supposition that, if mankind were agreed in considering utility to be the test of morality, they would remain without any agreement as to what is useful, and would take no measures for having their notions on the subject taught to the young, and enforced by law and opinion. There is no difficulty in proving any ethical standard whatever to work ill, if we suppose universal idiocy to be conjoined with it; but on any hypothesis short of that, mankind must by this time have acquired positive beliefs as to the effects of some actions on their happiness; and the beliefs which have thus come down are the rules of morality for the multitude, and for the philosopher until he has succeeded in finding better. That philosophers might easily do this, even now, on many subjects; that the received code of ethics is by no means of divine right; and that mankind have still much to learn as to the effects of actions on the general happiness, I admit, or rather, earnestly maintain. The corollaries from the principle of utility, like the precepts of every practical art, admit of indefinite improvement, and, in a progressive state of the human mind, their improvement is perpetually going on.

But to consider the rules of morality as improvable, is one thing; to pass over the intermediate generalisations entirely, and endeavour to test each individual action directly by the first principle, is another. It is a strange notion that the acknowledgment of a first principle is inconsistent with the admission of secondary ones. To inform a traveller respecting the place of his. ultimate destination, is not to forbid the use of landmarks and direction-posts on the way. The proposition that happiness is the end and aim of morality, does not mean that no road ought to be laid down to that goal, or that persons going thither should not be advised to take one direction rather than another. Men really ought to leave off talking a kind of nonsense on this subject, which

they would neither talk nor listen to on other matters of practical concernment. Nobody argues that the art of navigation is not founded on astronomy, because sailors cannot wait to calculate the Nautical Almanack. Being rational creatures, they go to sea with it ready calculated; and all rational creatures go out upon the sea of life with their minds made up on the common questions of right and wrong, as well as on many of the far more difficult questions of wise and foolish. And this, as long as foresight is a human quality, it is to be presumed they will continue to do. Whatever we adopt as the fundamental principle of morality, we require subordinate principles to apply it by; the impossibility of doing without them, being common to all systems, can afford no argument against any one in particular; but gravely to argue as if no such secondary principles could be had, and as if mankind had remained till now, and always must remain, without drawing any general conclusions from the experience of human life, is as high a pitch, I think, as absurdity has ever reached in philosophical controversy. . . .

CHAPTER 5. ON THE CONNECTION BETWEEN JUSTICE AND UTILITY

In all ages of speculation, one of the strongest obstacles to the reception of the doctrine that Utility or Happiness is the criterion of right and wrong, has been drawn from the idea of justice. The powerful sentiment, and apparently clear perception, which that word recalls with a rapidity and certainty resembling an instinct, have seemed to the majority of thinkers to point to an inherent quality in things; to show that the just must have an existence in Nature as something absolute, generically distinct from every variety of the Expedient, and, in idea, opposed to it, though (as is commonly acknowledged) never, in the long run, disjoined from it in fact.

In the case of this, as of our other moral sentiments, there is no necessary connection between the question of its origin, and that of its binding force.

That a feeling is bestowed on us by Nature, does not necessarily legitimate all its promptings. The feeling of justice might be a peculiar instinct, and might yet require, like our other instincts, to be controlled and enlightened by a higher reason. . . .

Now it is known that ethical writers divide moral duties into two classes, denoted by the ill-chosen expressions, duties of perfect and of imperfect obligation; the latter being those in which, though the act is obligatory, the particular occasions of performing it are left to our choice, as in the case of charity or beneficence, which we are indeed bound to practise, but not towards any definite person, nor at any prescribed time. In the more precise language of philosophic jurists, duties of perfect obligation are those duties in virtue of which a correlative right resides in some person or persons; duties of imperfect obligation are those moral obligations which do not give birth to any right. I think it will be found that this distinction exactly coincides with that which exists between justice and the other obligations of morality. In our survey of the various popular acceptations of justice, the term appeared generally to involve the idea of a personal right—a claim on the part of one or more individuals, like that which the law gives when it confers a proprietary or other legal right. Whether the injustice consists in depriving a person of a possession, or in breaking faith with him, or in treating him worse than he deserves, or worse than other people who have no greater claims, in each case the supposition implies two things—a wrong done, and some assignable person who is wronged. Injustice may also be done by treating a person better than others; but the wrong in this case is to his competitors, who are also assignable persons.

It seems to me that this feature in the case—a right in some person, correlative to the moral obligation—constitutes the specific difference between justice, and generosity or beneficence. Justice implies something which it is not only right to do, and wrong not to do, but which some individual person can claim from us as his moral right. No one has a moral right to our generosity or beneficence, because we are not morally bound to practise those virtues towards any given individual. And it will be found with respect to

this, as to every correct definition, that the instances which seem to conflict with it are those which most confirm it. For if a moralist attempts, as some have done, to make out that mankind generally, though not any given individual, have a right to all the good we can do them, he at once, by that thesis, includes generosity and beneficence within the category of justice. He is obliged to say, that our utmost exertions are due to our fellow creatures, thus assimilating them to a debt; or that nothing less can be a sufficient return for what society does for us, thus classing the case as one of gratitude; both of which are acknowledged cases of justice. Wherever there is right, the case is one of justice, and not of the virtue of beneficence: and whoever does not place the distinction between justice and morality in general, where we have now placed it, will be found to make no distinction between them at all, but to merge all morality in justice. . . .

To have a right, then, is, I conceive, to have something which society ought to defend me in the possession of. If the objector goes on to ask, why it ought? I can give him no other reason than general utility. If that expression does not seem to convey a sufficient feeling of the strength of the obligation, nor to account for the peculiar energy of the feeling, it is because there goes to the composition of the sentiment, not a rational only, but also an animal element, the thirst for retaliation; and this thirst derives its intensity, as well as its moral justification, from the extraordinarily important and impressive kind of utility which is concerned. The interest involved is that of security, to every one's feelings the most vital of all interests. All other earthly benefits are needed by one person, not needed by another; and many of them can, if necessary, be cheerfully foregone, or replaced by something else; but security no human being can possibly do without on it we depend for all our immunity from evil, and for the whole value of all and every good, beyond the passing moment; since nothing but the gratification of the instant could be of any worth to us, if we could be deprived of anything the next instant by whoever was momentarily stronger than ourselves. Now this most indispensable of all necessaries, after physical nutriment, cannot be had, unless the machinery for providing it is kept unintermittedly in active play. Our notion, therefore, of the claim we have on our fellow-creatures to join in making safe for us the very groundwork of our existence, gathers feelings around it so much more intense than those concerned in any of the more common cases of utility, that the difference in degree (as is often the case in psychology) becomes a real difference in kind. The claim assumes that character of absoluteness, that apparent infinity, and incommensurability with all other considerations, which constitute the distinction between the feeling of right and wrong and that of ordinary expediency and inexpediency. . . .

It appears from what has been said, that justice is a name for certain moral requirements, which, regarded collectively, stand higher in the scale of social utility, and are therefore of more paramount obligation, than any others; though particular cases may occur in which some other social duty is so important, as to overrule any one of the general maxims of justice. Thus, to save a life, it may not only be allowable, but a duty, to steal, or take by force, the necessary food or medicine, or to kidnap, and compel to officiate, the only qualified medical practitioner. In such cases, as we do not call anything justice which is not a virtue, we usually say, not that justice must give way to some other moral principle, but that what is just in ordinary cases is, by reason of that other principle, not just in the particular case. By this useful accommodation of language, the character of indefeasibility attributed to justice is kept up, and we are saved from the necessity of maintaining that there can be laudable injustice.

The considerations which have now been adduced resolve, I conceive, the only real difficulty in the utilitarian theory of morals. It has always been evident that all cases of justice are also cases of expediency: the difference is in the peculiar sentiment which attaches to the former, as contradistinguished from the latter. If this characteristic sentiment has been sufficiently accounted for; if there is no necessity to assume for it any peculiarity of origin; if it is simply the natural feeling of resentment, moralised by being made coextensive with the demands of social good; and if this feeling not only does but ought to exist in all the classes of cases to which the idea of justice corresponds; that idea no longer presents itself as a stumbling-block to the utilitarian ethics.

Justice remains the appropriate name for certain social utilities which are vastly more important, and therefore more absolute and imperative, than any others are as a class (though not more so than others may be in particular cases); and which, therefore, ought to be, as well as naturally are, guarded by a sentiment not only different in degree, but also in kind; distinguished from the milder feeling which attaches to the mere idea of promoting human pleasure or convenience, at once by the more definite nature of its commands, and by the sterner character of its sanctions.

DISCUSSION QUESTIONS

1. What philosophical problem is Mill's distinction between higher and lower pleasures supposed to solve? Do you think he successfully solves that problem? Why or why not?
2. Of the various objections to utilitarianism that Mill discusses in Chapter 2, which do you think is most important? Do you think Mill successfully replies to that objection? Why or why not?
3. Why, according to Mill, is it wrong to tell a lie to save yourself from momentary embarrassment?
4. What is the connection between justice and utility, according to Mill? What is his argument for the claim that they are connected in that way?

ARISTOTLE (384–322 BCE)
TRANSLATED BY TERENCE IRWIN

Nicomachean Ethics

Aristotle's *Nicomachean Ethics* offers one of the classic accounts of virtue ethics. In the excerpts presented here, Aristotle explains what he thinks the goal of ethics is, why he thinks that we should understand ethics in terms of virtue, and how he understands virtue in general. He also explains some specific virtues, such as courage and justice. As you read these excerpts, it may help to know that the translator has used the word happiness to translate the Greek word *eudaimonia*, which has a broader meaning in Greek than *happiness* does in English (see pp. 122–23).

GUIDING QUESTIONS

1. According to Aristotle, what are we trying to figure out when we do moral philosophy?
2. What is wrong with the "life of gratification," the "life of honor," and the life of the "moneymaker," according to Aristotle?
3. What is Aristotle's main claim about the best human life? What is his argument for that claim?
4. What is a virtue, according to Aristotle? How does one become virtuous?
5. What are some examples of virtues, and how do they illustrate his ideas about virtues and the "mean" between two extremes?
6. What are the two kinds of justice?
7. What is the best kind of life, according to Aristotle? What arguments does he give for this conclusion?

BOOK I

1. Every craft and every line of inquiry . . . seems to seek some good; that is why some people were right to describe the good as what everything seeks. But the ends [that are sought] appear to differ; some are activities, and others are products apart from the activities. . . .

Since there are many actions, crafts, and sciences, the ends turn out to be many as well; for health is the end of medicine, a boat of boat building, victory of generalship, and wealth of household management. But some of these pursuits are subordinate to some one capacity; for instance, bridle making and every other science producing equipment for horses are subordinate to horsemanship, while this and every action in warfare are, in turn, subordinate to generalship. . . . In all such cases, then, the ends of the ruling sciences are more choiceworthy than all the ends subordinate to them, since the lower ends are also pursued for the sake of the higher. . . .

2. Suppose, then, that the things achievable by action have some end that we wish for because of itself, and because of which we wish for the other things, and that we do not choose everything because of something else—for if we do, it will go on without

limit, so that desire will prove to be empty and futile. Clearly, this end will be . . . the best good.

Then does knowledge of this good carry great weight for [our] way of life, and would it make us better able, like archers who have a target to aim at, to hit the right mark? If so, we should try to grasp, in outline at any rate, what the good is, and which is its proper science. . . .

It seems proper to the most controlling science—the highest ruling science. And this appears characteristic of political science. For it is the one that prescribes which of the sciences ought to be studied in cities, and which ones each class in the city should learn, and how far; indeed, we see that even the most honored capacities—generalship, household management, and rhetoric, for instance—are subordinate to it. And since it uses the other sciences concerned with action, and moreover legislates what must be done and what avoided, its end will include the ends of the other sciences, and so this will be the human good. . . .

3. Our discussion will be adequate if we make things perspicuous enough to accord with the subject matter; for we would not seek the same degree of exactness in all sorts of arguments alike, any more than in the products of different crafts. Now, fine and just things . . . differ and vary so much as to seem to rest on convention only, not on nature. But [this is not a good reason, since] goods also vary in the same way, because they result in harm to many people—for some have been destroyed because of their wealth, others because of their bravery. And so, since this is our subject and these are our premises, we shall be satisfied to indicate the truth roughly and in outline; since our subject and our premises are things that hold good usually [but not universally], we shall be satisfied to draw conclusions of the same sort.

Each of our claims, then, ought to be accepted in the same way [as claiming to hold good usually]. For the educated person seeks exactness in each area to the extent that the nature of the subject allows; for apparently it is just as mistaken to demand demonstrations from a rhetorician as to accept [merely] persuasive arguments from a mathematician. Further, each person judges rightly what he knows, and

is a good judge about that; hence the good judge in a given area is the person educated in that area. . . .

This is why a youth is not a suitable student of political science; for he lacks experience of the actions in life. . . . Moreover, since he tends to follow his feelings, his study will be futile and useless; for the end [of political science] is action, not knowledge. . . . But for those who accord with reason in forming their desires and in their actions, knowledge of political science will be of great benefit. . . .

4. Let us, then, begin again. Since every sort of knowledge and decision pursues some good, what is the good that we say political science seeks? What, [in other words,] is the highest of all the goods achievable in action?

As far as its name goes, most people virtually agree; for both the many and the cultivated call it happiness, and they suppose that living well and doing well are the same as being happy. But they disagree about what happiness is, and the many do not give the same answer as the wise.

For the many think it is something obvious and evident—for instance, pleasure, wealth, or honor. Some take it to be one thing, others another. Indeed, the same person often changes his mind. . . .

5. For, it would seem, people quite reasonably reach their conception of the good, i.e., of happiness, from the lives [they lead]; for there are roughly three most favored lives: the lives of gratification, of political activity, and, third, of study.

The many, the most vulgar, would seem to conceive the good and happiness as pleasure, and hence they also like the life of gratification. In this they appear completely slavish, since the life they decide on is a life for grazing animals. Still, they have some argument in their defense, since many in positions of power feel as [the famously pleasure-loving Assyrian king] Sardanapallus felt, [and also choose this life].

The cultivated people, those active [in politics], conceive the good as honor, since this is more or less the end [normally pursued] in the political life. This, however, appears to be too superficial to be what we are seeking; for it seems to depend more on those who honor than on the one honored, whereas we intuitively believe that the good is something of our own and hard to take from us. Further, it would seem, they pursue honor to convince themselves that they are good; at any rate, they seek to be honored by prudent people, among people who know them, and for virtue. It is clear, then, that—in their view at any rate—virtue is superior [to honor].

Perhaps, indeed, one might conceive virtue more than honor to be the end of the political life. However, this also is apparently too incomplete [to be the good]. For it seems possible for someone to possess virtue but be asleep or inactive throughout his life, and, moreover, to suffer the worst evils and misfortunes. If this is the sort of life he leads, no one would count him as happy. . . .

The third life is the life of study, which we shall examine in [Book X].

The moneymaker's life is in a way forced on him [not chosen for itself]; and clearly wealth is not the good we are seeking, since it is [merely] useful, [choiceworthy only] for some other end. . . .

7. But let us return to the good we are looking for, and consider just what it could be. . . . Since there are apparently many ends, and we choose some of them (for instance, wealth, flutes, and, in general, instruments) because of something else, it is clear that not all ends are complete. But the best good is apparently something complete. And so, if only one end is complete, the good we are looking for will be this end; if more ends than one are complete, it will be the most complete end of these.

We say that an end pursued in its own right is more complete than an end pursued because of something else, and that an end that is never choiceworthy because of something else is more complete than ends that are choiceworthy both in their own right and because of this end. Hence an end that is always choiceworthy in its own right, never because of something else, is complete without qualification.

Now happiness, more than anything else, seems complete without qualification. For we always choose it because of itself, never because of something else. Honor, pleasure, understanding, and every virtue we certainly choose because of themselves, since we would choose each of them even if it had

no further result; but we also choose them for the sake of happiness, supposing that through them we shall be happy. Happiness, by contrast, no one ever chooses for their sake, or for the sake of anything else at all.

The same conclusion [that happiness is complete] also appears to follow from self-sufficiency. For the complete good seems to be self-sufficient [and] we regard something as self-sufficient when all by itself it makes a life choiceworthy and lacking nothing; and that is what we think happiness does. . . .

Happiness, then, is apparently something complete and self-sufficient, since it is the end of the things achievable in action.

But presumably the remark that the best good is happiness is apparently something [generally] agreed, and we still need a clearer statement of what the best good is. Perhaps, then, we shall find this if we first grasp the function of a human being. For just as the good, i.e., [doing] well for a flautist, a sculptor, and every craftsman, and, in general, for whatever has a function and [characteristic] action, seems to depend on its function, the same seems to be true for a human being, if a human being has some function.

Then do the carpenter and the leather worker have their functions and actions, but has a human being no function? Is he by nature idle, without any function? Or, just as eye, hand, foot, and, in general, every [bodily] part apparently has its function, may we likewise ascribe to a human being some function apart from all of these?

What, then, could this be? For living is apparently shared with plants, but what we are looking for is the special function of a human being; hence we should set aside the life of nutrition and growth. The life next in order is some sort of life of sense perception; but this too is apparently shared with horse, ox, and every animal.

The remaining possibility, then, is some sort of life of action of the [part of the soul] that has reason. One [part] of it has reason as obeying reason; the other has it as itself having reason and thinking. Moreover . . . we must take [a human being's special function to be] life as activity, since this seems to be called life more fully. We have found, then, that the human function is activity of the soul in accord with reason or requiring reason.

Now we say that the function of a [kind of thing]—of a harpist, for instance—is the same in kind as the function of an excellent individual of the kind—of an excellent harpist, for instance. And the same is true without qualification in every case, if we add to the function the superior achievement in accord with the virtue; for the function of a harpist is to play the harp, and the function of a good harpist is to play it well. Moreover, we take the human function to be a certain kind of life, and take this life to be activity and actions of the soul that involve reason; hence the function of the excellent man is to do this well and finely.

Now each function is completed well by being completed in accord with the virtue proper [to that kind of thing]. And so the human good proves to be activity of the soul in accord with virtue, and indeed with the best and most complete virtue, if there are more virtues than one. Moreover, in a complete life. For one swallow does not make a spring, nor does one day; nor, similarly, does one day or a short time make us blessed and happy. . . .

8. All the features that people look for in happiness appear to be true of the end described in our account. . . .

First, our account agrees with those who say happiness is virtue. . . .

Moreover, the life of these [virtuous] people is also pleasant in itself. . . . Each type of person finds pleasure in whatever he is called a lover of; a horse, for instance, pleases the horse-lover. . . . Similarly, what is just pleases the lover of justice, and in general what accords with virtue pleases the lover of virtue. . . .

Hence these people's life does not need pleasure to be added [to virtuous activity] as some sort of extra decoration; rather, it has its pleasure within itself. For besides the reasons already given, someone who does not enjoy fine actions is not good; for no one would call a person just, for instance, if he did not enjoy doing just actions, or generous if he did not enjoy generous actions, and similarly for other virtues. . . .

Nonetheless, happiness evidently also needs external goods to be added . . . since we cannot, or cannot easily, do fine actions if we lack the resources. For, first of all, in many actions we use friends, wealth, and political power just as we use instruments. Further, deprivation of certain [externals]—for instance, good birth, good children, beauty—mars our blessedness. . . .

BOOK II

1. Virtue . . . is of two sorts, virtue of thought and virtue of character. Virtue of thought arises and grows mostly from teaching; that is why it needs experience and time. Virtue of character results from habit. . . .

Hence it is also clear that none of the virtues of character arises in us naturally. For if something is by nature in one condition, habituation cannot bring it into another condition. . . . And so the virtues arise in us neither by nature nor against nature. Rather, we are by nature able to acquire them, and we are completed through habit.

Further, if something arises in us by nature, we first have the capacity for it, and later perform the activity. . . . Virtues, by contrast, we acquire, just as acquire crafts, by having first activated them. For we learn a craft by producing the same product that we must produce when we have learned it; we become builders, for instance, by building, and we become harpists by playing the harp. Similarly, then, we become just by doing just actions, temperate by doing temperate actions, brave by doing brave actions. . . .

That is why we must perform the right activities, since differences in these imply corresponding differences in the states [of character]. It is not unimportant, then, to acquire one sort of habit or another, right from our youth. On the contrary, it is very important, indeed all-important.

2. Our present discussion does not aim . . . at study; for the purpose of our examination is not to know what virtue is, but to become good, since otherwise

the inquiry would be of no benefit to us. And so we must examine the right ways of acting; for, as we have said, the actions also control the sorts of states we acquire. . . .

But let us take it as agreed in advance that every account of the actions we must do has to be stated in outline, not exactly. As we also said at the beginning, the type of accounts we demand should accord with the subject matter; and questions about action and expediency, like questions about health, have no fixed answers. . . .

First, then, we should observe that these sorts of states [of character] naturally tend to be ruined by excess and deficiency. We see this happen with strength and health. . . . For both excessive and deficient exercise ruin bodily strength, and, similarly, too much or too little eating or drinking ruins health, whereas the proportionate amount produces, increases, and preserves it.

The same is true, then, of temperance, bravery, and the other virtues. For if, for instance, someone avoids and is afraid of everything and stands firm against nothing, he becomes cowardly; if he is afraid of nothing at all and goes to face everything, he becomes rash. Similarly, if he gratifies himself with every pleasure and abstains from none, he becomes intemperate; if he avoids them all, as boors do, he becomes some sort of insensible person. Temperance and bravery, then, are ruined by excess and deficiency, but preserved by the mean.

But these actions are not only the sources and causes both of the emergence and growth of virtues and of their ruin; the activities of the virtues [once we have acquired them] also consist in these same actions. . . . For abstaining from pleasure makes us become temperate, and once we have become temperate we are most capable of abstaining from pleasures. It is similar with bravery; habituation in disdain for frightening situations and in standing firm against them makes us become brave, and once we have become brave we shall be most capable of standing firm.

3. But we must take someone's pleasure or pain following on his actions to be a sign of his state. For if someone who abstains from bodily pleasures enjoys the abstinence itself, he is temperate; if he is grieved by it, he is intemperate. Again, if he stands firm against terrifying situations and enjoys it, or at least does not find it painful, he is brave; if he finds it painful, he is cowardly. For virtue of character is about pleasures and pains. . . .

4. Someone might be puzzled, however, about what we mean by saying that we become just by doing just actions and become temperate by doing temperate actions. For [one might suppose] that if we do grammatical or musical actions, we are grammarians or musicians, and, similarly, if we do just or temperate actions, we are thereby just or temperate. . . .

But for actions in accord with the virtues to be done temperately or justly it does not suffice that they themselves have the right qualities. Rather, than agent must also be in the right state when he does them. First, he must know [that he is doing virtuous actions]; second, he must decide on them, and decide on them for themselves; and, third, he must also do them from a firm and unchanging state. . . .

Hence actions are called just or temperate when they are the sort that a just or temperate person would do. But the just and temperate person is not the one who [merely] does these actions, but the one who also does them in the way in which just or temperate people do them. . . .

6. It should be said . . . that every virtue causes its possessors to be in a good state and to perform their function well. . . . The virtue of a human being will . . . be the state that makes a human being good and makes him perform his function well. . . .

In everything continuous and divisible we can take more, less, and equal, and each of them either in the object itself or relative to us; and the equal is some intermediate between excess and deficiency. By the intermediate in the object I mean what is equidistant from each extremity; this is one and the same for all. But relative to us the intermediate is what is neither superfluous nor deficient; this is not one, and is not the same for all.

If, for instance, ten are many and two are few, we take six as intermediate in the object, since it exceeds [two] and is exceed [by ten] by an equal amount,

[four]. . . . But that is not how we must take the intermediate that is relative to us. For if ten pounds [of food], for instance, are a lot for someone to eat, and two pounds a little, it does not follow that the trainer will prescribe six, since this might also be either a little or a lot for the person who is to take it—for Milo [the athlete] a little, but for the beginner in gymnastics a lot. . . .

We can be afraid, for instance, or be confident, or have appetites, or get angry, or feel pity, and in general have pleasure or pain, both too much and too little, and in both ways not well. But having these feelings at the right times, about the right things, toward the right people, for the right end, and in the right way, is the intermediate and best condition, and this is proper to virtue. Similarly, actions also admit of excess, deficiency, and an intermediate condition.

Now virtue is about feelings and actions, in which excess and deficiency are in error and incur blame, whereas the intermediate condition is correct and wins praise, which are both proper to virtue. Virtue, then, is a mean, insofar as it aims at what is intermediate.

Moreover, there are many ways to be in error. . . . But there is only one way to be correct. That is why error is easy and correctness is difficult, since it is easy to miss the target and difficult to hit it. And so for this reason also excess and deficiency are proper to vice, the mean to virtue. . . .

Virtue, then, is a state that decides, consisting in a mean, the mean relative to us, which is defined by reference to reason, that is to say, to the reason by reference to which the prudent person would define it. It is a mean between two vices, one of excess and one of deficiency. . . .

Now not every action or feeling admits of the mean. For the names of some automatically include baseness—for instance, spite, shamelessness, envy [among feelings], and adultery, theft, murder, among actions. For all of these and similar things are called by these names because they themselves, not their excesses or deficiencies, are base. Hence in doing these things we can never be correct, but must be invariably in error. . . .

7. However, we must not only state this general account but also apply it to the particular cases. . . .

First, then, in feelings of fear and confidence the mean is bravery. The excessively fearless person is nameless (indeed many cases are nameless), and the one who is excessively confident is rash. The one who is excessive in fear and deficient in confidence is cowardly.

In pleasures and pains . . . the mean is temperance and the excess intemperance. People deficient in pleasure are not often found, which is why they also lack a name; let us call them insensible.

In giving and taking money the mean is generosity, the excess wastefulness and the deficiency ungenerosity. Here the vicious people have contrary excesses and defects; for the wasteful person is excessive in spending and deficient in taking, whereas the ungenerous person is excessive in taking and deficient in spending. . . .

In questions of money there are also other conditions. Another mean is magnificence; for the magnificent person differs from the generous by being concerned with large matters, while the generous person is concerned with small. The excess is ostentation and vulgarity, and the deficiency is stinginess. . . .

In honor and dishonor the mean is magnanimity, the excess something called a sort of vanity, and the deficiency pusillanimity. And just as we said that generosity differs from magnificence in its concern with small matters, similarly there is a virtue concerned with small honors, differing in the same way from magnanimity, which is concerned with great honors. For honor can be desired either in the right way or more or less than is right. If someone desires it to excess, he is called an honor-lover, and if his desire is deficient he is called indifferent to honor, but if he is intermediate he has no name. . . .

Anger also admits of an excess, deficiency, and mean. These are all practically nameless; but since we call the intermediate person mild, let us call the mean mildness. Among the extreme people, let the excessive person be irascible, and his vice irascibility, and let the deficient person be a sort of inirascible person, and his deficiency inirascibility. . . .

In truth-telling . . . let us call the intermediate person truthful, and the mean truthfulness; pretense that overstates will be boastfulness, and the person who has it boastful; pretense that understates will be self-deprecation, and the person who has it self-deprecating.

In sources of pleasure in amusements let us call the intermediate person witty, and the condition wit; the excess buffoonery and the person who has it a buffoon; and the deficient person a sort of boor and the state boorishness.

In the other sources of pleasure, those in daily life, let us call the person who is pleasant in the right way friendly, and the mean state friendliness. If someone does to excess with no [ulterior] aim, he will be ingratiating; if he does it for his own advantage, a flatterer. The deficient person, unpleasant in everything, will be a sort of quarrelsome and ill-tempered person.

There are also means in feelings and about feelings. Shame, for instance, is not a virtue, but the person prone to shame . . . receives praise. For here also one person is called intermediate, and another—the person excessively prone to shame, who is ashamed about everything—is called excessive; the person who is deficient in shame or never feels shame at all is said to have no sense of disgrace; and the intermediate one is called prone to shame.

Proper indignation is the mean between envy and spite; these conditions are concerned with pleasure and pain at what happens to our neighbors. For the properly indignant person feels pain when someone does well undeservedly; the envious person exceeds him by feeling pain when anyone does well, while the spiteful person is so deficient in feeling pain that he actually enjoys [other people's misfortunes]. . . .

9. We have said enough, then, to show that virtue of character is a mean . . . between two vices, one of excess and one of deficiency; and that it is a mean because it aims at the intermediate condition in feelings and actions.

That is why is it also hard work to be excellent. For in each case it is hard work to find the intermediate; for instance, not everyone, but only one who knows, finds the midpoint in a circle. So also getting angry, or giving and spending money, is easy and everyone can do it; but doing it to the right person, in the right amount, at the right time, for the right end, and in the right way is no longer easy, nor can everyone do it. Hence doing these things well is rare, praiseworthy, and fine.

That is why anyone who aims at the intermediate condition must first of all steer clear of the more contrary extreme. . . . For one extreme [e.g., cowardice] is more in error, the other [e.g., rashness] less. Since, therefore, it is hard to hit the intermediate extremely accurately, the second-best tack, as they say, is to take the lesser of the evils.

We must also examine what we ourselves drift into easily. For different people have different natural tendencies toward different goals, and we shall come to know our own tendencies from the pleasure or pain that arises in us. We must drag ourselves off in the contrary direction; for if we pull far away from error . . . we shall reach the intermediate condition. . . .

BOOK III

6. First let us discuss bravery. We have already made it apparent that there is a mean about feelings of fear and confidence. What we fear, clearly, is what is frightening, and such things are, speaking without qualification, bad things; hence people define fear as expectation of something bad.

Certainly we fear all bad things—for instance, bad reputation, poverty, sickness, friendlessness, death—but they do not all seem to concern the brave person. For fear of some bad things, such as bad reputation, is actually right and fine, and lack of fear is shameful; for if someone fears bad reputation, he is decent and properly prone to shame, and if he has no fear of it, he has no feeling of disgrace. Some, however, call this fearless person brave . . . for he has some similarity to the brave person. . . .

Then what sorts of frightening conditions concern the brave person? Surely the most frightening; for no one stands firmer against terrifying conditions. Now death is most frightening of all. . . . Still, not even death in all conditions—on the sea, for instance, or in sickness—seems to be the brave person's concern.

In what conditions, then, is death his concern? Surely in the finest conditions. Now such deaths are those in war, since they occur in the greatest and finest danger. This judgment is endorsed by the honors given in cities and by monarchs. Hence someone is called fully brave if he is intrepid in facing a fine death and the immediate dangers that bring death. And this is above all true of the dangers of war. . . .

7. The brave person is unperturbed [by frightening things], as far as a human being can be. Hence, though he will fear even the sorts of things that are not irresistible, he will stand firm against them, in the right way, as reason prescribes, for the sake of the fine, since this is the end aimed at by virtue.

It is possible to be more or less afraid of these frightening things, and also possible to be afraid of what is not frightening as though it were frightening. . . .

Hence whoever stands firm against the right things and fears the rights things, for the right end, in the right way, at the right time, and is correspondingly confident, is the brave person; for the brave person's actions and feelings accord with what something is worth, and follow what reason prescribes.

Every activity aims at actions in accord with the state of character. Now to the brave person bravery is fine; hence the end it aims at is also fine, since each thing is defined by its end. The brave person, then, aims at the fine when he stands firm and acts in accord with bravery.

Among those who go to excess the excessively fearless person has no name. . . . He would be some sort of madman, or incapable of feelings distress. . . .

The person who is excessively confident about frightening things is rash. . . . Moreover, rash people are impetuous, wishing for dangers before they arrive. . . . Brave people, on the contrary, are eager when in action, but keep quiet until then.

The person who is excessively afraid is the coward, since he fears the wrong things, and in the wrong way, and so on. Certainly, he is also deficient in confidence, but his excessive pain distinguishes him more clearly. Hence, since he is afraid of everything, he is a despairing sort. The brave person, on the contrary, is hopeful, since [he is confident and] confidence is proper to a hopeful person.

Hence the coward, the rash person, and the brave person are all concerned with the same things, but have different state related to them; the others are excessive or defective, but the brave person has the intermediate and right state.

BOOK V

1. Now it would seem that justice and injustice are both spoken of in more ways than one. . . . Let us, then, find the number of ways an unjust person is spoken of. Both the lawless person and the overreaching and unfair person seem to be unjust; and so, clearly, the lawful and the fair person will be just. Hence the just will be both the lawful and what is fair, and the unjust will be both the lawless and the unfair.

Since the unjust person is an overreacher, he will be concerned with goods. . . . Now the unjust person does not choose more in every case; in the case of what is bad . . . he actually chooses less. . . .

Since, as we saw, the lawless person is unjust and the lawful person is just, it clearly follows that whatever is lawful is in some way just. . . . Now the law instructs us to do the actions of a brave person—for instance, not to leave the battle-line, or to flee, or to throw away out weapons; of a temperate person—not to commit adultery or wanton aggression; or a mild person—not to strike or revile another; and similarly requires actions in accord with the other virtues, and prohibits actions in accord with the vices. The correctly established law does this correctly, and the less carefully framed one does this worse.

This type of justice, then, is complete virtue. . . . And that is why justice often seems to be supreme among the other virtues. . . .

2. But we are looking for the type of justice . . . that consists in a part of virtue [rather than complete virtue], and correspondingly for the type of injustice that is a part of vice. . . .

A sign that there is this type of justice and injustice is this: If someone's activities accord with the other vices—if, for instance, cowardice made him throw away his shield, or irritability made him revile someone, or ungenerosity made him fail to help someone with money—what he does is unjust, but not overreaching. But when someone acts from overreaching, in many cases his action accords with none of these vices—certainly not all of them; but it still accords with some type of wickedness, since we blame him, and [in particular] it accords with injustice.

Hence there is another type of injustice that is a part of the whole. . . . Further, if A commits adultery for profit and makes a profit, but B commits adultery because of his appetite, and spends money on it to his own loss, B seems intemperate rather than overreaching, but A seems unjust, not intemperate. Clearly, then, this is because A acts to make a profit.

Further, we can refer every other unjust action to some vice—to intemperance if someone committed adultery, to cowardice if he deserted his comrade in the battle-line, to anger if he struck someone. But if made an [unjust] profit, we can refer it to no other vice except injustice.

It is evident, then, that there is another type of injustice, special injustice, apart from injustice as a whole, [and which] is concerned with honor or wealth or safety . . . and aims at the pleasure that results from making a profit, whereas the concern of injustice as a whole is whatever concerns the excellent person. . . .

BOOK X

7. If happiness is activity in accord with virtue, it is reasonable for it to accord with the supreme virtue, which will be the virtue of the best thing. The best is understanding . . . and to understand what is fine and divine. . . . Hence complete happiness will be its activity in accord with its proper virtue; and . . . this activity is the activity of study. . . .

Besides, we think that pleasure must be mixed into happiness; and it is agreed that the activity in accord with wisdom is the most pleasant of the activities in accord with virtue. Certainly, philosophy seems to have remarkably pure and firm pleasures, and it is reasonable for those who have knowledge to spend their lives more pleasantly than those who seek it.

Moreover, the self-sufficiency we spoke of will be found in study more than in anything else. For admittedly the wise person, the just person, and the other virtuous people all need the good things necessary for life. Still, when these are adequately supplied, the just person needs other people as partners and recipients of his just actions; and the same is true of the temperate person, the brave person, and each of the others. But the wise person is able, and more able the wiser he is, to study even by himself; and though he presumably does it better with colleagues, even so he is more self-sufficient than any other [virtuous person].

Besides, study seems to be liked because of itself alone, since it has no result beyond having studied. But from the virtues concerned with action we try to a greater or lesser extent to gain something beyond the action itself.

Besides, happiness seems to be found in leisure; for we deny ourselves leisure so that we can be at leisure, and fight wars so that we can be at peace. Now the virtues concerned with action have their activities in politics or war, and actions here seem to require trouble. This seems completely true for actions in war, since no one chooses to fight a war, and no one continues it, for the sake of fighting a war; for someone would have to be a complete murderer if he made his friends his enemies so that there could be battles and killings. But the actions of the politician also deny us leisure; apart from political activities themselves, those actions seek positions of power and honors, or at least they seek happiness for the politician himself and for his fellow citizens. . . .

Hence among actions in accord with the virtues those in politics and wars are preeminently fine and great; but they require trouble, aim at some [further] end, and are choiceworthy for something other than themselves. But the activity of understanding, it seems, is superior in excellence because it is the activity of study, aims at no end apart from itself, and has its own proper pleasure, which increases the activity. Further, self-sufficiency, leisure, unwearied activity . . . and any other features ascribed to the blessed person, are evidently features of this activity. Hence a human being's complete happiness will be this activity. . . .

DISCUSSION QUESTIONS

1. What are the various kinds of lives that Aristotle considers as candidates for the best life? Do you find his arguments about these lives compelling? Why or why not?
2. Do you agree with Aristotle's basic idea about what makes a person's life as happy (or flourishing) as possible? Why or why not?
3. Aristotle famously argues that virtues are a mean between two extremes. Do you think this is always true? Why or why not?
4. What arguments does Aristotle give for thinking that the life of study is the best life for a human being? Do you find these arguments convincing? Why or why not?
5. Some people claim that because different cultures will understand virtues differently, Aristotle's ethics leads to a kind of cultural relativism (see pp. 98–102), according to which morality differs from one culture to another. Do you think that is true? If so, is it a problem for Aristotle's view? Why or why not?

STEPHANIE COLLINS

Care Ethics: The Four Key Claims

Stephanie Collins is a Lecturer in Politics at the University of Manchester in England. She writes about human rights, global justice, and feminist ethics. Collins explains four claims that form the core of the ethics of care.

GUIDING QUESTIONS

1. What are the four key claims that form the core of care ethics, according to Collins? (You won't be able to answer this question completely until the end of the paper, but keep it in mind as you read.)
2. What role(s) does Collins think principles should play in ethics? Why?
3. What kind of relationships are especially important, according to Collins? Why?
4. What is the difference between caring attitudes and caring actions? What role does each play in care ethics?

This chapter investigates a somewhat neglected moral theory: the theory of "care ethics." This theory can be traced back to Carol Gilligan, a 1980s psychologist who studied how women approach real-life moral dilemmas. In contrast to findings about men in earlier studies (Kohlberg 1973), Gilligan found women did not appeal to general principles or make categorical assertions about right and wrong. Instead, they focused "on the limitations of any particular resolution and describe[d] the conflicts that remain" (Gilligan 1982, 22). This seeming indecisiveness resulted from their perception of many conflicting responsibilities: to their family members, to their friends, to themselves, and those more distant. Paradigmatically, Gilligan described "Amy," a subject who saw the world as "a narrative of relationships that extends over time" in "a world that coheres through human connection rather than through systems of rules" (1982, 28–9). This contextually-embedded and relationship-oriented approach has driven care ethicists ever since.

But care ethicists are not just concerned with "what women think." Instead, they believe their theory can—indeed, should—guide all of us in moral decision-making, regardless of our gender and the particular dilemmas we face. Through reflection on the lived reality of ethical decision-making, care ethicists are led to the following ideas: that responsibilities derive from relationships between particular people, rather than from abstract rules and principles; that decision-making should be sympathy-based rather than duty- or principle-based; that personal relationships have a value that is often overlooked by other theories; that at least some responsibilities aim at fulfilling the needs of vulnerable persons (including their need for empowerment), rather than the universal rights of rational agents; and that morality demands not just one-off acts, but also ongoing patterns of actions and attitudes. Most importantly, care ethicists believe morality demands ongoing actions and attitudes of *care*, in addition to (or even in priority to) those of respect, non-interference, and tit-for-tat reciprocity—which care ethicists see as over-emphasised in other ethical theories. Importantly, though, care ethicists do not claim that other theories get nothing right: care ethics is not a theory of the *whole* of ethics or morality, but of important parts of it that have been inadequately appreciated by other theories (Engster 2007, 61–2; Held 2004, 65, 68; Tronto 1993, 126).

This chapter aims to crystallise the care ethical cluster of ideas, by describing, refining, and defending four key claims that constitute the central pillars of the theory.

1. SCEPTICISM ABOUT PRINCIPLES

1.1 Deliberation and Justification

Care ethicists view principles as insufficient at best—and distortive at worst—for proper ethical deliberation. We can think of principles as conditionals ("if, then" statements) with an imperative ("do this") in the "then" slot. Principles include: "if you've made a promise, then keep it"; "if you can save someone's life at low cost, then save their life"; "under all circumstances, don't murder." Care ethicists object that these generalise too much. The reasons you should keep a promise, or save someone's life, or even refrain from murder, are always unique to particular circumstances. We can't capture all those unique details in a general "if" or "under these circumstances" clause.

Care ethicists' ideas here can be divided into two camps: those regarding *deliberation*, and those regarding *justification*. Deliberation refers to the *procedures* we use when making ethical decisions. Justification refers to the outside-the-mind *reasons* why someone should do this-or-that. For example, suppose I can easily save a toddler from drowning in a shallow pond. When it comes to deliberation, I might just think: "The toddler's drowning! Act!" This is a sensible method of deliberation in the circumstances. But the method of providing a justification for my action will be quite different: my justification might refer to the value of human life, the fact that I would want someone to save me if they easily could, and so on. These abstract justificatory notions don't feature in the deliberation, and rightly so.

When care ethicists deride principles, sometimes they're arguing that we shouldn't use principles in deliberation. For example, in Selma Sevenhuijsen's version of care ethics, "[m]oral deliberation is . . . looking . . . at an issue from different perspectives and taking conflicting moral reactions and moral idioms as sources of morally relevant knowledge" (Sevenhuijsen 1998, 57; similarly Miller 2005, 139). At other times, care ethicists want to reject principles as justifications. Virginia Held gives the example of honouring one's parents, suggesting that the (justificatory) reason why a child should honour their father is because their particular father is worth honouring, for reasons that can only be spelled out by describing the details of that relationship over the years, and that cannot be captured in a general "if" clause (Held, 2006, 79–80; similarly Noddings 1984, 85; Ruddick 1980, 348–9; Tronto 1993, 27). In the next two sub-sections, I will assess care ethicists' views on deliberation and justification in turn.

1.2 Deliberation

Care ethicists are surely correct that wholly principle-based deliberation is not always best. As Ornaith O'Dowd puts it: if a child is drowning in a river, then "sitting down by the riverbank to stroke one's chin and ruminate on a particularly thought-provoking passage from [Immanuel Kant's] the *Metaphysics of Morals* is hardly justifiable . . ." (2012, 419). Not only that: if we went through life with principles always explicitly in mind, we would miss out on a lot of what's valuable—human connection, sympathy, and spontaneity, for example.

This would be irrelevant if there were no alternative to principle-based deliberation. But care ethics offers an alternative: sympathy. This involves appreciating someone else's situation from their perspective, and being moved to help them because of what one sees from that perspective. This requires giving full attention to the person, while attempting to see the world as *they* see it from their perspective—not to see the world as *you* would see it, if you were in their situation[1] (Kittay 1997, 236; Noddings 2010, ch. 2; Sevenhuijsen 1998, 62). This allows you to know

better what they need or want, why they need or want that thing, and how you might help them get it. It forces you to remove your self-interested goggles in approaching life. It is worth quoting Virginia Held at length on this:

> Kant famously argued that benevolent or sympathetic feelings lack moral worth; only the intention to act in accord with the moral law required by reason is morally rather than merely instrumentally of value. . . . Such theories miss the moral importance of actual, caring relations. They miss the importance of the emotions for understanding what we ought to do, and for motivating our morally recommended actions. Without empathetic awareness, one may not be able to meet another's needs in the way morality requires. Without feelings of concern, one may not take responsibility for responding to those in need. To the ethics of care, morality is less a matter of rational recognition and more a matter of taking responsibility for particular other persons in need. (Held 2014, 109)

Care ethicists often contrast this sympathetic mode of deliberation with a principle-based mode. For example, Nel Noddings says "[i]t is not just that highly mathematicized schemes are inevitably artificial . . . but they tend to fix our attention on their own gamelike quality. We become absorbed in the intricacies of the game instead of the plight of real people" (Noddings 2002, 60). Something is clearly lost in the deliberation Noddings describes. But should we deliberate with absolutely *no regard* for principles? Can't we have *both* principles *and* sympathy in our deliberation? Indeed, there are at least three reasons why care ethicists can, should, and sometimes do preserve some role for principles in deliberation.

First, principles are *compatible with sympathy*. Moral philosophers of all stripes give a role to sympathy in deliberation—alongside principles. Most obviously, virtue ethics give sympathy a central deliberative role, though the theory also includes principles or "virtue-rules" (Hursthouse 1999, Part II). Virtue ethics is the mainstream theory most similar to care ethics—some even see care ethics as a species of virtues ethics (Slote 2007), though this is a minority position. So care ethics can draw on this. Likewise, sophisticated consequentialists claim that deliberators should go back-and-forth, as circumstances allow, between an "indirect" sympathy-based deliberation and principle-based deliberation (Railton 1984; Driver 2005 on connecting this to care ethics). Care ethicists themselves have argued that Kantian ethics is consistent with a sympathetic approach to moral practice (Miller 2005; O'Dowd 2012). In sum, a combination of sympathy and principles is recommended by a range of mainstream ethical theories. Care ethicists can follow suit—and some already have.

Second, principles are *informative*. Sometimes, the results of sympathy are unclear or indeterminate: sympathy pulls you towards this person, and towards that person, with seemingly equal strength. Which one should you help? In such situations, conscientious carers need general principles to determine whose interests come first. Often, these decisions are made by likening the current situation to previous ones. This likening can occur only by referring to general features that the situations share. Recognizing these general features, and reacting to them consistently, brings order to our judgments: "[t]o argue that no two cases are ever alike is to invite moral chaos" (Held 1987, 119).

Third, principles sometimes *rightly overrule sympathy*. Consider parents engaging in "tough love," policymakers who must prioritise after funding cuts, or nurses deciding how to divide their time amongst patients. Here, principles serve to constrain the effects of sympathy. Sympathy is intentionally put to one side, in order to do what it best overall. This is in part because engaging in sympathy—considering another's situation from her point of view—sometimes blinds us to other morally relevant features of the situation.

In sum, we should endorse sympathy in deliberation, but not at the complete exclusion of principles. That is the most that care ethicists can credibly claim—but they are right to claim that much.

1.3 Justification

If we grant a role for principles in deliberation, this might just be because they are useful "rules of

thumb." If so, principles might have no role in *justifying* moral decisions. Along these lines, Noddings and Joan Tronto—two prominent care ethicists—both suggest that any principle general enough to be true will be too broad to be a full justification of particular actions. Noddings considers the principle "always act so as to establish, maintain or enhance caring relations" (2002, 30). Tronto considers the principle that "one should care" (1993, 153). They use these principles to demonstrate the *emptiness* of true, general, and universal principles for care ethical justifications of actions. Crucially, though, these unconditional principles are viewed by their authors as *true*. They are just not very rich justifications, since they don't say anything about why we should care.

This raises the question: are there rich principles of justification that ring true to care ethics? Yes. Here are three examples from the literature. First, Eva Feder Kittay's "principle of social responsibility for care": "*[t]o each according to his or her need for care, from each according to his or her capacity for care, and such support from social institutions as to make available resources and opportunities to those providing care, so that all will be adequately attended in relations that are sustaining*" (1999, 113, emphasis in original). Second, Daniel Engster's "principle of subsidiarity": "we should shift the actual delivery of care whenever possible to the most local and personal levels. We should care for others whenever possible by enabling them to care for themselves" (2007, 58). Third, my own "dependency principle": when an important interest is unfulfilled, and you're capable of fulfilling that interest, and fulfilling the interest will be not too costly, then you have a responsibility to fulfil the interest (Collins 2015, ch. 6). In short, some principles are empty and uninformative, while others are not. Informative principles might have a justificatory role within the best version of care ethics—we should leave this as an open possibility.

1.4 Conclusion: Claim 1

A key care ethical insight is that sympathy and direct attention to concrete particulars are important in deliberation. I have suggested that principles should also have some role in deliberation, and that care ethicists *can* preserve a place for principles in justification (though I haven't here argued that they *should* do this). We thus arrive at:

> *First Claim of Care Ethics.* Deliberation should include sympathy and direct attendance to concrete particulars.

2. PERSONAL RELATIONSHIPS

2.1 Three Claims About Relationship Importance

Care ethicists greatly value personal relationships, that is (roughly), relationships that are not formally contracted, that depend on a shared history (and/or predicted future) between the participants, and that are valued non-instrumentally by the participants. In personal relationships, participants tend to take one another's interests as their own: it is good *for me* when something good happens to my relative. Examples of such relationships include parents and children, siblings, friends, and spouses.

Care ethicists make three claims about personal relationships. First, personal relationships are paradigms for the rest of morality. We should take the same kind of attitude—sympathetic, compassionate—to everyone that we naturally take to personal relatives (even if not the same extent) (Noddings 2002, 2, 29; 2010, ch. 3). Second, some of the most morally valuable actions and attitudes are those that value, preserve, or promote personal relationships (Clement 1996, 15; Held 1987, 126; Noddings 1999, 3; Tronto 1993, 78). Third, some of the responsibilities that we have to all persons are weightier when had to personal relatives (Kittay 1997, 234; Bubeck 1995, 229–236).

Common-sense accords with these claims. Imagine a person who does not visit his lonely mother in a rest home, despite living nearby. We think that (a) this might indicate a general moral ineptitude; (b) he has more reason to value, preserve, or promote his relationship with his mother than his relationship with other lonely rest home residents; and (c) his responsibilities to visit his mother are weightier than any such responsibility he might have to other lonely residents.

But care ethicists do not think that the three claims of relationship importance apply to *all* personal relationships. Many relationships are abusive or disrespectful to participants, despite having the general characteristics of personal relationships mentioned above—simply consider abusive spousal relationships. So we need to specify the relationships to which the three claims apply.

2.2 Which Relationships?

One option is to say that the claims of relationship importance apply to those personal relationships that are valued by their participants. However, participants are not always good judges of whether personal relationships are worthy of emulation, preservation, and special attention. Taking this option would mask the power dynamics that limit some people's abilities to properly assess their relationships' value—most notably children, and in many societies women. Relationships so strongly inform our values, and do this in such a slow and creeping way, that it seems impossible to trust our own judgments of their value. Often, we're too enmeshed in them to judge (Minow and Shanley 1996).

A second option suggests that the social community—and its norms, expectations, and so on—could mark out the valuable relationships. But this gives too much power to norms and tradition, and not enough to marginalised voices, such as those of women and subordinated cultural groups. And if marginalised voices are given input, then we may be left with disagreement within the social community about which relationships are valuable. We would be left in a stalemate.

We can begin to resolve this by noting an assumption here: the assumption that "relationships are sources of moral importance." This is suspect. More plausibly, relationships—similarly to food, shelter, and security—are valuable in virtue of how they affect *persons* (Pettit 1997, 155). The relationship is not the thing *for the sake of which* we should take the claims of relationship importance to be true. Rather, we should take them to be true for the sake of the *people* in relationships.

Following this, I suggest the claims of relationship importance apply to all and only those personal relationships that have "value to" their participants. The idea of "value to" a person includes a subjective aspect: part of what adds value to a relationship is that participants *take* the relationship to be valuable to them. One might object to this, since, it seems, an abusive relationship's value is not enhanced by the fact that the abused participant *takes* the relationship to be valuable. But we can acknowledge the minimal value the subjective aspect adds in this case, while emphasising that the subjective aspect does not exhaust a relationship's value to its participants. Another part of what adds value to a relationship is that the relationship is in fact life-enhancing for them, whether they take it to be or not. This is the objective aspect. In an abusive relationship, the objective *dis*value greatly outweighs the subjective value, so that the relationship is disvaluable overall.

Why adopt this view of the relevant relationships? A powerful reason relates to the scope of care ethics. Contemporary care ethicists deny that their theory applies *only* to personal relationships. They instead emphasise that the responsibilities of care ethics are global: we have them to those at a great distance from us (Engster 2007; Held 2006; Kittay 2005; Miller 2010; Robinson 2011; Ruddick 1989). This has resulted in a tension within care ethics: on the one hand, personal relationships are still seen as important in the three ways outlined earlier. On the other hand, non-personal relationships are recognised as sources of imperatives to care. How can care ethicists account for the latter imperatives?

They can do it by saying that the importance of *any* relationship—personal or non-personal—is determined by that relationship's value to the individuals in that relationship. When our relationships to distant others have high value to us and to them, these non-personal relationships are moral paradigms, are worthy of

preservation, and give rise to weighty obligations. The first two claims of relationship importance—that the relationship is a paradigm and ought to be preserved—are true to the extent that the relationship is of value to participants.

For the last kind of relationship importance—that the relationship is a source of morally weighty duties—the story is more complicated. Here we want to say that a relationship that has *negative* value to its participants—such as an exploitative relationship—might give rise to weighty duties. Care ethicists do not disagree with this. But these are not duties *of care ethics*. Recall that care ethics is not a theory of the whole of morality. Morality includes duties that arise out of harming others, out of receiving benefits, out of making promises and contracts, and so on. It also includes duties not to interfere with others. These are all important duties—but they are not duties of care ethics. Neither are the duties that arise out of non-valuable relationships.

That said, the exaltation of "relationships that are valuable to participants" gets us a wider range of duties than might first meet the eye. This is because the claims of relationship importance—in particular, the second one about relationships being valued, protected, and promoted—properly apply not just to relationships that *already* have value to participants, but also to relationships that *would* have value to participants, *if* the relationship were formed. If we *could* create a relationship that would have value to participants, then care ethics says we have moral reasons to form—i.e., promote—that kind of relationship. Obviously, these reasons need to be balanced against moral reasons of all other kinds, including reasons to care for oneself. And—given what I said above about globalising the theory—*personal* relationships aren't the only kind of relationships that are relevant here. If we could form a "relationship" with an impoverished person that involved us contributing to institutional arrangements that benefited that person, and if that relationship would have value to them and/or us, then we have moral reason to form that relationship. This is part of promoting valuable relationships.

The suggestion, then, is that the importance of *any* relationship—actual or potential—is determined by that relationship's value to the participants. The special role of personal relationships within care ethics—as embodied in the three claims of relationship importance—is explained by personal relationships' high value to participants. But these are not the only relationships we should emulate, promote, and respond to. This interpretation allows us to exclude abusive personal relationships from being valuable, and, perhaps most importantly, to make sense of how we can globalise and institutionalise the demands of care ethics: we have moral reason to create all sorts of valuable relationships, even over long distances or mediated by institutions. In some cases, relationships can give rise to duties in other ways—such as if the relationship is exploitative—but this is not part of care ethics.

2.3 Conclusion: Claim 2

Care ethicists generally agree that personal relationships are moral paradigms that ought to be preserved and that generate weighty responsibilities. I suggested that we identify the relevant relationships by asking whether they have value to their participants. So we get Claim 2 of care ethics:

> *Second Claim of Care Ethics.* To the extent that they have value to individuals in the relationship, relationships ought to be (a) treated as moral paradigms, (b) valued, preserved, or promoted/formed, and (c) acknowledged as giving rise to weighty duties.

3. CARING ATTITUDES

3.1 What Are Caring Attitudes?

Unsurprisingly, care ethics calls upon agents to care. Care is multi-faceted. We can care about something—pay attention to it, emotionally invest in it, worry about it. We can care for something—tend to it, nurture it, help it thrive. We can take care around something—make sure it isn't disrupted, ensure it is left to go on without our interference. We care through directing our thoughts, through one-on-one interactions, through coordinated action with others,

by supporting other carers, and by contributing to institutions that care. Care can last a minute or go on for decades. It occurs on a multitude of levels, from the individual to the global. I'll divide care into two basic kinds: caring attitudes and caring actions. Some care ethicists run these together (Tronto 1993, 108; Held 2004, 60; Ruddick 1980, 348), but I will demonstrate that they each have value of their own. The present section focuses on attitudes, while Section 4 focuses on actions.

What are caring attitudes? In brief, to "care about" something is for it to matter to you—and for your emotions, desires, decisions, and attention to be influenced by how you believe things are going with it. The possible objects of caring attitudes are numerous: we can care about someone, something, some place, or some time. We can care about types or tokens: we might care about a type of thing ("interests"), or a type of person ("individuals with interests"). We might care about a type of event ("volcanic eruptions"), a type of state of affairs ("poverty"), or a type of property ("being ill"). Or we might just care about a particular token—a particular individual with interests, a particular volcanic eruption, a particular illness of a particular person, or similar. This type-token distinction matches onto a distinction made by Michael Slote and Virginia Held (respectively) between "generalised" (type-focused) and "specific" (token-focused) caring attitudes (Slote 1999, 2–3; Held 1993). Caring can be positively valenced (a pro-attitude, e.g., "I care about scientific discovery, so I want it to continue") or negatively valenced (a con-attitude, e.g., "I care about human rights abuses, so I want them to discontinue"). For you to genuinely not-care about something, you have to be entirely indifferent to it ("I don't care about what we have for dinner"). In short, caring attitudes are everywhere, and are easy to hold.

But presumably care ethics calls upon agents to have only those caring attitudes that are *morally valuable*. Which caring attitudes are these?

3.2 Morally Valuable Caring Attitudes

Plausibly, caring attitudes are like relationships: valuable in proportion to their value *to persons*. That value might lie in the attitude's being instrumental to a person's wellbeing, being partly constitutive of their wellbeing, or simply being a valuable attitude to them or for them, independently of their wellbeing. Thus caring attitudes have only *extrinsic* value—they are valuable in virtue of their relation to something else—but this doesn't mean that it only has *instrumental* value—that it is valued only as a means to some further end. Rather, caring attitudes might be non-instrumentally (but extrinsically) valued as *manifestations* of love, kindness, forgiveness, or so on—where these goods are intrinsically valuable to persons.

Care ethicists, though, are particularly concerned with caring attitudes that fulfil persons' needs (Bubeck 1995, 132; Engster 2007, 48; Held 2006, 10, 39; Kittay 1999, 133, 233; Miller 2010, 141, 150; Noddings 2010, ch. 7; Sevenhuijsen 1998, 60; Tronto 1993, 137–141). Needs are the most basic or vital constituents of, or means to, a minimally decent life. Should we *restrict* morally valuable instances of caring attitudes to those that fulfil needs? I suggest not. There may be a *stronger*, or *more urgent*, moral imperative to fulfil needs than other interests. But this does not exclude imperatives to fulfil less basic, urgent, or important interests. It is just that these imperatives will be of a weaker strength.

One plausible view of caring attitudes' moral value, then, is this. Morally valuable caring attitudes have as their object something that has, or that might affect something that has, interests, where the caring about is a pro-attitude to the fulfilment of those interests. This is consistent with us caring about things without interests, though such caring has no moral value. It is also consistent with us caring about things without interests (like medicine), where that caring has moral value, if the caring is nonetheless a pro-attitude to the fulfilment of interests (like the interests of people who need medicine). So, this is not to say that morally valuable caring attitudes are necessarily a positive response *to the object* of the caring. For example, to have a negative attitude to human rights abuses— that is, to be invested in such abuses discontinuing—is to respond positively to the interests of beings (humans) that are affected by that object.

Caring about human rights abuses in a negatively valenced way is morally valuable.

But can mere attitudes really be morally valuable? To answer this, imagine an aged father, Frank, who needs to have his house maintained. In one scenario, Frank's child, Sean, does this out of a personal, deep, long-lasting attitude of care for his father. In another scenario, a social worker, Wanda, does this because she's getting paid. Wanda cares about Frank to some extent—she wouldn't like to see Frank hurt. But Wanda's care doesn't affect her emotions, decisions, desires, attention, and so on nearly as much as, or in the way that, Sean's affects his. Wanda doesn't have the same kind of, or extent of, caring attitudes. Plausibly, Sean's assistance has value to Frank that Wanda's assistance does not.

How can we explain this? First, a caring attitude can be instrumentally valuable, by enabling attention to detail that generates knowledge of this particular person's interests and a motivation to fulfil those interests. Second, the caring attitude might have non-instrumental value, due to the attitude's relation to a fact whose truth they indicate—in this case, the fact that Sean loves Frank. Sean's attitude could have this value despite the fact that Wanda is equally disposed to recognise Frank's needs when they arise, equally recognising of the specificity of his needs, just as motivated to fulfil them (though motivated in a different way, i.e., money), and equally aware of the desirability of fostering caring attitudes within herself. This is not to say that Wanda's attitude is not caring: Wanda does take a pro-stance towards the fulfilment of Frank's interests. But our concern is the *moral value* of the two caring attitudes. Sean's attitude fares better in this regard.

We are now in a position to more carefully characterise the kinds of attitudes that are called for by care ethics. These are attitudes that (i) have as their object something that has interests, or something that might affect something that has interests; and that (ii) are a positive response (e.g. promoting, respecting, revering) to those interests; and that (iii) lead the agent's affects, desires, decisions, attention, or so on to be influenced by how the agent believes things are going with the interest-bearer. Clauses (i) and (ii) derive from the moral value of caring attitudes. Clause (iii) ensures that the attitude is one of caring, as charac-terised in the previous sub-section.

3.3 Responsibilities for Attitudes?

An objection arises: attitudes—and particularly the de-sires, emotions, and so on that might constitute, cause, or result from those attitudes, and generate their moral value—seem not to be under our voluntary control. It seems we can only have responsibilities to do things that are under our voluntary control. So, care ethics cannot say that we "should" have caring attitudes.

In reply: we can, in many circumstances, bring our-selves to have caring attitudes, including their motiva-tional and emotional aspects. We do this by consciously attending to the reasons we have to care about some-thing, downplaying the reasons against caring about the thing, or simply acting as if we care about the thing (with the aim that such actions will produce the atti-tude). And even if this is impossible, we can exercise long-term cultivation of dispositions and capacities to experience care emotions—so that the statement "you ought to care about suffering" (say) would translate into "you ought regularly to attend to others' suffering, do your best to ignore other demands on your atten-tion, place yourself in environments where suffering presents itself, remember or imagine yourself suffer-ing . . ." and so on. This is perfectly intelligible.

3.4 Conclusion: Claim 3

The attitude of care comes in many forms. Care ethics calls for those forms that have moral value, which, I have suggested, are those that are positively oriented towards interests. We now have:

> *Third Claim of Care Ethics.* Agents should have caring attitudes, that is, attitudes that: (i) have as their object something that has interests, or something that might affect something that has interests; and that (ii) are a positive response (e.g. promoting, respecting, revering) to those interests; and that (iii) lead the agent's affects, desires, decisions, attention, or so on to be influenced by how the agent believes things are going with the interest-bearer.

4. CARING ACTIONS

4.1 What Are Caring Actions?

In addition to having attitudes, we care by perform-ing, practicing, or giving care. I will use the phrases "caring for" (as opposed to "about"), "giving care," and "taking care of" synonymously, to refer to ac-tions of care. This includes actions that intend to leave alone, or not disturb, the thing we care for.

Caring actions differ from caring attitudes in a number of ways. First, the range of possible ob-jects is smaller. One does not *care for* a type of event ("volcanic eruptions," "human rights abuses," "scientific discoveries"), or a type of state of affairs ("poverty"), or a property ("having AIDS"). We might care for (as well care about) those who are *af-fected* by volcanic eruptions (human rights abuses, scientific discoveries, having AIDS), but then we are not caring for these things themselves. Also, care as an action is not open to a "pro" and "con" reading: to care for something is always to respond positively, rather than negatively, to that thing. And minimally caring actions are more costly to realise than mini-mally caring attitudes. While we care about anything we are not indifferent to, caring for something re-quires intentional actions or omissions.

Specifically, caring actions are intended in the manner "trying to do what I believe is good for this thing." Why just "trying" and "what I believe"? Con-sider a child who keeps a rock wrapped up in a blan-ket, carries the rock around with him, asks people to be quiet when he believes the rock is sleeping, and so on. He is asked whether he is caring for the rock, and he answers affirmatively. Does he actually care for the rock? He at least intends to. He intends to look after the rock, tend to it, enable it to live well, and so on. In short, he does what he believes is in the rock's interests.

I suggest that the boy does, in fact, care for the rock. He just does not do it very well. It is often dif-ficult to distinguish doing something badly from not doing it at all. If I get out paints and use them to rep-resent the bird outside my window, then I am paint-ing the bird even if the painting is unrecognisable as a bird. In such cases, my intentions (along with, perhaps, social conventions) are key to determining whether I am painting the bird. For caring, I suggest, it is *all* in the intentions. To care for someone is to do what you believe is in the interests of that thing— even if that thing, in fact, lacks interests, or even if you are incorrect about their interests. (Importantly, this is what it takes for an action to be *care* as opposed to *non-care*, not what it takes for an action to be *good care* as opposed to *bad care*.)

The intention is not a very strict condition. The carer need not consciously entertain their intention as "doing what I believe is in the recipient's interests" and they need not have a full-blown concept of interests. They just need an implicit belief that the action is good for the recipient in some way. Children, for example, can perfectly well care for their parents, without a hint of reflection on the fact. Moreover, fulfilling the person's interests need not be the final intention of the carer—the care can be intended to be instrumental to some other aim. Consider our social worker Wanda, who intends to fulfil Frank's interests only as a means to a paycheck. She cares *for* Frank, despite not caring much *about* Frank.

As a result, I will use the following definition of caring action (to be distinguished, in the next subsection, from *morally valuable* caring action):

> an action is caring if and only if it is performed under the (perhaps tacit) intention of fulfilling (or going some way to fulfilling) interest(s) that the agent perceives some perceived moral person (the recipient) to have.

4.2 Morally Valuable Caring Actions

The above definition is broad, and allows more specific definitions to be used for specific purposes. In particular, we should whittle this definition down so that it specifies only those caring actions that are called for by care ethics, that is, the morally valuable caring actions.

In defining caring action, I talked only about the *intentions* and *beliefs* of the caregiver. These things enhance moral value. But the *effects* matter greatly. Take the boy and his rock. The boy's actions do not

fulfil any interests of the rock. The rock does not *have* any interests. The boy's actions are caring. But they have less moral value than if the rock had interests that were being fulfilled. Effects matter.

One might object as follows. Imagine you and I each stumble upon injured dogs. We each attempt to drive our dog to the nearest vet. While your dog reaches the vet in time and is healed, I get caught in traffic and arrive five minutes too late. It seems odd, one might think, to say that your action is more valuable than mine. Your action had better effects, but this seems irrelevant for the *moral* assessment of the action.

However, we should distinguish: (i) the sources of an action's moral value, (ii) the conditions under which an agent morally ought to perform the action, (iii) the conditions under which the agent should be praised or blamed for performing the action. You and I deserve equal praise for our dog-saving efforts. And assuming that I couldn't reasonably have known about the traffic, we each had an equally weighty reason to do what we could for our respective dogs. But it is nonetheless true that your action was more valuable—was better care—than my action, through no fault of my own. That is to say, when we are retrospectively assessing the value of an action (as opposed to prospectively assessing whether the action should be performed, or retrospectively assessing the praiseworthiness or blameworthiness of the agent), its actual effects matter, alongside intentions and beliefs.

Additionally, some effects matter more than others. This point is frequently made by care ethicists, who, as we have seen, focus on persons' *needs*. While care might be directed at fulfilling any interest—however trivial—care will have value if it fulfils a more vital, important, or compelling interest (a need). By allowing that care is more valuable if it fulfils interests—and even more valuable if it fulfils the *most important* interests—we are able to avoid the "paternalism objection" to care ethics. This is the objection that care ethicists endorse actions that patronise, belittle, or otherwise undermine the autonomy of the care recipient—by fulfilling interests that are trivial, or not the ones the care recipient wants fulfilled. For morally valuable caring actions, it is not enough that the action is *intended* to fulfil important interests: to be valuable, the care must *actually* fulfil important interests. In many cases, these will be the interests *the recipient themselves endorses*, including empowerment, autonomy, independence (insofar as this is ever possible), and so on.

I suggest the following, then, about morally valuable caring actions. The *moral value* of caring action is a function of (1) how well that action fulfils the recipients' interests (where needs are more important than other interests), and (2) the strength of the agent's intentions to fulfil the recipient's interests. (2) is separable from (1). An action can be caring despite having little moral value, just as long as it has the right intentions (i.e. fulfilling perceived interests). Above this threshold, a caring action can have more or less moral value, as a function of (1) and (2).

4.3 Conclusion: Claim 4

Caring actions are actions performed with intentions to fulfil interests. These actions are morally valuable in proportion to the strength of the intention and the goodness of the effects. That is:

Fourth Claim of Care Ethics. (i) Agents should perform actions that are performed under the (perhaps tacit) intention of fulfilling (or going some way to fulfilling) interest(s) that the agent perceives some moral person (the recipient) to have; (ii) the strength of this "should" is determined by the moral value of action, which is a function of the strength of the intention, the likelihood that the action will fulfil the interest, and the extent to which the interest is appropriately described as a "need."

CONCLUSION

These four claims are merely the *normative* claims of care ethics. Many care ethicists make *descriptive* claims that support their overall outlooks. For example, many care ethicists endorse a relational view of autonomy, according to which autonomous

plans, projects, and purposes are inseparable from, and hugely influenced by, those around us. Many care ethicists emphasise that the world of ethics is constituted by complex webs of relationships between fragile, embodied human beings. With the four key normative claims now on the table, it is easy to see how they might arise out of a deep appreciation of these descriptive claims. But the four key claims are what make care ethics a *normative* ethical theory.

Although moral theorists who do not call themselves care ethicists may endorse the four claims, the claims are unlikely to be the central or most important parts of non-care ethical theories. Non-care ethicists are unlikely to be interested in intricately analysing actions of *care* in particular, or in vindicating sympathetic modes of deliberation in particular, as a central part of their theoretical edifice. It is the combination of these claims, and their status as the most important normative aspects of the theory, which makes care ethics distinctive.

REFERENCES

Bubeck, Diemut. 1995. *Care, Gender and Justice.* Oxford: Clarendon Press.

Clement, Grace. 1996. *Care, Autonomy, and Justice: Feminism and the Ethic of Care.* Boulder: Westview Press.

Collins, Stephanie. 2015. *The Core of Care Ethics.* Basingstoke: Palgrave Macmillan.

Driver, Julia. 2005. "Consequentialism and Feminist Ethics." *Hypatia* 20(4), 183–199.

Engster, Daniel. 2007. *The Heart of Justice: A Political Theory of Caring.* New York: Oxford University Press.

Gilligan, Carol. 1982. *In a Different Voice.* Cambridge, MA: Harvard University Press.

Held, Virginia. 1987. "Feminism and Moral Theory." Pp. 111–128 in E. F. Kittay and D. Meyers (eds), *Women and Moral Theory.* Totowa: Rowman & Littlefield.

Held, Virginia. 1993. *Feminist Morality.* Chicago: University of Chicago Press.

Held, Virginia. 2004. "Taking Care: Care as Practice and Value." Pp. 59–71 in C. Calhoun (ed.), *Setting the Moral Compass: Essays by Women Philosophers.* Oxford: Oxford University Press.

Held, Virginia. 2006. *The Ethics of Care: Personal, Political, and Global.* Oxford: Oxford University Press.

Held, Virginia. 2014. "The Ethics of Care as Normative Guidance: Comment on Gilligan." *Journal of Social Philosophy* 45(1), 107–115.

Hursthouse, Rosalind. 1999. *On Virtue Ethics*. Oxford: Oxford University Press.

Kittay, Eva Feder. 1997. "Human Dependency and Rawlsian Equality." Pp. 219–266 in D. T. Meyers (ed.), *Feminist Rethink the Self*. Colorado: Westview Press.

Kittay, Eva Feder. 1999. *Love's Labor: Essays on Women, Equality and Dependence*. New York: Routledge.

Kittay, Eva Feder. 2005. "Dependency, Difference and the Global Ethic of Longterm Care." *Journal of Political Philosophy* 13(4), 443–469.

Kohlberg, Lawrence. 1973. "The Claim to Moral Adequacy of a Highest Stage of Moral Judgment." *Journal of Philosophy* 70(18).

Miller, Sarah Clark. 2005. "Need, Care and Obligation." *Royal Institute of Philosophy* 80, supp. 57 (supplement on "The Philosophy of Need"), 137–160.

Miller, Sarah Clark. 2010. "Cosmopolitan Care." *Ethics and Social Welfare* special issue on "Care Ethics: New Theories and Applications" 4(2), 145–157.

Minow, Martha and Mary Lyndon Shanley. 1996. "Relational Rights and Responsibilities: Revisioning the Family in Liberal Political Theory and Law." *Hypatia* 11(1), 4–29.

Noddings, Nel. 1984. *Caring: A Feminine Approach to Ethics and Moral Education*. Berkeley: University of California Press.

Noddings, Nel. 1999. "Two Concepts of Caring." *Philosophy of Education* 1999, 36–39.

Noddings, Nel. 2002. *Starting at Home: Caring and Social Policy*. Los Angeles: University of California Press.

Noddings, Nel. 2010. *The Maternal Factor: Two Paths to Morality*. Los Angeles: University of California Press.

O'Dowd, Ornaith. 2012. "Care and Abstract Principles." *Hypatia* 27(2), 407–422.

Pettit, Philip. 1997. "Love and its Place in Moral Discourse." Pp. 153–163 in R. Lamb (ed.), *Love Analyzed*. Boulder: Westview Press.

Railton, Peter. 1984. "Alienation, Consequentialism, and the Demands of Morality." *Philosophy & Public Affairs* 13(2), 134–171.

Robinson, Fiona. 2011. *The Ethics of Care: A Feminist Approach to Human Security*. Philadelphia: Temple University Press.

Ruddick, Sara. 1980. "Maternal Thinking." *Feminist Studies* 6(2), 342–367.

Ruddick, Sara. 1989. *Maternal Thinking: Toward a Politics of Peace*. Boston: Beacon Press.

Sevenhuijsen, Selma. 1998. *Citizenship and the Ethics of Care: Feminist Considerations on Justice, Morality, and Politics*. New York: Routledge.

Slote, Michael. 1999. "Caring Versus the Philosophers." *Philosophy of Education* 1999, 25–35.

Slote, Michael. 2007. *The Ethics of Care and Empathy*. London: Routledge.

Tronto, Joan C. 1993. *Moral Boundaries: A Political Argument for an Ethic of Care*. London: Routledge.

NOTE

1. For present purposes, "sympathy" and "empathy" can be treated synonymously, though there are subtle distinctions that are relevant for other purposes.

DISCUSSION QUESTIONS

1. What are care ethicists' arguments against using principles in ethical deliberation? Do you find those arguments compelling? Why or why not?

2. What does Claim 2 (about the importance of relationships) mean for how we should live our lives? Would taking Claim 2 seriously dramatically affect how you live your life? Why or why not?

3. In what sense does Collins say the effects of one's caring actions matter morally? Do you agree with her claim about this? Why or why not?

4. In what ways are the key claims of care ethics at odds with deontology, consequentialism, and virtue ethics? In what ways do they overlap with those theories?

MENCIUS (CA. 372–289 BCE)
TRANSLATED BY BRYAN VAN NORDEN

Essential *Mengzi*: Selected Passages with Traditional Commentary

Mencius is known as Mengzi in Chinese; the book that records his discussions with various rulers and disciples in ancient China is also called *Mengzi*. Reading the *Mengzi* is a bit different than reading most Western philosophers because the text conveys Mencius's teachings by relating Mencius's aphorisms and stories about Mencius talking to other people. You sometimes need to know something about ancient Chinese history or culture to understand the point that Mencius is making in each passage. To help with that, even Chinese scholars have typically read the *Mengzi* along with traditional commentaries, such as those by the great twelfth-century philosopher Zhu Xi. In the excerpts below, the translator has included some of this commentary, along with his own, to help you understand the meaning of the various passages. You'll find these commentaries set off in the text next to the Chinese character 注 (zhù), which means "to annotate" or "to comment."

GUIDING QUESTIONS

1. What does Mencius mean by "profit"? What is his main criticism of focusing on profit?
2. In 1A3 (i.e., chapter 3 of Book 1A), Mencius compares King Hui to soldiers who flee from battle but turn around after fifty paces. What point is Mencius making with that analogy?
3. What skill is Mencius trying to encourage King Xuan to practice in 1A7?
4. What point is Mencius trying to make about human nature with the story about the child near the well in 2A6?
5. What is Mencius trying to say about virtue in 2A9? In what other passages does he make a similar point?
6. In what ways do the stories about Shun in 5A1, 5A2, and 5A3 seem inconsistent? What point is Mencius making by telling all three stories?
7. Does Mencius think that human nature is good or not good? What arguments does he give for his view in Book 6A?
8. What kinds of moral arguments do you see Mencius making in the text? For instance, is he appealing to obligations, consequences, or virtues? Is he making arguments by analogy or offering examples to support or undermine intermediate moral principles? (If you're not used to reading Chinese philosophy, Mencius might present some of these arguments in a slightly different way than you're used to seeing, but they're there!)

BOOK 1A

1. Mengzi had an audience with King Hui of Liang. The king said, "Venerable sir, you have not regarded hundreds of leagues too far to come, so you must have a way of profiting my state."

Mengzi replied, "Why must Your Majesty speak of 'profit'? Let there simply be benevolence [rén] and righteousness [yì]. If Your Majesty says, 'How can I profit my state?' the Chief Counselors will say, 'How can I profit my clan?' and the nobles and commoners will say, 'How can I profit my self?' Superiors and subordinates will seize profit from each other, and the state will be endangered. When the ruler in a state that can field ten thousand chariots is assassinated, it will invariably be by a clan that can field a thousand chariots. When the ruler in a state that can field a thousand chariots is assassinated, it will invariably be by a clan that can field a hundred chariots. To have a thousand out of ten thousand or a hundred out of a thousand is plenty. But when people put profit before righteousness, they cannot be satisfied without grasping for more.[1]

"Never have the benevolent left their parents behind. Never have the righteous put their ruler last. Let Your Majesty speak only of benevolence and righteousness. Why must one speak of 'profit'?"

注 Zhu Xi comments, "If one accords with the Heavenly Pattern, one will not seek profit, but one will naturally never fail to profit. If one submits to human desires, then one will never obtain profit though one seeks it, and harm will follow upon it. . . . This is the profound meaning with which the *Mengzi* begins. This is something learners should carefully examine and clearly understand."

Cheng Yi said, "A gentleman never fails to desire profit, but if one is single-mindedly focused on profit, then it leads to harm. If there is only benevolence and righteousness, then one will not seek profit, but one will never fail to profit."

[This passage] can be read as a criticism of Mohism, a consequentialist philosophy [in ancient China] that encouraged people to judge actions in terms of the benefits (or "profit") they bring to people in general and not just to oneself or one's group. . . . But Mengzi argues that this practice is self-undermining: aiming directly at profit is, paradoxically, unprofitable.

3. King Hui of Liang said, "We use our heart to the utmost for our state. When the region within the river has a famine, we move some of the people to the region to the east of river and move grain to the region within the river. When there is a famine in the region to the east of river, we do likewise. When we examine the governments of neighboring states, there are none that use their hearts to the utmost like we do. Why is it that the people of neighboring states do not grow fewer and our people do not grow more numerous?"

注 Zhu Xi explains, "He moves the people in order to get them to the food. He moves the grain to give it to those too old or young to move."

Mengzi replied, "Your Majesty is fond of war, so allow me to use war as an illustration. Thunderingly, the drums spur the soldiers on. Blades clash together. Casting aside their armor and weapons, they run. Some stop after running a hundred paces; some stop after running only fifty paces. How would it be if those who ran fifty paces were to laugh at those who ran a hundred paces?"

The king said, "That is not acceptable. They simply did not run a hundred paces. But this too is running."

Mengzi replied, "If Your Majesty understands this, then you will not expect your people to be more numerous than those of neighboring states. . . . "

注 Notice the subtle irony in Mengzi's comment, "Your Majesty is fond of war, so allow me to use war as an illustration." Mengzi's general point is that King Hui only understands a small part of good government. He goes on to explain other policies that the king needs to enact. . . .

7. King Xuan of Qi . . . said, "What must one's Virtue be like so that one can become King?"[2]

Mengzi said, "One cares for the people and becomes King. This is something no one can stop."

The king said, "Can one such as ourselves care for the people?

Mengzi said, "You can."

The king said, "How do you know that we can?"

Mengzi said, "I heard your attendant Hu He say,

While the king was sitting up in his hall, an ox was led past below. The king saw it and said, "Where is the ox going?" Hu He replied, "We are about to ritually anoint a bell with its blood." The king said, "Spare it. I cannot bear its frightened appearance, like an innocent going to the execution ground." Hu He replied, "So should we dispense with the anointing of the bell?" The king said, "How can that be dispensed with? Exchange it for a sheep."

Mengzi continued, "I do not know if this happened."

The king said, "It happened."

Mengzi said, "This heart is sufficient to become King. The commoners all thought Your Majesty was being stingy. But I knew that Your Majesty simply could not bear the suffering of the ox."

The king said, "That is so. There were indeed commoners who said that. But although Qi is a small state, how could I be stingy about one ox? It was just that I could not bear its frightened appearance, like an innocent going to execution ground. Hence, I exchanged it for a sheep."

Mengzi said, "Let Your Majesty not be surprised at the commoners taking you to be stingy. You took a [big] thing and exchanged it for a [small] thing. How could they understand it? If Your Majesty were pained at its being innocent and going to the execution ground, then what is there to choose between an ox and a sheep?"

The king laughed, saying, "What was this feeling, actually? It's not the case that I grudged its value and exchanged it for a sheep. But it makes sense that the commoners would say I was stingy."

注 Zhu Xi says, "This means that the ox and sheep are both going to die although innocent. In what ways

does one distinguish between them and exchange the sheep for the ox? Mengzi intentionally sets up this difficulty, desiring the king to examine himself and seek his fundamental heart. The king seems unable to do so. . . .

Mengzi said, "There is no harm. What you did was just a technique for (cultivating your) benevolence. You saw the ox but had not seen the sheep. Gentlemen cannot bear to see animals die if they have seen them living. If they hear their cries of suffering, they cannot bear to eat their flesh. Hence gentlemen keep their distance from the kitchen."

注 Zhu Xi comments, "On the one hand, killing the ox was something that the king could not bear to do. On the other hand, anointing the bell was something that could not be dispensed with. . . . When he saw the ox, this heart had already been expressed and could not be repressed. But he had not yet seen the sheep, so . . . there were no feelings to hinder. Hence, exchanging the sheep for the ox allowed for the two (i.e., the heart and the ritual) to be complete without harm. This is how it is a technique of benevolence. . . . Now, humans are the same as animals in being alive but are different categories of things. Hence, we use animals for rituals, and our heart that does not bear their suffering applies only as far as they are seen and heard. Keeping one's distance from the kitchen is a technique used to cultivate this heart and broaden one's benevolence."

The king was pleased and said, "The *Odes* say,

Another person had the heart,
I measured it.

This describes you, Master. I was the one who did it. I examined myself and sought to find my heart but failed to understand it. But when you discussed it, my heart was moved. So in what way does this heart accord with becoming King?"

注 Zhu Xi comments, "Because of Mengzi's words, the king's heart from the previous day sprouts again.

Consequently, he understands that this heart does not come from outside, but he still does not understand how to examine its root and extend it.

Mengzi said, "Suppose there were someone who reported to Your Majesty, 'My strength is sufficient to lift five hundred pounds, but not sufficient to lift one feather. My eyesight is sufficient to examine the tip of an autumn hair, but I cannot see a wagon of firewood.' Would your Majesty accept that?"

The king said, "No."

Mengzi said, "In the present case your kindness is sufficient to reach animals, but the effects do not reach the commoners. How is this different from the examples I just gave? Hence, one fails to lift a feather only because one does not use one's strength. One fails to see a wagon of firewood only because one does not use one's eyesight. The commoners fail to receive care only because one does not use one's kindness. Hence, Your Majesty fails to become King because you do not act, not because you are unable to act. . . ."

注 Zhu Xi comments, "People have the most valuable natures of anything in Heaven and Earth. Hence, people are in the same category as other people and are affectionate to each other. Consequently, the expression of compassion to the people is very immediate, but to animals it is slow. . . . In the present case, the king is already able to extend this heart [of benevolence] to animals. So his failure to care for the people and become King is not because he is unable to act. It only comes from his not being willing to act."

"Treat your elders as elders, and extend it to the elders of others; treat your young ones as young ones, and extend it to the young ones of others, and you can turn the world in the palm of your hand. . . . Hence, if one extends one's kindness, it will be sufficient to care for all within the Four Seas. . . ."

注 Zhu Xi explains, " 'To treat as elders' is to serve the elderly. 'Your elders' means your father and elder brothers. 'The elders of others' means the fathers and elder brothers of others. 'To treat as young ones' is to nurture young ones. 'Your young ones' means your children and younger brothers. 'The young ones of others' means the sons and younger brothers of others. . . ."

BOOK 1B

5. King Xuan of Qi asked, "People all tell me to destroy the Bright Tower. Should I destroy it or leave it?"

Mengzi replied, "The Bright Tower is the tower of a King. If your Majesty desires to put into effect Kingly government, do not destroy it."

The king said, "May I hear more about Kingly government?"

Mengzi replied, "In former times, King Wen ruled his state like this. For farmers, there was the nine-one system [of field management]. For those in positions of responsibility, there were stipends for their descendants. The customs officers of the roads and markets made inspections but levied no duties. The people were not prohibited from fishing in the ponds and weirs. Guilt for crime did not extent to the criminals' wives. The old without wives were called 'widowers,' the old without husbands were 'widows,' the old without children were 'bereft,' the young without fathers were 'orphans.' These four were the poorest among the people and had none to bring their cares to. King Wen, in applying benevolent government, put these four first. The *Odes* say,

> Fitting it is for those with funds
> To be sad for these wretched, lonely ones.

The king exclaimed, "What excellent teachings!"

Mengzi responded, "If Your Majesty regards them as excellent, then why do you not put them into effect?"

The king said, "We have a weakness. We are fond of wealth."

Mengzi responded, "In former times, Duke Liu of Zhou was fond of wealth. The *Odes* say,

They stacked, they stored,
Bundled up dried goods,
In bags, in sacks,
Thinking to gather together and bring glory.
His bows and arrows were displayed,
With shields, spears, and battle-axes,
He commenced the march against Bin.

Hence those who stayed at home had loaded granaries, and those who marched had full provisions. Only then could they 'commence the march.' If Your Majesty is fond of wealth but treats the commoners the same, what difficulty is there in becoming [a great] King?"[3]

注 Zhu Xi comments, "Mengzi means that Duke Liu's people were satisfied with their wealth because, although he was fond of wealth, he was able to extend his own heart so that it reached to the people. . . ."

The king said, "We have a weakness. We are fond of sex."

Mengzi responded, "In former times, King Tai of Zhou was fond of sex, and loved his wife. The *Odes* say,

The Ancient Duke Danfu
Came riding his horse in the morning,
Along the banks of the Western waters.
He came to the foot of Mount Qi,
With his Lady Jiang.
They came and both settled there.

At that time, there were no bitter women in private, or any unmarried men in public. If Your Majesty is fond of sex but treats the commoners the same, what difficulty is there in becoming [a great] King?"

注 Zhu Xi comments, "In my humble opinion, from the opening chapter of [Book 1B] down to this one, the general idea is the same. Whether it is the delights of making music (1B1), parks (1B2), touring (1B4), of the heart that is fond of courage (1B3), wealth, or sex (1B5), these are all part of the Heavenly Pattern that human feelings cannot lack. . . . To accord with the Pattern and be impartial to the world is the

manner in which sages fully use their natures. To give free reign to one's desires and be selfishly interested in oneself alone is the way in which the masses extinguish the Heavenly in themselves. . . ."

BOOK 2A

6. Mengzi said, "All humans have hearts that are not unfeeling toward others. . . .

"The reason why I say that all humans have hearts that are not unfeeling toward others is this. Suppose someone suddenly saw a child about to fall into a well: anyone in such a situation would have a feeling of alarm and compassion—not because one sought to get in good with the child's parents, not because one wanted fame among one's neighbors and friends, and not because one would dislike the sound of the child's cries.

注 Note that Mengzi does not say that every human would necessarily *act* to save the child. All he claims is that any human would have at least a momentary feeling . . . of genuine compassion, and that the reaction would occur "suddenly" (which shows that it is not the result of calculations of self-interest). This passage is, in part, a response to the "ethical egoist" Yang Zhu, who seems to have claimed that only self-interested motivations are part of human nature. . . .

"From this we can see that if one is without the feeling of compassion, one is not human. If one is without the feeling of disdain, one is not human. If one is without the feeling of deference, one is not human. If one is without the feeling of approval and disapproval, one is not human. The feeling of compassion is the sprout of benevolence. The feeling of disdain is the sprout of righteousness. The feeling of deference is the sprout of propriety. The feeling of approval and disapproval is the sprout of wisdom.

"People's having these four sprouts is like their having four limbs. To have these four sprouts, yet to claim that one is incapable (of Virtue), is to steal from oneself. To say that one's ruler is incapable is to steal from one's ruler. In general, having these four sprouts within oneself, if one knows to fill them all out, it will be like a fire starting up, a spring breaking through! If one can merely fill them out, they will be sufficient to care for all within the Four Seas. If one merely fails to fill them out, they will be insufficient to serve one's parents."

> 注 A "normal," healthy human has four limbs. Similarly, a normal human has the four "sprouts." But, as the comparison to limbs suggests, it is possible to lose the sprouts.
>   Mengzi thinks the capacity for virtue is innate in humans, but it must be cultivated ("filled out") in order for us to become fully virtuous. . . .

7. Mengzi said, "Is the arrow-maker less benevolent than the armor-maker? Yet the arrow-maker only fears that he may not harm people; the armor-marker only fears that he may harm people. The shaman-healer and the coffin-maker are the same way, respectively. Hence, one may not fail to be careful about one's choice of craft.

> 注 The arrow-maker and the coffin-maker are born with the same heart of benevolence as the armor-maker and the shaman-healer. But their choices of career and way of life determine whether they want humans to live or die.

"Kongzi said, 'To dwell in benevolence is beautiful; if one chooses to not dwell in benevolence, how can one be wise?' . . . If one is not benevolent though nothing prevents it, this is to fail to be wise. If one fails to be benevolent and fails to be wise, then one lacks propriety and righteousness. This is to be the lackey of other people. To be the lackey of other people yet to be ashamed of being a lackey is like being a bow-maker yet to be ashamed of making bows, or to be an arrow-maker yet to be ashamed of making arrows.

> 注 Zhu Xi explains this paragraph in the terms of the unity of the virtues: "Benevolence is the heart of

Heaven and Earth in giving birth to things. One gets it first of all, and it links all four virtues together. . . . Because one is not benevolent, one is not wise. Because one is not wise, one does not understand wherein propriety and righteousness lie."

"If you are ashamed of it, there is nothing as good as becoming benevolent. Benevolence is like archery. An archer corrects himself and only then shoots. If he shoots but does not hit the mark, he does not resent the one who defeats him but simply turns and seeks for it in himself."

> 注 Zhu Xi comments, "He does not discuss wisdom, propriety, and righteousness, because benevolence encompasses the entire substance. If one can become benevolent, then the other three are in its midst. . . ."

8. Mengzi said, "Kongzi's disciple Zilu was pleased if someone informed him of his faults. When King Yu heard good teachings he bowed down in thanks. The Great Shun was even greater than they. He was good at unifying himself with others. He put himself aside and joined with others. He delighted in copying from others in order to do good. From plowing, planting, making pottery, and fishing on up to being Emperor—he never failed to copy from others. To copy others when they do good is to do good with others. Hence, for a gentleman, nothing is greater than to do good with others."

> 注 Zhu Xi explains how the people mentioned form a hierarchy. "Zilu was pleased that he heard about his faults so he could reform them. Such was his courage in self-cultivation." Zhou Dunyi commented, "Nowadays, when people have a fault, they are not pleased to be corrected by others. This is like concealing an illness and shunning medicine." Zhu Xi continues, "In contrast, King Yu did not wait to have a fault, but was capable of humbling himself to accept what was good in the world." Finally, Shun was greater than Zilu or King Yu, because he did not await being *told* criticisms or *hearing* good advice. . . .

9. Mengzi said, "If someone was not Bo Yi's ruler, he would not serve him. If someone was not his friend, he would not treat him as a friend. . . . He looked upon taking a position at the court of a bad person or having a discussion with a bad person like wearing one's court cap and gown and sitting down in filth. He extended his heart of disdain for evil to the point that, if he stood with an ordinary villager whose cap was not on correctly, he would leave. . . as if he thought he was about to be defiled. For this reason, when the assorted lords came with fine rhetoric, he would not accept them. He would not accept them because he was adamant that going to serve them was not pure.

注 Bo Yi's disdain to do what is wrong is a manifestation of the heart of righteousness [but] he has extended his heart too far. . . .

"Liuxia Hui was not ashamed of a corrupt lord, and did not consider a petty office unworthy. In taking office, he did not conceal what was worthy but would necessarily act in accordance with the Way. When he was discharged, he was not bitter. In difficult and impoverished circumstances, he was not anxious. Hence, he said, 'You are you, and I am I. Even if you are stark naked beside me, how can you defile me?' Hence, contently, he was with others without losing himself. If constrained to remain, he would remain. He remained when constrained to remain because he was adamant that leaving was not pure.

注 Zhu Xi explains that "'without losing himself' is without losing his uprightness. Liuxia Hui's willingness to adapt to circumstances shows the "discretion" that is so central to Confucianism. However, he ends up compromising too much. . . .

Mengzi observed, "Bo Yi was too constrained; Liuxia Hui was not dignified. A gentleman is neither too constrained nor lacking in dignity."

注 Zhu Xi comments, "The actions of Bo Yi and Liuxia Hui definitely both reached the highest level. Nonetheless, since they have some biases, they definitely have an obscured view (of the Way). Hence, they cannot be followed as models.

BOOK 4A

11. Mengzi said, "The Way lies in what is near, but people seek it in what is distant; one's task lies in what is easy, but people seek it in what is difficult. If everyone would treat their parents as parents and their elders as elders, the world would be at peace."

27. Mengzi said, "The core of benevolence is serving one's parents. The core of righteousness is obeying one's elder brother. The core of wisdom is knowing these two and not abandoning them. The core of ritual propriety is the adornment of these two. The core of music is to delight in these two.

"If one delights in them, then they grow. If they grow, then how can they be stopped? If they cannot be stopped, then one does not notice one's feet dancing to them, one's hands swaying to them."

注 Mengzi holds that humans innately have incipient dispositions toward virtue. Benevolence is manifested in such things as spontaneous acts of feelings of compassion and love of one's parents. Righteousness is manifested in disdain to do shameful things, and respect or deference to elders. But these incipient feelings have to be cultivated so that they "grow" or "extend" to all relevantly similar situations. This passage suggests that part of what helps this growth is delighting in the manifestations of the sprouts. . . .

BOOK 5A

1. Mengzi's disciple Wan Zhang asked, "Shun 'went into the fields, and cried out and wept to the autumn sky.' Why did he cry out and weep?"

Mengzi replied, "He was bitter over the fact that he did not receive the affection of his parents. . . . Gongming Gao's disciple Zhang Xi asked him, 'I have heard your explanation of how Shun *went into the fields*. But I still do not understand the fact that he *cried out and wept to the autumn sky, and to his parents*.' Gongming Gao simply replied, 'This is not something that someone like you could understand.'

"Gongming Gao thought that the heart of a filial child could not be so indifferent that he would not cry. Shun thought, 'In exerting my strength to the utmost in plowing the fields, I have merely done my duty as a son. What have I done that my parents do not love me?!' The Emperor Yao directed his children . . . the various officials, the sacrificial oxen and sheep, the full storehouses and granaries, to serve Shun even while he toiled amid the plowed fields. Many of the nobles of the world went to him. The Emperor planned to oversee the world with him and eventually transfer it to him [by making Shun emperor]. But because he was not reconciled with his parents, Shun felt like a poor, homeless person. . . .

注 Gongming Gao was a disciple of Kongzi's disciple Zengzi. Yang Shi said, "Shun only feared that he was not agreeable to his parents. He never regarded himself as filial. If he had regarded himself as filial, then he would not have been filial." (Shun is a paradigm of filial piety.[4] But, paradoxically, the later tradition praises him for systematically underestimating his own virtue.)

"To have the nobles of the world delight in oneself is something people desire, but it was not sufficient to relieve his concern. To take pleasure in beauty is something people desire, and he married the Emperor's two daughters, but it was not sufficient to relive his concern. Wealth is something that people desire, and for wealth he had the whole world, but it was not sufficient to relieve his concern. . . . Others delighting in him, taking pleasure in beauty, wealth, esteem—none of these was sufficient to relieve his concern, because only being reconciled with his parents could relieve his concern. . . ."

2. Wan Zhang asked, "The *Odes* say

How should one handle taking a bride?
One must inform one's father and mother.

It seems that no one should be more faithful to such a teaching than Shun. So why did Shun take a bride without informing his father and mother?"

Mengzi responded, "He could not have taken a bride if he had informed them. For a man and a

woman to live together is the greatest of human roles. If he had informed his parents, then he would have had to abandon the greatest of human roles, which would have led to enmity with his father and mother. For this reason he did not inform them. . . ."[5]

3. Wan Zhang asked, "Shun's brother Xiang took it as his daily task to try to kill Shun, yet when Shun took office as Son of Heaven, he merely imprisoned him (rather than executing him). Why?"

Mengzi replied, "He actually gave him a territory to administer, although some mistakenly referred to it as 'imprisonment.'"

Wan Zhang continued, "Shun 'dismissed the Supervisor of Works to You Zhou and imprisoned Huan Dou on Mount Chong. He killed the rulers of the Three Miao in San Wei and executed Kun on Mount Yu. He punished these four and so all the world submitted.' This was because he was executing those who were not benevolent. Xiang was consummately lacking in benevolence, yet he gave him the territory of Youbi to administer. What crime did the people of Youbi commit?! Is a benevolent person inherently like this? In the case of other people, he punishes them. In the case of his younger brother, he gives him a territory to administer."

Mengzi replied, "Benevolent people do not store up anger nor do they dwell in bitterness against their younger brothers. They simply love and treat them as kin. Treating them as kin, they desire them to have rank. Loving them, they desire them to have wealth. He gave him Youbi to administer to give him wealth and rank. If he himself was the Son of Heaven [i.e., the Emperor], and his younger brother was a common fellow, could this be called loving and treating him as kin?"

Wan Zhang asked, "May I ask why some referred to it as 'banishment'?"

Mengzi replied, "Xiang did not have effective power in his state. The Son of Heaven instructed officials to administer the state and collect tribute and taxes. Hence, it was referred to as 'banishment.' So could Xiang have succeeded in being cruel to his subjects? Nonetheless, Shun desired to see him often. Hence, Xiang came to court as constantly as a flowing spring. . . ."

注 Zhu Xi comments, "By handling him this way, Shun did not lose the heart of treating as kin and loving, yet Xiang was unable to be cruel to the people of Youbi."[6] Wu Huo said, "Sages do not harm personal generosity for the sake of public righteousness, but they also do not harm public righteousness for personal generosity. Shun's relationship to Xiang was a case of both consummate benevolence and the utmost righteousness."

This passage illustrates the Confucian commitment to "differentiated love" [e.g., of family over others]. . . .

BOOK 6A

2. Gaozi said, "Human nature is like swirling water. Make an opening for it on the eastern side, then it flows east. Make an opening for it on the western side, then it flows west. Human nature not distinguishing between good and not good is like water not distinguishing between east and west."

Mengzi replied, "Water surely does not distinguish between east and west. But doesn't it distinguish between upward and downward?" Human nature being good is like water tending downward. There is no human who does not tend toward goodness. There is no water that does not tend downward.[7]

"Now, by striking water and making it leap up, you can cause it to go past your forehead. If you guide it by damming it, you can cause it to remain on a mountaintop. But is this the nature of water? It is only that way because of the circumstances. When humans are caused to not be good, it is only because their nature is the same way."

注 The key to appreciating this chapter (and the adjacent ones) is that the similes are not intended as mere rhetorical window dressing without cognitive content. Mengzi's objection is that Gaozi's simile fails to do justice to the natural characteristics of water, and thereby presents a misleading impression of human nature.

When humans become bad, it is due to artificial interference with their natural tendencies, similar to the manner in which water can be forced uphill.

6. Mengzi's disciple Gongduzi said, "Gaozi says, 'Human nature is neither good nor not good.' Some say, 'Human nature can become good, and it can become not good.' Therefore, when Wen and Wu

arose, the people were fond of goodness. When Tyrant You and Tyrant Li arose, the people were fond of destructiveness. Some say, 'There are natures that are good, and there are natures that are not good.' Therefore, with Yao as ruler, there was Shun's evil brother Xiang. With the Blind Man as a father, there was Shun. . . . Now, you say that human nature is good. Are all those others, then, wrong?"

Mengzi said, "As for what they are inherently, they can become good. This is what I mean by calling their natures good. As for their being not good, this is not the fault of their potential. Humans all have the feeling of compassion. Humans all have the feeling of disdain. Humans all have the feeling of respect. Humans all have the feeling of approval and disapproval. The feeling of compassion is benevolence. The feeling of disdain is righteousness. The feeling of respect is propriety. The feeling of approval and disapproval is wisdom. Benevolence, righteousness, propriety, and wisdom are not welded to us externally. We inherently have them. It is simply that we do not reflect upon them. Hence, it is said, 'Seek it and you will get it. Abandon it and you will lose it.' Some differ from others by two, five, or countless times—this is because they cannot fathom their potentials. . . .'"?

注 We find a similar account of the four feelings . . . and their correlation with Mengzi's four cardinal virtues in 2A6, except that the feelings are there said to be merely the "sprouts" of the virtues. Zhu Xi suggests that the difference in phrasing is because in the earlier passage Mengzi is stressing the need to cultivate these reactions, whereas here he is emphasizing the fact that they are innate. "Reflection" is focusing one's attention upon thinking about one's feelings and the situations that elicit them. It is an activity that involves feelings, thoughts, and perception. . . .

8. Mengzi said, "The trees of Ox Mountain were once beautiful. But because it bordered a large state, hatchets and axes besieged it. Could it remain verdant? Due to the respite it got during the day or night, and the moisture of rain and dew, there were sprouts and shoots growing there. But oxen and sheep came and grazed on them. Hence, it was as if it were barren. Seeing it barren, people believed that there had never been any timber there. But could this be the nature of the mountain?

注 Remember that Mengzi uses the metaphor of "sprouts" to describe our innate but incipient ethical inclinations.

"When we consider what is present in people, could they truly lack the hearts of benevolence and righteousness? The way that they discard their genuine hearts is like the hatchets and axes in relation to the trees. With them besieging it day by day, can it remain beautiful? With the respite it gets during the day or night . . . their likes and dislikes are sometimes close to those of others. But then what they do during the day again fetters and destroys it. If the fettering is repeated . . . then one is not far from an animal. Others see that he is an animal, and think that there was never any capacity there. But is this what a human is like inherently?

"Hence, if it merely gets nourishment, there is nothing that will not grow. If it merely loses its nourishment, there is nothing that will not vanish. . . .'

注 The story of Ox Mountain is Mengzi's reply to the objection that some people seem to lack the virtuous inclinations that he claims are part of human nature. Mengzi argues that such people . . . were born with a good nature, but it was stunted by some combination of a bad environment and their own repeated bad actions.

commanders of their armies because they delight in profit. . . . Those who are ministers will embrace profit in serving their rulers. Those who are children will embrace profit in serving their fathers. Those who are younger brothers will embrace profit in serving their elder brothers. This is for rulers and minsters, fathers and children, elder brothers and younger brothers to end up abandoning benevolence and righteousness. It has never happened that people embrace profit in their contact with one another yet fail to be destroyed.

"If you persuade the kings of Qin and Chu by means of benevolence and righteousness, the kings of Qin and Chu will set aside their armies because of their delight in benevolence and righteousness. . . . Those who are ministers will embrace benevolence and righteousness in serving their rulers. Those who are children will embrace benevolence and righteousness in serving their fathers. Those who are younger brothers will embrace benevolence and righteousness in serving their elder brothers. This is for rulers and ministers, fathers and children, elder brothers and younger brothers to abandon profit. It has never happened that people embrace benevolence and righteousness in their contact with one another, yet their ruler fails to become [a great] King. Why must one say 'profit'?"

BOOK 6B

4. When Song Keng was about to go to Chu, Mengzi encountered him at Stone Hill. Mengzi said, "Where are you about to go, venerable sir?"

Song Keng replied, "I have heard that Qin and Chu are at war. I plan to have an audience with the king of Chu, to persuade him to abandon this. If the king of Chu is not agreeable, I plan to have an audience with the king of Qin, to persuade him to abandon this. I shall certainly meet with success between the two kings."

Mengzi said, "I am not asking for details, but I wonder if I could hear the main point you will use in persuading them."

Song Keng said, "I shall explain the unprofitability of what they plan."

Mengzi said, "Your intention, venerable sir, is indeed great. But your slogan is unacceptable. If you persuade the kings of Qin and Chu by means of profit, the kings of Qin and Chu will set aside the

BOOK 7A

15. Mengzi said, "That which people are capable of without learning is their genuine capability. That which they know without pondering is their genuine knowledge. Among babes in arms there are none that do not know to love their parents. When they grow older, there are none that do not know to revere their elder brothers. Treating one's parents as parents is benevolence. Revering one's elders is righteousness. There is nothing else to do but extend these to the world.

注 This is Mengzi's philosophy of ethical cultivation in a nutshell. We are born with incipient tendencies toward benevolence and righteousness, which we must "extend" so that they reach all other relevantly similar cases. That is, we must feel compassion not only for our own parents but also for the parents of others. We must revere not only the elders of our family but also the elders of others. . . .

26. Mengzi said, "Yang Zhu favored being 'for one-self.' If plucking out one hair from his body would have benefited the whole world, he would not do it. Mozi favored 'impartial caring.' If scraping himself bare from head to heels would benefit the whole world, he would do it. Zimo held to the middle. Holding to the middle is close to it. But if one holds to the middle without discretion, that is the same as holding to one extreme. What I dislike about those who hold to one extreme is that they detract from the Way. They elevate one thing and leave aside a hundred others."

注 There is no simple formula for determining to what extent we should prioritize the interests of ourselves, our loved ones, and the world at large. . . . [Instead] we must use "discretion" to judge what is appropriate in each situation.

45. Mengzi said, "Gentleman, in relation to animals, are sparing of them but are not benevolent toward them. In relation to people, they are benevolent toward them but do not treat them as kin. They treat their kin as kin, and then are benevolent toward the people. They are benevolent toward the people, and then are sparing of animals."

注 This is a succinct statement of the Confucian doctrine of "differentiated love." . . . Virtuous people are very compassionate toward all humans, but without the special attachment they feel toward their own kin. They will not indiscriminately harm animals, but their concern for them is significantly less than for humans. Thus, King Xuan of Qi fails to be a true gentleman, because he shows more compassion to animals than to his own subjects. And Mohists [followers of Mozi, who advocated impartial caring for everyone,] fail to be true gentleman, because they are committed to showing equal concern to everyone, regardless of familial relationships.

BOOK 7B

5. Mengzi said, "A carpenter or a wheelwright can give another his compass or T-square, but he cannot make another skillful."

注 This is a criticism of those who, like the Mohists, wish to reduce ethical action to some precise procedure that does not require wisdom. . . .

31. Mengzi said, "People all have things that they will not bear. To extend this reaction to that which they will bear is benevolence. People all have things that they will not do. To extend this reaction to that which they will do is righteousness.

注 Zhu Xi comments, "People all have the hearts of compassion and disdain. Hence, no one fails to have things that he will not bear or will not do. These are the sprouts of benevolence and righteousness. Nonetheless . . . there are sometimes other cases in which people are unable to have these reactions. But if they extend what they are able to do so that they reach to what they were unable to do, then there will be nothing in which they are not benevolent and righteous."

"If people can fill out the heart that does not desire to harm others, their benevolence will be inexhaustible. If people can fill out the heart that will not trespass, their righteousness will be inexhaustible. . . ."

NOTES

1. The size of states and the strength of powerful families were typically measured in terms of how many war chariots they could field in battle.

2. "Virtue" [*dé*] is a sort of ethical charisma that induces others to submit without the need for coercion.

3. [This is the first time in these excerpts that we see Mencius using a story about a historical figure in the way that Western philosophers use thought experiments: He is using the example of Duke Liu to test the principle that being "fond of wealth" is "a weakness." Mencius uses this same kind of argument throughout the text. —DRM]

4. [Because Shun is a paradigm of filial virtue, Mencius uses surprising stories about him to investigate the nature of filial piety. The hidden premise in each argument here is that whatever Shun does correctly exhibits the virtue of filial piety. —DRM]

5. Shun's cruel parents would have opposed his marriage so that he would have no wife or children to inherit his property if he died. . . .

6. [This is an example of what the translator, in commenting on passage 4B24, calls "the Confucian fondness for seeking creative solutions to ethical problems." —DRM]

7. Although water is indifferent to flowing east and west, to make it flow either way, we must follow its natural disposition to flow downward. Likewise, to make humans good we must work with our natural dispositions.

DISCUSSION QUESTIONS

1. Do you agree with Mencius's conclusion about whether human nature is inherently good? Why or why not?
2. How, according to Mencius, do people become virtuous? How is that plan for ethical cultivation related to his views about whether human nature is "inherently good"?
3. What is the connection between Mencius's claims about the virtues in 2A7 and his criticisms of Bo Yi and Liuxia Hui in 2A9? Do you agree with Mencius that Bo Yi and Liuxia Hui are both ultimately flawed? Why or why not?
4. In 2A7, Mencius suggests that one's choice of profession can help or hinder a person in becoming virtuous. His reasons for thinking this are scattered through the rest of the text. Reconstruct, as well as you can, Mencius's argument for this claim. Do you find it convincing? Why or why not?
5. What is the Confucian doctrine of "differentiated love"? What arguments does Mencius give for that doctrine? Do you find these arguments convincing? Why or why not?

KWASI WIREDU

The Moral Foundations of an African Culture

Kwasi Wiredu is Distinguished University Professor Emeritus at the University of South Florida. Before coming to Florida, he taught at the University of Ghana for twenty-three years. He is one of the central figures in contemporary African philosophy. In this essay he explains some ethical concepts from the Akan culture in his native Ghana, focusing on the morally loaded Akan concept of personhood. Similar ideas arise in many sub-Saharan African cultures, as explained in this book's discussion of the ethics of *ubuntu* (see pp. 134–35).

GUIDING QUESTIONS

1. What are the two meanings of the Akan saying "*onipa na ohia*"?
2. What lessons do the Akan draw from the fact that each person is born into a particular community?
3. How does someone become "less of a person" in Akan ethical thought? What role does "striving after personhood" play in Akan ethics?
4. According to Wiredu, how does the Akan emphasis on "mutual aid" show up in everyday life?

Kwasi Wiredu. "The Moral Foundations of an African Culture," Person and Community (Ghanaian Philosophical Studies 1), Kwasi Wiredu and Kwame Gyekye, (eds.), 1992. Washington, D.C.: The Council for Research in Values and Philosophy.

INTRODUCTION

Morality in the strictest sense is universal to human culture. Indeed, it is *essential* to all human culture. Any society without a modicum of morality must collapse. But what is morality in this sense? It is simply the observance of rules for the harmonious adjustment of the interests of the individual to those of others in society. This, of course, is a minimal concept of morality. A richer concept of morality even more pertinent to human flourishing will have an essential reference to that special kind of motivation called the sense of duty. Morality in this sense involves not just the *de facto* conformity to the requirements of the harmony of interests, but also that conformity to those requirements which is inspired by an imaginative and sympathetic identification with the interests of others even at the cost of a possible abridgement of one's own interests. This is not a demand for a supererogatory altruism. But a certain minimum of altruism is absolutely essential to the moral motivation. In this sense too morality is probably universal to all human societies, though, most certainly, not to all known individuals.

The foregoing reflection still does not exclude the possibility of a legitimate basis for differentiating the morals of the various peoples of the world. This is so for at least three reasons. First of all, although morality in both of the senses just discriminated is the same wherever and whenever it is practiced, different peoples, groups and individuals have different understandings of it. The contrasting moral standpoints of humanism and supernaturalism, for example, illustrate this diversity. Secondly, the concrete cultural context in which a moral principle is applied may give it a distinctive coloring. Lastly, but most importantly, there is a broad concept of morals closely contiguous to the narrow one—which is what the two concepts of morality noted earlier on together amount to—in regard to which the contingencies of space, time and clime may play quite a constitutive role. This appertains to the domain that, speaking very broadly, may be called custom. In view here are such things as the prescriptions and proscriptions operative in a community regarding life and death, work and leisure, reward and retribution, aspirations and aversions, pleasure and pain, and the relationships between the sexes, the generations and other social categories and classes. The combined impact of such norms of life and thought in a society should give a distinctive impression of its morals.

AKAN HUMANISM

But let me start with the manner of conceiving morals. African conceptions of morals would seem generally to be of a humanistic orientation. Anthropological studies lend substantial support to this claim. Nevertheless, the accounts are not always philosophically inquisitive, and I prefer, in elaborating on this characterization, to rely on my own native knowledge of the life and thought of the Akans of Ghana. On this basis, I can affirm the humanism in question more uninhibitedly. The commonest formulation of this outlook is in the saying, which almost any Akan adult or even young hopeful will proffer on the slightest provocation, that it is a human being that has value: *Onipa na ohia.* The English translation just given of the Akan saying, though pertinent, needs supplementation, for the crucial term here has a double connotation. The word "(o)hia" in this context means both that which is of value and that which is needed. Through the first meaning the message is imparted that all value derives from human interests and through the second that human fellowship is the most important of human needs. When this last thought is uppermost in consciousness an Akan would be likely to add to the maxim under discussion an elucidation to the effect that you might have all the gold in the world and the best stocked wardrobe, but if you were to appeal to these in the hour of need they would not respond; only a human being will. *(Onipa ne asem: mefre sika a, sika nnye so; mefre ntama a, ntama nmye so; onipa ne asem.)* Already beginning to emerge is the great stress on human sociality in Akan thought, but before pursuing this angle of the subject let me tarry a while on the significance of Akan humanism.

One important implication of the founding of value on human interests is the independence of morality from religion in the Akan outlook: What is good in general is what promotes human interests. Correspondingly, what is good in the more narrowly ethical sense is, by definition, what is conducive to the harmonization of those interests. Thus, the will of God, not to talk of that of any other extra-human being, is logically incapable of defining the good. On the Akan understanding of things, indeed, God is good in the highest; but his goodness is conceptually of a type with the goodness of a just and benevolent ancestor, only in his case quality and scale are assumed to be limitless. The prospect of punishment from God or some lesser being may concentrate the mind on the narrow path of virtue, but it is not this that creates the sense of moral obligation. Similarly, the probability of police intervention might conceivably give pause to a would-be safe breaker, though if he or she had any sense of morals at all it would not be thanks to the collective will of the police or even the state.

This conceptual separation of morals from religion is, most likely, responsible in some measure for the remarkable fact that there is no such thing as an institutional religion in Akan culture. The procedures associated with the belief in sundry extra-human beings of varying powers and inclinations, so often given pride of place in accounts of African religions, are in fact practical utilitarian programs for tapping the resources of this world. The idea, in a nutshell, is that God invested the Cosmos with all sorts of potentialities, physical and quasi-physical, personal and quasi-personal, which human beings may bend to their purposes, if they learn how. Naturally, in dealing with beings and powers believed to be of a quasi-personal character, certain aspects of behavior patterns will manifest important analogies to the canons of ordinary human interactions. For example, if you wanted something from a being of superhuman repute who is open to persuasion mixed with praise, pragmatic common sense alone would recommend an attitude of demonstrative respect and

circumspection and a language of laudatory circumlocution reminiscent of worship, but the calculative and utilitarian purpose would belie any attribution of a specifically religious motivation. In fact, the Akans are known to be sharply contemptuous of "gods" who fail to deliver; continued respect is conditional on a high percentage of scoring by the Akan reckoning.

In total contrast to the foregoing is the Akan attitude to the Supreme Being, which is one of unconditional reverence and absolute trust. Absent here is any notion that so perfect a being requires or welcomes institutions for singing or reciting his praises. Nor, relatedly, are any such institutions felt to be necessary for the dissemination of moral education or the reinforcement of the will to virtue. The theater of moral upbringing is the home, at parents' feet and within range of kinsmen's inputs. The mechanism is precept, example and correction. The temporal span of the process is life-long, for, although upbringing belongs to the beginning of our earthly careers, the need for correction is an unending contingency in the lives of mortals. At adulthood, of course, as opposed to earlier stages in life, moral correction involves discourses of a higher level and may entail, besides the imposition of compensatory obligations (of which more later); but, at all stages, verbal lessons in morality are grounded in conceptual and empirical considerations about human well-being. All this is why the term "humanistic" is so very apt as a characterization of Akan moral thinking. At least in part, this is why it is correct to describe that ethic as non-supernaturalistic in spite of the sincere belief in a Supreme Being.

In so far, then, as the concept of religion is applicable to the Akan outlook on life and reality, it can refer only to the belief and trust in the Supreme Being. In this respect, Akan religion is purely intellectual. In this respect too it is purely personal, being just a tenet of an individual's voluntary metaphysic, devoid of social entanglements. In truth, most Akans espouse that metaphysic as a matter of course. Akan conventional wisdom actually holds that the existence of God is so obvious that it does not need to be taught even to a child. (*Obi nkyere akwadaa Nyame.*)

Nevertheless, skeptics are not unknown in Akan society, and a time-honored policy of peaceful laissez faire extends to them as to all others in matters of private persuasion.

DEFINING MORALITY

Morality too is intellectual, by Akan lights. Concrete moral situations in real life are frequently highly composite tangles of imponderables, and perceiving them in their true lineaments is a cognitive accomplishment in itself. So too is the sure grasping of first principles and their judicious application to the particulars of conduct. Morality is also personal, for in the last analysis the individual must take responsibility for his or her own actions. But surely morality is neither purely intellectual, for it has an irreducible passional ingredient, nor purely personal, for it is quintessentially social.

All these insights are encapsulated in various Akan maxims and turns of phrase. Recognition of the intellectual dimension of right conduct is evidenced in the Akan description of a person of ethical maturity as an *obadwenma*. This word means one possessed of high thinking powers. Literally, it says "child, thinking child," in other words, a thinking child of the species. The Akans are no less emphatic in their articulation of their sense of individual responsibility. According to a very popular proverb, it is because God dislikes injustice that he gave everyone their own name (thereby forestalling any misattribution of responsibility). Along with this clear sense of individual responsibility went an equally strong sense of the social reverberations of an individual's conduct. The primary responsibility for an action, positive or negative, rests with the doer, but a non-trivial secondary responsibility extends to the individual's family and, in some cases, to the environing community. This brings us to the social orientation of the Akan concept of a person. We will not be able to elaborate it fully in the present discussion, but a crucial consideration will be adduced here. It is that, for the Akans, a person is social not only because he or she lives in a community, which is the only context in which full development, or indeed any sort of human development is possible, but also because, by his original constitution, a human being is part of a social whole.

The underlying doctrine is this. A person consists of three elements. One of these comes *directly* from God and is, in fact, a speck of the divine substance. This is the life principle. In virtue of this constituent all human beings are one; they are all members of the universal family of humankind whose head and spring is God. *Nipa nyinaa ye Nyame mma: obiara nnye asaase ba.* Literally: all human beings are the children of God; none is the child of the earth. The two remaining elements are more mundane in origin. There is what might be called the blood principle which derives from the mother and, somewhat more stipulatively, there is what might be called the charisma principle which comes from the father. The blood from the mother is what principally gives rise to a person's body. The biological input from the father is responsible for the degree of personal presence that each individual develops at the appropriate stage. (This is what I would like the license to call the individual's degree of charisma.) The ontological classification of these elements is not exactly straightforward. Suffice it to warn that the physical/spiritual dichotomy is unlikely to be a source of light in this connection. In any case, our interest here is in the social significance of those components.

Both the maternal and paternal contributions to the make-up of a person are the bases of membership in specific social units. The Akans being a matrilineal group, it is the blood principle that situates a person in the most important kinship unit, namely, the lineage or, more extensively, the clan. Through the charisma principle one is a member of a grouping on the father's side which, although largely ceremonial, is nevertheless the framework of a lot of goodwill.

The point now is that, on this Akan showing, a person has a well-structured social identity even before birth. Thus, when an Akan maxim points out that when a human being descends from on high he or she alights in a town (*se onipa siane fi soro a obesi kuro mu*) the idea is that one comes into a community in which one already has well defined social affiliations. But society presupposes rules, and moral rules are the most essential of these. Since all rules have their rationale, a question that challenges the ethical imagination, especially one thoroughly impregnated with visions of the ineluctable sociality of human existence, is: What is the rationale of moral rules? Among the Akans some of the most profound philosophic conceptions are expressed by way of art motifs, and a celebrated answer to this question is offered in one such construct of fine art: a crocodile with one stomach and two heads locked in combat. Lessons: (1) Although human beings have a core of common interests, they also have conflicting interests that precipitate real struggles. (2) The aim of morality, as also derivatively of statesmanship, is to harmonize those warring interests through systematic adjustment and adaptation. The one stomach symbolizes not only the commonality of interests, but also a natural basis for the possibility of a solution to the existential antinomy.

Two levels of solution are distinguishable, corresponding to a distinction foreshadowed in our opening paragraph. There is the level of prudence or enlightened self-interest and there is that of pure moral motivation. Both species of thought and intention may be equally adapted to securing the social good, the first through cool and calm ratiocination, the second through both rational reflection and human sympathy. But they evoke different appraisals from people of goodwill. There will always be something unlovable about correctness of conduct bereft of passion. A Ghanaian comedian puts it even more strongly. Speaking with a deliberately unidiomatic bombast, he opines: "Ability without sentimentality is nothing short of barbarity." Nevertheless, it appears that teachers of morals everywhere have tended to find prudential considerations more psychologically efficacious in moral persuasion than abstract appeals to goodwill. Certainly, Akan ethical reflection does not stay immobile at this level of ethics, but Akan discourse abounds in prudential maxims. Here are a few.

1. If you do not allow your neighbor to reach nine you will never reach ten. *(Woamma wo yonko antwa nkrong a worentwa edu.)*

2. Somebody's troubles have arrived; those of another are on the way. *(Obi de aba; obi de nam kwan so.)*

3. It is a fool that says, "My neighbor is the butt of the attack not me." *(Kwasea na ose, "Ye de meyonko, yenne me.")*

4. The stick that was used to beat Takyi is the same that will be used to beat Nyankomago. *(Abaa a yede boo Takyi no aa na ye de bebo Nyankomago.)*

5. One person's path will intersect with another's before too long. *(Obi Kwan nkye na asi obi de mu.)*

That Akan ethics transcends this level of moral understanding is evident from other parts of their corpus of moral sayings. I will comment here on one particularly instructive form of moral expostulation. To a person whose conduct betrays obliviousness to the interests of others it is said, "Sticking into your neighbor's flesh, it might just as well be sticking into a piece of wood" *(Etua woyonko ho a etua dua mu)*, than which there can scarcely be a lower rating for a person's moral stature. On this reading of morals, the ultimate moral inadequacy consists in that lack of feeling which is the root of all selfishness. The implied imperative is: "In all inter-personal situations put yourself into the skin of the other and see if you can contemplate the consequences of your proposed action with equanimity." If we call the recommended frame of mind sympathetic impartiality, we may elicit from the Akan maxim under discussion the view that sympathetic impartiality is the first principle of all morals. This principle is the logical basis of the golden rule, or the obverse of it that is frequently heard in Akan ethical talk, namely, "Do not do onto others what you would not that they do onto you." *(Nea wo yonko de ye wo a erenye wo de no mfa nye no.* More literally: What you would not find acceptable if it were done to you by another, do not do to him or her.)* To be sure, this does not sound, even in our vernacular, as epigrammatic as the normal run of Akan apothegms, but it provides, nonetheless, a solid foundation for the definition of moral worth in its most edifying sense.

ETHICS AND PRACTICE

The foregoing account of the Akan perspective on moral first principles, however brief, must form the basis of our next question, which is: "In what basic ways do the Akans endeavor to translate their ethical understanding into practical fact?" In this regard the single most important consideration concerns the depth of the Akan sense of what we have called the sociality of human existence. Morality is, of course, necessarily social. Hence any group of humans that can be credited with any sense of morals at all—surely, a most minimal species credential—will have some sense of human sociality. But in the consciousness of moral humankind there is a finely graduated continuum of the intensity of this feeling which ranges, in an ascending order, from the austerely delimited social sympathies of rigorous individualism to the pervasive commitment to social involvement characteristic of communalism. It is a commonplace of anthropological wisdom that African social organization manifests the last type of outlook. Akan society is eminently true to this typology.

What this means, more amply, is that Akan society is of a type in which the greatest value is attached to communal belonging. And the way in which a sense of communal belonging is fostered in the individual is through the concentrated stress on kinship identity already adumbrated in our earlier allusions to the Akan concept of a person. Not only is there what might perhaps be called an ontological basis for this identity in terms of the constituents of personhood, but there is also a distinct normative layer of a profound social significance in that concept. Thus conceived, a human person is essentially the center of a thick set of concentric circles of obligations and responsibilities matched by rights and privileges revolving round levels of relationships irradiating from the consanguinity of household kith and kin, through the "blood" ties of lineage and clan, to the wider circumference of human familihood based on the common possession of the divine spark.

In consequence of this character of the Akan concept of a person, habitual default in duties and responsibilities could lead to a diminution in one's status as a person in the eyes of the community. Not, of course, that becoming less and less of a person implies being thought more and more unworthy of human rights. On the contrary, there is a strong sense of the irreducibility of human dignity in Akan thought. However socially inept an individual may be, he or she still remains a being begotten of a direct gift of God incarnated through the intimacy of man and woman. He or she remains, in other words, a human being and as such is deserving of a certain basic respect and sympathy. Indeed, as soon as confirmed social futility begins to look pathologically chronic, animadversion quickly turns into solicitude, and any previous efforts in hortatory correction or in the application of more concrete sanctions are redirected towards rehabilitation, usually with the aid of indigenous specialists in bodily and mental health.

Nevertheless, any Akan steeped in the culture or even just sensitive to surrounding social norms constantly watches and prays lest he or she be overtaken by the specter of loss of personhood (in any degree). More positively and also more optimistically, every cultivated Akan (*Okaniba*) sees life as a scenario of continual striving after personhood in ever increasing dimensions. The details of this life mission, so to speak, will also be the details of the Akan vision of the ethical life. We must here content ourselves with only broad outlines. But before going on let us note that since two paragraphs ago our focus has been on ethics or morals in the sense in which morality is a matter of *mores* rather than of the categorical imperative or even of the less hallowed canons of prudence.

What, then, in its social bearings, is the Akan ideal of personhood? It is the conception of an individual who through mature reflection and steady motivation is able to carve out a reasonably ample livelihood for self, "family" and a potentially wide group of kin dependents, besides making substantial contributions to the well-being of society at large. The communalistic orientation of the society in question means that an individual's image will depend rather crucially upon the extent to which his or her actions benefit others than himself, not, of course, by accident or coincidence but by design. The implied counsel, though, is not one of unrelieved self-denial, for the Akans are well aware that charity further afield must start at home. More pertinently, they are apt to point out that one cannot blow a horn on an empty stomach *(Yede ayaase na ehyen aben)*. Still an individual who remained content with self-regarding successes would be viewed as so circumscribed in outlook as not to merit the title of a real person.

Opportunities for other-regarding exertions in Akan society were legion in the past and remain so even now. By the very nature of the traditional economy, which was predominantly agricultural and based on individual self-employment, public works had, as a rule, to be done by voluntary communal labor. Habitual absences or malingering or half-hearted participation marked an individual down as a useless person *(onipa hunu)* or, by an easily deduced Akan equation, a non-person *(onye onipa)*. In contemporary Ghana (and Ivory Coast), where the Akans live, much of the public works are financed out of mandatory taxes and carried out by professionals with hired labor. Nevertheless, in the villages and small towns a significant portion of such work is still done by way of voluntary communal labor and a good proportion also through voluntary contributions of money and materials.

SOME CONTEMPORARY PROBLEMS

Here comes a contemporary complication: with the growth of commerce and industry, including the industry of modern politics, a non-negligible number of Akans have become very rich. In the Akan manner, they make voluntary contributions of unprecedented magnitudes to their communities; and the communities, for their part, reciprocate in fine eulogistic style and lionize them in other ways too, as is traditional. So far so good, except for the following circumstance. Some of these rich people are known to have come by their assets through debatable techniques of acquisition. The unfortunate effects of this situation on the ideals of the young

constitute some of the more intractable problems generated by the impact of industrialization on the Akan traditional ethic.

Another aspect of Akan communalism imperiled by modern conditions, through atrophy rather than adulteration, is the practice of neighborhood mutual aid. This practice had its foundation deep in the Akan conception of values. It is relevant here to recall the Akan adage: *Onipa na ohyia* quoted early in this discussion. It was interpreted as affirming, through the semantic fecundity of the word *hyia,* both that human interest is the basis of all value and that human fellowship is the most important of human needs. The concept of *Hyia* in the context of that adage is, in fact, a veritable mine of ethical meanings. In that context it also bears the seeds of another fundamental thought in the Akan philosophy of life, which is made explicit in the maxim: *Onipa hia moa,* meaning, by way of first approximation, "a human being needs help." The intent of the maxim, however, is not just to observe a fact, but also to prescribe a line of conduct. The imperative here is carried by the word *"hia,"* which in this context also has a connotation of entitlement: A human being deserves, ought, to be helped.

This imperative is born of an acute sense of the essential dependency of the human condition. The idea of dependency may even be taken as a component of the Akan conception of a person. "A human being" says a noted Akan proverb, "is not a palm tree so as to be self-sufficient": *Onipa nye abe na ne ho ahyia ne ho.* Indeed, at birth, a human being is not only not self-sufficient but also radically self-insufficient, if one may be permitted the expression: he or she is totally dependent on others. In due course, through growth and acculturation, acquired skills and abilities will reduce this dependency but will never eliminate it completely. Self-reliance is, of course, understood and recommended by the Akans, but its very possibility is predicated upon this ineliminable residue of human dependency. Human beings, therefore, at all times, in one way or another, directly or indirectly, need the help of their kind.

One very standard situation in Akan life in which this truth was continually illustrated was in traditional agriculture. As hinted earlier, this was generally based on small holdings worked by individual farmers and their households. In such a mode of production recurrent stages were easily foreseeable at which the resources of any one farmer would be insufficient to accomplish with the required dispatch a necessary task—be it the initial clearing of the ground or the scooping out of, say, cocoa beans from great heaps of pods. In such moments all that was necessary was for one to send word to one's neighbors indicating the time, place and the nature of help needed. Very much as day follows night, the people would assemble at the right time at the indicated place with their own implements of work and together help get the job done speedily and almost with festive enthusiasm, in full and warranted conviction that when their turn came the same gesture would be returned in exactly the same spirit. Anybody who availed himself of the benefits of this system and yet dragged his feet when the call came from others was liable to be convicted, at the bar of public opinion, of such fathomless degeneracy as to be branded a social outcast. The type of mutual aid here discussed probably occurs in varying intensities in rural communities all over the world, but in traditional Akan society it was so much and so palpably a part of working experience that the Akans actually came to think of life (obra) as one continuous drama of mutual aid (nnoboa). Obra ye nnoboa: Life is mutual aid, according to an Akan saying.

In recent times, however, amidst the exigencies of urbanization and the increasing—if not as yet preponderant—commercialization of agriculture, the ideology of mutual aid is losing some of its hold; and the spirit of neighborhood solidarity, though by no means extinguished, is finding fewer sweeping avenues of expression. It has not escaped some leaders of opinion that the traditional ethos of mutual aid might profitably be channelled into a strong movement of modern cooperatives, but as yet organized effort in this direction is halting in momentum and paltry in results.

Nevertheless, in countless small ways the sense of human solidarity continues to manifest itself quite pervasively in the daily life of the Akans and of the peoples of Ghana generally, of whom these moral characterizations remain true, if not to the letter, then at least to the syllable. Happily too, the threat of individualism posed by urbanization has not as yet proved unduly deleterious to this national trait. Thus, even now a Ghanaian on the countryside or in a large city, coming upon another human being, Ghanaian or foreigner, in some difficulty, will go well out of his way to help. As far as he or she is concerned, the bad person is exactly the one who would walk off on the excuse of some pressing business. Of course, if urbanization and other apparent concomitants of modernization are not controlled with conscious and rational planning based on the humane sensitivities of the communalistic ethic, then this fund of automatic good will dry up and African life will experience increasingly the Hobbesian rigors of a single-minded commercialism.

KINSHIP AND MORALITY

The allusion to foreigners in the last paragraph prompts a further observation. The sense of human solidarity which we have been discussing works particularly to the advantage of foreigners, who, in the deeply felt opinion of the Akans, are doubly deserving of sympathy; on grounds, first, of their common humanity and, second, of their vulnerability as individuals cut off for the time being, at any rate, from the emotional and material supports of their kinship environment. Accordingly, when some time ago an Akan guitarist and lyricist, Kwabena Onyina, sang *Akwantu mu sem: Akwantufo ye mmobo* (Think of the woes of travel: the plight of a traveller is rueful) he struck a sympathetic cord at the deepest reaches of the Akan consciousness. Gratified visitors to Ghana have often been quick to acknowledge the benefits accruing.

Again, to pursue an allusion in the preceding paragraph: the notion of kinship support just mentioned is of the highest importance in the Akan communal set-up, for it is the basis of the sense of belonging which gives the individual much of his psychological stability. (This, incidentally, is why a traveller bereft of it struck the Akan so much as a hardship case). It was also, *conversely,* the basis of a good proportion of the obligations in terms of which his moral standing was assessed. The smallest and the most intimate Akan kinship unit is the matrilineal household. This includes a person's mother and his mother's children, his mother's sisters and brothers, the children of the mother's sisters and, at the top, the grandmother. It is instructive to observe that the English words "aunt" and "cousin" fail to capture the depth of kinship feelings corresponding to the relations of mother's sister and mother's sister's children respectively, in spite of their mechanical correctness as translations. In the Akan language the words for mother and mother's children are the same as for mother's sisters and mother's sister's children. Since the relationships noted already comprehend quite a sizable community, especially if the grandmother concerned has been even averagely fertile, this guarantees that in the traditional setting an Akan child begins life with quite a large sense of belonging and a broad sweep of sympathies.

The next extension of the circle of the kinship relations just described brings us to the level of the lineage. Here the *basic* unit consists of a person's grandmother and her children and grandchildren together with the grandmother's brothers and sisters and the children and grandchildren of her sisters. This unit quickly swells up with the culturally legitimate addition of grandmother's maternal "cousins" and their descendants. From the point of view of a person's civic existence, this is the most significant circle of relations, for it was through the head of the lineage that, in traditional times, a person had his political representation. The lineage, as can easily be imagined, is a quite considerable group of people, but it is small in comparison with the maximal limit of kinship grouping, which is the set of all the people descending from one woman. The latter is the clan. For a quick idea of magnitude, consider that the Akans, now numbering in the region of seven million, trace their collective ancestry to seven women. Patently, individual Akans will never know all their relatives, but they can rest assured that they have a million of them.

For many practical purposes, however, it is the household and (basic) lineage circles of relations that have the most significance in terms of informal rights and obligations. Two illustrations must suffice

here. Adult members of the lineage may be called upon each to make financial contributions to rescue one of the fold fallen on hard times, say, threatening insolvency. In view of the powers of arithmetic, this did not necessarily take a heavy toll of individual pockets. Moreover, it was not lost upon the reflective individual that he or she might conceivably have been the beneficiary.

The next illustration has to do with a lugubrious subject matter. Bereavement is one of the severest trials of the human psyche; unfortunately, it is recurrent. By both precept and practice Akan traditional culture engages itself, pre-eminently, one might even say, with finding ways to soothe lacerated emotions in such crises. The lineage system incorporates in its arrangements just such a mechanism. In full operation everyone in the lineage is expected to play his part by word, song, dance and material resource. Nor does the culture leave this to the lineage alone. Friends, neighbors and even indirect acquaintances can always be counted upon to help in various ways to lighten the burden of sorrows. The framework for all this is the quite elaborate system of the Akan funeral. In spite of the excesses to which this institution has become subject through the rising tide of commercialism and egotistical exhibitionism, it remains an avenue for the expression of human solidarity at its most heartfelt depth. Proper participation thereto is, in Akan eyes, contributory proof of real personhood.

CONCLUSION

It is clear from the foregoing that socialization in the broad context of the lineage can be a veritable school for morality in its Akan acceptation. It is through the kinship channels of the lineage set-up that the Akan sense of the sociality of human beings finds its most natural expression. Moral life in the wider community is only an extension of a pattern of conduct inculcated at the lineage level. The fundamental values, some of which we have already outlined above, are the same on the two planes, and may be briefly summarized. A communalistic orientation will naturally prize social harmony. A characteristic Akan, and, as it seems, African way of pursuing this ideal is through decision-making by consensus rather than by majority opinion. In politics—traditional African politics, not the modern travesties rampant on the continent—this leads to a form of democracy very different from the Western variety.

A thoroughgoing consensual approach to social issues can be expected to lead to corresponding procedures in other areas of social life too. A particularly interesting case relates to the Akan reaction to wrong doing. Though the retributive spirit is not totally absent from reactions, especially at the state level, to some forms of wrong doing, the predominant tendency is to seek compensation or reconciliation or, in cases where extra-human forces are thought to be estranged, purification. I abstain from using the word "punishment" in this context advisedly, for given this last remark it may well be that there is no unproblematic rendition of this notion in the Akan conceptual framework. I cannot, however, pursue this question here.

A well-known feature of Akan morals is respect for age. This is intelligible not only from the fact that we are dealing with a society strongly based on kinship relations, which are naturally patterned into hierarchies based on age, but also because in traditional societies, which in part Akan society still remains, age is associated with knowledge, experience and wisdom. Akan moral thinking in regard to sex and marriage also deserves special mention. Here the humanistic and the communalistic aspects of the Akan outlook come into play with interesting results. Because only empirical considerations bearing on human interests are admitted in moral evaluation, such unconditional proscriptions of pre-marital sex as are found in Christian teaching are absent from the moral rules of the Akans. From their point of view, it would be irrational to stop a prospective couple from seeking full knowledge of each other, moral, psychological, sexual and so on. There is, of course, no sexual free-for-all; but, still, a non-furtive relationship between an unmarried man and an unmarried woman need not be restricted to hugging. The only proviso is that it should be above board. On the other hand, the high value placed on reproductive fertility in a communalistic society based on single-family-unit agriculture will predictably lead to the greatest emphasis being placed on the desirability of marriage and procreation. So much is this the case that being married with children well raised is part of the necessary conditions for personhood in the normative sense. A non-marrying, non-procreative person, however normal otherwise—not to talk of a Casanova equivalent—can permanently forget any prospect of this type of recognition in traditional Akan society. The only conceivable exceptions will be ones based on the noblest of alternative life commitments.

To understand all these facts about the Akan conception of morals is not necessarily to understand the culture in its entirety, but it is to have some sense of its foundations.

DISCUSSION QUESTIONS

1. Do you agree with both meanings of the saying, "*Onipa na ohia*" (i.e., "it is a human being that has value")? Why or why not?
2. Wiredu mentions five Akan "prudential maxims." What do you think each one means, and how do they relate to the emphasis on communal belonging and human fellowship in Akan ethics?
3. What does Wiredu mean when he says that in Akan thought, "a human being is part of a social whole" because of his or her "original constitution"? Why is this idea important for Akan ethics?
4. How does Akan ethics differ from the various theories of ethics derived from European philosophy? Do you find those differences appealing? Why or why not?

Moral Issues

Sex

YOLANDA ESTES

Mutual Respect and Sexual Morality

Yolanda Estes is a philosopher, writer, and painter who lives in Ecuador. She was formerly Associate Professor of Philosophy at Mississippi State University. In this chapter from a book on sex in college, Estes considers what the obligation to respect others means for the ethics of sex. She identifies ways to tell if a particular sexual interaction counts as mutually respectful and examines some moral issues that can arise in sexual relationships among college students, such as objectification, manipulation, and casual sex.

GUIDING QUESTIONS

1. What does Estes mean by "sex"?
2. What, according to Estes, are the criteria for mutually respectful sexual interaction?
3. Estes examines several different "moral issues associated with specific sexual relationships and activities." What are these relationships and activities? Does Estes consider all of them to be morally unacceptable?

SEXUAL MORALITY IS A REQUIRED COURSE

Sex is great. Enjoy it. But while you're doing it, put in some time and effort to make your college years a period of morally positive growth and sexually ful-filling development. I offer the following reflections on mutually respectful sexual interaction in the hope that my insights will prove useful to college students of many philosophical and sexual stripes. I hope my essay will illuminate your own thinking about sexual morality, but that is all I can accomplish here, so don't treat this essay as a college student's exhaustive or definitive manual to sex or sexual morality. When I talk about sex, I mean the vast range of possible inter-actions and relationships between human beings—however rare, weird, gross, brief, or tenuous—that arouse and satisfy someone's sex drive. It isn't actually relevant to my discussion whether your

Yolanda Estes. "Mutual Respect and Sexual Morality: How to Have College Sex Well." College Sex: Philosophy for Everyone, Michael Bruce and Robert M. Stewart (eds.), 2010, 209–219. © 2010 John Wiley & Sons, Inc.

individual notion of sex is heterosexual petting and kissing with your steady girl or guy, bisexual heavy flogging with a group of friends, or homosexual hula-hooping in a tub of green Jell-O with a perfect stranger. My message is that many of the sexual activities, interactions, and relationships a college student might have the opportunity to enjoy can be morally right but that sex poses serious moral quandaries for all of us and that we must address these difficulties before we have the right to enjoy ourselves sexually.

MORALITY AND SEXUALITY

As a philosopher, I regard human self-consciousness and freedom as fundamental to all other sorts of consciousness. In other words, I believe that our awareness of other things and other people depends on an immediate awareness of ourselves as thinking and active. From a moral perspective, I identify humanity with its free capacity to conceive and will its own goals. Unlike non-sentient or non-selfconscious organic and synthetic things (such as carrots, amoebas, bicycles, and computers), human beings freely determine their own goals (choose and plan what they want to be or to accomplish in the future) and freely will those goals (act to realize their concepts of the future). Thus, because human beings freely determine and will their own goals, they have dignity (or priceless worth as ends in themselves) as opposed to organic and synthetic things that have a price value (for which they might be bought and sold as mere means to an end).

A succinct, simplified account of my approach to morality would run as follows: first, human beings are free, so they have dignity; second, human beings have dignity, so they deserve respect; and third, human beings deserve respect, so they should always treat themselves and others with respect. We should eschew actions that undermine human freedom and dignity—and we should engage in actions that promote human freedom and dignity—in ourselves and in others. Instinctive, or common-sense, notions of basic human decency also suggest that all human relations—even the sexual relations between college students—should involve mutually respectful interactions.

We become familiar with our common human dignity by engaging in interactions with others that display mutual respect for our common human freedom. Some actions regarding ourselves and others preclude mutual respect. Manipulating (with lies or other deceptions) or coercing (with physical or psychological force) another person to perform an action she would not otherwise perform could not promote mutual respect. Seizing or damaging another person's things without his permission, or imprisoning or injuring his body, or attempting to control his psyche, would be disrespectful of his humanity. We would show no respect for ourselves if we compromised the freedom of our thoughts and deeds or sacrificed the integrity of our possessions, bodies, and minds. Mutual respect also requires some actions regarding ourselves and others. Helping (with tangible or intangible charity) or encouraging (with advice or persuasion) another to pursue her personally or humanly needful interests and to realize her morally obligatory goals would support mutual respect. Treating another person's possessions, body, or mind with consideration or benevolence is respectful of his humanity. We should show the same respect for ourselves by using our talents and other resources to their full potential and by caring for our possessions, bodies, and minds.

Your sexual interaction with others is one of many social contexts that you'll experience in college wherein you will come to know yourself as a human being, so your sexual interactions are not morally neutral ground. Our perceptions of ourselves and others as human beings are profoundly influenced by the integration of sexuality within our lives. Sex expresses our individual humanity, but not all sexual interactions involve mutual respect for our humanity. Some reflect an attempt to manipulate or coerce another person without promoting her dignity and freedom or to use another as a mere means without deferring to his humanity. We should avoid sexual actions that undermine human freedom and dignity—and we should engage in sexual actions that promote human freedom and dignity—in ourselves and others. Basic human decency also suggests that human sexual relations should involve mutually respectful sexual interaction.

Some sexual actions concerning ourselves and others exclude the possibility of mutual respect. Mutual respect also requires us to do certain things in our sexual interactions. Coercing another person to perform a sexual action he would not otherwise perform (e.g., by deceiving, manipulating, or drugging him) can't promote mutual respect. Sexually using another person without her permission (e.g., using bodily threat or force when she is unwilling to offer her sexual favors and having sex with her when she is too mentally or physically incapacitated to offer sexual favors) is disrespectful to her humanity. Engaging in sexual activities that pose significant risks to anyone's health and life (because we have not taken due precautions against disease or injury, because we are too incapacitated to exercise due prudence, or because the activities are inherently and unduly hazardous) or engaging in sexual activities that pose significant risk of pregnancy (because we have not taken due contraceptive precaution) for which we are unable or unwilling to take responsibility does wrong to ourselves and others. We show neither regard nor respect for ourselves if we fail to safeguard our consensual participation in sexual activities or to protect ourselves from physical and mental injury in our sexual activities. Helping or encouraging others to realize their personally and humanly needful goals or their morally obligatory goals while engaging in sexual activity supports mutual respect. Treating others' bodies or minds with consideration or benevolence while engaging in sexual activity is respectful of their humanity. We should show the same regard and respect for ourselves by caring for our bodies and minds within the sexual context.

CRITERIA OF MUTUALLY RESPECTFUL SEXUAL INTERACTION

Mutual respect requires that sexual partners give explicit, or at least implicit, expression of their voluntary participation in the sexual act. Additionally, it demands that each sexual partner exhibits concern for the other's interests and needs insofar as their wellbeing includes and extends beyond their sexual wellbeing. Finally, it compels that each sexual partner attend to the other's desires.

Reciprocal consent means that each partner shows that he chooses to engage in particular sexual activities with a particular partner at a particular time. It is necessary for mutual respect because without someone's indication that she is a willing sexual partner, we have every reason to suspect that she is the unwilling sexual victim of some compulsion or coercion. Reciprocal concern means that each partner demonstrates regard for his partner's personal, human, and moral wellbeing. It is essential for mutual respect because we cannot separate our sexuality from our personality, humanity, or general interests and needs. Without some evidence of each partner's consideration for the other's interests and needs, we have grounds for thinking that the sexual interaction could undermine at least one partner's wellbeing. Reciprocal desire means that each partner expresses complementary expectations and goals for her sexual interaction and that each partner attempts to satisfy those expectations and goals within her sexual interaction. It is necessary for mutual respect because sex without desire results in sensual or emotional dissatisfaction at best and physical or psychological trauma at worst.

We must communicate with our partner in order to assure that reciprocal consent, concern, and desire exist. Communication of consent, concern, and desire could be fairly direct, explicit, and specific or it could be fairly indirect, implicit, and vague. For example, you might say to some enticing somebody, "My, you're delicious; I'd love to jump your lovely bones right now" and this appealing, consenting partner might reply, "You're pretty scrumptious yourself: the condoms are in the bathroom." As you and your delightful partner begin to interact, he might suggest "I'm just crazy about giving oral sex," and you might respond desirously, "My favorite: enjoy." In the course of things, you might murmur, "This is so much fun, but I promised to help my friend with his homework tonight and I've got an early class tomorrow" and your concerned fellow enthusiast might exclaim "Aw, that's too bad: Maybe we can continue where we left off after your class tomorrow. Say, do you like green Jell-O?" Of course, many communications of consent, concern, and desire are not as clearly evident. You can probably imagine how this same series of communications could have been achieved more subtly. The issue is not how the communication was achieved, but that each partner possessed a reasonable, conscientious belief that reciprocal consent, concern, and desire existed.

Achieving mutually respectful sexual interaction would be easy if there were some fail-safe, trouble-free method for obtaining a reasonable, conscientious belief that reciprocal consent, concern, and desire existed. Unfortunately, there are no fail-safe, trouble-free methods. We can sometimes be uncertain about our own volition, needs, interests, and desires, so we can never be certain about our sexual partner's. Moreover, admiration, affection, or even love for a sexual partner fails to guarantee reciprocal consent, concern, and desire. We have only indicators, more or less precise, and signs, more or less ambiguous, to guide our deeds, which, ultimately, we must judge before the rational tribunal of our conscience. Despite these difficulties, we are morally obliged to make a strong effort to solicit, recognize, and interpret compelling evidence of our sexual partner's volition, interests, and desires.

Does this obligation imply that sexual partners must sign a legally binding contract that specifies their desires and expectations, describes their intended activities, and states their voluntary participation prior to every sexual interaction? No. Moreover, no legal contract could provide certain assurance of a partner's consent, concern, and desire. Does this obligation entail that a sexual partner must accommodate his partner's every sexual whim or devote every iota of his energy to making his partner personally, humanly, and morally fulfilled? No. Moreover, no effort could guarantee a partner's fulfillment. There are no certain assurances or guarantees, but there are ways to increase the possibility of reciprocal consent, concern, and desire. We can try to learn as much about our partner as possible by communicating with her about sexual desires, general interests, and other subjects. This reduces the chance of miscommunications and misunderstandings with our partner. We can take time to gain some sexual knowledge of our partner by proceeding cautiously and unhurriedly in the initial stages of a sexual relationship. This increases the chance of correctly interpreting and addressing expressions of consent, expectation, and desire. Before, during, and after sexual interactions, we can solicit more explicit, specific expressions of our partner's thoughts and feelings; observe our partner's reactions carefully; and reflect diligently on what we hear and see. This enhances the possibility of reciprocal consent, concern, and desire while improving our sexual technique and our opportunity for a repeat performance (or maybe even the addition of a hula-hoop or two).

An additional way of keeping sexually charged relationships and interactions in moral perspective is to compare them to analogous non-sexual relationships and interactions. If you were intoxicated, ill, distraught, exhausted, or if your capacity to choose and to communicate were otherwise compromised, would you think that you consented for someone to borrow your car or debit card simply because you left your keys or purse readily accessible? Probably not. Thus, you should probably question a sexual partner's consent if his capacity to choose and communicate is somehow impaired. For example, when the new-found object of your desires gets food-poisoning, flunks his physics exam, and spends the rest of the afternoon crying and drinking shots, you should probably put him to bed rather than take him to bed.

If you were involved in a relationship or interaction that served the other participant's needs and interests but undermined your wellbeing, would you believe that she was concerned about you? Most likely not. Thus, you should most likely doubt your own concern for a partner if your sexual relationship or interaction seems to undermine their needs and interests. For example, when aspects of your sexual relationship and interactions lead your main squeeze to neglect his studies, lose interest in the things that matter to him, abuse drugs, or tell lies, you should most likely change those aspects of your relationship or change sexual partners. If someone begged, threatened, pestered, bribed, or cajoled you into doing something for her that you didn't appear eager to do, would you consider that your expectations and desires had been addressed? Surely not.

Thus, you should surely suspect that your partner's expectations and desires were disregarded if you begged, threatened, pestered, bribed, or cajoled him into doing something sexual for you that he didn't appear eager to do. For example, when you express expectations and desires for things—like marriage, or anal sex, or green Jell-O—that your sexual buddy can't or won't give you or when your sexual partner never asks you for sex, tries to avoid sex, or seems ambiguous about their enjoyment of sex, you should surely revise your notion of what each of you is willing and able to do, have a thorough discussion about how each of you can better satisfy the other, or get out of that relationship.

MORAL ISSUES ASSOCIATED WITH SPECIFIC SEXUAL RELATIONSHIPS AND ACTIVITIES

Many seemingly innocuous activities could violate the criteria of reciprocal consent, concern, and desire, whereas many seemingly harmful activities could satisfy the standard of mutually respectful sex. In short, few sexual activities need preclude reciprocal consent, concern, and desire, but any might encumber mutual respect and most do pose specific challenges to those criteria. Every particular sexual interaction with a partner must be conscientiously evaluated with due attention to its unique characteristics. In the following paragraphs, I'll give just a few examples of the moral hazards associated with some sexual activities and relationships.

One example of a sexual behavior that is commonplace but morally problematic is objectification. Objectification involves treating a sexually appealing characteristic—such as an act, a prop, or a body part—as more important than the unique individual who has that characteristic. There is nothing bad about preferring buxom girls or tall boys, but if a sexual partner's arousing feature becomes indispensable while the partner becomes dispensable, i.e., if the appealing feature might as well be attached to

anyone at all, then he has been objectified. Most of us probably wouldn't consent to being depersonalized in this way. It is difficult both to objectify a person and show concern for her. Unless both partners are similarly obsessed with the sexually arousing feature, their desires aren't reciprocal. Objectification threatens the possibility of mutually respectful sexual interaction. Fetishism is a less commonplace sexual obsession with some act, prop, or body part that is important for sexual arousal and satisfaction. It can involve reciprocal consent, concern, and desire, but it presents a high risk for objectification. Whether a person merely prefers or fetishizes certain features is not morally important. The moral issue is whether a person regards their partner as a thing with a feature or as another human being who can share in his delight with that feature.

Another example of a mundane sexual behavior that includes moral hazards is manipulation. Manipulation involves misusing sexual favors to control another person's emotions and behaviors or misusing emotions and behaviors to extort another person's sexual favors. Our sexual interactions are usually contingent on the satisfaction we achieve in our general interactions with our partners. Sexual interaction is comforting and cathartic. It makes us feel valued and valuable. However, when we use sexual performance to reward and punish our partner's behavior, or to obtain gifts and niceties from our partner, and when we use emotions to extract sexual performance from our partner, we aren't showing respect. Many people use sex as a way of dominating their partner. Others turn dating into a barter of sex for gifts, entertainment, or other little luxuries and services. Some people take advantage of their prospective partner's sense of kindness and compassion (or his need for kindness and compassion) to get sex. These manipulative sexual activities indicate negligible reciprocity of concern or desire.

Some other examples of ordinary sexual behaviors that create moral problems include irreconcilability and inattentiveness. Irreconcilability and inattentiveness jeopardize reciprocal desire and concern. It is okay that everyone enters the bedroom with different expectations, unequal levels of lust, and disparate desires (e.g., one of you wants a little R&R after finals, and the other wants to feel like Homecoming Queen; or one of you is ready to take on the football team, and the other will settle for the school mascot; or one of you wants to try felching, and the other wants to try tantric yoga). It is wondrous that sexual interaction challenges us to cultivate our range of desires, to match our libido against another's, and to exert ourselves in the effort to please our partner. Nonetheless, when sexual partners' desires are profoundly incompatible, their sex drives are radically disproportionate, or their expectations are markedly opposed, they simply cannot have a sexual relationship based on mutual respect, because someone will always feel deprived or abused. It is normal to lose track of things (like your socks, your homework, or your wits) while you are enjoying sex. However, when you lose track of your partner's needs and interests, you are not treating him with concern. You must pay attention to your partner and your sexual interaction to achieve reciprocal consent, concern, and desire. Disregard for sexual incompatibility and inattention to sexual activity amount to a lack of mutual respect.

Casual sex and casual sexual relationships are examples of less traditional behaviors that can be morally acceptable but pose particular moral issues. Casual sex between almost total strangers seems to defy the criteria of reciprocal consent and concern. Likewise, casual sexual relationships between partners who are relative strangers outside the bedroom seem to imperil the criterion of mutual concern. The shorter, the shallower, or the narrower our sexual relationships, the more caution we must exercise in gauging the reciprocity of consent, concern, and desire. In the context of casual sex with strangers, this involves insisting upon very direct, explicit, and specific communication and avoiding scenarios and substances likely to impair good judgment and clear communication. In the context of casual sex with acquaintances, this involves soliciting direct, explicit, and specific affirmation that your partner's needs, expectations, and interests are being served by your relationship. So there's nothing intrinsically morally wrong with casual sexual interactions, but the participants must be morally responsible and honest enough to communicate openly and respond considerately.

Group sex and non-exclusive sexual relationships are other examples of sexual behaviors that can be mutually respectful but that involve specific moral complications. Group sex and non-exclusive sexual relationships also seem to threaten mutually respectful sexual interaction. There are some special moral risks associated with group sex and non-monogamous relationships. Each additional sexual partner complicates the dynamics of the sexual interaction and multiplies the difficulty of achieving mutual respect, so extra care is needed to achieve reciprocity of consent, concern, and desire between multiple partners. This requires extra communication between partners and extra attentiveness toward partners. Sexual relationships are always emotionally charged, which sometimes leads sexual partners to compromise their own or their partner's needs in order to achieve sexual satisfaction, preserve a relationship, or to serve other confused and confusing goals. Non-monogamous relationships can increase emotional tensions as well as possibilities of partners feeling jealous and neglected or otherwise discontented and dissatisfied. Extra care must be shown to assure reciprocity of consent, concern, and desire. This means especially candid communication about partners' needs, expectations, and interests. It also means especially frank discussion of limits (e.g., regarding temporal and emotional commitments or regarding disease and pregnancy prevention) and equity (e.g., regarding the fair extension of the liberties enjoyed by one partner to the others). So there's nothing intrinsically morally wrong with group sex or non-exclusive sexual relationships, but the participants must be emotionally sensitive, fair-minded, and morally diligent enough to address the needs, interests, and wellbeing of all of their sexual partners.

Sadomasochism is yet another example of a more unusual sexual behavior that can involve reciprocal consent, concern, and desire, but that does raise important special moral considerations. Sadomasochism involves taking sexual pleasure in inflicting or receiving pain. Sadomasochistic interactions pose many special hazards and responsibilities to the participants. Sexual partners sometimes change their minds about volition. For example, a partner might be initially eager to experience certain sensations and then might find those sensations unbearable, so it is crucial that both partners be communicative, attentive, and responsive lest they end up engaged in a non-consensual interaction. Sadomasochistic partners often communicate in seemingly ambiguous or contradictory ways. For example, a partner might cry out "Oh, please don't hurt me" when they really mean "Oh, please hurt me more," so it is important that the partners communicate in advance about their desires, that they quickly and accurately interpret ambiguous sexual gestures, and that they know each other well enough to respond properly to subtle signs of pleasure, satiation, fear, or distress.

Another very grave moral risk associated with sadomasochistic sex is physical danger. Even light sadomasochistic sex can result in serious injury or death, especially if the partners are uninformed or inexperienced. Concerned partners will become informed about risks and safety precautions and about their partner's specific health concerns (such as low or high blood pressure, sickle cell anemia, AIDS, or diabetes) in advance and will remain attentive to possible injuries during and after their sexual interaction. Since intense sensations can impair judgment, one partner must assume responsibility in advance for setting limits on physical risk and injury. A concerned partner must withhold additional stimulation even though their partner might very much like more when it poses some physical danger. Risks are multiplied when sadomasochistic sex is combined with inebriants that alter sensation, release inhibition, or impair judgment and communication. So there is nothing intrinsically morally wrong with sadomasochistic sex, but the partners must be morally conscientious enough to be well-informed and cautious about safety, communicative and attentive enough to respond promptly to their partner's needs, and psychologically mature enough to exercise self-control and good judgment.

A final example of a sexual behavior that is not necessarily odd but that ranges from humdrum delights to extreme thrills is the use of danger or substances to improve the sexual experience. Sexual pleasure can be enhanced by taking social or physical risks, or by using inebriating techniques or chemicals. For example, some people find the risks of having sex in public arousing, whereas some enjoy sex play with knives or guns. Others use electricity, piercing, hanging, or various forms of asphyxiation to produce pleasurable sensations. Of course, many people use chemicals, ranging from supposedly aphrodisiac foods, stimulating gels and lotions, alcohol, amyl nitrite, pot, or other drugs to increase arousal, reduce inhibition, or augment sensation. Most of these forms of sexual enhancement present some moral risks, which must be addressed responsibly if partners are to show mutual respect. Many of these activities, techniques, and chemicals create social or physical dangers, which could compromise reciprocal concern, whereas others impair sensation, judgment, or communication, which could compromise reciprocal consent and concern. Mutually respectful partners must be very well informed and must exercise extreme caution with risky techniques and dangerous chemicals. Many intelligent, informed, careful, and concerned people have injured or killed themselves or their partners using some of these techniques and chemicals. Some of these activities are simply too dangerous for morally responsible partners to do. Mutually respectful partners never use inebriants to impair a partner's judgment and obtain non-consensual sex or to deaden a partner's sensation to coerce them into performing sexual acts they find painful or loathsome. So there is nothing intrinsically morally wrong with sexual enhancements, but the participants must be intellectually informed and morally concerned enough to protect themselves and their partners from coercion and from social and physical danger.

DON'T FLUNK YOUR TEST

One of the most important things you can learn in college is that in order to have mutual respect between sexual partners everyone must assume responsibility for engaged, informed, communicative interaction. That might sound like it involves some embarrassment, a lot of physical and mental effort, or a great reduction of immediate sexual opportunity. It does. But if you aren't man or woman enough to communicate about sex and to exert yourself with consenting and eager partners, then you aren't man or woman enough to get laid. If you aren't prepared to be a morally conscientious sexual partner, start a vigorous exercise regimen, become a masturbatory virtuoso, or donate your time to a good charity, but don't muck up something as important as another person's sexual experience. Yes, being a good person is tough, but if there's someone somewhere in a tub of green Jell-O waiting around for a stranger with a hula-hoop, then there's probably someone somewhere waiting around for you. Be ready for that person.

DISCUSSION QUESTIONS

1. Why, according to Estes, does the general obligation to respect others lead to specific obligations connected with sex and sexual relationships?
2. Does Estes successfully identify the criteria for mutually respectful sexual interactions? If not, is it because there are additional criteria that she doesn't mention or is it because there are some kinds of mutually respectful sexual interactions that don't meet her criteria—or both?
3. Do you agree with Estes's conclusions about the ethics of casual sex? Why or why not?

TOM DOUGHERTY

Sex, Lies, and Consent

Tom Dougherty is a University Lecturer in Philosophy at Cambridge University. In this paper, Dougherty considers the connection between deception and sexual consent. In particular, he argues that it is seriously morally wrong for one person to deceive another person into having sex with him or her by lying (or otherwise misleading the other person) about something that would be a "deal-breaker" if the other person knew the truth. Such deception, Dougherty argues, makes it impossible for the other person to consent to sex with the deceiver.

GUIDING QUESTIONS

1. What, exactly, does Dougherty mean by "deceiving someone into sex"?
2. Dougherty gives two arguments for the claim that it is seriously wrong to have sex with someone without his or her morally valid consent. What are those two arguments?
3. Dougherty gives three arguments against the claim that someone who has been deceived into sex has given his or her morally valid consent to sex. What are those three arguments?
4. Why does Dougherty consider the "Harm Explanation" in Section II? Why does he consider the case of Stalin's skis in Section III?

Tom Dougherty. "Sex, Lies, and Consent." *Ethics*, 123(4) (July 2013), 717–744 © 2013 by the University of Chicago.

I. DECEITFUL SEDUCTION

According to a popular dating website, both men and women, on average, say that they are two inches taller and earn $20,000 more than one would expect.[1] Now it may be that these are innocent errors (though expensive ones for tax returns), or that rich and tall people find it particularly hard to meet partners in person. But in our more cynical moments, we may suspect that this is intentional deception. Why the tangled webs? Some may only want conversation over cappuccino, or a warm arm next to theirs in the movie theater. But others' aims will include sex. We might say that these people are "lying to get laid," if we wanted a snappy phrase. But it would be an inexact phrase insofar as the relevant moral phenomenon is deception, and some lies, understood as false assertions, do not deceive. In a notorious pickup joint where never a true word has been said, the regulars will not be fooled by tall tales, sweet nothings, and puffery. Indeed, in circumstances where lies are expected, telling the truth would itself be deceptive. Similarly, when certain expectations are in place, silence itself can be a form of communication and hence deceive.[2]

Deceiving someone into sex is wrong. No surprise here: mother told us as much. But *how* wrong? I speculate that most people think that the wrongness depends on the type of deception involved. Impersonating someone's spouse is seriously wrong but not so with run-of-the-mill falsehoods like "I'm not fussed about mess," "I'm 27 years old," "I went to Harvard," "I haven't had implants," "I *don't* want a relationship," "I *do* want a relationship," and even the simple "I like you." As Alan Wertheimer notes, "prevailing moral norms" are quite "permissive" with respect to sexual deception, and so while people "may think it sleazy if a male lies about his marital status, affections, or intentions in order to get a woman into bed, . . . many do not think this is a particularly serious matter." Along these lines, Jeffrie Murphy states that if a seducer misrepresents himself as "unusually sensitive and caring," then this involves "a minor kind of fraudulent misrepresentation . . . [that] is not utterly without moral taint," but he finds "it hard to get *deeply* indignant about these cases."[3] These are criticisms—no one would be proud to have brought up a sleazy child—but ones that are far milder than those made of serious sexual misconduct. I will attempt to persuade you that much more severe criticisms are in order, arguing against the following thesis:

> Lenient Thesis. It is only a minor wrong to deceive another person into sex by misleading her or him about certain personal features such as natural hair color, occupation, or romantic intentions.

We should understand this thesis as the claim that there are some trivial aspects of one's identity, about which it is not seriously wrong to deceive someone in order to get them into bed. Examples of this run-of-the-mill deception might include deception about one's sexual history, one's attitudes toward pets, or even how funny one finds the other person. Against the Lenient Thesis, I will argue that even with run-of-the-mill deception, culpably *deceiving another person into sex* is seriously wrong. In making this claim, I stipulate this italicized phrase to be understood as follows. First, the deception must concern the sexual encounter. Since each person is an essential part of the sexual encounter, one is deceived about the sexual encounter by deception about the other person. For example, this would include deception about whether this person is using birth control, about his or her profession, or about his or her mental attitudes.[4] Second, the deception must concern a *deal breaker*—a feature of the sexual encounter to which the other person's will is opposed. This requires more than concealing an undesirable feature. It must be the case that the other person is all things considered unwilling to engage in the sexual encounter, given that it has this feature. This is a significant qualification as it lets off the hook, for example, someone pretending to like a stranger's umbrella simply to strike up conversation that eventually leads to sex. (At least the qualification lets the deceiver off the hook, so long as knowing the truth about the other person's lukewarm opinions of the umbrella would not change the deceived person's willingness to have sex at the crucial moment.)

My argument is based on the fact that not only coercion can vitiate consent; deception can do so too.

Since coercion and deception are Kant's paradigms of "treating someone as a mere means," I think of this as a Kantian insight, though one that is acceptable to friends of other moral theories. To illustrate, suppose you tell me that you propose applying some chestnut brown hair dye to my hair. Excited at the prospect of brunette locks, I say that you may do so. However, you have been mischievously concealing the fact that it is really pink dye. Here I only gave you a moral permission to give my hair a chestnut color. Since the pink color of the dye was a deal breaker for me, I did not validly consent to what you did.[5] Similarly, I will argue that when someone is deceived into sex, the deception vitiates the victim's sexual consent. Since it is seriously wrong to have sex with someone without her morally valid consent, deceiving someone into sex is seriously wrong. Thus, my main argument runs:

1. Having sex with someone, while lacking her morally valid consent, is seriously wrong.
2. Deceiving another person into sex involves having sex with that person, while lacking her morally valid consent.
3. Therefore, deceiving someone into sex is seriously wrong.

A few people may already be sympathetic to a conclusion along these lines. For example, Wertheimer notes that "current social norms may understate the seriousness of sexual deception"[6] and suggests that sexual consent may be vitiated by deception about one's marital status, an affair with a partner's sister, one's views on contentious moral issues like abortion, one's feelings, or one's intentions to marry.[7] But many people will find my conclusion false, if not high-minded folly, and so I will attempt to defend it by offering subarguments for each premise in turn. Then I will discuss three important issues concerning my conclusion. First, it is not the deception that is seriously wrong but the sexual act. (To avoid confusion, it may help to stress that my term of art, "deceiving someone into sex," includes the sexual act.) Second, in addition to wrongness, there is a further issue of *culpability*. One can commit any wrong, even serious wrongs, in a blameless manner. So we may excuse those who act with a full excuse, such as

being reasonably ignorant about the deal breakers in question. Third, we can clarify the seriousness of the wrong in question by noting its commonalities with sex with an unwilling comatose person.

In making this argument, I will discuss general assumptions about moral rights. Specifically, I will address such issues as the implications of our right to bodily autonomy, the moral significance of harm, and the nature of consent and its relationship to intentions. To foreshadow, one issue that I will not be discussing is whether we should consider deceiving someone into sex as a form of rape. This turns on an orthogonal debate about whether we should apply the term "rape" to all forms of nonconsensual sex.[8] I leave this terminological choice to the reader. My interest is only in the substantive issue of serious wrongness. Another issue that I will not address is the legal issue of what laws we should have in place concerning sexual deception, since this issue brings in further practical complications. . . .[9]

II. WHY NONCONSENSUAL SEX IS SERIOUSLY WRONG

I will begin with the less controversial premise of my main argument—that having sex with someone who does not validly consent is seriously wrong. To be fully clear, the premise concerns only morally valid consent. This is defined as the consent that someone must have in order not to wrong the consenter by violating a right of hers. Consequently, it is the consent that makes permissible some actions that would otherwise be impermissible. Morally valid consent requires more than mere agreement. For example, agreement must be freely given, and so highly intoxicated agreement would not count as morally valid consent. Now I imagine many readers will be antecedently sympathetic to the claim that it is seriously wrong to have sex with someone while lacking her morally valid consent. For example, Robin West describes the claim that "nonconsensual sex is wrong in all circumstances, and so wrong as to be properly regarded as a serious crime" as a "basic moral claim."[10] Indeed, within the literature on sexual consent, the majority position is that this claim identifies "the wrong of rape."[11] Still the thesis requires defense, since an alternative, harms-based approach to the ethics of sex does not make consent foundationally important. Moreover, defending the premise will make clear the argumentative burden that will fall on my second premise—that someone does not give her morally valid consent to sex when she is deceived into sex.

The Rights-Based Argument

To introduce my first subargument, consider Joan McGregor's observation that the "moral wrongness of rape consists in violating an individual's autonomy right to control one's own body and one's sexual self-determination and the seriousness of rape derives from the special importance we attach to sexual autonomy."[12] Here McGregor has in mind coercive sex, but I am confident she would agree that her rationale extends to all forms of nonconsensual sex. In arguing for this claim, I make the following assumptions that are standard within rights theory.[13] We have moral claim-rights (henceforth "rights") over our persons and property. These include so-called negative rights against interference: the moral default is that others may not lay hands on, nor damage, our persons or property. These rights over our persons and property consist in more specific rights against particular actions by particular individuals. We move away from the default by giving other people our morally valid consent, thereby waiving some specific rights. For example, a customer may waive her rights against a hairdresser touching her hair but not other parts of her body. These waivers are typically revocable—at any point, the customer can take back her consent and reimpose her rights.

The moral significance of these rights is that typically it is morally impermissible for someone to wrong another person by infringing her rights.[14] How wrong it would be to violate a right depends on its stringency. The stringency of a right against a form of behavior depends on the importance to us of someone engaging in this behavior against our will.[15] Now controlling the sexual contact that others have with us is centrally important to us. This is not to say that sex has to be an active, emotionally meaningful part of someone's lifestyle. But it is crucially important that her sexual choices determine how her sex life goes. For example, the "prostitute and the celibate greatly value their integrity as sexual beings, even whilst they do not value the exercise of their sexuality."[16] And we can accept this point while leaving open the grounds of this importance—whether we contingently find sexual autonomy important, whether we are biologically hard wired to find it important, or whether it has an objective importance, even if we fail to recognize this importance.[17] This importance of sexual control explains the stringency of their sexual rights.[18] In light of this stringency, it is seriously wrong to violate someone's sexual rights. One would violate these rights unless one has her morally valid consent to sex.

The Argument from Serious Sexual Wrongs

My second subargument operates by inference to the best explanation. The explananda in question are the following two data. The first datum is that it is seriously wrong to have sex with someone by means of disguising the sexual nature of the encounter or by impersonating her spouse. Consider the following fictional examples. When naive and uneducated Dewey Dell arrived at a physician's seeking an abortion, it was seriously wrong for the assistant to cajole her into sex by telling her that the appropriate medical procedure was for him to penetrate her. When Milady mistook D'Artagnan for her lover in her ill-lit boudoir, it was seriously wrong of D'Artagnan knowingly to take advantage of her mistake to have sex with her.[19] The second datum is that it is seriously wrong to have sex with an unconscious person against her will. For example, in Pedro Almodóvar's *Hable Con Ella*, it was seriously wrong for the caregiver, Benigno, to have sex with the chronically comatose patient, Alicia. I maintain that the best explanation of each of these data, considered in isolation from the other, is that the offenders lacked their victim's morally valid consent. I will call this the "Consent Explanation":

> Consent Explanation. The seriousness of the wrongs both of sex by means of egregious deception and of sex with an unwilling unconscious person is explained by the fact that the victim did not validly consent to the sex.

Since it is uncontroversial that Alicia, Dewey Dell, and Milady did not offer morally valid consent to sex, the Consent Explanation correctly predicts that Benigno, the assistant, and D'Artagnan acted seriously wrongly.

Are other explanations at least as good? Alan Wertheimer outlines the main alternative: "As a first approximation, we might say that the wrongness of an act is a function of three factors: (1) its *expected* or *ex ante* harm to a victim, (2) A's culpability for that act, and (3) the actual harmful consequences of A's act, although (3) is controversial as it turns on the right view about moral luck."[20] I will call this view the "Harm Explanation":

> Harm Explanation. The seriousness of the wrongs both of sex by means of egregious deception and of sex with an unwilling unconscious person is explained by the harm suffered by the victim.

Thus stated, the explanation includes the view that the wrongness of a sexual offense depends only on harm; and it also includes the view that a sexual act can be wrong simply because it is nonconsensual, but the *seriousness* of the wrong is determined by the amount of harm. Now if a friend of the Harm Explanation considers violation of consent as a harm, then the Harm Explanation and the Consent Explanation are consistent. Therefore, if someone intends the Harm Explanation to be an alternative to the Consent Explanation, then the relevant harm cannot simply be the harm of having unwilling sex. Instead, one would have to point to harms like physical harms, experiential harms, and ensuing psychological harms. For Wertheimer, the crucial morally relevant type of harm is experiential harm, and so sexual deception is wrong when the action "is of a type that is likely to lead to experiential harm even though A's action has not harmed B in this case."[21]

Consequently, Wertheimer's view entails a view of deceiving someone into sex that is different from the one I am defending. Wertheimer takes a hard line with deception that is likely to result in experiential distress, but he is unwilling to judge that someone pretending to have a Harvard degree has committed a serious offense, even if his lie has "causal impact" on the victim's decision to have sex.[22]

The Harm Explanation is particularly attractive with respect to coercive sex, which is typically conceived of as sex obtained by physical force or threats of physical harm.[23] We cannot offer a proper account of the full extent of the wrong of violent rape, unless we mention the harms suffered by victims. This would appear to provide a strong motivation for the Harm Explanation.

However, the Harm Explanation is inadequate when it comes to explaining the serious wrongness of sex with the unconscious or by egregious forms of deception. The reason why is simple: as John Gardner and Stephen Shute have noted, there need be no harm involved.[24] The sex itself may not be physically damaging. Since the victims are unaware of having nonconsensual sex, they do not suffer experiential harms. And if these crimes remain undetected, then the victims will not suffer psychological harms later. Nonetheless, even when entirely harmless, sex with the unconscious and sex by means by egregious forms of deception are still seriously wrong.

On this point, Wertheimer has argued that sex with unconscious people is *likely* to be harmful.[25] But I am not aware of any investigation into whether this empirical claim about probabilities is correct. Indeed, I am doubtful that any such investigation could be carried out, given the obvious difficulties with getting good evidence about the frequency of harm caused by, say, sex with the comatose. Furthermore, I doubt that our robust judgment that nonconsensual sex with the comatose is seriously wrong is based on armchair speculation about these frequencies. Moreover, this judgment of ours is not hostage to the outcomes of an empirical investigation into this frequency. Even if, as an act-type, nonconsensual sex with the comatose turned out to be rarely detected and hence highly unlikely to be harmful, this discovery would not change our minds about it being seriously wrong. And the same is true of any token of this act-type. One could imagine a case of sex with a comatose person where the perpetrator took precautions that virtually ensured the sexual assault would be undetected. Nevertheless, this action would still be seriously wrong.[26]

Moreover, the Consent Explanation can accommodate the initial motivation for the Harm Explanation—the virtual platitude that harm is an important part of the explanation of why physically coercive sex is so bad. One can consistently hold that the nonconsensuality of physically coercive sex is sufficient for its being seriously wrong, while maintaining both that its particularly harmful nature is *also* sufficient for the action to be seriously wrong and that harm makes nonconsensual sex *even worse*. Indeed, as a fully general pattern, harm makes an action worse, even though its nonconsensuality is itself sufficient for the action's wrongness. If a stranger trespasses in your garden, then her action is wrong in virtue of the fact that she lacks your consent. But it is worse if she thereby ruins the flower beds. The Consent Explanation that I advocate here does not claim that harm never makes a moral difference. It merely maintains that if a sexual encounter is nonconsensual, then this feature makes it seriously wrong.

III. WHY THE DECEIVED DO NOT CONSENT

Before proceeding to defend my second premise—whenever someone is deceived into sex, she does not validly consent to the sex—let me rehearse the dialectic. I have so far argued for the claim that having non-consensual sex with someone is seriously wrong. By "nonconsensual sex," I intended sex without the victim's morally valid consent.[27] In doing so, I postponed much of the heavy lifting of the main argument to the defense of my second premise. This means that in this section I cannot simply claim that on one particular conception of consent, the deceived party does not consent to sex. I must make the

case that the deceived party does not give her *morally valid* consent to sex. Moreover, I suspect that few would antecedently agree since my target thesis seems right to many:

> Lenient Thesis. It is only a minor wrong to deceive another person into sex by misleading her or him about certain personal features such as natural hair color, occupation, or romantic intentions.

And I speculate that people hold this view because they think that the deceiver would have the victim's morally valid consent. I will offer three sub-arguments to the contrary.

The Argument Against Sexual Moralism

My first subargument aims to remove a key source of opposition to my second premise, by arguing that the Lenient Thesis cannot be grounded on an acceptable account of morally valid consent. To focus our discussion on run-of-the-mill deception, suppose that Chloe meets a hippie, Victoria, on a night out. Victoria makes it clear that she wants to have sex only with someone who shares her love of nature and peace. Consequently, Chloe falsely claims to have spent time in a war zone as a humanitarian, when in fact she was there on military service. When Victoria asks whether she likes animals, Chloe omits the truth—"only to eat or to hunt"—and pretends to love petting them and watching them in the wild. As a result of this deception, the two spent a night together. My claim is that Victoria did not validly consent to sex with Chloe. I expect that most friends of the Lenient Thesis will insist that Victoria did validly consent to sex, even if they disapprove of Chloe's deception on other grounds.

What account of morally valid consent could support the Lenient Thesis? A natural first thought is that Victoria consented because she was willing to have sex and indicated as much by means of speech or behavior. On this simpleminded account, if a competent person freely agrees to sex, then she consents. But this simpleminded account is implausible. For everyone should agree that Milady did not properly give her morally valid consent to the nocturnal poseur, D'Artagnan. To separate the cases of Milady and Victoria, the Lenient Thesis can only plausibly be based on a more sophisticated account of consent that makes a fundamental distinction between different features of a sexual encounter. On this view, someone does not validly consent to a sexual encounter when deceived about its "core" features, such as the interaction's not being is a genuine medical procedure or the other person's not being one's usual romantic partner. When someone is misled about these core features, then her will is not sufficiently implicated in the act for it to be consensual.[28] But on the other hand, someone may validly consent even when misled about the encounter's peripheral features, such as the other person's natural hair color, occupation, or romantic intentions.[29]

We can see the problem with this account of consent by starting to investigate how to draw the distinction between the core and periphery. There are some controversial borderline cases. A Cuban spy, masquerading as a dissident, marries a Florida woman but leaves her when his operational orders dictate. A British undercover policeman starts a relationship with an environmentalist in order to infiltrate her activist group. A Palestinian man pleads guilty to seducing an Israeli women by falsely telling her that he was unmarried and Jewish.[30] And the list goes on. Now I do not suppose that adherents of the Lenient Thesis will have uniform intuitions about whether the deceived person validly consents in each of these cases. People can agree that there is an important distinction between different features of a sexual encounter while disagreeing about how to draw this distinction. But what is important, for our purposes, is the nature of the debate about whether someone's religion, ethnicity, or political values count as a core feature of the sexual encounter. This is a debate about which features of a sexual encounter are objectively important enough to count as one of its core features. The lack of uniformity in people's intuitions about the cases simply reflects their differing views about the objective importance of religion, ethnicity, or political views for sex.

As such, the Lenient Thesis rests on an objectionably moralized conception of sex.[31] It assumes that some features of a sexual encounter are morally more important than others. In this way, our moral norms about sexual morality are skewed because of common assumptions that some reasons are good reasons for deciding not to have sex, but other reasons are not. Compare McGregor on legal norms: "It is worth speculating on the reasons for the law's unsympathetic reaction to victims of sexual fraud. . . . The general lack of sympathy [in cases such as someone impersonating a famous fashion photographer] is because it is believed that the women acted out of ignoble motives—the desire to get into the fashion industry, to have sex with famous people, and to exchange sex for an employment opportunity."[32] Though common, this appraisal of sexual motivations is a hangover from unacceptably moralistic views of sexuality and has survived into more enlightened times only because it has managed to avoid being subjected to proper critical scrutiny. For once we do call it into question, I hope that you will agree that it will not do. One of the key achievements of waves of sexual liberation has been the promotion of a sexual pluralism that allows each individual to pursue his or her own conception of the sexual good, so to speak. Appropriately valued, sexual autonomy permits "individuals to act freely on their own unconstrained conception of what their bodies and their sexual capacities are for."[33] As such, it is up to each individual to determine which features of a sexual encounter are particularly important to her. The religion of a sexual partner is an important part of a sexual encounter for someone if and only if that person decides that it is. Similarly, whether or not a partner's views about peace and animals are an important part of Victoria's sexual encounters is down to Victoria. In light of this point, it is not surprising that we can find counterexamples to a view of sexual consent based around the distinction between objectively core and peripheral features. Suppose that Jiang willingly engages in group sex with his boyfriend Isaiah and another man, Antonio. In doing so, Jiang consents to various kinds of sexual acts involving both men. At one point, Jiang mistakenly thinks that he is engaged in one of these kinds of acts with Isaiah, when in fact he is engaged in it with Antonio. Since Jiang is willing to have sex with Antonio at this point, the sex is consensual, even though Jiang is mistaken about a purportedly "core" feature of the encounter—whether it is sex with his boyfriend. The reason why it is consensual is that Jiang has decided that this feature is irrelevant in these specific circumstances. The moral significance of this feature, and indeed any feature, depends on Jiang.

This point may seem to call only for a minor revision to the view of consent that we are considering. It might seem that the problem lies only in positing objectively important features of a sexual encounter. Instead, one could make this importance a subjective matter, relativizing the distinction between core and peripheral features to each person in the circumstances in which she finds herself. For example, a partner's religion may be a core feature to someone with religious views; but whether a sexual partner is someone's ongoing romantic partner may be a peripheral feature to someone else on a particular occasion. Now there is nothing inherently problematic with this relativization. Indeed, I welcome movement in this direction. But the crucial point is that this relativization is scarcely, if at all, open to a friend of the Lenient Thesis. For how are we to distinguish between the core and peripheral features for each person? The most principled way to do so is to distinguish the features that someone considered relevant to her decision to have sex from those that she considered irrelevant.[34] In the language of the law, we might say that the core features are simply those that the victim considered "material" to her decision to have sex. But if we take this line, then we should conclude that someone does not consent to sex when she is deceived into sex. For, by my stipulative definition, someone is deceived into sex when she forms a false belief about a *deal breaker*: the deception conceals a feature of the sexual encounter that makes a decisive difference to the victim's decision to have sex.[35] To put this point in terms of our earlier example: the fact that Chloe is a soldier would count as a core feature of the sexual encounter precisely because this feature of Chloe is important enough to Victoria to make the difference between whether or not she is willing to have sex with her. So to resist my claim that someone fails to consent whenever she is deceived into sex, someone would have to find a different way of drawing the distinction between subjectively core and peripheral features. I am doubtful that anyone could find a systematic way of drawing the distinction, let alone that she could adequately motivate this way of doing so.[36]

The Argument from the Case of the Chihuahua

To introduce my second subargument, let us set aside sex for a moment and consider a different example. Suppose that Aisha asks me to let her dog into my apartment. Knowing that I loathe Chihuahuas, Aisha falsely says that it is a Great Dane, and I hand over my key. Imagine my surprise and fright, then, to come home to find a Chihuahua scuttling around my floor like an overgrown furry cockroach. I say to Aisha, reasonably enough, that this Chihuahua is not the agreed upon Great Dane. Aisha acknowledges the difference is undeniable. But she replies that I had consented to the arrangement since I had agreed to let her dog into my home. Aisha's reply will not do, I am afraid. Aisha has effectively trespassed upon my property. The fact that I agreed to admit *some dog* does not mean that I agreed to admit *that dog*.[37] What I consented to let into my home was a Great Dane, and that dog was not a Great Dane.

There are superficial differences between the cases—an apartment is not the same as a body and a dog's entrance is not the same as sexual contact. But the soldier and dog-owner cases are alike in all morally relevant respects, which are as follows. The victim has a right to control others' behavior within her personal space. The deceiver would act impermissibly if she invades the personal space without the victim's morally valid consent. The victim's will is opposed to what the deceiver in fact intends. The deceiver manages to obviate this obstacle to her plan by means of deception. This deception means that the victim's acquiescence does not count as morally valid consent. My aim here is to use the case of Aisha to illustrate this pattern, so that once we are primed, we will see it in the case of Chloe as well.

This is particularly clear if the deceived person explicitly thinks of, and voices, the restrictions on her consent. Suppose I say to Aisha, "You may bring in your dog as long as it isn't a Chihuahua—I won't stand to have such an unpredictable dog where I live." If I have thought and said this, then it is clear that I have not consented to her bringing in her Chihuahua. I have insisted on my moral right against having a Chihuahua in my apartment, and so Aisha would violate this right by bringing one in. Similarly, suppose that Victoria had explicitly said to Chloe, "I'm willing to have sex with you on the assumption that you love animals and have never been in the military; but I am unwilling to do so otherwise. You're an animal-lover and not a soldier, aren't you?" Since Chloe knows she is a soldier who is, at best, indifferent to animals' welfare, she cannot reasonably consider herself to have Victoria's morally valid consent if she deceives Victoria on these points. Victoria has insisted on her right against sexual contact with a soldier who is indifferent to animals, and so Chloe would violate this right by making such contact with her. But if this is right, then we must reject the view that someone consents to sex when she is deceived into sex by means of run-of-the-mill deception.

This point is enough to show that run-of-the-mill deception can vitiate sexual consent. So if you also agree that nonconsensual sex is seriously wrong, then you would have to reject the Lenient Thesis:

> Lenient Thesis. It is only a minor wrong to deceive another person into sex by misleading her or him about certain personal features such as natural hair color, occupation, or romantic intentions.

But I wish to press this line of objection further. The explicitness of the communicated consent shoves into the face of the deceiver the fact that she lacks the victim's morally valid consent. However, the explicitness is not necessary for the absence of this consent. It would also be sufficient that the deceiver knows about the victim's deal breakers. If Aisha knows that I am unwilling to have a Chihuahua in my apartment, then she cannot consider herself as having my morally valid consent when she hides the breed of her dog. Once we become alert to this fact, we will also see that if Chloe knows that Victoria is unwilling to sleep with soldiers, then she also cannot consider herself to have Victoria's morally valid consent.

Of course, knowledge of another person's deal breakers is hard to come by, particularly in light of the fact that someone's reasons for having sex can be opaque even to herself. But this knowledge also is unnecessary for a deceiver to lack a victim's valid consent. For suppose that Aisha is uncertain about whether I am against Chihuahuas in my apartment; still, she decides to deceive me about the breed of her dog *in case* I might refuse to admit a Chihuahua. Since her deception is aimed at the possibility that I am unwilling to admit a Chihuahua, and she knows this possibility actually obtains, she cannot reasonably consider herself to have my valid consent to admitting such a dog. And once more, when we are sensitive to this moral pattern, we will see the same is true with respect to sexual consent. Since Chloe deceives Victoria with the purpose of preventing Victoria's deal breakers getting in the way of sex, she cannot reasonably take herself to have Victoria's morally valid consent.

The Argument from a Substantive Account of Consent

My third subargument is the most controversial since it relies on a substantive account of consent. (But should you end up unpersuaded of this account, let me stress that the previous two subarguments do not rely on any particular substantive account of consent and are consistent with a less demanding account than the one I proceed to offer.)

I wish to motivate my account by leaning on the theory of rights I introduced earlier. We saw that we have (moral claim-)rights over our persons and our property, and we can waive specific rights against particular interactions with particular individuals. So what fixes the set of rights that we waive? I suggest the following answer:

> Intentions Thesis. The rights that we waive are the rights that we intend to waive.[38]

The animating thought behind this thesis is the familiar one that rights are intimately linked to our autonomy and agency. They mark out personal realms over which we have exclusive control, and our decisions determine exactly what may permissibly happen within these realms. Having these personal realms is crucial to our leading our lives in the ways that we should like. Fundamentally, this generates duties in other people to respect our wills: they must respect the choices that we make about what shall happen within these realms. If our choices are to maximally determine the permissibility of others' actions, then the rights that we waive must be the rights that we intend to waive. Only this arrangement leaves us fully sovereign over these realms.

In addition, the Intentions Thesis makes an account of consent continuous with the standard account of promise. It is uncontroversial that intentions fix the bounds of promises: the promises you make are those that you take yourself to be making. If there has been some confusion about a promisor's intentions, then the promisee must accept as final a sincere statement about what the promisor had in mind. (The promisee may have a separate complaint that the promisor has created in her a legitimate, but unfulfilled, expectation, but this takes us outside the ethics of promise, since promises are intentionally undertaken obligations.) Now consent and promise are closely related moral phenomena. By giving consent, we release others from obligations; by making promises, we place ourselves under obligations. We should expect these normative powers to operate on similar lines. The Intentions Thesis delivers this result.

Next we should observe that our intentions about waivers are typically both restrictive and extensive. Our intentions are *restrictive* insofar as we want to permit certain forms of behavior but not others. For example, we let hairdressers cut our hair but not stroke our hands. Meanwhile, our intentions are *extensive* insofar as there are always multiple courses of action that could realize the permitted behavior. There are countless permutations of snips that fall within any hairdresser's permitted range. Now, in general, the restrictions on our intentions are both explicit and implicit. Consider an intention unconnected to consent. Suppose Aisha intends to buy a puppy. She may explicitly have restricted herself to dogs in a shelter. But there will also be implicit

restrictions on her intention. If she is like most prospective dog owners, then Aisha will not have considered the possibility that puppies can have rabies. Despite this, unless she is quite the eccentric, she does not intend to buy a rabid puppy. This restriction on her intention is entirely implicit. This is a general feature of intentions, which is thus shared by our intentions for rights-waivers: these typically have both implicit and explicit restrictions. For example, when I intend to waive my rights against Aisha bringing around her dog, I do not intend to permit her to bring around a rabid dog, even if I do not explicitly consider or mention rabies.[39]

These points about intentions, in conjunction with the independently attractive Intentions Thesis, lead us to the following account of consent. In consenting, we intend to allow a restricted range of possibilities, where these restrictions are both implicit and explicit. Any actual interaction with our persons or property is consensual only if this interaction falls within this restricted range of permitted possibilities.[40] On this account of consent, if we object to events in virtue of *any* feature of them, then they lie outside the restricted range of possibilities to which we are consenting.[41] If these events nevertheless occur, then "what happened is not that for which consent was given."[42] This does not mean that we have to achieve the impossible feat of being aware of every feature of an event in order to consent to it. But it does mean that, were we aware of any of the features of the event, we would have to still be happy to go along with it. A consequence of this account is that it is not always transparent to people whether they are giving their morally valid consent to particular events in the world. But this is simply a consequence of the fact that the features of particular events are sometimes opaque to agents. And this is a welcome consequence: any account of consent must predict that Milady did not give her morally valid consent to sex with D'Artagnan even though at the time she thought she was properly consenting to what happened.

Applying this general account of consent to sex, people validly consent to sexual encounters only if they are willing to engage in these encounters, given all the features that these encounters have. Thus, this account of consent implies that when someone is deceived into sex, the sex is nonconsensual. For the deception has concealed a deal-breaking feature of the sexual encounter. As a result, the sexual encounter lies outside the range of possibilities that the victim intends to consent to. Therefore, whenever someone is deceived into sex, she does not validly consent to the sex, even in the case of run-of-the-mill deception, for example, about her partner's attitudes concerning peace and animals.

I have grounded this account of consent on the basis of three independently attractive motivations: a standard background theory of rights, the Intentions Thesis, and a general view of intentions. All of these are general motivations from outside of the sexual domain. They lead to an account of consent that entails that someone does not properly consent when deceived into sex. This result will seem counterintuitive to many, and this is some cost to the account. However, I would deny that an intuition that, say, Victoria consents to sex with Chloe deserves the status of a considered judgment around which we frame our ethical theory. For one, I have just offered two independent subarguments against such a claim. For another, we should be wary of our intuitions about sexual morality, since we often observe that recent generations' intuitions turn out to be mistaken. And we have excellent evidence that an intuition is mistaken if it conflicts both with the conclusion of the Chihuahua argument and with general considerations from other ethical domains, such as the ones that I have just used to motivate my favored account of consent.

That said, I would find it worrying if my account of consent has overly strong implications for the way consent functions in other aspects of our lives, and these implications contradicted relevant considered judgments of ours. Consider other aspects of our lives besides sex. Suppose Candace asks to store antique skis in Courtney's basement, and Courtney agrees. Unbeknownst to both parties, the skis were once owned by Josef Stalin. If Courtney had known about their former owner, then she would not have let Candace store them. Despite her opposition to this feature of the skis, are we really to say that Courtney did not validly consent to their presence in her basement?[43]

I take this to be the most troubling challenge to my account of consent. I fully accept that this account implies that Courtney does not properly consent, and it is clear that Candace behaved blamelessly. As a result, we might be tempted to say that the reason why is that Candace had Courtney's morally valid consent. But we must be cautious about jumping to conclusions too hastily, for the correct analysis of this case is more subtle. The feature that is priming us to judge Candace innocent is not the existence of Courtney's consent. Rather, it is the fact that Candace is justifiably ignorant of the skis' history. As such, she would have a full excuse for acting in the way she did. And we can see that it is this excuse that is guiding our intuitions, by imagining instead that Candace does know both of the skis' history and of Courtney's unwillingness to store sporting equipment once owned by bloodthirsty dictators. By making these modifications to the case, it structurally resembles the case in which Aisha tries to sneak her Chihuahua into my apartment. As such, I hope you agree that in this version of the case Candace does not have Courtney's valid consent, and that this explains why Candace acts wrongfully in storing the skis. Now whether Courtney validly consents depends on facts about Courtney—it depends on the nature of her mental attitudes or utterances. Whether Courtney validly consents does not depend on Candace's epistemic state. Since Courtney does not consent when Candace knows the skis were Stalin's, equally she does not consent when Candace is ignorant of this fact. As a result, we can see that Courtney does fail to properly consent in the original case, and our intuitions about Candace's innocence are explained fully by Candace's justifiable ignorance.

Still, we may have a related worry that is not tied to intuitions about cases. We might worry that in taking a strict line about what each party consents to, the account of consent forces us to forgo mutual benefits of cooperation. Since the scope of each party's consent is marked by their intentions, and both parties may permissibly be ignorant about whether an interaction is covered by these intentions, everyone may be worse off in virtue of being unable to form common knowledge about which interactions are consensual. As a result of failing to align their expectations about consensuality, they may bear unnecessary costs or forgo possible benefits.[44]

My response to this worry is threefold. First, we should take care not to overstate the scope of this concern. On my account of consent, it will often be possible to form these shared expectations through communication. So when consent is particularly important, as in the case of sexual rights, each party has more moral reason to communicate about their intentions. Admittedly, this response's force is limited by the fact that it would not cover cases in which each party is unable to discover whether the interaction is consensual. This may be particularly likely in the case of sexual consent if people are not always sure what their reasons for deciding to have sex are and what their deal breakers are.[45] Second, if a party has taken all reasonable measures to establish that the other party consents, and yet it turns out that she does not, then her justifiable ignorance provides her with a full excuse for moral wrongdoing. So considerations of her moral ledger would provide her with no significant dis-incentive to cooperation. Third, in the case of property rights, our choices of laws can take into account further benefits of mutual cooperation. To encourage this cooperation, we may prefer a property system that protects innocent people who act in good faith from bearing costs. Along these lines, someone might have legal protection if she has come to rely on a nonconsensual agreement, so long as the nonconsensuality arises from factors of which she could not reasonably be expected to be aware. Suppose Courtney is curious about why the letters "J. S." are engraved on the skis and, upon investigating, comes to discover their history; consequently, she objects to the arrangement as not being what she signed up for. One legal possibility is that if Candace has come to materially rely on the arrangement, then she may continue storing the skis, either for the terms of the lease or for enough time for her to make alternative arrangements. In order to offer an incentive for cooperation, we may prefer a property rights scheme that includes measures like this that aim to protect people who inadvertently partake in nonconsensual property transactions. Or we may not—the debates about various property schemes are complex, and I will not enter into them now. My point here is that if

we are particularly concerned with facilitating cooperation involving property, then we can so mold our property laws in these sorts of ways. But these considerations do not plausibly extend to bodily rights, since we are unwilling to trade bodily protection off against the possible benefits of mutual coordination and cooperation. Consequently, any acceptable legal system would require anyone to desist from a bodily interaction, upon discovery that the other party does not validly consent. As such, the rectificatory duties in the event of infringing bodily and property consent may diverge, and this is a consequence of valid bodily consent being significantly more morally important than valid property consent.

IV. BENIGN DECEPTION, CULPABILITY, AND THE SERIOUSNESS OF THE WRONG

So far I have defended both premises of my main argument, which together entail my conclusion that culpably deceiving someone into sex is seriously wrong:

1. Having sex with someone, while lacking her morally valid consent, is seriously wrong.
2. Deceiving another person into sex involves having sex with that person, while lacking her morally valid consent.
3. Therefore, deceiving someone into sex is seriously wrong.[46]

Having completed my argument, I wish now to discuss three points about my conclusion.

First, let me stress that the serious wrong here is the nonconsensual sex, rather than the deception in itself. Indeed, deception sometimes plays benign, and even desirable, roles in attraction and sexual relationships. Sarah Buss observes that in "many good human lives, the beloved falls in love with the lover because and only because he initially gives her a misleading impression of who he is and of his intentions."[47] Someone may harmlessly misrepresent how interested she is in her date's tales, and often one does best to conceal one's love until it is reciprocated.[48] Further, people may want to be deceived. Sometimes, we may want "to encounter reality indirectly, obliquely transformed" out of an enjoyment of the magic of romance.[49] And in relationships, we do not always endorse the way that we would react to certain truths about our partners, perhaps out of jealousy or insecurity. As a result, we may prefer that they lie to us so as not to incite these reactions in us.

These points are well taken. However, I deny, and Buss does not suggest, that these points legitimize deceiving someone into sex. For no matter how benign the deception in other respects, if it vitiates someone's sexual consent, then this leads to seriously wrong misconduct. The possible benefits of romance and relationships would not justify having nonconsensual sex with someone. So if someone deceives another person for the sake of their mutually falling in love, then the price she will have to pay is abstinence until she is sufficiently confident that the false beliefs are not part of the other person's reasons for having sex. Moreover, I speculate that much of the harmless or welcome subterfuge that features in attraction and relationships does not hide deal breakers and hence does not lead to deceiving people into sex. If someone would still choose to have sex with another person, were the veil of ignorance lifted, then her sexual consent is unaffected by the deception.

Second, in addition to the serious wrongness of acts, there is the further issue of agents' culpability for performing wrong acts. I am assuming the standard view of culpability, which includes deliberately doing wrong, being aware that one does wrong, and taking an excessive risk of doing wrong. Thus someone is culpable for serious wrongdoing if she deliberately aims to deceive another person into sex, if she foresees that her actions will lead to her deceiving another person into sex, and if she recklessly takes an excessive risk of deceiving someone into sex. These points about culpability are very familiar. But I want to briefly discuss the implications of recklessness for our topic. Suppose that Chloe lied about her career simply to avoid the conversation taking an awkward turn that might disrupt her smooth pickup technique. Still, Chloe should realize that she was taking a risk

that Victoria's belief that Chloe was an animal-loving humanitarian ends up a crucial part of her reason for consenting to sex. Indeed, when sexual partners deceive each other about themselves, there is frequently some risk, however small, of this deception leading to nonconsensual sex. This is because of the epistemic limitations people face. It is hard for people to know what other people's reasons are for deciding to have sex. Further, deception "is a pervasive possibility in sexual encounters and relationships" in light of "the peculiarly implicit nature of sexual communication," which makes miscommunication likely when "endearments and gestures of intimacy are not used to convey what they standardly convey."[50] Whether taking these risks counts as recklessness depends on how much risk it is acceptable to take. So how much of a risk may we take of deceiving another into sex? This is a difficult applied question, and I doubt that we can give it a precise answer in the abstract. Instead, the best we can do is to characterize the types of consideration to which we should attend when analyzing particular cases. On one side are the costs to a policy of avoiding deception. Honesty can come at a loss of privacy. Additionally, if people cautiously forgo sexual encounters, and it turns out that these would have been consensual, then they miss out on any benefits of these encounters. On the other side is the seriousness of the moral wrong of nonconsensual sex. We would have to weigh these considerations on a case-by-case basis.[51] But given the seriousness of the moral wrong, I suspect that we will often judge that people have strenuous duties to reduce the risk of deceiving another into sex, and it would be hard to justify the status quo in which "society, wisely or unwisely, generally expects [potential victims] to assume the risk of misrepresentation in intimate relationships."[52]

Third, a comparison between deceiving someone into sex and having sex with an unconscious person is enlightening because they are wrong for the same reason. Suppose that someone took highly effective precautions to ensure that his chronically comatose victim suffered no physical harm and never found out about his having sex with her. Why is his action wrong? My answer is twofold: the victim has a stringent right against sexual contact, which is based in the importance of her sexual autonomy, and he has violated this right by having nonconsensual sex with her. I have argued that these features are present when someone deceives another into sex. And so to avoid equating these cases, one would have to find a sufficiently morally important disanalogy. What could this be?

We can put to one side several irrelevant differences. First, there will be several counterfactual claims true of a victim of deception, such as "if the victim had inquired further, she might have avoided being attacked," and we might think that similar claims could not be made about an unconscious victim.[53] This points to the deceived victim's ability to avoid the fraud. However, some deception will be virtually undetectable, and some unconscious victims also have the ability to avoid attacks. If a victim passes out drunk, then one could say that "if the victim had drunk less, she would have avoided being attacked." But this does nothing to diminish the wrong she suffers. And this is a fully general point: wrongs are not diminished because victims could have avoided them. Stranger rape is no less bad simply because the victim could have avoided it "by never leaving home without a (reliable!) army."[54] Second, one might claim that victims of deception *ought* to have avoided deception, presumably in the prudential sense of "ought." But again, a similar point can be made of some unconscious victims. It is prudent not to drink so much that one passes out around people who are liable to have sex with unconscious victims. So there is no disanalogy and again, this point about prudence does not diminish the wrong perpetrated by offenders. Third, one might claim that some victims of deception can be complicit in their deception and thereby bear partial responsibility for it. For example, if Victoria wants to believe that Chloe is a humanitarian animal lover, then this may make her less skeptical than she would ordinarily be. However, this point would do nothing to improve our view of deceiving people into sex when the victims are not complicit in any way. And more importantly, someone's complicity does not diminish the other person's wrongdoing. We can see this if we consider cons. Suppose Carlo runs a Ponzi scheme. Some of his victims are entirely innocent of

any negligence on their parts; other victims believe Carlo partly because they want to believe him. I hope you agree that Carlo acts just as badly when he cons either type of victim. What this shows is that even if we grant for the sake of argument that some victims are responsible for their deception, this does not diminish the wrongdoing of the perpetrator. In the words of David Archard, we must avoid the "danger of having a zero-sum picture of responsibility for a crime. This picture imagines that the more that a person contributes by her behavior or negligence to bringing about the circumstances in which she is a victim of a crime, the less responsible is the criminal for the crime he commits. A crime is no less unwelcome or serious in its effects, or need it be any the less or malicious in its commission, for occurring in circumstances which the victim helped to realise."[55] This general point applies as much to sex as to Ponzi schemes.

There is, however, at least one morally important difference between the two types of nonconsensual sex. Victims of unconscious sex are likely to suffer a greater dignitary harm than victims of deceptive sex, insofar as the former victims are likely to feel that they have been more violated than the latter victims. However, I suggest that this is simply a consequence of the fact that the latter victims mistakenly accept the Lenient Thesis. Many people who are deceived into sex do not consider themselves to have suffered a serious moral wrong. In light of this, they do not consider themselves to be gravely disrespected. However, if it were more widely realized that the Lenient Thesis is false, then this difference between unconscious and deceptive sex would disappear. Both sets of victims would then realize that they have suffered a grave affront to their sexual autonomy. So there is a morally relevant difference, but one that would evaporate if the correct view of sexual deception were more widely accepted. Are there other differences beside? I cannot think of any, but for reasons of space, I will not pursue this inquiry further here. Instead, I will simply make the provocative suggestion that if everyone rejected the false Lenient Thesis, then deceiving someone into sex would be in the same moral ballpark as having sex with an unconscious person. If others wish to reject this rough moral equation, then I pass the challenge to them to find further moral differences.

V. CONCLUSION

To summarize, I have argued that deceiving someone into sex vitiates her consent to sex, and it is seriously wrong to have sex without someone's valid consent to sex. Therefore, deceiving someone into sex is seriously wrong. The seriousness of this wrong is widely recognized when the deception involves, say, spousal impersonation. But it is wrongly overlooked in the case of run-of-the-mill deception.

My conclusion may appear prudish or reactionary. But I would resist this characterization. Instead, it is the inevitable consequence of placing the proper value on our sexual autonomy. Ultimately, my stance is motivated by the thought that someone has the right to decide down to the very last detail what comes into sexual contact with her body, and this is a particularly important right. For example, Victoria's rights over her sex life extend to deciding the interests in animals or peace of the people she sleeps with, or for that matter their incomes or favorite colors. The Lenient Thesis goes wrong because it objectionably trivializes some of these choices. But the truth is that it is Victoria's prerogative to choose not to have sex with someone in virtue of any feature of her whatsoever, and "taking away the power to consent to sexual relationships, to control this most personal part of our domain, is an extremely grave and serious injury."[56] Since deceiving someone into sex involves disrespecting her sexual choices, my thesis calls for more autonomy in our sex lives. As such, we should not see it as a prudish or reactionary thesis but a liberating one.

NOTES

1. "The Big Lies People Tell in Online Dating," http://blog.okcupid.com/index.php /the-biggest-lies-in-online-dating/ (accessed on February 1, 2013).

2. For example, if it is common knowledge that someone is expected to disclose a sexually transmitted disease, then a failure to make any disclosure may communicate to the other person an absence of the disease. This is not to say that all forms of concealment are deception, though. I am currently omitting to mention the color of my eyes and hence concealing it from you, but I am not deceiving you about it.

3. Wertheimer himself rejects these norms. Peter Westen notes that a similar view is common concerning the related, though separate, legal issue, observing that "most judges and commentators [would] find it normatively untenable . . . that an actor, who entices a woman to engage in sexual intercourse by falsely telling her that he is a high-ranking executive . . . absent other defenses on his part, would be guilty of rape." Alan Wertheimer, *Consent to Sexual Relations* (Cambridge: Cambridge University Press, 2003), 193; Jeffrie Murphy, "Women, Violence and the Criminal Law," in *In Harm's Way: Essays in Honor of Joel Feinberg*, ed. Jules Coleman and Allen Buchanan (Cambridge: Cambridge University Press, 1994), 219; Peter Westen, *The Logic of Consent* (Aldershot: Ashgate, 2004), 200.

4. Some commentators have thought that promises, e.g., of marriage would not constitute deception about the sexual encounter, since the promises concern the future rather than the present sexual encounter. But this overlooks the fact that "one who makes a promise of love and marriage to another also conveys something much more concrete—a statement of fact about a matter of which the speaker has special knowledge. In avowing such feelings, the speaker represents that his heart and mind are at that moment filled with the committed intentions and deep emotions of which he speaks." Moreover, someone's intentions affect the nature of the sexual encounter: casual sex is different from sex where parties have further romantic intentions. Jane E. Larson, "Women Understand So Little, They Call My Good Nature 'Deceit': A Feminist Rethinking of Seduction," *Columbia Law Review* 93 (1993): 374–472, at 466–67.

5. There is an orthogonal controversy about whether consent consists in one's mental attitudes or one's communications. I will not engage in this debate here, but in passing I would note that this example shows that if the communications view is correct, then we must interpret someone's communications on the basis of her underlying intentions. If I say, "you may carry out your plans," then the phrase "your plans" concerns what you actually plan. But I do not properly consent because I do not intend to permit you to dye my hair pink. For "mental-attitude" accounts of consent, see Heidi Hurd, "The Moral Magic of Consent," *Legal Theory* 2 (1996): 121–46; Larry Alexander, "The

Moral Magic of Consent II," *Legal Theory* 2 (1996): 165–74. For "communication" accounts, see Wertheimer, *Consent to Sexual Relations*; Joan McGregor, *Is It Rape? On Acquaintance Rape and Taking Women's Consent Seriously* (Aldershot: Ashgate, 2005).

6. Wertheimer, *Consent to Sexual Relations*, 199.

7. Although claiming not to have "resolved the question as to when consent to sexual relations should be regarded as" morally valid (213), Wertheimer's position is close to the one I defend, as he maintains that as "a general principle, we might think that A's deception should generally undermine the moral and transformative power of consent because it precludes B from being able to decide whether engaging in sex with A is in her interests or compatible with her values. As a moral matter, I think this is basically correct" (193). Wertheimer leaves this judgment about sexual consent at the level of intuition, which is a controversial dialectical ploy, given the popularity of the Lenient Thesis. I hope to buttress this judgment by contributing arguments in its defense. However, as we will shortly see, Wertheimer would disagree with my claim that all nonconsensual sex is seriously wrong; instead, he maintains that the seriousness of the wrong depends on the expected harm involved to a victim. Wertheimer, *Consent to Sexual Relations*.

8. Catharine MacKinnon argues that rape laws should be reformed so that the concept of consent does not feature in them. On her proposal, rape should be conceived of as forced sex. MacKinnon, "Feminism, Marxism, Method and the State," *Signs: Journal of Women in Culture and Society* 8 (1982): 635–58, at 650, 655. However, perhaps the majority position is that rape should be defined in terms of the absence of consent. See, e.g., Susan Estrich, "Rape," *Yale Law Journal* 95 (1986): 1087–1184, at 1095–96, 1132–33; David Archard, "The Wrong of Rape," *Philosophical Quarterly* 57 (2007): 374–93; McGregor, *Is It Rape?*

9. Stephen Schulhofer argues that there are evidential problems in establishing whether someone culpably deceived another into sex, and there are difficulties in framing a law that penalizes only seriously wrong misconduct. Additionally, he suggests that the law may be influenced by the fact that victims of deception are partially self-deceived, believing and not believing at the same time, and they may indeed welcome some forms of deception as part of the fantasy of erotic experience. While these issues remain unresolved, Schulhofer suggests that "it may be too soon to reach a judgment about the kinds of misleading comments that should be considered illegal in matters of sexual intimacy. . . . It may be preferable [as a matter of law] to leave to the individual

the decision whether to believe, whether to rely, and whether to assume the risk of deception by trusting the other party." Similarly, Wertheimer maintains that the "permissive approach to sexual deception embodied in the law may derive in part from 'line-drawing' difficulties" concerning how to distinguish "morally serious deceptions" from "puffing" or "storytelling," and in part from "evidentiary difficulties" in establishing what the deceiver said and whether he was intending to deceive. In light of these points, with respect to the law, Wertheimer suggests that "for 'administrative reasons' it may be sensible to assign the burden of fraud to dispensers of information in the commercial arena and to the recipients of fraud in the sexual arena." Stephen Schulhofer, *Unwanted Sex* (Cambridge, MA: Harvard University Press, 1998), 154–58; Wertheimer, *Consent to Sexual Relations*, 199–204.

10. Robin West, "Sex, Law and Consent," in *The Ethics of Consent: Theory and Practice*, ed. Franklin G. Miller and Alan Wertheimer (Oxford: Oxford University Press, 2010), 221–50.

11. Estrich, "Rape"; John Gardner and Stephen Shute, "The Wrongness of Rape," in *Oxford Essays in Jurisprudence*, ed. J. Horder (Oxford: Oxford University Press, 2000); Archard, "The Wrong of Rape."

12. Joan McGregor, "Force, Consent, and the Reasonable Woman," in Coleman and Buchanan, *In Harm's Way*, 236. See also McGregor, *Is It Rape?*

13. Here I broadly follow Judith Jarvis Thomson's landmark account in her *The Realm of Rights* (Cambridge, MA: Harvard University Press, 1990).

14. Most rights theorists allow that there are usually some benefits that justify infringing a right, although they deny that maximizing utility is always a justification. But even when infringing is permissible, the right leaves a "moral residue" in the need for an apology and possible compensation; ibid., 84.

15. A fully detailed explanation of rights' stringency would take us into an orthogonal controversy between so-called interest theories and will theories about whether rights protect our interests or our choices. My point is neutral with respect to this debate. Both sides accept that our rights over our sex lives are more stringent than our rights over our lawns, and that this is explained in the fact that lawn trespass is less important to us than bodily trespass. For a recent discussion of the debate between these two theories, see Matthew H. Kramer, N. E. Simmonds, and Hillel Steiner, *A Debate over Rights* (Oxford: Oxford University Press, 1998).

16. Archard, "The Wrong of Rape," 391.

17. For the contingent view see Murphy, "Women, Violence and the Criminal Law"; Scott Anderson, "Prostitution and Sexual Autonomy," *Ethics* 112 (2002): 748–80, at 774; for the biological view, see Alan Wertheimer, "Consent and Sexual Relations," *Legal Theory* 2 (1996): 89–113, at 100; for the objective interest view, see Archard, "The Wrong of Rape."

18. For a related argument, see Archard, "The Wrong of Rape."

19. William Faulkner, *As I Lay Dying* (New York: Vintage, 1990); Alexandre Dumas, *The Three Musketeers*, trans. Lord Sudley (New York: Penguin, 1995). Patricia Falk documents real world analogues in her survey of legal cases in her "Rape by Fraud and Rape by Coercion," *Brooklyn Law Review* 64 (1998): 39–180.

20. Wertheimer, *Consent to Sexual Relations*, 96. For another view that ties "moral gravity" to "differences in degree of harm," see Joel Feinberg, "Victims' Excuses: The Case of Fraudulently Procured Consent," *Ethics* 96 (1986): 330–45, at 341.

21. Wertheimer, *Consent to Sexual Relations*, 203.

22. Ibid., 192.

23. But why only threats of *physical* harm? For an argument that threats of psychological harm can vitiate consent, see Sarah Conly, "Seduction, Rape, and Coercion," *Ethics* 115 (2004): 96–121.

24. Their counterexample to the Harm Explanation is drug-induced "utterly harmless rape perpetrated on a sexually aroused but somatic victim and leaving no trace on her memory or body." Gardner and Shute, "The rongness of Rape," 198.

25. Wertheimer, *Consent to Sexual Relations*.

26. The same points could be made about deception by means of spousal impersonation. However, cases of undetectable impersonation are rare, with twin impersonation cases being the most realistic. For an actual example of twin impersonation, see Falk, "Rape by Fraud," 67.

27. As such, this premise is acceptable to different theorists who operate with distinct conceptions of morally valid consent. Thanks to an anonymous reviewer for pressing me to address this point.

28. David Archard adopts an approach along these lines, which is based on a gradable notion of voluntariness: "There are aspects of a sexual act—what, why, and with whom—about which, and there are also degrees to which, a person may be misled in respect of that act. The more completely a person is misled, the less willingly she can be said to engage in that act, and the more wronged she is if she does engage in that act. She is wronged to the extent that her will is not implicated in the act and it does not express

her free choices" (50). This allows Archard to maintain that false proclamations of love need not vitiate sexual consent, on the grounds that this deception is slight enough that the will of the deceived is still sufficiently "implicated." But this analysis is inconsistent with Archard's own account of the requirement of informed consent. Here Archard states that "the person does not need to know everything, only everything that would make a real difference to whether or not she consented" (46). This claim is in tension with the gradable voluntariness approach since the claim implies that all forms of deceiving someone into sex are nonconsensual. This is because ignorance of any deal-breaker makes "a real difference to whether or not" one consents. So if false proclamations of love lead to someone being deceived into sex, then she does not validly consent. Her will is opposed to the encounter, given it is an encounter with someone who does not love her, and this is enough to make it the case that she does not validly consent. David Archard, *Sexual Consent* (Oxford: Westview, 1998).

29. This loosely parallels the legal distinction mentioned by Joel Feinberg between "deception about what is consented to and deception about collateral matters for the purpose of inducing the victim to consent." As Rollin Perkins puts it, deception about the nature of the sexual act—"fraud in the *factum*"—vitiates legal consent, on the grounds that "what happened is not that for which consent was given." But deception about collateral matters of fact—"fraud in the inducement"—does not vitiate legal consent. Stephen Schulhofer notes that in practice only two forms of deception are generally recognized as being punished by law—"fraud as to the nature of the act and impersonation of a woman's husband." Spousal impersonation counts on the grounds that it changes the nature of the sexual act into adultery. The law goes wrong, in my view, in ignoring the fact that the other person is a constituent of the sexual act. Rollin M. Perkins, *Perkins on Criminal Law*, 1st ed. (New York: Foundation, 1957), 856; Feinberg, "Victims' Excuses," 331; Stephen Schulhofer, "Taking Sexual Autonomy Seriously: Rape Law and Beyond," *Law and Philosophy* 11 (1992): 35–94, at 88.

30. Rick Bragg, "Ex-Wife Is Suing Cuba over a Spy's Deception," *New York Times*, August 15, 1999 (accessed on February 1, 2013 at http://www.nytimes.com/1999/08/15/us/ex-wife-is-suing-cuba-over-a-spy-s-deception.html); Rob Evans and Paul Lewis, "Former Lovers of Undercover Officers Sue Police over Deceit," *Guardian*, December 16, 2011 (accessed on February 1, 2013, at http://www.guardian.co.uk/uk/2011/dec/16/lovers-undercover-officers -sue-police); Jo Adetunji and Harriet Sherwood, "Arab Guilty of Rape after Consensual Sex with Jew," *Guardian*, July 21,

2010 (accessed on February 1, at http://www.guardian.co.uk /world/2010/jul/21/arab-guilty-rape-consensual-sex-jew).

31. Considering sex by means of false promises, Murphy tentatively makes this point explicitly: "We could coherently conceptualize as rape any sex obtained through fraudulent inducement so long as the nature of the inducement itself does not provide strong evidence that the victim does not value sexuality in the way characteristic of the norms we seek to protect. A woman trading sex for the promise of a mink coat would reveal such deviation and thereby reveal an interest less worthy of protection." Murphy, "Women, Violence, and the Criminal Law," 222 (italics removed from the original). An editor of *Ethics* has pointed out that there is a sense in which my own position rests on a moralized conception of sex, insofar as I take violations of sexual rights to be serious wrongs. But to be clear, what I am valuing here is not any particular form of sex but rather individuals' sexual *control* over whom they have sex with and how. And I remain neutral on the grounds of this value, so I am happy to ground it in the contingent fact that people happen to find this control highly important to them.

32. McGregor also speculates that "often what is at work is the suggestion that if these women are so gullible, naive, and stupid, then they get what they deserve when they consent to fraudulent claims," McGregor, *Is It Rape?*, 187.

33. Stephen Schulhofer is here discussing the appropriate "legal protection of autonomous choice" in his "Taking Sexual Autonomy Seriously," 70.

34. In proposing a new tort for sexual fraud, Jane Larson defends this standard for the "materiality" of a misrepresentation. "One who fraudulently makes a misrepresentation of fact, opinion, intention, or law, for the purpose of inducing another to consent to sexual relations in reliance upon it, is subject to liability to the other in deceit for serious physical, pecuniary, and emotional loss caused to the recipient by his or her justifiable reliance upon the misrepresentation." Thus what matters, on Larson's proposal, is whether the misrepresentation "substantially influenced" the victim's decision to have sex. Larson, "Women Understand So Little," 462–64.

35. One of the rankings that Feinberg considers for gradations of voluntariness focuses on the different effects that deception may have on a victim's decision making. However, he suggests that "a more interesting, and perhaps more useful, way of ranking the false beliefs that might be created and exploited by a deceiver" involves distinguishing whether inducements involved promises or threats and harms or nonbenefits. Feinberg, "Victims' Excuses," 341–44.

36. One possibility is to maintain that deception only vitiates morally efficacious consent when it is particularly unexpected. In the context of advocating reforms to rape law, Joan McGregor makes an "appeal to expectations in a potential sexual relationship" in order to ground a legal distinction between the exaggeration, promises, and flattery that are normal, expected parts of courtship from serious cases of deception. With respect to successful deception that affects someone's decision to have sex, McGregor states that "having sex with an imposter is not going to result in indifference on the part of the victim. On the other hand, finding out that your lover is not exactly the person you thought—he does not have a Harvard degree, does not come from a famous family, and is not rich—will not be met with such disbelief and deep sense of harm." While McGregor is here only addressing the legal issue of which laws should be in place, there is a parallel position to be taken on the moral issue: one could maintain that only unexpected deception vitiates consent. Along similar lines, one might hold that consenting to sex under circumstances in which one has good reason to think one may be the victim of deception is consenting to taking the risk that one is being deceived—even about "deal-breaking" facts. Either way, an appeal to expectations is unpromising in an account of morally valid consent because people's expectations are simply based on the frequency of the wrong in question, and this frequency has no intrinsic moral significance. If spousal impersonation became sufficiently widespread, with the consequence that victims did not react with "disbelief " upon learning that they had been deceived, then spousal impersonation would be no better for that fact, nor would it thereby become consensual. This is a pattern that we observe across the board. In nonsexual domains, the fact that a certain type of fraud is widespread and therefore expected does not make it the case that a genuinely deceived victim offers morally valid consent to a con. Thanks to an editor of *Ethics* for pressing me to address this point and for his or her formulation of it. McGregor, *Is It Rape?*, 181–89.

37. For elaboration of this general point, see, e.g., Alexander, "The Moral Magic of Consent II."

38. As well as waiving rights, we can also forfeit rights. This forfeiture can be unintentional. For example, a would-be murderer would unintentionally forfeit her right not to be killed if her victim acts in self-defense. Thanks to editors of Ethics for pressing me to address this point.

39. Explicit communication is unnecessary. If Aisha tells you that she intends to get a puppy, then you would infer that it is not the case that she wants to get a rabid puppy. We assume that conversational participants make utterances that are informative but will not waste everyone's

time with excessive detail. Since it is common ground that I would not want a rabid Great Dane in my apartment, I need not mention this explicitly to Aisha, when communicating the range of my consent to Aisha. Thanks to an anonymous reviewer for prompting me to address this point.

40. This point holds even when someone has bad reasons for refusing to have sex with someone. We can all agree that racist prejudice is a morally abhorrent reason for any action. Nonetheless, when racists only decide to have sex with people of their own race on the basis of this prejudice, then they are consenting only to sex with people of their own race. When it comes to consent, we must respect other people's wills as they actually are, not as they ought to be.

41. An anonymous reviewer has pointed out that one potential cost of this account of consent is that it would require our having a grip on how to individuate events and identify their features. But I doubt any full ethical theory can get away without ever having to individuate events, and in any event, I suggest that this cost is actually quite slight. Moreover, to make use of this account of consent, we do not need a fancy theory of the metaphysics of events. For the most part, we can rely simply on our intuitive judgments about what features an event has, and ask whether someone would have been happy to go along with the event, given that it has each of these features.

42. This principle often governs the law's view of consent when the deception amounts to "fraud in the factum"—deception concerning the "core nature" of the act. See n. 30. Perkins, *Perkins on Criminal Law*, 856.

43. Thanks to an anonymous reviewer for pressing this type of objection.

44. Thanks to an anonymous reviewer for prompting me to address this concern.

45. Thanks to an editor of *Ethics* for correcting me on this point.

46. Some people are surprised by an implication of the thesis that culpably deceiving someone into sex is seriously wrong: two individuals can simultaneously seriously wrong each other by mutually deceiving each other into sex. But even if this implication is unexpected, we should accept it. For people can simultaneously wrong each other in the same way. By analogy, consider a fistfight. Each person may lose the right to complain about the other's behavior. But from a bystander's perspective, we can see that each has acted badly in assaulting the other. We do not judge their behavior as morally neutral simply because the other is treating them in the same way.

47. Sarah Buss, "Valuing Autonomy and Respecting Persons: Manipulation, Seduction, and the Basis of Moral Constraints," *Ethics* 115 (2005): 195–235, at 220–21.

48. Ibid., 221.

49. Ibid., 226.

50. Onora O'Neill, "Between Consenting Adults," *Philosophy and Public Affairs* 14 (1985): 252–77, at 269.

51. This touches on an important issue that is linked to our main topic of deception: concealment. This raises the question of what duties people have to inform their sexual partners about themselves to avoid false beliefs about deal breakers. But this question is a nuanced one. Toward the goal of mutually consensual sex, some epistemic labor may be required on both sides. If someone has a highly idiosyncratic sexual preference—say, he only wants to sleep with people whose star sign is Pisces—then it may be his responsibility to disclose this preference, rather than his partner's responsibility to inquire into whether he has this preference.

52. Schulhofer, "Taking Sexual Autonomy Seriously," 54.

53. Thanks to an anonymous reviewer for stressing the need for me to address these putative disanalogies.

54. Judith Jarvis Thomson, "A Defense of Abortion," *Philosophy and Public Affairs* 1 (1971): 47–66, at 59.

55. Archard, *Sexual Consent*, 139.

56. McGregor, "Force," 235.

DISCUSSION QUESTIONS

1. Which of Dougherty's two arguments from Section II do you find more convincing? Why?
2. Which of Dougherty's three arguments from Section III do you find most convincing? Why?
3. Do you need to find all of Dougherty's arguments from Sections II and III convincing in order to find his main argument convincing? Why or why not?
4. Dougherty quotes David Archard as saying that we must avoid "the danger of having a zero-sum picture of responsibility for a crime." What does this mean, and what does it have to do with Dougherty's claims about being deceived into sex?

Anne W. Eaton

A Sensible Antiporn Feminism

Anne W. Eaton is Professor of Philosophy at the University of Illinois–Chicago. She studies ethics and the philosophy of art. In this paper, Eaton enters a long-running conversation about whether pornography harms women. Eaton aims to strengthen the argument that certain kinds of pornography harm women by clarifying the kinds of harm pornography can cause and the sense in which it is a cause of those harms. Among other things, this paper illustrates the importance of clarifying the concepts you use in your arguments and the need to look to other academic disciplines to support your argument.

GUIDING QUESTIONS

1. What kinds of pornography is Eaton referring to when she uses the word "pornography"?
2. What kinds of harms does Eaton think pornography causes?
3. In what sense does Eaton think that pornography might "cause" these harms?
4. What does Eaton think about the evidence that we currently have for or against the claim that pornography causes harm? What kind of evidence does she think we would need to establish that claim?

A recent article in *The Boston Globe* asks, "What happened to the anti-porn feminists?"[1] Although a political debate about pornography still rages in the United States, civil libertarians and cultural conservatives dominate the dispute, whereas antiporn feminists, who played a leading role in opposing pornography in the 1970s, have considerably less public presence. Antiporn feminism has similarly dwindled in the academy where sex-positive feminists like Laura Kipnis and feminist-identified porn artists such as Annie Sprinkle have gained favor in English, art history, and gender studies departments. Academics in the humanities today are more likely to critically analyze pornographic works than to protest against them.

Why has antiporn feminism (hereafter APF) lost ground, particularly among self-identified feminists? Our *Globe* writer suggests that it is at least in part the recent growth of the porn industry and,

in particular, the explosion of internet pornography that has weakened the antiporn case. Although these things certainly play some role, they cannot explain why antiporn feminism, in particular, has waned, while culturally conservative opponents of pornography are gaining influence.

I'd like to offer another explanation, namely, that over the years APF has gained a bad reputation. Nowadays "antiporn feminism" conjures images of imperious and censorial finger-waggers who mean to police every corner of our erotic imaginations. Their insistence that pornography is harmful to women is considered overly simplistic, while their proposed remedy for this putative harm is taken to flagrantly violate the First Amendment.

In some instances this caricature is well deserved. However, I make the case that on certain key issues this criticism rests on a misunderstanding. It is part of the point of this article to critically examine the

A.W. Eaton "A Sensible Antiporn Feminism." *Ethics* 117(4) (July 2007), 674–715 © 2007 by The University of Chicago. Notes have been amended and renumbered.

terms in which the pornography debate is framed and to expose confusions resulting from lack of precision on many levels. By clarifying terms like 'pornography', 'cause', and 'harm', I aim to sift out irrelevant and uncharitable criticisms of APF. But this is only part of my purpose here, for, as I mentioned, the caricature is partially warranted. I believe that APF has not presented its best arguments, has suffered from imprecision and subtlety in its delineation of pornography's harms, has refused to acknowledge the limits of its evidence for these putative harms, and has proposed remedies that are extreme, overly broad, and murky. In this article I will expose these flaws and point the way toward correcting them. In so doing, I hope to convince you that APF can be a sophisticated and reasonable position that is both supported by a powerful intuitive argument and sensitive to the complexities of the empirical data regarding pornography's effects. It can be, in a word, 'sensible'.

My investigation will take the following shape. Section I provides an argument for APF and outlines some of its central tenets. Section II disentangles the various sorts of injury that pornography is thought to cause, exposing a wide array of harms that vary considerably in their character and severity. Section III examines the most common criticisms of APF and argues that they can be deflected by attributing to APF a more sensible conception of causation. Section IV assesses the current state of the evidence for APF's case and outlines a path for future research. Section V addresses some lingering objections and suggests some problems for further reflection, while Section VI provides a brief conclusion.

I. THE HARM HYPOTHESIS

Let's begin with the vexing term 'pornography'. Some antiporn feminists construe the term so broadly as to encompass all forms and genres. This position has been justly criticized for ignoring the often liberatory power dynamics that characterize much gay and lesbian pornography, S/M (sadomasochistic) pornography, and pornography made by and for women. To account for such differences, a sensible APF restricts itself to *inegalitarian pornography*: sexually explicit representations that as a whole eroticize relations (acts, scenarios, or postures) characterized by gender inequity.[2] Although this category overlaps significantly with violent pornography, the two are not coextensive, since some pornography eroticizes sexual relations that are violent but not inegalitarian, while other pornography is deeply degrading to women but not at all violent.

Antiporn feminism connects inegalitarian pornography (hereafter simply "pornography") to harm in several ways. First, it distinguishes the harms occurring in the production of pornography (e.g., the various kinds of coercion, brutality, rape, and other exploitation sometimes inflicted upon women in making porn) from those that occur post-production. Second, among postproduction harms, some antiporn feminists distinguish the charge that pornographic materials themselves constitute harm, in the manner of hate speech,[3] from the claim that exposure to such representations causes harm. This article focuses on this last kind of harm, which is always indirect, that is, it is always mediated through a second party, namely, the consumer of pornography. The basic idea is that pornography shapes the attitudes and conduct of its audience in ways that are injurious to women. I shall refer to this as the "harm hypothesis."

The best argument for the harm hypothesis can be summed up in just a few steps as follows: [4]

i) Our society is marked by gender inequality in which women (and girls, although I shall say only "women" for ease of exposition) suffer many disadvantages as compared with men (and boys). This inequality is evident in both individuals' attitudes and conduct and in institutional practices.[5]

ii) This is a grave injustice.

iii) Whether or not it is natural, the subordination of women is not inevitable but rather is sustained and reproduced by a nexus of social factors that range from the explicit (as in the denial of rights and privileges and other overt discrimination) to the very subtle. An important example of these more subtle means of subordination are the many ways in which children are socialized from an early age to "appropriate" gender roles, according to which boys should be masculine (i.e., self-confident, independent, courageous, physically strong, assertive, and dominant) and girls should be feminine (i.e., demure, passive, submissive, delicate, and self-sacrificing). The modi operandi of this socialization include religion, the household division of labor, and the influence of various representational forms such as advertisements, television, movies, popular music and music videos, fashion magazines, and high art, all of which often promote masculinity and femininity as ideals for men and women, respectively. Violence and force (as well as the threat of violence and force) also play a significant active role in maintaining gender norms and the subordination of women; that is, sexual assault enforces gender inequality and is not merely a symptom of it.[6]

iv) Aspects of gender inequality have erotic appeal for many people. This can be seen, for example, in the way that gender stereotypes, such as dominance and strength for men and softness and submissiveness for women, standardly serve as markers of sexiness. At the extreme end of the spectrum of gender inequality, nonconsensual violence against women is sexually stimulating for many.

v) Like gender inequality itself, the erotic appeal of unequal relations between the sexes is not inevitable, regardless of whether it is natural. Rather, this particular form of sexual desire is fostered by various kinds of representations, from fashion magazines to high art.

vi) Eroticizing gender inequality—its mechanisms, norms, myths, and trappings—is a particularly effective mechanism for promoting and sustaining it.[7] Its efficacy stems from several factors: (a) Transforming gender inequality into a source of sexual gratification renders this inequality not just tolerable and easier to accept but also desirable and highly enjoyable. (b) This pleasure to which gender subordination is linked is one in which nearly all humans are intensely invested, thereby strengthening gender inequality's significance and broadening its appeal. (c) This eroticization makes gender inequality appealing to men and women alike. Insofar as women want to be attractive to men, they internalize the subordinating norms of attractiveness and thereby collaborate in their own oppression.[8] (d) Finally, sexualizing gender inequality enlists our physical appetites and sexual desires in favor of sexism. Since these are rarely, if ever, amenable to control via rational scrutiny, harnessing our appetites and desires to gender inequality is an effective way of psychologically embedding it.

vii) Pornography eroticizes the mechanisms, norms, myths, and trappings of gender inequality. Its fusing of pleasure with subordination has two components: (a) it does so in terms of its representational content by depicting women deriving sexual pleasure from a range of inegalitarian relations and situations, from being the passive objects of conquest to scenarios of humiliation, degradation, and sexual abuse; (b) inegalitarian pornography presents these representations of subordination in a manner aimed to sexually arouse.

The argument concludes that, by harnessing representations of women's subordination to a ubiquitous and weighty pleasure, pornography is especially effective at getting its audience to internalize its inegalitarian views. . . . Antiporn feminists hold that pornography perverts the emotional life of its audience by soliciting very strong positive feelings for situations characterized by gender inequality and in so doing plays a role in sustaining and reproducing a system of pervasive injustice.

It should be noted that this argument pertains to pornography's adverse consequences for women and that this starkly distinguishes it from the arguments of those who disapprove of pornography because it offends religious beliefs or social mores. The peculiarly feminist objection is not that pornography is sinful, obscene, impolite, lewd, shameful, or disgusting but instead that pornography causes women harm in the sense that it impairs or thwarts their capacity to pursue their interests. Before we can see just which interests inegalitarian pornography purportedly thwarts and how, I need to deflect some worries about the argument.

1. First, it is important to note that the problem with inegalitarian pornography is not simply that it depicts women being degraded and subordinated; rather, the problem is that inegalitarian pornography endorses and recommends women's subordination and degradation. This point is frequently misunderstood by critics of APF,[9] at least in part because some antiporn feminists themselves confuse mere representation with advocacy. But this is a mistake: a depiction of subordination or degradation is not by itself an endorsement of that subordination or degradation.

The pornographic endorsement of gender inequity has three essential ingredients, the first two of which pertain to representational content: (*a*) strong indications that subordinating, degrading, or objectifying acts are pleasurable both for the perpetrators and the women who are the objects of those acts and (*b*) the suggestion that such treatment is acceptable and even merited. But there is more to pornography's endorsement: (*c*) inegalitarian pornography also eroticizes this degrading and objectifying picture of women. By employing conventional signs and codes of erotic representation, for example, sexual explicitness conjoined with particular postures, scenarios, outfits, or music and sound (obviously not all apply to each medium), pornography aims to kindle carnal appetites and arouse sexual desire. In sum, pornography endorses by representing women enjoying, benefiting from, and deserving acts that are objectifying, degrading, or even physically injurious and rendering these things libidinally appealing on a visceral level. And, as any advertiser will tell you, making something sexy is among the most effective means of endorsement.

2. The argument is sensitive to the wide range of degrees of gender inequity that pornography eroticizes: whereas some nonviolent representations show women sexually stimulated by their own weakness, passivity, and domination by men, violent pornography represents women deriving sexual pleasure from

rape. A sensible APF does not assume, for instance, that all inegalitarian pornography leads to rape.

3. The argument does not hold that pornography is the only thing that promotes and sustains gender inequality but rather that it is exceptionally effective in this regard. Although other forms of representation are harmful to women—for instance, advertisements, movies, television, and music videos also promote deleterious stereotypes about women—pornography is thought to be especially harmful because it couches strongly inegalitarian messages in an intensely eroticizing format. This is important to note because, as discussed in Section III below, it means that although eliminating all inegalitarian pornography would be an important step toward gender equity, this would not eradicate gender inequality altogether.

4. The harm hypothesis need not appear within a social constructivist framework. It is true that most antiporn feminists hold that gender attributes and relations, as well as their erotic appeal, are not "natural," in the sense of biologically rooted, but are shaped by historical events, social forces, and ideology. However, the argument can remain agnostic about whether gender inequality and its erotic appeal are in some sense natural; it need only acknowledge that they are not inevitable.[10] In this way, the argument is amenable to both social constructivists and those, like Mill, who attribute gender inequality at least partially to males' superior physical strength.[11] The latter need not assume that our biological potentialities ordain the current state of affairs, since we compensate for all kinds of deficiencies by stimulating and nurturing some potentialities while hindering others. Further, it does not follow from the fact that something is biologically rooted that it is for that reason justified. Mill, for instance, insisted that biologically rooted inequality between the sexes does not justify an unequal social organization. For the purposes of our argument against pornography, one need only accept that gender inequality is unjust and that it can be reinforced, nurtured, and exacerbated through its eroticization; one need not accept the more radical claim that gender inequality is entirely socially constructed.

5. A related noteworthy aspect of this argument and a frequently overlooked feature of APF is that one need not understand pornography's role in promoting and sustaining gender inequality in active

terms. Sexualizing gender hierarchy can also reinforce or exacerbate already existing conditions of inequality, undermine prohibitions or other strictures against discriminatory behavior, and predispose an audience to internalize the psychology of gender inequality. According to the argument presented here, pornography need not actively solicit rape, for example, in order to be a significant force in promoting and sustaining gender inequality.

II. A TAXONOMY OF HARMS

Without further specification, the harm hypothesis remains futilely vague. To begin with, the alleged cause ranges from something as indefinite as prolonged exposure to pornography to something as specific as a single encounter with a particular representation. And the indirect postproduction harms are a motley assortment of adverse effects that differ significantly in their character, severity, and even kind of victim. When discussing pornography's purportedly harmful consequences, antiporn feminists have typically ignored such distinctions and treated the harms en masse, but this undermines the plausibility of the harm hypothesis and leads to confusions regarding what would count as evidence for it. I begin to resolve these problems by disentangling several levels of cause and effect operative in the harm hypothesis and delineating the many variables found at each level. This will not only refine the harm hypothesis and lend precision to feminism's case against pornography but also clarify our understanding of the remedies for its purported harms. Sharply defining these purported harms reveals that very few would be candidates for state intervention of any sort, thereby prying the harm hypothesis away from its association with censorship. As noted earlier, the harm hypothesis is concerned with the third-party harms that pornography purportedly causes. This little-noted yet conspicuous fact means that there are actually two stages of cause and effect. In the first stage, exposure to pornography (what I call the "stage 1 cause") has some impact on its consumers (the "stage 1 effect"), and, in the second

stage, this prompts the consumers to act (the "stage 2 cause") in a manner injurious to another party (the "stage 2 effect"). Below I map out the variables at each stage in order to lay bare the wide range of harms that pornography is alleged to cause (see fig. 1).

A. Stage 1 Causes

Exposure to pornography is of two sorts: a specifiable and limited number of discrete encounters with particular pornographic representations, which I call *singular* causes, and processes of wider temporal duration, such as prolonged exposure to a variety of pornographic representations, which I call *diffuse* causes. Several variables apply to each sort of encounter. First, one must consider the "strength" of the pornography, or the degree to which it is inegalitarian. Second, one must consider the duration of each encounter and, with respect to singular stage 1 causes, the total number of encounters. In the case of diffuse causes, one must also consider the frequency of encounters and the total period of pornography use. Finally, it is important to distinguish cases where pornography use is relatively localized in a population from those where it is widespread (the significance of this distinction will become clear when we turn to stage 2 effects).

Putting these stage 1 causal variables together begins to reveal the complexities involved in specifying the first term of the harm hypothesis. If pornography has an effect on its consumers, it will likely take the form of a dose-response relationship, where an increase in the level, intensity, duration, or total level of exposure to the cause increases the risk of an effect. Consider an analogy with smoking. When predicting a person's health, it is important to know not simply whether she is a regular smoker, as opposed to only having tried cigarettes a few times, but also how often she smokes, whether she smokes the entire cigarette, what strength of cigarette she prefers, and how long she has been a smoker. Whereas certain combinations of these variables will significantly raise a person's chances of getting cancer, others will not. We should think of pornography along the same lines: whereas one person might have occasionally encountered mildly inegalitarian pornography at some point in his life, another might have been a regular consumer of the most violent and inegalitarian pornography for years. Antiporn feminists and their critics have both overlooked the dose-response relationship, commonly speaking of exposure to pornography as if it were an all-or-nothing phenomenon. This fails to capture the subtlety of human interaction with representations and leads to extreme and implausible formulations of the harm hypothesis. A

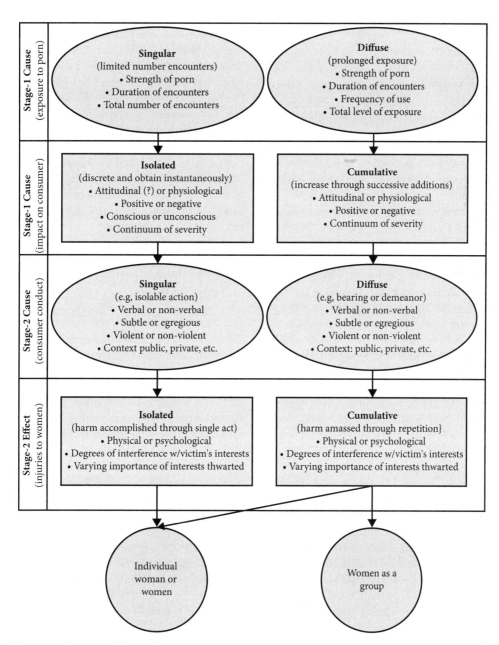

FIG. 1   Summary of purported harms

sensible APF begins by recognizing the many variables at play in the stage 1 causes.

B. Stage 1 Effects

Stage 1 effects (on consumers of pornography) also admit of many distinctions. *Singular* stage 1 causes, namely, particular encounters with individual works, yield isolated effects that are disconnected from other effects and obtain in an instant rather than amassing cumulatively. Most physiological responses to pornography are examples of such isolated effects (although, as we shall see below, there is dispute about whether discrete and limited encounters with pornography can yield isolated attitudinal effects). *Cumulative* effects which result from diffuse stage-1 causes, by contrast, increase gradually through successive encounters such that not any one encounter with pornography suffices to produce them. To return to our smoking analogy, ill effects like emphysema, heart disease, and lung cancer do not result from smoking just one or two cigarettes but instead are the aggregative result of long-term smoking. (The disanalogy here is that smoking is cumulatively harmful for the person who smokes, whereas pornography is purportedly harmful to a third party. Although this disanalogy is irrelevant to the isolated/cumulative distinction, it will become important in the last section of this article.)

Cutting across the distinction between isolated and cumulative stage 1 effects are a range of variables pertaining to the quality of these purported effects on consumers of pornography. First, we can distinguish *physiological* effects, such as training sexual responses to inegalitarian representations, from *attitudinal* effects. The latter can be well defined, as in conscious and explicit beliefs about women's inferiority, or diffuse, such as inclinations toward sexual situations where women are subordinate. Attitudes can be further divided into conscious and unconscious and positive and negative (e.g., positive attitudes toward rape as opposed to the breakdown of inhibitions against rape, as mentioned in the paragraph numbered 5 above).[12] Finally, stage 1 effects lie on a continuum of severity from mildly sexist attitudes to violent conduct.

C. Stage 2 Causes

A stage 2 cause is the outward public manifestation of a stage 1 effect that can be perceived by, and so affect, another. It is, in a word, conduct.

As one might expect, pornography's purported stage 2 causes reflect the diversity and complexity of the alleged stage 1 effects. First, as with stage 1 causes, they can be *singular*, as in an isolable action or series of actions, or *diffuse*, as with a general demeanor or bearing. Second, they vary tremendously in character: they can be verbal or nonverbal, violent or nonviolent, subtle or egregious. Third, they can appear in a variety of public and private contexts: from the family to the workplace, from sexual relations to a court of law. This broad spectrum of conduct ranges from something like a habit of openly glancing at women's bodies in professional contexts, to an unconscious disposition to be lenient with rapists on trial,[13] to an inability to distinguish coerced from consensual sex.

D. Stage 2 Effects

Finally we come to pornography's alleged injuries. As we have seen, antiporn feminists charge that pornography harms women by indirectly impairing or thwarting their interests. As one might expect, given the diversity and complexity in the chain of causes and effects seen thus far, these purportedly harmful effects vary significantly. First, the harms can result from particular acts or from dissipated activities without exact limits that do not lend themselves to precise measurement and definition; that is, in terms used earlier, the stage 2 effect can be *isolated* or *cumulative*. Second, the harms can be physical or psychological or both. Third, there are degrees of interference with women's interests, from mild interference to complete impairment. Finally, the interests that pornography purportedly thwarts vary in importance. Sexism is not an all-or-none phenomenon but rather exists on a continuum of severity. Sexual assault is an example of a severe injury that is accomplished through a single, isolable act. Constantly being treated as a sex object is considerably less severe cumulative harm: a few isolated instances rarely do lasting damage but regular un-invited sexual attention, however subtle, restricts a woman's participation in public life.[14]

Cutting across the variables just mentioned is a distinction between two kinds of injured party: individual women and women as a group. *Individual harms* occur when a particular person's interests are thwarted or set back. *Group harms*, by contrast, are not merely the aggregate of harms to individual women but instead result from diminishing the status of the group as a whole. The status of women is diminished when simply being a woman is sufficient to make one a potential target for harm—from underestimation of one's intellect to sexual assault. Although few feminists make this distinction explicitly, many attribute both individual and group harms to pornography. It is important to note that if group harms obtain, it is almost certainly only if pornography use is widespread in a society.[15]

E. Why a Taxonomy of Harms Matters

Pornography's allegedly harmful effect—gender inequality—has a broad range of manifestations and severities. Distinguishing between these is essential for a careful, nuanced, and verifiable formulation of the harm hypothesis in the following ways.

First, it helps us to assess APF's plausibility. Since, as we have seen, the variables of the harm hypothesis are manifold and complex, one should not assume that each kind of cause yields each kind of effect. Certain causal claims—for example, that one man's isolated encounter with a single piece of pornography could by itself lead to rape or to the diminished status of women as a whole—are so unlikely as to seem preposterous, and yet it is for such unreasonable connections that APF is routinely criticized. To avoid such misunderstandings, a sensible APF should clearly delineate the various purported causes and effects so as to correlate them correctly.

A second reason to stress these distinctions between kinds of harms is that they greatly affect the nature of APF's proposed remedies. There are at least four options for preventing and redressing pornography's purported harms: (*a*) criminalization, (*b*) civil action, (*c*) restrictions and other forms of state regulation, or (*d*) moral condemnation. Whereas the first three are matters of state regulation, the last has no necessary legal implications. If pornography is found to be on balance harmful in the ways that antiporn feminists allege, then it merits moral condemnation and perhaps even its public expression. On this point all antiporn feminists should agree. The question is whether pornography's harms license anything more, and the answer depends entirely on just which sorts of harms pornography causes. If pornography's harms are limited to things such as men's underestimation of women's intellects, then, although we should condemn this as genuine harm, our condemnation would not license state intervention of any sort. Many things that are harmful and wrong have no policy implications, for example, bigotry, selfishness, lying, needlessly hurting others' feelings, adultery, and name-calling. It is, then, a mistake to assume—as so many do—that feminist opponents of pornography necessarily support legal remedies, much less censorship. . . .

III. ASSESSING THE CAUSAL MODEL

The harm hypothesis lies at the center of the pornography debate. Given the elaborate empirical efforts on both sides to prove or disprove it, it is surprising that the term 'cause' and other causal language are left almost completely unspecified. Antiporn feminists (with one notable exception) do not define it, although causal vocabulary abounds in their indictment of pornography.[16] Likewise, their critics typically do not specify what they mean in denying a causal connection between pornography and harm. Both camps treat the term 'cause' as if it were self-evident and free from ambiguity. This is a mistake since ignoring the complexities of causal terminology leads the disputants to talk past one another on this key issue of whether pornography causes harm.

What are these complexities of causal terminology? Even before we subject the concept to philosophical scrutiny, our ordinary use of causal concepts appears to reveal several importantly different senses of the term. We say, for example, that kindling a flame under a pot of water will cause the contents to boil. If the water is reasonably pure and the altitude is close to sea level, then raising the temperature to 100°C will cause water to boil in every instance, and there is no other way to make water boil—at least in these circumstances. In philosophical parlance, we might say that raising water's temperature to 100°C is both necessary and sufficient to make it boil. To take another example, *Mycobacterium* is the cause of tuberculosis, yet although it is necessary for the disease, it is not sufficient, since some people carry the bacterium but remain entirely asymptomatic. Finally, everyone accepts that regular cigarette smoking causes lung cancer, among other things. Yet even in cases of extreme smoking, lung cancer affects only a small fraction while the disease regularly strikes in the absence of any smoking at all. Smoking is neither necessary nor sufficient for contracting the disease, yet there is nevertheless widespread agreement among both experts and lay people that smoking causes cancer.

The fact that our everyday conception of causation at least appears to comprise such different senses, coupled with the fact that antiporn feminists do not say just what they mean by 'cause', should give us pause with respect to the pornography debate. Just what do antiporn feminists mean when they assert that pornography causes harm, and what do proporn feminists and others mean in rejecting this proposition? I shall argue that whereas antiporn feminists mean one thing by 'cause' when they claim that pornography causes harm to women, their critics saddle them with a quite different and less tenable conception of causation. This confusion, which has gone unnoticed in the literature, leads the disputants to talk past one another, and this obscures the true stakes of the debate. To help resolve this confusion, I propose a philosophically sensible and scientifically respectable conception of causation to which a cautious APF should adhere.

With the general shape of the problem in mind, let us turn to the standard criticism of the harm hypothesis, which has two related prongs. First, critics charge that the harm hypothesis is overly deterministic; second, they claim that the harm hypothesis contradicts the evidence. By examining each in turn, I show that both criticisms implicitly attribute to APF the wrong model of causation.

A. Determinism?

First, it is common to criticize APF for claiming that pornography causally determines its audience to think and act in ways that are harmful to women.[17] This sentiment is captured by Deborah Cameron and Elizabeth Frazer who, in an influential and often-cited article, liken APF's characterization of the causal relationship between pornography and its audience to the interaction between billiard balls.[18] The idea is basically this: just as the cue ball strikes the eight ball and propels it on a trajectory from point x to point y that is fixed by strict mechanical laws, so pornography makes its consumers think, feel, or act in fixed ways that obtain in every context. Cameron and Frazer are understandably critical of such a picture of pornography: after all, "humans are not like billiard balls."[19] Although they are right to find the deterministic model inappropriate for explaining human action, they are wrong to assume that this is the model underlying the harm hypothesis.

Now, antiporn feminists do sometimes characterize the causal relationship between pornography and harm in a deterministic manner, and to that extent they merit the criticisms of Cameron and Frazer and others.[20] But there are key places where an altogether different picture is suggested. For instance, when she directly addresses the issue of causation in a footnote, MacKinnon hints at an altogether different conception of the causal relation: "Positivistic causality—linear, exclusive, unidirectional—has become the implicit standard for the validity of connection between pornography and harm. This standard requires the kind of control that can be achieved only, if at all, in laboratory settings. . . . In real-world settings, a relation of linear consequentiality between pornography and harm is seldom sufficiently isolable or uncontaminated. . . . I am suggesting that the positivistic model of causation may be inappropriate to the social reality of pornography."[21]

I suggest that what MacKinnon means by "positivistic linear causality" is a deterministic conception of causation where x is a *deterministic cause* of y if and only if (i) x is temporally prior to y and (ii) the occurrence of x is sufficient for the occurrence of y. Because MacKinnon finds a deterministic view inadequate to the task of describing social life, she calls for a "more complex causality,"[22] although she does not explain what this means. But there is a readily available conception of causality that provides an appropriate framework for the harm hypothesis, circumvents problems raised by the critics, and is scientifically respectable, namely, probabilistic causality.

Debates about the correct way to capture the notion of probabilistic causation need not concern us here.[23] The heart of the view is this: x is a cause of y if and only if (i) x occurs earlier than y and (ii) the probability of the occurrence of y is greater, given the occurrence of x, than the probability of the occurrence of y given not-x. That is, x bears positive statistical relevance to y in the sense that the occurrence of x makes the occurrence of y more likely. An important feature of this conception of causation is that it admits of degrees: causes can be more or less effective, and one measures the effectiveness of a cause by how much it raises the probability of the effects.

Probabilistic causation is a defensible, practical, and common conception of cause that any sensible APF should adopt. It's not only the conception of causation accepted and employed in all areas of science,[24] but it also fits our ordinary uses of the term 'cause': when we say, for example, that smoking causes cancer, we mean that the first phenomenon significantly raises the chances of the other. The fact that smoking does not guarantee cancer and other diseases does not undermine a causal connection between smoking and ill health effects.

Just as we conceive of smoking's harms in probabilistic terms, so the hypothesis that pornography causes harm holds that men's exposure to pornography significantly increases the risk of a variety of harms to women. As with smoking, since pornography's alleged harms are multiple and complex,

as discussed in Section II above, the risk of various injuries may differ; for instance, the risk of cumulative harms to women as a group may be greater than the risk of isolated harms to individuals. Section IV briefly considers how such determinations are made.

B. Evidence

The second and related prong of the standard criticism of the harm hypothesis is that it contradicts the evidence. This evidence comes from studies that (*a*) compare countries (or regions of countries) with strict controls on pornography to those with relaxed controls in terms of differentials in sex crime rates or gender equality or (*b*) compare differentials in sex crime rates within a single country whose regulations on pornography have changed. These comparative studies yield two types of result.

The first reveals that certain societies with high levels of pornography have low levels of sex crimes. For instance, a commonly cited set of studies on Denmark reveals a drop in sex crime rates after the repeal of its pornography law in 1969.[25] Another study that is frequently cited by critics of APF reveals a low incidence of reported rape in Japan as compared with that in the United States,[26] although violent pornography (the sort sexualizing rape and other violence against women) circulates more openly and widely in Japan than in the United States.[27] "If pornography increases misogyny—and indirectly rape," Richard Posner asks, "why is the incidence of rape so low in Japan?"[28]

The second kind of study shows that societies in which there are relatively low levels of pornography suffer from high levels of sexual assault or gender inequality. Some studies reveal that Singapore, which has very tight controls on pornography, experienced a greater increase in rape rates between 1964 and 1974 than did Stockholm, which has very liberal laws on pornography.[29] Several critics cite studies by Larry Baron showing that in the southern United States, circulation of pornography is at its lowest in the country despite the highest levels of social, political, and economic inequality between women and men.[30] Further, Baron finds a positive correlation between high pornography sales and high gender equality, and he suggests that both are due to political tolerance.

These potentially revealing studies are riddled with problems that appear to go unnoticed. First, the Danish study ignored changes in the legal definitions of sex crimes, so that, although the total number of lesser sex crimes dropped after the repeal of the pornography law in the Danish case, rape rates actually rose.[31] Second, some of these studies assume that legal restrictions on pornography correlate with the actual circulation of pornography. However, as Strossen herself points out, the censorship of pornography often increases its desirability and circulation on the black market. There are, after all, tight controls on pornography in Japan, and yet, as Abramson and Hayashi point out, violent pornography abounds.[32] Third, most of these studies rely on statistics of reported rather than actual rapes. This is especially problematic in the case of sex crimes like rape that are notoriously underreported. The Japan study is a case in point. There is a strong incentive for Japanese women to remain silent about sexual harassment, domestic abuse, and rape because those who fight back suffer strong retribution. This is evident in the first Japanese sexual harassment case in Fukuoka in 1989, where, although the victim eventually won, she had to conceal her identity because of so many threats of violence against her and her family. The fact that rape is even more grossly underreported in Japan than in the United States casts doubt on Abramson and Hayashi's widely cited study.

The most significant problem with these studies is that they risk what is often called the *ecologic fallacy*: ascribing characteristics to members of a group that they may not in fact possess as individuals.[33] The studies offer only statistics for the circulation of pornography in each country and the incidence of sex crimes for each country or the overall rating of gender equality for each region, thereby providing data only for groups and taking no account of variability among individuals in those regions with respect to pornography consumption. It is possible, given what is known about the Singapore case, for instance, that the few men who buy pornography are also the very same men who commit all or most of the rapes in the

country, a fact that (*a*) would be compatible with a decrease in overall rapes and a decrease in porn sales and (*b*) prima facie supports the feminist antiporn case. In order to tell whether these studies disprove an association between pornography and sex crimes, we also need exposure and outcome data for the individuals in the regions studied, something that APF's critics have not provided.

But let us imagine that the data for individuals corresponded to that for groups and that all other problems with these studies could be set right. What objections to the harm hypothesis do data of this sort raise? First, such studies show that gender inequality and violent sex crimes can result from other factors, such as the influence of professional sports, religion, television, or popular music. As Strossen puts it, pornography does not have "a corner on the sexism and violence market."[34] In other words, the studies of societies that impose tight restrictions on the circulation of pornography (assuming this in fact correlates with low circulation of pornography) yet suffer high levels of gender-based violence or gender inequality show that pornography is not necessary for sexual violence and gender inequality. Therefore it is, in the words of one critic, "absurd" to frame pornography as a cause and to conclude that restricting it in any way would prevent various harms to women.[35] Second, exposure to pornography does not, as Laura Kipnis puts it, "cause 100% guaranteed harm."[36] Pornography does not drive one to sexist behavior or to adopt sexist attitudes; plenty of people use pornography without any obvious ill effects. As indicated by the cases where pornography flourishes but levels of sex crimes are relatively low, pornography is not sufficient for sexual assault and other injuries. The third and final objection presented by these studies is that pornography's effects on its users are highly context dependent. If pornography is positively correlated with harms at all, the correlation is far from exceptionless. The critics of APF conclude that these studies "conclusively refute" the harm hypothesis.[37]

The first thing to note is that most of these studies focus exclusively on one sort of harm, namely, sexual assault, and so they have nothing to say about the many other purported isolated and cumulative harms to both individuals and women as a group. But even with respect to sexual assault, the studies cited above would "conclusively refute" the harm hypothesis only if it maintained that exposure to pornography were necessary or sufficient for rape. But this is not the right way to understand APF's harm hypothesis, which, I urge, is probabilistic in nature. This means that there may well be cases where pornography does not lead to rape or where rape is prevalent but pornography is not. This is not to say, however, that these studies entirely miss the point, for they do challenge a sensible APF to provide a plausible explanation for these and similar cases. Such an explanation should involve not only a detailed exposition of the errors mentioned above but also empirical justification of the harm hypothesis itself. We turn to the latter in the next section.

Another central aspect of a sensible harm hypothesis is that its causal connection holds ceteris paribus. We should expect that a man raised in a society like Denmark that has a high degree of gender equality would be less negatively affected by exposure to pornography than one living in a culture where women have few rights and men are socialized to dominate them. A host of variables that make up what one might call *context* can play a significant role in rape and other sexist conduct. But this does not mean that we should not consider pornography a cause of rape, for many factors can actively raise the probability of rape, each of which deserves to be considered a partial cause. To see what I mean, let us return to the analogy with diseases.

It is a central tenet of epidemiology, the modern study of the etiology of diseases, that the causes of diseases are neither singular nor simple; instead, multiple causes act together in an interdependent web of causal complements.[38] One cannot speak of "the cause" of heart disease, for example, since there are many: hereditary factors; dietary excesses of saturated fat, cholesterol, calories, or salt; obesity; stress; cigarette smoking; and lack of exercise, to name a few. Although none of these factors is necessary for heart disease and rarely is any single factor sufficient, several factors typically work together, often reinforcing each other to form a complex web-like causal mechanism. Imagine a familiar kind of case where smoking and stress cause a person to suffer a heart attack.

The facts that (*a*) the person's smoking did not act alone and (*b*) many nonsmokers suffer heart attacks means neither (*c*) that smoking was not a cause of the heart attack nor (*d*) that smoking is not a cause of heart attacks in general. There was a set of causal conditions, none of which was alone sufficient but each of which was necessary for the heart attack, that taken together were sufficient but not necessary for the heart attack. To say that these causal conditions are interdependent, then, is to say that the effects of the causal agent depend on the prevalence of its causal complements in the population. For instance, the effects of stress depend on the prevalence of smoking, serum cholesterol, and lack of exercise, to name only a few, in the group. Causes are in this way interdependent on other causal factors.

A sensible APF follows this model, conceiving of pornography as one key factor that actively raises the probability of harms rather than the element singly responsible for them. As antiporn feminists like Cass Sunstein and Larry May make clear, it is completely misguided to hold pornography single-handedly responsible for things like rape or gender inequality or to expect that these would disappear were pornography eliminated.[39] Rather, we hypothesize that exposure to pornography is a salient risk factor for a variety of harms.

Seeing pornography as one salient ingredient in a larger causal pie is not only in line with our best science but also fits with current legal practice in the realm of tort law. In an essay that has not received sufficient attention in the pornography debate, Don Adams notes that tort law adheres not to a single-cause model of injury but to a recipe model of causality, where two or more defendants can be held jointly and severally liable for a single injury—a practice referred to as the joint and several liability of concurrent tort-feasors.[40] To illustrate this, Adams offers the following actual case. A company left its parking lots unlit for many weeks, and one night a man was mugged. The man sued the company and won because, the judge reasoned, the company's negligence causally contributed to and so was partially responsible for the attack.[41] The judgment does not at all exculpate the assailant who would also have been held responsible had he been caught. In cases like this, responsibility can be divided among several parties and need not be limited to a singular cause. We should apply the same standards to pornography that reign in other areas of tort law, Adams reasons, making pornography a legitimate potential cause of rape in a legal sense. Just as a dark parking lot does not drive everyone to assault, so pornography does not drive everyone to rape, but in some cases pornography may be a significant ingredient in injurious conduct.

In short, a sensible APF should construe the causal relation between pornography and harm not in terms of necessary or sufficient conditions but rather as (a) probabilistic, (b) holding ceteris paribus, and (c) one salient component of a complex causal mechanism. This means that the purported injuries are not guaranteed to obtain in each instance of exposure to pornography and, further, that they can occur in the absence of such exposure. Although the comparative studies cited by critics of APF do reveal something about the conditions under which pornography does not have detrimental effects, they do not decisively refute, as Strossen and others would have it, the antiporn feminist case when sensibly framed.

IV. DISCOVERING CAUSES

This new formulation of the harm hypothesis may seem vague. If it merely asserts that pornography may sometimes increase the risk of various harms, then what sense does it make to speak of pornography causing harm at all? Further, how do we verify such a hypothesis? That is, how can we tell whether there is a significant risk of any kind of harm associated with exposure to pornography?

As I have been suggesting, the etiology of diseases is no simpler, since diseases are the cumulative effects of numerous factors. Even infectious disease agents do not act alone: two people identically exposed to the same infectious agent can experience different symptoms or no symptoms at all, depending on various agent, host, and environmental factors. Noninfectious diseases like cancer are even

more complicated, since there is no physical factor whose presence is necessary for the disease to occur. Nevertheless, epidemiologists have proven that regular smoking causes cancer. I suggest that feminists would do well to employ the methods of epidemiology in attempting to verify the harm hypothesis.

So how does one discover the causes of a given disease? The investigation begins with clinical observations of individuals, but it cannot stop there. For instance, the simple clinical observation that most lung cancer patients were regular smokers did not count as evidence that smoking causes cancer because the number of cases of the illness were not related to the population at risk. Given merely clinical data, it is possible (a) that there is no special association between smoking and cancer,[42] (b) that the causal connection goes the other direction (perhaps lung cancer creates a craving for cigarettes), or (c) that both lung cancer and cigarette smoking are collateral effects of a common cause. Mere correlation does not imply causation, even of the probabilistic sort.

This is important for the matter at hand because antiporn feminists have relied too heavily on data of the clinical sort to support the harm hypothesis. Testimony from both victims and perpetrators of sexual assault is regularly offered as evidence of pornography's harms in courts of law (esp. the MacKinnon-Dworkin hearings), governmental inquiries on the impact of pornography (the President's Commission on Obscenity and Pornography [1970], and the Meese Commission [1986]), as well as a variety of antipornography studies by both men and women.[43] These very upsetting accounts repeatedly reveal that sex crimes of various sorts are preceded or accompanied by use of pornography.

The sheer number of such accounts, combined with the intimate connection between pornography's representational content (i.e., what is represented in pornographic works) and the nature of the criminal acts in question, warrants suspicion about pornography's role in such crimes. But anecdotal evidence alone does not establish a meaningful positive association, much less a causal connection. The problem is not the anecdotal nature of the presumed evidence but rather that these accounts are not related to the population at risk. It may be that a large percentage of rapists also masturbate, but this would only be meaningful if we knew something about the habits of nonrapists. In order for the anecdotal evidence to be meaningful, we need to know the following: How many regular consumers of pornography never commit a sex crime of any sort? And how many sex offenders never use pornography? Although feminists are rightly alarmed by the many accounts of pornography's connection with sex crimes—particularly since it is often used as a tool in the crimes—it is a mistake to take this as conclusive, or even strong, evidence for the harm hypothesis. Instead, feminists should take the anecdotal evidence as a springboard for pursuing a meaningful positive association and, ultimately, a causal connection. How should we proceed?

In order to verify associations suggested by clinical data, epidemiologists move to the macro level to compare disease rates among very large groups with differing levels of exposure to the suspected cause. In ecologic studies, large populations are compared in terms of the incidence of exposure to a suspected cause and the incidence and prevalence of a disease. In proving a causal connection between smoking and lung cancer, for instance, many studies compared the United States, Norway, Poland, Israel, France, and Japan to find that, as smoking increases, lung cancer also increases. This was a crucial step in demonstrating a positive association between smoking and the disease.

Antiporn feminists have begun to compare the incidence and prevalence of exposure to pornography and of sex crimes in different populations. For example, Court provides evidence that variations in the availability of pornography correspond positively with changes in reported occurrences of rape; in particular, rape reports increase in places where pornography also increases.[44] Scott and Schwalm found a strong correlation between incidences of rape per capita and sales of magazines like *Playboy* and *Penthouse*.[45] This corroborated Baron and Straus's earlier findings that showed a positive correlation between rape rates and the circulation of sex magazines in regions in the United States.[46] Although these studies are suggestive, they are plagued by many of the same problems that undermine the ecologic studies proffered by APF's critics; for example, they assume that restrictions on pornography and reported rapes

correspond to the actual amount of pornography circulating and the actual number of rapes. More important, there have not been enough careful and thorough ecologic studies to conclusively support a strong positive association between pornography and sex crimes, nor have there been, to my knowledge, any empirical investigations of pornography's other more subtle purported harms. In order for the harm hypothesis to become more than a hypothesis, we need more careful ecologic studies.

If antiporn feminists could produce a coherent body of studies demonstrating a positive association between pornography and harm, this still would not by itself establish causation, since, as noted earlier, ecologic studies only provide data for groups and do not give exposure/effect data for individuals of a population. In the case of smoking research, for instance, ecologic studies do not tell us whether those who developed lung cancer are the same individuals who smoked. In order to establish a positive association, one also needs exposure and outcome data for individuals in the population. Since such data are typically missing from large-scale comparisons of populations, epidemiologists turn to studies of individual characteristics, such as case control and cohort studies. Sticking with our smoking example, a case control study compares the smoking histories of a group of lung cancer patients with the smoking histories of a group of patients without lung cancer. A cohort study compares smokers and nonsmokers and determines the rate of lung cancer in each group. Finally, when possible, one will perform clinical trials or community trials, although such experiments are usually only permissible when the suspected causal agents are neutral or beneficial.

Antiporn feminists and other critics of pornography have produced some studies of the case control and cohort sort, although the studies are problematic and the results inconclusive.[47] The bulk of evidence concerning individuals takes the form of clinical trials of various sorts that aim to test the impact of exposure to pornography.[48] These can be divided into (*a*) experiments that show how exposure to pornography can facilitate the formation and reinforcement of dimensions of sexist psychology (perceptions of and attitudes toward women) in both sexual and nonsexual contexts,[49] and (*b*) those that draw some connection between exposure to pornography and sexist conduct of various sorts.[50]

These experimental data are riddled with problems, some of which have been noticed by critics.[51] First, many of the studies concerned with pornography's potential to incite unwanted sexual violence measure its impact on audiences (stage 1 effects) but tell us nothing about how this translates into actual harms (stage 2 effects). If pornography has a tendency to make coercive sex attractive to its audience, as some studies show, this will not necessarily translate into conduct, since the effect might be counterbalanced or outweighed by the consumer's other attitudes and commitments, thereby inhibiting the expression of any such desire. Second, the studies that do attempt to measure pornography's effect on actual conduct must, for ethical reasons, be satisfied with things like willingness to administer electric shocks as substitutes for actual aggressive behavior, and it is dubious that such artificial conditions reveal anything about real-world conduct.[52] Third, the clinical trials are almost always performed on a small select group of people—namely, male college students—that is not randomized and so does not allow for extrapolation to the general population. Fourth, the clinical trials are also limited from a feminist perspective since (*a*) nearly all focus on sexual violence and do not attend to pornography's many other purported harms and (*b*) the experiments are restricted temporally and so cannot capture the effects of long-term exposure to pornography. Although smoking two packs of cigarettes in an afternoon might make me sick to my stomach, it won't give me lung cancer—and if it did, the disease wouldn't manifest itself for years. Likewise, we oughtn't expect short-term exposure to pornography to produce every sort of harmful effect, particularly those amassed cumulatively. If antiporn feminists like Larry May are right that pornography's effects are preponderantly cumulative, then the clinical trials are entirely misguided. For these reasons, a sensible APF would do better to focus on studies of the case control and cohort sort when attempting to produce data about individuals in the population supposedly at risk.

Finally, like most feminist research in this area, the clinical trials do not distinguish among kinds of pornography. We cannot tell from these data whether all forms of erotic material—and here we might include erotically explicit artworks—lead to sexist psychology and conduct or whether these harms result from a particular subset of erotic representation. I have urged that the best feminist argument against pornography focuses on the harms that arise due to the eroticization of inegalitarian relations between women and men. If this is right, then attempts to gather evidence for the harm hypothesis should concentrate on specifically inegalitarian pornography while using egalitarian pornography and erotica as controls. This would also have the benefit of prying feminist thought away from the apparent blanket condemnation of all erotic material.

Let us suppose that, through ecologic and case control studies, a meaningful positive correlation between inegalitarian pornography and various harms had been demonstrated. How do we get from this to establishing a causal relation? After all, it could be true that a large percentage of lung cancer patients were smokers and that lots of smokers get lung cancer and that the disease is much rarer among nonsmokers yet also true that (*a*) lung cancer causes the craving for smoking, rather than the converse, or (*b*) both smoking and lung cancer are collateral effects of some more primary cause. In order to determine whether an observed association is causal, epidemiologists standardly appeal to the following criteria:[53]

1. *Temporality*: exposure to the suspected causal factor must precede the onset of disease and the interval between exposure and disease must be considered.
2. *Strength*: strong associations provide firmer evidence of causality than weak ones. Strength of association is measured by relative risk or odds ratio.
3. *Quantal-dose relationship*: an increase in the level, intensity, duration, or total level of exposure to a causal agent leads to a progressive increase in risk of disease.
4. *Consistency*: replication of findings is particularly important.
5. *Plausibility*: the association should be plausible within the current state of knowledge.

6. *Consideration of alternate explanations*: in judging whether an observed association is causal, the extent to which investigators have taken account of alternate explanations is important.

7. *Cessation data*: if a factor is a cause of a disease, the risk of the disease should decline upon reduction or elimination of exposure to the factor.

Although many antiporn feminists are reluctant to admit it, we are far from providing evidence that meets these criteria. It is for this reason that I refer to our position as a hypothesis. At this point we have only a persuasive argument supported by suggestive bits of evidence. But this is not a reason to capitulate to our critics, for their evidence is equally flawed and inconclusive, and when the antiporn feminist position is sensibly framed, their criticisms are considerably less persuasive. It took a very long time and extensive experimentation and research to determine that smoking causes lung cancer and other diseases. Research on the effects of pornography is still in its infant stages, and it is too soon to pronounce on the matter.

V. OBJECTIONS AND PROBLEMS FOR FURTHER REFLECTION

Some lingering challenges to the harm hypothesis . . . cluster around the fact that, even if a strong positive association between pornography and harm could be established, this does not imply causation. This leads to three related difficulties.

First, it is plausible that the direction of causation goes in the other direction. This is most likely a problem in the case of diffuse stage 2 causes, where the putative effects of exposure to pornography include attitudes like the underestimation of women's intellects or the taste for female submissiveness. As mentioned above, the arguments about how pornography influences its users' attitudes and conduct appear to depend on the implicit premise that men will find pornography sexually stimulating in the first place, and this initial appeal is difficult to explain without assuming viewers' predisposition toward sexist perceptions of women. This suggests that, although pornography may cater to sexist attitudes and desires, it is these prior attitudes and desires that explain the production and consumption of pornography, not the converse.

The second objection is that the association between pornography and gender-based harms may not be causal at all, since both could be collateral effects of a common cause. Consider the case of sexual assault. Joel Feinberg argues that pornography does not cause sexual assault but rather that the "cult of macho"—ideals of manliness that centrally involve the domination of women—independently gives rise to both.[54]

Unlike the previous worries, the third objection concedes pornography's role in bringing about particular harms but worries that its role might be merely auxiliary. Perhaps pervasive gender inequality is the true cause of sexual violence against women and pornography is just what Richard Lewontin calls an agency: an alternative path of transmission for some more basic cause.[55] Although it is wrong to say that an agency is completely irrelevant to the harm in question, our efforts would be better spent, so the objection goes, attacking the true cause of the harms in question, whatever that cause may be.

These are substantial difficulties that a sensibly formulated APF can answer. To begin with, we need to acknowledge that, however useful for capturing the

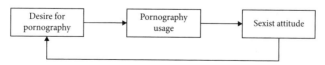

FIG. 2 Feedback effects of pornography for individual users

probabilistic nature of the causal connection, the disease analogy breaks down at some point, because its asymmetrical cause-and-effect picture does not capture the complex reciprocal relationship between pornography and its purported harms. Whereas the causal association between smoking and cancer is unidirectional, a sensible harm hypothesis holds that pornography and many of its harms encourage and reinforce one another in the manner of a positive feedback loop. At the level of an individual consumer, the feedback loop would look something like what is shown in figure 2.

Although some sexist attitudes (e.g., fantasies, desires, or beliefs) are required for pornography to be attractive in the first place, according to the harm hypothesis, regular exposure to pornography reinforces and exacerbates these attitudes and may generate others, thereby inciting the desire for more pornography. The fact that some prior sexist attitudes are required for pornography to initially attract its audience does not mean that pornography plays no causal role in the formation of sexist attitudes. As I have argued, the harm hypothesis holds that pornography is a significant component in a complex causal mechanism. We now must complicate this multifactored causal mechanism with the notion of a positive feedback loop in which the effects of exposure to pornography facilitate and accelerate the desire for more pornography. In some sense, the critics are right that the direction of causation does go the other way.

The second objection charged that pornography does not cause harm but rather that both pornography and its putative harms are collateral effects of some common cause. A sensible APF should remain open to this possibility which is always a concern when attempting to discover the causes of things. It is also just the sort of problem that epidemiological methods recommended here are designed to identify.[56]

VI. CONCLUSION

Does exposure to inegalitarian pornography cause sexist attitudes and behaviors? Does it lead men to underestimate, objectify, or discriminate against women? Does it provoke acts of physical violence or predispose its users to other antisocial behavior?

Such questions lie at the heart of the pornography debate. At first blush philosophical inquiry would seem useless in answering them, for either pornography causes harm or it does not, and nothing short of considerable empirical data can decide the matter. As we have seen, those on either side of the debate marshal evidence from cross-cultural studies, clinical trials, and personal testimony in order to support or deny a causal connection between pornography and harm, yet little attention has been paid to the terms in which the debate is framed. Both camps treat the terms 'pornography', 'cause', and 'harm' as if they were unambiguous, an imprecision that leads the disputants to talk past one another and that infects the arguments and the evidence on both sides: it is often unclear exactly what kind of harm one is trying to prove or deny or what sort of causal connection one is looking to establish or reject. It is here that philosophy can help by clarifying terms, sifting out irrelevant and uncharitable criticisms of positions, and providing the strongest arguments. In the end, however, we feminist philosophers can only go so far in our attempts to persuade others that pornography is, on balance, harmful or not. It is my view that we should welcome these limitations and do our best to offer precise yet nuanced positions to be empirically tested.

This article has tried to do just that by making a case for a sensible version of APF. By way of conclusion, here again are its central tenets. First, we are concerned not with the sweeping category of pornography in general but only with inegalitarian pornography. This allows for the possibility that some forms of pornography may be neutral or even beneficial with respect to gender equality. Second, we hold that the debate has for too long concentrated on pornography's purported connection with sexual assault, a focus that has naturally led to talk of state regulation and made APF appear alarmist and extremist in skeptics' eyes. As a remedy, this article offers a careful and nuanced delineation of pornography's alleged harms, recognizing a wide range of potential injuries that differ in terms of character and severity. Third, and related, we are sensitive to the entire range of pornography's putative harms when proposing means of prevention and redress. A sensible APF is cautious and judicious and not necessarily in favor of state regulation of pornography. Fourth, we understand the claim that pornography causes harm as a hypothesis that has yet to be conclusively proved (or refuted) and that must be tested empirically. This article proposes that APF employ the methods of epidemiology—our current best science of causes—in attempting to verify the harm hypothesis. Fifth, a sensible APF holds that gender inequality is the cumulative effect of multiple factors, of which inegalitarian pornography is just one. This is to say, we adhere to a multicomponent view of causality in which pornography is one factor in a complex causal mechanism. We do not hold pornography solely responsible for gender inequality, nor do we think that elimination of pornography would solve all our problems. Sixth, and related, we also construe the causal relation between pornography and its purported harms probabilistically and as holding ceteris paribus. This is to say, exposure to pornography is neither necessary nor sufficient for its putative injuries but rather raises the chances of harm depending on context. Seventh, and finally, we conceive of pornography's role in sexism on the model of a feedback loop: at the same time that inegalitarian pornography is the result of gender inequality, it also facilitates and accelerates this inequality, and it does so cumulatively.

NOTES

1. Drake Bennett, "What Happened to the Anti-porn Feminists?" *Boston Globe*, March 6, 2005.

2. A few points of clarification. A work that includes a few scenes that eroticize inegalitarian relations but in which these are balanced or outweighed by other kinds of scenes—imagine, e.g., a story of a heterosexual couple who take turns in submissive roles while the partner plays the dominant role—would not count as "inegalitarian pornography." Also, I use "gender inequality" in the standard way to refer to the subordination of women; it does not refer to situations where men are subordinate to women. . . .

3. In earlier works, Catharine MacKinnon suggests not just that exposure to pornography causes harm, but that pornography itself "is a harm" (*Feminism Unmodified: Discourses on Life and Law* [Cambridge, MA: Harvard University Press, 1987], 177) or is "an act of male supremacy" (ibid., 154). . . .

4. My outline has been influenced by Joshua Cohen's reconstruction of Catharine MacKinnon's argument (Joshua Cohen, "Freedom, Equality, and Pornography," in *Justice and Injustice in Law and Legal Theory*, ed. Austin Sarat and Thomas Kearns [Ann Arbor: University of Michigan Press, 1996], 99–137, esp. 103–5), although I depart from Cohen's reconstruction in several significant ways, noted below.

5. For example, women are discriminated against in employment and are on average paid less than men; they typically bear the greater burden of child care and household chores; their reproductive freedom is restricted or constantly under threat of restriction; they are subject to various forms of sexual harassment in the workplace and other public arenas; and they endure, or at the very least are under the constant threat of, rape, battery, and incest both inside and outside the home. These are just some of the ways that women, simply because they are women, occupy a subordinate position in our society.

6. Susan Brownmiller provided the first thorough and eloquent explanation of sexual violence's function as a means to keep women in a state of fear and thereby perpetuate male dominance in *Against Our Will: Men, Women and Rape* (New York: Simon & Schuster, 1975). . . .

7. This idea was first suggested by John Stuart Mill in *The Subjection of Women* (1869; Indianapolis: Hackett, 1988), although most antiporn feminists do not acknowledge this debt. . . .

8. This idea also goes back to Mill who noted that "the object of being attractive to men [has] become the polar star of feminine education and formation of character" (Mill, *The Subjection of Women*, 16). As a "means of holding women in subjection," he points to the representation of "meekness, submissiveness, and resignation of all individual will into the hands of a man, as an essential part of sexual attractiveness" (Mill, *The Subjection of Women*, 16). MacKinnon expresses a similar view when she notes that the sexualization of gender inequality "organizes women's pleasure so as to give us a stake in our own subordination" (MacKinnon, *Feminism Unmodified*, 7). Both are clearly thinking of heterosexual women, although the point also stands for bisexual women as well. . . .

9. For example, Lynne Segal makes this mistake when she writes: "We are, it is true, ubiquitously surrounded by images and discourses which represent women as passive, fetishised objects and men as active, controlling agents. . . . They saturate all scientific and cultural discourses of the last hundred years—from sexology,

embryology and psychoanalysis to literary and visual genres, high and low. . . . Men don't need pornography to encounter these 'facts' of crude and coercive, promiscuous male sexualities, or helpless and yielding, nurturing female sensitivities" (Lynne Segal, "Does Pornography Cause Violence? The Search for Evidence," in Church Gibson and Gibson, *Dirty Looks*, 5–21, 18–19).

10. As Ian Hacking makes clear, what's really at stake in social constructivism is to show that the phenomenon in question (i.e., the thing said to be socially constructed) is not inevitable, i.e., that the phenomenon in question could have been otherwise and so can perhaps be changed (Ian Hacking, *The Social Construction of What?* [Cambridge, MA: Harvard University Press, 1999], esp. 6ff.).

11. Mill, *The Subjection of Women*, 5–6. Although Mill does insist upon the biological roots of sex inequality, he warns that we should not likewise take all current aspects of gender subordination (including the stereotypical traits of femininity and masculinity) to be natural, in the sense of biologically rooted. We cannot know the nature of each sex, he says, because we all were formed under conditions of gender inequality. He writes: "What is now called the nature of women is an eminently artificial thing—the result of forced repression in some directions, unnatural stimulation in others" (Mill, *The Subjection of Women*, 22).

12. For research on pornography's purported disinhibitory effects, see Neil Malamuth, Maggie Heim, and Seymour Feshbach, "Sexual Responsiveness of College Students to Rape Depictions: Inhibitory and Disinhibitory Effects," *Journal of Personality and Social Psychology* 38 (1990): 399–408.

13. Andrew Taslitz has convincingly shown the ways that narratives marked by gender hierarchy shape trial outcomes and, in particular, how they undermine justice for rape victims. He examines representations (from high art, popular culture, and pornography) and argues that these influence how jurors gauge a rape survivor's truthfulness, complicity in the rape, and harm incurred by the rape. See Andrew E. Taslitz, *Rape and the Culture of the Courtroom* (New York: New York University Press, 1999).

14. For an excellent description of the role of sexual objectification in maintaining male dominance, see Sandra Bartky, "On Psychological Oppression," in her *Femininity and Domination: Studies in the Phenomenology of Oppression* (New York: Routledge, 1990), 22–32.

15. This distinction between individual and group harms is not the same as the distinction between isolated and cumulative effects. Although it is highly unlikely, as I say above, it is at least in principle possible that group harms result from widespread singular encounters with pornography. And it is more likely that some individual harms result from cumulative exposure to pornography. . . .

16. The exception is Diana Russell's well-known article, "Pornography and Rape: A Causal Model." We briefly consider her definition of cause below.

17. See, e.g., Judith Butler, *Excitable Speech: A Politics of the Performative* (New York: Routledge, 1997), and "The Force of Fantasy: Feminism, Mapplethorpe, and Discursive Excess," *Differences: A Journal of Feminist Cultural Studies* 2 (1990): 105–25; Edward de Grazia, *Girls Lean Back Everywhere: The Law of Obscenity and the Assault on Genius* (New York: Random House, 1992); Donald Downs, *The New Politics of Pornography* (Chicago: University of Chicago Press, 1989); Laura Kipnis, *Bound and Gagged: Pornography and the Politics of Fantasy in America* (Durham, NC: Duke University Press, 1999); Marcia Pally, *Sex and Sensibility: Reflections on Forbidden Mirrors and the Will to Censor* (Hopewell, NJ: Ecco, 1994); Richard Posner, *Sex and Reason* (Cambridge, MA: Harvard University Press, 1992), and "Obsession" (review of MacKinnon's *Only Words*), *New Republic* 209 (October 1993): 31–36; Segal, "Does Pornography Cause Violence?" 5–21; and Nadine Strossen, *Defending Pornography: Free Speech, Sex and the Fight for Women's Rights* (New York: New York University Press, 2000).

18. Deborah Cameron and Elizabeth Frazer, "On the Question of Pornography and Sexual Violence: Moving beyond Cause and Effect," originally published in Itzin, *Pornography: Women, Violence and Civil Liberties*, 240–53. . . .

19. Ibid., 368. . . .

20. For example, MacKinnon writes: "Sooner or later, in one way or another, the consumers want to live out the pornography further in three dimensions. Sooner or later, in one way or another, they do. *It* makes them want to" (MacKinnon, *Only Words*, 19). It's not just that pornography will inevitably cause its users to want to imitate the demeaning and subordinating acts it represents; some, like Diana Russell, insist that pornography is sufficient for harmful behavior (see Russell, *Pornography and Rape*, 64).

21. Catharine MacKinnon, "Francis Biddle's Sister: Pornography, Civil Rights, and Speech," in MacKinnon, *Feminism Unmodified*, 163–97, 187 n. 115.

22. MacKinnon, "Not a Moral Issue," 156. In the same essay, MacKinnon also mentions "an entirely new theory of social causality" (161).

23. For discussions of this problem, see Judea Pearl, *Causality: Models, Reasoning, and Inference* (Cambridge: Cambridge University Press, 2000); Wesley Salmon, *Causality and Explanation* (Oxford: Oxford University

Press, 1998); and Patrick Suppes, *Probabilistic Metaphysics* (Oxford: Blackwell, 1984).

24. On the prevalence of indeterminate causation in modern physics (particularly quantum mechanics), see G. E. M. Anscombe, "Causality and Determination" (1971) in *Causation*, ed. Ernest Sosa and Michael Tooley (Oxford: Oxford University Press, 1993); Mellor, *The Facts of Causation* (esp. 53ff.); Suppes, *Probabilitistic Metaphysics*; and Wesley Salmon's essay, "Determinism and Indeterminism in Modern Science," in his *Causality and Explanation*, 25–50. For arguments against the use of determinism in the field of genetics and biology, see Richard Lewontin, *The Triple Helix: Gene, Organism, Environment* (Cambridge, MA: Harvard University Press, 2000), and *Biology as Ideology* (New York: Harper Perennial, 1991).

25. Berl Kutchinsky, "Toward an Explanation of the Decrease in Registered Sex Crimes in Copenhagen," in *U.S. Commission on Obscenity and Pornography: Technical Report*, vol. 8 (Washington, DC: U.S. Government Printing Office, 1970), "Pornography and Its Effects in Denmark and the United States: A Rejoinder and Beyond," *Comparative Social Research: An Annual* 8 (1985): 301–30, "Deception and Propaganda," *Society* 24 (1987): 21–24, and "Pornography and Rape: Theory and Practice: Evidence from Crime Data in Four Countries Where Pornography Is Easily Available," *International Journal of Law and Psychiatry* 14 (1990): 40–64.

26. See, e.g., Strossen, *Defending Pornography*, 255–56; Pally, *Sex and Sensibility*, 57–61; and Posner, *Sex and Reason*, 369–70.

27. According to Paul Abramson and Haruo Hayashi, Japan reports a rape rate of 2.4 people per 100,000, as compared with 34.5 per 100,000 in the United States. See Paul Abramson and Haruo Hayashi, "Pornography in Japan: Cross Cultural and Theoretical Considerations," in *Pornography and Sexual Aggression*, ed. Neil Malamuth and Edward Donnerstein (Orlando, FL: Academic Press, 1984), 173–85. This matter is also discussed in Edward Donnerstein, Daniel Linz, and Steven Penrod, *The Question of Pornography: Research Findings and Policy Implications* (London: Collier Macmillan, 1987).

28. Posner, *Sex and Reason*, 370.

29. Donnerstein et al., *The Question of Pornography*.

30. See, e.g., Larry Barron, "Pornography and Gender Equality: An Empirical Analysis," *Journal of Sex Research* 27 (1990): 161–68.

31. See John Court, "Sex and Violence: A Ripple Effect," in Malamuth and Donnerstein, *Pornography and Sexual Aggression*, 143–72, 144ff.

32. Abramson and Hayashi ("Pornography in Japan," 177) note that at the time of their study it was illegal in Japan to show pubic hair and adult genitals in sexually explicit stimuli. Despite these restrictions, pornography, and especially violent pornography, was widely available.

33. For a clear and detailed explanation of the *ecologic fallacy*, see Leon Gordis, *Epidemiology* (Philadelphia: Saunders, 1996), 169ff.

34. Strossen (*Defending Pornography*, 249), Segal ("Does Pornography Cause Violence?"), Pally (*Sex and Sensibility*), and Kipnis (*Bound and Gagged*) level similar criticisms.

35. Kendrick, *The Secret Museum*, 253. Segal similarly asserts that "pornography is not the problem here, nor its elimination the solution" ("Does Pornography Cause Violence?" 16).

36. Kipnis, *Bound and Gagged*, 205.

37. Strossen, *Defending Pornography*, 254. Posner draws a similar conclusion in *Sex and Reason*, 371.

38. For a clear and insightful discussion of epidemiology's historical development from a single-agent conception of causation to a causal pie model, see B. Burt Gerstman, *Epidemiology Kept Simple: An Introduction to Traditonal and Modern Epidemiology*, 2nd ed. (New York: Wiley, 2003), 41ff.

39. Sunstein, Democracy and the Problem of Free Speech, 217, 219; May, Masculinity and Morality, 73.

40. Don Adams, "Can Pornography Cause Rape?" *Journal of Social Philosophy* 31 (2000): 1–43.

41. *Loeser v. Nathan Hale Gardens, Inc.*, 425 N.Y.S.2d 104 (1980). This is cited in Adams, "Can Pornography Cause Rape?" 11–12.

42. For instance, since it is also true that most smokers drink coffee, there is an association between coffee drinking and lung cancer. One cannot tell from the clinical data alone that coffee drinking is not a cause of lung cancer.

43. For testimony from victims of sexual assault and incest, see MacKinnon and Dworkin, *In Harms Way*. Diana Russell also questioned a sample of adult women in San Francisco and found that about 10 percent reported "upsetting sexual experiences with people who tried to get them to do something sexual they'd seen in pornography" (Russell, *Pornography and Rape*, 124). For testimony regarding pornography's injuries from male users, see Michael Kimmel, ed., *Men Confronting Pornography* (New York: Crown, 1990). For testimony from rapists, see Timothy Beneke, *Men on Rape* (New York: St. Martin's, 1982).

44. Court, "Sex and Violence."

45. See J. Scott and L. Schwalm, "Rape Rates and the Circulation of Adult Magazines," *Journal of Sex Research* 24 (1988): 241–50.

46. See L. Baron and M. Straus, "Four Theories of Rape: A Macrosociological Analysis," *Social Problems* 34 (1987): 467–89.

47. For instance, in the late 1960s five studies were performed for the U.S. Commission on Obscenity and Pornography that compare known sex criminals with those who were not known to have committed sex crimes in terms of exposure to pornography (not in the restricted sense of inegalitarian pornography but rather in the broader sense of "sexually explicit materials"). Of the five studies, one was inconclusive, three found less exposure to pornography in the group of known sex criminals than in the control group, and only one found greater exposure to pornography among sex criminals (*U.S. Commission on Obscenity and Pornography: Technical Report*). A few other studies compare the frequency of sex crimes committed by offenders who use pornography with the frequency of those committed by offenders who use none. One study found no difference (Gene Abel, M. S. Mittelman, and Judith Becker: "The Effects of Erotica on Paraphiliacs' Behavior," unpublished paper cited in Attorney General's Commission on Pornography, *Final Report*, U.S. Department of Justice, Washington, DC, 969–70, and also in Christensen, *Pornography*, 174 n. 7), while two others did find a positive correlation between pornography use and coercive sex acts (see summaries of studies by M. P. Marshall and K. E. Koss, in U.S. Commission on Obscenity and Pornography, *Final Report*, 950 and 961, cited in Christensen, *Pornography*, 174 n. 9). All of these studies are problematic for a variety of reasons. First, they rely on memory reports, which are highly fallible. Second, they deal only with convicted sex offenders, yet given that statistics on sexual assault and incest suggest that the number of actual sex offenders is much higher than those who are convicted, there is a good chance that some of participants of such studies are misclassified.

48. This vast literature is summarized in MacKinnon, *Sex Equality*, 1543ff.

49. For example, Zillmann and Bryant did a group of studies in which male and female college students were exposed to "standard" pornography (i.e., nonviolent) pornography regularly for a period of weeks. The studies revealed that, as compared with control groups, the "prolonged exposure group" tended to trivialize rape and recommended a significantly shorter incarceration period for a convicted rapist, reported greater acceptance of male dominance in intimate relationships, and demonstrated increased callousness toward female sexuality. See Dolf Zillman and Jennings Bryant, "Effects of Prolonged Consumption of Pornography on Family Values," *Journal of Family Issues* 9 (1998): 518–44, "Pornography's Impact on Sexual Satisfaction," in *Journal of Applied Social Psychology* 18 (1988): 438–53, "Effects of Massive Exposure to Pornography," in Malamuth and Donnerstein, *Pornography and Sexual Aggression*, 115–38, and "Pornography, Sexual Callousness and the Trivialization of Rape," *Journal of Communication* 32 (1982): 10–21. Studies by Malamuth and others show that prolonged exposure to pornography with "rape myth" scenarios (i.e., women portrayed as enjoying rape) resulted in increased acceptance of and positive attitudes toward violence against women, increased endorsement of rape myth perceptions, and had adverse affects on observers' perceptions of women in general and rape victims in particular (see, e.g., Neith Malamuth, "Aggression against Women: Cultural and Individual Differences," in Malamuth and Donnerstein, *Pornography and Sexual Aggression*, 19–52; Neil Malamuth and James Check, "Penile Tumescence and Perceptual Responses to Rape as a Function of Victims' Perceived Reactions," *Journal of Applied Social Psychology* 10 [1980]: 528–47, "The Effects of Mass Media Exposure on Acceptance of Violence against Women: A Field Experiment," *Journal of Research in Personality* 15 [1981]: 436–46, "Sexual Arousal to Rape Depictions: Individual Differences," *Journal of Abnormal Psychology* 92 [1983]: 55–67, and "The Effects of Aggressive Pornography on Beliefs in Rape Myths: Individual Differences," *Journal of Research in Personality* 19 [1985]: 299–320; Neil Malamuth, Scott Haber, and Seymour Feshbach, "Sexual Rsponsiveness of College Students to Rape Depictions: Inhibitory and Disinhibitory Effects," *Journal of Personality and Social Psychology* 19 [1980]: 399–408). For an excellent summary of these and of studies with similar results, see James Weaver, "Social and Psychological Research Evidence: Perceptual and Behavioral Consequences of Exposure to Pornography," in Itzin, *Pornography*, 284–309.

50. Many studies show that exposure to both violent and nonviolent pornography can cause aggressive behavior under certain circumstances (e.g., Dolph Zillman, *The Connection between Sex and Aggression* [Hillsdale, NJ: Erlbaum, 1984]; Kenneth E. Leonard and Stuart P. Taylor, "Exposure to Pornography, Permissive and Non-Permissive Cues, and Male Agression towards Females," *Motivation and Emotion* 7 [1983]: 291–99; Edward Donnerstein, "Erotica and Human Aggression," in *Aggression: Theoretical and Empirical Reviews*, ed. Edward Donnerstein and Russell Green [New York: Academic Press, 1983], and "Pornography: Its Effect on Violence against Women," in Malamuth and Donnerstein, *Pornography and Sexual Aggression*, 53–82). As Weaver

points out ("Social and Psychological Research Evidence," 301), it is for ethical reasons impossible to perform experiments that elicit the more violent types of sexist behavior. This means that many of these experiments are forced to rely on subjects' reports of psychological states and proxies, such as willingness to deliver electric shocks. Although these are serious limitations, Weaver insists that these data are "more informative and reliable than conventional wisdom, guessing, or ignorance" (301).

51. See Christensen, *Pornography*, 135–38, as well as F. M. Christensen, "Cultural Ideological Bias in Pornography Research," *Philosophy of the Social Sciences* 20 (1990): 351–75; Segal, "Does Pornography Cause Violence?"; Pally, *Sex and Sensibility*, esp. chap. 3.

52. As Donnerstein et al. (*The Question of Pornography*, 174) themselves admit, whether laboratory experiments tell us anything "about real-world aggression, such as rape, is still a matter for considerable debate."

53. These *Epidemiology Kept Simple* guidelines, sometimes referred to as *criteria* for causation, were first laid out by the Surgeon General's Advisory Committee on Smoking and Health and were later expanded by British scientist A. Bradford Hill in 1965. The guidelines are outlined in Gerstman, *Epidemiology Kept Simple*, 294ff., and Gordis, *Epidemiology*, 176ff.

54. Joel Feinberg, *Offense to Others: The Moral Limits of the Criminal Law* (Oxford: Oxford University Press, 1985), 150ff.

55. Lewontin, *The Triple Helix*, 101–5, and also his *Biology as Ideology*, 41ff. Lewontin illustrates the concept of *agency* with the following example. The chief "causes" of death in Europe at the end of the nineteenth century were infectious diseases, such as smallpox, tuberculosis, pneumonia, and measles. By the First World War, these deaths due to infectious disease had reduced dramatically. Interestingly, the reason for this dramatic change was not the discovery of pathogens (which had no observable effect on mortality rates), nor the development of modern drug treatments (because 90 percent of the reduction in death rates due to infectious disease had already occurred by the time of the discovery of antibiotics), nor changes in sanitation (since the principal diseases were airborne, not waterborne). The reason for the change was an increase in wages, which led to an improvement in nutrition, and a decrease in working hours, which lessened physiological stress. The real cause of the deaths in question, Lewontin argues, was a particular form of industrial capitalism that resulted in overwork and undernourishment; infectious diseases were simply the agencies of these deaths. Likewise, one could argue that pornography is a mere subsidiary pathway for the expression of the true cause, which we might call pervasive gender inequality.

56. Confounding is one of the most important problems in epidemiological studies. Confounding occurs when factor A was thought to be a cause of disease B, but factor X turns out to be a risk factor for both A and B, which explains the association between the latter. For a description of the statistical methods employed to detect confounding, see Gordis, *Epidemiology*, 185–89.

DISCUSSION QUESTIONS

1. How, according to Eaton, is inegalitarian pornography connected to gender inequality?
2. According to antiporn feminists, inegalitarian pornography does more than just depict women being subordinated and degraded; it "recommends women's subordination and degradation." Why does Eaton think it does this? Do you agree? Why or why not?
3. What does Eaton try to show by comparing the harms caused by pornography to the harms caused by smoking cigarettes?
4. Do you think that inegalitarian pornography is a cause of any of the kinds of harms that Eaton describes? Why or why not?

Race

J. L. A. GARCIA

The Heart of Racism

Jorge L. A. Garcia is Professor of Philosophy at Boston College. He writes on moral theory, race and racism, and various issues in applied ethics. In this paper, Garcia argues that we should understand racism in terms of virtues and vices. He then applies this understanding of racism to issues such as affirmative action and institutional racism.

GUIDING QUESTIONS

1. How does Garcia define racism? Why does he think that is a good way to understand racism?
2. How, according to Garcia, is racism related to virtues and vices?
3. What does Garcia mean when he says that "racial discrimination is not always racist discrimination"?
4. What is "Kiplingesque" racism? Why, according to Garcia, is it immoral?
5. What does Garcia conclude about the cases discussed by Judith Lichtenberg? What arguments does he give for his conclusions?
6. What, according to Garcia, is "institutional racism"? How is Garcia's view of institutional racism "both narrower and wider than some others that have been offered"?
7. How do Antony Flew and Anthony Skillen characterize institutional racism? What, according to Garcia, is wrong with their views?

The phenomenon of racism having plagued us for many centuries now, it is somewhat surprising to learn that the concept is so young. The second edition of *The Oxford English Dictionary* (1989) dates the earliest appearances of the term 'racism' only to the 1930s.[1] During that decade, as the shadow of Nazism lengthened across Europe, social thinkers coined the term to describe the ideas and theories of racial biology and anthropology to which the Nazi movement's intellectual defenders appealed in justifying its political program. Thus, Ruth Benedict, in a book published in 1940, called racism "the dogma that one ethnic group is condemned by nature to congenital inferiority and another group is destined to congenital superiority"[2] (Benedict, 1940).

These origins are reflected in the definition that the *O.E.D.* still offers: "The theory that distinctive human characteristics and abilities are determined by race."[3] Textbook definitions also echo this origin: "Racism— a doctrine that one race is superior" (Schaefer, 1990: p. 27). Recently, however, some have argued that these definitions no longer capture what people mean when they talk of racism in the moral and political discourse that has become the term's primary context. Some on the political left argue that definitions reducing racism to people's beliefs do not do justice to racism

J.L.A. Garcia. "The Heart of Racism." *Journal of Social Philosophy*, 27(1), Spring 1996, 5–45. © 1996 Journal of Social Philosophy.

as a sociopolitical reality. Robert Miles records the transition in the thought of Ambalvaner Sivanandan, director of Britain's Institute of Race Relations, who abandoned his earlier account of racism (1973) as "an explicit and systematic ideology of racial superiority" because later (1983) he came to think that "racism is about power not prejudice." Eventually (1985), he saw racism as "structures and institutions with power to discriminate" (1985). (Quoted at Miles, 1989: p. 54.)[4] From the right, the philosopher Antony Flew has suggested that, to identify racism with "negative beliefs" about "actual or alleged matters of fact" is a "sinister and potentially dangerous thing"—it "is to demand, irrespective of any evidence which might be turned up to the contrary, that everyone must renounce certain disapproved propositions."[5] Flew worries that this poses a serious threat to intellectual freedom, and proposes a behavioral understanding of 'racism' as "meaning the advantaging or disadvantaging of individuals for no better reason than that they happen to be members of this racial group rather than that."

I agree with these critics that in contemporary moral and political discourse and thought, what we have in mind when we talk of racism is no longer simply a matter of beliefs.[6] However, I think their proposed reconceptions are themselves inadequate. In this paper, I present an account of racism that, I think, better reflects contemporary usage of the term, especially its primary employment as both descriptive and evaluative, and I sketch some of this view's implications for the morality of race-sensitive discrimination in private and public life. I will also briefly point out some of this account's advantages over various other ways of thinking about racism that we have already mentioned—racism as a doctrine, as a socioeconomic system of oppression, or as a form of action. . . .

I. A VOLITIONAL CONCEPTION OF RACISM

Kwame Anthony Appiah rightly complains that, although people frequently voice their abhorrence of racism, "rarely does anyone stop to say what it is, or

what is wrong with it" (Appiah, 1990: 3). This way of stating the program of inquiry we need is promising, because, although racism is not essentially "a moral doctrine," *pace* Appiah, it is always a moral evil[7] (Appiah, 1990: 13). No account of what racism is can be adequate unless it at the same time makes clear what is wrong with it. How should we conceive racism, then, if we follow Appiah's advice "to take our ordinary ways of thinking about race and racism and point up some of their presuppositions"? (Appiah, 1990: 4) My proposal is that we conceive of racism as fundamentally a vicious kind of racially based disregard for the welfare of certain people. In its central and most vicious form, it is a hatred, ill-will, directed against a person or persons on account of their assigned race. In a derivative form, one is a racist when one either does not care at all or does not care enough (i.e., as much as morality requires) or does not care in the right ways about people assigned to a certain racial group, where this disregard is based on racial classification. Racism, then, is something that essentially involves not our beliefs and their rationality or irrationality, but our wants, intentions, likes, and dislikes and their distance from the moral virtues."[8] Such a view helps explain racism's conceptual ties to various forms of *hatred* and contempt. (Note that 'contempt' derives from 'to contemn'—not to care (about someone's needs and rights.)

It might be objected that there can be no such thing as racism because, as many now affirm, "there are no races." This objection fails. First, that 'race' is partially a social construction does not entail that there are no races. One might even maintain, though I would not, that race-terms, like 'person', 'preference', 'choice', 'welfare', etc., and, more controversially, such terms as 'reason for action', 'immoral', 'morally obligatory', etc. may be terms that, while neither included within nor translatable into, the language of physics, nevertheless arise in such a way and at such a fundamental level of social or anthropological discourse that they should be counted as real, at least, for purposes of political and ethical theory.'[9] Second, as many racial anti-realists concede, even if it were true that race is unreal, what we call racism could still be real (Appiah, 1992:

p. 45). What my account of racism requires is not that there be races, but that people make distinctions in their hearts, whether consciously or not on the basis of their (or others') racial classifications. That implies nothing about the truth of those classifications. . . .[10]

Thinking of racism as thus rooted in the heart fits common sense and ordinary usage in a number of ways. It is instructive that contemptuous White racists have sometimes called certain of their enemies 'Nigger-lovers.' When we seek to uncover the implied contrast-term for this epithet, it surely suggests that enemies of those who "love" Black people, as manifested in their efforts to combat segregation, and so forth, are those who hate Black people or who have little or no human feelings toward us at all. This is surely born out by the behavior and rhetoric of paradigmatic White racists.

This account makes racism similar to other familiar forms of intergroup animosity. Activists in favor of Israel and of what they perceive as Jewish interests sometimes call anti-Semites 'Jew-haters.' . . .What is important for us is to note that *hostility* toward Jews is the heart of anti-Semitism.

It is also worth noting that, immediately prior to the coining of the term 'racism', even some of the early anti-Nazi polemicists referred to their subject as 'race hatred'.[11] This suggests such thinkers may have realized that the true problem was not so much the doctrines of the scientists of race-biology and race-anthropology, but the antipathy these doctrines rationalized and encouraged.

Racism also seems, intuitively, to be structurally similar to xenophobia and the anti-homosexual malice sometimes called 'homophobia'. However, xenophobia is commonly understood not primarily as consisting in holding certain irrational beliefs about foreigners, but in *hatred* or disregard of them. This suggests that racism should, as I here claim, be considered a form of disaffection.[12] The gay activists Kirk and Madsen urge that we reclassify some so-called 'homophobes' as 'homohaters'. They cite studies indicating that many people who detest homosexuals betray none of the telltale physiological signs of phobia, and remind us that what is at stake is primarily a hostility toward homosexual persons on account of their homosexuality.[13] Again, by analogy, racism should be deemed a form of disregard.

On my account, racism retains its strong ties to intolerance. This tie is uncontroversial. Marable, for example, writes of "racism, and other types of intolerance, such as anti-Semitism . . . [and] homophobia. . ." (Marable, 1992: 3,10). Intolerant behavior is to be expected if racism is hatred.[14] How, after all, can one tolerate those whom one wants to injure, and why ought one to trouble oneself to tolerate those whom one disregards?

Such an account of racism as I propose can both retain and explain the link between the two "senses of" racism found in some dictionaries: (i) belief in superiority of R1s to R2s, and (ii) inter-racial 'antagonism'.[15] I suggest that we think of these as two elements within most common forms of racism. In real racists, I think, (ii) is normally a ground of (i) (though sometimes the reverse is true), and (i) is usually a rationalization of (ii). What is more important is that (i) may not be logically *necessary* for racism. (In some people, it may nonetheless be a psychological necessity.) However, even when (ii) is a result of (i), it is (ii) and not (i), that makes a person a racist. (Logically, not causally.)

My view helps explain why racism is always immoral. As Stephen Nathanson says, "Racism, as we ordinarily speak of it, . . . implies . . . a special disregard for other groups. Hence, there is a sense in which racism is necessarily immoral" (Nathanson, 1992: p. 9).[16] Its immorality stems from its being opposed to the virtues of benevolence and justice. Racism is a form of morally insufficient (i.e., vicious) concern or respect for some others. It infects actions in which one (a) tries to injure people assigned to a racial group because of their race, or (b) objectionably fails to take care *not* to injure them (where the agent accepts harm to R1s because she disregards the interests and needs of R1s because they are R1s). We can also allow that an action is racist in a derivative and weaker sense when it is less directly connected to racist disregard, for example, when someone (c) does something that (regardless of its intended, probable, or actual effects) stems in significant part from a belief or apprehension about other people, that one has (in significant part) because of one's disaffection toward them because of (what one thinks to be their) race. Racism, thus, will often offend against justice, not just against benevolence, because one sort of injury to another is withholding from her the respect she is owed and the deference and trust that properly express that respect. Certain forms of paternalism, while benevolent in some of their goals, may be vicious in the means employed. The paternalist may deliberately choose to deprive another of some goods, such as those of (licit) freedom and (limited) self-determination in order to obtain other goods for her. Here, as elsewhere, the good end need not justify the unjust means. Extreme paternalism constitutes an instrumentally malevolent benevolence: one harms A to help her. I return to this below in my discussion of 'Kiplingesque' racism. . . .

My account of racism suggests a new understanding of racist behavior and of its immorality. This view allows for the existence of *both* individual racism and institutional racism. Moreover, it makes clear the connection between the two, and enables us better to understand racism's nature and limits. . . .

Some think that institutions, etc. are racist when they are structures of racial domination, and that individual beliefs, etc. are racist when they express, support, or justify racial superiority. Both, of course, involve denying or violating the equal dignity and worth of all human beings independent of race. This sort of approach contains some insight. However, it leaves unclear how the two levels or types of racism are related, if they are related at all. Thus, such views leave us rather in the dark about what it is in virtue of which each is a form of racism. Some say that institutional racism is what is of central importance; individual racism, then, matters only inasmuch as it perpetuates institutional racism. I think that claim reverses the order of moral importance, and I shall maintain that the individual level has more explanatory importance.

At the individual level, it is in desires, wishes, intentions, and the like that racism fundamentally lies, not in actions or beliefs. Actions and beliefs are racist in virtue of their *coming from* racism in the desires, wishes, and intentions of individuals, not in virtue of their *leading to* these or other undesirable effects. Racism is, for this reason, an interesting case study

in what we might call 'infection' (or 'input-centered' or backward-looking) models of wrongdoing, in contrast to the more familiar consequentialist and other result-driven approaches. Infection models of wrongdoing—according to which an action is wrong because of the moral disvalue of what goes into it rather than the nonmoral value of what comes out of it—seem the best approach within virtues-based ethics. In such ethical systems, actions are immoral insofar as they are greedy, arrogant, uncaring, lustful, contemptuous, or otherwise corrupted in their motivational sources.[17] Finally, desires, wishes, and intentions *are* racist when they either are, or in certain ways reflect, attitudes that withhold from people, on the basis of their being assigned to a particular race, levels or forms of good-will, caring, and well-wishing that moral virtue demands.[18] At its core, then, racism consists in vicious attitudes toward people based on their assigned race. From there, it extends to corrupt the people, individual actions, institutional behavior, and systemic operations it infects. Some, however, seem not to think of racism in this way, as something that, like cruelty or stupidity, can escalate from its primary occurrence in individual people to infect collective thought and decision-making of organizations and, from there, to contaminate the behavior of institutions as well. So to think of it is to see the term as not merely descriptive and evaluative, but also as having some explanatory force.

How is institutional racism connected to racism within the individual? Let us contrast two pictures. On the first, institutional racism is of prime moral and explanatory importance. Individual racism, then, matters (and, perhaps, occurs) only insofar as it contributes to the institutional racism which subjugates a racial group. On the second, opposed view, racism within individual persons is of prime moral and explanatory import, and institutional racism occurs and matters because racist attitudes (desires, aims, hopes, fears, plans) infect the reasoning, decision-making, and action of individuals not only in their private behavior, but also when they make and execute the policies of those institutions in which they operate. I take the second view. Institutional racism, in the central sense of the term, occurs when institutional behavior stems from (a) or (b) above or, in an extended sense, when it stems from (c). Obvious examples would be the infamous Jim Crow laws that originated in the former Confederacy after Reconstruction. Personal racism exists when and insofar as a person is racist in her desires, plans, aims, etc., most notably when this racism informs her conduct. In the same way, institutional racism exists when and insofar as an institution is racist in the aims, plans, etc., that people give it, especially when their racism informs its behavior. Institutional racism begins when racism extends from the hearts of individual people to become institutionalized. What matters is that racist attitudes contaminate the operation of the institution; it is irrelevant what its original point may have been, what its designers meant it to do. If it does not operate from those motives (at time T1), then it does not embody institutional racism (at T1). On this view, some phenomena sometimes described as institutionally racist will turn out not to be properly so describable, but others not normally considered to be institutionally racist will fit the description. (I return to this below.)

Not only is individual racism of greater explanatory import, I think it also more important morally. Those of us who see morality primarily as a matter of suitably responding to other people and to the opportunities they present for us to pursue value will understand racism as an offense against the virtues of benevolence and justice in that it is an undue restriction on the respect and goodwill owed people. (Ourselves as well as others; racism, we must remember, can take the form of self-hate.) Indeed, as follows from what I have elsewhere argued, it is hard to render coherent the view that racist hate is bad mainly for its bad effects. The sense in which an action's effects are bad is that they are undesirable. But that it is to say that these effects are evil things to want and thus things the desire for which is evil, vicious. Thus, any claim that racial disadvantage is a bad thing presupposes a more basic claim that race-hatred is vicious. What is more basic morally is also morally more important in at least one sense of that term.[19] Of course, we should bear in mind that morality is not the same as politics. What is morally most important may not be the problem whose rectification is of greatest political urgency.

II. IMPLICATIONS AND ADVANTAGES

There are some noteworthy implications and advantages of the proposed way of conceiving of racism.

First, it suggests that prejudice, in its strict sense of 'pre-judgment', is not essential to racism, and that some racial prejudice may not be racist, strictly speaking. Racism is not, on this view, primarily a cognitive matter, and so it is not in its essence a matter of how or when one makes one's judgments. Of course, we can still properly call prejudiced-based beliefs racist in that they *characteristically* either are rooted in prior racial disregard, which they rationalize, or they foster such disregard.[20] Whether having such a belief is immoral in a given case will depend in large part on whether it is a rationalization for racial disaffection. It may depend on *why* the individual is so quick to think the worst of people assigned to the other racial group. Of course, even when the order is reversed and the prejudice does not whitewash a prior and independent racial disaffection, but causes a subsequent one, the person will still be racist because of that disaffection, even if she is not racist in holding that belief, that is, even if she does not hold it for what we might call 'racist reasons.' My guess is that, in most people who have been racists for some expanse of time, the belief and the disregard will reinforce each other.

A person may hold prejudices about people assigned to a race without herself being racist and without it being racist of her to hold those prejudices.[21] The beliefs themselves can be called 'racist' in an extended sense because they are characteristically racist. However, just as one may make a wise move without acting wisely (as when one makes a sound investment for stupid reasons), so one may hold a racist belief without holding it for racist reasons. One holds such a belief for racist reasons when it is duly connected to racial disregard: when it is held in order to rationalize that disaffection or when contempt inclines one to attribute undesirable features to people assigned to a racial group. One whose racist beliefs have no such connection to any racial disregard in her heart does not hold them in a racist way and if she has no such disregard, she is not herself a racist, irrespective of her prejudices.

Second, when racism is so conceived, the person with racist feelings, desires, hopes, fears, and dispositions is racist even if she never acts on these attitudes in such a way as to harm people designated as members of the hated race. (This is not true when racism is conceived as consisting in a system of social oppression.) It is important to know that racism can exist in (and even pervade) societies in which there is no systematic oppression, if only because the attempts to oppress fail. Even those who think racism important primarily because of its effects should find this possibility of inactive racism worrisome for, so long as this latent racism persists, there is constant threat of oppressive behavior.

Third, on this view, race-based preference (favoritism) need not be racist. *Preferential* treatment in affirmative action, while race-based, is not normally based on any racial disregard. This is a crucial difference between James Meredith's complaint against the University of Mississippi and Allan Bakke's complaint against the University of California at Davis Medical School (see Appiah, 1990: p. 15).* Appiah says that what he calls "Extrinsic racism has usually been the basis [1] for treating people worse than we otherwise might, [2] for giving them less than their humanity entitles them to" (Appiah, 1992: 18). What is important to note here is that (1) and (2) are not at all morally equivalent. Giving someone less than her humanity entitles her to is morally wrong. To give someone less than we could give her, and even to give her less than we would if she (or we, or things) were different is to treat her "*worse* [in the sense of 'less well'] than we otherwise might." However, the latter is not normally morally objectionable. Of course, we may not deny people even gratuitous favors out of hatred or contempt, whether or not race-based, but that does not entail that we may not licitly choose to bestow favors instead on those to

whom we feel more warmly. That I feel closer to A than I do to B does not mean that I feel hatred or callousness toward B. I may give A more than A has a claim to get from me and more than I give B, while nevertheless giving B everything to which she is entitled (and even more). Thus, race-based favoritism does not have to involve (2) and need not violate morality. . . .

Discrimination *on the basis of* race, then, need not be immoral. It is discrimination *against* people because of their racial assignment that cannot but be immoral. Christopher Jencks says "we need formal discrimination in favor of blacks to offset the effects of persistent informal discrimination against them."[22] Suppose Jencks' claim about our need for discrimination is true. Can racial favoritism ever be justified? It will help to remind ourselves that discriminating *in favor of* R1s need not entail discriminating *against* R2s.[23] The latter consists in acting either (i) with intention of harming R2s, or (ii) with hard-hearted racist indifference to the action's foreseeable ill effects on R2s,[24] or (iii) from racist beliefs held because of racist disaffection. Similarly, racial self-segregation need not be immoral. It may be especially suspect when White people do it, because we have good historical reason to be suspicious that what is presented as merely greater-than-morally-required concern for fellow White people really involves less-than-morally-required concern for Black people. It may also be ill-advised even when it is Black people who do it. However, in neither case must it be immoral.[25] In neither case must it be racist.

According to this conception of racism, *de jure racial segregation* violates political morality primarily because (and, therefore, when) it expresses a majority's (or minority's) racial indifference, contempt, or ill-will. It is therein vicious, offending against the virtues of both benevolence and justice. However, it

---

*James Meredith applied to the University of Mississippi in 1961, when state law barred black students from the university. The next fall, despite vigorous and sometimes violent opposition, Meredith became the first black student to enroll at the university. Allan Bakke, a white Vietnam veteran, applied to medical school at the University of California, Davis in 1973. The school rejected him (twice) while admitting some minority students with lesser academic qualifications. Bakke sued the school, arguing that the school's affirmative action policy had violated his constitutional rights. The U.S. Supreme Court eventually ruled in his favor. —DRM]

need not have such origin, a fact illustrated by recent suggestions to establish separate academies to deal with the educational challenges confronting young Black males, and by efforts to control the racial demography of public housing projects in order to avoid problems that have sometimes arisen when such projects became virtually all-Black or virtually all-White. Whatever the social merit of such proposals, in cases like these, even if the segregation in the end proves immoral, this is not intrinsic. There must be some special additional factor present that makes it immoral. De facto racial segregation (mere separation or disproportional representation) need not be morally problematic at all when it happens to result from decently and responsibly motivated individual or social actions.[26] However, it will be immoral if its bad effects on, say, Rls are accepted out of racist hardheartedness, that is, out of racist indifference to the harm done Rls. This will sometimes, but not always, be the case when harms are disproportionally distributed across the various racial groupings to which people are assigned.

Fourth, on this view of racism, racist discrimination need not always be conscious. The real reason why person P1 does not rent person P2 a room may be that P1 views P2 as a member of a racial group R2, to whose members P1 has an aversion. That may be what it is about P2 that turns P1 off, even if P1 convinces herself it was for some other reason that she did not rent. As racist discrimination need not always be conscious, so it need not always be intended to harm. Some of what is called 'environmental racism,' especially the location of waste dumps so as disproportionally to burden Black people, is normally not intended to harm anyone at all. Nevertheless, it is racist if, for example, the dumpers regard it as less important if it is 'only,' say, Black people who suffer. However, it will usually be the case that intentional discrimination based on racist attitudes will be more objectionable morally, and harder to justify, than is unintentional, unconscious racist discrimination. *Racial* discrimination is not always racist discrimination. The latter is always immoral, because racism is inherently vicious and it corrupts any differentiation that it infects. The former—racial discrimination—is not inherently immoral. Its moral

status will depend on the usual factors—intent, knowledge, motive, and so on—to which we turn to determine what is vicious.

This understanding of racism also offers a new perspective on the controversy over efforts to restrict racist "hate speech." Unlike racially *offensive* speech, which is defined by its (actual or probable) effects, racist *hate* speech is defined by its origins, i.e., by whether it expresses (and is thus an act of) racially directed hate. So we cannot classify a remark as racist hate speech simply on the basis of *what* was said, we need to look to why the speaker said it. Speech laden with racial slurs and epithets is presumptively hateful, of course, but merely voicing an opinion that members of R1 are inferior (in some germane way) will count as racist (in any of the term's chief senses, at least) only if, for example, it expresses an opinion held from the operation of some predisposition to believe bad things about R1s, which predisposition itself stems in part from racial disregard.[27] This understanding of racist hate speech should allay the fears of those who think that racial oversensitivity and the fear of offending the oversensitive will stifle the discussion of delicate and important matters beneath a blanket of what is called 'political correctness.' Racist hate speech is defined by its motive forces and, given a fair presumption of innocence, it will be difficult to give convincing evidence of ugly motive behind controversial opinions whose statement is free of racial insults.

III. SOME DIFFICULTIES

It may seem that my view fails to meet the test of accommodating clear cases of racism from history. Consider some members of the southern White aristocracy in the antebellum or Jim Crow periods of American history—people who would never permit racial epithets to escape their lips, and who *were* solicitous and even protective of those they considered 'their Negroes' (especially Black servants and their kin), but who not only acquiesced in, but actively and strongly supported the social system of racial separatism, hierarchy, and oppression. These people strongly opposed Black equality in the social, economic, and political realms, but they appear to have been free of any vehement racial hatred. It appears that we should call such people racists. The question is: Does the account offered here allow them to be so classified?[28]

This presents a nice difficulty, I think, and one it will be illuminating to grapple with. There is, plainly, a kind of hatred that consists in opposition to a person's (or group's) welfare. Hatred is the opposite of love and, as to love someone is to wish her well (i.e., to want and will that she enjoy life and its benefits), so one kind of hatred for her is to wish her ill (i.e., to want and will that she not enjoy them). It is important to remember, however, that not all hatred is wishing another ill for its own sake. When I take revenge, for example, I act from hate, but I also want to do my enemy ill for a purpose (to get even). So too when I act from envy. (I want to deprive the other of goods in order to keep her from being better off than I, or from being better off than I wish her to be.) I have sometimes talked here about racial "antipathy" ("animosity," "aversion," "hostility," etc.), but I do not mean that the attitude in question has to be especially negative or passionate. Nor need it be notably ill-mannered or crude in its expression. What is essential is that it consists in either opposition to the well-being of people classified as members of the targeted racial group or in a racially based callousness to the needs and interests of such people.

This, I think, gives us what we need in order to see part of what makes our patricians racists, for all their well-bred dispassion and good manners. They stand against the advancement of Black people (as a group, even if they make an exception for 'their Negroes'). They are averse to it as such, not merely doing things that have the *side* effect of setting back the interests of Black people.[29] Rather, they *mean* to retard those interests, to keep Black people "in their place" relative to White people. They may adopt this stance of active, conscious, and deliberate hostility to

Black welfare either simply to benefit themselves at the expense of Black people or out of the contemptuous belief that, because they are Black, they merit no better. In any event, these aristocrats and their behavior can properly be classified as racist.

Recall, too, that even if the central case of racism is racial hatred (male-volence), the racial disaffection that constitutes racism also extends to racial callousness, heartlessness, coldness, or uncaring. (We might group these as the vice of nonbenevolence.) These too are racism, for it is surely vicious morally to be so disposed toward people classified as belonging to a certain racial group that one does not care whether they prosper or suffer, and is thus indifferent to the way in which the side effects of one's action disadvantage them. Indeed, I think that, as described, our genteel, oppressive members of the gentry go beyond this to manifest a kind of practical hostility: they consciously and actively act to suppress Black people. However, even those who do not go that far are still racist. (Dr. King famously reminded us that to the extent that the good are silent in the face of evil, they are not (being) good). Morally, much will depend on what these agents mean to do. Do they seek to deprive Black people of various positions and opportunities precisely because they wish Black people not to have these things because the things are good? If so, this is a still deeper type of race malice.

It may not be clear how the understanding of racism offered here accommodates the common-sense view that the attitudes, rhetoric, behavior, and representatives of the mindset we might characterize as the 'white man's burden'-view count as racist.[30] One who holds such a Kiplingesque* view (let's call her K) thinks non-Whites ignorant, backward, undisciplined, and generally in need of a tough dose of European 'civilizing' in important aspects of their lives. This training in civilization may sometimes be harsh, but it is supposed to be for the good of the 'primitive' people. Moreover, it is important, for our purposes, to remember that K may think that, for all

---

*In his 1899 poem "The White Man's Burden," the British writer Rudyard Kipling urges his fellow whites to conquer the non-white peoples of the world as a way of allegedly improving their situation, since Kipling saw non-whites as backward and in need of enlightenment. —DRM

their ignorance, lack of discipline, and other intellectual and moral failings, individuals within the purportedly primitive people may in certain respects, and even on the whole, be moral superiors to certain of their European 'civilizers.' Thus, Kipling's notorious coda to "Gunga Din."[31]

The matter is a complex one, of course, but I think that, at least in extreme instances, such an approach can be seen to fit the model of racism whose adoption I have urged. What is needed is to attend to and apply our earlier remarks about breaches of respect and the vice of injustice. An important part of respect is recognizing the other as a human like oneself, including treating her like one. There can be extremes of condescension so inordinate they constitute degradation. In such cases, a subject goes beyond more familiar forms of paternalism to demean the other, treating her as utterly irresponsible. Plainly, those who take it upon themselves to conscript mature, responsible, healthy, socialized (and innocent) adults into a regimen of education designed to strip them of all authority over their own lives and make them into 'civilized' folk condescend in just this way.[32] This abusive paternalism borders on contempt and it can violate the rights of the subjugated people by denying them the respect and deference to which their status entitles them. By willfully depriving the oppressed people of the goods of freedom, even as part of an ultimately well-meant project of 'improving' them, the colonizers act with the kind of instrumentally malevolent benevolence we discussed above. The colonizers stunt and maim in order to help, and therein plainly will certain evils to the victims they think of as beneficiaries. Thus, their conduct counts as a kind of malevolence insofar as we take the term literally to mean willing evils.[33]

Of course, the Kiplingesque agent will not think of herself as depriving responsible, socialized people of their rights over their lives; she does not see them that way and thinks them too immature to have such rights. However, we need to ask why she regards Third World peoples as she does. Here, I suspect, the answer is likely to be that her view of them is influenced, quite possibly without her being conscious of it, by her interest in maintaining the social and economic advantages of having her group wield control over its subjects. If so, her beliefs are relevantly motivated and affected by (instrumental) ill-will, her desire to gain by harming others. When this is so, then her beliefs are racist not just in the weak sense that their content is the sort that characteristically is tied to racial disaffection, but in the stronger and morally more important sense that her own acceptance of these beliefs is partially motivated by racial disaffection. She is *being* racist in thinking as she does. I conclude that the account of racism offered here can allow that, and help explain why, many people who hold the 'white man's burden'-mentality are racist, indeed, why they maybe racist in several different (but connected) ways.

Having said all this about some who are what I have called Kiplingesque racists and about some 'well-meaning' southern aristocrats, I must admit that my account suggests that some people in these situations, some involved in racially oppressive social systems, will not themselves be racist in their attitudes, in their behavior, or even in their beliefs (at least, in the stronger sense of being racist in holding her beliefs). I do not shrink from this result, and think it should temper our reliance on the concept of collective responsibility. There are real cases where people share in both wrongdoing and blameworthiness, but collective responsibility for racism is philosophically problematic (in ways I cannot here pursue) and, I think, it is neither so common nor so important morally as some maintain (see May, 1992).

IV. SOME CASES

. . .

What should we say of a case Judith Lichtenberg raises, in which, acting from racial fear, a White person crosses the street to avoid Black pedestrians she perceives as possible dangers?[34] Lichtenberg thinks it acceptable for the fearful (and prejudiced?) White person to cross the street in order to avoid proximity with the Black teenagers who approach her at night (p. 4). She sensibly suggests that this is not racist if the person would respond in the same way with White teenagers. "She might well do the same if the teenagers were white. In that case her behavior does not constitute racial discrimination." . . . Helpfully, Lichtenberg cites several factors she thinks relevant to deciding when it is unjust to take race into account. How much harm does the victim suffer? How much does the agent stand to suffer if she does not discriminate? Is the person who discriminates acting in a public or official capacity?

Lichtenberg maintains that the Black teenagers suffer "a minimal slight—if it's even noticed." She even suggests that the White person might spare their feelings "by a display of ulterior motivation, like [pretending to] inspect the rosebushes on the other side" of the street in order to make it look as if it were her admiration for the flowers, and not her fear of Black people, that motivated her to cross the street. The latter pretense is, in my judgment, insulting and unlikely to succeed. More important, this appears to be a guilty response, as if the person is trying to cover up something she knows is wrong. I think that fact should cause Lichtenberg and her imagined agent to reconsider the claim that the action is unobjectionable. It is also quite wrong-headed to think that the harm of insult is entirely a matter of whether a person has hurt feelings. Does it make a difference that the victims suffer little direct and tangible harm? Some, but not much. After all, by that criterion, egregiously racist behavior such as engaging in caricatures or telling jokes that mock Black people would be justified if done in an all-White setting.

According to Lichtenberg, it is acceptable for the White woman to try to avoid the Black teenager on the street, but much harder to justify her racially discriminating when he applies for a job. It will be difficult to maintain this position, however. How is this woman—so terrified of contact with young Black males that she will not walk on the same side of the street with them—simply to turn off this uneasiness when the time comes for her to decide whether to offer a job to the Black male? Suppose that the job is to help out in her family's grocery store, and that this is likely to mean that the woman and the teenager will be alone in the store some evenings? Lichtenberg's advice, that the woman indulge her prejudice in her private life but rigorously exclude it from their official conduct, seems unstable. Indeed, Lichtenberg

seems to assume that the woman can take refuge in bureaucracy, that she will be the personnel officer who does the hiring, while it is other people who will actually have to work in proximity with the new employee. It is the worst of liberal bad faith, however, for this woman to practice her tolerance in official decision-making, but only on the condition that it is other people who will have to bear the burden of adjusting to the pluralistic environment those decisions create and of making that environment work. (Compare the liberal politician who boldly integrates the public schools while taking care to "protect" her own kids in all-White private schools.)

Lichtenberg assumes that private discrimination is less serious morally, but this is doubtful. The heart is where racism, like all immorality, begins and dwells. Even if some moral *virtue-traits* were differentially distributed along racial lines (and even if that were for genetic rather than historical reasons), each individual would still retain the right to be given the benefit of the probability that she is *not* herself specially inclined toward vice. Of course, this sort of racial discrimination need not be racist, since it can be entirely unconnected to any racial disaffection, just as it may not be irrational if it is a response to a genuine statistical disparity in risk. (Similarly, there need be nothing immoral in age-based discrimination should the woman seek to avoid being on dark streets alone with teenagers but not with the elderly.) Nevertheless, such conduct runs substantial risk of reinforcing some of the ugly racial stereotypes that are used to rationalize racial antipathy, and there is reason to avoid relying upon it.

Our view of institutional racism is both narrower and wider than some others that have been offered. To see how it is narrower, that is, less inclusive, let us consider the practice of 'word-of-mouth' job-recruitment, in which people assigned to a privileged racial group, who tend to socialize only with one another, distribute special access to employment benefits to social acquaintances similarly assigned. Some deem this institutional racism, because of its adverse impact on those considered members of the disadvantaged group. (See, for example, Ezorsky, 1991.) Miles protests against those who expansively identify institutional racism with, as he puts it, "all actions or processes (whatever their origin or motivation) which result in one group being placed or retained in a subordinate position by another." In his eyes, the practice of 'word-of-mouth' recruitment is not racist because, although it has an admittedly disproportionally adverse impact on people assigned to the disadvantaged racial group (e.g., African-Americans), it has similar impact on members of other groups—ethnic, gender, economic—that are underrepresented among the elite (Miles, 1989: pp. 52, 61).

One can, however, respond that this fact does not show the practice is not an instance of institutional racism. It may be an instance of institutional racism and, at the same time, an instance of institutional sexism, of institutional 'classism,' etc.[35] Miles' critics have a point. I think, however, what this shows is that we go wrong when we try to identify institutional racism merely by examining the effects of institutional practices. On the view taken here, the practice, while possibly undesirable and perhaps even unjust, is not racist unless it stems from racist antipathy or lack of empathy or from negative beliefs born of such disaffection, in the hearts of the people who carry out the practice.[36]

Consider, similarly, the so-called 'old boy network.'[37] Person F, upon hearing of an opening at his place of employment, tells the people he thinks of (who are all White males like himself) about the job and recommends one of them (Person G) to the boss, who hires him. Ignoring the exaggeration in calling anything so informal an 'institution,' let us explore whether this 'institution' of the 'old boy network' is racist. Is F (or F's behavior) racist? Is G (or G's behavior) racist? Some are ready to offer affirmative answers. What should we say? First, G cannot be racist just for receiving the job; that's not sufficiently active. What about G's act of *accepting* the job? That can be racist. I think, however, that it is racist only in the exceptional circumstance where the institutions are so corrupt that G should have nothing to do with them. Second, F may be racist insofar as his mental process skips over some possible candidates simply because the stereotypes he uses (perhaps to mask his racial disaffection from himself and others) keep him from thinking of them as possible job candidates. Third, one needs some further reason not yet given to label racist the practice of the 'old boy network.' It may work 'systematically' to the detriment of Black people. That, however, merely shows that, in our society, with our history of racism, Black people can be disadvantaged by many things other than race-based factors. (Glenn Loury offers several other examples of this, interestingly including the custom of endogamy among both White and Black people.[38]) What is important to note is that it is misleading to call all these things racist, because that terminology fails to differentiate the very different ways in which and reasons for which they disadvantage people. This classification and broad use of the term, then, fails adequately to inform us and, of more practical importance, it fails to direct our attention (and efforts) to the source of the difficulty. It doesn't identify for us *how* things are going wrong and thus *what* needs to be changed.

Some accounts of institutional racism threaten to be excessively broad in other ways. Some implicitly restrict institutional racism to operations *within* a society—they see it as one group maintaining its social control over the other.[39] This is too narrow, since it would exclude, for example, what seem to be some clear cases of institutional racism, such as discrimination in immigration and in foreign assistance policies. However, if this restriction to intra-group behavior is simply removed from these accounts, then they will have to count as instances of institutional racism some actions which do not properly fall within the class. Suppose, for example, the government of a hostile planet, free of any bigotry toward any Earthling racial group, but unenamored of all Earthlings, launches a missile to destroy the Earth. Suppose it lands in Africa. This institutional (governmental) action has a disproportionally adverse impact on Black people, but it is silly to describe it as racist. (It remains silly even if the aliens decide to target *all* their attacks on the same continent—say, because its size or subterranean mineral deposits make it easier for their tracking systems to locate—and the effect thus becomes 'systematic.') Talk of racism here is inane because the action, its motivation, and its agents are entirely untainted by any racial disaffection or prejudice. By the same token, however, although the agents of many earthly institutions *are* tainted by racism (e.g., in the U.S. government), that fact cannot suffice, even in combination with adverse impacts, to make its actions institutionally racist. The racism has first to *get into* the institutional conduct somehow by informing the conduct of individual agents. In contrast, proponents of expansive accounts of institutional racism, by focusing on the action's effects, end up in the untenable position of claiming that racism somehow *comes out of* institutional behavior, while simultaneously denying that it must ever even get into the action at the action's source in the aims, beliefs, desires, hopes, fears, and so on of the agents who execute institutional policy.[40]

We can also profitably turn our account to an interesting case Skillen offers. He writes:

> Suppose Dr Smythe-Browne's surgery has been ticking over happily for years until it is realized that few of the many local Asians visit him. It turns out that they travel some distance to Dr Patel's surgery. Dr Smythe-Browne and his staff are upset. Then they realise that, stupidly, he has never taken the trouble to make himself understood by or to understand the Asians in his area. His surgery practices have had the effect of excluding or at least discouraging Asians. Newly aware, he sets out to fix the situation.
>
> By the same token as his practices have been 'consequentially', not 'constitutively' discriminatory, they have been 'blind', lacking in awareness.
>
> The example shows the possibility of a certain sort of 'racism' that, if we must attribute blame, is a function of a lack of thought (energy, resources, etc.). If that lack of thought is itself to be described as 'discriminatory' it would need to be shown Dr Smy the-Browne showed no such lack of attention when one of the local streets became gentrified. .. In such cases, it is not racial sets as such that are the focus of attention, but race as culturally 'inscribed'. In other words, one is concerned with people in respect of how they identify themselves and are identified by others (for example, intimidating institutions or outright racists). (Skillen, p. 81)

Despite what Skillen implies, that an institution intimidates some racial groups ("sets") does not make it racist. Flew is right about the insufficiency (even the irrelevance) of mere effects to establish racism, as he is right about the sufficiency of racism to establish immorality.[41] Otherwise, the interplanetary attacks in our earlier example would count as instances of institutional racism. Moreover, that Smythe-Browne was thoughtless about what might be needed to attract

Asians in no way shows his conduct was racist, not even if he was more sensitive and interested in how to attract 'yuppies' brought close by local gentrification. Insensitivity to certain race-related differences is not racist, even if one is sensitive to class-related differences or to differences associated with other racial differences. Smythe-Browne does not so much "discourage" Asians as fail to encourage them. Psychologically and ontologically, that is a very different matter, and those differences are likely to correlate with moral differences as well. (Failure to encourage is likely merely to be at worst an offense of *non*benevolence rather of *male*volence.) *Perhaps* the Asians were 'invisible' to Smythe-Browne in a way that he is culpable for. To show this, however, more would need to be said about why he did not notice them, their absence, and their special interests. Is it that he cares so little about Asians and their *well-being? If there* is nothing like this involved, then there is no racism in Smythe-Browne's professional behavior, I say. And if there is something like this involved, then Smythe-Browne's conduct is not purely "'consequentially'. . . discriminatory." It is corrupted by its motivation in racial disaffection.

When it comes to defending racial preferences against Flew's strictures, however, Skillen shows more insight. He adds further detail to his case, asking us to suppose that Dr. Smythe-Browne "decides that the only way to cope with the situation is to get an Asian doctor, preferably female, onto the staff. He advertises the job and, finding a good person of the sort he needs, she joins the practice, whereas a number of, in other respects at least, equally good applicants (white, male for the most part) do not. Is this 'racism'?" Skillen thinks not, and I think he argues his point well. "Is it not, in Flew's terms, a case of 'discriminating in favour of a racially defined subset out of a total set'? Well, not necessarily. Dr. Smythe-Browne's criteria remain medical. His selection is legitimate insofar as we accept that medicine is a human and communicative 'art' in respect of which socially significant variables are relevant. In that sense it is simply not the case that bypassed candidates with better degree results were necessarily 'better candidates'" (Skillen, p. 82).

With this understanding and assessment, I agree wholeheartedly. Dr. Smythe-Brown's hiring preference here seems to me to exemplify the sort of race-based distinction that is in its nature and its morality quite different from racist discrimination.[42]

As I mentioned, this account of institutional racism is also more inclusive than some. Flew's account, for example, is too narrow in ways I shall point out below.[43] Usually, people apply the term institutional racism only to practices that reinforce existing inter-group power relations. However, a company of people, all of whom are assigned to an oppressed racial group, may harbor reactive racist attitudes toward all those designated as members of the dominant group, and may institutionalize their racism in such institutions as they control: excluding people considered members of the resented group from access to certain schools, scholarships, employment positions, memberships, etc., not out of fraternal/sororal solidarity with others similarly oppressed, nor out of a concern to realize more just distribution of benefits, but simply from resentful racial antipathy. That is racism in the operations of a social organization, institutionalized racism, and should therefore count as institutional racism. This bears out an observation of Randall Kennedy's. "Some argue that, at least with respect to whites, African Americans cannot be racist because, as a group, they lack the power to subordinate whites. Among other failings, this theory ignores nitty-gritty realities. Regardless of the relative strength of African-American and Jewish communities, the African Americans who beat Jews in Crown Heights for racially motivated reasons were, at the moment, sufficiently powerful to subordinate their victims. This theory, moreover, ignores the plain fact African Americans—as judges, teachers, mayors, police officers, members of Congress and army officers—increasingly occupy positions of power and influence from which they could, if so minded, tremendously damage clients, coworkers, dependents, and beyond, the society as a whole" (Kennedy, 1994).

The approach taken here opens the door to the sort of research H. L. Gates has recently called for. He writes, "[W]e have finessed the gap between rhetoric and reality by forging new and subtler definitions of the word 'racism.' Hence a new model of institutional racism is one that can operate in the absence of actual racists. By redefining our terms we can always say of the economic gap between black and white America:

the problem is still racism... and by stipulation it would be true. But the grip of this vocabulary has tended to foreclose the more sophisticated models of political economy we so desperately need" (Gates, 1994).

V. OTHER VIEWS

This way of understanding the nature of racism contrasts with certain other views from the literature. . . . Let us examine the views offered by Antony Flew and Anthony Skillen in the recent exchange to which we have already several times attended (Skillen, 1993; Flew, 1990). . . .

Racism has, according to Skillen, an "institutional character." "If it is the case that individuals, not institutions, have intentions or goals, we need to say that institutions operate through individuals, that our intentions are structured by institutions (going home, teaching, keeping the country or the club white and so on) . . . Racism, like sexism or confessional discrimination can be an implicit thing, taken for granted, a traditional part of the way we've always done things" (Skillen, p. 80).

"[A]s Flew's . . . objection charging the opponent of 'institutionalized racism' with definition in terms of 'consequences' bears out, his main concern is not with institutions whose racism is more or less constitutive of their identity [as in a club or school founded to give Whites refuge from integration], . . . [but] with regulative practices: tests, entry requirements, employment practices, which, *as it turns out,* result in poor outcomes for members of certain racial sets" (p. 81, original emphasis).

This is wrong-headed for reasons that should by now be clear. No institutional practices can be racist—nor malicious, dishonest, or in any other way morally vicious—merely because "as it turns out" they have undesirable effects. Flew is right that an institution can be racist in the way it is constituted, and Skillen is right that institutions can also be racist in their operations, even when innocently founded. However, Skillen goes too far that its effects alone can suffice to make an institution racist. Institutional racism exists, as we said, when the racism in individuals becomes institutionalized. To become institutionalized, racism must infect the institution's operations by informing the ends it adopts, or the means it employs, or the grounds on which it accepts undesirable side effects (as is normally the case in 'environmental racism'), or the assumptions on which it works. Failing any such basis, Skillen is unable to explain how racism gets into the institution to corrupt its behavior. Any suggestion that it gets into the institution and its behavior after the fact from the behavior's effects is incoherent. Skillen's error is to confuse output-driven concepts, such as being dangerous or harmful or lethal, with a moral concept such as racism. Output-driven concepts can be useful for moral judgment, because they help us to ask the right questions about why the agent (here: the institution) acted as it did and why it did not abandon its plans in in favor of some less harmful course of action. Answers to these questions can help us to decide whether the action is negligent or malicious or otherwise vicious. *However,* output-driven concepts cannot *suffice* to ground *assigning* any moral status, because vice and virtue are by nature tied to the action's motivation. Effects can only be (defeasible) evidence of motivation.[44]

Finally, Skillen is correct to observe that oftentimes institutions shape individual intentions and actions. Institutional racism will often exist in reciprocal relation to individual racism. The racism of some Individual (or individuals) first infects the institution, and the institution's resultant racism then reinforces racism in that individual or breeds it in others. Once individual racism exists, institutional racism can be a powerful instrument of its perpetuation. This reciprocity of causal influence, however, should not blind us to the question of origins. Individual racism can come into the world without depending on some prior institutionalization. (It could come to be, say, as a result of some twist in one person's temperament.) The converse is not true. Institutional racism can reinforce and perpetuate individual racism. Unless an institution is corrupted (in its ends, means, priorities, or assumptions) by a prior and independent racism in some individual's heart, however, institutional racism can never come to exist.

Nevertheless, we should take care not to overstate the dependence of institutional racism upon individual. Institutional racism appears to be capable of continuing after individual racism has largely died out. Think of a case where, for example, officials continue, uncomprehendingly, to implement policies originally designed, and still functioning, to disadvantage those assigned to a certain racial group. Indeed, I strongly doubt that the qualifier 'and still functioning' is necessary. Institutional racism can exist without actually functioning to harm anyone. Suppose, a few generations back, some Rls designed a certain institutional procedure P specifically to harm R2s, an oppressed racial group, though the designers were never explicit about this aim. Later, anti-R2 feeling among Rls faded away, and in time real social equality was achieved. The Rls, however, are a traditionalist lot, and they continue faithfully to execute P out of deference to custom and their ancestors. P no longer specially harms R2s. (Perhaps it excludes from various privileges those who come from some specific, traditionally poor R2 neighborhoods, and R2s are no longer disproportionally represented in those neighborhoods, which, perhaps, are also no longer disproportionally poor.)

In that case, it appears that the racism of the earlier generation persists in the institutional procedure P, even though P no longer specially harms R2s. This indicates that institutional racism, no less than individual racism, can be either effective or ineffective, either harmful or innocuous. Institutional racism, then, is a bad thing; but it is a bad thing not because of its actual effects, but sometimes merely because of its aims. The study of people's aims directs the social theorist's attention into their hearts, to what they care about, to what they have set themselves on having, or being, or making, or doing. Such is the stuff of the moral virtues, of course. Neither the social theorist nor the moral theorist can continue to neglect them if she wishes to understand the world. Or to change it.

VI. CONCLUSION

These reflections suggest that an improved understanding of racism and its immorality calls for a comprehensive rethinking of racial discrimination, of the preferential treatment programs sometimes disparaged as 'reverse discrimination,' and of institutional conduct as well. They also indicate the direction such a rethinking should take, and its dependence on the virtues and other concepts from moral psychology. That may require a significant change in the way social philosophers have recently treated these and related topics.

NOTES

1. The same dictionary dates the cognate 'racist', as both adjective and noun, to the same period, but places the first appearances of 'racialism' and 'racialist' three decades earlier.

2. Miles begins a summary of his review of the first uses of the term in the effort of certain intellectuals to attack the pseudo-scientific defenses of the Nazi movement by saying that "the concept of racism was forged largely in the course of a conscious attempt to withdraw the sanction of science from a particular meaning of the idea of 'race'"; and he chides these early critics on the grounds that their interpretation of racism, "by focusing on the product of nineteenth century scientific theorizing, tended to presume that racism was always, and therefore was only, a structured and relatively coherent set of assertions.... Such a definition [is problematic insofar as it] excludes less formally structured assertions, stereotypical ascriptions and symbolic representations. . . " (Miles, 1986: pp. 47, 48).

3. Merriam-Webster's *Ninth New Collegiate Dictionary* offers a secondary definition: "racial prejudice or discrimination."

4. For a negative appraisal of Sivanandan's thought, see David Dale, "Racial Mischief: The Case of Dr. Sivanandan," in Palmer, 1986: pp. 82–94.

5. Discussing an account of racism offered by Britain's Commission for Racial Equality, Flew writes: "[a] sinister and potentially dangerous thing here is the reference to actual or alleged matters of fact—to 'negative beliefs'. . . . For this is to demand, irrespective of any evidence which might be turned up to the contrary, that everyone must renounce certain disapproved propositions about average or universal differences and similarities as between races and racial groups: difference and similarities, that is, either in respect of biology or in respect of culture. To concede such a demand to the often Marxist militants of race relations is to open the door to purges: not only of libraries and of textbooks and of curricula; but also of people. It is not ten years since many a campus in the U.S.A. was ringing with calls to 'Sack' and even to 'Kill Jensen'—Jensen being a psychologist who dared to publish evidence suggesting that there may be genetically determined average differences between different races and

racial groups in respect of other than their racial defining characteristics" (Flew, 1986: p. 22). I critically examine Flew's view of racism at the end of this essay.

6. Banton suggests that we should restrict our usage of the term, withholding its application from many people we nowadays call racists. In his view, these people are not racists because they use arguments of cultural superiority in preference to the doctrines of biologically based superiority the term was coined to pick out (Banton, 1970). This proposal is unrealistic, and serves to illustrate what makes unacceptable the excessively conservative approach to word meaning of those who still insist that racism consists solely in certain beliefs, ideology, doctrines, and theories.

7. That is not to say that its definition must include a moral evaluation. The act-utilitarian must hold that nonoptimific behavior is always wrong simply in virtue of what it is and what morality is, but she need not think the term 'nonoptimific' includes a moral evaluation in its definition. Similarly, a divine command theorist may judge every act against God's will to be immoral *eo ipso,* without thinking this wrongness analytically derivable from the meaning of 'against God's will'.

8. According to Miles, the term 'racism' originally denoted certain pseudo-scientific doctrines. I think the term changed its meaning, and speculate that this change occurred as race became important less for the discredited beliefs than for attitudes and resultant social practices. (See Miles, 1989: chaps. 2, 3.) On the linguistic history, also see the *Oxford English Dictionary,* 2nd ed.

9. Compare David Wiggins and John McDowell on Kantian moral realism. (See Wiggins, "Truth, Invention, and the Meaning of Life," in Wiggins, 1987; and McDowell, 1986.)

Although in conversation with me he has denied any such dependence, there is reason to worry that Appiah's position may covertly rely on a form of scientism, the supposition that no serious use of a once-pseudo-scientific term is permissible if it plays no role within legitimate science. In any case, he seems to allow that neither the fact that the concept of 'race' is inexact in its criteria and extension, nor the fact that it was the subject of a discredited science, nor the fact that it was used to justify unjust social practices, is by itself sufficient to show that the notion must be banished from speech. (Perhaps he thinks they are jointly sufficient, but that remains to be shown.) Moreover, he is willing to talk informally of this person being Black and that one White, so he and I are not so far apart. I do not see why this informal, but acceptable, way of speaking cannot be extended to allow us to call such talk acceptable (albeit informal) racial classifications. Of course, informal talk of races cannot be accepted if racial terms must really be scientific. That, however, returns us to our question why anyone should think that.

Appiah's criticism of talk of races on the grounds that there are no "racial essences" suggests that he may presuppose a metaphysical essentialism that does not count against using racial terms on the looser bases of Wittgensteinian "family resemblances": perhaps a combination of surface and ancestral features, ordered in no one way, underlies the legitimate application of race terms to many but not all persons.

10. Miles objects to some early accounts of the nature of racism on the grounds that they "tended to remain inextricably entangled with, and consequently to legitimate, the idea of 'race'" (Miles, 1989: p. 48).

11. "Critics of scientific theories of race prior to this decade [the 1930s] did not use a concept of racism to identify their ideological object. For example, in a wide-ranging critique published in the late 1920s, Friedrich Hertz referred to 'race hatred'" (Miles, 1989: p. 42).

12. As I said at the outset, the term 'xenophobia' also suggests that this aversion to others is accompanied or caused by fear of them, but I do not think this association carries over to 'racism'.

13. They write, "'Homophobia' is a comforting word, isn't it? It suggests that . . . all who oppose, threaten, and persecute us [that is, homosexuals] are actually scared of us! [However, f]ear need have nothing to do with it. A well-designed study . . . demonstrat[ed] that although some 'homonegative' males respond to homosexual stimuli with the 'tell-tale racing heart' of phobia, plenty of others don't." Kirk and Madsen condemn "the specious 'diagnosis'" of homophobia as a "medically exculpatory euphemism," and offer a proposal: "Let's reserve the term 'homophobia' for the psychiatric cases to which it really applies, and find a more honest label for the attitudes, words, and acts of hatred that are, after all, the real problem." As for their own linguistic procedure, "when we really do mean 'fear of homosexuals,' [then] 'homophobia' it will be; when we're talking about hatred of homosexuals, we'll speak (without the hyphen) of 'homohatred,' 'homohating,' and 'homohaters.' We urge the reader to follow suit." (See Kirk and Madsen, 1989: pp. xxii–xxiii.) This is sensible advice, though some caveats are in order. First, we should bear in mind that not every fear is a phobia. Second, even the quasi-scientific term "homonegative" tends to lump together such very different matters as (i) a person's personal aversion to her own engaging in homosexual activities, (ii) her concern over perceived social effects of other peoples' homosexual conduct, and (iii) her holding the belief that such conduct is morally impermissible. Hatred of homosexual persons is immoral (although, as Kirk and Madsen point out, to

see it simply as a medical condition tends to exculpate). Moral disapproval of homosexual practices, whether on medical, moral, or religious grounds, is a different matter, however, and it may often be an unrelated one. Third, to use the prefix 'homo' to mean 'homosexual' is objectionable for obvious reasons, so it seems preferable to speak of 'homosexual-haters' and 'homosexual-hatred,' retaining the hyphen. This would also make it clear, as the term 'homophobia' does not, that what is to condemned is an attitude of ill-will or contempt toward certain people, and not a moral judgment on certain practices.

14. The Freudian theorist Elizabeth Young-Bruehl, in an unpublished paper, argues that anti-Semitism differs from racism in that anti-Semitism, which she thinks rooted in a combination of assumed male Gentile sexual superiority and economic and intellectual inferiority, aims to exterminate its targets, while racism, which she thinks rooted in assumed White male sexual inferiority, seeks to keep its victims around for humiliation (Young-Bruehl, 1992). I suspect all this is wrong-headed. For our purposes, what is important is that no such causality is essential to racism or anti-Semitism, because we should label haters of Jews or Black people anti-Semite and racists even if we knew their hatred had different causes.

15. I shall use such terms as 'R1' and 'R2' to refer to racial groups, and such expressions as 'R1s' and 'R2s' to refer to people assigned to such groups. This usage holds potential for some confusion, since the plural term 'R1s' is not the plural of the singular term 'R1', but I think the context will always disambiguate each instance of this usage.

16. Two caveats. First, since our interest is in the central sense(s) of the term 'racism', I see little reason to add Cottingham's qualifier "there is a sense in which" to our claim that racism must be illicit. Any sense of the term in which racism is not illicit must be decidedly peripheral. Second, Cottingham seems to think of this "disregard" as primarily a matter of negative evaluative beliefs, while I reject any such doxastic account and construe 'disregard' as disaffection or malice.

17. See Slote, 1994, and Garcia, forthcoming.

18. I will not try to identify minimal levels of good will such that having less is against the virtue of benevolence, nor minimal levels of respect such that less offends against justice. I doubt these levels can be identified in abstraction, and it will be difficult or impossible for us to determine them even in minutely described particular situations. Throughout, I generally restrict my talk of disrespect and other forms of disregard to cases where the levels are morally vicious, offending against the moral virtues of benevolence and justice, respectively.

19. See Garcia, 1986, and Garcia, 1987.

20. In a way similar to my nondoxastic account of racism, John Dewey seems to have offered an account of race-prejudice that is nondoxastic. Recent scholarship reminds us that, for Dewey, prejudice was not primarily a matter of hasty judgment, but of a fear of, and aversion to, what is unfamiliar. Gregory Pappas expounded Dewey's view in his paper, "Dewey's Philosophical Interpretation of Racial Prejudice," presented at a session of the 1992 Ford Fellows Conference in Irvine, California.

21. See Appiah, 1992.

22. Quoted in Hacker, "The New Civil War," p. 30.

23. Arguing against some writers who use the slogan "Preference is not prejudice" to support their view that moderate racial preference is permissible, Miles complains, "[T]o prefer is to rank and to choose to value something or person or group, and therefore necessarily to preclude some other thing, person or group." (Miles, 1989: 8) What Miles says is true, but it does nothing to prove the controverted point that excluding person S1 in the course of expressing greater-than-morally-required regard for S2 is the moral equivalent of excluding S1 out of less-than-morally-required concern for S1. That said, I do certainly not wish to associate myself with the further doctrines of the thinkers Miles is criticizing, who use the inflammatory example of preferring to marry within one race as an example of supposedly innocent preference. In a society such as ours, any such "preference" is likely to be informed by and to result in part from an aversion to interracial marriage as 'race-treachery' or 'miscegenation'. Such a preference is not at all innocent, in my view, having roots in deep-seated racial antipathy.

In personal correspondence, Glenn Loury has expressed misgivings about my view, reminding me that "what ends in personal viciousness towards the 'other' finds its beginning in the more benign celebration of the virtues of one's 'own kind'." I wonder whether, in fact, racial antipathy does *always* begin in such a benign attitude. However, even if it does, the danger that it may lead to racial antipathy is a reason to be cautious of racial favoritism. It is not a reason to condemn this partiality as malign nor, more to the point, as racist. Even the framers of a recent California measure proposing to outlaw racial preferences observe a distinction between discriminating against A and according B a preference. "The anti-affirmative action measure is essentially a simple declaration: 'Neither the State of California nor any of its political subdivisions shall use race, sex, color, ethnicity, or national origin as a criterion for either discriminating against or granting preferential treatment to, any individual or group in the operation of the state's system of public employment, public education, or public contracting'" (Schrag, 1995: p. 18). The drafters may, however, make the distinction merely to close a possible linguistic loophole, and not deem it a distinction that marks any genuine and morally significant difference. With that, of course, I disagree.

24. I say 'foreseeable' effects rather than 'foreseen' because S's racist contempt may be the reason she does not bother to find out, and thus does not foresee some of the bad effects of her behavior.

25. I think this undermines an argument recently offered by Gomberg. He argues against what has been called "moderate patriotism," which "includ[es limited] preference for fellow nationals," on the grounds that any argument in defense of it will also legitimize what he calls "moderate racism," which allows someone to "discriminate against black or Hispanic people or against immigrants" so long as one is careful not to "violate their fundamental rights" (p. 147). Assuming that such "moderate racism" is unjustifiable, then so too is moderate patriotism or any form of preference. The problem is that it is hard to see why Gomberg's "moderate racism" need be unjustifiable, or even why it is racism. His analogy with patriotism suggests that what Gomberg has in mind is merely a mild form of preference for people of one's own racial group. This will sometimes be suspicious morally, especially when the one discriminating on the basis of race belongs to a group that has enforced and benefited from forms of discrimination that are racist, that is, that are driven by racial disaffection. However, it is unclear that there is anything morally troubling in same-race favoritism by those on the bottom, or by those who live in a situation, unlike ours, where favoritism has been historically divorced from race hatred. Similarly, there seems to be nothing morally troubling in other-race favoritism; at least, there is nothing morally troubling where this favoritism is likely to be divorced from hatred of one's own racial group, as is the case with other-race favoritism by those from historically oppressing groups.

Indeed, while same-race favoritism by people considered members of the oppressing group and other-race favoritism by those allocated to the oppressed group are disturbing morally, I think that, to the extent this discomfort is legitimate, it will be rooted in our suspicion that it is really race-hatred masking as mere favoritism, or in our worry that such a practice, should it become widespread, will have the bad effect of exacerbating the comparatively disadvantaged position of those assigned to the historically oppressed group. The latter worry may be serious, but it is a concern about the general effects of a social (or personal) policy, not a concern that individuals may be treated unjustly. As such, it is much less significant morally.

(Since first writing this, I have seen a similar point made in Stephen Nathanson's response to Gomberg. Nathanson sensibly writes that "a racial preference might not be inherently wrong or evil. American Blacks have been an oppressed group that has needed special attention. Whites are not similarly oppressed as a group. Thus, a person with a special affection and concern for whites might not be equally justified in promoting their interests . . . " Actions done from such favoritism will even "be wrong if they require neglect of the much more pressing need of others", Nathanson, 1992: pp. 10,11).

In this connection, it is worth noting that Appiah rejects what he calls "intrinsic speciesism," adherents of which think it would be morally permissible "to kill cattle for beef, even if cattle exercised all the complex cultural skills of human beings" (Appiah, 1992: 19). Such a position is to be condemned, of course, but we can condemn it without necessarily rejecting the view ("moderate speciesism"?) that even in the world of Appiah's cosmopolitan cattle, we may, and perhaps even should, show greater concern for members of our own species simply because of their relation to us. The impermissibility of such favoritism does not follow from the recognition that there are moral limits on the ways in which we may treat the various others outside the favored group. I can think morality allows and even demands that I care specially for my family without thereby committing myself to thinking that we may slaughter, butcher, and eat the folks next door.

26. See Carter, 1991.

27. For a helpful discussion of the controversy surrounding efforts to identify and regulate hate speech, and of the different grounds offered for these restrictions, see Simon, 1991.

28. Lichtenberg reminds us that such figures are often seen as paradigms of racism, though, unfortunately, she ties this to her claim that Black people and White people tend to have fundamentally different understandings of the nature of racism. "The white picture of the racist is the old-time southern white supremicist" (p. 3). Sure it is not merely what is sometimes disparaged as "thinking White" to see such people as plausible instances of racism.

29. Contrast a religious school that (like the Westminster Academy, in the newspapers a few years back) refuses to hire non-Christians. This policy deprives those who would otherwise have been hired of prestige and salary. However, this deprivation is incidental to the policy's purpose, benign or benighted as it may be, of securing a certain sort of instruction by hiring only instructors with certain relevant convictions.

30. Philip Kitcher directed my attention to this topic.

31. "Though I've belted you and flayed you, By the livin' Gawd that made you, You're a better man than I am, Gunga Din." Rudyard Kipling, "Gunga Din," in Kipling:

a Selection of his Stories and Poems (Garden City: Doubleday, n.d.).

32. It is in the form of Kiplingesque, 'white man's burden'-racism that racism most nearly approaches the structure of sexism. Sexism is, of course, a form of social bias to which many assume racism is structurally similar, and those who introduced the notion of sexism as a concept of social explanation explicitly modeled it on (their understanding of) racism. In general, however, I think the similarity is not great. Sexism appears *normally* to be a form of condescension, wherein males deprive women of authority and power in order to protect them from the consequences of their supposed immaturity and weakness. This sort of disrespect can violate the virtue of justice in just the ways I have been describing. However, noticing that racism in certain peripheral forms can resemble what sexism seems to be in its most central forms helps reveal a significant dissimilarity between these two social vices. (For a sophisticated comparative account of racism and sexism, see Thomas, 1980.)

33. See Garcia, 1987.

34. Reflecting on this case should help inform our answers to related questions: What should we say of those, White or Black, who lock car doors when driving through Black neighborhoods but not White ones? Or of storeowners (again, White or Black) who will not admit Black teenagers to their premises?

35. It was Larry Blum who pointed out to me the availability of this line of response to Miles.

36. It is also doubtful whether such an informal practice, not tied to any organizational structure in particular and part of no determined policy, properly counts as institutional behavior at all. However, I will not pursue that classificatory matter here. Philosophers and other social thinkers nowadays use the term 'institution' in quite a broad and vague way, and this is not the place to try to correct that practice. (That 'institution'? For a step toward a more discriminate use, see the brief discussion of 'institutions' and 'practices' in MacIntyre, 1984, chap. 14.)

37. This phenomenon is closely related to that of word-of-mouth job recruiting. There are, however, some distinctions. The 'old boy network' is defined by an educational elite of private schools (which often embeds a still more restricted elite who are members of secret societies, dining halls, and special clubs). This educationally elite network may also extend its privileging beyond recruitment to include admission to restricted social occasions and establishments where business is conducted, employment advancement, informal help and advice, and the wielding of influence to gain preference in academic admissions and fellowships, the awarding of contracts and consultantships,

immunity from having to pay for misconduct, and other social and economic privileges.

38. Loury, 1992.

39. For instance, "[T]he essential feature of racism is . . . the *defense* of a system from which advantage is derived on the basis of race" (D. Wellman, quoted at Miles, 1989: p. 52, emphasis added).

40. This reflection illuminates a further example. Young-Bruehl says, "A current law [in the United States] which has as its known consequence that women using federally funded family planning clinics—a majority of whom are women of color—will be deprived of information to make informed reproductive choices is, simply, racist" (Young-Bruehl, 1992: p. 10). The law she seems to have had in mind was an executive order, which, because of court action, was never enforced and was later rescinded.

Young-Bruehl clearly assumes that this information would have been given outside the context of a clerisy of family planning professionals trying to encourage poor, predominantly Black, women to terminate their pregnancies for what the professionals see as their own good. She also seems to assume that it is somehow wrong for the state to try to discourage such choices and that withholding this information about where to get an abortion is objectionable in a way that depriving women of detailed information about the effects of abortion on the developing life within is not. She sees the effects of the regulation as a harm to poor, Black women as individuals, while it is, arguably, better to understand the provision as a protection of poor Black people as a group. I do not here challenge her assumptions. Permit me to observe only that she does not argue for them, that they are not at all obvious, and that I think them all implausible and some plainly false.

41. It is not clear what Skillen thinks about the latter point. I agree that some people with racist beliefs should not be condemned morally, but that is because I think that racist beliefs don't make one a real racist and that the beliefs are 'racist' only in a derivative sense. Does Skillen agree?

42. One must, however, take care not to proceed too far down this path. One must assure that the White candidates are not victims of reverse racism. For it would normally be wrong to keep out Black candidates even if the White patients related better to White physicians. One may not bow to primary racism by becoming illicitly collaborative in its workings. See the discussion in section IV above.

43. Throughout this discussion, I have had to rely on Skillen for a presentation of Flew's views. Flew's paper is difficult to locate and the periodical in which it appeared is no longer published. Fortunately, Skillen is aware of the difficulty, and takes extra care to present Flew's views at length, separating summary from interpretation or critique.

I follow his practice in presenting sometimes extensive verbatim passages quoted from Flew.

44. I am aware that the charge I here level against Skillen would also militate against all forms of direct, optimizing consequentialism, and against other result-driven accounts of wrongdoing, such as the satisficing consequentialism Slote discussed. (For more on this, see Garcia, 1990, Garcia, 1992, and Slote, 1985.

BIBLIOGRAPHY

Adams, Robert. "The Virtue of Faith." In Adams, *The Virtue of Faith*, pp. 9–24. Oxford: Oxford University Press, 1987.

Appiah, Anthony. "Racisms." In *Anatomy of Racism*, pp. 3–17. Ed. D. T. Goldberg. Minneapolis: University of Minnesota Press, 1990.

———. *In My Father's House: Africa in the Philosophy of Culture*. Oxford: Oxford University Press, 1992.

Banton, Michael. "The Concept of Racism." In *Race and Racialism*, pp. 17–34. Ed. Sami Zubaida. New York: Barnes & Noble, 1970.

——— and Robert Miles. "Racism." In *Dictionary of Race and Ethnic Relations*. 2nd ed. Ed. E. Ellis Cashmore. London: Routledge, 1988.

Blum, Lawrence. "Antiracism, Multiculturalism, and Interracial Community: Three Educational Values for a Multicultural Society." Office of Graduate Studies and Research, University of Massachusetts at Boston, 1991.

———. *Moral Perception and Particularity*. Cambridge: Cambridge University Press, 1994.

———. "Individual and Institutional Racism." Unpublished paper read at Smith College, February, 1993.

Carter, Stephen. *Reflections of an Affirmative Action Baby*. New York: Basic Books, 1991.

Castoriadis, Cornelius. "Reflections on Racism." *Thesis Eleven* No. 32 (1992): 112.

Cohen, Marshall, et al., eds. *Marx, Justice, and History*. Princeton: Princeton University Press, 1980.

Cottingham, John. "Partiality, Favouritism and Morality," *Philosophical Quarterly* 36 (1986): 357–73.

Ezorsky, Gertrude. *Racism and Justice*. Ithaca: Cornell University Press, 1991.

Flew, Antony. "Clarifying the Concepts." In Palmer, 1986, pp. 15–31.

———. "Three Concepts of Racism." *Encounter* 73 (September, 1990).

Garcia, J. L. A. "The Tunsollen, the Seinsollen, and the Soseinsollen," *American Philosophical Quarterly* 23 (1986): 267–76.

———. "Goods and Evils." *Philosophy and Phenomenological Research* 47 (1987): 385–412.

————. "The Primacy of the Virtuous." *Philosophia* 20 (1990): 69–91.

————. "African-American Perspectives, Cultural Relativism, and Normative Issues." In *African-American Perspectives on Biomedical Issues: Philosophical Issues,* pp. 11–66. Ed. Edmund Pellegrino and Harley Flack. Washington: Georgetown University Press, 1992.

————. "The New Critique of Anti-Consequentialist Moral Theory." *Philosophical Studies* 71 (1993): 1–32.

————. "Virtue Ethics." In *Cambridge Dictionary of Philosophy.* Ed. Robert Audi. Cambridge: Cambridge University Press, 1995.

————. "Current Conceptions of Racism." *Journal of Social Philosophy,* forthcoming.

Gates, Henry Louis, Jr. "Let Them Talk: a review of 'Words that Wound: Critical Race Theory, Assaultive Speech and the First Amendment,' by Mari J. Matsuda, Charles R. Lawrence III, Richard Delgado, and Kimberle Williams Crenshaw." *New Republic.* September 20 & 27, 1993 (double issue), pp. 37–49 at 48.

Gilligan, Carol. *In a Different Voice.* Cambridge: Harvard University Press, 1982.

Goldberg, David Theo. "The Social Formation of Racist Discourse." In *Anatomy of Racism,* pp. 295–318. Ed. D. T. Goldberg. Minneapolis: University of Minnesota Press, 1990.

————. "The Semantics of Race." *Ethnic and Racial Studies* 15 (1992): 543–69.

————. "Racist Exclusions." *Philosophical Forum* 26 (1994): 21–32.

Gomberg, Paul. "Patriotism Is Like Racism." *Ethics* 101 (1990): 144–50.

Green, Judith. "King's Historical Location of Political Concepts." *APA Newsletter on Philosophy and the Black Experience* 91 (1992): 12–14.

Hacker, Andrew. *Two Nations: Black and White, Separate, Hostile, Unequal.* New York: Scribner's, 1992.

————. "The New Civil War." *New York Review of Books.* April 23, 1992, pp. 30–33.

Hursthouse, Rosalind. "Virtue Theory and Abortion." *Philosophy and Public Affairs* 20 (1993): 223–46.

Kamm, F. M. "Non-Consequentialism, the Person as an End-in-Itself, and the Significance of Status." *Philosophy and Public Affairs* 21 (1992): 354–89.

Kennedy, Randall. "Some Good May Yet Come of This." *Time.* February 28, 1994, p. 34.

Kirk, Marshall, and Hunter Madsen. *After the Ball: How America Will Conquer Its Fear and Hatred of Gays in the '90s.* New York: Doubleday, 1989.

Larrabee, Mary Jane, ed. *An Ethic of Care.* New York: Routledge, 1993.

Lichtenberg, Judith. "Racism in the Head, Racism in the World." *Philosophy and Public Policy* (Newsletter of the Institute for Philosophy and Public Policy, University of Maryland), Vol. 12 (1992).

Loury, Glenn. "Why Should We Care About Group Inequality?" *Social Philosophy and Policy* 5 (1987–1988), pp. 249–71.

————. "The Economics of Discrimination." *Harvard Journal of African-American Public Policy* 1 (1992), pp. 91–110.

————. "The New Liberal Racism: a review of Andrew Hacker's *Two Nations." First Things* (January, 1993), pp. 39–42.

Lukes, Stephen. *Marxism and Morality.* Oxford: Oxford University Press, 1987.

Lyas, Colin, ed. *Philosophy and Linguistics.* New York; St. Martin's, 1969.

MacIntyre, Alasdair. *After Virtue.* 2nd ed. Notre Dame: University of Notre Dame Press, 1984.

Marable, Manning. *Black America: Multicultural Democracy in the Age of Clarence Thomas and David Duke.* Open Magazine Pamphlet Series, #16. Westfield, N. J., 1992.

May, Larry, ed. *Collective Responsibility.* Lanham, Maryland: Rowman and Littlefield, 1992.

McDowell, John. "Values and Secondary Qualities." In *Morality and Objectivity,* pp. 110–29. Ed. Ted Honderich. London: Humanities, 1985.

Miles, Robert. *Racism.* London: Routledge, 1989.

Murphy, Jeffrie, and Jean Hampton. *Forgiveness and Mercy.* New York: Cambridge University Press, 1988.

Nathanson, Stephen. "Is Patriotism Like Racism?" *APA Newsletter on Philosophy and the Black Experience* 91 (1992): 9–11.

Noddings, Nell. *Caring.* Berkeley: University of California Press, 1986.

Okin, Susan Miller. *Justice, Gender and the Family.* New York; Basic Books, 1989.

Palmer, Frank, ed. *Anti-Racism: an Assault on Education and Value.* London: Sherwood, 1986.

Piper, Adrian M. "Higher Order Discrimination." In *Identity, Character, & Morality,* pp. 285–309. Ed. Owen Flanagan and Amelie Rorty. Cambridge: MIT Press, 1990.

Rothenberg, Paula. *Racism and Sexism: an Integrated Study.* St. Martin's, 1988.

Schaefer, Richard. *Racial and Ethnic Groups.* 4th ed. Glenview: Scott, Foresman, 1990.

Schrag, Peter. "Son of 187." *New Republic.* January 30, 1995, pp. 16–19.

Sheehan, Thomas. "A Normal Nazi." *New York Review of Books.* January 14, 1992.

Simon, Thomas. "Fighting Racism: Hate Speech Detours." In *An Ethical Education: Community and Morality in the Multicultural University*. Ed. Mortimer Sellers. Oxford: Berg, 1994.

Skillen, Anthony. "Racism: Flew's Three Concepts of Racism." *Journal of Applied Philosophy*. vol. 10 (1993): 73–89. Skillen quotes from and cites A. G. N. Flew, "Three Concepts of Racism," *Encounter* 73 (September, 1990). I have had to rely on Skillen's careful summary for the presentation of Flew's views. The publication in which Flew's article appeared is no longer published and is difficult to find.

Slote, Michael. *Common-Sense Morality and Consequentialism*. London: Routledge & Kegan Paul, 1985.

———. "Agent-Based Virtue Ethics." A paper presented at a University of Santa Clara conference on virtue ethics, March, 1994.

Thomas, Laurence. "Racism and Sexism: Some Conceptual Differences." *Ethics* 90 (1980): 239–250.

Ture, Kwame, and Charles Hamilton. *Black Power*. New York: Vintage, 1992. (Reissue, with new afterword, of 1967 edition.)

West, Cornel. *Race Matters*. Boston: Beacon, 1993.

Wiggins, David. *Needs, Value, Truth*. New York: Blackwell, 1987.

Williams, Patricia. *The Alchemy of Race and Rights*. Cambridge: Harvard University Press, 1991.

Wistrich, Robert. *Antisemitism: The Longest Hatred*. New York: Pantheon, 1992.

Young, Iris. *Justice and the Politics of Difference*. Princeton: Princeton University Press, 1990.

Young-Bruehl, Elizabeth. "Kinds of Types of Prejudices." 1992. Unpublished.

DISCUSSION QUESTIONS

1. Do you think Garcia's definition of racism is a good way to understand the problem of racism? Why or why not?
2. Garcia claims that "discriminating in favor of [one race] need not entail discriminating against [another race]." What is his argument for this? Do you find it convincing? Why or why not?
3. What is "institutional racism" and how does it differ from "individual racism," according to Garcia? What is Garcia's argument that the latter is more important than the former? Do you find that argument convincing? Why or why not?
4. What is an example of a behavior or institution that you think is racist that would not count as racist on Garcia's account? Why is it racist? Alternatively, what is an example of a behavior or institution that counts as racist on Garcia's account, but that you think is not racist? Why isn't it racist?

LAURENCE THOMAS

What Good Am I?

Laurence Thomas is Professor of Philosophy and Political Science at Syracuse University. He has published extensively in moral and political philosophy, and his unorthodox teaching tactics have garnered notice in the New York Times and on his Wikipedia page. In this paper, Thomas takes up the issue of affirmative action in universities, arguing that a diverse faculty creates important educational and scholarly benefits.

GUIDING QUESTIONS

1. Thomas begins by considering and dismissing two arguments about affirmative action. What are they? Why does he dismiss them?
2. What is Thomas's main claim about the benefit that women and minority faculty members bring to a university? What is his argument for that claim?
3. How does Thomas respond to the point that "there are some women and minority students who will achieve no matter [how diverse] the environment"?
4. What objections to his view does Thomas consider? How does he respond to those objections?
5. What "concrete illustration" does Thomas offer to illustrate the benefits of a diverse faculty for the academy as a whole?

What good am I as a black professor? The raging debate over affirmative action surely invites me to ask this searching question of myself, just as it must invite those belonging to other so-called suspect categories to ask it of themselves. If knowledge is color blind, why should it matter whether the face in front of the classroom is a European white, a Hispanic, an Asian, and so on? Why should it matter whether the person is female or male?

One of the most well-known arguments for affirmative action is the role-model argument. It is also the argument that I think is the least satisfactory—not because women and minorities do not need role models—everyone does—but because as the argument is often presented, it comes dangerously close to implying that about the only thing a black, for instance, can teach a white is how not to be a racist. Well, I think better of myself than that. And I hope that all women and minorities feel the same about themselves. . . .

But even if the role-model argument were acceptable in some version or the other, affirmative action would still seem unsavory, as the implicit assumption about those hired as affirmative action appointments is that they are less qualified than those who are not. For, so the argument goes, the practice would be unnecessary if, in the first place, affirmative action appointees were the most qualified for the position, since they would be hired by virtue of their merits. I call this the counterfactual argument from qualifications.

Now, while I do not want to say much about it, this argument has always struck me as extremely odd. In a morally perfect world, it is no doubt true that if women and minorities were the most qualified they would be hired by virtue of their merits. But this truth tells me nothing about how things are in this world. It does not show that biases built up over decades and centuries do not operate in the favor of, say, white males over nonwhite males. It is as if one argued against feeding the starving simply on the grounds that in a morally perfect world starvation would not exist. Perhaps it would not. But this is no argument against feeding the starving now.

It would be one thing if those who advance the counterfactual argument from qualifications addressed the issue of built-up biases that operate against women and minorities. Then I could perhaps suppose that they are arguing in good faith. But for them to ignore these built-up biases in the name of an ideal world is sheer hypocrisy. It is to confuse what the ideal should be with the steps that should be taken to get there. Sometimes the steps are very simple or, in any case, purely procedural: instead of A, do B; or perform a series of well-defined steps that guarantee the outcome. Not so with nonbiased hiring, however, since what is involved is a change in attitude and feelings—not even merely a change in belief. After all, it is possible to believe something quite sincerely and yet not have the emotional wherewithal to act in accordance with that belief. . . .

The philosophical debate over affirmative action has stalled . . . because so many who oppose it, and some who do not, are unwilling to acknowledge the fact that sincere belief in equality does not entail a corresponding change in attitude and feelings in day-to-day interactions with women and minorities. Specifically, sincere belief does not eradicate residual and, thus, unintentional sexist and racist attitudes.[1] So, joviality among minorities may be taken by whites as the absence of intellectual depth or sincerity on the part of those minorities, since such behavior is presumed to be uncommon among high-minded intellectual whites. Similarly, it is a liability for academic women to be too fashionable in their attire, since fashionably attired women are often taken by men as aiming to be seductive.

Lest there be any misunderstanding, nothing I have said entails that unqualified women and minorities should be hired. I take it to be obvious, though, that whether someone is the best qualified is often a judgment call. On the other hand, what I have as much as said is that there are built-up biases in the hiring process that disfavor women and minorities and need to be corrected. I think of it as rather on the order of correcting for unfavorable moral head winds. It is possible to be committed to gender and racial equality and yet live a life in which residual, and thus unintentional, sexism and racism operate to varying degrees of explicitness.

I want to return now to the question with which I began this essay: What good am I as a black professor? I want to answer this question because, insofar as our aim is a just society, I think it is extremely important to see the way in which it does matter that the person in front of the class is not always a white male, notwithstanding the truth that knowledge, itself, is color blind.

Teaching is not just about transmitting knowledge. If it were, then students could simply read books and professors could simply pass out tapes or lecture notes. Like it or not, teachers are the object of intense emotions and feelings on the part of students solicitous of faculty approval and affirmation. Thus, teaching is very much about intellectual affirmation; and there can be no such affirmation of the student by the mentor in the absence of deep trust between them, be the setting elementary or graduate school. Without this trust, a mentor's praise will ring empty; constructive criticism will seem mean-spirited; and advice will be poorly received, if sought after at all. A student needs to be confident that he can make a mistake before the professor without being regarded as stupid in the professor's eyes and that the professor is interested in seeing beyond his weaknesses to his strengths. Otherwise, the student's interactions with the professor will be plagued by uncertainty; and that uncertainty will fuel the self-doubts of the student.

Now, the position that I should like to defend, however, is not that only women can trust women, only minorities can trust minorities, and only whites can trust whites. That surely is not what we want. Still, it must be acknowledged, first of all, that racism and sexism have very often been a bar to such trust between mentor and student, when the professor has been a white male and the student has been either a woman or a member of a minority group. Of course, trust between mentor and student is not easy to come by in any case. This, though, is compatible with women and minorities having even greater problems if the professor is a white male.

Sometimes a woman professor will be necessary if a woman student is to feel the trust of a mentor that makes intellectual affirmation possible; sometimes a minority professor will be necessary for a minority student; indeed, sometimes a white professor will be necessary for a white student. (Suppose the white student is from a very sexist and racist part of the United States, and it takes a white professor to undo the student's biases.)

Significantly, though, in an academy where there is gender and racial diversity among the faculty, that diversity alone gives a woman or minority student the hope that intellectual affirmation is possible. This is so even if the student's mentor should turn out to be a white male. For part of what secures our conviction that we are living in a just society is not merely that we experience justice, but that we see justice around us. A diverse faculty serves precisely this end in terms of women and minority students believing that it is possible for them to have an intellectually affirming mentor relationship with a faculty member regardless of the faculty's gender or race.

Naturally, there are some women and minority students who will achieve no matter what the environment. Harriet Jacobs and Frederick Douglass were slaves who went on to accomplish more than many of us will who have never seen the chains of slavery. Neither, though, would have thought their success a reason to leave slavery intact. Likewise, the fact that there are some women and minorities who will prevail in spite of the obstacles is no reason to leave the status quo in place.

There is another part of the argument. Where there is intellectual affirmation, there is also gratitude. When a student finds that affirmation in a faculty member, a bond is formed, anchored in the student's gratitude, that can weather almost anything. Without such ties there could be no "ole boy" network—a factor that is not about racism, but a kind of social interaction running its emotional course. When women and minority faculty play an intellectually affirming role in the lives of white male students, such faculty undermine a nonracist and nonsexist pattern of emotional feelings that has unwittingly served the sexist and racist end of passing the intellectual mantle from white male to white male. For what we want, surely, is not just blacks passing the mantle to blacks, women to women, and white males to white males, but a world in which it is possible for all to see one another as proper recipients of the intellectual mantle. Nothing serves this end better than the gratitude between mentor and student that often enough ranges over differences between gender and race or both.

Ideally, my discussion of trust, intellectual affirmation, and gratitude should have been supplemented with a discussion of nonverbal behavior. For it seems to me that what has been ignored by all of the authors is the way in which judgments are communicated not simply by what is said but by a vast array of nonverbal behavior. Again, a verbal and sincere commitment to equality, without the relevant change in emotions and feelings, will invariably leave nonverbal behavior intact. Mere voice intonation and flow of speech can be a dead giveaway that the listener does not expect much of substance to come from the speaker. Anyone who doubts this should just remind her- or himself that it is a commonplace to remark to someone over the phone that he sounds tired or "down" or distracted, where the basis for this judgment, obviously, can only be how the individual sounds. One can get the clear sense that one called at the wrong time just by the way in which the other person responds or gets involved in the conversation. So, ironically, there is a

sense in which it can be easier to convince ourselves that we are committed to gender and racial equality than it is to convince a woman or a minority person; for the latter see and experience our nonverbal behavior in a way that we ourselves do not. Specifically, it so often happens that a woman or minority can see that a person's nonverbal behavior belies their verbal support of gender and racial equality in faculty hiring—an interruption here, or an all too quick dismissal of a remark there. And this is to say nothing of the ways in which the oppressor often seems to know better than the victim how the victim is affected by the oppression that permeates her or his life, an arrogance that is communicated in a myriad of ways. This is not the place, though, to address the topic of social justice and nonverbal behavior.[2]

Before moving on let me consider an objection to my view. No doubt some will balk at the very idea of women and minority faculty intellectually affirming white male students. But this is just so much nonsense on the part of those balking. For I have drawn attention to a most powerful force in the lives of all individuals, namely trust and gratitude; and I have indicated that just as these feelings have unwittingly served racist and sexist ends, they can serve ends that are morally laudable. Furthermore, I have rejected the idea, often implicit in the role-model argument, that women and minority faculty are only good for their own kind. What is more, the position I have advocated is not one of subservience in the least, as I have spoken of an affirming role that underwrites an often unshakable debt of gratitude.

So, to return to the question with which I began this essay: I matter as a black professor and so do women and minority faculty generally, because collectively, if not in each individual case, we represent the hope, sometimes in a very personal way, that the university is an environment where the trust that gives rise to intellectual affirmation and the accompanying gratitude is possible for all, and between all peoples. Nothing short of the reality of diversity can permanently anchor this hope for ourselves and posterity.

This argument for diversity is quite different from those considered by some other writers. I do not advocate the representation of given viewpoints or the position that the ethnic and gender composition of faculty members should be proportional to their numbers in society. The former is absurd because it is a mistake to insist that points of view are either gender- or color-coded. The latter is absurd because it would actually entail getting rid of some faculty, since the percentage of Jews in the academy far exceeds their percentage in the population. If one day this should come to be true of blacks or Hispanics, they in turn would be fair game. . . .

I would like to conclude with a concrete illustration of the way in which trust and gratitude can make a difference in the academy. As everyone knows, being cited affirmatively is an important indication of professional success. Now, who gets cited is not just a matter of what is true and good. On the contrary, students generally cite the works of their mentors and the work of others introduced to them by their mentors; and, on the other hand, mentors generally cite the work of those students of theirs for whom they have provided considerable intellectual affirmation. Sexism and racism have often been obstacles to faculty believing that women and minorities can be proper objects of full intellectual affirmation. It has also contributed to the absence of women and minority faculty which, in turn, has made it well-nigh impossible for white male students to feel an intellectual debt of gratitude to women and minority faculty. Their presence in the academy cannot help but bring about a change with regard to so simple a matter as patterns of citation, the professional ripple effect of which will be significant beyond many of our wildest dreams.

If social justice were just a matter of saying or writing the correct words, then equality would have long ago been a *fait accompli* in the academy. For I barely know anyone who is a faculty member who has not bemoaned the absence of minorities and women in the academy, albeit to varying degrees. So, I conclude with a very direct question: Is it really possible that so many faculty could be so concerned that women and minorities should flourish in the academy, and yet so few do? You will have to forgive me for not believing that it is. For as any good Kantian knows, one cannot consistently will an end without also willing the means to that end. Onora O'Neill writes: "Willing, after all, is not just a matter of wishing that something were the case, but involves committing oneself to doing something to bring that situation about when opportunity is there and recognized. Kant expressed this point by insisting that rationality requires that whoever wills some end wills the necessary means insofar as these are available."[3] If Kant is right, then much hand-wringing talk about social equality for women and minorities can only be judged insincere.

NOTES

1. For a most illuminating discussion along this line, see Adrian M. S. Piper's very important essay, "Higher-Order Discrimination," in Owen Flanagan and Amelie Oksenberg Rorty, eds., *Identity, Character, and Morality: Essays in Moral Psychology* (Cambridge: MIT Press, 1990).

2. For an attempt, see my "Moral Deference," *Philosophical Forum* 24 (1992): 233–50.

3. Onora O'Neill, *Constructions of Reason: Explorations of Kant's Practical Philosophy* (Cambridge University Press, 1989), p. 90.

DISCUSSION QUESTIONS

1. What is the "counterfactual argument from qualifications"? How does Thomas respond to it? Do you find his response convincing? Why or why not?

2. Why, exactly, does Thomas think that having a diverse faculty will help women and minorities build good relationships with mentors? Do you agree with him? Why or why not?

3. What role does gratitude play in undermining sexist and racist social patterns, according to Thomas? How does this relate to his claim that a diverse faculty is also good for white male students?

4. Do Thomas's arguments extend to other settings besides universities (e.g., to hiring in corporations)? If so, how? If not, why not?

Xiaofei Liu

"No Fats, Femmes, or Asians"

Xiaofei Liu is Assistant Professor of Philosophy at Xiamen University in China, where he writes poetry and moral philosophy. In this paper, he takes up the question of whether it is morally permissible to refuse to date people of certain races. His starting point is a controversy in the American LGBT community that began with a blog post complaining about online dating profiles that exclude people of particular races from considerations as potential partners. Liu argues that such exclusionary racialized preferences are morally wrong, whereas "simple [non-racialized] looksism" is not.

GUIDING QUESTIONS

1. What are "racial looksism" and "simple looksism"? How are they relevant to preferences about whom to date? What is the main point that Liu wants to make about these two kinds of "looksism"?
2. What does Liu mean when he says that he understands racial looksism as a "personal preference" rather than a "personal policy"? What objection does he consider to this way of understanding racial looksism? How does he respond to that objection?
3. Why is racial looksism a kind of overgeneralization? Why, according to Liu, is it wrong to overgeneralize in this way?
4. What is "appreciation respect"? How does it differ from "recognition respect" and "appraisal respect"? What role do these kinds of respect play in Liu's argument?
5. What analogy does Liu draw between racial discrimination in hiring and admissions and racial discrimination in personal relationships?
6. What objections does Liu consider? How does he respond to them?

1   INTRODUCTION

In a recent article on a Lesbian, Gay, Bisexual and Transgender (LGBT) community website, LGBT activist Jimmy Nguyen complained about a frequent caveat in online dating profiles—"No Fats, Femmes, or Asians" (2011). Mr. Nguyen was frustrated at the bias against Asians in the American gay community. Although avoiding the accusation of racism, he channeled his frustration by calling it racial looksism.[1] The article sparked an interesting response. One commentator asked, "Mr. Nguyen, would you date a fat man?" The point is elegantly made: if *simple looksism* is acceptable, what's wrong with racial looksism?

This exchange highlights something perplexing about our attitudes toward discrimination. We object to certain forms of discrimination, yet at the same time take for granted some other forms. What might ground our discriminative treatment of discrimination? Is there any relevant difference between racial looksism and simple looksism?

"No fats, femmes, or Asians: the utility of critical race theory in examining the role of gay stock stories in the marginalization of gay Asian men," Xiaofei Liu, 2015 Contemporary Justice Review, reprinted by permission of the publisher (Taylor & Francis Ltd, http://www.tandfonline.com). Issues in Criminal, Social, and Restorative Justice.

These are interesting philosophical questions. However, the primary goal of this paper is not to differentiate between forms of discrimination. What's presumed in the commentator's response is a popular attitude: personal preferences or tastes are not objects of moral assessment—they are simply personal affairs. As the idiom says, "There is no accounting for taste." Thus, personal preferences, such as whom to date, whose birthday party to attend, whom to invite to a bar or restaurant, or whom to greet warmly in one's neighborhood, are usually not considered moral issues. The primary goal of this paper is to argue against this popular attitude. I argue that some personal preferences are moral issues and a preference like racial looksism is morally wrong. It is wrong because it is an overgeneralization that disrespects individuality by treating people as exchangeable tokens of one type, and such disrespect denies some of its objects appreciation that their dignity entitles them to. As it turns out, there is indeed, on my account, a relevant moral difference between racial looksism and simple looksism.

Defining complex social phenomena is often very difficult; yet, some clarification of the key concepts is necessary. I understand simple looksism as a preference that finds certain people aesthetically unappealing and thus sexually unattractive due to their having certain physical appearance.[2] Racial looksism, as stated in the caveat "No Fats, Femmes, or Asians," is a preference that finds certain people aesthetically unappealing and thus sexually unattractive due to their belonging to a certain race. However, despite the appearance that racial looksism picks on racial identity *per se*, what actually motivates this race-qua-race racial looksism is a weaker, race-qua-looks racial looksism, which discriminates against a certain race on the basis of some physical appearance typically associated with that race, such as dark skin color or epicanthic fold. In reality, a racial looksist views a certain racial group as unattractive often not by virtue of their racial identity per se, but by virtue of the looks that are believed to be characteristic of their race.

It is also worth pointing out that racial looksism can be understood as a preference or a personal policy. A safer thesis would treat racial looksism as a personal policy—something clearly subject to our voluntary control. However, for reasons that will become clear later, I will argue for a bolder thesis—racial looksism

is wrong, even as a personal preference. But I do want to make one note about a preference like this. A preference like racial looksism is an exclusionary preference—that is, a preference that excludes some people from a certain qualification (e.g. being aesthetically and sexually attractive), or a preference that ranks these people so low in that regard that they are virtually unqualified. It is exclusionary preference that I find objectionable, not just any kind of preference.[3]

2 A PRELIMINARY ARGUMENT

Before arguing for why a personal preference like racial looksism is morally wrong, I should address a preliminary issue first. It may be argued that even if preferences like racial looksism are wrong, we cannot help whom we are attracted to, and since preferences, unlike decisions or choices, are not under our control, the possession of them is not subject to moral appraisal.

This argument makes two problematic assumptions. First, it assumes that we are subject to moral appraisal only for things over which we have control. But this assumption has been called to question by many philosophers.[4] Second, and more importantly, it assumes that all preferences are beyond our control. It is well established that some preferences or biases[5] can be changed by various conditioning, including social conditioning (Blair et al. 2001; Dasgupta and Greenwald 2001; Rudman et al. 2001). For example, people came to like a social group that they previously disliked, after lengthy exposure to positive things about that group (Dasgupta and Greenwald 2001). People came to accept homosexuals by allowing homosexuals into their personal lives. Recent psychological research has shown that even the degree of one's sexual arousal can be altered by conditioning (Laan and Janssen 2007; Pfaus 2007). For example, some studies in social psychology show that repeated exposure to pornography can significantly reduce viewers' satisfaction with their intimate partners' affection, physical appearance, and so on (Zillmann and Bryant 1988). By choosing to indulge in pornography-viewing, these viewers put themselves in a position to form preferences that find their intimate partners less appealing. Such examples show that our preferences are not necessarily beyond our control and we often have a choice either to endorse and cultivate them or to resist and fight them.

The reason why we find members of a certain racial group unattractive is often a combination of lack of positive portraits of them in society and our own failure to allow them into our personal lives as equals. In such cases, we have a choice either to continue endorsing, or even cultivating, our preferences against that group, or to make an effort to invite them into our personal lives and put ourselves in a position to discover their attractive traits. If one chooses to keep excluding that group from one's personal life, such as proudly endorsing an exclusionary preference against them in one's public profiles, then his possession of the relevant preference is not beyond his control and thus can be subject to moral appraisal.[6]

Now that I have explained why the possession of preferences like racial looksism can be subject to moral appraisal, it is time to return to our main question: Are such preferences morally wrong?

3 RACIAL LOOKSISM AS OVERGENERALIZATION

The main problem with racial looksism is that it is an overgeneralization. An overgeneralization involves viewing, based on the fact that some people who share a common trait P have X, any individual with P as having X, while (1) in this process whether that individual actually has X is disregarded, and (2) an individual's having P is actually not directly contributive to his or her having X.

It is true that there is some statistical association between race and type of physical appearance; but it is also true that there is a great degree of variance within each race in terms of individual physical appearance. Take skin color as an example. Skin color is sometimes thought to be strictly correlated with race, but this race-to-skin-color identity has been seriously challenged by scientists, as well as by recent

social development. For example, according to anthropologist Alan H. Goodman and his colleagues, "all skin colors, whether dark or light, are due not to the static concept of race but to continual shifting adaptation of life under sun" (Goodman et al. 2012, 103). Individuals in the same racial group can vary significantly in terms of skin color. East Africans and West Africans can have quite different skin colors; the same is true for Northern and Southern Europeans, Northern and Southern Chinese, and so on. Genetic mixture through marriage has also rapidly outdated the idea of race-to-skin-color identity. Nowadays, many self-identified black Americans have a skin color lighter than a Caucasian American. The very fact that they identify themselves as blacks shows that race is not just a synonym for skin color, but used in a way that reflects various other factors—for example, cultural inheritance. Thus, to identify race with a specific skin color is both scientifically and sociologically ungrounded—it ignores a significant degree of variance.

Furthermore, two individuals of distinct races can even share great similarities in their physical appearance: similar facial configuration, similar body-shape, etc. For example, epicanthic fold, which is usually thought to be a characteristic trait of people from central and eastern Asia, can also be found in Native Americans and some Europeans (e.g. Scandinavians and Poles). It is not rare for people who frequently travel around the world to find similar faces in different races.

Thus, using race as the ground for judging individual physical appearance is an overgeneralization—it disregards how one individual actually looks, and one's racial identity is not directly contributive to one's having a particular physical appearance because of the variance within a race. Some people may find certain physical appearance, such as dark skin or epicanthic fold, aesthetically unappealing; let's grant that they are entitled to such personal opinions or attitudes. But their exclusion of every member of a racial group from being considered as aesthetically attractive by virtue of some alleged physical racial characteristics that they consider aesthetically unappealing is unwarranted. Race *as such* does not tell how an individual member of that race looks.

Many racist, sexist and other discriminatory attitudes are based on precisely such overgeneralization. Social psychologist Claude M. Steele described a frustrating experience of a young African-American student at the University of Chicago in his recent best-selling book—*Whistling Vivaldi*. When this young man walked down the streets of Chicago's Hyde Park neighborhood, he had to constantly suffer the humiliation of being looked at with fear and being avoided in the street, because of his skin color (2011, 6). Recently, instances of uncivilized behaviors of some mainland Chinese tourists agitated some Hong Kong residents and caused them to initiate anti-mainland protests and to label all tourists from mainland China derogatively as "locusts" (Mullany 2014). Such reaction only accelerated the tension between Hong Kong and mainland China, as many mainland Chinese felt unfairly criticized and demeaned.[7]

Such overgeneralization, especially when involving disadvantageous treatment, can be offensive. It is offensive first because it treats people as exchangeable tokens of a type and thus disregards their individuality. Everybody deserves to be treated based on what kind of person he or she is, not based on what kind of person other people are. It is offensive also because it unfairly denies these people respect that their individual qualities make appropriate.

Racial looksism is an overgeneralization—it differentiates on the basis of a certain physical trait said to be characteristic of one's race, regardless of whether it is true of a given individual. In contrast, when someone finds people of certain physical appearance (such as excessive obesity) aesthetically unappealing, this preference or opinion takes into account their relevant individual quality. Therefore, there is a relevant difference between racial looksism and simple looksism. And Mr. Nguyen has a valid point in raising concerns about racial looksism—such an exclusionary preference disregards people's individuality and, in doing so, it denies them appreciation that their individual qualities make appropriate.

However, being offensive and disrespectful does not necessarily make one thing morally wrong. One important gap that needs to be bridged is the often-noted dichotomy between the public realm and the private realm. Preferences such as how attractive I find another person and whom I like to invite to a bar are usually considered personal affairs. Unlike discrimination in employment or admission, such preferences do not seem to infringe anybody's rights or deprive anybody of access to important public resources. It may be offensive and hurtful to others that I do not find them attractive, but such preferences or opinions are totally within my own rights to hold. Whether or not I find others aesthetically appealing is, like whether or not I like a certain type of music, simply a matter of personal taste, not an issue of moral concern. So one may argue.

Intuitive as it sounds, this argument should be rejected. To see why, it is helpful to first borrow some terminology from the philosophical discussion on dignity and respect.[8] The dignity of a person, as Kant tells us, is that "by which" one "exacts *respect* for himself from all other rational beings" and because of which one "can . . . value himself on a footing of equality with them" (1996, 6:435, original emphasis). Dignity grants every person a fundamental equal moral status. To treat anyone as being fundamentally inferior to others is to disrespect that person's dignity and thus to violate the duty of equal respect.

Stephen Darwall (1977) further distinguishes between two kinds of respect: *recognition respect* and *appraisal respect*. Recognition respect, Darwall tells us, is the kind of respect that "consists in giving appropriate consideration or recognition to some feature of its object in deliberating about what to do" (1977, 38). An important subset of recognition respect is *moral recognition respect*—to respect something in this way is to "regard it as requiring restrictions on the moral acceptability of actions connected with it". (40) Since people are fundamentally equal, they are entitled to equal moral recognition respect—that is, there is a moral requirement that others' fundamental equal moral status be taken seriously and weighed appropriately in our deliberation about our action.

In contrast, appraisal respect is the kind of respect that "consists in an attitude of positive appraisal" of someone for his or her excellence either "as a person" (e.g. being honest) or "as engaged in some particular pursuit" (e.g. being a skilled basketball player) (38). This kind of respect is not universally owed. Rather, it is given on the basis of a person's having certain relevant excellence, and, according to Darwall, the relevant excellence must ultimately arise from one's moral character (38–39).

Because Darwall limits appraisal respect to only the kind of respect that ultimately arises from appraisal of one's moral character, I think we can add a third category—*appreciation respect*. This third type of respect arises from appreciation for non-moral-character-based excellence, such as natural beauty, sheer intelligence, and athletic gift. In many ways, appreciation respect resembles appraisal respect: it consists in a positive attitude toward someone (in this case, appreciation), it is not owed to everybody, and it should be given according to the object's relevant excellence.[9]

Based on our moral duty to give equal moral recognition respect to every person, one may be tempted to make the following argument against a preference like racial looksism: it denies some people appreciation that their individual qualities make appropriate, and thus violates the duty of equal respect. The problem with this inference is that, unlike moral recognition respect, appraisal and appreciation respects are not owed to everyone and not supposed to be morally constraining. For example, Darwall makes it clear that appraisal respect "does not essentially involve any conception of how one's behavior toward that person is appropriately restricted." (1977, 41) This remark echoes the aforementioned argument: how I appreciate or value other people seems to be my personal affair; I do not violate a moral duty if I fail to give someone appraisal or appreciation appropriate to his or her relevant individual quality.

I think accepting the moral constraints arising from equal moral recognition respect does entail accepting certain moral constraints on appraisal and appreciation respects. Here is my argument.

4 FROM RECOGNITION RESPECT TO APPRAISAL AND APPRECIATION RESPECTS

My argument starts with the premise that, without a reasonable justification, it is wrong to discriminate on the basis of race or sex in employment and admission. Some minimum form of equality of opportunity to work and to become educated needs to be honored and protected—even if that means restricting people's freedom to handle their own resources (e.g. a private business owner's freedom to decide whom to hire or a private school's freedom to decide whom to admit). If one does not accept this starting point, the rest of the argument will not be relevant.

Second, the reason why we put such emphasis on equality of opportunity in employment and admission could be due to either a deontological or a consequentialist consideration (Arneson 2002; Sect. 6). To disadvantage, without any good reason, people of a certain race or sex in their pursuit of work or education is wrong either because it violates the deontological requirement of equal treatment, or because it injures their basic wellbeing by limiting these important opportunities. Theorists still debate over which account best explains the wrongfulness of discrimination (Altman 2011). I believe these accounts are two sides of the same coin. At bottom is the idea that work and education are essential to wellbeing: most people need to work to satisfy their basic material needs and to receive education to satisfy their basic spiritual needs; and every person's pursuit of a life of basic wellbeing needs to be properly honored. We emphasize equality of opportunity in employment and admission ultimately because we ought to treat people as equally deserving of a life of basic wellbeing.

Admittedly, to treat people as equally deserving of a life of basic wellbeing does not mean to have absolute equality of opportunity when it comes to work and education. But it should mean at least that our society be structured in such a way that prevents blatant disrespect of people's fundamental equality. In the case of employment and education, it means, in part, to morally prohibit discrimination on the basis of race or sex—even if this prohibition would limit some people's freedom to use their personal resources.

If this is right, then a similar moral prohibition should also exist for personal relationships. Our wellbeing does not just mean satisfaction of basic material and spiritual needs, it also means satisfaction of basic relational needs, such as the need for love, friendship, and social esteem. Flourishing personal relationships—loving relationship, meaningful friendship, proper social esteem, and so on—are also important components of wellbeing. To many of us, these personal relationships may be even more important than work or education.

Thus, our pursuit of a life of basic wellbeing must include, among other things, the pursuit of these flourishing personal relationships. But these relationships require, as a pre-condition, certain attitudes of positive appraisal or appreciation, such as trust, gratitude, approval, and admiration. For example, romantic love requires, in the first place, an attitude of positive appraisal and appreciation of the beloved person for his or her moral and non-moral excellence. Therefore, to have flourishing personal relationships requires, in the first place, to be properly considered for these appraisal and appreciation respects.

Consequently, if respecting people as equally deserving of a life of basic well-being requires that we honor and protect some minimum form of equality of opportunity to work and to become educated, it should also require that we honor and protect some minimum form of proper consideration for appraisal and appreciation respects. The alleged gap between the public and the private realm may give us reason for lowering the bar of the minimum-level honoring and protection when we move from the public realm to the private realm, but I find it quite implausible that this gap should justify a complete annihilation of any need for proper honoring and protection when it comes to opportunity to satisfy basic relational needs.

What then should this minimum form of proper consideration for appraisal and appreciation respects consist of? Should it include a requirement that every person be given the same consideration, just like in employment and admission? But when employers consider whom to hire or admission officers consider whom to admit, they need only to consider those who have applied. When we consider potential candidates for appraisal or appreciation respect, there isn't exactly a pool of "applicants"; rather, the potential candidates include anyone whom we have encountered one way or another in our lives. It would be too demanding to ask us to give every such person the same consideration.

I shall not attempt a full account of duty to proper consideration for appraisal and appreciation respects in this paper. All I want to emphasize is that there are ways to honor and protect proper consideration for appraisal and appreciation respects without imposing unreasonable demands. In particular, the following two constraints strike me as quite reasonable.

First, when we are already considering someone for a certain personal relationship or some related appraisal or appreciation respect, it seems reasonable to require that we give that person a consideration that is fair. Second, it also seems reasonable to require that, among those whom we have encountered multiple times in our lives, we do not constantly deny some of them such consideration. For example, occasionally forgetting to invite people of a certain race to one's party need not indicate denial of equal respect. But if one constantly excludes people of that race from being considered as potential guests, he treats them as if they are less deserving of his friendship.

Therefore, if we accept the duty of equal moral recognition respect and believe that our basic wellbeing includes flourishing personal relationships, we should accept, at least, the following moral constraints on "what to do" when it comes to appraisal and appreciation respects: we ought not to intentionally deny a fair consideration to anyone whom we are already considering for appraisal or appreciation respect, and we ought not to constantly deny such consideration to someone whom we have encountered multiple times in our lives.

By fair consideration for appraisal or appreciation respect, I mean, first, a consideration based on a criterion that is equally applied to everyone. It is unfair to subject some people to a more demanding criterion while others are evaluated against a less demanding one.

Second, a fair consideration must be based on a criterion that has an appropriate justification. An appropriately justified criterion for appraisal or appreciation respect is one based on the object's relevant excellence.[10] Which excellence is relevant in a given context is usually determined by what kind of qualities is in fact directly contributive to the type of relationship at issue. For example, in the case of friendship, qualities such as honesty and compassion are directly contributive to good friendship. Thus, it is appropriate to value and trust an honest and compassionate friend more than a dishonest and indifferent friend. By contrast, it is usually unjustified to use height as the differentiating criterion in the case of friendship, for height is usually not directly contributive to good friendship.[11]

In addition, I think we should add that the justification of the criterion must not itself imply denial of equal moral recognition respect. It may seem reasonable, for instance, not to make friends with people of a certain race if doing so would incur social shame upon oneself—there is a real contributing relation between not incurring social shame and suitability for friendship in this context. But accepting this justification would imply acquiescence to an existing practice that already denies people equal moral recognition respect—it is equivalent to admitting that it is indeed shameful to make friends with them.[12]

To sum up, if the duty of equal moral recognition respect requires that we honor and protect some minimum form of equality of opportunity to work and to become educated since satisfaction of one's basic material and spiritual needs is essential to a life of basic wellbeing, it should also require that we honor and protect some minimum form of proper consideration for appraisal and appreciation respects that are important to basic relational wellbeing. We fail to give a person that minimum form of proper consideration if we intentionally or constantly deny that person a fair consideration, a consideration based on a criterion which is applied to everyone and which picks out qualities that are directly contributive to the type of relationship at issue.

Therefore, accepting the moral constraints arising from equal moral recognition respect does entail accepting certain moral constraints on "what to do" when it comes to appraisal and appreciation respects. Consequently, the alleged gap between the public and the private realm is not as big as it first appears. The same reason that moves us to oppose racial and sexual discrimination in the public realm should also move us to oppose a personal preference like racial looksism.

Racial looksism, as an overgeneralization, is based on a criterion[13] that is not directly contributive to the having of a particular physical appearance and thus irrelevant to assessing one's aesthetic appeal. Such a preference, thus, constantly denies some people a fair consideration for appreciation respect and violates the duty of equal respect. This is why racial looksism is not just offensive and disrespectful, but also morally wrong.

By contrast, simple looksism usually does not involve employment of a proxy like race; it is based directly on individual physical appearance. It thus does not deny the objects a consideration for appreciation respect that is fair in the given context. Of course, people may have different opinions regarding the aesthetic attractiveness of a particular physical trait—some may find fat people sexually attractive for example. But when a person finds fat people unattractive because, in his personal view, excessive weight is an aesthetic turnoff, he has a prima facie justification—it seems reasonable to believe that body shape and proportionality are directly contributive to aesthetic appeal.

Hence, there is a relevant difference between racial looksism and simple looksism: racial looksism is based on something not directly contributive to aesthetic appeal and thus denies people a fair consideration; whereas simple looksism is based on something directly contributive to aesthetic appeal and thus does not deny people a fair consideration. On this very score, we have reason to morally object to the former, but not the latter.

One may object: "What if some people indeed find a certain race an aesthetic turnoff for them, would that give them a prima facie justification?" But the problem is that such race-qua-race racial looksism would imply already denial of fundamental equality. Such a preference treats a whole racial group as simply aesthetically inferior, regardless of how each individual actually looks. It manifests a demeaning attitude that denies people of that race their fundamental equality.[14]

Of course, our current aesthetic preference against certain physical appearance might turn out involving denial of equality as well, or it might ultimately be proven unjustified. For example, some people may find fat people unattractive because they, mistakenly, take excessive weight as a sign of laziness. If one can show that an aesthetic preference indeed involves denial of fundamental equality or a false contributing relation, then such a preference will also be objectionable.[15] But until a sound argument to this effect is provided, simple looksism has at least a prima facie justification.

Finally, I should note that, even though I think some forms of simple looksism, as mere preferences, are morally acceptable, actually excluding people from relationships simply by virtue of their looks is usually not. To deny people friendship, for instance, simply because they are fat or thin is to ignore the traits relevant to friendship (such as moral characters) and thus to fail to give them a fair consideration.

5 RESPONSE TO OBJECTIONS

Let's consider some objections. First, one may find my focus on preferences objectionable. What seems to really matter for our wellbeing is how our interpersonal relationships actually turn out, not how our attractiveness is appreciated. One who does not find a certain group of people attractive can nevertheless develop a relationship with them. Therefore, our focus should not be preferences like racial looksism, but biases and prejudices in the actual dealing of relationship.

I have four responses. First, appreciation respect is an important part of our wellbeing. Imagine a female scholar who works in a male-dominated environment. Because of her sex, her intelligence is constantly underrated by her male colleagues. Even though she still enjoys her academic endeavor, it is easy to see how her sense of fulfillment can be greatly diminished by the lack of due appreciation from her peers.

Second, how we view others in their intellectual and aesthetic value is connected to how we value them as persons at a deeper level. A person who, for purely prudential reasons, discriminates against people of another race in relationship may nevertheless view them as fundamentally equal to him; but if a person views a whole race simply as aesthetically or intellectually inferior, chances are this person has a more fundamental disbelief in equality.

Third, the discrimination that one faces in actual relationships may be rooted in just those biases at the appreciation level. The reason why an employer discriminates against an Asian candidate of equal qualification may be precisely that he views Asians as less enjoyable people to invite to a bar or to a movie. Thus, unless biases at the appreciation level are properly addressed, discrimination in actual relationships is likely to persist. Focusing merely on discrimination in actual relationships is like treating the symptom without treating the disease.

Lastly, the reason why we are biased against a certain social group is often that we have failed to allow them into our personal lives. So, one recipe for treating such biases is to make an effort to invite members of that group into our personal lives, to interact with them, and to recognize the attractive traits in them.[16] Since preferences like racial looksism are precisely the kind of things that would prevent us from making such an effort, this is why it is especially important to address them. These are the reasons why I think it is important to bring to light a preference like racial looksism and to articulate unequivocally why it is morally objectionable.

Another objection may be directed at my focus on overgeneralization. It is well recognized that statistical discrimination, discrimination based on statistical evidence that a certain social group differ from other groups in some particular aspect, are not per se wrong (Alexander 1992; Lippert-Rasmussen 2007). For example, Lippert-Rasmussen (2007) points out that certain kinds of racial profiling, such as giving a closer scrutiny at the airport security checkpoint to people from regions where terrorism-risk is statistically much higher, can be justified. One may argue that this kind of racial profiling is also an overgeneralization: it is certainly not the case that every person from those regions is a terrorist, and thus being a resident of those regions is not directly contributive to being a terrorist. If racial looksism is morally wrong because it is an overgeneralization that denies its objects some important form of respect, wouldn't this be true for other kinds of statistical discrimination as well?

One important difference is that racial looksism is exclusionary. Statistical discrimination such as closer security scrutiny at the airport does not completely exclude people coming from high-risk regions from being considered for admission; rather, it takes into account relevant individual background in the consideration for admission. A total exclusion is much harder to justify than merely giving closer scrutiny to a certain group. Imagine that the airport security staff decides, based on the statistical fact that terrorism-risk in certain regions is high, to automatically deny entrance to every passenger coming from those regions, regardless of that person's actual background. No reasonable person would find such a decision acceptable. It is unacceptable precisely because it denies people from those regions a fair consideration.

Another type of statistical discrimination that is justified does involve total exclusion. Universities often, in their admission process, automatically turn down applicants whose test scores are below a certain threshold. The underlying rationale is usually that, statistically, students who score below a certain threshold are less likely to thrive academically. But, of course, not every student thus excluded would be doomed to fail in the university. Thus, if racial looksism is wrong, won't such practice be wrong too?

An important difference between the two is that the skills assessed by those academic tests are directly contributive to academic performance (or so we tend to believe), and thus using an applicant's individual scores as the differentiating criterion does offer the applicant a consideration based on his or her relevant individual qualities. By contrast, racial looksism disregards the relevant individual qualities. This is why statistical discrimination based on individual test scores is justified, but racial looksism is not. Admittedly, the academic tests currently relied on by university admission offices do not necessarily accurately measure every relevant aspect of academic potential. But this just means that we need to improve these tests and make them as fair and accurate as possible, for the very reason I am stressing.

Here is another case worth considering. Lippert-Rasmussen mentioned that it is often "permissible to not hire an alcoholic as a pilot given statistical information that most alcoholics from time to time fail to keep sober on the job" (2007, 395). One may argue that not all alcoholics have problems keeping sober on the job, and thus, if my reasoning is right, excluding them from being considered for a pilot job merely on the basis of the statistical fact that most alcoholics have such problems will also be wrong.

My response is that if the underlying rationale for such a hiring policy is based on what most alcoholics are like, regardless of whether a given individual is able to remain sober on the job, then this policy is indeed questionable. However, the rationale need not be based on some crude group statistic—i.e. statistic that looks superficially at how most individuals in a given group behave without attending to individual differences; it can be based on the fact that, for any individual alcoholic, it is more likely that he or she will turn up inebriated to work. In other words, addiction to alcohol can be something directly contributive to higher risk of intoxication at the individual level, and higher risk of intoxication is a relevant individual quality in the evaluation of whether a candidate is suitable for a pilot job. Exclusionary treatment based on crude group statistics often risks denial of a fair consideration to some members of that group; exclusionary treatment based on the relevant individual tendency, on the other hand, is usually free of such risk.[17]

In reality, however, there is often no way to determine individual tendency in the absence of group statistic. It is unrealistic, for instance, to follow each applicant to find out how many times he or she turns up inebriated to work. Often, we have to rely on group statistic. This is certainly true. My point here is not to discredit all group statistics. Rather, my point is to call our attention to two different kinds of group statistic from which we may draw conclusion about individual tendency. One type of group statistic is grounded on some common feature that is directly contributive to one's having certain individual tendency relevant in the given consideration. For example, one may find out that all alcoholics share a type of physical mechanism that is similarly vulnerable to alcohol-caused impairment to self-control. Consequently, statistical information on how most alcoholics are affected by this addiction can provide useful information on how a given individual will be affected, which is relevant in the consideration for hiring a pilot. The other type, crude group statistic, is grounded on some common feature that is not directly contributive to one's having certain individual tendency relevant in the given consideration. For example, being a male black living in Chicago's Hyde Park area is not directly contributive to being violent and crime-prone, even if the criminal rate of black people in that area is high; and being a tourist from mainland China is not directly contributive to being a walking disgrace in the streets of Hong Kong, even though a significant portion of those tourists do behave in an unpleasant way.

So, even though racial looksism and the hiring policy concerning alcoholics are both based on group statistics, the former ignores the relevant individual qualities but the latter need not. As we can see, not all statistical discriminations are wrong. A statistical discrimination is wrong only when the statistic fact about a group is used to deny a member of that group a consideration based on his or her relevant individual qualities.

Let's consider a third objection. Even if I refuse to develop a personal relationship with people of a certain race, they may still have plenty of opportunities to develop personal relationships with other people or with people of their own race. Thus, my refusal to be associated with them does not necessarily deprive them of their opportunity to have flourishing personal relationships.

But by the same reasoning, employers could also defend their discriminatory actions by arguing that "I have no personal obligation to treat you equally since your equal opportunity is already suitably protected by the society" or that "there are other employers out there and you still have plenty of opportunities to find a job in their places or in your own racial community." Injury to other people's wellbeing can be a reason why discrimination is wrong;[18] but there is also something intrinsically wrong about a preference like racial looksism—it disregards the victims' individuality and, by doing so, denies them a fair consideration.

The fourth objection is this: homosexuals are attracted only to people of the same sex and heterosexuals only to people of the opposite sex, but there are beautiful people in either sex, much like there are beautiful people in every race. If racial looksism is wrong because it is an overgeneralization, won't sexual preference also be wrong for the same reason?

The difference between sexual preference and racial looksism is that sex as such is directly contributive to sexual appeal whereas race as such is not. It matters to sexual appeal how good looking one is, to which sex is indeed irrelevant; but what also matters to sexual appeal is, as a biological fact, one's sexual characteristics. One's sexual characteristics are directly contributive to one's sexual appeal to a given person.[19] Thus, there is an appropriate justification for discriminating on the basis of sex in the context of assessing sexual appeal. Unlike racial looksism, sexual preference usually does not deny people a consideration that is fair in the given context.

Here is another objection. According to my account, racial looksism is wrong because race is an irrelevant factor in the given context and thus such a preference denies people a fair consideration. If this account is right, then there should be no difference between using an irrelevant factor like race as the differentiating criterion and using an irrelevant factor like, say, handedness as the differentiating criterion. But usually we don't find the latter as offensive.

I think the fundamental moral structure is identical in these two cases. Two factors make differential treatment based on race more offensive. First, certain races are historically associated with various negative stereotypes, most of which depict a certain race as servants, subordinates, or even animals. Thus, differential treatment motivated by such negative stereotyping often manifests a more grave disrespect of dignity. Second, as we mentioned earlier, the injury to its victims is also a reason why discrimination is wrong. Owing to those existing negative stereotypes, a race-based differential treatment is likely to invite the victims to think about those negative portraits of them and thus result in a much greater insult. By contrast, differential treatment based on handedness does not have such an unpleasant history and is not associated with many salient negative stereotypes. Consequently, differential treatment based on handedness often incurs less outrage and scrutiny.

The sixth objection goes like this. We often give louder applause to our family members, friends, and classmates for their achievement, even if their achievement is not greater than the achievement of a stranger. Does my theory also say that preferences of this kind are morally wrong?

As I clarified earlier, what I find objectionable is exclusionary preferences like racial looksism, not all preferences in personal relationships. There are certainly legitimate moral grounds for differential treatment in personal relationships. For example, being a family member usually means deeper attachment to other family members' wellbeing, and thus it is natural for us to feel more excited and appreciative if they succeed. Therefore, as long as we give people a fair consideration and show them appraisal or appreciation respect appropriate to their relevant qualities, we can be justified, on grounds other than equal respect, in giving additional appreciation to certain people.

Let's consider one last objection. Suppose someone posts the following conditional caveat: "No Asians, unless having such and such physical features." This partially exclusionary preference does take into consideration relevant factors—i.e. certain physical features, and thus is not an overgeneralization. But we may feel that even this conditional caveat is wrong. So, one may object that my overgeneralization account of why racial looksism is wrong does not quite capture its wrongfulness.

My first response is that overgeneralization is one reason why an exclusionary preference like racial looksism is wrong; but I do not claim that it is the only ground for thinking it is wrong. For example, one can also argue that an expression like "No Asians, unless having such and such physical features" tends to change the power dynamics concerning races in the society and thus suppress certain racial groups.[20] This could be another reason why such an expression is wrong. (Of course, on this ground, there will be no morally relevant difference between racial looksism and simple looksism.)

Does this show my account, which focuses on overgeneralization and equal respect and leaves out other moral considerations, is at least inadequate for explaining why racial looksism is wrong? Let us reflect more carefully on the intuition that a conditional caveat like "No Asians, unless having such and such physical features" is wrong. Is this intuition well-grounded? Depending on how we interpret it.

On one interpretation, the caveat can be taken as saying "Asians, by default, are unlikable, but my preference for certain physical appearance could still trump my general dislike for Asians." The caveat so understood implies a demeaning, race-qua-race racial looksism—viewing a whole race as simply aesthetically inferior (at least by default). I have explained earlier, by appealing to the duty of equal respect, why this strong form of racial looksism is wrong. So, if this is why we find the conditional caveat wrong, my account can perfectly accommodate our intuition.

On another interpretation, the caveat can be taken as saying "Asians with such and such physical appearance are likable; Asians with such and such physical appearance are unlikable." The caveat so understood will imply a straightforward simple looksism—it differentiates simply by means of physical appearance and the word "Asians" becomes less relevant and could be replaced by any other racial identity. Is there good reason for thinking that this simple looksism is definitely wrong? Given the discriminative nature of appraisal and appreciation respects, it is hard to see why it is. If a preference for certain physical strength in sports, say, is morally acceptable, why isn't a taste for certain physical appearance in dating? Appearance is as relevant to sexual appeal as athleticism to sport competition.

Of course, one may appeal to the alteration of the power dynamics concerning looks in society or maybe the harm resulting from some existing negative stereotypes to explain why that simple looksism is wrong. But even if the conditional caveat is wrong on these grounds, it will be wrong only contingently. We cannot provide, on these grounds, a more general account for why cases that share the same discriminative structure with this conditional caveat are wrong. For example, we would have great difficulty explaining why people would also frown at a caveat like "No right-handed or Caucasian."

This is why I chose to focus on overgeneralization and equal respect, which I believe provide a more general ground for explaining the intrinsic wrongfulness of discrimination.

6   CONCLUDING REMARKS

Dignity entitles every person to some equal respect at the fundamental level. Everyone's pursuit of a life of basic wellbeing, such as opportunities to work and to become educated, deserves to be equally respected. While this entitlement to equal respect does not mean absolute equal share of respect in every aspect of life, it does require us, when it comes differential treatment in appraisal and appreciation respects that are important to wellbeing, not to intentionally or constantly deny people who we have encountered in life a fair consideration—a consideration based on their relevant individual qualities. Appreciation respects, especially those involved in romantic relationship and friendship, are important for relational wellbeing, and thus a fair consideration for them should not be intentionally or constantly denied to any person that we have encountered in life. An overgeneralization like racial looksism treats a person not by his or her relevant individual quality, and thus constantly denies some people a fair consideration for some important form of appreciation. This is why racial lookism is morally wrong.

The tendency to generalize on the basis of some common feature may be something embedded in our genetics—it is easy to see the evolutionary advantage of having such a tendency. For example, a person who tends to learn to avoid snakes after being attacked by one is more likely to survive than a person who does not. But this does not mean such tendency is always morally justifiable when operating in other contexts. In cases of appraisal and appreciation respects that are important for basic wellbeing, for instance, treating a person merely on the basis of that person's social identity is often morally objectionable, as it tends to deny that person a fair consideration based on his or her relevant individual quality. In such contexts, the tendency to generalize is often something that we should try to constrain.

The value of equality and individuality has been the driving force behind many of our recent social and political changes. In this paper, I tried to argue that, to truly achieve the moral ideal in which everyone's individuality is properly respected and everyone genuinely enjoys an equality of opportunity to a life of basic wellbeing, change needs to be brought a step further—from the social and political level to the more personal level. While this argument may upset the received view on personal freedom—as people tend to think that whom to date or invite to a bar is a personal matter, I hope that my argument has at least succeeded in showing that, if we truly care about equality and individuality, there is some good reason to endure a "personal" upset.

Changing a personal preference such as racial looksism is difficult. But there are things we can do: we can put ourselves in a position that would lead us to change such a preference. For example, we can invite people of a different race into our personal lives and expose ourselves to their attractive traits. These are small steps that we can take to enable a big leap in the direction of greater equality. I hope that, by raising an issue like racial looksism, this paper will call attention to the biases and prejudices hidden in the corners of our private lives, which have, by and large, escaped the academic limelight.

NOTES

1. He wrote: "Gay men are not necessarily racist; instead, we are "look[s]ist," perhaps even more so than our straight counterparts. And the idealized vision of gay Adonis in the United States is white. . . . Asians seem relegated to the bottom of the attractiveness spectrum. . . . This is racial look[s]ism."

2. Sexual appeal can be affected by things other than appearance. For simplicity and because of the context in which the issue of racial looksism is raised, this paper focuses on appearance-based reason for sexual appeal.

3. One can further ask whether non-exclusionary preferences can also be questioned. I will consider two such cases (the last two objections) in Section 5.

4. A number of philosophers have argued that we can be morally responsible for behaviors over which we lack voluntary control. See, for example, Adams (1985), McKenna (2004), Sher (2006), and Smith (2008).

5. A quick clarification on terminology. I treat bias as a certain kind of preference, preference that ultimately lacks an appropriate justification. I further understand prejudice as a biased judgment.

6. Holroyd (2012) makes a similar point. Holroyd argues that individuals who are not responsible for being influenced by implicit bias can nevertheless meet sufficient conditions for responsibility, when they have "long range control" for taking actions to mitigate implicit biases or when their "reflective level beliefs and attitudes. . . . manifest implicit biases."

7. Sexism as an overgeneralization is also recognized by the U.S. Supreme Court. In the 1996 *U.S vs Virginia* case, the U.S. Supreme Court ruled against the male-only

admission policy of Virginia Military Institute on the basis that such a policy is an "overbroad generalization" and that a public policy "must not rely on overbroad generalizations about the different talents, capacities, or preferences of males and females."

8. Some theorists believe that discrimination like racism and sexism in employment or admission is wrong because it fails to give people equal respect. For respect-based theories, see, for example, Ely (1980), Dworkin (1985), Hellman (2008), and Shin (2009).

9. They differ in that, while appraisal respect responds to excellence typically resulting from one's moral characters, appreciation respect responds to excellence that is usually not a result of one's moral characters.

10. Some theorists hold similar views. For instance, Alan Goldman (1979) and Sidney Hook (1995) argue that hiring decisions based on race, sex, religion and other social categories are wrong because such decisions should be based on who is best qualified for the post. Although Hook and Goldman focus on decisions in employment, such decisions inevitably involve assessment of appraisal and appreciation respects.

11. These contributing relations, such as character traits to suitability for friendship and basketball skills to value of a basketball player, are not something that we can simply ignore or alter at will; rather, they are what any rational person needs to take into account in the planning for and the pursuit of a good life. Thus, these contributing relations constitute the normative fabric of our interpersonal relationships. A rational person would not subscribe to a differentiating criterion in interpersonal relationship that is not grounded on real contributing relations, and would not use it as the basis for his or her expectations of and plans for a good life. This is why differential treatment based on such a criterion is unfair.

12. There might be cases in which one decides not to make friends with members of another group not because he thinks it is shameful to make friends with them, but simply because he does not want to lose friends in his own group. How should I respond to such cases? One possible response is to insist that such an act does imply denial of equal moral recognition respect—acquiescence to one's fellow members' denial of equal respect is a form of denying equal respect. Another is to say that such an act does not imply denial of equal moral recognition respect and thus is not intrinsically wrong; but it can still be wrong because it injures members of the other group. I am not sure which response is better. However, offering a completely satisfactory answer to such cases is not essential to my main task. Thus, I will leave it as an unsettled issue in my account.

13. The criterion need not be consciously or explicitly employed. A preference may differentiate at a subconscious level.

14. For the same reason, it would be wrong for one to prefer country music to rap music for the sole reason that rap music is a type of music that black people like. Disliking a type of music for purely race-related reasons is equivalent to saying that one race is simply aesthetically inferior and any music they like is thus inferior. Such a musical taste manifests a demeaning attitude toward people of that race, one that denies them their fundamental equality. Musical taste is not always "just a personal matter"; it can be a moral issue.

15. It is also possible to have a case in which, even if some types of obesity appear aesthetically unattractive to an individual, not all types of obesity do. And if that individual excludes all fat people from being considered as attractive, he would also deny some of them a fair consideration. I agree that, in such cases, simple looksism is also wrong. However, in cases in which being fat is indeed an aesthetic turnoff to someone, that person does have an appropriate justification for this preference. This is in direct contrast with a race-qua-race racial looksism, which simply takes a whole race as unattractive and thus denies people of that race their fundamental equality and demeans them.

16. In a review of 203 studies from 25 countries, involving 90,000 participants, Thomas Pettigrew and Linda Tropp (2000) discovered that, 94% of the time, biases and prejudices diminished as intergroup contact increased.

17. One may object that individual tendency also does not guarantee that one will behave in the same way on every occasion, and thus also risks overgeneralization. But, in the case of pilot assessment, what's relevant is precisely the chances of intoxication on duty. This is why exclusionary treatment based on individual tendency in this case is not an overgeneralization.

18. One popular view on why racism or sexism is wrong is the *injury-based view*, according to which, racial or sexual discrimination in employment or admission is wrong because it undermines the victims' equal opportunity to access various social resources or because it injures the victims' deliberative freedoms. For accounts of this kind, see Fiss (1976), Gardner (1998), Pose (2000), Lippert-Rasmussen (2006), Moreau (2010), and Segall (2012).

19. For some people, such as bisexuals, sexual characteristics are less relevant to sexual appeal. If they, without any appropriate justification, exclude a certain sex from being considered as sexually attractive, I think there is also something objectionable. Likewise, if someone only likes men not because he is biologically attracted only to people with male sexual characteristics, but because he views

femininity as inferior to masculinity, and female bodily traits inferior to male bodily traits, I think there is something wrong about such a sexual preference.

20. I would like to thank Ruth E. Groenhout for raising this point.

REFERENCES

Adams, R. (1985) Involuntary sins. *The Philosophical Review* 93: 3–31.

Alexander, L. (1992) What makes wrongful discrimination wrong? Biases, preferences, stereotypes, and proxies. *University of Pennsylvania Law Review* 141: 149–219.

Altman, A. (2011) Discrimination. *Stanford Encyclopedia of Philosophy.* http://plato.stanford. edu/entries/discrimination/#WroDirDis. Accessed by March 4 2015.

Arneson, R. (2002) Equality of opportunity. *Stanford Encyclopedia of Philosophy.* http://plato.stanford.edu/entries/ equal-opportunity/#6. Accessed by October 1 2014.

Blair, I. V., Ma, J. E., Lenton, A. P. (2001) Imagining stereotypes away: the moderation of implicit stereotypes through mental imagery. *Journal of Personality and Social Psychology* 81: 828–841.

Darwall, S. (1977) Two kinds of respect. *Ethics* 88: 36–49.

Dasgupta, N., Greenwald, A. G. (2001) On the malleability of automatic attitudes: combating automatic prejudice with images of admired and disliked individuals. *Journal of Personality and Social Psychology* 81: 800–814.

Dworkin, R. (1985) *A matter of principle.* Cambridge: Harvard University Press.

Ely, J. (1980) *Democracy and distrust.* Cambridge: Harvard University Press.

Fiss, O. (1976) Groups and the equal protection clause. *Philosophy and Public Affairs* 5: 107–77.

Gardner, J. (1998) On the ground of her sex(uality). *Oxford Journal of Legal Studies* 18: 167–187.

Goldman, A. (1979) *Justice and reverse discrimination.* Princeton: Princeton University Press.

Goodman, A. H., Moses, Y. T., Jones, J. L. (2012) *Race: are we so different?* Oxford: Wiley-Blackwell.

Hellman, D. (2008) *Why is discrimination wrong?* Cambridge: Harvard University Press.

Holroyd, J. (2012) Responsibility for implicit bias. *Journal of Social Philosophy* 43: 274–306.

Hook, S. (1995) Reverse discrimination. In S. Cahn (ed.) *The affirmative action debate.* New York: Routledge, pp. 145–152.

Kant, I. (1996) The metaphysics of morals. In M. Gregor (trans & ed) *Practical philosophy.* Cambridge: Harvard University Press.

Laan, E., Janssen, E. (2007) How do men and women feel? Determinants of subjective experience of sexual arousal. In E. Janssen (ed.) *The psychophysiology of sex.* Bloomington: Indiana University Press, pp. 278–290.

Lippert-Rasmussen, K. (2006) The badness of discrimination. *Ethical Theory and Moral Practice* 9: 167–85.

Lippert-Rasmussen, K. (2007) Nothing personal: on statistical discrimination. *Journal of Political Philosophy* 15: 385–404.

McKenna, M. (2004) Responsibility and globally manipulated agents. *Philosophical Topics* 32: 169–82.

Moreau, S. (2010) What is discrimination. *Philosophy and Public Affairs* 38: 143–79.

Mullany, G. (2014) Backlash over Hong Kong's treatment of mainland visitors. *The New York Times.* http://sinosphere.blogs.nytimes.com/2014/04/23/backlash-over-hong-kongs-treatment-of-mainland-visitors/. Accessed October 11 2014.

Nguyen, J. (2011) Gaysians are beautiful. *The Advocate.* http://www.advocate.com/politics/commentary/2011/03/03/gaysians-are-beautiful-jimmy-nguyen. Accessed March 15 2013.

Pettigrew, T. F., Tropp, L. R. (2000) Does intergroup contact reduce prejudice? Recent meta-analytic findings. In S. Oskamp (ed.) *Reducing prejudice and discrimination.* Mahwah: Erlbaum, pp. 93–114.

Pfaus, J. G. (2007) Models of sexual motivation. In E. Janssen (ed.) The *psychophysiology of sex.* Bloomington: Indiana University Press, pp. 340–362.

Pose, R. (2000) Prejudicial appearances: the logic of American anti-discrimination law. *California Law Review* 88: 1–40.

Rudman, L. A., Ashmore, R. D., Gary, M. L. (2001) 'Unlearning' automatic biases: the malleability of implicit prejudice and stereotypes. *Journal of Personality and Social Psychology* 81: 856–868.

Segall, S. (2012) What's so bad about discrimination. *Utilitas* 24: 82–100.

Sher, G. (2006) Out of control. *Ethics* 116: 285–301.

Shin, P. (2009) The substantive principle of equal treatment. *Legal Theory* 15: 149–172.

Smith, A. (2008) Control, responsibility and moral assessment. *Philosophical Studies* 138: 367–92.

Steele, C. M. (2011) *Whistling Vivaldi: how stereotypes affect us and what we can do.* New York: W. W. Norton.

United States v. Virginia 518 U.S. 515 (1996). https://supreme.justia.com/cases/federal/us/ 518/515/. Accessed July 8 2013.

Zillmann, D., Bryant, J. (1988) Pornography's impact on sexual satisfaction. *Journal of Applied Social Psychology* 18: 438–453.

DISCUSSION QUESTIONS

1. Liu argues that even "mere preferences" are "subject to moral appraisal." What does he mean by this? How does he argue for that claim? Do you find his arguments convincing? Why or why not?
2. What is Liu's main argument for his conclusion that "racial looksism" is morally wrong, but that "simple looksism" is not? Do you find this argument convincing? Why or why not?
3. Of the various objections that Liu considers, which do you think is most important? How does he respond to that objection? Do you find his response convincing? Why or why not?
4. Do you think racial looksism is always racist? Why or why not? Would Jorge Garcia (the author of an earlier reading) agree with you? Why or why not?

Abortion

MARY ANNE WARREN (1946–2010)

On the Moral and Legal Status of Abortion

Mary Anne Warren was Professor Emerita of Philosophy at San Francisco State University. She helped establish applied ethics as a serious subfield of philosophy, writing mainly on ethical questions raised by reproductive issues, such as abortion. In this classic paper, Warren argues that although a fetus is a human being in a biological sense, it does not have the features that make something a person in the morally relevant sense.

GUIDING QUESTIONS

1. What is the main conclusion that Warren aims to establish? Why does she think that conclusion is important for thinking about the morality of abortion?
2. What is the "traditional" argument against abortion? According to Warren, what is the problem with that argument?
3. What criteria does Warren give for including something as a full-fledged member of the moral community? What role do those criteria play in her argument about abortion?
4. Warren considers two major objections to her main conclusion. What are those objections and how does Warren respond to them?

Mary Anne Warren. "On the Moral and Legal Status of Abortion." *The Monist* (1973) 57 (1): 43–61. © 1973 Oxford University Press. Article has been excerpted, and notes have been renumbered.

We will be concerned with both the moral status of abortion, which for our purposes we may define as the act which a woman performs in voluntarily terminating, or allowing another person to terminate, her pregnancy, and the legal status which is appropriate for this act. I will argue that . . . it is possible to show that, on the basis of intuitions which we may expect even the opponents of abortion to share, a fetus is not a person, and hence not the sort of entity to which it is proper to ascribe full moral rights.

Of course, while some philosophers would deny the possibility of any such proof others will deny that there is any need for it, since the moral permissibility of abortion appears to them to be too obvious to require proof. But the inadequacy of this attitude should be evident from the fact that both the friends and the foes of abortion consider their position to be morally self-evident. Because proabortionists have never adequately come to grips with the conceptual issues surrounding abortion, most if not all, of the arguments which they advance in opposition to laws restricting access to abortion fail to refute or even weaken the traditional antiabortion argument, i.e., that a fetus is a human being, and therefore abortion is murder.

These arguments are typically of one of two sorts. Either they point to the terrible side effects of the restrictive laws, e.g., the deaths due to illegal abortions, and the fact that it is poor women who suffer the most as a result of these laws, or else they state that to deny a woman access to abortion is to deprive her of her right to control her own body. Unfortunately, however, the fact that restricting access to abortion has tragic side effects does not, in itself, show that the restrictions are unjustified, since murder is wrong regardless of the consequences of prohibiting it; and the appeal to the right to control one's body, which is generally construed as a property right, is at best a rather feeble argument for the permissibility of abortion. Mere ownership does not give me the right to kill innocent people whom I find on my property, and indeed I am apt to be held responsible if such people injure themselves while on my property. It is equally unclear that I have any moral right to expel an innocent person from my property when I know that doing so will result in his death. . . .

But however we wish to construe the right to abortion, we cannot hope to convince those who consider abortion a form of murder of the existence of any such right unless we are able to produce a clear and convincing refutation of the traditional antiabortion argument, and this has not, to my knowledge, been done. With respect to the two most vital issues which that argument involves, i.e., the humanity of the fetus and its implication for the moral status of abortion, confusion has prevailed on both sides of the dispute. . . .

John Noonan is correct in saying that "the fundamental question in the long history of abortion is, How do you determine the humanity of a being?"[1] He summarizes his own antiabortion argument, which is a version of the official position of the Catholic Church, as follows:

> . . . it is wrong to kill humans, however poor, weak, defenseless, and lacking in opportunity to develop their potential they may be. It is therefore morally wrong to kill Biafrans. Similarly, it is morally wrong to kill embryos.[2]

Noonan bases his claim that fetuses are human upon what he calls the theologians' criterion of humanity: that whoever is conceived of human beings is human.

. . . In Section II, I will argue that a fetus cannot be considered a member of the moral community, the set of beings with full and equal moral rights, for the simple reason that it is not a person, and that it is personhood, and not genetic humanity, i.e., humanity as defined by Noonan, which is the basis for membership in this community. I will argue that a fetus, whatever its stage of development, satisfies none of the basic criteria of personhood, and is not even enough like a person to be accorded even some of the same rights on the basis of this resemblance. Nor, as we will see, is a fetus's potential personhood a threat to the morality of abortion, since, whatever the rights of potential people may be, they are invariably overridden in any conflict with the moral rights of actual people. . . .

II

The question which we must answer in order to produce a satisfactory solution to the problem of the moral status of abortion is this: How are we to define the moral community, the set of beings with full and equal moral rights, such that we can decide whether a human fetus is a member of this community or not? What sort of entity, exactly, has the inalienable rights to life, liberty, and the pursuit of happiness? Jefferson attributed these rights to all *men,* and it may or may not be fair to suggest that he intended to attribute them *only* to men. Perhaps he ought to have attributed them to all human beings. If so, then we arrive, first, at Noonan's problem of defining what makes a being human, and, second, at the equally vital question which Noonan does not consider, namely, What reason is there for identifying the moral community with the set of all human beings, in whatever way we have chosen to define that term?

1. On the Definition of 'Human'

One reason why this vital second question is so frequently overlooked in the debate over the moral status of abortion is that the term 'human' has two distinct, but not often distinguished, senses. This fact results in a slide of meaning, which serves to conceal the fallaciousness of the traditional argument that since (1) it is wrong to kill innocent human beings, and (2) fetuses are innocent human beings, then (3) it is wrong to kill fetuses. For if 'human' is used in the same sense in both (1) and (2) then, whichever of the two senses is meant, one of these premises is question-begging. And if it is used in two different senses then of course the conclusion doesn't follow.

Thus, (1) is a self-evident moral truth,[3] and avoids begging the question about abortion, only if 'human being' is used to mean something like "a full-fledged member of the moral community." (It may or may not also be meant to refer exclusively to members of the species *Homo sapiens.)* We may call this the *moral* sense of 'human.' It is not to be confused with what we will call the *genetic* sense, i.e., the sense in which *any* member of the species is a human being, and no member of any other species could be. If (1) is acceptable only if the moral sense is intended, (2) is non-question-begging only if what is intended is the genetic sense.

In "Deciding Who Is Human," Noonan argues for the classification of fetuses with human beings by pointing to the presence of the full genetic code, and the potential capacity for rational thought (p. 135). It is clear that what he needs to show, for his version of the traditional argument to be valid, is that fetuses are human in the moral sense, the sense in which it is analytically true that all human beings have full moral rights. But, in the absence of any argument showing that whatever is genetically human is also morally human, and he gives none, nothing more than genetic humanity can be demonstrated by the presence of the human genetic code. And, as we will see, the *potential* capacity for rational thought can at most show that an entity has the potential for *becoming* human in the moral sense.

2. Defining the Moral Community

Can it be established that genetic humanity is sufficient for moral humanity? I think that there are very good reasons for not defining the moral community in this way. I would like to suggest an alternative way of defining the moral community, which I will argue for only to the extent of explaining why it is, or should be, self-evident. The suggestion is simply that the moral community consists of all and only *people,* rather than all and only human beings;[4] and probably the best way of demonstrating its self-evidence is by considering the concept of personhood, to see what sorts of entity are and are not persons, and what the decision that a being is or is not a person implies about its moral rights.

What characteristics entitle an entity to be considered a person? This is obviously not the place to attempt a complete analysis of the concept of personhood, but we do not need such a fully adequate analysis just to determine whether and why a fetus is or isn't a person. All we need is a rough and approximate list of the most basic criteria of personhood, and some idea of which, or how many, of these an entity must satisfy in order to properly be considered a person.

In searching for such criteria, it is useful to look beyond the set of people with whom we are acquainted, and ask how we would decide whether a totally alien being was a person or not. (For we have no right to assume that genetic humanity is necessary for personhood.) Imagine a space traveler who lands on an unknown planet and encounters a race of beings utterly unlike any he has ever seen or heard of. If he wants to be sure of behaving morally toward these beings, he has to somehow decide whether they are people, and hence have full moral rights, or whether they are the sort of thing which he need not feel guilty about treating as, for example, a source of food.

How should he go about making this decision? If he has some anthropological background, he might look for such things as religion, art, and the manufacturing of tools, weapons, or shelters, since these factors have been used to distinguish our human from our prehuman ancestors, in what seems to be closer to the moral than the genetic sense of 'human'. And no doubt he would be right to consider the presence of such factors as good evidence that the alien beings were people, and morally human. It would, however, be overly anthropocentric of him to take the absence of these things as adequate evidence that they were not, since we can imagine people who have progressed beyond, or evolved without ever developing, these cultural characteristics.

I suggest that the traits which are most central to the concept of personhood, or humanity in the moral sense, are, very roughly, the following:

1. consciousness (of objects and events external and/or internal to the being), and in particular the capacity to feel pain;
2. reasoning (the *developed* capacity to solve new and relatively complex problems);
3. self-motivated activity (activity which is relatively independent of either genetic or direct external control);
4. the capacity to communicate, by whatever means, messages of an indefinite variety of types, that is, not just with an indefinite number of possible contents, but on indefinitely many possible topics;
5. the presence of self-concepts, and self-awareness, either individual or racial, or both.

Admittedly, there are apt to be a great many problems involved in formulating precise definitions of these criteria, let alone in developing universally valid behavioral criteria for deciding when they apply. But I will assume that both we and our explorer know approximately what (1)–(5) mean, and that he is also able to determine whether or not they apply. How, then, should he use his findings to decide whether or not the alien beings are people? We needn't suppose that an entity must have *all* of these attributes to be properly considered a person; (1) and (2) alone may well be sufficient for personhood, and quite probably (1)–(3) are sufficient. Neither do we need to insist that any one of these criteria is *necessary* for personhood, although once again (1) and (2) look like fairly good candidates for necessary conditions, as does (3), if 'activity' is construed so as to include the activity of reasoning.

All we need to claim, to demonstrate that a fetus is not a person, is that any being which satisfies *none* of (1)–(5) is certainly not a person. I consider this claim to be so obvious that I think anyone who denied it, and claimed that a being which satisfied none of (1)–(5) was a person all the same, would thereby demonstrate that he had no notion at all of what a person is—perhaps because he had confused the concept of a person with that of genetic humanity. If the opponents of abortion were to deny the appropriateness of these five criteria, I do not know what further arguments would convince them. We would probably have to admit that our conceptual schemes were indeed irreconcilably different, and that our dispute could not be settled objectively.

I do not expect this to happen, however, since I think that the concept of a person is one which is very nearly universal (to people), and that it is common to both proabortionists and antiabortionists, even though neither group has fully realized the relevance of this concept to the resolution of their dispute. Furthermore, I think that on reflection even the antiabortionists ought to agree not only that (1)–(5) are central to the concept of personhood, but also that it is a part of this concept that all and only people have full moral rights. The concept of a person is in part a moral concept; once we have admitted that *x* is a person we have recognized, even if we have not agreed to respect, *x's* right to be treated as a member of the moral community. It is true that the claim that *x* is a *human being* is more commonly voiced as part of an appeal to treat x decently than is the claim that x is a person, but this is either because 'human being' is here used in the sense which implies personhood, or because the genetic and moral senses of 'human' have been confused.

Now if (1)–(5) are indeed the primary criteria of personhood, then it is clear that genetic humanity is neither necessary nor sufficient for establishing that an entity is a person. Some human beings are not people, and there may well be people who are not human beings. A man or woman whose consciousness has been permanently obliterated but who remains alive is a human being which is no longer a person; defective human beings, with no appreciable mental capacity, are not and presumably never will be people; and a fetus is a human being which is not yet a person, and which therefore cannot coherently be said to have full moral rights. Citizens of the next century should be prepared to recognize highly advanced, self-aware robots or computers, should such be developed, and intelligent inhabitants of other worlds, should such be found, as people in the fullest sense, and to respect their moral rights. But to ascribe full moral rights to an entity which is not a person is as absurd as to ascribe moral obligations and responsibilities to such an entity.

3. Fetal Development and the Right to Life

Two problems arise in the application of these suggestions for the definition of the moral community to the determination of the precise moral status of a human fetus. Given that the paradigm example of a person is a normal adult human being, then (1) How like this paradigm, in particular how far advanced since conception, does a human being need to be before it begins to have a right to life by virtue, not of being fully a person as of yet, but of being *like* a person? and (2) To what extent, if any, does the fact that a fetus has the *potential* for becoming a person endow it with some of the same rights? Each of these questions requires some comment.

In answering the first question, we need not attempt a detailed consideration of the moral rights of organisms which are not developed enough, aware enough, intelligent enough, etc., to be considered people, but which resemble people in some respects. It does seem reasonable to suggest that the more like a person, in the relevant respects, a being is, the stronger is the case for regarding it as having a right to life, and indeed the stronger its right to life is. Thus we ought to take seriously the suggestion that, insofar as "the human individual develops biologically in a continuous fashion . . . the rights of a human person might develop in the same way."[5] But we must keep in mind that the attributes which are relevant in determining whether or not an entity is enough like a person to be regarded as having some of the same moral rights are no different from those which are relevant to determining whether or not it is fully a person—i.e., are no different from (1)–(5)—and that being genetically human, or having recognizably human facial and other physical features, or detectable brain activity, or the capacity to survive outside the uterus, are simply not among these relevant attributes.

Thus it is clear that even though a seven- or eight-month fetus has features which make it apt to arouse in us almost the same powerful protective instinct as is commonly aroused by a small infant, nevertheless it is not significantly more personlike than is a very small embryo. It is *somewhat* more personlike; it can apparently feel and respond to pain, and it may even have a rudimentary form of consciousness, insofar as its brain is quite active. Nevertheless, it seems safe to say that it is not fully conscious, in the way that an infant of a few months is, and that it cannot reason, or communicate messages of indefinitely many sorts, does not engage in self-motivated activity, and has no self-awareness. Thus, in the *relevant* respects, a fetus, even a fully developed one, is considerably less personlike than is the average mature mammal, indeed the average fish. And I think that a rational person must conclude that if the right to life of a fetus is to be based upon its resemblance to a person, then it cannot be said to have any more right to life than, let us say, a newborn guppy (which also seems to be capable of feeling pain), and that a right of that magnitude could never override a woman's right to obtain an abortion, at any stage of her pregnancy.

There may, of course, be other arguments in favor of placing legal limits upon the stage of pregnancy in which an abortion may be performed. Given the relative safety of the new techniques of artifically inducing labor during the third trimester, the danger to the woman's life or health is no longer such an argument. Neither is the fact that people tend to respond to the thought of abortion in the later stages of pregnancy with emotional repulsion, since mere emotional responses cannot take the place of moral reasoning in determining what ought to be permitted. Nor, finally, is the frequently heard argument that legalizing abortion, especially late in the pregnancy, may erode the level of respect for human life, leading, perhaps, to an increase in unjustified euthanasia and other crimes. For this threat, if it is a threat, can be better met by educating people to the kinds of moral distinctions which we are making here than by limiting access to abortion (which limitation may, in its disregard for the rights of women, be just as damaging to the level of respect for human rights).

Thus, since the fact that even a fully developed fetus is not personlike enough to have any significant right to life on the basis of its personlikeness shows that no legal restrictions upon the stage of pregnancy in which an abortion may be performed can be justified on the grounds that we should protect the rights of the older fetus; and since there is no other apparent justification for such restrictions, we may conclude that they are entirely unjustified. Whether or not it would be *indecent* (whatever that means) for a woman in her seventh month to obtain an abortion just to avoid having to postpone a trip to Europe, it would not, in itself, be *immoral,* and therefore it ought to be permitted.

4. Potential Personhood and the Right to Life

We have seen that a fetus does not resemble a person in any way which can support the claim that it has even some of the same rights. But what about its *potential,* the fact that if nurtured and allowed to develop naturally it will very probably become a person? Doesn't that alone give it at least some right to life? It is hard to deny that the fact that an entity is a potential person is a strong prima facie reason for

not destroying it; but we need not conclude from this that a potential person has a right to life, by virtue of that potential. It may be that our feeling that it is better, other things being equal, not to destroy a potential person is better explained by the fact that potential people are still (felt to be) an invaluable resource, not to be lightly squandered. Surely, if every speck of dust were a potential person, we would be much less apt to conclude that every potential person has a right to become actual.

Still, we do not need to insist that a potential person has no right to life whatever. There may well be something immoral, and not just imprudent, about wantonly destroying potential people, when doing so isn't necessary to protect anyone's rights. But even if a potential person does have some prima facie right to life, such a right could not possibly outweigh the right of a woman to obtain an abortion, since the rights of any actual person invariably outweigh those of any potential person, whenever the two conflict. Since this may not be immediately obvious in the case of a human fetus, let us look at another case.

Suppose that our space explorer falls into the hands of an alien culture, whose scientists decide to create a few hundred thousand or more human beings, by breaking his body into its component cells, and using these to create fully developed human beings, with, of course, his genetic code. We may imagine that each of these newly created men will have all of the original man's abilities, skills, knowledge, and so on, and also have an individual self-concept, in short that each of them will be a bona fide (though hardly unique) person. Imagine that the whole project will take only seconds, and that its chances of success are extremely high, and that our explorer knows all of this, and also knows that these people will be treated fairly. I maintain that in such a situation he would have every right to escape if he could, and thus to deprive all of these potential people of their potential lives; for his right to life outweighs all of theirs together, in spite of the fact that they are all genetically human, all innocent, and all have a very high probability of becoming people very soon, if only he refrains from acting.

Indeed, I think he would have a right to escape even if it were not his life which the alien scientists planned to take, but only a year of his freedom, or, indeed, only a day. Nor would he be obligated to stay if he had gotten captured (thus bringing all these people- potentials into existence) because of his own carelessness, or even if he had done so deliberately, knowing the consequences. Regardless of how he got captured, he is not morally obligated to remain in captivity for *any* period of time for the sake of permitting any number of potential people to come into actuality, so great is the margin by which one actual person's right to liberty outweighs whatever right to life even a hundred thousand potential people have. And it seems reasonable to conclude that the rights of a woman will outweigh by a similar margin whatever right to life a fetus may have by virtue of its potential personhood.

Thus, neither a fetus's resemblance to a person, nor its potential for becoming a person provides any basis whatever for the claim that it has any significant right to life. Consequently, a woman's right to protect her health, happiness, freedom, and even her life,[6] by terminating an unwanted pregnancy, will always override whatever right to life it may be appropriate to ascribe to a fetus, even a fully developed one. And thus, in the absence of any overwhelming social need for every possible child, the laws which restrict the right to obtain an abortion, or limit the period of pregnancy during which an abortion may be performed, are a wholly unjustified violation of a woman's most basic moral and constitutional rights.

NOTES

1. John Noonan, "Abortion and the Catholic Church: A Summary History," *Natural Law Forum*, 12 (1967), 125.

2. John Noonan, "Deciding Who Is Human," *Natural Law Forum*, 13 (1968), 134.

3. Of course, the principle that it is (always) wrong to kill innocent human beings is in need of many other modifications, e.g., that it may be permissible to do so to save a greater number of other innocent human beings, but we may safely ignore these complications here.

4. From here on, we will use 'human' to mean genetically human, since the moral sense seems closely connected to, and perhaps derived from, the assumption that genetic humanity is sufficient for membership in the moral community.

5. Thomas L. Hayes, "A Biological View," *Commonweal*, 85 (March 17, 1967), 677–78; quoted by Daniel Callahan, in *Abortion, Law, Choice, and Morality* (London: Macmillan & Co., 1970).

6. That is, insofar as the death rate, for the woman, is higher for childbirth than for early abortion.

DISCUSSION QUESTIONS

1. What is Warren's objection to the argument that abortion is permissible because a woman has a right to control her own body? How is her objection related to her main argument?

2. Do you agree that Warren's criteria for personhood would provide space explorers with a good way to tell which alien creatures had the same moral rights as adult humans? Why or why not?

3. How does Warren respond to the objection that a human fetus has the potential to become a person? Do you find her response convincing? Why or why not?

4. What do Warren's views about personhood imply about the moral rights of a newborn baby? Is this a problem for Warren's view? Why or why not?

Don Marquis

Why Abortion Is Immoral

Don Marquis is Professor of Philosophy at the University of Kansas. In this paper, Marquis argues that abortion is seriously morally wrong. His argument does not depend on religious claims or on claims about whether a fetus is a "person" in some technical, philosophical sense. Instead, it depends on the idea that a fetus has a "future of value."

GUIDING QUESTIONS

1. In Section I, Marquis sketches common pro-choice and anti-abortion arguments. What is he trying to show by doing so?
2. Why, according to Marquis, is it wrong to kill an adult human? What is his argument for his answer to that question? How does his answer to that question relate to this main argument against abortion?
3. In Section III, Marquis considers two "rival accounts of the ethics of killing." Why does he do that? What problems does he find with those accounts?
4. What three objections does Marquis consider in Section IV? How does he respond to each one?

The view that abortion is, with rare exceptions, seriously immoral has received little support in the recent philosophical literature. No doubt most philosophers affiliated with secular institutions of higher education believe that the anti-abortion position is either a symptom of irrational religious dogma or a conclusion generated by seriously confused philosophical argument. The purpose of this essay is to undermine this general belief. This essay sets out an argument that purports to show, as well as any argument in ethics can show, that abortion is, except possibly in rare cases, seriously immoral, that it is in the same moral category as killing an innocent adult human being.

The argument is based on a major assumption. Many of the most insightful and careful writers on the ethics of abortion—such as Joel Feinberg, Michael Tooley, Mary Anne Warren, H. Tristram Engelhardt, Jr., L. W. Sumner, John T. Noonan, Jr., and Philip Devine[1]—believe that whether or not abortion is morally permissible stands or falls on whether or not a fetus is the sort of being whose life it is

seriously wrong to end. The argument of this essay will assume, but not argue, that they are correct.

Also, this essay will neglect issues of great importance to a complete ethics of abortion. Some anti-abortionists will allow that certain abortions, such as abortion before implantation or abortion when the life of a woman is threatened by a pregnancy or abortion after rape, may be morally permissible. This essay will not explore the casuistry of these hard cases. The purpose of this essay is to develop a general argument for the claim that the overwhelming majority of deliberate abortions are seriously immoral.

I.

A sketch of standard anti-abortion and pro-choice arguments exhibits how those arguments possess certain symmetries that explain why partisans of

Don Marquis. "Why Abortion Is Immoral." *The Journal of Philosophy*, 86(4) (Apr. 1989), 183–202. Permission by author and The Journal of Philosophy.

those positions are so convinced of the correctness of their own positions, why they are not successful in convincing their opponents, and why, to others, this issue seems to be unresolvable. An analysis of the nature of this standoff suggests a strategy for surmounting it.

Consider the way a typical anti-abortionist argues. She will argue or assert that life is present from the moment of conception or that fetuses look like babies or that fetuses possess a characteristic such as a genetic code that is both necessary and sufficient for being human. Anti-abortionists seem to believe that (1) the truth of all of these claims is quite obvious, and (2) establishing any of these claims is sufficient to show that abortion is morally akin to murder.

A standard pro-choice strategy exhibits similarities. The pro-choicer will argue or assert that fetuses are not persons or that fetuses are not rational agents or that fetuses are not social beings. Pro-choicer seem to believe that (1) the truth of any of these claims is quite obvious, and (2) establishing any of these claims is sufficient to show that an abortion is not a wrongful killing.

In fact, both the pro-choice and the anti-abortion claims do seem to be true, although the "it looks like a baby" claim is more difficult to establish the earlier the pregnancy. We seem to have a standoff. How can it be resolved?

As everyone who has taken a bit of logic knows, if any of these arguments concerning abortion is a good argument, it requires not only some claim characterizing fetuses, but also some general moral principle that ties a characteristic of fetuses to having or not having the right to life or to some other moral characteristic that will generate the obligation or the lack of obligation not to end the life of a fetus. Accordingly, the arguments of the anti-abortionist and the pro-choicer need a bit of filling in to be regarded as adequate.

Note what each partisan will say. The anti-abortionist will claim that her position is supported by such generally accepted moral principles as "It is always prima facie seriously wrong to take a human life" or "It is always prima facie seriously wrong to end the life of a baby." Since these are generally accepted moral principles, her position is certainly not obviously wrong. The pro-choicer will claim that

her position is supported by such plausible moral principles as "Being a person is what gives an individual intrinsic moral worth" or "It is only seriously prima facie wrong to take the life of a member of the human community." Since these are generally accepted moral principles, the pro-choice position is certainly not obviously wrong. Unfortunately, we have again arrived at a standoff.

Now, how might one deal with this standoff? The standard approach is to try to show how the moral principles of one's opponent lose their plausibility under analysis. It is easy to see how this is possible. On the one hand, the anti-abortionist will defend a moral principle concerning the wrongness of killing which tends to be broad in scope in order that even fetuses at an early stage of pregnancy will fall under it. The problem with broad principles is that they often embrace too much. In this particular instance, the principle "It is always prima facie wrong to take a human life" seems to entail that it is wrong to end the existence of a living human cancer-cell culture, on the grounds that the culture is both living and human. Therefore, it seems that the anti-abortionist's favored principle is too broad.

On the other hand, the pro-choicer wants to find a moral principle concerning the wrongness of killing which tends to be narrow in scope in order that fetuses will *not* fall under it. The problem with narrow principles is that they often do not embrace enough. Hence, the needed principles such as "It is prima facie seriously wrong to kill only persons" or "It is prima facie wrong to kill only rational agents" do not explain why it is wrong to kill infants or young children or the severely retarded or even perhaps the severely mentally ill. Therefore, we seem again to have a standoff. The anti-abortionist charges, not unreasonably, that pro-choice principles concerning killing are too narrow to be acceptable; the pro-choicer charges, not unreasonably, that anti-abortionist principles concerning killing are too broad to be acceptable.

Attempts by both sides to patch up the difficulties in their positions run into further difficulties. The anti-abortionist will try to remove the problem in her position by reformulating her principle concerning killing in terms of human beings. Now we end up with: "It is always prima facie seriously wrong to end the life of a human being." This principle has the advantage of avoiding the problem of the human cancer-cell culture counterexample. But this advantage is purchased at a high price. For although it is clear that a fetus is both human and alive, it is not at all clear that a fetus is a human *being*. There is at least something to be said for the view that something becomes a human being only after a process of development, and that therefore first trimester fetuses and perhaps all fetuses are not yet human beings. Hence, the anti-abortionist, by this move, has merely exchanged one problem for another.[2]

The pro-choicer fares no better. She may attempt to find reasons why killing infants, young children, and the severely retarded is wrong which are independent of her major principle that is supposed to explain the wrongness of taking human life, but which will not also make abortion immoral. This is no easy task. Appeals to social utility will seem satisfactory only to those who resolve not to think of the enormous difficulties with a utilitarian account of the wrongness of killing and the significant social costs of preserving the lives of the unproductive.[3] A pro-choice strategy that extends the definition of 'person' to infants or even to young children seems just as arbitrary as an anti-abortion strategy that extends the definition of 'human being' to fetuses. Again, we find symmetries in the two positions and we arrive at a standoff.

There are even further problems that reflect symmetries in the two positions. In addition to counterexample problems, or the arbitrary application problems that can be exchanged for them, the standard anti-abortionist principle "It is prima facie seriously wrong to kill a human being," or one of its variants, can be objected to on the grounds of ambiguity. If 'human being' is taken to be a *biological* category, then the anti-abortionist is left with the problem of explaining why a merely biological category should make a moral difference. Why, it is asked, is it any more reasonable to base a moral conclusion on the number of chromosomes in one's cells than on the color of one's skin?[4] If 'human being', on the other hand, is taken to be a *moral* category, then the claim that a fetus is a human being cannot be taken to be a premise in the anti-abortion argument, for it is precisely what needs to be established. Hence, either the antiabortionist's main category is a morally irrelevant, merely biological category, or it is of no use to the anti-abortionist in establishing (noncircularly, of course) that abortion is wrong.

Although this problem with the anti-abortionist position is often noticed, it is less often noticed that the pro-choice position suffers from an analogous problem. The principle "Only persons have the right to life" also suffers from an ambiguity. The term 'person' is typically defined in terms of psychological characteristics, although there will certainly be disagreement concerning which characteristics are most important. Supposing that this matter can be settled, the pro-choicer is left with the problem of explaining why *psychological* characteristics should make a *moral* difference. If the pro-choicer should attempt to deal with this problem by claiming that an explanation is not necessary, that in fact we do treat such a cluster of psychological properties as having moral significance, the sharp-witted anti-abortionist should have a ready response. We do treat being both living and human as having moral significance. If it is legitimate for the pro-choicer to demand that the anti-abortionist provide an explanation of the connection between the biological character of being a human being and the wrongness of being killed (even though people accept this connection), then it is legitimate for the antiabortionist to demand that the pro-choicer provide an explanation of the connection between psychological criteria for being a person and the wrongness of being killed (even though that connection is accepted).[5] . . .

Passions in the abortion debate run high. There are both plausibilities and difficulties with the standard positions. Accordingly, it is hardly surprising that partisans of either side embrace with fervor the moral generalizations that support the conclusions they preanalytically favor, and reject with disdain the moral generalizations of their opponents as being subject to inescapable difficulties. It is easy to believe that the counterexamples to one's own moral principles are merely temporary difficulties that will dissolve in the wake of further philosophical research, and that the counterexamples to the principles of one's opponents are straightforward. This might suggest to an impartial observer (if there are any) that the abortion issue is unresolvable.

There is a way out of this apparent dialectical quandary. The moral generalizations of both sides are not quite correct. The generalizations hold for the most part, for the usual cases. This suggests that they are all *accidental* generalizations, that the moral claims made by those on both sides of the dispute do not touch on the *essence* of the matter.

This use of the distinction between essence and accident is not meant to invoke obscure metaphysical categories. Rather, it is intended to reflect the rather atheoretical nature of the abortion discussion. If the generalization a partisan in the abortion dispute adopts were derived from the reason why ending the life of a human being is wrong, then there could not be exceptions to that generalization unless some special case obtains in which there are even more powerful countervailing reasons. Such generalizations would not be merely accidental generalizations; they would point to, or be based upon, the essence of the wrongness of killing, what it is that makes killing wrong. All this suggests that a necessary condition of resolving the abortion controversy is a more theoretical account of the wrongness of killing. After all, if we merely believe, but do not understand, why killing adult human beings such as ourselves is wrong, how could we conceivably show that abortion is either immoral or permissible?

II.

In order to develop such an account, we can start from the following unproblematic assumption concerning our own case: it is wrong to kill *us*. Why is it wrong? Some answers can be easily eliminated. It might be said that what makes killing us wrong is that a killing brutalizes the one who kills. But the brutalization consists of being inured to the performance of an act that is hideously immoral; hence, the brutalization does not explain the immorality. It might be said that what makes killing us wrong is the great loss others would experience due to our absence. Although such hubris is understandable, such an explanation does not account for the wrongness of killing hermits, or those whose lives are relatively independent and whose friends find it easy to make new friends.

A more obvious answer is better. What primarily makes killing wrong is neither its effect on the murderer nor its effect on the victim's friends and relatives, but its effect on the victim. The loss of one's life is one of the greatest losses one can suffer. The loss of one's life deprives one of all the experiences, activities, projects, and enjoyments that would otherwise have constituted one's future. Therefore, killing someone is wrong, primarily because the killing inflicts (one of) the greatest possible losses on the victim. To describe this as the loss of life can be misleading, however. The change in my biological state does not by itself make killing me wrong. The effect of the loss of my biological life is the loss to me of all those activities, projects, experiences, and enjoyments which would otherwise have constituted my future personal life. These activities, projects, experiences, and enjoyments are either valuable for their own sakes or are means to something else that is valuable for its own sake. Some parts of my future are not valued by me now, but will come to be valued by me as I grow older and as my values and capacities change. When I am killed, I am deprived both of what I now value which would have been part of my future personal life, but also what I would come to value. Therefore, when I die, I am deprived of all of the value of my future. Inflicting this loss on me is ultimately what makes killing me wrong. This being the case, it would seem that what makes killing *any* adult human being prima facie seriously wrong is the loss of his or her future.[6]

How should this rudimentary theory of the wrongness of killing be evaluated? It cannot be faulted for deriving an 'ought' from an 'is', for it does not. The analysis assumes that killing me (or you, reader) is prima facie seriously wrong. The point of the analysis is to establish which natural property ultimately explains the wrongness of the killing, given that it is wrong. A natural property will ultimately explain the wrongness of killing, only if (1) the explanation fits with our intuitions about the matter and (2) there is no other natural property that provides the basis for a better explanation of the wrongness of killing. This analysis rests on the intuition that what makes killing a particular human or animal wrong is what it does to that particular human or animal. What makes killing wrong is some natural effect or other of the killing. Some would deny this. For instance, a divine–command theorist in ethics would deny it. Surely this denial is, however, one of those features of divine-command theory which renders it so implausible.

The claim that what makes killing wrong is the loss of the victim's future is directly supported by two considerations. In the first place, this theory explains why we regard killing as one of the worst of crimes. Killing is especially wrong, because it deprives the victim of more than perhaps any other crime. In the second place, people with AIDS or cancer who know they are dying believe, of course, that dying is a very bad thing for them. They believe that the loss of a future to them that they would otherwise have experienced is what makes their premature death a very bad thing for them. A better theory of the wrongness of killing would require a different natural property associated with killing which better fits with the attitudes of the dying. What could it be?

The view that what makes killing wrong is the loss to the victim of the value of the victim's future gains additional support when some of its implications are examined. In the first place, it is incompatible with the view that it is wrong to kill only beings who are biologically human. It is possible that there exists a different species from another planet whose members have a future like ours. Since having a future like that is what makes killing someone wrong, this theory entails that it would be wrong to kill members of such a species. Hence, this theory is opposed to the claim that only life that is biologically human has great moral worth, a claim which many antiabortionists have seemed to adopt. This opposition, which this theory has in common with personhood theories, seems to be a merit of the theory.

In the second place, the claim that the loss of one's future is the wrong-making feature of one's being killed entails the possibility that the futures of some actual nonhuman mammals on our own planet are sufficiently like ours that it is seriously wrong to kill them also. Whether some animals do have the same right to life as human beings depends on adding to the account of the wrongness of killing some additional account of just what it is about my future or the futures of other adult human beings which makes it wrong to kill us. No such additional account will be offered in this essay. Undoubtedly, the provision of such an account would be a very difficult matter. Undoubtedly, any such account would be quite controversial. Hence, it surely should not reflect badly on this sketch of an elementary theory of the wrongness of killing that it is indeterminate with respect to some very difficult issues regarding animal rights.

In the third place, the claim that the loss of one's future is the wrong-making feature of one's being killed does not entail, as sanctity of human life theories do, that active euthanasia is wrong. Persons who are severely and incurably ill, who face a future of pain and despair, and who wish to die will not have suffered a loss if they are killed. It is, strictly speaking, the value of a human's future which makes killing wrong in this theory. This being so, killing does not necessarily wrong some persons who are sick and dying. Of course, there may be other reasons for a prohibition of active euthanasia, but that is another matter. Sanctity-of-human-life theories seem to hold that active euthanasia is seriously wrong even in an individual case where there seems to be good reason for it independently of public policy considerations. This consequence is most implausible, and it is a plus for the claim that the loss of a future of value is what makes killing wrong that it does not share this consequence.

In the fourth place, the account of the wrongness of killing defended in this essay does straightforwardly entail that it is prima facie seriously wrong to kill children and infants, for we do presume that they have futures of value. Since we do believe that it is wrong to kill defenseless little babies, it is important that a theory of the wrongness of killing easily account for this. Personhood theories of the wrongness of killing, on the other hand, cannot straightforwardly account for the wrongness of killing infants and young children.[7] Hence, such theories must add special ad hoc accounts of the wrongness of killing the young. The plausibility of such ad hoc theories seems to be a function of how desperately one wants such theories to work. The claim that the primary wrong-making feature of a killing is the loss to the victim of the value of its future accounts for the wrongness of killing young children and infants directly; it makes the wrongness of such acts as obvious as we actually think it is. This is a further merit of this theory. Accordingly, it seems that this value of a future-like-ours theory of the wrongness of killing shares strengths of both sanctity-of-life and personhood accounts while avoiding weaknesses of both. In addition, it meshes with a central intuition concerning what makes killing wrong.

The claim that the primary wrong-making feature of a killing is the loss to the victim of the value of its future has obvious consequences for the ethics of abortion. The future of a standard fetus includes a set of experiences, projects, activities, and such which are identical with the futures of adult human beings and are identical with the futures of young children. Since the reason that is sufficient to explain why it is wrong to kill human beings after the time of birth is a reason that also applies to fetuses, it follows that abortion is prima facie seriously morally wrong.

This argument does not rely on the invalid inference that, since it is wrong to kill persons, it is wrong to kill potential persons also. The category that is morally central to this analysis is the category of having a valuable future like ours; it is not the category of personhood. The argument to the conclusion that abortion is prima facie seriously morally wrong proceeded independently of the notion of person or potential person or any equivalent. Someone may wish to start with this analysis in terms of the value of a human future, conclude that abortion is, except perhaps in rare circumstances, seriously morally wrong, infer that fetuses have the right to life, and then call fetuses "persons" as a result of their having the right to life. Clearly, in this case, the category of person is being used to state the *conclusion* of the analysis rather than to generate the *argument* of the analysis.

The structure of this anti-abortion argument can be both illuminated and defended by comparing it to what appears to be the best argument for the wrongness of the wanton infliction of pain on animals. This latter argument is based on the assumption that it is prima facie wrong to inflict pain on me (or you, reader). What is the natural property associated with the infliction of pain which makes such infliction

wrong? The obvious answer seems to be that the infliction of pain causes suffering and that suffering is a misfortune. The suffering caused by the infliction of pain is what makes the wanton infliction of pain on me wrong. The wanton infliction of pain on other adult humans causes suffering. The wanton infliction of pain on animals causes suffering. Since causing suffering is what makes the wanton infliction of pain wrong and since the wanton infliction of pain on animals causes suffering, it follows that the wanton infliction of pain on animals is wrong.

This argument for the wrongness of the wanton infliction of pain on animals shares a number of structural features with the argument for the serious prima facie wrongness of abortion. Both arguments start with an obvious assumption concerning what it is wrong to do to me (or you, reader). Both then look for the characteristic or the consequence of the wrong action which makes the action wrong. Both recognize that the wrong-making feature of these immoral actions is a property of actions sometimes directed at individuals other than postnatal human beings. If the structure of the argument for the wrongness of the wanton infliction of pain on animals is sound, then the structure of the argument for the prima facie serious wrongness of abortion is also sound, for the structure of the two arguments is the same. The structure common to both is the key to the explanation of how the wrongness of abortion can be demonstrated without recourse to the category of person. In neither argument is that category crucial. . . .

Of course, this value of a future-like-ours argument, if sound, shows only that abortion is prima facie wrong, not that it is wrong in any and all circumstances. Since the loss of the future to a standard fetus, if killed, is, however, at least as great a loss as the loss of the future to a standard adult human being who is killed, abortion, like ordinary killing, could be justified only by the most compelling reasons. The loss of one's life is almost the greatest misfortune that can happen to one. Presumably abortion could be justified in some circumstances, only if the loss consequent on failing to abort would be at least as great. Accordingly, morally permissible abortions will be rare indeed unless, perhaps, they occur so early in pregnancy that a fetus is not yet definitely an individual. Hence, this argument should be taken as showing that abortion is presumptively very seriously wrong, where the presumption is very strong—as strong as the presumption that killing another adult human being is wrong.

III.

How complete an account of the wrongness of killing does the value of a future-like-ours account have to be in order that the wrongness of abortion is a consequence? This account does not have to be an account of the necessary conditions for the wrongness of killing. Some persons in nursing homes may lack valuable human futures, yet it may be wrong to kill them for other reasons. Furthermore, this account does not obviously have to be the sole reason killing is wrong where the victim did have a valuable future. This analysis claims only that, for any killing where the victim did have a valuable future like ours, having that future by itself is sufficient to create the strong presumption that the killing is seriously wrong.

One way to overturn the value of a future-like-ours argument would be to find some account of the wrongness of killing which is at least as intelligible and which has different implications for the ethics of abortion. Two rival accounts possess at least some degree of plausibility. One account is based on the obvious fact that people value the experience of living and wish for that valuable experience to continue. Therefore, it might be said, what makes killing wrong is the discontinuation of that experience for the victim. Let us call this the *discontinuation account*.[8] Another rival account is based upon the obvious fact that people strongly desire to continue to live. This suggests that what makes killing us so wrong is that it interferes with the fulfillment of a strong and fundamental desire, the fulfillment of which is necessary for the fulfillment of any other desires we might have. Let us call this the *desire account*.[9]

Consider first the desire account as a rival account of the ethics of killing which would provide the basis for rejecting the anti-abortion position. Such an account will have to be stronger than the value of a future-like-ours account of the wrongness of abortion if it is to do the job expected of it. To entail the wrongness of abortion, the value of a future-like-ours account has only to provide a sufficient, but not a necessary, condition for the wrongness of killing. The desire account, on the other hand, must provide us also with a necessary condition for the wrongness of killing in order to generate a prochoice conclusion on abortion. The reason for this is that presumably the argument from the desire account moves from the claim that what makes killing wrong is interference with a very strong desire to the claim that abortion is not wrong because the fetus lacks a strong desire to live. Obviously, this inference fails if someone's having the desire to live is not a necessary condition of its being wrong to kill that individual.

One problem with the desire account is that we do regard it as seriously wrong to kill persons who have little desire to live or who have no desire to live or, indeed, have a desire not to live. We believe it is seriously wrong to kill the unconscious, the sleeping, those who are tired of life, and those who are suicidal. The value-of-a-human-future account renders standard morality intelligible in these cases; these cases appear to be incompatible with the desire account.

The desire account is subject to a deeper difficulty. We desire life, because we value the goods of this life. The goodness of life is not secondary to our desire for it. If this were not so, the pain of one's own premature death could be done away with merely by an appropriate alteration in the configuration of one's desires. This is absurd. Hence, it would seem that it is the loss of the goods of one's future, not the interference with the fulfillment of a strong desire to live, which accounts ultimately for the wrongness of killing.

It is worth noting that, if the desire account is modified so that it does not provide a necessary, but only a sufficient, condition for the wrongness of killing, the desire account is compatible with the value of a future-like-ours account. The combined accounts will yield an anti-abortion ethic. This suggests that one can retain what is intuitively plausible about the desire account without a challenge to the basic argument of this paper.

It is also worth noting that, if future desires have moral force in a modified desire account of the wrongness of killing, one can find support for an anti-abortion ethic even in the absence of a value of a future-like-ours account. If one decides that a morally relevant property, the possession of which is sufficient to make it wrong to kill some individual, is the desire at some future time to live—one might decide to justify one's refusal to kill suicidal teenagers on these grounds, for example—then, since typical fetuses will have the desire in the future to live, it is wrong to kill typical fetuses. Accordingly, it does not seem that a desire account of the wrongness of killing can provide a justification of a pro-choice ethic of abortion which is nearly as adequate as the value of a human-future justification of an anti-abortion ethic.

The discontinuation account looks more promising as an account of the wrongness of killing. It seems just as intelligible as the value of a future-like-ours account, but it does not justify an anti-abortion position. Obviously, if it is the continuation of one's activities, experiences, and projects, the loss of which makes killing wrong, then it is not wrong to kill fetuses for that reason, for fetuses do not have experiences, activities, and projects to be continued or discontinued. Accordingly, the discontinuation account does not have the antiabortion consequences that the value of a future-like-ours account has. Yet, it seems as intelligible as the value of a future-like-ours account, for when we think of what would be wrong with our being killed, it does seem as if it is the discontinuation of what makes our lives worthwhile which makes killing us wrong.

Is the discontinuation account just as good an account as the value of a future-like-ours account? The discontinuation account will not be adequate at all, if it does not refer to the *value* of the experience that may be discontinued. One does not want the discontinuation account to make it wrong to kill a patient who begs for death and who is in severe pain that cannot be relieved short of killing. (I leave open the question of whether it is wrong for other reasons.) Accordingly, the discontinuation account must be more than a bare discontinuation account. It must make some reference to the positive value of the patient's experiences. But, by the same token, the value of a future-like-ours account cannot be a bare future account either. Just having a future surely does not itself rule out killing the above patient. This account must make some reference to the value of the patient's future experiences and projects also. Hence, both accounts involve the value of experiences, projects, and activities. So far we still have symmetry between the accounts.

The symmetry fades, however, when we focus on the time period of the value of the experiences, etc., which has moral consequences. Although both accounts leave open the possibility that the patient in our example may be killed, this possibility is left open only in virtue of the utterly bleak future for the patient. It makes no difference whether the patient's immediate past contains intolerable pain, or consists in being in a coma (which we can imagine is a situation of indifference), or consists in a life of value. If the patient's future is a future of value, we want our account to make it wrong to kill the patient. If the patient's future is intolerable, whatever his or her immediate past, we want our account to allow killing the patient. Obviously, then, it is the value of that patient's future which is doing the work in rendering the morality of killing the patient intelligible.

This being the case, it seems clear that whether one has immediate past experiences or not does no work in the explanation of what makes killing wrong. The addition the discontinuation account makes to the value of a human future account is otiose. Its addition to the value-of-a-future account plays no role at all in rendering intelligible the wrongness of killing. Therefore, it can be discarded with the discontinuation account of which it is a part.

IV.

The analysis of the previous section suggests that alternative general accounts of the wrongness of killing are either inadequate or unsuccessful in getting around the anti-abortion consequences of the value of a future-like-ours argument. A different strategy for avoiding these anti-abortion consequences involves limiting the scope of the value of a future argument. More precisely, the strategy involves arguing that fetuses lack a property that is essential for the value-of-a-future argument (or for any anti-abortion argument) to apply to them.

One move of this sort is based upon the claim that a necessary condition of one's future being valuable is that one values it. Value implies a valuer. Given this one might argue that, since fetuses cannot value their futures, their futures are not valuable to them. Hence, it does not seriously wrong them deliberately to end their lives.

This move fails, however, because of some ambiguities. Let us assume that something cannot be of value unless it is valued by someone. This does not entail that my life is of no value unless it is valued by me. I may think, in a period of despair, that my future is of no worth whatsoever, but I may be wrong because others rightly see value—even great value— in it. Furthermore, my future can be valuable to me even if I do not value it. This is the case when a young person attempts suicide, but is rescued and goes on to significant human achievements. Such young people's futures are ultimately valuable to them, even though such futures do not seem to be valuable to them at the moment of attempted suicide. A fetus's future can be valuable to it in the same way. Accordingly, this attempt to limit the anti-abortion argument fails.

Another similar attempt to reject the anti-abortion position is based on Tooley's claim that an entity cannot possess the right to life unless it has the capacity to desire its continued existence. It follows that, since fetuses lack the conceptual capacity to desire to continue to live, they lack the right to life. Accordingly, Tooley concludes that abortion cannot be seriously prima facie wrong (*op. cit.,* pp. 46/7).

What could be the evidence for Tooley's basic claim? Tooley once argued that individuals have a prima facie right to what they desire and that the lack of the capacity to desire something undercuts the basis of one's right to it (*op. cit.,* pp. 44/5). This argument plainly will not succeed in the context of the analysis of this essay, however, since the point here is to establish the fetus's right to life on other grounds. Tooley's argument assumes that the right to life cannot be established in general on some basis other than the desire for life. This position was considered and rejected in the preceding section of this paper.

One might attempt to defend Tooley's basic claim on the grounds that, because a fetus cannot apprehend continued life as a benefit, its continued life cannot be a benefit or cannot be something it has a right to or cannot be something that is in its interest. This might be defended in terms of the general proposition that, if an individual is literally incapable of caring about or taking an interest in some X, then one does not have a right to X or X is not a benefit or X is not something that is in one's interest.[10]

Each member of this family of claims seems to be open to objections. As John C. Stevens[11] has pointed out, one may have a right to be treated with a certain medical procedure (because of a health insurance policy one has purchased), even though one cannot conceive of the nature of the procedure. And, as Tooley himself has pointed out, persons who have been indoctrinated, or drugged, or rendered temporarily unconscious may be literally incapable of caring about or taking an interest in something that is in their interest or is something to which they have a right, or is something that benefits them. Hence, the Tooley claim that would restrict the scope of the value of a future-like-ours argument is undermined by counterexamples.[12]

Finally, Paul Bassen[13] has argued that, even though the prospects of an embryo might seem to be a basis for the wrongness of abortion, an embryo cannot be a victim and therefore cannot be wronged. An embryo cannot be a victim, he says, because it lacks sentience. His central argument for this seems to be that, even though plants and the permanently unconscious are alive, they clearly cannot be victims. What is the explanation of this? Bassen claims that the explanation is that their lives consist of mere metabolism and mere metabolism is not enough to ground victimizability. Mentation is required.

The problem with this attempt to establish the absence of victimizability is that both plants and the permanently unconscious clearly lack what Bassen calls "prospects" or what I have called "a future life like ours." Hence, it is surely open to one to argue that the real reason we believe plants and the permanently unconscious cannot be victims is that killing them cannot deprive them of a future life like ours; the real reason is not their absence of present mentation.

Bassen recognizes that his view is subject to this difficulty, and he recognizes that the case of children seems to support this difficulty, for "much of what we do for children is based on prospects." He argues, however, that, in the case of children and in other such cases, "potentiality comes into play only where victimizability has been secured on other grounds" (*ibid.*, p. 333).

Bassen's defense of his view is patently question-begging, since what is adequate to secure victimizability is exactly what is at issue. His examples do not support his own view against the thesis of this essay. Of course, embryos can be victims: when their lives are deliberately terminated, they are deprived of their futures of value, their prospects. This makes them victims, for it directly wrongs them.

The seeming plausibility of Bassen's view stems from the fact that paradigmatic cases of imagining someone as a victim involve empathy, and empathy requires mentation of the victim. The victims of flood, famine, rape, or child abuse are all persons with whom we can empathize. That empathy seems to be part of seeing them as victims.[14]

In spite of the strength of these examples, the attractive intuition that a situation in which there is victimization requires the possibility of empathy is subject to counterexamples. Consider a case that Bassen himself offers: "Posthumous obliteration of an author's work constitutes a misfortune for him only if he had wished his work to endure" (*op cit.*, p. 318). The conditions Bassen wishes to impose upon the possibility of being victimized here seem far too strong. Perhaps this author, due to his unrealistic standards of excellence and his low self-esteem, regarded his work as unworthy of survival, even though it possessed genuine literary merit. Destruction of such work would surely victimize its author. In such a case, empathy with the victim concerning the loss is clearly impossible.

Of course, Bassen does not make the possibility of empathy a necessary condition of victimizability; he requires only mentation. Hence, on Bassen's actual view, this author, as I have described him, can be a victim. The problem is that the basic intuition that renders Bassen's view plausible is missing in the author's case. In order to attempt to avoid counterexamples, Bassen has made his thesis too weak to be supported by the intuitions that suggested it.

Even so, the mentation requirement on victimizability is still subject to counterexamples. Suppose a severe accident renders me totally unconscious for a month, after which I recover. Surely killing me while I am unconscious victimizes me, even though I am incapable of mentation during that time. It follows that Bassen's thesis fails. Apparently, attempts to restrict the value of a future-like-ours argument so that fetuses do not fall within its scope do not succeed.

V.

In this essay, it has been argued that the correct ethic of the wrongness of killing can be extended to fetal life and used to show that there is a strong presumption that any abortion is morally impermissible. If the ethic of killing adopted here entails, however, that contraception is also seriously immoral, then there would appear to be a difficulty with the analysis of this essay.

But this analysis does not entail that contraception is wrong. Of course, contraception prevents the actualization of a possible future of value. Hence, it follows from the claim that futures of value should be maximized that contraception is prima facie immoral. This obligation to maximize does not exist, however; furthermore, nothing in the ethics of killing in this paper entails that it does. The ethics of killing in this essay would entail that contraception is wrong only if something were denied a human future of value by contraception. Nothing at all is denied such a future by contraception, however.

Candidates for a subject of harm by contraception fall into four categories: (1) some sperm or other, (2) some ovum or other, (3) a sperm and an ovum separately, and (4) a sperm and an ovum together. Assigning the harm to some sperm is utterly arbitrary, for no reason can be given for making a sperm the subject of harm rather than an ovum. Assigning the harm to some ovum is utterly arbitrary, for no reason can be given for making an ovum the subject of harm rather than a sperm. One might attempt to avoid these problems by insisting that contraception deprives both the sperm and the ovum separately of a valuable future like ours. On this alternative, too many futures are lost. Contraception was supposed to be wrong, because it deprived us of one future of value, not two. One might attempt to avoid this problem by holding that contraception deprives the combination of sperm and ovum of a valuable future like ours. But here the definite article misleads. At the time of contraception, there are hundreds of millions of sperm, one (released) ovum and millions of possible combinations of all of these. There is no actual combination at all. Is the subject of the loss to be a merely possible combination? Which one? This alternative does not yield an actual subject of harm either. Accordingly, the immorality of contraception is not entailed by the loss of a future-like-ours argument simply because there is no nonarbitrarily identifiable subject of the loss in the case of contraception.

VI.

The purpose of this essay has been to set out an argument for the serious presumptive wrongness of abortion subject to the assumption that the moral permissibility of abortion stands or falls on the moral status of the fetus. Since a fetus possesses a property, the possession of which in adult human beings is sufficient to make killing an adult human being wrong, abortion is wrong. This way of dealing with the problem of abortion seems superior to other approaches to the ethics of abortion, because it rests on an ethics of killing which is close to self-evident, because the crucial morally relevant property clearly applies to fetuses, and because the argument avoids the usual equivocations on 'human life', 'human being', or 'person'. The argument rests neither on religious claims nor on Papal dogma. It is not subject to the objection of "speciesism." Its soundness is compatible with the moral permissibility of euthanasia and contraception. It deals with our intuitions concerning young children.

Finally, this analysis can be viewed as resolving a standard problem—indeed, *the* standard problem—concerning the ethics of abortion. Clearly, it is wrong to kill adult human beings. Clearly, it is not wrong to end the life of some arbitrarily chosen single human cell. Fetuses seem to be like arbitrarily chosen human cells in some respects and like adult humans in other respects. The problem of the ethics of abortion is the problem of determining the fetal property that settles this moral controversy. The thesis of this essay is that the problem of the ethics of abortion, so understood, is solvable.

NOTES

1. Feinberg, "Abortion," in *Matters of Life and Death: New Introductory Essays in Moral Philosophy,* Tom Regan, ed. (New York: Random House, 1986), pp. 256–293; Tooley, "Abortion and Infanticide," *Philosophy and Public Affairs,* ii, 1 (1972):37–65, Tooley, *Abortion and Infanticide* (New York: Oxford, 1984); Warren, "On the Moral and Legal Status of Abortion," *The Monist,* I, vii, 1 (1973):43–61; Engelhardt, "The Ontology of Abortion," *Ethics, I,* xxxiv, 3 (1974):217–234; Sumner, *Abortion and Moral Theory* (Princeton: University Press, 1981); Noonan, "An Almost Absolute Value in History," in *The Morality of Abortion: Legal and Historical Perspectives,* Noonan, ed. (Cambridge: Harvard, 1970); and Devine, *The Ethics of Homicide* (Ithaca: Cornell, 1978).

2. For interesting discussions of this issue, see Warren Quinn, "Abortion: Identity and Loss," *Philosophy and Public Affairs,* XIII, 1 (1984):24–54; and Lawrence C. Becker, "Human Being: The Boundaries of the Concept," *Philosophy and Public Affairs,* IV, 4 (1975):334–359.

3. For example, see my "Ethics and the Elderly: Some Problems," in Stuart Spicker, Kathleen Woodward, and David Van Tassel, eds., *Aging and the Elderly: Humanistic Perspectives in Gerontology* (Atlantic Highlands, NJ: Humanities, 1978), pp. 341–355.

4. See Warren, *op. cit.,* and Tooley, "Abortion and Infanticide."

5. This seems to be the fatal flaw in Warren's treatment of this issue.

6. I have been most influenced on this matter by Jonathan Glover, *Causing Death and Saving Lives* (New York: Penguin, 1977), ch. 3; and Robert Young, "What Is So Wrong with Killing People?" *Philosophy, I,* iv, 210 (1979):515–528.

7. Feinberg, Tooley, Warren, and Engelhardt have all dealt with this problem.

8. I am indebted to Jack Bricke for raising this objection.

9. Presumably a preference utilitarian would press such an objection. Tooley once suggested that his account has such a theoretical underpinning. See his "Abortion and Infanticide," pp. 44/5.

10. Donald VanDeVeer seems to think this is self-evident. See his "Whither Baby Doe?" in *Matters of Life and Death*, p. 233.

11. "Must the Bearer of a Right Have the Concept of That to Which He Has a Right?" *Ethics*, xcv, 1 (1984): 68–74.

12. See Tooley again in "Abortion and Infanticide," pp. 47–49.

13. "Present Sakes and Future Prospects: The Status of Early Abortion," *Philosophy and Public Affairs*, XI, 4 (1982): 322–326.

14. Note carefully the reasons he gives on the bottom of p. 316.

DISCUSSION QUESTIONS

1. Do you agree with Marquis's criticisms of standard pro-choice and anti-abortion arguments? Why or why not?
2. Do you agree with Marquis's "future of value" account of the ethics of killing? Why or why not?
3. Does a normally developing, healthy fetus have a "future of value," in Marquis's sense of that expression? Why or why not?
4. Of the three objections Marquis considers in Section IV, which do you think is the strongest? Do you think that Marquis's reply to that objection is successful? Why or why not?

JUDITH JARVIS THOMSON

A Defense of Abortion

Judith Jarvis Thomson is Professor Emerita of Philosophy at the Massachusetts Institute of Technology. She has written important philosophical work in several fields of philosophy, including applied ethics, normative ethics, metaethics, and metaphysics. In this paper, Thomson argues that even if a fetus does have a right to life, it is still morally permissible for a woman to abort a pregnancy.

GUIDING QUESTIONS

1. What anti-abortion argument does Thomson criticize in this paper?
2. What is the original point of Thomson's thought experiment involving the violinist and the Society of Music Lovers? What other points does Thomson make using that example later in the paper?
3. In Sections 3 and 4, Thomson argues for a particular way of understanding what it is to have a right to life. What are her arguments for this view? What does that view have to do with her main conclusion about abortion?

Republished with permission of John Wiley and Sons, Inc, from "A Defense of Abortion," Judith Jarvis Thomson, Philosophy and Public Affairs, 1, 1971; permission conveyed through Copyright Clearance Center, Inc.

4. How does Thomson respond to the claim that a woman who "voluntarily indulges in intercourse" may not get an abortion if she becomes pregnant because she is partially responsible for having become pregnant?
5. Does Thomson believe that there is never anything morally wrong with getting an abortion? Why or why not?

Most opposition to abortion relies on the premise that the fetus is a human being, a person, from the moment of conception. The premise is argued for, but, as I think, not well. Take, for example, the most common argument. We are asked to notice that the development of a human being from conception through birth into childhood is continuous; then it is said that to draw a line, to choose a point in this development and say "before this point the thing is not a person, after this point it is a person" is to make an arbitrary choice, a choice for which in the nature of things no good reason can be given. It is concluded that the fetus is, or anyway that we had better say it is, a person from the moment of conception. But this conclusion does not follow. Similar things might be said about the development of an acorn into an oak tree, and it does not follow that acorns are oak trees, or that we had better say they are. Arguments of this form are sometimes called "slippery slope arguments"—the phrase is perhaps self-explanatory—and it is dismaying that opponents of abortion rely on them so heavily and uncritically.

I am inclined to agree, however, that the prospects for "drawing a line" in the development of the fetus look dim. I am inclined to think also that we shall probably have to agree that the fetus has already become a human person well before birth. Indeed, it comes as a surprise when one first learns how early in its life it begins to acquire human characteristics. By the tenth week, for example, it already has a face, arms and legs, fingers and toes; it has internal organs, and brain activity is detectable.[1] On the other hand, I think that the premise is false, that the fetus is not a person from the moment of conception. A newly fertilized ovum, a newly implanted clump of cells, is no more a person than an acorn is an oak tree. But I shall not discuss any of this. For it seems to me to be of great interest to ask what happens if, for the sake of argument, we allow the premise. How, precisely, are we supposed to get from there to the conclusion that abortion is morally impermissible? Opponents of abortion commonly spend most of their time establishing that the fetus is a person, and hardly any time explaining the step from there to the impermissibility of abortion. Perhaps they think the step too simple and obvious to require much comment. Or perhaps instead they are simply being economical in argument. Many of those who defend abortion rely on the premise that the fetus is not a person, but only a bit of tissue that will become a person at birth; and why pay out more arguments than you have to? Whatever the explanation, I suggest that the step they take is neither easy nor obvious, that it calls for closer examination than it is commonly given, and that when we do give it this closer examination we shall feel inclined to reject it.

I propose, then, that we grant that the fetus is a person, from the moment of conception. How does the argument go from here? Something like this, I take it. Every person has a right to life. So the fetus has a right to life. No doubt the mother has a right to decide what shall happen in and to her body; everyone would grant that. But surely a person's right to life is stronger and more stringent than the mother's right to decide what happens in and to her body, and so outweighs it. So the fetus may not be killed; an abortion may not be performed.

It sounds plausible. But now let me ask you to imagine this. You wake up in the morning and find yourself back to back in bed with an unconscious violinist. A famous unconscious violinist. He has been found to have a fatal kidney ailment, and the Society of Music Lovers has canvassed all the available medical records and found that you alone have the right blood type to help. They have therefore kidnapped you, and last night the violinist's circulatory system was plugged into yours, so that your kidneys can be used to extract poisons from his blood as well as your own. The director of the hospital now tells you, "Look, we're sorry the Society of Music Lovers did this to you—we would never have permitted it if we had known. But still, they did it, and the violinist now is plugged into you. To unplug you would be to kill him. But never mind, it's only for nine months. By then he will have recovered from his ailment, and can safely be unplugged from you." Is it morally incumbent on you to accede to this situation? No doubt it would be very nice of you if you did, a great kindness. But do you *have* to accede to it? What if it were not nine months, but nine years? Or longer still? What if the director of the hospital says, "Tough luck, I agree, but you've now got to stay in bed, with the violinist plugged into you, for the rest of your life. Because remember this. All persons have a right to life, and violinists are persons. Granted you have a right to decide what happens in and to your body, but a person's right to life outweighs your right to decide what happens in and to your body. So you cannot ever be unplugged from him." I imagine you would regard this as outrageous, which suggests that something really is wrong with that plausible-sounding argument I mentioned a moment ago.

In this case, of course, you were kidnapped; you didn't volunteer for the operation that plugged the violinist into your kidneys. Can those who oppose abortion on the ground I mentioned make an exception for a pregnancy due to rape? Certainly. They can say that persons have a right to life only if they didn't come into existence because of rape; or they can say that all persons have a right to life, but that some have less of a right to life than others, in particular, that those who came into existence because of rape have less. But these statements have a rather unpleasant sound. Surely the question of whether you have a right to life at all, or how much of it you have, shouldn't turn on the question of whether or not you are the product of a rape. And in fact the people who oppose abortion on the ground I mentioned do not make this distinction, and hence do not make an exception in case of rape.

Nor do they make an exception for a case in which the mother has to spend the nine months of her pregnancy in bed. They would agree that would be a great pity, and hard on the mother; but all the same, all persons have a right to life, the fetus is a person, and so on. I suspect, in fact, that they would not make an exception for a case in which, miraculously enough, the pregnancy went on for nine years, or even the rest of the mother's life.

Some won't even make an exception for a case in which continuation of the pregnancy is likely to shorten the mother's life; they regard abortion as impermissible even to save the mother's life. Such cases are nowadays very rare, and many opponents of abortion do not accept this extreme view. All the same, it is a good place to begin: a number of points of interest come out in respect to it.

1. Let us call the view that abortion is impermissible even to save the mother's life "the extreme view." I want to suggest first that it does not issue from the argument I mentioned earlier without the addition of some fairly powerful premises. Suppose a woman has become pregnant, and now learns that she has a cardiac condition such that she will die if she carries the baby to term. What may be done for her? The fetus, being a person, has a right to life, but as the mother is a person too, so has she a right to life. Presumably they have an equal right to life. How is it supposed to come out that an abortion may not be performed? If mother and child have an equal right to life, shouldn't we perhaps flip a coin? Or should we add to the mother's right to life her right to decide what happens in and to her body, which everybody seems to be ready to grant—the sum of her rights now outweighing the fetus' right to life?

The most familiar argument here is the following. We are told that performing the abortion would be directly killing[2] the child, whereas doing nothing would not be killing the mother, but only letting her die. Moreover, in killing the child, one would be killing an innocent person, for the child has committed no crime, and is not aiming at his mother's death. And then there are a variety of ways in which this might be continued. (1) But as directly killing an innocent person is always and absolutely impermissible, an abortion may not be performed. Or, (2) as directly killing an innocent person is murder, and murder is always and absolutely impermissible, an abortion may not be performed.[3] Or, (3) as one's duty to refrain from directly killing an innocent person is more stringent than one's duty to keep a person from dying, an abortion may not be performed. Or, (4) if one's only options are directly killing an innocent person or letting a person die, one must prefer letting the person die, and thus an abortion may not be performed.[4]

Some people seem to have thought that these are not further premises which must be added if the conclusion is to be reached, but that they follow from the very fact that an innocent person has a right to life.[5] But this seems to me to be a mistake, and perhaps the simplest way to show this is to bring out that while we must certainly grant that innocent persons have a right to life, the theses in (1) through (4) are all false. Take (2), for example. If directly killing an innocent person is murder, and thus is impermissible, then the mother's directly killing the innocent person inside her is murder, and thus is impermissible. But it cannot seriously be thought to be murder if the mother performs an abortion on herself to save her life. It cannot seriously be said that she *must* refrain, that she *must* sit passively by and wait for her death. Let us look again at the case of you and the violinist. There you are, in bed with the violinist, and the director of the hospital says to you, "It's all most distressing, and I deeply sympathize, but you see this is putting an additional strain on your kidneys, and you'll be dead within the month. But you *have* to stay where you are all the same. Because unplugging you would be directly killing an innocent violinist, and that's murder, and that's impermissible." If anything in the world is true, it is that you do not commit murder, you do not do what is impermissible, if you reach around to your back and unplug yourself from that violinist to save your life.

The main focus of attention in writings on abortion has been on what a third party may or may not do in answer to a request from a woman for an abortion. This is in a way understandable. Things being as they are, there isn't much a woman can safely do to abort herself. So the question asked is what a third party may do, and what the mother may do, if it is mentioned at all, is deduced, almost as an afterthought, from what it is concluded that third parties may do. But it seems to me that to treat the matter in this way is to refuse to grant to the mother that very status of person which is so firmly insisted on for the fetus. For we cannot simply read off what a person may do from what a third party may do. Suppose you find yourself trapped in a tiny house with a growing child. I mean a very tiny house, and a rapidly growing child—you are already up against the wall of the house and in a few minutes you'll be crushed to death. The child on the other hand won't be crushed to death; if nothing is done to stop him from growing he'll be hurt, but in the end he'll simply burst open the house and walk out a free man. Now I could well understand it if a bystander were to say, "There's nothing we can do for you. We cannot choose between your life and his, we cannot be the ones to decide who is to live, we cannot intervene." But it cannot be concluded that you too can do nothing, that you cannot attack it to save your life. However innocent the child may be, you do not have to wait passively while it crushes you to death. Perhaps a pregnant woman is vaguely felt to have the status of house, to which we don't allow the right of self-defense. But if the woman houses the child, it should be remembered that she is a person who houses it.

I should perhaps stop to say explicitly that I am not claiming that people have a right to do anything whatever to save their lives. I think, rather, that there are drastic limits to the right of self-defense. If someone threatens you with death unless you torture someone else to death, I think you have not the right, even to save your life, to do so. But the case under consideration here is very different. In our case there are only two people involved, one whose life is threatened, and one who threatens it. Both are innocent: the one who is threatened is not threatened because of any fault, the one who threatens does not threaten because of any fault. For this reason we may feel that we bystanders cannot intervene. But the person threatened can.

In sum, a woman surely can defend her life against the threat to it posed by the unborn child, even if doing so involves its death. And this shows not merely that the theses in (1) through (4) are false; it shows also that the extreme view of abortion is false, and so we need not canvass any other possible ways of arriving at it from the argument I mentioned at the outset.

2. The extreme view could of course be weakened to say that while abortion is permissible to save the mother's life, it may not be performed by a third party, but only by the mother herself. But this cannot be right either. For what we have to keep in mind is

that the mother and the unborn child are not like two tenants in a small house which has, by an unfortunate mistake, been rented to both: the mother *owns* the house. The fact that she does adds to the offensiveness of deducing that the mother can do nothing from the supposition that third parties can do nothing. But it does more than this: it casts a bright light on the supposition that third parties can do nothing. Certainly it lets us see that a third party who says "I cannot choose between you" is fooling himself if he thinks this is impartiality. If Jones has found and fastened on a certain coat, which he needs to keep him from freezing, but which Smith also needs to keep him from freezing, then it is not impartiality that says "I cannot choose between you" when Smith owns the coat. Women have said again and again "This body is *my* body!" and they have reason to feel angry, reason to feel that it has been like shouting into the wind. Smith, after all, is hardly likely to bless us if we say to him, "Of course it's your coat, anybody would grant that it is. But no one may choose between you and Jones who is to have it."

We should really ask what it is that says "no one may choose" in the face of the fact that the body that houses the child is the mother's body. It may be simply a failure to appreciate this fact. But it may be something more interesting, namely the sense that one has a right to refuse to lay hands on people, even where it would be just and fair to do so, even where justice seems to require that somebody do so. Thus justice might call for somebody to get Smith's coat back from Jones, and yet you have a right to refuse to be the one to lay hands on Jones, a right to refuse to do physical violence to him. This, I think, must be granted. But then what should be said is not "no one may choose," but only "*I* cannot choose," and indeed not even this, but "*I* will not *act*," leaving it open that somebody else can or should, and in particular that anyone in a position of authority, with the job of securing people's rights, both can and should. So this is no difficulty. I have not been arguing that any given third party must accede to the mother's request that he perform an abortion to save her life, but only that he may.

I suppose that in some views of human life the mother's body is only on loan to her, the loan not being one which gives her any prior claim to it. One who held this view might well think it impartiality to say "I cannot choose." But I shall simply ignore this possibility. My own view is that if a human being has any just, prior claim to anything at all, he has a just, prior claim to his own body. And perhaps this needn't be argued for here anyway, since, as I mentioned, the arguments against abortion we are looking at do grant that the woman has a right to decide what happens in and to her body.

But although they do grant it, I have tried to show that they do not take seriously what is done in granting it. I suggest the same thing will reappear even more clearly when we turn away from cases in which the mother's life is at stake, and attend, as I propose we now do, to the vastly more common cases in which a woman wants an abortion for some less weighty reason than preserving her own life.

3. Where the mother's life is not at stake, the argument I mentioned at the outset seems to have a much stronger pull. "Everyone has a right to life, so the unborn person has a right to life." And isn't the child's right to life weightier than anything other than the mother's own right to life, which she might put forward as ground for an abortion?

This argument treats the right to life as if it were unproblematic. It is not, and this seems to me to be precisely the source of the mistake.

For we should now, at long last, ask what it comes to, to have a right to life. In some views having a right to life includes having a right to be given at least the bare minimum one needs for continued life. But suppose that what in fact *is* the bare minimum a man needs for continued life is something he has no right at all to be given? If I am sick unto death, and the only thing that will save my life is the touch of Henry Fonda's cool hand on my fevered brow, then all the same, I have no right to be given the touch of Henry Fonda's cool hand on my fevered brow. It would be frightfully nice of him to fly in from the West Coast to provide it. It would be less nice, though no doubt well meant, if my friends flew out to the West Coast and carried Henry Fonda back with them. But I have no right at all against anybody that he should do this for me. Or again, to return to the story I told earlier, the fact that for continued life that violinist needs the continued use of your kidneys does not establish that he has a right to be given the continued use of your kidneys. He certainly has no right against you that *you* should give him continued use of your kidneys. For nobody has any right to use your kidneys unless you give him such a right; and nobody has the right against you that you shall give him this right—if you do allow him to go on using your kidneys, this is a kindness on your part, and not something he can claim from you as his due. Nor has he any right against anybody else that *they* should give him continued use of your kidneys. Certainly he had no right against the Society of Music Lovers that they should plug him into you in the first place. And if you now start to unplug yourself, having learned that you will otherwise have to spend nine years in bed with him, there is nobody in the world who must try to prevent you, in order to see to it that he is given something he has a right to be given.

Some people are rather stricter about the right to life. In their view, it does not include the right to be given anything, but amounts to, and only to, the right not to be killed by anybody. But here a related difficulty arises. If everybody is to refrain from killing that violinist, then everybody must refrain from doing a great many different sorts of things. Everybody must refrain from slitting his throat, everybody must refrain from shooting him—and everybody must refrain from unplugging you from him. But does he have a right against everybody that they shall refrain from unplugging you from him? To refrain from doing this is to allow him to continue to use your kidneys. It could be argued that he has a right against us that *we* should allow him to continue to use your kidneys. That is, while he had no right against us that we should give him the use of your kidneys, it might be argued that he anyway has a right against us that we shall not now intervene and deprive him of the use of your kidneys. I shall come back to third-party interventions later. But certainly the violinist has no right against you that *you* shall allow him to continue to use your kidneys. As I said, if you do allow him to use them, it is a kindness on your part, and not something you owe him.

The difficulty I point to here is not peculiar to the right to life. It reappears in connection with all the other natural rights; and it is something which an adequate account of rights must deal with. For present purposes it is enough just to draw attention to it. But I would stress that I am not arguing that people do not have a right to life—quite to the contrary, it seems to me that the primary control we must place on the acceptability of an account of rights is that it should turn out in that account to be a truth that all persons have a right to life. I am arguing only that having a right to life does not guarantee having either a right to be given the use of or a right to be allowed continued use of another person's body—even if one needs it for life itself. So the right to life will not serve the opponents of abortion in the very simple and clear way in which they seem to have thought it would.

4. There is another way to bring out the difficulty. In the most ordinary sort of case, to deprive someone of what he has a right to is to treat him unjustly. Suppose a boy and his small brother are jointly given a box of chocolates for Christmas. If the older boy takes the box and refuses to give his brother any of the chocolates, he is unjust to him, for the brother has been given a right to half of them. But suppose that, having learned that otherwise it means nine years in bed with that violinist, you unplug yourself from him. You surely are not being unjust to him, for you gave him no right to use your kidneys, and no one else can have given him any such right. But we have to notice that in unplugging yourself, you are killing him; and violinists, like everybody else, have a right to life, and thus in the view we were considering just now, the right not to be killed. So here you do what he supposedly has a right you shall not do, but you do not act unjustly to him in doing it.

The emendation which may be made at this point is this: the right to life consists not in the right not to be killed, but rather in the right not to be killed unjustly. This runs a risk of circularity, but never mind: it would enable us to square the fact that the violinist has a right to life with the fact that you do not act unjustly toward him in unplugging yourself, thereby killing him. For if you do not kill him unjustly, you do not violate his right to life, and so it is no wonder you do him no injustice.

But if this emendation is accepted, the gap in the argument against abortion stares us plainly in the face: it is by no means enough to show that the fetus is a person, and to remind us that all persons have a right to life—we need to be shown also that killing the fetus violates its right to life, i.e., that abortion is unjust killing. And is it?

I suppose we may take it as a datum that in a case of pregnancy due to rape the mother has not given the unborn person a right to the use of her body for food and shelter. Indeed, in what pregnancy could it be supposed that the mother has given the unborn person such a right? It is not as if there were unborn persons drifting about the world, to whom a woman who wants a child says "I invite you in."

But it might be argued that there are other ways one can have acquired a right to the use of another person's body than by having been invited to use it by that person. Suppose a woman voluntarily indulges in intercourse, knowing of the chance it will issue in pregnancy, and then she does become pregnant; is she not in part responsible for the presence, in fact the very existence, of the unborn person inside her? No doubt she did not invite it in. But doesn't her partial responsibility for its being there itself give it a right to the use of her body?[6] If so, then her aborting it would be more like the boy's taking away the chocolates, and less like your unplugging yourself from the violinist—doing so would be depriving it of what it does have a right to, and thus would be doing it an injustice.

And then, too, it might be asked whether or not she can kill it even to save her own life: If she voluntarily called it into existence, how can she now kill it, even in self-defense?

The first thing to be said about this is that it is something new. Opponents of abortion have been so concerned to make out the independence of the fetus, in order to establish that it has a right to life, just as its mother does, that they have tended to overlook the possible support they might gain from making out that the fetus is *dependent* on the mother, in order to establish that she has a special kind of responsibility for it, a responsibility that gives it rights against her which are not possessed by any independent person—such as an ailing violinist who is a stranger to her.

On the other hand, this argument would give the unborn person a right to its mother's body only if her pregnancy resulted from a voluntary act, undertaken in full knowledge of the chance a pregnancy might result from it. It would leave out entirely the unborn person whose existence is due to rape. Pending the availability of some further argument, then, we would be left with the conclusion that unborn persons whose existence is due to rape have no right to the use of their mothers' bodies, and thus that aborting them is not depriving them of anything they have a right to and hence is not unjust killing.

And we should also notice that it is not at all plain that this argument really does go even as far as it purports to. For there are cases and cases, and the details make a difference. If the room is stuffy, and I therefore open a window to air it, and a burglar climbs in, it would be absurd to say, "Ah, now he can stay, she's given him a right to the use of her house—for she is partially responsible for his presence there, having voluntarily done what enabled him to get in, in full knowledge that there are such things as burglars, and that burglars burgle." It would be still more absurd to say this if I had had bars installed outside my windows, precisely to prevent burglars from getting in, and a burglar got in only because of a defect in the bars. It remains equally absurd if we imagine it is not a burglar who climbs in, but an innocent person who blunders or falls in. Again, suppose it were like this: people-seeds drift about in the air like pollen, and if you open your windows, one may drift in and take root in your carpets or upholstery. You don't want children, so you fix up your windows with fine mesh screens, the very best you can buy. As can happen, however, and on very, very rare occasions does happen, one of the screens is defective; and a seed drifts in and takes root. Does the person-plant who now develops have a right to the use of your house? Surely not—despite the fact that you voluntarily opened your windows, you knowingly kept carpets and upholstered furniture, and you knew that screens were sometimes defective. Someone may argue that you are responsible for its rooting, that it does have a right to your house, because after all you *could* have lived out your life with bare floors and furniture, or with sealed windows and doors. But this won't do—for by the same token anyone can avoid a pregnancy due to rape by having a hysterectomy, or anyway by never leaving home without a (reliable!) army.

It seems to me that the argument we are looking at can establish at most that there are *some* cases in which the unborn person has a right to the use of its mother's body, and therefore *some* cases in which abortion is unjust killing. There is room for much discussion and argument as to precisely which, if any. But I think we should sidestep this issue and leave it open, for at any rate the argument certainly does not establish that all abortion is unjust killing.

5. There is room for yet another argument here, however. We surely must all grant that there may be cases in which it would be morally indecent to detach a person from your body at the cost of his life. Suppose you learn that what the violinist needs is not nine years of your life, but only one hour: all you need do to save his life is to spend one hour in that bed with him. Suppose also that letting him use your kidneys for that one hour would not affect your health in the slightest. Admittedly you were kidnapped. Admittedly you did not give anyone permission to plug him into you. Nevertheless it seems to me plain you *ought* to allow him to use your kidneys for that hour—it would be indecent to refuse.

Again, suppose pregnancy lasted only an hour, and constituted no threat to life or health. And suppose that a woman becomes pregnant as a result of rape. Admittedly she did not voluntarily do anything to bring about the existence of a child. Admittedly she did nothing at all which would give the unborn person a right to the use of her body. All the same it might well be said, as in the newly emended violinist story, that she *ought* to allow it to remain for that hour—that it would be indecent of her to refuse.

Now some people are inclined to use the term "right" in such a way that it follows from the fact that you ought to allow a person to use your body for the hour he needs, that he has a right to use your body for the hour he needs, even though he has not been given that right by any person or act. They may say that it follows also that if you refuse, you act unjustly toward him. This use of the term is perhaps so common that it cannot be called wrong; nevertheless it seems to me to be an unfortunate loosening of what we would do better to keep a tight rein on. Suppose that box of chocolates I mentioned earlier had not been given to both boys jointly, but was given

only to the older boy. There he sits, stolidly eating his way through the box, his small brother watching enviously. Here we are likely to say "You ought not to be so mean. You ought to give your brother some of those chocolates." My own view is that it just does not follow from the truth of this that the brother has any right to any of the chocolates. If the boy refuses to give his brother any, he is greedy, stingy, callous—but not unjust. I suppose that the people I have in mind will say it does follow that the brother has a right to some of the chocolates, and thus that the boy does act unjustly if he refuses to give his brother any. But the effect of saying this is to obscure what we should keep distinct, namely the difference between the boy's refusal in this case and the boy's refusal in the earlier case, in which the box was given to both boys jointly, and in which the small brother thus had what was from any point of view clear title to half.

A further objection to so using the term "right" that from the fact that A ought to do a thing for B, it follows that B has a right against A that A do it for him, is that it is going to make the question of whether or not a man has a right to a thing turn on how easy it is to provide him with it; and this seems not merely unfortunate, but morally unacceptable. Take the case of Henry Fonda again. I said earlier that I had no right to the touch of his cool hand on my fevered brow, even though I needed it to save my life. I said it would be frightfully nice of him to fly in from the West Coast to provide me with it, but that I had no right against him that he should do so. But suppose he isn't on the West Coast. Suppose he has only to walk across the room, place a hand briefly on my brow—and lo, my life is saved. Then surely he ought to do it, it would be indecent to refuse. Is it to be said "Ah, well, it follows that in this case she has a right to the touch of his hand on her brow, and so it would be an injustice in him to refuse"? So that I have a right to it when it is easy for him to provide it, though no right when it's hard? It's rather a shocking idea that anyone's rights should fade away and disappear as it gets harder and harder to accord them to him.

So my own view is that even though you ought to let the violinist use your kidneys for the one hour he needs, we should not conclude that he has a right to do so—we should say that if you refuse, you are, like the boy who owns all the chocolates and will give none away, self-centered and callous, indecent in fact, but not unjust. And similarly, that even supposing a case in which a woman pregnant due to rape ought to allow the unborn person to use her body for the hour he needs, we should not conclude that he has a right to do so; we should conclude that she is self-centered, callous, indecent, but not unjust, if she refuses. The complaints are no less grave; they are just different. However, there is no need to insist on this point. If anyone does wish to deduce "he has a right" from "you ought," then all the same he must surely grant that there are cases in which it is not morally required of you that you allow that violinist to use your kidneys, and in which he does not have a right to use them, and in which you do not do him an injustice if you refuse. And so also for mother and unborn child. Except in such cases as the unborn person has a right to demand it—and we were leaving open the possibility that there may be such cases—nobody is morally *required* to make large sacrifices, of health, of all other interests and concerns, of all other duties and commitments, for nine years, or even for nine months, in order to keep another person alive.

6. We have in fact to distinguish between two kinds of Samaritan: the Good Samaritan and what we might call the Minimally Decent Samaritan. The story of the Good Samaritan, you will remember, goes like this:

> A certain man went down from Jerusalem to Jericho, and fell among thieves, which stripped him of his raiment, and wounded him, and departed, leaving him half dead.
>
> And by chance there came down a certain priest that way; and when he saw him, he passed by on the other side.
>
> And likewise a Levite, when he was at the place, came and looked on him, and passed by on the other side.
>
> But a certain Samaritan, as he journeyed, came where he was; and when he saw him he had compassion on him.
>
> And went to him, and bound up his wounds, pouring in oil and wine, and set him on his own beast, and brought him to an inn, and took care of him.
>
> And on the morrow, when he departed, he took out two pence, and gave them to the host, and said unto him,

> "Take care of him; and whatsoever thou spendest more, when I come again, I will repay thee."

(Luke 10:30–35)

The Good Samaritan went out of his way, at some cost to himself, to help one in need of it. We are not told what the options were, that is, whether or not the priest and the Levite could have helped by doing less than the Good Samaritan did, but assuming they could have, then the fact they did nothing at all shows they were not even Minimally Decent Samaritans, not because they were not Samaritans, but because they were not even minimally decent.

These things are a matter of degree, of course, but there is a difference, and it comes out perhaps most clearly in the story of Kitty Genovese, who, as you will remember, was murdered while thirty-eight people watched or listened, and did nothing at all to help her. A Good Samaritan would have rushed out to give direct assistance against the murderer. Or perhaps we had better allow that it would have been a Splendid Samaritan who did this, on the ground that it would have involved a risk of death for himself. But the thirty-eight not only did not do this, they did not even trouble to pick up a phone to call the police. Minimally Decent Samaritanism would call for doing at least that, and their not having done it was monstrous.

After telling the story of the Good Samaritan, Jesus said "Go, and do thou likewise." Perhaps he meant that we are morally required to act as the Good Samaritan did. Perhaps he was urging people to do more than is morally required of them. At all events it seems plain that it was not morally required of any of the thirty-eight that he rush out to give direct assistance at the risk of his own life, and that it is not morally required of anyone that he give long stretches of his life—nine years or nine months—to sustaining the life of a person who has no special right (we were leaving open the possibility of this) to demand it.

Indeed, with one rather striking class of exceptions, no one in any country in the world is *legally* required to do anywhere near as much as this for anyone else. The class of exceptions is obvious. My main concern here is not the state of the law in respect to abortion, but it is worth drawing attention to the fact that in no state in this country is any man compelled by law to be even a Minimally Decent Samaritan to any person; there is no law under which charges could be brought against the thirty-eight who stood by while Kitty Genovese died. By contrast, in most states in this country women are compelled by law to be not merely Minimally Decent Samaritans, but Good Samaritans to unborn persons inside them. This doesn't by itself settle anything one way or the other, because it may well be argued that there should be laws in this country—as there are in many European countries—compelling at least Minimally Decent Samaritanism.[7] But it does show that there is a gross injustice in the existing state of the law. And it shows also that the groups currently working against liberalization of abortion laws, in fact working toward having it declared unconstitutional for a state to permit abortion, had better start working for the adoption of Good Samaritan laws generally, or earn the charge that they are acting in bad faith.

I should think, myself, that Minimally Decent Samaritan laws would be one thing, Good Samaritan laws quite another, and in fact highly improper. But we are not here concerned with the law. What we should ask is not whether anybody should be compelled by law to be a Good Samaritan, but whether we must accede to a situation in which somebody is being compelled—by nature, perhaps—to be a Good Samaritan. We have, in other words, to look now at third-party interventions. I have been arguing that no person is morally required to make large sacrifices to sustain the life of another who has no right to demand them, and this even where the sacrifices do not include life itself; we are not morally required to be Good Samaritans or anyway Very Good Samaritans to one another. But what if a man cannot extricate himself from such a situation? What if he appeals to us to extricate him? It seems to me plain that there are cases in which we can, cases in which a Good Samaritan would extricate him. There you are, you were kidnapped, and nine years in bed with that violinist lie ahead of you. You have your own life to lead. You are sorry, but you simply cannot see giving up so much of your life to the sustaining of his. You cannot extricate yourself, and ask us to do

so. I should have thought that—in light of his having no right to the use of your body—it was obvious that we do not have to accede to your being forced to give up so much. We can do what you ask. There is no injustice to the violinist in our doing so.

7. Following the lead of the opponents of abortion, I have throughout been speaking of the fetus merely as a person, and what I have been asking is whether or not the argument we began with, which proceeds only from the fetus' being a person, really does establish its conclusion. I have argued that it does not.

But of course there are arguments and arguments, and it may be said that I have simply fastened on the wrong one. It may be said that what is important is not merely the fact that the fetus is a person, but that it is a person for whom the woman has a special kind of responsibility issuing from the fact that she is its mother. And it might be argued that all my analogies are therefore irrelevant—for you do not have that special kind of responsibility for that violinist, Henry Fonda does not have that special kind of responsibility for me. And our attention might be drawn to the fact that men and women both *are* compelled by law to provide support for their children.

I have in effect dealt (briefly) with this argument in section 4 above; but a (still briefer) recapitulation now may be in order. Surely we do not have any such "special responsibility" for a person unless we have assumed it, explicitly or implicitly. If a set of parents do not try to prevent pregnancy, do not obtain an abortion, and then at the time of birth of the child do not put it out for adoption, but rather take it home with them, then they have assumed responsibility for it, they have given it rights, and they cannot *now* withdraw support from it at the cost of its life because they now find it difficult to go on providing for it. But if they have taken all reasonable precautions against having a child, they do not simply by virtue of their biological relationship to the child who comes into existence have a special responsibility for it. They may wish to assume responsibility for it, or they may not wish to. And I am suggesting that if assuming responsibility for it would require large sacrifices, then they may refuse. A Good Samaritan would not refuse—or anyway, a Splendid Samaritan, if the sacrifices that had to be made were enormous. But then so would a Good Samaritan assume responsibility for that violinist; so would Henry Fonda, if he is a Good Samaritan, fly in from the West Coast and assume responsibility for me.

8. My argument will be found unsatisfactory on two counts by many of those who want to regard abortion as morally permissible. First, while I do argue that abortion is not impermissible, I do not argue that it is always permissible. There may well be cases in which carrying the child to term requires only Minimally Decent Samaritanism of the mother, and this is a standard we must not fall below. I am inclined to think it a merit of my account precisely that it does *not* give a general yes or a general no. It allows for and supports our sense that, for example, a sick and desperately frightened fourteen-year-old schoolgirl, pregnant due to rape, may *of course* choose abortion, and that any law which rules this out is an insane law. And it also allows for and supports our sense that in other cases resort to abortion is even positively indecent. It would be indecent in the woman to request an abortion, and indecent in a doctor to perform it, if she is in her seventh month, and wants the abortion just to avoid the nuisance of postponing a trip abroad. The very fact that the arguments I have been drawing attention to treat all cases of abortion, or even all cases of abortion in which the mother's life is not at stake, as morally on a par ought to have made them suspect at the outset.

Secondly, while I am arguing for the permissibility of abortion in some cases, I am not arguing for the right to secure the death of the unborn child. It is easy to confuse these two things in that up to a certain point in the life of the fetus it is not able to survive outside the mother's body; hence removing it from her body guarantees its death. But they are importantly different. I have argued that you are not morally required to spend nine months in bed, sustaining the life of that violinist; but to say this is by no means to say that if, when you unplug yourself, there is a miracle and he survives, you then have a right to turn round and slit his throat. You may detach yourself even if this costs him his life; you have no right to be guaranteed his death, by some other means, if unplugging yourself does not kill him. There are some people who will feel dissatisfied by this feature of my argument. A woman may be utterly devastated by the thought of a child, a bit of herself, put out for adoption and never seen or heard of again. She may therefore want not merely that the child be detached from her, but more, that it die. Some opponents of abortion are inclined to regard this as beneath contempt—thereby showing insensitivity to what is surely a powerful source of despair. All the same, I agree that the desire for the child's death is not one which anybody may gratify, should it turn out to be possible to detach the child alive.

At this place, however, it should be remembered that we have only been pretending throughout that the fetus is a human being from the moment of conception. A very early abortion is surely not the killing of a person, and so is not dealt with by anything I have said here.

NOTES

1. Daniel Callahan, Abortion: *Law, Choice and Morality* (New York, 1970), p. 373. This book gives a fascinating survey of the available information on abortion. The Jewish tradition is surveyed in David M. Feldman, *Birth Control in Jewish Law* (New York, 1968), Part 5; the Catholic tradition in John T. Noonan, Jr., "An Almost Absolute Value in History," in *The Morality of Abortion,* ed. John T. Noonan, Jr. (Cambridge, Mass., 1970).

2. The term "direct" in the arguments I refer to is a technical one. Roughly, what is meant by "direct killing" is either killing as an end in itself, or killing as a means to some end, for example, the end of saving someone else's life. See note 6, below, for an example of its use.

3. Cf. *Encyclical Letter of Pope Pius XI on Christian Marriage*, St. Paul Editions (Boston, n.d.), p. 32: "however much we may pity the mother whose health and even life is gravely imperiled in the performance of the duty allotted to her by nature, nevertheless what could ever be a sufficient reason for excusing in any way the direct murder of the innocent? This is precisely what we are dealing with here." Noonan (*The Morality of Abortion*, p. 43) reads this as follows: "What cause can ever avail to excuse in any way the direct killing of the innocent? For it is a question of that."

4. The thesis in (4) is in an interesting way weaker than those in (1), (2), and (3): they rule out abortion even in cases in which both mother and child will die if the abortion is not performed. By contrast, one who held the view

expressed in (4) could consistently say that one needn't prefer letting two persons die to killing one.

5. Cf. the following passage from Pius XII, *Address to the Italian Catholic Society of Midwives*: "The baby in the maternal breast has the right to life immediately from God.—Hence there is no man, no human authority, no science, no medical, eugenic, social, economic or moral 'indication' which can establish or grant a valid juridical ground for a direct deliberate disposition of an innocent human life, that is a disposition which looks to its destruction either as an end or as a means to another end perhaps

in itself not illicit.—The baby, still not born, is a man in the same degree and for the same reason as the mother" (quoted in Noonan, *The Morality of Abortion*, p. 45).

6. The need for a discussion of this argument was brought home to me by members of the Society for Ethical and Legal Philosophy, to whom this paper was originally presented.

7. For a discussion of the difficulties involved, and a survey of the European experience with such laws, see *The Good Samaritan and the Law*, ed. James M. Ratcliffe (New York, 1966).

DISCUSSION QUESTIONS

1. What are the different arguments that Thomson makes using the violinist example? Which of them do you think are successful? Which are not? Why?
2. Thomson discusses two different views about what it means to have a right to life. What do each of these views imply about moral issues other than abortion? Do these implications make them more or less plausible?
3. What are the thought experiments involving the burglar and the "people-seeds" supposed to show? Do you think those arguments succeed? Why or why not?
4. What is the main point of Thomson's discussion of the Good Samaritan in Section 6? Do you think her arguments in that section succeed? Why or why not?

Euthanasia

Susan M. Wolf

Physician-Assisted Suicide

Susan M. Wolf is the McKnight Presidential Professor of Law, Medicine & Public Policy at the University of Minnesota, as well as the Faegre Baker Daniels Professor of Law and a Professor of Medicine. In this paper, she explains several different kinds of physician-assisted death and summarizes key moral and legal arguments for and against those different practices.

Clinics in Geriatric Medicine 21(1) (2005), 179–192.

DISCUSSION QUESTIONS

1. Wolf distinguishes three different practices that are sometimes lumped together under the label "euthanasia." What are these practices? Describe each one briefly in your own words.
2. Wolf sketches three main arguments in support of physician-assisted suicide and/or euthanasia. What are they?
3. Wolf sketches three main arguments against physician-assisted suicide and/or euthanasia. What are they?

Debate over the acceptability of physician-assisted suicide in the United States has intensified in the past decade. Discussion of the practice dates back thousands of years; Hippocratic writings enjoined physicians to give no "deadly drug" even if asked [1]. Arguments over the wisdom of allowing physicians to assist patients in committing suicide have waxed and waned since then [2]. However, a number of developments have recently increased the intensity of debate.

First, improved clinical capacity to extend life has led to concern over how to assure competent, humane, and responsive care at the end of life [3]. Thus, a tremendous amount of work has been devoted to securing for patients the right to refuse unwanted life-sustaining treatment, the option of using advance directives to govern care after loss of decisional capacity, and access to effective pain relief and palliative care. Efforts to secure these rights and options have predictably led to debate over whether patients should have the option, and indeed the right, to assistance from a physician in committing suicide.

Second, some physicians have publicly revealed that they have provided such assistance to patients. An anonymous 1988 account of doing so in "It's Over, Debbie" plus Dr. Timothy Quill's 1991 account fueled national discussion [4,5]. Dr. Jack Kevorkian fueled debate as well by repeatedly assisting suicide and performing euthanasia, until he was successfully prosecuted for second-degree murder and jailed in 1999 [6].

Legal changes have fired debate as well. In a series of decisions that began in 1973, courts in the Netherlands carved out categories of cases in which both physician-assisted suicide and euthanasia would be allowed [7]. In 1995, the Dutch Ministry of Justice and the Royal Dutch Medical Association codified the cases in which both practices would be allowed and the applicable procedures [8]. In 2001, the Dutch

parliament formally legalized both practices [9,10]. Dutch researchers have studied clinical practice as the law has evolved, producing important empirical studies that have added to the debate [11–18].

In 1997, Oregon legalized physician-assisted suicide by lethal prescription [19]. Although the United States Department of Justice then attempted to block prescription of controlled substances for this purpose, claiming it violated the Federal Controlled Substances Act [20], the courts rejected this challenge [21]. We now see 6 years of reported experience with the Oregon statute and data on practice to date [22–31].

In 1994, a group of patients and physicians brought a constitutional challenge to the state statutes prohibiting physician-assisted suicide in New York and Washington State [32,33]. These became the first cases to go to the United States Supreme Court on the question of whether state prohibitions violate patients' rights to due process and equal protection under the United States Constitution. These two cases engendered an outpouring of briefs, articles, and media coverage. In 1997, the Court decided that state prohibitions did not violate patients' constitutional rights, leaving individual states free to maintain their prohibitions or permit the practice. Only Oregon has thus far legalized physician-assisted suicide.

The effect of this recent history has been an upsurge in attention to the practice. Numerous polls and studies have attempted to ascertain the state of public opinion and attitudes among health professionals [34–45]. Many commentators, however, have urged caution in interpreting those data, given substantial variation in how questions are phrased and uncertainty about how informed respondents are [44,46].

This article articulates the major arguments for and against permitting physicians to assist suicide. It then offers concrete recommendations for addressing concerns about end-of-life care that have surfaced in the assisted-suicide debate. Reasoned debate starts, however, with careful definition of the practice.

DEFINITIONS

The debate over physician-assisted suicide has long been plagued by confusion. Early in the debate, "euthanasia" was used to refer to termination of life-sustaining treatment (sometimes called "passive euthanasia"), assistance in suicide, and a physician directly taking a patient's life (sometimes called "active euthanasia"). It is now widely recognized that lumping those three practices together is confusing, as there is a separate clinical, ethical, and legal discussion of each.

Termination of life-sustaining treatment refers to withholding or withdrawing any life-sustaining treatment—from artificial ventilation, to in-hospital CPR, to antibiotics—at the request of a patient with decisional capacity or the appropriate surrogate of a patient without such capacity. Health professionals are not only permitted to honor such requests, there is broad legal, ethical, and clinical consensus that professionals should do so [47–49]. The United States Supreme Court has recognized a constitutional right to refuse unwanted life-sustaining treatment [50].

Physician-assisted suicide requires a suicide. This means the patient himself or herself must perform the death-causing act, typically by ingesting lethal medication. However, the physician provides prior assistance, typically by prescribing the lethal drugs knowing that the patient may use them to commit suicide. The physician may also instruct the patient on how to assure lethality.

In contrast to the broad consensus supporting physicians' honoring requests to terminate treatment, there is no consensus on physician-assisted suicide. Organized medical and nursing societies have condemned the practice, and many states have explicit legal prohibitions [51–53]. Debate over whether to lift those prohibitions continues.

In the case of euthanasia, the physician performs the death-causing act, directly and intentionally ending the patient's life. Typically, the physician administers a lethal injection. Discussion of euthanasia distinguishes among voluntary, involuntary, and nonvoluntary euthanasia [54]. The first has been requested by the patient, the second is administered over the patient's objection, and in the third case the patient's preference has not been elicited or the patient lacks decisional capacity to choose.

No state in the United States permits euthanasia; it is widely prohibited as a species of homicide [49,55]. Although the Dutch permit physician-assisted suicide and euthanasia, discussion and proposals in the United States have sharply contrasted the two practices. Though there has been substantial support for allowing physician-assisted suicide, there has been much less support for permitting euthanasia. A major reason has been that physician-assisted suicide is less subject to abuse; because the patient takes the last, fatal step, there is greater assurance that the patient is genuinely choosing to die and has not changed his or her mind. Documentation of nonvoluntary euthanasia in the Netherlands, involving euthanasia of incompetent adults and children, has added to concern that euthanasia may be more readily abused than physician-assisted suicide [11, 56–60].

These definitions merely offer a starting place for debate. Many of those challenging the continued prohibition of physician-assisted suicide and euthanasia proceed by arguing that there is no principled distinction between licit practices, such as terminating life-sustaining treatment and aggressive pain relief, and practices widely deemed illicit, such as physician-assisted suicide and euthanasia. All four practices, they maintain, may lead to death. They argue that physicians may intend and cause death in each case. They claim that distinctions between causing death by omission (of life-sustaining treatment) and commission (providing a lethal prescription or injection, for instance) make little difference.

A hefty philosophical literature now debates these claims. As a legal matter, however, the Supreme Court in the physician-assisted suicide cases found it rational and constitutional for state legislatures to distinguish between forgoing life-sustaining treatment and physician-assisted suicide [32,33].

Thus, states may treat the former practice as legal and may facilitate forgoing treatment through statutes recognizing advance directives, for example, while making assisted suicide illegal. American law has long recognized a common law and constitutional right to be free of unwanted bodily invasion, even if the bodily invasion is life-sustaining and the foreseeable consequence of refusal is death. Courts have concluded that respecting the patient's freedom to refuse unwanted bodily invasion is essential to a constitutional scheme of ordered liberty. Yet the freedom to refuse invasion does not seem to cover assisted suicide, the demand for the means to perform bodily invasion on oneself for the explicit purpose of dying. Indeed, the law recognizes no right to commit suicide or to demand another's help; anyone assisting a suicide risks criminal prosecution. So the question in law is whether physicians should be exempt from this broad prohibition. The general answer thus far has been "no."

The debate about the difference between forgoing treatment and assisting suicide has focused recently on the claim that there are intermediate practices—specifically, aggressive pain relief leading to death and what has been called "terminal sedation," that challenge the continued viability of a distinction. An observer would be able to distinguish classic cases of forgoing treatment (say, by withdrawing artificial ventilation) from assisting suicide (say, by providing a lethal prescription). The claim, however, is that it would be harder to distinguish two practices from assisted suicide or euthanasia: first, pain relief that may suppress respiration and hasten death, and second, sedation combined with withdrawal of artificial nutrition. On the former, there is wide agreement that patients are entitled to expert pain relief and palliative care. Even pain relief that may risk respiratory depression and hastening death is widely accepted under three conditions: (1) there is no less dangerous way to provide effective pain relief; (2) the patient with decisional capacity or incompetent patient's surrogate is informed of the risks and accepts them; and (3) the physician's goal is therapeutic, that is, to provide pain relief, not end the patient's life. If those conditions are met, then pain relief that risks hastening death joins the roster of many interventions

that physicians and surgeons offer every day that aim to achieve a therapeutic goal but risk causing death. Mere risk of causing death does not make a practice assisted suicide or euthanasia. That said, there is an empirical debate over whether expert techniques to alleviate pain actually do risk hastening death [61–63]; if they do not, then the distinction between aggressive pain relief and assisted suicide or euthanasia becomes even clearer.

The second practice, "terminal sedation," raises a different issue—there is no agreement on what this term means. The term gained currency during the pendency of the Supreme Court cases on assisted suicide; briefs in support of those challenging the state prohibitions on assisted suicide argued that an already accepted practice of terminal sedation was indistinguishable. Yet the emerging literature offers different definitions.

A definition often encountered is that terminal sedation involves sedating a patient to unconsciousness while withholding artificial nutrition [64–66]. The claim is that clinicians doing this are intentionally causing death. However, if sedation to unconsciousness is required to achieve good pain relief and palliative care, and artificial nutrition is withdrawn at the request of a patient with capacity or the incompetent patient's surrogate, then this combination of practices is readily distinguished from assisted suicide and euthanasia. Providing good pain relief and palliative care is a fundamental obligation of clinicians; so is honoring the patient's wish (or appropriate surrogate's choice) to be free of unwanted life-sustaining treatment, whether artificial nutrition, ventilation, or another invasive modality. The combination of these practices remains distinguishable from providing a lethal prescription or injection for the purpose of directly and immediately causing death.

This section has distinguished among a set of practices in order to allow normative discussion on whether to legitimize physician-assisted suicide. Normative discussion is impossible without some sense of what the terms mean. But this section has also suggested the controversy that has plagued efforts to define these practices, including arguments over the difference between withholding and withdrawing treatment, acts and omissions, and intending the patient's death versus foreseeing it. Although those arguments continue, what allows meaningful debate is that at some common-sense, observable level, we actually do know which practice is which.

ARGUMENTS IN FAVOR OF PHYSICIAN-ASSISTED SUICIDE

Advocates for legitimating physician-assisted suicide rest their arguments chiefly on patients' rights of autonomy and liberty, physicians' duties to treat symptoms, such as pain and discomfort at the end of life, and the claim that killing (or helping the patient kill himself or herself) is not morally worse than allowing to die. Not all arguments for legitimating physician-assisted suicide or euthanasia call for outright legalization. One proposal, for example, would create an affirmative defense of "mercy killing" to a criminal prosecution for homicide [67].

American bioethics and law have a long history of championing a patient's moral and legal rights of autonomy and liberty. There is wide consensus in ethics, law, and clinical care that those rights entitle the patient to refuse unwanted life-sustaining treatment. The question is whether those rights also create an entitlement to a willing physician's assistance in committing suicide.

The Supreme Court has rejected the claim that the United States Constitution protects such a legal right. Debate continues, however, on whether a moral right exists and whether individual states should follow Oregon's lead and create a right protected by statute.

Supporters of a right to assisted suicide argue that the right to refuse unwanted treatment is best understood as part of a broader right to decide how to die. They maintain that this is a fundamental part of choosing what happens to your body and the trajectory of your life. They argue that rights of autonomy and liberty are weak if they are only negative rights to refuse treatment. They claim there is no principled basis for insisting that a patient endure a protracted and burdensome death by refusal of treatment and depriving the patient of the option of a faster death in the patient's control by physician-assisted suicide.

This leads to a second argument, that physicians have a duty to make assisted suicide available. This argument rests on physician duties of beneficence and nonmaleficence (ie, physician duties to care for patients and do no harm to them). The claim here is in part empirical, that patients seeking assisted suicide are suffering pain, discomfort, and burdens that can be relieved only by assisted suicide. A related claim is that physicians who have brought patients to the brink of death through the rigors of treatment (life-sustaining and otherwise) but then deny requested assistance with suicide wrongfully abandon those patients [68].

Beauchamp and Childress [69] make a weaker claim, that physicians are not obligated to assist suicide but that they may be permitted to do so in some circumstances. They articulate a set of criteria necessary to justify assistance, including an informed, voluntary, and durable request made by a competent patient, together with rejection of the alternatives, in the context of an ongoing doctor-patient relationship. They thus focus on the nature of the patient's request, the physician's motives, and the act's consequences to decide if such aid in dying is justified. At the same time, they recognize that creating a rule allowing physician-assisted suicide requires not only that some cases of it be justified, but that a widely applied rule and its likely consequences be acceptable.

Beauchamp and Childress [69] are among a number of authors rejecting the persuasiveness of distinctions between killing and allowing to die. Such challenges to the distinction between killing and allowing to die have often been animated by Rachels's [70] argument that the actions of a greedy relative who allows a cousin to drown so he can inherit are no worse than if he killed the cousin to inherit. However, in both of Rachels's scenarios, the relative intends and strives to produce his cousin's death; there is no other goal driving him. Yet in effectuating a patient's wish to forgo treatment, the physician is striving to respect the patient's right to bodily integrity and authority to exclude unwanted bodily invasion. Further, death may or may not eventuate, depending on the clinical situation. Thus, Rachels's argument is open to challenge and remains controversial.

Much as some advocates for physician-assisted suicide have challenged on philosophical grounds the distinction between honoring refusals of life-sustaining treatment and assisting suicide, others have recently challenged the distinction by claiming that some practices deemed acceptable under the prior rubric are difficult to distinguish from more active aid in dying, such as euthanasia. They point in particular to what some call "terminal sedation" [64–66]. Though the term is used inconsistently, it frequently refers to sedation to unconsciousness plus termination of artificial nutrition. However, when a patient with decisional capacity or incompetent patient's surrogate properly authorizes termination of artificial nutrition as an exercise of the right to be free of unwanted bodily invasion, and sedation to unconsciousness is clinically warranted and properly consented to, it is difficult to see this as equivalent to lethal prescription or injection. The fact that a practice predictably brings on death does not determine whether it is licit or not; that distinction hinges on the underlying patient rights, patient or surrogate authorization, and physician motives.

Finally, empirical data from the Netherlands and now Oregon have fueled competing assessments. Though some claim the Dutch data show a viable practice of assisted suicide and euthanasia, others have expressed concern over data showing significant violations of the Dutch requirement of voluntary, competent patient consent [60,71]. This is most obvious in data showing euthanasia of children and incompetent adults [13,56,57,71–73]. Further, data showing that a substantial number of Dutch physicians fail to comply with the reporting rules, thus thwarting effective oversight, have raised questions about how any regime of assisted suicide and euthanasia can be effectively controlled [14,58,74]. In reality, there is a broader debate about the applicability of the Dutch experience to the United States context. Significant differences between the two countries suggest that the problems plaguing the Dutch experience would be worse in the United States, with a far larger and more diverse population,

no universal health care insurance, and health care more often rendered by a physician with little or no prior relationship with the patient [75–78].

The Oregon data may thus be more readily generalized to the rest of the country than the Dutch data, but remain sparse. In 6 years of reported experience, physicians have written 265 lethal prescriptions, and 171 patients have used these prescriptions to commit suicide [27]. However, the Oregon data rely on physician reports, and physicians in Oregon (as in the Netherlands) may underreport or may report compliance with the rules when the rules have been violated. As some commentators have pointed out, what is not reported in Oregon we have no way to know [79].

ARGUMENTS AGAINST PHYSICIAN-ASSISTED SUICIDE

Key arguments against legitimating physician-assisted suicide are that the traditional rejection of this as part of the physician's role is important to the integrity of the medical profession; that legitimating the practice will lead to error, abuse, and negative consequences for patients; and that the practice is actually not clinically necessary to provide humane care at the end of life.

Many commentators have expressed deep concern that the traditional Hippocratic injunction to physicians to refuse to assist suicide and perform euthanasia remains essential to the ethical integrity of the medical profession [80–83]. Physicians routinely wield power over life and death almost unmatched by others in our society. A commitment to use those powers only to comfort and heal, avoiding use of those powers to intentionally cause death, helps orient the profession toward beneficence and nonmaleficence. Thus, avoiding assisted suicide and euthanasia becomes part of a larger ethical commitment to do no harm. Psychologically, a prohibition on assisting suicide and performing euthanasia may help prevent physicians from acting out ambivalence toward the dying patient by deliberately ending that patient's life [84]. Practically speaking, the prohibition may help avoid erroneously or abusively taking life.

One response to these arguments has been that a modern physician is committed not only to care and cure but to respect patient autonomy. Thus, it is argued, a physician should respect and assist the voluntary and competent choice of a patient, even if the patient chooses suicide or euthanasia. The problem with this argument is that a physician is not morally obligated to do everything a patient wants; to hold otherwise would reduce the physician to the patient's puppet and suggest there is no ethical limit to what a physician may do. Patients may request unapproved or inappropriate medications, nontherapeutic and even injuring procedures, and experimental procedures that pose excessive risk. In all of these cases, the physician's job is not simply to accede to the patient's request. The physician has duties that may include saying no.

The more specific question, then, is, What are the physician's duties at the end of life? Many commentators have argued that a physician has duties to respect a patient's right to be free of unwanted invasive treatment and to meet a patient's need for pain relief and palliative care, but that these do not translate into a duty to deliberately cause the patient's death through lethal prescription or injection [85,86]. A physician is morally and legally obligated to respect a patient's right to refuse treatment, even if the foreseeable consequence of honoring the refusal is likely to be death; that much is widely agreed. A physician caring for a patient at the end of life is also obligated to strive competently to relieve pain and provide palliation, even if the pain relief required carries a foreseeable risk of hastening death; that, too, is widely agreed. The argument is that there is an important distinction between (1) respecting the right to forgo treatment and meeting the need for pain relief with the goal of caring and (2) supplying lethal medication or injection to deliberately end life.

A related set of arguments points to the likely consequences of permitting physicians to assist suicide. Those who favor assisted suicide often assume that they can design a process free of error and abuse, but

were an MD a license to prescribe lethal medication, it would be unrealistic to assume such perfection. Physicians are human beings. They make mistakes. In the United States, they often do not know their patient well and may not appreciate what concerns are contributing to a patient's request for assisted suicide or the range of options that exist for addressing those concerns.

In a country of tremendous disparities in health status, access to care, and quality of care, there is substantial concern that physician-assisted suicide would be subject to significant error and abuse [76]. Over 40 million Americans entirely lack the health care insurance necessary to cope with serious illness [87,88]; others may face limited and unappealing choices in dealing with illness or disability, including a limited choice of setting. One may cogently argue that what these individuals need is access to good care and supportive settings, not a lethal prescription. Individuals with disabilities may properly worry that they are especially vulnerable to error and abuse [89]. Too often, their quality of life may be undervalued. It may be far easier for clinicians to respond to a disabled individual's situation with a lethal prescription than to address the underlying problems and to open options.

Finally, those opposing physician-assisted suicide argue that the practice is not necessary to provide humane care at the end of life. They point out that many of those advocating physician-assisted suicide mistakenly argue that the practice is needed to address pain. Yet as long as physicians can provide aggressive pain relief and palliative care, including sedating to unconsciousness if necessary, pain is not the primary argument for physician-assisted suicide. Data reveal that most patients interested in assisted suicide are not motivated by pain [27–29,31,44]. Instead, concerns about losing autonomy, dignity, and control, as well as depression and helplessness, loom large. Physicians, of course, are not all-powerful deities who can simply remove all of those concerns; some of these are part of the human condition and the reality of death. But the literature suggests that physicians skilled in care at the end of life, with good hospice options to offer and a skilled team can usually provide what Emanuel and Emanuel call a "good death" [90].

NEXT STEPS

Whether one supports or opposes legitimating physician-assisted suicide, there are substantial steps that can be taken to improve care at the end of life and reduce the perceived need for the practice [91]. Expert pain relief and palliative care, including sedation to unconsciousness when necessary, should be widely available. Ready access to hospice and other supportive settings and services is important. Work remains to be done to make recognized rights to forgo life-sustaining treatment a clinical reality. When patients are forgoing life-sustaining treatment, clinicians versed in the art of caring for the dying should manage symptoms and provide support effectively. The particular barriers to good care confronting dying patients who are uninsured or underinsured must be addressed.

If significant headway were made on these fronts, it is difficult to say how much demand for physician-assisted suicide would remain. Thus, advancing thinking on assisted suicide demands not only continued ethical, legal, and clinical debate plus ongoing empirical study as in Oregon, but also concrete improvement in care at the end of life.

SUMMARY

The debate over physician-assisted suicide is complex and multidisciplinary, requiring attention to ethical, legal, clinical, and empirical arguments. Indeed, the complexity of the debate has engendered skepticism about the wisdom of ballot measures and other means of simply polling the population for the answer [46]. Progress may instead require improvement in end-of-life care coupled with careful analysis of those cases in which patients seem interested in assisted suicide despite good care. Ultimately, there is no avoiding searching debate about the nature and limit of patient autonomy, the duties and proper role of the physician, and the likely impact of allowing assisted suicide when the barriers to good end-of-life care remain so high.

REFERENCES

1. Kass LR, Lund N. Courting death: assisted suicide, doctors, and the law. Commentary 1996; 102(6):17–29, 19.

2. Emanuel EJ. The history of euthanasia debates in the United States and Britain. Ann Intern Med 1994;121(10):793–802.

3. Doukas DJ, Brody H. Care at the twilight: ethics and end-of-life care. Am Fam Physician 1995; 52(5):1294–9.

4. Anonymous. It's over, Debbie. JAMA 1988; 259(2):272.

5. Quill TE. Death and dignity: a case of individualized decision making. N Engl J Med 1991; 324(10):691–4.

6. Murphy B, Swickard J. Convicted of murder. Detroit Free Press, 1999. Available at: http:// www.freep.com/news/extra2/qkevo272.htm. Accessed September 20, 2004.

7. Keown J. Law and practice of euthanasia in the Netherlands. Law Q Rev 1992;108(Jan):51–78.

8. Angell M. Helping desperately ill people to die. In: Emanuel LL, editor. Regulating how we die: the ethical, medical, and legal issues surrounding physician-assisted suicide. Cambridge (MA): Harvard University Press; 1998. p. 3–20, 15.

9. Dutch Ministry of Justice. Euthanasia and assisted suicide control act takes effect on 1 April 2002. Available at: http://www.justitie.nl/english/press/press_releases/archive/archive_2002/ euthanasia_and_assisted_suicide_control_act_takes_effect_on_1_april_2002.asp. Accessed September 20, 2004.

10. Euthanasia and assisted suicide control act: summary of the bill. Available at: http://www. justitie.nl/english/themes/euthanasia/summary_of_the_bill.asp. Accessed September 20, 2004.

11. Van der Maas PJ, Van Delden JJ, Pijnenborg L. Euthanasia and other medical decisions concerning the end of life: an investigation performed upon request of the Commission of Inquiry into the Medical Practice Concerning Euthanasia. Health Policy 1992;21(1–2): 1–262.

12. Van der Wal G, Van Eijk JTM, Leenen HJJ, Spreeuwenberg C. Euthanasia and assisted suicide. I. How often is it practiced by family doctors in the Netherlands? Fam Pract 1992;9(2):130–4.

13. Van der Maas PJ, Van der Wal G, Haverkate I, et al. Euthanasia, physician-assisted suicide, and other medical practices involving the end of life in the Netherlands, 1990–1995. N Engl J Med 1996;335(22):1699–705.

14. Van der Wal G, Van der Maas PJ, Bosma JM, et al. Evaluation of the notification procedure for physician-assisted death in the Netherlands. N Engl J Med 1996; 335(22):1706–11.

15. Groenewoud JH, Van der Heide A, Onwuteaka-Philipsen BD, et al. Clinical problems with the performance of euthanasia and physician-assisted suicide in the Netherlands. N Engl J Med 2000;342(8):551–6.

16. Veldink JH, Wokke JHJ, Van der Wal G, et al. Euthanasia and physician-assisted suicide among patients with amyotrophic lateral sclerosis in the Netherlands. N Engl J Med 2002;346(21): 1638–44.

17. Marquet RL, Bartelds A, Visser GJ, et al. Twenty-five years of requests for euthanasia and physician assisted suicide in Dutch general practice: trend analysis. BMJ 2003;327(7408):201–2.

18. Groenewoud JH, Van der Heide A, Tholen AJ, et al. Psychiatric consultation with regard to requests for euthanasia or physician-assisted suicide. Gen Hosp Psychiatry 2004;26(4):323–30.

19. Oregon Death with Dignity Act, Or Rev Stat §§ 127.800–127.897 (2001).

20. 21 USC §§ 801–904 (2000).

21. Oregon v Ashcroft, 192 F Supp 2d 1077, 1092 (D Or 2002), review granted by 368 F3d 1118, 1125 (9th Cir 2004).

22. Oregon Department of Human Resources. Oregon's Death with Dignity Act: the first year's experience. 1999. Available at: http://www.dhs.state.or.us/publichealth/chs/pas/year1/ar-index. cfm. Accessed September 22, 2004.

23. Oregon Department of Human Services. Oregon's Death with Dignity Act: the second year's experience. 2000. Available at: http://www.dhs.state.or.us/publichealth/chs/pas/year2/ar-index. cfm. Accessed September 22, 2004.

24. Oregon Department of Human Services. Oregon's Death with Dignity Act: three years of legalized physician-assisted suicide. 2001. Available at: http://www.dhs.state .or.us/publichealth/ chs/pas/year3/ar-index.cfm. Accessed September 22, 2004.

25. Oregon Department of Human Services. Fourth annual report on Oregon's Death with Dignity Act. 2002. Available at http://www.dhs.state.or.us/publichealth/chs/pas/year4/ar-index.cfm. Accessed September 22, 2004.

26. Oregon Department of Human Services. Fifth annual report on Oregon's Death with Dignity Act. 2003. Available at: http://www.dhs.state.or.us/publichealth/chs/pas/year5/ar-index.cfm. Accessed September 22, 2004.

27. Oregon Department of Human Services. Sixth annual report on Oregon's Death with Dignity Act. 2004. Available at: http://www.dhs.state.or.us/publichealth/chs/pas/ar-index.cfm. Accessed September 22, 2004.

28. Chin AE, Hedberg K, Higginson GK, Fleming DW. Legalized physician-assisted suicide in Oregon—the first year's experience. N Engl J Med 1999;340(7):577–83.

29. Sullivan AD, Hedberg K, Fleming DW. Legalized physician-assisted suicide in Oregon—the second year. N Engl J Med 2000;342(8):598–604.

30. Ganzini L, Nelson HD, Schmidt TA, et al. Physicians' experiences with the Oregon Death with Dignity Act. N Engl J Med 2000;342(8):557–63.

31. Ganzini L, Harvath TA, Jackson A, et al. Experiences of Oregon nurses and social workers with hospice patients who requested assistance with suicide. N Engl J Med 2002;347(8):582–8.

32. Vacco v Quill, 521 US 793 (1997).

33. Washington v Glucksberg, 521 US 702 (1997).

34. Blendon RJ, Szalay US, Knox RA. Should physicians aid their patients in dying? The public perspective. JAMA 1992;267(19):2658–62.

35. Jacobson JA, Kasworm EM, Battin MP, et al. Decedents' reported preferences for physician-assisted death: a survey of informants listed on death certificates in Utah. J Clin Ethics 1995; 6(2):149–57.

36. Black AL, Wallace JI, Starks HE, Pearlman RA. Physician-assisted suicide and euthanasia in Washington state: patient requests and physician response. JAMA 1996;275(12):919–25.

37. Breitbart W, Rosenfeld BD, Passik SD. Interest in physician-assisted suicide among ambulatory HIV-infected patients. Am J Psych 1996;153(2):238–42.

38. Emanuel EJ, Fairclough DL. Euthanasia and physician-assisted suicide: attitudes and experiences of oncology patients, oncologists, and the public. Lancet 1996; 347(9018):1805–10.

39. Ganzini L, Fenn DS, Lee MA, et al. Attitudes of Oregon psychiatrists toward physician-assisted suicide. Am J Psych 1996;153(11):1469–75.

40. Schmidt TA, Zechnich AD, Tilden VP, et al. Oregon emergency physicians' experiences with, attitudes toward, and concerns about physician-assisted suicide. Acad Emerg Med 1996;3(10): 938–45.

41. Emanuel EJ, Fairclough DL, Emanuel LL. Attitudes and desires related to euthanasia and physician-assisted suicide among terminally ill patients and their caregivers. JAMA 2000; 284(19):2460–8.

42. Ganzini L, Nelson HD, Lee MA, et al. Oregon physicians' attitudes and experiences with end-of-life care since passage of the Oregon Death with Dignity Act. JAMA 2001;285(18):2363–9.

43. Miller PJ, Mesler MA, Eggman ST. Take some time to look inside their hearts: hospice social workers contemplate physician-assisted suicide. Soc Work Health Care 2002;35(3):53 –64.

44. Emanuel EJ. Euthanasia and physician-assisted suicide: a review of the empirical data from the United States. Arch Intern Med 2002;162:142–52.

45. Sprung CL, Cohen SL, Sjokvist P, et al. End-of-life practices in European intensive care units. JAMA 2003;290(6):790–7.

46. Wolf SM. Pragmatism in the face of death: the role of facts in the assisted suicide debate. Minn Law Rev 1998;82(4):1063–101, 1086 n.93.

47. Johnson SH. From medicalization to legalization to politicization: O'Connor, Cruzan, and refusal of treatment in the 1990s. Conn Law Rev 1989;21(3):685–722.

48. Dubler NN. Commentary: balancing life and death—proceed with caution. Am J Public Health 1993;83(1):23–5.

49. Meisel A, Cerminara KL. The right to die: the law of end-of-life decisionmaking. 3rd edition. New York: Aspen; 2004.

50. Cruzan v Director, Missouri Dept of Health, 497 US 261 (1990).

51. American Medical Association. Policy E-2.211: Physician-assisted suicide. Available at: http://www.ama-assn.org/apps/pf_new/pf_online?f_n=browse &doc=policyfiles/HnE/E-2.211.HTM. Accessed September 21, 2004.

52. American Nurses Association. Position statements: assisted suicide. Available at: http:// nursingworld.org/readroom/position/ethics/etsuic.htm. Accessed October 4, 2004.

53. Marzen TJ, O'Dowd MK, Crone D, Balch TJ. Suicide: a constitutional right? Duquesne Law Rev 1985; 24(1):1–242.

54. Beauchamp TL, Childress JF. Principles of biomedical ethics. 5th edition. New York: Oxford University Press; 2001. p. 145.

55. Cantor NL. Legal frontiers of death and dying. Bloomington (IN)7 Indiana University Press; 1987. p. 32.

56. Van der Maas PJ, Van Delden JJM. Euthanasia and other medical decisions concerning the end of life. Lancet 1991;338(8768):669–74.

57. Pijnenborg L, Van der Maas PJ. Life-terminating acts without explicit request of patient. Lancet 1993;341 (8854):1196–9.

58. Muller MT, Van der Wal G, Van Eijk JT, Ribbe MW. Voluntary active euthanasia and physician-assisted suicide in Dutch nursing homes: Are the requirements for prudent practice properly met? J Am Geriatr Soc 1994;42(6):624–9.

59. Van der Wal G, Muller MT, Christ LM, et al. Voluntary active euthanasia and physician-assisted suicide in Dutch nursing homes: requests and administrations. J Am Geriatr Soc 1994;42(6):620–3.

60. Angell M. Euthanasia in the Netherlands—good news or bad? N Engl J Med 1996;335(22): 1676–8.

61. Sykes N, Thorns A. The use of opioids and sedatives at the end of life. Lancet Oncol 2003; 4(5):312–8.

62. Muller-Busch HC, Andres I, Jehser T. Sedation in palliative care—a critical analysis of 7 years experience. BMC Palliat Care 2003;2(1):2–9.

63. Rietjens JAC, Van der Heide A, Vrakking AM, et al. Physician reports of terminal sedation without hydration or nutrition for patients nearing death in the Netherlands. Ann Intern Med 2004;141(3):178–85.

64. Mount B. Morphine drips, terminal sedation, and slow euthanasia: definitions and facts, not anecdotes. J Palliat Care 1996;12(9):31–7.

65. Quill TE, Lo B, Brock DW. Palliative options of last resort: a comparison of voluntarily stopping eating and drinking, terminal sedation, physician-assisted suicide, and voluntary active euthanasia. JAMA 1997;278(23):2099–104.

66. Orentlicher D. Matters of life and death: making moral theory work in medical ethics and the law. Princeton (NJ)7 Princeton University Press; 2001. p. 49–51.

67. Rachels J. The end of life: euthanasia and morality. New York: Oxford University Press; 1986. p. 185.

68. Miller FG, Brody H. Professional integrity and physician-assisted death. Hastings Cent Rep 1995;25(3):8–17.

69. Beauchamp TL, Childress JF. Principles of biomedical ethics. 5th edition. New York: Oxford University Press; 2001. p. 146–52.

70. Rachels J. Active and passive euthanasia. N Engl J Med 1975;292(2):78–80.

71. Cohen-Almagor R. Non-voluntary and involuntary euthanasia in the Netherlands: Dutch perspectives. Issues Law Med 2003;18(3):239–57.

72. Wolf SM. Facing assisted suicide and euthanasia in children and adolescents. In: Emanuel LL, editor. Regulating how we die: the ethical, medical, and legal issues surrounding physician-assisted suicide. Cambridge (MA): Harvard University Press; 1998. p. 92–119, 274–94.

73. Fenigsen R. Dutch euthanasia: the new government ordered study. Issues Law Med 2004; 20(1):73–9.

74. Sheldon T. Dutch reporting of euthanasia cases falls—despite legal reporting requirements. BMJ 2004; 328(7448):1336.

75. Emanuel LL. A question of balance. In: Emanuel LL, editor. Regulating how we die: the ethical, medical, and legal issues surrounding physician-assisted suicide. Cambridge (MA): Harvard University Press; 1998. p. 234–60, 246–7.

76. Bok S. Physician-assisted suicide. In: Dworkin G, Frey RG, Bok S, editors. Euthanasia and physician-assisted suicide: for and against. Cambridge, England: Cambridge University Press; 1998. p. 128–39, 135.

77. Green K. Physician-assisted suicide and euthanasia: safeguarding against the "slippery slope"— the Netherlands versus the United States. Indiana Int Comp Law Rev 2003;13:639–81, 673–6.

78. Wolf SM. Gender, feminism, and death: physician-assisted and euthanasia. In: Wolf SM, editor. Feminism and bioethics: beyond reproduction. New York: Oxford University Press; 1996. p. 282–317.

79. Foley K, Hendin H. The Oregon report: don't ask, don't tell. Hastings Cent Rep 1999;29(3): 37–42.

80. Kass LR. Neither for love nor money: why doctors must not kill. Public Interest 1989;94: 25–46.

81. Gaylin W, Kass LR, Pellegrino ED, Siegler M. Doctors must not kill. JAMA 1988;259(14): 2139–40.

82. Kass LR. Why doctors must not kill. Commonwealth 1991;118(14 Suppl):472–6.

83. Baumrin B. Physician, stay thy hand! In: Battin MP, Rhodes R, Silvers A, editors. Physician-assisted suicide: expanding the debate. New York: Routledge; 1998. p. 177–81.

84. Burt RA. Death is that man taking names: intersections of American medicine, law, and culture. Berkeley (CA)7 University of California Press; 2002. p. 162–3.

85. Gert B, Culver CM, Clouser KD. An alternative to physician-assisted suicide: a conceptual moral analysis. In: Battin MP, Rhodes R, Silvers A, editors. Physician-assisted suicide: expanding the debate. New York: Routledge; 1998. p. 182–202.

86. Pellegrino ED. The false promise of beneficient killing. In: Emanuel LL, editor. Regulating how we die: the ethical, medical, and legal issues surrounding physician-

assisted suicide. Cambridge (MA): Harvard University Press; 1998. p. 71–91.

87. DeNavas-Walt C, Proctor BD, Mills RJ. Income, poverty, and health insurance coverage in the United States: 2003. US Census Bureau 2004;14. Available at: http://www.census.gov/prod/ 2004pubs/p60-226.pdf. Accessed September 29, 2004.

88. How many people lack health insurance and for how long? Congress of the United States. Congressional Budget Office. 2003;vii. Available at: http://www.cbo.gov/ftpdocs/42xx/doc4210/ 05-12-Uninsured.pdf. Accessed September 29, 2004.

89. Siegel MC. Lethal pity: the Oregon Death with Dignity Act, its implications for the disabled, and the struggle for equality in an able-bodied world. Law Inequal 1998;16(1): 259–88.

90. Emanuel EJ, Emanuel LL. The promise of a good death. Lancet 1998;351(9114):SII21–9.

91. Foley KM. Competent care for the dying instead of physician-assisted suicide. N Engl J Med 1997;336(1):53–8.

DISCUSSION QUESTIONS

1. How, exactly, are patients' rights of autonomy and liberty supposed to support a moral right to physician-assisted suicide? Do you find that argument convincing? Why or why not?

2. Wolf sketches three arguments for a moral right to physician-assisted death. Which of these arguments support only physician-assisted suicide? Which also support euthanasia?

3. How is the physician's special obligation to "do no harm" related to the arguments that Wolf sketches against physician-assisted suicide?

4. Based on the data and arguments presented in Wolf's paper, do you think that allowing physician-assisted suicide and/or euthanasia would lead to "error, abuse, and negative consequences for patients"? If so, is that a compelling reason to prohibit either or both of those practices?

JAMES RACHELS (1941–2005)

Active and Passive Euthanasia

James Rachels was Professor of Philosophy at the University of Alabama at Birmingham. He wrote on a wide range of topics in applied ethics but is perhaps best known for his widely used textbooks on moral philosophy. In this paper, Rachels argues that there is no moral difference between killing someone and letting someone die. Therefore, he argues, there is no good reason to believe that active euthanasia is morally forbidden while passive euthanasia is morally permissible.

GUIDING QUESTIONS

1. What moral claim is Rachels criticizing in this paper?
2. What point is Rachels trying to make with the examples of the patient with throat cancer and the baby with Down's syndrome?
3. What is the thought experiment involving Smith and Jones intended to show? How is this related to the main argument about active and passive euthanasia?
4. How does Rachels respond to the objection that in passive euthanasia, "the doctor does not do anything to bring about the patient's death," but in active euthanasia, he or she does?

The distinction between active and passive euthanasia is thought to be crucial for medical ethics. The idea is that it is permissible, at least in some cases, to withhold treatment and allow a patient to die, but it is never permissible to take any direct action designed to kill the patient. This doctrine seems to be accepted by most doctors, and it is endorsed in a statement adopted by the House of Delegates of the American Medical Association on December 4, 1973:

> The intentional termination of the life of one human being by another—mercy killing—is contrary to that for which the medical profession stands and is contrary to the policy of the American Medical Association.
>
> The cessation of the employment of extraordinary means to prolong the life of the body when there is irrefutable evidence that biological death is imminent is the decision of the patient and/or his immediate family. The advice and judgment of the physician should be freely available to the patient and/or his immediate family.

However, a strong case can be made against this doctrine. In what follows I will set out some of the relevant arguments, and urge doctors to reconsider their views on this matter.

To begin with a familiar type of situation, a patient who is dying of incurable cancer of the throat is in terrible pain, which can no longer be satisfactorily alleviated. He is certain to die within a few days, even if present treatment is continued, but he does not want to go on living for those days since the pain is unbearable. So he asks the doctor for an end to it, and his family joins in the request.

Suppose the doctor agrees to withhold treatment, as the conventional doctrine says he may. The justification for his doing so is that the patient is in terrible agony, and since he is going to die anyway, it would be wrong to prolong his suffering needlessly.

But now notice this. If one simply withholds treatment, it may take the patient longer to die, and so he may suffer more than he would if more direct action were taken and a lethal injection given. This fact provides strong reason for thinking that, once the initial decision not to prolong his agony has been made active euthanasia is actually preferable to passive euthanasia, rather than the reverse. To say otherwise is to endorse the option that leads to more suffering rather than less, and is contrary to the humanitarian impulse that prompts the decision not to prolong his life in the first place.

Part of my point is that the process of being "allowed to die" can be relatively slow and painful, whereas being given a lethal injection is relatively quick and painless. Let me give a different sort of example. In the United States about one in 600 babies is born with Down's syndrome. Most of these babies are otherwise healthy—that is, with only the usual pediatric care, they will· proceed to an otherwise normal infancy. Some, however, are born with congenital defects such as intestinal obstructions that require operations if they are to live. Sometimes, the parents and the doctor will decide not to operate, and let the infant die. Anthony Shaw describes what happens then:

> When surgery is denied [the doctor] must try to keep the infant from suffering while natural forces sap the baby's life away. As a surgeon whose natural inclination is to use the scalpel to fight off death, standing by and watching a salvageable baby die is the most emotionally exhausting experience I know. It is easy at a conference, in a theoretical discussion, to decide that such infants should be allowed to die. It is altogether different to stand by in the nursery and watch as dehydration and infection wither a tiny being over hours and days. This is a terrible ordeal for me and the hospital staff—much more so than for the parents who never set foot in the nursery.[1]

I can understand why some people are opposed to all euthanasia, and insist that such infants must be allowed to live. I think I can also understand why other people favor destroying these babies quickly and painlessly. But why should anyone favor letting "dehydration and infection wither a tiny being over hours and days"? The doctrine that says that a baby may be allowed to dehydrate and wither, but may not be given an injection that would end its life without suffering, seems so patently cruel as to require no further refutation. The strong language is not intended to offend, but only to put the point in the clearest possible way.

My second argument is that the conventional doctrine leads to decisions concerning life and death made on irrelevant grounds.

Consider again the case of the infants with Down's syndrome who need operations for congenital defects unrelated to the syndrome to live. Sometimes, there is no operation, and the baby dies, but when there is no such defect, the baby lives on. Now, an operation such as that to remove an intestinal obstruction is not prohibitively difficult. The reason why such operations are not performed in these cases is, clearly, that the child has Down's syndrome and the parents and doctor judge that because of that fact it is better for the child to die.

But notice that this situation is absurd, no matter what view one takes of the lives and potentials of such babies. If the life of such an infant is worth preserving, what does it matter if it needs a simple operation? Or, if one thinks it better that such a baby

should not live on, what difference does it make that it happens to have an unobstructed intestinal tract? In either case, the matter of life and death is being decided on irrelevant grounds. It is the Down's syndrome, and not the intestines, that is the issue. The matter should be decided, if at all, on that basis, and not be allowed to depend on the essentially irrelevant question of whether the intestinal tract is blocked.

What makes this situation possible, of course, is the idea that when there is an intestinal blockage, one can "let the baby die," but when there is no such defect there is nothing that can be done, for one must not "kill" it. The fact that this idea leads to such results as deciding life or death on irrelevant grounds is another good reason why the doctrine should be rejected.

One reason why so many people think that there is an important moral difference between active and passive euthanasia is that they think killing someone is morally worse than letting someone die. But is it? Is killing, in itself, worse than letting die? To investigate this issue, two cases may be considered that are exactly alike except that one involves killing whereas the other involves letting someone die. Then, it can be asked whether this difference makes any difference to the moral assessments. It is important that the cases be exactly alike, except for this one difference, since otherwise one cannot be confident that it is this difference and not some other that accounts for any variation in the assessments of the two cases. So, let us consider this pair of cases:

In the first, Smith stands to gain a large inheritance if anything should happen to his six-year-old cousin. One evening while the child is taking his bath, Smith sneaks into the bathroom and drowns the child, and then arranges things so that it will look like an accident.

In the second, Jones also stands to gain if anything should happen to his six-year-old cousin. Like Smith, Jones sneaks in planning to drown the child in his bath. However, just as he enters the bathroom Jones sees the child slip and hit his head, and fall face down in the water. Jones is delighted; he stands by, ready to push the child's head back under if it is necessary, but it is not necessary. With only a little thrashing about, the child drowns all by himself, "accidentally," as Jones watches and does nothing.

Now Smith killed the child, whereas Jones "merely" let the child die. That is the only difference between them. Did either man behave better, from a moral point of view? If the difference between killing and letting die were in itself a morally important matter, one should say that Jones's behavior was less reprehensible than Smith's. But does one really want to say that? I think not. In the first place, both men acted from the same motive, personal gain, and both had exactly the same end in view when they acted. It may be inferred from Smith's conduct that he is a bad man, although that judgment may be withdrawn or modified if certain further facts are learned about him—for example, that he is mentally deranged. But would not the very same thing be inferred about Jones from his conduct? And would not the same further considerations also be relevant to any· modification of this judgment? Moreover, suppose Jones pleaded, in his own defense, "After all, I didn't do anything except just stand there and watch the child drown. I didn't kill him; I only let him die." Again, if letting die were in itself less bad than killing, this defense should have at least some weight. But it does not. Such a "defense" can only be regarded as a grotesque perversion of moral reasoning. Morally speaking, it is no defense at all.

Now, it may be pointed out, quite properly, that the cases of euthanasia with which doctors are concerned are not like this at all. They do not involve personal gain or the destruction of normal healthy children. Doctors are concerned only with cases in which the patient's life is of no further use to him, or in which the patient's life has become or will soon become a terrible burden. However, the point is the same in these cases: the bare difference between killing and letting die does not, in itself, make a moral difference. If a doctor lets a patient die, for humane reasons, he is in the same moral position as if he had given the patient a lethal injection for humane reasons. If his decision was wrong—if, for example, the patient's illness was in fact curable—the decision would be equally regrettable no matter which method was used to carry it out. And if the doctor's decision was the right one, the method used is not in itself important.

The AMA policy statement isolates the crucial issue very well; the crucial issue is "the intentional termination of the life of one human being by another." But after identifying this issue, and forbidding

"mercy killing," the statement goes on to deny that the cessation of treatment is the intentional termination of a life. This is where the mistake comes in, for what is the cessation of treatment, in these circumstances, if it is not "the intentional termination of the life of one human being by another?" Of course it is exactly that, and if it were not, there would be no point to it.

Many people will find this judgment hard to accept. One reason, I think, is that it is very easy to conflate the question of whether killing is, in itself, worse than letting die, with the very different question of whether most actual cases of killing are more reprehensible than most actual cases of letting die. Most actual cases of killing are clearly terrible (think, for example, of all the murders reported in the newspapers), and one hears of such cases every day. On the other hand, one hardly ever hears of a case of letting die, except for the actions of doctors who are motivated by humanitarian reasons. So one learns to think of killing in a much worse light than of letting die. But this does not mean that there is something about killing that makes it in itself worse than letting die, for it is not the bare difference between killing and letting die that makes the difference in these cases. Rather, the other factors—the murderer's motive of personal gain, for example, contrasted with the doctor's humanitarian motivation—account for different reactions to the different cases.

I have argued that killing is not in itself any worse than letting die; if my contention is right, it follows that active euthanasia is not any worse than passive euthanasia. What arguments can be given on the other side? The most common, I believe, is the following: "The important difference between active and passive euthanasia is that, in passive euthanasia, the doctor does not do anything to bring about the patient's death. The doctor does nothing, and the patient dies of whatever ills already afflict him. In active euthanasia, however, the doctor does something to bring about the patient's death: he kills him. The doctor who gives the patient with cancer a lethal injection has himself caused his patient's death; whereas if he merely ceases treatment, the cancer is the cause of the death."

A number of points need to be made here. The first is that it is not exactly correct to say that in passive euthanasia the doctor does nothing, for he does do one thing that is very important: he lets the patient die. "Letting someone die" is certainly different, in some respects, from other types of action—mainly in that it is a kind of action that one may perform by way of not performing certain other actions. For example, one may let a patient die by way of not giving medication, just as one may insult someone by way of not shaking his hand. But for any purpose of moral assessment, it is a type of action nonetheless. The decision to let a patient die is subject to moral appraisal in the same way that a decision to kill him would be subject to moral appraisal: it may be assessed as wise or unwise, compassionate or sadistic, right or wrong. If a doctor deliberately let a patient die who was suffering from a routinely curable illness, the doctor would certainly be to blame for what he had done, just as he would be to blame if he had needlessly killed the patient. Charges against him would then be appropriate. If so, it would be no defense at all for him to insist that he didn't "do anything." He would have done something very serious indeed, for he let his patient die.

Fixing the cause of death may be very important from a legal point of view, for it may determine whether criminal charges are brought against the doctor. But I do not think that this notion can be used to show a moral difference between active and passive euthanasia. The reason why it is considered bad to be the cause of someone's death is that death is regarded as a great evil—and so it is. However, if it has been decided that euthanasia—even passive euthanasia—is desirable in a given case, it has also been decided that in this instance death is no greater an evil than the patient's continued existence. And if this is true, the usual reason for not wanting to be the cause of someone's death simply does not apply.

Finally, doctors may think that all of this is only of academic interest—the sort of thing that philosophers may worry about but that has no practical bearing on their own work. After all, doctors must be concerned about the legal consequences of what they do, and active euthanasia is clearly forbidden by the law. But even so, doctors should also be concerned with the fact that the law is forcing upon them a moral doctrine that may well be indefensible, and has a considerable effect on their practices. Of course, most doctors are not now in the position of being coerced in this matter, for they do not regard themselves as merely going along with what the law requires. Rather, in statements such as the AMA policy statement that I have quoted, they are endorsing this doctrine as a central point of medical ethics. In that statement, active euthanasia is condemned not merely as illegal but as "contrary to that for which the medical profession stands," whereas passive euthanasia is approved. However, the preceding considerations suggest that there is really no moral difference between the two, considered in themselves (there may be important moral differences in some cases in their *consequences,* but, as I pointed out, these differences may make active euthanasia, and not passive euthanasia, the morally preferable option). So, whereas doctors may have to discriminate between active and passive euthanasia to satisfy the law, they should not do any more than that. In particular, they should not give the distinction any added authority and weight by writing it into official statements of medical ethics.

NOTES

1. Shaw A: 'Doctor, Do We Have a Choice?' *The New York Times Magazine,* January 30, 1972, p54.

DISCUSSION QUESTIONS

1. Do you find the thought experiment involving Smith and Jones convincing? Why or why not?
2. Why, according to Rachels, do people think that killing is worse than letting die? Do you find his explanation convincing? Why or why not?
3. Suppose that we accept Rachels's claim that killing someone is no morally worse than letting someone die. What would this imply for moral issues other than physician-assisted death? Do these implications make Rachels's claim more or less plausible?
4. Has Rachels successfully argued that active euthanasia is morally permissible? Why or why not? Was he trying to argue that it is morally permissible?

J. GAY-WILLIAMS

The Wrongfulness of Euthanasia

In this short paper, J. Gay-Williams argues that active euthanasia is morally wrong. After specifying what counts as active euthanasia, the paper presents three independent arguments for its main conclusion.

GUIDING QUESTIONS

1. What is Gay-Williams's main conclusion in this paper? How is that conclusion related to James Rachels's conclusion about active and passive euthanasia?
2. What, exactly, does Gay-Williams mean by "euthanasia"?
3. What are the three main arguments that Gay-Williams presents against euthanasia? Do you need to find all of them convincing to accept the paper's main conclusion?

My impression is that euthanasia—the idea, if not the practice—is slowly gaining acceptance within our society. Cynics might attribute this to an increasing tendency to devalue human life, but I do not believe this is the major factor. The acceptance is much more likely to be the result of unthinking sympathy and benevolence. Well-publicized, tragic stories like that of Karen Quinlan elicit from us deep feelings of compassion. We think to ourselves, "She and her family would be better off if she were dead." It is an easy step from this very human response to the view that if someone (and others) would be better off dead, then it must be all right to kill that person. Although I respect the compassion that leads to this conclusion, I believe the conclusion is wrong. I want to show that euthanasia is wrong. It is inherently wrong, but it is also wrong judged from the standpoints of self-interest and of practical effects.

Before presenting my arguments to support this claim, it would be well to define "euthanasia." An essential aspect of euthanasia is that it involves taking a human life, either one's own or that of another. Also, the person whose life is taken must be someone who is believed to be suffering from some disease or injury from which recovery cannot reasonably be expected. Finally, the action must be deliberate and intentional. Thus, euthanasia is intentionally taking the life of a presumably hopeless person. Whether the life is one's own or that of another, the taking of it is still euthanasia.

It is important to be clear about the deliberate and intentional aspect of the killing. If a hopeless person is given an injection of the wrong drug by mistake and this causes his death, this is wrongful killing but not euthanasia. The killing cannot be the result of accident. Furthermore, if the person is given an injection of a drug that is believed to be necessary to treat his disease or better his condition and the person dies as a result, then this is neither wrongful killing nor euthanasia. The intention was to make the patient well, not kill him. Similarly, when a patient's condition is such that it is not reasonable to hope that any medical procedures or treatments will save his life, a failure to implement the procedures or treatments is not euthanasia. If the person dies, this will be as a result of his injuries or disease and not because of his failure to receive treatment.

The failure to continue treatment after it has been realized that the patient has little chance of benefitting from it has been characterized by some as "passive euthanasia." This phrase is misleading and mistaken. In such cases, the person involved is not killed (the first essential aspect of euthanasia), nor is the death of the person intended by the withholding of additional treatment (the third essential aspect of euthanasia). The aim may be to spare the person additional and unjustifiable pain, to save him from the indignities of hopeless manipulations, and to avoid increasing the financial and emotional burden on his family. When I buy a pencil it is so that I can use it to write, not to contribute to an increase in the gross national product. This may be the unintended consequence of my action, but it is not the aim of my action. So it is with failing to continue the treatment of a dying person. I intend his death no more than I intend to reduce the GNP by not using medical supplies. His is an unintended dying, and so-called "passive euthanasia" is not euthanasia at all.

1. THE ARGUMENT FROM NATURE

Every human being has a natural inclination to continue living. Our reflexes and responses fit us to fight attackers, flee wild animals, and dodge out of the way of trucks. In our daily lives we exercise the caution and care necessary to protect ourselves. Our bodies are similarly structured for survival right down to the molecular level. When we are cut, our capillaries seal shut, our blood clots, and fibrogen is produced to start the process of healing the wound. When we are invaded by bacteria, antibodies are produced to fight against the alien organisms, and their remains are swept out of the body by special cells designed for clean-up work.

Euthanasia does violence to this natural goal of survival. It is literally acting against nature because all the processes of nature are bent towards the end of bodily survival. Euthanasia defeats these subtle mechanisms in a way that, in a particular case, disease and injury might not.

It is possible, but not necessary, to make an appeal to revealed religion in this connection. Man as trustee of his body acts against God, its rightful possessor, when he takes his own life. He also violates the commandment to hold life sacred and never to take it without just and compelling cause. But since this appeal will persuade only those who are prepared to accept that religion has access to revealed truths, I shall not employ this line of argument.

It is enough, I believe, to recognize that the organization of the human body and our patterns of behavioral responses make the continuation of life a natural goal. By reason alone, then, we can recognize that euthanasia sets us against our own nature. Furthermore, in doing so, euthanasia does violence to our dignity. Our dignity comes from seeking our ends. When one of our goals is survival, and actions are taken that eliminate that goal, then our natural dignity suffers. Unlike animals, we are conscious through reason of our nature and our ends. Euthanasia involves acting as if this dual nature—inclination towards survival and awareness of this as an end—did not exist. Thus, euthanasia denies our basic human character and requires that we regard ourselves or others as something less than fully human.

2. THE ARGUMENT FROM SELF-INTEREST

The above arguments are, I believe, sufficient to show that euthanasia is inherently wrong. But there are reasons for considering it wrong when judged by standards other than reason. Because death is final and irreversible, euthanasia contains within it the possibility that we will work against our own interest if we practice it or allow it to be practiced on us.

Contemporary medicine has high standards of excellence and a proven record of accomplishment, but it does not possess perfect and complete knowledge. A mistaken diagnosis is possible, and so is a mistaken prognosis. Consequently, we may believe that we are dying of a disease when, as a matter of fact, we may not be. We may think that we have no hope of recovery when, as a matter of fact, our chances are quite good. In such circumstances, if euthanasia were permitted, we would die needlessly. Death is final and the chance of error too great to approve the practice of euthanasia.

Also, there is always the possibility that an experimental procedure or a hitherto untried technique will pull us through. We should at least keep this option open, but euthanasia closes it off. Furthermore, spontaneous remission does occur in many cases. For no apparent reason, a patient simply recovers when those all around him, including his physicians, expected him to die. Euthanasia would just guarantee their expectations and leave no room for the "miraculous" recoveries that frequently occur.

Finally, knowing that we can take our life at any time (or ask another to take it) might well incline us to give up too easily. The will to live is strong in all of us, but it can be weakened by pain and suffering and feelings of hopelessness. If during a bad time we allow ourselves to be killed, we never have a chance to reconsider. Recovery from a serious illness requires that we fight for it, and anything that weakens our determination by suggesting that there is an easy way out is ultimately against our own interest. Also, we may be inclined towards euthanasia because of our concern for others. If we see our sickness and suffering as an emotional and financial burden on our family, we may feel that to leave our life is to make their lives easier. The very presence of the possibility of euthanasia may keep us from surviving when we might.

3. THE ARGUMENT FROM PRACTICAL EFFECTS

Doctors and nurses are, for the most part, totally committed to saving lives. A life lost is, for them, almost a personal failure, an insult to their skills and knowledge. Euthanasia as a practice might well alter this. It could have a corrupting influence so that in any case that is severe doctors and nurses might not try hard enough to save the patient. They might decide that the patient would simply be "better off dead" and take the steps necessary to make that come about.

This attitude could then carry over to their dealings with patients less seriously ill. The result would be an overall decline in the quality of medical care.

Finally, euthanasia as a policy is a slippery slope. A person apparently hopelessly ill may be allowed to take his own life. Then he may be permitted to deputize others to do it for him should he no longer be able to act. The judgment of others then becomes the ruling factor. Already at this point euthanasia is not personal and voluntary, for others are acting "on behalf of" the patient as they see fit. This may well incline them to act on behalf of other patients who have not authorized them to exercise their judgment. It is only a short step, then, from voluntary euthanasia (self-inflicted or authorized), to directed euthanasia administered to a patient who has given no authorization, to involuntary euthanasia conducted as part of a social policy. Recently many psychiatrists and sociologists have argued that we define as "mental illness" those forms of behavior that we disapprove of. This gives us license then to lock up those who display the behavior. The category of the "hopelessly ill" provides the possibility of even worse abuse. Embedded in a social policy, it would give society or its representatives the authority to eliminate all those who might be considered too "ill" to function normally any longer. The dangers of euthanasia are too great to all to run the risk of approving it in any form. The first slippery step may well lead to a serious and harmful fall.

I hope that I have succeeded in showing why the benevolence that inclines us to give approval of euthanasia is misplaced. Euthanasia is inherently wrong because it violates the nature and dignity of human beings. But even those who are not convinced by this must be persuaded that the potential personal and social dangers inherent in euthanasia are sufficient to forbid our approving it either as a personal practice or as a public policy.

Suffering is surely a terrible thing, and we have a clear duty to comfort those in need and to ease their suffering when we can. But suffering is also a natural part of life with values for the individual and for others that we should not overlook. We may legitimately seek for others and for ourselves an easeful death. Euthanasia, however, is not just an easeful death. It is a wrongful death. Euthanasia is not just dying. It is killing.

DISCUSSION QUESTIONS

1. Why, according to Gay-Williams, isn't "passive euthanasia" really a form of euthanasia? Do you find this argument convincing? Why or why not?
2. Do you agree with Gay-Williams that euthanasia "sets us against our own nature"? Why or why not?
3. How might someone object to Gay-Williams's argument from self-interest? How do you think Gay-Williams would respond to that objection?
4. What would Susan Wolf (the author of an earlier paper in this section) say about Gay-Williams's argument from practical effects?
5. Of Gay-Williams's three main arguments against euthanasia, which do you find most convincing? Why? Which do you find least convincing? Why?

Capital Punishment

ERNEST VAN DEN HAAG (1914–2002)

The Ultimate Punishment: A Defense

Ernest van den Haag was John M. Olin Professor of Jurisprudence and Public Policy at Fordham University. In this paper, he argues in support of capital punishment (often called the death penalty), both by explaining his reasons for supporting it and by trying to refute arguments commonly given against it.

GUIDING QUESTIONS

1. What does van den Haag mean by "maldistribution" of the death penalty? What arguments does he give for thinking that maldistribution is not a good reason to oppose the death penalty?
2. Does van den Haag think that the death penalty deters crime? Is this important for him? Why or why not?
3. What is van den Haag's main reason for supporting the death penalty?
4. Van den Haag considers "two moral objections" to the death penalty. What are they? How does he respond to them?

In an average year about 20,000 homicides occur in the United States. Fewer than 300 convicted murderers are sentenced to death. But because no more than thirty murderers have been executed in any recent year, most convicts sentenced to death are likely to die of old age. Nonetheless, the death penalty looms large in discussions: it raises important moral questions independent of the number of executions.

The death penalty is our harshest punishment.[1] It is irrevocable: it ends the existence of those punished, instead of temporarily imprisoning them. Further, although not intended to cause physical pain, execution is the only corporal punishment still applied to adults.[2] These singular characteristics contribute to the perennial, impassioned controversy about capital punishment.

I. DISTRIBUTION

Consideration of the justice, morality, or usefulness, of capital punishment is often conflated with objections to its alleged discriminatory or capricious distribution among the guilty. Wrongly so. If capital punishment is immoral *in se,* no distribution among the guilty could make it moral. If capital punishment is moral, no distribution would make it immoral. Improper distribution cannot affect the quality of what is distributed, be it punishments or rewards. Discriminatory or capricious distribution thus could not justify abolition of the death penalty. Further, maldistribution inheres no more in capital punishment than in any other punishment.

Maldistribution between the guilty and the innocent is, by definition, unjust. But the injustice does not lie in the nature of the punishment. Because of the finality of the death penalty, the most grievous maldistribution occurs when it is imposed upon the innocent. However, the frequent allegations of discrimination and capriciousness refer to maldistribution among the guilty and not to the punishment of the innocent .

Maldistribution of any punishment among those who deserve it is irrelevant to its justice or morality. Even if poor or black convicts guilty of capital offenses suffer capital punishment, and other convicts equally guilty of the same crimes do not, a more equal distribution, however desirable, would merely be more equal. It would not be more just to the convicts under sentence of death.

Punishments are imposed on persons, not on racial or economic groups. Guilt is personal. The only relevant question is: does the person to be executed deserve the punishment? Whether or not others who deserved the same punishment, whatever their economic or racial group, have avoided execution is irrelevant. If they have, the guilt of the executed convicts would not be diminished, nor would their punishment be less deserved. To put the issue starkly, if the death penalty were imposed on guilty blacks, but not on guilty whites, or, if it were imposed by a lottery among the guilty, this irrationally discriminatory or capricious distribution would neither make the penalty unjust, nor cause anyone to be unjustly punished, despite the undue impunity bestowed on others.

Equality, in short, seems morally less important than justice. And justice is independent of distributional inequalities. The ideal of equal justice demands that justice be equally distributed, not that it be replaced by equality. Justice requires that as many of the guilty as possible be punished, regardless of whether others have avoided punishment. To let these others escape the deserved punishment does not do justice to them, or to society. But it is not unjust to those who could not escape. . . .

Recent data reveal little direct racial discrimination in the sentencing of those arrested and convicted of murder.[3] The abrogation of the death penalty for rape has eliminated a major source of racial discrimination. Concededly, some discrimination based on the race of murder victims may exist; yet, this discrimination affects criminal victimizers in an unexpected way. Murderers of whites are thought more likely to be executed than murderers of blacks. Black victims, then, are less fully vindicated than white ones. However, because most black murderers kill blacks, black murderers are spared the death penalty more often than are white murderers. They fare better than most white murderers.[4] The motivation behind unequal distribution of the death penalty may well have been to discriminate against blacks, but the result has favored them. Maldistribution is thus a straw man for empirical as well as analytical reasons.

II. MISCARRIAGES OF JUSTICE

In a recent survey Professors Hugo Adam Bedau and Michael Radelet found that 7000 persons were executed in the United States between 1900 and 1985 and that 25 were innocent of capital crimes.[5] Among the innocents they list Sacco and Vanzetti as well as Ethel and Julius Rosenberg. Although their data may be questionable, I do not doubt that, over a long enough period, miscarriages of justice will occur even in capital cases.

Despite precautions, nearly all human activities, such as trucking, lighting, or construction, cost the lives of some innocent bystanders. We do not give up these activities, because the advantages, moral or material, outweigh the unintended losses.[6] Analogously, for those who think the death penalty just, miscarriages of justice are offset by the moral benefits and the usefulness of doing justice. For those who think the death penalty unjust even when it does not miscarry, miscarriages can hardly be decisive.

III. DETERRENCE

Despite much recent work, there has been no conclusive statistical demonstration that the death penalty is a better deterrent than are alternative punishments.[7] However, deterrence is less than decisive for either side. Most abolitionists acknowledge that they would continue to favor abolition even if the death penalty were shown to deter more murders than alternatives could deter.[8] Abolitionists appear to value the life of a convicted murderer or, at least, his non-execution, more highly than they value the lives of the innocent victims who might be spared by deterring prospective murderers.

Deterrence is not altogether decisive for me either. I would favor retention of the death penalty as retribution even if it were shown that the threat of execution could not deter prospective murderers not already deterred by the threat of imprisonment.[9] Still, I believe the death penalty, because of its finality, is more feared than imprisonment, and deters some prospective murderers not deterred by the threat of imprisonment. Sparing the lives of even a few prospective victims by deterring their murderers is more important than preserving the lives of

convicted murderers because of the possibility, or even the probability, that executing them would not deter others. Whereas the lives of the victims who might be saved are valuable, that of the murderer has only negative value, because of his crime. Surely the criminal law is meant to protect the lives of potential victims in preference to those of actual murderers.

Murder rates are determined by many factors; neither the severity nor the probability of the threatened sanction is always decisive. However, for the long run, I share the view of Sir James Fitzjames Stephen: "Some men, probably, abstain from murder because they fear that if they committed murder they would be hanged. Hundreds of thousands abstain from it because they regard it with horror. One great reason why they regard it with horror is that murderers are hanged."[10] Penal sanctions are useful in the long run for the formation of the internal restraints so necessary to control crime. The severity and finality of the death penalty is appropriate to the seriousness and the finality of murder.[11]

IV. INCIDENTAL ISSUES:
COST, RELATIVE SUFFERING,
BRUTALIZATION

Many nondecisive issues are associated with capital punishment. Some believe that the monetary cost of appealing a capital sentence is excessive.[12] Yet most comparisons of the cost of life imprisonment with the cost of execution, apart from their dubious relevance, are flawed at least by the implied assumption that life prisoners will generate no judicial costs during their imprisonment. At any rate, the actual monetary costs are trumped by the importance of doing justice.

Others insist that a person sentenced to death suffers more than his victim suffered, and that this (excess) suffering is undue according to the *lex talionis* (rule of retaliation).[13] We cannot know whether the murderer on death row suffers more than his victim suffered; however, unlike the murderer, the victim deserved none of the suffering inflicted. Further, the limitations of the *lex talionis* were meant to restrain private vengeance, not the social retribution that has taken its place. Punishment—regardless of the motivation—is not intended to revenge, offset, or compensate for the victim's suffering, or to be measured by it. Punishment is to vindicate the law and the social order undermined by the crime. This is why a kidnapper's penal confinement is not limited to the period for which he imprisoned his victim; nor is a burglar's confinement meant merely to offset the suffering or the harm he caused his victim; nor is it meant only to offset the advantage he gained.[14]

Another argument heard at least since [eighteenth-century Italian legal thinker Cesare] Beccaria[15] is that, by killing a murderer, we encourage, endorse, or legitimize unlawful killing. Yet, although all punishments are meant to be unpleasant, it is seldom argued that they legitimize the unlawful imposition of identical unpleasantness. Imprisonment is not thought to legitimize kidnapping; neither are fines thought to legitimize robbery. The difference between murder and execution, or between kidnapping and imprisonment, is that the first is unlawful and undeserved, the second a lawful and deserved punishment for an unlawful act. The physical similarities of the punishment to the crime are irrelevant. The relevant difference is not physical, but social.[16]

V. JUSTICE, EXCESS, DEGRADATION

We threaten punishments in order to deter crime. We impose them not only to make the threats credible but also as retribution (justice) for the crimes that were not deterred. Threats and punishments are necessary to deter and deterrence is a sufficient practical justification for them. Retribution is an independent moral justification.[17] Although penalties can be unwise, repulsive, or inappropriate, and those punished can be pitiable, in a sense the infliction of legal punishment on a guilty person cannot be unjust. By committing the crime, the criminal volunteered to assume the risk of receiving a legal punishment that he could have avoided by not committing the crime. The punishment he suffers is the punishment he voluntarily risked suffering and, therefore, it is no more unjust to him than any other event for which one knowingly

volunteers to assume the risk. Thus, the death penalty cannot be unjust to the guilty criminal.[18]

There remain, however, two moral objections. The penalty may be regarded as always excessive as retribution and always morally degrading. To regard the death penalty as always excessive, one must believe that no crime—no matter how heinous—could possibly justify capital punishment. Such a belief can be neither corroborated nor refuted; it is an article of faith.

Alternatively, or concurrently, one may believe that everybody, the murderer no less than the victim, has an imprescriptible (natural?) right to life. The law therefore should not deprive anyone of life. I share Jeremy Bentham's view that any such "natural and imprescriptible rights" are "nonsense upon stilts."[19]

Justice Brennan has insisted that the death penalty is "uncivilized," "inhuman," inconsistent with "human dignity" and with "the sanctity of life,"[20] that it "treats members of the human race as nonhumans, as objects to be toyed with and discarded,"[21] that it is "uniquely degrading to human dignity"[22] and "by its very nature, [involves] a denial of the executed person's humanity."[23] Justice Brennan does not say why he thinks execution "uncivilized." Hitherto most civilizations have had the death penalty, although it has been discarded in Western Europe, where it is currently unfashionable probably because of its abuse by totalitarian regimes.

By "degrading," Justice Brennan seems to mean that execution degrades the executed convicts. Yet philosophers, such as Immanuel Kant and G. F. W. Hegel, have insisted that, when deserved, execution, far from degrading the executed convict, affirms his humanity by affirming his rationality and his responsibility for his actions. They thought that execution, when deserved, is required for the sake of the convict's dignity. (Does not life imprisonment violate human dignity more than execution, by keeping alive a prisoner deprived of all autonomy?)[24]

Common sense indicates that it cannot be death—our common fate—that is inhuman. Therefore, Justice Brennan must mean that death degrades when it comes not as a natural or accidental event, but as a deliberate social imposition. The murderer learns through his punishment that his fellow men have found him unworthy of living; that because he has murdered, he is being expelled from the community of the living. This degradation is self-inflicted. By murdering, the murderer has so dehumanized himself that he cannot remain among the living. The social recognition of his self-degradation is the punitive essence of execution. To believe, as Justice Brennan appears to, that the degradation is inflicted by the execution reverses the direction of causality.

Execution of those who have committed heinous murders may deter only one murder per year. If it does, it seems quite warranted. It is also the only fitting retribution for murder I can think of.

NOTES

1. Some writers, for example, Cesare Bonesana, Marchese di Beccaria, have thought that life imprisonment is more severe. *See C. Beccaria, Dei Delitti e Delle Pene* 62–70 (1764). More recently, Jacques Barzun, has expressed this view. *See* Barzun, *In Favor of Capital Punishment,* in *The Death Penalty in America* 154 (H. Bedau ed. 1964). However, the overwhelming majority of both abolitionists and of convicts under death sentence prefer life imprisonment to execution.

2. For a discussion of the sources of opposition to corporal punishment, see E. van den Haag, *Punishing Criminals* 196–206 (1975).

3. *See* Bureau Of Justice Statistics, U.S. Dep't Of Justice, Bulletin No. NCJ-98,399, Capital Punishment 1984, at 9 (1985); Johnson, *The Executioner's Bias,* Nat'l Rev., Nov. 15, 1985, at 44.

4. It barely need be said that any discrimination against (for example, black murderers of whites) must also be discrimination *for* (for example, black murderers of blacks).

5. Bedau & Radelet, *Miscarriages of Justice in Potentially Capital Cases* (1st draft, Oct. 1985) (on file at Harvard Law School Library).

6. An excessive number of trucking accidents or of miscarriages of justice could offset the benefits gained by trucking or the practice of doing justice. We are, however, far from this situation.

7. For a sample of conflicting views on the subject, see Baldus & Cole, A Comparison of the Work of Thorsten Sellin and Isaac Ehrlich on the Deterrent Effect of Capital Punishment, 85 YALE L.J. 170 (1975); Bowers & Pierce, Deterrence or Brutalization: What Is the Effect of Executions?, 26 Crime & Delinq. 453 (1980); Bowers & Pierce, The Illusion of Deterrence in Isaac Ehrlich's Research on Capital Punishment, 85 Yale L. J. 187 (1975); Ehrlich, Fear of Deterrence: A Critical Evaluation of the "Report of the Panel on Research on Deterrent

and Incapacitative Effects", 6 J. Legal Stud. 293 (1977); Ehrlich, The Deterrent Effect of Capital Punishment: A Question of Life and Death, 65 Am. Econ. Rev. 397, 415–16 (1975); Ehrlich & Gibbons, On the Measurement of the Deterrent Effect of Capital Punishment and the Theory of Deterrence, 6 J. Legal Stud. 35 (1977).

8. For most abolitionists, the discrimination argument, *see supra* pp. 1662-64, is similarly nondecisive: they would favor abolition even if there could be no racial discrimination.

9. If executions were shown to increase the murder rate in the long run, I would favor abolition. Sparing the innocent victims who would be spared, *ex hypothesi,* by the nonexecution of murderers would be more important to me than the execution, however just, of murderers. But although there is a lively discussion of the subject, no serious evidence exists to support the hypothesis that executions produce a higher murder rate. *Cf.* Phillips, *The Deterrent Effect of Capital Punishment: New Evidence on an Old Controversy,* 86 Am. J. Soc. 139 (1980) (arguing that murder rates drop immediately after executions of criminals).

10. H. Gross, A Theory Of Criminal Justice 489 (1979) (attributing this passage to Sir James Fitzjames Stephen).

11. Weems v. United States, 217 U.S. 349 (1910), suggests that penalties be proportionate to the seriousness of the crime—a common theme of the criminal law. Murder, therefore, demands more than life imprisonment, if, as I believe, it is a more serious crime than other crimes punished by life imprisonment. In modern times, our sensibility requires that the range of punishments be narrower than the range of crimes—but not so narrow as to exclude the death penalty.

12. *Cf.* Kaplan, *Administering Capital Punishment,* 36 U. Fla. L. Rev. 177, 178, 190–91 (1984) (noting the high cost of appealing a capital sentence).

13. For an example of this view, see A. Camus, Reflections On The Guillotine 24–30 (1959). On the limitations allegedly imposed by the *lex talionis,* see Reiman, *Justice, Civilization, and the Death Penalty: Answering van den Haag,* 14 PHIL. & PUB. AFF. 115, 119–34 (1985).

14. Thus restitution (a civil liability) cannot satisfy the punitive purpose of penal sanctions, whether the purpose be retributive or deterrent.

15. See *supra* note 3.

16. Some abolitionists challenge: if the death penalty is just and serves as a deterrent, why not televise executions? The answer is simple. The death even of a murderer, however well-deserved, should not serve as public entertainment. It so served in earlier centuries. But in this respect our sensibility has changed for the better, I believe. Further, television unavoidably would trivialize executions, wedged in, as they would be, between game shows, situation comedies

and the like. Finally, because televised executions would focus on the physical aspects of the punishment, rather than the nature of the crime and the suffering of the victim, a televised execution would present the murderer as the victim of the state. Far from communicating the moral significance of the execution, television would shift the focus to the pitiable fear of the murderer. We no longer place in cages those sentenced to imprisonment to expose them to public view. Why should we so expose those sentenced to execution?

17. *See* van den Haag, *Punishment as a Device for Controlling the Crime Rate,* 33 Rutgers 1. Rev. 706, 719 (1981) (explaining why the desire for retribution, although independent, would have to be satisfied even if deterrence were the only purpose of punishment.)

18. An explicit threat of punitive action is necessary to the justification of any legal punishment: *nulla poena sine lege* (no punishment without [preexisting] law). To be sufficiently justified, the threat must in turn have a rational and legitimate purpose. "Your money or your life" does not qualify; nor does the threat of an unjust law; nor, finally, does a threat that is altogether disproportionate to the importance of its purpose. In short, preannouncement legitimizes the threatened punishment only if the threat is warranted. But this leaves a very wide range of justified threats. Furthermore, the punished person is aware of the penalty for his actions and thus volunteers to take the risk even of an unjust punishment. His victim, however, did not volunteer to risk anything. The question whether any self-inflicted injury—such as a legal punishment—ever can be unjust to a person who knowingly risked it is a matter that requires more analysis than is possible here.

19. *The Works Of Jeremy Bentham* 105 (J. Bowring ed. 1972). However, I would be more polite about prescriptible natural rights, which Bentham (described as "simple nonsense." Id. (It does not matter whether natural rights are called "moral" or "human" rights as they currently are by most writers.)

20. The Death Penalty In America 256-63 (H. Bedau ed.. 3d ed. 1982) (quoting Furman v. Georgia, 408 U.S. 238, 286, 305 (1972) (Brennan, J., concurring).

21. *Id.* at 272–73; *see also* Gregg v. Georgia, 428 U.S. I53. 230 (1976) (Brennan, J., dissenting).

22. Furman v. Georgia, 408 U.S. 238, 291 (1972) (Brennan, J., concurring).

23. *Id.* at 290.

24. *See* Barzun, *supra* note 3, *passim.*

DISCUSSION QUESTIONS

1. Do you agree with van den Haag that "[j]ustice requires as many of the guilty to be punished, regardless of whether others have avoided punishment"? Why or why not?
2. What does van den Haag think is the most important reason to punish criminals? Do you agree? Why or why not?
3. Do you agree with van den Haag that the mere possibility of deterrence provides a strong reason for supporting the death penalty? Why or why not?
4. Do you agree with van den Haag's implied claim that there are at least *some* crimes that are so heinous that the criminal deserves to die? If not, why not? If so, what kinds of crimes would you put in that category? Why?

STEPHEN NATHANSON

An Eye for an Eye? The Morality of Punishing by Death

Stephen Nathanson is Professor Emeritus in Philosophy at Northeastern University. He has written on a range of topics in moral and political philosophy. In this excerpt from his book *An Eye for an Eye? The Morality of Punishing by Death,* Nathanson criticizes some moral principles that are often used to argue for capital punishment.

GUIDING QUESTIONS

1. What is the principle of "an eye for an eye," according to Nathanson? What are his two main criticisms of it?
2. Why does Nathanson believe the principle of an "eye for an eye" gives "either . . . wrong answers or no answers at all" to questions about how to punish various crimes?
3. What is the "principle of proportionality"? How is it better than the principle of an "eye for an eye," according to Nathanson? Why, according to Nathanson, does it fail to support the death penalty?
4. What general point is Nathanson trying to make with the four imaginary scenarios in which one person saves another from drowning? How does this point relate to his arguments about the death penalty?

AN EYE FOR AN EYE?

Suppose we try to determine what people deserve from a strictly moral point of view. How shall we proceed?

The most usual suggestion is that we look at a person's actions because what someone deserves would appear to depend on what he or she does. A person's actions, it seems, provide not only a basis for a moral appraisal of the person but also a guide to how he should be treated. According to the *lex talionis* or principle of "an eye for an eye," we ought to treat people as they have treated others. What people deserve as recipients of rewards or punishments is determined by what they do as agents.

This is a powerful and attractive view, one that appears to be backed not only by moral common sense but also by tradition and philosophical thought. The most famous statement of philosophical support for

this view comes from Immanuel Kant, who linked it directly with an argument for the death penalty. Discussing the problem of punishment, Kant writes,

> What kind and what degree of punishment does legal justice adopt as its principle and standard? None other than the principle of equality . . . the principle of not treating one side more favorably than the other. Accordingly, any undeserved evil that you inflict on someone else among the people is one that you do to yourself. If you vilify, you vilify yourself; if you steal from him, you steal from yourself; if you kill him, you kill yourself. Only the law of retribution (*jus talionis*) can determine exactly the kind and degree of punishment.[1]

Kant's view is attractive for a number of reasons. First, it accords with our belief that what a person deserves is related to what he does. Second, it appeals to a moral standard and does not seem to rely on any particular legal or political institutions. Third, it seems to provides a measure of appropriate punishment that can be used as a guide to creating laws and instituting punishments. It tells us that the punishment is to be identical with the crime. Whatever the criminal did to the victim is to be done in turn to the criminal.

In spite of the attractions of Kant's view, it is deeply flawed. When we see why, it will be clear that the whole "eye for an eye" perspective must be rejected.

PROBLEMS WITH THE EQUAL PUNISHMENT PRINCIPLE

There are two main problems with this view. First, appearances to the contrary, it does not actually provide a measure of moral desert. Second, it does not provide an adequate criterion for determining appropriate levels of punishment.

Let us begin with the second criticism, the claim that Kant's view fails to tell us how much punishment is appropriate for particular crimes. We can see this, first, by noting that for certain crimes, Kant's view recommends punishments that are not morally acceptable. Applied strictly, it would require that we rape rapists, torture torturers, and burn arsonists whose acts have led to deaths. In general, where a particular crime involves barbaric and inhuman treatment, Kant's principle tells us to act barbarically and inhumanly in return. So, in some cases, the principle generates unacceptable answers to the question of what constitutes appropriate punishment.

This is not its only defect. In many other cases, the principle tells us nothing at all about how to punish. While Kant thought it obvious how to apply his principle in the case of murder, his principle cannot serve as a general rule because it does not tell us how to punish many crimes. Using the Kantian version or the more common "eye for an eye" standard, what would we decide to do to embezzlers, spies, drunken drivers, airline hijackers, drug users, prostitutes, air polluters, or persons who practice medicine without a license? If one reflects on this question, it becomes clear that there is simply no answer to it. We could

not in fact design a system of punishment simply on the basis of the "eye for an eye" principle.

In order to justify using the "eye for an eye" principle to answer our question about murder and the death penalty, we would first have to show that it worked for a whole range of cases, giving acceptable answers to questions about amounts of punishment. Then, having established it as a satisfactory general principle, we could apply it to the case of murder. It turns out, however, that when we try to apply the principle generally, we find that it either gives wrong answers or no answers at all. Indeed, I suspect that the principle of "an eye for an eye" is no longer even a principle. Instead, it is simply a metaphorical disguise for expressing belief in the death penalty. People who cite it do not take it seriously. They do not believe in a kidnapping for a kidnapping, a theft for a theft, and so on. Perhaps "an eye for an eye" once was a genuine principle, but now it is merely a slogan. Therefore, it gives us no guidance in deciding whether murderers deserve to die.

In reply to these objections, one might defend the principle by saying that it does not require that punishments be strictly identical with crimes. Rather, it requires only that a punishment produce an amount of suffering in the criminal which is equal to the amount suffered by the victim. Thus, we don't have to hijack airplanes belonging to airline hijackers, spy on spies, etc. We simply have to reproduce in them the harm done to others.

Unfortunately, this reply really does not solve the problem. It provides no answer to the first objection, since it would still require us to behave barbarically in our treatment of those who are guilty of barbaric crimes. Even if we do not reproduce their actions exactly, any action which caused equal suffering would itself be barbaric. Second, in trying to produce equal amounts of suffering, we run into many problems. Just how much suffering is produced by an airline hijacker or a spy? And how do we apply this principle to prostitutes or drug users, who may not produce any suffering at all? We have rough ideas about how serious various crimes are, but this may not correlate with any clear sense of just how much harm is done.

Furthermore, the same problem arises in determining how much suffering a particular punishment would produce for a particular criminal. People vary in their tolerance of pain and in the amount of unhappiness that a fine or a jail sentence would cause them. Recluses will be less disturbed by banishment than extroverts. Nature lovers will suffer more in prison than people who are indifferent to natural beauty. A literal application of the principle would require that we tailor punishments to individual sensitivities, yet this is at best impractical. To a large extent, the legal system must work with standardized and rather crude estimates of the negative impact that punishments have on people.

The move from calling for a punishment that is identical to the crime to favoring one that is equal in the harm done is no help to us or to the defense of the principle. "An eye for an eye" tells us neither what people deserve nor how we should treat them when they have done wrong.

PROPORTIONAL RETRIBUTIVISM

The view we have been considering can be called "equality retributivism," since it proposes that we repay criminals with punishments equal to their crimes. In the light of problems like those I have cited, some people have proposed a variation on this view, calling not for equal punishments but rather for punishments which are *proportional* to the crime. In defending such a view as a guide for setting criminal punishments, Andrew von Hirsch writes:

> If one asks how severely a wrongdoer deserves to be punished, a familiar principle comes to mind: Severity of punishment should be commensurate with the seriousness of the wrong. Only grave wrongs merit severe penalties; minor misdeeds deserve lenient punishments. Disproportionate penalties are un-deserved—severe sanctions for minor wrongs or vice versa. This principle has variously been called a principle of "proportionality" or "just deserts"; we prefer to call it commensurate deserts.[2]

Like Kant, von Hirsch makes the punishment which a person deserves depend on that person's actions, but he departs from Kant in substituting proportionality

for equality as the criterion for setting the amount of punishment.

In implementing a punishment system based on the proportionality view, one would first make a list of crimes, ranking them in order of seriousness. At one end would be quite trivial offenses like parking meter violations, while very serious crimes such as murder would occupy the other. In between, other crimes would be ranked according to their relative gravity. Then a corresponding scale of punishments would be constructed, and the two would be correlated. Punishments would be proportionate to crimes so long as we could say that the more serious the crime was, the higher on the punishment scale was the punishment administered.

This system does not have the defects of equality retributivism. It does not require that we treat those guilty of barbaric crimes barbarically. This is because we can set the upper limit of the punishment scale so as to exclude truly barbaric punishments. Second, unlike the equality principle, the proportionality view is genuinely general, providing a way of handling all crimes. Finally, it does justice to our ordinary belief that certain punishments are unjust because they are too severe or too lenient for the crime committed.

The proportionality principle does, I think, play a legitimate role in our thinking about punishments. Nonetheless, it is no help to death penalty advocates, because it does not require that murderers be executed. All that it requires is that if murder is the most serious crime, then murder should be punished by the most severe punishment on the scale. The principle does not tell us what this punishment should be, however, and it is quite compatible with the view that the most severe punishment should be a long prison term.

This failure of the theory to provide a basis for supporting the death penalty reveals an important gap in proportional retributivism. It shows that while the theory is general in scope, it does not yield any specific recommendations regarding punishment. It tells us, for example, that armed robbery should be punished more severely than embezzling and less severely than murder, but it does not tell us how much to punish any of these. This weakness is, in effect, conceded by von Hirsch, who admits that if we want to implement the "commensurate deserts" principle, we must supplement it with information about what level of punishment is needed to deter crimes.[3] In a later discussion of how to "anchor" the punishment system, he deals with this problem in more depth, but the factors he cites as relevant to making specific judgments (such as available prison space) have nothing to do with what people deserve. He also seems to suggest that a range of punishments may be appropriate for a particular crime. This runs counter to the death penalty supporter's sense that death alone is appropriate for some murderers.[4]

Neither of these retributive views, then, provides support for the death penalty. The equality principle fails because it is not in general true that the appropriate punishment for a crime is to do to the criminal what he has done to others. In some cases this is immoral, while in others it is impossible. The proportionality principle may be correct, but by itself it cannot determine specific punishments for specific crimes. Because of its flexibility and open-endedness, it is compatible with a great range of different punishments for murder.[5]

A MORE SERIOUS OBJECTION

So far, in looking at these versions of retributivism, I have tried to show that they do not help us to determine the appropriate punishment for specific crimes. That is, they do not really tell us what sort of treatment is deserved by people who have acted in certain ways.

There is a more serious defect of both versions of the theory, however. Neither one succeeds in basing punishment on what a person morally deserves. Why is this? Because both theories focus solely on the action that a person has performed, and this action is not the proper basis for determining moral desert. We cannot tell what a person deserves simply by examining what he has done.

While it may sound odd to say that a person's degree of moral desert is not determined by his actions, the point is actually a matter of common sense morality. We can see this by considering the following examples, all of which are cases of rescuing a drowning person.

1. A and B have robbed a bank, but B has hidden the money from A. A finds B at the beach and sees that he is drowning. A drags B from the water, revives him, finds out the location of the money, and then shoots him, leaving him for dead. The shot, however, is not fatal. A has saved B's life.

2. C recognizes D, a wealthy businessman, at the beach. Later, she sees D struggling in the water and, hoping to get a reward, she saves him. C would not have saved D if she had not thought that a reward was likely.

3. E is drowning at the beach and is spotted by F, a poor swimmer. F leaps into the water and, at great risk to her own life, manages to save E.

4. G is drowning at the beach but is spotted by Superman, who rescues him effortlessly.

In each of these cases, the very same act occurs. One person saves another from drowning. Yet, if we attempt to assess what each rescuer morally deserves, we will arrive at very different answers for each case. This is because judgments of desert are moral judgments about people and not just about their actions or how they should be treated. Our moral judgments about A, C, F, and Superman in the examples above are quite different, in spite of the similarity of their actions. From a moral point of view, we would not rate A as being praiseworthy at all because he had no concern for B's well-being and in fact wished him dead. C, the rescuer motivated by the prospect of a reward, wished D no harm but is also less praiseworthy because her act was not motivated by genuine concern for D's well-being. Finally, while F, the poor swimmer, and Superman both acted from benevolent motives, F is more deserving of praise because of the greater risk which she took and the greater difficulties she faced in accomplishing the rescue.

What these cases make clear is that there is no direct connection between what a person does and his or her degree of moral desert. To make judgments of moral desert, we need to know about a person's intentions, motivations, and circumstances, not just about the action and its result. Since both Kant and von Hirsch base their judgments concerning appropriate punishments simply on the act that has been committed, they do not succeed in basing their recommended punishments on what a person morally deserves, for what a person deserves depends on factors which they do not consider.

It is quite ironic that Kant overlooks this and provides an exclusively act-oriented account of assessing people in his discussion of punishment. In other writings, Kant insists that the fact that an action is harmful or helpful does not by itself tell us how to assess the moral value of the agent's performing it.[6] He lays great stress on the significance of motivation, claiming that the moral value of actions depends *entirely* on whether they are done from a moral motive.

"PAYBACK" RETRIBUTIVISM

With this criticism in mind, it is instructive to look back at the passage from Kant about the need to execute murderers. What is striking about the passage is that Kant does not talk about desert at all. He does not say that a person deserves to die because he has killed and therefore that he ought to be executed. Rather, he says that a person should be executed simply because he has killed.

The lack of any reference to moral desert in this passage is more than just a linguistic oversight by Kant. It reflects the existence of a form of retributivism that is related to but different from the view that I have been discussing. I have assumed that the central retributivist ideal is that people ought to get what they deserve. But there is another view of retribution, according to which justice is done when a person is paid back for what he does. In this famous passage, Kant expresses the "payback" version of retributivism rather than a form of the view that focuses on moral desert. Why this is I do not know, but in any case, Kant is not alone in thinking that retribution has been achieved when a person has been treated as he has treated others.

Although retribution is often cited as a goal of the criminal law, this "payback" conception is weak and unattractive. First, it provides no justification for punishment. We want to know why it is morally permissible to punish someone who has committed a crime, and the answer of the "payback" retributivist is simply that it is permissible to pay people back for

their deeds by doing to them what they have done to others. This reply begs the question by offering no independent reason for punishing. By contrast, one who justifies punishment by saying that the person being punished deserves this treatment appears to be offering a substantive, independent reason for punishing, making this view much more attractive than the "payback" conception. He is pointing to some feature of the person which makes the punishment appropriate.

Second, the "payback" retributivist defines the actions people have committed by reference to the *results* of those actions. If we consider this view, however, it is easy to generate conclusions that the retributivist himself would find unacceptable. When people who believe in "an eye for an eye" say that those who kill must be killed in turn, this cannot possibly be their final word on the matter. If it were, then they would be committed to the view that those who kill accidentally must be killed. More absurdly, they would have to hold that whenever the death penalty is imposed, the executioner of the murderer would in turn have to be killed because he has killed, as would the executioner of the executioner and so on.

These absurd conclusions can, of course, be avoided by describing actions in more sophisticated ways. Doing this makes it possible to deny that accidental and intentional killings are the same. It allows us to distinguish the intentional killing done by the original murderer from the intentional killing performed by the executioner. Having done this, we can call one of these acts murder, a second accidental homicide, and the third a legal execution. Furthermore, we then say that it is only murderers—and not those who commit accidental homicide or perform legal executions—who should be paid back for their deeds. Once we do this, however, we have moved away from the "payback" version of retributivism and its simple focus on the results of actions. In distinguishing these various killings, we have been forced to look at motives, intentions, and circumstances and not just to consider actions and results. To do this is to leave behind "payback" retributivism and to return to the more complex "giving people what they deserve" version of the theory. Indeed, this is the most plausible version of the theory. Retributivism without desert is simply too crude a view to be plausible.

Any reasonable principle, then, will recognize that not all killings are murders and hence that not all who kill deserve to die. This is, in fact, the view of common sense morality, which sanctions some types of killing (for example, killing in self-defense) and thus allows that one who kills may even be morally blameless. Furthermore, even among those killings that are illegitimate and that we want to classify as murder, not all are equally reprehensible. This is reflected in the Supreme Court's judgment that mandatory death sentences for murder are unconstitutional.[7] Though the Court often speaks the language of retribution, its decisions depart from the simplicity of "payback" retributivism.

CONCLUSIONS

In this chapter, I have examined some of the arguments that might be used to defend the view that murderers deserve to die. I have tried to show why these arguments fail. The traditional versions of retributivism do not justify death as a specific punishment for murder. Moreover, in their usual forms, they omit factors that are essential to determining what a person deserves. Paradoxically, one cannot tell what a person deserves simply by knowing what he has done. In particular, it is not enough to know that someone has killed someone else or even that he has done so unjustifiably. The examples of the various rescuers show that we must consider more than a person's deeds to determine what he or she deserves.

At this point, one might suggest that I have been unfair to advocates of the death penalty. After all, the standard homicide laws require that we take account of motives, intentions, and other features of a criminal's actions and character that are relevant to desert.

If we consider these factors, perhaps we can distinguish between those killers who deserve to die and those who do not.

Death penalty advocates might charge that I have only shown that not all who kill deserve to die, but if we define murder properly, we may be able to show that at least some of those who murder deserve to die. Let us see whether this proposal can be carried out.

NOTES

1. Kant, *Metaphysical Elements of Justice,* translated by John Ladd (Indianapolis: Bobbs-Merrill, 1965), 101.

2. Doing *Justice* (New York: Hill & Wang, 1976), 66; reprinted in *Sentencing,* edited by H. Gross and A. von Hirsch (Oxford University Press, 1981), 243. For a more recent discussion and further defense by von Hirsch, see his *Past or Future Crimes* (New Brunswick, N.J.: Rutgers University Press, 1985).

3. Von Hirsch, *Doing Justice,* 93–94. My criticisms of proportional retributivism are not novel. For helpful discussions of the view, see Hugo Bedau, "Concessions to Retribution in Punishment," in *Justice and Punishment,* edited by J. Cederblom and W. Blizek (Cambridge, Mass.: Ballinger, 1977), and M. Golding, *Philosophy of Law* (Englewood Cliffs, N.J.: Prentice Hall, 1975), 98–99.

4. See von Hirsch, *Past and Future Crimes,* ch. 8.

5. For more positive assessments of these theories, see Jeffrey Reiman, "Justice, Civilization, and the Death Penalty," *Philosophy and Public Affairs* 14 (1985): 115–48; and Michael Davis, "How to Make the Punishment Fit the Crime," *Ethics* 93 (1983).

6. Consider the following more representative statement by Kant: "To be beneficent when we can is a duty; and besides this, there are many minds so sympathetically constituted that . . . they find a pleasure in spreading joy around them, and can take delight in the satisfaction of others so far as it is their own work. But I maintain that in such a case an action of this kind, however proper, however amiable it may be, has nevertheless no true moral worth. . . . For the maxim lacks the moral import, namely, that such actions be done *from duty,* not from inclination." See *Fundamental Principles of the Metaphysic of Morals,* translated by T. Abbott (New York: Liberal Arts Press, 1949), 15–16.

7. The Court struck down mandatory death sentences in Woodson v. *North Carolina,* 428 U.S. 280–324 (1976).

DISCUSSION QUESTIONS

1. Do you think the principle of "an eye for an eye" can be fixed to meet Nathanson's initial criticisms of it? If so, how? If not, why not?
2. Nathanson argues that the principle of proportionality does not *by itself* justify capital punishment. Do you think that there are other plausible premises that can be combined with the principle of proportionality to justify capital punishment? If so, what are they? If not, why not?
3. Nathanson argues that neither "an eye for an eye" nor the principle of proportionality adequately accounts for the motivations or circumstances of a crime. How might a supporter of these principles reply to this objection?
4. Do you agree with Nathanson that "an eye for an eye" must take into account what a criminal deserves? Why or why not?

THADDEUS METZ

African Values and Capital Punishment

Thaddeus Metz is Distinguished Professor of Philosophy at the University of Witwatersrand in South Africa. He has been influential in promoting a philosophical understanding of the ethics of *ubuntu*. In this paper, Metz argues that traditional African values support the abolition of capital punishment.

GUIDING QUESTIONS

1. What does Metz mean by "African values"?
2. What three arguments against the death penalty does Metz criticize? What problems does he find with them?
3. What is the purpose of Metz's thought experiment involving the two machete-wielding men chasing an elderly woman?
4. What is Metz's argument against the death penalty? How does it relate to distinctively African values?

INTRODUCTION

What is the strongest argument grounded in African values for abolishing capital punishment? In this chapter, I defend a particular answer to this question, one that invokes an under-theorized conception of human dignity. Roughly, I maintain that the death penalty is nearly always morally unjustified, and should therefore be abolished, because it degrades people's special capacity for communal relationship. To defend this claim, I proceed by: first, clarifying what I aim to achieve in this essay; second, criticizing existing objections to the death penalty that ethicists, jurists and others have proffered on "African" grounds; third, advancing a new, dignity-based objection with an African pedigree that I take to be the most promising; and, fourth, making some concluding remarks about related work that should be undertaken if my argumentation in this essay is sound.

From: Gerard Walmsley (ed.), *African Philosophy and the Future of Africa*. Council for Research in Values and Philosophy 83–90.

CLARIFYING MY AIM

I have said that I aim to answer the question, "What is the most promising way to object to the death penalty, when appealing to African values?" This question is naturally understood to assume, for the sake of argument, *that* the death penalty is immoral, and seeks the best explanation of *why* it is. Many readers, however, might be initially unconvinced that the death penalty is immoral. Indeed, capital punishment is legal in more than two dozen states below the Sahara, and often majorities in sub-Saharan abolitionist states would like to see it legalized.[1] However, such readers will find good reason to change their minds, if, as I expect, they find the argument I make against capital punishment to be independently attractive.

I maintain, in fact, that many African readers will find my argument against capital punishment to be attractive for appealing to certain ideas implicit in views they already hold. I argue that characteristically African values provide good reason to reject the death penalty, regardless of whether that has been appreciated up to now. By "African values," I mean ideas about good/bad and right/wrong that have been salient among the black peoples in the sub-Saharan region in a way they have tended not to be elsewhere in the world. Such a construal of the word "African" implies neither that such values are held by *everyone below the Sahara,* nor that *no one beyond the Sahara* does so. Instead, this word is meant to connote properties that have been recurrently exemplified in that region among those not of European, Arab or Asian descent and that have not been instantiated most other places on the globe. My claim is that there are ideas about the dignity of persons, the value of community, and the justifiability of violence that are common in the moral-philosophical worldviews of traditional black sub-Saharan societies and that, upon philosophical clarification and refinement, can be seen to entail that capital punishment should be abolished.

I use the terms "death penalty" and "capital punishment" interchangeably to indicate the state's intentional killing of a person that expresses disapproval of a crime that has been judged to have been committed. So stated, the death penalty, imposed by the judicial branch of government, must be distinguished from deadly force, employed by the executive branch. To use deadly force (or to do so justifiably) is for the police or army to employ coercion, which has a good chance of killing its target, in order to prevent harm to innocent parties. Deadly force is "prospective," by which I mean that it is by definition deployed before a crime or other aggression has been committed, and is (justifiably) used to stop the harmful act from being done. The death penalty, in contrast, is "retrospective" in that it is a response to harm or a wrong that has already been done (or has been perceived to have been). A second major difference between the two is that the death penalty is meant to censure certain wrongful behaviour, whereas deadly force need not be condemnatory, e.g., it may sometimes (rightfully!) be employed against "innocent threats," i.e., persons who, for no fault of their own, would otherwise harm other persons. Below I argue that one major problem with the existing African arguments against the death penalty is that they counterintuitively entail that deadly force is unjustified in cases where it clearly is not.

In claiming that certain African values entail that the death penalty "should be abolished," I mean to say that it is nearly always an injustice. Of course, "nearly always" is not the same as "always." Below I admit that there are rare cases in which imposing the death penalty would be justified by the sub-Saharan rationale I provide. However, they would be so infrequently encountered, and it would be so difficult to prove that they meet the relevant criteria, that I suspect that the most reasonable course for a state to take would be to abolish the death penalty altogether, rather than to make allowance for the very odd exception.

CONSEQUENTIALIST ARGUMENTS

I have not encountered anyone appealing to African considerations who systematically argues that abolishing the death penalty would promote the general welfare more than retaining the death penalty. However, I have found those who have contended that retaining the death penalty would not promote the general welfare more than abolishing it. That is, some African abolitionists have sought to object to a consequentialist argument for the death penalty by contending that the results of abolishing it, with regard to crime rates and the like, would be no worse than those of retaining it. Typically, the debate has focused on deterrence, with abolitionists, such as the important Nigerian philosopher Segun Gbadegesin, pointing out that, for decades, criminologists were unable to find real evidence that the death penalty deters more than say life in prison.[2]

The "African"' source of this consequentialist debate is straightforwardly understood to be the fact that sub-Saharans characteristically prize community, and that punishment is justified insofar as it will prevent either members of the community from being harmed or communal norms from being violated. Some African philosophers have explicitly argued for stringent penalties such as the death penalty based on the idea that the end of protecting the community justifies the means (at least if the party being severely punished is guilty of a serious crime).[3] African abolitionists have replied to this argument by contending that the community would be no less protected if the state no longer used the death penalty.

There is one serious problem with this rationale against the death penalty: there have been studies conducted in the past 10 years that purport to provide new, strong evidence that the death penalty can deter, and has indeed deterred, crime more than its absence.[4] Of course, these studies have been questioned. However, while it was a truism in the 20th century that there was no good evidence for the deterrent capacity of the death penalty, in the 21st it is debatable whether there is. Insofar as the consequences of the retention of the death penalty relative to its abolition are unclear, one is not yet justified in rejecting the death penalty for consequentialist considerations.

EXTANT DIGNITY-BASED ARGUMENTS

The objection that capital punishment is degrading of human dignity neatly side-steps the problem facing a consequentialist criticism of it. A dignity-based objection does not appeal to the results of the death penalty, but rather maintains that there is something about it "in itself" that is morally wrong. To have a dignity is, roughly, to have a superlative final value, i.e., to be a certain entity that is good for its own sake to a degree higher than anything else in the animal, vegetable and mineral kingdoms.[5] I first present and reject two dignity-based objections to the death penalty that have been prominently made from an African perspective, before presenting a new one that I maintain is a clear improvement on them.

First, one encounters the argument that human beings have a dignity of a sort that would be degraded were an innocent person executed, an argument that Moses Òkè has made most thoroughly from an African standpoint.[6] He points out that it has been common among traditional Yorubas, a people in Western Africa, to believe that all or most human beings have a dignity. I add that the same is true of traditional African societies more generally, with many of them holding that human beings have a dignity in virtue of being a spiritual offshoot of God, the source of all vitality. Supposing that the state must above all not degrade people's dignity, that an innocent person's dignity would be degraded if he were executed, and that the state can never be certain that those it executes are guilty,[7] it follows that the state should abolish the death penalty.

I mention a prima facie problem with this rationale, before presenting what I think is a decisive reason to reject it. One might point out that certainty is not expected anywhere else in our moral reasoning, and that a weaker, but still robust, standard of proof beyond a reasonable doubt both is more sensible and can sometimes be satisfied. If one has proof beyond a reasonable doubt that someone deserves to die for his misdeeds, then one arguably does not *degrade* him upon putting him to death, or does not do so in a way that warrants blame or guilt, even if he is in fact innocent and does not deserve execution.

While this problem with Òkè 's argument is worth considering, I think the most damning consideration against it is that it oddly entails that the use of deadly force is unjustified in cases where it plainly is not. If "respect for the dignity of all (is) not in sync with either the policy or the practice of judicially killing offenders or alleged offenders in the community, especially when it (is) granted that the judicial system (is) always vulnerable to error,"[8] then all intentional killing must be considered impermissibly disrespectful. However, that would mean that it is wrong ever to use deadly force in defence of oneself or of others. Elsewhere, I have maintained that the following case, "Ethnic Cleansing," shows this implication to be deeply counterintuitive:[9]

> You are a peacekeeper who sees two men chasing an innocent, elderly woman with machetes, trying to kill her merely because she has a different ethnicity. You have a machine gun. After firing a warning shot to deter the men (that you see they have recognized as a warning), they are not scared off and continue after the woman. You shoot the two aggressors, reasonably judging it to be necessary and sufficient to protect the one innocent. They die, and she lives.

I claim that the use of deadly force is morally justified in the case of "Ethnic Cleansing," *despite the lack of certainty* that the men will continue aggressing or will succeed in seriously harming the woman. And most African readers will agree. Pacifism is far from the dominant approach to violence in sub-Saharan moral thinking, and it is instead widely accepted that violence in self- or other-defence can be justified. In sum, if certainty of guilt for serious harm were necessary for intentional killing to be justified, then deadly force would always be unjustified, but it is not. Hence, Òkè 's objection to the death penalty is fatally (so to speak) flawed.

The same problem applies to a second, somewhat more common African- and dignity-based argument against the death penalty. Members of the Constitutional Court of the Republic of South Africa, among others, have maintained that human life has an inherent dignity that confers an inalienable right to life on all of us. As the death penalty would violate a person's right to life, even if he were guilty, it would be an impermissible degradation. As one justice of the Court has said:

> [There is a need to] recognise the right to and protection of human dignity as a right concomitant to life itself and inherent in all human beings, so that South Africans may also appreciate that even the vilest criminal remains a human being *(Furman v Georgia, supra)*. In my view, life and dignity are like two sides of the same coin. The concept of *ubuntu* embodies them both.[10]

"*Ubuntu*" is the Nguni term for humanness that is understood by many in southern Africa to encapsulate morality. To have *ubuntu* is to live a genuinely human or ethical way of life, which one does, roughly, by prizing community with other persons.[11] The Court takes others to merit communal relationship by virtue of the dignity they have as human beings, and for such relating to include upholding everyone's right to life regardless of what they have done.

However, the problem with this rationale against the death penalty is that it counterintuitively also rules out the use of any deadly force. If one's vile actions are not enough to forfeit one's right to life, then even the aggressors in Ethnic Cleansing retain theirs, making it prohibitively degrading for the peacekeeper to shoot them. However, I presume the reader agrees with me that deadly force would be justified in such a case, meaning that the present objection to the death penalty is not the right one to make.[12]

A NEW DIGNITY-BASED ARGUMENT

I now present a third, dignity-based argument against the death penalty that is grounded in African values, one that avoids both the problematic appeal to the consequences of its imposition and the counterintuitive implication that deadly force is invariably impermissible. Part of this new rationale includes the idea that human beings have a dignity just insofar as they are capable of communal relationships, where these are understood to be relationships in which one both shares a way of life with others and cares about their quality of life.[13] To share a way of life with others and to care about their quality of life is more or less what English-speakers mean by "friendship" or "love" in a broad sense. By this account of dignity, then, if one had to choose between killing a cat or a person, one should spare the latter because it has a capacity to love that makes it intrinsically worth more than the former.

Now, what would it mean to degrade someone who has a dignity in virtue of her capacity for communal or friendly relationships?[14] On the face of it, unfriendly or unloving behaviour is what would treat others as incapable of community or as less than special for being so capable. More specifically, degradation often consists of unfriendly behaviour toward someone that is not meant to counteract her unfriendliness. Respect for the capacity for community or love means treating a person in accordance with the way she has exercised it. Roughly, those who have been friendly do not warrant unfriendly treatment, whereas those who have been unfriendly do warrant unfriendly treatment, if necessary to protect those threatened by their comparable unfriendliness. If one is unfriendly toward another because one must be in order to prevent his proportionate unfriendliness, then one is not disrespecting his capacity for friendliness, which he has misused.

This account of the way to degrade, and conversely to respect, individuals capable of friendship or community grounds a straightforward explanation of why the death penalty would be degrading but deadly force would not. Aggressors in (clearly justified) other-defence cases are, by virtue of being killed, *being forced to correct their own proportionately unfriendly relationships,* whereas killing offenders in the case of capital punishment would not serve this function.

This rationale against the death penalty is not vulnerable to purported counterexamples that one might be tempted to suggest. For instance, although capital punishment might, as above, serve the function of deterrence and hence prevent unfriendliness proportionate to what the offender has done, it would not be necessary to end any proportionate unfriendliness that the *offender* is engaging in or responsible for. The person on death row is no longer torturing, mutilating or killing, and so the death penalty would not help those threatened by *his* comparable unfriendliness. Furthermore, even if execution were to (m)end unfriendly relationships that the offender still has or harm that he has caused, e.g., with regard to the victim's family, this unfriendliness would not be *proportionate* to the grossly unfriendly action of execution.[15]

CONCLUSION

In this chapter I have critically discussed objections to the death penalty that have been made by appealing to values salient below the Sahara desert. I have argued that the most promising sub-Saharan rationale for abolishing capital punishment invokes the underanalyzed idea that human dignity inheres in our capacity for communal relationships, understood as the combination of sharing a way of life and caring for others' quality of life, or as friendliness. This capacity of an offender would be degraded, I argued, if the state put him to death, insofar as doing so would not be necessary to correct any proportionate misuse of the capacity for community, viz., unfriendliness, on his part. However, I contended that the capacity of aggressors to enter into community with others would not be degraded if the state used deadly force against them, since doing so would be necessary to counteract a comparable unfriendliness on their part.

In other work, it would be worthwhile considering how this objection to capital punishment compares to other objections to it, ones that are not necessarily grounded in salient African ideas. In particular, if I have indeed identified the best way to criticize the death penalty by appeal to sub-Saharan values, it would be worth considering how this criticism weighs up against, say, one grounded on a more Western, and specifically Kantian, understanding of dignity. According to the Kantian, human beings have a dignity insofar as they are capable of autonomy. Which conception of dignity, one grounded on autonomy or community, is more likely to entail that the death penalty is unjust and to give the best explanation of why it is? And which conception of dignity is more plausible on the whole? Such questions deserve answers in future research.

NOTES

1. See Dirk van Zyl Smit, "The Death Penalty in Africa," *African Human Rights Law Journal* (2004) 4: 1-16. Cf. Lilian Chenwi, *Towards the Abolition of the Death Penalty in Africa: A Human Rights Perspective* (Pretoria: Pretoria University Law Press, 2007).

2. Segun Gbadegesin, "Can There Be an Adequate Justification for Capital Punishment?," in Jan Broekman *et al.* (eds.) *Social Justice and Individual Responsibility in the Welfare State* (Stuttgart: Frans Steiner Verlag, 1985), pp. 227–233 at 231–233; M. Adekunle Owoade, "Capital Punishment: Philosophical Issues and Contemporary Problems in Nigeria," *Second Order* (New Series) (1988) 1: 41–61 at 47–57; Constitutional Court of the Republic of South Africa, *The State versus T Makwanyone and M Mchunu,* Case No. CCT/3/94 (1995), http://www.saflii.org/.

3. For two examples, see Egbeke Aja, "Crime and Punishment: An Indigenous African Experience," *The Journal of Value Inquiry* (1997) 31: 353-368; and Oladele Abiodun Balogun, "A Philosophical Defence of Punishment in Traditional African Legal Culture: The Yoruba Example," *The Journal of Pan African Studies* (2009) 3: 43–54.

4. For some of the key papers, see Hashem Dezhbakhsh *et al.,* "Does Capital Punishment have a Deterrent Effect? New Evidence from Postmoratorium Panel Data," *American Law and Economics Review* (2003) 5: 344–376; H. Naci Mocan and R. Kaj Gittings, "Getting Off Death Row: Commuted Sentences and the Deterrent Effect of Capital Punishment," *Journal of Law and Economics* (2003) 46: 453–478; Joanna Shepherd, "Murders of Passion, Execution Delays, and the Deterrence of Capital Punishment," *Journal of Legal Studies* (2004) 33: 283–321.

5. I have spelled out the concept of dignity with much more care in Thaddeus Metz, "African Conceptions of Human Dignity," *Human Rights Review* (2011) DOI: 10.1007/s 12142-011-0200-4.

6. Moses, Òkè, "An Indigenous Yoruba-African Philosophical Argument against Capital Punishment," *The Journal of Philosophy, Science and Law* (2007) 7, http://www.miami.edu/ethics/jpsl.71.

7. And, furthermore, that the state cannot compensate someone (or at least not adequately!) if he has been wrongfully put to death.

8. Òkè, (note 6).

9. See Thaddeus Metz, "Human Dignity, Capital Punishment, and an African Moral Theory: Toward a New Philosophy of Human Rights," *Journal of Human Rights* (2010) 9: 81–99 at 86.

10. Constitutional Court of the Republic of South Africa, (note 2), para. 311; see also para. 313, 229, as well as Gbadegesin (note 2), p. 227, and P. M. Maduna, "The Death Penalty and Human Rights," *South African Journal on Human Rights* (1996) 12: 193–213 at 207–213.

11. For what 1 take to be the most philosophically appealing facets of *ubuntu,* see Thaddeus Metz, "Toward an African Moral Theory," *Journal of Political Philosophy* (2007) 15: 321–341.

12. I first made this argument in Metz, (note 9), pp. 86, 88–89. There are additional African-based arguments against the death penalty from the Court that are not as prominent, but there I argue that they all fall prey to the same problem of implying that deadly force is impermissible.

13. I have done the most to spell out this conception of dignity in Metz (notes 5, 9), but one can find related ideas in H. R. Botman, "The OIKOS in a Global Economic Era," in J. R. Cochrane *et al.* (eds.) *Sameness and Difference* (Washington, D.C.: The Council for Research in Values and Philosophy, 2000), http://www.crvp.org/book/Series02/ II-6/chapter_x.htm; and Bénézet Bujo, *Foundations of an African Ethic* (New York: Crossroad, 2001), p. 88.

14. The next few paragraphs borrow from Metz (note 9), pp. 92–93.

15. There are some unusual situations in which the death penalty would counteract the offender's proportionate unfriendliness, when, say, he is responsible for organizing terrorist activities and the only way to stop his followers from engaging in them would be to execute him. For more discussion see Metz, (note 9), p. 93.

DISCUSSION QUESTIONS

1. Metz raises two objections to Moses Òkè's dignity-based argument against the death penalty. How might Òkè respond to Metz's first objection?

2. Metz argues that both dignity-based arguments against the death penalty are subject to the same objection. What is it? How might supporters of those arguments respond to Metz's objection?

3. Explain Metz's main argument against the death penalty in your own words. Why, according to Metz, isn't capital punishment a justifiable way of "counteracting [a murderer's] unfriendliness"?

Torture

HENRY SHUE

Torture

Henry Shue is Professor Emeritus of Politics and International Relations at the University of Oxford. He is best known for his work on basic rights and on the ethics of climate change. In this paper, Shue argues that torture is morally forbidden. Although the paper was written in 1978, it has received renewed attention in light of controversy over American treatment of detainees in Iraq, Afghanistan, and Guantánamo Bay.

GUIDING QUESTIONS

1. Why does Shue introduce the argument comparing torture to "just-combat killing"?
2. What is the difference between "terroristic torture" and "interrogational torture," according to Shue?
3. What is the argument that torture amounts to an "assault on the defenseless"? Does Shue think it applies to "interrogational torture"? Why or why not?
4. Other than the argument that it amounts to an assault on the defenseless, what is Shue's argument that "terroristic torture" could never be morally permissible?
5. Toward the end of this paper, Shue imagines a scenario in which interrogational torture would be justified. What is his argument that we should not draw conclusions about ordinary cases based on this extraordinary, imaginary case?

Whatever one might have to say about torture, there appear to be moral reasons for not saying it. Obviously I am not persuaded by these reasons, but they deserve some mention. Mostly, they add up to a sort of Pandora's Box objection: if practically everyone is opposed to all torture, why bring it up, start people thinking about it, and risk weakening the inhibitions against what is clearly a terrible business?

Torture is indeed contrary to every relevant international law, including the laws of war. No other practice except slavery is so universally and unanimously condemned in law and human convention. Yet, unlike slavery, which is still most definitely practiced but affects relatively few people, torture is widespread and growing. According to Amnesty International, scores of governments are now using some torture—including governments which are widely viewed as fairly civilized—and a number of governments are heavily dependent upon torture for their very survival.[1]

So, to cut discussion of this objection short, Pandora's Box is open. Although virtually everyone continues ritualistically to condemn all torture publicly, the deep conviction, as reflected in actual policy, is in many cases not behind the strong language. In

Henry Shue. "Torture." *Philosophy & Public Affairs* (7)2 (Winter 1978), 124–143. Philosophy & Public Affairs © 1978 Wiley. Reproduced with permission of BLACKWELL PUBLISHING, INC. in the format Book via Copyright Clearance Center.

addition, partial justifications for some of the torture continue to circulate.[2]

One of the general contentions that keeps coming to the surface is: since killing is worse than torture, and killing is sometimes permitted, especially in war, we ought sometimes to permit torture, especially when the situation consists of a protracted, if undeclared, war between a government and its enemies. I shall try first to show the weakness of this argument. To establish that one argument for permitting some torture is unsuccessful is, of course, not to establish that no torture is to be permitted. But in the remainder of the essay I shall also try to show, far more interestingly, that a comparison between some types of killing in combat and some types of torture actually provides an insight into an important respect in which much torture is morally worse. This respect is the degree of satisfaction of the primitive moral prohibition against assault upon the defenseless. Comprehending how torture violates this prohibition helps to explain—and justify—the peculiar disgust which torture normally arouses.

The general idea of the defense of at least some torture can be explained more fully, using "just-combat killing" to refer to killing done in accord with all relevant requirements for the conduct of warfare.[3] The defense has two stages.

A Since (1) just-combat killing is total destruction of a person,

(2) torture is—usually—only partial destruction or temporary incapacitation of a person, and

(3) the total destruction of a person is a greater harm than the partial destruction of a person is,

then (4) just-combat killing is a greater harm than torture usually is;

B Since (4) just-combat killing is a greater harm than torture usually is, and

(5) just-combat killing is sometimes morally permissible,

then (6) torture is sometimes morally permissible.

To state the argument one step at a time is to reveal its main weakness. Stage B tacitly assumes that if a greater harm is sometimes permissible, then a lesser harm is too, at least sometimes. The mistake is to assume that the only consideration relevant to moral permissibility is the amount of harm done. Even if one grants that killing someone in combat is doing him or her a greater harm than torturing him or her (Stage A), it by no means follows that there could not be a justification for the greater harm that was not applicable to the lesser harm. Specifically, it would matter if some killing could satisfy other moral constraints (besides the constraint of minimizing harm) which no torture could satisfy.[4]

A defender of at least some torture could, however, readily modify the last step of the argument to deal with the point that one cannot simply weigh amounts of "harm" against each other but must consider other relevant standards as well by adding a final qualification:

(6') torture is sometimes morally permissible, provided that it meets whichever standards are satisfied by just-combat killing.

If we do not challenge the judgment that just-combat killing is a greater harm than torture usually is, the question to raise is: Can torture meet the standards satisfied by just-combat killing? If so, that might be one reason in favor of allowing such torture. If not, torture will have been reaffirmed to be an activity of an extremely low moral order.

ASSAULT UPON THE DEFENSELESS

The laws of war include an elaborate, and for the most part long-established, code for what might be described as the proper conduct of the killing of other people. Like most codes, the laws of war have been constructed piecemeal and different bits of the code serve different functions.[5] It would almost certainly be impossible to specify any one unifying purpose served by the laws of warfare as a whole. Surely major portions of the law serve to keep warfare within one sort of principle of efficiency by requiring that the minimum destruction necessary to the attainment of legitimate objectives be used.

However, not all the basic principles incorporated in the laws of war could be justified as serving the purpose of minimizing destruction. One of the most basic principles for the conduct of war (*jus in bello*) rests on the distinction between combatants and noncombatants and requires that insofar as possible, violence not be directed at noncombatants.[6] Now, obviously, there are some conceptual difficulties in trying to separate combatants and noncombatants in some guerrilla warfare and even sometimes in modern conventional warfare among industrial societies. This difficulty is a two-edged sword; it can be used to argue that it is increasingly impossible for war to be fought justly as readily as it can be used to argue that the distinction between combatants and noncombatants is obsolete. In any case, I do not now want to defend or criticize the principle of avoiding attack upon noncombatants but to isolate one of the more general moral principles this specific principle of warfare serves.

It might be thought to serve, for example, a sort of efficiency principle in that it helps to minimize human casualties and suffering. Normally, the armed forces of the opposing nations constitute only a fraction of the respective total populations. If the casualties can be restricted to these official fighters, perhaps total casualties and suffering will be smaller than they would be if human targets were unrestricted.

But this justification for the principle of not attacking noncombatants does not ring true. Unless one is determined a priori to explain everything in terms of minimizing numbers of casualties, there is little reason to believe that this principle actually functions primarily to restrict the number of casualties rather than, as its own terms suggest, the *types* of casualties.[7] A more convincing suggestion about the best justification which could be given is that the principle goes some way toward keeping combat humane, by protecting those who are assumed to be incapable of defending themselves. The principle of warfare is an instance of a more general moral principle which prohibits assaults upon the defenseless.[8]

Nonpacifists who have refined the international code for the conduct of warfare have not necessarily viewed the killing involved in war as in itself any less terrible than pacifists view it. One fundamental function of the distinction between combatants and noncombatants is to try to make a terrible combat fair, and the killing involved can seem morally tolerable to nonpacifists in large part because it is the outcome of what is conceived as a fair procedure. To the extent that the distinction between combatants and noncombatants is observed, those who are killed will be those who were directly engaged in trying to kill their killers. The fairness may be perceived to lie in this fact: that those who are killed had a reasonable chance to survive by killing instead. It was kill or be killed for both parties, and each had his or her opportunity to survive. No doubt the opportunities may not have been anywhere near equal—it would be impossible to restrict wars to equally matched opponents. But at least none of the parties to the combat were defenseless.

Now this obviously invokes a simplified, if not romanticized, portrait of warfare. And at least some aspects of the laws of warfare can legitimately be criticized for relying too heavily for their justification on a core notion that modern warfare retains aspects of a knightly joust, or a duel, which have long since vanished, if ever they were present. But the point now is not to attack or defend the efficacy of the principle of warfare that combat is more acceptable morally if restricted to official combatants, but to notice one of its moral bases, which, I am suggesting, is that it allows for a "fair fight" by means of protecting the utterly defenseless from assault. The resulting picture of war—accurate or not—is not of victim and perpetrator (or, of mutual victims) but of a winner and a loser, each of whom might have enjoyed, or suffered, the fate of the other. Of course, the satisfaction of the requirement of providing for a "fair fight" would not by itself make a conflict morally acceptable overall. An unprovoked and otherwise unjustified invasion does not become morally acceptable just because attacks upon noncombatants, use of prohibited weapons, and so on are avoided.

At least part of the peculiar disgust which torture evokes may be derived from its apparent failure to satisfy even this weak constraint of being a "fair fight." The supreme reason, of course, is that torture begins only after the fight is—for the victim—finished. Only losers are tortured. A "fair fight" may even in fact already have occurred and led to the capture of the person who is to be tortured. But now that the torture victim has exhausted all means of defense and is powerless before the victors, a fresh assault begins. The surrender is followed by new attacks upon the defeated by the now unrestrained conquerors. In this respect torture is indeed not analogous to the killing in battle of a healthy and well-armed foe; it is a cruel assault upon the defenseless. In combat the other person one kills is still a threat when killed and is killed in part for the sake of one's own survival. The torturer inflicts pain and damage upon another person who, by virtue of now being within his or her power, is no longer a threat and is entirely at the torturer's mercy.

It is in this respect of violating the prohibition against assault upon the defenseless, then, that the manner in which torture is conducted is morally more reprehensible than the manner in which killing would occur if the laws of war were honored. In this respect torture sinks below even the well-regulated mutual slaughter of a justly fought war.

TORTURE WITHIN CONSTRAINTS?

But is all torture indeed an assault upon the defenseless? For, it could be argued in support of some torture that in many cases there is something beyond the initial surrender which the torturer wants from the victim and that in such cases the victim could comply and provide the torturer with whatever is wanted. To refuse to comply with the further demand would then be to maintain a second line of defense. The victim would, in a sense, not have surrendered—at least not fully surrendered—but instead only retreated. The victim is not, on this view, utterly helpless in the face of unrestrainable assault as long as he or she holds in reserve an act of compliance which would satisfy the torturer and bring the torture to an end.

It might be proposed, then, that there could be at least one type of morally less unacceptable torture. Obviously the torture victim must remain defenseless in the literal sense, because it cannot be expected that his or her captors would provide means of defense against themselves. But an alternative to a capability for a literal defense is an effective capability for surrender, that is, a form of surrender which will in fact bring an end to attacks. In the case of torture the relevant form of surrender might seem to be a compliance with the wishes of the torturer that provides an escape from further torture.

Accordingly, the constraint on the torture that would, on this view, make it less objectionable would be this: the victim of torture must have available an act of compliance which, if performed, will end the torture. In other words, the purpose of the torture must be known to the victim, the purpose must be the performance of some action within the victim's power to perform, and the victim's performance of the desired action must produce the permanent cessation of the torture. I shall refer to torture that provides for such an act of compliance as torture that satisfies the constraint of possible compliance. As soon becomes clear, it makes a great difference what kind of act is presented as the act of compliance. And a person with an iron will, a great sense of honor, or an overwhelming commitment to a cause may choose not to accept voluntarily cessation of the torture on the terms offered. But the basic point would be merely that there should be some terms understood so that the victim retains one last portion of control over his or her fate. Escape is not defense, but it is a manner of protecting oneself. A practice of torture that allows for escape through compliance might seem immune to the charge of engaging in assault upon the defenseless. Such is the proposal.

One type of contemporary torture, however, is clearly incapable of satisfying the constraint of possible compliance. The extraction of information from the victim, which perhaps—whatever the deepest motivations of torturers may have been—has historically been a dominant explicit purpose of torture is now, in world practice, overshadowed by the goal of the intimidation of people other than the victim.[9] Torture is in many countries used primarily to intimidate potential opponents of the government from actively expressing their opposition in any form considered objectionable by the regime. Prohibited forms of expression range, among various regimes, from participation in terroristic guerrilla movements to the publication of accurate news accounts. The extent of the suffering inflicted upon the victims of the torture is proportioned, not according to the responses of the victim, but according to the expected impact of news of the torture upon other people over whom the torture victim normally has no control. The function of general intimidation of others, or deterrence of dissent, is radically different from the function of extracting specific information under the control of the victim of torture, in respects which are central to the assessment of such torture. This is naturally not to deny that any given instance of torture may serve, to varying degrees, both purposes—and, indeed, other purposes still.

Terroristic torture, as we may call this dominant type, cannot satisfy the constraint of possible compliance, because its purpose (intimidation of persons other than the victim of the torture) cannot be accomplished and may not even be capable of being influenced by the victim of the torture. The victim's suffering—indeed, the victim—is being used entirely as a means to an end over which the victim has no control. Terroristic torture is a pure case—the purest possible case—of the violation of the Kantian principle that no person may be used *only* as a means. The victim is simply a site at which great pain occurs so that others may know about it and be frightened by the prospect. The torturers have no particular reason not to make the suffering as great and as extended as possible. Quite possibly the more terrible the torture, the more intimidating it will be— this is certainly likely to be believed to be so.

Accordingly, one ought to expect extensions into the sorts of "experimentation" and other barbarities documented recently in the cases of, for example, the Pinochet government in Chile and the Amin government in Uganda.[10] Terroristic torturers have no particular reason not to carry the torture through to the murder of the victim, provided the victim's family or friends can be expected to spread the word about the price of any conduct compatible with disloyalty. Therefore, terroristic torture clearly cannot satisfy even the extremely mild constraint of providing for the possibility of compliance by its victim.[11]

The degree of need for assaults upon the defenseless initially appears to be quite different in the case of torture for the purpose of extracting information, which we may call *interrogational torture.*[12] This type of torture needs separate examination because,

however condemnable we ought in the end to consider it overall, its purpose of gaining information appears to be consistent with the observation of some constraint on the part of any torturer genuinely pursuing that purpose alone. Interrogational torture does have a built-in end-point: when the information has been obtained, the torture has accomplished its purpose and need not be continued. Thus, satisfaction of the constraint of possible compliance seems to be quite compatible with the explicit end of interrogational torture, which could be terminated upon the victim's compliance in providing the information sought.

In a fairly obvious fashion the torturer could consider himself or herself to have completed the assigned task—or probably more hopefully, any superiors who were supervising the process at some emotional distance could consider the task to be finished and put a stop to it. A pure case of interrogational torture, then, appears able to satisfy the constraint of possible compliance, since it offers an escape, in the form of providing the information wanted by the torturers, which affords some protection against further assault.

Two kinds of difficulties arise for the suggestion that even largely interrogational torture could escape the charge that it includes assaults upon the defenseless. It is hardly necessary to point out that very few actual instances of torture are likely to fall entirely within the category of interrogational torture. Torture intended primarily to obtain information is by no means always in practice held to some minimum necessary amount. To the extent that the torturer's motivation is sadistic or otherwise brutal, he or she will be strongly inclined to exceed any rational calculations about what is sufficient for the stated purpose. In view of the strength and nature of a torturer's likely passions—of, for example, hate and self-hate, disgust and self-disgust, horror and fascination, subservience toward superiors and aggression toward victims—no constraint is to be counted upon in practice.

Still, it is of at least theoretical interest to ask whether torturers with a genuine will to do so could conduct interrogational torture in a manner which would satisfy the constraint of possible compliance. In order to tell, it is essential to grasp specifically what compliance would normally involve. Almost all torture is "political" in the sense that it is inflicted by the government in power upon people who are, seem to be, or might be opposed to the government. Some torture is also inflicted by opponents of a government upon people who are, seem to be, or might be supporting the government. Possible victims of torture fall into three broad categories: the ready collaborator, the innocent bystander, and the dedicated enemy.

First, the torturers may happen upon someone who is involved with the other side but is not dedicated to such a degree that cooperation with the torturers would, from the victim's perspective, constitute a betrayal of anything highly valued. For such a person a betrayal of cause and allies might indeed serve as a form of genuine escape.

The second possibility is the capture of someone who is passive toward both sides and essentially uninvolved. If such a bystander should happen to know the relevant information—which is very unlikely—and to be willing to provide it, no torture would be called for. But what if the victim would be perfectly willing to provide the information sought in order to escape the torture but does not have the information? Systems of torture are notoriously incompetent. The usual situation is captured with icy accuracy by the reputed informal motto of the Saigon police, "If they are not guilty, beat them until they are."[13] The victims of torture need an escape not only from beatings for what they know but also from beatings for what they do not know. In short, the victim has no convincing way of demonstrating that he or she cannot comply, even when compliance is impossible. (Compare the reputed dunking test for witches: if the woman sank, she was an ordinary mortal.)

Even a torturer who would be willing to stop after learning all that could be learned, which is nothing at all if the "wrong" person is being tortured, would have difficulty discriminating among pleas. Any keeping of the tacit bargain to stop when compliance has been as complete as possible would likely be undercut by uncertainty about when the fullest possible compliance had occurred. The difficulty of demonstrating that one had collaborated as much as one could might in fact haunt the collaborator as well as the innocent, especially if his or her collaboration had struck the torturers as being of little real value.

Finally, when the torturers succeed in torturing someone genuinely committed to the other side, compliance means, in a word, betrayal; betrayal of one's ideals and one's comrades. The possibility of betrayal cannot be counted as an escape. Undoubtedly some ideals are vicious and some friends are partners in crime—this can be true of either the government, the opposition, or both. Nevertheless, a betrayal is no escape for a dedicated member of either a government or its opposition, who cannot collaborate without denying his or her highest values.[14]

For any genuine escape must be something better than settling for the lesser of two evils. One can always try to minimize one's losses—even in dilemmas from which there is no real escape. But if accepting the lesser of two evils always counted as an escape, there would be no situations from which there was no escape, except perhaps those in which all alternatives happened to be equally evil. On such a loose notion of escape, all conscripts would become volunteers, since they could always desert. And all assaults containing any alternatives would then be acceptable. An alternative which is legitimately to count as an escape must not only be preferable but also itself satisfy some minimum standard of moral acceptability. A denial of one's self does not count.

Therefore, on the whole, the apparent possibility of escape through compliance tends to melt away upon examination. The ready collaborator and the innocent bystander have some hope of an acceptable escape, but only provided that the torturers both (a) are persuaded that the victim has kept his or her part of the bargain by telling all there is to tell and (b) choose to keep their side of the bargain in a situation in which agreements cannot be enforced upon them and they have nothing to lose by continuing the torture if they please. If one is treated as if one is a dedicated enemy, as seems likely to be the standard procedure, the fact that one actually belongs in another category has no effect. On the other hand, the dedicated enemies of the torturers, who presumably tend to know more and consequently are the primary intended targets of the torture, are provided with nothing which can be considered an escape and can only protect themselves, as torture victims always have, by pretending to be collaborators or innocents, and thereby imperiling the members of these two categories.

MORALLY PERMISSIBLE TORTURE?

Still, it must reluctantly be admitted that the avoidance of assaults upon the defenseless is not the only, or even in all cases an overriding, moral consideration. And, therefore, even if terroristic and interrogational torture, each in its own way, is bound to involve attacks upon people unable to defend themselves or to escape, it is still not utterly inconceivable that instances of one or the other type of torture might sometimes, all things considered, be justified. Consequently, we must sketch the elements of an overall assessment of these two types of torture, beginning again with the dominant contemporary form: terroristic.

Anyone who thought an overall justification could be given for an episode of terroristic torture would at the least have to provide a clear statement of necessary conditions, all of which would have to be satisfied before any actions so extraordinarily cruel as terroristic torture could be morally acceptable. If the torture were actually to be justified, the conditions would, of course, have to be met in fact. An attempt to specify the necessary conditions for a morally permissible episode of terroristic torture might include conditions such as the following. A first necessary condition would be that the purpose actually being sought through the torture would need to be not only morally good but supremely important, and examples of such purposes would have to be selected by criteria of moral importance which would themselves need to be justified. Second, terroristic torture would presumably have to be the least harmful means of accomplishing the supremely important goal. Given how very harmful terroristic torture is, this could rarely be the case. And it would be unlikely unless the period of use of the torture in the society was limited in an enforceable manner. Third, it would have to be absolutely clear for what purpose the terroristic torture was being used, what would constitute achievement of that purpose, and thus, when the torture would end. The torture could not become a standard practice of government for an indefinite duration. And so on.

But is there any supremely important end to which terroristic torture could be the least harmful means? Could terroristic torture be employed for a brief interlude and then outlawed? Consider what would be involved in answering the latter question. A government could, it might seem, terrorize until the terror had accomplished its purpose and then suspend the terror. There are few, if any, clear cases of a regime's voluntarily renouncing terror after having created, through terror, a situation in which terror was no longer needed. And there is considerable evidence of the improbability of this sequence. Terroristic torture tends to become, according to Amnesty International, "administrative practice": a routine procedure institutionalized into the method of governing.[15] Some bureaus collect taxes, other bureaus conduct torture. First a suspect is arrested, next he or she is tortured. Torture gains the momentum of an ingrained element of a standard operating procedure.

Several factors appear to point in the direction of permanence. From the perspective of the victims, even where the population does not initially feel exploited, terror is very unsuitable to the generation of loyalty. This would add to the difficulty of any transition away from reliance on terror. Where the population does feel exploited even before the torture begins, the sense of outrage (which is certainly rationally justified toward the choice of victims, as we have seen) could often prove stronger than the fear of suffering. Tragically, any unlikelihood that the terroristic torture would "work" would almost guarantee that it would continue to be used. From the perspective of the torturers, it is rare for any entrenched bureau to choose to eliminate itself rather than to try to prove its essential value and the need for its own expansion. This is especially likely if the members of the operation are either thoroughly cynical or thoroughly sincere in their conviction that they are protecting "national security" or some other value taken to be supremely important. The greater burden of proof rests, I would think, on anyone who believes that controllable terroristic torture is possible.

Rousseau says at one point that pure democracy is a system of government suitable only for angels—ordinary mortals cannot handle it. If Rousseau's assumption is that principles for human beings cannot ignore the limits of the capacity of human beings, he is surely right. (This would mean that political philosophy often cannot be entirely nonempirical.) As devilish as terroristic torture is, in a sense it too may be a technique only for angels: perhaps only angels could use it within the only constraints which would make it permissible and, then, lay it aside. The partial list of criteria for the acceptable use of terroristic torture sketched above, in combination with strong evidence of the uncontrollability of terroristic torture, would come as close to a reductio ad absurdum as one could hope to produce in political philosophy. Observance of merely the constraints listed would require a degree of self-control and self-restraint, individual and bureaucratic, which might turn out to be saintly. If so, terroristic torture would have been shown to be justifiable only if it could be kept within constraints within which it could almost certainly not be kept.

But if the final objection against terroristic torture turned out to be empirical evidence that it is probably uncontrollable, would not the philosophical arguments themselves turn out to have been irrelevant? Why bother to show that terroristic torture assaults the defenseless, if in the end the case against it is going to rest on an empirical hypothesis about the improbability of keeping such torture within reasonable bounds?

The thesis about assault upon the defenseless matters, even though it is not in itself conclusive, because the uncontrollability thesis could only be probable and would also not be conclusive in itself. It could not be shown to be certain that terroristic torture will become entrenched, will be used for minor purposes, will be used when actually not necessary, and so on. And we sometimes go ahead and allow practices which might get out of hand. The relevance of showing the extent of the assault upon defenseless people is to establish how much is at stake if the practice is allowed and then runs amok. If the evidence for uncontrollability were strong, that fact plus the demonstration of extreme cruelty would constitute a decisive case against terroristic torture. It would, then, never be justified.

Much of what can be said about terroristic torture can also be said about instances involving interrogational torture. This is the case primarily because in practice there are evidently few pure cases of interrogational torture.[16] An instance of torture which is to any significant degree terroristic in purpose ought to be treated as terroristic. But if we keep in mind how far we are departing from most actual practice, we may, as before, consider instances in which the *sole* purpose of torture is to extract certain information and therefore the torturer is willing to stop as soon as he or she is sure that the victim has provided all the information which the victim has.

As argued in the preceding section, interrogational torture would in practice be difficult to make into less of an assault upon the defenseless. The supposed possibility of escape through compliance turns out to depend upon the keeping of a bargain which is entirely unenforceable within the torture situation and upon the making of discriminations among victims that would usually be difficult to make until after they no longer mattered. In fact, since any sensible willing collaborator will cooperate in a hurry, only the committed and the innocent are likely to be severely tortured. More important, in the case of someone being tortured because of profoundly held convictions, the "escape" would normally be a violation of integrity.

As with terroristic torture, any complete argument for permitting instances of interrogational torture would have to include a full specification of all necessary conditions of a permissible instance, such as its serving a supremely important purpose (with criteria of importance), its being the least harmful means to that goal, its having a clearly defined and reachable endpoint, and so on. This would not be a simple matter. Also as in the case of terroristic torture, a considerable danger exists that whatever necessary conditions were specified, any practice of torture once set in motion would gain enough momentum to burst any bonds and become a standard operating procedure. Torture is the ultimate shortcut. If it were ever permitted under any conditions, the temptation to use it increasingly would be very strong.

Nevertheless, it cannot be denied that there are imaginable cases in which the harm that could be prevented by a rare instance of pure interrogational torture would be so enormous as to outweigh the cruelty of the torture itself and, possibly, the enormous potential harm which would result if what was intended to be a rare instance was actually the breaching of the dam which would lead to a torrent of torture. There is a standard philosopher's example which someone always invokes: suppose a fanatic, perfectly willing to die rather than collaborate in the thwarting of his own scheme, has set a hidden nuclear device to explode in the heart of Paris. There is no time to evacuate the innocent people or even the movable art treasures—the only hope of preventing tragedy is to torture the perpetrator, find the device, and deactivate it.

I can see no way to deny the permissibility of torture in a case *just like this*. To allow the destruction of much of a great city and many of its people would be almost as wicked as purposely to destroy it, as the Nazis did to London and Warsaw, and the Allies did to Dresden and Tokyo, during World War II. But there is a saying in jurisprudence that hard cases make bad law, and there might well be one in philosophy that artificial cases make bad ethics. If the example is made sufficiently extraordinary, the conclusion that the torture is permissible is secure. But one cannot easily draw conclusions for ordinary cases from extraordinary ones, and as the situations described become more likely, the conclusion that the torture is permissible becomes more debatable.

Notice how unlike the circumstances of an actual choice about torture the philosopher's example is. The proposed victim of our torture is not someone we suspect of planting the device: he *is* the perpetrator. He is not some pitiful psychotic making one last play for attention: he *did* plant the device. The wiring is not backwards, the mechanism is not jammed: the device *will* destroy the city if not deactivated.

Much more important from the perspective of whether general conclusions applicable to ordinary cases can be drawn are the background conditions that tend to be assumed. The torture will not be conducted in the basement of a small-town jail in the provinces by local thugs popping pills; the prime minister and chief justice are being kept informed; and a priest and a doctor are present. The victim will not be raped or forced to eat excrement and will not collapse with a heart attack or become deranged before talking; while avoiding irreparable damage, the antiseptic pain will carefully be increased only up to the point at which the necessary information is divulged, and the doctor will then immediately administer an antibiotic and a tranquilizer. The torture is purely interrogational.[17]

Most important, such incidents do not continue to happen. There are not so many people with grievances

against this government that the torture is becoming necessary more often, and in the smaller cities, and for slightly lesser threats, and with a little less care, and so on. Any judgment that torture could be sanctioned in an isolated case without seriously weakening existing inhibitions against the more general use of torture rests on empirical hypotheses about the psychology and politics of torture. There *is* considerable evidence of all torture's metastatic tendency. If there is also evidence that interrogational torture can sometimes be used with the surgical precision which imagined justifiable cases always assume, such rare uses would have to be considered.

Does the possibility that torture might be justifiable in some of the rarefied situations which can be imagined provide any reason to consider relaxing the legal prohibitions against it? Absolutely not. The distance between the situations which must be concocted in order to have a plausible case of morally permissible torture and the situations which actually occur is, if anything, further reason why the existing prohibitions against torture should remain and should be strengthened by making torture an international crime. An act of torture ought to remain illegal so that anyone who sincerely believes such an act to be the least available evil is placed in the position of needing to justify his or her act morally in order to defend himself or herself legally. The torturer should be in roughly the same position as someone who commits civil disobedience. Anyone who thinks an act of torture is justified should have no alternative but to convince a group of peers in a public trial that all necessary conditions for a morally permissible act were indeed satisfied. If it is reasonable to put someone through torture, it is reasonable to put someone else through a careful explanation of why. If the situation approximates those in the imaginary examples in which torture seems possible to justify, a judge can surely be expected to suspend the sentence. Meanwhile, there is little need to be concerned about possible injustice to justified torturers and great need to find means to restrain totally unjustified torture.

NOTES

1. See Amnesty International, *Report on Torture* (New York: Farrar, Straus and Giroux, 1975). pp. 21–33.

2. I primarily have in mind conversations which cannot be cited, but for a written source see Roger Trinquier, *La Guerre Moderne* (Paris: La Table Ronde, *Philosophy & Public Affairs* 7, no. 2 © 1978 by Princeton University Press *00048-3915/78/0702-0124$01.00/1* 1961), pp. 39, 42, 187–191. Consider the following: "Et c'est tricher que d'admettre sereinement que l'artillerie ou l'aviation peuvent bombarder des villages où se trouvent des femmes et des enfants qui seront inutilement massacrés, alors que le plus souvent les ennemis visés auront pu s'enfuir, et refuser que des spécialistes en interrogeant un terroriste permettent de se saisir des vrais coupables et d'épargner les innocents" (p. 42).

3. By "just combat" I mean warfare which satisfies what has traditionally been called *jus in bello,* the law governing how war may be fought once underway, rather than *jus ad bellum,* the law governing when war may be undertaken.

4. Obviously one could also challenge other elements of the argument—most notably, perhaps, premise (3). Torture is usually humiliating and degrading—the pain is normally experienced naked and amidst filth. But while killing destroys life, it need not destroy dignity. Which is worse, an honorable death or a degraded existence? While I am not unsympathetic with this line of attack, I do not want to try to use it. It suffers from being an attempt somehow just to intuit the relative degrees of evil attached respectively to death and degradation. Such judgments should probably be the outcome, rather than the starting point, of an argument. The rest of the essay bears directly on them.

5. See James T. Johnson, *Ideology, Reason, and the Limitation of War: Religious and Secular Concepts 1200–1740* (Princeton: Princeton University Press, 1975). Johnson stresses the largely religious origins of *jus ad bellum* and the largely secular origins of *jus in bello.*

6. For the current law, see Geneva Convention Relative to the Protection of Civilian Persons in Time of War, 12 August 1949 [1955], 6 U.S.T. 3516; T.I.A.S. No. 3365; 75 U.N.T.S. 287. Also see United States, Department of the Army, *The Law of Land Warfare,* Field Manual 27-10 (Washington: Government Printing Office, 1956), Chap. 5, "Civilian Persons"; and United States, Department of the Air Force, *International Law—The Conduct of Armed Conflict and Air Operations,* Air Force Pamphlet 110–31 (Washington: Government Printing Office, 1976), Chap. 3, "Combatants, Noncombatants and Civilians." This Convention was to be revised at a Geneva Conference in 1977; of considerable interest are the recommendations for greater protection of civilians advanced in Sub-comm. on International Organizations of the House Comm. on Foreign Affairs, 93d Cong., 2d Sess. (1974), *Human Rights in the World Community; A Call for U.S. Leadership,* p. 38.

For the history, see Johnson, especially pp. 32–33 and 42–46, although I am interested here in the justification which could be given for the principle today, not the original justification (insofar as it was different).

The prohibition against attack upon noncombatants is considered by some authorities to be fundamental. See, for example, Jean Pictet, *The Principles of International Humanitarian Law* (Geneva: International Committee of the Red Cross, 1966), p. 53: "This general immunity of the civilian population has not been clearly defined in positive law, but it remains, in spite of many distortions, the basis of the laws of war." It is often assumed by others that the exigencies of a stable form of mutual assured destruction (MAD) make unavoidable the targeting of a nuclear deterrent on the enemy's civilian population and that therefore priority on avoidance of civilian casualties is impossible in nuclear war. For a persuasive contrary view, see Bruce M. Russett, "Assured Destruction of What? A Counter-combatant Alternative to Nuclear MADness," *Public Policy* 22 (1974): 121–138.

7. This judgment is supported by Stockholm International Peace Research Institute, *The Law of War and Dubious Weapons* (Stockholm: Almqvist & Wiksell, 1976), p. 9: "The prohibition on deliberately attacking the civilian population as such is not based exclusively on the principle of avoiding unnecessary suffering."

8. To defend the bombing of cities in World War II on the ground that *total* casualties (combatant and noncombatant) were thereby reduced is to miss, or ignore, the point.

9. See Amnesty International, 69.

10. See United Nations, General Assembly, Report of the Economic and Social Council, *Protection of Human Rights in Chile* (UN Document A/31/253, 8 October 1976, 31st Session), p. 97; and *Uganda and Human Rights: Reports to the UN Commission on Human Rights* (Geneva: International Commission of Jurists, 1977), p. 118.

11. A further source of arbitrariness is the fact that there is, in addition, no natural limit on the "appropriate" targets of terroristic torture, since the victim does not need to possess any specific information, or to have done anything in particular, except possibly to have acted "suspiciously." Even the latter is not necessary if the judgment is made, as it apparently was by the Nazis, that random terror will be the most effective.

It has been suggested that there might be a category of "deserved" terroristic torture, conducted only after a fair trial had established the guilt of the torture victim for some heinous crime. A fair procedure for determining who is to be tortured would transform the torture into a form of deterrent punishment—doubtless a cruel and unusual one.

Such torture would stand only with a general deterrent theory of punishment according to which *who* is punished depends upon guilt, but *how much* he or she is punished depends upon supposed deterrent effects. I would think that any finding that terroristic torture could be fitted within a deterrent theory of punishment (provided the torture was preceded by a fair trial) could cut either way and would be at least as plausible a reason for rejecting the general theory as it would be for accepting the particular case of terroristic torture. But I will not pursue this because I am not aware of any current practice of reserving torture as the sentence for people after they are convicted by a trial with the usual safeguards. Torture customarily precedes any semblance of a trial. One can, of course, imagine various sorts of torture other than the two common kinds discussed here.

12. These two categories of torture are not intended to be, and are not, exhaustive. See previous note.

13. Amnesty International, 166.

14. Defenders of privilege customarily portray themselves as defenders of civilization against the vilest barbarians. Self-deception sometimes further smooths the way to treating whoever are the current enemies as beneath contempt and certainly unworthy of equal respect as human beings. Consequently, I am reluctant to concede, even as a limiting case, that there are probably rare individuals so wicked as to lack integrity, or anyway to lack any integrity worthy of respect. But, what sort of integrity could one have violated by torturing Hitler?

Any very slight qualification here must not, however, be taken as a flinging wide open of the doors. To be beyond the pale in the relevant respect must involve far more than simply serving values which the torturers find abhorrent. Otherwise, license has been granted simply to torture whoever are one's greatest enemies—the only victims very many torturers would want in any case. Unfortunately, I cannot see a way to delimit those who are genuinely beyond the pale which does not beg for abuse.

15. I am assuming the unrestrained character of terroristic torture as it is actually practiced. Besides the general study by Amnesty International cited above and below, Amnesty International regularly issues studies of individual countries.

Of particular interest, perhaps, is: *Report on Allegations of Torture in Brazil,* 3d ed. (London: Amnesty International Publications, 1976). The Committee on International Relations of the United States House of Representatives has published during 1975–1977 extensive hearings on torture in dozens of countries. And other nongovernmental organizations, such as the International Commission of Jurists and the International League for Human Rights, have published careful accounts of the nature of the torture practiced in various particular countries. I believe that the category of terroristic torture used in this article is an accurate reflection of a very high proportion of the actual cases of contemporary torture. It would be tedious to document this here, but see, for example, Amnesty International, pp. 21, 26, 103, 199.

Nevertheless, it can be granted that terroristic torture is not necessarily un-restrained. It is conceivable for torture to fail to be constrained by the responses of its victim but to be subject to other constraints: to use brutality of only a certain degree, to conduct torture of unlimited (or limited) brutality but for only a limited time, to select victims who "deserve" it (compare note 11), etc. I have not discussed such a category of "constrained terroristic torture" because I believe it to be empty -for very good psychological and political reasons. On the methodological question here, see the concluding paragraphs of this article.

16. Amnesty International, pp. 24–25, 114–242.

17. For a realistic account of the effects of torture, see *Evidence of Torture: Studies by the Amnesty International Danish Medical Group* (London: Amnesty International Publications, 1977). Note in particular: "Undoubtedly the worst sequelae of torture were psychological and neurological" (p. 12). For suggestions about medical ethics for physicians attending persons being tortured, see "Declaration of Tokyo: Guidelines for Medical Doctors Concerning Torture," in United Nations, General Assembly, Note by the Secretary-General, *Torture and other Cruel, Inhuman or Degrading Treatment or Punishment in relation to Detention and Imprisonment* (UN Document A/31/234, 6 October 1976, 31st Session), Annex II.

DISCUSSION QUESTIONS

1. What is Shue's argument about whether "interrogational torture" counts as an "assault against the defenseless"? Do you find his argument convincing? Why or why not?

2. What is Shue's argument that "terroristic torture" is "uncontrollable"? Do you find this argument convincing? Why or why not?

3. Do you agree with Shue's claim that interrogational torture would be justified in the imaginary scenario involving the "fanatic" who is about to blow up Paris? Do you agree with Shue's claims about what conclusions we can draw from that thought experiment? Why or why not?

ALAN M. DERSHOWITZ

Should the Ticking Time Bomb Terrorist Be Tortured?

Alan Dershowitz is Professor Emeritus at Harvard Law School. As a lawyer, Dershowitz has worked on a number of prominent criminal cases. As a legal scholar and author, he has written books on civil liberties, the Israeli-Palestinian conflict, and many other topics. In this excerpt from his book *Why Terrorism Works,* Dershowitz argues for a well-defined legal structure for authorizing torture in certain kinds of cases.

GUIDING QUESTIONS

1. What is Dershowitz's basic argument that non-lethal torture is sometimes morally permissible?
2. What basic objection does Dershowitz raise against his own argument?
3. Dershowitz identifies four options that democratic governments have for handling torture. What are they, and what are the three basic values that make it hard to choose between them?
4. Which of the four options does Dershowitz claim is best? How does he use discussions of torture in sixteenth-century England, wiretapping warrants, and the wartime internment of Japanese Americans to support that claim?

HOW THE CURRENT TORTURE DEBATE BEGAN

Before September 11, 2001, no one thought the issue of torture would ever reemerge as a topic of serious debate in this country. Yet shortly after that watershed event, FBI agents began to leak stories suggesting that they might have to resort to torture to get some detainees, who were suspected of complicity in al-Qaeda terrorism, to provide information necessary to prevent a recurrence. An FBI source told the press that because "we are known for humanitarian treatment" of arrestees, we have been unable to get any terrorist suspects to divulge information about possible future plans. "We're into this thing for 35 days and nobody is talking," he said in obvious frustration. "Basically we're stuck." A senior FBI aide warned that "it could get to the spot where we could

go to pressure, . . . where *we won't have a choice,* and we are probably getting there."[1] But in a democracy there is *always* a choice.

In 1978 a terrorist group kidnapped Italy's former prime minister Aldo Moro and threatened to kill him. A summary of the case described the decision not to resort to torture: "During the hunt for the kidnappers of Aldo Moro, an investigator for the Italian security services proposed to General Carlo Della Chiesa [of the State Police] that a prisoner who seemed to have information on the case be tortured. The General rejected the idea, replying, 'Italy can survive the loss of Aldo Moro, but it cannot survive the introduction of torture.'" The terrorists eventually murdered Moro.[2]

The Supreme Court of Israel made the choice to disallow even moderate forms of physical pressure, despite claims that such nonlethal torture was necessary to save lives. Whether to employ any particular form of pressure on a suspect is always a matter of choice. It is the essence of democracy that we always have a choice, and we have appropriate institutional mechanisms for making choices, even—perhaps especially—choices among evils.

Constitutional democracies are, of course, constrained in the choices they may lawfully make. The Fifth Amendment prohibits compelled self-incrimination, which means that statements elicited by means of torture may not be introduced into evidence against the defendant who has been tortured.[3] But if a suspect is given immunity and then tortured into providing information about a future terrorist act, his privilege against self-incrimination has not been violated.[4] (Nor would it be violated if the information were elicited by means of "truth serum," as Judge William Webster, the former head of the FBI and the CIA, has proposed—as long as the information and its fruits were not used against him in a criminal trial.) Nor has his right to be free from "cruel and unusual punishment," since that provision of the Eighth Amendment has been interpreted to apply solely to punishment after conviction.[5] The only constitutional barriers would be the "due process" clauses of the Fifth and Fourteenth Amendments, which are quite general and sufficiently flexible to permit an argument that the only process "due" a terrorist suspected of refusing to disclose information necessary to prevent a terrorist attack is the requirement of probable cause and some degree of judicial supervision.[6]

In addition to possible constitutional constraints, we are also limited by our treaty obligations, which have the force of law. The Geneva Convention Against Torture prohibits all forms of torture and provides for no exceptions. It defines torture so broadly as to include many techniques that are routinely used around the world, including in Western democracies:

> For the purposes of this Convention, the term "torture means any act by which severe pain or suffering, whether physical or mental, is intentionally inflicted on a person for such purposes as obtaining from him or a third person information or a confession, punishing him for an act he or a third person has committed or is suspected of having committed, or intimidating or coercing him or a third person, or for any reason based on discrimination of any kind, when such pain or suffering is inflicted by or at the instigation of or with the consent

or acquiescence of a public official or other person acting in an official capacity.[7]

Many nations that routinely practice the most brutal forms of torture are signatories to this convention, but they hypocritically ignore it. The United States adopted the convention, but with a reservation: we agreed to be bound by it "only to the extent that it is consistent with . . . the Eighth Amendment." Decisions by U.S. courts have suggested that the Eighth Amendment may not prohibit the use of physical force to obtain information needed to save lives; so if the United States chose to employ nonlethal torture in such an extreme case it could arguably remain in technical compliance with its treaty obligation. Our courts routinely refuse to apply the convention to "mental" or "psychological" torture, which is commonplace.[8]

In any event, there are legal steps we could take, if we chose to resort to torture, that would make it possible for us to use this technique for eliciting information in dire circumstances. Neither the presence nor the absence of legal constraints answers the fundamental moral question: should we? This is a choice that almost no one wants to have to make. Torture has been off the agenda of civilized discourse for so many centuries that it is a subject reserved largely for historians rather than contemporary moralists (though it remains a staple of abstract philosophers debating the virtues and vices of absolutism). I have been criticized for even discussing the issue, on the ground that academic discussion confers legitimacy on a practice that deserves none. I have also been criticized for raising a red herring, since it is "well known" that torture does not work—it produces many false confessions and useless misinformation, because a person will say anything to stop being tortured.[9]

This argument is reminiscent of the ones my students make in desperately seeking to avoid the choice of evils by driving the hypothetical railroad train off the track. The tragic reality is that torture sometimes works, much though many people wish it did not. There are numerous instances in which torture has produced self-proving, truthful information that was necessary to prevent harm to civilians. The *Washington Post* has recounted a case from 1995 in which Philippine authorities tortured a terrorist into disclosing information that may have foiled plots to assassinate the pope and to crash eleven commercial airliners carrying approximately four thousand passengers into the Pacific Ocean, as well as a plan to fly a private Cessna filled with explosives into CIA headquarters. For sixty-seven days, intelligence agents beat the suspect "with a chair and a long piece of wood [breaking most of his ribs], forced water into his mouth, and crushed lighted cigarettes into his private parts"—a procedure that the Philippine intelligence service calls "tactical interrogation." After successfully employing this procedure they turned him over to American authorities, along with the lifesaving information they had beaten out of him.[10]

It is impossible to avoid the difficult moral dilemma of choosing among evils by denying the empirical reality that torture *sometimes* works, even if it does not always work.[11] No technique of crime prevention always works.

It is also sometimes argued that even when torture does produce accurate information that helps to foil a terrorist plot as the Philippine torture apparently did—there is no hard evidence that the *total amount* of terrorism is thereby reduced. The foiling of any one plot may simply result in the planning of another terrorist act, especially given the unlimited reservoir of potential terrorists. This argument may have some merit in regard to recurring acts of retail terrorism, such as the suicide bombings in Israel. Preventing one bombing may not significantly reduce the total number of civilian deaths, though it does, of course, make a difference to those who would have been killed in the thwarted explosion. But the argument is much weaker when it comes to acts of mega-terrorism, such as those prevented by the Philippine torture or the attacks perpetrated on September 11, 2001. It is the prospect of such mega-acts—and the possibility of preventing them—that raises the stakes in the torture debate.

It is precisely because torture sometimes does work and can sometimes prevent major disasters that it still exists in many parts of the world and has been totally eliminated from none. It also explains why the U.S. government sometimes "renders" terrorist suspects to nations like Egypt and Jordan, "whose intelligence services have close ties to the CIA and where they can be subjected to interrogation tactics—

including torture and threats to families—that are illegal in the United States," as the *Washington Post* has reported. "In some cases, U.S. intelligence agents remain closely involved in the interrogation. . . . 'After September 11, these sorts of movements have been occurring all of the time,' a U.S. diplomat said. 'It allows us to get information from terrorists in a way we can't do on U.S. soil.'" As former CIA counterintelligence chief Vincent Cannistraro observed: "Egyptian jails are full of guys who are missing toenails and fingernails." Our government has a "don't ask, don't tell" policy when it comes to obtaining information from other governments that practice torture.[12] All such American complicity in foreign torture violates the plain language of the Geneva Convention Against Torture, which explicitly prohibits torture from being inflicted not only by signatory nations but also "at the instigation of or with the consent or acquiescence of" any person "acting in an official capacity." As we began to come to grips with the horrible evils of mass murder by terrorists, it became inevitable that torture would return to the agenda, and it has. The recent capture of a high-ranking al-Qaeda operative, possibly with information about terrorist "sleeper cells" and future targets, has raised the question of how to compel him to disclose this important information. We must be prepared to think about the alternatives in a rational manner. We cannot evade our responsibility by pretending that torture is not being used or by having others use it for our benefit.

Accordingly, this chapter considers torture as an example of how to think about the kinds of tragic choices we are likely to confront in the age of biological, chemical, and nuclear terrorism. . . .

THE CASE FOR TORTURING THE TICKING BOMB TERRORIST

The arguments in favor of using torture as a last resort to prevent a ticking bomb from exploding and killing many people are both simple and simple-minded. Bentham constructed a compelling hypothetical case to support his utilitarian argument against an absolute prohibition on torture:

> Suppose an occasion were to arise, in which a suspicion is entertained, as strong as that which would be received as a sufficient ground for arrest and commitment as for felony—a suspicion that at this very time a considerable number of individuals are actually suffering, by illegal violence inflictions equal in intensity to those which if inflicted by the hand of justice, would universally be spoken of under the name of torture. For the purpose of rescuing from torture these hundred innocents, should any scruple be made of applying equal or superior torture, to extract the requisite information from the mouth of one criminal, who having it in his power to make known the place where at this time the enormity was practising or about to be practised, should refuse to do so? To say nothing of wisdom, could any pretence be made so much as to the praise of blind and vulgar humanity, by the man who to save one criminal, should determine to abandon 100 innocent persons to the same fate?[13]

If the torture of one guilty person would be justified to prevent the torture of a hundred innocent persons, it would seem to follow—certainly to Bentham—that it would also be justified to prevent the murder of thousands of innocent civilians in the ticking bomb case. Consider two hypothetical situations that are not, unfortunately, beyond the realm of possibility. In fact, they are both extrapolations on actual situations we have faced.

Several weeks before September 11, 2001, the Immigration and Naturalization Service detained Zacarias Moussaoui after flight instructors reported suspicious statements he had made while taking flying lessons and paying for them with large amounts of cash.[14] The government decided not to seek a warrant to search his computer. Now imagine that they had, and that they discovered he was part of a plan to destroy large occupied buildings, but without any further details. They interrogated him, gave him immunity from prosecution, and offered him large cash rewards and a new identity. He refused to talk. They then threatened him, tried to trick him, and employed every lawful technique available. He still refused. They even injected him with sodium pentothal and other truth serums, but to no avail. The attack now appeared to be imminent, but the FBI still had no idea what the target was or what means would be used to attack it. We could not simply evacuate all buildings indefinitely. An FBI agent proposes the use of nonlethal torture—say, a sterilized needle inserted under the fingernails to produce unbearable pain without any threat to health or life, or the method used in the film *Marathon Man,* a dental drill through an unanesthetized tooth.

The simple cost-benefit analysis for employing such nonlethal torture seems overwhelming: it is surely better to inflict nonlethal pain on one guilty terrorist who is illegally withholding information needed to prevent an act of terrorism than to permit a large number of innocent victims to die.[15] Pain is a lesser and more remediable harm than death; and the lives of a thousand innocent people should be valued more than the bodily integrity of one guilty person. If the variation on the Moussaoui case is not sufficiently compelling to make this point, we can always raise the stakes. Several weeks after September 11, our government received reports that a ten-kiloton nuclear weapon may have been stolen from Russia and was on its way to New York City, where it would be detonated and kill hundreds of thousands of people. The reliability of the source, code named Dragonfire, was uncertain, but assume for purposes of this hypothetical extension of the actual case that the source was a captured terrorist—like the one tortured by the Philippine authorities—who knew precisely how and where the weapon was being bought into New York and was to be detonated. Again, everything short of torture is tried, but to no avail. It is not absolutely certain torture will work, but it is our last, best hope for preventing a cataclysmic nuclear devastation in a city too large to evacuate in time. Should nonlethal torture be tried? Bentham would certainly have said yes.

The strongest argument against any resort to torture, even in the ticking bomb case, also derives from Bentham's utilitarian calculus. Experience has shown that if torture, which has been deemed illegitimate by the civilized world for more than a century, were now to be legitimated—even for limited use in one extraordinary type of situation—such legitimation would constitute an important symbolic setback in the worldwide campaign against human rights abuses. Inevitably, the legitimation of torture by the world's leading democracy would provide a welcome justification for its more widespread use in other parts of the world. Two Bentham scholars, W. L. Twining and P. E. Twining, have argued that torture is unacceptable even if it is restricted to an extremely limited category of cases:

> There is at least one good practical reason for drawing a distinction between justifying an isolated act of torture in an extreme emergency of the kind postulated above and justifying the *institutionalisation* of torture as a regular practice. The circumstances are so extreme in which most of us would be prepared to justify resort to torture, if at all, the conditions we would impose would be so stringent, the practical problems of devising and enforcing adequate safeguards so difficult and the risks of abuse so great that it would be unwise and danger-ous to entrust any government, however enlightened, with such a power. Even an out-and-out utilitarian can support an absolute prohibition against institutionalised torture on the ground that no government in the world can be trusted not to abuse the power and to satisfy in practice the conditions he would impose.[16]

Bentham's own justification was based on *case* or *act* utilitarianism—a demonstration that in a *particular case,* the benefits that would flow from the limited use of torture would outweigh its costs. The argument against any use of torture would derive from *rule* utilitarianism—which considers the impli-cations of establishing a precedent that would inevi-tably be extended beyond its limited case utilitarian justification to other possible evils of lesser mag-nitude. Even terrorism itself could be justified by a case utilitarian approach. Surely one could come up with a singular situation in which the targeting of a small number of civilians could be thought necessary to save thousands of other civilians—blowing up a German kindergarten by the relatives of inmates in a Nazi death camp, for example, and threatening to repeat the targeting of German children unless the death camps were shut down.

The reason this kind of single-case utilitarian justification is simple-minded is that it has no inherent limiting principle. If nonlethal torture of one person is justified to prevent the killing of many important people, then what if it were necessary to use lethal torture—or at least torture that posed a substantial risk of death? What if it were necessary to torture the suspect's mother or children to get him to divulge the information? What if it took threatening to kill his family, his friends, his entire village?[17] Under a simple-minded quantitative case utilitarianism, anything goes as long as the number of people tortured or killed does not exceed the number that would be saved. This is morality by numbers, unless there are other constraints on what we can properly do. These other constraints can come from rule utilitarianism or other principles of morality, such as the prohibition against deliberately punishing the innocent. Unless we are prepared to impose some limits on the use of torture or other barbaric tactics that might be of some use in preventing terrorism, we risk hurtling down a slippery slope into the abyss of amorality and ultimately tyranny. Dostoevsky captured the complexity of this dilemma in *The Brothers Karamazov* when he had Ivan pose the following question to Alyosha: "Imagine that you are creating a fabric of human destiny with the object of making men happy in the end, giving them peace at least, but that it was essential and inevitable to torture to death only one tiny creature—that baby beating its breast with its fist, for instance—and to found that edifice on its unavenged tears, would you consent to be the architect on those conditions? Tell me the truth."

A willingness to kill an innocent child suggests a willingness to do anything to achieve a necessary result. Hence the slippery slope.

It does not necessarily follow from this under-standable fear of the slippery slope that we can never consider the use of nonlethal infliction of pain, if its use were to be limited by acceptable principles of morality. After all, imprisoning a witness who refuses to testify after being given immunity is designed to be punitive—that is painful. Such imprisonment can, on occasion, produce more pain and greater risk of death than nonlethal torture. Yet we continue to threaten and use the pain of imprisonment to loosen the tongues of reluctant witnesses.[18]

It is commonplace for police and prosecutors to threaten recalcitrant suspects with prison rape. As one prosecutor put it: "You're going to be the boyfriend of a very bad man." The slippery slope is an argument of caution, not a debate stopper, since virtually every compromise with an absolutist approach to rights carries the risk of slipping further. An appropriate response to the slippery slope is to build in a principled break. For example, if nonlethal torture were legally limited to convicted terrorists who had knowledge of future massive terrorist acts, were given immunity, and still refused to provide the information, there might still be objections to the use of torture, but they would have to go beyond the slippery slope argument.[19]

The case utilitarian argument for torturing a ticking bomb terrorist is bolstered by an argument from analogy—an *a fortiori* argument. What moral principle could justify the death penalty for past individual murders and at the same time condemn nonlethal torture to prevent future mass murders? Bentham posed this rhetorical question as support for his argument. The death penalty is, of course, reserved for convicted murderers. But again, what if torture was limited to convicted terrorists who refused to divulge information about future terrorism? Consider as well the analogy to the use of deadly force against suspects fleeing from arrest for dangerous felonies of which they have not yet been convicted. Or military retaliations that produce the predictable and inevitable collateral killing of some innocent civilians. The case against torture, if made by a Quaker who opposes the death penalty, war, self-defense, and the use of lethal force against fleeing felons, is understandable. But for anyone who justifies killing on the basis of a cost-benefit analysis, the case against the use of nonlethal torture to save multiple lives is more difficult to make. In the end, absolute opposition to torture—even nonlethal torture in the ticking bomb case—may rest more on historical and aesthetic considerations than on moral or logical ones.

In debating the issue of torture, the first question I am often asked is, "Do you want to take us back to the Middle Ages?" The association between any form of torture and gruesome death is powerful in the minds of most people knowledgeable of the history of its abuses. This understandable association makes it difficult for many people to think about nonlethal torture as a technique for *saving* lives.

The second question I am asked is, "What kind of torture do you have in mind?" When I respond by describing the sterilized needle being shoved under the fingernails, the reaction is visceral and often visible—a shudder coupled with a facial gesture of disgust. Discussions of the death penalty on the other hand can be conducted without these kinds of reactions, especially now that we literally put the condemned prisoner "to sleep" by laying him out on a gurney and injecting a lethal substance into his body. There is no breaking of the neck, burning of the brain, bursting of internal organs, or gasping for breath that used to accompany hanging, electrocution, shooting, and gassing. The executioner has been replaced by a paramedical technician, as the aesthetics of death have become more acceptable. All this tends to cover up the reality that death is forever while nonlethal pain is temporary. In our modern age death is underrated, while pain is overrated.

I observed a similar phenomenon several years ago during the debate over corporal punishment that was generated by the decision of a court in Singapore to sentence a young American to medically supervised lashing with a cane. Americans who support the death penalty and who express little concern about inner-city prison conditions were outraged by the specter of a few welts on the buttocks of an American. It was an utterly irrational display of hypocrisy and double standards. Given a choice between a medically administered whipping and one month in a typical state lockup or prison, any rational and knowledgeable person would choose the lash. No one dies of welts or pain, but many inmates are raped, beaten, knifed, and otherwise mutilated and tortured in American prisons. The difference is that we don't see—and we don't want to see—what goes on behind their high walls. Nor do we want to think about it. Raising the issue of torture makes Americans think about a brutalizing and unaesthetic phenomenon that has been out of our consciousness for many years.[20]

THE THREE—OR FOUR—WAYS

The debate over the use of torture goes back many years, with Bentham supporting it in a limited category of cases, Kant opposing it as part of his categorical imperative against improperly using people as means for achieving noble ends, and Voltaire's views on the matter being "hopelessly confused."[21] The modern resort to terrorism has renewed the debate over how a rights-based society should respond to the prospect of using nonlethal torture in the ticking bomb situation. In the late 1980s the Israeli government appointed a commission headed by a retired Supreme Court justice to look into precisely that situation. The commission concluded that there are "three ways for solving this grave dilemma between the vital need to preserve the very existence of the state and its citizens, and maintain its character as a law-abiding state." The first is to allow the security services to continue to fight terrorism in "a twilight zone which is outside the realm of law." The second is "the way of the hypocrites: they declare that they abide by the rule of law, but turn a blind eye to what goes on beneath the surface." And the third, "the truthful road of the rule of law," is that the "law itself must insure a proper framework for the activity" of the security services in seeking to prevent terrorist acts.[22]

There is of course a fourth road: namely to forgo any use of torture and simply allow the preventable terrorist act to occur.[23] After the Supreme Court of Israel outlawed the use of physical pressure, the Israeli security services claimed that, as a result of the Supreme Court's decision, at least one preventable act of terrorism had been allowed to take place, one that killed several people when a bus was bombed.[24] Whether this claim is true, false, or somewhere in between is difficult to assess.[25] But it is clear that if the preventable act of terrorism was of the magnitude of the attacks of September 11, there would be a great outcry in any democracy that had deliberately refused to take available preventive action, even if it required the use of torture. During numerous public appearances since September 11, 2001, I have asked audiences for a show of hands as to how many would support the use of nonlethal torture in a ticking bomb case. Virtually every hand is raised. The few that remain down go up when I ask how many believe that torture would actually be used in such a case.

Law enforcement personnel give similar responses. This can be seen in reports of physical abuse directed against some suspects that have been detained following September 11, reports that have been taken quite seriously by at least one federal judge.[26] It is confirmed by the willingness of U.S. law enforcement officials to facilitate the torture of terrorist suspects by repressive regimes allied with our intelligence agencies. As one former CIA operative with thirty years of experience reported: "A lot of people are saying we need someone at the agency who can pull fingernails out. Others are saying, 'Let others use interrogation methods that we don't use.' The only question then is, do you want to have CIA people in the room?" The real issue, therefore, is not whether some torture would or would not be used in the ticking bomb case—it would. The question is whether it would be done openly, pursuant to a previously established legal procedure, or whether it would be done secretly, in violation of existing law.[27]

Several important values are pitted against each other in this conflict. The first is the safety and security of a nation's citizens. Under the ticking bomb scenario this value may require the use of torture, if that is the only way to prevent the bomb from exploding and killing large numbers of civilians. The second value is the preservation of civil liberties and human rights. This value requires that we not accept torture as a legitimate part of our legal system. In my debates with two prominent civil libertarians, Floyd Abrams and Harvey Silverglate, both have acknowledged that they would want nonlethal torture to be used if it could prevent thousands of deaths, but they did not want torture to be officially recognized by our legal system. As Abrams put it: "In a democracy sometimes it is necessary to do things off the books and below the radar screen." Former presidential candidate Alan Keyes took the position that although torture might be *necessary* in a given situation it could never be *right*. He suggested that a president *should* authorize the torturing of a ticking bomb terrorist, but that this act should not be legitimated by the courts or incorporated into our legal system. He argued that wrongful and indeed unlawful acts might sometimes be necessary to preserve the nation, but that no aura of legitimacy should be placed on these actions by judicial imprimatur.

This understandable approach is in conflict with the third important value: namely, open accountability and visibility in a democracy. "Off-the-book actions below the radar screen" are antithetical to the theory and practice of democracy. Citizens cannot approve or disapprove of governmental actions of which they are unaware. We have learned the lesson of history that off-the-book actions can produce terrible consequences. Richard Nixon's creation of a group of "plumbers" led to Watergate, and Ronald Reagan's authorization of an off-the-books foreign policy in Central America led to the Iran-Contra scandal. And these are only the ones we know about!

Perhaps the most extreme example of such a hypocritical approach to torture comes—not surprisingly—from the French experience in Algeria. The French army used torture extensively in seeking to prevent terrorism during a brutal colonial war from 1955 to 1957. An officer who supervised this torture, General Paul Aussaresses, wrote a book recounting what he had done and seen, including the torture of dozens of Algerians. "The best way to make a terrorist talk when he refused to say what he knew was to torture him," he boasted. Although the book was published decades after the war was over, the general was prosecuted—but not for what he had done to the Algerians. Instead, he was prosecuted for *revealing* what he had done, and seeking to justify it.[28]

In a democracy governed by the rule of law, we should never want our soldiers or our president to take any action that we deem wrong or illegal. A good test of whether an action should or should not be done is whether we are prepared to have it disclosed—perhaps not immediately, but certainly after some time has passed.

No legal system operating under the rule of law should ever tolerate an "off-the-books" approach to necessity. Even the defense of necessity must be justified lawfully. The road to tyranny has always been paved with claims of necessity made by those responsible for the security of a nation. Our system of checks and balances requires that all presidential actions, like all legislative or military actions, be consistent with governing law. If it is necessary to torture in the ticking bomb case, then our governing laws must accommodate this practice. If we refuse to change our law to accommodate any particular action, then our government should not take that action.[29]

Only in a democracy committed to civil liberties would a triangular conflict of this kind exist. Totalitarian and authoritarian regimes experience no such conflict, because they subscribe to neither the civil libertarian nor the democratic values that come in conflict with the value of security. The hard question is: which value is to be preferred when an inevitable clash occurs? One or more of these values must inevitably be compromised in making the tragic choice presented by the ticking bomb case. If we do not torture, we compromise the security and safety of our citizens. If we tolerate torture, but keep it off the books and below the radar screen, we compromise principles of democratic accountability. If we create a legal structure for limiting and controlling torture, we compromise our principled opposition to torture in all circumstances and create a potentially dangerous and expandable situation.

In 1678, the French writer François de La Rochefoucauld said that "hypocrisy is the homage that vice renders to virtue." In this case we have two vices: terrorism and torture. We also have two virtues: civil liberties and democratic accountability. Most civil libertarians I know prefer hypocrisy, precisely because it appears to avoid the conflict between security and civil liberties, but by choosing the way of the hypocrite these civil libertarians compromise the value of democratic accountability. Such is the nature of tragic choices in a complex world. As Bentham put it more than two centuries ago: "Government throughout is but a choice of evils." In a democracy, such choices must be made, whenever possible, with openness and democratic accountability, and subject to the rule of law.[30]

Consider another terrible choice of evils that could easily have been presented on September 11, 2001—and may well be presented in the future: a hijacked passenger jet is on a collision course with a densely occupied office building; the only way to prevent the destruction of the building and the killing of its occupants is to shoot down the jet, thereby killing its innocent passengers. This choice now seems easy, because the passengers are certain to die anyway and their somewhat earlier deaths will save numerous lives. The passenger jet must be shot down. But what if it were only *probable,* not certain, that the jet would crash into the building? Say, for example, we know from cell phone transmissions that passengers are struggling to regain control of the hijacked jet, but it is unlikely they will succeed in time. Or say we have no communication with the jet and all we know is that it is off course and heading toward Washington, D.C., or some other densely populated city. Under these more questionable circumstances, the question becomes *who* should make this life and death choice between evils—a decision that may turn out tragically wrong?

No reasonable person would allocate this decision to a fighter jet pilot who happened to be in the area or to a local airbase commander—unless of course there was no time for the matter to be passed up the chain of command to the president or the secretary of defense. A decision of this kind should be made at the highest level possible, with visibility and accountability.

Why is this not also true of the decision to torture a ticking bomb terrorist? Why should that choice of evils be relegated to a local policeman, FBI agent, or CIA operative, rather than to a judge, the attorney general, or the president?

There are, of course, important differences between the decision to shoot down the plane and the decision to torture the ticking bomb terrorist. Having to shoot down an airplane, though tragic, is not likely to be a recurring issue. There is no slope down which to slip.[31] Moreover, the jet to be shot down is filled with our fellow citizens—people with whom we can identify. The suspected terrorist we may choose to torture is a "they"—an enemy with whom we do not identify but with whose potential victims we do identify. The risk of making the wrong decision, or of overdoing the torture, is far greater, since we do not care as much what happens to "them" as to "us."[32] Finally, there is something different about torture—even nonlethal torture—that sets it apart from a quick death. In addition to the horrible history associated with torture, there is also the aesthetic of torture. The very idea of deliberately subjecting a captive human being to excruciating pain violates our sense of what is acceptable. On a purely rational basis, it is far worse to shoot a fleeing felon in the back and kill him, yet every civilized society authorizes shooting

such a suspect who poses dangers of committing violent crimes against the police or others. In the United States we execute convicted murderers, despite compelling evidence of the unfairness and ineffectiveness of capital punishment. Yet many of us recoil at the prospect of shoving a sterilized needle under the finger of a suspect who is refusing to divulge information that might prevent multiple deaths. Despite the irrationality of these distinctions, they are understandable, especially in light of the sordid history of torture.

We associate torture with the Inquisition, the Gestapo, the Stalinist purges, and the Argentine colonels responsible for the "dirty war." We recall it as a prelude to death, an integral part of a regime of gratuitous pain leading to a painful demise. We find it difficult to imagine a benign use of nonlethal torture to save lives.

Yet there was a time in the history of Anglo-Saxon law when torture was used to save life, rather than to take it, and when the limited administration of nonlethal torture was supervised by judges, including some who are well remembered in history.[33] This fascinating story has been recounted by Professor John Langbein of Yale Law School, and it is worth summarizing here because it helps inform the debate over whether, if torture would in fact be used in a ticking bomb case, it would be worse to make it part of the legal system, or worse to have it done off the books and below the radar screen.

In his book on legalized torture during the sixteenth and seventeenth centuries, *Torture and the Law of Proof,* Langbein demonstrates the trade-off between torture and other important values. Torture was employed for several purposes. First, it was used to secure the evidence necessary to obtain a guilty verdict under the rigorous criteria for conviction required at the time—either the testimony of two eyewitnesses or the confession of the accused himself. Circumstantial evidence, no matter how compelling, would not do. As Langbein concludes, "no society will long tolerate a legal system in which there is no prospect in convicting unrepentant persons who commit clandestine crimes. Something had to be done to extend the system to those cases. The two-eyewitness rule was hard to compromise or evade, but the confession invited 'subterfuge.'" The subterfuge that was adopted permitted the use of torture to obtain confessions from suspects against whom there was compelling circumstantial evidence of guilt. The circumstantial evidence, alone, could not be used to convict, but it was used to obtain a torture warrant. That torture warrant was in turn used to obtain a confession, which then had to be independently corroborated—at least in most cases (witchcraft and other such cases were exempted from the requirement of corroboration).[34]

Torture was also used against persons already convicted of capital crimes, such as high treason, who were thought to have information necessary to prevent attacks on the state.

Langbein studied eighty-one torture warrants, issued between 1540 and 1640, and found that in many of them, especially in "the higher cases of treasons, torture is used for discovery, and not for evidence." Torture was "used to protect the state" and "mostly that meant preventive torture to identify and forestall plots and plotters." It was only when the legal system loosened its requirement of proof (or introduced the "black box" of the jury system) and when perceived threats against the state diminished that torture was no longer deemed necessary to convict guilty defendants against whom there had previously been insufficient evidence, or to secure preventive information.[35]

The ancient Jewish system of jurisprudence came up with yet another solution to the conundrum of convicting the guilty and preventing harms to the community in the face of difficult evidentiary barriers. Jewish law required two witnesses and a specific advance warning before a guilty person could be convicted. Because confessions were disfavored, torture was not an available option. Instead, the defendant who had been seen killing by one reliable witness, or whose guilt was obvious from the circumstantial evidence, was formally acquitted, but he was then taken to a secure location and fed a concoction of barley and water until his stomach burst and he died. Moreover, Jewish law permitted more flexible forms of self-help against those who were believed to endanger the community.[36]

Every society has insisted on the incapacitation of dangerous criminals regardless of strictures in the formal legal rules. Some use torture, others use informal sanctions, while yet others create the black box of a jury, which need not explain its commonsense verdicts. Similarly, every society insists that, if there are steps that can be taken to prevent effective acts of terrorism, these steps should be taken, even if they require some compromise with other important principles.

In deciding whether the ticking bomb terrorist should be tortured, one important question is whether there would be less torture if it were done as part of the legal system, as it was in sixteenth- and seventeenth-century England, or off the books, as it is in many countries today. The Langbein study does not definitively answer this question, but it does provide some suggestive insights. The English system of torture was more visible and thus more subject to public accountability, and it is likely that torture was employed less frequently in England than in France. "During these years when it appears that torture might have become routinized in English criminal procedure, the Privy Council kept the torture power under careful control and never allowed it to fall into the hands of the regular law enforcement officers," as it had in France. In England "no law enforcement officer . . . acquired the power to use torture without special warrant." Moreover, when torture warrants were abolished, "the English experiment with torture left no traces." Because it was under centralized control, it was easier to abolish than it was in France, where it persisted for many years.[37]

It is always difficult to extrapolate from history, but it seems logical that a formal, visible, accountable, and centralized system is somewhat easier to control than an ad hoc, off-the-books, and under-the-radar-screen nonsystem. I believe, though I certainly cannot prove, that a formal requirement of a judicial warrant as a prerequisite to nonlethal torture would decrease the amount of physical violence directed against suspects. At the most obvious level, a double check is always more protective than a single check. In every instance in which a warrant is requested, a field officer has already decided that torture is justified and, in the absence of a warrant requirement, would simply proceed with the torture. Requiring that decision to be approved by a judicial officer will result in fewer instances of torture even if the judge rarely turns down a request. Moreover, I believe that most judges would require compelling evidence before they would authorize so extraordinary a departure from our constitutional norms, and law enforcement officials would be reluctant to seek a warrant unless they had compelling evidence that the suspect had information needed to prevent an imminent terrorist attack. A record would be kept of every warrant granted, and although it is certainly possible that some individual agents might torture without a warrant, they would have no excuse, since a warrant procedure would be available. They could not claim "necessity," because the decision as to whether the torture is indeed necessary has been taken out of their hands and placed in the hands of a judge. In addition, even if torture were deemed totally illegal without any exception, it would still occur, though the public would be less aware of its existence.

I also believe that the rights of the suspect would be better protected with a warrant requirement. He would be granted immunity, told that he was now compelled to testify, threatened with imprisonment if he refused to do so, and given the option of providing the requested information. Only if he refused to do what he was legally compelled to do—provide necessary information, which could not incriminate him because of the immunity—would he be threatened with torture. Knowing that such a threat was authorized by the law, he might well provide the information.[38] If he still refused to, he would be subjected to judicially monitored physical measures designed to cause excruciating pain without leaving any lasting damage.

Let me cite two examples to demonstrate why I think there would be less torture with a warrant requirement than without one. Recall the case of the alleged national security wiretap placed on the phones of Martin Luther King by the Kennedy administration in the early 1960s. This was in the days when the attorney general could authorize a national security wiretap without a warrant. Today no judge would issue a warrant in a case as flimsy as that one. When Zacarias Moussaoui was detained after raising suspicions while trying to learn how to fly an airplane, the government did not even seek a national security wiretap because its lawyers believed that a judge would not have granted one. If Moussaoui's computer could have been searched without a warrant, it almost certainly would have been.

It should be recalled that in the context of searches, our Supreme Court opted for a judicial check on the discretion of the police, by requiring a search warrant in most cases. The Court has explained the reason for the warrant requirement as follows: "The informed and deliberate determinations of magistrates. . . are to be preferred over the hurried action of officers."[39] Justice Robert Jackson elaborated:

> The point of the Fourth Amendment, which often is not grasped by zealous officers, is not that it denies law enforcement the support of the usual inferences which reasonable men draw from evidence. Its protection consists in requiring that those inferences be drawn by a neutral and detached magistrate instead of being judged by the officer engaged in the often competitive enterprise of ferreting out crime. Any assumption that evidence sufficient to support a magistrate's disinterested determination to issue a search warrant will justify the officers in making a search without a warrant would reduce the Amendment to nullity and leave the people's homes secure only in the discretion of police officers.[40]

Although torture is very different from a search, the policies underlying the warrant requirement are relevant to the question whether there is likely to be more torture or less if the decision is left entirely to field officers, or if a judicial officer has to approve a request for a torture warrant. As Abraham Maslow once observed, to a man with a hammer, everything looks like a nail. If the man with the hammer must get judicial approval before he can use it, he will probably use it less often and more carefully.

There are other, somewhat more subtle, considerations that should be factored into any decision regarding torture. There are some who see silence as a virtue when it comes to the choice among such horrible evils as torture and terrorism. It is far better, they argue, not to discuss or write about issues of this sort, lest they become legitimated. And legitimation is an appropriate concern. Justice Jackson, in his opinion in one of the cases concerning the detention of Japanese-Americans during World War II, made the following relevant observation:

> Much is said of the danger to liberty from the Army program for deporting and detaining these citizens of Japanese extraction. But a judicial construction of the due process clause that will sustain this order is a far

more subtle blow to liberty than the promulgation of the order itself. A military order, however unconstitutional, is not apt to last longer than the military emergency. Even during that period a succeeding commander may revoke it all. But once a judicial opinion rationalizes such an order to show that it conforms to the Constitution, or rather rationalizes the Constitution to show that the Constitution sanctions such an order, the Court for all time has validated the principle of racial discrimination in criminal procedure and of transplanting American citizens. The principle then lies about like a loaded weapon ready for the hand of any authority that can bring forward a plausible claim of an urgent need. Every repetition imbeds that principle more deeply in our law and thinking and expands it to new purposes. All who observe the work of courts are familiar with what Judge Cardozo described as "the tendency of a principle to expand itself to the limit of its logic." A military commander may overstep the bounds of constitutionality, and it is an incident. But if we review and approve, that passing incident becomes the doctrine of the Constitution. There it has a generative power of its own, and all that it creates will be in its own image.[41]

A similar argument can be made regarding torture: if an agent tortures, that is "an incident," but if the courts authorize it, it becomes a precedent. There is, however, an important difference between the detention of Japanese-American citizens and torture. The detentions were done openly and with presidential accountability; torture would be done secretly, with official deniability. Tolerating an off-the-book system of secret torture can also establish a dangerous precedent.

A variation on this "legitimation" argument would postpone consideration of the choice between authorizing torture and forgoing a possible tactic necessary to prevent an imminent act of terrorism until after the choice—presumably the choice to torture—has been made. In that way, the discussion would not, in itself, encourage the use of torture. If it were employed, then we could decide whether it was justified, excusable, condemnable, or something in between. The problem with that argument is that no FBI agent who tortured a suspect into disclosing information that prevented an act of mass terrorism would be prosecuted—as the policemen who tortured the kidnapper into disclosing the whereabouts of his victim were not prosecuted. In the absence of a prosecution, there would be no occasion to judge the appropriateness of the torture.

I disagree with these more passive approaches and believe that in a democracy it is always preferable to decide controversial issues in advance, rather than in the heat of battle. I would apply this rule to other tragic choices as well, including the possible use of a nuclear first strike, or retaliatory strikes—so long as the discussion was sufficiently general to avoid giving our potential enemies a strategic advantage by their knowledge of our policy.

Even if government officials decline to discuss such issues, academics have a duty to raise them and submit them to the marketplace of ideas. There may be danger in open discussion, but there is far greater danger in actions based on secret discussion, or no discussion at all.

Whatever option our nation eventually adopts—no torture even to prevent massive terrorism, no torture except with a warrant authorizing nonlethal torture, or no "officially" approved torture but its selective use beneath the radar screen—the choice is ours to make in a democracy. We do have a choice, and we should make it—before local FBI agents make it for us on the basis of a false assumption that we do not really "have a choice."

NOTES

1. Walter Pincus, "Silence of 4 Terror Probe Suspects Poses a Dilemma for FBI," *Washington Post*, 10/21/2001 (emphasis added).

2. Elizabeth Fox, "A Prosecution in Trouble," *Atlantic Monthly*, 3/1985, p. 38.

3. But see the case of *Leon v. Wainright* 734 F.2d 770 (11th Circuit 1984), holding that a *subsequent* statement made by a man who had *previously* been tortured into revealing the whereabouts of a kidnap victim could be introduced into evidence.

4. *Kastigar v. United States*, 406 U.S. 441 (1972).

5. The relevant portion of the Supreme Court decision in *Ingraham v. Wright* 430 U.S. 651, 664 (1971) reads: "An examination of the history of the [Eighth] Amendment and the decisions of this Court construing the proscription against cruel and unusual punishment confirms that it was designed to protect those convicted of crimes. We adhere to this long-standing limitation."

6. See *Leon v. Wainwright*. I have written previously on how the due process clauses could allow torture in certain circumstances. [See] Alan M. Dershowitz, "Is There a Torturous Road to Justice?" *Los Angeles Times*, 11/8/2011. . . .

7. "Convention Against Torture and Other Cruel, Inhuman or Degrading Treatment of Punishment," adopted by the U.N. General Assembly, 12/10/1984, an in effect since 6/26/1987, after it was ratified by twenty nations.

8. Samuel Francis, "Son of New World Order," *Washington Times*, 10/24/1990; *USA v. Cobb* 1 S.C.R. 587 (2001). Relevant decisions include the above-cited *Ingraham v. Wright* and *Leon v. Wainwright*.

9. William F. Buckley, among others, points to the case of the person who was tortured by Philippine authorities and confessed to having taken part in the Oklahoma City bombing, but of course no one believed him. Compare this to the account described in the next paragraph of the tortured suspect whose information may have prevented a serious act of terrorism.

10. Matthew Brzezinski, "Bust and Boom: Six Years Before the September 11 Attacks, Philippine Police Took Down an al Qaeda Cell That Had Been Plotting, Among Other Things, to Fly Explosives-Laden Planes into the Pentagon—and Possibly Some Skyscrapers," *Washington Post*, 12/30/2001. See also Alexander Cockburn, "The Wide World of Torture," *Nation*, 11/26/2001; Dough Struck, Howard Schneider, Karl Vick, and Peter Baker, "Bin Laden Followers Reach Across the Globe," *Washington Post*, 9/23/2001.

11. There can be no doubt that torture sometimes works. Jordan apparently broke the most notorious terrorist of the 1980s, Abu Nidal, by threatening his mother. Philippine police reportedly helped crack the 1993 World Trade Center bombings by torturing a suspect. Steve Chapman, "No Tortured Dilemma," *Washington Times*, 11/5/2001. It is, of course, possible that judicially supervised torture will work less effectively than unsupervised torture, since the torture will know that there are limits to the torture being inflicted. At this point in time, any empirical resolution of this issue seems speculative.

12. Rajiv Chandrasekaran and Peter Finn, "U.S. Behind Secret Transfer of Terror Suspects," *Washington Post*, 3/11/2002; Kevin Johnson and Richard Willing, "Ex-CIA Chief Revitalizes 'Truth Serum' Debate," *USA Today*, 4/26/2002.

13. Quoted in W. L. Twining and P. E. Twining, "Bentham on Torture," *Northern Ireland Legal Quarterly*, Autumn 1973, p. 347. Bentham's hypothetical question does not distinguish between torture inflicted by private persons and by governments.

14. David Johnson and Philip Shenon, "F.B.I. Curbed Scrutiny of Man Now a Suspect in the Attacks," *New York Times*, 10/6/2001.

15. It is illegal to withhold relevant information from a grand jury after receiving immunity. See *Kastigar v. U.S.* 406 U.S. 441 (1972).

16. Twining and Twining, "Bentham on Torture," pp. 348–49. The argument for the limited use of torture in the ticking bomb case falls into a category of argument know as "argument from the extreme case," which is a useful heuristic to counter arguments for absolute principles.

17. To demonstrate that this is not just in the realm of the hypothetical: "The former CIA officer said he also suggested the agency begin targeting close relatives of known terrorists and use them to obtain intelligence. 'You get the mothers and their brothers and their sisters under your complete control, and then you make that known to the target,' he said. 'You imply or you directly threaten [that] his family is going to pay the price if he makes the wrong decision.' " Bob Drogin and Greg Miller, "Spy Agencies Facing Questions of Tactics," *Los Angeles Times*, 10/28/2001.

18. One of my clients, who refused to testify against the mafia, was threatened by the government that if he persisted in his refusal the government would "leak" false information that he was cooperating, thus exposing him to mob retaliation.

19. *USA v. Cobb*.

20. On conditions in American prisons, see Alan M. Dershowitz, "Supreme Court Acknowledges Country's Other Rape Epidemic," *Boston Herald*, 6/12/1994. . . .

21. John Langbein, *Torture and the Law of Proof* (Chicago: University of Chicago Press, 1977), p. 68. Voltaire generally opposed torture but favored it in some cases.

22. A special edition of the *Israel Law Review* in 1989 presented a written symposium on the report of the Landau Commission, which investigated interrogation practices of Israel's General Security Services from 1987 to 1989.

23. A fifth approach would be simply to never discuss the issue of torture—or to postpone any such discussion until after we actually experience a ticking bomb case—but I have always believed that it is preferable to consider and discuss tragic choices before we confront them, so that the issue can be debated without recriminatory emotions and after-the-fact finger-pointing.

24. "The Supreme Court of Israel left the security services a tiny window of opportunity in extreme cases. Citing the traditional common-law defense of necessity, the Supreme Court left open the possibility that a member of the security service who honestly believed that rough interrogation was the only means available to save lives in imminent danger could raise this defense. This leaves each individual member of the security services in the position of having to guess how a court would ultimately resolve his case. That is extremely unfair to such investigators. It would have been far

better had the court required any investigator who believed that torture was necessary in order to save lives to apply to a judge. The judge would then be in a position either to authorize or refuse to authorize a 'torture warrant.' Such a procedure would requires judges to dirty their hands by authorizing torture warrants or bear the responsibility for failing to do so. Individual interrogators should not have to place their liberty at risk by guessing how a court might ultimately decide a close case. They should be able to get an advance ruling based on the evidence available at the time. . . ."

25. Charles M. Sennot, "Israeli High Court Bans Torture in Questioning; 10,000 Palestinians Subject to Tactics," *Boston Globe*, 9/7/1999.

26. Osama Awadallah, a green-card holder living in San Diego, has made various charges of torture, abuse, and denial of access to a lawyer. Shira Scheindlin, a federal district judge in New York, has confirmed the seriousness and credibility of the charges, saying Awadallah may have been "unlawfully arrested, unlawfully searched, abused by law enforcement officials, denied access to his lawyer and family." [Anthony Lewis, "Taking Our Liberties," *New York Times*, 3/9/2002.]

27. Drogin and Miller, "Spy Agencies Facing Questions of Tacics." Philip Heymann is the only person I have debated thus far who is willing to take the position that no form of torture should ever be permitted—or used—even if thousands of lives could be saved by its use. Philip B. Heymann, "Torture Should Not Be Authorized," *Boston Globe*, 2/16/2002. Whether he would act on that principled view if he were the responsible government official who was authorized to make this life and death choice—as distinguished from an academic with the luxury of expressing views without being accountable for their consequences—is a more difficult question. He has told me that he probably would authorize torture in an actual ticking bomb case, but that it would be wrong and he would expect to be punished for it.

28. Suzanne Daley, "France Is Seeking a Fine in Trial of Algerian War General," *New York Times*, 11/29/2001.

29. The necessity defense is designed to allow interstitial action to be taken in the absence of any governing law and in the absence of time to change the law. It is for the nonrecurring situation that was never anticipated by the law. The use of torture in the ticking bomb case has been debated for decades. It can surely be anticipated. See [Alan M. Dershowitz, *Shouting Fire* (New York: Little, Brown, 2002),], pp. 474–76.

Indeed, there is already one case in [American] jurisprudence in which this has occurred and the courts have considered it. In the 1984 case of *Leon v. Wainwright*, Jean Leon and an accomplice kidnapped a taxicab driver and held him for ransom. Leon was arrested while trying [to]

collect the ransom but refused to disclose where he was holding the victim. At this point, several police officers threatened him and then twisted his arm behind his back and choked him until he told them the victim's whereabouts. Although the federal appellate court disclaimed any wish to "sanction the use of force and coercion, by police officers" the judges went out of their way to state that this was not the act of "brutal law enforcement agents trying to obtain a confession." "This was instead a group of concerned officers acting in a reasonable manner to obtain information they needed in order to protect another individual from bodily harm or death." Although the court did not find it necessary to invoke the "necessity defense," since no charges were brought against the policemen who tortured the kidnapper, it described the torture as having been "motivated by the immediate *necessity* to find the victim and save his life." *Leon v. Wainwright* 734 F.2d 770, 772–73 (11th Circuit 1984) (emphasis added). If an appellate court would so regard the use of police brutality—torture—in a case involving one kidnap victim, it is not difficult to extrapolate to a situation in which hundreds or thousands of lives might hang in the balance.

30. Quoted in Twining and Twining, "Bentham on Torture," p. 345.

31. For an elaboration of this view, see Dershowitz, *Shouting Fire*, pp. 97–99.

32. [One of the pilots] who would have been responsible for [taking] down the hijacked plane heading from Pennsylvania to Washington, D.C., on September 11, 2001, has praised the passengers who apparently struggled with the hijackers, causing the plane to crash. These brave passengers spared him the dreadful task of [taking] down a plane full of fellow Americans. The stakes are different when it comes to torturing enemy terrorists.

33. Sir Edward Coke was "designated in commissions to examine particular suspects under torture." Langbein, *Torture and the Law of Proof*, p. 73.

34. Ibid., p. 7.

35. Ibid., p. 90, quoting Bacon.

36. Din Rodef, or Law of the Pursuer, refers to the halachic principle [i.e., principle in Jewish law] that one may kill a person who is threatening someone else's life. This rule was set forth in the twelfth century by Moses Maimonides, a great Talmudic scholar [and philosopher].

37. Lanbegin, *Torture and the Law of Proof*, pp. 136–37, 139.

38. When it is known that torture is a possible option, terrorists sometimes provide the information and then claim they have been tortured, in order to be able to justify their complicity to their colleagues.

39. *U.S. v. Lefkowitz*, 285 U.S. 452, 464 (1932). The Fourth Amendment provides that "The right of the people to be secure in their persons, houses, papers, and effects, against unreasonable searches and seizures, shall not be violated, and no Warrants shall issue, but upon probable cause, supported by Oath or affirmation, and particularly describing the place to be searched, and the persons or things to be seized." There are numerous exceptions to the warrant requirement. When there are exigent circumstances, for example, or when a person with authority consents to the search, the police do not need a warrant. Also, police officers can search someone without a warrant if they have lawfully arrested the person. If the police arrest someone inside a car, they can also search the interior of the car and any containers inside the car.

40. *Johnson v. U.S.* 333 U.S. 10, 13–14 (1948).

41. *Korematsu v. U.S.* 323 U.S. 214, 245–46 (1944) (Jackson, J., dissenting).

DISCUSSION QUESTIONS

1. Dershowitz describes two hypothetical scenarios in which he thinks non-lethal torture would be justified. What are they? Do you agree that non-lethal torture would be justified in those circumstances? Why or why not?
2. How does Dershowitz respond to the rule-utilitarian objection to torturing people in ticking bomb–type cases? Do you find his responses convincing? Why or why not?
3. Of the four options that Dershowitz identifies for dealing with torture in a democratic society, which do you think is best? Why?
4. What are Dershowitz's arguments for thinking that there would be less torture if there were a system to issue warrants for torture? Do you find them convincing? Why or why not?

JEFF MCMAHAN

Torture in Principle and in Practice

Jeff McMahan is White's Professor of Moral Philosophy at the University of Oxford. He has published widely in applied ethics and is especially well known for his writings on the ethics of war. In this paper, he argues that while there are hypothetical scenarios in which torture would be permissible in principle, it would still be wrong to allow torture in practice.

GUIDING QUESTIONS

1. What is "moral absolutism"? What arguments does McMahan give against moral absolutism in general?
2. What two justifications does McMahan offer for torturing a terrorist in a "ticking bomb" scenario?
3. What is McMahan's argument that even if torture is permissible in principle, it nonetheless ought to be forbidden as a matter of law?

Jeff McMahan. "Should the Ticking Bomb Terrorist Be Tortured?" *Public Affairs Quarterly*, 22(2) (Apr. 2008), 91–108. By permission of the author.

I. AGAINST MORAL ABSOLUTISMS

Those of us who oppose torture, and who are acutely conscious of the grave wrongs being committed in our name by our current government, had better be clear and convincing about the basis of our opposition. . . . I believe that the case against torture cannot plausibly take an absolutist form and that effective opposition to torture is ill-served by appeals to unexplicated and ultimately unserviceable notions such as that torture violates the victim's human dignity and undermines the perpetrator's humanity. We fail to take the problem of torture sufficiently seriously if we treat it as a simple matter of civilization versus barbarism, or a choice between respect for human dignity and a collapse into moral degradation and defilement.

In this section I will explain in a quite general way why I believe that absolute prohibitions of act-types such as torture and killing are unacceptable. In the second section, I will elucidate the grounds on which torture can be morally permissible in principle. In the third and final section, I will argue that the moral justifiability of torture in principle is virtually irrelevant in practice and that it is morally necessary that the law, both domestic and international, should prohibit the practice of torture absolutely—that is, without exceptions.

One surprising feature of the debate about torture is that a great many opponents of torture adopt the view that torture is in principle absolutely prohibited by morality.[1] Nothing, on this view, could ever justify torture. What is surprising about this is that most of these people seem to reject absolutism in all other areas of morality. Most of them, for example, are not absolutists about killing. And it is easy to see why if we survey the more prominent variants of the view that killing is absolutely prohibited by morality.

One view is that it is absolutely impermissible to kill an innocent person. Stated this simply, however, such a view is doubtfully coherent, since it seems possible that there could be cases in which whatever a person does, she will kill an innocent person. So perhaps this first version of absolutism about killing should instead be that whenever there is an option

that does not involve killing an innocent person, it is absolutely prohibited to kill an innocent person.

Note that this view applies to all instances of killing, whether the killing is intended or merely foreseen but unintended. Because of this, it provides the basis for what I think is the most plausible version of pacifism, which claims that war is invariably wrong because it always involves the killing of innocent people. This is not an absolutist form of pacifism because it does not rule out a war that would not involve any killing of innocent people—for example, a war at sea or in outer space, assuming that combatants on neither side were innocent in the relevant sense. But it is a form of pacifism because it rules out all wars that we are ever likely to fight.

The problem with this form of absolutism about killing is that it attributes excessive weight to the significance of the distinction between killing and letting die, and no weight at all to the distinction between intended killing and killing that is unintended though foreseen. Suppose that there is a single military base from which a group of bombers will fly to drop bombs on a city in which 100,000 innocent people live. Suppose further that one can save all these people by destroying the base before the bombers can take off, but that in doing so one will unavoidably kill one innocent person as a side effect. The view that an avoidable killing of an innocent person can never be permissible implies that one ought to allow the 100,000 innocent people to be killed. Although I accept that the distinction between what we do and what we allow to happen has moral significance, it is hard to believe that it is sufficiently significant to make the destruction of the base morally impermissible.

A more plausible absolutist view about killing is that it is absolutely impermissible to kill innocent people *intentionally*. Yet most of us reject this view on intuitive grounds. Suppose that, for whatever reason, the only means of preventing the destruction of the city with its 100,000 innocent inhabitants is to kill one innocent person. To suppose that it would be permissible to kill this person as a side effect, as in the previous version of the example, but absolutely impermissible to kill him intentionally, is to attribute excessive significance to intention. Although I accept that in general it is more seriously objectionable to harm a person intentionally than to cause him the same harm foreseeably but unintentionally, it is hard to believe that what an agent intends in acting can make as much difference as this form of absolutism assumes.

This is, of course, merely an appeal to intuition. But there is a more serious problem for this form of absolutism about killing. (The same problem arises for the previous version as well.) Assume that innocence is all-or-nothing, that is, that innocence is not a matter of degree. And assume further that what it is for a person to be innocent, in the sense relevant to the permissibility of killing, is that the person bears no moral responsibility for a wrong, such as a threat of wrongful harm, that might be prevented or corrected by killing him. (I believe that this is the correct substantive sense of the term in this context, though I cannot argue for that here.) Given these assumptions, noninnocence must be a matter of degree, since moral responsibility comes in degrees. Next consider two people, each of whom poses a threat to a large number of innocent people. One bears no moral responsibility whatsoever for the threat he poses (he may have been involuntarily administered a drug that has rendered him irresistibly susceptible to suggestion), while the other bears only the slightest possible degree of responsibility for the threat he poses. The view that it is absolutely impermissible intentionally to kill an innocent person, but not necessarily impermissible to kill a relevantly noninnocent person, prohibits the killing of the first threatening person, no matter how much harm he will otherwise cause, but allows that it may be permissible to kill the second, even if the harm he would cause would be of a substantially lesser magnitude.

Some may think that this objection is easy to evade because on what they regard as a more plausible conception of innocence, noninnocence is also all-or-nothing. For example, many people believe that to be innocent in war is simply to pose no threat to others, so that to be noninnocent is to pose a threat; and a person either poses a threat or he does not. But whatever conception of innocence one adopts, there remains a similar problem: the problem of uncertainty. Suppose that one could save many people's lives by killing one person, but that one cannot be certain whether this person is innocent in the relevant sense. On some conceptions of innocence it may be hard to imagine cases in which this is true. But I suspect that such cases are always possible. If, for example, we accept the common view that a person is noninnocent in the relevant sense if he poses a threat to others, we can imagine a case in which we are uncertain whether a person actually poses a threat but are confident that, if he does, killing him will eliminate the threat, and that, if he does not, killing him will nevertheless eliminate the threat in a different way. Suppose that in such a case it is reasonable to believe that there is a 60 percent probability that he does not pose a threat and is therefore innocent. It is hard to see how a theory that implies that it could be permissible to kill him could be said to assert an absolute prohibition of the intentional killing of the innocent. Yet the same seems true even as we progressively lower the probability that he is innocent. Even if there is only a 5 percent probability that he is innocent, how can a theory that implies that it is permissible to kill him count as absolutely prohibiting the intentional killing of the innocent?

It seems that an absolutist prohibition of the intentional killing of the innocent must insist that the intentional killing of a person can be permissible only if it is certain that the person is noninnocent. Yet in practice this would be tantamount to an absolute prohibition of the intentional killing of persons, whether innocent or noninnocent, since one can never in practice be *certain* of a person's noninnocence.

Some pacifists do claim that the intentional killing of any person is absolutely prohibited. So do some others who are not pacifists because they believe that it is possible to participate in war intending only to incapacitate one's enemies, though foreseeing that one's means of incapacitating them may also kill them as a side effect. But the price of accepting this view is the rejection of fundamental principles of justice. If a man is on the verge of killing an innocent child and the only way one can prevent him from doing it is to kill him, it is permissible as a matter of justice to kill him, even with the *intention* of killing him. By his own voluntary action he has made it the case that either he or the child will be killed. It is a matter of justice in the distribution of harm that he should pay the cost of his own wrongful action. Given what he has done, he cannot reasonably object to being killed, and he will not be wronged if he is killed.

Absolutists about torture must also reject these same demands of justice. If one could prevent a man from torturing an innocent child only by torturing the man, absolutists insist that it would be wrong to torture him, even if the torture one would inflict on him would be less bad than that which he would inflict on the child.[2] Questions about the just distribution of harm simply do not arise.

I will return to this problem later. Before concluding this section, it is worth noting one further objection to absolutism that is particularly acute in the case of an absolute prohibition of torture. All moral theories have line-drawing problems, but absolutist theories are particularly vulnerable, for they have to draw a line between acts that are absolutely forbidden—impermissible no matter what the alternative might be—and acts that can be permissible. Torture, no matter how it is defined, involves the deliberate infliction of harm. How severe the harm must be to count as torture is of course a question that is much debated, and to which the Bush administration's "Bybee memo" gave a preposterous answer. The important point here, however, is that if the act-type "torture" is supposed to be absolutely impermissible, it must be defined in such a way that it is plausible to say that any act that counts as torture is absolutely impermissible. Absolutism about torture would be intuitively unsustainable if, for example, twisting a person's arm to cause him pain were to count as torture. Indeed, in order for their view to seem at all plausible, absolutists are under pressure to set the threshold for torture rather high. But suppose they are able to define the threshold with some precision, so that the deliberate infliction of any degree of pain or suffering above that threshold counts as torture, provided other relevant conditions are also satisfied. They then face the question: "Why is the deliberate infliction of pain just above the threshold incapable of justification, while the infliction of pain just below it can be permissible, given that the difference between the two degrees of pain is so slight?" I doubt that there is any satisfactory response to this challenge.

2. TORTURE IN PRINCIPLE

In the debate about torture, the notorious "ticking bomb" argument enlists our intuitions against absolutism. This argument deploys the familiar hypothetical example in which we have captured a terrorist who we know has planted a nuclear bomb in a city. The bomb will detonate soon unless we disable it, but the terrorist will not tell us where it is hidden. Our only hope of finding it is to torture him.

If nothing else, this example exposes the intuitive implausibility of absolutism about torture. Opponents of torture are often evasive in addressing the question whether torture would be morally permissible in this case. I do not, however, think that it aids the credibility of the anti-torture case either to deny that torture would be permissible in this example or to refuse to address the question, as many opponents of torture do. We should concede that torture would be morally permissible, or perhaps even morally required, in this hypothetical case and then ask what implications that concession has for matters of policy and law. I will shortly try to show that advocates and opponents of torture alike tend to exaggerate the significance of the example and to misinterpret its intuitive force.

Opponents of torture tend to argue that the ticking bomb example is unrealistic, as indeed it is. It presupposes a high degree of reliability in the belief that there really is a nuclear bomb that will otherwise detonate, that the person we hold captive planted it, or at least knows where it is, that torture will be effective in getting him to reveal its location, and so on. But pointing out that actual cases have neither the epistemic features nor the all-or-nothing character of the make-believe example leaves it open that actual cases may nevertheless raise similar challenges.

There have been and will continue to be times when people who are attempting to protect innocent people from terrorism will capture a person they reasonably and indeed correctly believe to be guilty of a terrorist atrocity. They will also believe, and not wholly without reason, that by torturing this person they *might* obtain information that they could not otherwise obtain, and that might enhance their ability to prevent other terrorist acts.

These people will want, and need, moral guidance. Could we honestly tell them that they really face no moral dilemma at all, since it should be luminously obvious that to engage in torture would be absolutely impermissible, odious, and barbaric? Would it be illuminating or persuasive to tell them that torture is ruled out because it is disrespectful of human dignity? What if, following our guidance, they were to refrain from torturing their captive, only to discover later that he did indeed have knowledge of an impending terrorist act that subsequently killed thousands of innocent people and that they might have been able to prevent had they tortured him? On what grounds could we reassure them that, even so, it would have been wrong for them to torture him?

There is in fact a good answer to this question but it is not the facile answer offered by absolutism. I will offer this answer at the end of the paper. But before I can state it, I need to say more about the conditions in which torture might in principle be morally justified.

I have claimed that defenders and opponents of torture alike tend to misinterpret the significance of the ticking bomb case. Defenders of torture usually take it to show that torture can be justified as the lesser evil, or that it can have what in law is called a justification of necessity, and opponents of torture often follow them in making this assumption.[3] The lesser-evil justification is subject to different interpretations. According to the consequentialist interpretation, the intentional infliction of harm is justified whenever it prevents a greater evil, even when the evil prevented would be only slightly greater than the evil caused. There is, however, a "threshold deontological" interpretation of the lesser-evil justification according to which there are moral constraints against the intentional infliction of harm that can be overridden only when the evil averted is *substantially greater* than the one inflicted. This latter interpretation of the lesser-evil justification is intuitively more plausible than the consequentialist interpretation, but the ticking bomb case is designed to ensure that both interpretations agree that the constraint against torture is overridden by the magnitude of the harm that could be expected to be prevented only by torturing the terrorist.

As I noted, most opponents of torture are not absolutists about the prohibition of killing—even, I suspect, about the prohibition of the intentional killing of the innocent. They accept, in other words, that one or both of these lesser-evil justifications explain certain exceptions to the prohibition of killing. With respect to torture, however, they worry that even the threshold deontological justification affords insufficient protection against torture. For the essential vagueness of the notion of a "substantially greater" evil makes it difficult to challenge the claim by proponents of torture in any particular case that the threshold has been passed—that is, that the evil to be averted is great enough to justify torture. In practice, therefore, the vagueness of this notion tends to vitiate the distinction between the consequentialist and threshold deontological interpretations of the lesser-evil justification. In practice, the lesser-evil justification tends to be almost limitlessly permissive. If the ticking bomb case is understood as supporting the lesser-evil justification for torture, it becomes readily comprehensible why enthusiastic advocates of torture are fond of it, while opponents fear it.

Suppose that in the ticking bomb case the probability of compelling the terrorist to divulge the location of the bomb would be higher if we were to torture his small child before his eyes rather than torture him. A pure lesser-evil justification does not distinguish between torturing the terrorist and torturing his child. Suppose that we could be confident of breaking the terrorist's will in time either by torturing him or by torturing his child, but that his will would break much sooner if we torture the child. If torturing the child would inflict less suffering overall, despite the fact that this would in effect involve torturing two people rather than one, a pure lesser-evil justification might *require* that we torture the child. That seems to me clearly wrong, though it is testimony to the intuitive force of the threshold deontological version of the lesser-evil justification that if the stakes were high enough in the ticking bomb case, most people agree that it could be *permissible* to torture the child if that offered the best chance of saving the city, which itself, we might suppose, is home to more than a million children who would otherwise be killed.

But of course the stakes have never actually been nearly this high. To the best of my knowledge, there has never been an actual instance of torture that has been justifiable by appeal to a lesser-evil justification with a high threshold for overriding the constraint against the intentional torture of the innocent. Perhaps there will be such a case in the future. But the mere possibility that such a case will arise is no basis for the formulation of law or policy, both of which have to be focused on the cases that people actually confront. If a ticking bomb case, in which it would be morally permissible to torture a terrorist or his child, were ever actually to occur, people would not look to law or policy or even moral theory for guidance. In these conditions, it would hardly matter what our law or policy might be, and people would not need a moral theory to tell them that torture would be permissible. For people are, as we know, often greatly tempted by torture even in cases in which the stakes are minor in comparison with those in the ticking bomb case. One contingency that we really do not need to worry about is that people will be inhibited by moral scruples, or even fear of legal penalties, from engaging in torture in a ticking bomb case and will thus allow a city to be destroyed.

When I said earlier that people have missed the significance of the ticking bomb case, I meant that they have taken the lesson of the case to be that there can be a lesser-evil justification for torture. While that is true, it is uninteresting, for it is really nothing more than a rejection of moral absolutism. What people have often overlooked is that there is another and better explanation of why it would be permissible to torture the terrorist in that case. This is that the terrorist, by virtue of his responsibility for a threat of wrongful harm to innocent people, has made himself *liable* to be tortured if that is a necessary and proportionate means of preventing his having planted the bomb from killing those people. To say that he is liable to be tortured is to say that torturing him would not wrong him or violate his rights, in the circumstances.

The appeal to liability is a more familiar and less controversial justification for harming people than the appeal to the lesser evil. In criminal law, the infliction of punishment is justified on the ground that the criminal has made himself liable to be punished by virtue of his moral responsibility for a criminal act, usually involving harm to the innocent. In tort law, the imposition of a burden of compensation is usually justified on the ground that the tortfeasor has, through

her own fault, made herself liable to compensate the victim or victims of her action. And the best account of permissible defense is that it is justified because the aggressor has made himself liable by virtue of his moral responsibility for a threat of wrongful harm to another. In each case, the justification for the intentional harming of the person who is liable is a matter of justice in the distribution of harm. In criminal law, the usual view is that it is a demand of retributive justice to inflict on wrongdoers the harm that they deserve (even if the *aim* of punishment is to prevent or deter further criminal action). In tort law, it is typically thought to be a matter of corrective justice that harms should be redistributed ex post in accordance with people's responsibility for their occurrence. And in the law of self-defense, it is a matter of preventive justice that inevitable harms should be distributed ex ante to those who are morally responsible for the fact that others will otherwise be wrongfully harmed.

In the ticking bomb case, the torture of the terrorist could be justified as a matter of preventive justice. Because of his own previous wrongful action and his present wrongful refusal to avert the effects of his earlier act, he is morally responsible for having made it inevitable either that millions of innocent people will be killed or that he will be tortured. Justice requires that what is, for us, an unavoidable harm be distributed to him rather than being allowed to be inflicted by him upon the innocent. While the fact that the harm we inflict is much the lesser of the two evils effectively guarantees that our action is proportionate, it is not a necessary condition of the permissibility of our action. We would be justified in torturing the terrorist even if all we would thereby avert was the equivalent torture of only one innocent person which the terrorist's previous action had made otherwise inevitable. It is, indeed, a commonplace in the theory of justified defense that a person acting culpably can be liable to suffer a *greater* harm than that which the defensive action averts.

Note also that in this latter case involving a choice between tortures, the justification for torturing the terrorist does not extend to the torture of his child. While the terrorist's action has made him liable to be harmed, his child is entirely innocent. The child has done nothing to lose his right not to be tortured as a means of preventing even the more severe torture of another innocent person. Those who reject moral absolutism must concede that the child's right not to be tortured is capable of being overridden, but it is not overridden in this case. Neither is the terrorist's right overridden; rather, the terrorist has forfeited his right not to be tortured as a means of preventing an innocent person from being tortured.

It is also worth emphasizing that the claim here is only that the terrorist is *liable* to be tortured, not that he *deserves* to be. The claim that a person deserves to be harmed in a certain way entails that it is intrinsically good that he should suffer that particular harm. Although I accept that people can deserve to suffer, I do not accept that a person can deserve to be tortured. I do not, however, have a principled account of the upper limits of deserved suffering.[4]

I have canvassed two forms of justification for harming people—that the harming is the lesser evil and that the victim has made himself morally liable to be harmed—and have suggested that most people accept the lesser evil justification in cases in which the harm that is caused is greatly exceeded in magnitude by the harm that is prevented. This extends, in principle, even to the worst forms of torture—for example, most people would accept that it would be permissible to torture one innocent person for a year if this were the only way to prevent a billion innocent people from being tortured in an equivalent way for an equivalent period. The right not to be tortured is thus not absolute because it can in principle be overridden. . . .

I will conclude this section by noting a point that emerges when we consider the possibility of justifying torture by appeal to the victim's liability rather than by claiming that torture is the lesser evil. Discussions of interrogational torture often focus, quite rightly, on the uncertainties facing those who would practice it, and on the way these uncertainties are blithely stipulated away in hypothetical examples, such as the ticking bomb case.[5] In actual cases in which interrogational torture might be used to gain information about terrorist activity, the uncertainties and thus the possibilities for mistake are legion. The person tortured might not be a terrorist at all; even if he is, his organization may have no plans for further terrorist activity; even if it does have such plans,

he may know nothing about them; even if he knows about them, he may lie, simply saying whatever he judges his captors want to hear, in order to stop the torture; he may die under the stress; and so on.

Of these uncertainties, one is morally more significant than the others. Consider two possible types of case.

1. We are certain, beyond any possibility of reasonable doubt, that there is a terrorist plot against us, and that an attack is impending. We have captured a person of whom we reasonably believe that there is a significant probability that he is a terrorist and has knowledge that might enable us to prevent the attack. But in fact this person is not a terrorist and has no relevant knowledge.

2. We have captured a person who we are certain is a terrorist. (Suppose that there are videos, taken independently by unrelated observers, of this person throwing a grenade into a school bus filled with children, and that we later subdued and captured him as he was entering a crowded restaurant with bombs strapped beneath his overcoat.) We reasonably believe that there is a high probability of an impending terrorist attack by members of his group and that he has knowledge of the plot. But in fact (2i) there is no plot, or (2ii) while there is a plot, he has no knowledge of it.

Suppose that, in both cases, we torture the captive in an unavailing effort to gain information. In both cases, our action is objectively wrong, for we have tortured a person without any possibility that something good could come of it, though we could not have known this in advance. In both cases, it is possible that our action is *subjectively* permissible, in the sense that if our factual beliefs, which I have stipulated are reasonable or epistemically justified, were all true, then our action would be objectively permissible. Our action might be subjectively permissible if in the first case the probability of an impending, large-scale attack were very high, or if in the second case the probability that our captive is a terrorist with knowledge of the impending attack were very high.

There is nevertheless an important difference between the cases that makes it significantly more difficult to justify interrogational torture in the first case than in the second. This is that in the first case our action clearly wrongs the victim, or infringes his rights, whereas that may not be true in the second. In the second case, our captive has freely acted in ways that have now created a situation in which we reasonably believe that we must choose between torturing him and allowing a large number of innocent people to remain at significant risk of being killed by action in which he is complicit and for which he would therefore be jointly responsible. In reality, our epistemically justified belief that we face this dilemma is false. But it is the terrorist's fault, not ours, that we are in this situation. By his own culpable action, he is responsible for our justified, though false, belief that he continues to pose a threat to innocent people. He cannot reasonably expect us to accept his assertion that he has no knowledge of any further plot. He has therefore imposed on us the subjective necessity of acting in the absence of relevant knowledge. In these conditions, he has no justified complaint if we choose to try to reduce what we reasonably perceive to be the great risks that he and his confederates pose to numerous innocent people by inflicting grave harm on him.

3. TORTURE IN PRACTICE

Thus far I have argued that interrogational torture can in principle be morally justified in a way that is continuous with the primary justification for self-defense and defense of others. But having made this concession, I will now argue that it is of virtually no practical significance.[6] Whether torture can be morally permissible is less significant as a question of individual or personal morality than it is as a question of institutional morality—that is, the moral principles governing the design and functioning of social institutions. This is not to deny that the question whether it is morally permissible to participate or engage in torture arises with considerable urgency for some individuals. But I suspect that the vast majority of those who are in a position in which this question might arise are not much interested in morality and are thus disinclined to consider the question at all. For the minority who

may wrestle with the question, deliberation is likely to be conducted principally by reference to the law; that is, they will look to the law for moral guidance. And in any case, the fact that interrogational torture is not a private activity but a political one means that morality must govern the practice not primarily through appeals to individual conscience but by dictating what law and policy should say about it.

What, then, does morality imply about how the law should treat the practice of torture? In conditions in which we could expect full compliance with the law of torture but not with other areas of the law, or with morality, the law should of course permit torture on those rare occasions when it would be morally justified—that is, when the victim is liable, the stakes high, and the uncertainties minimal—and prohibit it in all other cases. But these are obviously not the conditions in which we live. In the conditions in which it is our misfortune to live, a law that would simply restate the permissions and prohibitions of morality would be wholly infeasible. In these conditions, state officials contemplating the use of torture are their own judges, and those whose goals are unjust are likely to believe that they are just. And even when they are aware that their goals are unjust, they are unlikely to have scruples about means and will claim moral justification whenever torture seems expedient. Even those whose goals are just will be tempted to perceive or to concoct a moral justification when none exists.

If we could give a precise account of the conditions of moral justification for interrogational torture and could effectively enforce a law that simply prohibited torture in all cases in which those conditions were not met, so that all those who used torture in the absence of moral justification could expect to receive punishment, then such a law might be practicable. But even if we could produce a determinate set of conditions in which interrogational torture would be morally justified, a law that permitted torture only in those conditions would not be enforceable. States would shield their own torturers and states themselves, or at least the more powerful ones, would be shielded by our general inability to bring effective sanctions against them.

It seems, therefore, that if we grant any legal permission to use torture, particularly one that attempts to capture the complex conditions of moral justification, it will be exploited by those whose aims are unjust and either abused or interpreted overly generously even by those whose aims are just. Throughout human history, torture has been very extensively employed, but the proportion of cases in which the use appears to have been morally justified seems almost negligible. Part of the reason for this is that morally decent people are naturally repelled by the practice of torture and are reluctant to use it; thus it tends to be used far more frequently by those who are both unjust and cruel.[7] This does not mean that it is uncommon among peoples that subject themselves to democratic constraints. What has been called "clean torture"—torture that leaves no marks—has been employed by Western, democratic states far more often than most of us suspect.[8] But this brings out another important point, which is that the forms of torture used by undemocratic states tend to be even more hideous than the "clean" forms favored by states with provisions for democratic accountability. The tortures inflicted at Abu Ghraib and Guantanamo are in general (at least so far as we know at present) quite tame compared to the techniques used, for example, by the fascist regimes in Latin America that the U.S. supported during the 1970s and 1980s—though these regimes were, admittedly, more interested in torture for terrorist rather than interrogational purposes, and so were free to be as imaginative as they liked.

The crucial points are these. When torture has been practiced, it has been unjustified far more often than it has been morally justified. In part this is because it is more often used by the unjust against the just than by the just against the unjust. The forms that it takes in the hands of those whose aims are unjust tend, moreover, to be the most horrible forms imaginable. It therefore seems that anything that makes it easier for governments to use torture is almost certain to have terrible effects quite generally, and in particular to result in far more violations of human rights than would otherwise occur. Any legal permission to use torture, however restricted, would make it easier for governments to use torture, and would therefore have terrible effects overall, including more extensive violations of fundamental human rights. The legal prohibition of torture must therefore be absolute.

This may strike most of us as plausible in the case of international law. Few of us, after all, would like to see loopholes that could be exploited by regimes such as the former Ba'athist government in Iraq. But some people, known as "exceptionalists," argue that the U.S. is different and that we can safely have highly circumscribed provisions for the legal use of torture without precipitating the widespread practice of torture by vicious and undemocratic regimes, which will probably use it to the extent that they find it expedient no matter what we do. But this is a delusion. The Bush administration has provided ample proof, if any were needed, that we cannot be trusted to use torture only on those very rare occasions on which it would be morally justified. More importantly, we cannot proceed with torture the way we have with nuclear weapons—that is, by permitting it to ourselves while denying it to others by means of security guarantees, economic rewards, and other measures designed to make abstention in the interests of all. If we permit ourselves to use torture, we thereby forfeit any ability we might otherwise have to prevent its use by others. Any efforts we might make would be no more effective than a proselytizing defense of vegetarianism by someone complacently enjoying a steak. Our only hope of being able to impose legal and other constraints on the use of torture in the service of unjust ends by vicious and cruel regimes is to deny the option to ourselves as well, even in cases in which we believe it would be permissible.

If we are to deny ourselves the option of torture, we must reject it not only legally but institutionally. We must make it transparent to external observers that we do not train our interrogators in techniques of torture, do not permit them the use of special equipment for torture, and will hold them liable to harsh punishments if they ever do use torture, even with higher authorization.

A total legal prohibition of torture, both domestically and internationally, will not, of course, prevent its use. But it can make it costlier for governments to practice torture, and anything that makes torture harder to practice is important.

It is also obvious that a legal prohibition of torture does not preclude an effective defense against terrorism. I think we should concede that there may be occasions on which obedience to a law prohibiting interrogational torture will make innocent people more vulnerable than they would otherwise be. But that is compatible with its being the case that we and others will be more secure overall if, in an effort to eliminate torture altogether, we refrain from using it even when it would in fact help us, at least in the short term.

There is an analogy here with an effective policy of gun control. If we could be largely successful in eliminating the private possession of handguns, we would, in general, be substantially more secure than we are with widespread private possession, even when most people's motives for keeping a gun are defensive. It is true that effective gun control would leave some guns in the hands of criminals and that there would be occasions when the policy would deny the most effective means of self-defense to a person confronted by an armed criminal. But we should simply accept the inevitability of those occasions as the price of a policy that would greatly reduce the occasions when self-defense would be necessary, thereby greatly enhancing people's security overall. It would be irrational to prefer a more effective means of defense in the event of an attack, if the cost were that one would be more likely to be attacked, and therefore far more likely to be killed than if one were denied the more effective defense.

At the end of the first section of this paper I raised the question what we could say to people who have refrained from torture only to find that if they had used it they could probably have averted a tragedy. On most occasions—that is, in cases in which the certainties about threat, liability, effectiveness, and so on that characterize the ticking bomb case are absent—what we can say to them is this:

> What you did was *subjectively* right—that is, it was what you ought to have done given the beliefs you reasonably held at the time. There was no rational basis available to you for doing otherwise than you did. In the great majority of situations epistemically indistinguishable from the one you were in, torture would have been unnecessary or ineffective and thus would have been objectively wrong. You were simply unlucky that your reasonable beliefs turned out, improbably, to be mistaken. If you could have known all the facts, it *might* have been permissible for you to use torture despite

the effect that might have had in eroding respect for the taboo against torture that we must continue to work to establish. But the level of certainty about the relevant facts that would have provided that justification was simply not available to you. In the circumstances in which you had to act, you did exactly as you ought to have done.

There are many objections to the argument of this paper that I cannot address in the space allotted to me here. But I will conclude by noting and briefly responding to one. One might accept that moral absolutism about torture is mistaken and yet believe that people generally will be more likely to repudiate the use of torture if they believe that it is absolutely prohibited by morality than if they believe that it can sometimes be permissible. If that were true, it is arguable that morality itself would require that we try to deceive ourselves and others into accepting the absolutist position. I am reasonably confident that a world without torture but in which people held mistaken absolutist beliefs would be better than a world in which people held the view for which I have argued but were insufficiently motivated by it, so that torture continued to be used. But I do not think that we face this choice. I think the case I have advanced against torture is in fact quite strong. It is simple without being simple-minded, and its simplicity makes it accessible and frees it from reliance on rhetoric for its impact. Indeed, I think it will actually be more convincing than the absolutist position to ordinary people, whose modes of thought tend to be more receptive to pragmatic considerations than to high-minded moral doctrines that they may find more suited to guiding the conduct of saints than to determining the policies of states.[9]

NOTES

1. There are many examples, of whom Juratowitch and Mayerfeld are only two. [See Ben Juratowitch, "Torture Is Always Wrong," *Public Affairs Quarterly*, vol. 22, no. 2 (April 2008), pp. 81–90; Jamie Mayerfeld, "In Defense of the Absolute Prohibition on Torture," *Public Affairs Quarterly*, vol. 22, no. 2 (April 2008), pp. 109–128.] Another is Kim Lane Scheppele, who writes, "I do in fact believe that torture is always and absolutely wrong, given the position we should accord to human dignity, even that

of terrorists." She does not, however, argue for this view but instead develops a strong pragmatic case against the practice of torture. See Kim Lane Scheppele, "Hypothetical Torture in the 'War on Terrorism,'" *Journal of National Security Law and Policy,* vol. 1 (2005), pp. 285–340, p. 287.

2. See Jeff McMahan, "Torture, Morality, and Law," *Case Western Reserve Journal of International Law,* vol. 37 (2006), pp. 241-248, pp. 243–244.

3. For example, Juratowitch (p. 81) takes the ticking bomb case to support "the consequentialist case for torture," and Scheppele (p. 293) contends that "hiding behind this hypothetical is an implicit consequentialist argument that torture would be justified if the consequences of *not* torturing were serious enough."

4. I am waiting for Shelly Kagan's much-anticipated book, *The Geometry of Desert,* to discipline and instruct my unruly intuitions about desert.

5. See, for example, Scheppele, "Hypothetical Torture in the 'War on Terrorism'"; David Luban, "Liberalism, Torture, and the Ticking Bomb," *Virginia Law Review,* vol. 91 (2005), pp. 1425–1461; and Henry Shue, "Torture in Dreamland: Disposing of the Ticking Bomb," *Case Western Reserve Journal of International Law,* vol. 37 (2006), pp. 231–239.

6. Here I am in agreement with Luban, Scheppele, Shue, and many others.

7. In the immediate aftermath of World War II, General Douglas MacArthur negotiated a secret amnesty for the Japanese perpetrators of atrocities involving medical experimentation on captives. He offered them immunity from prosecution for war crimes in exchange for exclusive access to the data derived from the experiments, which he judged would be useful to the U.S. military in future conflicts. What is noteworthy here is that he judged even so shameful an act as this to be preferable to obtaining the Japanese files by means of torture. Thus, in acquiescing in the exchange, he remarked to a subordinate: "Well, if you feel that you cannot draw out the information, we are not given to torture." See Hal Gold, *Unit 731 Testimony* (Tokyo: Tuttle Publishing, 1996), p. 97.

8. See Darius Rejali, *Torture and Democracy* (Princeton, N.J.: Princeton University Press, 2007).

9. I am immensely grateful to Jamie Mayerfeld for pressing me relentlessly to be attentive not only to the validity of my arguments but also to the ways in which they might be misinterpreted or misused. Although he will still disagree with it, this paper is much better for my exposure to his passionate concern about this issue.

DISCUSSION QUESTIONS

1. What is the "line-drawing problem" that McMahan identifies at the end of Section 1? Do you think absolutist opponents of torture can solve that problem? If so, how? If not, why not?
2. McMahan alludes to objections that "the ticking bomb example is unrealistic." In what ways is it unrealistic? Why does McMahan find such objections inadequate? Do you agree with him? Why or why not?
3. McMahan argues that a terrorist has, through his or her actions, made himself or herself liable to be tortured. What is his argument for this claim? Do you find it convincing? Why or why not?
4. How do you think Alan Dershowitz (the author of the previous reading) would respond to McMahan's argument that torture ought to be illegal?

War

JEFF MCMAHAN

The Ethics of Killing in War*

Jeff McMahan is White's Professor of Moral Philosophy at the University of Oxford. He has published widely in applied ethics and is especially well known for his writings on the ethics of war. In this paper, he challenges three of the central claims of traditional just war theory, which provides rules for when a country may go to war and how soldiers ought to act in war.

GUIDING QUESTIONS

1. What is the difference between the principles of "*jus ad bellum*" and those of "*jus in bello*"? Which of those principles determine whether a soldier is a "just combatant" or an "unjust combatant," as McMahan uses those terms?
2. What are the three tenets of the "traditional theory" of just war? Does McMahan believe that this traditional theory follows from the "permissibility of defense force" in war? Why or why not?
3. Does McMahan believe that unjust combatants are justified in fighting wars? Why or why not?
4. What is McMahan's argument for the claim that *jus in bello* is not independent of *jus ad bellum*?
5. What is the thought experiment of "The Implacable Pursuer" supposed to show? How is that relevant to McMahan's conclusions about the "requirement of discrimination"?
6. What is McMahan's "responsibility criterion"? Does McMahan think that the "laws of war" should use the responsibility criterion to determine who counts as a legitimate target in war? Why or why not?

THE TRADITIONAL THEORY OF THE JUST WAR

The traditional theory of the just war comprises two sets of principles, one governing the resort to war (*jus ad bellum*) and the other governing the conduct of war (*jus in bello*). The two set of principles are regarded, in Michael Walzer's words, as "logically independent. It is perfectly possible for a just war to be fought unjustly and for an unjust war to be fought in strict accordance with the rules" (Walzer, 1977, p 21).[1] Let us say that those who fight in a just war are *just combatants,* while those who fight in a war that is unjust because it lacks a just cause are *unjust combatants*. (A just cause is an aim that can contribute to the justification for war and that may permissibly be pursued by means of war.) The most important implication of the idea that *jus in bello* is independent of *jus ad bellum* is that it makes no difference to the permissibility of an unjust combatant's

*This is an abridged version of a paper that originally appeared in Ethics 114 (2004): 693–733. . . . Acknowledgments of my intellectual debts appear in the original version.

From Philosophia (2006) 34: 23–41.

conduct in war that he fights without a just cause. Unjust combatants do not do wrong merely by participating in an unjust war. They do wrong only if they violate the principles of *jus in bello*. So the moral position of unjust combatants is indistinguishable from that of just combatants—a condition that Walzer refers to as "the moral equality of soldiers" (Walzer, 1977, p 34). Both just and unjust combatants have "an equal right to kill" (Walzer, 1977, p 41).

They do not, of course, have a right to kill just anyone. According to the traditional theory, combatants are permitted to kill only opposing combatants. This is, indeed, the traditional understanding of the central requirement of *jus in bello*: the requirement of discrimination. All combatants, just and unjust alike, must discriminate between combatants and noncombatants, intentionally attacking only the former and not the latter.

In this paper I will challenge all three foundational tenets of the traditional theory I have identified: (1) that the principles of *jus in bello* are independent of those of *jus ad bellum*, (2) that unjust combatants can abide by the principles *of jus in bello* and do not act wrongly unless they fail to do so, and (3) that combatants are permissible targets of attack while noncombatants are not. I will begin by examining certain arguments that have been offered in support of these tenets. I will then argue that the tenets cannot be correct. Finally, I will sketch the outlines of a revisionist understanding of the just war that I believe is more consistent and plausible, as well as better grounded, than the traditional theory.

THE PRESUMED PERMISSIBILITY OF DEFENSIVE FORCE

According to the traditional theory, we are all initially "morally immune" to attack. Those who do nothing to lose their right against attack are commonly said to be *innocent*. Yet, as Thomas Nagel observes, in the tradition "'innocent' means 'currently harmless,' and it is opposed not to 'guilty' but to 'doing harm'" (Nagel, 1985, p 69). Those who retain their immunity

to attack are therefore those who are not threatening. In the context of war, the innocent are those who do not contribute to the prosecution of the war—that is, noncombatants. The noninnocent are those who pose a threat to others—that is, combatants. They lose their immunity and are liable to attack.

These observations help to reveal how the three tenets of the traditional theory follow from a general principle of the permissibility of defensive force. Because just combatants threaten unjust combatants, they are noninnocent and lose their right not to be attacked. For "that right," according to Walzer, "is lost by those who bear arms 'effectively' because they pose a danger to other people" (Walzer, 1977, p 145). It does not matter that they have done no wrong: "Simply by fighting," just combatants lose "their title to life and liberty, . . . even though, unlike aggressor states, they have committed no crime" (Walzer, 1977, p 136). This is why unjust combatants do no wrong in attacking them. But just combatants are also permitted, for the same reason, to attack the unjust combatants who threaten them. The fact that just combatants fight in a just war while unjust combatants do not is irrelevant to their respective justifications for fighting; hence the independence of *jus in bello* from *jus ad bellum*. Finally, the distinction between combatants and noncombatants is significant because combatants pose a threat and so may be the target of defensive force, while noncombatants do not pose a threat and thus cannot be the target of defensive force (though of course they can be used instrumentally in defensive efforts directed against threats posed by others).

The attempt to ground the tenets of just war theory in the permissibility of defensive force cannot succeed, however, because it is simply false that all defensive force is permissible. Consider a case at the individual level of a surprise attack. Suppose a villain attacks you, entirely without justification or excuse, but that the initial attack fails to overcome you. Rightly believing that he will otherwise kill you, you justifiably attack him in self-defense. If all necessary and proportionate defensive force is permissible, the fact that you now pose a threat to your attacker makes it permissible for him to attack you—even to kill you if your defensive counterattack threatens his life. Hobbes accepted this conclusion, but he was one of the last people to accept it. Most find it impossible to believe that, by unjustifiably attacking you and thereby making it justifiable for you to engage in self-defense, your attacker can create the conditions in which it becomes permissible for him to attack you. Most of us believe that, in these circumstances, your attacker has no right not to be attacked by you, that your attack would not wrong him in any way, and that he therefore has no right of self-defense against your justified, defensive attack (McMahan, 1994a, p 257). But if your attacker has no right of self-defense, then not all defensive force is permissible.

Walzer recognizes this. He implicitly rejects the suggestion that the three foundational tenets of the traditional theory derive from a principle of the permissibility of defensive force. Indeed, he supplies his own counterexample to such a principle: "In the course of a bank robbery, a thief shoots a guard reaching for his gun. The thief is guilty of murder, even if he claims that he acted in self-defense. Since he had no right to rob the bank, he also had no right to defend himself against the bank's defenders" (Walzer, 1977, p 128).[2] In general, Walzer believes, there is no right to self-defense in the course of criminal activity. And he concedes that "aggression is . . . a criminal activity" (Walzer, 1977, p 128). Yet he contends that participation in unjust, aggressive war differs in a morally significant way from participation in domestic criminal activities. In the domestic context, "the idea of necessity doesn't apply to criminal activity: it was not necessary to rob the bank in the first place" (Walzer, 1977, p 128). But the idea of necessity does, he argues, apply to war, and this makes a difference to the morality of participation in an unjust war. "Personal choice," he contends, "effectively disappears as soon as fighting becomes a legal obligation and a patriotic duty. . . . For the state decrees that an army of a certain size be raised, and it sets out to find the necessary men, using all the techniques of coercion and persuasion at its disposal" (Walzer, 1977, p 28). Because those who become combatants are subject to a variety of forces that compel their will—manipulation, deception, coercion, their own sense of the moral authority of the government that

commands them to fight, uncertainty about the conditions of justice in the resort to war, and so on—they cannot be held responsible for merely participating in an unjust war. As Walzer puts it, "their war is not their crime"; for "the war itself, . . . soldiers are not responsible" (Walzer, 1977, pp 37–38).

These claims about the necessity of participation in an unjust war support the contention that such participation differs *in permissibility* from ordinary criminal activity *only* if they provide a basis for claiming that participation is *justified*. But it seems that they are best understood as *excuses*. They may show that a particular unjust combatant is not a criminal and is not to be blamed or punished for what he does, but they do not show that he acts permissibly. If, however, unjust combatants are at best merely excused for fighting, while just combatants are justified, two of the central tenets of traditional just war theory must be rejected. It is false that unjust combatants do no wrong to fight provided they respect the rules of engagement. And it is false, a fortiori, that *jus in bello* is independent of *jus ad bellum*.

ARE UNJUST COMBATANTS JUSTIFIED IN FIGHTING?

The best argument of which I am aware for the claim that participation in an unjust war can be morally justified appeals to institutional considerations. There are institutions that are necessary to achieve certain important social goods—for example, coordinated decision-making, security, and so on. We therefore have moral reason to support these institutions. But they cannot operate to produce social goods unless people are willing to participate in them even when they require that people do what they believe to be wrong, and may actually *be* wrong. For example, democratic decision-making may require voting, but voting is pointless unless people will abide by the outcome of the vote, even if it commits them to support policies or participate in activities they believe to be wrong. Similarly, domestic security requires laws that, to be effective, must be enforced. Police, judges, prison officials, and others must therefore enforce the laws, including those they believe, perhaps rightly, to be unjust. For the legal system could not function if individuals were permitted selectively to enforce only those laws they believed to be just.

Similar considerations apply to participation in military institutions. It may be rational both epistemically and practically to establish an institutional division of moral labor that assigns responsibility for important decisions such as whether to go to war to those who have access to the relevant information, are positioned to coordinate an effective response to external threats, and can be held accountable for their decisions. Military institutions themselves may thus demand that only those with the assigned authority should make decisions pertaining to *jus ad bellum*. If the institutions are to survive and carry out their functions, others within them must fulfill their assigned roles even if they disagree with the decisions reached by those responsible for matters of *jus ad bellum*.

By participating in such institutions as the legal system and the military, individuals risk becoming instruments of injustice. But if the institutions are sufficiently important, this is a risk that individuals morally ought to take.

This argument, while forceful, cannot vindicate the traditional view that unjust combatants do wrong only if they violate the rules of *jus in bello*. For it grounds an unjust combatant's justification for fighting in his duty to support certain institutions and in his duties to his fellow participants in these institutions; but these duties arise only in the case of institutions that are genuinely just and important. Thus when unjust combatants are compelled by governments or military organizations that lack legitimacy to fight in wars that lack democratic authorization, they have no institutional obligations that can justify their fighting. According to this argument, therefore, some unjust combatants are justified in fighting while others are not. And this is not what the traditional view claims.

Can the appeal to institutional obligations show that at least *some* unjust combatants are justified in fighting? It seems clear that there are cases in which

such considerations as the importance of an institution in securing social goods, the importance of the individual's contribution to the survival and integrity of the institution, and the individual's obligations to other participants in the institution together make it permissible, all things considered, for the individual to do what would otherwise be wrong, and may be unjust to those who are victims of the action. In such cases, the conflict between the individual's duties is resolved in favor of the institutional duties, though the individual may also be morally required to call attention to and protest against the malfunctioning of the institution.

There are, however, some types of act that are so seriously objectionable that they cannot become permissible even if they are demanded by institutions that are both just and important. For example, while it may be permissible or even obligatory for agents of a legal system that is just overall to enforce an unjust law (especially when people can choose whether to accept the risks involved in violating that law), it may not be permissible for them to punish, and would certainly be impermissible for them to execute, a person they know to be innocent of violating the law, even if that is what their institutional role requires. The same is true of the sorts of act required by participation in an unjust war—namely, killing people who have done no wrong, collaborating in the destruction of their political institutions and way of life, and so on. These acts are beyond the limits of what can be made permissible by a person's institutional obligations. This is in part because of the gravity of the harms inflicted; but it is also, and equally essentially, because of the moral status of the victims. Just combatants, in taking up arms in a just cause—most commonly, defense against unjust aggression—do nothing to lose their right not to be attacked or killed or to make themselves morally liable to attack; they are innocent in the relevant sense. Merely posing a threat to the unjust combatants who have attacked them is, as we have seen, not enough to make them liable. So in fighting against just combatants, unjust combatants would be attacking and killing the innocent. It is generally believed to be wrong, except in the direst circumstances, to kill the innocent even as a means of averting a greater evil. How, then, could it be permissible to kill the innocent as a means of achieving aims that are *unjust*?

It is often suggested that if some soldiers or draftees refuse on moral grounds to fight in an unjust war, this could compromise the efficient functioning and perhaps even threaten the survival of valuable institutions to which these people would rightly be committed. But even if this is true, those who create, serve, and are served by valuable institutions must themselves bear the burdens when those institutions malfunction, thereby causing or threatening unjust harm to others. It would be unjust to impose the costs of their own mistakes or wrongdoing on others.

Yet the consequences for just institutions of people refusing to fight in unjust wars are unlikely to be calamitous. If the refusal to cooperate were sufficiently extensive or widespread, it could seriously degrade the ability of the aggressor (as I will call a country that fights an unjust war) to prosecute the unjust war and could even contribute to its defeat. This might be bad for the aggressor overall, but there are reasons for doubting whether it would be bad for the aggressor's just institutions—and it is just institutions rather than overall national self-interest that is the focus of the argument we are considering. Victory in an unjust war may serve the national interest but is likely on balance to have a corrupting effect on just institutions. Would just institutions in Germany, for example, have benefited from victory in World War II?

WHY *JUS IN BELLO* CANNOT BE INDEPENDENT OF *JUS AD BELLUM*

Recall that the *jus ad bellum* requirement of just cause is a constraint on the *type* of good that may permissibly be pursued by means of war. Just cause is an extrapolation into the domain of war of the insistence that one may not seriously harm or kill another person except for certain highly specific reasons, such as to defend oneself or another against an unjust threat of extreme gravity. Just as one may not kill a person as a means of promoting certain goods,

no matter how great those goods would be, so there are many goods—for example, economic growth—that may not be pursued by means of war, no matter how effective war would be in promoting them.[3]

I will argue that whether people fighting in a war have a just cause makes a great difference to whether their acts of war can satisfy the *jus in bello* requirement of proportionality. This requirement holds that for an act of war to be permissible, its bad effects must not be out of proportion to its good effects. Yet, if the requirement of just cause specifies the types of good that may legitimately be pursued by means of war, it is hard to see how, in the absence of a just cause, there can be *any* goods to weigh against the harms that the acts of unjust combatants cause. For goods that may not legitimately be pursued by means of war cannot contribute to the justification for an act of war and thus cannot figure in the proportionality calculation for that act of war.

There are, however, some goods that combatants may legitimately pursue in the course of war even when their war aims are otherwise unjust. These are the goods that would be secured by preventing just combatants from engaging in acts of war that would be wrong. There are two basic ways in which just combatants may act wrongly in fighting. One is to pursue their just cause by wrongful means—that is, by force or violence that is unnecessary, excessive, disproportionate, or indiscriminate. The other is to pursue a subordinate aim that is unjust within a war that is just overall because its guiding aims are just. As an example of the former, suppose that just combatants were to attempt to coerce the surrender of their opponents by attacking a population of innocent civilians. It would be permissible, if necessary, for unjust combatants to use military force against the just combatants to prevent this. By posing an unjust threat by their own belligerent action, the just combatants would, as I will argue later, make themselves liable to attack. In these circumstances, the good that the unjust combatants' action would achieve—saving the lives of innocents—would weigh against the harm it would cause to the just combatants, thereby making the action proportionate. This, therefore, is an act of war by unjust combatants against just combatants that is proportionate and permissible.

This, however, is of negligible significance for the defense of the traditional theory of the just war. For unjust war cannot consist entirely, or even predominantly, of acts that prevent wrongful acts by just combatants. In practice only a small proportion of the acts constitutive of an unjust war could be of this sort. If this is right, then an unjust war *cannot* be fought "in strict accordance with the rules." For except in the limited range of cases in which unjust combatants act to prevent wrongful acts by just combatants, their acts of war cannot satisfy the proportionality requirement, and satisfaction of this requirement is a necessary condition of permissible conduct in war.[4] In general, therefore, unjust combatants cannot participate in war without doing wrong. Since this is not true of just combatants, *jus in bello* cannot be independent of *jus ad bellum*. In short, the first two foundational tenets of the traditional theory are mistaken.

If the range of goods that can make the action of unjust combatants proportionate is restricted to the prevention of harms that would otherwise be unjustly inflicted by just combatants, what have just war theorists been assuming when they have claimed that acts of war by unjust combatants can be proportionate in the same way that acts of war of just combatants can? What goods have they thought might weigh against the harms caused?

Sidgwick gives a neutral statement of the requirement of proportionality, one he assumes can be satisfied by just and unjust combatants alike. He states that the "moral combatant" will seek as his end "to disable his opponent, and force him into submission," but that he must not "do him . . . any mischief of which the conduciveness to the end is slight in comparison with the amount of the mischief" (Sidgwick, 1891, p 254). Walzer interprets this passage as claiming that the "mischief" caused by an act of war must be weighed against the act's contribution to "the end of victory" (Walzer, 1977, p 129). And this is the orthodox view: the harm caused must be weighed against the "military value" of the act, which is measured by its contribution to the defeat of the enemy.

But one cannot weigh the bad effects that one would cause against the contribution one's act would make to the end of victory without having some sense of what the good effects of victory would be.

Without that, it is hard to see how there can be any constraint at all. One cannot evaluatively weigh the "mischief" caused by an act of war against the contribution the act would make to the probability of a mere *event*; one must also have some sense of the importance or value of the event. If one's cause is unjust, the value of the event—victory—would presumably be negative, not positive. How, for example, could a Nazi soldier weigh the harms he would cause to enemy combatants against the end of victory by the Nazis without assigning any value to that victory? If he believes a Nazi victory would be a great good, he is mistaken.

Perhaps some have assumed that, given the inevitable uncertainties about just cause, it is important to encourage all combatants to exercise restraint by keeping their action proportionate to what they *believe* will be its good effects. This is indeed plausible but, so understood, the requirement of proportionality is, in its application to unjust combatants, not a genuine moral requirement but merely a device that serves the moral purpose of limiting the violence of those who ought not to be engaged in warfare at all.

Another possibility is that what proportionality requires is just a neutral comparison between the harm an act of war inflicts and that which it averts *on the battlefield*. It is not concerned with the larger aims of the war at all but weighs the harms inflicted on enemy forces against the magnitude of the threat they pose to one's own forces in combat.

This view does not, however, match most people's intuitions—even though these intuitions favor the view that proportionality is a neutral requirement that can be satisfied or violated by just and unjust combatants alike. Most people believe, for example, that it would be permissible to kill ten enemy combatants (or twenty, or a hundred) to prevent the killing of a single member of one's own forces. This is in part because the threat from enemy combatants is not confined to the threat they pose to one's own forces; they also threaten the aims one has in fighting.

This view is tantamount to the claim that the good to be weighed in the proportionality calculation is the self-preservation of the unjust combatants themselves. But unjust combatants are entitled to weigh the good of their own preservation against the harms they might cause only if this good is one that it is permissible for them to pursue in the circumstances. And the assumption that it is permissible for them to use force even in self-defense is precisely what I have challenged. Those they have attacked, and who in consequence now threaten them in return, have done nothing to lose their right not to be attacked. Recall that in the individual case a culpable attacker has no right of self-defense against the defensive force of his victim. This should be true of unjust combatants as well unless the circumstances of war fundamentally alter the morality of defensive force.[5] I believe that the morality of defense in war is continuous with the morality of individual self-defense. Indeed, justified warfare just is the collective exercise of individual rights of self- and other-defense in a coordinated manner against a common threat.[6]

Two further points deserve mention here. First, self-defense by unjust combatants in general fails to meet the necessity requirement for permissible self-defense. They need not kill in order to avoid harm to themselves when they have the option of surrender. They are unjustified in killing in self-defense when they could preserve their lives simply by stopping their own wrongful action.

Second, even if acts of war by unjust combatants could in some instances be proportionate because the goods secured by self-defense would outweigh the harms caused, it remains true that no unjust war could consist entirely in justified acts of individual self- and other-defense. While a series of acts of individual self-defense might in combination count as war, it would in the nature of the case be a just rather than unjust war. Even if there can be just wars of aggression, an unjust war of defense would involve resistance to the aggressor's just cause and not just the defense of individual lives.

In summary, it is still rather mysterious what traditional just war theorists have been assuming in their supposition that unjust combatants can satisfy the requirement of proportionality in the same way that just combatants can. If, as I have argued, unjust combatants can satisfy that requirement in only a narrow range of cases, and if, as just war theorists assert, the satisfaction of the proportionality requirement is a necessary condition of permissible conduct

in war, it follows that in practice no unjust war can be fought in a permissible manner, that in general unjust combatants do wrong merely by fighting, and that because a just war can be fought entirely in a permissible manner, *jus in bello* cannot be independent of *jus ad bellum*.

THE REQUIREMENT OF DISCRIMINATION

The arguments I have advanced also challenge the third foundational tenet of the traditional theory: the requirement of discrimination. They do not challenge that requirement in its most generic formulation, which is simply that combatants must discriminate between legitimate and illegitimate targets. Rather, they challenge the assumption that the distinction between legitimate and illegitimate targets coincides with that between combatants and noncombatants. For I have argued that it is *not* permissible for unjust combatants to attack just combatants, except to prevent just combatants from engaging in wrongdoing that makes them morally liable to attack. For unjust combatants, therefore, there are, with few exceptions, *no* legitimate targets of belligerent action. In general, noncombatants *and just* combatants are alike impermissible targets for unjust combatants.

What, then, is the correct interpretation of the requirement? There must be one, for even if in general there are no legitimate targets for unjust combatants, there must, unless pacifism is true, be legitimate targets for just combatants, but also limits to what they may permissibly attack. That a just combatant's action may serve a just cause does not mean that he or she may treat anyone as fair game.

One possibility is that even if the traditional requirement is unacceptable in its application to unjust combatants, it is nevertheless correct in its application to just combatants. It might be, in other words, that just combatants are permitted to attack unjust combatants but not to conduct intentional attacks against noncombatants.[7] This view has, moreover, an obvious foundation in a more general and seemingly compelling principle. This principle is a significantly qualified variant of the principle rejected earlier that asserts the permissibility of defensive force. The qualified principle holds that, if other things are equal, it is permissible to use defensive force against anyone who poses an *unjust* threat. Because unjust combatants pose an unjust threat (except on those occasions when they are defending themselves or others against wrongful action by just combatants) but enemy noncombatants do not, it follows from the qualified general principle that enemy combatants are in general legitimate targets for just combatants but that enemy noncombatants are not.

This position has the clear advantage of being able to recognize the impermissibility of self-defense against what I have elsewhere called a Just Attacker—that is, a person who is justified in attacking another and whose victim lacks a right not to be attacked by him and is therefore not wronged by the attack. Thus, whereas the more orthodox view of Walzer and most others in the just war tradition has to assert that the conditions of war fundamentally alter the morality of defensive force, this alternative position holds that the same basic principle—the permissibility of defensive force against unjust threats—applies equally and without modification both in domestic society and in war. And although this alternative view is fundamentally antagonistic to the more orthodox view because it offers no justification for most acts of war by unjust combatants, it, or at least something very close to it, is not unfamiliar in the just war tradition.[8]

I will, however, argue against this alternative understanding as well, despite its greater plausibility. I will argue that even in its application to just combatants, the requirement of discrimination cannot take the relevant distinction to be that between combatants and noncombatants.

This alternative understanding of the requirement of discrimination asserts that it is *posing an unjust threat* that makes a person morally liable to defensive force or, to put it another way, makes the person lack a right not to be attacked in self- or other-defense. I claim, by contrast, that posing an unjust threat is neither necessary nor sufficient for liability. It is possible to pose an unjust threat without being liable to attack and possible to be liable to attack without posing an unjust threat, and indeed without posing a threat at all.

How could it be that one could pose an unjust threat to another without losing one's right not to be attacked—that is, without it becoming permissible for one's potential victim to attack in self-defense? I believe—though I concede that the implications are counterintuitive—that one does not lose one's right not to be attacked by posing an unjust threat to another *if one is in no way morally responsible for this fact.*

Consider an example drawn from science fiction:

The Implacable Pursuer A person is drugged and kidnapped while sleeping by a villain who then implants a device in her brain that *irresistibly* directs her will to the task of killing you. As a result, she will implacably pursue your death until she kills you, at which time the device will automatically deactivate itself.

Let us stipulate that the original person will continue to exist throughout the period in which her will is controlled by the device. Indeed it seems coherent to suppose that, while she pursues you, a part of her conscious mind could observe her own behavior with horror but be powerless to exert control over the movements of her body.

I claim that the Pursuer, who is what I call a *Non-Responsible Threat,* has done nothing to lose any rights or to make herself morally liable to attack. Although she is causally implicated in the threat to you, that is a wholly external fact about her position in the local causal architecture. It has no more moral significance than the fact that an innocent bystander might, through no fault of her own, occupy a position in the causal architecture that makes your killing her the only means by which you could save your own life. If you would not be permitted to kill the innocent bystander as a means of self-preservation, you are also not permitted to kill the Non-Responsible Threat in self-defense. For a Non-Responsible Threat is morally indistinguishable from an innocent bystander.[9] (There *are* lesser harms you could permissibly inflict on an innocent bystander as a means of self-preservation. Whatever harms you would be permitted to inflict on an innocent bystander in order to save your life, you would also be permitted to inflict on a Non-Responsible Threat in self-defense.)

The claim that one may not kill a Non-Responsible Threat in self-defense is contrary to common sense. It is not, however, directly relevant to the requirement of discrimination or to the morality of war, since unjust combatants are almost invariably morally responsible at least to some degree for the unjust threats they pose. Nevertheless, the case of the Pursuer does suggest that moral responsibility is important to liability. If the Pursuer were in some measure responsible for the unjust threat she poses, that would establish an obviously relevant moral asymmetry between you and her and would constitute a sufficient basis for the permissibility of your killing her if that were necessary to defend your life.

We ought not to conclude, however, that it is a person's being responsible for posing an unjust threat that makes it permissible to use force against that person in order to eliminate the threat. For a person may be morally liable to such force simply by virtue of being morally responsible for an unjust threat, even if he does not himself *pose* the threat. Consider again the case of the Pursuer. Suppose that the person who programmed and implanted the mind-control device—call him the *Initiator*—has suffered an accident and is now bedridden and tethered to a respirator. You go to plead with him only to discover that he is powerless to stop the Pursuer.[10] At that point, you see the approach of the Pursuer, who has followed you to the Initiator's house. You have only two options for saving yourself. One is to shoot the Pursuer as she approaches. The other is to flee in the Initiator's car. This car, however, is battery-powered and the only available battery is the one that is supplying power to the respirator. In order to flee the Pursuer, you must remove the power supply from the Initiator's respirator, thereby killing him.

What ought you to do: allow yourself to be killed, kill the Pursuer, who poses an unjust threat but is not responsible, or kill the Initiator, who now poses no threat but is morally responsible for the threat posed by the Pursuer? It would be permissible for you to allow yourself to be killed but in the circumstances that is not morally required. The view that asserts the permissibility of defense against unjust threats implies that you may kill the Pursuer but not the Initiator. Intuitively, however, it seems that if you must kill one or the other to save your life, you *must* kill the Initiator rather than the Pursuer. Because the Initiator is the one who is morally responsible for the fact that someone must die, he should, as a matter of justice, bear the costs of his own voluntary and culpable action. (We can assume that, if you evade the Pursuer on this occasion, she can be subdued by the police and the device can then be removed from her brain.)

In summary, what the case of the Implacable Pursuer suggests is that *posing* an unjust threat is neither necessary nor sufficient for moral liability to force or violence that is necessary to eliminate the threat. Rather, what makes a person morally liable to force or violence that is necessary to eliminate an unjust threat is *moral responsibility* for initiating or sustaining the threat (or perhaps, in some cases, for failing to eliminate the threat).

THE CRITERION OF LIABILITY AND ITS APPLICATION TO UNJUST COMBATANTS

This account of the basis of liability to defensive force has implications for the nature of the requirement of discrimination. If it is moral responsibility for an unjust threat that is the principal basis of liability to defensive (or preservative) force, it seems to follow that what makes a person a legitimate target in war is moral responsibility for an unjust threat. This assumes that permissible force in war always involves defense against an unjust threat; but it may be that there are some types of just cause for war that are not defensive, such as offensive action to recover territory or other goods that were lost to previous unjust aggression. To accommodate these possibilities, our claim should be broadened to assert that what makes a person a legitimate target in war is moral responsibility for an unjust threat or, more generally, for a wrong that provides a just cause for war. The requirement of discrimination should then hold that combatants must discriminate between those who are morally responsible for an unjust threat, or for a wrong that provides a just cause, and those who are not. It should state that while it is permissible to attack the former, it is not permissible intentionally to attack the latter—or if, more plausibly, we think that the requirement should not be absolute, it should state that there is a strong moral presumption against the permissibility of intentionally attacking those who are not responsible for an unjust threat or for a wrong that provides a just cause.

According to this understanding of the requirement of discrimination, all unjust combatants who are morally responsible for posing an unjust threat are legitimate targets of defensive or preservative attack by just combatants. This means that virtually all unjust combatants are legitimate targets because virtually all are moral agents, and because even those who are in rear areas or are asleep and are therefore not presently attacking nevertheless pose a threat by virtue of their participation in a continuing attack that has many phases coordinated over time.

It is important for understanding these claims to note that the understanding of "responsibility" employed here is eccentric.[11] Responsibility—for an unjust threat, for instance—is often assumed to require some degree of culpability, which involves both fault in the act and fault in the agent. As I will use the term, however, responsibility does not presuppose or entail culpability. If a morally responsible agent—that is, an agent with the capacity for autonomous deliberation and action—creates an unjust threat through voluntary action that is wrongful but fully excused, she is to some extent responsible for that threat even though she is not blamable.[12] In such a case there is fault in the act but not in the agent. I believe, moreover, that there can be responsibility even in the absence of fault in the act—that is, even when a person acts permissibly. If, for example, a person voluntarily engages in a permissible but foreseeably risk-imposing activity, such as driving a car, that person will be responsible if, contrary to reasonable expectation and through no fault on the part of the agent, that activity creates a threat or causes harm to which the victim is in no way liable. It is important to bear these points in mind; for it is sometimes thought that if we reject the view that the innocent in war are simply those who pose no threat, the alternative must be to accept that innocence means *moral* innocence, which contrasts

with moral guilt or culpability. According to this latter view, it is *culpable* responsibility for an unjust threat that is the basis of moral liability to defensive force. This, however, is not the view defended here.[13]

Unjust combatants pose an unjust threat. But they may, as we noted earlier, have one or more of a variety of excuses: for example, they may have been deceived, manipulated, indoctrinated, or coerced or compelled by threats, or perhaps they just believed, reasonably but mistakenly, in the moral authority of their government. In some cases, these excusing conditions will be strong enough to absolve an unjust combatant of all culpability for participation in an unjust war. But conditions of this sort are never sufficient to absolve him of *all responsibility* for his participation, or for the unjust threat he poses. Thus, even if he is *morally* innocent, he is not innocent in the sense that is relevant to the requirement of discrimination. Only the absence of a capacity for moral agency could absolve him of all responsibility for his action and thus make him innocent in the latter sense.[14]

Moral responsibility, however, is a matter of degree and the degree of an unjust combatant's responsibility for posing an unjust threat is reduced by such excuses as nonculpable ignorance and duress. And it is reasonable to assume that the extent to which a person is morally liable to defensive force varies with the degree of his responsibility for the existence of, or for posing, an unjust threat. But how are we to understand the idea that liability varies in degree? It seems that either a person is a legitimate target or he is not; either it is permissible to attack him or it is not.

A person becomes a legitimate target in war by being to some degree morally responsible for an unjust threat, or for a wrong that provides a just cause for war. But there are various constraints, such as minimal force and proportionality, that apply even to attacks on legitimate targets. The way that variations in the degree of a person's liability to defensive force are manifested is in variations in the strength or stringency of these constraints. For example, a level of harm that it might be proportionate to inflict on unjust combatants who are culpable might not be proportionate if inflicted on unjust combatants known to be largely innocent.

It may be objected that, while this might be true in principle, it is irrelevant in practice since it is normally impossible to know, of any particular unjust combatant, the degree to which he is morally responsible for the unjust threat he poses or for whatever grievance constitutes the just cause for war. This is largely true. But, as in the case of individual self-defense, reasonable agents in war have to act on the basis of presumptions that are as well grounded as possible in the circumstances. And there is occasionally good reason to presume that one group of unjust combatants bears a greater degree of liability than another. In the first American war against Iraq, for example, all Iraqi combatants were unjust combatants because they fought to resist the reversal of their country's unjust invasion and occupation of Kuwait. Yet some bore a greater degree of responsibility than others. It was reasonable to assume that members of the Iraqi Republican Guard, a highly-paid, elite volunteer force loyal to the regime, were responsible for their action to a higher degree than poorly armed conscripts who had been compelled by threats to themselves and their families to take up positions in the desert. I believe that the proportionality requirement applied differently to attacks against these different groups. Forces of the coalition against Iraq were entitled to inflict as much harm on the Republican Guard as was necessary to eliminate the threat the guard posed to them; but they may have been morally required to accept greater risks to themselves to reduce the harm inflicted on conscripts, in something like the way that combatants are obliged to accept greater risks in order to minimize incidental harm to innocent civilians.

More generally, it is true of most unjust combatants that their conduct is excused to varying degrees by the sorts of consideration Walzer mentions in arguing that they are not criminals and that these excuses diminish their liability to varying degrees. This is in itself an important consideration that affects the way that the requirements of minimal force and proportionality apply to the use of force even in a just war. Even just wars should be fought with more restraint than might be required if it were reasonable to assume that unjust combatants were criminals or villains rather than the victims of duress and delusion.

NONCOMBATANT LIABILITY

Recall that the example of the Initiator offers intuitive support for the claim that one need not pose an unjust threat or currently be part of that threat in order to be morally responsible for it. And it should be obvious that in war there are some who occupy a position analogous to that of the Initiator: namely, noncombatants who bear significant responsibility for initiating or sustaining an unjust war, or for the wrong whose redress is the just cause for war. Some of these may be responsible to a greater degree than any combatant. In 1954, for example, executives of the United Fruit Company persuaded the Eisenhower administration to organize and direct a coup that overthrew the democratic government of Guatemala and installed a new regime that returned to the company some uncultivated lands that had been nationalized in an effort to aid the peasants. This is a paradigm of an unjust war and it is reasonable to suppose that the executives bore at least as great a degree of responsibility for the killing and the violation of national self-determination as the soldiers who carried it out.[15] According to the understanding of the requirement of discrimination I have advanced—which I will refer to as the *responsibility criterion*—the executives were liable; they were legitimate targets. If attacking them would have been as effective as attacking soldiers in preventing the coup, the responsibility criterion implies that, other things being equal, it would have been permissible to attack them, and that that might have been preferable to attacking combatants, particularly if it would have meant that fewer people had to be killed.

The responsibility criterion denies both the permission and the prohibition asserted by the traditional requirement. Because it claims that it is in general impermissible for unjust combatants to attack just combatants, it denies the traditional claim that all combatants are permissible targets; because it claims that some noncombatants are permissible targets, it denies the traditional prohibition of intentional attacks on noncombatants.

Perhaps some may not find it appalling to suppose that in the case of United Fruit, certain civilians could be morally liable to attack. But for most people, the general suggestion that civilians can be legitimate targets in war will seem pernicious. The best way to address this understandable reaction is to respond to a couple of the more obvious objections to the responsibility criterion.[16]

One worry is that because moral responsibility is a matter of degree, it is difficult to identify a lower bound or threshold for responsibility for an unjust threat or other grievance that provides a just cause for war. Because of this, the responsibility criterion threatens to be utterly promiscuous in its assignment of liability in war. For in an unjust war many voters and perhaps all taxpayers must surely bear some *degree* of responsibility for their country's action. But if the responsibility criterion implies that a great many or even most ordinary citizens in a country fighting an unjust war are legitimate targets, it can hardly be regarded as a principle of *discrimination* at all.

The first part of the reply to this objection is that the same objection applies in a more seriously damaging way to the traditional requirement of discrimination. According to the traditional requirement of discrimination, noncombatants are those who are not threatening, who do not contribute to the threat posed by their country. The problem of drawing the line between those who contribute to the threat and those who do not is a familiar one in the just war literature. The typical response is to try to find a basis for drawing the distinction between combatants and noncombatants in a way that limits liability in war to soldiers, those who directly supply them with the instruments of war (including, perhaps, workers in munitions factories, but *only* while they are at work), and those who occupy positions in the military chain of command.[17] It is sometimes said, for instance, that if a person who makes a material contribution to the war is doing the same thing she would be doing if war were not in progress, she is not a combatant. But such criteria of combatant status never correspond to the tradition's own generic notion of a combatant, which is simply the notion of a person who poses a threat or contributes to the threat his country poses—the latter clause being necessary for the inclusion of military personnel who occupy roles that do not involve participation in combat or the firing of weapons. And the class of those who contribute, even quite directly, to their country's war effort is in fact considerably more extensive than the class of military personnel. It includes, for example, doctors who heal wounded soldiers and return them to combat.

So the line-drawing problem is not unique to the responsibility criterion. But on what basis can I claim that this problem is more seriously damaging to the traditional requirement of discrimination? The reason is that on the traditional view, the criterion of liability is all-or-nothing: either one is a combatant or one is not, a legitimate target or not a legitimate target. There are no degrees of liability. The only constraints on attacking legitimate targets (combatants) are the requirements of necessity, minimal force, and proportionality, and the proportionality calculation takes account of only two variables: the gravity of the threat that the combatant poses and the magnitude of the harm that defensive force would inflict. According to the responsibility criterion, by contrast, the proportionality calculation has to take account of *three* variables: The gravity of the threat, the amount of harm that would be inflicted, and the degree of the potential target's moral liability. Thus a use of force that would be proportionate according to the traditional requirement of discrimination might be disproportionate according to the responsibility criterion if the person at whom it would be directed was only weakly responsible for the threat (or other wrong) that was the basis of his liability. In short, even though the responsibility criterion (like the traditional requirement) implies that many civilians are permissible targets in *principle,* in the vast majority of cases a civilian's degree of liability will be so low that to attack him or her *militarily* would be wholly disproportionate. While voters or taxpayers might be morally liable, for example, to the effects of certain kinds of economic sanction, they would not be appropriate targets for military force. This conclusion is reinforced by the fact that, in contrast to unjust combatants, even morally responsible noncombatants normally make only a very slight causal contribution to their country's unjust war, so that attacking them would do little to diminish the threat their country poses or to advance the just cause.

A second objection is that, just as it is normally impossible to have accurate information about an unjust combatant's responsibility for the threat he poses, so it is normally impossible to have detailed information about whether and to what extent a particular noncombatant is responsible for her country's unjust war. Again, this is true. But it does not show that noncombatants cannot be liable, but only that just combatants can seldom know which ones are responsible or to what extent they are responsible. And this drastically restricts the practical significance of the responsibility criterion's implication that some noncombatants may be legitimate targets in war. For, while a few noncombatants may bear a high degree of responsibility for their country's unjust war and many may be responsible to a much weaker degree, there are also many others who are not responsible at all. Because one cannot normally distinguish among the highly responsible, the minimally responsible, and those who are not responsible at all, just combatants should in general err on the side of caution by acting on the presumption that noncombatants are innocent—that is, devoid of responsibility for their country's unjust war (just as just combatants may act on the presumption that unjust combatants *are* responsible for the threat they pose). And even if, on some occasions, just combatants were to have sufficient information to be able to distinguish between responsible and nonresponsible noncombatants, the responsible ones would normally be intermingled among the nonresponsible, making it impossible to direct force, or even economic sanctions, against the responsible ones only. And this is a further reason why military action can very rarely if ever be proportionate against civilian targets. In this respect, attacks on civilian populations are again importantly different from attacks against groups of unjust combatants, for *all* of the latter are (or may reasonably be presumed to be) to some degree liable to defensive force.

THE LAWS OF WAR

Doubtless most readers retain a strong sense that opening the door to intentional attacks on noncombatants is profoundly dangerous. As with the other three objections I have canvassed, this is true. It is important that combatants should always experience deep inhibitions against attacking noncombatants. As I have argued, it is very seldom permissible, even according to the responsibility criterion, to attack noncombatants. Yet the temptation to attack them is very strong, both among those with political grievances who lack military power and among those who control powerful military forces. Because most soldiers, just and unjust alike, believe their cause is just, they will be strongly disposed to kill civilians if they believe that it is permissible to kill enemy civilians who are responsible for an unjust war. It therefore seems better to discourage even those few attacks on noncombatants that could in principle be morally justified.

This suggests that there is indeed a role for the traditional requirement of discrimination. Although it is false as a criterion of moral liability to attack in war, it ought nevertheless to be upheld as a convention to which all combatants are bound. Thus far in this essay I have focused on what I will refer to as the "deep" morality of war: the criterion of moral liability to attack, the relation between just cause and the *jus in bello* requirement of proportionality, and so on. But there is another dimension to the morality of war that I have not explored: the laws of war, or conventions established to mitigate the savagery of war. It is in everyone's interests that such conventions be recognized and obeyed. But, although the conventions have their point in considerations of consequences, they can have a role even in a nonconsequentialist account of the morality of war, such as the one I offer here. Given that general adherence to certain conventions is better for everyone, all have a moral reason to recognize and abide by these conventions. For it is rational for each side in a conflict to adhere to them only if the other side does. Thus if one side breaches the understanding that the conventions will be followed, it may cease to be rational or morally required for the other side to persist in its adherence to them. A valuable device for limiting the violence will thereby be lost, and that will be worse for all.

It is important to understand that the account I have developed of the deep morality of war is *not* an account of the laws of war. The formulation of the laws of war is a wholly different task, one that I have not attempted and that has to be carried out with a view to the consequences of the adoption and enforcement of the laws or conventions. It is, indeed, entirely clear that the laws of war must diverge significantly from the deep morality of war as I have presented it. Perhaps most obviously, the fact that most combatants believe that their cause is just means that the laws of war must, at least for the most part, be neutral between just and unjust combatants, as the traditional theory insists that the requirements of *jus in bello are.* Consider, for example, the question of punishment in the aftermath of a war. I have argued that according to the deep morality of war, unjust combatants in general cannot obey certain requirements of *jus in bello* and therefore act wrongly by participating in an unjust war. While many are fully excused, some may be culpable to varying degrees, and some may even deserve punishment, even if they have confined their attacks to military targets. But it would be counterproductive and indeed disastrous to permit the punishment of ordinary soldiers merely for their participation in an unjust war. This is so for several reasons.

First, it is simply impossible for one country, or even an international body, to provide fair trials for all the members of an army. Second, there is the problem of "victor's justice": the winning side will declare its war to have been just and will be tempted to seek vengeance against vanquished soldiers under the guise of punishment. Finally, if all combatants have to fear this fate, they may be deterred from surrendering; and it is irrational to establish incentives to protract wars rather than to terminate them.

It is, however, important to be able to punish just combatants who act wrongly in the way they conduct a war. The solution, it seems, must be to reserve punishment for infractions of the conventions or laws of war, which must be neutral between just and unjust combatants, rather than for violations of the deeper principles of *jus in bello,* which are not neutral.

It is possible that the traditional rules of *jus in bello* coincide rather closely with the laws that would be optimal for regulating conduct in battle. These rules have evolved over many centuries and have been refined, tested, and adapted to the experience of war as the nature of war has itself evolved. They may, in particular, be well suited to the regulation of the conduct of war in conditions in which there are few institutional constraints, so that the restraining effects have to come from the content of the rules rather than from institutions in which the rules might be embedded.[18]

It is also possible that these rules are not ideal. They are the products not only of modern battlefields but also of ancient chivalric engagements, religious wars, and Medieval Catholic philosophy. (Just war theory is unique in contemporary practical ethics in two respects. It is widely and uncritically accepted and differs very little in content from what Western religious thinkers have believed from the Middle Ages to the present.) The account of the deep morality of war I have sketched provides a basis for the reevaluation of the rules we have inherited. Ideally we should establish laws of war best suited to get combatants on both sides to conform their action as closely as possible to the constraints imposed by the deep morality of war. Yet it is dangerous to tamper with rules that already command a high degree of allegiance. The stakes are too high to allow for much experimentation with alternatives.

There are, moreover, objections to the idea that we can distinguish between the deep morality of war and the laws of war. One such objection has been forcefully stated by Walzer: "No limit is accepted simply because it is thought that it will be useful. The war convention must first be morally plausible . . . ; it must correspond to our sense of what is right."[19]

This may not be a problem for some of the conventional laws of war. The idea that it is wrong to attack noncombatants, for instance, already corresponds to most people's sense of what is right. Moreover, it *does* seem that people can accept limits, even in war, on the ground that respect for these limits serves everyone's interests. It is not obvious, for example, that poison gas is inherently more objectionable morally than artillery, provided that its use is confined to the battlefield; yet the convention that prohibits its use is widely obeyed, mainly because we all sense that it would be worse for everyone, ourselves included, were the taboo to be breached.

Suppose, however, that I am wrong about this and that, in general, if combatants are to be sufficiently motivated to obey certain rules in the conduct of war, they will have to believe that those rules really do constitute the deep morality of war. If it is imperative to get them to respect certain conventions, must we present the conventions as the deep morality of war and suppress the genuine deeper principles? Must the morality of war be self-effacing in this way?[20] I confess that I do not know what to say about this, though my inclination is to think that what is most important is not that the correct account of the morality of war should meet the publicity condition, or that combatants not be deceived, but that wars, when inevitable, should be fought as decently and with as little harm, especially to the innocent, as possible.

One further objection to distinguishing between the deep morality of war and the laws of war is that there are bound to be circumstances in which the deeper morality and the conventions will conflict—for example, when morality requires an attack on noncombatants while the conventional requirement of discrimination forbids it. How ought such conflicts to be resolved? In order for morality to require the violation of the convention in a particular case, it must take into account not only the positive reasons for attacking noncombatants but also the effect that the violation of the convention would be likely to have on general respect for the convention. For it is widely accepted that the violation of a convention by one side tends to release the other side from its commitment to respect the convention. If, however, this consideration is factored in and morality still requires the violation of the convention, it seems that the convention ought to be violated. Yet there is so much scope for self-deception in these matters that this is a conclusion that one ought never to accept with complacency.

If, despite these problems, it is right that there must be laws of war that diverge from the deep morality of war, then war is normatively governed by two sets of principles that operate at different levels. It may seem, however, that it is really the conventions that must be action-guiding in the conduct of war and, if so, that raises the question whether the deeper morality of war has any practical significance at all. Are the judgments it issues of merely academic interest?

I think not. If nothing else, the deep morality of war is a guide to individual conscience. It demands of potential volunteers, potential conscripts, and active military personnel that they consider with the utmost seriousness whether any war in which they might fight is just and to refuse to fight unless they can be confident that it is. The effects of this demand are hard to predict. It might simply prompt governments to become ever more subtle and clever in the lies they tell their citizens. If so, it is a corollary of the account I have offered that greater efforts must be made to ensure openness in government. Yet I think that the main effect would be to make it harder for governments to fight unjust wars.

NOTES

1. Compare Henry Sidgwick's claim that "the rules which civilised opinion should attempt to impose on combatants . . . must abstract from all consideration of the justice of the war" (Sidgwick, 1891, pp 253–254).

2. See also the discussion on Walzer's pp. 38–39.

3. Here I draw on the argument in McMahan and McKim (1993), pp. 502–506, 512–513.

4. I believe that in the same cases in which they cannot satisfy the requirement of proportionality, unjust combatants also cannot satisfy the requirement of discrimination. But this claim presupposes a conception of the requirement of discrimination different from the orthodox conception. I will defend the alternative conception in the following section.

5. In an earlier paper, I claimed that "a case can perhaps be made" for the view that morally innocent unjust combatants can be "justified in engaging in self-defense against the defensive counterattack by the victims of their initial attack" (McMahan, 1994b). Because I now attribute less significance than I did earlier to the distinction between moral innocence and moral culpability, I believe that this earlier claim is mistaken. Two philosophers who have argued persuasively against my earlier position on self-defense by morally innocent unjust combatants against just combatants are Richard Arneson ("Just Warfare Theory and Noncombatant Immunity," manuscript) and McPherson (2004).

6. This is, of course, a controversial claim that I lack space to defend here, though I do so in a manuscript in progress called The Ethics of Killing: Self-Defense, War, and Punishment. I defend the claim against important objections in McMahan (2004).

7. I believe, contrary to the traditional assumption, that there can be rare instances in which both sides in a war have a just cause and are justified in fighting. For present purposes I leave it an open question what the requirement of discrimination should say about attacks by just combatants against just combatants in such cases.

8. See, for example, Anscombe (1981), p. 53.

9. A mistaken variant of this claim is defended in McMahan (1994a). A better argument is in McMahan (2002). Others who argue that there is no right of self-defense against a Non-Responsible Threat are Zohar (1993), Otsuka (1994) and Rodin (2002).

10. I am indebted to Monsignor Stuart Swetland and to Richard Arneson for making me see the importance of this detail. If the Initiator could eliminate the threat to you, he could be regarded as continuing to pose the threat by having set it in motion and then refusing to stop it. For an ancestor of this kind of case that differs from it in that the person in the position of the Initiator remains a necessary cause of the threat, see Alexander (1985), p. 100.

11. For further elucidation, see McMahan (2002), pp. 402–403.

12. Since writing the longer version of this paper, I have modified my view about the conditions for moral responsibility for an unjust threat. I now believe that in cases in which a morally responsible agent poses an unjust threat through voluntary action but was not engaging in a risk-imposing activity and could not have foreseen that he would pose a threat, he is not responsible for the threat. See McMahan (2005).

13. It is, however, the view I defended in both "Self-Defense and the Problem of the Innocent Attacker" (McMahan, 1994a) and "Innocence, Self-Defense, and Killing in War" (McMahan, 1994b).

14. Again, my view is no longer quite so strong. See Footnote 12.

15. For a brief but more detailed description of this episode, see McMahan (1985), pp. 13–14.

16. Some of these responses indicate ways in which the account of the morality of war I have developed in this paper is superior to the cruder account I advanced in "Innocence, Self-Defense, and Killing in War" (McMahan, 1994b), which invites similar objections but cannot answer them in the ways suggested here.

17. For representative examples, see Nagel (1985), pp. 69–70, Walzer (1977), pp. 144–146, Finnis et al. (1987), pp. 86–90, and Oderberg (2000), pp. 217–219.

18. I am indebted here to Allen Buchanan.

19. Walzer (1977), p. 133.

20. I have been helpfully pressed to confront this and related problems by Charles Beitz, Gilbert Harman, Philip Pettit, and Peter Singer. They will be disappointed by my anemic and noncommittal response.

REFERENCES

Alexander, L. (1985). Self-Defense and the Killing of Noncombatants. In Beitz, Charles R. et al. (Eds.) *International Ethics*. Princeton: Princeton University Press, pp. 98–105.

Anscombe, E. (1981). *Ethics, Religion, and Politics: Collected Philosophical Papers,* vol. 3. Minneapolis: University of Minnesota Press.

Finnis, J., Boyle, J., & Grisez, G. (1987). *Nuclear Deterrence, Morality, and Realism.* Oxford: Oxford University Press.

McMahan, J. (1985). *Reagan and the World: Imperial Policy in the New Cold War.* New York: Monthly Review Press.

McMahan, J. (1994a). Self-Defense and the Problem of the Innocent Attacker. Ethics 104, pp. 252–290.

McMahan, J. (1994b). Innocence, Self-Defense, and Killing in War. *Journal of Political Philosophy* 2, pp. 193–221.

McMahan, J. (2002). *The Ethics of Killing: Problems at the Margins of Life.* New York: Oxford University Press.

McMahan, J. (2004). War as Self-Defense. Ethics and International Affairs 18, pp. 75–80.

McMahan, J. (2005). The Basis of Moral Liability to Defensive Killing. *Philosophical Issues* 15, pp. 386–405.

McMahan, J., & McKim, R. (1993). The Just War and the Gulf War. *Canadian Journal of Philosophy* 23, pp. 501–541.

McPherson, L. (2004). Innocence and Responsibility in War. *Canadian Journal of Philosophy* 34, pp. 485–506.

Nagel, T. (1985). War and Massacre. In Beitz, Charles R. et al. (Eds.) *International Ethics.* Princeton: Princeton University Press pp. 53–74.

Oderberg, D. (2000). *Applied Ethics.* Oxford: Blackwell.

Otsuka, M. (1994). Killing the Innocent in Self-Defense. *Philosophy and Public Affairs* 23, pp. 74–94.

Rodin, D. (2002). *War and Self-Defense.* Oxford: Clarendon Press.

Sidgwick, H. (1891). *The Elements of Politics.* London: Macmillan.

Walzer, M. (1977). *Just and Unjust Wars.* Harmondsworth: Penguin.

Zohar, N. (1993). Collective War and Individual Self-Defense: Against the Conscription of "Self-Defense." *Political Theory* 21, pp. 606–622.

DISCUSSION QUESTIONS

1. What arguments does McMahan give against the traditional assumption that "unjust combatants" are typically justified in trying to kill just combatants? Do you find these arguments convincing? Why or why not?

2. What is McMahan's argument that "posing an unjust threat is neither necessary nor sufficient for moral liability to . . . violence"? Do you find his argument convincing? Why or why not?

3. What is McMahan's argument that some noncombatants are legitimate targets for just combatants? Of the various objections he considers, which do you think is the most important? Do you find his response to that objection convincing? Why or why not?

4. What do McMahan's arguments imply about whether American soldiers should have fought in the Iraq War (formally known as Operation Iraqi Freedom)? Do you agree? Why or why not?

CHERYL ABBATE

Assuming Risk: A Critical Analysis of a Soldier's Duty to Prevent Collateral Casualties

Cheryl Abbate teaches philosophy at University of Colorado–Boulder. She writes about environmental ethics, animal ethics, and military ethics. In this paper, she argues against the idea that individual soldiers or their commanders have an obligation to take great risks to protect all innocent civilians during war.

GUIDING QUESTIONS

1. What is the "principle of risk" that Abbate criticizes in this paper? How is it connected to the Doctrine of Double Effect?
2. How, according to Abbate, does a soldier's obligation to obey lawful orders undermine the "principle of risk"?
3. How, according to Abbate, does a soldier's duty of loyalty to his or her fellow soldiers undermine the "principle of risk"?
4. Which civilians count as "protected civilians," according to Abbate, and why do soldiers have greater responsibilities toward them than toward "unprotected civilians"?
5. Why does Abbate consider whether military commanders are justified in ordering soldiers to assume additional risks to protect civilians? Does she think they are justified? Why or why not?

INTRODUCTION

Within the just war tradition, considerable attention is afforded to the issue of how to fight justly once engaged *in* war. A central tenet of just fighting involves adhering to a principle of non-combatant immunity, which prohibits soldiers from taking direct aim at non-combatants in a military attack. Soldiers are thus commanded to discriminate cautiously between enemy threats and innocent civilians in order to minimize, or ideally eliminate, occasions of collateral damage. Yet, despite the caution that is employed by soldiers, destruction of non-military property and harm to innocent civilians appear to be an inevitable side effect of war, and decisions regarding the lives of innocent civilians must often be weighed against military objectives. In such situations, one important line of thought relies on an appeal to the doctrine of double effect (DDE), a moral doctrine that is used to draw a moral distinction between the intended effects and the unintended (but foreseen) effects of a voluntary action.

The intending/foreseeing distinction of the DDE is used to justify, while at the same time minimize, the killing of non-combatants in wartime operations by Lichtenberg (1994), Kaufman (2003), Ramsey (1961), Miller (1991) and Hurka (2005), while other just war theorists such as McKeogh (2002) and Bica (1998) reject the intending/foreseeing distinction altogether, claiming that even the foreseen killing of a

Journal of Military Ethics, "Assuming Risk: A Critical Analysis of a Soldier's Duty to Prevent Collateral Casualties," 13(1), 2014, 70–93, Cheryl Abbate, Copyright © 2014, Taylor and Francis. With permission of Springer.

civilian is a violation of justice. According to Rodin (2004) and Holmes (1989), the DDE essentially grants a license to kill a significant number of human beings, while Thomson (1991) maintains that the killing of civilians is justified only by an appeal to self-defense.

Certain just war theorists such as Walzer (1977, 2004), Christopher (1994), Lee (2004), Coady (2008) and Schwenkenbecher (2014), in an attempt to preserve the foreseeing/intending distinction while at the same time criticizing the DDE in its traditional form, on the grounds that it is too permissive, have revised (or more strictly interpreted) the DDE so that it encompasses a "double intention," which demands of soldiers that they foster a high standard of care that involves, at the very least, the intention to try not to harm civilians. In his revision of the DDE, Walzer (1977: 152–156) goes so far as to claim that soldiers have a duty to assume certain risks in order to protect the lives of *all* innocent civilians.

I offer a critical response to this principle of risk by first considering whether the principle of risk can be justified as a guiding principle for individual soldiers on the battlefield. Ultimately, I argue that such a principle cannot be justified, since adherence to it would require soldiers to neglect their strict duties and obligations, as required by the role of military professionals, and furthermore, it would obligate soldiers to go above and beyond what is required by the role of the soldier. I first discuss the soldiers' strict duties of obedience to their chain of command, illustrating how assuming certain risks would require soldiers to challenge authority, thus undermining the command structure of the military. Next, I draw attention to the special duty that soldiers have to not endanger or jeopardize the safety of their comrades by assuming certain risks. Lastly, although I acknowledge that soldiers have a duty to prevent harm or save lives even when doing so involves a significant risk, I argue that this duty vis-à-vis civilians is owed *only* to those civilians who are what I will refer to as "protected civilians": that is, civilians whom soldiers (or the soldier's nation) voluntarily promise to protect, such as co-nationals, to-be-liberated civilians and allied civilians.[1] After concluding that the principle of risk is not justified as a normative principle that should guide the conduct of soldiers

on the battlefield, I then consider whether the principle of risk is justified as a principle for commanders to adhere to during mission planning. I consider the obligation of commanding officers to provide for the safety and welfare of their subordinates and to achieve victory, both of which require commanders not to put their soldiers in risky situations in order to save "unprotected" civilians. I thus conclude that, given the current goals and values of the US military, the *principle of risk* is an unjustified constraint on soldiers and commanders in the US Armed Forces.[2]

I close by suggesting that, in order for soldiers to be reasonably expected to assume risks in order to save the lives of all civilians, the military itself is arguably in need of a radical transformation: a transformation that demands a significant revision regarding militaristic goals, values, strategies, policies, warrior codes and expectations of service members.

PRELIMINARY REMARKS ON COLLATERAL DAMAGE, *JUS IN BELLO* AND THE DOCTRINE OF DOUBLE EFFECT

Collateral damage is defined by the US Department of Defense as the "unintentional or incidental injury or damage to persons or objects that would not be lawful military targets in the circumstances ruling at the time. Such damage is not unlawful so long as it is not excessive in light of the overall military advantage anticipated from the attack" (Joint Chiefs of Staff 2002: A-2). Collateral damage, then, is always *incidental* or *unintentional* (although perhaps foreseen), which is the result of a legitimate military attack directed at enemy forces or facilities. In the case of military operations, collateral damage generally refers to civilian property and non-combatant casualties or injuries. Thus, a given attack in wartime may involve two effects: (1) one that is the direct, intended or primary effect (which would be considered to be the *good* effect—e.g. the destruction of an enemy bomb-making facility); and (2) a secondary effect that is unintended (but perhaps foreseeable) and is usually a bad effect, such as the death or harm of innocent civilians.

For the purpose of this paper, I will focus solely on collateral casualties: a more restrictive notion than collateral damage (collateral damage pertaining to both casualties and property). "Collateral casualties," then, refers to the incidental killing or injury of non-combatants during a lawful military attack. Although the destruction of civilian property is not inconsequential, the debate, as it is framed by Walzer (1977, 2004), Lee (2004) and Christopher (1994), presents a significant concern for civilian life and physical welfare.[3]

Considerations for collateral casualties has been addressed in the just war tradition, an influential approach to the ethics of war and peace that employs a set of universal, moral rules that provide a moral framework for evaluating the justice of all aspects of war.[4] The concern for collateral casualties is addressed in the principles fundamental to *jus in bello*, which is the just war doctrine that stipulates the use of force *in* armed combat, which directly concerns military officers and soldiers who are responsible for the actual fighting.[5]

The DDE, which is described as a way of reconciling the killing of innocents with lawful wartime operations, is often invoked in describing and determining certain rules of *jus in bello* (such as *no means mala in se*, military necessity, discrimination/distinction and proportionality).[6] By drawing a moral distinction between the intended effects of an action and the unintended, but perhaps foreseen, effects of an action, the DDE provides normative guidance regarding how soldiers fighting in war should approach the issue of collateral casualties. According to the traditional formulation of the DDE, the killing or injury of non-combatants is said to be justified or permissible so long as the following four conditions are met:

1. The act is good in itself or at least indifferent, which means, for our purposes, that it is a legitimate act of war (*No means mala in se*).
2. The direct effect is morally acceptable—the destruction of military supplies, for example, or the killing of enemy soldiers (*Military necessity*).

3. The intention of the actor is good, that is, he or she aims only at the acceptable effect; the evil effect is not one of his or her ends, nor is it a means to his ends (*Discrimination/ distinction*).
4. The good effect is sufficiently good to compensate for allowing the evil effect; it must be justified under Sidgwick's proportionality rule (*Proportionality*). (Walzer 1977: 153).

In order to understand the discrimination restraint that forbids the direct targeting of civilians (wanton or not), consider the following scenarios:

1. There is an influential terrorist leader who is primarily responsible for planning, motivating and executing a number of terrorist attacks. It is his leadership that encourages and inspires others to conduct acts of terrorism. It just so happens that we are able to locate the homes of his family and closest friends (who have no apparent involvement in conducting acts of terror). We begin, one by one, to bomb these homes, killing the residents, in order to encourage the terrorist leader to turn himself in. The terrorist, who loves and cares for his family and friends, turns himself in and, in the absence of his leadership, all acts of terrorism from this particular terrorist group come to an immediate halt.
2. A team of soldiers has been ordered to enter a civilian home in order to capture two influential, violent terrorist leaders. When the soldiers enter the home, the terrorists fire at the soldiers and as a result, the soldiers return fire. A child who was in the room is unintentionally shot dead in the midst of the firefight.

The key distinction between these two scenarios involves intention: in the first scenario, the innocent civilians were directly targeted and the soldiers who bombed the home intended for the civilians to die, while in the second scenario, the soldiers did not take direct aim at the child, nor did they intend for the child to die. Furthermore, these scenarios represent an important distinction between direct and indirect killing: "in direct killing, death is the intended goal of an act, or an intended means to an intended goal; in indirect killing, death is a side effect caused by an act that has some other intended goal" (Lackey 1989: 66). According to Kaufman (2003), the dominant position in just war theory is that, while the intentional, direct killing of innocents can never be justified (even if it would lead to desirable consequences), a military act that causes the unintended, indirect killings of innocents can be justified, so long as the act is necessary for military success and the negative effects were proportional to the good effects obtained.

THE PRINCIPLE OF DOUBLE INTENTION AND THE PRINCIPLE OF RISK

Walzer criticizes the traditional form of the DDE, as it concerns wartime operations, on the ground that it is "darkly permissive"; it allows for a "blanket justification" for collateral casualties when, in many cases, the death and/or injuries could have been prevented (Walzer 1977: 153). In particular, Walzer is troubled by the third condition, which he claims fails to capture the full extent of a soldier's moral obligations in war. His central claim is that the principle of discrimination merely instructs soldiers to foster a "negative" intention not to intend the death or injury of non-combatants, while failing to further command soldiers to foster a positive intention to preserve, protect or save civilian lives. Lee echoes Walzer's concern as he writes:

> the doctrine of double effect is too lenient [as it applies to military operations]; it does not capture the extent to which combatants should seek to avoid harming civilians. Not only should combatants not try to harm civilians; they should try not to harm them. (Lee 2004: 234)

In *Just and Unjust Wars*, Walzer provides an example to illustrate the failure of the DDE. In a memoir of the First World War, Frank Richards recalls the bombing of dugouts or cellars (which were frequently used as hiding places by enemy German soldiers). Typically, soldiers would throw bombs into the cellars and look around the cellars for casualties after the bombs went off. However, Richards and his men were aware that civilians would often hide in these cellars, so they would shout down into the cellar prior to throwing the bombs. In one case, a woman and her family were saved by the verbal warnings of the soldiers (Walzer 1977: 152).

Yet, as Walzer points out, none of the principles of the DDE morally obliged Richards to issue a verbal warning prior to throwing the bombs into the cellars. Rather, the DDE would have permitted him to throw the bombs into the cellars without warning, thus justifying the death of non-combatants who may have been hiding in the cellars. This is because:

1. The act Richards engaged in (blowing up cellars) was a legitimate military act.
2. The direct effect was good and a military necessity (destruction of enemy hideouts).
3. The intention was good: Richards clearly intended the destruction of enemy hideouts and not the civilian deaths.
4. The good effect was sufficiently good in comparison to the evil effect; the elimination of enemy hideouts would, presumably, outweigh the possible civilian deaths.

According to Walzer, the simplistic conclusion that no moral harm would have been done in this scenario is a bit troubling. That is, we should not be so quick to judge it morally acceptable to throw bombs into enemy hideouts before yelling out *even if* the success of the mission would be proportional to the lost civilian lives. This is because the soldiers could have prevented an additional harm—the loss of innocent civilian lives. Hence, Walzer argues that Richards and his men acted as moral men *ought* to act by issuing a verbal warning before blowing up the cellars, even given the possible risks associated with shouting out (e.g. the German soldiers could have scrambled out of the cellar, firing as they came) (Walzer 1977: 154). Walzer ultimately concludes that "if saving civilian lives means risking soldiers' lives, the risk must be accepted" (156).[7] Thus, Walzer amends the third principle of the DDE in order to include a *positive intention* to reduce harm to noncombatants:

> (3) the intention of the actor is good, that is, he aims narrowly at the acceptable effect; the evil effect is not one of his ends, nor is it a means to his ends, and, aware of the evil involved, he seeks to minimize it, accepting costs to himself. (155)

Essentially, the demand is for a *double intention*: (1) that the good be aimed at; and (2) that the soldier mitigates the foreseeable evil as far as possible, that is, soldiers should intend *not* to harm civilians (Lee 2004). Let us refer to this as the *principle of double intention*.[8] From the principle of double intention, a second principle is said to be entailed: the *principle of risk*, which requires soldiers to mitigate civilian harm or death even when doing so involves significant risks to the actor (Walzer 1977: 155, 2004: 17).

THE MILITARY ETHIC

In the following analysis of the principle of risk as both a principle that guides individual soldiers on the battlefield and as a principle that guides commanders during operational planning, I will consider the strict obligations that are imparted to a soldier *qua* someone inhabiting the role of the soldier (or commander *qua* someone inhabiting the role of the commander). My critique stems from considerations of "role morality": the idea that special rights and obligations attach to certain social or professional roles that differ from the rights and obligations of "common morality" that governs the behavior of people not inhabiting such roles (Luban 1988). The roles of soldier and commander are examples of such roles that entail special and unique obligations or, as Hartle (1989: 5) describes it, "role-differentiated behavior." This is to say that the military has a unique status; it stands outside the scope of ordinary morality and any attempt to make normative judgments or critiques of military professionals without giving due reflection to the special status and demands of the military will

be problematic. Thus, consideration of what ought to be done, when making normative judgments regarding military soldiers and commanders, must take into account the special role of the soldier and commander, which in turn depends directly on the function of the military itself.

Since the central goal of the military profession is the security of the state, and an important means of attaining a secure state is fighting and winning wars, soldiers and commanders are both obligated to foster the values, attitudes and dispositions that are instrumental to achieving a secure state and winning wars (so long as by doing so, they do not violate the law of war) (Hartle 1989: 30). It is my central claim that it is deeply problematic to command military professionals to embrace normative principles that directly conflict with their special roles and unique duties. In the following discussion, I will illustrate how the principle of risk is such a principle that would require both soldiers and commanders to violate their unique roles that they undertake as military professionals.

ANALYSIS OF THE *PRINCIPLE OF RISK* AS A GUIDING PRINCIPLE FOR SOLDIERS ON THE BATTLEFIELD

In the following section, I will provide an account of the core military virtues that are essential for sustained and effective military operations. In doing so, I will focus considerable attention on the military virtues of obedience, loyalty, duty, sacrifice, courage and selflessness that are required at a very high, complex level in everyday military operations due to the *role or nature* of the individual soldier who executes ground operations. I will then illustrate how the principle of risk is not justified as a guiding principle for individual soldiers on the battlefield because it would require soldiers: (1) to undermine the core virtues that are central to the role of the soldier; and (2) to go above and beyond what is required by the role of the soldier.[9]

Obedience to Lawful Orders

The command structure of the military limits the freedom of individual soldiers to make their own decisions in tactical situations where risk or danger inevitably follows. That is, fundamental to military success is a rigid command structure and a corresponding demand for obedience to that structure. The commanding officer makes all final tactical decisions, including decisions regarding target selection and how to respond to civilian presence on the battlefield, while subordinate soldiers are obligated to obey the commander's decisions.

In any given mission, soldiers are provided with the commander's intent, which stipulates the commander's overall vision and general guidance as to how to accomplish the respective mission. In providing guidance that addresses the potential of civilian encounters, the commander will order soldiers to fight in one of two ways: (1) in such a way that requires soldiers to assume risk in order to save civilian lives; or (2) in such a way that requires soldiers to complete a mission with minimal risks that entails that soldiers avoid all unnecessary risks, including the risks involved in protecting civilians. After using the commander's intent as guidance for mission development, platoon leaders, squad leaders and team leaders (who are responsible for leading and conducting ground operations) develop battle plans that are rehearsed extensively before execution of the operation. During these rehearsals, soldiers are informed of the commander's intent, which stipulates the appropriate response to potential civilian encounters.[10]

Given this basic overview of military planning, let us reconsider Walzer's example of Richards and the enemy cellars. Prior to execution of this mission, the soldiers would have rehearsed specific actions on the objective (in this case, the cellars). Since battle rehearsals always take into account civilian considerations, the soldiers would have been informed of whether or not they should assume the dangers and risks of shouting out before blowing up the cellars. If the commander demands for minimal risk to friendly forces, then this would entail that soldiers should not engage in extra-risky actions, such as shouting out before blowing up the cellar. Thus, prior to mission execution, Richards and his men would have

been instructed by their leader whether or not they should call out a warning order before throwing in the grenade.

Note that it would not have been *unlawful* for Richards' leader to order the soldiers to refrain from shouting out a warning before blowing up the cellar. It is not criminal or unlawful to order one's troops to refrain from taking risks to save civilian lives. Rather, the Law of War forbids only the direct killing of unarmed individuals, and furthermore, it permits soldiers to conduct missions that may put civilians at risk based on the principle of *military necessity*.[11] In cases where collateral damage is "rendered absolutely necessary by military operations" or "offers a definite military advantage," the destruction of property and indirect killing of innocents is permitted, without the further requirement that a soldier assume a certain risk to reduce the damage.[12] War crimes or unlawful acts of war concern only the *direct* use of violence against non-combatants, such as "murder, the ill-treatment or deportation of civilian residents of an occupied territory to slave labor camps, the murder or ill-treatment of prisoners of war, the killing of prisoners, the wanton destruction of cities, towns and villages, and any devastation not justified by military necessity" (Solis 2010: 301–303).

The question then remains whether a soldier is justified in disobeying a lawful order in order to protect innocent civilians. In the US military, disobeying *lawful* orders can be prosecuted as a felony under the Uniform Code of Military Justice (US Army 1956: 182–183). That is, soldiers have a *legal* duty to obey *lawful orders* from their superiors.[13] Huntington takes this consideration of obeying lawful orders a step further, arguing that so long as an order is lawful, soldiers have a moral obligation to obey it. This is because:

> For the [military] profession to perform its function, each level within it must be able to command the instantaneous and loyal obedience of subordinate levels. Without these relationships, military professionalism is impossible. Consequently, loyalty and obedience are the highest military virtues. . . . When a military man receives a legal order from an authorized superior, he does not argue, he does not hesitate, he does not substitute his own views; he obeys instantly. (Huntington 1957: 73)

Huntington's central point is that one act of disobedience can upset the entire command structure of the military, which is dependent on an unwavering obedience to lawful orders. The success of the military is intrinsically connected to a rigid structure of command and leadership: obedience to orders is an integral part of soldier training and mission success, such as in combat situations where life or death depends on instant obedience.[14] When individual soldiers challenge or undermine the decisions made by their higher command in combat, even for what they believe to be moral reasons, disorder is inevitable. That is, if we allow one soldier to question or defy authority for what he or she believes to be moral reasons, we open the door to, and furthermore incite, the next soldier to defy authority for his or her own reasons, and so on. The end result would be an unmanageable, chaotic and un-cooperative military that invites soldiers to challenge authority, even in life or death situations.

Let us reconsider Walzer's cellar example to illustrate this point. For argument's sake, imagine that when Richards decided to issue a warning call to potential civilians, an enemy soldier who was in one of the nearby bunkers heard the warning call and immediately exited the bunker, firing his weapon all the way. Meanwhile, Richards' team leader, who specifically instructed his team to exercise stealth in conducting the mission, was caught off guard by the noise that Richards was making and instantly reacted by reprimanding him and, as a result, he was unable to react quickly enough to defend himself against the enemy soldier who fired directly at him.

This example illustrates the possible detrimental effect of individual decision-making in combat situations. Encouraging individual soldiers to take risks on their own undermines unit integrity and the authority of the leader; it upsets the tactical ambiance and arouses confusion, distraction and disorder throughout the ranks. Rather than granting soldiers individual authority to deviate from tactical plans as they see fit, concern for civilians and the risks or costs associated with saving civilian lives should be addressed in the unit's battle rehearsals prior to mission execution. If a soldier chooses to adhere to the principle of risk, and in doing so, disregards the

commanding officer's instruction, the whole command structure of the military, which is fundamental to mission success, would be undermined.

It may be objected that the character trait of unwavering obedience is not to be valorized, even in a military setting. If a soldier is conditioned to be unquestionably obedient to the military's command structure, the soldier may fail to question authority when faced with an unlawful order. That is, a soldier may be either: (1) too afraid to challenge orders because of the emphasis on obedience in the military; or (2) unaware that the order is unlawful, and out of obedience, performs the unlawful action.

The *US Field Manual* (FM) 100-1 enumerates the values central to the profession that reinforce, strengthen and promote the professional Army ethic: loyalty, duty, selflessness, service, integrity, courage, candor, competence and commitment (US Army 1976). *Courage* can be identified as either physical or moral courage, moral courage being of significant importance to the issue at hand. Miller (2000: 254) defines moral courage as: "the capacity to overcome the fear of shame and humiliation in order to admit one's mistakes, to confess a wrong, to reject evil conformity, to denounce injustice, and to defy immoral or imprudent orders." Olsthoorn (2007: 275) points to the soldiers in Lt. Calley's platoon who refused to participate in the My Lai massacre as paradigmatic examples of individuals who exemplify the trait of moral courage. Although the nature of the military may appear to demand conformism, soldiers are required by the professional military ethic to foster the trait of moral courage in order to refuse to obey unlawful orders. This is demanded by the role of the soldier, whose ultimate aim is to uphold the constitution, even when doing so requires that he challenge authority.

Furthermore, the value of competence requires that soldiers "develop and maintain the highest possible level of professional knowledge and skill" (Hartle 1989: 53). Soldiers are not only obligated to demonstrate competency of the field manuals that govern combat operations, but they are also required to know, understand and "adhere to the laws of war and the regulations of their service in performing their professional functions" (53). Soldiers must then be capable of distinguishing lawful from unlawful orders by familiarizing themselves with the Law of War that governs the military profession. Ignorance, then, is not an excuse for blindly obeying unlawful orders. Thus, in addition to fostering the trait of obedience (to lawful orders), the role of the soldier requires the virtue of moral courage, in order to renounce unlawful orders, and the virtue of competence, which demands an understanding of the Laws of War and of which actions violate this body of law.

Loyalty to Fellow Comrades

As a member of a team, soldiers have a unique or special obligation to protect and safeguard the lives of their fellow comrades. This consideration is derived from the ethics of care, which maintains that "the central focus of the ethics of care is on the compelling moral salience of attending to and meeting the needs of the particular others for whom we take responsibility" (Held 2006: 10). This same valuing and prioritizing of relationships that is central to care ethics is inseparable from the successful development of relationships within the military, where we find teams of soldiers who form relationships or bonds with each other, which is often referred to as a band of "brothers" or "sisters." Because of the deep relationships that are formed through team-bonding, it seems uncontroversial to maintain that soldiers impart on themselves a deep obligation to their fellow comrades, especially when it comes to preserving their lives. This duty or obligation can be characterized as a form of loyalty, which Coleman characterizes as a:

> loyalty that service members tend to feel for each other, reflected in the desire to protect each other from harm and to defend each other from attack, whatever form that attack may take, and wherever that attack may be thought to be coming from. (Coleman 2009: 109)

The virtue of loyalty is of considerable importance because soldiers operate under the faith that their fellow comrades will do whatever it takes (so long as it is lawful) to save one another and "leave no soldier behind." As Coleman (2009: 111) points out,

military personnel put themselves at risk in performing their duty in combat situations, expecting that their fellow comrades will demonstrate "extreme, possibly unlimited, loyalty." If there were no special commitment to loyalty that encouraged service members to promote the safety and welfare of each other, the military could not function as it does today: soldiers would live in a constant state of fear, anxiety and uncertainty, questioning whether their teammates would make a decision that jeopardizes their lives. To illustrate this point, consider the following scenario:

> Specialist (SPC) Engels, a mounted gunner, is part of a convoy that must drive through a civilian part of town. When his vehicle passes through the local town, it is surrounded by a crowd of civilians. As he patrols the area, he spots a man with an energy formed projectile (EFP), whose body language suggests that he is about to launch it at Engel's vehicle. If the EFP is successfully launched, SPC Engels' whole vehicle will explode, killing not only himself, but the other soldiers in his vehicle. SPC Engels has a choice: (1) he can fire his primary weapon (which is already mounted): an M249, a light machine gun that fires indiscriminately and most certainly will kill innocent civilians in the area, but also will certainly take out the man with the EFP; or (2) he can take the extra time to switch to his secondary weapon, an M4, which is used for more accurate targeting, although the chances of taking out this man are unlikely, given the fact that SPC Engels is in a moving vehicle, and furthermore, the man may launch the EFP before he has time to even switch to his alternate weapon.

SPC Engels can assume a risk by switching to his alternate weapon, yet at the same time, he increases the likelihood that his vehicle will be blown to pieces along with himself and his teammates. If he were to assume such a risk, SPC Engels would violate one of his core duties as a soldier: to protect and promote the lives and safety of his comrades. If SPC Engel's teammates cannot trust him to perform his military duty (in this case, to ensure the safety of his vehicle), then the foundation of trust, which is critical to military success, is undermined. Soldiers would constantly be on guard not only against enemy troops, but against their fellow comrades, fearing that their fellow comrades might deviate from the rehearsed battle plan and engage in risky behavior in order to protect civilians. SPC Engels cannot forget that he is a member of a team that he is uniquely obligated to protect, and assuming a risk in order to protect civilians endangers not only himself, but his fellow comrades who have placed their lives in his hands.

One might point out that cultivating a virtue of "unlimited" loyalty towards one's fellow comrades may compel soldiers to demonstrate loyalty to a soldier who has performed an unlawful act of war and requests another soldier to either help cover it up or keep quiet about the event. We can think of detainee abuse as a prime example. If a soldier refuses to keep quiet about the abuse, he or she might be branded as disloyal. Coleman presents an interesting response to this problem, claiming that:

> given that the original act of misconduct is itself a form of disloyalty, [it is disloyal to the soldier's oath of enlistment and to the aims and ideals of the military], it seems odd in such a case to accuse the second [soldier] of being disloyal; odd to even suggest that loyalty could or should be requested or even demanded by someone who is demonstrating a lack of loyalty at the time. (Coleman 2009: 110)

The military, then, seems to require a qualified sense of loyalty: loyalty to actions and persons who are loyal and moral themselves.

Duties to Civilians (Protected vs Unprotected)

Unpredictable situations may arise that present soldiers with a decision to assume a certain risk in order to protect civilians that: (1) is not addressed by their commander's guidance; and (2) does not endanger their teammates. Consider the following scenario:

> Sergeant (Sgt) Gibson is part of an explosive ordnance disposal (EOD) team whose mission is to dismantle improvised explosive devices (IEDs). On one particular mission, Sgt Gibson takes off by himself to dismantle an IED while the rest of his team stays a considerable distance back. While he is at the IED site, Sgt Gibson sees three individuals running towards him: two men who are firing automatic weapons at him and one child who is dragged along by the men. Because Sgt Gibson has a protective mask on, he is unable to use the only weapon on him: an M4 that requires careful targeting and sight picture alignment in order to successfully take out specific targets. Sgt Gibson has a choice: he can throw a hand grenade at the group, which will take out all three individuals, or he could take off his protective mask and try to take out only the combatants by carefully targeting them with his M4, yet in doing so, he leaves himself vulnerable to the bullets that continue to fire in his direction.

I argue that even in such a scenario, the soldier remains under no obligation to assume an additional risk to protect this child, so long as the child is not a "protected civilian." Yet, I concede that the role of the soldier requires that soldiers assume risks in order to prevent harm to civilians who belong to the "protected civilians" category, which includes co-nationals, to-be-liberated civilians and allied civilians. This is because these civilians have a particular *claim* to protection that "unprotected civilians" do not have.

Before considering this argument, let us return to Walzer's claim that a soldier should employ the principle of risk in his engagements with *all* civilians. The support for this claim stems from the theory that "the structure of rights stands independently of political allegiance; it establishes obligations that are owed, so to speak, to humanity itself and to particular human beings and not merely to one's fellow citizens" (Walzer 1977: 158). Furthermore, since "soldiers are in the business of risking their lives," meaning that it is in the nature of the soldier to take risks, they should be prepared to risk their own lives and demonstrate personal courage and selflessness in order to reduce risk to innocents when acting in their combat roles (Coleman 2009: 104). Christopher (1994: 177) reinforces these claims, maintaining that the purpose of the military force is to "protect the civilian population."

Note that there are two central claims that motivate the principle of risk. The first is that all civilians, as human beings, have a moral status that entitles them to the right not to be attacked, harmed or killed that does not depend upon their nationality (Lee 2004,

Walzer 1977). As Primoratz (1997: 224) writes, "every human being is an individual, a person separate from other persons," which entitles each human being to a high level of respect. This consideration is substantiated by McMahan (2009) and Shue (1980), who rightly point to the moral wrongness of killing innocents, which entails that soldiers have, at the very least, a *negative* duty to avoid harming them.

The second claim that is implied by the principle of risk is that the nature or role of the soldier requires soldiers to risk their lives in order to promote the lives of other human beings, which entails the positive duty to prevent harm or, as Walzer (1977: 156) puts it, it requires soldiers to foster a "positive commitment" to "save civilian lives." Note that the discussion regarding the duty to assume an additional risk to prevent harm to innocents arises specifically in discussions surrounding military operations. Thus, the claim that soldiers, and not civilians, are required to risk their lives in order to promote civilian welfare seems to entail that there is something unique about the role of the soldier that confers on them a special obligation to assume a risk in order to prevent harm.[15]

From these two claims, it is assumed that soldiers should foster a willingness to assume a level of risk to *equally* protect *all* innocents who are present on the battlefield. Since it is respect for the human being that imparts the duty to assume risk on the soldier, Christopher (1994: 104) concludes that "a good rule of thumb might be that enemy civilians (innocents) should be subjected intentionally to no greater risk than to which one is willing to subject one's own innocent population." Soldiers thus are assumed to have an *equal* obligation to prevent harm to all civilians, regardless of their nation membership.

Protected Civilians: Co-Nationals

The view that soldiers have an equal *positive* obligation to protect *all* innocents is rejected by Fleury (1998), who draws what he believes to be a morally relevant distinction between two types of civilians, which results in two different sets of duties and obligations that a soldier might have: (1) negative duties not to harm civilians from the state or country that one's country is at war with; and (2) negative duties not to harm *and* positive duties to protect civilians from one's own nation:

> A distinction should be made between one's own innocents and the innocent citizens of an enemy nation in terms of the moral duty not to intentionally harm noncombatants. Certainly, soldiers do not have the same *positive* duty to protect innocents among the enemy population, as they have to protect their own population, although they have an obligation not to harm innocents intentionally regardless of their nationality. (Fleury 1998: 12; emphasis added by author)

In this passage, Fleury rightly points out that soldiers have an equal moral and legal obligation to refrain from directly harming *any* civilian. That is, regardless of one's national membership, one has a certain moral standing that should be respected due to one's moral status as a human being. Yet, Fleury makes an additional claim: soldiers have an additional duty or obligation to *only* co-nationals. This special duty entails that soldiers assume a *positive* obligation to protect or save co-nationals, even when doing so requires that they put themselves at risk. A clear example where this positive duty was realized is the Iran Hostage Crisis of 1979–81, where, after negotiation attempts with Iran failed to secure the release of American hostages, the military conducted a dangerous rescue attempt, Operation Eagle Claw, which resulted in the death of eight American soldiers. In this situation, American soldiers were said to have a positive duty to save civilian lives, even when doing so posed a significant danger. Yet it is not clear why an American soldier would have this same positive duty if the captives were not Americans, and instead, were from a nation with which the USA was engaged in a defensive war.[16]

This idea that we have special obligations to co-nationals stems from an appeal to what Hurka (1997) refers to as agent-relative national partiality. Such a view is an extension of moral particularism: the view that morality involves particular relations with particular people, which entails that one owes special obligations to those whom one forms relationships with, such as friends, family and, in this case, nation.

As Hurka (2005: 60) points out, "the relations among citizens of a nation are not as close as between parents and children, and the partiality they justify is not as strong. But common sense still calls for some partiality toward fellow citizens." This attitude of partiality to one's co-nationals, if justified, could invoke on soldiers a duty to assume risk in order to protect civilians from their own country.

Hurka maintains that this moderate form of nationalism, partiality to co-nationals (as opposed to full-blooded nationalism, an impersonal partiality that concerns impersonal goals such as the survival and flourishing of one's nation), is justified so long as there is a special tie that warrants agent-relative national partiality. According to Hurka (1997), there are two components of this special tie: (1) a nation having good qualities (like an individual can have good qualities); and (2) co-nationals having a shared-history-of-the-right-kind of doing good together or suffering evil or oppression together. So, American soldiers can be said to be justified in endorsing a form of nationalism, since: (1) the USA has good qualities, such as freedom, equality and so forth, and these qualities define both America and its citizens; and (2) Americans have a shared-history-of-the-right-kind: Americans have bonded together to overcome a number of tragedies, such as the terrorist attacks of 9/11 (Hurka 1997).

This sense of agent-relative national partiality is supported by the motto of the US Military Academy: duty-honor-country (Sorley 1986: 141). Hartle (1989: 49) points out that the country is the object to which the performance of duty and the maintenance of honor are devoted. In the US military enlistment oath, soldiers pledge to protect the constitution against all enemies, foreign and domestic (US Army 2013). Service to the nation or country, then, is the *primary* goal of the military profession: soldiers vow to engage in battle and wars in order to promote their country, which includes both protecting the qualities or traits of the nation (freedom and democracy) and protecting the actual constituents of the state with whom they have a shared history. All of this is to say that soldiers indeed have unique obligations to citizens from their own nation, but not necessarily to every other civilian.

This idea that soldiers have a unique obligation to co-nationals is confirmed by the Soldier's Creed, which embodies the core duties and obligations fundamental to the role of the American soldier: "I am a warrior and a member of a team"; "I serve the people of the United States"; "I will never leave a fallen comrade."[17] These phrases indicate that the Soldier's Creed specifically enumerates the core obligations of a solider: to defend *America* and the *people of the United States*. In evaluating the obligations that soldiers specifically volunteer for and willfully commit to, we will find that they do not necessarily commit themselves to risking their own life to protect *all* civilians, such as those who live in a nation with which the USA is engaged in a defensive war. To dictate further obligations of risk, beyond what a soldier actually agrees to when enlisting in the Armed Forces, is to undermine the soldier's original, voluntary and most sacred commitments.

Protected Civilians: To-Be-Liberated Civilians

The notion of "protected civilians," then, certainly includes civilians from a soldier's own nation (co-nationals). Yet, this notion might also be extended to refer to civilians from other nations, depending on the proclaimed purpose of the particular conflict. As mentioned previously, the *primary* purpose of the US Armed Forces is to protect the constitution against all enemies. Yet, the military can be (and is often) used for other purposes, such as humanitarian interventions where the protection of the USA is not at stake and the publicly proclaimed goal of military action is the ending of human rights violations or the destruction of a corrupt and evil regime. In fact, in the 2002 National Security Strategy, President Bush proclaimed that the USA would "champion aspirations for human dignity" through "special efforts," which presumably include military efforts. This commitment to providing humanitarian relief was re-emphasized later in President Obama's 2010 National Security Strategy and his 2012 review entitled "Sustaining U.S. Global Leadership: Priorities for 21st Century Defense." These reports indicate that the protection of the state evidently is not the exclusive goal of the military: humanitarian and peacekeeping efforts are often the publicly proclaimed goals of the US Armed Forces, as evident in Operation Restore Hope (the 1992–93 humanitarian intervention in Somalia), the Kosovo intervention, and Operation Provide Comfort (the 1991 humanitarian relief for the Kurds in northern Iraq).

Keeping the goal of humanitarian interventions in mind, we might challenge Fleury's claim that, in any given conflict, soldiers have special obligations and duties *only* to co-nationals. Rather, the nature of the respective conflict and the proclaimed goal of the nation determines to whom we owe special duties. As Tripodi (2006: 229) points out, we must draw a distinction between the "warrior ethos" and "peace-keeping ethos"; while the warrior is focused primarily on the protection of the interests of his state and the state's constituents, the peacekeeper is concerned with protecting *all* human beings.

For example, "to-be-liberated civilians," those civilians whom we aim to liberate in a humanitarian intervention, clearly are owed special moral protection since the very goal of the nation's participation in the respective conflict is to reduce civilian harm: not to increase it.[18] As Lucas (2003: 93) points out, intervening forces must be willing to put themselves in harm's way for the sake of the moral ideas that they aim to promote. The point is that it is counterproductive to be motivated to engage in a humanitarian conflict by a principle of reducing harm to civilians, while achieving victory through a violation of such a principle.

Protected Civilians: Allied Civilians

The 2002 and 2010 National Security Strategies do not limit military protection to only those civilians involved in humanitarian interventions. In addition, allies, those nations who join us in mutual benefit in order to achieve a common military goal, are also offered special protection. As it is written in the National Security Strategies of both 2002 and 2010, the USA has a special obligation and commitment to prevent enemies from threatening allies and friends.

Practically speaking, if the military refused to protect and promote the lives of allied civilians, they would open themselves up to conflict with their own allies, whose support they are dependent on for mission success. Keeping in mind that the highest priority of the military is to defend the nation, the military should be committed to ensuring the high morale of its allies by deterring threats against and promoting the welfare of its citizens, even when doing so requires soldiers to assume additional risk.

What all "protected civilians" have in common is this: soldiers and/or the state voluntarily avow to protect them. Thus, the special obligation to assume risk on behalf of "protected civilians" arises from a promissory or contractual obligation. For instance, when considering the special obligation to "protected civilians," we will find that the obligation to assume a risk on their behalf is grounded in the consideration that when soldiers voluntarily enlist in the military and each time they recite the Soldier's Creed, they raise the expectation of those to whom they pledge to protect, namely their fellow comrades, the state, the state's constituents, and also those civilians whom the USA vows to protect and liberate. The constituents of the state and other nations "protected" by the USA thus have a right that their expectation of being protected is met by the soldier, given that the soldier and/or the USA voluntarily raised their expectations.

Furthermore, when soldiers participate in humanitarian interventions, they act as agents of the state that vows to protect the civilians who are exploited by a corrupt or evil regime. By engaging in a humanitarian intervention, the state voluntarily raises the expectation of the civilians who reside in such a regime, thus, as agents of the state, soldiers are bound to fulfill this expectation. Likewise, since the state vows to protect allies, soldiers, as agents of the state, assume a special obligation to protect allied civilians.

Note that neither the state nor the soldier has voluntarily raised the expectations of what I refer to as "unprotected civilians" (which includes, but is not limited to, third-country nationals and civilians from nations that the United States of America is at war with for non-humanitarian reasons) by pledging to save them or reduce harm to them when doing so entails a risk. Since this particular obligation depends upon a voluntary promise, and given the fact that a soldier has not voluntarily promised to protect these civilians, the soldier is, according to this logic, not obligated to assume increased risk in order to promote their welfare.

ANALYSIS OF THE *PRINCIPLE OF RISK* AS A GUIDE FOR COMMANDERS IN DECISION-MAKING

Thus far, I have argued that the principle of risk is not justified as a principle that should guide individual soldier conduct on the battlefield. Although it seems that the decision to assume a risk should not be made at the individual soldier level, this leaves open the possibility that the principle of risk is justified as a principle that guides the commander, who makes the final tactical decisions regarding target selection and civilian encounters during decision-making and planning. Thus one final question remains: is a commander justified in ordering soldiers to assume risk for "unprotected civilians," and if so, under what circumstances?

In order to answer this question, we must first determine the primary duties of a commander. As mentioned earlier, in order to develop an appropriate military ethic, we must first determine the central goal of that profession (Miller 2004: 201). We have already identified that the central goal of the military profession is the security of the state, and one of the means of attaining a secure state is fighting and winning wars (Hartle 1989: 30). Thus, commanders should embrace the virtues and principles that enable them to achieve their defined purpose of accomplishing assigned missions and winning battles. If ordering soldiers to assume extra risks in any way threatens the mission, the commander is obligated to order his soldiers to not assume such risks, regardless of the innocent lives that could potentially be saved.[19]

An example is provided by Walzer that is useful for illustrating this point: in Korea, American troops would automatically use tanks and call for artillery fire and air support in order to return fire into the hillside when they were pinned down and fired upon by enemy troops. The tactic of the American military resulted in "saving" the lives of many American soldiers, but civilians were indiscriminately killed (Walzer 1977: 154–155). Walzer argues that, in this scenario, the soldiers should have sent out a patrol to outflank the enemy rather than use tanks and artillery fire, despite the greater risks that would have been involved (155). Yet, the decision to attack on foot, which Walzer fails to acknowledge, would have been made by the commanding officer. Thus the question remains: should the commander have ordered a patrol to outflank the enemy rather than use tanks and artillery fire? In answering this question, I will defer to a critique by Cohen (1989: 28), who points out that requiring soldiers to set out on foot to outflank the enemy would require the troops to leave their cover in order to advance to root out the enemy and they would be exposed and fired upon while unable to return fire. Assuming such a risk compromises the whole mission, thus the commander, in order to fulfill his duty of ensuring military victory, should have made the decision to call in for artillery fire.

Keep in mind that commanders are not only required by their role as military professionals to win battles, but they are also required to *command* subordinates. Commanding soldiers involves not only delegating and ordering soldiers to fight in certain battles; it also comes with an incredible amount of responsibility over soldiers, their welfare and their lives. That is, as leaders, commanders are responsible for providing for the safety and promoting the welfare of each and every soldier under their command. Furthermore, the responsibility that they have for their soldiers takes priority over any obligation they owe to civilians. This line of thought is substantiated by Article 5947, Title 10, US Code, which states that "commanding officers and others in authority shall take all necessary and proper action . . . to promote and safeguard the morale, physical well-being, and general welfare of the officers and enlisted men under their command and charge" (US Army 2008: 2), and the US Army

& Marine Corps Counterinsurgency Field Manual, which states that soldiers are not obligated "to take so much risk that they fail in their mission or forfeit their lives" (US Army & Marine Corps 2007: 245). Thus, the role of the commander requires that he first and foremost defend his country by winning battles, and second, that he ensures the safety of the troops that he commands by not subjecting them to risks that threaten their lives. . . .

A RE-EVALUATION OF INSTITUTIONAL POLICIES, VALUES AND WARRIOR CODES

Although the fundamental goal of this article is to cast doubt upon the principle of risk as it applies to both soldiers and commanders in the US military, I by no means intend to discount the contemporary concern for collateral damage in the just war literature, nor do I intend to challenge the claim that it is imperative that militaries minimize the harmful effects of war on innocent civilians—protected or unprotected. Rather, what I hope I have illustrated is that, given the US Armed Forces' current policies, values, warrior codes, expectations of service members and proclaimed goals, we cannot reasonably expect soldiers or commanders in the US military to adhere to the principle of risk.

Since the military is responsible for defining both the role of the commander and the role of the soldier, individuals who voluntarily serve in the military are obligated to adhere to the requirements of these respective roles. Yet, neither the role of the soldier nor the role of the commander currently permits military professionals to embrace the principle of risk, since doing so would undermine the stated priorities of the US Armed Forces (i.e. the security of the state). What we need, then, is a radical re-evaluation of political and military priorities: not a new principle for individual soldiers and commanders to embrace that would require them to undermine their roles as defined by the military. . . .

CONCLUSION

Although I have illustrated that, given the current policies, strategies and goals of the US military, the principle of risk undermines both the role of the soldier and commander, Walzer has incited a provocative discussion that, at the very least, should encourage us to challenge the priorities and strategies of the institution of the US military that, for the most part, arguably promote nationalism and narrowly focuses on self-interested goals. Birkeland (1993) claims that the armed forces exist as an icon that represents masculine ethics, with oppressive values and goals. If that is true, and we are able to transform this masculine ethic, we might be able to reassess what we can reasonably demand from combat soldiers and commanders serving in the US Armed Forces.

NOTES

1. This is not necessarily an exhaustive list of all possible civilians who could be classified as "protected civilians," yet it will suffice for the purpose of the following discussion.

2. In this article, my attention is limited to a discussion of the US Armed Forces. My argument fundamentally relies on an analysis of the virtues emphasized in the US military; since other militaries might promote different military virtues, the arguments included in this paper may not be applicable to those militaries.

3. Walzer (1977), Christopher (1994) and Lee (2004) are concerned with the principle of discrimination as it should be used to prevent harm to civilians and protect human rights.

4. For a more in-depth discussion of just war theory, see Toner (2010).

5. The scope of this paper is limited to considerations of *jus in bello*, which addresses the principles of fighting justly once engaged in war. I bracket the issues concerning *jus ad bellum* (the justice of resorting to war in the first place) or *jus post bellum* (considerations of peace agreements and the termination phase of the war), assuming that soldiers are morally obligated to adhere to the principles of *jus in bello* regardless of whether the war is just or unjust.

6. For examples, see Lee (2004), Walzer (1977) and Coady (2008), who are three among many who describe the relationship between just war theory and the DDE. The

noted principles of *jus in bello* (*no means mala in se*, military necessity, discrimination/distinction, proportionality) are described in the Law of War (also known as the Law of Armed Combat), which is derived from international treaties. For example, see: 1949 Geneva Convention (IV): Relative to the Protection of Civilian Persons in Time of War and 1907 Hague Convention: Respecting the Rights and Duties of Neutral Powers and Persons in Case of War on Land (Hague V). The principles of *jus in bello* can also be found in the US Army's *Rule of Land Warfare* (1914: 130, para. 366).

7. Note that in describing the double intention, Walzer (1977) indicates that it requires soldiers to foster a "positive" (159) effort to minimize or reduce harms to civilians (155) and to "save civilian lives" (156). It is unclear if Walzer equates reducing harm with saving lives, but it is clear that he believes that the double effect covers both possibilities (if they are separate categories). Thus some of the examples I give to illustrate my points will be of "reducing harms" and "saving lives," since it appears that Walzer believes that both are entailed by the principle of double intention and risk. It is outside the scope of my paper to argue if there is a moral distinction between the two. However, one could argue that Walzer meant that preventing a harm that might have happened is in fact an instance of saving a life. Also note that neither Lee nor Christopher mention the duty to "save lives"; rather, they speak in terms of "minimizing harms." A special thank you to Helen Frowe who encouraged me to consider how the distinction between "saving lives" and "reducing harms" would apply to this discussion.

8. This comes from Lee (2004).

9. See Van de Pitte (2007) and Hartle (1989:46–47) for extensive discussions of this issue.

10. Note that a commander is restrained by the Rules of Engagement (ROE), which are the primary tools for regulating force. See CJCSI 3121.01B (2005), Standing Rules of Engagement/Standing Rules for the Use of Force for US Forces.

11. See The Hague: *The Convention (Iv) Respecting the Laws and Customs of War on Land and its Annex: Regulations concerning the Laws and Customs of War on Land*, Article 23; Article 27; Article 52 (1907); and the Additional Protocol I, *Protocols to the Geneva Convention*, Article 51 (1977).

12. See the Fourth Geneva Convention: *The Protection of Civilian Persons in Time of War*, Article 52 (1949), and the Additional Protocol I, *Protocols to the Geneva Convention*, Article 51 (1977).

13. *Lawful* order is key here. This rules out the "obligation" of soldiers to partake in morally heinous actions such as torturing or raping another human being.

14. This is not to say that soldiers should be unquestioningly obedient: soldiers are required to challenge, disobey and report unlawful orders, such as those that violate the Law of War.

15. For a thorough discussion of why soldiers are said to be held to a higher standard than ordinary civilians, see Ficarrotta (2010).

16. Keep in mind that this is a clear instance of "saving lives" (which Walzer argues is entailed by the principle of double intention). We can also imagine instances where soldiers are required to assume a risk in order to "minimize harm" to "protected civilians," such as co-nationals. For instance, imagine that several American journalists are held hostage by a terrorist group in a building that American troops are directed to clear. In such a situation, the troops would be required to attack on foot so that while destroying the enemy, they could also prevent the death of the American journalists, as opposed to attacking by an air strike, which would pose an imminent threat to the journalists. It appears that there is a significant difference between how the situation would be handled, and furthermore should be handled, if there were "enemy civilians" in the building rather than co-nationals, in this case American journalists.

17. The Soldier's Creed is the standard that all US Army personnel are encouraged to live by. It accurately summarizes the core duties of a soldier. It is taught at basic training and recited at all training events, ceremonies, and so forth.

18. This terminology (to-be-liberated) is borrowed from Overland (2011). However, the usage differs: Overland draws a further distinction between to-be-liberated civilians and regime-supporting civilians, where the term to-be-liberated civilians refers to only those civilians in a corrupt regime who refuse support of the regime. I use the phrase to-be-liberated to refer to *all* civilians who live in a corrupt regime, in that our aim is still to liberate (and perhaps educate) the oppressed, regardless of how they respond to the intervention.

19. I will, at times, refer to the soldier or commander as "he," since when writing this paper, the Direct Combat Exclusion Rule (DCER), which prohibits females from serving in infantry units below the brigade level and combat Military Occupational Specialties, was still in effect in the US military. Although I recognize that females may still engage in combat under the old DCER, many of the scenarios I describe are that of an infantry unit below the brigade level. With the DCER rescinded in 2013, these arguments will now come to apply to female soldiers and commanders as well.

REFERENCES

Bica, Camillo. (1998) Interpreting Just War Theory's *Jus in Bello* Criterion of Discrimination, *Public Affairs Quarterly*, 12(2), pp. 157–168.

Birkeland, Janis. (1993) Ecofeminism: Linking Theory and Practice, in: Greta Gaard (Ed), *Ecofeminism*, pp. 13–59 (Philadelphia, PA: Temple University Press).

Christopher, Paul. (1994) *The Ethics of War and Peace* (Upper Saddle River, NJ: Prentice Hall).

Coady, C. A. J. (Tony). (2008) *Morality and Political Violence* (New York: Cambridge University Press).

Cohen, Sheldon. (1989) *Arms and Judgment* (Boulder, CO: Westview Press).

Coleman, Stephen. (2009) The Problems of Duty and Loyalty, *Journal of Military Ethics*, 8(2), pp. 105–115. doi:10.1080/15027570903037892.

Ficarrotta, J. Carl. (2010) *Kantian Thinking about Military Ethics* (Farnham: Ashgate).

Fleury, J. G. Col. (1998) Jus in Bello and Military Necessity, *Advanced Military Studies Course 1*, Department of National Defense, accessed 4 April 2014, available at: http://www.cfc. forces.gc.ca/259/260/261/fleury2.pdf; Internet

Geneva Conventions. (1949) Convention (IV) relative to the Protection of Civilian Persons in Time of War, *International Committee at the Red Cross*, accessed 4 April 2014, available at: http://www.icrc.org/ihl.nsf/INTRO/380; Internet.

Geneva Conventions. (1977) Protocol Additional to the Geneva Conventions of 12 August 1949, and Relating to the Protection of Victims of International Armed Conflicts (Protocol I), *International Committee at the Red Cross*, accessed 4 April 2014, available at: http://www. icrc.org/ihl.nsf/INTRO/470; Internet.

Hartle, Anthony. (1989) *Moral Issues in Military Decision Making* (St. Lawrence, KS: University Press of Kansas).

Held, Virginia. (2006) *The Ethics of Care: Personal, Political, and Global* (New York: Oxford University Press).

Hodge, Hope. (2012) Rules of Engagement: Reevaluation Much Needed, *Human Events*, 25 September, accessed 4 April 2014, available at: http://www.humanevents.com/2012/09/25/rules-of-engagement-reevaluation-much-needed/; Internet.

Holmes, Robert. (1989) *On War and Morality* (Princeton, NJ: Princeton University Press).

Huntington, Samuel. (1957) *The Soldier and the State: The Theory and Politics of Civil-Military Relations* (Cambridge, MA: The Belknap Press of Harvard University).

Hurka, Thomas. (1997) The Justification of National Partiality, in: Robert McKim & Jeff McMahan (Eds), *The Morality of Nationalism*, pp. 139–157 (New York: Oxford University Press).

Hurka, Thomas. (2005) Proportionality in the Morality of War, *Philosophy & Public Affairs*, 33(1), pp. 34–66. doi:10.1111/j.1088-4963.2005.00024.x.

Joint Chiefs of Staff. (2002) *Joint Doctrine for Targeting: Joint Publication 3-60* (Washington, DC: Department of Defense).

Joint Chiefs of Staff. (2005) *Standing Rules of Engagement/Standing Rules for the Use of Force for U.S. Forces CJCSI 3121.01B.* (Washington, DC: Department of Defense).

Kasher, Asa. (2007) The Principle of Distinction, *Journal of Military Ethics*, 6(2), pp. 152–167. doi:10.1080/15027570701436841.

Kaufman, Whitley. (2003) What Is the Scope of Civilian Immunity in Wartime? *Journal of Military Ethics*, 2(3), pp. 186–194. doi:10.1080/15027570310000685.

Lackey, Douglas. (1989) *The Ethics of War and Peace* (Englewood Cliffs, NJ: Prentice Hall).

Lee, Steven. (2004) Double Effect, Double Intention, and Asymmetric Warfare, *Journal of Military Ethics*, 3(3), pp. 233–254. doi:10.1080/15027570410006183.

Lichtenberg, Judith. (1994) War, Innocence, and the Doctrine of Double Effect, *Philosophical Studies*, 74(3), pp. 347–368. doi:10.1007/BF00989700.

Luban, David. (1988) *Lawyers and Justice: An Ethical Study* (Princeton, NJ: Princeton University Press).

Lucas, George. (2003) From *Jus ad Bellum* to *Jus ad Pacem*, in: Deen Chatterjee and Don Scheid (Eds), *Ethics and Foreign Intervention*, pp. 72–96 (Cambridge: Cambridge University Press).

McKeogh, Colm. (2002) *Innocent Civilians: The Morality of Killing in War* (Basingstoke: Palgrave Macmillan).

McMahan, Jeff. (2009) *Killing in War* (Oxford: Clarendon Press).

Miller, Joseph. (2004) Squaring the Circle: Teaching Philosophical Ethics in the Military, *Journal of Military Ethics*, 3(3), pp. 199–215. doi:10.1080/15027570410006219.

Miller, Richard. (1991) *Interpretations of Conflict* (Chicago, IL: University of Chicago Press).

Miller, William. (2000) *The Mystery of Courage* (Cambridge, MA: Harvard University Press).

Olsthoorn, Peter. (2007) Courage in the Military: Physical and Moral, *Journal of Military Ethics* 6(4), pp. 270–279. doi:10.1080/15027570701755471.

Overland, Gerhard. (2011) High-Fliers: Who Should Bear the Risk of Humanitarian Intervention?, in: Paolo Tripodi & Jessica Wolfendale (Eds), *New Wars and New Soldiers*, pp. 69–86 (Burlington, VT: Ashgate).

Plaw, Avery. (2010) Upholding the Principle of Distinction in Counter-Terrorist Operations: A Dialogue, *Journal of Military Ethics*, 9(1), pp. 3–22. doi:10.1080/15027570903523073.

Primoratz, Igor. (1997) What is Terrorism?, *Journal of Applied Philosophy*, 14(3), pp. 221–233. doi:10.1111/1468-5930.00059.

Ramsey, Paul. (1961) *War and the Christian Conscience: How Shall Modern War Be Conducted?* (Durham, NC: Duke University Press).

Rodin, David. (2004) Terrorism without Intention, *Ethics*, 114, pp. 752–771. doi:10.1086/383442.

Schwenkenbecher, Anne. (2014) Collateral Damage and the Principle of Due Care, *Journal of Military Ethics* 13(1). doi:10.1080/15027570.2014.910015.

Shue, Henry. (1980) *Basic Rights: Subsistence, Affluence and US Foreign Policy* (Princeton, NJ: Princeton University Press).

Smith, Herschel. (2007) Politically Correct Rules of Engagement Endanger Troops, *The Captain's Journal*, accessed 4 April 2014 available at: http://www.captainsjournal.com/2006/12/06/politically-correct-rules-of-engagement-endanger-troops; Internet.

Solis, Gary. (2010) *The Law of Armed Conflict: International Humanitarian Law in War* (Cambridge: Cambridge University Press).

Sorley, Lewis. (1986) Duty, Honor, Country: Practice and Precept, in: Malham M. Wakin (Ed), *War, Morality, and the Military Profession*, pp. 140–156 (Boulder, CO: Westview Press).

Szoldra, Paul. (2012) Marine: Strict Rules of Engagement Are Killing more Americans than Enemy in this Lost War, *Business Insider*, 24 August, accessed 4 April 2014, available at: http://www.businessinsider.com/one-marines-views-on-afghanistan-2012-8; Internet.

The Hague. (1907) Convention (IV) Respecting the Laws and Customs of War on Land and its Annex: Regulations Concerning the Laws and Customs of War on Land, *International Committee at the Red Cross*, accessed 4 April 2014, available at: http://www.icrc.org/applic/ihl/ihl.nsf/INTRO/195; Internet.

Thomson, Judith Jarvis. (1991) Self Defense, *Philosophy and Public Affairs*, 20(4), pp. 283–310.

Toner, Christopher. (2010) The Logical Structure of Just War Theory, *Journal of Ethics*, 14(2), pp. 81–102.

Tripodi, Paolo. (2006) Peacekeepers, Moral Autonomy, and the Use of Force, *Journal of Military Ethics*, 5(3), pp. 214–232. doi:10.1080/15027570600913338.

Tunnell, Harry, Col. (2010) Open Door Policy – Report from a Tactical Commander (Memorandum for the Honorable John McHugh, Secretary of the Army), 20 August, accessed 4 April 2014, available at: http://www.michaelyon-online.com/images/pdf/secarmy_redactedredux.pdf; Internet.

US Army. (1914) *Rule of Land Warfare* (Washington, DC: United States War Department).

US Army. (1956) *The Law of Land Warfare: FM 27-10* (Washington, DC: Department of the Army).

US Army. (1976) *The Army: FM 100-1* (Washington, DC: Department of the Army).

US Army. (2008) *Command Policy Army Regulation: FM 600-20* (Washington, DC: Department of the Army).

US Army. (2013) *Army Doctrine Reference Publication ADRP 1: The Army Profession* (Washington, DC: Department of the Army).

US Army & Marine Corps. (2007) *US Army & Marine Corps Counterinsurgency Field Manual: FM 3-24* (Washington, DC: Department of the Army).

Van de Pitte, Margaret. (2007) What Is Wrong with a Military Career?, *Peace Review*, 19(2), pp. 183–189.

Walzer, Michael. (1977) *Just and Unjust Wars* (New York: Basic Books).

Walzer, Michael. (2004) *Arguing about War* (New Haven, CT: Yale University Press).

DISCUSSION QUESTIONS

1. Do you agree with Michael Walzer that the Doctrine of Double Effect is too permissive with respect to collateral casualities? Why or why not?

2. Abbate claims that "the military has a unique status" and that soldiers and commanders are "outside the scope of ordinary morality." What role does this claim play in her argument? Do you agree with that claim? Why or why not?

3. Abbate describes a hypothetical scenario in which the fictional Sgt. Gibson must decide how much risk to take in order to protect a child while responding to an attack on his life. What does Abbate conclude about Gibson's obligations in this scenario? What is her argument for that conclusion? Do you find it convincing? Why or why not?

4. Do Abbate's arguments entail that soldiers are *never* obligated to undertake *any* additional risk to avoid harm to "unprotected civilians"? Why or why not?

BRADLEY JAY STRAWSER

Moral Predators: The Duty to Employ Uninhabited Aerial Vehicles

Bradley Jay Strawser is Assistant Professor of Philosophy at the Naval Postgraduate School in Monterey, California, and a Research Associate at the Oxford Institute for Ethics, Law, and Armed Conflict at the University of Oxford. In this paper, Strawser considers and rejects various arguments against the military use of uninhabited aerial vehicles (UAVs), more commonly known as "drones." He then argues that, under certain circumstances, the military is actually obligated to use UAVs rather than other means of warfare.

GUIDING QUESTIONS

1. What kinds of weapons, exactly, does Strawser include under the label "uninhabited aerial vehicles"? What kinds of weapons does he explicitly exclude?
2. What is the "principle of unnecessary risk (PUR)" and what reasons does Strawser give for accepting it?
3. What is Strawser's main conclusion? What is his basic argument for that conclusion?

INTRODUCTION

Lethal employment of uninhabited aerial vehicles (UAVs) has risen precipitously by a few Western nation-states (most notably the United States) across several theaters of operation (Afghanistan, Pakistan, Yemen, and other locations).[1] The emergence of this technology has sparked widespread debate over the ethical justification of its use. Some claim these drones create a particularly asymmetrical form of warfare that is somehow ignoble or dishonorable. Others contend that UAVs impede certain *jus in bello* principles. Some claim that drones create psychological conflicts for their operators (who are often thousands of miles away) causing unacceptable cognitive dissonance in the mindset of the warrior. Still others raise concerns over drones carrying

out targeted killings by non-military government agencies (such as the CIA) and other concerns over their present employment. There is a worry that UAVs could lead to autonomous weapons that make lethal decisions on their own. Finally, some argue that by removing the pilot from the theater of combat a degree of asymmetrical warfare is attained such that the risk threshold for a given state is lowered too far—that it becomes too easy for a state using drones to go to war; thus, their use is ethically pernicious.

In this paper I argue that there is an ethical obligation to use UAVs. Indeed, I hold that, in principle, there is no need for special ethical concern for this weapons system as opposed to any other more standard weapon technology. All of the concerns just listed either miss their mark and do not challenge the ethical obligation to employ UAVs in principle or else do not rise to the level needed to override

Journal of Military Ethics, "Moral Predators: The Duty to Employ Uninhabited Aerial Vehicles", 9(4), 2010, 342–368, Bradley Jay Strawser, Copyright © 2010, Taylor and Francis. With permission of Springer.

the principles which form the basis of ethical obligation for UAV employment. I argue that remotely controlled weapons systems are merely an extension of a long historical trajectory of removing a warrior ever farther from his foe for the warrior's better protection. UAVs are only a difference in degree down this path; there is nothing about their remote use that puts them in a different ethical category.

My argument rests on the premise that if an agent is pursuing a morally justified yet inherently risky action, then there is a moral imperative to protect this agent if it possible to do so, unless there exists a countervailing good that outweighs the protection of the agent. Thus, I will contend that, as a technology that better protects (presumably) justified warriors, UAV use is ethically obligatory, not suspicious. After some preliminaries, I will first present the argument for the ethical obligation to use remotely controlled weapons. Then I will walk through the various ethical concerns which are supposed problems for UAV implementation and show how each of these worries is misplaced or fails to adequately counter the ethical obligation for their use.

REMOTE WEAPONS AS ETHICALLY OBLIGATORY

Media coverage and public debate over the military use of uninhabited remotely controlled weapons is currently *en vogue*.[2] It is surprising then, given such a backdrop, that the case for the ethical obligation to employ UAVs has yet to have been definitively made. That is precisely what I intend to do. First, some distinctions must be made regarding what the target of my claims in this paper will be. Primarily, I am referencing those aircraft presently employed by the United States (and other) militaries commonly known as "Unmanned Aerial Vehicles" or drones. To avoid unnecessary gender bias I prefer the locution of Uninhabited Aerial Vehicles (UAVs) which I will use throughout.[3] Examples include the General Atomics MQ-1 Predator and the General Atomics MQ-9

Reaper.[4] UAVs have been employed for some time as reconnaissance aircraft, but only fairly recently have such platforms been used for lethal engagement. Critically, when referencing UAVs I only intend those aircraft which are under human control for, at the minimum, any particular lethal action the machine executes. Autonomous weapon systems, which can execute lethal actions apart from a human decision to do so—that can operate "on their own"—will be addressed below in Objection 1. Finally, my discussion here regarding the ethical obligation to employ UAVs could be applied, with the necessary changes, to any remotely controlled lethal weapon system, including land- or sea-based remotely controlled weapons.[5]

I contend that in certain contexts UAV employment is not only ethically permissible, but is, in fact, ethically obligatory. The basis for this claim rests upon what I call the principle of unnecessary risk (PUR). PUR proceeds as follows: If X gives Y an order to accomplish good goal G, then X has an obligation, other things being equal, to chose a means to accomplish G that does not violate the demands of justice, make the world worse, or expose Y to potentially lethal risk unless incurring such risk aids in the accomplishment of G in some way that cannot be gained via less risky means. That is, it is wrong to command someone to take on *unnecessary* potentially lethal risks in an effort to carry out a just action for some good; any potentially lethal risk incurred must be justified by some strong countervailing reason. In the absence of such a reason, ordering someone to incur potentially lethal risk is morally impermissible. Importantly, PUR is a demand not to order someone to take unnecessary risk *on par* with alternative means to accomplish some goal G. This is what the other things being equal clause is meant to capture. That is, in some cases, the only possible way to accomplish G will be to order Y to undertake a particular means which exposes Y to potentially lethal risk. In such cases, PUR is not directly applicable; whether or not the order is justified must be determined on other grounds. PUR simply demands that no *more* risk than is required for the accomplishment of G (no unnecessary risk) is ordered by X to be incurred by Y.

I take PUR to be uncontroversial. In fact, it is possible that an even stronger form of PUR could be developed that morally bars not only potentially lethal risk, but any risk of bodily harm whatsoever. Further, there may be a reflexive form of PUR available that could entail self-regarding duties not to incur potentially lethal risk unnecessarily. But some may complain that an individual has the moral permission to incur lethal risk in carrying out act X in pursuit of good A even if the risk in no way aids the accomplishment of A (or some other good B) nor is demanded by justice. To avoid such controversy, I employ here the more modest form of PUR as I have developed it. So even if some wish to contend that it is morally permissible for an individual to take unnecessary potentially lethal risks upon his or herself in accomplishing some good, it still seems that PUR holds with no problems, focused as it is upon commanding others to action.[6] That is, if some argue that there are no moral prohibitions against recklessly endangering one's own life for no good reason, certainly morality demands that there is a strong moral prohibition against unnecessarily endangering another's life.[7]

Another important argument can be used for the obligation to employ UAVs over inhabited aerial vehicles. Namely, UAVs are, on par, cheaper to produce and deploy than inhabited planes that accomplish similar missions. Thus, the argument could run, we are obligated to spend as little shared resources as are necessary on any given collective venture (such as a military undertaking), since those resources are scarce and could be used for other worthy goals. A principle of unnecessary waste of scarce resources (PUWSR) could be formulated to capture the normative appeal of such an approach.[8] PUWSR would contend that by not employing UAVs to the greatest extent possible militaries are wasting scarce resources and that UAVs should, therefore, be used in place of inhabited aircraft so as to be better stewards of said shared resources. For, after all, any money not spent on a military venture could be allocated towards other important demands of social justice, such as (say) an egalitarian concern for equal opportunity of welfare.[9] Such a principle, then, could be used to put normative pressure on the financial budgets of Western militaries and demand that efficiency of cost is an important moral issue.

I laud such approaches—and find financial concerns to be particularly relevant in the case of UAV underemployment—but in this paper I set aside such arguments and focus instead on what I see as the stronger normative principle of unnecessarily risking an agent performing a morally justified act. I do this because appeals to principles like PUWSR, while legitimate, are often more easily overridden by other competing normative concerns. That is, even a relatively significant cost difference between two competing methods for carrying out a given act could quickly become moot were there any relevant differences warranting moral concern between the two courses of action. Of course, in this case (UAVs versus inhabited aircraft) whether there are such differences will often be an empirical question. And if, as I assume in this paper, UAVs can carry out similar missions without any significant loss in capability, then concerns over cost would apply just as well. But I still view PUR as a stronger moral claim—one that demands a higher justificatory bar to override—than principles such as the PUWSR; thus, it is upon PUR that I base my central claims in this paper.

Returning then to PUR, an example may help demonstrate its modest moral demands and *prima facie* appeal. Imagine a group of soldiers are fighting in a just war against an unjust enemy. The (unjust) enemy soldiers are, say, invading the just soldiers' country and committing horrific crimes against humanity in the process. In the defensive effort a group of just soldiers, led by Captain Zelda, engage the enemy who are a short 50 yards away. Assume that engaging these enemy soldiers is a just action in pursuit of some good (in this case the good of defending their homes, families, themselves, and other innocents). Captain Zelda has an idea. She decides to remove her bullet-proof vest, throw down her rifle, and charge the enemies with nothing more than a large rock and chutzpa. She turns to the troops under her command and orders them to do likewise. Set aside whether or not such an action is morally permissible for Captain Zelda to pursue individually. Also assume that charging the enemy in this fashion would in no way aid in accomplishing the good of successfully attacking the enemies yet would dramatically increase the lethal risk her troops incur. PUR says that it is morally impermissible for her to order her fellow troops in her squad to take off their bullet-proof vests, throw down their rifles, and charge the enemy with only a rock since there is no good reason to do so. PUR holds that it is morally impermissible for Captain Zelda to endanger the lives of her troops any more than is necessary for the accomplishment of good A. My argument below for the moral obligation to employ UAVs rests on PUR as a sound moral principle.

Note that such an action as Captain Zelda's planned foolhardy charge *may* contribute to some other thing, Q, which she takes as a good, such as an adrenaline rush or perceived valor gained by taking such inordinate risks. In such a case, one could try to argue that the act passes PUR since it aims at some other (purported) good. But PUR is not in the business of determining whether or not certain goals are goods worthy of being sought. It is a structural principle that functions on permissible commands to others only after it has been determined what the morally proper good to pursue should be. So, granting a proper good, PUR demands that one commands others to incur lethal risk (or increased lethal risk) only in pursuit of that good (or some equal or greater good) if it is necessary in the way defined. That is, the risk one orders another to incur must track exactly with the necessity of that risk in relation to the accomplishment of the purported good. In this case, we are agreeing that the good sought (or the good that *should* be sought) is the successful attacking of the enemy; hence, Captain Zelda's actions are impermissible by way of PUR for they do not aid in the accomplishment of the proper good nor are they demanded by justice or some other good. If Captain Zelda engages in reckless warfare and orders others to do likewise not because of necessity but because of some personal pleasure gained by the excitement of risk-taking and combat, then we would conclude her actions to be morally impermissible for other reasons outside PUR. That is, it may very well be that Captain Zelda orders her troops to make such a brash charge in the pursuit of something she takes as a good. In that case, the reason her action is wrong is not due to PUR but because she is mistaken that this is a good worthy of being sought and ordering others to seek (the adrenaline rush of risky combat, say). But, if we agree that the good that *should* be sought is attacking the enemy, her orders are impermissible via PUR because her commands in no way help in this aim even though they cause her troops to incur (greater) lethal risk.

Granting PUR then, consider the following claim, OP:

(OP) For any just action taken by a given military, if it is possible for the military to use UAV platforms in place of inhabited aerial vehicles without a significant loss of capability, then that military has an ethical obligation to do so.

I argue that OP is true. It could, of course, very well turn out that OP is only vacuously true because the antecedent is false. This paper will not primarily be arguing for or against the truth of OP's antecedent, but instead assume it is true and argue that the normative consequent follows.[10] The antecedent of OP could be false for any number of reasons. First, it could turn out to be technologically infeasible to transition some military aircraft into remotely piloted vehicles without a significant loss of capability, for various reasons.[11] Or it could be near impossible to do so due to budgetary constraints.[12] Further, it could be that the antecedent of OP is false because remotely controlled weapon systems cannot practice target discrimination as effectively as inhabited vehicles can; and this would constitute a significant loss of capability. Or it could turn out that for some as of yet unforeseen reason remotely piloted weapon systems are not as capable in some other manner as inhabited vehicles. In any such case, the antecedent is false and OP is vacuously true.

There are very good reasons to believe, however, that the antecedent of OP could be true and even likely, as will be mentioned at points below. The central aim of this paper, however, is to establish that the normative consequent follows if the antecedent is true. Further, the antecedent of these claims is an empirical question—one that can be tested for its veracity. What I am investigating is whether there is any principled reason for not employing UAVs. I contend that there is not, and further (based on PUR) that there is a strong moral obligation to use them in place of inhabited aircraft. If there is such an obligation, then OP follows.[13]

Note that the "in place of" criterion of OP is crucial for its derivation from PUR. A given commander in a combat context is obligated by PUR to order her troops to use weapon Z in place of W if and only if Z reduces the risk placed on that soldier in comparison with and as an alternative to W. It is the risk differential between options Z and W that is the source of the obligation. To put it another way, because Z exists and is presently available for the commander to order her troops to use *in place of* W, the commander is obligated *not* to order the use of W so long as Z is a viable alternative that meets the other criteria (such as not violating the demands of justice). That is to say, the ordering to use Z is (presumably) permissible in a just warfighting context; it becomes obligatory only as an *alternative* to W. But, if only W exists (or is the only option for other reasons, such as the demands of justice), then it could very well be permissible to order the use of W. Both W and the less-risky Z must be viable options for the obligation to use Z to instantiate via PUR.

To build the case for OP's consequent, consider the following scenario. Two small towns, Prudentville and Recklessville, each have a local police force that includes a highly trained "bomb squad." Each bomb squad has been very successful in disarming and disposing of malicious explosive ordnance throughout the years with few (but some) casualties. Recently, both towns acquired remotely controlled robots that can be used to disarm explosives while being operated from afar. Under the control of a trained explosive ordnance disposal (EOD) technician, these robots are just as capable at disarming bombs as the EOD technicians are themselves working "hands on." And with the robots, of course, the EOD technicians are not at any risk of injury or death. After some initial experimentation to ensure use of the robots did not cost them any bomb-disarming capability, Prudentville decides to have their bomb squad use the robots in any situation where it was possible to do so. They viewed the decision as a "no-brainer": saving the life of even one bomb-technician would be well worth the cost of using the robot. Recklessville decides not to have their EOD technicians use the robots, even though they have them available and are capable of doing so. Thus, they put their bomb technicians at risk for no reason (or no *good* reason, at any rate) and violate PUR.

Take the above story as a guiding normative analogy for claim OP.[14] If it is possible for the bomb squad to use a robot to defuse the bomb remotely, with no significant or relevant loss of capability, then via PUR the bomb squad has a clear ethical obligation to use the robot in place of a human handling the bomb directly. The situation is relevantly analogous with the current and future use of remotely controlled military aircraft. That is, if it is possible for a state to have its military use remotely controlled weapon systems to carry out combat missions instead of inhabited weapon systems, with no significant or relevant loss of capability, then via PUR (assuming military missions carry potentially lethal risks) the state has a clear ethical obligation to do so. This is simply because by operating at a much greater distance from combat, the operator of the weapon system is exposed to significantly less risk. And if there is no compelling reason to expose a soldier to risk, then it is wrong to do so. Hence, OP.

One important caveat: The justification of remotely controlled weapons in war here assumes that their employment is done as part of a fully justified war effort meeting both *jus ad bellum* and *jus in bello* criteria. Thus, if the military in question is justified in a particular military strike in the first place, they should protect the just warrior carrying out the action to the greatest extent as is possible—up until protecting the warrior impedes his/her ability to behave justly in combat, as will be argued below. Granted, if a given military action is unjustified, then it is unjustified whether it is done by a pilot flying an aircraft remotely or otherwise. That is, my argument that the employment of UAVs is ethically obligatory follows out of PUR in that a given military action in question must be a proper good in the first place. If the act is morally unjustified to begin with, then it is morally impermissible for other reasons outside of the scope of PUR. Notice, for example, that this leaves open the possibility that universal pacifism may be the correct moral outlook towards warfare and yet

OP still holds (although vacuously, because a pacifist will hold that there simply are no justified military actions).

A related point is that some may here object that my analogy between a bomb squad and a military force fails for the bomb squad is trying to disarm a bomb, and thereby *prevent* the loss of life, whereas a military strike is attempting to *take* life. Yet the point of connection for the analogy is not what, specifically, the given action is attempting to carry out (be it disarming a bomb or delivering a bomb), but simply that a particular action is justified and aiming towards *some* worthy good combined with being inherently risky to the agent engaging in the action. Again, the analogy to UAV use rests on a presumption that a given military strike employing a UAV is justified to start with—if it is not, then the UAV strike is morally impermissible, of course.[15] So the case with the bomb squad is intended to focus on the moral principle of unnecessary risk in the execution of *some* good. The bomb squad, commanded by their town, undertakes morally justified but risky action F aiming to accomplish good goal G. If G can be accomplished just as effectively but with less risk to the bomb squad by a means other than F (such as by using a robot), then there is a moral obligation to use the robot.

The same reasoning applies, with the necessary changes, for a given military force. A military, commanded by their state, undertakes morally justified but risky action F aiming to accomplish good goal G. If G can be accomplished equally as effectively but with less risk to the military members (such as by using an uninhabited drone), then there is a moral obligation to use the drone. That the good G for the bomb squad case is the protection of life while in the UAV case G is the taking of life is not a relevant difference for the analogy. What matters is that G is a good worthy of pursuit.

To put the position another way still: ordering a warfighter to take on risk in any activity must be justified. If a given action can be equally well accomplished via two different methods, one of which incurs less risk for the warfighter's personal safety than the other, then a justification must be given for why this safer method is not used. If there is no good reason not to use it, then we are obligated to employ the safer method. For all cases of ordering a warfighter to undertake any given risky action, there should be a reason that demonstrates why the risk is necessary for the accomplishment of the given objective. If one grants that removing a pilot from the theater of combat by using a UAV instead of an inhabited weapon platform greatly reduces the risk to that pilot, then there should be a presumption for using a UAV (or any remote weapon) whenever it is possible to do so in a way that does not compromise the capability of a given warrior to behave justly. The burden of proof, then, is on those who argue that we should not employ UAVs or similar remote technology. Such a position needs to justify why we should have pilots take on such risk. As mentioned above, there are a variety of objections usually offered as to why UAV employment is ethically suspicious. I shall now review each of these in turn and show why they fail to overcome the claim that UAVs are, in principle, ethically obligatory.[16]

OBJECTION 1: THE MOVE TO INDEPENDENT AUTONOMOUS WEAPONS SYSTEMS

Some worry that UAVs lead us down a road toward independent autonomous weapons (IAWs); robots that make lethal decisions on their own.[17] Where to draw the line when a weapon system is "autonomous" is notoriously difficult.[18] For simplicity's sake here, I refer to any weapon that makes a decision on its own accord to launch a particular lethal attack as "independently autonomous" (or "fully" autonomous as is sometimes used). Thus, a cruise missile that guides itself to a target would not be an IAW because a human agent made the decision to launch it and for it to go attack the given target, but a Predator drone programmed so as to make the particular decision to fire on a specific target of its own accord would become an IAW. So long as there is a "human in the loop" (to use the common military parlance) for each particular lethal decision, I consider it non-autonomous for the purposes of this paper. That is, so long as a human agent makes the decision whether or not to employ lethal force, the weapon is not an IAW as I use the term. The argument against the employment of UAVs runs like this: IAWs are morally impermissible. UAV development will lead to IAWs. Therefore, UAV development is impermissible.

RESPONSE

As an objection against UAV usage goes, this fails to counter the moral obligation for their employment. In fact, we can grant the first premise (that "IAWs are morally impermissible") but dispatch the objection by arguing that its second premise is presently unsubstantiated (that "UAV development will lead to IAWs"). One could agree with the objection that we should not develop IAWs and that we should not allow development of UAVs to lead us down the road towards IAWs. Indeed, it is plausible that it could be difficult to stop such a progression, but it is not true that the development of UAVs will *necessarily* lead to the development of IAWs. Thus, we need empirical evidence to show that this is the case. The objection is a kind of slippery slope objection because it assumes that the development and employment of UAVs must lead to the development and deployment of IAWs. Slippery slope objections are problematic because they fail to acknowledge a plausible middle ground stopping point. Namely, this objection misses the possibility of maintaining the employment of UAVs while at the same time working for the banning of IAWs (something I recommend Western nation-states do). Thus, at present, this objection fails as an argument against the ethical obligation to employ (and develop) UAV technology.

I raise this objection first so as to make an important distinction for the scope of this paper. In this paper I am only arguing for the moral obligation to use remote weapons that are explicitly non-autonomous, at least regarding any lethal decisions. On my view, the distinction between IAWs and non-autonomous

remote weapons is of paramount importance in this debate and is often neglected. One reason it is so important is that if this distinction is neglected and, even more importantly, if this distinction is not enforced and efforts to develop IAWs are not stopped, then objection 1 stands (assuming that one grants its first premise). That is, to be clear, it is entirely possible that the use of UAVs will in fact lead to the use of IAWs. If this can be shown to be the case and if it cannot be stopped, then, since I do grant the first premise, I see it as a legitimate objection against the employment of UAVs. But my hope is that the development of IAWs can be stopped even while UAVs are employed and developed. I do not here have space to argue against the moral permissibility of IAWs—that has been done effectively elsewhere (see Sparrow 2007; Asaro 2006, 2007; Himma 2007).[19]

Some may object that my acceptance of the premise that "IAWs are morally impermissible" is inconsistent with my use of PUR to ground the moral obligation to use UAVs. The objection would contend that many weapon systems which could (arguably) be considered IAWs offer far better protection of a just warfighter and are thereby obligatory via PUR. Examples could be weapons systems such as the Phalanx Close In Weapon System or the SeaRAM employed by the US Navy when they are used in fully autonomous mode. Without such weapon systems many sailors would potentially be at unnecessary risk, or so this objection claims.[20] But this objection fails to appreciate that PUR, although a strong at first view moral principle, can be overridden by a strong enough countervailing normative reason. In this case, although I do not argue for it here, I find the principled objections to IAWs to be sufficiently strong such that they override the moral demands of PUR. That is to say, it is perfectly compatible and in no way logically inconsistent to hold (as I do) that some non-autonomous weapon systems (such as UAVs) are obligatory via PUR and at the same time hold that IAWs are impermissible on grounds specific to their autonomous nature which overrides PUR. In any case, regardless of whether or not one accepts the first premise of objection 1, the objection on the whole fails because it is a slippery slope argument that is inadequately substantiated.

OBJECTION 2: UAV LIMITATIONS LEAD TO *JUS IN BELLO* VIOLATIONS

Some grant that remotely controlled weapons better protect the just warfighter but argue that they do so at the cost of a decreased ability to discriminate combatants from noncombatants and other *jus in bello* compromises.

RESPONSE

Certainly, if an UAV operator engaging the battlefield from thousands of miles away through a video feed is unable to properly adhere to the *jus in bello* principles of discrimination and proportionality, then such drones should not be used. Indeed, if using a UAV in place of an inhabited weapon platform in anyway whatsoever decreases the ability to adhere to *jus in bello* principles, then a UAV should not be used. This is consistent with OP since adhering to principles of discrimination and proportionality are key aspects of a weapon system's capability. And the just warrior's increased protection (which a UAV provides) should not be bought at an increased risk to noncombatants. Martin Cook (2004) makes this point effectively when he discusses the 1999 NATO air campaign waged in Kosovo. It seemed to some that by conducting missions at a minimum of 15,000 feet, NATO was more concerned with force-protection than noncombatant discrimination (see Cook 2004: 126–127). Had the combat missions been flown at a lower altitude they would have put the pilots at more risk but would have been significantly better at discriminating between, say, an ambulance and a military transport. It is the duty of the just warfighter, I contend, to take additional risk upon him/herself if such risk is required in order to better shield innocents from harm.[21] Thus, in arguing for OP, part of the assumption of the antecedent is that the use of UAVs does not hamper the warfighter's (technical) ability to discriminate between combatants and noncombatants nor make judicious decisions of proportionality. Such a technical weakness would constitute a "significant loss of capability."

However, there is good reason to think just the opposite is true: that UAV technology actually *increases* a pilot's ability to discriminate. For example, the Israeli government-owned Rafael Armament Development Authority claims that with the new Spike Extended Range precision missile, which is designed to be used by UAVs, they have achieved "urban warfare precision" (Rafael Advanced Defense Systems 2010). The missile can be launched in a fire, observe, and update mode (as opposed to a "fire and forget" mode) that "allows the UAV operator to update the missile, aim, point, or steer the missile off course if the intended target turns out to be a civilian" (Rafael Advanced Defense Systems 2010). The report goes on to quote an Israeli pilot who has used the weapon system: "The beauty of this seeker is that as the missile gets closer to the target, the picture gets clearer. . . . The video image sent from the seeker via the fiber-optic link appears larger in our gunner's display. And that makes it much easier to distinguish legitimate from non-legitimate targets" (Rafael Advanced Defense Systems 2010).[22]

And recent studies bear out that UAVs appear to have, in fact, greater technical capabilities at making determinations of combatant status. Avery Plaw (2010) has recently compiled a database combining reports from a variety of sources on the results of United States UAV attacks carried out in Pakistan from 2004 to 2007. This data shows that UAV strikes were far better at noncombatant discrimination than all other methods used for engaging Taliban fighters in the region. For example, the UAV strikes resulted in a ratio of over 17 to 1 of intended militant targets to civilian deaths compared with a 4 to 1 ratio for Pakistan Special Weapons and Tactics Teams team offensives or a nearly 3 to 1 for Pakistan Army operations in the same region during the same time period. Or, compare the 17 to 1 ratio for the UAV employment to the shocking 0.125 to 1 militant to civilian casualty ratio estimate for all armed conflict worldwide for the year 2000 (Plaw 2010).[23] If these numbers are even close to accurate, it seems that there is strong evidence which directly contradicts the central premise of objection 2. That is, UAVs are better, not worse, at noncombatant discrimination.

Regardless, however, whether or not UAVs are as technically capable of making determinations of proper target discrimination is an empirical question. If it turns out that UAVs are not as capable, then OP's antecedent is false and the claim is vacuously true. At present, however, all available evidence points strongly towards there being no reduction in the technical ability of UAV pilots to discriminate as opposed to inhabited aircraft pilots' ability. But, this being an empirical matter, there is no in-principle objection here to UAVs being ethically obligatory for military use.

OBJECTION 3: COGNITIVE DISSONANCE FOR UAV OPERATORS

This objection worries that the use of drones leads to psychological conflicts for their operators causing cognitive dissonance in the mindset of the warrior. The worry can manifest two separate ethical concerns, first that it is wrong to do this to UAV operators—for them to kill the enemy from their "desk" at work and then go home to dinner and their child's soccer match—that this places an unjust psychological burden on them. The second and greater concern is that this cognitive dissonance will weaken the operator's will to fight justly in several ways (e.g. the operators not taking the warfare as "real" or serious enough but instead viewing it as a video game; the operators suffering mental problems and post traumatic stress disorder which, because of their distance from the battlefield, could go untreated and unrecognized, causing further problems and leading to inappropriate decisions; and so forth.)[24]

RESPONSE

The argument that the ethical justification for UAVs is threatened if UAV operators are more likely to behave unjustly in their combat actions due to this cognitive dissonance is unsound. First, it can be argued that the temptation for the warfighter to commit *jus in bello* violations would actually lessen, perhaps significantly so, once the warfighter is not at risk. The remote pilot can take more time in evaluating a target before firing—to ensure that target is an enemy combatant—than they would be able to otherwise; for in the worst case scenario a machine is lost, not a human pilot. Returning to the bomb squad analogy, in using a robot the EOD technicians do not experience the same level of stress because there is no danger to themselves; thus, they are not as nervous and, presumably, more successful. The same could hold true for UAV pilots making judicious decisions in combat. Once fear for their own safety is not a pressing concern, one would assume the operator would be more capable, not less, of behaving justly.

But perhaps this is not the case. Maybe the distance and disjunct of this level of remote weaponry does create a significant and genuinely new kind of stress on warfighters that might compromise their abilities to behave justly. There is significant empirical work here yet to be done. But even if we grant that displaced combat harms UAV pilots' abilities, first note that there are means of overcoming this problem and, second, that this issue is not a knock against the ethical justification of UAVs themselves. If necessary we could, for example, move all UAV operators much closer to the theater of combat; forcing them to live in a deployed environment, along the same time-zone as the combat, and under more standard battlefield conditions and stresses.[25]

Further, note that all UAV action has the ability to be recorded and monitored. By default since it is remotely controlled, whatever data feed a UAV pilot received can easily be overseen by many others simultaneously and later for review and critique. This added level of accountability could be used to get, if necessary, further added layers of scrutiny over lethal decisionmaking—even demanding more than one officer agree to a kill, for example. Indeed, an entire team of officers and human rights lawyers could oversee every single lethal decision made by a UAV, if desired or deemed necessary. The point is that there are a variety of ways to overcome any concerns that the pilots of UAVs would be somehow less judicious on average than inhabited weapon systems would be. All of this argues against this cognitive dissonance problem as being somehow insurmountable, much less negating the ethical obligation for UAV use in principle. Moreover, even if there is some psychological harm done to UAV pilots that we cannot overcome, it certainly seems that such harm would be less damaging than the expected harm that could come about via inhabited flights.

OBJECTION 4: TARGETED KILLING BY UAVS

Recent media coverage has raised concerns over the use of UAVs for targeted killings, particularly as is currently being done by the Central Intelligence Agency (CIA) in Pakistan, Yemen, and other theaters of operation.[26] The specific objection is that assassinations fall outside the bounds of acceptable just-war theory/practice and that UAVs somehow make this practice too easy or contribute to it in some unacceptable manner.

RESPONSE

Although I will not argue for the position here, I wholeheartedly share the ethical concerns over assassinations.[27] I further share the underlying concerns regarding a non-military government agency carrying out independent lethal operations in a foreign theater. But none of these concerns are restricted in any significant way to remotely controlled weapon systems. The CIA could be carrying out these same missions with a trained sniper or an inhabited aircraft. It is this particular *policy* that is of proper ethical concern here, not UAV technology or use in general.

Some might argue, however, that the UAV makes targeted killing of this sort particularly pernicious

because, first, an aerial vehicle flying over airspace is in some principled way different than sending in a ground special forces unit. Second, the objection claims that the battle for the "hearts and minds" of local nationals in a given theater is significantly worsened by what they view as ignoble warfare; UAVs are thought to be "cowardly." And, third, the objection continues, there are some ways in which UAV technology makes such policies easier to execute because of the abilities unique to current UAV platforms.

As to the first concern, this is admittedly an interesting case that could appear to be peculiar to UAVs. Namely, if a nation-state sends a UAV over another sovereign nation-state's airspace they have not sent an actual person or agent over the airspace. This could perhaps leave room for a contrived argument that because no actual person crossed a border no infringement of national sovereignty occurred. Although intrigued by this distinction for UAV weaponry, I do not find it persuasive. For a UAV strike in terms of sovereignty issues is analogous to a long-distance artillery shell fired across the border or other forms of attack that do not involve an agent crossing an actual geographic border such as cyber-warfare.[28] In such cases, yes, no actual person violated the territorial integrity of the sovereign state in question, but, of course, all nations would still (rightly) view such acts as a direct violation of their sovereignty. So, contra the worry, UAVs do not create a special class of weapons that can escape traditional just-war theory scrutiny or respect for territorial integrity and national sovereignty through an odd loophole.

As for the second concern, two points are in order. First, I would argue that it is at least possible that if UAVs are used in line with the rules of warfare, and civilian casualities are not increased (and perhaps even lessened) due to their usage, then there might be no *greater* resistance from a local populace than would be encountered for more conventional weapons. There is some empirical evidence (albeit limited) to back up this possibility (Plaw 2010). Further, the possibility has some intuitive plausibility when we note that the majority of hostile responses to UAVs by local populaces have come, as usual, when they have inadvertently hit civilian targets—but we have seen this same response in other conflicts when similar strikes were delivered from (say) a B-52 bomber flying at altitude dropping munitions. Again, this seems to point to the possibility that the particular platform dropping the bomb (inhabited or uninhabited) is not what generates a hostile response from the people below, but whether the attack was justified and hits legitimate targets. But perhaps this response fails. There is, admittedly, some strong empirical evidence suggesting just the opposite: that local populaces' particular resistance to UAVs is precisely due to the fact that they are uninhabited. But so be it. For even if the first response fails, recall that my argument for the ethical justification of UAVs requires that there be no reduction in just warfighting capability. So even if it does turn out that in a given theater of operation UAVs do, in fact, cause significantly greater resistance from the local populace as compared to the resistance that similar inhabited vehicles would generate (perhaps because the population thinks they are cowardly or some similar response), then they should not be used on OP grounds. Such a limitation would clearly fall under the "significant loss of capability" clause of OP. And, of course, this is an empirical question, not an in-principle objection to UAVs.[29]

The third concern—that UAV technology makes such actions easier to carry out—similarly does not offer a principled objection to the moral obligation to use UAVs.[30] It is true that the extended ability of platforms such as the Predator to "hover" and stay in a localized area for long hours, even days, and observe targets, is a clear combat advantage. Many inhabited aircraft do not have such capacities. And, further, some of the remote areas where such strikes are carried out by UAVs are such that they would be inaccessible to similar inhabited weapon platforms. But these facts about the superior capabilities of UAVs do not count against OP. Just as the advent of airpower brought with it many new and often superior ways warfighters could engage in combat (both justified and not), such advantages do not imply anything inherently wrong with airpower as airpower. Further, the mere existence of such advantages does not force policymakers to misuse these capabilities. Certainly, it would be impossible to drop bombs on innocent

civilians if planes did not exist. But that some drop bombs on innocent civilians does not make airplanes morally suspicious, but rather those who so use them to drop bombs. The same holds true for the new capabilities brought about by UAVs.

Thus, there is nothing peculiar to UAVs in regards to the ethical concerns over their present use in targeted killings around the globe. It is the morality of the United States' recent policy of targeted killings we must debate here; not the ethical justification of UAVs.[31]

OBJECTION 5: UAVS CREATE UNJUST ASYMMETRY IN COMBAT

This objection normally runs as follows: The use of remotely controlled weapons by one force against another force that does not have similar technology crosses an asymmetry threshold that makes the combat inherently ignoble. That is, the extent of asymmetry in the combat abilities between two opposing sides becomes so great when one side employs remote weapons that the fight is intrinsically unfair and that, in turn, makes the use of said remote weapons morally impermissible. This position is usually held because in such circumstances one side literally does not take *any* life-or-death risks whatsoever (or nearly so, since its warfighters are not even *present* in the primary theater of combat) whereas the opposing side carries all the risk of combat.

RESPONSE

As an objection against the ethical justification for remotely controlled weapons broadly, and UAVs in particular, this commonly heard argument fails. First, if someone holds that justified combat should be a "fair fight" between sides, at least to some degree, then I wouldd argue that contemporary military engagements crossed that threshold long ago. How fair is the present fight between an F-22 pilot flying at altitude delivering a precision missile and a tribal warrior wielding a rocket-propelled grenade? If there is a moral problem here due to asymmetry, it seems to have occurred long before UAV implementation and is not endemic to them. But, second, even if the actual removal of the warrior from the theater of combat represents a truly new level of asymmetry in combat (and perhaps it does), this alone is still no argument against doing it.[32] This is because if one combatant is ethically justified in their effort, and the other is not, then it is good that the just warrior has the advantage and is better protected.[33]

Here I am following Jeff McMahan's recent work rejecting the moral equality of combatants (see McMahan 2009). That is, the warrior fighting for a just cause is morally justified to take the life of the enemy combatant, whereas the unjust fighter is not justified, even if they follow the traditional principles of *jus in bello* such as only targeting combatants and the like, to kill the justified fighter. Thus, there is no chivalrous reason for a just combatant to "equal the playing field" or "fight fair." If combatant A fights under a just cause, while combatant B fights for an unjust cause, combatant A owes nothing to combatant B by way of exposing his/herself to some minimal threshold of risk. Thus, it is *right* for combatant A to reduce the risk in an engagement with the unjust enemy.

But even if one disagrees with McMahan's position and the rejection of the MEC, there are still no grounds to object to the protecting of a soldier under the "fair fight" objection. A MEC advocate would still presumably agree that armed forces pursuing a justified action as part of a just war is justified to do all they can to protect their soldier so long as that protection does not hinder the soldier's ability to follow *jus in bello* principles. The only difference is that a MEC advocate will think the unjust aggressor state enjoys the same allowance to protect their warfighter similarly.[34] That is, even if one thinks that soldiers enjoy a symmetrical position of the right to individual defensive measures in a given conflict, this in no way prevents either side from maximizing their personal defense so long as it is not at the cost of *jus in bello* precepts; indeed, such precepts (under MEC) would explicitly allow it.[35]

Thus, again, the argument for a "fair fight" fails on two counts. First, it is already overcome by earlier technological advancements because present military operations are already far from fair even without the asymmetry of UAV weapon systems and thus the issue here is not with UAVs properly speaking. And, second, the desire for a "fair fight" is simply a weak claim in the first place; something akin to an archaic demand of military commanders in eighteenth century warfare to line up their troops across from one another for a "dignified battle." There is simply no normatively compelling reason to think a justified military force need have a fair fight anymore than we would think a police force ought not use bullet-proof vests to offer dangerous criminals a fair fight.[36]

But perhaps this still does not give the objection its due. Paul Bloomfield once remarked that simply the idea of "being killed by remote control" is powerful and disturbing.[37] The intuition seems to be that killing someone in such a manner is profoundly disrespectful; that a human being deserves to be able to at least point at his or her killers (and condemn them, if they are unjust) even if his or her killers are cruising 20,000 feet above in a plane. The thought is that at least a human being in a plane high above is less of a "faceless" death wrought upon someone than a robot being operated remotely would be. Or consider the sentiment Uwe Steinhoff raises in discussing remote weaponry generally and how the odd risk asymmetry it creates (making the targets of attack "defenseless") does not feel like "honorable" warfare:

> To be sure, I do not deny that there is something fishy about attacking the defenseless. What is fishy about it might be captured very well in this passage: "The pilot of a fighter-bomber or the crew of a man-of-war from which the Tomahawk rockets are launched are beyond the reach of the enemy's weapons. War has lost all features of the classical duel situation here and has approached, to put it cynically, certain forms of pest control" (Steinhoff 2006: 7).[38]

It must be admitted that there does appear something ignoble or dishonorable in such a vision of warfare as "pest control" that Münkler's quote describes. Perhaps it is that such distance makes warfare seem too clinical or cold-hearted.[39] Many will have sympathy with such a sentiment when envisioning UAV warfare—myself included. But whatever this sentiment is, it does not amount to a normative argument; such a "feeling" does not constitute a moral reason for rejecting UAV use. Something being disturbing does not by itself make it wrong. This sense of the ignobility must be elucidated into a coherent and compelling ethical argument against using UAVs; mere displeasure at imagining their employment does not help us. As Steinhoff writes,

> Judged from a traditional warrior's code of honor, a code that emphasizes, among other things, courage, there is nothing honorable in killing off defenseless enemies (whether it is therefore already *dis*honorable is yet another question). But honor and morality are not the same, and honor and the laws of war are not either. In short, the prohibition of assaults upon the defenseless is neither an explicit nor an implicit principle of the laws of war or of just war theory (Steinhoff 2006: 8).

Steinhoff is certainly right in this. I would add that a crucial element in how one "feels" about imagining such warfare depends on whether or not the precision missile strike in the picture envisioned is justified or not. Is it a military strike as part of a fully justified defense against an aggressing, unjustified, destructive enemy force? Is the strike hitting a legitimate and morally culpable target? If it is, such factors temper our view of the strike considerably and move us away from the "pest control" picture. In such a case, we should desire that the just warrior be well protected from any possible threat that this enemy might proffer—protection that the UAV affords.

OBJECTION 6: REDUCTION OF THE *JUS AD BELLUM* THRESHOLD

The worry here is that the asymmetry in combat abilities created by the advanced technology of UAVs, and in particular by the massive reduction of risk to the UAV pilot, makes it too easy for the nation employing UAVs to go to war.[40] That is, the asymmetry

created by UAVs lowers the *jus ad bellum* threshold such that more unjust wars might be conducted because the risks of war to a nation-state could become so minimal.[41]

RESPONSE

This objection, on first glance, may appear to be the strongest objection to the implementation of UAVs. The worry that it will be easier to go to war if we have technology X, and thus more tempting to enter into unjust wars (making more unjust wars more likely), is intuitively plausible. But this kind of argument ultimately fails for the objection does not succeed in negating the present moral imperative to use UAVs as derived from PUR. To see why this is, consider two possible worlds, Alpha and Beta. In Alpha, nation-state Zandar has developed the technology to make bullet-proof vests for its military members to wear in combat which significantly decreases the risks they incur in battle. Zandar, in accordance with PUR, produces these bullet-proof vests and has its military members wear them. In world Beta, nation-state Zandar has developed the same technology and has the bullet-proof vests available. However, it reasons that if it uses these bullet-proof vests, war would "cost" it less in terms of risks to its own troops and, thus, be easier (and thus more tempting) to wage. In such circumstances, Beta-world-Zandar worries, more unjust wars are more likely. So it decides not to use bullet-proof vests in order to make war more costly to wage (by intentionally increasing the risk to its soldiers) in the hopes that this will lessen the likelihood that Zandar will engage in an unjust war in the future. Aside from this one decision, the worlds Alpha and Beta are identical.

Let us assume that it turns out Beta-world-Zandar's reasoning was correct. That is, going forward from this juncture there does, indeed, end up being some greater number of unjust wars waged in world Alpha than in world Beta. The use of the bullet-proof vests in some way lowered the threshold for going to war for Alpha-world-Zandar enough that it made a positive difference on the total number of wars fought—which included some unjust wars. I still contend that Beta-world-Zandar's decision was morally impermissible. This is because the normative force of PUR upon present actions is too strong to overcome such weak predictive calculations of future possibilities.[42]

I will show why this is shortly, but first note that the scope of this issue far exceeds UAVs and bulletproof vests, of course, but strikes at *any* asymmetry in military technological development whatsoever. Any improvement to a given military's capabilities that gives it an advantage over its potential enemies will face the same objection offered here against UAVs. But that would mean that this objection could be used to block the development and implementation of *any* military technology that creates any asymmetry. Further, the objection could actually be employed to work backwards: that current militaries should intentionally reduce military capabilities in order to make war more costly to them since doing so would place their soldiers at greater risk. Following this logic could even lead to the conclusion that a state should have their militaries throw away their weaponry and all defensive technology, for certainly a neutered military would be less likely to engage in unjust wars in the future.

I grant that this worry about asymmetry created by improvements in military technology making it easier to go to war may well be a legitimate concern. But it is a logic that quickly runs to demanding no military technology whatsoever in the hopes of avoiding future unjust wars. Perhaps this is correct. Perhaps there should be no militaries. But notice that we are now a far cry from arguing over UAV technology. We are arguing over the existence of any military weaponry or advancement whatsoever. If so, then this is not actually an objection *specific* to UAVs in principle. Moreover, if objection 6 is correct in this way, then OP still stands—it is just a vacuous claim: as would be *any* claim about the possibility of justified use of military weaponry of any kind.

But the problems with the objection run even deeper. As I alluded to above, the reasoning by Beta-world-Zandar not to use the vests, notice, rests on epistemically dubious calculations that are predictive about *themselves* doing something wrong in the future ("we might be more likely to do wrong action X down the road") over epistemically solid calculations to protect their own just warfighters presently ("our soldiers will be safer *today* if they wear the vests"). Notice what odd moral reasoning would be occurring were objection 6 to work: *because* we will most likely behave unjustly in the future, we should behave unjustly in the present (by violating PUR in choosing not to protect our warriors as best we can) in order to try to prevent ourselves from acting unjustly in the future. If that holds, we have a strange account of moral epistemology at work, to say the least. We should forego taking presently morally correct action A in order to help restrain our future selves from the likelihood of committing morally wrong action B. In other words, we should do something wrong now in order to (hopefully) better stop ourselves from doing something wrong in the future.

This seems odd, although there could perhaps be cases where such decisions are the right actions—the lesser of two evils, perhaps. But notice that the Beta-world-Zandar decision is not a straightforward case of present self-restraint to limit future potential wrongdoing for, presumably, *usual* cases of present self-restraint are not acts that are themselves impermissible. For example, imagine a man, Tom, who knows he tends to get very angry and do intemperate things. Tom decides he should lock up his gun in a safe and give the key to it to a trusted friend. Tom does this present act to restrain his future self from doing something wrong. But Tom's locking up his gun is not an impermissible act viewed on its own. Violating PUR by not protecting just warfighters is a presently impermissible act viewed in isolation. Thus what makes the reasoning of Beta-world-Zandar's decision so strange: they are intentionally putting their soldiers at greater risk now (which would be considered impermissible in isolation) in order to restrain themselves from doing something impermissible in the future. The comparison back to Tom would be if Tom decides to punch his friend Sam now (which is impermissible) because it will help him not do something worse in the future (such as kill Bob). If that is actually the case, then this *could* be the right thing to do. But notice that we would require a rather high level of epistemic certitude for Tom's knowledge of this scenario—and that there is no other means to avoid killing Bob—in order to deem his act justifiable. That is, if Tom has near *certainty* that the only way to prevent himself from killing Bob in the future is by punching Sam now, then perhaps it is a justified act. But one wonders how Tom could *ever* have such epistemic certitude predicting future acts. The same is true for Beta-world-Zandar.

But perhaps it is still possible that such a decision is justified. This is because, one could argue, I am here equivocating on the moral weight of the present wrong of failing to protect just warfighters and the future potential wrong of more unjust wars. If they are of vastly different moral significance and consequence, then perhaps it is justifiable to do a lesser wrong now in order to increase even the slightest chance of avoiding a much greater wrong in the future. I grant this possibility. Indeed, one could argue that such a decision is directly in accord with PUR since the good of avoiding future wars is a greater good than the present protection of just soldiers (that is, some would argue that such a calculus is demanded by justice).

The trouble with applying this to our present case is the high degree of epistemic uncertainty we have in predicting future states of affairs, particularly future decisions to go to war. That is, even if the wrong of sacrificing the protection afforded to just soldiers is a lesser evil than the possibility of future unjust wars, we have complete confidence in the *present* wrong occurring but we would be far less than certain of the future wrong occurring. In other words, the *odds* of that future wrong occurring will matter and it is unclear how we could reliably predict such odds. The odds need not be equal between the wrongs, of course. If the greater evil was great enough, we could perhaps need only a relatively small chance of its occurrence to outweigh even the certainty of a lesser evil. But, again, it is unclear if we can even have *that* small level of epistemic confidence that a given weapon technology (be it bullet-proof vests, M-16 rifles, or UAVs) would lead to greater instances of unjust wars; or at least not the level of confidence we would need to trump the demand not to commit the present wrong.

So even if it turns out that future worlds would be ones with less war were we to intentionally limit our own military technological development, we cannot have enough epistemic certainty in knowing this presently to overcome the demands to protect the just warfighter. Short of a crystal ball, I cannot imagine how we could ever have the level of certainty for predictive knowledge claims of future group behavior that would be necessary to claim that the future *possible* good should outweigh our present moral duty not to unnecessarily risk others. Perhaps it can be done, but this must be demonstrated before we intentionally bring unnecessary risk upon others. That is, one would have to show how we can have such epistemic confidence that we are not violating PUR (via the demands of justice override) in not presently protecting just warfighters. The burden of proof will be on those claiming that we must presently undertake an act that we would usually consider impermissible in isolation in order to avoid a future evil that we do not have complete confidence in. Hence, although it is certainly possible that use of UAVs could lower the costs of going to war for a given state and, thereby, lower the threshold for going to war such that a state might have an increased likelihood of engaging in a war that is unjust, such predictions cannot be the basis for demanding an intentional violation of PUR given our present epistemic limitations.

This is an unhappy conclusion. While I have great sympathy for the worry, it seems PUR is too strong to overcome with such shaky future predictions as to the unethical decisions a future state would make. And, again, if we allow this block against UAVs it would set in motion a moral principle that would not stop at UAVs but encompass all military technology—not just its future development but retroactively demand that present military technology creating force asymmetry be intentionally reduced.[43] If this is sound we could eventually be back at demanding that Captain Zelda *should* be required to fight with no bullet-proof vest, no rifle, and with only a rock in order to make war "cost us more" so that we would be less likely to engage in an unjust one. But this is absurd. If a war is just, we are obligated to protect the just warfighters engaging in it. UAVs do precisely that.

CONCLUSION

UAVs will have an increasingly large presence in military operations on all levels; this much appears increasingly inevitable. Here I have made the case that any new technology that better protects the just warfighter is at least a *prima facie* ethical improvement and is morally required to be used unless there are strong countervailing reasons to give up that protection. I have argued that if using UAVs (as a particular kind of remote weapon) does not incur a significant loss of capability—particularly the operators' ability to engage in warfare in accordance with *jus in bello* principles—then there is an ethical obligation to use them and, indeed, transition entire military inventories to UAVs anywhere it is possible to do so. In fact, I endorse the stronger claim that such a proposed transition would not only be feasible without a significant loss of capability but would actually *increase* weapons systems capability *and* the ability to fight justly.[44] All of the concerns regarding UAVs presently on offer do not negate this ethical obligation to use uninhabited weapon systems and should be properly viewed instead as indictments against mistaken policy decisions and specific instances of force application—not as principled objections against UAVs themselves for none of the concerns are endemic to UAVs in any significant way.

Finally, I note that this paper is in the odd position of arguing for the ethical obligation to use UAVs for a putatively just military action in the current context wherein much, if not all, *actual* UAV employment is part of military actions that are morally questionable or outright impermissible. The particular contemporary circumstances and misuses of UAVs, however, do not trump the moral principles underlying the ethical obligation to employ UAVs for *just* actions. Indeed, this highlights the central point well: the first question for the morally permissible use of *any* weapon technology is, of course, whether the military action itself is morally justified. If it is not a justified undertaking in the first place, then it does not matter if it is carried out via a crossbow, a sniper rifle, or a UAV; it is morally impermissible regardless. If the act is morally justified, however, we are obliged

via the demands of PUR to protect the agent ordered to carry out that action as best we can; be it a police officer apprehending a dangerous criminal, an EOD technician disarming a bomb, or a just warrior fighting an unjust enemy. Hence, the ethical obligation to employ UAVs.

NOTES

1. And there are other locations where it is presumed (although not verified) that lethal UAV employment has taken place, such as in Gaza by the Israel Defense Forces. In this paper I will refer to these remotely controlled weapon systems primarily as UAVs (Uninhabited Aerial Vehicles) and occasionally as drones. UAVs that are used for lethal combat purposes are sometimes referred UCAVs (Uninhabited Combat Aerial Vehicles), but I will not use that locution here. See below for further clarification of these terms and some important distinctions. For a far more in-depth classification of various types and kinds of remote weapon systems see Sparrow (2009).

2. Singer (2009) gained wide press and much of his work discusses these ethical concerns over drones. Recent events such as the potential *jus in bello* violations wrought by Predator drones in Afghanistan—have received international media attention. Various human rights watchdog groups raised alarm over recent Israeli strikes in Gaza using the Predator platform supposedly against noncombatants. In the past year alone, publications such as The New Yorker, The Atlantic, the Washington Post, Scientific American, the New York Times, and media outlets such as National Public Radio and Public Broadcasting Systems, have all had substantial reports and several highly critical opinion pieces on the use of UAVs. Additionally, there are many in the United States military community itself who do not question the efficacy of UAV usage but rather have principled worries concerning their use such as those mentioned above. It is currently a "hot topic" at professional military ethics and development conferences.

3. Occasionally, such aircraft are instead referred to as Remotely Piloted Vehicles (RPVs). This is especially the case in present US Air Force usage which could be due to public relations concerns over worries regarding autonomous weapon systems. That is, "RPV" emphasizes that these vehicles are still controlled by human pilots. That we see a move away from the UAV moniker back to the RPV idiom in common discourse is telling of the felt need by some in the military community to emphasize that these aircraft still require human pilots (particularly the pilot community in the US Air Force). For more on this phenomenon

see Fitzsimonds and Mahnken (2007). See Sparrow (2009) for more fine-grained distinctions on the kinds of uninhabited weapon systems and their classifications. Also see Sparrow (2007).

4. See all of the following for good expositions of the historical trail leading to present day lethal UAVs: Singer (2009), Card (2007), Mustin (2002). For a good overview of the planned future of UAVs, see Office of the Under Secretary of Defense (2006). Note that technically speaking, UAVs are not individual aircraft but weapon systems involving several aircraft and ground control stations.

5. Such as the land-based Foster-Miller's Special Weapons Observation Remote Direct-Action System (SWORDS) or Qiniteq's Modular Advanced Armed Robotic System (MAARS) weapons. See Arkin (2009) for a good overview of such weapons.

6. Some argue that PUR as presented here is false due to the possibility of someone entering into a foolish agreement with another. Imagine if X signs a contract with Y to follow his commands no matter how stupid or irrational they may be. In such a case, if Y orders X to incur potentially lethal risk for no good reason, then X cannot claim that his right is infringed. Assuming X entered into the agreement with informed consent and was not under coercion or exploited, one could argue that Y's order is not morally impermissible. (Thanks to Stephen Kershnar for this objection.) If one were to grant this is possibility, then PUR can be amended to reflect those relationships where X enters under the authority of Y on the assumption that Y will not order him to take on risk for no good reason; that is, X assumes Y will follow PUR. At any rate, I think most military members in Western militaries implicitly expect their commanders not to risk their lives unnecessarily.

7. That is, in my view there may very well be a self-regarding duty to oneself that is entailed by PUR, but I set aside the possibility here to avoid libertarian objections and paternalism concerns. I am strongly inclined to think, however, that there is a self-regarding form of PUR that could hold up against many libertarian objections so several initially apparent counter-examples to PUR would not actually hold. For example, some may offer the activity of skydiving as a morally permissible act to undertake even though it involves incurring potentially lethal risk. But PUR would allow for the moral permissibility of this action for, presumably, the lethal risk involved in skydiving is actually a necessary part of the good sought by the action. In this case, the good is the thrill and excitement of the act of jumping out of an airplane. Thus, the "rush" sought after by such skydivers (among other possible goods they seek when undertaking the activity) requires taking on the

risk. So, according to a self-regarding PUR, it would be morally permissible for an agent to take on the risk of skydiving because that risk directly contributes to the good sought. Whether or not seeking out death-defying activities for the sake of an adrenaline rush is a good that should be sought (or a good at all) is another matter. The PUR does not resolve disputes over what is and is not a good to seek, but rather only the moral demand not to unnecessarily incur lethal risk in seeking an established putative good.

8. Thanks to an anonymous reviewer for suggesting such a principle.

9. Indeed, I think there are strong arguments that can be made against resource expenditures for military ventures in general when it is shown the plethora of other good ways such resources could be alternatively spent. It is an empirical question, certainly, but it is not implausible in the least to imagine that, for example, the roughly $750 billion dollars the United States has spent thus far on the war in Iraq could not have been spent in other ways that would have done far more good in the world. But that is a debate for another paper. For an interesting presentation of the various trade-offs military expenditures impose on a populace, see the National Priorities Project (2010) for the literal financial cost of war.

10. Notice that, if true, then OP carries with it a corollary to pursue the development of and transition to an all-UAV military force: (OPT) For any given state, if it is possible to transition its entire military inventory of inhabited aerial vehicles to UAVs without a significant loss of capability, then that state has an ethical obligation to do so.

11. Although it certainly appears to be technologically possible since there are already UAVs in operation. See below for some discussion on this.

12. Although, granting the ethical obligation to protect the just warfighter I lay out below, this would have to be a truly astronomical cost—particularly in relative comparison to the amount presently spent on defense budgets. Of course, it's entirely possible that morality demands resources be spent on other things entirely outside of defense costs, such as education, development, and the like. But that is another matter.

13. Notice that although this paper is focused on lethal UAVs, the corollary claim of OPT (see note 10) would hold for all aircraft. That is, even cargo planes and the like (even those used to transport soldiers), should be transitioned to UAVs. The idea is simple: risking one less person on the flight (the pilot or pilots) is better than risking them if not necessary. However, of course, it is quite possible that troops would refuse to fly on a plane without a present pilot. If that is the case, then that would be a "significant

loss of capability" and so, perhaps, UAVs are not equally capable as inhabited aircraft in the case of troop transporting cargo planes. An example of such platforms for small cargo loads is the Mist Mobility Integrated Systems Technology (MMIST) CQ-10A SnowGoose which is already operationally capable.

14. Singer (2009) also discusses the use of bomb-disarming robots and the connection between their use and the use of remote robots and weaponry more broadly by military forces.

15. Thus, while it is true that UAV usage is ethically impermissible in such instances, so too would any kind of strike via any kind of weapon system (inhabited or uninhabited) be impermissible; the impermissibility does not derive from UAV-specific employment. That is, it is not the UAV qua UAV that makes such a strike impermissible.

16. I will note briefly that I am not even airing objections that claim UAV employment is "weak" or somehow not "tough enough" or "cowardly." These responses against UAVs derived from some type of wrong-headed machismo are certainly common but, one hopes, are not taken seriously by any military policy decisionmakers. See below for discussion on how the perception of the UAV by enemy forces, however, could have an impact on determining its capability.

17. Some worry over this development and others laud it. Arkin (2009), for example, sees the development of UAVs as in-line with the development of IAWs and focuses his work on how to develop such autonomous systems to follow the Laws of Armed Conflict and various Rules of Engagement (how to give the machines an "ethics upgrade"). Arkin contends that such developments are moral improvements and should be pursued with vigor.

18. For some helpful efforts to this end, see Sparrow (2007).

19. Indeed, precisely because I do agree with the first premise of objection 1, I argue that now is the time to institute policies that would block IAW development even while we develop UAV and other remote weapon systems that are human controlled.

20. Many thanks to an anonymous reviewer for this objection.

21. This position is controversial and widely discussed. Or, better, the entire notion of who should bear risks in any conflict is greatly contested, but most of the debate hinges on questions of liability, debates over the doctrine of the moral equality of combatants (MEC), and distinction issues. If a just warrior was fighting in a truly just war and the innocents in question were truly innocent and in no way liable, some will argue their moral status (the just combatant and the innocent) is equal. And, thus, while just warriors should do all they can to shield the innocent from harm, they should not treat the noncombatants' worth as above their own safety. And once the doctrine of the moral equality of combatants is disposed of (see below on McMahan), it can become difficult to sustain my view (that the just warrior ought to bear the burden for shielding innocents from harm) for all cases, particularly once strict boundaries between combatants and noncombatants are questioned. Seth Lazar has argued that McMahan's position becomes untenable in precisely this way because liability will extend to far too many noncombatants in ways that should make them justifiable targets in McMahan's rubric. See Lazar (2010). Steinhoff (2008) has challenged McMahan on his rejection of MEC by using claims from within McMahan's own theory. See McMahan (2008) for a thorough response.

22. Nota bene: In this objection I am focusing solely on the technical ability of UAVs to discriminate properly; I will consider the impact on the psychology of the warfighter (and subsequent *in bello* worries therein) below in objection 2.

23. And see Plaw (2010) cited above for all the various references used in creating the database. Regarding the estimate for the global causality ratio, see Osiel (2009: 143) and Kaldor (1999: 8).

24. Many thanks to several UAV pilots for firsthand accounts and discussion of these phenomena (their identification is withheld by request). See Wallach and Allen (2009) and Singer (2009) where the cavalier attitude of treating UAV operations like a video game is discussed.

25. Militaries could even go so far as to force UAV operators to live in bunkers and set off fake mortar rounds and so forth around the compound in order to make it feel more "real" if such effects were shown to help overcome this supposed problem of cognitive dissonance caused by being too far from the battlefield.

26. See, for example, Mayer (2009). Notice that nowhere in this long article does the author ever discuss the ethical justification of UAVs themselves. As nearly all recent discussions of UAVs in the public square do, it goes into great detail regarding the ethical concerns raised by targeted killings, sovereignty issues regarding operations in Pakistan, worries over military functions being carried out by a non-military department of the government (the CIA), and so forth, without ever discussing the ethical justification of UAVs in principle.

27. For an interesting discussion of the justification of assassination see Kaufman (2007). See also Kershnar (2004). For an argument that many leaders should not

be treated with non-combatant immunity but are legitimate targets, see Kershnar (2005). Presumably, the UAV-targeted leaders of Al-Qaeda and the Taliban would fit as such targets under Kershnar's argument. Gross (2006) gives the argument that targeted killings cannot fit into a proper moral category. If they are an extension of law enforcement, they fail due process, and assassination as self-defense seems implausible, or so Gross argues.

28. For a helpful account of the future of this new form of warfare, see Dipert (2010).

29. I will note, however, that such an empirical question would be very difficult to determine in many contexts. That is, the question is not if a given local populace would display resistance to munitions being dropped by UAVs (that is likely). Rather the empirical question that would have to be determined is if that resistance to UAVs is significantly greater than what resistance would be encountered via an inhabited aircraft. And that would be hard to determine, to say the least.

30. This kind of objection is raised by Phythian (2010).

31. For a helpful discussion of this point see Kolff (2003).

32. A further reason to think that the removal of the warrior from the theater of combat in itself is nothing particularly new is the existence of Intercontinental Ballistic Missile operators and the like who are certainly removed from the theater of combat where their munitions would be delivered. (Thanks to an anonymous reviewer for this point.)

33. An important point to note here is that the operators of UAVs would be considered combatants under the traditional just-war theory rubric. (Thanks to Uwe Stienhoff for raising this point.) I'll remain neutral on this point (if for no other reason than that I reject the moral equality of combatants thesis), but note that whatever one's division of combatants, the UAV pilots would certainly still qualify. This has the (perhaps odd) result of meaning the UAV operators would be legitimate targets under most just-war accounts, even though they would be conducting operations from their office thousands of miles away (at places like Nellis Air Force Base, Nevada). So be it.

34. Interestingly, McMahan holds that those who fight without a just cause cannot, in principle, ever satisfy the *jus in bello* principle of proportionality. See McMahan (2004). But a traditional advocate of MEC would disagree, of course. For an attempt to defend some of the traditional elements entailed by MEC, see Benbaji (2008).

35. For a good discussion of some of the complexities and difficulties of symmetrical rights to personal defensive measures enjoyed by soldiers on the traditional just-war theory model (contra the asymmetry of a right to personal

defensive measures in individual self-defensive cases where culpability is included in such determinations) see Emerton and Handfield (2009). For a good note on this issue of liability and defense see McMahan (2005: 10) and McMahan (2009).

36. Additionally, there is a different concern with the asymmetry created by advanced technology which worries that the asymmetry makes it too easy to go to war and thus lowers a nation's *jus ad bellum* threshold too far. I will address this separate concern below.

37. Paul Bloomfield, personal correspondence, 12 July 2010 and discussions held at the University of Connecticut ethics reading group, summer 2010.

38. Steinhoff is quoting from Münkler (2003: 234), Steinhoff's translation. In the original paper Steinhoff is discussing the general lack of bravery involved in attacking the defenseless as part of the debate over torture. The quote is referencing an attitude against any remote weaponry where the warrior has effectively removed his/herself from risk, and, as such, can easily be applied to UAV usage. Note that it further affirms the point above that if there is some kind of dishonorable fight for UAVs due to the asymmetry of the combat, the threshold was crossed long before UAVs (as in Münkler's referencing Tomahawk missiles) and is therefore not endemic to them, in particular, but to modern warfare across the board. The use of the phrase "pest control" to describe what is seen as this particularly noncourageous form of warfare was discussed in my panel at the 7th Global Conference on War and Peace, 2010, Prague, Czech Republic. Many thanks to Uwe Steinhoff for permission to use the remark and directing me toward Münkler's work.

39. Bloomfield argues that the root of the "pest control" worry is our aversion to being treated as pests ourselves were we to be attacked via remote control. If UAVs were used by our enemies against us, we would think they are wronging us in some way to kill us in this manner (wronging us over-and-above the killing itself, that is.) Thus, the thought runs, we should extend this respect for all people into all contexts, even against the unjust enemy: that is, all humans deserve the respect of not being killed via such remotely controlled "pest control" measures.

40. Notice I say the "massive reduction in risk" not total reduction for, presumably, on most just-war theory accounts, the UAV operators would still be considered liable targets for attack since they would most certainly be combatants. For more on UAV operators being legitimate targets, see Singer (2009: 386).

41. Thanks to the audience at the 2010 International Society of Military Ethics Annual Conference in San Diego for the thorough discussion of this objection.

42. It could be objected here that this analogy does not hold because of different obligations that arise from "purely" defensive military technologies (such as bullet-proof vests) as opposed to those offensive weapons that serve to increase defensive capabilities (such as UAVs). The distinction between offensive versus defensive military capabilities is contentious for many reasons. For one, anything (such as a vest) that increases a soldier's defensive abilities will thereby increase that person's value as an offensive force. But, I will not argue this point here. If one is convinced that my story regarding Zandar does not apply to UAVs due to the offensive/defensive distinction, then the entire thought experiment could be re-cast with the use of eighteenth century muskets versus the use of contemporary M-16 rifles as the competing choices. The muskets (clearly offensive weapons) would reduce the troops' defensive capabilities because they take longer to load, are less accurate, etc. After replacing vests with M-16s, the results of this thought experiment, mutatis mutandis, would be the same. Thanks to Donald Joy for helping to develop this point.

43. I should note, of course, that there is a long history of arguments for disarmament that proceed precisely along these grounds; particularly for nuclear weapons. Notice, however, that the strongest arguments of this type are advanced against particular technologies that are viewed as ethically problematic in principle in isolation from other evils. That is, there is something wrong with (say) nuclear weapons or landmines in principle (the inability to discriminate, etc.) that provides an impetus for banning them in the first place, wholly apart from what future harms they could make more likely. Additionally, by reducing them we reduce the future chance of their unjust use. But this is precisely because any future use of them would be unjust so we can have a certainty that if they were ever used in the future, such use would be unjust. This is entirely different for UAVs, which can be used justly in some circumstances.

44. Although I have not fully argued for this stronger claim here. Again, see Plaw (2010) cited above. Of course, if this stronger claim is true, it would press an even greater ethical obligation to employ UAVs and transition military inventories to all-UAV forces.

REFERENCES

Arkin, R. (2009) *Governing Lethal Behavior in Autonomous Robots* (New York: Chapman & Hall).

Asaro, P. (2006) What Should We Want From a Robot Ethic? *International Review of Information Ethics*, 6, pp. 9–16.

Asaro, P. (2007) How Just Could a Robot War Be? Paper presented at 5th European Computing and Philosophy Conference, Twenthe, NL, June.

Asaro, P. (2007) Robots and Responsibility from a Legal Perspective. Paper presented at IEEE International Conference on Robotics and Automation, Rome.

Benbaji, Y. (2008) A Defense of the Traditional War Convention, *Ethics,* 118, pp. 464–495.

Card, J. (2007) Killer Machines, *Foreign Policy,* May, p. 92.

Cook, M. (2004) *The Moral Warrior* (Albany, NY: SUNY Press).

Dipert, R. (2010) The Ethics of Cyberwarfare. Paper presented at International Society of Military Ethics Annual Conference, San Diego, CA, January.

Emerton, P. & Handfield, T. (2009) Order and Affray: Defensive Privileges in Warfare, *Philosophy and Public Affairs,* 37, pp. 382–414.

Fitzsimonds, J. R. & Mahnken, T. G. (2007) Military Officer Attitudes Toward UAV Adoption: Exploring Institutional Impediments to Innovation, *Joint Forces Quarterly,* 46, pp. 96–103.

Gross, M. (2006) Assassination and Targeted Killing: Law Enforcement, Execution, or Self-Defence? *Journal of Applied Philosophy,* 23(3), pp. 323–335.

Himma, K. (2007) Artificial Agency, Consciousness, and the Criteria for Moral Agency: What Properties Must an Artificial Agent Have to be a Moral Agent? Paper presented at 7th International Computer Ethics Conference, San Diego, CA, July.

Kaldor, M. (1999) *New and Old Wars* (Palo Alto, CA: Stanford University Press).

Kaufman, W. R. P. (2007) Rethinking the Ban on Assassination, in: M. W. Brough, J. W. Lango & H. van der Linden (Eds), *Rethinking the Just War Tradition* (Albany, NY: SUNY Press).

Kershnar, S. (2004) The Moral Argument for a Policy of Assassination, *Reason Papers,* 27, pp. 45–67.

Kershnar, S. (2005) Assassination and the Immunity Theory, *Philosophia,* 33(4), pp. 129–147.

Kolff, D. W. (2003) Missile Strike Carried Out with Yemeni Cooperation—Using UCAVs to Kill Alleged Terrorists: A Professional Approach to the Normative Basis of Military Ethics, *Journal of Military Ethics,* 2(3), pp. 240–244.

Lazar, S. (2009) Responsibility, Risk, and Killing in Self-Defense, *Ethics,* 199, pp. 699–728.

Lazar, S. (2010) The Responsibility Dilemma for Killing in War: A Review Essay, *Philosophy and Public Affairs,* 38(2), pp. 180–213.

Mayer, J. (2009) The Predator War: What are the risks of the CIA's covert drone program? *The New Yorker*, October, accessed 26 October 2010, available at: http://www.newyorker.com/reporting/2009/10/26/091026fa_fact_mayer; Internet.

McMahan, J. (2004) The Ethics of Killing in War, *Ethics*, 114(4), pp. 708–718.

McMahan, J. (2005) Just Cause for War, *Ethics and International Affairs*, 19(3), pp. 1–21.

McMahan, J. (2008) Debate: Justification and Liability in War, *Journal of Political Philosophy*, 16(2), pp. 227–244.

McMahan, J. (2009) *Killing in War* (New York: Oxford University Press).

Münkler, H. (2003) *Die neuen Kriege* (Reinbek at Hamburg: Rowohlt).

Mustin, J. (2002) Future Employment of Unmanned Aerial Vehicles, *Air and Space Power Journal*, 16(2), pp. 86–97.

National Priorities Project (2010) *Cost of War*, accessed 1 September 2010, available at: http://www. nationalpriorities.org/costofwar_home; Internet.

Office of the Under Secretary of Defense (2006) *Unmanned Aircraft Systems Roadmap: 2005–2030* (Washington, DC: Office of the Under Secretary of Defense).

Osiel, M. (2009) *The End of Reciprocity* (Cambridge: Cambridge University Press).

Phythian, M. (2010) Ethics and Intelligence: The Implications of the Rise of the Armed Drone. Paper presented at 7th Global Conference on War and Peace, Prague, 30 April.

Plaw, A. (2010) Sudden Justice. Paper presented at 7th Annual Global Conference on War and Peace, Prague, 1 May.

Rafael Advanced Defense Systems (2010) *Spike ER Precision Missile*, accessed 1 June 2010, available at: http://www.rafael.co.il/marketing/sip storage/files/0/600.pdf; Internet.

Singer, P. W. (2009) *Wired for War: The Robotics Revolution and Conflict in the 21st Century* (New York: Penguin Press).

Sparrow, R. (2007) Killer Robots, *Journal of Applied Philosophy*, 24(1), pp. 63–77.

Sparrow, R. (2009) Building a Better Warbot: Ethical Issues in the Design of Unmanned Systems for Military Applications, *Science and Engineering Ethics*, 15, pp. 169–187.

Steinhoff, U. (2006) Torture: The Case for Dirty Harry and against Alan Dershowitz, *Journal of Applied Philosophy*, 23(3), pp. 337–353.

Steinhoff, U. (2008) Jeff McMahan on the Moral Inequality of Combatants, *Journal of Political Philosophy*, 16(2), pp. 220–226.

Wallach, W. & Allen, C. (2009) *Moral Machines: Teaching Robots Right from Wrong* (New York: Oxford University Press).

DISCUSSION QUESTIONS

1. Do you find Strawser's basic argument for his main conclusion compelling? Why or why not?
2. What is Strawser's response to the objection that UAVs lead to more noncombatant deaths? Do you find his response convincing? Why or why not?
3. Strawser discusses the concern that the availability of UAVs makes it easier to carry out ethically problematic targeted killings. How does Strawser respond to that concern? Do you find his response convincing? Why or why not?
4. Of the six objections that Strawser considers, which do you find most important? Why? Do you think that Strawser adequately responds to that objection? Why or why not?

Animals

PETER SINGER

All Animals Are Equal[1]

Peter Singer is the Ira W. DeCamp Professor of Bioethics at Princeton University and Laureate Professor at the University of Melbourne in Australia. He has written widely on applied ethics and is most famous for his work on global poverty and the treatment of animals. In this paper, which Singer published in 1974, he argues that we are obligated to "extend to other species the basic principle of equality" that we apply to all humans.

GUIDING QUESTIONS

1. What, exactly, does Singer mean when he says that we are obligated to treat all animals as equals? What does he mean when he says that our current attitudes toward non-human animals are "speciesist"?
2. What point is Singer making by discussing Thomas Taylor's reply to Mary Wollstonecraft's *Vindication of the Rights of Women*?
3. Does Singer believe that we ought to oppose racism and sexism because "there are no differences between the races and sexes *as such*"? Why or why not?
4. What does Singer think determines whether we are obligated to take something's interests into account? Why?
5. Why does Singer think that appealing to the "intrinsic dignity" of humans is "obscurantist mumbo-jumbo"?
6. What point is Singer making in his discussion about humans with severe and permanent mental impairments?

In recent years a number of oppressed groups have campaigned vigorously for equality. The classic instance is the Black Liberation movement, which demands an end to the prejudice and discrimination that has made blacks second-class citizens. The immediate appeal of the black liberation movement and its initial, if limited success made it a model for other oppressed groups to follow. We became familiar with liberation movements for Spanish-Americans, gay people, and a variety of other minorities. When a majority group—women—began their campaign, some thought we had come to the end of the road. Discrimination on the basis of sex, it has been said, is the last universally accepted form of discrimination, practiced without secrecy or pretense even

in those liberal circles that have long prided themselves on their freedom from prejudice against racial minorities.

One should always be wary of talking of "the last remaining form of discrimination." If we have learnt anything from the liberation movements, we should have learnt how difficult it is to be aware of latent prejudice in our attitudes to particular groups until this prejudice is forcefully pointed out.

A liberation movement demands an expansion of our moral horizons and an extension or reinterpretation of the basic moral principle of equality. Practices that were previously regarded as natural and inevitable come to be seen as the result of an unjustifiable prejudice. Who can say with confidence that all his

From *Philosophic Exchange*, Vol. 5 (1974) No. 1, Article 6.

or her attitudes and practices are beyond criticism? If we wish to avoid being numbered amongst the oppressors, we must be prepared to re-think even our most fundamental attitudes. We need to consider them from the point of view of those most disadvantaged by our attitudes, and the practices that follow from these attitudes. If we can make this unaccustomed mental switch we may discover a pattern in our attitudes and practices that consistently operates so as to benefit one group—usually the one to which we ourselves belong—at the expense of another. In this way we may come to see that there is a case for a new liberation movement. My aim is to advocate that we make this mental switch in respect of our attitudes and practices towards a very large group of beings: members of species other than our own—or, as we popularly though misleadingly call them, animals. In other words, I am urging that we extend to other species the basic principle of equality that most of us recognise should be extended to all members of our own species.

All this may sound a little far-fetched, more like a parody of other liberation movements than a serious objective. In fact, in the past the idea of "The Rights of Animals" really has been used to parody the case for women's rights. When Mary Wollstonecroft, a forerunner of later feminists, published her *Vindication of the Rights of Women* in 1792, her ideas were widely regarded as absurd, and they were satirized in an anonymous publication entitled *A Vindication of the Rights of Brutes*. The author of this satire (actually Thomas Taylor, a distinguished Cambridge philosopher) tried to refute Wollstonecroft's reasonings by showing that they could be carried one stage further. If sound when applied to women, why should the arguments not be applied to dogs, cats and horses? They seemed to hold equally well for these "brutes"; yet to hold that brutes had rights was manifestly absurd; therefore the reasoning by which this conclusion had been reached must be unsound, and if unsound when applied to brutes, it must also be unsound when applied to women, since the very same arguments had been used in each case.

One way in which we might reply to this argument is by saying that the case for equality between men and women cannot validly be extended to non-human animals. Women have a right to vote, for instance, because they are just as capable of making rational decisions as men are; dogs, on the other hand, are incapable of understanding the significance of voting, so they cannot have the right to vote. There are many other obvious ways in which men and women resemble each other closely, while humans and other animals differ greatly. So, it might be said, men and women are similar beings, and should have equal rights, while humans and non-humans are different and should not have equal rights.

The thought behind this reply to Taylor's analogy is correct up to a point, but it does not go far enough. There *are* important differences between humans and other animals, and these differences must give rise to *some* differences in the rights that each have. Recognizing this obvious fact, however, is no barrier to the case for extending the basic principle of equality to non-human animals. The differences that exist between men and women are equally undeniable, and the supporters of Women's Liberation are aware that these differences may give rise to different rights. Many feminists hold that women have the right to an abortion on request. It does not follow that since these same people are campaigning for equality between men and women they must support the right of men to have abortions too. Since a man cannot have an abortion, it is meaningless to talk of his right to have one. Since a pig can't vote, it is meaningless to talk of its right to vote. There is no reason why either Women's Liberation or Animal Liberation should get involved in such nonsense. The extension of the basic principle of equality from one group to another does not imply that we must treat both groups in exactly the same way, or grant exactly the same rights to both groups. Whether we should do so will depend on the nature of the members of the two groups. The basic principle of equality, I shall argue, is equality of consideration; and equal consideration for different beings may lead to different treatment and different rights.

So there is a different way of replying to Taylor's attempt to parody Wollstonecroft's arguments, a way which does not deny the differences between humans and non-humans, but goes more deeply into the question of equality, and concludes by finding nothing absurd in the idea that the basic principle of equality applies to so-called "brutes." I believe that we reach this conclusion if we examine the basis on which our opposition to discrimination on grounds of race or sex ultimately rests. We will then see that we would be on shaky ground if we were to demand equality for blacks, women, and other groups of oppressed humans while denying equal consideration to non-humans.

When we say that all human beings, whatever their race, creed or sex, are equal, what is it that we are asserting? Those who wish to defend a hierarchical, inegalitarian society have often pointed out that by whatever test we choose, it simply is not true that all humans are equal. Like it or not, we must face the fact that humans come in different shapes and sizes; they come with differing moral capacities, differing intellectual abilities, differing amounts of benevolent feeling and sensitivity to the needs of others, differing abilities to communicate effectively, and differing capacities to experience pleasure and pain. In short, if the demand for equality were based on the actual equality of all human beings, we would have to stop demanding equality. It would be an unjustifiable demand.

Still, one might cling to the view that the demand for equality among human beings is based on the actual equality of the different races and sexes. Although humans differ as individuals in various ways, there are no differences between the races and sexes as *such*. From the mere fact that a person is black, or a woman, we cannot infer anything else about that person. This, it may be said, is what is wrong with racism and sexism. The white racist claims that whites are superior to blacks, but this is false— although there are differences between individuals, some blacks are superior to some whites in all of the capacities and abilities that could conceivably be relevant. The opponent of sexism would say the same: a person's sex is no guide to his or her abilities, and this is why it is unjustifiable to discriminate on the basis of sex.

This is a possible line of objection to racial and sexual discrimination. It is not, however, the way that someone really concerned about equality would choose, because taking this line could, in some circumstances, force one to accept a most inegalitarian

society. The fact that humans differ as individuals, rather than as races or sexes, is a valid reply to someone who defends a hierarchical society like, say, South Africa, in which all whites are superior in status to all blacks. The existence of individual variations that cut across the lines of race or sex, however, provides us with no defence at all against a more sophisticated opponent of equality, one who proposes that, say, the interests of those with IQ ratings above 100 be preferred to the interests of those with IQs below 100. Would a hierarchical society of this sort really be so much better than one based on race or sex? I think not. But if we tie the moral principle of equality to the factual equality of the different races or sexes, taken as a whole, our opposition to racism and sexism does not provide us with any basis for objecting to this kind of inegalitarianism.

There is a second important reason why we ought not to base our opposition to racism and sexism on any kind of factual equality, even the limited kind asserts that variations in capacities and abilities are spread evenly between the different races and sexes: we can have no absolute guarantee that these abilities and capacities really are distributed evenly, without regard to race or sex, among human beings. So far as actual abilities are concerned, there do seem to be certain measurable differences between both races and sexes. These differences do not, of course, appear in each case, but only when averages are taken. More important still, we do not yet know how much of these differences is really due to the different genetic endowments of the various races and sexes, and how much is due to environmental differences that are the result of past and continuing discrimination. Perhaps all of the important differences will eventually prove to be environmental rather than genetic. Anyone opposed to racism and sexism will certainly hope that this will be so, for it will make the task of ending discrimination a lot easier; nevertheless it would be dangerous to rest the case against racism and sexism on the belief that all significant differences are environmental in origin. The opponent of, say, racism who takes this line will be unable to avoid conceding that if differences in ability did after all prove to have some genetic connection with race, racism would in some way be defensible.

It would be folly for the opponent of racism to stake his whole case on a dogmatic commitment to one particular outcome of a difficult scientific issue which is still a long way from being settled. While attempts to prove that differences in certain selected abilities between races and sexes are primarily genetic in origin have certainly not been conclusive, the same must be said of attempts to prove that these differences are largely the result of environment. At this stage of the investigation we cannot be certain which view is correct, however much we may hope it is the latter.

Fortunately, there is no need to pin the case for equality to one particular outcome of this scientific investigation. The appropriate response to those who claim to have found evidence of genetically-based differences in ability between the races or sexes is not to stick to the belief that the genetic explanation must be wrong, whatever evidence to the contrary may turn up: instead we should make it quite clear that the claim to equality does not depend on intelligence, moral capacity, physical strength, or similar matters of fact. Equality is a moral ideal, not a simple assertion of fact. There is no logically compelling reason for assuming that a factual difference in ability between two people justifies any difference in the amount of consideration we give to satisfying their needs and interests. The principle of the equality of human beings is not a description of an alleged actual equality among humans: it is a prescription of how we should treat humans.

Jeremy Bentham incorporated the essential basis of moral equality into his utilitarian system of ethics in the formula: "Each to count for one and none for more than one." In other words, the interests of every being affected by an action are to be taken into account and given the same weight as the like interests of any other being. A later utilitarian, Henry Sidgwick, put the point in this way: "The good of any one individual is of no more importance, from the point of view (if I may say so) of the Universe, than the good of any other."[2] More recently, the leading figures in contemporary moral philosophy have shown a great deal of agreement in specifying as a fundamental presupposition of their moral theories some similar requirement which operates so as to give everyone's interests equal consideration—although they cannot agree on how this requirement is best formulated.[3]

It is an implication of this principle of equality that our concern for others ought not to depend on what they are like, or what abilities they possess—although precisely what this concern requires us to do may vary according to the characteristics of those affected by what we do. It is on this basis that the case against racism and the case against sexism must both ultimately rest; and it is in accordance with this principle that speciesism is also to be condemned. If possessing a higher degree of intelligence does not entitle one human to use another for his own ends, how can it entitle humans to exploit non-humans?

Many philosophers have proposed the principle of equal consideration of interests, in some form or other, as a basic moral principle; but, as we shall see in more detail shortly, not many of them have recognised that this principle applies to members of other species as well as to our own. Bentham was one of the few who did realize this. In a forward-looking passage, written at a time when black slaves in the British dominions were still being treated much as we now treat non-human animals, Bentham wrote:

> The day *may* come when the rest of the animal creation may acquire those rights which never could have been witholden from them but by the hand of tyranny. The French have already discovered that the blackness of the skin is no reason why a human being should be abandoned without redress to the caprice of a tormentor. It may one day come to be recognised that the number of the legs, the villosity of the skin, or the termination of the *os sacrum,* are reasons equally insufficient for abandoning a sensitive being to the same fate. What else is it that should trace the insuperable line? Is it the faculty of reason, or perhaps the faculty of discourse? But a full-grown horse or dog is beyond comparison a more rational, as well as a more conversable animal, than an infant of a day, or a week, or even a month, old. But suppose they were otherwise, what would it avail? The question is not, Can they reason? nor Can they *talk?* but, *Can they suffer?*[4]

In this passage Bentham points to the capacity for suffering as the vital characteristic that gives a being the right to equal consideration. The capacity for suffering—or more strictly, for suffering and/or enjoyment or happiness—is not just another characteristic like the capacity for language, or for higher mathematics. Bentham is not saying that those who try to mark "the insuperable line" that determines whether the interests of a being should be considered happen to have selected the wrong characteristic. The capacity for suffering and enjoying things is a pre-requisite for having interests at all, a condition that must be satisfied before we can speak of interests in any meaningful way. It would be nonsense to say that it was not in the interests of a stone to be kicked along the road by a schoolboy. A stone does not have interests because it cannot suffer. Nothing that we can do to it could possibly make any difference to its welfare. A mouse, on the other hand, does have an interest in not being tormented, because it will suffer if it is.

If a being suffers, there can be no moral justification for refusing to take that suffering into consideration. No matter what the nature of the being, the principle of equality requires that its suffering be counted equally with the like suffering—in so far as rough comparisons can be made—of any other being. If a being is not capable of suffering, or of experiencing enjoyment or happiness, there is nothing to be taken into account. This is why the limit of sentience (using the term as a convenient, if not strictly accurate, shorthand for the capacity to suffer or experience enjoyment or happiness) is the only defensible boundary of concern for the interests of others. To mark this boundary by some characteristic like intelligence or rationality would be to mark it in an arbitrary way. Why not choose some other characteristic, like skin color?

The racist violates the principle of equality by giving greater weight to the interests of members of his own race, when there is a clash between their interests and the interests of those of another race. Similarly the speciesist allows the interests of his own species to override the greater interests of members of other species.[5] The pattern is the same in each case. Most human beings are speciesists. I shall now very briefly describe some of the practices that show this.

For the great majority of human beings, especially in urban, industrialized societies, the most direct form of contact with members of other species is at meal-times: we eat them. In doing so we treat them purely as means to our ends. We regard their life and well-being as subordinate to our taste for a particular kind of dish. I say "taste" deliberately—this is purely a matter of pleasing our palate. There can be no defence of eating flesh in terms of satisfying nutritional needs, since it has been established beyond doubt that we could satisfy our need for protein and other essential nutrients far more efficiently with a diet that replaced animal flesh by soy beans, or products derived from soy beans, and other high-protein vegetable products.[6]

It is not merely the act of killing that indicates what we are ready to do to other species in order to gratify our tastes. The suffering we inflict on the animals while they are alive is perhaps an even clearer indication of our speciesism than the fact that we are prepared to kill them.[7] In order to have meat on the table at a price that people can afford, our society tolerates methods of meat production that confine sentient animals in cramped, unsuitable conditions for the entire durations of their lives. Animals are treated like machines that convert fodder into flesh, and any innovation that results in a higher "conversion ratio" is liable to be adopted. As one authority on the subject has said, "cruelty is acknowledged only when profitability ceases."[8] So hens are crowded four or five to a cage with a floor area of twenty inches by eighteen inches, or around the size of a single page of the *New York Times*. The cages have wire floors, since this reduces cleaning costs, though wire is unsuitable for the hens' feet; the floors slope, since this makes the eggs roll down for easy collection, although this makes it difficult for the hens to rest comfortably. In these conditions all the birds' natural instincts are thwarted: they cannot stretch their wings fully, walk freely, dust-bathe, scratch the ground, or build a nest. Although they have never known other conditions, observers have noticed that the birds vainly try to perform these actions. Frustrated at their inability to do so, they often develop what farmers call "vices," and peck each other to death. To prevent this, the beaks of young birds are often cut off.

This kind of treatment is not limited to poultry. Pigs are now also being reared in cages inside sheds.

These animals are comparable to dogs in intelligence, and need a varied, stimulating environment if they are not to suffer from stress and boredom. Anyone who kept a dog in the way in which pigs are frequently kept would be liable to prosecution, in England at least, but because our interest in exploiting pigs is greater than our interest in exploiting dogs, we object to cruelty to dogs while consuming the produce of cruelty to pigs. Of the other animals, the condition of veal calves is perhaps worst of all, since these animals are so closely confined that they cannot even turn around or get up and lie down freely. In this way they do not develop unpalatable muscle. They are also made anaemic and kept short of roughage, to keep their flesh pale, since white veal fetches a higher price; as a result they develop a craving for iron and roughage, and have been observed to gnaw wood off the sides of their stalls, and lick greedily at any rusty hinge that is within reach.

Since, as I have said, none of these practices cater for anything more than our pleasures of taste, our practice of rearing and killing other animals in order to eat them is a clear instance of the sacrifice of the most important interests of other beings in order to satisfy trivial interests of our own. To avoid speciesism we must stop this practice, and each of us has a moral obligation to cease supporting the practice. Our custom is all the support that the meat industry needs. The decision to cease giving it that support may be difficult, but it is no more difficult than it would have been for a white Southerner to go against the traditions of his society and free his slaves; if we do not change our dietary habits, how can we censure those slaveholders who would not change their own way of living?

The same form of discrimination may be observed in the widespread practice of experimenting on other species in order to see if certain substances are safe for human beings, or to test some psychological theory about the effect of severe punishment on learning, or to try out various new compounds just in case something turns up. People sometimes think that all this experimentation is for vital medical purposes, and so will reduce suffering overall. This comfortable belief is very wide of the mark. Drug companies test new shampoos and cosmetics that they are intending to put on the market by dropping them into the eyes of rabbits, held open by metal clips, in order to observe what damage results. Food additives, like artificial colorings and preservatives, are tested by what is known as the "LD50"—a test designed to find the level of consumption at which 50% of a group of animals will die. In the process, nearly all of the animals are made very sick before some finally die, and others pull through. If the substance is relatively harmless, as it often is, huge doses have to be force-fed to the animals, until in some cases sheer volume or concentration of the substance causes death.

Much of this pointless cruelty goes on in the universities. In many areas of science, non-human animals are regarded as an item of laboratory equipment, to be used and expended as desired. In psychology laboratories experimenters devise endless variations and repetitions of experiments that were of little value in the first place. To quote just one example, from the experimenter's own account in a psychology journal: at the University of Pennsylvania, Perrin S. Cohen hung six dogs in hammocks with electrodes taped to their hind feet. Electric shock of varying intensity was then administered through the electrodes. If the dog learnt to press its head against a panel on the left, the shock was turned off, but otherwise it remained on indefinitely. Three of the dogs, however, were required to wait periods varying from 2 to 7 seconds while being shocked before making the response that turned off the current. If they failed to wait, they received further shocks. Each dog was given from 26 to 46 "sessions" in the hammock, each session consisting of 80 "trials" or shocks, administered at intervals of one minute. The experimenter reported that the dogs, who were unable to move in the hammock, barked or bobbed their heads when the current was applied. The reported findings of the experiment were that there was a delay in the dogs' responses that increased proportionately to the time the dogs were required to endure the shock, but a gradual increase in the intensity of the shock had no systematic effect in the timing of the response. The experiment was funded by the National Institutes of Health, and the United States Public Health Service.[9]

In this example, and countless cases like it, the possible benefits to mankind are either non-existent or fantastically remote; while the certain losses to members of other species are very real. This is, again, a clear indication of speciesism.

In the past, argument about vivesection has often missed this point, because it has been put in absolutist terms: would the abolitionist be prepared to let thousands die if they could be saved by experimenting on a single animal? The way to reply to this purely hypothetical question is to pose another: would the experimenter be prepared to perform his experiment on an orphaned human infant, if that were the only way to save many lives? (I say "orphan" to avoid the complication of parental feelings, although in doing so I am being overfair to the experimenter, since the nonhuman subjects of experiments are not orphans.) If the experimenter is not prepared to use an orphaned human infant, then his readiness to use nonhumans is simple discrimination, since adult apes, cats, mice and other mammals are more aware of what is happening to them, more self-directing and, so far as we can tell, at least as sensitive to pain, as any human infant. There seems to be no relevant characteristic that human infants possess that adult mammals do not have to the same or a higher degree. (Someone might try to argue that what makes it wrong to experiment on a human infant is that the infant will, in time and if left alone, develop into more than the nonhuman, but one would then, to be consistent, have to oppose abortion, since the fetus has the same potential as the infant—indeed, even contraception and abstinence might be wrong on this ground, since the egg and sperm, considered jointly, also have the same potential. In any case, this argument still gives us no reason for selecting a nonhuman, rather than a human with severe and irreversible brain damage, as the subject for our experiments.)

The experimenter, then, shows a bias in favor of his own species whenever he carries out an experiment on a nonhuman for a purpose that he would not think justified him in using a human being at an equal or lower level of sentience, awareness, ability to be self-directing, etc. No one familiar with the kind of results yielded by most experiments on animals can have the slightest doubt that if this bias were eliminated the number of experiments performed would be a minute fraction of the number performed today.

Experimenting on animals, and eating their flesh, are perhaps the two major forms of speciesism in our society. By comparison, the third and last form of speciesism is so minor as to be insignificant, but it is perhaps of some special interest to those for whom this paper was written. I am referring to speciesism in contemporary philosophy.

Philosophy ought to question the basic assumptions of the age. Thinking through, critically and carefully, what most people take for granted is, I believe, the chief task of philosophy, and it is this task that makes philosophy a worthwhile activity. Regrettably, philosophy does not always live up to its historic role. Philosophers are human beings and they are subject to all the preconceptions of the society to which they belong. Sometimes they succeed in breaking free of the prevailing ideology: more often they become its most sophisticated defenders. So, in this case, philosophy as practiced in the universities today does not challenge anyone's preconceptions about our relations with other species. By their writings, those philosophers who tackle problems that touch upon the issue reveal that they make the same unquestioned assumptions as most other humans, and what they say tends to confirm the reader in his or her comfortable speciesist habits.

I could illustrate this claim by referring to the writings of philosophers in various fields—for instance, the attempts that have been made by those interested in rights to draw the boundary of the sphere of rights so that it runs parallel to the biological boundaries of the species *homo sapiens,* including infants and even mental defectives, but excluding those other beings of equal or greater capacity who are so useful to us at mealtimes and in our laboratories. I think it would be a more appropriate conclusion to this paper, however, if I concentrated on the problem with which we have been centrally concerned, the problem of equality.

It is significant that the problem of equality, in moral and political philosophy, is invariably formulated in terms of human equality. The effect of this is that the question of the equality of other animals does not confront the philosopher, or student, as an issue in itself—and this is already an indication of the failure of philosophy to challenge accepted beliefs. Still, philosophers have found it difficult to discuss the issue of human equality without raising, in a paragraph or two, the question of the status of other animals. The reason for this, which should be apparent from what I have said already, is that if humans are to be regarded as equal to one another, we need some sense of "equal" that does not require any actual, descriptive equality of capacities, talents or other qualities. If equality is to be related to any actual characteristics of humans, these characteristics must be some lowest common denominator, pitched so low that no human lacks them—but then the philosopher comes up against the catch that any such set of characteristics which covers *all* humans will not be possessed *only by humans.* In other words, it turns out that in the only sense in which we can truly say, as an assertion of fact, that all humans are equal, at least some members of other species are also equal—equal, that is, to each other and to humans. If, on the other hand, we regard the statement "All humans are equal" in some non-factual way, perhaps as a prescription, then, as I have already argued, it is even more difficult to exclude non-humans from the sphere of equality.

This result is not what the egalitarian philosopher originally intended to assert. Instead of accepting the radical outcome to which their own reasonings naturally point, however, most philosophers try to reconcile their beliefs in human equality and animal inequality by arguments that can only be described as devious.

As a first example, I take William Frankena's well-known article "The Concept of Social Justice."[10] Frankena opposes the idea of basing justice on merit, because he sees that this could lead to highly inegalitarian results. Instead he proposes the principle that:

> . . . all men are to be treated as equals, not because they are equal, in any respect but simply because they are human. They are human because they have emotions and desires, and are able to think, and hence are capable of enjoying a good life in a sense in which other animals are not.

But what is this capacity to enjoy the good life which all humans have, but no other animals? Other animals have emotions and desires, and appear to be capable of enjoying a good life. We may doubt that they can think—although the behavior of some apes, dolphins and even dogs suggests, that some of them can—but what is the relevance of thinking? Frankena goes on to admit that by "the good life" he means "not so much the morally good life as the happy or satisfactory life," so thought would appear to be unnecessary for enjoying the good life; in fact to emphasise the need for thought would make difficulties for the egalitarian since only some people are capable of leading intellectually satisfying lives, or morally good lives. This makes it difficult to see what Frankena's principle of equality has to do with simply being *human.* Surely every sentient being is capable of leading a life that is happier or less miserable than some alternative life, and hence has a claim to be taken into account. In this respect the distinction between humans and non-humans is not a sharp division, but rather a continuum along which we move gradually, and with overlaps between the species, from simple capacities for enjoyment and satisfaction, or pain and suffering, to more complex ones.

Faced with a situation in which they see a need for some basis for the moral gulf that is commonly thought to separate humans and animals, but can find no concrete difference that will do the job without undermining the equality of humans philosophers tend to waffle. They resort to high-sounding phrases like "the intrinsic dignity of the human individual."[11] They talk of the "intrinsic worth of all men" as if men (humans?) had some worth that other beings did not,[12] or they say that humans, and only humans, are "ends in themselves," while "everything other than a person can only have value for a person."[13]

This idea of a distinctive human dignity and worth has a long history; it can be traced back directly to the Renaissance humanists, for instance to Pico della Mirandola's *Oration on the Dignity of Man.* Pico and other humanists based their estimate of human dignity on the idea that man possessed the central, pivotal position in the "Great Chain of Being" that led from the lowliest forms of matter to God himself; this view of the universe, in turn, goes back to both classical and Judeo-Christian doctrines. Contemporary philosophers have cast off these metaphysical and religious shackles and freely invoke the dignity of mankind without needing to justify the idea at all. Why should we not attribute "intrinsic dignity" or "intrinsic worth" to ourselves? Fellow-humans are unlikely to reject the accolades we so generously bestow on them, and those to whom we deny the honor are unable to object. Indeed, when one thinks only of humans, it can be very liberal, very progressive, to talk of the dignity of all human beings. In so doing, we implicitly condemn slavery, racism, and other violations of human rights. We admit that we ourselves are in some fundamental sense on a par with the poorest, most ignorant members of our own species. It is only when we think of humans as no more than a small sub-group of all the beings that inhabit our planet that we may realize that in elevating our own species we are at the same time lowering the relative status of all other species.

The truth is that the appeal to the intrinsic dignity of human beings appears to solve the egalitarian's problems only as long as it goes unchallenged. Once we ask *why* it should be that all humans—including infants, mental defectives, psychopaths, Hitler, Stalin and the rest–have some kind of dignity or worth that no elephant, pig or chimpanzee can ever achieve, we see that this question is as difficult to answer as our original request for some relevant fact that justifies the inequality of humans and other animals. In fact, these two questions are really one: talk of intrinsic dignity or moral worth only takes the problem back one step, because any satisfactory defence of the claim that all and only humans have intrinsic dignity would need to refer to some relevant capacities or characteristics that all and only humans possess. Philosophers frequently introduce ideas of dignity, respect and worth at the point at which other reasons appear to be lacking, but this is hardly good enough. Fine phrases are the last resource of those who have run out of arguments.

In case there are those who still think it may be possible to find some relevant characteristic that distinguishes all humans from all members of other species, I shall refer again, before I conclude, to the existence of some humans who quite clearly are below the level of awareness, self-consciousness, intelligence, and sentience, of many non-humans.

I am thinking of humans with severe and irreparable brain damage, and also of infant humans. To avoid the complication of the relevance of a being's potential, however, I shall henceforth concentrate on permanently retarded humans.

Philosophers who set out to find a characteristic that will distinguish humans from other animals rarely take the course of abandoning these groups of humans by lumping them in with the other animals. It is easy to see why they do not. To take this line without re-thinking our attitudes to other animals would entail that we have the right to perform painful experiments on retarded humans for trivial reasons; similarly it would follow that we had the right to rear and kill these humans for food. To most philosophers these consequences are as unacceptable as the view that we should stop treating non-humans in this way.

Of course, when discussing the problem of equality it is possible to ignore the problem of mental defectives, or brush it aside as if somehow insignificant.[14] This is the easiest way out. What else remains? My final example of speciesism in contemporary philosophy has been selected to show what happens when a writer is prepared to face the question of human equality and animal inequality without ignoring the existence of mental defectives, and without resorting to obscurantist mumbo-jumbo. Stanley Benn's clear and honest article "Egalitarianism and Equal Consideration of Interests"[15] fits this description.

Benn, after noting the usual "evident human inequalities" argues, correctly I think, for equality of consideration as the only possible basis for egalitarianism. Yet Benn, like other writers, is thinking only of "equal consideration of human interests." Benn is quite open in his defence of this restriction of equal consideration:

> . . . not to possess human shape *is* a disqualifying condition. However faithful or intelligent a dog may be, it would be a monstrous sentimentality to attribute to him interests that could be weighed in an equal balance with those of human beings . . . if, for instance, one had to decide between feeding a hungry baby or a hungry dog, anyone who chose the dog would generally be reckoned morally defective, unable to recognize a fundamental inequality of claims.

This is what distinguishes our attitude to animals from our attitude to imbeciles. It would be odd to say that we ought to respect equally the dignity or personality of the imbecile and of the rational man . . . but there is nothing odd about saying that we should respect their interests equally, that is, that we should give to the interests of each the same serious consideration as claims to considerations necessary for some standard of well-being that we can recognize and endorse.

Benn's statement of the basis of the consideration we should have for imbeciles seems to me correct, but why should there be any fundamental inequality of claims between a dog and a human imbecile? Benn sees that if equal consideration depended on rationality, no reason could be given against using imbeciles for research purposes, as we now use dogs and guinea pigs. This will not do: "But of course we do distinguish imbeciles from animals in this regard," he says. That the common distinction is justifiable is something Benn does not question; his problem is how it is to be justified. The answer he gives is this:

> . . . we respect the interests of men and give them priority over dogs not *insofar* as they are rational, but because rationality is the human norm. We say it is *unfair* to exploit the deficiencies of the imbecile who falls short of the norm, just as it would be *unfair,* and not just ordinarily dishonest, to steal from a blind man. If we do not think in this way about dogs, it is because we do not see the irrationality of the dog as a deficiency or a handicap, but as normal for the species. The characteristics, therefore, that distinguish the normal man from the normal dog make it intelligible for us to talk of other men having interests and capacities, and therefore claims, of precisely the same kind as we make on our own behalf. But although these characteristics may provide the point of the distinction between men and other species, they are not in fact the qualifying conditions for membership, or the distinguishing criteria of the class of morally considerable persons; and this is precisely because a man does not become a member of a different species, with its own standards of normality, by reason of not possessing these characteristics.

The final sentence of this passage gives the argument away. An imbecile, Benn concedes, may have no characteristics superior to those of a dog; nevertheless this does not make the imbecile a member of "a different species" as the dog is. *Therefore* it would be "unfair" to use the imbecile for medical research as we use the dog. But why? That the imbecile is not rational is just the way things have worked out, and the same is true of the dog–neither is any more responsible for their mental level. If it is unfair to take advantage of an isolated defect, why is it fair to take advantage of a more general limitation? I find it hard to see anything in this argument except a defence of preferring the interests of members of our own species because they are members of our own species. To those who think there might be more to it, I suggest the following mental exercise. Assume that it has been proven that there is a difference in the average, or normal, intelligence quotient for two different races, say whites and blacks. Then substitute the term "white" for every occurrence of "men" and "black" for every occurrence of "dog" in the passage quoted; and substitute "high I.Q." for "rationality" and when Benn talks of "imbeciles" replace this term by "dumb whites"–that is, whites who fall well below the normal white I.Q. score. Finally, change "species" to "race." Now re-read the passage. It has become a defence of a rigid, no-exceptions division between whites and blacks, based on I.Q. scores, *not withstanding an admitted overlap* between whites and blacks in this respect. The revised passage is, of course, outrageous, and this is not only because we have made fictitious assumptions in our substitutions. The point is that in the original passage Benn was defending a rigid division in the amount of consideration due to members of different species, despite admitted cases of overlap. If the original did not, at first reading strike us as being as outrageous as the revised version does, this is largely because although we are not racists ourselves, most of us are speciesists. Like the other articles, Benn's stands as a warning of the ease with which the best minds can fall victim to a prevailing ideology.

NOTES

1. Passages of this article appeared in a review of *Animals, Men and Morals,* edited by S. and R. Godlovitch and J. Harris (Gollancz and Taplinger, London 1972) in *The New York Review of Books*, April 5 , 1973. The whole

direction of my thinking on this subject I owe to talks with a number of friends in Oxford in 1970–71. especially Richard Keshen, Stanley Godlovitch, and, above all, Roslind Godlovitch.

2. *The Methods of Ethics* (7th Ed.) p. 382.

3. For example, R. M. Hare. *Freedom and Reason* (Oxford, 1963) and J. Rawls, *A Theory of Justice* (Harvard, 1972); for a brief account of the essential agreement on this issue between these and other positions, see R. M. Hare, "Rules of War and Moral Reasoning," *Philosophy and Public Affairs,* vol. I. no. 2 (1972).

4. *Introduction to the Principles of Morals and Legislation,* ch. XVII.

5. I owe the term "speciesism" to Dr. Richard Ryder.

6. In order to produce 1 1b. of protein in the form of beef or veal, we must feed 21 lbs. of protein to the animal. Other forms of livestock are slightly less inefficient, but the average ratio in the U.S. is still 1:8. It has been estimated that the amount of protein lost to humans in this way is equivalent to 90% of the annual world protein deficit. For a brief account, see Frances Moore Lappe, *Diet for a Small Planet* (Friends of The Earth/Ballantine, New York 1971) pp. 4–11.

7. Although one might think that killing a being is obviously the ultimate wrong one can do to it, I think that the infliction of suffering is a clearer indication of speciesism because it might be argued that at least part of what is wrong with killing a human is that most humans are conscious of their existence over time, and have desires and purposes that extend into the future—see, for instance, M. Tooley, "Abortion and Infanticide," *Philosophy and Public Affairs,* vol. 2, no. 1 (1972). Of course, if one took this view one would have to hold—as Tooley does—that killing a human infant or mental defective is not in itself wrong, and is less serious than killing certain higher mammals that probably do have a sense of their own existence over time.

8. Ruth Harrison, *Animal Machines* (Stuart, London, 1964). This book provides an eye-opening account of intensive farming methods for those unfamiliar with the subject.

9. *Journal of the Experimental Analysis of Behavior,* vol. 13, no. 1 (1970). Any recent volume of this journal, or of other journals in the field, like the *Journal of Comparative and Physiological Psychology,* will contain reports of equally cruel and trivial experiments. For a fuller account. see Richard Ryder, "Experiments on Animals" in *Animals, Men and Morals.*

10. In R. Brandt (ed.) *Social Justice* (Prentice Hall, Englewood Cliffs, 1962); the passage quoted appears on p. 19.

11. Frankena, *op. cit.,* p. 23.

12. H. A. Bedau, "Egalitarianism and the Idea of Equality" in *Nomos IX: Equality,* ed. J. R. Pennock and J. W. Chapman, New York 1967.

13. G. Vlastos. "Justice and Equality" in Brandt, *Social Justice,* p. 48.

14. E. G. Bernard Williams, "The Idea of Equality," in *Philosophy, Politics and Society* (second series) ed. P. Laslett and W. Runciman (Blackwell, Oxford, 1962) p. 118; J. Rawls. A *Theory of Justice*, p, pp. 509-10.

15. *Nomos IX: Equality;* the passages quoted are on pp. 62ff.

DISCUSSION QUESTIONS

1. What is Singer's main argument for regarding all animals as equals? Do you find that argument convincing? Why or why not?

2. Singer discusses various attempts to explain why humans deserve greater moral consideration than non-human animals. Do you find any of those attempts convincing, despite Singer's criticisms? If so, why? If not, can you think of any other ways to argue that humans deserve greater moral consideration?

3. Suppose that a critic of animal equality accepted the claim that human infants and severely mentally handicapped adults did not have the same "intrinsic worth" as normal adult humans. How might such a person argue that it is still wrong to, e.g., perform medical experiments on orphaned infants?

4. Singer considers a few different versions of the objection that humans have a special moral worth or dignity that non-humans lack. In your words, explain whichever version of this objection you think is the strongest. How does Singer reply to it? Do you find his reply convincing? Why or why not?

BONNIE STEINBOCK

Speciesism and the Idea of Equality

Bonnie Steinbock is Professor Emerita of Philosophy at the University at Albany. She has written extensively on bioethics and animal ethics. In this paper, Steinbock responds to Peter Singer's argument (in the previous reading) that "all animals are equal." She argues that while all animals' interests count, humans' interests count more than non-human animals' interests.

GUIDING QUESTIONS

1. Steinbock begins by explaining and even defending Singer's claims about speciesism. At what point in the paper does she begin to disagree with Singer?
2. What is Steinbock's central point of disagreement with Singer that leads her to reject his conclusion?
3. What relevant differences does Steinbock identify between humans and non-human animals? Which difference(s) does she see as the real basis of humans' greater moral importance? Why?
4. Given Steinbock's views about what makes human lives more valuable than animal lives, are there any humans whose lives are less valuable than some animal lives? If so, how does Steinbock think we should treat those humans? Why?

Most of us believe that we are entitled to treat members of other species in ways which would be considered wrong if inflicted on members of our own species. We kill them for food, keep them confined, use them in painful experiments. The moral philosopher has to ask what relevant difference justifies this difference in treatment. A look at this question will lead us to re-examine the distinctions which we have assumed make a moral difference.

It has been suggested by Peter Singer[1] that our current attitudes are "speciesist," a word intended to make one think of "racist" or "sexist." The idea is that membership in a species is in itself not relevant to moral treatment, and that much of our behaviour and attitudes towards non-human animals is based simply on this irrelevant fact.

There is, however, an important difference between racism or sexism and "speciesism." We do not subject animals to different moral treatment simply because they have fur and feathers, but because they are in fact different from human beings in ways that could be morally relevant. It is false that women are incapable of being benefited by education, and therefore that claim cannot serve to justify preventing them from attending school. But this is not false of cows and dogs, even chimpanzees. Intelligence is thought to be a morally relevant capacity because of its relation to the capacity for moral responsibility.

What is Singer's response? He agrees that non-human animals lack certain capacities that human animals possess, and that this may justify different *treatment*. But it does not justify giving less consideration to their needs and interests. According to Singer, the moral mistake which the racist or sexist makes is not essentially the factual error of thinking that blacks or women are inferior to white men. For

Bonnie Steinbock. "Speciesism and the Idea of Equality" *Philosophy*, 53(204) (April 1978), 247–256 © 1978 The Royal Institute of Philosophy. Reprinted with the permission of Cambridge University Press.

even if there were no factual error, even if it were true that blacks and women are less intelligent and responsible than whites and men, this would not justify giving less consideration to their needs and interests. It is important to note that the term "speciesism" is in one way like, and in another way unlike, the terms "racism" and "sexism." What the term "speciesism" has in common with these terms is the reference to focusing on a characteristic which is, in itself, irrelevant to moral treatment. And it is worth reminding us of this. But Singer's real aim is to bring us to a new understanding of the idea of equality. The question is, on what do claims to equality rest? The demand for *human* equality is a demand that the interests of all human beings be considered equally, unless there is a moral justification for not doing so. But why should the interests of all human beings be considered equally? In order to answer this question, we have to give some sense to the phrase, "All men (human beings) are created equal." Human beings are manifestly *not* equal, differing greatly in intelligence, virtue and capacities. In virtue of what can the claim to equality be made?

It is Singer's contention that claims to equality do not rest on factual equality. Not only do human beings differ in their capacities, but it might even turn out that intelligence, the capacity for virtue, etc., are not distributed evenly among the races and sexes:

> The appropriate response to those who claim to have found evidence of genetically based differences in ability between the races or sexes is not to stick to the belief that the genetic explanation must be wrong, whatever evidence to the contrary may turn up; instead we should make it quite clear that the claim to equality does not depend on intelligence, moral capacity, physical strength, or similar matters of fact. Equality is a moral ideal, not a simple assertion of fact. There is no logically compelling reason for assuming that a factual difference in ability between two people justifies any difference in the amount of consideration we give to satisfying their needs and interests. The principle of equality of human beings is not a description of an alleged actual equality among humans: it is a prescription of how we should treat humans.[2]

In so far as the subject is human equality, Singer's view is supported by other philosophers. Bernard Williams, for example, is concerned to show that

demands for equality cannot rest on factual equality among people, for no such equality exists.[3] The only respect in which all men are equal, according to Williams, is that they are all equally men. This seems to be a platitude, but Williams denies that it is trivial. Membership in the species *homo sapiens* in itself has no special moral significance, but rather the fact that all men are human serves as a *reminder* that being human involves the possession of characteristics that are morally relevant. But on what characteristics does Williams focus? Aside from the desire for self-respect (which I will discuss later), Williams is not concerned with uniquely human capacities. Rather, he focuses on the capacity to feel pain and the capacity to feel affection. It is in virtue of these capacities, it seems, that the idea of equality is to be justified.

Apparently Richard Wasserstrom has the same idea as he sets out the racist's "logical and moral mistakes" in "Rights, Human Rights and Racial Discrimination."[4] The racist fails to acknowledge that the black person is as capable of suffering as the white person. According to Wasserstrom, the reason why a person is said to have a right not to be made to suffer acute physical pain is that we all do in fact value freedom from such pain. Therefore, if anyone has a right to be free from suffering acute physical pain, *everyone* has this right, for there is no possible basis of discrimination. Wasserstrom says, "For, if all persons do have equal capacities of these sorts and if the existence of these capacities is the reason for ascribing these rights to anyone, then all persons ought to have the right to claim equality of treatment in respect to the possession and exercise of these rights."[5] The basis of equality, for Wasserstrom as for Williams, lies not in some uniquely human capacity, but rather in the fact that all human beings are alike in their capacity to suffer. Writers on equality have focused on this capacity, I think, because it functions as some sort of lowest common denominator, so that whatever the other capacities of a human being, he is entitled to equal consideration because, like everyone else, he is capable of suffering.

If the capacity to suffer is the reason for ascribing a right to freedom from acute pain, or a right to well being, then it certainly looks as though these rights must be extended to animals as well. This is the conclusion Singer arrives at. The demand for human equality rests on the equal capacity of all human beings to suffer and to enjoy well being. But if this is the basis of the demand for equality, then this demand must include all beings which have an equal capacity to suffer and enjoy well being. That is why Singer places at the basis of the demand for equality, not intelligence or reason, but sentience. And equality will mean, not equality of treatment, but "equal consideration of interests." The equal consideration of interests will often mean quite different treatment, depending on the nature of the entity being considered. (It would be as absurd to talk of a dog's right to vote, Singer says, as to talk of a man's right to have an abortion.)

It might be thought that the issue of equality depends on a discussion of rights. According to this line of thought, animals do not merit equal consideration of interests because, unlike human beings, they do not, or cannot, have rights. But I am not going to discuss rights, important as the issue is. The fact that an entity does not have rights does not necessarily imply that its interests are going to count for less than the interests of entities which are right-bearers. According to the view of rights held by H. L. A. Hart and S. I. Benn, infants do not have rights, nor do the mentally defective, nor do the insane, in so far as they all lack certain minimal conceptual capabilities for having rights.[6] Yet it certainly does not seem that either Hart or Benn would agree that *therefore* their interests are to be counted for less, or that it is morally permissible to treat them in ways in which it would not be permissible to treat right-bearers. It seems to mean only that we must give different sorts of reasons for our obligations to take into consideration the interests of those who do not have rights.

We have reasons concerning the treatment of other people which are clearly independent of the notion of rights. We would say that it is wrong to punch someone because doing that infringes his rights. But we could also say that it is wrong because doing that hurts him, and that is, ordinarily, enough of a reason not to do it. Now this particular reason extends not only to human beings, but to all sentient creatures. One has a *prima facie* reason not to pull the cat's tail (whether or not the cat has rights) because it hurts the cat. And this is the only thing, normally, which is relevant in this case. The fact that the cat is not a "rational being," that it is not capable of moral responsibility, that it cannot make free choices or shape its life— all of these differences from us have nothing to do with the justifiability of pulling its tail. Does this show that rationality and the rest of it are irrelevant to moral treatment?

I hope to show that this is not the case. But first I want to point out that the issue is not one of cruelty to animals. We all agree that cruelty is wrong, whether perpetrated on a moral or non-moral, rational or non-rational agent. Cruelty is defined as the infliction of unnecessary pain or suffering. What is to count as necessary or unnecessary is determined, in part, by the nature of the end pursued. Torturing an animal is cruel, because although the pain is logically necessary for the action to be torture, the end (deriving enjoyment from seeing the animal suffer) is monstrous. Allowing animals to suffer from neglect or for the sake of large profits may also be thought to be unnecessary and therefore cruel. But there may be some ends, which are very good (such as the advancement of medical knowledge), which can be accomplished by subjecting animals to pain in experiments. Although most people would agree that the pain inflicted on animals used in medical research ought to be kept to a minimum, they would consider pain that cannot be eliminated "necessary" and therefore not cruel. It would probably not be so regarded if the subjects were non-voluntary human beings. Necessity, then, is defined in terms of human benefit, but this is just what is being called into question. The topic of cruelty to animals, while important from a practical viewpoint, because much of our present treatment of animals involves the infliction of suffering for no good reason, is not very interesting philosophically. What is philosophically interesting is whether we are justified in having different standards of necessity for human suffering and for animal suffering.

Singer says, quite rightly I think, "If a being suffers, there can be no moral justification for refusing to take that suffering into consideration."[7] But he thinks that the principle of equality requires that, no matter what the nature of the being, its suffering be counted equally with the like suffering of any other being. In other words sentience does not simply provide us with reasons for acting; it is the *only* relevant consideration for equal consideration of interests. It is this view that I wish to challenge.

I want to challenge it partly because it has such counter-intuitive results. It means, for example, that feeding starving children before feeding starving dogs is just like a Catholic charity's feeding hungry Catholics before feeding hungry non-Catholics. It is simply a matter of taking care of one's own, something which is usually morally permissible. But whereas we would admire the Catholic agency which did not discriminate, but fed all children, first come, first served, we would feel quite differently about someone who had this policy for dogs and children. Nor is this, it seems to me, simply a matter of a sentimental preference for our own species. I might feel much more love for my dog than for a strange child—and yet I might feel morally obliged to feed the child before I fed my dog. If I gave in to the feelings of love and fed my dog and let the child go hungry, I would probably feel guilty. This is not to say that we can simply rely on such feelings. Huck Finn felt guilty at helping Jim escape, which he viewed as stealing from a woman who had never done him any harm. But while the existence of such feelings does not settle the morality of an issue, it is not clear to me that they can be explained away. In any event, their existence can serve as a motivation for trying to find a rational justification for considering human interests above non-human ones.

However, it does seem to me that this *requires* a justification. Until now, common sense (and academic philosophy) have seen no such need. Benn says, "No one claims equal consideration for all mammals— human beings count, mice do not, though it would not be easy to say *why* not. . . . Although we hesitate to inflict unnecessary pain on sentient creatures, such as mice or dogs, we are quite sure that we do not need to show good reasons for putting human interests before theirs."[8]

I think we do have to justify counting our interests more heavily than those of animals. But how? Singer is right, I think, to point out that it will not do to refer vaguely to the greater value of human life, to human worth and dignity:

> Faced with a situation in which they see a need for some basis for the moral gulf that is commonly thought to separate humans and animals, but can find no concrete difference that will do this without undermining the equality of humans, philosophers tend to waffle. They resort to high-sounding phrases like "the intrinsic dignity of the human individual." They talk of "the intrinsic worth of all men" as if men had some worth that other beings do not have or they say that human beings, and only human beings, are "ends in themselves," while "everything other than a person can only have value for a person." . . . Why should we not attribute "intrinsic dignity" or "intrinsic worth" to ourselves? Why should we not say that we are the only things in the universe that have intrinsic value? Our fellow human beings are unlikely to reject the accolades we so generously bestow upon them, and those to whom we deny the honour are unable to object.[9]

Singer is right to be sceptical of terms like "intrinsic dignity" and "intrinsic worth." These phrases are no substitute for a moral argument. But they may point to one. In trying to understand what is meant by these phrases, we may find a difference or differences between human beings and non-human animals that will justify different treatment while not undermining claims for human equality. While we are not compelled to discriminate among people because of different capacities, if we can find a significant difference in capacities between human and non-human animals, this could serve to justify regarding human interests as primary. It is not arbitrary or smug, I think, to maintain that human beings have a different moral status from members of other species because of certain capacities which are characteristic of being human. We may not all be equal in these capacities, but all human beings possess them to some measure, and non-human animals do not. For example, human beings are normally held to be responsible for what they do. In recognizing that someone is responsible for his or her actions, you accord that person a respect which is reserved for those possessed of moral autonomy, or capable of achieving such autonomy. Secondly, human beings can be expected to reciprocate in a way that non-human animals cannot. Non-human animals cannot be motivated by altruistic or moral reasons; they cannot treat you fairly or unfairly. This does not rule out the possibility of an animal being motivated by sympathy or pity. It does rule out altruistic motivation in the sense of motivation due to the recognition that the needs and interests of others provide one with certain reasons for acting.[10] Human beings are capable of altruistic motivation in this sense. We are sometimes motivated simply by the recognition that someone else is in pain, and that pain is a bad thing, no matter who suffers it. It is this sort of reason that I claim cannot motivate an animal or any entity not possessed of fairly abstract concepts. (If some non-human animals do possess the requisite concepts—perhaps chimpanzees who have learned a language— they might well be capable of altruistic motivation.) This means that our moral dealings with animals are necessarily much more limited than our dealings with other human beings. If rats invade our houses, carrying disease and biting our children, we cannot reason with them, hoping to persuade them of the injustice they do us. We can only attempt to get rid of them. And it is this that makes it reasonable for us to accord them a separate and not equal moral status, even though their capacity to suffer provides us with some reason to kill them painlessly, if this can be done without too much sacrifice of human interests. Thirdly, as Williams points out, there is the "desire for self-respect": "a certain human desire to be identified with what one is doing, to be able to realize purposes of one's own, and not to be the instrument of another's will unless one has willingly accepted such a role."[11] Some animals may have some form of this desire, and to the extent that they do, we ought to consider their interest in freedom and self-determination. (Such considerations might affect our attitudes toward zoos and circuses.) But the desire for self-respect *per se* requires the intellectual capacities of human beings, and this desire provides us with special reasons not to treat human beings in certain ways. It is an affront to the dignity of a human being to be a slave (even if a well-treated one); this cannot be true for a horse or a cow. To point this out is of course only to say that the justification for the treatment of an entity will depend on the sort of entity in question. In our treatment of other entities, we must consider the desire for autonomy, dignity and respect, but only where such a desire exists. Recognition of different desires

and interests will often require different treatment, a point Singer himself makes.

But is the issue simply one of different desires and interests justifying and requiring different treatment? I would like to make a stronger claim, namely, that certain capacities, which seem to be unique to human beings, entitle their possessors to a privileged position in the moral community. Both rats and human beings dislike pain, and so we have a *prima facie* reason not to inflict pain on either. But if we can free human beings from crippling diseases, pain and death through experimentation which involves making animals suffer, and if this is the only way to achieve such results, then I think that such experimentation is justified because human lives are more valuable than animal lives. And this is because of certain capacities and abilities that normal human beings have which animals apparently do not, and which human beings cannot exercise if they are devastated by pain or disease.

My point is not that the lack of the sorts of capacities I have been discussing gives us a justification for treating animals just as we like, but rather that it is these differences between human beings and non-human animals which provide a rational basis for different moral treatment and consideration. Singer focuses on sentience alone as the basis of equality, but we can justify the belief that human beings have a moral worth that non-human animals do not, in virtue of specific capacities, and without resorting to "high-sounding phrases."

Singer thinks that intelligence, the capacity for moral responsibility, for virtue, etc., are irrelevant to equality, because we would not accept a hierarchy based on intelligence any more than one based on race. We do not think that those with greater capacities ought to have their interests weighed more heavily than those with lesser capacities, and this, he thinks, shows that differences in such capacities are irrelevant to equality. But it does not show this at all. Kevin Donaghy argues (rightly, I think) that what entitles us human beings to a privileged position in the moral community is a certain minimal level of intelligence, which is a prerequisite for morally relevant capacities.[12] The fact that we would reject a hierarchical society based on degree of intelligence does not show that a minimal level of intelligence cannot be used as a cut-off point, justifying giving greater consideration to the interests of those entities which meet this standard.

Interestingly enough, Singer concedes the rationality of valuing the lives of normal human beings over the lives of non-human animals.[13] We are not required to value equally the life of a normal human being and the life of an animal, he thinks, but only their suffering. But I doubt that the value of an entity's life can be separated from the value of its suffering in this way. If we value the lives of human beings more than the lives of animals, this is because we value certain capacities that human beings have and animals do not. But freedom from suffering is, in general, a minimal condition for exercising these capacities, for living a fully human life. So, valuing human life more involves regarding human interests as counting for more. That is why we regard human suffering as more deplorable than comparable animal suffering.

But there is one point of Singer's which I have not yet met. Some human beings (if only a very few) are less intelligent than some non-human animals. Some have less capacity for moral choice and responsibility. What status in the moral community are these members of our species to occupy? Are their interests to be considered equally with ours? Is experimenting on them permissible where such experiments are painful or injurious, but somehow necessary for human well being? If it is certain of our capacities which entitle us to a privileged position, it looks as if those lacking those capacities are not entitled to a privileged position. To think it is justifiable to experiment on an adult chimpanzee but not on a severely mentally incapacitated human being seems to be focusing on membership in a species where that has no moral relevance. (It is being "speciesist" in a perfectly reasonable use of the word.) How are we to meet this challenge?

Donaghy is untroubled by this objection. He says that it is fully in accord with his intuitions, that he regards the killing of a normally intelligent human being as far more serious than the killing of a person so severely limited that he lacked the intellectual capacities of an adult pig. But this parry really misses the point. The question is whether Donaghy thinks that the killing of a human being so severely limited that he lacked the intellectual capacities of an adult pig would be less serious than the killing of that pig. If superior intelligence is what justifies privileged status in the moral community, then the pig who is smarter than a human being ought to have superior moral status. And I doubt that this is fully in accord with Donaghy's intuitions.

I doubt that anyone will be able to come up with a concrete and morally relevant difference that would justify, say, using a chimpanzee in an experiment rather than a human being with less capacity for reasoning, moral responsibility, etc. Should we then experiment on the severely retarded? Utilitarian considerations aside (the difficulty of comparing intelligence between species, for example), we feel a special obligation to care for the handicapped members of our own species, who cannot survive in this world without such care. Non-human animals manage very well, despite their "lower intelligence" and lesser capacities; most of them do not require special care from us. This does not, of course, justify experimenting on them. However, to subject to experimentation those people who depend on us seems even worse than subjecting members of other species to it. In addition, when we consider the severely retarded, we think, "That could be me." It makes sense to think that one might have been born retarded, but not to think that one might have been born a monkey. And so, although one can imagine oneself in the monkey's place, one feels a closer identification with the severely retarded human being. Here we are getting away from such things as "morally relevant differences" and are talking about something much more difficult to articulate, namely, the role of feeling and sentiment in moral thinking. We would be *horrified* by the use of the retarded in medical research. But what are we to make of this horror? Has it moral significance or is it "mere" sentiment, of no more import than the sentiment of whites against blacks? It is terribly difficult to know how to evaluate such feelings.[14] I am not going to say more about this, because I think that the treatment of severely incapacitated human beings does not pose an insurmountable objection to the privileged status principle. I am willing to admit that my horror at the thought of experiments being performed on severely mentally incapacitated human beings in cases in which

I would find it justifiable and preferable to perform the same experiments on non-human animals (capable of similar suffering) may not be a moral emotion. But it is certainly not wrong of us to extend special care to members of our own species, motivated by feelings of sympathy, protectiveness, etc. If this is speciesism, it is stripped of its tone of moral condemnation. It is not racist to provide special care to members of your own race; it is racist to fall below your moral obligation to a person because of his or her race. I have been arguing that we are morally obliged to consider the interests of all sentient creatures, but not to consider those interests equally with human interests. Nevertheless, even this recognition will mean some radical changes in our attitude toward and treatment of other species.[15]

NOTES

1. Peter Singer, *Animal Liberation* (A New York Review Book, 1975).

2. Singer, 5.

3. Bernard Williams, "The Idea of Equality," *Philosophy, Politics and Society* (Second Series), Laslett and Runciman (eds.) (Blackwell, 1962), 110–131, reprinted in *Moral Concepts*, Feinberg (ed.) (Oxford, 1970), 153–171.

4. Richard Wasserstrom, "Rights, Human Rights, and Racial Discrimination" *Journal of Philosophy* 61, No. 20 (1964), reprinted in *Human Rights*, A. I. Melden (ed.) (Wadsworth, 1970), 96–110.

5. Ibid., 106.

6. H. L. A. Hart, "Are There Any Natural Rights?" *Philosophical Review* 64 (1955), and S. I. Benn, "Abortion, Infanticide, and Respect for Persons" *The Problem of Abortion,* Feinberg (ed.) (Wadsworth, 1973), 92-–104.

7. Singer, 9.

8. Benn, "Equality, Moral and Social" *The Encyclopedia of Philosophy* 3, 40.

9. Singer, 266-–267.

10. This conception of altruistic motivation comes from Thomas Nagel's *The Possibility of Altruism* (Oxford, 1970).

11. Williams, op. cit., 157.

12. Kevin Donaghy, "Singer on Speciesism'," *Philosophic Exchange* (Summer 1974).

13. Singer, 22.

14. We run into the same problem when discussing abortion. Of what significance are our feelings toward the unborn when discussing its status? Is it relevant or irrelevant that it looks like a human being?

15. I would like to acknowledge the help of, and offer thanks to, Professor Richard Arneson of the University of California, San Diego; Professor Sidney Gendin of Eastern Michigan University; and Professor Peter Singer of Monash University, all of whom read and commented on earlier drafts of this paper.

DISCUSSION QUESTIONS

1. What is Steinbock's main argument that "human lives are more valuable than animal lives"? Do you find that argument convincing? Why or why not?

2. How does Steinbock respond to the objection that some non-human animals have greater mental capacities than some humans? Do you find her response convincing? Why or why not?

3. Steinbock discusses several differences between humans and non-humans that she might have used as the basis for humans' greater moral value. Could she have given a better response to the objection about mentally impaired humans if she had chosen another difference as the basis for humans' greater moral value?

4. Given that Steinbock agrees with Singer that non-human animals' interests matter, what practices do you think she and Singer would both want to change (e.g., keeping animals as pets, eating meat, using animals in medical research, testing cosmetics on animals, etc.)? On what practices would Steinbock and Singer disagree? Why?

ALASTAIR NORCROSS

Puppies, Pigs, and People: Eating Meat and Marginal Cases

Alastair Norcross is Associate Professor of Philosophy at University of Colorado–Boulder. A self-described "card-carrying, no-holds-barred, act utilitarian," Norcross mostly writes about ethical theory, but he has also written on topics in applied ethics. In this intentionally provocative paper, Norcross argues that eating factory-farmed meat is morally forbidden, paying special attention to arguments about the similarities and differences between severely mentally handicapped humans and non-human animals.

GUIDING QUESTIONS

1. Norcross begins by describing a hypothetical scenario in which Fred mistreats some puppies. To what, exactly, does Norcross compare Fred's behavior?
2. Norcross considers four differences between Fred's behavior and that of "most Americans [who] consume meat." What are those differences? Does Norcross believe that any of them are morally relevant? Why or why not?
3. What is "the rationality gambit" and how is it connected to "the argument from marginal cases"? How does Norcross respond to that argument?
4. According to Norcross, what is "the most serious flaw" in attempts to justify factory farming and similar practices?

1. FRED'S BASEMENT

Consider the story of Fred, who receives a visit from the police one day. They have been summoned by Fred's neighbors, who have been disturbed by strange sounds emanating from Fred's basement. When they enter the basement they are confronted by the following scene: Twenty-six small wire cages, each containing a puppy, some whining, some whimpering, some howling. The puppies range in age from newborn to about six months. Many of them show signs of mutilation. Urine and feces cover the bottoms of the cages and the basement floor. Fred explains that he keeps the puppies for twenty-six

weeks, and then butchers them while holding them upside-down. During their lives he performs a series of mutilations on them, such as slicing off their noses and their paws with a hot knife, all without any form of anesthesia. Except for the mutilations, the puppies are never allowed out of the cages, which are barely big enough to hold them at twenty-six weeks. The police are horrified, and promptly charge Fred with animal abuse. As details of the case are publicized, the public is outraged. Newspapers are flooded with letters demanding that Fred be severely punished. There are calls for more severe penalties for animal abuse. Fred is denounced as a vile sadist.

Finally, at his trial, Fred explains his behavior, and argues that he is blameless and therefore

Alastair Norcross. "Puppies, Pigs, and People: Eating Meat and Marginal Cases." *Philosophical Perspectives*, 18(1) (2004), 229–245. Copyright © 2004, John Wiley and Sons.

deserves no punishment. He is, he explains, a great lover of chocolate. A couple of years ago, he was involved in a car accident, which resulted in some head trauma. Upon his release from hospital, having apparently suffered no lasting ill effects, he visited his favorite restaurant and ordered their famous rich dark chocolate mousse. Imagine his dismay when he discovered that his experience of the mousse was a pale shadow of its former self. The mousse tasted bland, slightly pleasant, but with none of the intense chocolaty flavor he remembered so well. The waiter assured him that the recipe was unchanged from the last time he had tasted it, just the day before his accident. In some consternation, Fred rushed out to buy a bar of his favorite Belgian chocolate. Again, he was dismayed to discover that his experience of the chocolate was barely even pleasurable. Extensive investigation revealed that his experience of other foods remained unaffected, but chocolate, in all its forms, now tasted bland and insipid. Desperate for a solution to his problem, Fred visited a renowned gustatory neurologist, Dr. T. Bud. Extensive tests revealed that the accident had irreparably damaged the godiva gland, which secretes cocoamone, the hormone responsible for the experience of chocolate. Fred urgently requested hormone replacement therapy. Dr. Bud informed him that, until recently, there had been no known source of cocoamone, other than the human godiva gland, and that it was impossible to collect cocoamone from one person to be used by another. However, a chance discovery had altered the situation. A forensic veterinary surgeon, performing an autopsy on a severely abused puppy, had discovered high concentrations of cocoamone in the puppy's brain. It turned out that puppies, who don't normally produce cocoamone, could be stimulated to do so by extended periods of severe stress and suffering. The research, which led to this discovery, while gaining tenure for its authors, had not been widely publicized, for fear of antagonizing animal welfare groups. Although this research clearly gave Fred the hope of tasting chocolate again, there were no commercially available sources of puppy-derived cocoamone. Lack of demand, combined with fear of bad publicity, had deterred drug companies from getting into the puppy torturing business. Fred appeals to the court to imagine

his anguish, on discovering that a solution to his severe deprivation was possible, but not readily available. But he wasn't inclined to sit around bemoaning his cruel fate. He did what any chocolate lover would do. He read the research, and set up his own cocoamone collection lab in his basement. Six months of intense puppy suffering, followed by a brutal death, produced enough cocoamone to last him a week, hence the twenty-six cages. He isn't a sadist or an animal abuser, he explains. If there were a method of collecting cocoamone without torturing puppies, he would gladly employ it. He derives no pleasure from the suffering of the puppies itself. He sympathizes with those who are horrified by the pain and misery of the animals, but the court must realize that human pleasure is at stake. The puppies, while undeniably cute, are mere animals. He admits that he would be just as healthy without chocolate, if not more so. But this isn't a matter of survival or health. His life would be unacceptably impoverished without the experience of chocolate.

End of story. Clearly, we are horrified by Fred's behavior, and unconvinced by his attempted justification. It is, of course, unfortunate for Fred that he can no longer enjoy the taste of chocolate, but that in no way excuses the imposition of severe suffering on the puppies. I expect near universal agreement with this claim (the exceptions being those who are either inhumanly callous or thinking ahead, and wish to avoid the following conclusion, to which such agreement commits them). No decent person would even contemplate torturing puppies merely to enhance a gustatory experience. However, billions of animals endure intense suffering every year for precisely this end. Most of the chicken, veal, beef, and pork consumed in the US comes from intensive confinement facilities, in which the animals live cramped, stress-filled lives and endure unanaesthetized mutilations.[1] The vast majority of people would suffer no ill health from the elimination of meat from their diets. Quite the reverse. The supposed benefits from this system of factory farming, apart from the profits accruing to agribusiness, are increased levels of gustatory pleasure for those who claim that they couldn't enjoy a meat-free diet as much as their current meat-filled diets. If we are prepared to condemn Fred for torturing puppies merely to enhance his gustatory experiences, shouldn't we similarly condemn the millions who purchase and consume factory-raised meat? Are there any morally significant differences between Fred's behavior and their behavior?

2. FRED'S BEHAVIOR COMPARED WITH OUR BEHAVIOR

The first difference that might seem to be relevant is that Fred tortures the puppies himself, whereas most Americans consume meat that comes from animals that have been tortured by others. But is this really relevant? What if Fred had been squeamish and had employed someone else to torture the puppies and extract the cocoamone? Would we have thought any better of Fred? Of course not.

Another difference between Fred and many consumers of factory-raised meat is that many, perhaps most, such consumers are unaware of the treatment of the animals, before they appear in neatly wrapped packages on supermarket shelves. Perhaps I should moderate my challenge, then. If we are prepared to condemn Fred for torturing puppies merely to enhance his gustatory experiences, shouldn't we similarly condemn those who purchase and consume factory-raised meat, in full, or even partial, awareness of the suffering endured by the animals? While many consumers are still blissfully ignorant of the appalling treatment meted out to meat, that number is rapidly dwindling, thanks to vigorous publicity campaigns waged by animal welfare groups. Furthermore, any meat-eating readers of this article are now deprived of the excuse of ignorance.

Perhaps a consumer of factory-raised animals could argue as follows: While I agree that Fred's behavior is abominable, mine is crucially different. If Fred did not consume his chocolate, he would not raise and torture puppies (or pay someone else to do so). Therefore Fred could prevent the suffering of the puppies. However, if I did not buy and consume factory-raised meat, no animals would be spared lives of misery. Agribusiness is much too large to respond to the behavior of one consumer. Therefore

I cannot prevent the suffering of any animals. I may well regret the suffering inflicted on animals for the sake of human enjoyment. I may even agree that the human enjoyment doesn't justify the suffering. However, since the animals will suffer no matter what I do, I may as well enjoy the taste of their flesh.

There are at least two lines of response to this attempted defense. First, consider an analogous case. You visit a friend in an exotic location, say Alabama. Your friend takes you out to eat at the finest restaurant in Tuscaloosa. For dessert you select the house specialty, "Chocolate Mousse à la Bama," served with a small cup of coffee, which you are instructed to drink before eating the mousse. The mousse is quite simply the most delicious dessert you have ever tasted. Never before has chocolate tasted so rich and satisfying. Tempted to order a second, you ask your friend what makes this mousse so delicious. He informs you that the mousse itself is ordinary, but the coffee contains a concentrated dose of cocoamone, the newly discovered chocolate-enhancing hormone. Researchers at Auburn University have perfected a technique for extracting cocoamone from the brains of freshly slaughtered puppies, who have been subjected to lives of pain and frustration. Each puppy's brain yields four doses, each of which is effective for about fifteen minutes, just long enough to enjoy one serving of mousse. You are, naturally, horrified and disgusted. You will certainly not order another serving, you tell your friend. In fact, you are shocked that your friend, who had always seemed to be a morally decent person, could have both recommended the dessert to you and eaten one himself, in full awareness of the loathsome process necessary for the experience. He agrees that the suffering of the puppies is outrageous, and that the gain in human pleasure in no way justifies the appalling treatment they have to endure. However, neither he nor you can save any puppies by refraining from consuming cocoamone. Cocoamone production is now Alabama's leading industry, so it is much too large to respond to the behavior of one or two consumers. Since the puppies will suffer no matter what either of you does, you may as well enjoy the mousse.

If it is as obvious as it seems that a morally decent person, who is aware of the details of cocoamone production, couldn't order Chocolate Mousse à la

Bama, it should be equally obvious that a morally decent person, who is aware of the details of factory farming, can't purchase and consume factory-raised meat. If the attempted excuse of causal impotence is compelling in the latter case, it should be compelling in the former case. But it isn't.

The second response to the claim of causal impotence is to deny it. Consider the case of chickens, the most cruelly treated of all animals raised for human consumption, with the possible exception of veal calves. In 1998, almost 8 billion chickens were slaughtered in the US,[2] almost all of them raised on factory farms. Suppose that there are 250 million chicken eaters in the US, and that each one consumes, on average, 25 chickens per year (this leaves a fair number of chickens slaughtered for nonhuman consumption, or for export). Clearly, if only one of those chicken eaters gave up eating chicken, the industry would not respond. Equally clearly, if they all gave up eating chicken, billions of chickens (approximately 6.25 billion per year) would not be bred, tortured, and killed. But there must also be some number of consumers, far short of 250 million, whose renunciation of chicken would cause the industry to reduce the number of chickens bred in factory farms. The industry may not be able to respond to each individual's behavior, but it must respond to the behavior of fairly large numbers. Suppose that the industry is sensitive to a reduction in demand for chicken equivalent to 10,000 people becoming vegetarians. (This seems like a reasonable guess, but I have no idea what the actual numbers are, nor is it important.) For each group of 10,000 who give up chicken, a quarter of a million fewer chickens are bred per year. It appears, then, that if you give up eating chicken, you have only a one in ten thousand chance of making any difference to the lives of chickens, unless it is certain that fewer than 10,000 people will ever give up eating chicken, in which case you have no chance. Isn't a one in ten thousand chance small enough to render your continued consumption of chicken blameless? Not at all. While the chance that your behavior is harmful may be small, the harm that is risked is enormous. The larger the numbers needed to make a difference to chicken production, the larger the difference such numbers would make. A one in ten thousand chance of saving

250,000 chickens per year from excruciating lives is morally and mathematically equivalent to the certainty of saving 25 chickens per year. We commonly accept that even small risks of great harms are unacceptable. That is why we disapprove of parents who fail to secure their children in car seats or with seat belts, who leave their small children unattended at home, or who drink or smoke heavily during pregnancy. Or consider commercial aircraft safety measures. The chances that the oxygen masks, the lifejackets, or the emergency exits on any given plane will be called on to save any lives in a given week, are far smaller than one in ten thousand. And yet we would be outraged to discover that an airline had knowingly allowed a plane to fly for a week with nonfunctioning emergency exits, oxygen masks, and lifejackets. So, even if it is true that your giving up factory raised chicken has only a tiny chance of preventing suffering, given that the amount of suffering that would be prevented is in inverse proportion to your chance of preventing it, your continued consumption is not thereby excused.

But perhaps it is not even true that your giving up chicken has only a tiny chance of making any difference. Suppose again that the poultry industry only reduces production when a threshold of 10,000 fresh vegetarians is reached. Suppose also, as is almost certainly true, that vegetarianism is growing in popularity in the US (and elsewhere). Then, even if you are not the one, newly converted vegetarian, to reach the next threshold of 10,000, your conversion will reduce the time required before the next threshold is reached. The sooner the threshold is reached, the sooner production, and therefore animal suffering, is reduced. Your behavior, therefore, does make a difference. Furthermore, many people who become vegetarians influence others to become vegetarian, who in turn influence others, and so on. It appears, then, that the claim of causal impotence is mere wishful thinking, on the part of those meat lovers who are morally sensitive enough to realize that human gustatory pleasure does not justify inflicting extreme suffering on animals.

Perhaps there is a further difference between the treatment of Fred's puppies and the treatment of animals on factory farms. The suffering of the puppies is a necessary means to the production of gustatory pleasure, whereas the suffering of animals on factory farms is simply a by-product of the conditions dictated by economic considerations. Therefore, it might be argued, the suffering of the puppies is *intended as a means* to Fred's pleasure, whereas the suffering of factory raised animals is merely *foreseen* as a side-effect of a system that is a means to the gustatory pleasures of millions. The distinction between what is intended, either as a means or as an end in itself, and what is "merely" foreseen is central to the Doctrine of Double Effect. Supporters of this doctrine claim that it is sometimes permissible to bring about an effect that is merely foreseen, even though the very same effect could not permissibly be brought about if intended. (Other conditions have to be met in order for the Doctrine of Double Effect to judge an action permissible, most notably that there be an outweighing good effect.) Fred acts impermissibly, according to this line of argument, because he intends the suffering of the puppies as a means to his pleasure. Most meat eaters, on the other hand, even if aware of the suffering of the animals, do not intend the suffering.

In response to this line of argument, I could remind the reader that Samuel Johnson said, or should have said, that the Doctrine of Double Effect is the last refuge of a scoundrel.[3] I won't do that, however, since neither the doctrine itself, nor the alleged moral distinction between intending and foreseeing can justify the consumption of factory-raised meat. The Doctrine of Double Effect requires not merely that a bad effect be foreseen and not intended, but also that there be an outweighing good effect. In the case of the suffering of factory-raised animals, whatever good could plausibly be claimed to come out of the system clearly doesn't outweigh the bad. Furthermore, it would be easy to modify the story of Fred to render the puppies' suffering "merely" foreseen. For example, suppose that the cocoamone is produced by a chemical reaction that can only occur when large quantities of drain-cleaner are forced down the throat of a conscious, unanaesthetized puppy. The consequent appalling suffering, while not itself a means to the production of cocoamone, is nonetheless an unavoidable side-effect of the means. In this variation of the story, Fred's behavior is no less abominable than in the original.

One last difference between the behavior of Fred and the behavior of the consumers of factory-raised meat is worth discussing, if only because it is so frequently cited in response to the arguments of this paper. Fred's behavior is abominable, according to this line of thinking, because it involves the suffering of *puppies*. The behavior of meat-eaters, on the other hand, "merely" involves the suffering of chickens, pigs, cows, calves, sheep, and the like. Puppies (and probably dogs and cats in general) are morally different from the other animals. Puppies *count* (morally, that is), whereas the other animals don't, or at least not nearly as much.

So, what gives puppies a higher moral status than the animals we eat? Presumably there is some morally relevant property or properties possessed by puppies but not by farm animals. Perhaps puppies have a greater degree of rationality than farm animals, or a more finely developed moral sense, or at least a sense of loyalty and devotion. The problems with this kind of approach are obvious. It's highly unlikely that any property that has even an outside chance of being ethically relevant[4] is both possessed by puppies and not possessed by any farm animals. For example, it's probably true that most puppies have a greater degree of rationality (whatever that means) than most chickens, but the comparison with pigs is far more dubious. Besides, if Fred were to inform the jury that he had taken pains to acquire particularly stupid, morally obtuse, disloyal and undevoted puppies, would they (or we) have declared his behavior to be morally acceptable? Clearly not. This is, of course, simply the puppy version of the problem of marginal cases (which I will discuss later). The human version is no less relevant. If their lack of certain degrees of rationality, moral sensibility, loyalty, devotion, and the like makes it permissible to torture farm animals for our gustatory pleasure, it should be permissible to do the same to those unfortunate humans who also lack those properties. Since the latter behavior isn't permissible, the lack of such properties doesn't justify the former behavior.

Perhaps, though, there is something that separates puppies, even marginal puppies (and marginal humans) from farm animals—our sympathy. Puppies count more than other animals, because we care more about them. We are outraged to hear of puppies abused in scientific experiments, but unconcerned at the treatment of laboratory rats or animals on factory farms. Before the 2002 World Cup, several members of the England team sent a letter to the government of South Korea protesting the treatment of dogs and cats raised for food in that country. The same players have not protested the treatment of animals on factory farms in England. This example, while clearly illustrating the difference in attitudes towards cats and dogs on the one hand, and farm animals on the other, also reveals one of the problems with this approach to the question of moral status. Although the English footballers, and the English (and US) public in general, clearly care far more about the treatment of cats and dogs than of farm animals, the South Koreans, just as clearly, do not. Are we to conclude that Fred's behavior would not be abominable were he living in South Korea, where dogs and cats are routinely abused for the sake of gustatory pleasure? Such relativism is, to put it mildly, hard to swallow. Perhaps, though, we can maintain the view that human feelings determine the moral status of animals, without condoning the treatment of dogs and cats in South Korea (and other countries). Not all human feelings count. Only the feelings of those who have achieved exactly the right degree of moral sensibility. That just so happens to be those in countries like the US and Britain who care deeply for the welfare of dogs and cats, but not particularly for the welfare of cows, chickens, pigs, and other factory-raised animals. Dog and cat eaters in South Korea are insufficiently sensitive, and humane farming advocates in Britain and the US are overly so. But, of course, it won't do simply to insist that this is the right degree of moral sensibility. We need an explanation of why this is the right degree of sensibility. Moral sensibility consists, at least in part, in reacting differently to different features of situations, actions, agents, and patients. If the right degree of moral sensibility requires reacting differently to puppies and to farm animals, there must be a morally relevant difference between puppies and farm animals. Such a difference can't simply consist in the fact that (some) people do react differently to them. The appeal to differential human sympathy illustrates a purely descriptive psychological difference

between the behavior of Fred and that of someone who knowingly consumes factory-raised meat. It can do no serious moral work.

I have been unable to discover any morally relevant differences between the behavior of Fred, the puppy torturer, and the behavior of the millions of people who purchase and consume factory-raised meat, at least those who do so in the knowledge that the animals live lives of suffering and deprivation. If morality demands that we not torture puppies merely to enhance our own eating pleasure, morality also demands that we not support factory farming by purchasing factory-raised meat.

3. THE TEXAN'S CHALLENGE

Perhaps what I have said thus far is enough to convince many that the purchase and consumption of factory-raised meat is immoral. It is clear that the attribution of a different (and elevated) moral status to puppies from that attributed to farm animals is unjustified. But, one philosopher's *modus ponens*, as they say, is another Texan's *modus tollens*. Here is the *modus ponens* I have been urging:

1. If it's wrong to torture puppies for gustatory pleasure, it's wrong to support factory farming.
2. It is wrong to torture puppies for gustatory pleasure.
3. Therefore it's wrong to support factory farming.

But some may be so convinced that supporting factory farming is not wrong that they may substitute that conviction for the second premise, and conclude that it is not wrong to torture puppies for gustatory pleasure. Thus we are confronted with the Texan's *modus tollens*:

(T1) If it's wrong to torture puppies for gustatory pleasure, then it's wrong to support factory farming.
(T2) It's not wrong to support factory farming.
(T3) Therefore it's not wrong to torture puppies for gustatory pleasure.

I'm not saying that there is a large risk that many people, even Texans, will start breeding puppies for food (outside of those countries where it is already accepted practice). What they may do (and have done when I have presented them with this argument) is explain their reluctance to do so as a mere sentimental preference, as opposed to a morally mandated choice. They may claim, in a somewhat Kantian spirit, that someone who can treat puppies like that may be more likely to mistreat humans. They may agree that all animals deserve equal consideration of their interests. They may then justify their different treatment of animals either on the grounds that they are simply giving some animals *more* than they deserve, or that they are attending to their own interests. If the former, they could claim that morality mandates minimal standards of conduct, but that nothing prevents us from choosing to go beyond the requirements of morality when we feel like it. If the latter, they could claim that their sentimental attachment to puppies, kittens, and the like, makes it in their own interests not to raise and kill them for food. Nonetheless, they may insist, in terms of moral status, there is a clear difference between humans and other animals. Humans have a moral status so far above that of other animals that we couldn't even consider raising humans for food (even humanely), or experimenting on them without their consent, even though we routinely do such things to other animals.

4. HUMANS' VERSUS ANIMALS' ETHICAL STATUS—THE RATIONALITY GAMBIT

For the purposes of this discussion, to claim that humans have a superior ethical status to animals is to claim that it is morally right to give the interests of humans greater weight than those of animals in deciding how to behave. Such claims will often be couched in terms of rights, such as the rights to life, liberty or respect, but nothing turns on this terminological matter. One may claim that it is generally

wrong to kill humans, but not animals, because humans are rational, and animals are not. Or one may claim that the suffering of animals counts less than the suffering of humans (if at all), because humans are rational, and animals are not. These claims may proceed through the intermediate claim that the rights of humans are more extensive and stronger than those (if any) of animals. Alternatively, one may directly ground the judgment about the moral status of certain types of behavior in claims about the alleged natural properties of the individuals involved. Much of the debate over the moral status of abortion proceeds along these lines. Many opponents of abortion appeal to features that fetuses have in common with adult humans, in order to argue that it is, at least usually, just as seriously wrong to kill them as it is to kill us. For example, John Noonan claims that it is the possession of a full human genetic code that grounds the attribution to fetuses of this exalted ethical status. Such an argument may, but doesn't have to, proceed through the intermediate claim that anything that possesses a full human genetic code has a right to life. Many proponents of the moral permissibility of abortion, on the other hand, claim features such as self-consciousness or linguistic ability as necessary conditions of full moral status, and thus deny such status to fetuses.

What could ground the claim of superior moral status for humans? Just as the defender of a higher moral status for puppies than for farm animals needs to find some property or properties possessed by puppies but not by farm animals, so the defender of a higher moral status for humans need to find some property or properties possessed by humans but not by other animals. The traditional view, dating back at least to Aristotle, is that rationality is what separates humans, both morally and metaphysically, from other animals. With a greater understanding of the cognitive powers of some animals, recent philosophers have often refined the claim to stress the kind and level of rationality required for moral reasoning. Let's start with a representative sample of three. Consider first these claims of Bonnie Steinbock:

> While we are not compelled to discriminate among people because of different capacities, if we can find

a significant difference in capacities between human and non-human animals, this could serve to justify regarding human interests as primary. It is not arbitrary or smug, I think, to maintain that human beings have a different moral status from members of other species because of certain capacities which are characteristic of being human. We may not all be equal in these capacities, but all human beings possess them to some measure, and non-human animals do not. For example, human beings are normally held to be responsible for what they do. . . . Secondly, human beings can be expected to reciprocate in a way that non-human animals cannot. . . . Thirdly, . . . there is the "desire for self-respect."[5]

Similarly, Mary Anne Warren argues that "the rights of persons are generally stronger than those of sentient beings which are not persons." Her main premise to support this conclusion is the following:

[T]here is one difference [between human and non-human nature] which has a clear moral relevance: people are at least sometimes capable of being moved to action or inaction by the force of reasoned argument.[6]

Carl Cohen, one of the most vehement modern defenders of what Peter Singer calls "speciesism" states his position as follows:

Between species of animate life, however—between (for example) humans on the one hand and cats or rats on the other—the morally relevant differences are enormous, and almost universally appreciated. Humans engage in moral reflection; humans are morally autonomous; humans are members of moral communities, recognizing just claims against their own interest. Human beings do have rights, theirs is a moral status very different from that of cats or rats.[7]

So, the claim is that human interests and/or rights are stronger or more important than those of animals, because humans possess a kind and level of rationality not possessed by animals. How much of our current behaviour towards animals this justifies depends on just how much consideration should be given to animal interests, and on what rights, if any, they possess. Both Steinbock and Warren stress that animal interests need to be taken seriously into account. Warren claims that animals have important rights, but not as important as human rights. Cohen, on the other hand, argues that we should actually *increase* our use of animals.

5. THE CHALLENGE OF MARGINAL CASES

One of the most serious challenges to this defense of the traditional view involves a consideration of what philosophers refer to as "marginal cases." Whatever kind and level of rationality is selected as justifying the attribution of superior moral status to humans will either be lacking in some humans or present in some animals. To take one of the most commonly-suggested features, many humans are incapable of engaging in moral reflection. For some, this incapacity is temporary, as is the case with infants, or the temporarily cognitively disabled. Others who once had the capacity may have permanently lost it, as is the case with the severely senile or the irreversibly comatose. Still others never had and never will have the capacity, as is the case with the severely mentally disabled. If we base our claims for the moral superiority of humans over animals on the attribution of such capacities, won't we have to exclude many humans? Won't we then be forced to the claim that there is at least as much moral reason to use cognitively deficient humans in experiments and for food as to use animals? Perhaps we could exclude the only temporarily disabled, on the grounds of potentiality, though that move has its own problems. Nonetheless, the other two categories would be vulnerable to this objection.

I will consider two lines of response to the argument from marginal cases. The first denies that we have to attribute different moral status to marginal humans, but maintains that we are, nonetheless, justified in attributing different moral status to animals who are just as cognitively sophisticated as marginal humans, if not more so. The second admits that, strictly speaking, marginal humans are morally inferior to other humans, but proceeds to claim pragmatic reasons for treating them, at least usually, *as if* they had equal status.

As representatives of the first line of defense, I will consider arguments from three philosophers, Carl Cohen, Alan White, and David Schmidtz. First, Cohen:

> [the argument from marginal cases] fails; it mistakenly treats an essential feature of humanity as though it were a screen for sorting humans. The capacity for moral judgment that distinguishes humans from animals is not a test to be administered to human beings one by one. Persons who are unable, because of some disability, to perform the full moral functions natural to human beings are certainly not for that reason ejected from the moral community. The issue is one of kind. . . . What humans retain when disabled, animals have never had.[8]

Alan White argues that animals don't have rights, on the grounds that they cannot intelligibly be spoken of in the full language of a right. By this he means that they cannot, for example, claim, demand, assert, insist on, secure, waive, or surrender a right. This is what he has to say in response to the argument from marginal cases:

> Nor does this, as some contend, exclude infants, children, the feeble-minded, the comatose, the dead, or generations yet unborn. Any of these may be for various reasons empirically unable to fulfill the full role of right-holder. But . . . they are logically possible subjects of rights to whom the full language of rights can significantly, however falsely, be used. It is a misfortune, not a tautology, that these persons cannot exercise or enjoy, claim, or waive, their rights or do their duty or fulfil their obligations.[9]

David Schmidtz defends the appeal to typical characteristics of species, such as mice, chimpanzees, and humans, in making decisions on the use of different species in experiments. He also considers the argument from marginal cases:

> Of course, some chimpanzees lack the characteristic features in virtue of which chimpanzees command respect as a species, just as some humans lack the characteristic features in virtue of which humans command respect as a species. It is equally obvious that some chimpanzees have cognitive capacities (for example) that are superior to the cognitive capacities of some humans. But whether every human being is superior to every chimpanzee is beside the point. The point is that

we can, we do, and we should make decisions on the basis of our recognition that mice, chimpanzees, and humans are relevantly different *types*. We can have it both ways after all. Or so a speciesist could argue.[10]

There is something deeply troublesome about the line of argument that runs through all three of these responses to the argument from marginal cases. A particular feature, or set of features, is claimed to have so much moral significance that its presence or lack can make the difference to whether a piece of behavior is morally justified or morally outrageous. But then it is claimed that the presence or lack of the feature in any *particular* case is not important. The relevant question is whether the presence or lack of the feature is *normal*. Such an argument would seem perfectly preposterous in most other cases. Suppose, for example, that ten famous people are on trial in the afterlife for crimes against humanity. On the basis of conclusive evidence, five are found guilty and five are found not guilty. Four of the guilty are sentenced to an eternity of torment, and one is granted an eternity of bliss. Four of the innocent are granted an eternity of bliss, and one is sentenced to an eternity of torment. The one innocent who is sentenced to torment asks why he, and not the fifth guilty person, must go to hell. Saint Peter replies, "Isn't it obvious Mr. Ghandi? You are male. The other four men— Adolph Hitler, Joseph Stalin, George W. Bush, and Richard Nixon—are all guilty. Therefore the normal condition for a male defendant in this trial is guilt. The fact that you happen to be innocent is irrelevant. Likewise, of the five female defendants in this trial, only one was guilty. Therefore the normal condition for female defendants in this trial is innocence. That is why Margaret Thatcher gets to go to heaven instead of you."

As I said, such an argument is preposterous. Is the reply to the argument from marginal cases any better? Perhaps it will be claimed that a biological category such as a species is more "natural," whatever that means, than a category like "all the male (or female) defendants in this trial." Even setting aside the not inconsiderable worries about the conventionality of biological categories, it is not at all clear why this distinction should be morally relevant. What if it turned out that there were statistically relevant differences in the mental abilities of men and women?

Suppose that men were, on average, more skilled at manipulating numbers than women, and that women were, on average, more empathetic than men. Would such differences in what was "normal" for men and women justify us in preferring an innumerate man to a female math genius for a job as an accountant, or an insensitive woman to an ultra-sympathetic man for a job as a counselor? I take it that the biological distinction between male and female is just as real as that between human and chimpanzee.

A second response to the argument from marginal cases is to concede that cognitively deficient humans really do have an inferior moral status to normal humans. Can we, then, use such humans as we do animals? I know of no-one who takes the further step of advocating the use of marginal humans for food (though R.G. Frey has made some suggestive remarks concerning experimentation). How can we advocate this second response while blocking the further step? Warren suggests that "there are powerful practical and emotional reasons for protecting non-rational human beings, reasons which are absent in the case of most non-human animals."[11] It would clearly outrage common human sensibilities, if we were to raise retarded children for food or medical experiments.[12] Here is Steinbock in a similar vein:

> I doubt that anyone will be able to come up with a concrete and morally relevant difference that would justify, say, using a chimpanzee in an experiment rather than a human being with less capacity for reasoning, moral responsibility, etc. Should we then experiment on the severely retarded? Utilitarian considerations aside, we feel a special obligation to care for the handicapped members of our own species, who cannot survive in this world without such care. . . . In addition, when we consider the severely retarded, we think, "That could be me." It makes sense to think that one might have been born retarded, but not to think that one might have been born a monkey. . . . Here we are getting away from such things as "morally relevant differences" and are talking about something much more difficult to articulate, namely, the role of feeling and sentiment in moral thinking.[13]

This line of response clearly won't satisfy those who think that marginal humans really do deserve equal moral consideration with other humans. It is also a very shaky basis on which to justify our current practices.

What outrages human sensibilities is a very fragile thing. Human history is littered with examples of widespread acceptance of the systematic mistreatment of some groups who didn't generate any sympathetic response from others. That we do feel a kind of sympathy for retarded humans that we don't feel for dogs is, if true, a contingent matter. To see just how shaky a basis this is for protecting retarded humans, imagine that a new kind of birth defect (perhaps associated with beef from cows treated with bovine growth hormone) produces severe mental retardation, green skin, and a complete lack of emotional bond between parents and child. Furthermore, suppose that the mental retardation is of the same kind and severity as that caused by other birth defects that don't have the other two effects. It seems likely that denying moral status to such defective humans would not run the same risks of outraging human sensibilities as would the denial of moral status to other, less easily distinguished and more loved defective humans. Would these contingent empirical differences between our reactions to different sources of mental retardation justify us in ascribing different direct moral status to their subjects? The only difference between them is skin color and whether they are loved by others. Any theory that could ascribe moral relevance to differences such as these doesn't deserve to be taken seriously.[14]

Finally, perhaps we could claim that the practice of giving greater weight to the interests of all humans than of animals is justified on evolutionary grounds. Perhaps such differential concern has survival value for the species. Something like this may well be true, but it is hard to see the moral relevance. We can hardly justify the privileging of human interests over animal interests on the grounds that such privileging serves human interests!

6. AGENT AND PATIENT—THE SPECIESIST'S CENTRAL CONFUSION

Although the argument from marginal cases certainly poses a formidable challenge to any proposed criterion of full moral standing that excludes animals, it doesn't, in my view, constitute the most serious flaw in such attempts to justify the status quo. The proposed criteria are all variations on the Aristotelian criterion of rationality. But what is the moral relevance of rationality? Why should we think that the possession of a certain level or kind of rationality renders the possessor's interests of greater moral significance than those of a merely sentient being? In Bentham's famous words "The question is not, Can they reason? nor Can they talk? But, Can they suffer?"[15]

What do defenders of the alleged superiority of human interests say in response to Bentham's challenge? Some, such as Carl Cohen, simply reiterate the differences between humans and animals that they claim to carry moral significance. Animals are not members of moral communities, they don't engage in moral reflection, they can't be moved by moral reasons, *therefore* (?) their interests don't count as much as ours. Others, such as Steinbock and Warren, attempt to go further. Here is Warren on the subject:

> Why is rationality morally relevant? It does not make us "better" than other animals or more "perfect." . . . But it is morally relevant insofar as it provides greater possibilities for cooperation and for the nonviolent resolution of problems.[16]

Warren is certainly correct in claiming that a certain level and kind of rationality is morally relevant. Where she, and others who give similar arguments, go wrong is in specifying what the moral relevance amounts to. If a being is incapable of moral reasoning, at even the most basic level, if it is incapable of being moved by moral reasons, claims, or arguments, then it cannot be a moral agent. It cannot be subject to moral obligations, to moral praise or blame. Punishing a dog for doing something "wrong" is no more than an attempt to alter its future behavior. So long as we are undeceived about the dog's cognitive capacities, we are not, except metaphorically, expressing any moral judgment about the dog's behavior. (We may, of course, be expressing a moral judgment about the behavior of the dog's owner, who didn't

train it very well.) All this is well and good, but what is the significance for the question of what weight to give to animal interests? That animals can't be moral *agents* doesn't seem to be relevant to their status as moral *patients*.* Many, perhaps most, humans are both moral agents and patients. Most, perhaps all, animals are only moral patients. Why would the lack of moral agency give them diminished status as moral patients? Full status as a moral patient is not some kind of reward for moral agency. I have heard students complain in this regard that it is *unfair* that humans bear the burdens of moral responsibility, and don't get enhanced consideration of their interests in return. This is a very strange claim. Humans are subject to moral obligations, because they are the kind of creatures who *can* be. What grounds moral agency is simply different from what grounds moral standing as a patient. It is no more unfair that humans and not animals are moral agents, than it is unfair that real animals and not stuffed toys are moral patients.

One other attempt to justify the selection of rationality as the criterion of full moral standing is worth considering. Recall the suggestion that rationality is important insofar as it facilitates cooperation. If we view the essence of morality as reciprocity, the significance of rationality is obvious. A certain twisted, but all-too-common, interpretation of the Golden Rule is that we should "do unto others in order to get them to do unto us." There's no point, according to this approach, in giving much, if any, consideration to the interests of animals, because they are simply incapable of giving like consideration to our interests. In discussing the morality of eating meat, I have, many times, heard students claim that we are justified in eating meat, because "the animals would eat us, if given half a chance." (That they say this in regard to our practice of eating cows and chickens is depressing testimony to their knowledge of the animals they gobble up with such gusto.) Inasmuch as there is a consistent view being expressed here at all, it concerns self-interest, as opposed to morality. Whether it serves my interests to give the

---

*[A "moral agent" is, roughly, someone or something that has moral obligations. A "moral patient" is, roughly, someone or something toward which moral agents could have moral obligations. Normal adult humans are both moral agents and moral patients. Human infants are moral patients but not moral agents. —DRM]

same weight to the interests of animals as to those of humans is an interesting question, but it is not the same question as whether it is *right* to give animals' interests equal weight. The same point, of course, applies to the question of whether to give equal weight to my interests, or those of my family, race, sex, religion, etc. as to those of other people.

Perhaps it will be objected that I am being unfair to the suggestion that the essence of morality is reciprocity. Reciprocity is important, not because it serves *my* interests, but because it serves the interests of all. Reciprocity facilitates cooperation, which in turn produces benefits for all. What we should say about this depends on the scope of "all." If it includes all sentient beings, then the significance of animals' inability to reciprocate is in what it tells us about *how* to give their interests equal consideration. It certainly can't tell us that we should give less, or no, consideration to their interests. If, on the other hand, we claim that rationality is important for reciprocity, which is important for cooperation, which is important for benefiting humans, which is the ultimate goal of morality, we have clearly begged the question against giving equal consideration to the interests of animals.

It seems that any attempt to justify the claim that humans have a higher moral status than other animals by appealing to some version of rationality as the morally relevant difference between humans and animals will fail on at least two counts. It will fail to give an adequate answer to the argument from marginal cases, and, more importantly, it will fail to make the case that such a difference is morally relevant to the status of animals as moral patients as opposed to their status as moral agents.

I conclude that our intuitions that Fred's behavior is morally impermissible are accurate. Furthermore, given that the behavior of those who knowingly support factory farming is morally indistinguishable, it follows that their behavior is also morally impermissible.[17]

NOTES

1. For information on factory farms, see, for example, Jim Mason and Peter Singer, *Animal Factories*, 2d ed. (New York: Harmony Books, 1990), Karen Davis, *Prisoned Chickens, Poisoned Eggs: An Inside Look at the Modern Poultry Industry* (Summertown, TN: Book Publishing Co., 1996), John Robbins, *Diet for a New America* (Walpole, NH: Stillpoint, 1987).

2. *Livestock Slaughter 1998 Summary*, NASS, USDA (Washington, D.C.: March 1999), 2; and *Poultry Slaughter*, NASS, USDA (Washington, D.C.: February 2, 1999), 1f.

3. For a fine critique of the Doctrine of Double Effect, see Jonathan Bennett, *The Act Itself*, (Oxford 1995), ch. 11.

4. If someone were to assert that "puppyishness" or simply "being a puppy" were ethically relevant, I could do no more than favor them with an incredulous stare.

5. Bonnie Steinbock, "Speciesism and the Idea of Equality," *Philosophy* 53, no. 204 (April 1978). Reprinted in *Contemporary Moral Problems*, 5th edition, James E. White (ed.) (West, 1997) 467–468.

6. Mary Anne Warren, "Difficulties with the Strong Animal Rights Position," *Between the Species* 2, no. 4, 1987. Reprinted in *Contemporary Moral Problems*, 5th edition, James E. White (ed.) (West. 1997), 482.

7. Carl Cohen, "The Case for the Use of Animals in Biomedical Research," *The New England Journal of Medicine*, vol. 315, 1986. Reprinted in *Social Ethics*, 4th edition, Thomas A. Mappes and Jane S. Zembaty, (eds.) (New York: McGraw-Hill, 1992) 463.

8. Cohen, Op. cit. 461.

9. Alan White, *Rights*, (OUP 1984). Reprinted in *Animal Rights and Human Obligations*, 2nd edition, Tom Regan and Peter Singer (eds.) (Prentice Hall, 1989), 120.

10. David Schmidtz, "Are all Species Equal?," *Journal of Applied Philosophy*, Vol. 15, no. 1 (1998), 61, my emphasis.

11. Warren, op. cit. 483.

12. For a similar argument, see Peter Carruthers, *The Animals Issue: Moral Theory in Practice*. (Cambridge University Press, 1992.)

13. Steinbock, op. cit. 469–470.

14. Certain crude versions of the so-called ethics of care do seem to entail that the mere fact of being loved gives a different ethical status.

15. Jeremy Bentham, *Introduction to the Principles of Morals and Legislation*, (Various) chapter 17.

16. Warren, op. cit. 482.

17. This paper, in various forms, has been presented in more places than I can remember, and has benefited from the comments of more people than I can shake a stick at. I particularly wish to thank, for their helpful comments, Doug Ehring, Mylan Engel, Mark Heller, and Steve Sverdlik.

DISCUSSION QUESTIONS

1. Which of the differences between Fred's behavior and eating factory-farmed meat do you think is most morally significant? Why? Do you think that this difference undermines Norcross's argument by analogy? Why or why not?
2. How does Norcross respond to "the claim of causal impotence" in the case of factory-farmed meat? Do you find his responses convincing? Why or why not?
3. What are the two different ways that Norcross responds to the argument from marginal cases? Do you find his responses convincing? Why or why not?
4. Do Norcross's arguments imply that it is wrong to hunt animals for food? Why or why not?

Global Poverty

ONORA NELL

Lifeboat Earth

Baroness Onora O'Neill, who published this paper under the name Onora Nell, is Emeritus Professor of Philosophy at the University of Cambridge. She has long been actively involved in various scholarly organizations and philanthropic foundations and organizations and has served in the British Parliament's House of Lords since 1999. In this paper, written shortly after a terrible famine in the African Sahel, she argues that people in wealthier countries have a moral obligation to try to prevent deaths from famine in poor countries.

GUIDING QUESTIONS

1. How does Nell interpret the right not to be killed and the duty not to kill? In particular, in what kinds of cases does Nell think that the right not to be killed can be overridden?
2. What point is Nell trying to make with the various hypothetical scenarios she gives in the section on "Justifiable Killings in Lifeboats"?
3. How does Nell distinguish between "killing" and "allowing to die"? What is her argument that withholding food from someone on a well-provisioned lifeboat amounts to killing that person rather than allowing him or her to die?
4. What is Nell's argument for the claim that "[e]ven on a sufficiently equipped earth some persons are killed by others' distribution decisions"?
5. What arguments does Nell give for thinking that individual people, especially in wealthy countries, bear some responsibility for the deaths caused by "others' distribution decisions"?

If in the fairly near future millions of people die of starvation, will those who survive be in any way to blame for those deaths? Is there anything which people ought to do now, and from now on, if they are to be able to avoid responsibility for unjustifiable deaths in famine years? I shall argue from the assumption that persons have a right not to be killed unjustifiably to the claim that we have a duty to try to prevent and postpone famine deaths. A corollary of this claim is that if we do nothing we shall bear some blame for some deaths.

JUSTIFIABLE KILLING

I shall assume that persons have a right not to be killed and a corresponding duty not to kill. I shall make no assumptions about the other rights persons may have. In particular, I shall not assume that persons have a right not to be allowed to die by those who could prevent it or a duty to prevent others' deaths whenever they could do so. Nor will I assume that persons lack this right.

Even if persons have no rights other than a right not to be killed, this right can justifiably be overridden in certain circumstances. Not all killings are unjustifiable. I shall be particularly concerned with two sorts of circumstances in which the right not to be killed is justifiably overridden. The first of these is the case of unavoidable killings; the second is the case of self-defense.

Unavoidable killings occur in situations where a person doing some act causes some death or deaths which he could not avoid. Often such deaths will be unavoidable because of the killer's ignorance of some relevant circumstance at the time of his decision to act. If B is driving a train, and A blunders onto the track and is either unnoticed by B or noticed too late for B to stop the train, and B kills A, then B could not have avoided killing A, given his decision to drive the train. Another sort of case of unavoidable killing occurs when B could avoid killing A or could avoid killing C, but cannot avoid killing one of the two. For example, if B is the carrier of a highly contagious and invariably fatal illness, he might find

himself so placed that he cannot avoid meeting and so killing either A or C, though he can choose which of them to meet. In this case the unavoidability of B's killing someone is not relative to some prior decision B made. The cases of unavoidable killings with which I want to deal here are of the latter sort, and I shall argue that in such cases B kills justifiably if certain further conditions are met.

A killing may also be justifiable if it is undertaken in self-defense. I shall not argue here that persons have a right of self-defense which is independent of their right not to be killed, but rather that a minimal right of self-defense is a corollary of a right not to be killed. Hence the notion of self-defense on which I shall rely is in some ways different from, and narrower than, other interpretations of the right of self-defense. I shall also assume that if A has a right to defend himself against B, then third parties ought to defend A's right. If we take seriously the right not to be killed and its corollaries, then we ought to enforce others' rights not to be killed.

The right of self-defense which is a corollary of the right not to be killed is a right to take action to prevent killings. If I have a right not to be killed then I have a right to prevent others from endangering my life, though I may endanger their lives in so doing only if that is the only available way to prevent the danger to my own life. Similarly if another has the right not to be killed then I should, if possible, do something to prevent others from endangering his life, but I may endanger their lives in so doing only if that is the only available way to prevent the danger to his life. This duty to defend others is *not* a general duty of beneficence but a very restricted duty to enforce others' rights not to be killed.

The right to self-defense so construed is quite narrow. It includes no right of action against those who, though they cause or are likely to cause us harm, clearly do not endanger our lives. (However, specific cases are often unclear. The shopkeeper who shoots a person who holds him up with a toy gun was not endangered, but it may have been very reasonable of him to suppose that he was endangered.) And it includes no right to greater than minimal preventive action against a person who endangers one's life. If B is chasing A with a gun, and A could save his life either by closing a bullet-proof door or by shooting *B*, then if people have only a right not to be killed and a minimal corollary right of self-defense, *A* would have no right to shoot *B*. (Again, such cases are often unclear—*A* may not know that the door is bullet-proof or not think of it or may simply reason that shooting *B* is a better guarantee of prevention.) A right of proportionate self defense which might justify *A* in shooting *B*, even were it clear that closing the door would have been enough to prevent *B*, is not a corollary of the right not to be killed. Perhaps a right of proportionate retaliation might be justified by some claim such as that aggressors lose certain rights, but I shall take no position on this issue.

In one respect the narrow right of self-defense, which is the corollary of a right not to be killed, is more extensive than some other interpretations of the right of self-defense. For it is a right to take action against others who endanger our lives whether or not they do so intentionally. *A*'s right not to be killed entitles him to take action not only against aggressors but also against those "innocent threats"[1] who endanger lives without being aggressors. If *B* is likely to cause *A*'s death inadvertently or involuntarily, then *A* has, if he has a right not to be killed, a right to take whatever steps are necessary to prevent *B* from doing so, provided that these do not infringe *B*'s right not to be killed unnecessarily. If *B* approaches *A* with a highly contagious and invariably lethal illness, then *A* may try to prevent *B* from getting near him even if *B* knows nothing about the danger he brings. If other means fail, *A* may kill *B* in self-defense, even though *B* was no aggressor.

This construal of the right of self-defense severs the link between aggression and self-defense. When we defend ourselves against innocent threats there is no aggressor, only somebody who endangers life. But it would be misleading to call this right a right of self-preservation. For self-preservation is commonly construed (as by Locke) as including a right to subsistence, and so a right to engage in a large variety of activities whether or not anybody endangers us. But the right which is the corollary of the right not to be killed is a right only to prevent others from endangering our lives, whether or not they intend to do so, and to do so with minimal danger to their lives.

Only if one takes a Hobbesian view of human nature and sees others' acts as always completely threatening will the rights of self-defense and self-preservation tend to merge and everything done to maintain life be done to prevent its destruction. Without Hobbesian assumptions the contexts where the minimal right of self-defense can be invoked are fairly special, yet not, I shall argue, rare.

There may be various other circumstances in which persons' rights not to be killed may be overridden. Perhaps, for example, we may justifiably kill those who consent to us doing so. I shall take no position on whether persons can waive their rights not to be killed or on any further situations in which killings might be justifiable.

JUSTIFIABLE KILLINGS ON LIFEBOATS

The time has come to start imagining lurid situations, which is the standard operating procedure for this type of discussion. I shall begin by looking at some sorts of killings which might occur on a lifeboat and shall consider the sorts of justifications which they might be given.

Let us imagine six survivors on a lifeboat. There are two possible levels of provisions:

(1) Provisions are on all reasonable calculations sufficient to last until rescue. Either the boat is near land, or it is amply provisioned or it has gear for distilling water, catching fish, etc.

(2) Provisions are on all reasonable calculations unlikely to be sufficient for all six to survive until rescue.

We can call situation (1) the *well-equipped lifeboat situation;* situation (2) *the under-equipped lifeboat situation.* There may, of course, be cases where the six survivors are unsure which situation they are in, but for simplicity I shall disregard those here.

On a well-equipped lifeboat it is possible for all to survive until rescue. No killing could be justified as unavoidable, and if someone is killed, then the justification could only be self-defense in special situations. Consider the following examples:

(1A) On a well-equipped lifeboat with six persons, *A* threatens to jettison the fresh water, without which some or all would not survive till rescue. *A* may be either hostile or deranged. *B* reasons with *A,* but when this fails, shoots him. *B* can appeal to his own and the others' right of self-defense to justify the killing. "It was him or us," he may reasonably say, "for he would have placed us in an under-equipped lifeboat situation." He may say this both when *A* acts to harm the others and when *A* acts as an innocent threat.

(1B) On a well-equipped lifeboat with six persons, *B, C, D, E,* and *F* decide to withhold food from *A,* who consequently dies. In this case they cannot appeal to self-defense—for all could have survived. Nor can they claim that they merely let *A* die—"We didn't *do* anything"—for *A* would not otherwise have died. This was not a case of violating the problematic right not to be allowed to die but of violating the right not to be killed, and the violation is without justification of self-defense or of unavoidability.

On an under-equipped lifeboat it is not possible for all to survive until rescue. Some deaths are unavoidable, but sometimes there is no particular person whose death is unavoidable. Consider the following examples:

(2A) On an under-equipped lifeboat with six persons, *A* is very ill and needs extra water, which is already scarce. The others decide not to let him have any water, and *A* dies of thirst. If *A* drinks, then not all will survive. On the other hand it is clear that *A* was killed rather than allowed to die. If he had received water he might have survived. Though some death was unavoidable, *A*'s was not and selecting him as the victim requires justification.

(2B) On an under-equipped lifeboat with six persons, water is so scarce that only four can

survive (perhaps the distillation unit is designed for supplying four people). But who should go without? Suppose two are chosen to go without, either by lot or by some other method, and consequently die. The others cannot claim that all they did was to allow the two who were deprived of water to die—for these two might otherwise have been among the survivors. Nobody had a greater right to be a survivor, but given that not all could survive, those who did not survive were killed justifiably if the method by which they were chosen was fair. (Of course, a lot needs to be said about what would make a selection procedure fair.)

(2C) The same situation as in (2B) holds, but the two who are not to drink ask to be shot to ease their deaths. Again the survivors cannot claim that they did not kill but at most that they killed justifiably. Whether they did so is not affected by their shooting rather than dehydrating the victims, but only by the unavoidability of some deaths and the fairness of procedures for selecting victims.

(2D) Again the basic situation is as in (2B). But the two who are not to drink rebel. The others shoot them and so keep control of the water. Here it is all too clear that those who died were killed, but they too may have been justifiably killed. Whether the survivors kill justifiably depends neither on the method of killing nor on the victims' cooperation, except insofar as cooperation is relevant to the fairness of selection procedures.

Lifeboat situations do not occur very frequently. We are not often confronted starkly with the choice between killing or being killed by the application of a decision to distribute scarce rations in a certain way. Yet this is becoming the situation of the human species on this globe. The current metaphor "spaceship Earth" suggests more drama and less danger; if we are feeling sober about the situation, "lifeboat Earth" may be more suggestive.

Some may object to the metaphor "lifeboat Earth." A lifeboat is small; all aboard have equal claims to be there and to share equally in the provisions. Whereas the earth is vast and while all may have equal rights to be there, some also have property rights which give them special rights to consume, while others do not. The starving millions are far away and have no right to what is owned by affluent individuals or nations, even if it could prevent their deaths. If they die, it will be said, this is a violation at most of their right not to be allowed to die. And this I have not established or assumed.

I think that this could reasonably have been said in times past. The poverty and consequent deaths of far-off persons was something which the affluent might perhaps have done something to prevent, but which they had (often) done nothing to bring about. Hence they had not violated the right not to be killed of those living far off. But the economic and technological interdependence of today alters this situation.[2] Sometimes deaths are produced by some persons or groups of persons in distant, usually affluent, nations. Sometimes such persons and groups of persons violate not only some persons' alleged right not to be allowed to die but also their more fundamental right not to be killed.

We tend to imagine violations of the right not to be killed in terms of the killings so frequently discussed in the United States today: confrontations between individuals where one directly, violently, and intentionally brings about the other's death. As the lifeboat situations have shown, there are other ways in which we can kill one another. In any case, we do not restrict our vision to the typical mugger or murderer context. B may violate A's right not to be killed even when

(a) B does not act alone.
(b) A's death is not immediate.
(c) It is not certain whether A or another will die in consequence of B's action.
(d) B does not intend A's death.

The following set of examples illustrates these points about killings:

(aa) A is beaten by a gang consisting of B, C, D, etc. No one assailant single-handedly killed him, yet his right not to be killed was violated by all who took part.

(bb) A is poisoned slowly by daily doses. The final dose, like earlier ones, was not, by itself, lethal. But the poisoner still violated A's right not to be killed.

(cc) B plays Russian roulette with A, C, D, E, F, and G, firing a revolver at each once, when he knows that one firing in six will be lethal. If A is shot and dies, then B has violated his right not to be killed.

(dd) Henry II asks who will rid him of the turbulent priest, and his supporters kill Becket. It is reasonably clear that Henry did not intend Becket's death, even though he in part brought it about, as he later admitted.

These explications of the right not to be killed are not too controversial taken individually, and I would suggest that their conjunction is also uncontroversial. Even when A's death is the result of the acts of many persons and is not an immediate consequence of their deeds, nor even a certain consequence, and is not intended by them, A's right not to be killed may be violated.

FIRST CLASS VERSUS STEERAGE ON LIFEBOAT EARTH

If we imagine a lifeboat in which special quarters are provided for the (recently) first-class passengers, and on which the food and water for all passengers are stowed in those quarters, then we have a fair, if crude, model of the present human situation on lifeboat Earth. For even on the assumption that there is at present sufficient for all to survive, some have control over the means of survival and so, indirectly, over others' survival. Sometimes the exercise of control can lead, even on a well-equipped lifeboat, to the starvation and death of some of those who lack control. On an ill-equipped lifeboat some must die in any case and, as we have already seen, though some of these deaths may be killings, some of them may be justifiable killings. Corresponding situations can, do, and will arise on lifeboat Earth, and it is to these that we should turn our attention, covering both the presumed present situation of global sufficiency of the means of survival and the expected future situation of global insufficiency.

Sufficiency Situations

Aboard a well-equipped lifeboat any distribution of food and water which leads to a death is a killing and not just a case of permitting a death. For the acts of those who distribute the food and water are the causes of a death which would not have occurred had those agents either had no causal influence or done other acts. By contrast, a person whom they leave in the water to drown is merely allowed to die, for his death would have taken place (other things being equal) had those agents had no causal influence, though it could have been prevented had they rescued him.[3] The distinction between killing and allowing to die, as here construed, does not depend on any claims about the other rights of persons who are killed. The death of the shortchanged passenger of example (1B) violated his property rights as well as his right not to be killed, but the reason the death was classifiable as a killing depended on the part which the acts of the other passengers had in causing it. If we suppose that a stowaway on a lifeboat has no right to food and water and is denied them, then clearly his property rights have not been violated. Even so, by the above definitions he is killed rather than allowed to die. For if the other passengers had either had no causal influence or done otherwise, his death would not have occurred. Their actions—in this case distributing food only to those entitled to it—caused the stowaway's death. Their acts would be justifiable only if property rights can sometimes override the right not to be killed.

Many would claim that the situation on lifeboat Earth is not analogous to that on ordinary lifeboats, since it is not evident that we all have a claim, let alone an equal claim, on the earth's resources. Perhaps some of us are stowaways. I shall not here assume that we do all have some claim on the earth's resources, even though I think it plausible to suppose that we do. I shall assume that even if persons have unequal property rights and some people own nothing, it does not follow that B's exercise of his property rights can override A's right not to be killed.[4] Where our activities lead to others' deaths which would not have occurred had we either done something else or had no causal influence, no claim that the activities were within our economic rights would suffice to show that we did not kill.

It is not far-fetched to think that at present the economic activity of some groups of persons leads to others' deaths. I shall choose a couple of examples of the sort of activity which can do so, but I do not think that these examples do more than begin a list of cases of killing by economic activities. Neither of these examples depends on questioning the existence of unequal property rights; they assume only that such rights do not override a right not to be killed. Neither example is one for which it is plausible to think that the killing could be justified as undertaken in self-defense.

Case one might be called the *foreign investment situation*. A group of investors may form a company which invests abroad—perhaps in a plantation or in a mine—and so manage their affairs that a high level of profits is repatriated, while the wages for the laborers are so minimal that their survival rate is lowered, that is, their expectation of life is lower than it might have been had the company not invested there. In such a case the investors and company management do not act alone, do not cause immediate deaths, and do not know in advance who will die; it is also likely that they intend no deaths. But by their involvement in the economy of an underdeveloped area they cannot claim, as can another company which has no investments there, that they are "doing nothing." On the contrary, they are setting the policies which determine the living standards which determine the survival rate. When persons die because of the lowered standard of living established by a firm or a number of firms which dominate a local economy and either limit persons to employment on their terms or lower the other prospects for employment by damaging traditional economic structures, and these firms could either pay higher wages or stay out of the area altogether, then those who establish these policies are violating some persons' rights not to be killed. Foreign investment which *raises* living standards, even to a still abysmal level, could not be held to kill, for it causes no additional deaths, unless there are special circumstances, as in the following example.

Even when a company investing in an underdeveloped country establishes high wages and benefits and raises the expectation of life for its workers, it often manages to combine these payments with high profitability only by having achieved a tax-exempt status. In such cases the company is being subsidized by the general tax revenue of the underdeveloped economy. It makes no contribution to the infrastructure—e.g. roads and harbors and airports—from which it benefits. In this way many underdeveloped economies have come to include developed enclaves whose development is achieved in part at the expense of the poorer majority.[5] In such cases, government and company policy combine to produce a high wage sector at the expense of a low wage sector; in consequence, some of the persons in the low wage sector, who would not otherwise have died, may die; these persons, whoever they may be, are killed and not merely allowed to die. Such killings may sometimes be justifiable—perhaps, if they are outnumbered by lives saved through having a developed sector—but they are killings nonetheless, since the victims might have survived if not burdened by transfer payments to the developed sector.

But, one may say, the management of such a corporation and its investors should be distinguished more sharply. Even if the management may choose a level of wages, and consequently of survival, the investors usually know nothing of this. But the investors, even if ignorant, are responsible for company policy. They may often fail to exercise control, but by law they have control. They choose to invest in a company with certain foreign investments; they profit from it; they can, and others cannot, affect company policy in fundamental ways. To be sure the investors are not murderers—they do not intend to bring about the deaths of any persons; nor do the company managers usually intend any of the deaths company policies cause. Even so, investors and management acting together with the sorts of results just described do violate some persons' rights not to be killed and usually cannot justify such killings either as required for self-defense or as unavoidable.

Case two, where even under sufficiency conditions some persons' economic activities result in the deaths of other persons, might be called the *commodity pricing* case. Underdeveloped countries often depend heavily on the price level of a few commodities. So a sharp drop in the world price of coffee or sugar or cocoa may spell ruin and lowered survival rates for whole regions. Yet such drops in price levels are not in all cases due to factors beyond human control. Where they are the result of action by investors, brokers, or government agencies, these persons and bodies are choosing policies which will kill some people. Once again, to be sure, the killing is not singlehanded, it is not instantaneous, the killers cannot foresee exactly who will die, and they may not intend anybody to die.

Because of the economic interdependence of different countries, deaths can also be caused by rises in the prices of various commodities. For example, the present near-famine in the Sahelian region of Africa and in the Indian subcontinent is attributed by agronomists partly to climatic shifts and partly to the increased prices of oil and hence of fertilizer, wheat, and other grains.

> The recent doubling in international prices of essential foodstuffs will, of necessity, be reflected in higher death rates among the world's lowest income groups, who lack the income to increase their food expenditures proportionately, but live on diets near the subsistence level to begin with.[6]

Of course, not all of those who die will be killed. Those who die of drought will merely be allowed to die, and some of those who die because less has been grown with less fertilizer will also die because of forces beyond the control of any human agency. But to the extent that the raising of oil prices is an achievement of Arab diplomacy and oil company management rather than a windfall, the consequent deaths are killings. Some of them may perhaps be justifiable killings (perhaps if outnumbered by lives saved within the Arab world by industrialization), but killings nonetheless.

Even on a sufficiently equipped earth some persons are killed by others' distribution decisions. The causal chains leading to death-producing distributions are often extremely complex. Where they can be perceived with reasonable clarity we ought, if we take seriously the right not to be killed and seek not merely to avoid killing others but to prevent third parties from doing so, to support policies which reduce deaths. For example—and these are only examples—we should support certain sorts of aid policies rather than others; we should oppose certain sorts of foreign investment; we should oppose certain sorts of commodity speculation, and perhaps support certain sorts of price support agreements for some commodities (e.g. those which try to maintain high prices for products on whose sale poverty stricken economies depend).

If we take the view that we have no duty to enforce the rights of others, then we cannot draw so general a conclusion about our duty to support various economic policies which might avoid some unjustifiable killings. But we might still find that we should take action of certain sorts either because our own lives are threatened by certain economic activities of others or because our own economic activities threaten others' lives. Only if we knew that we were not part of any system of activities causing unjustifiable deaths could we have no duties to support policies which seek to avoid such deaths. Modern economic causal chains are so complex that it is likely that only those who are economically isolated and self-sufficient could know that they are part of no such systems of activities. Persons who believe that they are involved in some death-producing activities will have some of the same duties as those who think they have a duty to enforce others' rights not to be killed.

Scarcity Situations

The last section showed that sometimes, even in sufficiency situations, some might be killed by the way in which others arranged the distribution of the means of subsistence. Of far more importance in the long run is the true lifeboat situation—the situation of scarcity. We face a situation in which not everyone who is born can live out the normal span of human life and, further, in which we must expect today's normal life-span to be shortened. The date at which serious scarcity will begin is not generally agreed upon, but even the more optimistic prophets place it no more than decades away.[7] Its arrival will depend on factors such as the rate of technological

invention and innovation, especially in agriculture and pollution control, and the success of programs to limit human fertility.

Such predictions may be viewed as exonerating us from complicity in famine deaths. If famine is inevitable, then—while we may have to choose whom to save—the deaths of those whom we do not or cannot save cannot be seen as killings for which we bear any responsibility. For these deaths would have occurred even if we had no causal influence. The decisions to be made may be excruciatingly difficult, but at least we can comfort ourselves that we did not produce or contribute to the famine.

However, this comforting view of famine predictions neglects the fact that these predictions are contingent upon certain assumptions about what people will do in the prefamine period. Famine is said to be inevitable *if* people do not curb their fertility, alter their consumption patterns, and avoid pollution and consequent ecological catastrophes. It is the policies of the present which will produce, defer, or avoid famine. Hence if famine comes, the deaths that occur will be results of decisions made earlier. Only if we take no part in systems of activities which lead to famine situations can we view ourselves as choosing whom to save rather than whom to kill when famine comes. In an economically interdependent world there are few people who can look on the approach of famine as a natural disaster from which they may kindly rescue some, but for whose arrival they bear no responsibility. We cannot stoically regard particular famine deaths as unavoidable if we have contributed to the emergence and extent of famine.

If we bear some responsibility for the advent of famine, then any decision on distributing the risk of famine is a decision whom to kill. Even a decision to rely on natural selection as a famine policy is choosing a policy for killing—for under a different famine policy different persons might have survived, and under different prefamine policies there might have been no famine or a less severe famine. The choice of a particular famine policy may be justifiable on the grounds that once we have let it get to that point there is not enough to go around, and somebody must go, as on an ill-equipped lifeboat. Even so, the famine policy chosen will not be a policy of saving some but not all persons from an unavoidable predicament.

Persons cannot, of course, make famine policies individually. Famine and prefamine policies are and will be made by governments individually and collectively and perhaps also by some voluntary organizations. It may even prove politically impossible to have a coherent famine or prefamine policy for the whole world; if so, we shall have to settle for partial and piecemeal policies. But each person who is in a position to support or oppose such policies, whether global or local, has to decide which to support and which to oppose. Even for individual persons, inaction and inattention are often a decision—a decision to support the famine and prefamine policies, which are the status quo whether or not they are "hands off" policies. There are large numbers of ways in which private citizens may affect such policies. They do so in supporting or opposing legislation affecting aid and foreign investment, in supporting or opposing certain sorts of charities or groups such as Zero Population Growth, in promoting or opposing ecologically conservative technology and lifestyles. Hence we have individually the onus of avoiding killing. For even though we

(a) do not kill single-handedly those who die of famine

(b) do not kill instantaneously those who die of famine

(c) do not know which individuals will die as the result of the prefamine and famine policies we support (unless we support something like a genocidal famine policy)

(d) do not intend any famine deaths

we nonetheless kill and do not merely allow to die. For as the result of our actions in concert with others, some will die who might have survived had we either acted otherwise or had no causal influence. . . .

NOTES

1. Cf. Robert Nozick, *Anarchy State and Utopia* (New York, 1974), p. 34. Nozick defines an innocent threat as "someone who is innocently a causal agent in a process such that he would be an aggressor had he chosen to become such an agent."

2. Cf. Peter Singer, "Famine, Affluence, and Morality," *Philosophy & Public Affairs* 1, no. 3 (Spring 1972): 229–243, 232. I am in agreement with many of the points which Singer makes, but am interested in arguing that we must have some famine policy from a much weaker set of premises. Singer uses some consequentialist premises: starvation is bad; we ought to prevent bad things when we can do so without worse consequences; hence we ought to prevent starvation whether it is nearby or far off and whether others are doing so or not. The argument of this article does not depend on a particular theory about the grounds of obligation, but should be a corollary of any nonbizarre ethical theory which has any room for a notion of rights.

3. This way of distinguishing killing from allowing to die does not rely on distinguishing "negative" from "positive" acts. Such attempts seem unpromising since any act has multiple descriptions of which some will be negative and others positive. If a clear distinction is to be made between killing and letting die, it must hinge on the *difference* which an act makes for a person's survival, rather than on the description under which the agent acts.

4. The point may appear rather arbitrary, given that I have not rested my case on one theory of the grounds of obligation. But I believe that almost any such theory will show a right not to be killed to override a property right. Perhaps this is why Locke's theory can seem so odd—in moving from a right of self-preservation to a justification of unequal property rights, he finds himself gradually having to reinterpret all rights as property rights, thus coming to see us as the owners of our persons.

5. Cf. P.A. Baron, *The Political Economy of Growth* (New York, 1957), especially chap. 5, "On the Roots of Backwardness"; or A.G. Frank, *Capitalism and Underdevelopment in Latin America* (New York, 1967). Both works argue that underdeveloped economies are among the products of developed ones.

6. Lester R. Brown and Erik P. Eckholm, "The Empty Breadbasket," *Ceres* (F.A.O. Review on Development), March–April 1974, p. 59. See also N. Borlaug and R. Ewell, "The Shrinking Margin," in the same issue.

7. For discussions of the time and extent of famine see, for example, P.R. Ehrlich, *The Population Bomb,* rev. ed. (New York, 1971); R.L. Heilbroner, *An Inquiry into the Human Prospect* (New York, 1974); *Scientific American,* September 1974, especially R. Freedman and B. Berelson, "The Human Population"; P. Demeny, "The Populations of the Underdeveloped Countries"; R. Revelle, "Food and Population."

DISCUSSION QUESTIONS

1. Why do you think Nell uses such a narrow understanding of the right not to be killed? How does that strengthen her argument?
2. How does Nell defend the analogy between a well-equipped lifeboat with two "classes" and the present situation on Earth as a whole? Do you find her argument by analogy convincing? Why or why not?
3. Assume, for the sake of argument, that Nell is right that people in wealthy countries *are* killing people who die of famines. Do you think Nell is correct that individuals in wealthy countries therefore have a moral obligation to try to prevent those famine deaths? Why or why not?
4. Do Nell's arguments imply that people in wealthy countries have a moral obligation to relieve global poverty even in times and places where there is no famine? Why or why not?

PETER SINGER

Famine, Affluence, and Morality

Peter Singer is the Ira W. DeCamp Professor of Bioethics at Princeton University and Laureate Professor at the University of Melbourne in Australia. He has written widely on applied ethics and is most famous for his work on global poverty and the treatment of animals. In this paper, Singer argues that most people in wealthy countries, such as the United States, have a moral obligation to donate a substantial fraction of their income to fight global poverty. Singer has continued to write on these topics, including in a recent popular book called *The Life You Can Save*.

GUIDING QUESTIONS

1. What are the two basic premises with which Singer begins his argument? What are the two different versions of his second premise? Which version does he use in his main argument?
2. What is the original purpose of the drowning child thought experiment in Singer's paper? In what other ways does Singer use that example?
3. What is the main conclusion of Singer's paper?
4. After considering various objections, how much of a wealthy country's national income does Singer ultimately think should be devoted to fighting poverty?

Peter Singer. "Famine, Affluence, and Morality." Philosophy & Public Affairs, 1(3) (Spring 1972), 229–243. Philosophy & Public Affairs © 1975 Wiley. Reproduced with permission of BLACKWELL PUBLISHING, INC. in the format Book via Copyright Clearance Center.

As I write this, in November 1971, people are dying in East Bengal from lack of food, shelter, and medical care.* The suffering and death that are occurring there now are not inevitable, not unavoidable in any fatalistic sense of the term. Constant poverty, a cyclone, and a civil war have turned at least nine million people into destitute refugees; nevertheless, it is not beyond the capacity of the richer nations to give enough assistance to reduce any further suffering to very small proportions. The decisions and actions of human beings can prevent this kind of suffering. Unfortunately, human beings have not made the necessary decisions. At the individual level, people have, with very few exceptions, not responded to the situation in any significant way. Generally speaking, people have not given large sums to relief funds; they have not written to their parliamentary representatives demanding increased government assistance; they have not demonstrated in the streets, held symbolic fasts, or done anything else directed toward providing the refugees with the means to satisfy their essential needs. At the government level, no government has given the sort of massive aid that would enable the refugees to survive for more than a few days. Britain, for instance, has given rather more than most countries. It has, to date, given £14,750,000. For comparative purposes, Britain's share of the nonrecoverable development costs of the Anglo-French Concorde project is already in excess of £275,000,000, and on present estimates will reach £440,000,000. The implication is that the British government values a supersonic transport more than thirty times as highly as it values the lives of the nine million refugees. Australia is another country which, on a per capita basis, is well up in the "aid to Bengal" table. Australia's aid, however, amounts to less than one-twelfth of the cost of Sydney's new opera house. The total amount given, from all sources, now stands at about £65,000,000. The estimated cost of keeping the refugees alive for one year is £464,000,000. Most of the refugees have now been in the camps for more than six months. The World Bank has said that India needs a minimum of £300,000,000 in assistance from other countries before the end of the year. It

seems obvious that assistance on this scale will not be forthcoming. India will be forced to choose between letting the refugees starve or diverting funds from her own development program, which will mean that more of her own people will starve in the future.[1]

These are the essential facts about the present situation in Bengal. So far as it concerns us here, there is nothing unique about this situation except its magnitude. The Bengal emergency is just the latest and most acute of a series of major emergencies in various parts of the world, arising both from natural and from man-made causes. There are also many parts of the world in which people die from malnutrition and lack of food independent of any special emergency. I take Bengal as my example only because it is the present concern, and because the size of the problem has ensured that it has been given adequate publicity. Neither individuals nor governments can claim to be unaware of what is happening there.

What are the moral implications of a situation like this? In what follows, I shall argue that the way people in relatively affluent countries react to a situation like that in Bengal cannot be justified; indeed, the whole way we look at moral issues—our moral conceptual scheme —needs to be altered, and with it, the way of life that has come to be taken for granted in our society.

In arguing for this conclusion I will not, of course, claim to be morally neutral. I shall, however, try to argue for the moral position that I take, so that anyone who accepts certain assumptions, to be made explicit, will, I hope, accept my conclusion.

I begin with the assumption that suffering and death from lack of food, shelter, and medical care are bad. I think most people will agree about this, although one may reach the same view by different routes. I shall not argue for this view. People can hold all sorts of eccentric positions, and perhaps from some of them it would not follow that death by starvation is in itself bad. It is difficult, perhaps impossible, to refute such positions, and so for brevity I will henceforth take this assumption as accepted. Those who disagree need read no further.

---

*[The people Singer mentions were refugees fleeing the Bangladesh War of Independence.—DRM]

My next point is this: if it is in our power to prevent something bad from happening, without thereby sacrificing anything of comparable moral importance, we ought, morally, to do it. By "without sacrificing anything of comparable moral importance" I mean without causing anything else comparably bad to happen, or doing something that is wrong in itself, or failing to promote some moral good, comparable in significance to the bad thing that we can prevent. This principle seems almost as uncontroversial as the last one. It requires us only to prevent what is bad, and not to promote what is good, and it requires this of us only when we can do it without sacrificing anything that is, from the moral point of view, comparably important. I could even, as far as the application of my argument to the Bengal emergency is concerned, qualify the point so as to make it: if it is in our power to prevent something very bad from happening, without thereby sacrificing anything morally significant, we ought, morally, to do it. An application of this principle would be as follows: if I am walking past a shallow pond and see a child drowning in it, I ought to wade in and pull the child out. This will mean getting my clothes muddy, but this is insignificant, while the death of the child would presumably be a very bad thing.

The uncontroversial appearance of the principle just stated is deceptive. If it were acted upon, even in its qualified form, our lives, our society, and our world would be fundamentally changed. For the principle takes, firstly, no account of proximity or distance. It makes no moral difference whether the person I can help is a neighbor's child ten yards from me or a Bengali whose name I shall never know, ten thousand miles away. Secondly, the principle makes no distinction between cases in which I am the only person who could possibly do anything and cases in which I am just one among millions in the same position.

I do not think I need to say much in defense of the refusal to take proximity and distance into account. The fact that a person is physically near to us, so that we have personal contact with him, may make it more likely that we *shall* assist him, but this does not show that we *ought* to help him rather than another who happens to be further away. If we accept any principle of impartiality, universalizability, equality, or whatever, we cannot discriminate against someone merely because he is far away from us (or we are far away from him). Admittedly, it is possible that we are in a better position to judge what needs to be done to help a person near to us than one far away, and perhaps also to provide the assistance we judge to be necessary. If this were the case, it would be a reason for helping those near to us first. This may once have been a justification for being more concerned with the poor in one's own town than with famine victims in India. Unfortunately for those who like to keep their moral responsibilities limited, instant communication and swift transportation have changed the situation. From the moral point of view, the development of the world into a "global village" has made an important, though still unrecognized, difference to our moral situation. Expert observers and supervisors, sent out by famine relief organizations or permanently stationed in famine-prone areas, can direct our aid to a refugee in Bengal almost as effectively as we could get it to someone in our own block. There would seem, therefore, to be no possible justification for discriminating on geographical grounds.

There may be a greater need to defend the second implication of my principle—that the fact that there are millions of other people in the same position, in respect to the Bengali refugees, as I am, does not make the situation significantly different from a situation in which I am the only person who can prevent something very bad from occurring. Again, of course, I admit that there is a psychological difference between the cases; one feels less guilty about doing nothing if one can point to others, similarly placed, who have also done nothing. Yet this can make no real difference to our moral obligations.[2] Should I consider that I am less obliged to pull the drowning child out of the pond if on looking around I see other people, no further away than I am, who have also noticed the child but are doing nothing? One has only to ask this question to see the absurdity of the view that numbers lessen obligation. It is a view that is an ideal excuse for inactivity; unfortunately most of the major evils—poverty, overpopulation, pollution—are problems in which everyone is almost equally involved.

The view that numbers do make a difference can be made plausible if stated in this way: if everyone in circumstances like mine gave £5 to the Bengal Relief Fund, there would be enough to provide food, shelter, and medical care for the refugees; there is no reason why I should give more than anyone else in the same circumstances as I am; therefore I have no obligation to give more than £5. Each premise in this argument is true, and the argument looks sound. It may convince us, unless we notice that it is based on a hypothetical premise, although the conclusion is not stated hypothetically. The argument would be sound if the conclusion were: if everyone in circumstances like mine were to give £5, I would have no obligation to give more than £5. If the conclusion were so stated, however, it would be obvious that the argument has no bearing on a situation in which it is not the case that everyone else gives £5. This, of course, is the actual situation. It is more or less certain that not everyone in circumstances like mine will give £5. So there will not be enough to provide the needed food, shelter, and medical care. Therefore by giving more than £5 I will prevent more suffering than I would if I gave just £5.

It might be thought that this argument has an absurd consequence. Since the situation appears to be that very few people are likely to give substantial amounts, it follows that I and everyone else in similar circumstances ought to give as much as possible, that is, at least up to the point at which by giving more one would begin to cause serious suffering for oneself and one's dependents—perhaps even beyond this point to the point of marginal utility, at which by giving more one would cause oneself and one's dependents as much suffering as one would prevent in Bengal. If everyone does this, however, there will be more than can be used for the benefit of the refugees, and some of the sacrifice will have been unnecessary. Thus, if everyone does what he ought to do, the result will not be as good as it would be if everyone did a little less than he ought to do, or if only some do all that they ought to do.

The paradox here arises only if we assume that the actions in question—sending money to the relief funds—are performed more or less simultaneously, and are also unexpected. For if it is to be expected that everyone is going to contribute something, then clearly each is not obliged to give as much as he would have been obliged to had others not been giving too. And if everyone is not acting more or less simultaneously, then those giving later will know how much more is needed, and will have no obligation to give more than is necessary to reach this amount. To say this is not to deny the principle that people in the same circumstances have the same obligations, but to point out that the fact that others have given, or may be expected to give, is a relevant circumstance: those giving after it has become known that many others are giving and those giving before are not in the same circumstances. So the seemingly absurd consequence of the principle I have put forward can occur only if people are in error about the actual circumstances—that is, if they think they are giving when others are not, but in fact they are giving when others are. The result of everyone doing what he really ought to do cannot be worse than the result of everyone doing less than he ought to do, although the result of everyone doing what he reasonably believes he ought to do could be.

If my argument so far has been sound, neither our distance from a preventable evil nor the number of other people who, in respect to that evil, are in the same situation as we are, lessens our obligation to mitigate or prevent that evil. I shall therefore take as established the principle I asserted earlier. As I have already said, I need to assert it only in its qualified form: if it is in our power to prevent something very bad from happening, without thereby sacrificing anything else morally significant, we ought, morally, to do it.

The outcome of this argument is that our traditional moral categories are upset. The traditional distinction between duty and charity cannot be drawn, or at least, not in the place we normally draw it. Giving money to the Bengal Relief Fund is regarded as an act of charity in our society. The bodies which collect money are known as "charities." These organizations see themselves in this way—if you send them a check, you will be thanked for your "generosity." Because giving money is regarded as an act of charity, it is not thought that there is anything wrong with not giving. The charitable man may be praised, but the man who is not charitable is not condemned. People do not feel in any way ashamed or guilty about spending money on new clothes or a new car instead of giving it to famine relief. (Indeed, the alternative does not occur to them.) This way of looking at the matter cannot be justified. When we buy new clothes not to keep ourselves warm but to look "well-dressed" we are not providing for any important need. We would not be sacrificing anything significant if we were to continue to wear our old clothes, and give the money to famine relief. By doing so, we would be preventing another person from starving. It follows from what I have said earlier that we ought to give money away, rather than spend it on clothes which we do not need to keep us warm. To do so is not charitable, or generous. Nor is it the kind of act which philosophers and theologians have called "supererogatory"—an act which it would be good to do, but not wrong not to do. On the contrary, we ought to give the money away, and it is wrong not to do so.

I am not maintaining that there are no acts which are charitable, or that there are no acts which it would be good to do but not wrong not to do. It may be possible to redraw the distinction between duty and charity in some other place. All I am arguing here is that the present way of drawing the distinction, which makes it an act of charity for a man living at the level of affluence which most people in the "developed nations" enjoy to give money to save someone else from starvation, cannot be supported. It is beyond the scope of my argument to consider whether the distinction should be redrawn or abolished altogether. There would be many other possible ways of drawing the distinction—for instance, one might decide that it is good to make other people as happy as possible, but not wrong not to do so.

Despite the limited nature of the revision in our moral conceptual scheme which I am proposing, the revision would, given the extent of both affluence and famine in the world today, have radical implications. These implications may lead to further objections, distinct from those I have already considered. I shall discuss two of these.

One objection to the position I have taken might be simply that it is too drastic a revision of our moral scheme. People do not ordinarily judge in the way I have suggested they should. Most people reserve their moral condemnation for those who violate some moral norm, such as the norm against taking another person's property. They do not condemn those who indulge in luxury instead of giving to famine relief. But given that I did not set out to present a morally neutral description of the way people make moral judgments, the way people do in fact judge has nothing to do with the validity of my conclusion. My conclusion follows from the principle which I advanced earlier, and unless that principle is rejected, or the arguments shown to be unsound, I think the conclusion must stand, however strange it appears.

It might, nevertheless, be interesting to consider why our society, and most other societies, do judge differently from the way I have suggested they should. In a well-known article, J. O. Urmson suggests that the imperatives of duty, which tell us what we must do, as distinct from what it would be good to do but not wrong not to do, function so as to prohibit behavior that is intolerable if men are to live together in society.[3] This may explain the origin and continued existence of the present division between acts of duty and acts of charity. Moral attitudes are shaped by the needs of society, and no doubt society needs people who will observe the rules that make social existence tolerable. From the point of view of a particular society, it is essential to prevent violations of norms against killing, stealing, and so on. It is quite inessential, however, to help people outside one's own society.

If this is an explanation of our common distinction between duty and supererogation, however, it is not a justification of it. The moral point of view requires us to look beyond the interests of our own society. Previously, as I have already mentioned, this may hardly have been feasible, but it is quite feasible now. From the moral point of view, the prevention of the starvation of millions of people outside our society must be considered at least as pressing as the upholding of property norms within our society.

It has been argued by some writers, among them Sidgwick and Urmson, that we need to have a basic moral code which is not too far beyond the capacities of the ordinary man, for otherwise there will be a general breakdown of compliance with the moral code.

Crudely stated, this argument suggests that if we tell people that they ought to refrain from murder and give everything they do not really need to famine relief, they will do neither, whereas if we tell them that they ought to refrain from murder and that it is good to give to famine relief but not wrong not to do so, they will at least refrain from murder. The issue here is: Where should we draw the line between conduct that is required and conduct that is good although not required, so as to get the best possible result? This would seem to be an empirical question, although a very difficult one. One objection to the Sidgwick-Urmson line of argument is that it takes insufficient account of the effect that moral standards can have on the decisions we make. Given a society in which a wealthy man who gives five percent of his income to famine relief is regarded as most generous, it is not surprising that a proposal that we all ought to give away half our incomes will be thought to be absurdly unrealistic. In a society which held that no man should have more than enough while others have less than they need, such a proposal might seem narrow-minded. What it is possible for a man to do and what he is likely to do are both, I think, very greatly influenced by what people around him are doing and expecting him to do. In any case, the possibility that by spreading the idea that we ought to be doing very much more than we are to relieve famine we shall bring about a general breakdown of moral behavior seems remote. If the stakes are an end to widespread starvation, it is worth the risk. Finally, it should be emphasized that these considerations are relevant only to the issue of what we should require from others, and not to what we ourselves ought to do.

The second objection to my attack on the present distinction between duty and charity is one which has from time to time been made against utilitarianism. It follows from some forms of utilitarian theory that we all ought, morally, to be working full time to increase the balance of happiness over misery. The position I have taken here would not lead to this conclusion in all circumstances, for if there were no bad occurrences that we could prevent without sacrificing something of comparable moral importance, my argument would have no application. Given the present conditions in many parts of the world,

however, it does follow from my argument that we ought, morally, to be working full time to relieve great suffering of the sort that occurs as a result of famine or other disasters. Of course, mitigating circumstances can be adduced—for instance, that if we wear ourselves out through overwork, we shall be less effective than we would otherwise have been. Nevertheless, when all considerations of this sort have been taken into account, the conclusion remains: we ought to be preventing as much suffering as we can without sacrificing something else of comparable moral importance. This conclusion is one which we may be reluctant to face. I cannot see, though, why it should be regarded as a criticism of the position for which I have argued, rather than a criticism of our ordinary standards of behavior. Since most people are self-interested to some degree, very few of us are likely to do everything that we ought to do. It would, however, hardly be honest to take this as evidence that it is not the case that we ought to do it.

It may still be thought that my conclusions are so wildly out of line with what everyone else thinks and has always thought that there must be something wrong with the argument somewhere. In order to show that my conclusions, while certainly contrary to contemporary Western moral standards, would not have seemed so extraordinary at other times and in other places, I would like to quote a passage from a writer not normally thought of as a way-out radical, Thomas Aquinas.

> Now, according to the natural order instituted by divine providence, material goods are provided for the satisfaction of human needs. Therefore the division and appropriation of property, which proceeds from human law, must not hinder the satisfaction of man's necessity from such goods. Equally, whatever a man has in superabundance is owed, of natural right, to the poor for their sustenance. So Ambrosius says, and it is also to be found in the *Decretum Gratiani:* "The bread which you withhold belongs to the hungry; the clothing you shut away, to the naked; and the money you bury in the earth is the redemption and freedom of the penniless."[4]

I now want to consider a number of points, more practical than philosophical, which are relevant to the application of the moral conclusion we have reached.

These points challenge not the idea that we ought to be doing all we can to prevent starvation, but the idea that giving away a great deal of money is the best means to this end.

It is sometimes said that overseas aid should be a government responsibility, and that therefore one ought not to give to privately run charities. Giving privately, it is said, allows the government and the non-contributing members of society to escape their responsibilities.

This argument seems to assume that the more people there are who give to privately organized famine relief funds, the less likely it is that the government will take over full responsibility for such aid. This assumption is unsupported, and does not strike me as at all plausible. The opposite view—that if no one gives voluntarily, a government will assume that its citizens are uninterested in famine relief and would not wish to be forced into giving aid—seems more plausible. In any case, unless there were a definite probability that by refusing to give one would be helping to bring about massive government assistance, people who do refuse to make voluntary contributions are refusing to prevent a certain amount of suffering without being able to point to any tangible beneficial consequence of their refusal. So the onus of showing how their refusal will bring about government action is on those who refuse to give.

I do not, of course, want to dispute the contention that governments of affluent nations should be giving many times the amount of genuine, no-strings-attached aid that they are giving now. I agree, too, that giving privately is not enough, and that we ought to be campaigning actively for entirely new standards for both public and private contributions to famine relief. Indeed, I would sympathize with someone who thought that campaigning was more important than giving oneself, although I doubt whether preaching what one does not practice would be very effective. Unfortunately, for many people the idea that "it's the government's responsibility" is a reason for not giving which does not appear to entail any political action either.

Another, more serious reason for not giving to famine relief funds is that until there is effective population control, relieving famine merely postpones starvation. If we save the Bengal refugees now, others, perhaps the children of these refugees, will face starvation in a few years' time. In support of this, one may cite the now well-known facts about the population explosion and the relatively limited scope for expanded production.

This point, like the previous one, is an argument against relieving suffering that is happening now, because of a belief about what might happen in the future; it is unlike the previous point in that very good evidence can be adduced in support of this belief about the future. I will not go into the evidence here. I accept that the earth cannot support indefinitely a population rising at the present rate. This certainly poses a problem for anyone who thinks it important to prevent famine. Again, however, one could accept the argument without drawing the conclusion that it absolves one from any obligation to do anything to prevent famine. The conclusion that should be drawn is that the best means of preventing famine, in the long run, is population control. It would then follow from the position reached earlier that one ought to be doing all one can to promote population control (unless one held that all forms of population control were wrong in themselves, or would have significantly bad consequences). Since there are organizations working specifically for population control, one would then support them rather than more orthodox methods of preventing famine.

A third point raised by the conclusion reached earlier relates to the question of just how much we all ought to be giving away. One possibility, which has already been mentioned, is that we ought to give until we reach the level of marginal utility—that is, the level at which, by giving more, I would cause as much suffering to myself or my dependents as I would relieve by my gift. This would mean, of course, that one would reduce oneself to very near the material circumstances of a Bengali refugee. It will be recalled that earlier I put forward both a strong and a moderate version of the principle of preventing bad occurrences. The strong version, which required us to prevent bad things from happening unless in doing so we would be sacrificing something of comparable moral significance, does seem to require reducing ourselves to the level of marginal utility. I should also say that the strong version seems to me to be the correct one. I proposed the more moderate version—that we should prevent bad occurrences unless, to do so, we had to sacrifice something morally significant—only in order to show that even on this surely undeniable principle a great change in our way of life is required. On the more moderate principle, it may not follow that we ought to reduce ourselves to the level of marginal utility, for one might hold that to reduce oneself and one's family to this level is to cause something significantly bad to happen. Whether this is so I shall not discuss, since, as I have said, I can see no good reason for holding the moderate version of the principle rather than the strong version. Even if we accepted the principle only in its moderate form, however, it should be clear that we would have to give away enough to ensure that the consumer society, dependent as it is on people spending on trivia rather than giving to famine relief, would slow down and perhaps disappear entirely. There are several reasons why this would be desirable in itself. The value and necessity of economic growth are now being questioned not only by conservationists, but by economists as well.[5] There is no doubt, too, that the consumer society has had a distorting effect on the goals and purposes of its members. Yet looking at the matter purely from the point of view of overseas aid, there must be a limit to the extent to which we should deliberately slow down our economy; for it might be the case that if we gave away, say, forty percent of our Gross National Product, we would slow down the economy so much that in absolute terms we would be giving less than if we gave twenty-five percent of the much larger GNP that we would have if we limited our contribution to this smaller percentage.

I mention this only as an indication of the sort of factor that one would have to take into account in working out an ideal. Since Western societies generally consider one percent of the GNP an acceptable level for overseas aid, the matter is entirely academic. Nor does it affect the question of how much an individual should give in a society in which very few are giving substantial amounts.

It is sometimes said, though less often now than it used to be, that philosophers have no special role to play in public affairs, since most public issues depend primarily on an assessment of facts. On questions of fact, it is said, philosophers as such have no special expertise, and so it has been possible to engage in philosophy without committing oneself to any position on major public issues. No doubt there are some issues of social policy and foreign policy about which it can truly be said that a really expert assessment of the facts is required before taking sides or acting, but the issue of famine is surely not one of these. The facts about the existence of suffering are beyond dispute. Nor, I think, is it disputed that we can do something about it, either through orthodox methods of famine relief or through population control or both. This is therefore an issue on which philosophers are competent to take a position. The issue is one which faces everyone who has more money than he needs to support himself and his dependents, or who is in a position to take some sort of political action. These categories must include practically every teacher and student of philosophy in the universities of the Western world. If philosophy is to deal with matters that are relevant to both teachers and students, this is an issue that philosophers should discuss.

Discussion, though, is not enough. What is the point of relating philosophy to public (and personal) affairs if we do not take our conclusions seriously? In this instance, taking our conclusion seriously means acting upon it. The philosopher will not find it any easier than anyone else to alter his attitudes and way of life to the extent that, if I am right, is involved in doing everything that we ought to be doing.

At the very least, though, one can make a start. The philosopher who does so will have to sacrifice some of the benefits of the consumer society, but he can find compensation in the satisfaction of a way of life in which theory and practice, if not yet in harmony, are at least coming together.

NOTES

1. There was also a third possibility: that India would go to war to enable the refugees to return to their lands. Since I wrote this paper, India has taken this way out. The situation is no longer that described above, but this does not affect my argument, as the next paragraph indicates.

2. In view of the special sense philosophers often give to the term, I should say that I use "obligation" simply as the abstract noun derived from "ought," so that "I have an obligation to" means no more, and no less, than "I ought to." This usage is in accordance with the definition of "ought" given by the *Shorter Oxford English Dictionary:* "the general verb to express duty or obligation." I do not think any issue of substance hangs on the way the term is used; sentences in which I use "obligation" could all be rewritten, although somewhat clumsily, as sentences in which a clause containing "ought" replaces the term "obligation."

3. J. O. Urmson, "Saints and Heroes," in *Essays in Moral Philosophy,* ed. Abraham I. Melden (Seattle and London, 1958), p. 214. For a related but significantly different view see also Henry Sidgwick, *The Methods of Ethics,* 7th edn. (London, 1907), pp. 220–221, 492–493.

4. *Summa Theologica,* II-II, Question 66, Article 7, in *Aquinas, Selected Political Writings,* ed. A. P. d'Entreves, trans. J. G. Dawson (Oxford, 1948), p. 171.

5. See, for instance, John Kenneth Galbraith, *The New Industrial State* (Boston, 1967); and E. J. Mishan, *The Costs of Economic Growth* (London, 1967).

DISCUSSION QUESTIONS

1. Singer argues that neither distance from the needy nor the fact that many others can help undermine the obligation to prevent very bad things from happening. What are his arguments for these claims? Do you find them convincing? Why or why not?
2. What two objections arise from the "radical implications" of his conclusion, according to Singer? How does he respond to these objections? Which objection do you find most important? Why?
3. Singer raises three objections based on practical concerns. What are these objections? Do you find his responses convincing? Why or why not?
4. What sacrifices would you have to make if you accepted the weaker version of Singer's argument (i.e., the one using the weaker version of his second premise)? Do you regard these sacrifices as too great a price to pay for preventing someone else's death and suffering from lack of food, shelter, and medical care? Why or why not?

FIONA WOOLLARD

Saving Strangers: What Does Morality Demand?

Fiona Woollard is Associate Professor of Philosophy at the University of Southampton in England. She writes on both normative and applied ethics, including topics such as the distinction between killing and letting die and the philosophy of pregnancy and sex. In this paper, she applies her ideas about the distinction between killing and letting die to Peter Singer's argument (in the previous reading) that people in wealthy countries have an obligation to donate a large fraction of our income to fight global poverty.

From: *Dialogue: A Journal of Religion and Philosophy* 38 (April 2012), pp. 41–46.

GUIDING QUESTIONS

1. What is the point of contrasting Peter Unger's "Envelope" case with Singer's "Pond" case?
2. Woollard reports two arguments that Peter Unger gives to undermine a difference between his "Envelope" case and Singer's "Pond" case. What are these arguments? How does Woollard respond to each argument?
3. Why, according to Woollard, does morality "contain a restricted requirement to aid"?
4. What is Woollard's argument that one's proximity to someone who needs help is morally relevant to one's obligation to aid that person?
5. Does Woollard's argument show that people in wealthy countries have *no* obligation to give money to fight global poverty?

Each year, millions of children die from starvation, malnutrition or easily-treatable illnesses. UNICEF estimates that in Niger and West Africa alone over a million children need to be treated for life-threatening malnutrition. It is relatively cheap to help: "Just £5 will help UNICEF feed a child for a week. With the right treatment, a child can recover in six weeks." (http://www.unicef.org.uk Accessed 13.02.2012). If we take these figures at face value, then it seems as if we can save a child's life for £30.

How should we respond to this fact? This may be one of the most important questions in applied moral philosophy. While few of us actually have to choose whether to kill in self-defence or when to go to war, if you are an ordinary member of an affluent nation, you face this question. How you respond is, quite literally, a matter of life and death. In addition to its huge practical import, the issue is of great philosophical interest. To answer it, we must confront apparent conflicts between some of our most firmly held moral beliefs. Our commonsense understanding of this issue seems to be full of contradictions.

THE EXTREME DEMAND

In November 1971, a young philosopher called Peter Singer wrote a very famous paper, "Famine, Affluence and Morality" (*Philosophy & Public Affairs,* Vol. 1, No. 3: 229-243). Singer argues that we need to radically revise our response to the facts about

preventable death noted above. A typical person living in the West is morally required to respond to these facts by giving away around half of her money and assets to organisations like UNICEF. This is not something that it would be "nice" or "admirable" for us to do. It is not an optional extra. It is a moral duty and we are doing something very wrong if we fail to live up to that duty.[1]

Singer's conclusion is radical, but his argument is relatively simple. He claims that we all intuitively agree with the following principle: "If it is in our power to prevent something bad from happening, without thereby sacrificing anything of comparable moral importance, we ought, morally, to do it" (Singer, p. 231). I'll call this Singer's principle. Singer claims that his principle is supported by the following case:

> Pond: You are on your way to work when you see a child drowning in a pond. If you do not stop and pull her out, she will die (Singer, p. 231).

You clearly must pull the child out of the pond. You are required to do so even if this will be quite costly to you. You must save the child even if you will ruin your expensive new shoes, miss an important business meeting or even risk some physical harm, such as a broken leg. These costs pale into insignificance when compared to what the child stands to lose—his life.

The life of the child dying of poverty is no less important than the life of the child in the pond. So you are morally required to save him too, even if it costs £30. But then there is another child to save, and another, and another. You must keep giving away money and saving children until you stand to lose something of comparable moral importance. You must give away most of your money. This has come to be known as the Extreme Demand.

Of course, if everyone in the West gave away most of their money, this might cause more harm than good. Singer is looking at what an individual must do in the current situation, knowing that most people are not going to do much to save the starving. Because most people do so little, the morally conscientious individual must take up the slack.

Singer's argument was later developed by Peter Unger (*Living High and Letting Die*, Oxford University Press, 1996). Unger noted that many people are unconvinced by Singer's appeal to the Pond case. Although the Pond case seems to support Singer's Principle, other cases seem to contradict it. Consider:

> Envelope: you receive a letter from UNICEF asking you to place as much as you can in the handy return envelop and donate it to be used to save the lives of children who will otherwise die soon (Unger, p. 9).[2]

According to most people, you don't do anything wrong if you throw the letter straight in the bin. This suggests that we do not intuitively believe Singer's principle. Unger concludes that Singer's argument is incomplete. To complete the argument, we must show that our intuitive reaction to the Envelope case is wrong.

Unger attempts to do this by arguing that there is no morally relevant difference between Pond and Envelope. If there is no morally relevant difference between the cases, then the same moral requirements should apply in both cases. If you are required to help in Pond, you are required to help in Envelope – and in all the subsequent Envelope cases. Those who want to deny Singer's conclusion must say that you are not required to help in Pond. Almost no one is happy to say that.

Unger considers which features we might appeal to when trying to explain why we are required to help in Pond but not in Envelope. Some people appeal to proximity: "The child in Pond is right there in front of you!" Others suggest that it matters whether you are the unique potential saviour or one of many potential saviours: "You're the only one who can save the child in Pond!"

Unger uses two strategies to convince us that each candidate distinction is not morally relevant—and thus cannot ground a difference in our obligations. First, he appeals to our intuitive reactions to particular cases. Second, he appeals to what he calls our "general moral common sense", our views after reflection about whether the feature in question should make a moral difference (Unger, p. 28). As Unger goes through a long list of candidate distinctions, I cannot consider all his arguments. I will focus on his discussion of proximity.

PROXIMITY 1: INTUITIONS ABOUT CASES

In Pond, the child is very close, in Envelope, he is far away. Could this explain why we think you have to help in Pond but not in Envelope? To try to show that proximity cannot explain the difference in our intuitive reactions, Unger asks us to consider a Pond-type case where we are far away from the person who needs help:

> CB Radio: The child is drowning in a sinking boat ten miles away. He manages to get through to you on your CB Radio. You are able to determine his location and could drive to him and rescue him (Unger, p. 34).

Intuitively, you are still required to save the child—even if this will be quite costly to you.

Unger also asks us to consider an Envelope-type case where the people who need help are close to you.

> Bungalow Compound: You arrive at your holiday bungalow to find an appeal from a local charity, accompanied by a handy return envelope, asking for money to save the sick children next door (Unger, p. 34).

Unger suggests that, intuitively, Bungalow Compound is just like Envelope. You do not have to help the children.

So, Unger says, it cannot be proximity that explains the difference between our reactions to Pond and Envelope. In a Pond case without proximity you are still required to help. In an Envelope case with proximity, you are not required to help. Our intuitions about cases treat proximity as morally irrelevant.

I do not think that Unger has shown that our intuitive reactions to cases treat proximity as morally irrelevant.

First, there might be more than one morally relevant factor. In CB Radio, even though you are far away from the drowning child, you have spoken to him. You have had a personal encounter with him. Perhaps you have to aid if *either* you are close by *or* you have had a personal encounter with the victim. CB Radio does not show that distance is morally irrelevant.

Second, I do not think Unger is right that Bungalow Compound is intuitively morally equivalent to Envelope. It is not okay to sit beside your pool, sipping a pina colada, knowing that the children are dying next door and doing nothing to help. However, I think that the requirement to help is affected by the fact that there is an ongoing stream of nearby children who need your help. The case is equivalent to a version of Pond in which you see a drowning child every time you step outside. You are not required to keep making big sacrifices every time you face this kind of appeal. But you do have a stronger obligation to help these children than you would have had if you had stayed at home.

PROXIMITY 2: GENERAL MORAL COMMON SENSE

I have suggested that Unger has failed to show that our intuitive reactions to cases are not affected by proximity. However, Unger believes that many of our intuitive reactions to particular cases are unreliable. What matters is whether a factor should make a difference to our obligations.

Unger suggests that reflection will show that proximity should not make any difference to our obligations: ". . . unlike many physical forces, the strength of a moral force doesn't diminish with distance. Surely, our moral common sense tells us that much" (Unger, p. 33).

It does seem strange that proximity should make a moral difference. Why should the fact that someone happens to be far away mean that we do not have to help him?

I will argue that proximity is morally relevant. The core of my argument is that this moral relevance must be assessed from within an understanding of the need for a restricted requirement to aid. Unger has misunderstood the moral significance of factors like proximity. Unger seems to start from an assumption that there is a default obligation to aid in all cases and then ask how that obligation could be diminished by features such as physical distance. This is misguided.

I suggest that morality needs to contain a requirement to make substantial sacrifices to aid in some, but not all, cases. Given the need for such a restricted requirement to aid, we need a criterion to distinguish between cases where agents are required to aid and cases where the agent is not required to aid. I suggest that proximity is appropriate to form such a criterion.

Why does morality need to contain a restricted requirement to aid? The reason that morality should contain a requirement to aid is obvious. It matters morally that children are dying. If a person can prevent a child's death, she has a strong moral reason to do so. If morality did not contain any requirement to aid, it would fail to recognise the importance of human life.

So why must this requirement be restricted? Why can't we accept Singer's principle: "If it is in our power to prevent something bad from happening, without thereby sacrificing anything of comparable moral importance, we ought, morally, to do it" (Singer, p. 231).

Philosophers have given several different arguments that the requirement to aid must be restricted. Some appeal to demandingness. Morality cannot, as a matter of course, require us to make substantial sacrifices for others. A morality that makes such extreme demands as part of everyday life is simply too hard to live up to.

When considering this argument it is important to remember that we are talking about moral *requirements* not supererogatory acts. We are looking at what we are required to do to aid others, what it would be wrong to fail to do. We are not looking at what a morally perfect person would do. Singer and Unger claim that we behave *wrongly* if we do not live up to Singer's principle. Moral requirements should be something that it is generally reasonable to expect people to live up to.

My own argument for the restricted requirement is slightly different. It is based on what is needed for a person's body and other resources to genuinely belong to her. Suppose that before using "my" car I must check to see if anyone else needs it more than me. In this case, it is not really my car. For a resource to genuinely belong to me, it must be, substantially enough, at my use and not at the use of others. This applies to my body as well as to other resources.

This does not mean that I can never be required to use my body or other resources to prevent harm. A car can still belong to me if I must use it to drive someone to the hospital if they have a heart attack right in front of me—even if this will seriously damage the car. But if I am routinely required to give up the use of my car in ways that are very costly to me, then it is not really my car. For example, a requirement to spend all my time acting as an ambulance service whenever anyone in Hampshire has a heart attack does not treat my body or my car as genuinely belonging to me. Such a requirement treats my body and my car as common resources.

I suggest that a requirement to make substantial sacrifices to save in all cases like Envelope does not treat my body and other resources as genuinely belonging to me. Under such a requirement, I can expect to regularly have to give the use of my body and resources to others, even though this is very costly to me. My body and others resources are not substantially enough at my use. However, a restricted requirement to aid, in which we are required to make substantial sacrifices to aid only in certain rare cases, does leave my body and other resources substantially enough at my use.

I have not argued here that morality must recognise that a person's body and other resources genuinely belong to him. Until this is established, the conclusion is conditional: *if* morality is to recognise that a person's body and other resources belong to him, then the requirement to aid must be restricted. Nonetheless, the claim that this is *my* body in a morally significant way is very appealing. To show that my opponent must deny this is an important step forward.

This argument suggests that there should be a stringent duty to aid in, and only in, a small subset of cases. This should be a set of cases that we are likely to encounter rarely, if at all. However, if an agent does encounter such a case, she will be required to aid even if this will be very costly to her. We need some way of picking out the set of cases in which the agent is required to make such substantial sacrifices.[3]

I suggest that it is morally appropriate for the agent to be required to make substantial sacrifices to save strangers in those cases in which he is close to the victim. That a victim is near the agent makes the victim's need strongly associated with the agent. As Frances Kamm observes, "we are locatable beings, positioned at the centre of our world" (Frances Kamm, *Intricate Ethics,* Oxford University Press, 2007, p. 387.) This fact about our nature affects the way that we relate to the world, making what is physically close to us psychologically close too. These cases stand out from the general mass of opportunities to aid strangers because the agent seems strongly connected to the victim and his needs. It makes sense for the criterion for stringent duties to aid to be based on the connection between the agent and the victim or need. In taking such a criterion, morality shapes itself around the agent's point of view.

I have looked at proximity, but as suggested earlier, I believe that there are other morally relevant differences between the Pond case and the Envelope case. I suggest that the agent will be required to make substantial sacrifices to aid in those cases, and only those cases, where he is strongly connected to the victim or need. Proximity is one factor that creates a close connection. Other factors, such as having had a personal encounter with the victim, may have the same effect.

I have argued against Singer and Unger. The Pond case cannot be used to show that a typical person living in the affluent West is morally required to give away around half of her money and assets to organisations like UNICEF. There are morally significant differences between Pond and Envelope. However, I do not want to argue for complacency. A requirement to make a non-trivial regular contribution in response to ongoing need is compatible with the arguments for the restricted requirement to aid. This requirement is not overly demanding. It leaves your resources for the most part at your own use. There are strong moral considerations in favour of such a requirement – for it could save lives. The issue is also complicated in that a significant part of the responsibility for the plight of many in extreme poverty can be laid at the door of more affluent nations, whether through the imperialist actions of the past or our current contributions to climate change. Thus efforts to prevent poverty-related deaths may be more properly seen as reparations than aid. Overall, it is likely that most of us should do far more than we currently do. My argument is simply that Singer and Unger fail to show that the Extreme Demand follows from the simple fact that there are preventable deaths. I include some useful contact details, for those who wish to increase their regular contributions to preventing deaths.

USEFUL CONTACT DETAILS

- Singer's organisation: The Life You Can Save (www.thelifeyoucansave.com)
- GiveWell (http://givewell.org/)
- UNICEF UK (www.unicef.org.uk/)
- OXFAM (www.oxfam.org.uk)

NOTES

1. Singer's work has not only generated huge amounts of philosophical discussion, it has also had an astounding real world impact. In the month after Singer gave this argument in the New York Times, UNICEF and OXFAM claimed to have received a total of about $660,000 more than they usually took in from the phone numbers given in the piece. . . .

2. I have made some adjustments to Unger's original presentation of the case.

3. The suggestion is not that each person should have to sacrifice a set, limited, amount over her lifetime to aid others. The sacrifices we can be required to make in Pond cases are greater than the total lifetime contribution to e.g. UNICEF required of most people. The requirement to make such substantial sacrifices in Pond cases is acceptable because most people are unlikely to ever encounter such a case.

DISCUSSION QUESTIONS

1. Woollard and Unger disagree about whether the "Bungalow Compound" case is "intuitively equivalent" to the "Envelope" case. Whose intuitive judgments are closer to your own? Why?

2. What is Woollard's argument for the claim that if your body and resources genuinely belong to you, then the requirement to aid others must be restricted?

3. In this paper, Woollard does not argue for the claim that your body and resources genuinely belong to you. Do you think this claim is correct? Why or why not?

4. Do you think that the strength of an agent's "connection" to a needy person is an appropriate way to restrict an agent's requirement to aid others? Why or why not? If so, do you think proximity provides the right kind of "connection"? Why or why not?

Climate Change

WALTER SINNOTT-ARMSTRONG

It's Not *My* Fault: Global Warming and Individual Moral Obligations

Walter Sinnott-Armstrong is the Chauncey Stillman Professor of Practical Ethics at Duke University. He has published widely in moral theory and epistemology (the theory of knowledge) and is currently pursuing projects in neuroethics, moral psychology, and the philosophy of law. His free online critical thinking course, Think Again, enrolled almost a quarter of a million students in 2012. In this paper, Sinnott-Armstrong argues that even though our collective greenhouse gas emissions are driving dangerous climate change, individuals do nothing wrong in emitting greenhouse gases.

GUIDING QUESTIONS

1. What does Sinnott-Armstrong think that governments ought to do about climate change? What, if anything, does he think this implies about what individuals ought to do about climate change?
2. Exactly what question does Sinnott-Armstrong want to answer? What answer is he inclined to give to that question? Why does he want to find a moral principle to support that answer?
3. Why, according to Sinnott-Armstrong, does each of the principles in Sections 3–6 fail to imply that it is wrong to "drive a gas guzzler just for fun"? (You may need to give different answers for different principles.)
4. Does Sinnott-Armstrong take himself to have proven that it is morally permissible to drive a gas guzzler just for fun? Why or why not?
5. What obligations does Sinnott-Armstrong think individuals *do* have in connection with climate change?

1. ASSUMPTIONS

To make the issue stark, let us begin with a few assumptions. I believe that these assumptions are probably roughly accurate, but none is certain, and I will not try to justify them here.* Instead, I will simply take them for granted for the sake of argument.[1]

---

*[Scientists have learned much more about climate change since Sinnott-Armstrong wrote this paper, giving us an even better idea about the impacts he mentions in the following paragraphs. For more up-to-date information, see the latest reports by the Intergovernmental Panel on Climate Change (IPCC). —DRM]

Walter Sinnott-Armstrong (2005), "It's Not My Fault: Global Warming and Individual Moral Obligations", in Walter Sinnott-Armstrong, Richard B. Howarth (ed.) Perspectives on Climate Change: Science, Economics, Politics, Ethics (Advances in the Economics of Environmental Resources, Volume 5) Emerald Group Publishing Limited, pp. 285–307. © Emerald Group Publishing Limited all rights reserved.

First, global warming[†] has begun and is likely to increase over the next century. We cannot be sure exactly how much or how fast, but hot times are coming.[2]

Second, a significant amount of global warming is due to human activities. The main culprit is fossil fuels.

Third, global warming will create serious problems for many people over the long term by causing climate changes, including violent storms, floods from sea level rises, droughts, heat waves, and so on. Millions of people will probably be displaced or die.

Fourth, the poor will be hurt most of all. The rich countries are causing most of the global warming, but they will be able to adapt to climate changes more easily.[3] Poor countries that are close to sea level might be devastated.

Fifth, governments, especially the biggest and richest ones, are able to mitigate global warming.[4] They can impose limits on emissions. They can require or give incentives for increased energy efficiency. They can stop deforestation and fund reforestation. They can develop ways to sequester carbon dioxide in oceans or underground. These steps will help, but the only long-run solution lies in alternatives to fossil fuels. These alternatives can be found soon if governments start massive research projects now.[5]

Sixth, it is too late to stop global warming. Because there is so much carbon dioxide in the atmosphere already, because carbon dioxide remains in the atmosphere for so long, and because we will remain dependent on fossil fuels in the near future, governments can slow down global warming or reduce its severity, but they cannot prevent it. Hence, governments need to adapt. They need to build seawalls. They need to reinforce houses that cannot withstand storms. They need to move populations from low-lying areas.[6]

Seventh, these steps will be costly. Increased energy efficiency can reduce expenses, adaptation will create some jobs, and money will be made in the research and production of alternatives to fossil fuels. Still, any steps that mitigate or adapt to global warming will slow down our economies, at least in the short run.[7] That will hurt many people, especially many poor people.

Eighth, despite these costs, the major governments throughout the world still morally ought to take some of these steps. The clearest moral obligation falls on the United States. The United States caused and continues to cause more of the problem than any other country. The United States can spend more resources on a solution without sacrificing basic necessities. This country has the scientific expertise to solve technical problems. Other countries follow its lead (sometimes!). So the United States has a special moral obligation to help mitigate and adapt to global warming.[8]

2. THE PROBLEM

Even assuming all of this, it is still not clear what I as an individual morally ought to do about global warming. That issue is not as simple as many people assume. I want to bring out some of its complications.

It should be clear from the start that "individual" moral obligations do not always follow directly from collective moral obligations. The fact that your government morally ought to do something does not prove that you ought to do it, even if your government fails. Suppose that a bridge is dangerous because so much traffic has gone over it and continues to go over it. The government has a moral obligation to make the bridge safe. If the government fails to do its duty, it does not follow that I personally have a moral obligation to fix the bridge. It does not even follow that I have a moral obligation to fill in one crack in the bridge, even if the bridge would be fixed if everyone filled in one crack, even if I drove over the bridge many times, and even if I still drive over it every day. Fixing the bridge is the government's job, not mine. While I ought to encourage the government to fulfill its obligations,[9] I do not have to take on those obligations myself.

All that this shows is that government obligations do not always imply parallel individual obligations. Still, maybe sometimes they do. My government has a moral obligation to teach arithmetic to the children in my town, including my own children. If the government fails in this obligation, then I do take on a moral

---

[†][Sinott-Armstrong uses the narrower term "global warming" to describe the effects of accumulating greenhouse gases, such as carbon dioxide. Since warming the planet leads to other kinds of changes in the climate, most scientists now prefer the broader term "climate change."—DRM]

obligation to teach arithmetic to my children.[10] Thus, when the government fails in its obligations, sometimes I have to fill in, and sometimes I do not.

What about global warming? If the government fails to do anything about global warming, what am I supposed to do about it? There are lots of ways for me as an individual to fight global warming. I can protest against bad government policies and vote for candidates who will make the government fulfill its moral obligations. I can support private organizations that fight global warming, such as the Pew Foundation,[11] or boycott companies that contribute too much to global warming, such as most oil companies. Each of these cases is interesting, but they all differ. To simplify our discussion, we need to pick one act as our focus.

My example will be wasteful driving. Some people drive to their jobs or to the store because they have no other reasonable way to work and eat. I want to avoid issues about whether these goals justify driving, so I will focus on a case where nothing so important is gained. I will consider driving for fun on a beautiful Sunday afternoon. My drive is not necessary to cure depression or calm aggressive impulses. All that is gained is pleasure: Ah, the feel of wind in your hair! The views! How spectacular! Of course, you could drive a fuel-efficient hybrid car. But fuel-efficient cars have less "get up and go." So let us consider a gas-guzzling sport utility vehicle. Ah, the feeling of power! The excitement! Maybe you do not like to go for drives in sport utility vehicles on sunny Sunday afternoons, but many people do.

Do we have a moral obligation not to drive in such circumstances? This question concerns driving, not buying cars. To make this clear, let us assume that I borrow the gas-guzzler from a friend. This question is also not about legal obligations. So let us assume that it is perfectly legal to go for such drives. Perhaps it ought to be illegal, but it is not. Note also that my question is not about what would be "best." Maybe it would be better, even morally better, for me not to drive a gas-guzzler just for fun. But that is not the issue I want to address here. My question is whether I have a moral obligation not to drive a gas-guzzler just for fun on this particular sunny Sunday afternoon.

One final complication must be removed. I am interested in global warming, but there might be other moral reasons not to drive unnecessarily. I risk causing an accident, since I am not a perfect driver. I also will likely spew exhaust into the breathing space of pedestrians, bicyclists, or animals on the side of the road as I drive by. Perhaps these harms and risks give me a moral obligation not to go for my joyride. That is not clear. After all, these reasons also apply if I drive the most efficient car available, and even if I am driving to work with no other way to keep my job. Indeed, I might scare or injure bystanders even if my car gave off no greenhouse gases or pollution. In any case, I want to focus on global warming. So my real question is whether the facts about global warming give me any moral obligation not to drive a gas-guzzler just for fun on this sunny Sunday afternoon.

I admit that I am inclined to answer, "Yes." To me, global warming does seem to make such wasteful driving morally wrong.

Still, I do not feel confident in this judgment. I know that other people disagree (even though they are also concerned about the environment). I would probably have different moral intuitions about this case if I had been raised differently or if I now lived in a different culture. My moral intuition might be distorted by overgeneralization from the other cases where I think that other entities (large governments) do have moral obligations to fight global warming. I also worry that my moral intuition might be distorted by my desire to avoid conflicts with my environmentalist friends.[12] The issue of global warming generates strong emotions because of its political implications and because of how scary its effects are. It is also a peculiarly modern case, especially because it operates on a much grander scale than my moral intuitions evolved to handle long ago when acts did not have such long-term effects on future generations (or at least people were not aware of such effects). In such circumstances, I doubt that we are justified in trusting our moral intuitions alone. We need some kind of confirmation.[13]

One way to confirm the truth of my moral intuitions would be to derive them from a general moral principle. A principle could tell us why wasteful driving is morally wrong, so we would not have to depend on bare assertion. And a principle might be supported by more trustworthy moral beliefs. The problem is which principle?

3. ACTUAL ACT PRINCIPLES

One plausible principle refers to causing harm. If one person had to inhale all of the exhaust from my car, this would harm him and give me a moral obligation not to drive my car just for fun. Such cases suggest:

The harm principle: We have a moral obligation not to perform an act that causes harm to others.

This principle implies that I have a moral obligation not to drive my gas-guzzler just for fun if such driving causes harm.

The problem is that such driving does not cause harm in normal cases. If one person were in a position to inhale all of my exhaust, then he would get sick if I did drive, and he would not get sick if I did not drive (under normal circumstances). In contrast, global warming will still occur even if I do not drive just for fun. Moreover, even if I do drive a gas-guzzler just for fun for a long time, global warming will not occur unless lots of other people also expel greenhouse gases. So my individual act is neither necessary nor sufficient for global warming.

There are, admittedly, special circumstances in which an act causes harm without being either necessary or sufficient for that harm. Imagine that it takes three people to push a car off a cliff with a passenger locked inside, and five people are already pushing. If I join and help them push, then my act of pushing is neither necessary nor sufficient to make the car go off the cliff. Nonetheless, my act of pushing is a cause (or part of the cause) of the harm to the passenger. Why? Because I intend to cause harm to the passenger, and because my act is unusual. When I intend a harm to occur, my intention provides a reason to pick my act out of all the other background circumstances and identify it as a cause. Similarly, when my act is unusual in the sense that most people would not act that way, that also provides a reason to pick out my act and call it a cause.

Why does it matter what is usual? Compare matches. For a match to light up, we need to strike it so as to create friction. There also has to be oxygen. We do not call the oxygen the cause of the fire, since oxygen is usually present. Instead, we say that the friction causes the match to light, since it is unusual for that friction to occur. It happens only once in the life of each match. Thus, what is usual affects ascriptions of causation even in purely physical cases.

In moral cases, there are additional reasons not to call something a cause when it is usual. Labeling an act a cause of harm and, on this basis, holding its agent responsible for that harm by blaming the agent or condemning his act is normally counterproductive when that agent is acting no worse than most other people. If people who are doing no worse than average are condemned, then people who are doing much worse than average will suspect that they will still be subject to condemnation even if they start doing better, and even if they improve enough to bring themselves up to the average. We should distribute blame (and praise) so as to give incentives for the worst offenders to get better. The most efficient and effective way to do this is to reserve our condemnation for those who are well below average. This means that we should not hold people responsible for harms by calling their acts causes of harms when their acts are not at all unusual, assuming that they did not intend the harm.

The application to global warming should be clear. It is not unusual to go for joyrides. Such drivers do not intend any harm. Hence, we should not see my act of driving on a sunny Sunday afternoon as a cause of global warming or its harms.

Another argument leads to the same conclusion: the harms of global warming result from the massive quantities of greenhouse gases in the atmosphere. Greenhouse gases (such as carbon dioxide and water vapor) are perfectly fine in small quantities. They help plants grow. The problem emerges only when there is too much of them. But my joyride by itself does not cause the massive quantities that are harmful.

Contrast someone who pours cyanide poison into a river. Later someone drinking from the river downstream ingests some molecules of the poison. Those molecules cause the person to get ill and die. This is very different from the causal chain in global warming, because no particular molecules from my car cause global warming in the direct way that particular molecules of the poison do cause the drinker's death. Global warming is more like a river that is going to flood downstream because of torrential rains. I pour a quart of water into the river upstream (maybe just because I do not want to carry it). My act of pouring the quart into the river is not a cause of the flood. Analogously, my act of driving for fun is not a cause of global warming.

Contrast also another large-scale moral problem: famine relief. Some people say that I have no moral obligation to contribute to famine relief because the famine will continue and people will die whether or not I donate my money to a relief agency. However, I could help a certain individual if I gave my donation directly to that individual. In contrast, if I refrain from driving for fun on this one Sunday, there is no individual who will be helped in the least.[14] I cannot help anyone by depriving myself of this joyride.

The point becomes clearer if we distinguish global warming from climate change. You might think that my driving on Sunday raises the temperature of the globe by an infinitesimal amount. I doubt that, but, even if it does, my exhaust on that Sunday does not cause any climate change at all. No storms or floods or droughts or heat waves can be traced to my individual act of driving. It is these climate changes that cause harms to people. Global warming by itself causes no harm without climate change. Hence, since my individual act of driving on that one Sunday does not cause any climate change, it causes no harm to anyone.

The point is not that harms do not occur from global warming. I have already admitted that they do. The point is also not that my exhaust is overkill, like poisoning someone who is already dying from poison. My exhaust is not sufficient for the harms of global warming, and I do not intend those harms. Nor is it the point that the harms from global warming occur much later in time. If I place a time bomb in a building, I can cause harm many years later. And the point is not that the harm I cause is imperceptible. I admit that some harms can be imperceptible because they are too small or for other reasons.[15] Instead, the point is simply that my individual joyride does not cause global warming, climate change, or any of their resulting harms, at least directly.

Admittedly, my acts can lead to other acts by me or by other people. Maybe one case of wasteful driving creates a bad habit that will lead me to do it again and again. Or maybe a lot of other people look up to me and would follow my example of wasteful driving. Or maybe my wasteful driving will undermine my commitment to environmentalism and lead me to stop supporting important green causes or to harm the environment in more serious ways. If so, we could apply:

The indirect harm principle: We have a moral obligation not to perform an act that causes harm to others indirectly by causing someone to carry out acts that cause harm to others.

This principle would explain why it is morally wrong to drive a gas-guzzler just for fun if this act led to other harmful acts.

One problem here is that my acts are not that influential. People like to see themselves as more influential than they really are. On a realistic view, however, it is unlikely that anyone would drive wastefully if I did and would not if I did not. Moreover, wasteful driving is not that habit forming. My act of driving this Sunday does not make me drive next Sunday. I do not get addicted. Driving the next Sunday is a separate decision.[16] And my wasteful driving will not undermine my devotion to environmentalism. If my argument in this chapter is correct, then my belief that the government has a moral obligation to fight global warming is perfectly compatible with a belief that I as an individual have no moral obligation not to drive a gas-guzzler for fun. If I keep this compatibility in mind, then my driving my gas-guzzler for fun will not undermine my devotion to the cause of getting the government to do something about global warming.

Besides, the indirect harm principle is misleading. To see why, consider David. David is no environmentalist. He already has a habit of driving his gas-guzzler for fun on Sundays. Nobody likes him, so nobody follows his example. But David still has a moral obligation not to drive his gas-guzzler just for fun this Sunday, and his obligation has the same basis as mine, if I have one. So my moral obligation cannot depend on the factors cited by the indirect harm principle.

The most important problem for supposed indirect harms is the same as for direct harms: even if I create a bad habit and undermine my personal environmentalism and set a bad example that others follow, all of this would still not be enough to cause climate change if other people stopped expelling greenhouse gases. So, as long as I neither intend harm nor do anything unusual, my act cannot cause climate change even if I do create bad habits and followers. The scale of climate change is just too big for me to cause it, even "with a little help from my friends."

Of course, even if I do not cause climate change, I still might seem to contribute to climate change in the sense that I make it worse. If so, another principle applies:

The contribution principle: We have a moral obligation not to make problems worse.

This principle applies if climate change will be worse if I drive than it will be if I do not drive.

The problem with this argument is that my act of driving does not even make climate change worse. Climate change would be just as bad if I did not drive. The reason is that climate change becomes worse only if more people (and animals) are hurt or if they are hurt worse. There is nothing bad about global warming or climate change in itself if no people (or animals) are harmed. But there is no individual person or animal who will be worse off if I drive than if I do not drive my gas-guzzler just for fun. Global warming and climate change occur on such a massive scale that my individual driving makes no difference to the welfare of anyone.

Some might complain that this is not what they mean by "contribute." All it takes for me to contribute to global warming in their view is for me to expel greenhouse gases into the atmosphere. I do "that" when I drive, so we can apply:

The gas principle: We have a moral obligation not to expel greenhouse gases into the atmosphere.

If this principle were true, it would explain why I have a moral obligation not to drive my gas-guzzler just for fun.

Unfortunately, it is hard to see any reason to accept this principle. There is nothing immoral about greenhouse gases in themselves when they cause no harm. Greenhouse gases include carbon dioxide and water vapor, which occur naturally and help plants grow. The problem of global warming occurs because of the high quantities of greenhouse gases, not because of anything bad about smaller quantities of the same gases. So it is hard to see why I would have a moral obligation not to expel harmless quantities of greenhouse gases. And that is all I do by myself.

Furthermore, if the gas principle were true, it would be unbelievably restrictive. It implies that I have a moral obligation not to boil water (since water vapor is a greenhouse gas) or to exercise (since I expel carbon dioxide when I breathe heavily). When you think it through, an amazing array of seemingly morally acceptable activities would be ruled out by the gas principle. These implications suggest that we had better look elsewhere for a reason why I have a moral obligation not to drive a gas-guzzler just for fun.

Maybe the reason is risk. It is sometimes morally wrong to create a risk of a harm even if that harm does not occur. I grant that drunk driving is immoral, because it risks harm to others, even if the drunk driver gets home safely without hurting anyone. Thus, we get another principle:

The risk principle: We have a moral obligation not to increase the risk of harms to other people.[17]

The problem here is that global warming is not like drunk driving. When drunk driving causes harm, it is easy to identify the victim of this particular drunk driver. There is no way to identify any particular victim of my wasteful driving in normal circumstances.

In addition, my earlier point applies here again. If the risk principle were true, it would be unbelievably restrictive. Exercising and boiling water also expel greenhouse gases, so they also increase the risk of global warming if my driving does. This principle implies that almost everything we do violates a moral obligation.

Defenders of such principles sometimes respond by distinguishing significant from insignificant risks or increases in risks. That distinction is problematic, at least here. A risk is called significant when it is "too" much. But then we need to ask what makes this risk too much when other risks are not too much. The reasons for counting a risk as significant are then the real reasons for thinking that there is a moral obligation not to drive wastefully. So we need to specify those reasons directly instead of hiding them under a waffle-term like "significant."

4. INTERNAL PRINCIPLES

None of the principles discussed so far is both defensible and strong enough to yield a moral obligation not to drive a gas-guzzler just for fun. Maybe we can do better by looking inward.

Kantians claim that the moral status of acts depends on their agents' maxims or "subjective principles of volition"[18]–roughly what we would call motives or intentions or plans. This internal focus is evident in Kant's first formulation of the categorical imperative:

The universalizability principle: We have a moral obligation not to act on any maxim that we cannot will to be a universal law.

The idea is not that universally acting on that maxim would have bad consequences. (We will consider that kind of principle below.) Instead, the claim is that some maxims "cannot even be thought as a universal law of nature without contradiction."[19] However, my maxim when I drive a gas-guzzler just for fun on this sunny Sunday afternoon is simply to have harmless fun. There is no way to derive a contradiction from a universal law that people do or may have harmless fun. Kantians might respond that my maxim is, instead, to expel greenhouse gases. I still see no way to derive a literal contradiction from a

universal law that people do or may expel greenhouse gases. There would be bad consequences, but that is not a contradiction, as Kant requires. In any case, my maxim (or intention or motive) is not to expel greenhouse gases. My goals would be reached completely if I went for my drive and had my fun without expelling any greenhouse gases. This leaves no ground for claiming that my driving violates Kant's first formula of the categorical imperative.

Kant does supply a second formulation, which is really a different principle:

The means principle: We have a moral obligation not to treat any other person as a means only.[20]

It is not clear exactly how to understand this formulation, but the most natural interpretation is that for me to treat someone as a means implies my using harm to that person as part of my plan to achieve my goals. Driving for fun does not do that. I would have just as much fun if nobody were ever harmed by global warming. Harm to others is no part of my plans. So Kant's principle cannot explain why I have a moral obligation not to drive just for fun on this sunny Sunday afternoon.

A similar point applies to a traditional principle that focuses on intention:

The doctrine of double effect: We have a moral obligation not to harm anyone intentionally (either as an end or as a means).

This principle fails to apply to my Sunday driving both because my driving does not cause harm to anyone and because I do not intend harm to anyone. I would succeed in doing everything I intended to do if I enjoyed my drive but magically my car gave off no greenhouse gases and no global warming occurred.

Another inner-directed theory is virtue ethics. This approach focuses on general character traits rather than particular acts or intentions. It is not clear how to derive a principle regarding obligations from virtue ethics, but here is a common attempt:

The virtue principle: We have a moral obligation not to perform an act that expresses a vice or is contrary to virtue.

This principle solves our problem if driving a gas-guzzler expresses a vice, or if no virtuous person would drive a gas-guzzler just for fun.

How can we tell whether this principle applies? How can we tell whether driving a gas-guzzler for fun "expresses a vice"? On the face of it, it expresses a desire for fun. There is nothing vicious about having fun. Having fun becomes vicious only if it is harmful or risky. But I have already responded to the principles of harm and risk. Moreover, driving a gas-guzzler for fun does not always express a vice. If other people did not produce so much greenhouse gas, I could drive my gas-guzzler just for fun without anyone being harmed by global warming. Then I could do it without being vicious. This situation is not realistic, but it does show that wasteful driving is not essentially vicious or contrary to virtue.

Some will disagree. Maybe your notions of virtue and vice make it essentially vicious to drive wastefully. But why? To apply this principle, we need some antecedent test of when an act expresses a vice. You cannot just say, "I know vice when I see it," because other people look at the same act and do not see vice, just fun. It begs the question to appeal to what you see when others do not see it, and you have no reason to believe that your vision is any clearer than theirs. But that means that this virtue principle cannot be applied without begging the question. We need to find some reason why such driving is vicious. Once we have this reason, we can appeal to it directly as a reason why I have a moral obligation not to drive wastefully. The side step through virtue does not help and only obscures the issue.

Some virtue theorists might respond that life would be better if more people were to focus on general character traits, including green virtues, such as moderation and love of nature.[21] One reason is that it is so hard to determine obligations in particular cases. Another reason is that focusing on particular obligations leaves no way to escape problems like global warming. This might be correct. Maybe we should spend more time thinking about whether we have green virtues rather than about whether we have specific obligations. But that does not show that we do have a moral obligation not to drive gas-guzzlers just for fun. Changing our focus will not bring any moral obligation into existence. There are other important moral issues besides moral obligation, but this does not show that moral obligations are not important as well.

5. COLLECTIVE PRINCIPLES

Maybe our mistake is to focus on individual persons. We could, instead, focus on institutions. One institution is the legal system, so we might adopt:

The ideal law principle: We have a moral obligation not to perform an action if it ought to be illegal.

I already said that the government ought to fight global warming. One way to do so is to make it illegal to drive wastefully or to buy (or sell) inefficient gas-guzzlers. If the government ought to pass such laws, then, even before such laws are passed, I have a moral obligation not to drive a gas-guzzler just for fun, according to the ideal law principle.

The first weakness in this argument lies in its assumption that wasteful driving or gas-guzzlers ought to be illegal. That is dubious. The enforcement costs of a law against joyrides would be enormous. A law against gas-guzzlers would be easier to enforce, but inducements to efficiency (such as higher taxes on gas and gas-guzzlers, or tax breaks for buying fuel-efficient cars) might accomplish the same goals with less loss of individual freedom. Governments ought to accomplish their goals with less loss of freedom, if they can. Note the "if." I do not claim that these other laws would work as well as an outright prohibition of gas-guzzlers. I do not know. Still, the point is that such alternative laws would not make it illegal (only expensive) to drive a gas-guzzler for fun. If those alternative laws are better than outright prohibitions (because they allow more freedom), then the ideal law principle cannot yield a moral obligation not to drive a gas-guzzler now.

Moreover, the connection between law and morality cannot be so simple. Suppose that the government morally ought to raise taxes on fossil fuels in order to reduce usage and to help pay for adaptation to global warming. It still seems morally permissible for me and for you not to pay that tax now. We do not have any moral obligation to send a check to the government for the amount that we would have to pay if taxes were raised to the ideal level. One reason is that our checks would not help to solve the problem, since others would continue to conduct business as usual. What would help to solve the problem is for the taxes to be increased. Maybe we all have moral obligations to try to get the taxes increased. Still, until they are increased, we as individuals have no moral obligations to abide by the ideal tax law instead of the actual tax law.

Analogously, it is actually legal to buy and drive gas-guzzlers. Maybe these vehicles should be illegal. I am not sure. If gas-guzzlers morally ought to be illegal, then maybe we morally ought to work to get them outlawed. But that still would not show that now, while they are legal, we have a moral obligation not to drive them just for fun on a sunny Sunday afternoon.

Which laws are best depends on side effects of formal institutions, such as enforcement costs and loss of freedom (resulting from the coercion of laws). Maybe we can do better by looking at informal groups.

Different groups involve different relations between members. Orchestras and political parties, for example, plan to do what they do and adjust their actions to other members of the group in order to achieve a common goal. Such groups can be held responsible for their joint acts, even when no individual alone performs those acts. However, gas-guzzler drivers do not form this kind of group. Gas-guzzler drivers do not share goals, do not make plans together, and do not adjust their acts to each other (at least usually).

There is an abstract set of gas-guzzler drivers, but membership in a set is too arbitrary to create moral responsibility. I am also in a set of all terrorists plus me, but my membership in that abstract set does not make me responsible for the harms that terrorists cause.

The only feature that holds together the group of people who drive gas-guzzlers is simply that they all perform the same kind of act. The fact that so many people carry out acts of that kind does create or worsen global warming. That collective bad effect is supposed to make it morally wrong to perform any act of that kind, according to the following:

The group principle: We have a moral obligation not to perform an action if this action makes us a member of a group whose actions together cause harm.

Why? It begs the question here merely to assume that, if it is bad for everyone in a group to perform acts of a kind, then it is morally wrong for an individual to perform an act of that kind. Besides, this principle is implausible or at least questionable in many cases. Suppose that everyone in an airport is talking loudly. If only a few people were talking, there would be no problem. But the collective effect of so many people talking makes it hard to hear announcements, so some people miss their flights. Suppose, in these circumstances, I say loudly (but not too loudly), "I wish everyone would be quiet." My speech does not seem immoral, since it alone does not harm anyone. Maybe there should be a rule (or law) against such loud speech in this setting (as in a library), but if there is not (as I am assuming), then it does not seem immoral to do what others do, as long as they are going to do it anyway, so the harm is going to occur anyway.[22]

Again, suppose that the president sends everyone (or at least most taxpayers) a check for $600. If all recipients cash their checks, the government deficit will grow, government programs will have to be slashed, and severe economic and social problems will result. You know that enough other people will cash their checks to make these results to a great degree inevitable. You also know that it is perfectly legal to cash your check, although you think it should be illegal, because the checks should not have been issued in the first place. In these circumstances, is it morally wrong for you to cash your check? I doubt it. Your act of cashing your check causes no harm by itself, and you have no intention to cause harm. Your act of cashing your check does make you a member of a group that collectively causes harm, but that still does not seem to give you a moral obligation not to join the group by cashing your check, since you cannot change what the group does. It might be morally good or ideal to protest by tearing up your check, but it does not seem morally obligatory.

Thus, the group principle fails. Perhaps it might be saved by adding some kind of qualification, but I do not see how.[23]

6. COUNTERFACTUAL PRINCIPLES

Maybe our mistake is to focus on actual circumstances. So let us try some counterfactuals about what would happen in possible worlds that are not actual. Different counterfactuals are used by different versions of rule-consequentialism.[24]

One counterfactual is built into the common question, "What would happen if everybody did that?" This question suggests a principle:

The general action principle: I have a moral obligation not to perform an act when it would be worse for everyone to perform an act of the same kind.[25]

It does seem likely that, if everyone in the world drove a gas-guzzler often enough, global warming would increase intolerably. We would also quickly run out of fossil fuels. The general action principle is, thus, supposed to explain why it is morally wrong to drive a gas-guzzler.

Unfortunately, that popular principle is indefensible. It would be disastrous if every human had no children. But that does not make it morally wrong for a particular individual to choose to have no children. There is no moral obligation to have at least one child.

The reason is that so few people want to remain childless. Most people would not go without children even if they were allowed to. This suggests a different principle:

The general permission principle: I have a moral obligation not to perform an act whenever it would be worse for everyone to be permitted to perform an act of that kind.

This principle seems better because it would not be disastrous for everyone to be permitted to remain childless. This principle is supposed to be able to explain why it is morally wrong to steal (or lie, cheat, rape, or murder), because it would be disastrous for everyone to be permitted to steal (or lie, cheat, rape, or murder) whenever (if ever) they wanted to.

Not quite. An agent is permitted or allowed in the relevant sense when she will not be liable to punishment, condemnation (by others), or feelings of guilt for carrying out the act. It is possible for someone to be permitted in this sense without knowing that she is permitted and, indeed, without anyone knowing that she is permitted. But it would not be disastrous for everyone to be permitted to steal if nobody knew that they were permitted to steal, since then they would still be deterred by fear of punishment, condemnation, or guilt. Similarly for lying, rape, and so on. So the general permission principle cannot quite explain why such acts are morally wrong.

Still, it would be disastrous if everyone knew that they were permitted to steal (or lie, rape, etc.). So we simply need to add one qualification:

The public permission principle: I have a moral obligation not to perform an act whenever it would be worse for everyone to know that everyone is permitted to perform an act of that kind.[26]

Now this principle seems to explain the moral wrongness of many of the acts we take to be morally wrong, since it would be disastrous if everyone knew that everyone was permitted to steal, lie, cheat, and so on.

Unfortunately, this revised principle runs into trouble in other cases. Imagine that 1000 people want to take Flight 38 to Amsterdam on October 13, 2003, but the plane is not large enough to carry that many people. If all 1,000 took that particular flight, then it would crash. But these people are all stupid and stubborn enough that, if they knew that they were all allowed to take the flight, they all would pack themselves in, despite warnings, and the flight would crash. Luckily, this counterfactual does not reflect what actually happens. In the actual world, the airline is not stupid. Since the plane can safely carry only 300 people, the airline sells only 300 tickets and does not allow anyone on the flight without a ticket. If I have a ticket for that flight, then there is nothing morally wrong with me taking the flight along with the other 299 who have tickets. This shows that an act is not always morally wrong when it would (counterfactually) be disastrous for everyone to know that everyone is allowed to do it.[27]

The lesson of this example applies directly to my case of driving a gas-guzzler. Disaster occurs in the airplane case when too many people do what is harmless by itself. Similarly, disaster occurs when too many people burn too much fossil fuel. But that does not make it wrong in either case for one individual to perform an individual act that is harmless by itself. It only creates an obligation on the part of the government (or airline) to pass regulations to keep too many people from acting that way.

Another example brings out another weakness in the public permission principle. Consider open marriage. Max and Minnie get married because each loves the other and values the other person's love. Still, they think of sexual intercourse as a fun activity that they separate from love. After careful discussion before they got married, each happily agreed that each may have sex after marriage with whomever he or she wants. They value honesty, so they did add one condition: every sexual encounter must be reported to the other spouse. As long as they keep no secrets from each other and still love each other, they see no problem with their having sex with other people. They do not broadcast this feature of their marriage, but they do know (after years of experience) that it works for them.

Nonetheless, the society in which Max and Minnie live might be filled with people who are very different from them. If everyone knew that everyone is permitted to have sex during marriage with other people as long as the other spouse is informed and agreed to the arrangement, then various problems would arise. Merely asking a spouse whether he or she would be willing to enter into such an agreement would be enough to create suspicions and doubts in the other spouse's mind that would undermine many marriages or keep many couples from getting

married, when they would have gotten or remained happily married if they had not been offered such an agreement. As a result, the society will have less love, fewer stable marriages, and more unhappy children of unnecessary divorce. Things would be much better if everyone believed that such agreements were not permitted in the first place, so they condemned them and felt guilty for even considering them. I think that this result is not unrealistic, but here I am merely postulating these facts in my example.

The point is that, even if other people are like this, so that it would be worse for everyone to know that everyone is permitted to have sex outside of marriage with spousal knowledge and consent, Max and Minnie are not like this, and they know that they are not like this, so it is hard to believe that they as individuals have a moral obligation to abide by a restriction that is justified by other people's dispositions. If Max and Minnie have a joint agreement that works for them, but they keep it secret from others, then there is nothing immoral about them having sex outside of their marriage (whether or not this counts as adultery). If this is correct, then the general permission principle fails again.

As before, the lesson of this example applies directly to my case of driving a gas-guzzler. The reason why Max and Minnie are not immoral is that they have a right to their own private relationship as long as they do not harm others (such as by spreading disease or discord). But I have already argued that my driving a gas-guzzler on this Sunday afternoon does not cause harm. I seem to have a right to have fun in the way I want as long as I do not hurt anybody else, just like Max and Minnie. So the public permission principle cannot explain why it is morally wrong to drive a gas-guzzler for fun on this sunny Sunday afternoon.[28]

One final counterfactual approach is contractualism, whose most forceful recent proponent is Tim Scanlon.[29] Scanlon proposes:

The contractualist principle: I have a moral obligation not to perform an act whenever it violates a general rule that nobody could reasonably reject as a public rule for governing action in society.

Let us try to apply this principle to the case of Max and Minnie. Consider a general rule against adultery, that is, against voluntary sex between a married person and someone other than his or her spouse, even if the spouse knows and consents. It might seem that Max and Minnie could not reasonably reject this rule as a public social rule, because they want to avoid problems for their own society. If so, Scanlon's principle leads to the same questionable results as the public permission principle. If Scanlon replies that Max and Minnie can reasonably reject the anti-adultery rule, then why? The most plausible answer is that it is their own business how they have fun as long as they do not hurt anybody. But this answer is available also to people who drive gas-guzzlers just for fun. So this principle cannot explain why that act is morally wrong.

More generally, the test of what can be rejected "reasonably" depends on moral intuitions. Environmentalists might think it unreasonable to reject a principle that prohibits me from driving my gas-guzzler just for fun, but others will think it reasonable to reject such a principle, because it restricts my freedom to perform an act that harms nobody. The appeal to reasonable rejection itself begs the question in the absence of an account of why such rejection is unreasonable. Environmentalists might be able to specify reasons why it is unreasonable, but then it is those reasons that explain why this act is morally wrong. The framework of reasonable rejection becomes a distracting and unnecessary side step.[30]

7. WHAT IS LEFT?

We are left with no defensible principle to support the claim that I have a moral obligation not to drive a gas-guzzler just for fun. Does this result show that this claim is false? Not necessarily.

Some audiences[31] have suggested that my journey through various principles teaches us that we should not look for general moral principles to back up our moral intuitions. They see my arguments as a *reductio ad absurdum* of principlism, which is the view that moral obligations (or our beliefs in them) depend on principles. Principles are unavailable, so we should focus instead on particular cases, according to the opposing view called particularism.[32]

However, the fact that we cannot find any principle does not show that we do not need one. I already gave my reasons why we need a moral principle to back up our intuitions in this case. This case is controversial, emotional, peculiarly modern, and likely to be distorted by overgeneralization and partiality. These factors suggest that we need confirmation for our moral intuitions at least in this case, even if we do not need any confirmation in other cases.

For such reasons, we seem to need a moral principle, but we have none. This fact still does not show that such wasteful driving is not morally wrong. It only shows that we do not know whether it is morally wrong. Our ignorance might be temporary. If someone comes up with a defensible principle that does rule out wasteful driving, then I will be happy to listen and happy if it works. However, until some such principle is found, we cannot claim to know that it is morally wrong to drive a gas-guzzler just for fun.

The demand for a principle in this case does not lead to general moral skepticism. We still might know that acts and omissions that cause harm are morally wrong because of the harm principle. Still, since that principle and others do not apply to my wasteful driving, and since moral intuitions are unreliable in cases like this, we cannot know that my wasteful driving is morally wrong.

This conclusion will still upset many environmentalists. They think that they know that wasteful driving is immoral. They want to be able to condemn those who drive gas-guzzlers just for fun on sunny Sunday afternoons.

My conclusion should not be so disappointing. Even if individuals have no such moral obligations, it is still morally better or morally ideal for individuals not to waste gas. We can and should praise those who save fuel.

We can express our personal dislike for wasting gas and for people who do it. We might even be justified in publicly condemning wasteful driving and drivers who waste a lot, in circumstances where such public rebuke is appropriate. Perhaps people who drive wastefully should feel guilty for their acts and ashamed of themselves, at least if they perform such acts regularly; and we should bring up our children so that they will feel these emotions. All of these re-actions are available even if we cannot truthfully say that such driving violates a moral "obligation." And these approaches might be more constructive in the long run than accusing someone of violating a moral obligation.

Moreover, even if individuals have no moral obli-gations not to waste gas by taking unnecessary Sunday drives just for fun, governments still have moral ob-ligations to fight global warming, because they can make a difference. My fundamental point has been that global warming is such a large problem that it is not individuals who cause it or who need to fix it. In-stead, governments need to fix it, and quickly. Finding and implementing a real solution is the task of govern-ments. Environmentalists should focus their efforts on those who are not doing their job rather than on those who take Sunday afternoon drives just for fun.

This focus will also avoid a common mistake. Some environmentalists keep their hands clean by withdrawing into a simple life where they use very little fossil fuels. That is great. I encourage it. But some of these escapees then think that they have done their duty, so they rarely come down out of the hills to work for political candidates who could and would change government policies. This attitude helps nobody. We should not think that we can do enough simply by buying fuel-efficient cars, insulat-ing our houses, and setting up a windmill to make our own electricity. That is all wonderful, but it nei-ther does little or nothing to stop global warming, nor does this focus fulfill our real moral obligations, which are to get governments to do their job to pre-vent the disaster of excessive global warming. It is better to enjoy your Sunday driving while working to change the law so as to make it illegal for you to enjoy your Sunday driving.

NOTES

1. For skeptics, see Lomborg (1998, chapter 24) and Singer (1997). A more reliable partial skeptic is Richard S. Lindzen, but his papers are quite technical. If you do not share my bleak view of global warming, treat the rest of this essay as conditional. The issue of how individual moral obli-gations are related to collective moral obligations is interest-ing and important in its own right, even if my assumptions about global warming turn out to be inaccurate.

2. See Mahlman (2005), Schlesinger (2005), and Weatherly (2005).

3. See Shukla (2005).

4. See Bodansky (2005).

5. See Shue (2005).

6. See Jamieson (2005).

7. See Toman (2005).

8. See Driver (2005).

9. If I have an obligation to encourage the government to fulfill its obligation, then the government's obligation does impose some obligation on me. Still, I do not have an obligation to do what the government has an obligation to do. In short, I have no parallel moral obligation. That is what is at issue here.

10. I do not seem to have the same moral obligation to teach my neighbors' children when our government fails to teach them. Why not? The natural answer is that I have a special relation to my children that I do not have to their children. I also do not have such a special relation to future people who will be harmed by global warming.

11. See Claussen (2005).

12. Indeed, I am worried about how my environmental-ist friends will react to this essay, but I cannot let fear stop me from following where arguments lead.

13. For more on why moral intuitions need confirma-tion, see Sinnott-Armstrong (2005).

14. Another difference between these cases is that my failure to donate to famine relief is an inaction, whereas my driving is an action. As Bob Fogelin put it in conversation, one is a sin of omission, but the other is a sin of emission. But I assume that omissions can be causes. The real ques-tion is whether my measly emissions of greenhouse gases can be causes of global warming.

15. Cf. Parfit (1984, pp. 75–82).

16. If my act this Sunday does not cause me to drive next Sunday, then effects of my driving next Sunday are not consequences of my driving this Sunday. Some still might say that I can affect global warming by driving wastefully many times over the course of years. I doubt this, but I do not need to deny it. The fact that it is morally wrong for me to do all of a hundred acts together does not imply that it is morally wrong for me to do one of those hundred acts. Even if it would be morally wrong for me to pick all of the flowers in a park, it need not be morally wrong for me to pick one flower in that park.

17. The importance of risks in environmental ethics is a recurrent theme in the writings of Kristin Shrader-Frechette.

18. Kant (1785/1959, p. 400, n. 1).

19. *Ibid*, 424. According to Kant, a weaker kind of contradiction in the will signals an imperfect duty. However, imperfect duties permit "exception in the interest of inclination" (421), so an imperfect obligation not to drive a gas-guzzler would permit me to drive it this Sunday when I am so inclined. Thus, I assume that a moral obligation not to drive a gas-guzzler for fun on a particular occasion would have to be a perfect obligation in Kant's view.

20. *Ibid*, 429. I omit Kant's clause regarding treating others as ends because that clause captures imperfect duties, which are not my concern here (for reasons given in the preceding note).

21. Jamieson (2007).

22. Compare also standing up to see the athletes in a sporting event, when others do so. Such examples obviously involve much less harm than global warming. I use trivial examples to diminish emotional interference. The point is only that such examples share a structure that defenders of the group principle would claim to be sufficient for a moral obligation.

23. Parfit (1984, pp. 67 86) is famous for arguing that an individual act is immoral if it falls in a group of acts that collectively cause harm. To support his claim Parfit uses examples like the Harmless Torturers (p. 80). But torturers intend to cause harm. That's what makes them torturers. Hence, Parfit's cases cannot show anything wrong with wasteful driving, where there is no intention to cause any harm. For criticisms of Parfit's claims, see Jackson (1997).

24. Cf. Sinnott-Armstrong (2003) and Hooker (2003).

25. Cf. Singer (1971).

26. Cf. Gert (2005). Gert does add details that I will not discuss here. For a more complete response, see Sinnott-Armstrong (2002).

27. The point, of course, depends on how you describe the act. It would not be disastrous to allow everyone "with a ticket" to take the flight (as long as there are not too many tickets). What is disastrous is to allow everyone (without qualification) to take the flight. Still, that case shows that it is not always morally wrong to do X when it would be disastrous to allow everyone to do X. To solve these problems, we need to put some limits on the kinds of descriptions that can replace the variable X. But any limit needs to be justified, and it is not at all clear how to justify such limits without begging the question.

28. The examples in the text show why violating a justified public rule is not sufficient for private immorality. It is also not necessary, since it might not be disastrous if all

parents were permitted to kill their children, if no parent ever wanted to kill his or her children. The failure of this approach to give a necessary condition is another reason to doubt that it captures the essence of morality.

29. Scanlon (1998).

30. Scanlon's framework still might be useful as a heuristic, for overcoming partiality, as a pedagogical tool, or as a vivid way to display coherence among moral intuitions at different levels. My point is that it cannot be used to justify moral judgments or to show what makes acts morally wrong. For more, see Sinnott-Arm-strong (in press, chap. 8).

31. Such as Bill Pollard in Edinburgh.

32. Developed by Dancy (1993, 2004). For criticisms, see Sinnott-Armstrong (1999).

REFERENCES

Dancy, J. (1993). *Moral reasons.* Oxford: Blackwell.

Dancy, J. (2004). *Ethics without principles.* New York: Oxford University Press.

Gert, B. (2005). *Morality: Its nature and justification* (Revised ed.). New York: Oxford University Press.

Hooker, B. (2003). Rule consequentialism. In: *The Stanford Encyclopedia of Philosophy.* Available at: http://plato.stanford.edu/entries/consequentialism-rule

Jackson, F. (1997). Which effects? In: J. Dancy (Ed.), *Reading Parfit* (pp. 42–53). Oxford: Blackwell.

Jamieson, D. (2007). When utilitarians should be virtue theorists. *Utilitas* 19: 160–183.

Kant, I. (1959). *Foundations of the metaphysics of morals* (L. W. Beck, Trans.). Indianapolis, IN: Bobbs-Merrill. (Original work published in 1785).

Lomborg, B. (1998). *The skeptical environmentalist.* New York: Cambridge University Press.

Parfit, D. (1984). *Reasons and persons.* Oxford: Clarendon Press.

Scanlon, T. (1998). *What we owe to each other.* Cambridge, MA: Harvard University Press.

Singer, M. (1971). *Generalization in ethics.* New York: Atheneum.

Singer, S. F. (1997). *Hot talk, cold science.* Oakland, CA: The Independent Institute.

Sinnott-Armstrong, W. (1999). Some varieties of particularism. *Metaphilosophy, 30,* 1–12.

Sinnott-Armstrong, W. (2002). Gert contra consequentialism. In: W. Sinnott-Armstrong & R. Audi (Eds), *Rationality, rules, and ideals: Critical essays on Bernard Gert's moral theory* (pp. 145–163). Lanham, MD: Rowman and Littlefield.

Sinnott-Armstrong, W. (2003). Consequentialism. In: *The Stanford Encyclopedia of Philosophy*. Available at: http://plato.stanford.edu/entries/consequentialism

Sinnott-Armstrong, W. (2005). Moral intuitionism and empirical psychology. In: T. Horgan & M. Timmons (Eds), *Metaethics after Moore* (pp. 339–365). New York: Oxford University Press.

Sinnott-Armstrong, W. (2006). *Moral skepticisms*. New York: Oxford University Press.

DISCUSSION QUESTIONS

1. Sinnott-Armstrong claims that an individual's emitting greenhouse gases by driving does not harm anyone and does not make climate change any worse than it otherwise would be. How do these claims fit into his larger argument? What are his arguments for them? Do you find them convincing? Why or why not?
2. For each of the fifteen principles that he considers, Sinnott-Armstrong offers reasons to think that the principle fails to entail an individual obligation to refrain from emitting greenhouse gases unnecessarily. Which of his responses do you think is the weakest? Why?
3. State a principle, other than one that Sinnott-Armstrong discusses, that might be taken to entail an individual obligation not to emit greenhouse gases unnecessarily. How might someone argue that it does not entail any such obligation?
4. What do Sinnott-Armstrong's arguments imply for the weaker conclusion that it would be morally better for an individual to avoid emitting greenhouse gases unnecessarily? Why?

JOHN BROOME

Private Morality and Climate Change

John Broome is Emeritus White's Professor of Moral Philosophy at the University of Oxford. He began his career as an economist and has been writing about the intersection of climate policy and moral philosophy for more than two decades. In this excerpt from his book *Climate Matters: Ethics in a Warming World*, Broome argues that our greenhouse gas emissions unjustly harm others and that, as a result, we have a moral obligation to reduce our "carbon footprint" to zero through lifestyle changes and carbon offsets.

GUIDING QUESTIONS

1. What is Broome's argument that your greenhouse gas emissions cause serious harm?
2. What is Broome's argument that the harm you cause through your greenhouse gas emissions is unjust?
3. What objections does Broome consider in the section about "complications caused by governments' actions"? How does he respond to those objections?
4. What is Broome's argument that you should offset your emissions?
5. What objections to offsetting does Broome consider? How does he respond to each objection?

Should you stop flying to distant places on vacation? Should you install a windmill in your garden? If not, should you at least buy your electricity from a green supplier? If you are hoping for answers to questions like these from this book, you are lucky. They are in this chapter. As a moral philosopher, I am surprised to find myself giving definite answers to such practical questions. Moral philosophy generally involves a lot of "on the one hand . . . and on the other. . . ." Giving moral instruction is not normally part of the discipline. But in thinking through questions about the private morality of climate change, I found definite answers emerging that seem to me inescapable.

This chapter does not describe all the duties that fall on you as a result of climate change. Fulfilling the duties of justice described in this chapter will alleviate to only a small extent the harms caused by greenhouse gas. Significant progress can be achieved only by governments, because only governments have the power to get all their people to change their behavior. Governments have the moral duty to respond to climate change, and you as a citizen have a duty to do what you can through political action to get your government to fulfil them. Governments' duties are for later chapters, and those will determine your duties as a citizen. This chapter is about your duties as a private individual, rather than as a citizen.

YOUR EMISSIONS CAUSE SERIOUS HARM

The private morality of climate change starts by recognizing that your own individual emissions of greenhouse gas do serious harm. You might at first think your own emissions have a negligible effect because they are so minute in comparison to emissions around the world. You would be wrong.

If you live a normal life in a rich country, you cause many tonnes of carbon dioxide to be emitted each year. If you fly from New York to London and back, that single trip will emit more than a tonne. An average person from a rich country born in 1950 will emit around 800 tonnes in a lifetime.[1] You can see the harmfulness of these amounts in various ways. The World Health Organization publishes estimates of the number of deaths and the amount of disease that will be caused by global warming.[2] On the basis of the WHO's figures, it can be estimated very roughly that your lifetime emissions will wipe out more than six months of healthy human life.[3] Each year, your annual emissions destroy a few days of healthy life in total. These are serious harms.

Or look at it in terms of money. Economists have calculated a money value for the "social cost of carbon," which is the damage done by a tonne of carbon dioxide dumped into the atmosphere. Their estimates vary greatly. The British government's report *The Stern Review* estimates that the figure is between $25 and $85 per tonne, depending on how radically the world responds to the need to reduce emissions.[4] These numbers are an attempt to put a money value on the total of all the harms that will be caused by a tonne of carbon dioxide, irrespective of when they occur.

Another authoritative source, *A Question of Balance* by William Nordhaus, gives the much lower figure of $7.40 per tonne of carbon dioxide.[5] But Nordhaus is in effect measuring something different. His figure gives the amount of money you would need to set aside now in order to pay fully for all the harms when they arise, or compensate the people who are harmed. He supposes that the money is invested at an interest rate of 5.5 percent.[6] Since many of the harms will occur far in the future, there is plenty of time for the money to grow at compound interest; at 5.5 percent it grows 250-fold in a century. Nordhaus confirms that, if he were to adjust his calculation to cut out this element of increase at compound interest, he would reach a figure for the social cost of carbon that is close to Stern's.[7] This degree of agreement suggests that *The Stern Review's* figures may be about right.

On these figures, the monetary value of the harm you do over a lifetime ranges between $19,000 and $65,000, or between 65 cents and over $2 per day for every day you are alive. However you look at it, your emissions do serious harm.

You might not be convinced. Whatever harm you do, it is spread over the whole globe. The harm you do to each particular person is minuscule. If you live in a rich country, your contribution over your lifetime to global warming is half a billionth of a degree.[8] Nobody would ever notice it. So you might think your personal emissions are insignificant.

But a great many minuscule, imperceptible harms add up to a serious harm. If you doubt that, think of the recipients of harm. Each one receives harm from the emissions of billions of people. The amount each receives from each emitter is minuscule and imperceptible. Yet some recipients are already suffering serious harm in total. Some are even being killed by global warming. This shows that adding up vast numbers of minuscule amounts can amount to a serious harm. Similarly, although each emitter harms each recipient only imperceptibly, the amounts add up. The harm each emitter does to all the people together is large.

Still, you might think you cannot be absolutely certain that your emissions do harm. It is true that you cannot be absolutely certain, but it is overwhelmingly likely. There is no significant chance that your emissions do no harm.

Greenhouse gas harms people in multifarious ways. Each of them is chancy to some extent. A particular storm will be harmful only if the water rises above the flood defences. Each increase in the amount of greenhouse gas in the air slightly increases the quantity of rain, but it will be a matter of chance whether the particular quantity of gas you emit this year will be enough to cause a flood on any particular occasion. Your emission increases the likelihood of a flood, but it might not actually cause any particular flood. So it is true that your particular emissions may do no harm in a single event. But during the centuries they are in the air they will have the chance of causing harm on innumerable occasions. It is extraordinarily unlikely that they will do no harm at all. There is no real uncertainty there.

There is a different source of chanciness in the harms you cause. It is sometimes a matter of chance whether a particular act of yours leads to an emission of greenhouse gas. If you decide to fly between London and New York, you will probably occupy a seat that would otherwise have been left empty. The plane would probably have gone anyway, and your weight adds little to its emissions. So there is a good chance that a particular flight of yours makes little difference to total emissions.

However, the airline will adjust its schedules to meet demand. As demand increases, there has to come a point where it puts on an extra flight or sends a larger plane. Just one extra passenger will push it across that boundary. Just by chance, your single decision might have that effect. If so, it leads to a great many tonnes of emissions. So your decision might have little effect, but it might have a very big effect. The figure I gave for your emissions–over a tonne for a round trip between London and New York–is an average. It can happen that one single trip emits little, but on average a trip emits a lot.

There is no such chanciness in the effect of many or your acts. You can be sure that much of what you do cause emissions. When you drive a car powered by fossil fuel, it is certain that carbon dioxide will spew from its exhaust pipe. In any case, even if you are not always sure that what you do causes emissions, this is no reason to doubt that every bit of emission that you do cause is harmful.

You might have a different, fatalistic reason for thinking your emissions do no harm. You might think it is already too late to do anything about climate change: nothing you can do now will prevent a disaster. You may be right. The process of climate change triggers positive feedbacks, which accelerate the process. An example is the melting of snow: warming causes snow to melt, and that in turn contributes to warming, because land that is clear of snow absorbs more heat from the sun. Some feed-backs may accelerate global warming to the point where it cannot be stopped. Triggering one of those would be catastrophic. The most worrying possibility arises from the vast amounts of methane that are trapped in permafrost on land and under the sea around the Arctic. The warming of the atmosphere is already causing some of this methane to escape. Since methane is an extremely powerful greenhouse gas, it causes further warming. There is enough methane there to destroy us all, and it is possible that we have already passed the tipping point for all of it to escape.

If we have indeed passed it, your own emissions make no difference in the long run. There will be catastrophe whether you make them or not. But this should not make you think they are harmless. If we are on track to disaster, your emissions accelerate us along the way. They bring the disaster nearer, and that is harmful. If there is to be a catastrophe, the later the better. So even fatalism does not give you a good reason to doubt that your emissions are harmful.

One more reason for doubt is that climate science is uncertain, in the way in which all of science is uncertain. Scientists recognize that new discoveries in the future may force them to revise even the best-established scientific theories. Nevertheless, some theories, such as quantum mechanics or the theory of relativity, are supported by such strong evidence that there is no real doubt that they are at least close to the truth. The evidence that man-made climate change is in progress is by now overwhelming, and there is overwhelming evidence that it is harmful. The amount of harm that greenhouse gas will do remains uncertain, but there is no significant doubt that it is harmful to some extent.

YOUR EMISSIONS ARE UNJUST

Moreover, the harm your emissions do is done to people; . . . in the case of your individual emissions, you cannot shelter behind any excuse from the nonidentity effect. Your emissions also meet other conditions . . . which imply that they are unjust. The harm they do results from an action of yours; it is serious; it is not accidental; you do not make restitution (I assume); you act for your own benefit (I assume); it is not fully reciprocated; and you could easily reduce it. This last point is explained in detail in this chapter.

Is this conclusion affected by the minute possibility that your emissions do no harm? We might take either of two different views about this possibility, but they both lead to the same result. One view is that to impose a risk of harm on someone is to do her an injustice. The other is that you do an injustice only if you actually harm someone, but it is morally wrong to act in a way that risks doing an injustice. Either way, you ought not to cause greenhouse gas to be emitted, at least without compensating the people who are harmed, and this duty is derived from justice. This conclusion is particularly compelling because the risk of harm is very great; there is only the tiniest possibility that your emissions harm no one.

So each of us in under a duty of justice not to cause the emission of greenhouse gas without compensating the people who are harmed as a result. Your carbon footprint ought to be zero, unless you make restitution. This is strong advice. But I find I cannot avoid drawing this conclusion. Fortunately, it will turn out to be less onerous than it may at first appear to be.

By what means should you satisfy this requirement? You might try to do it by compensating the people you harm. If you can invest money at 5.5 percent interest, compensation would in principle be remarkably cheap. I quoted William Nordhaus's estimate that the harm done by a tonne of carbon dioxide could be compensated for by $7.40 if it is invested at 5.5 percent. However, I do not recommend this method of achieving justice, because it will fail. Remember that duties of justice are owed to particular people. Your emissions of greenhouse gas are an injustice done to a large fraction of the world's population. You will not be able to compensate each of them individually.

You might try and make restitution through a collective international scheme of some sort. That way, you will not compensate all the individuals you harm, but you might manage some sort of surrogate compensation, by compensating large populations rather than individuals. Possibly justice may be satisfied by surrogate compensation; this is a matter for argument. But there remains another problem. You do not know how much compensation you actually owe. None of us knows how much harm we cause by our emissions. We may be able to compute how much gas we emit, but the harm that gas does is very uncertain. I have mentioned some figures for the social cost of carbon, but they are not very reliable.

You would do much better not to make the emissions in the first place; no compensation will then be required. This is possible. True, you could not live in a way that does not cause the emission of any greenhouse gas at all, but you can cancel out your emissions. Virtually anything you buy has been produced using energy from fossil fuels. Even if you use electricity produced from renewable sources such as wind or sunlight, the machinery that produces the electricity will have been built using some fossil fuels. You can certainly reduce your emissions, of course. We all know what steps to take. Do not live wastefully. Be frugal with energy in particular. Switch off lights. Do not waste water. Eat less meat. Eat local food. And so on. Many of these are steps you can take at little or no cost to yourself, and you should certainly take those ones. But your most effective way of reducing your emissions to zero is to cancel or *offset* the emissions that you will still be causing after you have taken those steps. I shall examine offsetting in some detail later in this chapter.

I am not telling you this as a way to solve the problem of climate change. If everyone did it, it would solve the problem, but not everyone can do it. Reducing your individual emissions of greenhouse gas is not the most effective way for you to make the world a better place. Your duty to have a zero carbon footprint does not derive from your duty of goodness. You must do it to avoid injustice–simply that.

So far as solving the problem of climate change is concerned, your best route is through political action to induce your government to do what it should. Reducing your carbon footprint to zero may contribute indirectly to that effort. It expresses your own commitment to reducing emissions. You should do it on grounds of justice, but it may also have this beneficial political side effect.

COMPLICATIONS CAUSED BY GOVERNMENTS' ACTIONS

Before we come to offsetting, we need to take account of two complications. Each is caused by an interaction between governments' efforts to slow climate change and the actions of individuals.

The first complication affects anyone who lives in the European Union or in any country that imposes a cap on greenhouse gas emissions.[9] Suppose at present you consume electricity bought from a company that generates it partly or wholly from fossil fuels. Now suppose you switch your consumption of electricity to a green source. You might start buying electricity from a company that uses only renewable energy, or cover your roof with solar panels.

If you live in a country where the emissions of the electricity industry are capped, your previous supplier will have permits that allow it to emit greenhouse gas up to a certain quantity. It will not have been wasting its valuable permits, so it will certainly have been emitting up to its limit. It will probably continue emitting to the same limit when it loses your custom. It now produces less electricity, but it will probably continue to use its fossil fuel generators as before, and reduce its production from renewable sources. If it uses no renewable sources, or alternatively if it chooses to reduce its production from fossil fuels rather than from renewable resources, it will find itself holding surplus emission permits. It will sell them to some other company, and that company will use them to increase its emissions. Since the number of emissions permits is not reduced, the quantity of emissions will not be reduced.

As a result, when you free yourself from electricity generated from fossil fuels, I am sorry to say you do not reduce your country's overall emissions of greenhouse gas one whit. You bring no benefit to the climate, in fact. The same applies to other ways of reducing your emissions besides changing your electricity supply. In a country where emissions are capped, the overall quantity of emissions is fixed by the number of permits that have been issued. When you reduce emissions, other people's emissions will correspondingly increase. The total remains the same. The only exceptions to this rule are in industries outside the capping scheme. As things stand in the European Union, reducing plane travel reduce emissions, because airlines are not capped.

This is not a criticism of cap and trade. It is the international community's way of reducing emissions overall. If all goes well, caps will progressively be reduced. It is the cap imposed from above that will in due course drive down each industry's emissions. The system happens to have the side effect that individual actions from below will not reduce emissions.

Individual actions may still have an indirect political effect. Switching to a green supplier is a way of indicating conspicuously that you care about reducing emissions. When you and other people make the switch, it may encourage your government to reduce the cap on the electricity industry. Indeed it is built into Australia's proposed cap and trade scheme that, when people switch to green electricity, the cap is automatically reduced by a corresponding amount.[10] So what I say does not apply to the Australian proposal.

However, even though switching to green energy does not reduce overall emissions, one important thing remains true. When you reduce emissions, you move closer to meeting your duty of justice not to cause emissions yourself. You move closer to justice, even though you do no good.

That may seem paradoxical. Compare two ways you might conduct your life in a country with a cap. In one you generate your own electricity from renewable sources. In the other you buy electricity from a supplier who generates it from fossil fuels. In the first case, you are harming no one by your use of electricity. In the second case, you are harming people. That is an injustice. Yet I have just said that in the second case you cause no more people to be harmed than in the first case. Am I not speaking paradoxically?

I am not. In the second case you harm people, even though you cause no more people to be harmed. Here is a parallel example, adapted from a story made famous by the moral philosopher Bernard Williams.[11] Jim, travelling in a lawless country, stumbles across a soldier who is about to execute an innocent peasant. The soldier offers to pay Jim a fee if he, Jim, executes the peasant instead. Either way, the peasant will be killed. Should Jim accept the fee and kill the peasant? He should not. If he does, he will kill the peasant, which is to harm him. True, he will cause no more harm to be done since the peasant will anyway be killed. But if he kills the peasant the harm will be done by him, Jim. It is an injustice done by Jim: the injustice consists in harming not in merely causing more harm to be

done. If promoting good was the only thing that mattered, it would not be wrong for Jim to kill the peasant. But because justice also matters, it is wrong.

Similarly, on grounds of justice you should not harm people by emitting greenhouse gas, even though, if you do not make those emissions, the people will still be harmed. You can move closer to justice by taking your electricity supply from green sources. However, you have another way of moving closer to justice, and this way also does some good. It is offsetting. Although it is justice, not goodness, that requires you to avoid emitting greenhouse gas, you should take notice of goodness in choosing your means of satisfying this requirement. I therefore do not recommend switching to green in a country (except perhaps Australia in the future) where the energy industry is capped.

The second complication caused by governments' actions is this. In a country that is making a serious effort to slow climate change, emitting greenhouse gas will bear a cost known as a "carbon price." . . . It may be that companies pay a tax to the government for emissions. Alternatively, there may be trading in emission permits, so that companies have to pay a price for permits (or forgo the opportunity to sell permits) when they emit. Either way, if you live in a country with a carbon price, when you buy goods, a part of their price will reflect the emissions that have been made in manufacturing them. Ideally, the carbon price should be equal in value to the harm that emissions do, so that when you buy a product, you pay the full value of the harm that is done in the course of producing it. What difference does this make to your duty of justice?

Does it mean you do no injustice when you cause emissions by buying goods? It does if the carbon price you pay is used to compensate the individual people whom your emissions harm. But that is not likely. Even if your government participates in some scheme to recompense the victims of that climate change, it is unlikely that the victims of your own emissions will be properly recompensed. Despite the price you pay, it remains likely your emissions will harm people who are not properly compensated. So they remain unjust. You should offset them.

WHAT IS OFFSETTING?

Offsetting your emissions means ensuring that, for every unit of greenhouse gas you cause to be added to the atmosphere, you also cause a unit to be subtracted from it. If you offset, on balance you add nothing. Offsetting does not remove the very molecules that you emit, but the climate does not care which particular molecules are warming it. If you successfully offset all your emissions, you do no harm by emissions. You therefore do no justice by them.

It will not be easy to calculate the offset you need. You must make sure you offset: not just the gas that is directly emitted by your own actions, but also the gas that supplied the energy used in making everything you consume. The average emissions in your own country will not be a good guide, because much of what you consume will have been manufactured abroad. It would be safest to overestimate. In any case, this calculation is much simpler that trying to calculate the harm your emissions do, with the aim of compensating people for them. This adds to the reasons for preferring offsetting to compensating.

How do you offset in practice? You may be able to subtract gas from the atmosphere yourself. One way of doing so is to grow some trees. As they grow, trees remove carbon from the atmosphere to build their bodies: they take in carbon dioxide molecules, keep the carbon, and release the oxygen. But you would need to make sure that the trees' carbon is permanently kept out of the atmosphere, and that would be hard to achieve. Eventually your trees will die and decompose, and their carbon will return to the air again. Somehow you will have to ensure your forest will be replanted and replanted again perpetually even after your death. For that reason, effective do-it-yourself offsetting is difficult.

Indeed, actually subtracting carbon from the air is difficult by any means. There is a chemical explanations of why. Oxidizing carbon to produce carbon dioxide releases energy. That is why we do it in the first place; it is our way of getting energy. Turning carbon dioxide back into elemental carbon absorbs the same amount of energy. It would be futile to make energy by oxidizing carbon and then use that same amount of artificial energy to turn the resulting carbon dioxide back into carbon. Returning the carbon to elemental form is sensible only if the energy is drawn from a renewable source that cannot be used in other ways. Trees do this for us: they use energy from the sun that would otherwise be wasted.

There are some artificial means of taking carbon dioxide from the air and storing it, rather than converting it to carbon. It has to be stored in a place from which it cannot escape back into the atmosphere. One option is deep underground in geological formations. At present, methods of doing this are too expensive to be a practical means of offsetting.

Apart from planting trees, presently available practical means are "preventive," as I shall call them. Instead of taking carbon dioxide out of the atmosphere, they make sure that less gets into the atmosphere in the first place. They prevent gas that would have been emitted from getting emitted.

Plenty of commercial organizations offer to do this for you as an individual. You pay them a fee per tonne of offsetting you ask them to do. They use your money to finance projects that diminish emissions somewhere in the world. Most projects are located in developing countries. Most of them create sources of renewable energy. For instance, they build hydroelectric power stations or wind farms. Other projects promote the efficient use of energy. One example is a project that installs efficient cooking stoves in people's homes in Africa and Asia. Cooking with firewood is an important cause of carbon emissions. Using efficient stoves reduces emissions, and has the added health benefit of making homes less smoky.

Preventive offsetting is genuine offsetting, provided it leads to a real reduction in the global emission of greenhouse gas. If you offset all your emissions by this means, you make sure that your presence in the world causes no greenhouse gas to be added to the atmosphere. You therefore do no harm to anyone through emissions. But we need to recognize that it is difficult to be sure that the reduction in emissions you pay for really happens. You have to compare what happens, given the project you pay for, with what would have happened otherwise. What would have happened otherwise is bound to be a bit indefinite. Suppose a project builds a new biomass power station. Who knows whether, had the power station not been built with offsetting money, the local government would have decided to do it anyway within a few years? This problem of ensuring that the reduction is in addition to what would have happened anyway is known in the carbon business as the problem of "additionality."

It is well illustrated by a program known as REDD (Reducing Emissions from Deforestation and Forest Degradation), which is supported by the UNFCCC as an offset mechanism. It aims to reduce emissions from deforestation in developing countries. Developing countries are to be paid for leaving their forests standing, rather than felling them. Companies can buy a patch of forest as an offset for the amount of carbon that is contained in that patch. But if the offset is to be genuine, the world's total emissions of carbon must be reduced by that amount as a result. The particular patch that is purchased will not be felled, we hope. But how do we know it would have been felled otherwise? And even if it would have been, how do we know that the purchase will not simply cause a different patch of forest to be felled instead? REDD would serve as a convincing offset mechanism only if all forests in a particular country would be felled unless the country is paid not to fell them. For most countries, that is not true.

REDD is a good idea for separate reasons. Standing trees have a value for the world, since they lock up carbon. It is therefore a good idea to pay developing countries not to fell their forests. Moreover, paying for forests is a means of redistributing wealth from rich countries to poorer ones; . . . redistribution from rich to poor is generally an improvement. But REDD is dubious as an offset mechanism. You cannot safely ensure that you are not committing an injustice in emitting carbon dioxide by purchasing a patch of forest as an offset. I do not recommend this method of offsetting.

But as a private person, you are not likely to participate in REDD anyway. REDD is supposed to supply offsets to companies and nations. You will be dealing with smaller offsetting companies. There are independent organizations that verify and certify the projects of these companies, to make sure they are truly "additional." I think we can rely on their work to an extent. By judicious choice of an offsetting company, by attention to its certification, and perhaps by overbuying offsets to allow a safety margin, you can make yourself reasonably confident that you are making a genuine offset. That way you can save yourself from committing an injustice. You might not be fully confident, and this is perhaps a reason to go further in reducing your own direct emissions that you otherwise would do.

OBJECTIONS TO OFFSETTING

Nevertheless, some environmentalists object to offsetting. In 2007, the leading environmental organization Greenpeace issued a strong statement opposing it. It said:

> The truth is, once you've put a tonne of CO_2 into the atmosphere, there's nothing offsetting can do to stop it changing our climate.[12]

This is disingenuous. True, once you have put a tonne of carbon dioxide molecules into the atmosphere, those molecules will wreak their damage. However, if at the same time you remove the same number of other carbon dioxide molecules, you prevent those ones from wreaking damage. Your overall effect is zero. As far as the climate is concerned, emitting a tonne of carbon dioxide and offsetting it is exactly as good as not emitting it in the first place, providing the offset is genuine.

Does Greenpeace have a sound objection to offsetting? One of its concerns is that not all offsets are genuinely "additional." I agree this is a real concern, and we have to rely on good certification. Is there a sound objection beyond that? The Greenpeace statement went on to say:

> Offsets shift the responsibility for reducing our carbon footprint from western governments to ordinary people in the developing world.

Greenpeace is evidently concerned that offsets allow people in the rich countries to carry on emitting greenhouse gas as they always have, whereas the world needs to reduce its emissions. What it the truth in that?

The first truth is that offsetting is remarkably cheap. This is one of the reasons I recommend it as a better way to avoid injustice than trying to compensate the people whom your emissions harm. Reputable companies offer offsets at a price of around $10 per tonne of carbon dioxide. Compare this with *The Stern Review*'s figure of $25 to $85 for the value of the harm emissions do. I shall soon explain why the price is so low.

Suppose an average American causes 30 tonnes a year to be emitted. Her annual emission could be offset for a mere $300. Given this cheap price, we can except most inhabitants of rich countries to prefer to offset most of their emissions, rather than reduce them much. Earlier, I recommended you to reduce your emissions in obvious and cheap ways, but to offset the rest. If you follow my advice, I do not expect you to change your own activities much. You will behave as Greenpeace predicts.

However, since you will offset your emissions, the net effect of your behaviour will be a zero emission. Until you offset, you were emitting gas; now you have reduced global emissions by the whole amount that previously you emitted.

Could you do better for the climate? Not by emitting less and correspondingly offsetting less. If you did that, your net emissions would once again be zero, which is no better for the climate. You could do better by emitting less, and continuing to spend the same on offsets, or by continuing to emit as before and spending more on offsets. In effect, this would make your carbon footprint negative. It would be going beyond your duty of justice to avoid harming people. But since it would make the world a better place, it might potentially be a duty of goodness.

However, making your carbon footprint negative is in competition with all the other ways of improving the world that are available to you. . . .It is not the most effective. If you wish to use your resources to improve the world, you can save a life for a few hundred dollars. You cannot save a life as cheaply as that by carbon offsetting. So far as the climate is concerned, you are not under any duty of goodness to

go beyond what justice requires of you. You should reduce your carbon footprint to zero, but no more is required.

Since offsetting does less good than using your money in other ways, should you offset at all? Should you not take the money you would have used for offsetting, and instead send it to a charity that will make better use of it? You should not. If you did, you would be acting unjustly by emitting greenhouse gas that harms people. True, you would be doing more good, but morality does not normally permit you to act unjustly for the sake of doing greater good. There are exceptions to this rule, but yours is not one. Remember that you yourself are the main beneficiary of your unjust act. Your emissions benefit you, and only a small part of your benefit will be canceled out by the money you send to charity.

But what if you are an altruist, and devote all your resources to doing good? That is different. If you do not yourself benefit from your emissions, they are not so clearly unjust. Even if they are unjust, their injustice is plausibly made morally permissible by the much greater good that results from them. An altruist has a good case for not offsetting her emissions.

Is offsetting morally dubious? Greenpeace says that offsetting your emissions is passing on the responsibility for reducing emissions to developing countries. It appears to be suggesting that this is morally dubious. Is it right?

To answer this question, I must start by explaining why offsetting is so cheap. It is because of the very thing that causes the problem of climate change in the first place. Greenhouse gases are an externality. The harm done by emitting them is not borne by the emitter. Consequently, people have been happily emitting greenhouse gas even though they could easily have emitted less just by taking some easy steps. Now that offsetting companies offer them money to emit less, they can easily accept the offer and take those steps. Because the steps are easy, they will not demand to be paid much for making them.

As yet, very little offsetting is taking place in the world, so easy steps are enough to meet the present demand for offsetting. You can at present fulfill your duty of justice cheaply just because other people are not fulfilling theirs, but if people start to offset more, the price of doing so will rise. If all the people in rich countries were to achieve zero net emissions by offsetting, the price would rise a great deal. It would reach a level where those people would find it beneficial to reduce their direct emissions too, so as to reduce the amount of offsetting they have to do.

In the meantime, most of the offsetting reductions will occur in the developing countries rather than the rich ones. Most offsetting projects are located in those countries for two reasons. One is that it helps ensure they are truly additional. Most rich countries are committed by the Kyoto Protocol and its successors to meet a particular target for emissions. If an offsetting project took place in one of those countries, the country would probably count it as helping to meet its target. It would therefore compensate itself by emitting more in some other way. The second reason is that it is generally cheaper to reduce emissions in developing countries. Many rich countries have already started reducing their emissions, so the cheapest opportunities for reductions in those countries have already been taken up. In addition, labor is cheaper in poorer countries.

As a general rule, it is better for the world if things are done where they can be done most cheaply. That is the way to achieve a result with the least use of resources. But is there something morally wrong with reducing emissions, in particular, where it can be done most cheaply? Doing so may seem reminiscent of certain other activities that raise moral questions. One is disposing of toxic waste. Exporting toxic waste from a rich country to a poor country is morally dubious, even though it may be the cheapest way of disposing of the waste. Indeed, the practice is now banned by the Basel Convention, which came into force in 1992. Greenpeace's statement may be hinting that shifting the burden of reducing emissions from rich countries to poor ones is morally similar to exporting toxic waste.

The objection to exporting toxic waste is that it harms the population of the country that imports it. A fee may be paid to the importing one, but the particular people who receive the fee rarely suffer the harm that comes with it. On the other hand, carbon offsetting does not harm the people of the country that does it. It generally benefits them by giving them employment or in other ways. For instance, installing efficient cooking stoves benefits their health. There is no objection on these grounds.

True, part of the reason offsetting is so cheap is that the people of the countries that do it are far poorer than the people who pay for the offsets. The rich offsetters are taking advantage of the poverty of the poor, therefore. Is that morally wrong? I take it for granted that the world's gross inequality is morally bad. But offsetting carbon emissions transfers wealth from the rich to the poor, so it reduces the inequality a little. I therefore cannot see how the world's inequality can make offsetting morally wrong. Still, it remains true that the rich who use cheap offsets are taking advantage of other people's poverty. This may give them a moral reason to contribute more to relieving poverty.

Does offsetting delay progress on climate change?
Greenpeace recognizes that, if the world is to get climate change under control, the rich countries will have to cut their emissions. It is concerned that offsetting will allow them to delay doing so. I think this is a genuine worry.

However, it is a worry about governments rather than individuals. I am not recommending offsetting to governments; I am recommending it only to individuals as a way of acting justly. Significant progress on reducing emissions—progress on a scale that makes the world significantly better—is going to have to come from governments. Governments are in one way or another going to have to make their populations emit less greenhouse gas. But governments like to make promises in public, and then privately avoid carrying them out fully and honestly. Offsetting may offer them a useful smokescreen for evading their responsibilities.

Large-scale offsetting is available to governments and large organizations as part of the cap and trade system. An offsetting project can apply to be certified under something called the Clean Development Mechanism (CDM) of the UNFCCC. The certificate asserts that it is genuinely "additional": it prevents the emission of greenhouse gas that would otherwise have been emitted. Once a project is certified under the CDM, the amount of emission it saves can be sold on the market as a "carbon credit." A carbon credit has the same effect as an emission permit; its holder is allowed to emit as much greenhouse gas as the offsetting project saves. This creates the opportunity for shenanigans.

For example, there is a plan to include REDD under the CDM. If that happens, it will throw huge quantities of new carbon credits on the market, pushing down the carbon price. Each patch of tropical forest will be salable as a credit. Rich countries, and companies within rich countries, will buy up these credits and so get themselves permission to make new emissions up to the level of the credit. REDD is a good idea in principle, but it will simply lead to extra global emissions unless any new carbon credits it produces are balanced by a corresponding cut in emission permits around the world. The international process being what it is, that may not happen.

This chapter is not about the shenanigans of companies and nations. It is about the morality of individuals. When you as an individual buy carbon offsets, you are trading in the carbon market. The offsets you buy are not the same as the ones that are bought by nations and corporations. You need not be involved in REDD. Greenpeace may well be right about the manipulation of the large-scale market, but I do not think its objections carry over to the informal market.

I do not think Greenpeace has a correct objection to offsetting by individuals. Private offsetting is a means by which each person can avoid causing harm to others. It allows us each to act justly in this respect.

SUMMARY

Each of us had a clear duty to emit no greenhouse gas. Emitting greenhouse gas does serious harm to others for our own benefit, and that is morally impermissible. It is an injustice. The duty to emit no greenhouse gas is stringent, but even so it can be satisfied easily and effectively by offsetting. Offsetting is not morally dubious, as some environmental organizations suggest it is.

Reducing our emissions to zero, whether by offsetting or in other ways, will not go far toward solving the problem of climate change. We should do it on grounds of justice, not because it is a good way to improve the world. To improve the world, we shall have to adopt political means. We shall have to work through our governments, because only governments can take action on the large scale that is required.

NOTES

1. David J. Frame, "Personal and intergenerational carbon footprints," forthcoming.

2. World Health Organization, *Global Health Risks: Mortality and Burden of Disease Attributable to Selected Major Risks,* 2009. The calculations are adapted from David Frame's.

3. I base this figure on estimates in Frame, "Personal and intergenerational carbon footprints."

4. Nicholas Stern et al., *The Economics of Climate Change: The Stern Review* (Cambridge: Cambridge University Press, 2007), 304.

5. William Nordhaus, *A Question of Balance: Weighing the Options on Global Warming Policies* (New Haven: Yale University Press, 2008), 196.

6. Ibid., 178.

7. Ibid., 186.

8. Frame, "Ethics and personal carbon footprints."

9. Thanks here to Cameron Hepburn.

10. Ross Garnaut, *The Garnaut Review 2011: Australia in the Global Response to Climate Change* (Cambridge: Cambridge University Press, 2011), 76.

11. Bernard Williams, "A critique of utilitarianism," in *Utilitarianism: For and Against,* by J. J. C. Smart and Bernard Williams (Cambridge: Cambridge University Press, 1973), 77–150.

12. Statement by Charlie Kronick of Greenpeace, January 17, 2007, available at: http://www.greenpeace.uk/media/press-releases/greenpeace-statement-on-carbon-off-setting.

DISCUSSION QUESTIONS

1. Are you convinced by Broome's argument that your greenhouse gas emissions harm others unjustly? Why or why not?
2. Why, according to Broome, are you obligated to reduce your greenhouse gas emissions even if doing so has no effect on the total amount of greenhouse gases emitted? Do you find his argument convincing? Why or why not?
3. Broome considers several objections to the practice of offsetting your greenhouse gas emissions. Which of those objections do you think is most important? Do you find Broome's reply convincing? Why or why not?
4. How do you think Walter Sinnott-Armstrong (the author of the previous reading) would respond to Broome's main argument? Whose argument do you think is stronger? Why?

SARAH KRAKOFF

Parenting the Planet

Sarah Krakoff is Professor of Law at the University of Colorado–Boulder. She writes mainly on American Indian law and natural resource law. In this paper, Krakoff argues that the time has come to think of humans' relationship with Earth in a new way. We are, she argues, almost like parents to the planet now, and that parenting the planet well requires a certain set of virtues that will enable us to tackle problems like climate change.

GUIDING QUESTIONS

1. What, according to Krakoff, is this paper's main goal?
2. What benefits does Krakoff identify for thinking of the stages of human psychological development as a metaphor for our relationship to the Earth?
3. What point is Krakoff trying to make by describing various activities of organizations that are trying to address climate change?
4. What specific virtues does Krakoff think people should exhibit toward the environment? How does she think those virtues will help people address environmental problems like climate change?

INTRODUCTION

The Earth is under our thumb. Global warming is the latest example of how human activity has reached every nook and cranny of the Earth's natural systems, but it is not the only one. The effects on the ozone layer, the collapse of fisheries throughout the world, and the accelerated species extinction rate, among many other phenomena, indicate the planetary scope of human impacts. As Nobel Prize winner Paul Crutzen has put it, we have entered the "Anthropocene," the era of ubiquitous human influence on the Earth's geological systems.[1] Robert H. Socolow similarly suggested that today we might think of ourselves as "planetarians," due to our wide-ranging impacts and, arguably, correspondingly broad responsibilities.[2] This stage, the Anthropocene, the Planetarian, or whatever label we choose to apply, provides the occasion to reconsider our relationship with the natural world. Just as importantly, it provides the occasion to dwell on what it means to be human and the legacy that we would like to leave behind. Despite the need for sophisticated technological solutions to address the many challenges of global climate change, ultimately our decisions will reflect our moral and ethical commitments to other humans and to the natural world, even if they will not reflect them perfectly.

Since the Industrial Revolution, progress has gone hand-in-hand with technological innovation. For roughly the past forty years (dating, somewhat arbitrarily, from the first Earth Day in 1970), technology has, in significant measure, also allowed us to rein in some of the negative environmental consequences of industrialization. The Western developed world made substantial progress toward addressing, for example, air and water pollution through a mix of regulation and technology. Even in less obviously technology-dominant areas such as species preservation, the combination of scientific knowledge and human ingenuity resulted in important conservation victories, such as bringing the bald eagle, the California condor, and other less telegenic species back from the brink of extinction. These technological and scientific successes have been dominated by technological frames of thought, including welfare economics, market liberalism, and other rationalist/individualist approaches, that have monopolized politics and decision making in much of the Western developed world. These frames have in common an outlook of perpetual growth that is dependent on unstated assumptions about boundless resources. The appeal of these frames is obvious. But the benefits of perpetuating a vision of the good life that is bound up in these frames may be receding.

What I want to explore in this chapter is the possibility of a conception of how we relate to the planet that might supplant the dominant frames with a timelier and perhaps more enduring vision of ourselves

and our obligations. The seemingly intractable collective action features of climate change, which render it a commons problem of global and intergenerational proportions, make it all the more ripe for a conception of ourselves that does not depend predominately on individual rational self-interest to explain human motivation. An appropriate, though admittedly not perfect, metaphor for this new stage is that of parenting. The features of global climate change, like the features of parenting in the ordinary sense, are such that daily and indefinite behavior change is called for, and personal and hedonistic desires may have to be set aside when necessary; and yet, with any luck, we will derive deep satisfaction and joy in our new role even if we glance with occasional longing at the more libertine phase we have left behind. And finally, parenting the planet will require us to accept that, even if, or perhaps *especially* if, we do the best we can and all goes as well as possible, we will never know the end of the story. To be a parent is inherently tragic in this sense, even while parenting also has the potential to magnify the best aspects of the human experience—love, joy, passion—all gained through the necessary loss of displacing the self as the center of the universe. Finally, parenting captures the paradox that taking on the challenge of displacing one's own needs requires the willingness to recognize that one has a monopoly on how to control and influence the needs of others. Like parents, we as a species are in the driver's seat. Whether we exercise our control and influence to allow the flourishing of others (including other human communities, other species, and future generations) or not is up to us.

Philosophers have provided an array of theories and arguments in support of an ethical relationship with the natural world. Some are grounded in utilitarian theories, some in deontological approaches, and some in theories of virtue or character. Indeed, there is a burgeoning literature in the third category.[3] The interest in virtue-based accounts of an ethical relationship with nature might reflect an emerging sense that in the Anthropocene, positive environmental outcomes depend, more than ever before, on the fulfillment of human moral potential. The renewed interest in virtue may also reflect an inchoate sense that positive environmental outcomes are more elusive than ever before, and that we need a reason to be good that does not depend on them. The idea developed in this chapter—that we need a conception of ourselves and our relationship with nature that is in step with the Anthropocene—is akin to the virtue-based approaches for these reasons. Unlike virtue theory, however, my point is not to provide a philosophically convincing basis for an environmental ethic. Rather, my goal is to provide an accurate and bracing description of the stage that human beings are in with respect to our dominance of the planet, and then to sketch the ethical implications and possibilities. Being a parent, after all, is not itself a virtue. It is just a description of a very distinctive relationship. To be a good parent requires, at the very least, recognition of the particular power and influence that one is capable of wielding. The road to virtue may follow from that recognition, or not. But it certainly will not follow without it.

1. THE STAGES OF HUMAN PSYCHOLOGICAL DEVELOPMENT AS A METAPHOR

The psychoanalyst Erik Erikson outlined eight stages of human psychological development, starting with infancy and ending with old age. Later, when Erikson's wife and collaborator Joan lived a bit beyond even "old age," she sketched a ninth stage, which she did not name. Whether in eight or nine stages, the Eriksons' central idea, refined and modified by others since, is that human psychology is not static, and that we resolve certain psychological conflicts in order to meet the challenges of each phase of life. Erikson's approach is not strictly biological; his theory does not depend on a handful of immutable characteristics that can be universally applied regardless of time or circumstance. Rather, he is careful to say, "Wherever we begin . . . the central role that the stages are playing in our psychosocial theorizing will lead us ever deeper into the issues of *historical relativity.*"[4] In other words, the stages provide a useful framework for asking the right questions. Those questions include: What are the central conflicts that we face, and what virtues might

be cultivated to address those conflicts? The answers to those questions, however, are not automatic or universal, but rooted in the norms and values of particular cultures.

Erikson's insights, like Freud's and Jung's, now may seem somewhat basic. Just as most people accept as a general matter the role of unconscious motivation, most people in our culture accept that the mind of a child is not the same as the mind of an adolescent, and that the developmental issues we face as very young adults are different from those we face in middle age. What I want to borrow from this now familiar framework is the idea that different circumstances have different essential conflicts, and therefore call for the cultivation of different virtues and different behaviors. In the Anthropocene, the implications of attitudes and actions towards the environment are quite different than in previous eras, when human activity was capable of only the most ephemeral effects on the world.

Conceptualizing our relationship with the natural world in stages also has the following two interrelated benefits. First, this conceptual framework allows us to think, perhaps more objectively and less judgmentally, about the ways in which laws about the environment both reflect and reinforce the essential virtues and conflicts of a particular time and place. Thinking about stages may help us to see how laws generated during a previous stage, even laws that are protective of the environment, no longer are sufficient because they do not facilitate resolution of the essential conflicts we face today. To use an analogy to the human stages, we do not apply the same legal standards to the behavior of children that we do to the behavior of adults. We adjust our regulatory schemes and our expectations for behavior based on a sense of developmental appropriateness. Related to this, but going beyond legal reform, using the metaphor of stages (hopefully loosely, and not so dogmatically that I attempt to explain everything in terms of an elaborate Eriksonian developmental chart) may liberate us to think about our current situation in ways that make us feel hopeful, engaged, and ready to do our best rather than depressed, apathetic, frightened, or, maybe worst of all, like pretending that nothing is going on that warrants rethinking. Consider, for example, how strange and frustrating it would be to grapple with the challenges of adolescence equipped only with the conceptual tools and vocabulary of a preschooler. Clarity about the challenges and conflicts one faces at least provides the possibility for meaningful engagement with them, whereas uncertainty results in disorientation, confusion, and the potential for actions that are futile given the circumstances. A teenager cannot navigate the complex social environment of junior high school with the "will you play with me?" approach that worked in elementary school, and we cannot solve global warming by relying on the pollution-control strategies of the past.

Second, conceptualizing our relationship with the nonhuman world in terms of stages sidesteps the problem of whether we are distinct from or a part of "nature," or "wilderness." Taking a meta-view of how we see ourselves and our role in different periods, the question instead becomes one of both history and values. Have we *acted* as if we are members of the natural world, or have we *acted* as if the natural world is an object that is distinct from us? And what do our different attitudes and behaviors mean about our values? If we are indeed in the Anthropocene era, then the focus should appropriately shift from what is or is not "natural" to what we value and why.

This is, perhaps, all an elaborate way of saying that it is good to know where you are. We have, I believe, not yet grappled with where we are as a species in relationship with the rest of the natural world. Despite having entered the Anthropocene, we have not embarked on a widespread project of reconsidering what this might mean in terms of our obligations to other species, future generations, or even the many human beings who are on the short end of our effects on natural systems.

2. SOME FACTS ABOUT GLOBAL WARMING

So where are we? The scientific facts about global warming are covered in earlier [readings] and so I will not review them all here. Instead I will provide

a very brief summary, highlighting the aspects of climate change that lend themselves to a shift to a parenting conception of our relationship with the planet.

In terms of what we know about global warming, we now have roughly two decades of accumulated scientific studies. These studies are regularly reviewed by the [Intergovernmental] Panel on Climate Change (IPCC). In January 2007, the IPCC issued its fourth set of assessment reports on global warming. The IPCC concluded that "warming of the climate system is unequivocal,"[5] and also expressed "very high confidence" that human emissions of carbon dioxide (hereafter CO_2) and other heat-trapping gases (methane, nitrous oxide, various hydrofluorocarbons, various perfluorocarbons, and sulfur hexafluoride) since 1750 have caused the Earth's surface temperature to rise.[6] During that time, CO_2, the most important of the anthropogenic greenhouse gases, increased from a pre-industrial level of roughly 280 parts per million (ppm) to 382 ppm in 2007.[7]

CO_2, methane, and the other heat-trapping gases work in the following way. The sun's energy passes through the atmosphere in short, powerful waves. The Earth reflects the sun's energy back, but in longer heat waves. These longer waves are too big, molecularly speaking, to make it back through the "blanket" of CO_2 and other heat-trapping gases. This blanket keeps the Earth warmer than it would be if the heat energy were simply reflected back into space. If there were no heat-trapping gases in the layers of our atmosphere, the Earth's average surface temperature would be about 5°F (-15°C), far too cold for most of us. So the Earth is habitable thanks to greenhouse gases, but other planets are uninhabitable because they have atmospheres that trap too much heat. Venus, for example, has an atmosphere composed of 98 percent CO_2 and its surface temperature is 891°F (477°C). According to the scientist and author Tim Flannery, "if even 1 percent of Earth's atmosphere" were CO_2, it would, all other things being equal, "bring the surface temperature of the planet to boiling point."[8] Like Goldilocks, we want our atmosphere to be "just right." For millennia, it has been. But today, CO_2 and other gases are at levels that are far higher than they have been since the dawn of life as we now know it. Therefore, we may be fast approaching the point where global average surface temperatures are becoming, like Papa Bear's bowl of porridge, too hot.

The theory of global warming is not new. It has been with us since the 1890s, when a Swedish chemist demonstrated that a decrease in atmospheric CO_2 could have brought about an ice age, and further speculated that increasing levels of CO_2 due to coal burning would have a future warming effect.[9] Global warming advanced beyond the theoretical in the late 1950s, when scientists began to document the concern that human activities, including significant increases in CO_2 emissions, might be changing the way the atmosphere traps heat. In 1958, the scientists Roger Revelle and Charles Keeling established a research station at the top of Mauna Loa in Hawaii, from which they launched weather balloons and measured the amount of CO_2 in the atmosphere.[10] The measurements revealed a striking trend of annual increases in CO_2 concentrations, which, coupled with the physics of how CO_2 and other greenhouse gases trap heat, provided factual support for the hypothesis that human emissions would cause increases in the Earth's temperature.

Since this time, more and more evidence has been filling in. In retrospect, the scientific story is one of a sound hypothesis evolving year by year into an increasingly solid, and now all but indisputable, reality. There have been, and continue to be, distracting sideshows about the precision with which we know things. For example, a *Newsweek* story provides a nice summary of how the "denial machine," which the author describes as a "well-coordinated, well-funded campaign by contrarian scientists, free-market think tanks and industry," created a "paralyzing fog of doubt around climate change," for nearly two decades.[11] These efforts were funded by the American Petroleum Institute, the Western Fuels Association, and ExxonMobil Corporation. The denial machine is still in operation, but we are largely over the narrative of scientific doubt, at least in most mainstream circles. Instead, the doubt has shifted from whether humans are causing climate change to whether it is worth it economically to do anything serious to curb emissions.[12] We will come back to this later.

3. A BRIEF TOUR THROUGH THE EFFECTS

Warming's effects are also well covered in other chapters in this volume, and so I will not dwell on them for long. There are two aspects of global warming's impacts that I want to highlight, however, because they are particularly relevant to the idea of shifting to a new stage in terms of our conception of planetary obligations. First, global warming's effects on other species are, in many instances, already quite clear. While many know about the risk to the polar bear from the dramatic decrease in Arctic sea ice,[13] I suspect few have heard of the gradual displacement of a furry creature closer to my home, the pika. Pika live in colonies at high altitude, typically in skree fields on mountainsides. They are social, and communicate with one another through high-pitched squeaks or whistles. Pika require chilly temperatures, but, unlike humans, they cannot respond to the increasing heat by turning on the air conditioning. Instead, they have been migrating further up-slope to capture the high altitude benefit of cooler air. Yet some pika populations in the area known as the Great Basin, between the Sierra Nevada and the Rocky Mountains, have already disappeared because, presumably, they ran out of up.[14] At this point, it is tempting to reel off the many other species that are already at risk due to climate change. But I want to keep my promise not to dwell too long on these effects. We can think of the pika as a stand-in for the many other species that will not be able to adapt. Their loss will not be felt in any immediate, daily way, but they join the list of casualties to a process that we have set in motion.

Second, the effects of global warming are being, and will continue to be, felt disproportionately by developing nations and by poor people in general. As the IPCC Fourth Assessment Report concludes, "Africa is one of the continents most vulnerable to climate variability and change because of multiple stresses and low adaptive capacity."[15] The IPCC and other sources report a similarly disparate vulnerability for virtually all underdeveloped and developing regions. For example, a report by the Natural Resources Law Center at the University of Colorado documents disparate effects on Native American communities within the USA, including Native villages in Alaska, tribes throughout the increasingly arid Southwest, the salmon tribes of the Pacific Northwest, and the two Florida tribes.[16] Indeed, some Alaskan Native villages are already being forced to relocate due to global warming. Decreased sea ice has allowed more waves to pound the shore, and higher surface temperatures have made the shoreline less stable, causing coastal villages literally to slip into the ocean. The Native village of Kivalina, for example, used to comprise 54 acres. Erosion of the shoreline has shrunk the village to 27 acres. In 2006, the US Army Corps of Engineers concluded that in ten years the village would be uninhabitable. Relocation plans have estimated the costs of removal to range from $95 million to $400 million. Kivalina has filed a lawsuit against ExxonMobil and other corporate defendants, alleging nuisance theories as well as conspiracy to conceal facts about global warming and to mislead the public about its causes and effects.[17] Raising an even broader array of climate change's effects on Native life and culture, the Inuit Circumpolar Conference filed a petition before the Inter-American Commission on Human Rights alleging various human rights violations by the USA.[18] As in the context of effects on non-human species, this section could be the beginning of a much longer recitation of the disparate effects on poor and indigenous communities throughout the world, but this handful of examples will serve here to make the point.

To summarize, global warming is already having negative effects on other species, and not just the telegenic polar bear. And global warming is also either already affecting or likely to affect poor people everywhere, and particularly poor people in poor regions of the Southern Hemisphere as well as indigenous communities whose ways of life are tied to place. The ethical dimensions of climate change thus include obligations to other species and justice to the world's poor and indigenous peoples. This does not necessarily distinguish climate change from other global environmental problems. But the collective action features of climate change, outlined below, heighten the necessity as well as the difficulty of a truly global response.

4. THE POTENTIALLY TRAGIC STRUCTURE OF GLOBAL WARMING: TEMPORAL LAGS AND SPATIAL DISPERSION

If the reader is getting that bleak feeling, unfortunately we have to go a little bit further down before we can start climbing up. We have to discuss why global warming is different from other environmental problems, even if, at least compared to some, it is different only in magnitude. These, the potentially tragic features of global warming, are that it is both a temporally lagged and spatially dispersed phenomenon.

4.1 Temporal Lags

Global warming is a severely temporally lagged phenomenon because CO_2 stays in the atmosphere for hundreds of years, so most of the molecules added since the dawn of industrialization are still hanging around. As a practical matter, every molecule we add is one that is increasing the "thickness" of our atmospheric blanket because none are going away within a time-frame that matters. This results in a lag between emissions increases and the effects on warming. The effects from today's blanket will be felt throughout the rest of the century (meaning increased warming and so on) even if we were to stop all carbon emissions today. Likewise, we are now feeling the effects not of our own emissions, but those of our parents and grandparents. The problem compounds over time, because even if we begin to reduce emissions, we are reducing relative to a base with significant longevity. Reflecting this, a study by Susan Solomon and others found that changes in surface temperature, rainfall, and sea level are largely irreversible for more than 1,000 years after emissions are completely stopped.[19]

One challenge presented by the time lag is one of perception. It is understandable that we have a hard time experiencing today's daily activities as contributing to an increasingly intractable global problem

when the effects of these normal, culturally reinforced activities (driving, heating our homes with
fossil fuels, flying to visit relatives) will be felt decades from now. A related challenge is that it puts us
in the position of setting targets for emissions based
on predictions about the future rather than certainties
about the here and now. For example, there is a worrisome range of scientific assessments regarding safe
levels of global CO_2. James Hansen and several scientific coauthors are calling for reductions and stabilization at 350 ppm of atmospheric CO_2 in order to
avoid perpetual climate catastrophes.[20] Not very long
ago, the working assumption was that stabilization
somewhere between 450 and 550 ppm would suffice.[21] Today's levels, measured as recently as 2008,
are already at around 384 ppm. Given current rates of
emissions, we have a very small window (estimates
vary and depend on trends in the next few years, but
sometime between now and midcentury) to decrease
and then zero out our emissions.[22] So, to summarize,
the temporal features of global warming are such that
(1) we feel the effects tomorrow of our actions today,
(2) tomorrow will be with us for a long time, and
(3) the best plan for tomorrow is to start dramatically
reducing emissions today, even if we never achieve
100 percent consensus on the non-catastrophic level
of emissions.

4.2 Spatial Dispersion

Spatial dispersion is what makes global warming a
problem requiring a truly global solution. The atmosphere is a global commons. No matter where in
the world you are, your emissions contribute to the
increasing insulating properties of the atmosphere.
And the atmosphere is not and cannot be compart-
mentalized. So the fact that the USA has the highest
historical greenhouse gas emissions does not mean
that our atmosphere is "thicker" and our effects from
global warming are proportionally higher than other
countries. (In fact, in terms of effects, the contrary
is true. Regions that have contributed the least are
likely to feel the most severe effects.[23]) The spatial
dispersion means that reductions in one part of the
globe can be rendered meaningless by increases in

another part of the globe. If the total parts per million
of CO_2 continues to rise overall, it doesn't matter
where the parts come from. The "commons" nature
of global warming is what makes policymakers say
things like "What about China and India? If they
are not part of a global regime to reduce emissions,
we may be tightening our carbon belts for nothing."
Nobody wants to be a dupe. Rational choice and collective action theorists label this kind of commons
problem a prisoner's dilemma.[24] Each entity, acting
in its "rational self-interest" has an incentive not to
curb emissions even though the interests of all would
be served if we would agree to reduce emissions.

The temporal and spatial dispersion together
heighten the nature of this challenge. As Stephen
Gardiner has put it, they create a true intergenerational collective action problem.[25] Each generation
has an incentive, under rational choice assumptions,
not to reduce emissions because the "burdens" of reduction will be felt now and the "benefits" of curb-
ing emissions will be felt by subsequent generations.
If we look around at our behavior over the last two
decades, and even now as we dither about whether
to do anything serious at the national or global level
about mitigating emissions, we might find ourselves
persuaded by the rational choice description: rational
self-interest in our own well-being (which is heavily
dependent on our carbon economy) has led us not to
act for the benefit of future generations, other species,
and less well-off human communities, even though
the moral case for doing so is heightened by the
fact that we are the generation that could make the
biggest difference. As Gardiner has articulated,
the "perfect moral storm" that makes global warming
an acute yet elusive moral issue leads to behaviors
characterized by "moral corruption," which include
distraction, complacency, unreasonable doubt, selective attention, delusion, pandering, false witness, and
hypocrisy.[26] Indeed, these behaviors have all been
evident in the reaction to climate change at the national level. And yet, is the "we have done nothing,"
mother-of-all collective action descriptions accurate?
Have "we" been doing nothing? And furthermore, is
our conception of ourselves limited to a being that
calculates benefits and costs and acts "rationally"
on them?

5. ETHICS FOR A POTENTIALLY TRAGIC AGE

The remarkable thing is that despite the potentially tragic structure of global warming and the fact that warming's effects fall disproportionately on poor people, other species, and future generations, people all over the world, including the developed world, are trying to do something about it. Are they acting in a consequentialist and rationalist way, because they hope to succeed? In part they must be. But they likely also know that they may not succeed, for the reasons just described, and furthermore that they will never know if in fact they do. So while participants in various local arrangements to reduce greenhouse gas emissions want their actions to be part of a larger and ultimately successful movement, their behavior also reflects other values and motivations. What follows is a very impressionistic survey of some of the things happening around the world. I want to suggest that what is going on in these communities is neither silly, idealistic delusion nor grim self-denial in sacrifice to a preservationist goal. I want to suggest that there are pockets of humanity fashioning an alternative subjective identity, an identity whose meaning derives from participating in the daily tasks of parenting the planet. This identity is in part an end in itself, a way of constructing a meaningful and even joyous life in the face of tragic circumstances, even while it also has both existential and even potentially consequentialist implications.

There are too many individual and local initiatives on climate change to provide a comprehensive account. Instead, I will provide a brief overview of activities at the subnational level, spending a little more time on particularly salient examples. The overview starts at the highest subnational level of coordination and moves down the scale from there.

5.1 US States and Regions

At the state level, there is a great deal of activity.[27] Thirty-six states have completed "climate actions plans," which are initial documents laying out steps for reducing emissions and preparing for the already inevitable effects of warming. Forty-three states have greenhouse gas inventories, allowing them to track emissions. More impressively, twenty-one states have emissions reduction targets, and a number of those have an actual carbon cap and offset program for power plants. Twenty-nine states, plus the District of Columbia, have renewable portfolio standards, which require that a certain percentage of the state's electric needs come from renewable sources. In Colorado, the legislature recently raised the percentage of renewables in our renewable portfolio standard, requiring that we achieve 20 percent renewable sources by 2020.

California has been the leader in all of these efforts, and in 2006 enacted a law setting the goal of reducing the state's greenhouse gas emissions to 1990 levels by 2020.[28] The legislation authorizes the California Air Resources Board to adopt a market-based system to regulate greenhouse gases, and mandates enforcement of emissions standards against regulated sources.[29] In addition to action by individual states, there are several regional initiatives throughout the country, in which states (sometimes together with Canadian provinces) have combined to address climate change and in some cases are working toward regional cap-and-trade systems. The Regional Greenhouse Gas Initiative, which was the first of the regional efforts, includes ten states in its mandatory cap on emissions from the power sector.

5.2 Cities

Moving down the scale, cities have been very engaged with enacting climate policies. In 1993, Portland, Oregon, became the first city to adopt a strategy for reducing emissions of CO_2. In June 2005, Portland issued a "Progress Report" which concluded that the city and surrounding county had reduced per capita emissions by 12.5 percent since 1993.[30] Other cities including Seattle, Washington, and Salt Lake City, Utah, have joined Portland in establishing emissions reduction targets. To unite and further catalyze these efforts, Mayor Greg Nickels of Seattle created the US Mayors Climate Protection Agreement. The agreement urges federal and state governments to enact policies that meet or surpass the Kyoto target of reducing global warming pollution to 7 percent below 1990 levels by 2012 and also calls on Congress to pass greenhouse gas reduction legislation. The agreement states that signatory mayors will strive to meet or exceed the Kyoto targets within their own communities by creating an inventory of emissions in their cities, setting reduction targets, and increasing use of alternative energy sources. More than 800 mayors have signed the agreement.[31] All this activity demonstrates that governments at the local level are taking a leading role in setting and meeting greenhouse gas emissions reduction goals. My own hometown, Boulder, Colorado, has even managed to pass the country's first relatively modest carbon tax. The tax is imposed on residential and commercial energy customers, and is collected by the local electric utility. The charge is based on electricity use, and wind energy customers are exempt.

The tax is low, costing the average household only $1.33 per month, and is designed to fund Boulder's Climate Action Plan, a multi-faceted effort to increase efficiency and transition to renewable energy sources in order to meet Boulder's goals of complying with Kyoto's emissions reduction targets.

5.3 Non-Governmental Community Efforts

Beyond the governmental realm, there are also many examples of norms and practices emerging from within different local cultural communities. The following three examples highlight the impressive diversity among these efforts. First, the Inuit of the Arctic Circle, who have developed a culture over millennia of living low-carbon lives, now find that they must engage in international legal efforts to preserve that way of life. Second, a subsect of evangelical Christians has fashioned a religiously based movement to reduce emissions and care for the poor as well as other species. Third, neighbors in some countries are banding together to pledge to reduce their individual carbon footprints.

The Inuit Community

It is understandable that the Inuit, residents of the Arctic Circle, where warming is twice that of the global average, are very engaged with climate change. The Inuit Circumpolar Conference is a non-governmental organization representing "approximately 150,000 Inuit of Alaska, Canada, Greenland and Chukotka (Russia)."[32] Sheila Watt-Cloutier, an Inuit and member of the conference, filed a human rights petition (hereafter the Inuit petition) against the USA in the Inter-American Court of Human Rights in 2005.[33]

The petition intersperses scientific data with direct observations by Inuit people, including clear and poignant descriptions of how natural cycles are changing far faster than human culture can adapt, and how those changes are causing the loss of key cultural practices.[34] It also describes in vivid detail the many signs that other species are struggling, and perhaps heading toward extinction.[35]

The Inuit community, as viewed through the prism of their involvement with the Inuit petition and other efforts to participate in international climate discussions, embraces moral commitments to place and to future generations, and simultaneously engages with the highly technocratic and bureaucratic forms of science and international law. The Inuit, through these varied commitments and strategies, are attempting to preserve their place-dependent cultures while simultaneously integrating themselves into the global web of legal and technical relationships that will be required for them to succeed. Their efforts, although necessitated by dire circumstances, are therefore also imbued with hope and a sense of optimism.

The Evangelical Climate Community

The culture of mega churches with Christian rock groups and Bible study classes may seem a far cry from the culture of seal and whale hunting, igloo building, and fine-tuned reading of ice and snow, but global warming highlights their similarities. Like the Inuit, the evangelical climate community is engaged in a modern, multi-faceted campaign rooted in cultural and spiritual values. Those values extend care and obligation both forward in time, to the inheritors of the world that evangelicals believe that they are charged with "stewarding," and outward in space, to the residents of other nations who will feel most acutely global warming's effects.

While the evangelical climate community is less rooted in a particular geography than the Inuit communities, there are otherwise some interesting parallels. Like the Inuit, the evangelical impetus to address global warming grows out of a spiritual worldview. And also like the Inuit, the evangelical climate community embraces the science documenting global warming as well as the need for comprehensive legislative solutions. This is evident in the Evangelical Climate Initiative (ECI) statement, "Climate Change: An Evangelical Call to Action."[36] The statement describes the scientific consensus that global warming is real and human-induced, and argues that Christian moral convictions demand a response to the problem. The statement urges policymakers both to mitigate climate change and provide aid to the poor in order to help them adapt to the changes already underway.[37] Lastly, the statement calls on the USA to pass national legislation requiring reductions in CO_2 emissions through market-based mechanisms.[38] The evangelical climate movement has also attempted to draw attention to individual activities that can reduce greenhouse gas emissions. In 2002, the group formed a campaign entitled "What Would Jesus Drive" (WWJD), arguing that transportation choices are moral choices.[39]

CRAGS

The third and final community-based example is even further down the scale of size and organization. In the UK and the USA, small groups have formed whose members pledge to one another to live low-carbon lives. Carbon Rationing Action Groups, or CRAGS, as they are called, are communities that keep one another true to their principles by formulating a yearly limit of emissions for members and then meeting regularly to monitor one another. There are currently 160 people active in some 20 CRAGS across the UK, with another 13 in the formulation stage. These have been joined by two working CRAGS in Canada, three in the USA, and others in various start-up phases.[40]

The goal for the majority of CRAGS in the UK is to reduce personal carbon footprints by roughly 10 percent each year to achieve a reduction of 90 percent of current levels by 2030. To meet their goals, members are changing their daily habits, including using less light and different sources of fuel. According to a *New York Times* article, CRAG member "Jacqueline Sheedy has turned the former coal barge where she lives into a shrine to energy efficiency: She reads by candlelight in midwinter, converts the waste from her toilet into fertilizer, and hauls freshwater home on a trailer attached to her bicycle. Now Ms. Sheedy has set herself a new goal: to stop burning coal for heat and instead use wood from renewable resources."[41] Similar groups are forming all over, including in New York, Oregon, Maryland, and even Texas, which has the highest per capita emissions of any state in the USA.[42] In Boulder, Colorado, at least two CRAG-like groups have also formed, aided by the leadership and support of the City's Climate Action Program.

6. VIRTUES AND PRACTICES FOR A WARMING WORLD

From a rational choice/welfare economics perspective, all of these subglobal initiatives might be described as irrational. When we consider the spatial and intergenerational collective action features of global warming, people and communities are denying themselves a benefit in order to achieve a goal which may be undermined by increased carbon emissions by their neighbor the next house down, or the next city over, the next state over, and, even more threateningly, subsequent generations. Furthermore, conventional understandings of human empathy and planning—that near-empathy is more powerful than abstractions, and that the human time horizon does not reach much beyond two generations—are called into question by these local carbon mitigation activities.

What all of this activity might reflect is a shift in the way that we conceive of our role on the planet, and the identities that we are constructing to make our lives have meaning. In the face of a potentially tragic problem, we are not merely slotting in a strong preference for a better long-term outcome and acting on it, which could be a rational choice explanation for this behavior. Rather we are creating daily habits and rituals that make our lives feel good and meaningful, irrespective of whether we will succeed at stabilizing our greenhouse gas emissions at levels that could avoid severe and volatile outcomes. Consistent with virtue theory, we are fashioning an ethic that does not depend solely on a narrow version of rationality or consequences, but rather on an account of a fully realized human life. Moreover, we are acting ethically in the face of potential futility. Doing so may reflect a transition from a stage of control and dominance to one of care-taking and wisdom. Love, care, and wisdom are, according to Erikson, the central virtues of adulthood.[43] Analogously, virtue theorists have suggested that love, care, and wisdom, as well as a string of other virtues associated with communion, environmental activism, and sustainability, are central to good environmental character.[44] Perhaps the actions being taken across the globe are signs that we, as a species, are growing up.

The motivations to make this shift are as varied as the people and the communities that are making it. For some, like the Inuit, this conception of life as daily tending to the Earth has deep and ancient roots in culture and religion. As the late Justice William Brennan once put it: "[many indigenous] religions regard creation as an on-going process in which they are morally and religiously obligated to participate."[45] The Inuit have adopted this view of their role in the new challenge. For others, like the ECI and its members, the motivation is their own religious worldview. For all, there are, I suspect, some common threads. One recurring theme is that people want to be seen by subsequent generations as people who tried their best. They do not want to leave a legacy of indifference behind, even if they also are aware that what they are trying to do may not be enough. For example, Thomas R. Carper, a US Senator from Delaware, was quoted as saying that he "did not want his children and grandchildren chastising him for inaction in decades to come. 'I don't want them to say, "What did you do about it? What did you do about it when you had an opportunity?

Weren't you in the Senate?"' Carper said, adding that he hoped to tell them, 'I tried to move heaven and Earth to make sure we took a better course.'"[46] What is particularly telling about this quotation is that it assumes that the Senator has failed in his efforts. So his hope is not just that he succeeds politically. Surely he hopes that, but also that he is seen as someone who tried his hardest to avert harm to future generations, even if his work was unavailing.

Another theme is that daily engagement with something linked to a higher purpose is itself meaningful. One of the CRAG members put it this way, "I don't want our credits to be like taxes that we only think about once a year . . . I want them to be the lifeblood of the way we operate every day."[47] The Maryland Craggers state in their website that "we felt like we were part of something that mattered and could help other people."[48] Like parents, these politicians and ordinary folks are acting every day for the next generation. And like parents, CRAG members and others have found meaning and enjoyment in their new practices, even if occasionally they wish they could just turn up the darned heat. Also like parents, they will not know if their contributions, in the end, have had a happy conclusion. For parents in the usual sense, of course, do not hope to outlive their children, making the best end of the parenting story an inevitable unknown. (When parents in fact know the end, because their children have predeceased them, it is therefore an awful one.)

What all this may point to is that we are on the verge of a very different way to think about success, security, meaning, and happiness than the dominant ways of thinking about such things, at least in the Western developed world, for the last couple of centuries. And this all might be, not just a fine thing, but a wonderful, joyful thing. We may be developing a more dispersed and global sense of identity and obligation, and accompanying flexible attitudes and behaviors regarding how to measure contentment and satisfaction.

On a darker but not unrealistic note, these are the same attitudes that our children and grandchildren will need if our generation continues to fail to address climate change, and they are living in a world where formulating ethics in the face of natural resource devastation will be the presiding challenge.[49] That possibility is hardly indistinct, given the ongoing failure of the UN-sponsored process to formulate an enforceable multilateral climate treaty and the tenuousness of any substitute political arrangements between the USA, China, and India. Our political ingenuity seems to lag behind our technological prowess, leaving future generations and the natural world with the legacy of the Anthropocene as an atmospheric, geologic, and ecological matter, but not with respect to constructing an enduring and enforceable legal regime that can match these pervasive effects. The prospect of political failure at the global level serves only to heighten the importance of cultivating virtue locally. Without a personal and identity-based sense of why to care about nature, other species, or future generations, the very idea of an environmental ethic may simply slip away. Tragedy thus haunts environmental virtue as a theoretical and practical matter. Moreover, the tragedy is of human origin. The parenting metaphor captures this in a way that other virtue-oriented metaphors do not. There is nothing inherently dominating or tragic about friendship or stewardship. But, parenting, as a matter of description and potential, has these features. We might not like to think of our species as having overwhelming influence on the planet, and even if we recognize our control and influence, we might also prefer to believe that we have the intelligence and skill to fix everything. Yet climate change, the paradigmatic evidence of the Anthropocene, gives the lie to both. Parenting as a metaphor captures these aspects of control and tragedy, which is not to say that others may not do just as well. But a metaphor that lacks these features will leave us ill-equipped to confront current and future realities.

7. GROWING UP IS NOT THE ONLY OPTION

As suggested at the outset, the decisions we make at this crossroads in our relationship with the planet will depend on our values, our conception of ourselves, and the role we would like to play. They also depend on our sense of the ontology of the planet (which itself is a matter of background values). What is the planet? If viewed as an endlessly malleable resource, which, when we apply our dazzling ingenuity to it, can yield ever increasing wealth for humans, then the choice to address climate change by reducing emissions is not at all obvious. This view of the planet, which is the one that underlies the logic both of consumer capitalism and its supporting academic disciplines, including welfare economics and rational choice theories generally,[50] lends itself to skepticism about whether it is worth it economically to change our consumption patterns and energy infrastructure. This skepticism has two components. First, we are likely to fail to rein in emissions enough to avoid dramatic effects from climate change anyway. Second, we may be able to engineer our way out of the gravest difficulty.[51]

If, on the other hand, the planet is viewed as a bounded system with resources that are by definition limited, and further that there is beauty, meaning, and value in the way the Earth's flora and fauna (including the human fauna) interact, then putting that same dazzling human ingenuity to work to place humanity within, rather than above, the rest of the planet has greater appeal. At bottom, many of the disputes about how much mitigation (i.e., emissions reduction) to do to address climate change, versus how much to rely on geo-engineering, sequestration, and other technology-only fixes, come down to this difference in views about the world. Accompanying these different senses of the Earth's ontology are different outlooks on the human experience. If the Earth is a small, limited system that landed, for whatever set of reasons (and senses of this vary depending on religious and metaphysical orientation), in our hands, then part of being human is to care for it. If the Earth is, like Mary Poppins' magical bag, a source of endless material for satisfaction of human needs, then the predominant human mission is to exercise our powers to extract use out of that material.

Global warming may nudge more people to see the Earth as a bounded system, but it is not automatic that it will do so. The facts about global warming, like the facts about almost anything, can play a role in shaping values and worldviews, but they can also be slotted into pre-existing frames.[52] Further, there is a point at which the facts simply run out. Will geo-engineering solutions, such as spraying particulate matter into the stratosphere or seeding the ocean with iron to grow more algae,[53] work seamlessly, with no down-side effects on ecosystems or even human health? We may have factually based reasons to have serious doubts, but we do not know for certain, which is why we rely on background values to adopt rules of decision. For those in the "Earth as bounded system" camp, the rules that tend to rein in actions with potentially harmful, even if uncertain, effects on natural systems are preferred. For those in the "Earth as malleable resource" account, some version of cost-benefit analysis, with discounts for future generations, is the preferred rule. The rules we adopt are based ultimately on our sense of ourselves and how we want to spend our time here on earth, which brings us back to the metaphor of developmental stages. According to Erikson's account, the central virtues of childhood include hope, will, purpose, and competence.[54] These virtues seem eerily resonant with the view of the Earth as an infinitely malleable resource: "In the individual here and now [an exclusive condition of hopefulness] would mean a *maladaptive optimism.* For true hope leads inexorably into conflicts between the rapidly developing self-will and the will of others from which the rudiments of will must emerge."[55] Will, purpose, and competence, like hope, provide the necessary groundwork for mastering the world. What is lacking in these virtues, however, is a quality of sustaining love or obligation, as well as a sense of balancing one's own assertions of will with the world's many limitations. Those virtues arise later, first in adolescence, with fidelity, and then in adulthood, when, if the cultural and ideological framework is there to reinforce them, the virtues of care, love, and wisdom come to the fore.[56] The adult virtues build on each other, adding dimensions of obligation and widening concern.[57] Love "pervades the intimacy of individuals and is thus the basis of ethical concern," but can also become "a joint selfishness in the service of some territoriality, be it bed or home, village or country."[58] Care, then, extends beyond this potential for mutual narcissism. According to Erikson,

Care is a quality essential for psychosocial evolution, for we are the teaching species. Only man . . . can and must extend his solicitude over the long, parallel and overlapping childhoods of numerous offspring united in households and communities. As he transmits the rudiments of hope, will, purpose, and competence . . . he conveys a logic much beyond the literal meaning of the words he teaches, and he gradually outlines a particular world image and style of fellowship. All of this is necessary to complete in man the analogy to the basic, ethological situation between parent animal and young animal . . . Once we have grasped this interlocking of human life stages, we understand that adult man is so constituted as to *need to be needed* lest he suffer the mental deformation of self-absorption, in which he becomes his own infant and pet.[59]

Displacement of the self by taking on the care of others is the key to moving beyond the "mental deformation of self-absorption." To carry this to the species and planetary level, perhaps now is the moment when humanity must choose either to remain static, suspended in a state of self-love, or to move on to a stage of caring for the planet we live on and the many lives, human and otherwise, that it sustains. Finally, of wisdom, Erikson has this to say:

For if there is any responsibility in the cycle of life it must be that one generation owes the next that strength by which it can come to face ultimate concerns in its own way—unmarred by debilitating poverty or by the neurotic concerns caused by emotional exploitation.[60]

Wisdom, which is the knowledge accumulated over a lifetime of reflecting on the human condition, enables the broadest view of human responsibility. Wisdom entails an acceptance of one's own decline and mortality while seeing the needs of the coming generations.[61] "Wisdom, then, is detached concern with life itself, in the face of death itself."[62] Wisdom, like climate change, has a tragic structure. It may take a virtue wrought from tragic circumstances to match a structurally tragic commons problem.

These virtues—love, care, and wisdom—are the grown-up ones. They are the virtues necessary to accept a role of care-taking, of reducing our own demands on the Earth in order to cultivate the conditions for *all* human communities, in company with other species, to make their way.

We may not be entering a stage in which these virtues predominate. We may, as a world community, be too entrenched, too dispersed, and too path-dependent on the dominant technological frames to make the leap. Whether, as a whole, we are making that transition or not, certain factions of humanity, including but not limited to the ones described above, already are. And it may well be that these factions become the subcultures from which the rest of the world will have to learn, when and if we reach the bleaker stages of global warming that many scientists predict in the absence of immediate and radical action.[63]

CONCLUSION

Vice President Al Gore has made much of the fact that the Chinese word for *crisis* comprises two characters, the first the symbol for "danger" and the second the symbol for "opportunity."[64] In the film and book, *An Inconvenient Truth,* Gore catalogues the dangers of the "climate crisis," and also outlines the two kinds of opportunity it presents, both practical and moral. As to the latter, Gore writes that what we are presented with is the opportunity "of knowing: *a generational mission;* the exhilaration of a compelling *moral purpose . . . the opportunity to rise.*"[65] In an interesting parallel, Erikson theorizes that the move from one stage of human development to another is prompted by a crisis of personality. According to Erikson,

> Crisis once meant a turning point for better or for worse, a crucial period in which a decisive turn *one way or another* is unavoidable . . . Such crises occur in man's total development sometimes more noisily, as it were, when new instinctual needs meet abrupt prohibitions, sometimes more quietly when new capacities yearn to match new opportunities, and when new aspirations make it more obvious how limited one (as yet) is.[66]

We appear to be experiencing a crisis in this Eriksonian sense of an unavoidable turn. We have put the conditions in motion to alter the atmosphere of the planet in dramatic and pervasive ways. Whether we choose to respond by attempting to match our moral and emotional capacities to these circumstances or

not, our actions will affect the fate of the entire Earth and its future. Another way in which Erikson's version of crisis seems apt is that, in the course of a human life cycle, crises are normal; just part of growing up. It takes a crisis to prompt the transition to the next stage. It is normal, in other words, to confront the limits of a previous frame. Seeing it this way might dampen the fear of judgment that creeps into many discussions about obligations to less well-off human communities and other species. Were we bad and wrong to have emitted greenhouse gases in the way that we did? The question is somewhat irrelevant to figuring out how to react today. The normality of the Eriksonian version of crisis is helpful in one final way. If crises are normal, then we must learn to live with them for the long haul. The global climate crisis, rather than being experienced as a sudden conflagration, will be felt in myriad and dispersed ways, often not viscerally traceable to our emissions patterns. Despite this, the crisis calls for us to respond, one way or another, to the astounding ways in which we have put ourselves in the position, wittingly or not, of parenting the planet.

NOTES

1. Paul Crutzen and Eugene F. Stoermer, "The Anthropocene," *Global Change Newsletter* 41 (2000), 17–18.

2. Robert H. Socolow and Mary R. English, "Living Ethically in a Greenhouse," in *The Ethics of Global Climate Change*, Denis G. Arnold, ed. (New York: Cambridge University Press, 2011).

3. Recent works on virtue-based environmental ethics include Ronald Sandler, *Character and Environment* (New York: Columbia University Press, 2007), and Ronald Sandler and Philip Cafaro, *Environmental Virtue Ethics* (Oxford: Rowman & Littlefield, 2005).

4. Erikson and Erikson, *The Life Cycle Completed,* 12–13 (emphasis in original).

5. Intergovernmental Panel on Climate Change, "Climate Change 2007, the Physical Science Basis, Summary for Policy Makers," 4 (2007), available at www.ipcc.ch. [Hereafter "IPCC PSB Summary 2007."]

6. Ibid. at 3. The authors define "very high confidence" as at least a 90 percent chance. Ibid., n.7.

7. Ibid. at 2.

8. Tim Flannery, *The Weather Makers: How Man Is Changing the Climate and What It Means for Life on Earth* (New York: Atlantic Monthly Press, 2005), 23–4.

9. Ibid. at 39–42.

10. Al Gore, *An Inconvenient Truth: The Planetary Emergency of Global Warming and What We Can Do About It* (New York: Rodale, 2006), 38–39; Flannery, *The Weather Makers,* 24–5.

11. Sharon Begley, "Global Warming Is a Hoax*," *Newsweek* (August 2007).

12. One prominent example is Bjorn Lomborg, *Cool It: The Skeptical Environmentalist's Guide to Global Warming* (New York: Random House, 2007) (advocating some measures to reduce carbon emissions, but claiming that spending too much displaces other social and environmental priorities).

13. See Proposed Final Rule: Endangered and Threatened Wildlife and Plants; Determination of Threatened Status for the Polar Bear (*Ursus maritimus*) Throughout Its Range, 50 C.F.R. Part 17 (May 14, 2008).

14. Erik A. Beever, Peter F. Brussard, and Joel Berger, "Patterns of Apparent Extirpation Among Isolated Populations of Pikas (*Ochotona princeps*) in the Great Basin," *Journal of Mammology* 84, no. 1 (2003), 37–54; Sean F. Morrison and David S. Hik, "Demographic Analysis of a Declining Pika *Ochotona collaris* Population: Linking Survival to Broad-Scale Climate Patterns via Spring Snowmelt Patterns," *Journal of Animal Ecology* 76, no. 5 (2007), 899–907.

15. IPCC, "Climate Change 2007: Climate Change Impacts, Adaptation and Vulnerability," 8.

16. Jonathan Hanna, "Native Communities and Climate Change: Protecting Tribal Resources as Part of National Climate Policy," Natural Resources Law Center Publications, University of Colorado Law School (2007), available at www.colorado.edu/law/centers/nrlc/publications.

17. *Native Village of Kivalina v. ExxonMobil Corp.,* No. 08–1138 (N.D. CA, filed February 27, 2008).

18. Petition to the Inter-American Commission on Human Rights Seeking Relief from Violations Resulting from Global Warming Caused by Acts and Omissions of the United States (2005) (hereafter "Inuit petition").

19. Susan Solomon *et al.,* "Irreversible Climate Change Due to Carbon Dioxide Emissions," *PNAS* 106 (February 10, 2009), 1704–9.

20. Available at www.columbia.edu/-jeh1/2008/TargetCO₂_20080407.pdf.

21. Stephen Pacala and Robert Socolow, "Stabilization Wedges: Solving the Climate Problem for the Next 50 Years with Current Technologies," *Science* 305 (August 13, 2004), 968.

22. James Hansen *et al.,* "Target Atmospheric CO_2: Where Should Humanity Aim?," *The Open Atmospheric Science Journal* 2 (2008), 217–31, www.columbia.edu/-jeh1/2008/TargetCO₂_20080407.pdf.

23. Sarah Krakoff, "Ethical Perspectives on Resources Law and Policy: Global Warming and Our Common Future" in *The Evolution of Natural Resources Law,* Larry Macdonald and Sarah Van de Wetering, eds. (New York: ABA Publications, 2009).

24. Stephen Gardiner, "The Real Tragedy of the Commons," *Philosophy and Public Affairs* 30 (2001), 387.

25. Stephen Gardiner, A Perfect Moral Storm: Climate Change, Intergenerational Ethics and the Problem of Corruption," *Environmental Values* 15 (August 2006), 397.

26. Ibid. at 407–8.

27. For an overview of state and regional initiatives and programs, see www.pewclimate.org/states-regions.

28. California Global Warming Solutions Act, California Health and Safety Code, Div. 25.5 (signed into law on September 27, 2006).

29. Ibid.

30. Portland Online, "A Progress Report on the City of Portland and Multnomah County Local Action Plan on Global Warming," www.portlandonline.com.

31. "The U.S. Conference of Mayors Climate Protection Page," www.usmayors.org.

32. Inuit petition.

33. Ibid., 9.

34. Ibid., 48–9 (describing cultural loss, including passing on to future generations how to build an igloo).

35. Ibid., 212 (describing effects on seal pups and polar bears); 47 (describing effects on caribou); 4–5 ("For Inuit, warming is likely to disrupt or even destroy their hunting and food sharing culture as reduced sea ice causes the animals on which they depend on to decline, become less accessible and possibly extinct.") (citation omitted).

36. Evangelical Climate Initiative, "Climate Change: An Evangelical Call to Action."

37. Ibid.

38. Ibid.

39. Discussion Resources and Fact Sheets, available at http://whatwouldjesusdrive.info/intro.php.

40. See CRAG Homepage at www.carbonrationing.org.uk.

41. James Kanter, "Members of New Group in Britain Aim to Offset Their Own Carbon Output," *New York Times,* October 21, 2007.

42. US CRAG Groups, available at www.carbonrationing.org.uk/groups?country=us.

43. Erik H. Erikson, *Insight and Responsibility* (New York: W. W. Norton & Co., 1972.), 115.

44. Sandler, *Character and Environment,* 22.

45. *Lyng v. Northwest Cemetery Ass'n,* 485 U.S. 439, 460 (1988), Brennan, J. dissenting.

46. Juliet Eilperin, "Lawmakers on Hill Seek Consensus on Warming," *Washington Post,* January 31, 2007.

47. Kanter, "Members of New Group in Britain."

48. www.carbonrationing.org.uk/maryland

49. Two fictional renderings of such a world include Cormac McCarthy, *The Road* (New York: Vintage International, 2006), and James Howard Kunstler, *World Made by Hand* (New York: Atlantic Monthly Press, 2008). Both books explore what life might look like after catastrophic global events that eliminate modern technology. In *The Road,* life is reduced to its barest elements, and nearly all animal and plant species have been eliminated, leaving humans to wander the scorched Earth in search of sustenance. Kunstler's version of the post-apocalypse is slightly more familiar. Local flora and fauna have survived in some regions, and though all infrastructure from the energy economy is gone, there are vestiges of technology and engineering from which to build premodern communities.

50. For a good summary and critique of rational choice theories generally, see Michael Taylor, *Rationality and the Ideology of Disconnection* (New York: Cambridge University Press, 2006). For a similarly critical assessment of the modern discipline of economics in particular, see Stephen A. Marglin, *The Dismal Science: How Thinking Like a Scientist Undermines Community* (Cambridge, MA: Harvard University Press, 2008).

51. For different versions of this view, see Alan Carlin, "Why a Different Approach Is Required if Global Climate Change Is to Be Controlled Efficiently or Even at All," *William & Mary Environmental Law & Policy Review* 685 (2008), 32 (arguing that geo-engineering solutions are far preferable to emissions reduction approaches); and Lomborg, *Cool It* (arguing that the costs of mitigation are too high, and that adaptation and poverty relief should instead be the dominant policies).

52. There is a large and growing body of literature on this, including Dan Kahan and Donald Braman,"Cultural Cognition and Public Policy," *Yale Law & Policy Review* 149 (2006), 24.

53. Sid Perkins, "Scientists Work to Put Greenhouse Gas in Its Place," *Science News* 173, no. 16 (May 10, 2008), www.sciencenews.org/view/feature/id/31431 (describing ocean seeding and sequestration possibilities); Philip J. Rasch *et al.,* "Exploring the Geoengineering of Climate Using Stratospheric Sulfate Aerosols: The Role of Particle Size," *Geophysical Research Letters* 35, LO2809 (2008) (exploring spraying aerosols into the stratosphere to block incoming heat radiation).

54. Erikson, *Insight and Responsibility,* 115.

55. Ibid., 118 (emphasis added).

56. Ibid., 131–4.

57. Ibid.

58. Ibid., 130.

59. Ibid., 131.

60. Ibid., 133.

61. Ibid.

62. Ibid.

63. For a survey of the data on the likelihood of cataclysmic effects, see Michael C. MacCracken *et al.* (eds.), *Sudden and Disruptive Climate Change* (London: Earthscan, 2008).

64. See Gore, *An Inconvenient Truth,* 10.

65. Ibid., 11.

66. Erikson, *Insight and Responsibility,* 139 (emphasis in original).

DISCUSSION QUESTIONS

1. Why, according to Krakoff, is it better for us to think about climate change in terms of virtues rather than consequences or obligations?

2. Krakoff describes various "subglobal initiatives" to address climate change and remarks that they "might be described as irrational." Is it appropriate to describe them as "irrational"? Why or why not?

3. Given Krakoff's summary of the effects of climate change, how would people have to change their behavior to exhibit the "adult" or "parental" virtues that Krakoff mentions?

4. Especially when it comes to climate change and other environmental problems, do you think it is helpful and appropriate to think of humanity as "parenting the planet"? Why or why not?

INDEX

Page references followed by a *t* indicate tables; *f* indicate figures.

Abbate, Cheryl, 430–43

Abortion, 103, 139, 485n14; Bassen
on, 328–29; Catholic Church
on, 342n5; contraception and,
329–30; desire account, 326;
discontinuation account, 327;
fetus and, 314, 317–18, 332;
future-like-ours argument,
325–26, 328; Good Samaritan
story and, 339–40, 341;
human definition, 315, 340;
Hursthouse on ethics of, 47;
intermediate moral principle
and, 59; Marquis on immorality of, 143, 320–30; moral and
legal status of, 313–19; moral
community definition, 315–17;
moral generalization and,
322–23; no one may choose
argument, 335; potential
personhood and right to life,
318–19; pregnancy due to rape
and, 333; right to, 314; to save
woman's life, 333–34; slippery
slope argument and, 332;
Stevens on, 328; Thomson on
defense of, 331–41; Tooley on,
328; virtue ethics, 47; wrongness of killing, 323–25. *See
also* Anti-abortion argument

Abrams, Floyd, 395

Abramson, Paul, 271n27, 271n32

Acceptability, of premises, 9–10

Actions: affirmative, in universities,
294–98; being permitted
vs. morally permissible, 16;
caring, 201–3; conformable
to principle of utility, 172;
facing consequences of, 37;
hypothetical, categorical
imperatives and, 166; maxims
and universal law, 166–67;
morally permissible, 15–17,
16*f*; relevantly similar, 69–70;
vices and virtues evaluation
of, 51–53; virtues and, 188–90

Active euthanasia, 352–56

Active voice, in sentences, 148

Actual act principles, of global
warming: contribution
principle, 526; gas principle,
526; harm principle, 524–25;
indirect harm principle,
525–26; risk principle, 526–27

Act utilitarianism, 115–16, 116n5

Ad hominem fallacy, 83

Adventures of Huckleberry Finn
(Twain), 104

"Advertising and Behavior Control"
(Arrington), 29

Aesthetic claims, 17, 18*f*

Affirmative action, in universities,
294; counterfactual argument
from qualifications, 295–96;
intellectual affirmation, 297;
mentor relationships, 296;

role-model argument, 295;
trust and gratitude, 297–98

Affluence, morality, famine and,
508–15

African culture. *See* Akan African
culture

African philosophy, 134–35; on
ethics of caring, 53. *See also
Ubuntu*

African Sahel famine, 498

African values, capital punishment
and, 372–76, 377n15

Agent-relative national particularism, Hurka on, 439–40

Akan African culture: contemporary
problems, 222–23; ethics and
practice, 221–22; humanism,
217–19; on individual responsibilities, 219; introduction
to, 217; kinship and morality,
223–24; maxims of, 219–20,
222; moral foundations of,
216–25; morality defined,
219–20; neighborhood mutual
aid, 222; *onipa na ohia*, 216,
217–18; religion independence
from morality, 218; respect for
age, 225; on social identity,
219–21, 224–25; on Supreme
Being, 218; wealth and, 222

Alcoholics, statistical discrimination
and, 307–8

Alfano, Mark, 50*t*

Allied civilians, 431, 441–42

Allowing to die, justifiable killing and, 499, 501, 502, 503, 504, 506n3

Altruistic motivations, of human beings, 483

American Medical Association (AMA), on euthanasia, 355

American Psychological Association (APA) citation style, 147

Amnesty International, 378

Analects (Confucius), 99, 132

Analogies: Cameron and Hoffenberg on organ donations, 72–73; case studies, 74–75; evolving, 70–71; exaggerated, 72; Godwin's law of Nazi, 72; reasoning by, 67–75; refutation on logical, 73–74; to respond to moral arguments, 72–74. *See also* Argument by analogy

Anderson, Roger, 126

Animals: de-extinction of, 158; global warming effects on, 550–51; nature case studies and, 157–58

Animals, equality of, 468–71, 478–79; desire for self-respect and, 483; Donaghy on intelligence and, 483–84; experimentation on, 157, 473–74, 485, 494, 495; humans' versus animals' ethical status, 492–93; intrinsic worth and dignity, 476; meat eating and, 472–73; philosophy on, 474–76; suffering of, 472–73, 478n7, 481, 483–84, 486–88

Anthropocene age, 546–48, 557

Anti-abortion argument, 321; consequences, 327–28; psychological characteristics of person, 322

Anti-porn feminists (APF): causes discovery, 264–67; gender inequality, 253–54, 269n2, 269n8, 273n55; harm hypothesis, 253–56, 267f; on rape, 255–56, 259, 263, 265; taxonomy of harms, 256–59, 257f; weakening of, 252–53

Anti-porn feminists (APF) causal model, 259, 263–64; determinism in, 260–61; evidence in, 261–62

Anti-Semitism, 276, 289n14

APA. *See* American Psychological Association

APF. *See* Anti-porn feminists

Appealing to ignorance fallacy, 11

Appiah, Kwame Anthony, 275, 279, 288n9, 290n25

Applied ethics, 114

Appraisal respect, 302–6, 311n9

Appreciation respect, 303–6, 309, 310, 311n9, 311n10

Aquinas, Thomas, 127, 512; on virtues, 49; virtues and vices list, 50t

Archard, David, 249n28

Argument analysis, 5, 8, 325

Argument by analogy: Carr on bluffing in business, 69–70; comparisons, 70; evaluation of, 68–70; relevantly similar actions, 69–70; Singer on drowning child, 70–71, 71n2, 509, 516–18; structure of, 67–68

Argument evaluation, 8; cogency, soundness and validity, 12–13, 12f, 80; premise acceptability, 9–10; relevance, 10; sufficiency, 11

Arguments, 2, 9–13; Aristotle and, 7–8; brainstorming, 81–82; claims in, 3, 7; conclusion of, 3, 325; for cultural relativism, 100; ethics paper well-developed, 142–43; explanations vs., 4; goal for, 4; for and against identification, in moral questions method, 81–82, 86–88; for moral skepticism, 92, 93, 95; numbered list of premises and claims for, 3; objections identified and evaluated, 82–85, 88; structures, 6–8; understanding, 5–8

Arguments, moral: abortion and, 325–26, 328, 332, 335;

analogies to respond to, 72–74; animals and, 482–83; anti-abortion, 321–22, 327–28; capital punishment and, 373–76; euthanasia and, 358–60; moral claims and, 14–17; nonconsensual sex and, 236–44; physician-assisted suicide and, 346–48

Aristotle, 184; argument of, 7–8; on bravery, 190–91; golden mean and, 49; on happiness, 185–86; on justice and injustice, 191–92; on understanding, 192–93; on virtues, 49, 50, 50f, 187–90

Armstrong, Lance, 67

Arrington, Robert, 29

Asians, bias against, 299, 306, 310n1

Assassination, justification of, 464n27

Assault upon defenseless, in torture, 379–81, 384, 385, 387n6

Audi, Robert, 30t

Audience, premise acceptability and, 9, 10

Awadallah, Osama, 402n26

Axiological claims, 15, 15n2, 17, 17n3, 18f

Aztecs, 100–102, 112–13

Background information, in ethics paper, 140–42

Bakke, Allan, 279

Banton, Michael, 288n6

Baron, Larry, 261–62

Bassen, Paul, 328–29

Battin, Margaret, 113

Beauchamp, T. L., 346–47

Beccaria, Cesare, 363

Bedau, Hugo Adam, 361–62

Begging the question. *See* Circular reasoning

Being permitted, morally permissible actions vs., 16

Belfort, Jordan, 123

Beliefs, moral, 94n3; general beliefs, 102; inconsistency in, 96–97; reflective equilibrium and, 97–98; specific beliefs, 102

Benevolence. *See* Rén

Benign deception, 244–47

Benn, Stanley, 476–77, 481, 482

Bentham, Jeremy, 363, 396, 401n13; cost-benefit analysis of, 40, 394; felicific calculus of, 40, 171, 173–74, 392; on pleasure and pain in moral reasoning, 40, 171, 173–74; on right to equal consideration, 471–72; on torture, 393–94

Bergdahl, Bowe, 153–54

Bias, 300, 310n5

Bisexuals, 311n19

Biting the bullet, 64

Black Liberation movement, 468

Bloomfield, Paul, 458, 465n39

Blue Jasmine, 74–75

Boston Marathon, 2013, 34

Brainstorming arguments, 81–82

Bravery, Aristotle on, 190–91

Brennan, Jason, 52, 363–64

Brighouse, Harry, 60

Broome, John, 535–45

The Brothers Karamazov (Dostoevsky), 111

Brownmiller, Susan, 269n6

Bryant, Jennings, 272n49

Bush, George W., 440

Business: Carr on bluffing in, 69–70; money case studies and, 151–52

Buss, Sarah, 244–45

Callahan, Daniel, 28–29

Cameron, Deborah, 72–73, 260

Cameron, J. Stewart, 72–73

Capital punishment: Beccaria on, 363; Bedau and Radelet on innocence and, 361–62; distribution, 361; equal punishment principle, 367–68; incidental issues, 362–63; justice, excess, degradation in, 363–64, 376; *lex talionis* and, 362–63, 366–71; maldistribution, 361; miscarriages of justice, 361–62, 364n6; Nathanson on morality of, 366–71; objection to, 369–70; payback retributivism, 370–71; proportional retributivism, 368–69;

restitution and, 364n14; van den Haag on, 360–64. *See also* Death penalty

Capital punishment, African values and: communal friendly relationships and, 376, 377n15; community protection, 374; consequentialist arguments, 373–74; deadly force compared to, 373; degradation, 363–64, 376; dignity-based argument, 375–76; extant dignity-based arguments, 374–75; morally unjustified, 372; objections to, 373

Carbon Rationing Action Groups (CRAGS), 555, 556

Care ethics, 130–31, 193, 200–203; military and, 437; principles skepticism, 194–97; relationships, 197–99; Sevenhuijsen on, 195; virtue ethics compared to, 195–96; in Western, Chinese and African philosophies, 53

Caring: executive, 52–53; in interpersonal relationships, 131; virtue of, 52–53, 131

Caring actions: caring attitudes compared to, 201; intentions and, 201–2; moral value of, 202–3

Caring attitudes: caring actions compared to, 201; instrumental and non-instrumental value, 200; moral value of, 199–200; needs fulfillment for, 200; responsibilities for, 201; Slote and Held on, 199; type-token distinction, 199

Carr, Albert, 69–70

Case studies: for analogies, 74–75; animals and nature, 157–58; business and money, 151–52; for consequences, 45; for counterexamples, 65–66; crime and punishment, 154; film and fiction, 154–55; medicine and biotechnology, 158–59; for moral obligations, 34; for moral reasoning, 103–4; for normative theories,

125–26; for principles, 65–66; for religion, 112–13; technology, 155–56; war and peace, 152–54

Cassidy, R. Michael, 54

Casual sex, 231

Categorical imperatives, 119, 166; Formula of End-in-Itself, 121–22, 167–69, 170n9; Formula of Humanity, 121–22, 167–69, 170n2, 170n9, 382

Catholic tradition: on abortion, 342n5; natural law theory and, 127

Causal impotence claim, for factory farms, 488–89

Causal standards criteria, in epidemiological studies, 266–67

CDM. *See* Clean Development Mechanism

Central Intelligence Agency (CIA), targeted killings by, 456

Ceteris paribus clause. *See* Other things being equal clause

Charitable acts, 511, 513

Charity, duty compared to, 511–12

Cheating. *See* College cheating

Cheating Lessons (Lang), 86

The Chicago Manual of Style (Chicago style), 146

Childress, J. F., 346–47

Chinese philosophy: care ethics and, 53; counterexamples in, 61; Mencius on ancient ethics, 63–64. *See also* Mencius

CIA. *See* Central Intelligence Agency

Circular reasoning, 21

Citation of sources, in ethics paper: Chicago and MLA style, 147; footnotes and endnotes, 147, 147n21; management software for, 147

Cities, global warming ethics and, 553–54

Civilian casualties, in war, 430; collateral damage, 431–33, 443n5; DDE, 431–33; institutional policies, values, warrior codes, 443; *jus in bello* and, 431–33, 443n5; military ethic,

434; principle of double intention, 433–34; principle of risk, 433–42

Civilians, 443n1; allied, 431, 441–42; co-nationals protected, 431, 439–40; discrimination restraint for targeting, 432, 443n3; protected vs. unprotected duties to, 438–39; to-be-liberated protected, 431, 440–41, 448n18

Claims: for argument conclusion, 3, 325; factory farms causal impotence, 488–89; numbered list for, 3, 7, 11; relationships between, 18f; sexual consent fraudulent, 250n32; support of, 3

Claims, moral: axiological, 15, 15n2, 17, 17n3, 18f; deontic, 15, 15n2, 18f; moral arguments and, 14–17

Clarke, Judy, 34

Clean Development Mechanism (CDM), 544–45

Climate change, 142, 144; private morality and, 535–45; problems from global warming, 522

Coercion, 227, 235

Cogency, 12–13, 12f, 80

Cognitive dissonance, for UAVs operators, 455–56, 464n25

Cohen, Carl, 493, 494, 496

Cohen, Sheldon, 442, 493

Coleman, Stephen, 437

Collateral damage, in war, 431–33, 443n5

Collective moral obligations, 522–23

Collective principles, of global warming: group principle, 529–30; ideal law principle, 528–29

College cheating example, of moral questions, 76, 85–89

Collins, Stephanie, 193–203

Combat, unjust asymmetry, from UAVs, 457–59

Combatants, in war: just, 379, 387n3, 414–15; unjust, 416–18, 422–24

Combs, Justin, 45

Commanders, in decision-making, 442–43

Commission for Racial Equality, Britain, 288n5

Commission on Obscenity and Pornography, U.S., 272n47

Commodity pricing case, in Lifeboat Earth, 504–5

Communal friendly relationships, African values and, 376, 377n15

Communications view, in deception and sex, 234, 247n5

Community: African values of protection, 374; interest of, 172; LGBT, 299; moral, 315–17; non-governmental, global warming efforts, 554–56; relationships within social, 197–98

Comparisons, argument by analogy and, 70

Compassion, Mencius on, 209

Co-national protected civilians, 431, 439–40

"The Concept of Social Justice" (Frankena), 475

Concluding section, in ethics paper, 145

Conclusion: of argument, 3, 325; argument analysis identification of, 5; claim for, 3; final, in moral questions method, 85, 89; indicators, 5, 6–7

Conduct of war. *See Jus in bello*

Confirmation bias, 77–78

Confounding, in epidemiological studies, 273n56

Confucian ethics, 132–33, 205–15

Confucius, 98, 99

Congenital defects, euthanasia and, 353–54

Consent Explanation, in sexual consent, 236–38

Consequences: acts and rules, 43–44; case studies, 45; comparing, 36, 37–38; counterintuitive, 62; euthanasia legal, 356; facing of actions, 37; measuring, 36, 38–40; other

things being equal clause, 36; reasoning with, 35–46; uncertainty, 36, 41–43

Consequentialism, 36, 48; act utilitarianism, 115–16, 116n5; on capital punishment, 373–74; natural law theory compared to, 128; Railton and, 117; rule utilitarianism, 116–17, 116n5; variations of, 117

Consistency, reflective equilibrium and, 96–98

Constitution amendments, U.S., on torture, 390

Contraception, 329–30

Contractarianism, 129–30

Contractualism, 129–30

Contractualist principle, of global warming, 531–32

Contribution principle, of global warming, 526

Cook, Martin, 454

Cortés, Hernán, 100–102

Cost-benefit analysis, of Bentham, 40, 394

Cottingham, John, 289n16

Counterexamples: case studies, 65–66; eye for an eye, 60–61, 62, 366–67; Foot responding to, 63; reasoning and, 57–66, 165–66; responding to, 63–64; thought experiments and, 60–63

Counterfactual argument from qualifications, 295–96

Counterfactual principles, of global warming: contractualist principle, 531–32; general action principle, 530; general permission principle, 530; public permission principle, 530–31

Counterintuitive consequences, 62

CRAGS. *See* Carbon Rationing Action Groups

Crime and punishment case studies, 154

Criminal activity, Walzer on self-defense and, 416

CRISPR cell editing, 159

Crutzen, Paul, 546

Culpability, 234, 235, 244–47, 423

Cultural relativism: arguments for, 100; descriptive, 98; normative, 98–99, 100; relativistic pattern in, 100–101; slavery and, 101, 102

Cybersecurity in cars, 156

Dall-Leighton, Josh, 136

The Dark Knight, 125–26

Darwall, Stephen, 302–3

DDE. *See* Doctrine of double effect

Deadly force, African values and, 373

Death penalty: Brennan on, 363–64; deterrence and, 21–22, 362, 364n16, 374; *Woodson v. North Carolina* on mandatory, 271n8

Deaths: in East Bengal, 508–10; famine, 505–6; foreign investment and standards of living, 503–4

Deception, sex and, 251n52; benign, 244–47; communications view, 234, 247n5; deceitful seduction, 234–35; Feinberg on, 249n29; Gardner and Shute on, 237; Harm Explanation, 249n24; infringement of rights and, 248n14; interest and will theories, 248n15; Larson on sexual fraud, 250n34; legal issue of, 247n3; Lenient thesis, 234, 238–41, 245, 246, 248n7; Perkins on, 249n29; promises and, 247n4; Schulhofer on laws and, 248n9, 249n29, 250n33; sexually transmitted disease disclosure, 247n2; spousal impersonation, 249n26; Wertheimer on, 234, 235, 237, 247n3, 248n7, 248n9

De-extinction, of animals, 158

Defensive force, in war, 415–16; liability criteria in, 422–24

Degradation: capital punishment and, 363–64, 376; torture and, 387n4

De jure racial segregation, 279–80

Deliberation, 194–96

Deontic claims, 15, 15n2, 16*f*

Deontological constraints, 36

Deontology, 27, 82, 117; Kantian, 119–22, 120n11, 288n9, 376; Rossian, 118, 118n8; virtues, axiology and, 46–48

Dependency principle, of Collins, 196

Dershowitz, Alan, 389–400

Descriptive claims, 17–18, 18*f*

Descriptive cultural relativism, 98

Desire account, abortion and, 326

Destruction, laws of war and minimization of, 379–80

Deterrence, death penalty and, 21–22, 362, 364n16, 374

Dignity-based argument, capital punishment and, 375–76

Discontinuation account, abortion and, 327

Discrimination: alcoholics statistical, 307–8; *de jure* racial segregation, 279–80; Jencks on, 279; requirement in war, 420–22, 423, 425, 428n4; restraint, for targeting civilians, 432, 443n3; statistical, 306–7; unconscious, 280; women employment, 269n5, 296

Divine command theory, 111

Doctors Without Borders, 152

Doctrine of double effect (DDE), 59, 430; conditions for, 432; factory farms and, 490; on global warming, 527; intending and foreseeing in, 490; *jus in bello* and, 443n6; military necessity, 432; *no means mala in se*, 432; proportionality, 432; Walzer revision of, 431, 433–34

Dolphin hunting, 104

Donaghy, Kevin, 483–84

Doping, defense of, 67–68

Dostoevsky, Fyodor, 111

Dotcom, Kim, 152

Dougherty, Tom, 78, 140, 143, 233–47

Douglass, Frederick, 101, 102, 296–97

Dray, Rinat, 158

Drones. *See* Uninhabited aerial vehicles

Drowning child analogy, of Singer, 70–71, 71n2, 509, 516–18

Duty: charity compared to, 511–12; good will and, 165; imperatives, 166, 511; morality and, 198, 511, 516–17; in physician-assisted suicide, 346; preservation of life, 165; protected vs. unprotected, to civilians, 438–39; proximity and, 517–20; utilitarianism and rule of, 179

Duva-Rodriguez, Tatiana, 154

East Bengal, deaths in, 508–10

Eaton, Anne W., 252–69

Ecologic fallacy, 262

Education, equality of opportunity in, 303, 310

"Egalitarianism and Equal Consideration of Interests" (Benn), 476–77

Egypt, interrogational torture in, 391

Elgin marbles, 66

Elonis, Anthony, 156

Employment: equality of opportunity in, 303, 310; women discrimination in, 269n5, 296

End-in-itself, in Kant Formula of Humanity, 121–22, 167–69, 170n9

End-in-itself formulation, 121–22, 167–69, 170n9

Endnotes, 147

English system, of torture, 398

Engster, Daniel, 196

Enron fraudulent accounting practices, 151

EOD. *See* Explosive ordnance disposal

Epicureans, 175–76

Epidemiological studies, 264–65; causal standards criteria, 266–67

Epidemiology Kept Simple, 273n53

Epistemological claims, 17, 18*f*

Equal consideration: Bentham on right to, 471–72; for mentally deficient, 476–77; Wasserstrom on, 380

Equality: of opportunity, 303, 305, 310; retributivism, 366–69;

speciesism and, 479–85. *See also* Animals, equality of; Gender inequality

Equal punishment principle, for capital punishment, 367–68

Erikson, Erik, 548–49, 556

Estes, Yolanda, 78, 226–33

Ethical cultivation, Mencius on, 214–15

Ethical obligation, for UAVs use, 448–52

Ethics of care. *See* Care ethics

Ethics paper: background information, 140–42; citation of sources, 147; concluding section, 145; goals of, 138–39; introduction writing, 139–40; key terms definition, 140–42; objections explanation, 143–45; paraphrasing, 145–46; plagiarism, 145–46; quotations, 145–46; stylish academic writing, 148–49; well-developed argument, 142–43

Ethnic cleansing, 375

Eudaimonia (happiness), 123, 184

Euthanasia, 141, 158–59, 347; active and passive, 352–56; AMA on, 355; argument from nature, 358; argument from practical effect, 359–60; argument from self-interest, 358–59; Callahan on, 28–29; congenital defects and, 353–54; defined, 344, 357; Down's Syndrome and, 353, 354; Gay-Williams on wrongfulness of, 357–59; legal consequences of, 356; Marquis on, 64; patient pain and, 348, 353; Quinlan and, 357; Rachels on, 61; slippery slope argument on, 359. *See also* Physician-assisted suicide

Euthyphro (Plato), 111

Evaluation. *See* Argument evaluation

Evaluative claims. *See* Normative claims

Evangelical climate community global warming efforts, 554–55

Excess, capital punishment and, 363–64, 376

Exclusionary preference, of racial looksism, 300–301, 306, 308–9

Executive caring, 52–53

Expected value, 41–42, 42n5

Expediency, utilitarianism and, 180–83

Experimentation, on animals, 157, 473–74, 485, 494, 495

Explanations, arguments vs., 4

Explosive ordnance disposal (EOD) technician, 451, 455

Expressivism, 94n3

Extant dignity-based arguments, for capital punishment: ethnic cleansing, 375; Òkè on, 374–75; pacifism, 375

Extrinsic racism, 279

Eye for an eye counterexample, 60–61, 62, 366–67

Facebook, 75, 156

FaceFirst, 155–56

Facing consequences of actions, 37

Factory farms: animal suffering in, 486–88; causal impotence claim, 488–89; consumer unaware of animal treatment in, 488; DDE and, 490; eating meat from, 486–97; humans' versus animal's ethical status, 492–93; marginal cases and, 493–95; meat-free diets and, 486–89; *modus ponens* and *modus tollens*, 491–92; moral agent and moral patient, 495–97; rationality moral relevance, 495–97; reciprocity and, 497; Rossi and Garner on, 95–96

Fallacies: *ad hominem*, 83; appealing to ignorance, 11; circular reasoning, 21; ecologic, 262; of equivocation, 80; is/ought, 19, 19n4, 20; naturalistic, 19n4; objections and, 85; slippery slope, 38; strawman, 83; wishful thinking, 11

False promises, for sexual consent, 250n31

Family planning, 292n40

Famines, 515n2; affluence and morality, 507–15; African Sahel, 498; deaths, 505–6; moral obligation for relief of, 525, 533n14; policies and prefamine policies, 506; Singer on, 506n2, 507–15

Feinberg, Joel, 249n29, 250n35, 267

Felicific calculus, of Bentham, 40, 171, 173–74, 392

Fetus: abortion and, 314, 317–18, 332; human beings definition and, 315, 340; Noonan on classification of, 315, 492; personhood criteria, 316–17

Filial piety, Mencius on, 212, 215n4

Film and fiction case studies, 154–55

Final conclusion, in moral questions method, 85, 89

Finnis, John, 128

Fleury, J. G., 439, 441

Flew, Antony, 275, 285–87, 288n5, 292n43

FM. *See U.S. Field Manual*

Fondness of wealth, Mencius on, 208–9, 215n3

Foot, Philippa, 63

Footnotes, 147, 147n21

Foreign investment, death and standards of living, 503–4

Forfeiture of rights, 250n38

Formula of End-in-Itself formula, of Kant, 121–22, 167–69, 170n9

Formula of Humanity, of Kant, 170n2; end-in-itself, 121–22, 167–69, 170n9; merely as a means, 121–22, 167–69, 382

Formula of Kingdom of Ends, of Kant, 168, 169, 170n11

Formula of Law of Nature, of Kant, 166, 170n3

Formula of Universal Law, of Kant, 120–21, 120n11, 166–69, 170n2

Fossil fuels, global warming from, 522

Frankena, William, 475

Fraudulent claims, for sexual consent, 250n32

Frazer, Elizabeth, 260

Frey, R. G., 495

Future-like-ours argument, abortion and, 325–26, 328

Future of value, Marquis on, 58–59, 62, 64

Garcia, J. L. A., 274–88

Gardiner, Stephen, 552

Gardner, John, 237

Garner, Samual, 95–96

Garry, Ann, 31–32

Gas principle, of global warming, 526

Gates, H. L., 286

Gay-Williams, J., 357–59

Gaza Strip, 153

Gender hierarchy, Taslitz on, 270n13

Gender inequality, 253–55, 267, 269n2, 269n7, 269n8, 270n11, 273n55

General action principle, of global warming, 530

General beliefs, 102

General permission principle, of global warming, 530

Genetic screening, 57, 57n1

Geneva Convention Against Torture, 390, 391

Gert, Bernard, 30t

Get Hard, 155

Gilligan, Carol, 194

The Girl with the Dragon Tattoo, 155

Globalization, morality impacted by, 509

Global relationships, 198

Global warming, 546; actual act principles on, 524–27; assumptions on, 521–22; climate change problems from, 522; collective principle on, 528–30; costs to mitigate, 522; counterfactual principles, 530–32; effects on animals and poor countries, 550–51; facts, 549–50; from fossil fuels, 522; government moral obligation to mitigate, 522, 533n9; internal principle on, 527–28; lack of prevention of, 522; poor countries impact

from, 522; problem of, 522–23; Sinnott-Armstrong on, 521–33; theory of, 550; virtues and practices, 555–57; wealthy governments mitigation of, 522. *See also* Climate change; Greenhouse emissions

Global warming ethics: in cities, 553–54; non-governmental community efforts, 554–55; in U.S. States and regions, 553

Global warming structure: spatial dispersion, 552–53; temporal lags, 551–52

Goals, 4; of ethics paper, 138–39; torture intimidation, 381–82

God: morality and knowledge of, 129; utilitarianism and, 179–80

Godwin's law of Nazi analogies, 72

Golden mean, 49

Goldman, Alan, 311n10

Gomberg, Paul, 290n25

Good: effects pursuit, in wars, 418–19, 431–32; as honor, 185–86; knowledge of, 185; political science and, 185; seeking after, 184

Goodman, Alan H., 301

Goodness. *See Rén*

Good Samaritan story, abortion and, 339–40, 341

Good things pursuit and bad things avoidance principle, 128

Good will, 289n18; duty and, 165; Kant on, 164–65; *Ubuntu* shared identity and, 135

Gore, Al, 599

Governments: charitable acts responsibility, 513; global warming mitigated by wealthy, 522; greenhouse emissions complications from, 539–40; measure of, 172; moral obligation for global warming, 522, 533n9

Greatest Happiness Principle, 175–78

Greenhouse emissions, 535; government actions complications on, 539–40; harm from,

536–38; Hiller undercutting objection on, 84; Krakoff rebutting objection on, 83–84; Nordhaus on, 536; offsetting, 541–45; Sinnott-Armstrong on, 83; *The Stern Review* on, 536; unjustness of, 538–39

Greenpeace, offsetting objection by, 542–43, 545

Grounding for the Metaphysics of Morals (Kant), 164–70

Group harms, 270n15

Group principle, of global warming, 529–30

Group sex, 231

Guan Yu, 153

H5N1 flu virus, 75

Hacking, Ian, 270n10

Han dynasty, 153

Hansen, James, 552

Happiness: Aristotle on, 185–86; Greatest Happiness Principle, 175–78; justice and, 181; pleasure and, 176–77, 176–78; sacrifice of personal, 178–79; short- and long-term effect on, 40; virtue and, 178–79. *See also Eudaimonia*

Happiness calculus. *See* Felicific calculus

Harlan, John Marshall, 26, 26n2

Harm: explanation, of sexual consent, 237, 249n24; from greenhouse emissions, 536–38

Harman, Gilbert, 62

Harm hypothesis, APF and: objections and problems, 267–68; pornography consumers cause and effects, 256–58; pornography feedback efforts, 267f; public manifestation causes, 258; public manifestation effects, 258–59; subordination of women, 253–54; unequal relations erotic appeal, 254

Harm principle, for global warming, 524–25

Harsanyi, John, 44

Hart, H. L. A., 481

Hate speech, 280, 291n27
Hauser, Daniel, 75
Hauser, Jacques, 125
Hayashi, Haruo, 271n27, 271n32
Held, Virginia, 195, 199
Heymann, Philip, 402n27
Heyward, Bryant, 66
Hidden premise, 20–22
Hiller, Avram, 84
Hiring process: based on race, sex, 311n10; women and minorities disfavored in, 269n5, 296
Hitler, Adolf, 72
HIV/AIDS, 152
Hobbes, Thomas, 129
Hoffenberg, Raymond, 72–73
Holroyd, J., 310n6
Homophobia, 276, 289n13
Homosexuality, 308
Hook, Sidney, 311n19
Horwitz, Don, 53
Hui (king), 206
Human beings: altruistic motivations of, 483; animals' ethical status compared to, 492–93; fetus definition and, 315, 340
Human dignity and worth, 475–76
Human inequalities, Benn on, 476–77
Humanism, in Akan African culture, 217–19
Human nature: Mencius on, 209–10, 213–14, 215n7; moral law from, 128
Human-ness. See Ubuntu
Human psychological development, of Erikson, 548–49
Human value. See Onipa na ohia
Hume, David, 20, 43
Hume's Law, of is/ought fallacy, 19, 19n4, 20
Huntington, Samuel, 435
Hurka, Thomas, 439–40
Hursthouse, Rosalind, 47
Hypothetical imperative, 119, 166

IAWs. See Independent autonomous weapons
Ideal law principle, of global warming, 529

Identification: argument analysis, 5; in moral questions method, 79–88; of values and vices, 49–51
If, then statements, for principles, 194
Immorality: of abortion, Marquis on, 143, 320–30; of racism, 276–77, 279–80; of torture, Shue on, 35–36
Imperatives: of duty, 166, 511; hypothetical, 119, 166; maxims and, 165–66, 170n1. See also Categorical imperatives
Imperfect obligations, 170n7, 170n8, 182, 534n19; perfect vs., 33, 170n4
Implicit bias, 310n6
Inclinations, universal law and, 167–68, 170n4
Inconsistent beliefs, 96–97
An Inconvenient Truth (Gore), 559
Independent autonomous weapons (IAWs), UAVs move toward, 452–53, 464n17, 464n19
Indirect harm principle, of global warming, 525–26
Individual moral obligations, 522–23
Individual racism, 277–78
Individual tendency, 311n17
Information gathering, in moral questions method, 77–78
Informative principles, 196
Infringement of rights, 236, 248n14
Inglorious Basterds, 45
Ingraham v. Wright, 400n5
In Harms Way (MacKinnon and Dworkin), 271n43
Injury-based view, 311n18
Innocent threat, 64, 373, 490, 501, 506n1
Institutional obligations, unjust combatants and, 416–17
Institutional racism, 277–78, 283–387
Intellectual affirmation, 297
Intentions, caring actions and, 201–2
Intentions thesis, 241–43
Interest of community, 172
Interest theories, 248n15

Intergovernmental Panel on Climate Change (IPCC), 521
Intermediate moral principles: abortion and, 59; Brighouse and Swift on, 60; Marquis on future of value, 58–59, 62, 64. See also Doctrine of double effect
Internal principles, of global warming: DDE, 527; means principle, 527; universalizability principle, 527; virtue principle, 527–28
International law, torture condemnation, 378, 387n6, 411
Internet, 138
Interrogational torture, 382, 385, 410–12; in Egypt, 391; escape possibility through, 383–84
Intrinsic dignity, 476, 482
Intrinsic speciesism, of Appiah, 290n25
Intrinsic worth, 476, 482
Introduction to Principles of Morals and Legislation (Bentham), 40, 171–74
Introduction writing, in ethics paper, 139–40
Intuitions, moral: on global warming, 523; Harman on, 62; Unger on, 517–18
Inuit Circumpolar Conference, 551
Inuit of Arctic Circle, global warming efforts, 554, 556
IPCC. See Intergovernmental Panel on Climate Change
Iran Hostage Crisis, 439
Irreconcilability and inattentiveness, in sexual relationships, 230–31
Irreducible obligations, 118
Is/ought fallacy, 19, 19n4, 20

Jackson, Robert, 399–400
Jacobs, Harriet, 296–97
Japan: pornography in, 271n32; rape in, 261–62, 271n27
Jencks, Christopher, 279
Job recruiting, racism and, 291n37, 294

Johnson, Rebecca, 148
Judgments, moral, 22–23
Jury nullification, 26–27
Jus ad bellum (Resort to war): *jus in bello* dependence with, 418–20; threshold reduction, from UAVs, 459–62
Jus in bello (Conduct of war), 427; collateral damage and, 431–33, 443n5; DDE and, 443n6; *jus ad bellum* dependence with, 418–20; UAVs and, 447, 454–55
Just and Unjust Wars (Walzer), 433
Just combatants, in war, 387n3; torture compared to killing, 379; unjust compared to, 414–15; Walzer on, 414–15
Justice: Aristotle on injustice and, 191–92; capital punishment and, 363–64, 376; miscarriage of, 361–62, 364n6; utility connection with, 181–83
Justifiable killing: allowing to die and, 499, 501, 502, 503, 504, 506n3; on lifeboats, 500–502; right to self-defense, 499–500; unavoidable killings, 499
Justification, 194; of assassination, 464n27; Collins' dependency principle, 196; Engster's principle of subsidiarity, 196; Kittay's principle of social responsibility for care, 196; *Prima facie*, 305; single-case utilitarian, 393, 394
Just war theory, 414–15, 432, 433

Kagan, Shelly, 41–42, 42n5
Kamm, Frances, 519
Kant, Immanuel, 117; on eye for an eye, 366–67; Formula of End-in-Itself formula, 121–22, 167–69, 170n9; Formula of Kingdom of Ends, 168, 169, 170n11; Formula of Law of Nature, 166, 170n3; Formula of Universal Law, 120–21, 120n11, 166–69, 170n2; on good will, 164–65; natural law

theory of, 164–70; on punishment, 366–67, 370, 371n7; on respect for persons, 31–32; on sympathetic feelings, 195, 196; on torture, 394–95
Kantian deontology, 122, 376; categorical imperatives, 119; hypothetical imperatives, 119, 166; maxim, 119–21, 120n11; on moral realism, 288n9
Kaufman, Whitley, 433
Kennedy, Randall, 286
Kevorkian, Jack, 343
Keyes, Alan, 395
Key terms definition, in ethics paper, 140–42
Killings: abortion and wrongness of, 323–25; justifiable, 499–504, 506n3; moral absolutism about, 404–5; pacifism on, 405; physician assisted mercy, 346, 355; targeted, 456–57, 464n27; unavoidable, 499. *See also* Wars, ethics of killing in
King, Martin Luther, Jr., 48–49
Kinship and morality, in Akan African culture, 223–24
Kipling, Rudyard, 282–83, 291n32
Kipnis, Laura, 252, 262
Kirk, Marshall, 276, 289n13
Kittay, Eva Feder, 196
Kivimaki, Julius, 125
Knowledge: of God, 129; of good, 185
Knowlton, Corey, 157–58
Kosovo, Cook on, 454
Krakoff, Sarah, 83–84, 142, 546–61

Landa, Hans, 45
Lang, James, 86
Langbein, John, 397–98
Larson, Jane, 250n34
Law: global warming ideal law principle, 528–29; Godwin's of Nazi analogies, 72; Hume's, of is/ought fallacy, 19, 19n4, 20; international, torture condemnation, 378, 387n6, 411; moral, 18, 128, 169–70; natural law theory, 127–29, 164–70;

rape, 235, 248n8, 250n36; Schulhofer on deception and sex, 248n9, 249n29, 250n33; universal, 166–68, 170n4
Laws of war, 435, 437, 443n6, 444n14; minimizing destruction and, 379–80; morality of war compared to, 426–28; noncombatants attack avoided, 379–81
Lay, Kenneth, 151
Legal reasoning, precedents and analogies in, 68
Lenient thesis, 234, 238–41, 245, 246, 248n7
Leon v. Wainwright, 401n6, 402n29
Lesbian, Gay, Bisexual and Transgender (LGBT) community, 299
"Letter from a Birmingham Jail" (King), 48
Leviathan (Hobbes), 129
Lex talionis (Rule of retaliation), 362–63, 366–71
LGBT. *See* Lesbian, Gay, Bisexual and Transgender
Lĭ (Rites, ritual propriety), 132, 133
Liability criteria, in war defensive force, 422–24
Lichtenberg, Judith, 282–83, 291n28
Lifeboat Earth, 143, 498; claim on earth's resources, 503; commodity pricing case, 504–5; economic policies for, 505; exercise of control on, 502–3; famine deaths, 505–6; first class versus steerage quarters, 502–6; foreign investment situation, 503–4; justifiable killing, 499–500; justifiable killing on lifeboats, 500–502; scarcity situations, 505–6; sufficiency situations, 503–5
"Lifeboat Earth" (Nell), 143
Lincoln, Abraham, 123–24
Lippert-Rasmussen, K., 306, 307
Liu Bei, 153
Lives: of gratification, 185–86; of political activity, 185–86; of study, 186

Loury, Glenn, 284, 290n23
Love one's neighbor as oneself
    principle, 128
Loyalty to fellow comrades, by
    soldiers, 437–38
Lucas, George, 441

MacArthur, Douglas, 413n7
MacKinnon, Catharine, 248n8,
    260–61, 269n3, 269n8, 270n20
Madison, Ashley, 151
Madsen, Hunter, 276, 289n13
Make Your Home Among Strangers,
    154–55
Maldistribution, in capital punish-
    ment, 361
Malik, Jamal, 45
Manipulations, 227, 230
Manipulative advertising, Arrington
    on, 29–30
Manning, Bradley, 152
Marginal cases, 493, 495; Cohen, C.,
    on, 494; Schmidtz on animal
    experimentation, 494; White
    on, 494
Marquis, Don: on abortion immoral-
    ity, 143, 320–30; on eutha-
    nasia, 64; on future of value,
    58–59, 62, 64
Maslow, Abraham, 399
Maxims, 119; of Akan culture,
    219–20, 222; Formula of Uni-
    versal Law, 120–21, 120n11,
    166–69, 170n2; imperatives
    and, 165–66, 170n1; principles
    of, 170
McGregor, Joan, 236, 239, 250n36
McMahan, Jeff, 458; on killing in
    war ethics, 414–28; on torture,
    403–12
Means principle, of global
    warming, 527
Measure of government, 172
Meat eating, 472–73, 486–97
Meat-free diets, animal suffering
    and, 486–89
MEC. *See* Moral equality of
    combatants
Medicine and biotechnology case
    studies, 158–59

Megaupload, 152
Mencius, 132, 205; on ancient
    Chinese etiquette, 63–64;
    on benevolence, 206–15; on
    compassion, 209; counterex-
    amples and, 61, 63; on ethical
    cultivation, 214–15; on filial
    piety, 212, 215n4; on fondness
    of wealth, 208–9, 215n3; on
    human nature, 209–10, 213–
    14, 215n7; on profit, 206; on
    virtues, 49, 206–7, 211, 215n2;
    virtues and vices lists, 50t
Mengzi (Mencius), 205–15
Mentally deficient, 495; equal con-
    sideration for, 476–77; Hart
    and Benn on rights of, 481
Mercy killing, 346, 355
Meredith, James, 279
Merely as a means formulation,
    121–22, 167–69, 382
Metaethics, 94n3
Metz, Thaddeus, 134, 372–76
Miles, Robert, 288n2, 288n8,
    289n10, 290n23
Military ethics, 434, 442; care ethics
    and, 437; Strawser on, 37–38
Military necessity, 432, 435
Mill, John Stuart, 40, 175–83; gender
    inequality by, 255, 269n7,
    269n8, 270n11
Mirandola, Pico della, 475
Miscarriage of justice, 361–62,
    364n6
Les Misérables (Hugo), *prima facie*
    obligation in, 118
Misleading truth, 58
MLA. *See* Modern Language
    Association
Moderate racism, 290n25
Modern Language Association
    (MLA) citation style, 147
Modus ponens and *modus tollens*,
    491–92
Moral absolutisms: about killing,
    404–5; torture and, 404–6
Moral agent, 495–97
Moral arguments. *See*
    Arguments, moral
Moral beliefs. *See* Beliefs, moral

Moral claims. *See* Claims, moral
Moral code, Sidgwick and Urmson
    on, 511–12
Moral community: definition
    of, 315–17; personhood
    criteria, 316–17
Moral courage, Miller on, 436
Moral equality of combatants
    (MEC), 458, 464n21, 465n34
Moral equality of soldiers, Walzer
    on, 414–15
Moral intuitions. *See*
    Intuitions, moral
Morality: Akan African culture
    definition of, 219–20;
    charitable acts, 511, 513;
    climate change and private,
    535–45; duties and, 198, 511,
    516–17; famine and affluence,
    508–15; globalization impact
    on, 509; kinship and, Akan
    African culture on, 223–24;
    knowledge of God and, 129;
    law and, 18; proximity and
    distance refusal, 509, 517; reli-
    gion independence, Akan on,
    218; saving strangers, 515–20;
    social contract creation of,
    129; of war, 429n16
Moral judgments. *See* Judgments,
    moral
Morally bad action, facing conse-
    quences and, 37
Morally indifferent morally permis-
    sible actions, 15–16
Morally obligatory actions, 15, 16
Morally permissible actions: being
    permitted vs., 16; indifferent,
    15–16, 16f; supererogatory, 15,
    16–17, 16f
Morally wrong actions, 15, 16
Moral patient, 495–97
Moral questions. *See* Questions,
    moral
Moral questions method: for and
    against arguments identifica-
    tion, 81–82, 86–88; final
    conclusion, 85, 89; informa-
    tion gathering, 76–78, 86;
    objections identification and

evaluation, 82–85, 88; salient answers identification, 79–80, 86; specific moral question identification, 78–79, 86

Moral reasoning. *See* Reasoning, moral

Moral recognition respect, 302, 304, 305

Moral relativism, cultural relativism and, 98–102

Moral rights. *See* Rights, moral

Moral value: of caring actions, 202–3; of caring attitudes, 199–200

Moro, Aldo, 389

Moussaoui, Zacarias, 392, 399

Multi-track dispositions, virtues as, 54

Münkler, H., 458, 465n38

Murphy, Jeffrie, 234, 250n31

Mutually respectful sexual interaction: coercion and, 227; criteria for, 228–30; manipulations and, 227; reciprocal concern, 228–29; reciprocal consent, 228–29; reciprocal desire, 228–29

"Mutual Respect and Sexual Ethics" (Estes), 78

My Lai massacre, 436

Nagel, Thomas, 415

Nathanson, Stephen, 60–61, 62, 276, 366–71

National Security Strategy, 441; of Bush, 440; of Obama, 440

Native American communities, global warming effects on, 550–51

Naturalistic fallacy, 19n4

Natural law theory, 127, 129; consequentialism compared to, 128; of Kant, 164–70; universal law and, 166

Nazi analogies, 72

Needs fulfillment, 200

Nell, Onora, 298, 498–506

Nguyen, Jimmy, 299

Nguyen, Thao, 112

Nicomachean Ethics (Aristotle), 184–93

Nihilism, moral, 92–94

Noddings, Nel, 195, 196

No means mala in se, 432

Non-aesthetic axiological claims, 17

Non-aggression, Nozick on, 62, 63, 64

Noncombatants: laws of war attack avoided, 379–81; liability in war, 424–26

Nonconsensual sex, 235; chihuahua case argument, 240–41; right-based argument, 236; serious sexual wrongs argument, 236–38; sexual moralism argument, 238–40; substantive account of consent argument, 241–44

Nondoxastic account of racism, 290n20

Non-exclusive sexual relationships, 231

Non-governmental community efforts, on global warming: CRAGS, 555, 556; Evangelical climate community, 554–55; Inuit of Arctic Circle, 554, 556

Nonlethal torture, 389–90, 392–95, 397, 398, 400

Non-moral axiological claims, 17

Nonoptimific behavior, in racism, 288n7

Non-responsible threat, in self-defense, 421–22

Noonan, John, 314, 315, 341n3, 492

No one may choose argument, for abortion, 335

Norcross, Alastair, 486–97

Nordhaus, William, 536

Normative claims: aesthetic, 17; of care ethics, 193–203; deontic, 15, 15n2, 16f; descriptive, 17–18, 18f; epistemological, 17; prudential, 17

Normative cultural relativism, 98–99, 100

Normative ethics, 114

Normative premise, 36, 81

Normative theories, 114, 136; care ethics, 53, 130–31, 193–203, 437; case studies, 125–26;

Confucian ethics, 132–33, 206; consequentialism, 36, 48, 115–17, 116n5, 128, 373–74; contractarianism, 129–30; contractualism, 129–30; deontology, 27, 46–48, 117–22, 118n8, 120n11, 288n9, 376; natural law theory, 127–29, 164–70; *Ubuntu*, 134–35, 375; virtue ethics, 48, 50, 82, 122–24, 178–79, 184, 195–96

"Notes for a Law Lecture" (Lincoln), 123

Nozick, Robert, 62, 63, 64

Nuclear weapons, 466n43

Obama, Barack, 440

Obedience to lawful orders, by soldiers, 435–37, 444n13

Obesity, 311n15

Objectification, 230, 255, 270n14

Objections, 144; to capital punishment, African values and, 373; fallacies and, 85; identification and evaluation, in moral questions method, 82–85, 88; Krakoff rebutting objection to greenhouse emissions, 83–84; racial personal preferences, 306–7; rebutting, 82–84; replies to, 84–85; Sinnott-Armstrong on greenhouse emissions, 83; undercutting, 83, 84

Objections explanation, in ethics paper, 143–45

Objective obligation, subjective obligation vs., 107, 165–66, 170n1

Objectivity, moral, 102–3

Obligations, moral, 26n2, 130; case studies, 34; in famine and affluence, 509, 515n2; for famine relief, 525, 533n14; on global warming, 522–33; of governments to mitigate global warming, 522, 533n9; individual compared to collective, 522–23; irreducible, 118; justice and, 182; perfect vs. imperfect, 33; *prima facie*, 118, 118n8; proximity and, 517–20; reasoning with, 26–34; unorderable, 118

O'Dowd, Ornaith, 195

The Odyssey, 80

O.E.D. See The Oxford English Dictionary

Offsetting, of greenhouse emissions, 541; CDM and, 544–45; Greenpeace object to, 542–43, 545; objections to, 542–45; REDD, 542, 545

Off-the-books approach, to torture, 395–96

Òkè, Moses, 374–75

O'Neill, Onora. *See* Nell, Onora

Onipa na ohia (human value), in Akan African culture, 216, 217–18

Online dating case study, 151

Online dating profiles racial exclusion: appraisal, 302–6, 311n9; appreciation respects, 303–6, 309, 310, 311n9, 311n10; Asians bias in, 299; introduction, 299–300; personal preference, 300; preliminary argument, 300–301; racial looksism as overgeneralization, 301–3; recognition respect, 303–6; response to objections, 306–9

Operation Red Wings, 34

Opinions, moral judgments and, 23

Oration on the Dignity of Man (Mirandola), 475

Oregon, physician-assisted suicide legalization, 343, 346, 347

Oregon National Primate Research Center, 157

Organ donations, Cameron and Hoffenberg on, 72–73

Other things being equal clause, 36

The Oxford English Dictionary (*O.E.D.*), on racism, 274

Pacifism, 375, 405

Pain, in moral reasoning, 40, 173

Palmer, Walter, 156

Paraphrase, in ethics paper, 145–46

Parenting of planet metaphor, 546, 560–61; effects of global warming, 550–51; ethics for, 552–55; facts of global warming, 549–50; growing up, 557–59; stages in, 548–49; structure of global warming, 551–52; virtues and practices in global warming, 555–57

Passive euthanasia, 352–56

Passive voice, in sentence, 148

Payback retributivism, capital punishment and, 370–71

Penney, Heather, 153

Perfect obligations, 170n5, 170n6, 182; imperfect vs., 33, 170n4

Perkins, Rollin, 249n29

Person: Kant on respect for, 31–32; psychological characteristics of, 322

Personhood criteria, for fetus, 316–17

Pettigrew, Thomas, 311n16

Philippines torture case, 390–91, 401n9, 401n11

Philosophy, tips on reading, 162–63

Physician-assisted suicide, 141, 342, 349; arguments against, 347–48; arguments in favor of, 346–47; Beauchamp and Childress on, 346–47; bodily invasion, 345; definitions, 344–46; error and abuse of, 348; legal changes for, 343; life extension capacity improved, 343; mercy killing, 346, 355; Oregon legalization of, 343, 346, 347; patient autonomy and liberty rights, 346, 348; patient pain and, 348, 353; physician beneficent and nonmaleficence duties, 346; physician ethical integrity and, 347–48; by Quill and Kevorkian, 343; state decision for, 343, 344–45. *See also* Euthanasia

Plagiarism, ethics paper and, 145–46

Planetarian stage, 547

Plato, 8, 50

Plaw, Avery, 454

Pleasure: happiness and, 176–77; higher and lower, 177; Mill on, 175–83; in moral reasoning, 40, 173; quality in, 176

Poor countries, global warming impact on, 522, 550–51

Pornography, 154, 300–301; Garry on, 31–32; gender inequality endorsement by, 255; Harm hypothesis, APF and, 256–58, 267f; in Japan, 271n32; MacKinnon on, 269n3; Russell on, 271n43; studies on, 261–62, 272n47, 272n49, 272n50

Posner, Richard, 261

Practical reasoning: good things pursuit and bad things avoidance principle, 128; love one's neighbor as oneself principle, 128; will and, 165

Practical wisdom, 53, 124, 128

Preferences, 310n5; exclusionary, in racial looksism, 300–301, 306, 308–9; not prejudice and, 278–79, 290n23; personal, in racial looksism, 300, 302, 306–7, 310; race-based, 279; sexual, racial looksism and, 308

Pregnancy, due to rape, 333, 337, 338

Premises, 7; acceptability, 9–10; argument analysis identification of, 5; indicators, 5, 6; numbered list for, 3; relevance, 10; sufficiency, 11

Premises, moral, 18; hidden premise, 20–22; Hume's Law, 19–22

Preservation of life, as duty, 165

Prima facie justification, 305

Prima facie obligations, 118, 118n8

Prima facie wrongness, 321, 324–25, 328

Primoratz, Igor, 439

Principle of risk, 433; for commanders in decision-making, 442–43; for soldiers in battlefield, 434–42; Walzer on, 438

Principle of unnecessary risk (PUR), UAVs and, 448–51, 453, 460–61, 463n6, 463n7

Principle of unnecessary waste of scarce resources (PUWSR), 449

Principles: care ethics skepticism about, 194–97; case studies, 65–66; counterintuitive consequences, 62; deliberation and, 194–96; of double intention, 434, 444n16; if, then statements for, 194; informative, 196; intermediate moral, 58–60, 62; justification and, 194–96; moral, 97; overruling of sympathy, 196; reasoning with, 57–66, 165–66; Savulescu on genetic screening, 57, 57n1; of social responsibility, of Kittay, 196; of subsidiarity, of Engster, 196; sympathy compatibility with, 195; of utility, of Bentham, 171–72

Pro-choice argument, 321–22

Profit, Mencius on, 206

Proportionality: DDE and, 432; McMahan on, 465n34

Proportional retributivism, capital punishment and, 368–69

Prosecutors, Cassidy on honest, 54

Prosperity profit, Brennan on, 52

Proximity, moral duty and, 517–20

Prudential claims, 17, 18f

Public permission principle, of global warming, 530–31

Punishment: Kant on, 366–67, 370, 371n7; von Hirsch on, 368–69

PUR. See Principle of unnecessary risk

PUWSR. See Principle of unnecessary waste of scarce resources

A Question of Balance (Nordhaus), 536

Questions, moral, 90; college cheating example, 76, 85–89; specific identification, in moral questions method, 78–79, 86

Quill, Timothy, 343

Quinlan, Karen, 357

Quotations, ethics paper and, 145–46

Rachels, James, 61, 63, 352–56

Racial looksism: Asians, 299, 306, 310n1; exclusionary preference of, 300–301, 306, 308–9; as morally wrong, 300, 307–8; as overgeneralization, 301–3; overgeneralization in, 300; personal preference, 300, 302, 306–7, 310; physical appearance, 301–2, 309; sexual preference and, 308; simple looksism compared to, 305–6

Racial profiling, 306

Racism, 470–71; Appiah on, 275, 279, 288n9, 290n25; Banton on cultural superiority, 288n6; Bentham on, 471; capital punishment and, 361; cases, 282–86; Cottingham on, 289n16; difficulties on view of, 280–82; extrinsic, 279; Gomberg on moderate, 290n25; immorality of, 276–77, 279–80; implications and advantages to, 278–80; individual, 277–78, 282–83; institutional, 277–78, 283–87; job recruiting, 284, 291n37; Kantian moral realism, 288n9; Kiplingesque view of, 282–83; Lichtenberg on White understanding of, 291n28; Miles on, 275, 283–84, 288n2, 288n8, 289n10, 290n23; Nathanson on immorality of, 276; nondoxastic account of, 290n20; nonoptimific behavior, 288n7; preference is not prejudice, 278–79, 290n23; principle of equality violated by, 472; race-based preference, 279; Skillen on, 292n41, 292n43; social oppression, 279; term use, 274, 288n2; view of, 286–87; volitional conception of, 275–78

Radelet, Michael, 361–62

Railton, Peter, 117

Rape, 246, 273n52; APF on, 255–56, 259, 263, 265; in Japan, 261–62, 271n27; laws, 235, 248n8, 250n36; McGregor on, 236; pregnancy due to, 333, 337, 338

Reasoning, 2, 7–8; by analogy, 67–75; with consequences, 35–46; fallacies of circular, 21; legal, 68; with moral obligation, 26–34; practical, 128, 165; with principles and counterexamples, 57–66, 165–66; with virtues and vices, 46–56

Reasoning, moral: Bentham on pleasure and pain in, 40, 171, 173–74; case studies, 103–4; cultural relativism and, 100–102; moral objectivity and, 102–3; religion and, 105–13

Rebuts, 144

Rebutting objection, 82–84, 83n6, 88

Reciprocal concern, 228–29

Reciprocal consent, sexual morality and, 228–29

Reciprocal desire, 228–29

Reciprocity, 497

Recognition respect, 302

REDD. See Reducing Emissions from Deforestation and Forest Degradation

Reducing Emissions from Deforestation and Forest Degradation (REDD), 542, 545

Reflective equilibrium, consistency and, 96–98

Reform Act of 1832, 40

Refutation on logical analogy, Thomson on unprotected sex, 73–74

Relationships: caring in interpersonal relationships, 131; between claims, 18f; communal friendly, African values and, 376, 377n15; Confucian ethics and types of, 133; global, 198; importance claims, 197–98; mentor, in universities, 296; sexual, 230–32; within social community, 197–98; of value, 197, 198–99; weighty duties of, 198

Relativistic pattern, in cultural relativism, 100–102

Relevance, 10n7; of premises, 10

Relevantly similar actions, 69–70

Religion: Akan on morality independence from, 218; case studies, 112–13; diversity of traditions, 106; divine command theory, 111; Euthyphro dilemma, 111; moral reasoning and, 105–13; objective vs. subjective obligation, 107

Remotely Piloted Vehicles (RPVs), 462n3

Rén (Goodness or Benevolence), 132, 206, 210, 211, 215

Reservoir Dogs, 155

Resort to war. *See Jus ad bellum*

Respect-based theories, 311n8

Respect for persons, 33; Garry on pornography, 31–32; Kant on, 31–32, 121–22, 167–69

Responsibility, sexual morality and, 232–33

Restitution, 364n14

Retributivism: equality, 366–69; payback, 370–71; proportional, 368–69

Richards, Frank, 433, 435, 436

Righteousness. *See Yì*

Rights: -based argument, on nonconsensual sex, 236; equality and, 481; forfeiture of, 250n38; of humans compared to animals, 492–93; infringement of, 236, 248n14; interest and will theories on, 248n15; White on animals lack of, 494

Rights, moral, 182

"Rights, Human Rights and Racial Discrimination" (Wasserstrom), 480

Rights theorists, 248n14

Right to equal consideration, Bentham on, 471–72

Right to life, 332–35; fetal development and, 317–18; killing

unjustly, 336–37; potential personhood and, 318–19

Ringling Bros. and Barnum & Bailey circus, 157

Risk principle, of global warming, 526–27

Rites, ritual propriety. *See Lǐ*

Role-based obligations: euthanasia, 28–29; Foot on, 63

Role-model argument, for affirmative action, 295

Romeo and Juliet (Shakespeare), 136

Ross, W. D., 30t, 117

Rossi, John, 95–96

Rossian deontology, 118, 118n8

Rousseau, Jean-Jacques, 384–85

Royles, Christine, 136

RPVs. *See Remotely Piloted Vehicles*

Rukundo, Noela, 154

Rule of retaliation. *See Lex talionis*

Rules, Harsanyi on, 44

Rule utilitarianism, 116–17, 116n5

Russell, Diana, 271n43

Sacrifice, of personal happiness, 178–79

Sadler, Brooke, 87–88

Sadomasochism, 231–32

Salient answers: identification, in moral questions method, 79–80, 86; reasons for, 80

Sasseville, Marc, 153

Savulescu, Julian, 57, 57n1

Scarcity situations, 505–6

Schmidtz, David, 494

Schulhofer, Stephen, 248n9, 249n29, 250n33

Schuman, Rebecca, 138

Segal, Lynne, 269n9

Self awareness, sexual morality and, 227

Self-defense, 419–20, 428n5; Hobbes on, 415; justifiable killing and, 499–500; non-responsible threat in, 421–22; requirement of discrimination and, 421; Walzer on criminal activity and, 416

September 11, 2001, 143, 292, 389, 395, 396–97

Sevenhuijsen, Selma, 195

"Sex, Lies, and Consent" (Dougherty), 78, 140, 143, 233–47

Sexism, 470–71, 479–80

Sexual appeal, 310n2

Sexual consent: Archard's voluntariness grades, 249n28; Feinberg's voluntariness grades, 250n35; fraudulent claims, 250n32; harm explanation of, 237, 249n24; Murphy on false promises, 250n31; nonconsensual, 235–38; racist prejudice, 251n40; rape laws and, 248n8; reciprocal, 228–29; unconscious people and, 237, 246; Wertheimer on, 234, 235, 237, 247n3, 248n7, 248n9

Sexual fraud, 250n34

Sexual moralism, argument against, 238–40

Sexual morality, 226; coercion and, 227; manipulations, 227, 230; mutually respectful sexual interaction criteria, 228–30; responsibility, 232–33; self awareness, 227; sexual relationships and activities, 230–32

Sexual preference, racial looksism and, 308

Sexual relationships and activities: casual sex, 231; group sex and non-exclusive, 231; irreconcilability and inattentiveness, 230–31; manipulation, 230; mutual respect and, 228; objectification, 230; sadomasochism, 231–32; use of danger or substance, 232

Sexual violence, 262–63, 266, 269n6

Shared identity, social harmony and, 134–35

Shia Islam, 112

Shifting responsibilities, facing consequences and, 37

Shue, Henry, 35–36, 378–86

Shute, Stephen, 237

Sidgwick, Henry, 419, 428n1, 471, 511–12

Silverglate, Harvey, 395

Simola, Sheldene, 53

Simple looksism, 299, 311n15; racial looksism compared to, 305–6

Singer, Peter, 468–78, 579; on drowning child analogy, 70–71, 71n2, 509, 516–18; on famine, 506n2, 507–15; on suffering, 481–82

Single-case utilitarian justification, 393, 394

Sinnott-Armstrong, Walter, 142, 521–33

Skepticism, moral, 92; bad argument for, 93, 95; moral disagreement and, 93

Skillen, Anthony, 285–87, 292n41, 292n43

Slavery, 280–81, 297; cultural relativism and, 101, 102; Douglass on, 101, 102

Slippery slope argument, 38, 453; on abortion, 332; on euthanasia, 359; on torture, 393–94

Slippery slope fallacy, 38

Slote, Michael, 199

Slumdog Millionaire, 45, 114, 124; brothers consequences summary, 115, 115t; maxim and, 120

Social community, relationships within, 197–98

Social conditioning, bias and, 300

Social contract, morality created by, 129

Social deviance class, of Adler, 65–66

Social harmony, shared identity and solidarity, 134–35

Social identity, Akan African culture on, 219–21, 224–25

Socolow, Robert H., 547

Socrates, 8, 50

Soldier's Creed, 441, 444n17

Soldiers in battlefield, principle of risk and, 434, 442; competency demonstration, 436–37; loyalty to fellow comrades, 437–38; moral courage, 436; obedience to lawful orders, 435–37; protected co-nationals civilians, 431, 439–40; protected to-be-liberated civilians, 431, 440–41; protected vs. unprotected duties to civilians, 438–39

Solidarity in ubuntu, social harmony and, 134–35

Soling, Cevin, 87

Soundness, 12–13, 12f

Sparf and Hansen v. U.S., 26, 26n2

Spatial dispersion, in global warming, 552

Speciesism: animal experimentation, 157, 473–74, 485, 494, 495; Cohen, C., defense of, 493; equality and, 479–85; meat eating, 472–73, 474

Specific beliefs, 102

Spires, Jasper, 154

Spousal impersonation, 249n26

Sprinkle, Annie, 252

State of affairs, 36

State of nature, 129

Statistical discrimination, 306; alcoholics and, 307–8; total exclusion in, 307

Steele, Claude M., 302

Steinbock, Bonnie, 479–85, 495, 496

Steinhoff, Uwe, 458, 459, 464n21, 465n38

Stephen, James Fitzjames, 362

The Stern Review, on greenhouse emissions, 536

Stevens, John C., 328

Stoltzfoos, Christ, 136

Strater, Amy, 125

Strawman fallacy, 83

Strawser, Bradley, 37–38, 141, 144, 447–62

Strossen, Nadine, 262–64

Stylish academic writing, ethics paper and, 148–49, 148n22

Subconclusion, 7

The Subjection of Women (Mill), 269n7, 269n8, 270n11

Subjective obligation, objective obligation vs., 107, 165–66, 170n1

Subjectivism, moral, 94, 94n3; Rossi and Garner on factory farms, 95–96; tolerance, 95

Subordination, of women, 253–55

Suffering: of animals, 472–73, 478n7, 481, 483–84, 486–88; Bentham on, 472; Singer on, 481–82, 484; Wasserstrom on human, 480

Sufficiency: of premises, 11; situations, in Lifeboat Earth, 503–5

Sunderland, Abby, 45

Sunni Islam, 112

Supererogatory morally permissible actions, 15, 16–17, 16f

Supreme Being, Akan culture on, 218

Supreme Court of Israel, on torture, 389–90, 395, 401n24

Sutherland, Kevin, 154

Swift, Adam, 60

Sword, Helen, 148–49

Sympathy: deliberation and, 195; Kant on, 195, 196; principles compatibility with, 195; principles overruling of, 196

Targeted killings, 464n27; by CIA, 456; from UAVs, 456–57

Taslitz, Andrew, 270n13

Taylor, Thomas, 469–70

Technology case studies, 155–56

Temporal lags, in global warming, 551–52

Terminal sedation, 345, 347

Termination of life-sustaining treatment, 344, 345, 357–58

Terroristic torture, 381–82, 384–85, 387n11, 387n15, 406–9

Therefore, as conclusion indicator, 6–7

Thesis statement, 140

Thick ethical terms, 48

Thin ethical terms, 48

Thomas, Laurence, 294–98

Thomson, Judith Jarvis, 73–74, 331–41

Thought experiments: counterexamples and, 60–63; Nozick on non-aggression, 62–63; Rachels on euthanasia, 61

Ticking bomb terrorist, 391–94, 406–9, 413n3

Tindall, Daniel, 136

To-be-liberated civilians, 431, 440–41, 444n18

To Kill a Mockingbird, 34

Tolerance, moral subjectivism and, 95

Tooley, Michael, 328

Torture, 387n4, 388n14; appeal to liability, 408; assault upon defenseless, 379–81, 384, 385, 387n6; Bentham and, 393–94; within constraints, 381–82; debate on, 389–91; Dershowitz on, 389–400; English system of, 398; extraction of information by, 381–82; Heymann on, 402n27; history of, 397–99; institutionalisation of, 393; international law condemnation of, 378, 390, 411; interrogational, 382–85, 391, 410–12; intimidation goal, 381–82; just combatants killing compared to, 379; Kant and, 394–95; Keyes on, 395; legal permission to use, 410–12; MacArthur on, 413n7; McMahan on, 403–12; against moral absolutism, 404–6; morally permissible, 384–86; Moussaoui and, 392, 399; nonlethal, 389–90, 392–95, 397, 398, 400; off-the-books approach to, 395–96; Philippine case of, 390–91, 401n9, 401n11; in practice, 410–12; in principle, 406–10; September 11, 2001 and, 389; slippery slope argument on, 393–94; Supreme Court of Israel on, 389–90, 395, 401n24; terroristic, 381–82, 384–85, 387n11, 387n15, 406–9; of ticking bomb terrorist, 391–94, 406–9, 413n3; Twining, W. L., and P. E., on, 393; U.S. Constitutional amendments on, 390, 400n5; victim act of compliance, 381; Voltaire and, 395; warrant requirement, 399

Torture and the Law of Proof (Langbein), 397

Total exclusion, in statistical discrimination, 307

A Treatise of Human Nature (Hume), 20

Triangle Shirtwaist Fire, 151

Tripodi, Paolo, 441

Tronto, Joan, 196

Tropp, Linda, 311n16

The Truman Show, 34

Tsarnaev, Tamerlan, 34

Twain, Mark, 104

Twining, P. E., 393

Twining, W. L., 393

Type-token distinction, of caring attitudes, 199

UAVs. *See* Uninhabited aerial vehicles

Ubuntu (human-ness), 375; shared identity and good will, 135; social harmony, 134–35

Unavoidable killings, 499

Uncertainty, consequences and, 36, 41–43

Unconscious people, sexual consent and, 237, 246

Undercutting objection, 83, 84, 88

Understanding, Aristotle on, 192–93

Unger, Peter, 517–18

UNICEF, 516, 520, 520n1

Uninhabited aerial vehicles (UAVs), 37–38, 141, 144, 156, 462n1, 477n42; Bloomfield on, 458, 465n39; cognitive dissonance for operators of, 455–56, 464n25; cost factor, 449; EOD technicians, 451, 455; ethical obligation for use of, 448–52; IAWs move from, 452–53, 464n17, 474n19; *jus ad bellum* threshold reduction, 459–502; *jus in bello* and, 447, 454–55; Plaw on Pakistan attacks by, 454; PUR and, 448–51, 453, 460–61, 463n6, 463n7; PUWSR and, 449; Singer on, 462n2, 464n14; Steinhoff on, 458, 459, 464n21,

465n38; targeted killing by, 456–57; unjust asymmetry in combat, 457–59

Universalizability principle, of global warming, 527

Universal law, 166–68, 170n4

Universal obligations, 31; Audi, Gert, Ross on, 30t; manipulative advertising, 29–30

Unjust combatants, in war, 418; institutional obligations and, 416–17; just compared to, 414–15; liability criteria, 422–24; moral responsibility, 423–24

Unjustness, of greenhouse emissions, 538–39

Unorderable obligations, 118

Urmson, J. O., 511–12

U.S. Field Manual (FM), 436

U.S. v. Lefkowitz, 403n39

U.S. v. Virginia, 310n7

Utilitarianism, 171, 471; defined, 175–81; Epicureans and, 175–76; expediency and, 180–83; God and, 179–80; Greatest Happiness Principle in, 175–78; justice and utility connection, 181–83; rule of duty and, 179; single-case justification, 393, 394

Utilitarianism (Mill), 175–83

Utility, justice connection with, 181–83

Vaccination, of children, 158

Validity, 12–13, 12f

Value, relationships of, 197, 198–99

van den Haag, Ernest, 360–64

van Norden, Bryan, 99

Vegetarianism. *See* Meat-free diets

Verbessem, Eddy, 158

Verbessem, Marc, 158

Vices, 124, 528; for actions evaluation, 51–53; Alfano, Aquinas, Aristotle, Mencius list of, 50t; golden mean between two, 49; identification of, 49–51; reasoning with virtues and, 46–56; virtues associated with, 51t, 189–90

Vindication of the Rights of Brutes (Taylor), 469

Vindication of the Rights of Women (Wollstonecraft), 469

Virtue ethics, 48, 50, 82; care ethics compared to, 195–96; *eudaimonia*, 123, 184; practical wisdom and, 124; utilitarianism on happiness, 178–79; vice and, 124; *The Wolf of Wall Street* and, 122–23

Virtue principle, of global warming, 527–28

Virtues, 123; abortion ethics, 47; for actions evaluation, 51–53; actions with, 188–90; Alfano, Aquinas, Aristotle, Mencius list of, 50*t*; Aristotle on, 49, 50, 187–90; Brennan on profit for prosperity, 52; of caring, 52–53, 131; Cassidy on honest prosecutors, 54; of character, 187–88; deontology, axiology and, 46–48; for global warming, 555–57; golden mean between two vices, 49; identification of, 49–51; Mencius on, 49, 206–7, 211, 215n2; as multi-track dispositions, 54; racism and moral, 275; reasoning with vices and, 46–56; thick and thin ethical terms, 48; of thought, 187–88; vices associated with, 51*t*, 189–90

von Hirsch, Andrew, 368–69

Walzer, Michael, 419–21, 438, 444n7, 444n16; DDE revision, 431, 433–34; on just combatants, 414–15; on self-defense, 416

War and peace case studies, 152–54

Warner, John, 138

Warrant requirement, for torture, 399

Warren, Mary Anne, 313–19, 493, 495, 496

Warrior codes, 443

Wars: case studies, 152–54; civilian casualties in, 430–43; classified information leaks, 152

Wars, ethics of killing in: defensive force in, 415–16, 422–24; discrimination requirement, 420–22, 423, 425, 428n4; good effects pursuit, 418–19, 431–32; immunity to attack in, 415; *jus in bello* and *jus ad bellum*, 419–20; just compared to unjust combatants, 414–15; just war theory, 414–15, 432, 433; laws of war, 379–81, 426–28, 435, 437, 443n6, 444n15; McMahan on, 414–28; moral equality of soldiers, 414–15; noncombatant liability, 424–26; proportionality requirement in, 418–20, 423–24, 425, 428n4; self-defense, 415–16, 419–20, 428n5; Sidgwick on proportionality requirement, 419, 428n1; unjust combatants, 416–18, 422–24; Walzer on, 419, 421. *See also* Military ethics

Wassterstrom, Richard, 380, 480

Watkins, Sharon, 151

Wealth: Akan culture and, 222; of governments, global warming mitigated by, 522; Mencius on fondness of, 208–9, 215n3

Weems v. United States, 364n11

Weighty duties, of relationship, 198

Well-developed argument, in ethics paper, 142–43

Wertheimer, Alan, 234, 235, 237, 247n3, 248n7, 248n9

Westen, Peter, 247n3

Western philosophy, care ethics and, 53

"What to a Slave Is the Fourth of July" (Douglass), 101

Whistling Vivaldi (Steele), 302

White, Alan, 494

Wikileaks, 152

Williams, Bernard, 480, 483

Will theories, 248n15

Wishful thinking fallacy, 11

Wolf, Susan, 141, 342–49

The Wolf of Wall Street, virtue ethics and, 122–23

Wollstonecroft, Mary, 469

Women: employment discrimination, 269n5, 296; subordination of, 253–55. *See also* Abortion; Anti-porn feminists; Deception, sex and; Rape

Woodson v. North Carolina, 271n7

Woollard, Fiona, 515–20

"The Wrongs of Plagiarism: Ten Quick Arguments" (Sadler), 87–88

Xenophobia, 289n12

Xiaofei Liu, 299–310

Xuan (king), 206–7, 208

Yì (Righteousness), 132–33, 206

Young-Bruehl, Elizabeth, 289n14, 292n40

Zero Population Growth, 506

Zhang Fei, 153

Zhu Xi comments in *Mengzi*, 205–15

Zillman, Dolf, 272n49

Zombie nouns, Sword on, 148–49